PRAISE FOR

THE RISE OF THEODORE ROOSEVELT

"Reading Morris's comprehensive, necessarily breathless account of Roosevelt's rise is like riding a cannonball express through the Rockies, the peaks whipping past, one exceeding another in magnificence."

—MORDECAI RICHLER

"Morris has written a monumental work in every sense of the word. . . . The result is a book of pulsating and well-written narrative, documented by well over 100 pages of minute, immaculate notes. An average reader will take a long time to read and absorb it all. But read it he will. The tale never lags, like its unique human subject."

—EDWIN TETLOW, *The Christian Science Monitor*

"His prose is elegant and at the same time hard and lucid, and his sense of narrative flow is nearly flawless. . . . The author recreates a sense of the scene and an immediacy of the situation that any skilled writer should envy and the most jaded reader should find a joy."

—DARDEN A. PYRON, *Miami Herald*

"It is a big volume, but it is exciting enough to thrill any reader. Morris has an exceptional dexterity with words. . . . This book will undoubtedly become the standard study of Roosevelt's rise to power."

—THOMAS CONWAY, *The Boston Sunday Globe*

"To his task Morris brings imposing assets. . . . He is scrupulous in the use of his material and notably fair-minded, . . . [and] he can tell a very good story."

—ELTING E. MORISON, *The Washington Post Book World*

"This highly entertaining, immensely readable book is an extraordinary portrait of a most amazing man, Theodore Roosevelt. . . . Edmund Morris is scrupulously fair. He is not judgmental; he draws no sweeping conclusions. Sympathetic, amused, and understanding, he is neither adoring nor worshipful."

—CAREY MCWILLIAMS, *Chicago Sun-Times*

"*Theodore Roosevelt is one of those figures who cannot be fully calibrated without the distance of history and the views of an outsider. This towering biography is the first to answer both requisites. . . . Orchestrating his material with a certainty and lightness of touch, Morris shuns facile psychohistory and lets Roosevelt's life build its own edifice.*"

—EDWIN WARNER, *Time*

"*If you want a classic Teddy biography, one that hews close to the Theodore Roosevelt of patriotic legend, this entertaining and colorful book is for you. . . . TR would have enjoyed this version of his life, not only because it's exciting, particularly the cowboy tales, but because it's morally correct. . . . In no other Roosevelt biography do we get a more lively and lifelike picture of the pre-presidential Roosevelt.*"

—NICHOLAS VON HOFFMAN, *Chicago Tribune*

"*A huge book, but one that is so full of action that the reader will have difficulty putting it down. . . . A monumental piece of writing . . . one of the most interesting biographies to appear in many a moon.*"

—JAMES H. JESSE, *The Nashville Banner*

"*The documentation is almost overwhelming and the description of both events and personalities is unusually detailed and complete. Morris reveals the developing personality, the complex and often contradictory character, and the multiplicity of associations of this most ubiquitous of statesmen. His political career, literary activity, life as a rancher and soldier, and personal life are all abundantly covered. This may well become the definitive life.*"

—RALPH ADAMS BROWN, *Library Journal*

"*If a novelist were to create a character as multidimensional as Theodore Roosevelt, his credibility would be severely strained. One cannot finish Edmund Morris's sympathetic study of the 26th President's early years without feeling that if TR isn't one of our history's greatest men, he is surely one of the more fascinating ones.*"

—RICHARD SAMUEL WEST, *The Philadelphia Inquirer*

"*Morris has crafted a magnificent biography, carefully researched and gracefully written. He has a keen eye for just the right quotation to enliven an incident or bring a personality to life, and his own sense of humor sparkles through.*"

—ALLEN J. SHARE, Louisville *Courier-Journal*

"Morris faces all the problems and contradictions. . . . If he were less sympathetic than he is, his treatment of these aspects might make for distortion, but as it is, it only makes for fuller understanding.

"He is also, I must not fail to restate, a magnificent writer. You can read this book with the absorption with which you would read a great novel. . . . So great is Morris's skill that the reader follows the story as breathlessly as if he did not already know the outcome."

—EDWARD WAGENKNECHT, Waltham-Newton *News-Tribune*

"Readers of this first volume of a biography that takes Roosevelt to his first White House term will get some of the feeling of having received a series of doses of electric voltage."

—MAURICE DOLBIER, Providence *Sunday Journal*

"This volume leaves us on Sept. 2, 1901. President McKinley has been shot. . . . America would move into the 20th century with an activist President at its helm, a man who would set the pace of a strong, involved federal government. Morris is now writing that part of the story, and its publication is an event to anticipate eagerly."

—HARRY STEINBERG, *Newsday*

"This irresistible biography is a lot more than a string of dramatic anecdotes. For example, there's the magnificent prose picture of the disastrous Western winter of 1886–87. . . . Time and again, Mr. Morris seizes such relatively minor incidents and blows them up to fill the imaginative landscape of his study. . . .

"What does the total picture of Roosevelt add up to? . . . Mr. Morris's refusal to interpret analytically pays rich dividends. We get to see the many contradictory sides of Theodore Roosevelt—the killer of big game and the passionate conservationist; the indefatigable writer of historical potboilers and the scholar who produced the definitive naval history of the War of 1812; the sentimental family man and the tub-thumping advocate of imperialism—the list could go on forever. . . . For the time being, we can count our curiosity over them among the many reasons for looking forward to the second volume of this wonderfully absorbing biography."

—CHRISTOPHER LEHMANN-HAUPT, *The New York Times*

BY EDMUND MORRIS

The Rise of Theodore Roosevelt

Dutch: A Memoir of Ronald Reagan

Theodore Rex

Beethoven: The Universal Composer

Colonel Roosevelt

This Living Hand: And Other Essays

The Rise of Theodore Roosevelt

THE RISE OF THEODORE ROOSEVELT

Edmund Morris

RANDOM HOUSE TRADE PAPERBACKS
NEW YORK

Author's Note

This Random House Trade Paperback edition of *The Rise of Theodore Roosevelt* does not differ substantially from the first edition published in 1979, although many passages have been recast. Important material deriving from recent Roosevelt scholarship has been added to the text and the documentation throughout. The book has been redesigned to conform with *Theodore Rex,* and some illustrations have been replaced. There are no major deletions.

2010 Random House Trade Paperback Edition

Published in the United States by Random House Trade Paperbacks, an imprint of The Random House Publishing Group, a division of Random House, Inc., New York, and simultaneously in Canada by Random House of Canada Limited, Toronto.

RANDOM HOUSE TRADE PAPERBACKS and colophon are trademarks of Random House, Inc.

This work was originally published, in slightly different form, by Coward, McCann & Geoghegan in 1979.

LIBRARY OF CONGRESS CATALOGING-IN-PUBLICATION DATA

Morris, Edmund.
The rise of Theodore Roosevelt / Edmund Morris.
p. cm.
Originally published: New York: Coward, McCann & Geoghegan, © 1979.
Includes bibliographical references and index.
ISBN 0-375-75678-7

1. Roosevelt, Theodore, 1858–1919. 2. Presidents—United States—Biography. 3. United States—Politics and government—1901–1909. 4. New York (State)—Politics and government—1865–1950. I. Title.

E757 .M883 2001
973.91'1'092—dc21
[B] 2001030520

www.atrandom.com

Printed in the United States of America

27 29 30 28 26

Book design by Barbara M. Bachman

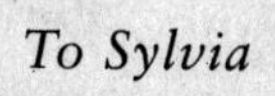
To Sylvia

CONTENTS

Prologue: New Year's Day, 1907 xi

PART ONE: 1858–1886

1: The Very Small Person 3
2: The Mind, But Not the Body 30
3: The Man with the Morning in His Face 54
4: The Swell in the Dog-Cart 80
5: The Political Hack 115
6: The Cyclone Assemblyman 140
7: The Fighting Cock 168
8: The Dude from New York 187
9: The Honorable Gentleman 213
10: The Delegate-at-Large 235
11: The Cowboy of the Present 261
12: The Four-Eyed Maverick 289
13: The Long Arm of the Law 313
14: The Next Mayor of New York 339

Interlude: Winter of the Blue Snow, 1886–1887 363

PART TWO: 1887–1901

15: The Literary Feller 371

16: The Silver-Plated Reform Commissioner 400

17: The Dear Old Beloved Brother 438

18: The Universe Spinner 470

19: The Biggest Man in New York 494

20: The Snake in the Grass 534

21: The Glorious Retreat 563

22: The Hot Weather Secretary 588

23: The Lieutenant Colonel 618

24: The Rough Rider 646

25: The Wolf Rising in the Heart 661

26: The Most Famous Man in America 695

27: The Boy Governor 723

28: The Man of Destiny 747

Epilogue: September 1901 775

Acknowledgments 781

Bibliography 783

Notes 789

Illustrations 891

Index 895

PROLOGUE: NEW YEAR'S DAY, 1907

AT ELEVEN O'CLOCK PRECISELY the sound of trumpets echoes within the White House, and floats, through open windows, out into the sunny morning. A shiver of excitement strikes the line of people waiting four abreast outside Theodore Roosevelt's front gate, and runs in serpentine reflex along Pennsylvania Avenue as far as Seventeenth Street, before whipping south and dissipating itself over half a mile away. The shiver is accompanied by a murmur: "The President's on his way downstairs."[1]

There is some shifting of feet, but no eager pushing forward. The crowd knows that Roosevelt has hundreds of bejeweled and manicured hands to shake privately before he grasps the coarser flesh of the general public. Judging by last year's reception, the gate will not be unlocked until one o'clock, and even then it will take a good two hours for everybody to pass through. Roosevelt may be the fastest handshaker in history (he averages fifty grips a minute), but he is also the most conscientious, insisting that all citizens who are sober, washed, and free of bodily advertising be permitted to wish the President of the United States a Happy New Year.[2]

On a day as perfect as this, nobody minds standing in line—with the possible exception of those unfortunates in the blue shadow of the State, War, and Navy Building. Already the temperature is a springlike 55 degrees. It is "Roosevelt weather," to use a popular phrase.[3] Ladies carry bunches of sweet-smelling hyacinths. Gentlemen refresh their thirst at dray-wagons parked against the sidewalk. A reporter, strolling up and down the line, notices that the weather

"All citizens who are sober, washed, and free of bodily advertising."

Theodore Roosevelt receives the American people on New Year's Day.

has brought out an unusual number of children, some of whom seem determined to enter the White House on roller skates.[4]

More music seeps into the still air. This time it is "The Star-Spangled Banner," played with dignified restraint by the Marine Band. (The President has had occasion to complain, in previous years, of too loud a welcome as he arrives in the vestibule.) After only one strophe, the anthem fades into silence, and another murmur runs down the line: "He's taking his position in the Blue Room." Now a German march. "He's begun to receive the ambassadors."[5]

FOR THE LAST half hour they have been rolling up in their glossy carriages—viscounts, barons, and knights bearing the greetings of emperors and kings to a plain man in a frock coat. A sizable crowd has gathered outside the East Gate to watch them alight under the porte cochère. Their Excellencies teeter down, almost crippled by the weight of full court dress. Plumed helmets wobble precariously, while silver nose-straps tweak at their mustaches. Great bars of medals tangle with their swaying epaulets, gold braid stiffens their trousers, and swords of honor slap against their thigh-length patent-leather boots. Officers of the White House detail, themselves as brilliant as butterflies, hurry across the sunny gravel to assist. Screened through the tall pickets of the White House fence, all this awkward pageantry dissolves into an impressionistic shimmer, and the crowd watches fascinated until the last diplomat has hobbled inside.[6]

Thousands of other onlookers throng Sixteenth Street and Connecticut Avenue to watch the cavalcade of Washington society converging upon the White House. Justices of the Supreme Court creak by in dignified four-wheelers. Congressional couples display themselves to the electorate in open broughams (necks crane for a glimpse of "Princess Alice" Longworth, the President's beautiful daughter, in apricot satin and diamonds). A silver-helmeted military attaché steers his own electric runabout. Two energetic little mules haul a mud-spattered bus full of Army ladies.[7]

Inspired by the balmy weather, many of the President's guests arrive on foot. Lafayette Square is crowded with elegant young men and women. Naval officers march five abreast, their plumes frothing in unison. Chinese grandees drag heavy silk robes. Grizzled veterans of the Civil War stomp along with tinkling medals, and the crowd parts respectfully before them. The air is full of high-spirited conversation and laughter, while the music pouring out of the White House (a continuous medley, now, of jigs and Joplin rags) creates an irresistible holiday mood. A newspaperman is struck by the happiness he sees everywhere, on this, "the best and fairest day President Roosevelt ever had."[8]

SUCH SUPERLATIVES in praise of the weather are mild in comparison with those being lavished on the state of the union. "On this day of our Lord, January 1, 1907," the Washington *Evening Star* reports, "we are the richest people in the world." The national wealth "has been rolling up at the rate of $4.6 billion per year, $127.3 million per day, $5.5 million per hour, $88,430 per minute, and $1,474 per second" during President Roosevelt's two Administrations.[9] Never have American farmers harvested such tremendous crops; railroads are groaning under the weight of unprecedented payloads; shipyards throb with record construction; the banks are awash with a spring-tide of money. Every one of the forty-five states has enriched itself since the last census, and in per capita terms Washington, D.C., is now "the Richest Spot on Earth."[10]

Politically, too, it has been a year of superlatives, many of them supplied, with characteristic immodesty, by the President himself. "No Congress in our time has done more good work," he fondly told the fifty-ninth, having battered it into submission with the sheer volume of his social legislation.[11] He calls its first session "the most substantial" in his experience of public affairs. Joseph G. Cannon, the Speaker of the House, agrees, with one reservation about the President's methods. "Roosevelt's all right," says Cannon, "but he's got no more use for the Constitution than a tomcat has for a marriage license."[12]

"Theodore the Sudden" has been accused of having a similar contempt for international law, ever since the afternoon in 1903 when he allowed a U.S. warship to "monitor" the Panamanian

Revolution. If he loses any sleep over his role in that questionable coup d'état, he shows no sign. On the contrary, he glories in the fact that America is now actually *building* the Panama Canal "after four centuries of conversation"[13] by other nations. A few weeks ago he visited the Canal Zone (the first trip abroad by a U.S. President in office), and the colossal excavations there moved him to Shakespearean hyperbole. "It shall be in future enough to say of any man 'he was connected with digging the Panama Canal' to confer the patent of nobility on that man," Roosevelt told his sweating engineers. "From time to time little men will come along to find fault with what you have done . . . they will go down the stream like bubbles, they will vanish; but the work you have done will remain for the ages."[14]

Few, indeed, are the little men who can find fault with the President on this beautiful New Year's Day, but they are correspondingly shrill. Congressman James Wadsworth, a battered opponent of Roosevelt's Pure Food Act (which goes into effect today), growls that "the bloody hero of Kettle Hill" is "unreliable, a faker, and a humbug."[15] The editor of the *St. Louis Censor,* who has never forgiven Roosevelt for inviting a black man to dine in the White House, warns that he is now trying to end segregation of Orientals in San Francisco schools. "Almost every week his Administration has been characterized by some outrageous act of usurpation . . . he is the most dangerous foe to human liberty that has ever set foot on American soil."[16] Another Southerner, by the name of Woodrow Wilson, is tempted to agree: "He is the most dangerous man of the age."[17] Mark Twain believes that the President is "clearly insane . . . and insanest upon war and its supreme glories."[18]

Roosevelt is used to such criticism. He has been hearing it all his life. "If a man has a very decided character, has a strongly accentuated career, it is normally the case of course that he makes ardent friends and bitter enemies."[19] Yet even impartial observers will admit there is a grain of truth in Twain's assertions. The President certainly has an irrational love of battle. He ceaselessly praises the joys of righteous killing, most recently in his annual message to Congress: "A just war is in the long run far better for a man's soul than the most prosperous peace."

Yet the fact about this most pugnacious of Presidents is that his two terms in office have been almost completely tranquil. (If he had not inherited an insurrection in the Philippines from William McKinley, he could absolve himself of any military deaths.) He is currently being hailed around the world as a flawless diplomat, and the man who has done more to advance the cause of peace than any other. If all Eastern Asia—and for that matter most of Western Europe—is not embroiled in conflict, it is largely due to peace settlements delicately mediated by Theodore Roosevelt. At the same time he has managed, without so much as firing one American pistol, to elevate his country to the giddy heights of world power.[20]

He never tires of reminding people that his famous aphorism "Speak Softly and Carry a Big Stick" proceeds according to civilized priorities. Persuasion should come before force. In any case it is the *availability* of raw power, not the use of it, that makes for effective diplomacy. Last summer's rebellion in Cuba, which left the island leaderless, provided Roosevelt with a textbook example. Acting as usual with lightning swiftness, he invoked an almost forgotten security agreement and proclaimed a U.S.-backed provisional government within twenty-four hours of the collapse of the old. While Secretary of War William H. Taft worked "to restore order and peace and public confidence," American warships steamed thoughtfully up and down the Cuban coastline. The rebels disbanded, Taft returned to Washington, and the big white ships followed. Cuba is now assured of regaining her independence, and the Big Stick has been laid down unbloodied.[21]

Roosevelt hopes the episode will put to an end, once and for all, rumors that he is still at heart an expansionist. "I have about as much desire to annex more islands," he declares, "as a boa-constrictor has to swallow a porcupine wrong end to."[22]

Two or three political clouds, perhaps, mar the perfect blue of Theodore Roosevelt's New Year. Japan is not convinced that his efforts to end discrimination against her citizens in California are sincere, and there are veiled threats of war; "but," as yesterday's Washington *Star* noted confidently, "President Roosevelt thinks he can settle them." The stock market, despite the booming economy, seems paralyzed. Wall Street billionaires are predicting that Roosevelt-style railroad rate regulation will sooner or later bring about financial catastrophe. And there is an ominous paucity of blacks on line today—only fourteen, by one count—indicating that race resentment is growing against his dishonorable discharge of three companies of colored soldiers for an unproved riot in Brownsville, Texas.[23]

As yet, these clouds do not loom very large. Roosevelt is free to enjoy the sensation of near-total control over "the mightiest republic on which the sun ever shone,"—his own phrase, much repeated.[24] Youngest and most vigorous man ever to enter the White House, he exults in what today's *New York Tribune* calls "an opulent efficiency of mind and body." He loves power, loves publicity for the added power it brings, and so far at least seems to have disproved the Actonian theory of corruption. Curiously, the more power Roosevelt acquires, the calmer and sweeter he becomes, and the more willing to step down in two years' time, although a third term is his for the asking. Until then he intends to exercise to the full his constitutional rights to cleave continents, place struggling poets on the federal payroll, and treat with crowned heads on terms of complete equality. Henry Adams calls him "the best herder of Emperors since Napoleon."[25] Expert opinion rates his influence over Congress as greater than that of Kaiser Wilhelm II over the Reichstag.[26] He commands a twenty-four-seat majority in the Senate, a hundred-seat majority in the House, and the frank adoration of the American public. A cornucopia of gifts pours daily into the White House mail-room: hams shaped to match the Rooseveltian profile, crates of live coons, Indian skin paintings, snakes from a traveling sideshow, chairs, badges, vases, and enough Big Sticks to dam the Potomac. One million "Teddy" bears are on sale in New York department stores. Countless small boys, including a frail youngster named Gene Tunney, are doing chest exercises in the hope of emulating their hero's physique. David Robinson, a bootblack from Lackawanna County, Pennsylvania, has just arrived in Washington, bearing letters of recommendation from judges and members of Congress, and begs the privilege of shining the President's shoes for nothing.[27]

Nor is Roosevelt-worship confined to the United States. In England, King Edward VII and ex–Prime Minister Balfour consider him to be "the greatest moral force of the age."[28] Serious British journals rank him on the same level as Washington and Lincoln. Even the august London *Times,* in a review of his latest "very remarkable" message to Congress, admits "It is hard not to covet such a force in public life as our American cousins have got in Mr. ROOSEVELT."[29]

All over the world Jews revere him for his efforts to halt the persecution of their co-religionists in Russia and Rumania, and for making Oscar Solomon Straus Secretary of Commerce and Labor, the first Jewish Cabinet officer in American history.[30] France's Ambassador to the United States, Jules Jusserand, says publicly that "President Roosevelt is the greatest man in the Western Hemisphere—head and shoulders above everyone else."[31]

And from Christiania, Norway, comes the ultimate accolade: an announcement that Theodore Roosevelt, world peacemaker, has become the first American to win the Nobel Prize.[32]

TWELVE-THIRTY HAS COME and gone, but the White House gates are still firmly shut. He must have shaken at least a thousand hands already. . . . Fob watches flash in the sun as students of Washington protocol calculate how long it will take him to work his way down through the social strata. Twenty minutes are generally enough for all the ambassadors, ministers, secretaries, and chargés d'affaires, assuming that each flatters the President for no longer than thirty seconds; ten minutes for the Supreme Court Justices and other members of the judiciary; a quarter of an hour for Senators, Representatives, and Delegates in Congress (he'll probably spend a minute or two talking to old Chaplain Edward Everett Hale, who hasn't missed a reception in sixty-two years); a good half-hour, knowing Roosevelt's priorities, for officers of the Navy and Army; then five minutes apiece for the Smithsonian Institution, the Civil Service, and the Attorney General's office . . . which means the Grand Army of the Republic should be going through about now. Last in the order of official precedence will be veterans of the Spanish-American War, including the inevitable Rough Riders, some of whom are very rough indeed. One of today's newspapers complains about the President's habit of inviting "thugs and assassins of Idaho and Montana to be his guests in the White House."[33] But Roosevelt has never been able to turn away the friends of his youth. After assuming the Presidency he sent out word that "the cowboy bunch can come in whenever they want to." When a doorkeeper mistakenly refused admission to one leathery customer, the President was indignant. "The next time they don't let you in, Sylvane, you just shoot through the windows."[34]

Twelve fifty-five. A stir at the head of the line. Bonnets are adjusted, with much bobbing of artificial fruit; ties are straightened, vests brushed free of popcorn. The gates swing open, and two bowler-hatted policemen lead the way down the White House drive. As the crowd approaches the portico, nine-year-old Quentin Roosevelt waves an affable greeting from his upstairs window. The officers eye him sternly: Young "Q" has a habit of dropping projectiles on men in uniform, including one gigantic, cop-flattening snowball that narrowly missed his father.[35]

The music grows louder as the public steps into the brilliantly lit vestibule. Sixty scarlet-coated bandsmen, hedged around with holly and poinsettia, maintain a brisk, incessant rhythm: Roosevelt knows that this makes his callers unconsciously move faster. Ushers jerk white-gloved thumbs in the direction of the Red Room. "Step lively now!"[36]

Shuffling obediently through shining pillars, past stone urns banked with Christmas-flowering plants, the crowd has a chance to admire Mrs. Roosevelt's interior restorations, begun in 1902 and only recently completed.[37] (One of her husband's first acts, as President, had been to ask Congress to purge the Executive Mansion of Victorian bric-a-brac and restore it to its original "stately simplicity.") These changes come as a shock to older people in line who remember the cozy, shabby, half-house, half–office building of yesteryear, with its dropsical sofas and brass spittoons. Now all is spaciousness and austerity. Regal red furnishings accentuate the gleaming coldness of stone halls and stairways. Roman bronze torches glow with newfangled electric light. The traditional floral displays, which used to make nineteenth-century receptions look like horticultural exhibitions, have been drastically reduced. Rare palms tower in wall niches; vases of violets and American Beauty roses perfume the air.[38]

Here the Roosevelts live in a style which, to their critics, seems "almost more than royal dignity."[39] Formality unknown since the days of George Washington governs the conduct of the First Family. Even the President's sisters have to make appointments to see him. During the official diplomatic season, beginning today, the White House will be the scene of banquets and receptions of an almost European splendor. (The President spends his entire $50,000 salary on entertaining.)[40] Roosevelt's practice, on such occasions, of making dramatic entrances at the stroke of the appointed hour, offering his arm to the lady who will sit at his right, looks like imperial pomp to some. "The President," says Henry James, "is distinctly tending—or trying—to make a court."[41]

Roosevelt himself scoffs cheerfully at such gibes. "They even say I want to be a prince myself! Not I! I've seen too many of them!"[42] He is merely performing, with meticulous correctness, the duties of a head of state. Within the confines of protocol he remains the most democratic of men. He refuses to use obsequious forms of address when writing to foreign rulers, preferring the informal second person, as a gentleman among gentlemen. Nor is he impressed when they address him as "Your Excellency" in return. "They might just as well call me His Transparency for all I care."[43]

Yet some citizens are bent on killing this "first of American Caesars." Last year a man walked into the President's office with a needle-sharp blade up his sleeve. Ever since then, White House security has been tight.[44] Uniformed aides confiscate bundles, inspect hats, draw pocketed hands into open view. All along the corridor, Secret Service men stand like statues. Only their eyes flicker: by the time a caller reaches the Blue Room, he has been scrutinized from head to foot at least three times. Roosevelt does not want to leave office a day too soon.

"I enjoy being President," he says simply.[45]

NO CHIEF EXECUTIVE has ever had so much fun. One of Roosevelt's favorite expressions is "dee-lighted"—he uses it so often, and with such grinning emphasis, that nobody doubts his sincerity. He indeed delights in every aspect of his job: in plowing through mountains of state documents, memorizing whole chunks and leaving his desk bare of even a card by lunchtime; in matching wits with the historians, zoologists, inventors, linguists, explorers, sociologists, actors, and statesmen who daily crowd his table; in bombarding Congress with book-length messages (his latest, a report on his trip to Panama, uses the novel technique of illustrated presentation); in setting aside millions of acres of unspoiled land at the stroke of a pen; in appointing struggling literati to jobs in the U.S. Treasury, on the tacit understanding they are to stay away from the office; in being, as one of his children humorously put it, "the bride at every wedding, and the corpse at every funeral."[46]

He takes an almost mechanistic delight in the smooth workings of political power. "It is fine to feel one's hand guiding great machinery."[47] Ex-President Grover Cleveland, himself a man of legendary ability, calls Theodore Roosevelt "the most perfectly equipped and most effective politician thus far seen in the Presidency."[48] Coming from a Democrat and longtime Roosevelt-watcher, this praise shows admiration of one virtuoso for another.

With his clicking efficiency and inhuman energy, the President seems not unlike a piece of engineering himself. Many observers are reminded of a high-speed locomotive. "I never knew a man with such a head of steam on," says William Sturgis Bigelow. "He never stops running, even while he stokes and fires," another acquaintance marvels, adding that Roosevelt presents "a dazzling, even appalling, spectacle of a human engine driven at full speed—the signals all properly set beforehand (and if they aren't, never mind!)." Henry James describes the engine as "destined to be overstrained perhaps, but not as yet, truly, betraying the least creak . . . it functions astonishingly, and is quite exciting to see."[49]

At the moment, Roosevelt can only be heard, since the first wave of handshakers, filing through the Red Room into the Blue, obscures him from view. He is in particularly good humor today, laughing heartily and often, in a high, hoarse voice that floats over the sound of the band.[50] It is an irresistible laugh: an eruption of mirth, rising gradually to falsetto chuckles, that convulses everybody around him. "You don't smile with Mr. Roosevelt," writes one reporter, "you shout with laughter with him, and then you shout again while he tries to cork up more laugh, and sputters, 'Come, gentlemen, let us be serious. This is most unbecoming.' "[51]

Besides being receptive to humor, the President produces plenty of it himself. As a raconteur, especially when telling stories of his days among the cowboys, he is inimitable, making his audiences laugh until they cry and ache. "You couldn't pick a hallful," declares the cartoonist Homer Davenport, "that could sit with faces straight through his story of the blue roan cow."[52] Physically, too, he is funny—never more so than when indulging his passion for eccentric exercise. Senator Henry Cabot Lodge has been heard yelling irritably at a portly object swaying in the sky, "Theodore! if you knew how ridiculous you look on top of that tree, you would come down at once."[53] On winter evenings in Rock Creek Park, strollers may observe the President of the United States wading pale and naked into the ice-clogged stream, followed by shivering members of his Cabinet.[54] Thumping noises in the White House library indicate that Roosevelt is being thrown around the room by a Japanese wrestler; a particularly seismic crash, which makes the entire mansion tremble, signifies that Secretary Taft has been forced to join in the fun.[55]

Mark Twain is not alone in thinking the President insane. Tales of Roosevelt's unpredictable behavior are legion, although there is usually an explanation. Once, for instance, he hailed a hansom cab on Pennsylvania Avenue, seized the horse, and mimed a knife attack upon it. On another occasion he startled the occupants of a trolley-car by making hideous faces at them from the Presidential carriage. It transpires that in the former case he was demonstrating to a companion the correct way to stab a wolf; in the latter he was merely returning the grimaces of some small boys, one of whom was the ubiquitous Quentin.[56]

Roosevelt can never resist children. Even now, he is holding up the line as he rumples the hair of a small boy with skates and a red sweater. "You must always remember," says his English friend Cecil Spring Rice, "that the President is about six."[57] Mrs. Roosevelt has let it be known that she considers him one of her own brood, to be disciplined accordingly. Between meetings he loves to sneak upstairs to the attic, headquarters of Quentin's "White House Gang," and thunder up and down in pursuit of squealing boys. These romps leave him so disheveled he has to change his shirt before returning to his duties.[58]

A very elegant old lady moves through the door of the Blue Room and curtsies before the President. He responds with a deep bow whose grace impresses observers.[59] Americans tend to forget that Roosevelt comes from the first circle of the New York aristocracy; the manners of Gramercy Park, Harvard, and the great houses of Europe flow naturally out of him. During the Portsmouth Peace Conference in 1905, he handled Russian counts and Japanese barons with such delicacy that neither side was able to claim preference. "The man who had been represented to us as impetuous to the point of rudeness," wrote one participant, "displayed a gentleness, a kindness, and a tactfulness that only a truly great man can command."[60]

Roosevelt's courtesy is not extended only to the well-born. The President of the United States leaps automatically from his chair when any woman enters the room, even if she is the governess of his children. Introduced to a party of people who ignore their own chauffeur, he protests: "I have not met this gentleman." He has never been able to get used to the fact that White House stewards serve him ahead of the ladies at his table, but accepts it as necessary protocol.[61]

For all his off-duty clowning, Roosevelt believes in the dignity of the Presidency. As head of state, he considers himself the equal, and on occasion the superior, of the scepter-bearers of Europe. "No person living," he curtly informed the German Ambassador, "precedes the President of the United States in the White House." He is quick to freeze anybody who presumes to be too familiar. Although he is resigned to being popularly known as "Teddy," it is a mistake to call him that to his face. He regards it as an "outrageous impertinence."[62]

CORDS OF OLD GOLD velvet channel the crowd into single file at the entrance to the Blue Room. Since the President stands just inside the door, on the right, there is little time to admire the oval chamber, with its silk-hung walls and banks of white roses; nor the beauty of the women invited "behind the line"—a signal mark of Presidential favor—and who now form a rustling backdrop of chiffon and lace and satin, their pearls aglow in the light of three sunny windows.[63] Roosevelt is shaking hands at top speed, so the observer has only two or three seconds to size him up.

A FEW SECONDS, surprisingly, are enough. Theodore Roosevelt is a man of such overwhelming physical impact that he stamps himself immediately on the consciousness. "Do you know the two most wonderful things I have seen in your country?" says the English statesman John Morley. "Niagara Falls and the President of the United States, both great wonders of nature!"[64] Their common quality, which photographs and paintings fail to capture, is a perpetual flow of torrential energy, a sense of motion even in stillness.[65] Both are physically thrilling to be near.

Although Theodore Roosevelt stands three inches short of six feet, he seems palpably massive.[66] Two hundred pounds of muscle—those who think it fat have not yet been bruised by contact with it—thicken his small-boned frame. (The only indications of the latter are tapered hands and absurdly small shoes.) A walrus-like belt of muscle strains against his stiff collar. Muscles push through the sleeves of his gray frock coat and the thighs of his striped trousers. Most muscular of all, however, is the famous chest, which small boys, on less formal occasions, are invited to pummel. Members of the White House Gang admit to "queer sensations" at the sight of this great barrel bearing down upon them, and half expect it to burst out of the Presidential shirt. Roosevelt has spent many thousands of hours punishing a variety of steel springs and gymnastic equipment, yet his is not the decorative brawn of a mere body-builder. Professional boxers testify that the President is a born fighter who repays their more ferocious blows with interest. "Theodore Roosevelt," says his heavyweight sparring partner, "is a strong, tough man; hard to hurt and harder to stop."[67]

The nerves that link all this mass of muscle are abnormally active. Roosevelt is not a twitcher—in moments of repose he is almost cataleptically still—but when talking his entire body mimes the rapidity of his thoughts. The right hand shoots out, bunches into a fist, and smacks into the left palm; the heels click together, the neck bulls forward, then, in a spasm of amusement, his face contorts, his head tosses back, spectacle-ribbons flying, and he shakes from head to foot with laughter. A moment later, he is listening with passionate concentration, crouching forward and massaging the speaker's shoulder as if to wring more information out of him. Should he hear something not to his liking, he recoils as if stung, and the blood rushes to his face.[68]

Were it not for his high brow, and the distracting brilliance of his smile, Roosevelt would unquestionably be an ugly man. His head is too big and square (one learned commentator calls it brachycephalous),[69] his ears too small, his jowls too heavy. The stiff brown hair is parted high and clipped unflatteringly short. Rimless pince-nez squeeze the thick nose, etching a tiny, perpetual frown between his eyebrows. The eyes themselves are large, wide-spaced, and very pale blue. Although Roosevelt's gaze is steady, the constant movement of his head keeps slicing the pince-nez across it, in a series of twinkling eclipses that make his true expression very hard to gauge. Only those who know him well are quick enough to catch the subtler messages Roosevelt sends forth. William Allen White occasionally sees "the shadow of some inner femininity deeply suppressed."[70] Owen Wister has detected (and Adolfo Muller-Ury painted) a sort of blurry wistfulness, a mixture of "perplexity and pain . . . the sign of frequent conflict between what he knew, and his wish not to know it, his determination to grasp his optimism tight, lest it escape him."[71]

His ample mustache does not entirely conceal a large, pouting underlip, on the rare occasions when that lip is still. Mostly, however, the mustache gyrates about Roosevelt's most celebrated feature—his dazzling teeth. Virtually every published description of the President, including those of provincial reporters who can catch only a quick glimpse of him through the window of a campaign train, celebrates his dental display. Cartoonists across the land have sketched them into American folk-consciousness, so much so that envelopes ornamented only with teeth and spectacles are routinely delivered to the White House.[72]

At first sight the famous incisors are, perhaps, disappointing, being neither so big nor so prominent as the cartoonists would make out. But to watch Roosevelt talking is to be hypnotized by them. White and even, they chop every word into neat syllables, sending them forth perfectly formed but separate, in a jerky *staccatissimo* that has no relation to the normal rhythms of speech. The President's diction is indeed so syncopated, and accompanied by such surprise thrusts of the head, that there are rumors of a youthful impediment, successfully conquered.[73] His very voice seems to rasp out of the tips of his teeth. "I always think of a man biting tenpenny nails when I think of Roosevelt making a speech," says an old colleague.[74] Others are reminded of engines and light artillery. Sibilants hiss out like escaping steam; plosives drive the lips apart with an audible *pfft.*[75]

Hearing him close up, one can understand his constant use of "dee-*lighted*." Phonetically, the word is made for him, with its grinning vowels and snapped-off consonants. So, too, is that other staple of the Rooseveltian vocabulary, "I." He pronounces it "*Aieeeee,*" allowing the final e's to rise to a self-satisfied pitch which never fails to irritate Henry Adams.[76]

The force of Roosevelt's utterance has the effect of burying his remarks, like shrapnel, in the memory of the listener. Years after meeting him, an Ohio farmer will lovingly recall every inflection of some such banality as "Are you German? Congratulations—I'm German too!" (His ability to find common strains of ancestry with voters has earned him the nickname of "Old Fifty-seven Varieties.")[77] Children are struck by the tenderness with which he enunciates his wife's name—"Edith."[78] H. G. Wells preserves, as if filmed and recorded, an interview with the President in the White House garden last summer. "I can see him now, and hear his unmusical voice saying, 'the effort's worth it, the effort's worth it,' and see the . . . how can I describe it? The friendly peering snarl of his face, like a man with sun in his eyes."[79]

The British author declares, in a *Harper's Weekly* article, that Roosevelt is as impressive mentally as physically. "His range of reading is amazing. He seems to be echoing with all the thought of the time, he has receptivity to the pitch of genius."[80] Opinions are divided as to whether the President possesses the other aspect of genius, originality. His habit of inviting every eminent man within reach to his table, then plunging into the depths of that man's specialty (for Roosevelt has no small talk), exposes but one facet of his mind at a time, to the distress of some finely tuned intellects. The medievalist Adams finds his lectures on history childlike and superficial; painters and musicians sense that his artistic judgment is coarse.[81]

Yet the vast majority of his interlocutors would agree with Wells that Theodore Roosevelt has "the most vigorous brain in a conspicuously responsible position in all the world."[82] Its variety is protean. A few weeks ago, when the British Embassy's new councillor, Sir Esmé Howard, mentioned a spell of diplomatic duty in Crete, Roosevelt immediately and learnedly began to discuss the archeological digs at Knossos. He then asked if Howard was by any chance descended from "Belted Will" of Border fame—quoting Scott on the subject, to the councillor's mystification.[83] The President is also capable of declaiming German poetry to Lutheran preachers, and comparing recently resuscitated Gaelic letters with Hopi Indian lyrics. He is recognized as the world authority on big American game mammals, and is an ornithologist of some note. Stooping to pick a speck of brown fluff off the White House lawn, he will murmur, "Very early for a fox sparrow!"[84] Roosevelt is equally at home with experts in naval strategy, forestry, Greek drama, cowpunching, metaphysics, protective coloration, and football techniques. His good friend Mrs. Henry Cabot Lodge cherishes the following Presidential document, dated 11 March 1906:

> *Dear Nannie* Can you have me to dinner either Wednesday or Friday? Would you be willing to have Bay and Bessie also? Then we could discuss the Hittite empire, the Pithecanthropus, and Magyar love songs, and the exact relations of the Atli of the *Volsunga Saga* to the Etzel of the *Nibelungenlied*, and of both to Attila—with interludes by Cabot about the rate bill, Beveridge, and other matters of more vivid contemporary interest. *Ever yours,*
>
> THEODORE ROOSEVELT[85]

There is self-mockery in this letter, but nobody doubts that Roosevelt could (and probably did) hold forth on such subjects in a single evening. He delights like a schoolboy in parading his knowledge, and does so so loudly, and at such length, that less vigorous talkers lapse into weary silence. John Hay once calculated that in a two-hour dinner at the White House, Roosevelt's guests were responsible for only four and a half minutes of conversation; the rest was supplied by the President himself.[86]

He is, fortunately, a superb talker, with a gift for *le mot juste* that stings and sizzles. Although he hardly ever swears—his intolerance of bad language verges on the prissy—he can pack such venom into a word like "swine" that it has the force of an obscenity, making his victim feel more swinish than a styful of hogs.[87] Roosevelt has a particular gift for humorous invective. Old-timers still talk about the New York Supreme Court Justice he pilloried as "an amiable old fuzzy-wuzzy with sweetbread brains." Critics of the Administration's Panama policy are "a small bunch of shrill eunuchs"; demonstrators against bloodsports are "logical vegetarians of the flabbiest Hindoo type." President Castro of Venezuela is "an unspeakably villainous little monkey," President Marroquín of Colombia is a "pithecanthropoid," and Senator William Alfred Peffer is immortalized as "a well-meaning, pin-headed, anarchistic crank, of hirsute and slabsided aspect."[88] When delivering himself of such insults, the President grimaces with glee. Booth Tarkington detects "an undertone of Homeric chuckling."[89]

Theodore Roosevelt is now only one handshake away. His famous "presence" charges the air about him. It is, in the opinion of one veteran politician, "unquestionably the greatest gift of personal magnetism ever possessed by an American."[90] Other writers grope for metaphors ranging from effervescence to electricity. "One despairs," says William Bayard Hale, "of giving a conception of the constancy and force of the stream of corpuscular personality given off by the President . . . It begins to play on the visitor's mind, his body, to accelerate his blood-current, and set his nerves tingling and his skin aglow."[91]

The word "tingle" appears again and again in descriptions of encounters with Roosevelt. He has, as Secretary Straus observes, "the quality of vitalizing things,"[92] and some people take an almost sensual pleasure in his proximity. Today, the President radiates even more health and vigor than usual—he has spent the last five days pounding through wet Virginia forests in search of turkey. His stiff hair shines, his complexion is a ruddy brown, his body exudes a clean scent of cologne.[93]

He stands with tiny feet spraddled, shoulders thrown back, chest and stomach crescent as a peacock, his left thumb comfortably hooked into a vest pocket. For what must be the three thousandth time, his right arm shoots out. "Dee-*lighted!*" Unlike his predecessors, Theodore Roosevelt does not limply allow himself to be shaken. He seizes on the fingers of every guest, and wrings them with surprising power. "It's a very full and very firm grip," warns one newspaper, "that might bring a woman to her knees if she wore her rings on her right hand."[94] The grip is accompanied by a discreet, but irresistible sideways pull, for the President, when he lets go, wishes to have his guest already well out of the way.[95] Yet this lightning moment of contact is enough for him to transmit the full voltage of his charm.

Insofar as charm can be analyzed, Roosevelt's owes its potency to a combination of genuine warmth and the self-confidence of a man who, in all his forty-eight years, has never encountered a character stronger than his own—with the exception of one revered person, with the same name as himself.

Women find the President enchanting. "I do delight in him," says Edith Wharton. The memory of every Rooseveltian encounter glows within her "like a tiny morsel of radium."[96] Another woman writes of meeting him at a reception: "The world seemed blotted out. I seemed to be enveloped in an atmosphere of warmth and kindly consideration. I felt that, for the time being, I was the sole object of his interest and concern."[97] If he senses any sexual interest in him, Theodore Roosevelt shows no sign: in matters of morality he is as prudish as a dowager. That small hard hand has caressed only two women. One of them stands beside him now, and the other, long dead, is never mentioned.

Men, too, feel the power of his charm. Even the bitterest of his political enemies will allow that he is "as sweet a man as ever scuttled a ship or cut a throat."[98] Senator John Spooner stormed into his office the other day "angry as a hornet" over Brownsville, and emerged "liking him again in spite of myself." Henry James, who privately considers Roosevelt to be "a dangerous and ominous jingo," is forced to recognize "his amusing likeability."[99]

His friends are frank in their adoration. "Theodore is one of the most lovable as well as one of the cleverest and most daring men I have ever known," says Henry Cabot Lodge, not normally given to hyperbole. Crusty John Muir "fairly fell in love" with the President when he visited Yosemite, and Jacob Riis claims the years he spent with Roosevelt were the happiest of his life.[100]

Yet, for all the warmth of the handshake, and the squeaking sincerity of the "Dee-*lighted!*" there is something automatic about that gray-blue gaze. One almost hears the whir of a shutter. "While talking," notes the *Philadelphia Independent,* "the camera of his mind is busy taking photographs."[101] If Roosevelt senses the presence of somebody who is likely to be of use to him, either politically or socially, he will instantly file the photograph, and with half a dozen sentences ensure that his guest, in turn, never forgets him. Ten years later is not too long a time for Roosevelt to call upon that man, in the sure knowledge that he has a friend.[102]

Theodore Roosevelt's memory can, in the opinion of the historian George Otto Trevelyan, be compared with the legendary mechanism of Thomas Babington Macaulay.[103] Authors are embarrassed, during Presidential audiences, to hear long quotes from their works which they themselves have forgotten. Congressmen know that it is useless to contest him on facts and figures. He astonishes the diplomat Count Albert Apponyi by reciting, almost verbatim, a long piece of Hungarian historical literature: when the Count expresses surprise, Roosevelt says he has neither seen nor thought of the document in twenty years. Asked to explain a similar performance before a delegation of Chinese, Roosevelt explains mildly: "I remembered a book that I had read some time ago, and as I talked the pages of the book came before my eyes."[104] The pages of his speeches similarly swim before him, although he seems to be speaking impromptu. When confronted with a face he does not instantly recall, he will put a hand over his eyes until it appears before him in its previous context.[105]

The small hard hand relaxes its grip, and the line moves on. Guests barely have time to greet the First Lady, who stands aloof and smiling in brown brocaded satin at her husband's elbow. She holds a bouquet of white roses, effectively discouraging handshakes. The White House's most brilliant entertainer since Dolley Madison, Edith Kermit Roosevelt is also its most puzzlingly private. Nobody knows what power she wields over the President, but rumor says it is considerable, particularly in the field of appointments. For all his political cunning, Roosevelt is not an infallible judge of men.[106]

"More lively please!" an usher calls at the door of the Green Room. The velvet ropes lead on through the East Room, down a curving stairway, then out into the sunshine.[107] The crowd disperses with the dazed expressions of a theater audience. There are some perfunctory remarks about the diplomatic display, but mostly the talk is about the man in the Blue Room. "You go to the White House," writes Richard Washburn Child, "you shake hands with Roosevelt and hear him talk—and then you go home to wring the personality out of your clothes."[108]

THE PRESIDENT CONTINUES to pump hands with such vigor that his last caller passes through the Blue Room shortly after two o'clock. Mrs. Roosevelt, and most of the receiving party, have long since excused themselves for lunch. Considering the exercise to which he has been put, Roosevelt is doubtless hungry too; yet even now he cannot rest. Wheeling in search of more victims, he grabs the hands of Agriculture Secretary James Wilson, who has stayed behind to keep him company. "Mr. Secretary," croaks Roosevelt, "to you I wish a very, *very* happy New Year!"[109] The fact that he has done so once already does not seem to occur to him. Still unsatisfied, the President proceeds to shake the hands of every aide, usher, and policeman in sight. Only then does he retire upstairs and scrub himself clean.[110]

Events which he cannot foresee will reduce the total of his callers next year. Never again will Theodore Roosevelt, or any other President, enjoy such homage. The journalists may add another superlative to their praises. On this first day of January 1907, the President has shaken 8,150 hands, more than any other man in history. As a world record, it will remain unbroken almost a century hence.[111]

LATER IN THE AFTERNOON, the President, his wife, and five of his six children are seen cantering off for a ride in the country. Although reporters cannot follow him through the rest of the day, enough is known of Roosevelt's domestic habits to predict its events with some accuracy.[112] Returning for tea, which he will swig from an outsize cup, Roosevelt will take advantage of the holiday quietness of his dark-green office to do some writing. Besides being President of the United States, he is also a professional author. The Elkhorn Edition of *The Works of Theodore Roosevelt,* just published, comprises twenty-three volumes of history, natural history, biography, political philosophy, and essays. At least two of his books, *The Naval War of 1812* and the four-volume *Winning of the West,* are considered definitive by serious historians.[113] He is also the author of many scientific articles and literary reviews, not to mention an estimated total of fifty thousand letters—the latest twenty-five of which he dashed off this morning.[114]

In the early evening the President will escort his family to No. 1733 N Street, where his elder sister Bamie will serve chocolate and whipped cream and champagne. After returning to the White House, the younger Roosevelts will be forcibly romped into bed, and the elder given permission to roller-skate for an hour in the basement. As quietness settles down over the Presidential apartments, Roosevelt and his wife will sit by the fire in the Prince of Wales Room and read to each other. At about ten o'clock the First Lady will rise and kiss her husband good night. He will continue to read in the light of a student lamp, peering through his one good eye (the other is almost blind) at the book held inches from his nose, flicking over the pages at a rate of two or three a minute.[115]

This is the time of the day he loves best. "Reading with me is a disease."[116] He succumbs to it so totally—on the heaving deck of the Presidential yacht in the middle of a cyclone, between whistle-stops on a campaign trip, even while waiting for his carriage at the front door—that he cannot hear his own name being spoken. Nothing short of a thump on the back will regain his attention. Asked to summarize the book he has been leafing through with such apparent haste, he will do so in minute detail, often quoting the actual text.[117]

The President manages to get through at least one book a day even when he is busy. Owen Wister has lent him a book shortly before a full evening's entertainment at the White House, and been astonished to hear a complete review of it over breakfast. "Somewhere between six one evening and eight-thirty next morning, beside his dressing and his dinner and his guests and his sleep, he had read a volume of three-hundred-and-odd pages, and missed nothing of significance that it contained."[118]

On evenings like this, when he has no official entertaining to do, Roosevelt will read two or three books entire.[119] His appetite for titles is omnivorous and insatiable, ranging from the the *Histories* of Thucydides to the *Tales of Uncle Remus*. Reading, as he has explained to Trevelyan, is for him the purest imaginative therapy. In the past year alone, Roosevelt has devoured all the novels of Trollope, the complete works of De Quincey, a *Life of Saint Patrick,* the prose works of Milton and Tacitus ("until I could stand them no longer"), Samuel Dill's *Roman Society from Nero to Marcus Aurelius,* the seafaring yarns of Jacobs, the poetry of Scott, Poe, and Longfellow, a German novel called *Jörn Uhl,* "a most satisfactorily lurid Man-eating Lion story," and Foulke's *Life of Oliver P. Morton,* not to mention at least five hundred other volumes, on subjects ranging from tropical flora to Italian naval history.[120]

The richness of Roosevelt's knowledge causes a continuous process of cross-fertilization to go on in his mind. Standing with candle in hand at a baptismal service in Santa Fe, he reflects that his ancestors, and those of the child's Mexican father, "doubtless fought in the Netherlands in the days of Alva and Parma." Watching a group of American sailors joke about bedbugs in the Navy, he is reminded of the freedom of comment traditionally allowed to Roman legionnaires after battle. Trying to persuade Congress to adopt a system of simplified spelling in Government documents, he unself-consciously cites a treatise on the subject published in the time of Cromwell.[121]

Tonight the President will bury himself, perhaps, in two volumes Mrs. Lodge has just sent him for review: Gissing's *Charles Dickens, A Critical Study,* and *The Greek View of Life,* by Lowes Dickinson.

He will be struck, as he peruses the latter, by interesting parallels between the Periclean attitude toward women and that of present-day Japan, and will make a mental note to write to Mrs. Lodge about it.[122] He may also read, with alternate approval and disapproval, two articles on Mormonism in the latest issue of *Outlook*. A five-thousand-word essay on "The Ancient Irish Sagas" in this month's *Century* magazine will not detain him long, since he is himself the author.[123] His method of reading periodicals is somewhat unusual: each page, as he comes to the end of it, is torn out and thrown onto the floor.[124] When both magazines have been thus reduced to a pile of crumpled paper, Roosevelt will leap from his rocking-chair and march down the corridor. Slowing his pace at the door of the presidential suite, he will tiptoe in, brush the famous teeth with only a moderate amount of noise, and pull on his blue-striped pajamas. Beside his pillow he will deposit a large, precautionary revolver.[125] His last act, after turning down the lamp and climbing into bed, will be to unclip his pince-nez and rub the reddened bridge of his nose. Then, there being nothing further to do, Theodore Roosevelt will energetically fall asleep.

Part One

1858–1886

The epigraphs at the head of every chapter are taken from Theodore Roosevelt's favorite poem, *The Saga of King Olaf*, by Longfellow.

"Such loveliness of line and tinting . . .
such sweet courtesy of manner."

Martha Bulloch Roosevelt at twenty-two.

CHAPTER 1

The Very Small Person

Then King Olaf entered,
Beautiful as morning,
Like the sun at Easter
Shone his happy face.

ON THE LATE afternoon of 27 October 1858, a flurry of activity disturbed the genteel quietness of East Twentieth Street, New York City.[1] Liveried servants flew out of the basement of No. 28, the Roosevelt brownstone, and hurried off in search of doctors, midwives, and stray members of the family—a difficult task, for it was now the fashionable visiting hour. Meanwhile Mrs. Theodore Roosevelt lay tossing in her satinwood bed, awaiting the arrival of her second child and first son.

Gaslight was flaring on the cobbles by the time a doctor arrived. The child was born at a quarter to eight, emerging so easily that neither chloroform nor instruments were needed. "Consequently," reported his grandmother, "the dear little thing has no cuts nor bruises about it." Theodore Roosevelt, Junior, was "as sweet and pretty a young baby as I have ever seen."

Mittie Roosevelt, inspecting her son the following morning, disagreed. She said, with Southern frankness, that he looked like a terrapin.[2]

Apart from these two contradictory images, there are no further visual descriptions of the newborn baby. He weighed eight and a half pounds, and was more than usually noisy.[3] When he reappears in the family chronicles ten months later, he has acquired a milk-crust and a nickname, "Teedie." At eighteen months the milk-crust has gone, but the nickname has not. He is now "almost a little beauty."[4]

Scattered references in other letters indicate a bright, hyperactive infant. Yet already the first of a succession of congenital ailments was beginning to weaken him. Asthma crowded his lungs, depriving him of sleep. "One of my memories," the ex-President wrote in his *Autobiography,* "is of my father walking up and down the room with me in his arms at night when I was a very small person, and of sitting up in bed gasping, with my father and mother trying to help me."[5] Even more nightmarish was the recollection of those same strong arms holding him, as the Roosevelt rig sped through darkened city streets, forcing a rush of air into the tiny lungs.[6]

THEODORE ROOSEVELT, SENIOR, was no stranger to childhood suffering. Gifted himself with magnificent health and strength—"I never seem to get tired"—he overflowed with sympathy for the small, the weak, the lame, and the poor. Even in that age when a certain amount of charitable work was expected of well-born citizens, he was remarkable for his passionate efforts on behalf of the waifs of New York. He had what he called "a troublesome conscience."[7]

Every seventh day of his life was dedicated to teaching in mission schools, distributing tracts, and interviewing wayward children. Long after dark he would come home after dinner at some such institution as the Newsboys' Lodging-House, or Mrs. Sattery's Night School for Little Italians. One of his prime concerns, as a founder of the Children's Aid Society, was to send street urchins to work on farms in the West. His charity extended as far as sick kittens, which could be seen peeking from his pockets as he drove down Broadway.[8]

At the time of Teedie's birth, Theodore Senior was twenty-seven years old, a partner in the old importing firm of Roosevelt and Son, and already one of the most influential men in New York. Handsome, wealthy, and gregarious, he was at ease with millionaires and paupers, never showing a trace of snobbery, real or inverse, in his relations with either class. "I can see him now," remembered a society matron years later, "in full evening dress, serving a most generous supper to his newsboys in the Lodging-House, and later dashing off to an evening party on Fifth Avenue."[9]

A photograph taken in 1862 shows deep eyes, leonine features, a glossy beard, and big, sloping shoulders. "He was a large, broad, bright, cheerful man," said his nephew Emlen Roosevelt, ". . . deep through, with a sense of abundant strength and power." The word "power" runs like a leitmotif through other descriptions of Theodore Senior: he was a person of inexorable drive. "A certain expression" on his face, as he strode breezily into the offices of business acquaintances, was enough to flip pocketbooks open. "How much this time, Theodore?"[10]

For all his compulsive philanthropy, he was neither sanctimonious nor ascetic. He took an exuberant, masculine joy in life, riding his horse through Central Park "as though born in the saddle," exercising with the energy of a teenager, waltzing all night long at society balls. Driving his four-in-hand back home in the small hours of the morning, he rattled through the streets at such a rate that his grooms allegedly "fell out at the corners."[11]

Such a combination of physical vitality and genuine love of humanity was rare indeed. His son called Theodore Senior "the best man I ever knew," adding, ". . . but he was the only man of whom I was ever really afraid."[12]

IN ALL RESPECTS except their intense love for each other, Theodore and Martha Roosevelt were striking opposites. Where he was big and disciplined and manly, "Mittie" was small, vague, and feminine to the point of caricature. He was the archetypal Northern burgher, she the Southern belle eternal, a lady about whom there always clung a hint of white columns and wisteria bowers. Born and raised in the luxury of a Georgia plantation, she remained, according to her son, "entirely unreconstructed until the day of her death."[13]

Of her beauty, especially in her youth (she was twenty-three when Teedie was born), contemporary accounts are unanimous in their praise. Her hair was fine and silky black, with a luster her French hairdresser called *noir doré*. Her skin was "more moonlight-white than cream-white," and in her cheeks there glowed a suggestion of coral.[14] Every day she took two successive baths, "one for cleaning, one for rinsing," and she dressed habitually in white muslin, summer and winter. "No dirt," an admirer marveled, "ever stopped near her."[15]

On Mittie's afternoons "at home" she would sit in her pale blue parlor, surrounded always by bunches of violets, while "neat little maids in lilac print gowns" escorted guests into her presence. Invariably they were enchanted. "Such loveliness of line and tinting . . . such sweet courtesy of manner!" gushed Mrs. Burton Harrison, a memoirist of the period. Of five or six gentlewomen whose "birth, breeding, and tact" established them as the flowers of New York society, "Mrs. Theodore Roosevelt seemed to me easily the most beautiful."[16]

Her exquisite looks were balanced by exquisite taste. Not surprisingly, for someone who made such a delicate pastel picture of herself, she was a connoisseur of painting and sculpture. She filled her house with the finest furniture and porcelain, and her need for "everything that was beautiful" is said to have strained even the considerable Roosevelt resources. Theodore Senior acknowledged that her palate for wine was superior to his own, and never paid for a consignment until she had personally approved it.[17]

Mittie was a woman of considerable wit. Her letters, written in a delicate Italian hand, show flashes of inventive humor.[18] As a storyteller, especially when recounting what her enraptured children called "slave tales," she revealed great gifts of mimicry. One evening, at a family party, she grimaced her way through a piece called "Old Bess in a Fit," while Theodore Senior, who could not bear seeing her lovely face distorted, tried in vain to stop her. Eventually he was reduced to picking her up like a doll and carrying her out of the room on his shoulder.[19]

FROM HIS FATHER, young Teedie inherited the sturdy Dutch character of Klaes Martenszen van Rosenvelt, one of the early settlers of New Amsterdam, who stepped ashore sometime in 1649. From that day on for the next two centuries, every generation of Roosevelts—Teedie being the seventh—was born on Manhattan Island.[20]

Oom Klaes had been a farmer, but subsequent Roosevelts ascended rapidly in the social scale, becoming manufacturers, merchants, engineers, and bankers. A Roosevelt had served in the New York State Senate and helped ratify the Constitution with Alexander Hamilton. Another had received his bride from the hands of General Lafayette. Industrious and honest, the family amassed a comfortable fortune. Teedie's grandfather Cornelius van Schaack Roosevelt was worth half a million dollars at a time when the average daily wage was fifty to seventy-five cents.[21]

The only non-Dutch infusion that Teedie received through his father was that of Grandmother Roosevelt, but it was a rich admixture of Welsh, English, Irish, Scotch-Irish, and German strains traceable back to immigrant Quakers. Strangely enough, she, and not old Cornelius, taught Teedie the only Dutch he ever knew, a nursery song:

Trippel trippel toontjes,
Kippen in de boontjes . . .

Fifty years later, when he went hunting in Africa, he sang this song to Boer settlers and found that they recognized it. "It was interesting," he wrote, "to meet these men whose ancestors had gone to the Cape about the time that mine went to America two and a half centuries previously, and to find that the descendants of the two streams of emigrants still crooned to their children some at least of the same nursery songs."[22]

From his mother, Teedie acquired several refined French traits. Although her forebears were predominantly Scots—James Bulloch of Glasgow emigrated to Charleston in 1729—they had early married into the Huguenot family of de Veaux.[23] Mittie, with her rococo beauty and elegance of manner, could have been mistaken for a Frenchwoman, and she passed on to Teedie a certain Gallic volubility.

The Bullochs also contributed aristocratic qualities, not shared by the Roosevelts. Whereas *Oom* Klaes had been a man of the soil, ranking far below Governor Pieter Stuyvesant, James Bulloch was a learned planter who could entertain Governor James Edward Oglethorpe on equal terms.[24] Unlike the Roosevelts, who with two or three exceptions preferred the security of commerce to the glamor of politics,[25] the Bullochs stepped naturally into positions of power. Among his direct maternal ancestors Teedie could count six distinguished politicians, including Archibald Bulloch, the first President of Revolutionary Georgia.[26]

Few Americans, surely, have been born into such a perfectly balanced home environment as the son of Theodore and Mittie Roosevelt. There was a harmony of Southern refinement and Northern vigor, feminine humor and masculine seriousness, and—later on—the rewards of privilege and the responsibilities of charity. Through the front window of the house Teedie looked down on carriages and cobblestones, and heard coming from Broadway and Fifth Avenue the rumble and throb of a great city. Through the rear window he gazed out into another world, an enormous, block-wide garden full of trees and flowers, roamed by ornamental peacocks.[27] Were it not for the weight of asthma in his lungs, he might consider himself a child of Paradise.

But then, five months after his second birthday, Southern cannons fired upon Fort Sumter, and the harmonies of 28 East Twentieth Street were jarred into discord.

WHEN WAR WAS DECLARED, on 12 April 1861, Teedie and his six-year-old sister Anna ("Bamie") had been joined by a fourteen-month-old brother, Elliott ("Ellie"), and Mittie Roosevelt was already pregnant with her final child, Corinne ("Conie"), who arrived in the fall. No sooner had the last been born than Theodore Senior left home, and sadness filled the house.[28]

He had spent most of the summer agonizing, to the tramp of mustering regiments, over what role he should play in the war. Although he was not yet thirty, and in prime physical shape, his domestic situation was such that he could not contemplate taking up arms. Under his roof lived three women—Grandmother Bulloch, Mittie, and her sister Annie—who owned slaves and a plantation and were passionate in their support of the Confederacy. (Mittie allegedly once hung out the Stars and Bars after a Southern victory.) Two of Mrs. Bulloch's sons were fighting for the South. Could he fire upon, or receive the bullets of, his brothers-in-law? In anguish Theodore Senior did what many of his wealthy friends were doing. He hired a substitute soldier.[29]

Yet as a strong Lincoln Republican, his "troublesome conscience" would not let him rest. A certain strain developed between himself and his wife, although their mutual love never wavered. "I wish we sympathized together on this question of so vital moment to our country," he told her gently. "I know you cannot understand my feelings and of course do not expect it."[30] Eventually he announced that he had decided to aid the war effort in a civilian capacity, and, true to his nature, soon found a charitable cause.

Already, in these early days of war, millions of government dollars were flowing through the pockets of Union soldiers and into the hands of sutlers, who infested military camps, hawking bottles of liquor hidden in loaves of bread. The sutlers charged such exorbitant prices that their customers soon had no money left to send home to their families. It was to right this wrong that Theodore Senior set off to Washington, and, conquering his natural distaste for politics, began to lobby for remedial legislation.

With two colleagues, he drafted a bill for the appointment of unpaid Allotment Commissioners, who would visit all military camps and persuade soldiers to set aside voluntary pay deductions for family support. This proposal, which eventually became standard military practice, seemed eccentric, if not downright suspect, in 1861, as a family friend recalled many years later:

> For three months they worked in Washington to secure the passage of this act—delayed by the utter inability of Congressmen to understand why anyone should urge a bill from which no one could selfishly secure an advantage. When this was passed he was appointed by President Lincoln one of the three Commissioners from this State. For long, weary

> months, in the depth of a hard winter, he went from camp to camp, urging the men to take advantage of this plan; on the saddle often six to eight hours a day, standing in the cold and mud as long, addressing the men and entering their names. This resulted in sending many millions of dollars to homes where it was greatly needed, kept the memory of wives and children fresh in the minds of the soldiers, and greatly improved their morale. Other States followed, and the economical results were very great.[31]

Lincoln's private secretary, a round-headed, slant-eyed youth named John Hay, proved a willing conduit to the President, and Theodore Senior made the most of his assistance. "It is a great luxury to feel I am at last doing something tangible for the country," he wrote Mittie. Homesickness nevertheless tugged at him. "I cannot," he confessed, "get Bammie's and Tedee's [*sic*] faces, as they bid me goodbye at the door, out of my mind."[32]

It is significant that Theodore Junior, when he came to write his own autobiography, made no mention whatsoever of his father's role in the Civil War—his invariable practice being to leave painful memories unspoken, "until they are too dead to throb."[33] To serve in mufti was, in his opinion, something less than manly, and his tacit disapproval of the episode is the only indication that Theodore Senior was ever less than a god to him. Many biographers, including his own sister, have suggested that guilt over that substitute soldier explains the future Rough Rider's almost desperate desire to wage war. He himself, at the age of three, made no bones about his wish to be at the front. "Teedie was really excited," wrote Annie Bulloch, "when I said to him, 'Darling, I must fit this zouave suit . . .' his little face flushed up and he said, 'Are me a soldier laddie?' I immediately took his own suggestion and told him he was and that I was the Captain."[34]

His liveliness, abnormal even for a small boy, was something of a trial to the languid Mittie. Six weeks after Theodore Senior's departure she complained: "Teedie is the most affectionate and endearing little creature in his ways, but begins to require Papa's discipline rather sadly. He is brimming full of mischief and has to be watched all the time."[35]

Yet the child was simultaneously sinking into what seemed like chronic invalidism. From the moment his father left home, the catalog of Teedie's ailments became continuous. He suffered from coughs, colds, nausea, fevers, and a congenital form of nervous diarrhea which the family euphemized as *cholera morbus*.[36] "I feel badly," he told his mother one morning, "—I have toothache in my stomach." On top of all this, his asthma was worsening. "Rarely, even at his best, could he sleep without being propped up in bed or in a big chair," remembered Corinne. Lack of appetite brought about symptoms of malnutrition. At one stage his whiteness and fragility were such that Annie Bulloch compared him to a very pale azalea. It seemed that he would not live to see his fourth birthday.[37]

The other children were not much healthier. Bamie, who had been dropped as a baby, suffered from a spinal defect that obliged her to wear a harness; Elliott was prone to colds and rushes of blood to the head; even little Corinne was ailing, and would soon fall victim to asthma as well.[38]

To Theodore Senior, sloughing tirelessly through the freezing mud of military camps, Mittie's letters made depressing reading. He was plainly bewildered by the fact that two such beautiful physical specimens had produced such a sickly brood of children. "I cannot help feeling," he wrote early in 1862, "that there must be something about the furnace or something that prevents them all from being healthy." With characteristic optimism he hoped for improvements in the summer, when he would be home for a visit, and exhorted his wife: "Remember to enjoy yourself just as much as you can."[39]

How much Teedie's asthma was aggravated by the absence of his father may be inferred from some remarks he made thirty-seven years later to Lincoln Steffens, after a steeplechase which left the reporter breathless:

> Handsome dandy that he was, the thought of him now and always has been a sense of comfort. I could breathe, I could

> sleep, when he had me in his arms. My father—he got me breath, he got me lungs, strength—life.[40]

WHEN THEODORE SENIOR FINALLY came home, on leave of absence from Washington, the garden behind 28 East Twentieth Street was lush with summer, the children were better, and his own mood had improved. He was able to tell stories of rides with President and Mrs. Lincoln, who had apparently fallen victim—as everybody did sooner or later—to his charm. The First Lady even took him shopping and asked him to choose bonnets for her.[41]

The effect of his lusty reappearance in the household was like a tonic to his women and children. The latter especially worshiped him "as though he were a sort of benevolent Norse god."[42] During morning prayers they would compete for the privilege of sitting in the "cubby-hole"—a favored stretch of sofa between his body and the mahogany arm. Later in the day, when he was away at work, they would wait for him on the piazza behind the house, until his key rattled in the latch and he burst upon them, laden with ice cream and peaches. He would feed the fruit to them as they lay spread-eagled on the edge of the piazza, letting the juice drip down into the garden. Afterward they would troop into his room to look on while he undressed, eagerly watching his pockets for the "treasures"—heavy male trinkets which he would solemnly deposit in the box on his dressing-table, or, on occasion, present to a lucky child.[43] This ritual would one day be faithfully reproduced by the President of the United States before his own children.

Despite the joy Theodore Senior felt at being at home again, he lost no time in restoring paternal discipline. It was during this summer that naughty Teedie felt for the first time the weight of his father's hand.

> I bit my elder sister's arm. I do not remember biting her arm, but I do remember running down to the yard, perfectly conscious that I had committed a crime. From the yard I went into the kitchen, got some dough from the cook, and crawled under the kitchen table. In a minute or

two my father entered from the yard and asked where I was. The warm-hearted Irish cook had a characteristic contempt for "informers," but although she said nothing she compromised between informing and her conscience by casting a look under the table. My father immediately dropped on all fours and darted at me. I feebly heaved the dough at him, and, having the advantage of him because I could stand up under the table, got a fair start for the stairs, but was caught halfway up them. The punishment that ensued fitted the crime, and I hope—and believe—that it did me good.[44]

THEODORE SENIOR never chastised his son again. It was not necessary. There hung about his big, relaxed body an ever-present threat of violence, like that of a lion who, dozing, will suddenly flick out a lethal paw. His reaction to any form of wrong—in particular "selfishness or cruelty, idleness, cowardice, or untruthfulness"—was so quick, and so certain, that nobody, child or adult, crossed him more than once. "Be sure to make the children obey your *first* order," he told Mittie.[45] Although her success was indifferent, they nevertheless came to understand "that the same standard of clean living was demanded for the boys as for the girls; that what was wrong in a woman could not be right in a man."[46]

ABOUT THE TIME Teedie turned four in October 1862, he began dimly to realize that his parents were not one in their views about the Civil War. These differences had been for the most part diplomatically concealed from the children during the summer, although Bamie recalled nights when Mittie would dine alone in her room rather than be exposed to the brutal Unionism of male conversation downstairs. "She must have been homesick for her own people until her heart bled in those early days . . . it was out of the very fulness of her heart that she used to tell us of home."[47]

Mittie, however, was not entirely alone. The flames of Southern patriotism burned as high in the breasts of her sister and mother, who, fond as they were of Theodore Senior, felt some embarrassment at having to live under the roof of a Lincoln Republican. As soon as their host left home these scruples vanished, and the three women busied themselves in support of the Confederacy. There were "days of hushed and thrilling excitement" when little Teedie helped the ladies of the house pack mysterious boxes, "to run the blockade."[48]

As Teedie became aware of the intensity of their feelings, he learned to play upon them, with some cruelty. "Once, when I felt I had been wronged by maternal discipline during the day, I attempted a partial vengeance by praying with loud fervor for the success of Union arms, when we all came to say our prayers before my mother in the evening." Mittie's sense of humor neutralized this moment of truculence, so Teedie tried the same trick on Aunt Annie, who was much less amused. She said she would never forget "the fury in the childish voice when he would plead with Divine Providence to 'grind the Southern troops to powder.' "[49]

Annie Bulloch had volunteered to pay for her bed and board by giving all the Roosevelt children their first lessons, an offer her lethargic sister was only too happy to accept. Perhaps with some trepidation, she now undertook the education of Teedie. It was on her knee that he learned the three Rs, and showed a decided preference for the first two at the expense of the third. Aunt Annie was a born teacher: energetic, practical, and kindly, with a dramatic flair that enlivened the dullest fact. Often as not—for she was an even better storyteller than her sister—the lessons would drift into reminiscences of the Old South. A mood of spinsterish melancholy colored Aunt Annie's tales of life on the Georgia plantations: of minuets under the mistletoe, and coach lamps drowned in warm darkness, as lovesick young men drove away—forever; of cock-fights and turkey-wrestling; of horses that had been named after, or (to a child who had only recently confused God with a fox) perhaps *were* Daniel Boone and Davy Crockett; of the famous fighting Bullochs and their exploits during the American Revolution; of Bre'r Rabbit, the Tar Baby, and "queer goings-on in the Negro quarters."[50]

Teedie thus, at a very early age, acquired a love for legend and anecdote, and inherited a nostalgia for a way of life he had never known. The key to his imagination had been unlocked by a woman to whom the past was more real than the present. As an adult reader of history, and as a professional writer of it, he always showed a tendency to "live" his subject; he always looked for narrative which was "instinct with the truth that both charms and teaches."[51]

Since Aunt Annie had three other children to take care of, she could not spend all her time satisfying Teedie's lust for information, which rapidly became insatiable. Confined indoors by ill health and winter weather, he wheezed restlessly from room to room in search of further entertainment. For a while he amused himself with *objets d'art* in the parlor: a Russian moujik pulling a tin sledge across a snowfield of malachite; a carved Swiss hunter chasing chamois goats around an improbably small mountain; and floor-to-ceiling mirrors in which he could exchange stares with a small, blond, stern-faced boy. Dominating his little universe, like some remote yet brilliant galaxy, was a gas chandelier coruscating with cut-glass prisms. "These prisms struck me as possessing peculiar magnificence," he wrote in later life. "One of them fell off one day, and I hastily grabbed it and stowed it away, passing several days of furtive delight in the treasure, a delight always alloyed with fear that I would be found out and convicted of larceny."[52]

The splendors of the parlor soon palled. There was little to detain him in the dining room, except at mealtimes; besides, its black haircloth furniture scratched his bare legs. The kitchen was *terra non grata* to pesky children. Eventually he was forced to explore the most forbidding room in the house: a windowless library, with tables, chairs, and gloomy bookcases.[53] Chancing upon a ponderous edition of David Livingstone's *Missionary Travels and Researches in Southern Africa,* Teedie opened it, and found within a world he could happily inhabit the rest of his days.

Although the book's pages of print meant nothing to him, its illustrations were copious, explicit, and strangely thrilling. Here were rampant hippopotami with canoes on their backs, horizon-filling herds of zebra, a magnified tsetse fly, as big as his hand, and an elephant so spiked with assegais as to resemble an enormous porcupine. For weeks Teedie dragged the volume, which was almost as big as he was, around the library, and begged his elders to fit stories to the pictures.[54]

Among the first books Teedie learned to decipher for himself were an unscientific study of mammals by Mayne Reid, and two natural histories by the English biologist J. G. Wood.[55] He pored endlessly over these in the library, curled up in a tiny chair which became his favorite article of furniture. Softly upholstered in red velvet, and fringed with long tassels, it seemed designed to comfort the scrawny angles of his body. For years the boy and his "tassel chair" were so inseparable it even accompanied him to the photographer's studio for his formal birthday portraits.

The library's gloom vanished at night, when gas lamps began to hiss, and the coal fire made its rugs and tapestries glow a rich, romantic red. Teedie was given free access to all the books on the shelves, save only a racy novel by Ouida, *Under Two Flags*. "I did read it, nevertheless, with greedy and fierce hope of coming on something unhealthy; but as a matter of fact all the parts that might have seemed unhealthy to an older person made no impression on me. . . . I simply enjoyed in a rather confused way the general adventures."[56]

As his reading abilities developed, and his ill-health continued, he turned more and more to stories of outdoor action, in which he could identify with heroes larger than life: the novels of Ballantyne, the sea-yarns of Captain Marryat, Cooper's tales of the American frontier. Epic poetry, too, inspired him—above all Longfellow's *Saga of King Olaf*, with its wild warlocks, blaring horns, and shields shining like suns.

> I was nervous and timid. Yet from reading of the people I admired,—ranging from the soldiers of Valley Forge, and Morgan's riflemen, to the heroes of my favorite stories—and from hearing of the feats performed by my Southern forefathers and kinsfolk, and from knowing my father, I felt a great admiration for men who were fearless and could hold their own in the world, and I had a great desire to be like them.[57]

IN THE SPRING of 1863 Theodore Senior, whose voluntary war services were now more and more concentrated in New York State, transported his ailing family to Loantaka, a country place in Madison, New Jersey. The children reacted to their rural surroundings with such delight, and with such general improvement to their health, that Loantaka remained the Roosevelt summer home for four consecutive seasons.

Here the bookish Teedie became aware of the "enthralling pleasures" of building wigwams in the woods, gathering hickory nuts and apples, hunting frogs, haying and harvesting, and scampering barefoot down long, leafy lanes. Despite his frail physique and asthma, he seemed to have an inexhaustible fund of nervous energy. This, combined with the ability to improvise countless stories about his environment, caused him to be accepted as an unquestioned leader by Corinne and Elliott, and such family friends as came to stay. (Bamie's four-year seniority, along with a certain adult seriousness of manner, disqualified her from membership in his gang.) Even on days when illness confined him to bed, the other children would forsake the fields in order to be entertained by the prodigal Teedie. His stories, remembered by Corinne into old age, were "about jungles and bold, mighty and imaginary fights with strange beasts . . . there was always a small boy in the stories . . . who understood the language of animals and would translate their opinions to us."[58]

Even in these early years, his knowledge of natural history was abnormal. No doubt much of it was acquired during his winters in the "tassel chair," but it was supplemented, every summer, by long hours of observation of the flora and fauna around him. The other children noticed that their leader "also led a life apart from us, seriously studying birds, their habits and their notes."[59] At first this study was haphazard, and Teedie made no attempt to document his observations, beyond filing them in his retentive memory. Not until he was seven years old, and back in New York City, did his formal career as a zoologist begin.

> I was walking up Broadway, and as I passed the market to which I used sometimes to be sent before breakfast to get strawberries, I suddenly saw a dead seal laid out on a slab of wood. That seal filled me with every possible feeling of

> romance and adventure. I asked where it was killed, and was informed in the harbor . . . As long as that seal remained there I haunted the neighborhood of the market day after day. I measured it, and I recall that, not having a tape measure, I had to do my best to get its girth with a folding pocket foot-rule, a difficult undertaking. I carefully made a record of the utterly useless measurements, and at once began to write a natural history of my own, on the strength of that seal. This, and subsequent natural histories, were written down in blank books in simplified spelling, wholly unpremeditated and unscientific. I had vague aspirations of in some way or another owning that seal, but they never got beyond the purely formless stage. I think, however, I did get the seal's skull, and with two of my cousins promptly started what we ambitiously called the "Roosevelt Museum of Natural History."[60]

His next major thesis was entitled "The Foregoing Ant." According to Corinne, it was inspired by a passing reference in Wood's *Natural History.* Teedie assumed that the adjective was physiological, perhaps referring to the ant's gait, and his subsequent essay on the subject was read aloud to a circle of mystified adults.[61]

Unfortunately for posterity, neither the Broadway Seal nor the Foregoing Ant appear in surviving records of Teedie's museum. There exists, however, a rather more learned opus, entitled "Natural History on Insects," which dates from his ninth year. "All the insects that I write about in this book," the author declares, "inhabbit North America. Now and then a friend has told me something about them but mostly I have gained their habbits from ofserv-a-tion." He discusses and illustrates various species of ants, spiders, lady-bugs, fireflies, horned "beetlles," and dragonflies. Then, with a fine disregard for the limitations of his title, he moves on to the study of hawks, minnows, and crayfish. The latter rather defeats his childish powers of description: "Look at a lobster," he suggests, "and you have its form."[62]

Apart from such lapses, Teedie's "ofserv-a-tion" is amazingly keen. A paragraph on the tree-spider, for example, notes that it is "grey spoted with black," and lives "in communitys of about 20" under patches of loosened bark; its web "looks exactly like some cotten on the top but if you take that off you will see several small little webs, all in a 'gumble' as we children yoused to call it, each having several little occupants." Even more remarkable, for a nine-year-old boy, is the methodical arrangement of classifications, and the patient indexing.

Teedie's interest in all "curiosities and living things" became something of a trial to his elders. Meeting Mrs. Hamilton Fish on a streetcar, he absentmindedly lifted his hat, whereupon several frogs leaped out of it, to the dismay of fellow passengers. Houseguests at No. 28 learned to sit on sofas warily, and to check their water-pitchers for snakes before pouring. When Mittie, in great disgust, threw out a litter of field-mice, her son loudly bemoaned "the loss to Science—the loss to Science."[63]

From time to time, members of the domestic staff threatened to give notice. A protest by a chambermaid forced Teedie to move the Roosevelt Museum of Natural History out of his bedroom and into the back hall upstairs. "How can I do the laundry," complained the washerwoman, "with a snapping turtle tied to the legs of the sink?" Finally, when a noxious odor permeated the entire house, even the good-natured cook issued her ultimatum: "Either I leave or the woodchuck does." Teedie had killed a fine specimen for anatomical study and ordered her to boil the animal, fur and all, for twenty-four hours.[64]

ON 28 APRIL 1868, Teedie wrote a letter to Mittie, who was paying a visit to Savannah along with Theodore Senior and Corinne. It is the earliest of his 150,000 letters to survive, yet there glitters, in virtually every sentence, a facet of his mature personality.

> *My Dear Mamma* I have just received your letter! What an excitement. What long letters you do write. I don't see how you can write them. My mouth opened wide with astonish when I heard how many flowers were sent in to you. I could revel in the buggie ones. I jumped with delight when I found you heard the mocking-bird, get some of its feathers if you

can. Thank Johnny for the feathers of the soldier's cap, give him my love also. We cried when you wrote about Grand-Mamma. Give my love to the good-natured (to use your own expresion) handsome lion, Conie, Johnny, Maud and Aunt Lucy. I am sorry the trees have been cut down. Aunt Annie, Edith, and Ellie send their love to you and all I sent mine to . . . In the letter you write me tell me how many curiosities and living things you have got for me. I miss Conie very much. I wish I were with you and Johnny for I could hunt for myself . . . *Yours loveingly.*

THEODORE ROOSEVELT

P.S. I liked your peas so much that I ate half of them.[65]

Promptness, excitability, warmth, histrionics, love of plants and animals, physical vitality, "dee-light," sensitivity to birdsong, fascination with military display, humor, family closeness, the conservationist, the natural historian, the hunter—all are here. Teedie mentions, *passim,* the name of his future wife, and there is a hint of the two-hundred-pound President in the embarrassed postscript. Even the large, childish handwriting is touchingly similar to that of the dying Colonel Roosevelt, scrawling his last memorandum half a century later.

DURING THE SUMMER of 1868, about the same time he was completing his "Natural History on Insects," Teedie began to keep a diary.[66] The Roosevelts were then living in their new country place at Barrytown-on-Hudson, New York, and the little volume is full of the joys of bird-nesting, swimming, hiking, and long rides through grass "up to the ponys head." Apart from one reference to "an attack of the Asmer" on 10 August, the diary reads like that of any normal nine-year-old. Yet Teedie's health was as bad as ever: he was never well for more than ten days at a time. So accustomed was he, by now, to recurrences of illness that he rarely bothered to record them.

Theodore Senior grew seriously worried as the summer went by, and Teedie, for all his hyperactivity, remained pasty-faced and skeletal. The other children were blooming in comparison—but only with their brother. Bamie's crippled spine, Elliott's tendency to rushes of blood in the head, and little Corinne's own asthma tormented all his protective feelings. Yet another cause for alarm was the strange decline of Mittie Roosevelt.

A certain wistfulness, combined with increasing fragility and indolence, had begun to affect this exquisite woman since the end of the Civil War. It was as if Sherman's looting of her ancestral home, and the simultaneous death of her mother, not to mention the banishment overseas of her two Secessionist brothers,[67] had cut the Southern lifelines that hitherto sustained her. Gradually she sank into a kind of gentle invalidism which was something not unlike a second childhood. Always helpless and fluttery, she grew incapable of running the house, and was treated by her children as one of its prettier ornaments—a doll in the parlor, whom they could pet when they chose. "Sweet little china Dresden mother," Elliott used to call her affectionately. Coaches summoned to take her for her three o'clock drive would creak up and down Twentieth Street for hours while Mittie made flustered attempts to get ready. Often as not she would never emerge at all.[68] Although she remained beautiful, charming, and witty, Theodore Senior was saddened to see yet another blossom wilt upon his boughs.

When Mittie herself suggested in the winter of 1868–69 that a trip to Europe might do the whole family good, he welcomed the idea. His business was prospering, and after the hard grind of his war work, a Grand Tour of Europe sounded like a welcome diversion. It would be of immense educational value to the children, none of whom had yet received outside schooling. With characteristic enthusiasm, Theodore Senior sat down and drafted an itinerary that must have given his wife pause, for it covered nine countries and a whole year of traveling time. The children reacted with even more dismay. They had been hoping to return to the Hudson Valley that summer. Theodore Senior turned a deaf ear to their pleas, and went ahead with the bookings. On 12 May 1869, he escorted his tearful brood aboard the paddle-steamer *Scotia*, bound for Liverpool.[69]

Although Teedie later declared that he "cordially hated" the Roosevelt Grand Tour, he recorded it at great length in his diaries. During all the 377 days he was away from home, he did not miss a single entry, with the exception of one stormy week on the return crossing. The spelling, in these cheap, battered notebooks, is that of a child, but the density of remembered detail would be extraordinary even in an adult. Some entries read like miniature museum catalogs. Evidently the cornucopia of Europe awakened his faculty of near-total recall.

The diaries begin on an enigmatic note. "It was verry hard parting from our friend," Teedie writes, confessing that he "cried a great deal." This mysterious person was almost certainly a seven-year-old girl named Edith Carow. For as far back as he could remember, quiet, steady-eyed little "Edie" had been his most intimate acquaintance outside the family circle. Indeed, it seemed at times that she lived within it, for her father's house was on Union Square, only a few blocks away from 28 East Twentieth Street, and she had come to regard the latter as her second home. Edith and Corinne had been born within weeks of each other, and were wheeled side by side in their baby carriages. When Aunt Annie began giving lessons to the younger Roosevelts, it was natural that Edith should be included. Although she was, in these early years, more attached to Corinne than anyone else, it was plain that a special relationship was developing between herself and Teedie. He was permitted to play "house" with her, whereas Elliott was not. They shared a passionate interest in books, and their characters complemented each other. Where he was ardent and impulsive, feverish in his enthusiasms, she was sensitive and cautious, a cooling breeze across his sometimes overheated landscape.[70]

Seasickness and homesickness were added to Teedie's normal quota of ills, as the *Scotia* thrashed her way slowly across the Atlantic. He remained aloof from the deck-games of other children on board, burying himself in books, or else gazing vaguely at gulls and passing ships, "a tall, thin lad," someone remembered, "with bright eyes and legs like pipe-stems."[71] During the latter part of the voyage he made friends with a learned gentleman from the West

Indies, and had long conversations with him on the subject of natural history. Late on the evening of 21 May the ship docked at Liverpool, and Teedie set foot in "Briten" for the first time.[72]

WHILE MITTIE PLUNGED INTO an ecstatic, ten-day reunion with her exiled brothers, the younger Roosevelts "jumped and romped" on the chilly English seashore. Theodore Senior, however, had not brought them abroad to play, and began to expose them to the bewildering variety of English history and architecture. Trips were made to the Duke of Devonshire's country seat at Chatsworth, and "Haden hall an old feudeul castle of the 11th century," where Teedie admired "the Leathern jacket in which a lord received his death wound." In early June they proceeded north via "furnace abby" and the Lake District to "Edinbourg." Despite the inevitable Scottish rain Teedie overcame an attack of asthma and greatly enjoyed visits to Walter Scott's mansion at Abbotsford, "the tweed (quite a decent brook)," and "Loch Lomend . . . where the poem 'Lady of the lake' was lade." The pace of sight-seeing intensified as the Roosevelts swung south via York to Oxford, by which time the young diarist had developed a formidable headache. "I have a tendency to headache," he noted in London five days later, apparently still suffering. He was "a little disappointed" at the range of fauna in the Zoological Gardens, but had fun playing in "hide park" and visiting "Westnubster abby." The "rare and beautiful specimens" in the British Museum fascinated him, as did the "christal palace" with its "imitations of egyptian, roman, greek etc. marbles," and the ancient Tower of London, where "I put my head on the block where so many had been beheaded." During this stay a doctor examined him and pronounced his lungs perfect. Teedie was immediately stricken with asthma so violent he had to be rushed to Hastings for three days of sea air.[73]

On 13 July the Roosevelts sailed down the Thames, "a verry, verry small river or a large creek," and crossed the English Channel to Antwerp. Teedie prided himself on being the last of his family to vomit, and "the first one that got on the continent." From Antwerp they began a leisurely tour of the Netherlands and northern Germany. While traveling up the Rhine, Teedie began to wheeze and cough: a rainy visit to Strasbourg made him "verry sick" and he spent the next morning in bed. In Switzerland he suffered alternate attacks of gastroenteritis, toothache, and asthma, yet showed amazing bursts of energy in between. He climbed an eight-thousand-foot mountain at Chamonix, scorning mules, walked nineteen miles across "the tatenwar" (La Tête Noire), thirteen miles around Visp, twenty miles through the Grimsel Pass, and ascended alone the steep hill of Wallenstein. "It is 3—and 3 miles back, and I went and came in 1 hour." Such incredible statistics might be dismissed as boyish exaggeration were it not for the fact that Theodore Senior frequently accompanied him and confirmed them. In his diaries, as in all his later writings, Teedie was a scrupulously accurate reporter.

Despite recurring moments when the boy was "verry verry home sick," he continued to stare seriously at everything around him, sketching the plan of a grotto in Geneva, comparing live Swiss chamois with the carved ones at home in East Twentieth Street, exploring the "gloomey dungeons" of Chillon Castle, researching everything he saw in guidebooks and geographies. In lighter moments he clowned raucously with Elliott and Corinne, gorged himself on fresh berries and cream, and waged war upon "several cross chambermaids."

On 9 September, Teedie and his father hiked over the crest of the Splügen Pass. The other Roosevelts followed in a carriage. "Soft balmy Italy of the poets," Teedie noted sarcastically, "is cold dreary smelly." However the "sceneerry" around "lake Coma" soon improved his attitude, and after a row across the lake "by the light of a golden moon" he himself began to wax poetical. "I strayed from the rest and now in the wood around the villa Colata . . . with no sound save the waterfall and the Italian breeze on my cheek, I all alone am writing my Journal."

The moon changed to "silver" over Lake Lugano, and Isola Bella, on Lake Maggiore, was "the most beautiful creation of mans, with lemons cactuses camphor trees lemons bamboos sugar cane in sight of snow white alps." Here a particularly vicious attack of asthma struck. "It came to a point," wrote Mittie to her sister, "where he had to sit up in bed to breathe. After taking a strong cup of black coffee the spasmodic part of the attack ceased and he slept . . . Had the coffee not taken effect he would have gone on struggling through the night, and been a complete wreck the next morning, in which condition you have so often seen him."[74]

Teedie's dormant literary talents were stimulated afresh by Venice. "We saw the moonlight on the water and I contrasted it with the black gondola's darting about like water goblins." Although the weather here was clear and dry, he became so "dreadfully ill" that on 20 September he collapsed in total exhaustion.

During the next two weeks his attacks of diarrhea and asthma were incessant. One night on the Austrian border, "I sat up for 4 successive hours and Papa made me smoke a cigar." This unorthodox remedy seems to have had temporary effect, for the following day he climbed the Adelsberg for two hours "in the broiling sun." But the long train trip to Vienna laid him low yet again. Theodore Senior, whose compassion for his son was tempered by an aggressive attitude to illness, refused to mollycoddle him. After only a day in bed Teedie was whisked off to the Treasury to see "the crowns of Charlamang and Roudolph the 2d rudly carved jewels and pearls yellow with age contrasting strangly with the polished pearls and sparkling gems of moddern times. Then Father and I went to a Natural history museum. It is a most interesting place, but I was hurried."

Throughout Teedie's diaries the masterful, all-capable figure of Theodore Senior strides with giant steps, tirelessly encouraging, comforting, supervising, and protecting his family. Handsome and resplendent in evening dress, he escorts Mittie and Bamie to the Vienna Opera. He leaps like a tiger upon a monk who shoves Teedie aside, and hurls him bodily into the crowd. Determined to picnic in an attractive orange grove, he overcomes the hostility of peasants and proprietor, and ends up gaily entertaining all comers to chicken, champagne, and honey. Only once, in the entire twelvemonth tour, does he lose patience with his children, and angrily call them "bothers." Even this mild imprecation is enough to make Teedie miserable for a whole evening.

As autumn settled over the Alps, the frequency of Teedie's

asthma attacks increased until they were rarely more than three days apart.[75] His diaries become poignant reading. In Salzburg, "I had a nightmare dreaming that the devil was carrying me away and have collerer morbos." In Munich, "I was verry sick . . . Mama was so kind telling me storrys and rubing me with her delicate fingers." In Dresden somebody more vigorous massaged his chest until "the blood came out." Yet the touring and sightseeing relentlessly continued. Teedie calculated that the Roosevelt Grand Tour was not yet half over, and he was overcome by a paroxysm of homesickness.

> October 17th Sunday [Dresden] I am by the fire with not another light but it . . . It is now after 5. All was dark excep the fire. I lay by it and listened to the wind and thought of the times at home in the country when I lay by the fire with some hickory nuts until like the slave who
>
> *Again he is king by the banks of the niger*
> *Again he can hear the wild roar of the tiger*
>
> Again I was lying by the roaring fire (with the cold October wind shrieking outside) in the cheerful lighted room and I turned around half expecting to see it all again and stern reality forced itself upon me and I thought of the time that would come never, never, never.

His misery lasted through visits to Berlin and Cologne, where he noted gloomily that 27 October was "the first of my birthdays that it snowed on." However, the Roosevelts celebrated the occasion with their customary blend of warmth and formality, donning full evening dress for dinner and showering him with such splendid gifts that his mood noticeably improved.

Five days into his twelfth year, the child gives the first of several indications that the man is beginning to develop within him: "We went to a shoe makers [in Brussels] and I saw a girl . . . the most beautiful but ferocious girl I have ever seen in my life." Another, more emotional entry, written three weeks later in Paris, records that "Mama showed me the portrait of Eidieth Carow and her face stired up in me homesickness and longings for the past which will come again never, alack never."

TEEDIE REMAINED DEPRESSED and ill in Paris. A doctor was summoned to his bedside three times, and three times changed his medicine; but neither this nor frequent "russian baths" had any effect. When at the end of November the Roosevelts started south to winter on the Riviera, his melancholy spilled out in tears: "I cried for homesickness and a wish to get out of the land where friends (or as I think them enemies) who can not speak my language are forced on me."

But the inexorable Theodore Senior pressed on down the Route Napoléon. On 6 December, Teedie was cheered by his first "decent" hill-climb in months, but his health was still a cause for concern: "I read till mama came in and then she lay down and I stroked her head and she felt my hands and nearly cried because they were feverish." As they proceeded east along the Riviera, his powers of observation revived. The diaries have vignettes of cruelty to animals, the military might of Monaco ("a few gendarmes and some dismounted cannon"), primitive house paintings, and a "verry romantic" sunset on the Italian border.

At Finale the Roosevelts amused themselves in jingoistic fashion with a crowd of Italian beggars:

> We hired one to keep off the rest. Then came some more fun. Papa bought two baskets of doughey cakes. A great crowd of boys girls and women. We tossed the cakes to them and we fed them like chickens with small pieces of cake and like chickens they ate it. Mr Stevens [a fellow traveler] kept guard with a whip with which he pretended to whip a small boy. We made them open their mouths and tossed cake into it. For a "Coup de Grace" we threw a lot of them in a place and a writhing heap of human beings . . . We made the crowds . . . give us three cheers for U.S.A. before we gave them cakes.[76]

Unfazed by such alarming evidence of Italian poverty, Teedie once again rhapsodized over the beauties of the Mediterranean landscape. His diary entries double or triple in length, to as much as a thousand words a day.

Moving leisurely down the Ligurian coast via Genoa and "Piza," the Roosevelt family arrived in Rome in time for Christmas. "Hip! hip! hurrah!!!!" rejoiced Teedie. "The presents passed our upmost expectations."[77] Rome, on the other hand, did not: his first impression of it, through rainy windows, was a dirty jumble of old buildings. But when the weather improved he explored the city and its environs enthusiastically, from the depths of the Catacombs to the heights of "rockety papa" (Rocca di Papa).

He showed similar conscientiousness on an excursion to Naples and Pompeii. The temptingly precipitous and icy slopes of Vesuvius enabled him to work off his superabundant energy on the last day of 1869. Reaching the summit long before other members of the family, Teedie happily inhaled sulfur fumes until his bronchii rebelled, and threw pebbles into the lava, careless of the turbulence that spewed them back into his face.

New Year's Day 1870 came and went, and, from the children's point of view, the worst part of the Grand Tour was over. Although several months of winter in Europe yet remained, spring was on its way, and the longed-for recrossing of the Atlantic no longer wavered in the impossible distance, like a mirage. For six weeks in Rome, while the elder Roosevelts socialized with fashionable American expatriates, they became ball-playing regulars on Pincian Hill.

Here, one glistening January day, "suddenly there came a stir—an unexpected excitement seemed everywhere." Gorgeously robed *sampetrini* approached, carrying an august Personage in a sedan-chair. Teedie, conscious of his Dutch Reformed heritage, hissed frantically that "he didn't believe in popes—that no real American would." As Corinne later recalled:

> The Pope . . . his benign face framed in white hair and the close cap which he wore, caught sight of the group of eager little children craning their necks to see him pass; and he

> smiled and put out one fragile, delicate hand toward us, and, lo! the late scoffer who, in spite of the ardent Americanism that burned in his eleven-year-old soul, had as much reverence as militant patriotism in his nature, fell upon his knees and kissed the delicate hand, which for a brief moment was laid upon his fair curly hair.[78]

Teedie, recording the incident in his diary that night, was much less sentimental. "We saw the Pope and we walked along and he extended his hand to me and I kissed it!! hem!! hem!!"

The rest of his stay in Rome was happy, educational, and comparatively free from illness. So were two subsequent weeks spent touring the galleries of Florence, Bologna, and Turin. Teedie revealed a precocious sensitivity to art, commenting in his diary on as many as fifty-seven items in a single day.[79] He was particularly moved by "the most beautiful of all beautiful pictures St. Cecelia listingning to the heavenly music."

On 10 March 1870, Theodore Senior took his family back to Paris for seven more weeks of sight-seeing. Damp and snowy weather aggravated Teedie's asthma, necessitating quick excursions out of town to Fontainebleau. As spring came in, the air warmed and sweetened, and he enjoyed "the happiest Easter I ever spent." At the end of April, Bamie, who was to stay in France for a year of finishing school, bade everybody a tearful good-bye.[80]

Recrossing the Channel for a final fortnight in England, the Roosevelts embarked from Liverpool on 14 May in a calm shower of rain. As they drew near to America, a joyous escort of whales sprayed Teedie with water. Sandy Hook drifted into view; the spires of Manhattan grew tall against the sky, dipped, swayed, and came to rest. "New York!!! Hip! Hurrah! What a bustle we had geting off."

CHAPTER 2

The Mind, But Not the Body

Then, with a smile of joy defiant
On his beardless lip,
Scaled he, light and self-reliant,
Eric's dragon-ship.

TEEDIE'S FIRST ADOLESCENT STIRRINGS, stimulated by the overwhelming impact of Europe, relapsed into dormancy in the familiar surroundings of New York City and the Hudson Valley. He was once again, through the long summer and fall of 1870, a bookish, bug-loving boy. His diary entries dwindle to single portmanteau sentences:

July 16 I hunted for birds nests and in the Afternoon went swimming and got caught in the rain.
July 17 Went to Sunday school wrote a letter and played about.
July 18 Hunted for birds nests and went over to the Harraymans for tea and had a nice time.[1]

He does not even bother to record the arrival, one squally September evening, of a very important guest. "Mittie," said Theodore Senior, as the family clustered around, "I want to present to you a young man who in the future, I believe, will make his name

"My father was the best man I ever knew."

Theodore Roosevelt Senior, aged about forty-five.

well-known in the United States. This is Mr. John Hay, and I wish the children to shake hands with him."[2] Teedie obeyed, and for a moment looked gravely into the eyes of his future Secretary of State.

The boy's only sign of physical development, as his twelfth birthday approached, was a rapid increase in height unaccompanied by any muscular filling out. His resemblance to a stork was accentuated by a habit of reading on one leg, while supporting a book on the jibbed thigh of the other. His health was, if anything, worse than ever: at least three times during the summer Theodore Senior had to take him across state for changes of air.[3] When the Roosevelts returned to East Twentieth Street in late September, Teedie was subjected to a thorough medical examination.

Dr. A. D. Rockwell found him "a bright, precocious boy . . . by no means robust," and recommended "plenty of fresh air and exercise."[4] This advice seemed superfluous (for Teedie was, on his good days, almost frenziedly active out-of-doors) but it related in particular to the development of his chest. The lungs crammed into that narrow cavity were themselves crammed with asthma, and the mere act of breathing placed a strain on his heart. Theodore Senior pondered Rockwell's diagnosis, and decided the time had come to present a major challenge to his son. Accordingly he sent for him.

"THEODORE," THE BIG MAN SAID, eschewing boyish nicknames, "you have the mind but you have not the body, and without the help of the body the mind cannot go as far as it should. You must *make* your body. It is hard drudgery to make one's body, but I know you will do it."

Mittie, who was an eyewitness, reported that the boy's reaction was the half-grin, half-snarl which later became world-famous. Jerking his head back, he replied through clenched teeth: "I'll make my body."[5]

The promise, once made, was adhered to with bulldog tenacity. Teedie began to make daily visits to Wood's Gymnasium, where he swung chest-weights with such energy that his mother wondered aloud "how many horse-power he was expending." At home, Theodore Senior fitted out the second-floor piazza with an arsenal of athletic equipment, and encouraged Teedie to spend all his spare time out there exercising.[6]

The piazza was a pleasant place for a city boy to work out. It faced south across the enormous Goelet garden, whence floated a constant supply of plant-purified air. Since the row of houses opposite, on the far side of Nineteenth Street, was low, sunshine poured down all day, all year round. Here, to the caw of peacocks and magpies, and the occasional moo of a cow, Teedie pushed and pulled and stretched and swung, working himself into the rhythmic trance of the true body-builder. "For many years," wrote Corinne afterward, "one of my most vivid recollections is seeing him between horizontal bars, widening his chest by regular, monotonous motion—drudgery indeed."[7]

Drudgery it may have seemed to the little girl, but to a boy of such hyperactive temperament as Teedie, the work was both a release and a pleasure. He exercised throughout the winter and spring of 1870–71. Fiber by fiber, his muscles tautened, while the skinny chest expanded by degrees perceptible only to himself. But the overall results were dramatic.[8] There is not a single mention of illness in his diary throughout August of 1871—his longest spell of health in years.

Glorying in his newfound strength, he plunges into the depths of icy rapids, and clambers to the heights of seven mountains (one of them twice on the same day). Along with this physical exuberance, he develops a more studious interest in nature. Observed species are now identified by their full zoological names. Paddling across Lake Regis, Teedie discovers flocks of *Aythya americana* and *Colymbus torquatus*. A *beryle alcyon* dives for fish and a *Putorious vison* swims across his path, while coveys of *Orytx virginianus* and *Bonasa umbellus* rise from the banks on either side. Riding behind a stagecoach to Au Sable Forks, he jumps off whenever he sees "a particularly beautiful lichen or moss," and collects several hundred specimens for preservation in the Roosevelt Museum of Natural History.[9]

TEEDIE'S THIRTEENTH WINTER and spring were much the same as his twelfth, except that the weights on the chest machine were heavier and his hours on the piazza longer. Meanwhile he continued to read voraciously. A friend of the period remembered him as "the most studious little brute I ever knew in my life."[10] Private tutors coached him in English, French, German, and Latin (there were rumors of another "terrible trip" to Europe), and a white-haired old gentleman who had been an associate of the great Audubon gave him lessons in taxidermy.[11] This smelly subject quickly became his major passion, restrained only by the supply of available carcasses. Then, in the summer of 1872, Teedie acquired his first gun.

It was, in his later description, "a breech-loading, pin-fire double-hyphen barrel of French manufacture . . . an excellent gun for a clumsy and often absent-minded boy. There was no spring to open it, and if the mechanism became rusty it could be opened with a brick without serious damage. When the cartridges stuck they could be removed in the same fashion. If they were loaded, however, the result was not always happy, and I tattooed myself with partially unburned grains of powder more than once."[12]

Although Teedie blazed away determinedly at the fauna of the Lower Hudson Valley (the Roosevelts had taken a summer house at Dobbs Ferry), he found, to his bewilderment, that he could not hit anything. Even more puzzling was the fact that his friends, using the same gun, seemed to be able to bag the invisible: they fired into the blue blur of the sky, or the green blur of the trees, whereupon specimens mysteriously dropped out of nowhere. The truth was slow to dawn on him:

> One day they read aloud an advertisement in huge letters on a distant billboard, and I then realized that something was the matter, for not only was I unable to read the sign, but I could not even see the letters. I spoke of this to my father, and soon afterwards got my first pair of spectacles, which literally opened an entirely new world to me. I had no idea how beautiful the world was until I got those spectacles . . . while much of my clumsiness and awkwardness was doubtless due to general characteristics, a good deal of it was due to the fact that I could not see, and yet was wholly ignorant that I was not seeing.[13]

It is impossible to overestimate the importance of this event on the boy's maturing sensibilities. Through the miraculous little windows that now gripped his nose, the world leaped into pristine focus, disclosing an infinity of detail, of color, of nuance, and of movement just when the screen of his mind was at its most receptive. One of the best features of his adult descriptive writing—an unsurpassed joy in things seen—dates back to this moment; while another—his abnormal sensitivity to sound—is surely the legacy of the myopic years that came before.[14]

Another revelatory experience occurred later that summer, and it was considerably less pleasant.

> Having an attack of asthma, I was sent off by myself to Moosehead Lake. On the stage-coach ride thither, I encountered a couple of other boys who were about my own age, but very much more competent and also much mischievous . . . They found that I was a foreordained and predestined victim, and industriously proceeded to make life miserable for me. The worst feature was that when I finally tried to fight them I discovered that either one singly could not only handle me with easy contempt, but handle me so as not to hurt me much and yet prevent my doing any damage whatever in return.[15]

The humiliation forced him to realize that his two years of body-building had achieved only token results. No matter how remarkable his progress might seem to himself, by the harsh standards of the world he was still a weakling. There and then he decided to join what he would later call "the fellowship of the doers." If he had exercised hard before, he must do so twice as hard now. He must also learn how to give and take punishment. "Accordingly, with my father's hearty approval, I started to learn to box."[16]

ON 16 OCTOBER 1872, the Roosevelts sailed to Liverpool on the first stage of another foreign tour—this time featuring Egypt and the Holy Land—with varied degrees of enthusiasm. Theodore

Senior was as usual full of cheery optimism. Having been appointed American commissioner to the Vienna Exposition the following spring, he looked forward to an enjoyable winter cruising the Nile and the Mediterranean. His lazy wife was quite content to recline on deck-chairs, as on sofas at home, or hammocks in the country. Bamie, already at seventeen the family's surrogate mother, clumped about arranging everything with a certain grim enjoyment. The two youngest Roosevelts dreaded another year away from their friends, but for a while the excitement of an ocean voyage muted their complaints. Teedie, for his part, took a serious, almost professorial view of the trip. As proprietor of the Roosevelt Museum, he was determined to treat his visit to the Nile as a scientific expedition and had already printed a quantity of pink labels for the identification of specimens. His new spectacles had focused his general interest in animals to an almost total obsession with birds. Hitherto his near sight had forced him to confine his observations to large, slow creatures that inhabited *terra firma*. Now he was able to record the ascent of hawks to ecstatic heights and sit for hours watching flocks of ibises settling on a distant island, until "the tops of trees would be whitened with immense multitudes perching on them."[17]

As Teedie turned fourteen, he blossomed into a grotesque flower of adolescence, offensive alike to eye, ear, and nostril. Mittie Roosevelt, fresh and crackling in her perpetual white silks and muslin, could hardly have contemplated him without despair. Apart from the owlish spectacles and snarling teeth, there was the overlong hair, its childish yellow darkening now to dirty blond; the bony wrists and ankles, which protruded every day a little farther from his carefully tailored suit; the fingers stained with ink and chemicals, the clumsy movements and too-quick reflexes. His voice had not so much broken as taken on a new undertone of harshness, while its shrill upper frequencies remained. Mittie described his laugh as a "sharp, ungreased squeak" which almost crushed her eardrums.[18] For much of the time he reeked of the laboratory: on days when he had been disemboweling as well as skinning his specimens, it was best to stand upwind of him.

Teedie alone seemed to be unaware of his eccentric appearance. "Pestered fearfully" by street-boys in Liverpool, he assumed it was because he was a Yankee, and was puzzled by a shopkeeper's refusal to sell him, on sight, a full pound of arsenic. "I was informed that I must bring a witness to prove that I was not going to commit murder, suicide or any such dreadfull thing, before I could have it!" he wrote in his new travel diary.[19] Presumably a witness was found, for within a couple of days he was skinning some snipe and partridge. All the way south, through England and Europe, Teedie continued his scientific labors.

Although he had a few words of praise for Continental scenery—the mossy roofs and distant windmills of Belgium, the "wild and picturesque" hills of Switzerland—his viewpoint was on the whole chauvinistic. Railroads, museums, even sanitation systems were unfavorably compared with those of America. Not until Egypt hove over the Mediterranean horizon, on 28 November 1872, did Teedie respond emotionally to his surroundings.

> How I gazed upon it! It was Egypt, the land of my dreams; Egypt the most ancient of all countries! A land that was old when Rome was bright, was old when Troy was taken! It was a sight to awaken a thousand thoughts, and it did.

His diary entries immediately become lengthy and enthusiastic. The descriptions of street life in Alexandria are as dense with visual detail and sound effects as film scenarios. Only in front of Pompey's Pillar did words fail him. "On seeing this stately remain of former glory, I *felt* a great deal but I *said* nothing. You can not express yourself on such an occasion."

Passing through the Nile Delta en route to Cairo, Teedie munched sugarcane and gazed in rapture at a multitude of exotic species: humped, long-haired zebus, delicate waders, great flapping, shrieking zic-zacs, kites and vultures floating on spirals of hot air, water buffaloes wallowing in the chocolate mud. As soon as he arrived in the capital he bought an ornithological directory and began to study Egyptian birds, "whose habits I was able to watch quite well through my spectacles." From now on the pages of his diary seem to come alive with squawks and fluttering wings. Even when going the rounds of historic buildings, he searched every nook and cranny for birds, discovering swallows under the dome of Mahommet Ali's mosque, and "perfectly distinguishable" species of geese in an ancient mosaic at Boulag.

There is evidence that this obsession with feathered creatures was something of a trial to the more "normal" members of the family. "When he does come into the room, you always hear the words 'bird' and 'skin,'" little Corinne complained. "It certainly is great fun *for him*."[20] Even the sweet-tempered Elliott revolted against having to share a hotel room with a brother who stored entrails in the basin. Theodore Senior, while sympathetic, was too wise a father to discourage his son's scientific tendencies. The career of natural historian, to which Teedie was obviously headed, was a respectable one, if not as profitable as a partnership in Roosevelt and Son.[21]

No doubt his businessman's eye had already discerned that this absentminded and unorthodox youth would be a disaster in the world of commerce, while questions of health and physical frailty would disqualify him from the Army and Navy. He could see, too, that Teedie, for all his scholarly single-mindedness, had not retreated from life. The boy still exercised regularly, read a wide variety of books and poetry, and showed a healthy interest in people and places. Watching while he eagerly surveyed the Sahara from the summit of the Great Pyramid, or timed the contortions of a group of howling dervishes, or stared at a beautiful *houri* in a Cairo window, Theodore Senior could relax, knowing that his son was educating himself.

On 12 December 1872, the Roosevelts moved out of Cairo on the first stage of their cruise up the Nile. Their home for the next two months was to be a privately chartered *dahabeah*. "It is the nicest, cosiest, pleasantest little place you ever saw," Teedie wrote in delight. There were—to Elliott's relief—individual staterooms for each member of the family, plus a spacious dining salon and a panoramic, shaded deck. For all its modern trimmings, the vessel was little different from those that, four thousand years before, had carried Pharaohs from one palace to another.[22]

The *dahabeah*'s progress, as they pushed south against the current, was almost hypnotically slow. Often, when the weak wind died, the crew was obliged to wade ashore with tackle and haul the houseboat along. None of the Roosevelts seems to have minded this Oriental form of locomotion. They watched the bronzed backs of the *fellaheen* curving against the tow-rope, listened to their "curious crooning songs," and luxuriated in the brilliant sunshine, "with never a moment's rain." Mittie in particular enjoyed herself. Traveling at speeds of two to three miles an hour exactly suited her temperament; she was also flattered by the attentions of four young Harvard men, who had chartered another *dahabeah* and were sailing upriver in convoy. Frequent stops enabled the children to explore riverside ruins and native villages.[23]

THE FIRST DAY ON THE NILE was a momentous one for Teedie. He coordinated the lenses of his crooked spectacles, and the sights of his battered rifle, well enough to bag a small warbler. It was "the first bird I ever shot and I was proportionately delighted." Throughout the twelve-hundred-mile trip to Aswân and back, Teedie ecstatically watched and listened to birds on the wing, and then as ecstatically killed them—a total, according to his own vague estimate, of "between one and two hundred."[24]

On Christmas Day his father presented him with a double-barreled breech-loading shotgun, and the boy's delight knew no bounds. "He is a most enthusiastic sportsman," wrote Theodore Senior, "and has infused some of his spirit into me. Yesterday I walked the bogs with him at the risk of sinking hopelessly and helplessly, for hours . . . but I felt that I must keep up with Teedie."[25]

No matter how sluggish the pace of the *dahabeah,* he managed to keep busy all day long. After breakfast he joined his younger brother and sister for two hours of lessons with Bamie. She discovered that Teedie knew a great deal more than she did on most subjects. Later, "he would put on a large pair of spectacles and swing his gun over his shoulder and start on whatever small donkey was provided at the place we had stopped, and ruthlessly lope after whatever object he had in view, the donkey almost invariably crowding between any other two who might be riding together." His habit, during these lopes, of allowing the loaded gun to bump and bounce about freely aroused considerable nervousness among his fellow hunters.

Throughout the broiling afternoons, Corinne recalled, he would sit under the canopy on deck "surrounded by the brown-faced and curious sailors . . . and skin and stuff the products of his sport."[26] At sunset, when breezes cooled the desert, he would join the family in tours of the stupendous ruins that regularly drifted into view.

One such expedition, early in the New Year of 1873, shattered him.

> In the evening we visited Harnak [sic] by moonlight. It was not beautiful only, it was grand, magnificent, and awe-inspiring. It seemed to take me back thousands of years, to the time of the Pharohs and to inspire thought which can never be spoken, a glimpse of the ineffable, of the unutterable. . . .[27]

With adolescent determination not to waste good purple prose, he repeated this entire passage, complete with ineffables and unutterables, in a letter to Aunt Annie two weeks later. Rather more characteristic of his mature humor is a postscript on Egyptian rural fashions: "I may as well mention that the dress of the inhabitants up to ten years of age is—nothing. After that they put on a shirt descended from some remote ancestor and never take it off until the day of their death."[28]

The Roosevelts enjoyed their southward cruise so much that they were tempted, upon reaching the First Aswân Cataract, to continue on into the heartland of North Africa.[29] But time was running out for Commissioner Roosevelt: he still had to escort his family through Palestine, Syria, Turkey, and Greece, before reporting for duty on 1 May at the Vienna Exposition. Reluctantly, he gave the order to turn downstream.

SIX DAYS LATER, after one of those sudden changes of pace and scene in which Theodore Senior delighted, the Roosevelts found themselves cantering on hired horses across the green fields of Palestine. They were accompanied on this leg of their Grand Tour by Nathaniel Thayer and August Jay, two of the young Harvard men they had met on the Nile. A pleased sense of adventure hung over the little party. Ahead of them lay a month's exploration of the Levant, most of it on horseback. Tonight would be spent in a monastery, and most of the next few days in a Jerusalem hotel; but after that they planned to live like nomads, camping out in the wilderness.[30]

Toward sunset the party arrived at its destination, the Convent of Ramle, about fifteen miles inland from Jaffa. Theodore Senior had made reservations here, but the monks took one look at his women and curtly announced there was "no room." This was not the sort of Biblical parallel he was looking for in the Holy Land, and he reacted with his usual aggressiveness. "A long talk ensued," Teedie reported. "At last the monks said that they had rooms for the gentlemen but that ladies could not go inside the inner walls . . . this difficulty was also overcome in time."[31]

A minor incident, perhaps, yet it haunts the imagination. Six tired women and children, two bewildered students; a gate, a darkening landscape, scowling bearded faces, and—dominating the whole scene—one determined man. Time and again Teedie was convinced, by experiences like this, that his father was all-powerful and irresistible; that forceful talk, combined with personal charm, would vanquish any opposition.

Riding on eastward the next day, Teedie began to get the feel of his horse. "He has some Arab blood in him, and is very swift, pretty, and spirited." After so many summers spent on the placid back of an American pony, it was thrilling to crouch over this lean body as it drummed tirelessly across the plain. Mr. Jay was challenged to a race and beaten. In great good humor, Teedie galloped up to a ridge of hills, and was suddenly confronted with Jerusalem. "Just what I expected it to be," he decided, "except that it was remarkably small."[32]

Apart from a single expression of "awe" on Calvary, Teedie's account of his travels through Palestine and Syria is free of conventional piety. He bathed irreverently in the Jordan ("what we should call a small creek in America"), noted that bribery alone gained access to the birthplace of Christ, and "killed two very pretty little finches" in the vicinity of Abraham's Oak. His pantheistic soul seems to have been stirred more by the bird-haunted glades around Jericho, the desolate grandeur of the Moab escarpment, and the ruins of Baalbek. "They gave me the same feeling as to contemplate the mighty temples of Thebes." Other, more primitive emotions surged when he came across a pair of jackals outside Damascus:

> I had just given the gun to Bootross [the under-dragoman], while I arranged my bridle when the jackals came in sight and he was off like a flash while I followed, shouting for my gun. He did not hear me and kept on. Bootross was on bad ground and could not get near the beasts. They separated, and I went after the largest, thinking to ride over him and then kill him with a club. On we went over hills, and through gulleys, where none but a Syrian horse could go. I gained rapidly on him and was within a few yards of him when he leaped over a cliff some fifteen feet high, and while I made a detour around he got in among some rocky hills where I could not get at him. I killed a large vulture afterwards.[33]

Apart from a cat he had shot near Jaffa "in mistake for a rabbit," this was his first attempt to hunt animals for sport, rather than science.

Toward the end of the Roosevelts' Levantine wanderings, Teedie recorded his first "bad attack of Asthma and Cholera Morbus" since leaving America five months previously. It was brought on by a freezing night in the mountains of Lebanon, and no doubt served to remind him that his battle for health was still not won. The clear dry air of the desert, and a diet of yogurt and salads, had given him a period of easy breathing and untroubled digestion; but now, as the prospect of "returning to civilization" loomed nearer, he knew he would have to take up the fight again.

He was "very seasick" during a short cruise to Greece (whose ruins did not impress him), "very sick" with colic in Constantinople, "very seasick" in the Black Sea, and "had the asthma" again while sailing up the Danube. By the time the Roosevelts arrived in Vienna on 19 April 1873, he was plainly depressed. Boredom weighed down heavily as his father plunged into preparations for the opening of the exposition, and his mother fussed over Bamie's European debut. "I bought a black cock and used up all my arsenic on him," wrote Teedie on 28 April, and on 11 May: "the last few weeks have been spent in the most dreary monotony. If I stayed here much longer I should spend all my money on books and birds *pour passer le temps.*"

But his parents had arranged a better way for him to pass his time. "At 10 P.M. on the 14th we two boys (with Father) left for Dresden, where we are to stay in a German Family for the summer."

It was Theodore Senior's typically bold intention to scatter the Roosevelts across Europe while he himself completed his duties in Vienna and returned to America ahead of them. Perhaps he sensed that a period of mutual independence was necessary. Years of close-knit domesticity, and the enforced claustrophobia of travel, had brought them rather too much under his wing. The boys in particular would benefit. A certain coziness, verging on effeminacy, was discernible in their relations with their sisters and "little Motherling," and it was high time they were off on their own. He had accordingly arranged, through the American consul in Dresden, that they would study German and French there privately for five months. Mittie and Bamie would take the cures at Carlsbad and Frankensbad, and shop in London and Paris. Eleven-year-old Corinne was told that she, too, was going to Dresden, but would live apart from Teedie and Elliott, "so that the brothers and sister would not speak too much English together." Theodore Senior soon came to regret this unconsciously cruel decision, and allowed the heart-stricken little girl to move in with the boys.[34]

DRESDEN WAS, in that peaceful heyday of the German Empire, one of the loveliest cities in the world. Its domes and spires and bridges, tremblingly reflected in the River Elbe, gave way on the one hand to mellow clusters of medieval housing, and on the other to the spacious estates of the rich. Beyond lay hills striped with vines and crowned with lush forests. The city's museums and libraries were full of masterpieces by Michelangelo, Raphael, Dante, and Goethe; its Court Opera had known the batons of Weber and Wagner; its zoological and mineralogical collections were unsurpassed in Europe. A general atmosphere of elegance and culture justly earned it the title of "Florence on the Elbe."[35]

Here, "in the finer part" of town (Mittie was pleased to note), lived a genteel family named Minkwitz, who agreed to accommodate and instruct the young Roosevelts through the summer. Theodore Senior could not have found a more typically Teutonic household. *Herr Hofsrath* Minkwitz was a member of the German Reichstag, imperious and stiffly formal. His wife was pink, plump, and hearty, a fount of cream teas and cakes. Their three daughters were "gay, well-educated, and very temperamental," and their two sons were fierce-looking university students, much slashed about the face. Teedie was predictably fascinated by this macabre pair. "One, a famous swordsman, was called *Der Rothe Herzog* (the Red Duke), and the other was nicknamed *Herr Nasehorn* (Sir Rhinoceros) because the tip of his nose had been cut off in a duel and sewn on again."[36]

The Minkwitz family proved to be both hospitable and conscientious. No sooner had Theodore Senior left town than they plunged the boys into a rigorous teaching schedule. "The plan of the day is this," wrote Teedie at the end of the first month. "Halfpast six, up and breakfast which is through at halfpast seven, when we study till nine; repeat till half past twelve, have lunch, and study till three, when we take coffee and have till tea (at seven) free. After tea we study till ten, when we go to bed. It is harder than I have ever studied before in my life, but I like it for I really feel that I am making considerable progress."[37]

Fräulein Anna, the Minkwitzes' eldest daughter, was placed in charge of Teedie and Elliott, teaching them German grammar and arithmetic with "unwearied patience." The rest of the family made a point of speaking German at all times, whether their young guests could understand them or not. Teedie, it soon transpired, understood better than they realized. He caught several personal observations about the elder Roosevelts, and gleefully retailed them by mail.[38] Although he developed a fair measure of spoken fluency, he never was as easy with German prose as he was with French. However, he grew to love and enjoy German poetry almost as much as he did English. It was during this summer that he discovered the *Nibelungenlied*, whose *Sturm und Drang* evoked vague folk-memories of his own Germanic ancestors.[39]

At first, Teedie did not make a very agreeable impression upon his hosts. They looked askance at his long, wavy hair, his ink-spattered hands, and ill-fitting clothes, from whose greasy recesses he was at any moment likely to produce a dead bat.[40] "My scientific pursuits cause the family a good deal of consternation," he reported sadly. "My arsenic was confiscated and my mice thrown (with the tongs) out of the window."[41] Undeterred, he continued to flay, pickle, and stuff a variety of local fauna. Whenever he could get out in the country he "collected specimens industriously and enlivened the household with hedgehogs and other small beasts and reptiles which persisted in escaping from partially closed bureau drawers."[42] The skins of these unfortunate animals were allowed to festoon the exterior of the house, with fine disregard for aesthetic effect. One night, during a thunderstorm so violent the Minkwitzes hid between their mattresses, Teedie was heard to murmur in his sleep: "Oh, it is raining and my hedgehog will be all spoiled."[43]

During their free evenings and weekends, the young Roosevelts happily explored the parks and shops of Dresden, and attended frequent performances of Shakespeare at the German Theater. By coincidence, their cousins John and Maud Elliott were also living in the city,[44] and the five little Americans soon became a gang, meeting every Sunday afternoon. Lest Theodore Senior frown upon this socializing in English, they affected a cultural veneer, calling themselves the Dresden Literary American Club. Corinne spelled out their various creative roles: "I . . . keep up the poetry part, Elliott and Johnny the tragical, and Teedie the funny." Evidently the last was beginning to fancy himself as a wit: his contributions to the club's copybooks, which have been preserved, strive mightily to imitate Dickens and Lewis Carroll, but the best that can be said of them is that they are long.[45]

His letters of the same period, written with the promptness and regularity that would always characterize him as a correspondent, are full of adolescent drollery, and since they are more spontaneous than his formal efforts, can still be read with pleasure. One of them, addressed to his mother, describes himself suffering from a familiar boyhood ailment:

> Picture to yourself an antiquated woodchuck with his cheeks filled with nuts, his face well-oiled, his voice hoarse from gargling and a cloth resembling in texture and cleanliness a second-hand dustman's castoff stocking around his head; picture to yourself that, I say, and you will have a good like likeness of your hopeful offspring while suffering from an attack of the mumps.[46]

Mittie may have been amused by that, but references in the same letter to recurring asthma and violent headaches were not so funny. She informed her husband that she would visit Dresden in August, and "if I find Teedie still with asthmatic feelings, I think I shall take him with me to Salzburg."[47] Theodore Senior was reluctant to interrupt the boy's studies, but he had just received a "humorous" letter himself, and it made poignant reading.

> I am at present suffering under a very slight attack of Asthma; however it is but a small attack and except for the fact that I cannot speak, without blowing up like an abridged edition of a hippopotamus, it does not inconvenience me much. We are now studying hard . . . (Excuse my writing; the asthma has made my hand tremble awfully).[48]

When Mittie arrived in Dresden she found he was sitting up to sleep again, just as he had as a child; his wheeze was perpetual and his color was not good.[49] She promptly bundled him off to a resort in the Swiss mountains, where his breathing cleared, only to be replaced by an ugly cough. It took three weeks in the pine-scented air of the Alps before he was well enough to return to his studies.

He compensated for time lost to ill health by asking Fräulein Anna to speed up his lessons. "Of course I could not be left behind," Elliott reported, "so we are working harder than ever in our lives." Teedie was already showing the determination, and inspirational qualities, of a born leader. The Minkwitzes, who had gotten over their misgivings about him, openly admired his ability to concentrate on his books and his specimens to the exclusion of physical suffering. "I wonder what will become of my Teedie," pondered Mittie, as she prepared to depart again for England. "You need not be anxious about him," replied Fräulein Anna. "He will surely one day be a great professor, or who knows, he may become even President of the United States."[50]

Mittie was scornfully amused and unbelieving, but Fräulein Anna prided herself, in her old age, on being the first to predict Teedie's future glory.

RECROSSING THE ATLANTIC in late October, Teedie turned fifteen. He was now, if not yet a man, then at least a youth of more than ordinary experience of the world. He had traveled exhaustively in Britain, Europe, North Africa, and the Middle East, visiting their great cities time and again and actually living in some for long periods. He had plumbed the Catacombs and climbed the Great Pyramid, slept in a monastery and toured a harem. He had hunted jackals on horseback, kissed the Pope's hand, stared into a volcano, traced an ancient civilization to its source, and followed the wanderings of Jesus. He had been exposed to much of the world's greatest art and architecture, become conversant in two foreign languages, and felt as much at home in Arab bazaars as at a German *kaffeeklatsch,* or on the shaven lawns of an English estate.

As is frequently the case with globetrotting children, the very variety of Teedie's knowledge put him at something of a disadvantage when it came to the requirements of formal education. His ambition was to enter Harvard in the fall of 1876, which meant he would have to be ready, by the summer of 1875, to take a series of stiff entrance examinations. Strong as he might be in science, history, geography, and modern languages, he was weak in Latin, Greek, and mathematics. For the next one and a half years he would have to apply himself to these uncongenial subjects. Also he would have to complete the building of his body. He was still too frail to think of going to boarding school;[51] to go to Harvard he must be able to compete, physically and mentally, with the finest young men in America. Theodore Senior was confident, on the record of Teedie's past accomplishments, that this challenge would be met and overcome. He had already retained an eminent tutor, Arthur Hamilton Cutler, to take charge of the boy's education.[52]

Nothing is known of the Roosevelts' reunion on the docks of Lower Manhattan, save that it took place on 5 November 1873. We may assume that it was joyous, and that Teedie's mood, as their carriage clattered up Broadway, was expectant.

INSTEAD OF TURNING EAST toward the familiar row of brownstones on Twentieth Street, the horses continued north to the distant green of Central Park. Theodore Senior had spent the last five months supervising the construction of a mansion at 6 West Fifty-seventh Street, on the outer fringes of New York City. Now in the prime of life—he was forty-two, a millionaire twice over, a founder of the Metropolitan and Natural History museums, a patron of the New York Orthopedic Hospital and many charities—he wished to establish himself in appropriately grand surroundings. "It seems like another landmark reached on my life's journey," he wrote Mittie after his first night in the new house. "We have now probably one abiding-place for the rest of our days."[53]

The mansion was designed by Russell Sturgis, New York's most fashionable architect. Although its blocky facade conformed with the town-house style of the period, its interior furnishings were unusually rich, with heavy Persian rugs in every hall, sumptuous furniture, and much ornamental woodwork, including a hand-carved staircase. Knowing his wife's intolerance of anything artificial, Theodore Senior had even gone to the length of ripping out a "beautifully finished" plaster ceiling and replacing it with real oak beams. There was a large museum in the garret for Teedie, and a fully equipped gymnasium on the top floor for all the children.[54]

Teedie lost no time in plunging into his new studies. He took an instant liking to Mr. Cutler, who in turn registered approval of "the alert, vigorous character of young Roosevelt's mind." At first Elliott and West Roosevelt, a cousin, joined in the lessons, but Teedie, working from six to eight hours a day, soon left them behind, and they dropped out the following summer. From then on he studied entirely alone. "The young man never seemed to know what idleness was," wrote Cutler, long after his pupil had become President. "Every leisure moment would find the last novel, some English classic, or some abstruse book on Natural History in his hand." Although Teedie showed predictable excellence in science, history, German, and French, "he did not neglect mathematics or the dry ancient languages."[55] None of these, however, ever came easily to him. Throughout life he was to mourn his inability to read Virgil and Homer in the original.

He continued to study with such passion that Theodore Senior worried about the effect on his health.[56] Yet Teedie could not be restrained. Harvard, with its age-old aura of masculinity, intellectualism, and social success, floated ever nearer. He seemed to sense that, if the grail eluded his reach, he might not have the strength to grasp it again.

IN THE SPRING OF 1874 the Roosevelts moved, as was their custom, into the country. Theodore Senior's growing desire to put down roots, symbolized by the town house on West Fifty-seventh Street, led him this time in the direction of Oyster Bay, Long Island, where his father and brothers had long since established a family colony by the sea. Here he rented a gracious, plantation-style residence whose white columns and wide veranda no doubt appealed to Mittie's Southern taste.[57] The house, which was to become their permanent summer home, was called Tranquillity.

This name caused considerable amusement among friends and neighbors, for the Roosevelt way of life was anything but tranquil. From dawn to dusk both house and garden resounded with activity. At any hour of the day, including breakfast-time, Theodore Senior might call upon his children for off-the-cuff speeches or recitations, whereupon they would roaringly oblige. Amateur theatricals were always being rehearsed or performed, practical jokes plotted, and violent obstacle races improvised, at great danger to life and limb. Teedie and Elliott took delight in blackening each other's eyes in boxing matches, and collapsing, at unpredictable moments, into wrestling bouts which would continue until they were too exhausted to disentangle themselves. Invariably, these explosions of energy were followed by a general dash into the waters of Oyster Bay. "We were all absolutely amphibious," recalled Bamie, "and one of the old fishermen used to say he was pretty sure dem Roosevelts were web-footed, as no one ever knew when we were in or out of the water." In the evening they would read aloud from classics of history or literature, prompting discussions which would last far into the night. An extraordinary intimacy seemed to bind them together: they unashamedly hugged and kissed one another in spasms of mutual affection which Mittie called "melts."[58]

Since the children were all growing up rapidly, their individual personalities became more and more defined in this first summer at Tranquillity. Bamie was kindly, capable, and domineering, already at nineteen a poised hostess and socialite. Teedie, not yet sixteen, was still something of a scholarly recluse, yet, when not bent over his books and birds, high-spirited and unaffected. Fourteen-year-old Elliott was "the most lovable of the Roosevelts,"[59] a budding Apollo with an eye for the girls, and twelve-year-old Corinne, mercurial and gushy, had already begun her lifelong career as a composer of sentimental poetry.

Understandably, some of the more staid members of New York society considered the Roosevelts eccentric. Others, such as the teenage Fanny Smith, an early admirer of Teedie, found them a family "so rarely gifted that it seemed touched with the flame of 'divine fire.' "[60] With Edith Carow—ripening now into attractive adolescence—she became one of the many "regulars" who stayed at Oyster Bay every summer, and attended a weekly dance class at Dodsworth's Ballroom during the New York social season.

Although it may be presumed that Teedie was not insensitive to the appeal of the opposite sex in 1874 and 1875 (he makes approving references to girls in his letters, and admits that he enjoys dancing) his main interests continued to be study and exercise.[61] Not even his triumph in the preliminary Harvard entrance examinations of July 1875 ("Is it not splendid! . . . I passed in all the eight subjects I tried") was allowed to affect the inflexible program he had devised for himself. Four times a year he took a recess of a week to ten days, but even these breaks were doggedly purposeful: he would head for the lakes of the Adirondacks, or the woods of Long Island and New Jersey, collecting specimens and data and loping for miles, gun in hand, after wild game.[62] He described one such excursion to Edith's summer place at Sea Bright as being full of "ornithological enjoyment and reptilian rapture."[63]

His battle for health would appear to have been mostly won by the end of 1875. A sporting calendar has been preserved which records that from 21 August through 11 December he engaged his brother and several male cousins in a series of fifteen athletic contests—running, jumping, vaulting, wrestling, and boxing—and won fourteen of them, drawing the other one. On 1 November he noted his physical measurements:

Chest	34	in
Waist	26½	"
Thigh	20	"
Calf	12½	"
Neck	14½	"
Shoulders	41	"
Arms up	10½	"
" straight	9¾	"
Fore arm	10	"
Weight	124 lbs	
Height	5 ft 8 in[64]	

From this, and from the descriptions of others, we can conjure up the picture of a skinny, sunburned boy, just seventeen years old, with wiry muscles and a clean glow of health about him. Occasional attacks of asthma still came and went, but did not bother him unduly. He affected a pair of side-whiskers, which emphasized the hard thrust of his jaw; his mouth, during moments of thoughtfulness, clamped "like a band of blued steel."[65] At other times, when he allowed his natural humor to bubble over, it seemed to consist of nothing but perfectly white teeth.

Although he was not handsome, he was an attractive youngster, and Fanny Smith, for one, adored him unashamedly. She was convinced that he would become President, and said as much to her sister; but the prophecy seems to have been as skeptically received as

Fräulein Anna's, two years before. In particular Fanny worshiped his courage and "high-mindedness." Some of her friends found him priggish, but she felt only a sunny charm, which still warmed her when she was an old woman of eighty-nine:

> As I look back to those early days perhaps the characteristic that made at the time the strongest appeal was the unquenchable gaiety which seemed to emanate from his whole personality. This quality was a noticeable family trait, but in Theodore it seemed to reach its height and to invigorate the atmosphere about him to an unusual degree. As a young girl I remember dreading to sit next to him at any formal dinner lest I become so convulsed with laughter at his whispered sallies as to disgrace myself and be forced to leave the room.[66]

That Fanny herself was something of a rival to Edith Carow is implied in another passage from her memoirs. She describes a winter afternoon when Elliott, always more forthcoming than Teedie, paid her and her sisters a courtly visit. While chatting in a window seat she suddenly noticed Teedie, "looking blue with cold," walking rapidly up and down outside.

> "Why, Elliott, do you see Theodore out there? Why *doesn't* he come in!" I exclaimed.
>
> Elliott replied—and to this day the incident remains a mystery—that Theodore also had planned a visit but that suddenly he had been overcome by bashfulness and had decided to remain outside. We brought him in, where he became—as always—"the life and soul of the party." But the incident reminds me of the unexpected strain of self-depreciation which surprised one through the years.[67]

MUCH LESS IS KNOWN of the relationship between Edith and Teedie, except that it deepened steadily into intimacy during the summer of 1876, his last before entering college. Having completed the equivalent of three years of college preparation in less than two,[68] he could finally relax and allow his social personality to develop. He would gallantly row her across Oyster Bay, "in the hottest sun, over the roughest water, in the smallest boat,"[69] and Edith tolerated it with her usual inscrutable sweetness. They would read and recite endlessly to each other, Edith showing a decided preference for *belles-lettres*, Teedie for rhythmic poetry and warlike, heroic prose.

Years after, family tradition would hold that these two "had an understanding"[70] by the time he went up to Harvard in the fall, but if so, there is no formal record of it. Nevertheless, seeds had been sown, and some sort of future flowering seemed assured.

CHAPTER 3

The Man with the Morning in His Face

Trained for either camp or court,
Skilful in each manly sport,
Young and beautiful and tall;
Art of warfare, craft of chases,
Swimming, skating, snow-shoe races
Excellent alike in all.

ON THE NIGHT OF 26 October 1876, the normally quiet streets of Cambridge, Massachusetts, were disturbed by the roars of a student demonstration. Freshman supporters of the Republican candidate for President stamped on the cobblestones and echoed a shout that could be heard in electoral districts across the nation: "*Hurrah for Hayes and Honest Ways!!*" Torchlight flickered redly on their optimistic faces and waving banners. After eight years of governmental scandals under the Grant Administration, it seemed at last that Civil Service Reform, so dear to the hearts of young progressives, was on the way. The United States, just one century old, stood thrillingly poised, like themselves, at the threshold of maturity. There was a crackle of excitement in the fall air, a promise

"Iron self-discipline had become a habit with him."

Theodore Roosevelt the Harvard freshman, 1877.

of power and future glory. The demonstrators were in great good humor, and not altogether in earnest: one lopsided banner called for FREE TRADE, FREE PRESS, AND FREE BEER.[1]

All at once, from a second-story window, came the jeering voice of a Democratic senior: "Hush up, you blooming freshmen!" Albert Bushnell Hart, who was in the crowd, noted the effect of this insult upon his classmates, and upon one of them in particular:

> Every student there was profoundly indignant. I noticed one little man, small but firmly knit. He had slammed his torch to the street. His fists quivered like steel springs and swished through the air as if plunging a hole through a mattress: I had never seen a man so angry before. "It's Roosevelt from New York," some one said. I made an effort to know Roosevelt better from that moment.[2]

According to other accounts, a potato came whizzing in the little man's direction, and his language in reply was unprintable.[3] A trifling incident, perhaps, but the Hayes demonstration was the first sign of any political interest in young Theodore. It happened to occur on the eve of his eighteenth birthday. He had been at Harvard for only one month.

CAMBRIDGE IN 1876 was essentially the same peaceful village it had been for more than two hundred years. The occasional shriek of a horsecar's wheels around a sharp corner, the slap of cement on bricks, the hiss of hydraulic dredges down by the marsh, warned that a noisier age was on its way, but as yet these sounds only accentuated the general sleepy calm, so soothing to academic nerves. In the center of the village stood the ivy-hung buildings of Harvard Yard, widely spaced with lawns and gravel walks, securely surrounded with iron railings, an oasis within an oasis. Through these railings could be glimpsed the intellectual elite of New England, men whose very nomenclature suggested the social exclusiveness, and inbred quality, of America's oldest cultural institution.[4]

The eight hundred students of Harvard College echoed, in their dress, mannerisms, and behavior, the general parochial atmosphere. Although President Eliot's revolutionary new administrative policies had freed them from the hidebound conformity of former years, they still tended to wear the same soft round hats and peajackets, quote the same verses of Omar Khayyhám, smoke the same *meerschaum* pipes, walk with the Harvard "swing" (actually an indolent saunter), and speak with the Harvard "drawl," with its characteristic hint of suppressed yawns. Their pose of fashionable languor was dropped only on evenings "across the river," when they would drink huge quantities of iced shandygaff in Bowdoin Square, and make loud nuisances of themselves at variety shows in the Globe Theater.[5] They cultivated a laissez-faire attitude to the outside world and its problems, elegantly summarized by George Pellew, class poet of Theodore's senior year, in his "Ode to Indifference":

We deem it narrow-minded to excel.
We call the man fanatic who applies
His life to one grand purpose till he dies.
Enthusiasm sees one side, one fact,
We try to see all sides, but do not act.
. . . We long to sit with newspapers unfurled,
Indifferent spectators of the world.[6]

These lines do not appear to have offended the future apostle of the Life Strenuous, when he heard them recited at the Hasty Pudding Club. He had other things on his mind at the time. Even so, it is surprising that he did not react to them as furiously as he did to the jeer, and the whizzing potato, of the Hayes demonstration. No philosophy, certainly, could be more foreign to his ardent nature than that of Indifference; as President he would wax apoplectic over much milder material.

The truth is that "Roosevelt from New York" was much more comfortable with the languid fops of Harvard than his apologists would admit. He not only relished the company of rich young men, but moved at once into the ranks of the richest and most arrogantly fashionable. Within a week of his arrival in Cambridge, he forsook the bread-slinging camaraderie of meals at Commons and joined a dining-club composed almost exclusively of Boston Brahmins.[7] Showing the self-protective instinct of a born snob, he carefully researched the "antecedents" of potential friends. "On this very account," he wrote Corinne, "I have avoided being very intimate with the New York fellows."[8]

Although his class numbered some 250—each of whom could, on graduation day, consider himself privileged above fifty thousand American youths—Theodore considered only a minute fraction to be the "gentleman-sort,"[9] and took little notice of the rest. But his personality was too warm, and his manners too good, for him to ignore them completely. "Roosevelt was perfectly willing to talk to others," recalled a member of the lower orders, "when the occasion arose."[10]

As a result of this attitude, his popularity at Harvard was confined to the minority who could call him "Teddy." Partly because he gave so little of himself to the majority, and partly because the variety of his interests kept him constantly on the move, vignettes of him during those early days at Cambridge are sketchy and dissimilar. Yet all are vivid. He trots around Holmes Field in a bright red football jersey, "the man with the morning in his face." Flushing with indignation, he leaps to his feet during roll call, and protests harshly the mispronunciation of his name; he drops from a horsecar in the Square, "thin-chested, spectacled, nervous and frail"; he hunches over a book in a roomful of noisy students, frowning with absorption, oblivious to horseplay around his chair, and to the fact that his boots are being charred by the fire; he stands in the door of Memorial Hall, talking vehemently, stammering, baring his teeth; he actually *runs* from one recitation to another, although it is not considered Harvard form to move at more than walking speed; again and again he leaps to his feet at lectures, challenging statements and demanding clarifications, until a professor shouts angrily, "See here, Roosevelt, let me talk. *I'm* running this course."[11]

Perhaps the most revealing anecdote is that of Richard Welling, who was, at this time, the strongest student in the records of Harvard Gymnasium. His first impression of Theodore was "a youth in the kindergarten stage of physical development," drearily swinging between vertical poles. Later that winter, when the youth invited him to go skating in bitter weather, Welling changed his mind. Theodore escorted him to Fresh Pond, which was

> too big and too unprotected from the furious winds to be good skating ground, rough ice, dull skates, wretched skaters scuffling about, mostly arms waving like windmills in a gale—and when any sane man would have voted to go home, as the afternoon's sport was clearly a flop, Roosevelt was exclaiming, "Isn't this bully!"—and the harder it blew, and the more we skated, the more often I had to hear, "Isn't this bully!" There was no trace of shelter where we could rub our ears, restore our fingers to some resemblance of feeling, or prevent our toes from becoming perhaps seriously frostbitten. Never in college was my own grit so put to the test, and yet I would not be the first to suggest "home."
>
> Nearly three hours passed before Roosevelt finally said: "It's too dark to skate any more," (as though, if there had been a moon, we could have gone on to midnight) . . . I recall my numbed fingers grasping the key to my room and unable to make a turn in the lock. That afternoon of so-called sport made me realize Roosevelt's amazing vitality.[12]

Theodore Senior, admitting to an "almost sinful" interest in his son's progress, worried sometimes about the physical phenomenon he had helped create. "His energy seems so superabundant that I fear it may get the better of him in one way or another."[13]

Clearly, the young man was going to have to do something about his temper. Arguments at his eating club provoked him to furious volleys of food-throwing, and on one occasion he slammed a whole pumpkin down on the head of an adversary. He reacted to personal abuse with instant fisticuffs, even punching friends who tried to restrain him.[14]

At first the social butterflies of Harvard did not know what to make of this hornet in their midst. His name was too foreign, his manner too "bumptious" to win instant acceptance. However, it did not take the Minots and Saltonstalls and Chapins long to discover that he was the brother of Bamie Roosevelt, the charming Knickerbocker who had summered in Bar Harbor, Maine, the last few years, and that his bumptiousness was a side-effect of his uncontrolled enthusiasms. They found it hard to dislike someone so supremely unconscious of his own peculiarity. "Teddy" happened to be a fascinating, if spluttery, talker: he could analyze lightweight boxing techniques, discuss the aerodynamics of birds and the protective coloration of animals, quote at will from the *Nibelungenlied* and the speeches of Abraham Lincoln, and explain what it was like trying to remain submerged in the Dead Sea. He was "queer," he was "crazy," he was "a bundle of eccentricities," but he was wholly interesting.[15]

It was the custom in those days for members of Harvard's more exclusive clubs to wander through the streets after election meetings, and serenade each new addition to their rolls. At least a dozen times, during the years 1876–80, the name that floated up through the night air was that of Theodore Roosevelt, Jr.[16]

FEARING THE DAMPNESS OF ground-floor dormitories, to which freshmen were traditionally assigned, Theodore took a room on the second floor of Mrs. Richardson's boardinghouse at 16 Winthrop Street, about halfway between the Yard and the Charles River. Furnished and decorated by Bamie, it was already "just as cosy and comfortable as it could look" when he moved in on 27 September 1876. Four big windows, facing north and east, supplied all the light an amateur taxidermist could wish for. The walls were tastefully papered, the carpet deep and warm. Cushions and a heavy fur rug awaited him on the chaise longue. There were his birds under domes of glass, and his bowie knives crossed over the mantel. A massively carved table stood in the center of the room, under the gas jet, along with the hard, bare chair which New Englanders considered appropriate for study. Theodore gazed about him in delight. "When I get my pictures and books," he assured Bamie, "I do not think there will be a room in College more handsome."[17]

As he settled in, and felt for the first time the joy of adulthood, he overflowed with gratitude to the parents who had brought him thus far. "It seems perfectly wonderful," he wrote Mittie, "looking back over my eighteen years of existence, to see how I have literally never spent an unhappy day, unless by my own fault. When I think of this and also of my intimacy with you all (for I hardly know a boy who is on as intimate and affectionate terms with his family as I am) I feel I have an immense amount to be thankful for."[18] Another letter dating from the early months of his freshman year is full of documentary detail:

> Perhaps you would like me to describe completely one day of college life; so I shall take last Monday. At half past seven my scout, having made the fire and blacked the boots, calls me, and I get round to breakfast at eight. Only a few of the boys are at breakfast, most having spent the night in Boston. Our quarters now are nice and sunny, and the room is prettily papered and ornamented. For breakfast we have tea or coffee, hot biscuits, toast, chops or beef steak, and buckwheat cakes. After breakfast I study till ten, when the mail arrives and is eagerly inspected. From eleven to twelve there is a Latin recitation with a meek-eyed Professor, who calls me Rusee-felt (hardly any one can get my name correctly, except as Rosy). Then I go over to the gymnasium, where I have a set-to with the gloves with "General" Lister, the boxing master—for I am training to box among the lightweights in the approaching match for the championship of Harvard. Then comes lunch, at which all the boys are assembled in an obstreperously joyful condition; a state of mind which brings on a free fight, to the detriment of Harry Jackson, who, with a dutch cheese and some coffee cups is put under the table; which proceeding calls forth dire threats of expulsion from Mrs. Morgan. Afterwards studying and recitation took up the time till halfpast four; as I was then going home, suddenly I heard "Hi, Ted! Catch!" and a baseball whizzed by me. Our two "babies," Bob Bacon and Arthur Hooper, were playing ball behind one of the buildings. So I stayed and watched them, until the ball went

> through a window and a proctor started out to inquire—when we abruptly separated. That evening I took dinner with Mr. and Mrs. Tudor, and had a very pleasant home-like time . . . When I returned I studied for an hour, and then, it being halfpast ten, put on my slippers, which are as comfortable as they are pretty, drew the rocking chair up to the fire, and spent the next half hour toasting my feet and reading Lamb.[19]

From time to time, as Theodore sat writing, he could glance over his shoulder and see the firelight reflected in the eyes of salamanders. He had established an impromptu vivarium in the corner of the room, where animals awaiting execution had an opportunity to review their past lives. At first this collection was small enough to reassure his landlady, but its population gradually expanded to include snakes, lobsters, and a giant tortoise. The latter managed to escape from its pen while Theodore was out, and wandered through the house in search of freedom: Mrs. Richardson, stumbling upon it, was frightened into hysterics. Rooseveltian eloquence presumably saved the day, for Theodore continued to reside at 16 Winthrop Street throughout his college career.[20]

In addition to boxing, wrestling, body-building, and his daily hours of recitation, the young freshman attended weekly dancing-classes, hunted in the woods around Cambridge, taught in Sunday school, stuffed and dissected his specimens, organized a whist club, took part in poetry-reading sessions, followed the Harvard football team to Yale ("The fellows . . . seem to be a much more scrubby set than ours"), and, in time-honored undergraduate fashion, caroused with his friends, making the night hideous with his harsh, unmusical singing.[21] He developed a sudden, and ardent, interest in the girls of Boston, and, thanks to his excellent local connections, was soon seeing many of them. Hardly a week went by, in those early months of 1877, without its round of matinees, theater parties, and balls. Theodore reported them all enthusiastically to his family, along with assurances that he was not neglecting his studies, and at least one guilty protestation that he remained faithful to Edith Carow.[22]

Although he had not lacked for female company hitherto in his life, it had been confined mostly to the Roosevelt family circle. Even his intimacy with Edith had the quality of a brother-sister relationship. Sickly and reclusive as a child, preoccupied with travel and self-improvement in his teens, he had had little opportunity to knock on strange doors. Now, doors were opening of their own accord, disclosing scores of fresh faces and alluring young figures. Understandably Theodore was dazzled. Almost every girl he met is described in his letters as "sweet," "bright," or "pretty."

What the girls thought of him, with his crooked spectacles, grinning teeth, and alarmingly frank conversation, was another matter. The evidence is that they tolerated him (to one debutante, he was "studious, ambitious, eccentric—not the sort to appeal at first") until they found they had grown fond of him.[23]

It might be mentioned here that neither during his student years, nor indeed at any time in his life, did Theodore show the slightest tolerance for women (or for that matter men) who were anything but "rigidly virtuous." His judgments of people lower down the moral or social scale could be particularly prudish. "Have just received a letter telling me that [cousin] Cornelius has distinguished himself by marrying a French actress!" he wrote in his diary one day. "He is a disgrace to the family—the vulgar brute."[24] Sex, to him, was part of the mystical union of marriage, and, however pleasurable as an act of love, its function was to procreate. Outside marriage, as far as he was concerned, it simply did not exist.[25]

Of the inclinations that naturally beset a young man when he returns, hot from the intimacies of a sleigh-ride, to his private room, it is perhaps unnecessary to speak. There are erasures and pages torn out of Theodore's diaries, yet also the ecstatic declaration, when he finally fell in love, "Thank Heaven, I am . . . perfectly pure."[26]

At the same time that he became a ladies' man, he developed into something of a fashion plate, or, as he preferred to describe himself, "very swell." Invited away for the weekend, he was suddenly ashamed of his hat, and sent home for a beaver. Selecting a new wardrobe, he agonized for days over his afternoon coat, "being undecided whether to have it a frock or a cutaway." He complained that his washerwoman did not act squarely "on the subject of white cravats."[27] He sported one necktie so brilliant it cast a glow upon his cheeks, and combed his whiskers until they swayed in the breeze. Sniggers could be heard in the Yard, as he marched dazzlingly by. But Theodore, in the manner of all dandies, pretended not to notice he was being noticed.[28]

WHEN HE ASSURED his parents that he was not neglecting his studies, he was telling the truth. Indeed, he got through prodigious quantities of work. Iron self-discipline had become a habit with him, and he plotted every day with the methodism of a Wesleyan minister. The amount of time he spent at his desk was comparatively small—rarely more than a quarter of the day—but his concentration was so intense, and his reading so rapid, that he could afford more time off than most. Even these "free" periods were packed with mental, physical, or social activity. "He was forever at it," said one classmate. Another marveled: "Never have I seen or read of a man with such an amazing array of interests."[29] Tumbling into bed at midnight or in the small hours, Theodore could luxuriate in healthy tiredness, satisfied that he had wasted not one minute of his waking hours.

His regimen was flexible, but balanced. Any overindulgence in sport or flirtation would be immediately compensated for by extra study. When an attack of measles laid him low in February 1877, he made up for lost time by canceling his Easter vacation in New York, secluding himself on a friend's farm, and finishing in five days "the first book of Horace, the sixth book of Homer, and the *Apology* of Socrates."[30]

It must not be assumed that Theodore struck any of the Harvard faculty as intellectually remarkable during this stage of his academic career. On the contrary, he was regarded as "an average B man . . . not in any way distinguished."[31] He paled in comparison with the scintillating, sixteen-year-old Bob Bacon, and at least half a dozen of his classmates surpassed him in composing themes. "Roosevelt's writing was to the point," said one instructor, "but did not have their air of cultivation."[32] Like many voluble men, he was a slow writer, painfully hammering out sentences which achieved force and clarity at the expense of polite style.

Neither this nor the pessimism of professors prevented him from scoring an average of 75 at the end of his freshman year, with honor grades in five out of seven subjects.[33] If it could not be counted a "distinguished" performance, for a boy who had largely educated himself, then it would do for the time being.

BEFORE LEAVING HARVARD for the summer of 1877, Theodore played host to several guests from New York, including Edith Carow. The latter, perhaps aware that she had local rivals, flirted with him and his classmates so successfully that he exclaimed afterward, "I don't think I ever saw Edith looking prettier; everyone . . . admired her little Ladyship intensely, and she behaved as sweetly as she looked." He begged Corinne to pass on the word that "I enjoyed *her* visit *very* much indeed."[34]

But within a day or two he was praising other girls again. When college broke up on 21 June, he hurried, not to the parlors of New York City, but to the lonely forests of the Adirondacks, "so as to get the birds in as good plumage as possible."[35] Possibly Edith, hearing this, heaved a quiet sigh. She could compete with the belles of Boston, but what were her charms compared with those of the orange-throated warbler, red-bellied nuthatch, and hairy woodpecker?

IN MID-JULY, THEODORE joined his family at Tranquillity, and soon afterward published his first printed work, *The Summer Birds of the Adirondacks.* This scientific catalog was the fruit of three expeditions dating back to August 1874, on the last of which he had been briefly joined by Harry Minot, his best friend from Harvard. Minot contributed a few observations and was listed as co-author, but the title-page typography left no doubt as to who took full credit. Ninety-seven species—some unknown even to longtime residents of the area—were described in precise thumbnail sketches, remarkable for their emphasis on song as well as plumage. Theodore's acute ear had been ravished, in the Adirondacks, by a wealth of melody such as he had never heard before. His notebooks, upon which *Birds* was based, are so full of auditory observations that visual ones are sometimes forgotten. Spectacles or no spectacles, sound always meant more to him than color. One rhapsodic passage shows how sensuously he reacted to it:

> Perhaps the sweetest bird music I have ever listened to was uttered by a hermit thrush. It was while hunting deer on a small lake, in the heart of the wilderness; the night was dark, for the moon had not yet risen, but there were clouds, and as we moved over the surface of the water with the perfect silence so strange and almost oppressive to the novice in this sport, I could distinguish dimly the outlines of the gloomy and impenetrable pine forests by which we were surrounded. We had been out for two or three hours but had seen nothing; once we heard a tree fall with a dull, heavy crash, and two or three times the harsh hooting of an owl had been answered by the unholy laughter of a loon from the bosom of the lake, but otherwise nothing had occurred to break the death-like stillness of the night; not even a breath of air stirred among the tops of the tall pine trees. Wearied by our unsuccess we at last turned homeward when suddenly the quiet was broken by the song of a hermit thrush; louder and clearer it sang from the depths of the grim and rugged woods, until the sweet, sad music seemed to fill the very air and to conquer for the moment the gloom of the night; then it died away and ceased as suddenly as it had begun. Perhaps the song would have seemed less sweet in the daytime, but uttered as it was, with such surroundings, sounding so strange and so beautiful amid these grand but desolate wilds, I shall never forget it.

This Keatsian passage, composed when Theodore was only eighteen, foreshadows the best of his mature writing in its simplicity and atmospheric effects. Yet he kept it and other such effusions strictly private: in his published works he seemed determined to be scholarly. *Summer Birds* was followed in due course by a similar study, *Notes on Some of the Birds of Oyster Bay.* Thirty-five years later, when the ex-President was writing his memoirs, he would look back fondly on these "obscure ornithological publications," which formally launched him on his career as a professional natural historian.[36]

That career was the subject of a solemn discussion between father and son during the late summer of 1877. Theodore's courses in his freshman year had all been prescribed; now, as his sophomore year loomed, he could choose some of his own—and begin to follow his future course in life. *Summer Birds,* which was favorably reviewed, must have convinced Theodore Senior that his son was already one of the most knowledgeable young naturalists in the United States.[37] The boy's collection of birds and skins, now numbering well into the hundreds, was probably unequaled in variety and quality by any American of his age. He was regarded as "a very promising taxidermist, appeared in a national directory of biologists, and very likely had no peer, as a teenage ornithologist, in his knowledge of bird coloration, courtship, flight, and song.[38] His future as a scientist would therefore seem to be assured. Yet Theodore Senior gave him surprisingly little encouragement.

> My father . . . told me that if I wished to be a scientific man I could do so. He explained that I must be sure that I really intensely desired to do scientific work, because if I went into it I must make it a serious career; that he had made enough money to enable me to take up such a career and do non-remunerative work of value *if I intended to do the very best work that was in me;* but that I must not dream of taking it up as a dilettante. He also gave me a piece of advice that I have always remembered, namely, that, if I was not going to earn money, I must even things up by not spending it. As he expressed it, I had to keep the fraction constant, and if I was not able to increase the numerator, then I must reduce the denominator. In other words, if I went into a scientific career, I must definitely abandon all thought of the enjoyment that could accompany a money-making career, and must find my pleasures elsewhere.
>
> After this conversation I fully intended to make science my life-work.[39]

Returning to Harvard as a sophomore in the fall of 1877, Theodore elected two courses in natural history: elementary botany, and comparative anatomy and physiology of vertebrates. (His instructor in this course, which he found "extremely interesting," was William James.) He also chose two courses of German and one of French, and was prescribed courses in rhetoric, constitutional history, and themes. In this demanding schedule he was to surpass the record of his freshman year with an excellent average of 89. He scored 96 and 92 in German, 94 in rhetoric, 89 in botany, and 79 in anatomy. His average would have been even higher, but for a hairsbreadth 51 in "that villainous French." Even so, with six honor grades out of eight, he once again confounded his academic critics, and there was no more talk of scholastic mediocrity. "He distinctly belonged," said Thomas Perry, instructor in themes, "to the best twenty-five in a very brilliant class."[40]

With respect to the other two hundred and twenty, Theodore gradually relaxed his rather snobbish standards. "My respect for the quality of my classmates has much increased lately," he wrote Corinne, "as they no longer seem to think it necessary to confine their conversation exclusively to athletic subjects. I was especially struck by this the other night, when after a couple of hours spent in boxing and wrestling with Arthur Hooper and Ralph Ellis, it was proposed to finish the evening by reading aloud from Tennyson, and we became so interested in *In Memoriam* that it was past one o'clock when we separated."[41] His best friend continued to be Harry Minot, but as time went on he showed an increasing fondness for Richard Saltonstall, a large, shy boy from the highest ranks of Boston society. With Bob Bacon, too, he maintained an easy friendship, and was invited with him to join the prestigious Institute of 1770.[42]

About the time he turned nineteen in October 1877, Theodore was informed that his father had been appointed Collector of Customs to the Port of New York by President Hayes. He dutifully expressed "the greatest interest" in subsequent movements toward confirmation by the Senate, but the interest was personal rather than political.[43] Since his appearance at the Hayes demonstration a year before, he had shown no further concern for politics; his letters of the period, so full of bubbling curiosity about other aspects of life, are bare of any reference to national affairs. Now, however, events conspired to force politics brutally upon his attention.

Theodore Senior, who had himself just turned forty-six, was as politically naive as his son. He assumed at first that the Collectorship was a reward for distinguished services to New York City, but disillusionment came rapidly. President Hayes, it turned out, had chosen him merely as a symbol of the Administration's commitment to Civil Service Reform. By elevating this decent and incorruptible man up to public office, Hayes hoped to embarrass Senator Roscoe Conkling, boss of the corrupt New York State Republican machine, who was demanding the reappointment of Chester A. Arthur as Collector. The fact that Arthur was himself decent and incorruptible only increased the savagery of the resultant battle for Senate confirmation. Roosevelt lay helpless as a pawn between the clashing forces of Old Guard "Spoils-men" and Reform Republicans.

Since Boss Conkling happened to sit on the Senate committee that must consider the appointment, it was subjected to endless delaying tactics. Yet Hayes would not withdraw his nomination, and Roosevelt, as a patriotic citizen, had no choice but to remain at the President's disposal.[44] He loathed Conkling with all his soul, and felt contaminated by any contact with the machine. Theodore Senior belonged to a class and a generation that considered politics to be a dirty business, best left, like street cleaning, to malodorous professionals. Humiliated by the scrutiny of his inferiors, exhausted by week after week of worry, he began to deteriorate physically under the strain. He was racked by mysterious intestinal cramps, which worsened as the struggle dragged on into December. By then the "Collectorship row" was making nationwide headlines, and while the nomination seemed doomed, suspense continued to torture the nominee.

His son, following daily developments in Cambridge, grew increasingly worried. "Am very uneasy about Father," he wrote on 16 December, after the nomination had been finally rejected in the Senate by a vote of 25 to 31. "Does the Doctor think it is anything serious?"[45] Two days later Theodore Senior collapsed with what was diagnosed as acute peritonitis. For a while he lay desperately ill, but as Christmas approached he began to recover. The Roosevelts celebrated with exhausted relief, vowing to have no more to do with politics.[46]

BACK AT HARVARD early in the New Year, Theodore recorded in a private diary his father's parting assurance "that after all I was the dearest of his children to him."[47] As always, the deep voice and all-seeing eyes inspired a determination to be worthy of "the best and most loving of men." He was cramming hard for his semiannual examinations when, late on the afternoon of Saturday, 9 February, an urgent summons arrived from New York.[48] Theodore ran to catch the overnight train, knowing that his father must have suffered a relapse, yet unaware that screams of agony were echoing through the Roosevelt town house. Theodore Senior's "peritonitis" was in reality a malignant fibrous tumor of the bowel, and since its brief period of remission over Christmas it had grown so rapidly that it was now strangling his intestines. The pain that he suffered had, in a matter of weeks, turned his dark hair gray; even now, as his elder son rushed to his bedside, it was all the other children could do to hold him down. "He was so mad with pain," Elliott recorded, "that beyond groans and horrible writhes and twists he could do nothing. Oh my God my Father what agonies you suffered."[49]

Theodore arrived on Sunday morning to find the flags of New York City flying at half-mast. "Greatheart" had died shortly before midnight.[50]

Alone in his room later that day, the new head of the Roosevelt family drew a thick slash down the margin of his diary for 9 February 1878 and wrote: "My dear Father. Born Sept. 23, 1831." Here his pen wavered and stopped.

WHEN THEODORE RESUMED writing on 12 February, the words flowed tumultuously, as if to wash away his grief.

> He has just been buried. I shall never forget these terrible three days; the hideous suspense of the ride on; the dull, inert

sorrow, during which I felt as if I had been stunned, or as if part of my life had been taken away, and the two moments of sharp, bitter agony, when I kissed the dear dead face and realized that he would never again on this earth speak to me or greet me with his loving smile, and then when I heard the sound of the first clod dropping on the coffin holding the one I loved dearest on earth. He looked so calm and sweet. I feel that if it were not for the certainty, that as he himself has so often said, "he is not dead but gone before," I should almost perish.

None of the Roosevelts, least of all Theodore himself, could have foreseen how shattered he would be by the premature loss of his father. "He was everything to me." For a while, it seemed as if the youth could not survive without him. Like a fledgling shoved too soon from the bough, he tumbled nakedly through the air; some of his diary entries are not so much expressions of sorrow as squawks of fright.

They give the impression of a sensitivity so extreme it verges on mental imbalance. For month after month Theodore pours a flood of anguish into his diary, although his letters remain determinedly cheerful. Only in private can he allow his despair to overflow, yet the effect is therapeutic. By the end of April he is able to note: "I am now getting over the first sharpness of grief." With perhaps unconscious symbolism, he shaves off his whiskers, and in consequence is "endlessly chaffed by the boys." On the first day of May, with the smell of spring in the air, he is surprised to find that his thoughts of Theodore Senior have suddenly become "pleasant" ones.[51]

His grief, however, was by no means over. It continued to flow well into the summer, and spasmodically through the fall. Purged of terror, it became sweetened with nostalgia. Memories of his father surfaced in the form of dreams and hallucinations of almost photographic vividness. "All through the sermon," he wrote one Sunday, "I was thinking of Father. I could see him sitting in the corner of the pew as distinctly as if he were alive, in the same dear old attitude, with his funny little 'warlike curl', and his beloved face. Oh, I feel so sad when I think of the word 'never.' "[52]

Never—it was the word he had repeated over and over again in his childhood diaries, when longing for the unrecoverable past. Inevitably, his earliest and most poignant memory floated up: "I remember so well how, years ago, when I was a weak, asthmatic child, he used to walk up and down with me in his arms for hours together, night after night, and oh, how my heart pains me when I think that I never was able to do anything for him in his last illness!"[53]

This, of course, was not his fault—early news of Theodore Senior's relapse had actually been withheld from him so as not to affect his studies—but it did not stop him reproaching himself, often in tones of bitter self-contempt. "I often feel badly that such a wonderful man as Father should have had a son of so little worth as I am. . . . How little use I am, or ever shall be in the world . . . I realize more and more every day that I am as much inferior to Father morally and mentally as physically."[54]

After the terror and the nostalgia, it was desire that eventually healed him. Longing for the man who had been his best friend in life was translated into an even more desperate longing to be worthy of him in death. "How I wish I could ever do something to keep up his name!"[55] In this ambition he would succeed so well that the name of Theodore Roosevelt would one day become the most famous in the world; ironically its very luster would obliterate the memory of its original bearer. But the large, kindly spirit of Theodore Senior hovered always over the shoulder of his son.

"Years afterward," Corinne recalled, "when the college boy of 1878 was entering upon his duties as President of the United States, he told me frequently that he never took any serious step or made any vital decision for his country without thinking first what position his father would have taken on the question."[56]

ON 23 FEBRUARY 1878, his first night back at Harvard after the funeral, Theodore noted casually: "I am left about $8000 a year: comfortable though not rich." No doubt, as he penned these words, his mind harked back to the conversation he had had with Theodore Senior the previous summer, when he had been promised enough

money to subsidize his career as a natural historian. Now here it was. It had arrived shockingly soon, but his duty was clear. Grief or no grief, he must balance the numerator of independence with the denominator of work. With remarkable self-discipline, given the hysteria of his private emotions, he at once resumed his studies, and within a week had scored 90 percent in two semiannual examinations. Invitations poured in from sympathetic friends in Boston, but he would accept none until May, and kept "grinding like a Trojan" for the rest of his sophomore year. At the same time he continued faithfully to exercise and teach in Sunday school, obedient to a precept of his father's, which he had never forgotten: "Take care of your morals first, your health next, and finally your studies."[57]

The excellence of his results in the annual examinations was achieved at much physical cost to himself. He was "unwell and feverish" during the latter part of May, and blamed his poor showing in French on "being forced to sit up all night with the asthma."[58] The ordeal was over at last on 5 June. Theodore caught the afternoon express to New York, and next morning began what he hoped would be a summer of "nude happiness . . . among the wilds of Oyster Bay."[59]

NUDE THE SUMMER certainly was—at least in the restricted Victorian sense of the term. Theodore was soon "mahogany from the waist up, thanks to hours of bare-chested rowing." But happiness was long kept at bay by unavoidable associations between Tranquillity and Theodore Senior. In every idle moment the skinny student might see the big, bearded man laughing, praying, snoozing in the shade, jumping into his trap at the station and driving off at a rattling pace, his white linen duster bagging behind him like a balloon. "Oh Father, how bitterly I miss you and long for you!"[60]

Just as he had distracted himself in college with work, Theodore now whipped himself into a frenzy of physical activity. Throughout July he rowed and portaged such exhausting distances, over such dreary wastes of water and mud-flats, that just to read his diary is to tire. On one occasion he rowed clear across Long Island Sound to Rye Beach, a total of over twenty-five miles in a single day. Rowing, as opposed to the more leisurely sport of sailing, was deeply satisfying to him. As Corinne remarked, "Theodore craved the actual effort of the arms and back, the actual sense of meeting the wave close to." Yet he loved riding even more, and spurred his horse Lightfoot to prodigious feats of endurance, including one twenty-mile gallop. In between rows and rides, Theodore would burn off his excess energy by running at speed through the woods, boxing and wrestling with Elliott, hiking, hunting, and swimming. His diary constantly exults in physical achievement, and never betrays fear that he might be overtaxing his strength. When forced to record an attack of *cholera morbus* in early August, he precedes it with the phrase, "Funnily enough . . ."[61]

Evidence that his heart, if not his body, was repairing itself came on 9 August. "It being Edith Carow's 17th birthday, I sent her a *bonbonièrre*." The young lady made her annual appearance at Oyster Bay a week later, and Theodore paid her his annual attentions, rowing her to Lloyds Neck, lunching out at Yellowbanks, and picking water lilies with her in Coldspring Harbor. Without reading more into the diary than is actually there, it is possible to discern the mounting excitement he felt in her proximity. On 22 August he let off steam by thundering off on a wild ride "that I am afraid . . . may have injured my horse." Later the same day Edith joined him for a sailing trip, and in the evening they went to a family party together. "Afterwards," his diary entry concludes, "Edith and I went up to the summer house."[62]

With this enigmatic remark, a curtain of blank paper descends, and Edith is not mentioned again for months. Whatever happened in the summerhouse, it seems to have kindled some sort of rage in Theodore. Only two days later he was bothered, while riding, by a neighbor's dog; drawing his revolver, he shot it dead, "rolling it over very neatly as it ran alongside the horse."[63] On a cruise up Long Island Sound with some male cousins, he blazed away with the same gun at anything he saw in the water, "from bottles or buoys to sharks and porpoises."[64]

With the first chill of fall in the air, Theodore's thoughts turned again to Harvard, and to his future. The uncertainty he had felt ever since committing himself to a scientific career was beginning to worry him, so much so he turned to an uncle for reassurance. But the old gentleman, while sympathetic, was unhelpful, and Theodore's bewilderment increased. "I have absolutely no idea what I should do when I leave college," he wrote in despair. "Oh Father, my Father, no words can tell how I shall miss your counsel and advice!"[65]

AS IF TO SEEK REFUGE from his doubts, he decided to spend the last few weeks of his vacation in the wilds of Aroostook County, in northern Maine. Arthur Cutler had hunted in the area—one of the last stands of virgin forest in the Northeast—and had suggested that Theodore might like to do the same. There was a backwoodsman there, said Cutler, named Bill Sewall; he kept open house for hunters, and was emphatically "a man to know." Huge, bearded, and full of lust for life, Sewall loved to shout poetry as he fought his canoe through white water, or slammed his ax into shuddering pine trees. No doubt Cutler sensed that this magnificent specimen of manhood might satisfy Theodore's cravings for a father figure. And since Sewall was humbly born, he might rub off some of the boy's veneer of snobbism before it toughened into impenetrable bark.

Island Falls, where Sewall had his headquarters, was so remote from New York City that Theodore took two full days to get there, completing the last thirty-six miles in a buckboard. Two cousins, Emlen and West Roosevelt, and a Doctor W. Thompson accompanied him. The strain of the journey, coming on top of his frenetic summer, caused him to suffer a bad attack of asthma, and when he arrived at Sewall's homestead, late on the evening of 7 September, he was wheezing. Sewall's first impression of him was "a thin, pale youngster with bad eyes and a weak heart."

Doctor Thompson took the backwoodsman aside. "He's not strong, but he's all grit. He'll kill himself before he'll even say he's tired." Sewall agreed that Theodore looked "mighty pindlin'," but soon found out that his appearance was deceptive.[66]

> We traveled twenty-five miles afoot one day on that first visit of his, which I maintain was a good fair walk for any

> common man. We hitched well, somehow or other, from the start. He was different from anybody that I had ever met; especially, he was fair-minded. . . . Besides, he was always good-natured and full of fun. I do not think I ever remember him being "out of sorts." He did not feel well sometimes, but he never would admit it.
>
> I could see not a single thing that wasn't fine in Theodore, no qualities that I didn't like. Some folks said that he was headstrong and aggressive, but I never found him so except when necessary; and I've always thought being headstrong and aggressive, on occasion, was a pretty good thing. He wasn't a bit cocky as far as I could see, though others thought so. I will say that he was not remarkably cautious about expressing his opinion.[67]

Theodore, for his part, found Sewall to be a figure straight out of *The Saga of King Olaf*. The backwoodsman agreed. "I don't know but what my ancestors *were* vikings."[68]

Tramping through the woods together, they were an oddly matched yet complementary pair: Sewall slow and purposeful, advancing with bearlike tread; Theodore wiry and nervous, cocking his gun at any hint of movement in the trees, stopping every now and again to pick up bugs. Since both men loved epic poetry, and could recite it by the yard, the squirrels of Aroostook County were entertained to many ringing declamations, including Sewall's favorite lines:

> *Who are the nobles of the earth,*
> *The true aristocrats,*
> *Who need not bow their heads to kings*
> *Nor doff to lords their hats?*
> *Who are they but the men of toil*
> *Who cleave the forest down*
> *And plant amid the wilderness*
> *The forest and the town?*[69]

The words may have been familiar to Theodore, yet falling from the lips of a man whose father had been a carpenter and whose mother a seamstress, they took on new, defiantly democratic overtones, which were not lost on the scion of the Roosevelts.[70]

ON 27 SEPTEMBER 1878, Theodore was welcomed back to Cambridge by his classmates, and to his surprise "was offered the Porcellian." Membership in this club was the highest social honor Harvard could bestow, and he was acutely embarrassed to refuse it. His scruples had nothing to do with the possible disapproval of a Bill Sewall. It was just that he had already been offered the A.D., and had accepted that instead.[71] Greatly regretting his hastiness, for he wished very much to be "a Porc man," he turned to the more important business of choosing a schedule for his junior year.

It proved to be an ambitious one, covering nine subjects and at least twenty hours a week of classroom and laboratory work. His electives were once again German and two natural history courses (zoology and geology), plus Italian and philosophy. Those prescribed were themes, forensics, logic, and metaphysics. In this formidable curriculum he was to score the best marks of his academic career, averaging 87 and standing thirteenth in a class of 166.[72] In two of his electives—philosophy and natural history—he stood first.[73]

No sooner had Theodore settled down to his familiar routine of recitations, study, exercise, and "sprees" than the Porcellian once more opened its doors to him. Early in October there happened to be a drunken quarrel in the Yard, during which a Porc man told an A.D. man that Teddy Roosevelt, given the chance, would have chosen *his* club first. When the taunt became public, the A.D. announced that as its new member had not yet signed in, he was free to reconsider his acceptance. "Of course by this arrangement I *have* to hurt somebody's feelings," Theodore wrote agitatedly in his diary. ". . . I have rarely felt as badly as I have during the last 24 hours; it is terribly hard to know what the honorable thing is to do." He decided that honor lay in the direction of the more prestigious club, and accepted the Porc's offer on 6 October. "I am delighted to be in," he told Bamie. ". . . There is a billiard table, magnificent library, punch-room &c, and my best friends are in it."[74]

Perhaps the best of these "best friends," now that Harry Minot had dropped out of Harvard to study law, was Dick Saltonstall, whose family mansion on Chestnut Hill became a second home to Theodore in the fall and winter of 1878. The first invitation to this bastion of Boston society came on Friday, 18 October. The two young men drove out of Cambridge in Saltonstall's buggy, crossed the river, and headed west into a brilliant fall landscape.[75]

Chestnut Hill lay six miles away. As the buggy creaked toward it, through increasingly luxuriant woods, Theodore could sense the waves of peace and security which flow around the enclaves of the very rich. A private lane curved up the hillside to where Leverett Saltonstall's house lay, huge and rambling, backed by chestnut trees, and fronting on an immense sweep of lawn. The lawn was shared by another, equally imposing mansion, the home of George Cabot Lee; a mere twenty yards of grass, and a token garden gate, separated the one property from the other.[76] Dick had doubtless already explained to Theodore that the Lees and Saltonstalls were more than mere neighbors. Mr. Lee was his uncle by marriage, and seventeen-year-old Alice Lee was the inseparable companion of his sister, Rose Saltonstall.[77] Theodore met both girls that evening. In his diary he described them with his usual vague adjectives, "sweet," "pretty," and "pleasant"—the last being reserved for Rose, who was decidedly the more homely of the two.

He greatly enjoyed himself that weekend, walking through the woods with Alice and Rose, attending church with both families on Sunday morning, and "chestnutting" alone with Alice in the afternoon.[78] As always, his soul responded to people of his own class, conversation on his own level, manners whose every nuance was familiar to him. Only a month ago Bill Sewall had convinced him that "the nobles of the earth" were "men of toil"—and probably would convince him again, as he intended to return to Island Falls one day. But in the meantime, the Lees and Saltonstalls were aristocracy enough for Theodore Roosevelt.

ON 27 OCTOBER, AS HIS second decade came to an end, the young man's thoughts turned to the past, and his grief for his father surged up afresh. To distract himself he took a ramble through the woods with his gun. His diary entry for that night proves, with unconscious humor, that his heart had at last healed: "Oh Father, sometimes I feel as though I would give half my life to see you but for a moment! Oh, what loving memories I have of you! 2 grey squirrel."

ON 2 NOVEMBER 1878, Theodore was initiated into the Porcellian.[79] It seems the honor rather went to his head. "Was 'higher' with wine than ever before—or will be again," he wrote. "Still, I could wind up my watch." Then, in a revealing afterword: "Wine makes me awfully fighty."[80] A throbbing hangover confirmed his lifelong resolve never to get drunk again, and the evidence is he never did. He continued to enjoy "sprees" at the Porc, including the traditional suppers of partridge and burgundy, and champagne breakfasts on Sundays; but he remained severely teetotal on most of these occasions, and abstemious on the others. As for smoking, he had promised his father to abstain from that manly practice until he was twenty-one, with the result that when the time came he had lost all interest in it. The third vice that appeals to most undergraduates was beneath his contemplation: he remained "perfectly pure" throughout his bachelor years.[81]

His second visit to Chestnut Hill occurred on 11 November, when he drove over to take tea with the Saltonstalls and their ubiquitous visitor from next door, who was "as sweet and pretty as ever." So, of course, was practically every girl that Theodore met. But Alice Lee seems to have merited his praise rather more than any other. When he saw her again, he was a houseguest for Thanksgiving, and already so much a part of the Chestnut Hill circle that she allowed him to call her "Alice."[82] As her own first "Teddy" lingered softly in his ears, he vowed, with all the strength of his passionate nature, that he would marry her.[83]

CHAPTER 4

The Swell in the Dog-Cart

A little bird in the air
Is singing of Thyri the fair,
The sister of Svend, the Dane;
And the song of the garrulous bird
In the streets of the town is heard,
And repeated again and again.
Hoist up your sails of silk,
And flee away from each other.

ALICE HATHAWAY LEE was just seventeen when Theodore first saw her on 18 October 1878. "As long as I live," he wrote afterward, "I shall never forget how sweetly she looked, and how prettily she greeted me."[1] With his photographic memory, he no doubt carried that first vision of her pristine to the grave. Alice blushing must indeed have been an unforgettable sight, and not only to eyes as worshipful as Theodore's. Contemporary testimonials to her beauty are as unanimous as those in praise of her charm. She was "an enchanting creature" of "singular loveliness"; of "quick intelligence," "endearing character," and "unfailing sunny temperament"; she was "gay," "exceptionally bright," and "the life of the

"She seems like a star of heaven . . . my pearl, my pure flower."

Alice Hathaway Lee when Theodore Roosevelt first met her.

party."[2] Images of sunshine and light recur so often in descriptions of her that one can understand how quickly she bedazzled Theodore, as indeed she bedazzled everybody.

The imagination, stimulated by such universal praise, delights to picture Alice Lee coming through that garden gate more than a century ago: an exquisite, willowy blonde, smiling shyly, moving with the "long, firm step" of a natural athlete. She wears a dress of white brocade that glows in the late-afternoon light.[3] Through Theodore's spectacles, as it were, we see, as she draws nearer, that she is tall—five foot seven, only two inches shorter than he—yet holds herself proudly erect. Her hair, drawn up to expose a graceful neck, is honey-colored, but when the sun strikes the water-curls that cling to her temples, or the thick ropes piled high on her head, unexpected highlights of gold shimmer in it. Her eyes are similarly chromatic: at times they seem a very pale blue, at others a pearly gray. Heavy lashes, when she glances down demurely, brush cheeks whose pinkness, blending into a soft pocket of shadow in the corner of her mouth, make her irresistibly kissable. She is, in short, as ravishing a beauty as ever walked across a Boston lawn, or through the pages of any Victorian novel. Theodore, drinking her in at every pore, fell in love with her there and then. Just two more meetings were enough to convince him "that win her I would, if it were possible," and to affirm that "I had never before cared . . . a snap of my finger for any girl."[4]

So much for Edith Carow. Theodore, when he wrote those words, was in such rapture over Alice that he probably exaggerated his indifference to other women. But whatever spark Edith had kindled in his heart was obliterated by the firestorm of passion which now consumed him. After only one weekend at Chestnut Hill he could afford to be sarcastic about his childhood sweetheart: ". . . give my love to Edith—if she's in a good humour; otherwise my respectful regards." The suspicion grows that his last interview with that strong-willed young lady, in the summerhouse at Oyster Bay, had been a stormy one. "If she seems particularly good-tempered," Theodore went on, "tell her that I hope that when I see her at Xmas it will not be on what you might call one of her off days."[5] With that he cast her from his mind, and dedicated himself to the "eager, restless, passionate pursuit of one all-absorbing object."[6]

GIVEN HER EXTREME YOUTH, and the protective aura of wealth and privilege that had always surrounded her, Alice not surprisingly proved to be as elusive a prize as Theodore had ever hunted. His ardor was so violent—in courtship as in everything else—that he periodically frightened her away, like a nervous doe; then he would have to restrain himself, and with soft words and soothing gestures coax her near again. She found him by no means a romantic attraction. The slight stench of arsenic that emanated from his clothes; the tickly whiskers and glittering glasses; the manic bursts of energy which left him white and sick with exhaustion; his geyser-like garrulousness, choked by stammers which would inevitably explode under the pressure of more words boiling up inside him; his exuberant hopping on the dance-floor, so perilous to lace pantaloons; the bloodcurdling stories of wolves and bears; the black eyes from boxing, the nervous diarrhea, the alarming hiss of asthma in his lungs—these were not the things a girl of polite background dreamed about, except perhaps in nightmares. Yet Alice could not help being intrigued by him, and flattered by his adoration. How different he was from those boring young Boston Brahmins—and, so far as she knew, from everybody else in the human race. How sidesplitting he could be, when he told jokes in that curious falsetto of his! Her quick mind rejoiced in his intelligence, and her body, when they skated together, to the masculine hardness of his arms. Even as she sprang away from him, she took care not to spring too far; not that there was any risk of him abandoning the chase. Theodore, like his father before him, "almost always got what he wanted."[7]

NO SOONER HAD the lovesick junior returned to Winthrop Street after Thanksgiving than he formally entered in his diary the vow that he would marry Alice Lee.[8] To make it doubly formal, he arranged a "tintype spree," or trip to the photographer's, so that he

"Bewhiskered and slim as a reed, he sits between the two girls."
Alice Lee, Theodore Roosevelt, and Rose Saltonstall, 1878.

might pose beside his beloved at the very onset of their courtship. Clearly it would be improper to suggest that Alice come to the studio alone, so Rose Saltonstall was roped in as a convenient third party. There is more than a hint of nervousness in Theodore's first letter to Alice, reminding her of their rendezvous. Even at this stage he seems afraid that his doe might wander.

PORCELLIAN CLUB

December 6, 1878

Dear Alice, I have been anxiously expecting a letter from you and Rose for the last two or three days; but none has come. You *must* not forget our tintype spree; I have been dextrously avoiding forming any engagements for Saturday . . . Tell Rose that I never passed a pleasanter Thanksgiving than at her house.

Judging from the accounts I have received the new dress for the party at New Bedford must have been a complete success.

YOUR FELLOW-CONSPIRATOR[9]

Alice did not forget, and the group portrait, so momentous to Theodore, survives. Bewhiskered and slim as a reed, he sits between the two girls, carefully clutching his hat and cane. Alice, seated lower, leans toward him, almost touching his right thigh. Her skirts droop sexily over his shoe. She wears a lace-fronted dress and high feathered hat. Her gray eyes gaze dreamily into the camera: she seems unaware of the giant resolve looming next to her.[10]

By now Alice Lee was occupying Theodore's thoughts through every waking hour, and would continue to do so, according to his own testimony, for the next year and a quarter. At times her girlish waywardness would drive him to despair; in one particular moment of frustration he ripped the pages containing the Thanksgiving vow bodily out of his diary.[11] There is a suggestion of sexual torment in Theodore's entry for 11 December 1878, when he asks God's help in staying virtuous, as his father would have wished, "and to do nothing I would have been ashamed to confess to him. I am very . . ." Here the eager researcher turns the page, only to find a huge blot of ink. Somehow its very blackness and monstrous shape convey more of Theodore's misery than whatever words he had scribbled beneath it.[12]

Such fits of depression were, however, rare in the early days of his courtship. "Teddy" continued to be welcome at Chestnut Hill, and Alice was quick to atone, with a soft word or look, for any bruise she may have inflicted upon him. At any such sign of favor he positively radiated with joy, and would exult, when alone with his diary, in his youth, his social and academic success, and the luck which had led him to Chestnut Hill. "Truly," he wrote, as 1878 passed into 1879, "these are the golden years of my life."[13]

IT MUST NOT BE SUPPOSED that Theodore's obsession with Alice Lee caused him to neglect his studies, or that he ceased to partake of the clubby delights of Harvard. "I have enjoyed quite a burst of popularity since I came back," he boasted in a letter home, "having been elected into several different clubs."[14] Apart from the Porc and its partridge suppers, he attended regular meetings of the Institute of 1770, and its secret caucus, "the old merry brutal ribald orgiastic natural wholesome Dickey."[15] He presented papers to the Harvard Natural History Society on such subjects as "The Gills of Crustaceans" and "Coloration of Birds." He lectured learnedly on sparrows at the Nuttall Ornithological Club (whose middle-aged members, discomfited by his knowledge, accused him of being vain and "cocksure"). He was put up for the Hasty Pudding early in the New Year, and won election as fifth man in the first nine.[16] When his instructor in political economy asked him to form a Finance Club, he not only did so immediately, but wrote a joint paper, with Bob Bacon, on "Municipal Taxation," and presented it at the club's inaugural meeting.

"We little suspected," wrote Professor J. Laurence Laughlin many years later, "that we were being addressed by a future President of the United States and his Secretary of State."[17]

Thus, in February of 1879, Theodore Roosevelt revealed that the political animal within him was at last beginning to stir. About the same time he made his first public speech, at the annual dinner of the *Harvard Crimson*. It was an awkward effort, yet vividly remembered by William Roscoe Thayer:

> Since entering college I had met him casually many times and had heard of his oddities and exuberance; but throughout I came to feel that I knew him. On being called to speak he seemed very shy and made, what I think he said, was his maiden speech. He still had difficulty in enunciating clearly or even in running off his words smoothly. At times he could hardly get them out at all, and then he would rush on for a few sentences, as skaters redouble their pace over thin ice. He told the story of two old gentlemen who stammered, the point of which was, that one of them, after distressing contortions and stoppages, recommended the other to go to Dr. X, adding, "He cured me."
>
> A trifling bit of thistledown for memory to have preserved after all these years; but still it is interesting to me to recall that this was the beginning of the public speaking of the man who later addressed more audiences than any other orator of his time and made a deeper impression by his spoken word.[18]

Although Theodore continued to dream of being a natural historian when he left college, he confessed that the prospect of three extra years of overseas study—a necessary academic requirement—made him "perfectly blue."[19] Politics, on the other hand, was beginning to appeal to him so strongly that he asked Professor Laughlin if he should not perhaps make that his career instead. Laughlin replied that the halls of American government were much more in need of idealistic young men than were zoological laboratories.[20] Still, Theodore clung to his imagined vocation, until a softer, more influential voice persuaded him to abandon the chimera forever.

Whether it was the prospect of losing her beau to some foreign university for three years, or simply his distressing tendency to produce creepy-crawlies, Alice Lee did not relish the idea of Theodore becoming Professor or Doctor Roosevelt. Her disapproval of his collecting was probably the reason for a startling remark he made to Harry Minot at the end of his sophomore year: "As you know, I don't approve of too much slaughter." Much later Theodore himself admitted that courting Alice "brought about a change in my ideas as regards science."[21]

Their intimacy ripened slowly during the early weeks of 1879. There were polite teas with the Saltonstalls and dances at the Lees', winter walks and coasting parties (Alice occasionally allowing him to share her toboggan) on the crisp slopes of Chestnut Hill. "I like the two girls more and more every day," he told Bamie, "especially pretty Alice."[22] Determined to make himself as irresistible as possible, he nurtured his reddish whiskers to the size of powder puffs, and grew increasingly resplendent in his dress, with high glossy collars, silk cravats and cameo pins, fobbed watch chains, and coats rakishly cut away to show off the uncreased, cylindrical trousers of a man of fashion.[23]

TOWARD THE END OF FEBRUARY, Theodore began to suffer from a surfeit of polite conversation. The drawing-rooms of Chestnut Hill suddenly became claustrophobic to him: he decided to clear his head, and his lungs, with another vacation in Maine.[24] When he reached Mattawamkeag Station on 1 March, Bill Sewall was waiting in a sleigh to escort him to Island Falls, thirty-six miles away.

For hour after hour, as they hissed north over a three-foot shroud of snow, Theodore marveled at a landscape wondrously changed from the one he had explored six months before. "I have never seen a grander or more beautiful sight than the northern woods in winter," he told his mother afterward. "The evergreens laden with snow make the most beautiful contrast of green and white, and when it freezes after a rain all the trees look as though they were made of crystal."[25]

At Island Falls, he renewed his acquaintance with Sewall's nephew and partner Wilmot Dow, whom he had met only briefly the previous September. Dow, just twenty-three, was as big a man as

Sewall, and, by the latter's admission, "a better guide . . . better hunter, better fisherman, and the best shot of any man in the country." In time this impassive, smooth-faced youth would become as good a friend to Theodore as his uncle.[26]

For the first few days in Aroostook County, the subzero temperatures troubled Theodore's asthma, or "guffling," as Sewall called it. But after a pung trip to a lumber camp at Oxbow, even deeper in the wilderness, he breathed clear again, and "enjoyed every minute" of his stay.[27] The Aroostook lumbermen, many of whom were unlettered, and had spent all their lives in the woods, were the roughest human beings he had yet encountered. Sewall noted how he charmed them and held their interest.

> Of course he did not understand the woods, but on every other subject he was posted. The reason that he knew so much about everything, I found, was that wherever he went he got right in with the people . . . Theodore enjoyed them immensely. He told me after he left the camp how glad he was that he had met them. He said that he could read about such things, but here he had got first hand accounts of backwoods life from the men who had lived it and knew what they were talking about. Even then he was quick to find the real man in very simple men.[28]

No doubt the emerging politician got great satisfaction out of his ability to converse, on equal terms, with backwoodsmen as well as Boston Brahmins. He asked Bill Sewall, as he had Professor Laughlin, whether he should go into science or politics after he graduated. "You may laugh, but I have a presentiment that some time I may be President."[29]

More intent on the here and now, Theodore the hunter exulted in chasing a caribou for thirty-six hours through the snowy forest, with neither tent nor blankets to protect him. The naturalist collected specimens, while the sometime invalid worked up "enough health to last me till next summer."[30] Last but not least, King Olaf trapped a lynx, and swore that its fur would soon warm the pretty feet of his beloved.

In mid-March, Theodore was back at Harvard, "doing double work to make up for my holiday."[31] Within a week he had breezed through his semiannuals with an average of over 85, and could turn once more to the courtship of Alice Lee. Determined to reenter her life in dramatic fashion, he chose as his stage the floor of the college gymnasium.

THE OCCASION WAS THE spring meeting of the Harvard Athletic Association on 22 March 1879. T. Roosevelt, Jr., weighing in at 135 pounds, was entered for the semifinal bout of the lightweight boxing championship, against W. W. Coolidge, at 133¼ pounds. The winner would presumably take on the defending champion, C. S. Hanks, entered at 133½ pounds.[32] Theodore, who was known to possess a wicked right hand, had given Coolidge "a tremendous thrashing" the year before,[33] no doubt hoped to repeat the performance now for the benefit of Alice Lee. She sat in the gallery with a party of other Boston girls, prettily wrapped in furs, for the gymnasium was freezing.[34]

The first bout went well for Theodore. According to the *Harvard Advocate,* he "displayed more coolness and skill than his opponent," and had no trouble in dispatching Coolidge. There was a ripple of delicate applause from the gallery, and he retired to sponge off for the final bout. When he came out, Hanks (who had duly won the other semifinal) was waiting for him. Again to quote the *Advocate,* "a spirited contest followed, in which Mr. Hanks succeeded in getting the best of his opponent by his quickness and power of endurance."

These terse words might have been the only record of the afternoon's fighting, except that some students in the audience were so impressed by Theodore's performance that they talked about it the rest of their lives. One of them was the future novelist Owen Wister, destined, like William Roscoe Thayer, to become a biographer of the skinny figure in the ring. His description of the bout has made it perhaps the most celebrated episode in Theodore's Harvard career:

> We freshmen on the floor and those girls in the gallery witnessed more than a spirited contest; owing to an innocent

> mistake of Mr. Hanks, we saw that prophetic flash of the Roosevelt that was to come.
>
> Time was called on a round, Roosevelt dropped his guard, and Hanks landed a heavy blow on his nose, which spurted blood. Loud hoots and hisses from gallery and floor were set up, whereat Roosevelt's arm was instantly flung out to command silence, while his alert and slender figure stood quiet.
>
> "It's all right," he assured us eagerly, his arm still in the air to hold the silence; then, pointing to the time-keeper, "he didn't hear him," he explained, in the same conversational but arresting tone. With bleeding nose he walked up to Hanks and shook hands with him.[35]

According to another spectator, Hanks said good-naturedly, "Hadn't we better stop?" Theodore shook his head like a terrier, bared his teeth, and began punching again. The rest of the bout was "distinctly gory." It was plain that the smaller man was outclassed. Hanks had a much longer reach; his eyesight, moreover, was normal, whereas Theodore was obliged to box without spectacles. "It was no fight at all," another student remembered. ". . . You should have seen that little fellow staggering about, banging the air. Hanks couldn't put him out and Roosevelt wouldn't give up. It wasn't a fight, but, oh, he showed himself a fighter!"[36]

One wonders if Alice Lee, shuddering into her furs, admired the bloody Theodore as much as his classmates, however. At any rate, he succeeded in drawing himself to her attention again. As soon as his cuts and bruises healed she accepted an invitation to "a little lunch party" in his rooms. Five other girls and college boys were present, under the benign chaperonage of Mrs. Saltonstall. The lynx rug was presented with great ceremony. Alice announced that she would make Teddy a pair of slippers.[37] Their relationship was moving into an intimate, more serious phase, and Mrs. Saltonstall surely reported this fact back to Chestnut Hill. But the Lees did not seem to fear losing a daughter who, at the tender age of seventeen, had yet to make her debut.

With spring sweetening the air, and Alice growing increasingly receptive to his advances, Theodore decided to pay court to her on horseback, in the style of a true gallant. Lightfoot was accordingly shipped to Cambridge. All at once Chestnut Hill seemed so much closer that Theodore took to galloping over the river almost daily, looking (in his own words) "very swell, with hunting crop and beaver."[38] He took long walks with Alice, taught Alice the five-step waltz, played whist with Alice, told Alice ghost stories, wrote endlessly in his diaries about Alice, Alice, Alice. The very shape of the word, as it uncurled from his pen, seemed to give him pleasure. All through April and May, he overflowed with happiness as intense as his grief of the previous year. "What a royally good time I am having . . . I can't conceive of a fellow possibly enjoying himself more."[39]

BY RISING EARLY and working before breakfast, Theodore was able to pack six to eight hours of study into the first half of the day, leaving his afternoons and evenings free for romance. Although he defined this as "a life of most luxurious ease," poor Lightfoot cannot have agreed. The animal was not only thundering constantly along the hard road to Chestnut Hill, but had to help Theodore work off his exuberance afterward with marathon gallops through the countryside. When, on 13 May, Theodore was invited to dinner at the Lees', he whipped Lightfoot up to such a pace that he nearly killed both horse and himself. "I rode like Jehu, both coming and going, and as it was pitch dark when I returned (about 10:15) we fell, while galloping downhill—a misadventure which I thoroughly deserve for being a fool." For weeks it seemed that the crippled horse might not recover, and Theodore was obliged to visit his beloved on foot—a twelve-mile tramp every time.[40]

By early June, however, he was once again in the saddle. Pausing only to register a preoccupied 87 percent in his annual examinations,[41] Theodore braced himself for the final phase of his courtship of Alice Lee. It was now or never. Only two weeks remained until Harvard shut its doors for the summer. Then, for almost three months, he would be hundreds of miles away from her—while other suitors, perhaps, strolled the lawns of Chestnut Hill. Alice had already given disturbing hints that she liked to flirt. If he did not secure her by Class Day, she might be wooed away.

It comes as a surprise to flick through Theodore's diary for these momentous final weeks of his junior year and find no hint of crisis in its bland pages. Since ripping out his written vow to marry Alice, he had begun what was to become a lifelong habit, that of simply not recording what was ominous, unresolved, or disgraceful. Triumph was worth the ink; tragedy was not. Until Alice was his, he would continue merely to list the trivial details of their relationship, so that if he failed, posterity would not know it, and even he, in time, might forget his aching desire for her.

His letters home are just as guarded, although one cannot help but admire how subtly, since the New Year, Theodore has made the Roosevelts aware of Alice Lee, and prepared them, subconsciously as it were, for his possible engagement. Casually he suggests the entire family might like to come up to Harvard for Class Day, 20 June. "I want you particularly to know some of my girlfriends now."[42] How convenient to have both them and the Lees at hand, should he wish to make an announcement—at the conclusion of his junior year, at the blossoming climax of spring!

Although it is not certain that Theodore asked Alice to marry him on Class Day, he afterward confirmed that he proposed to her sometime in June, and his unerring sense of place and time would seem to make the evening of the twentieth inevitable.[43] He had been tense as a wire the night before, at the D.K.E. Strawberry festivities: "I got into a row with a mucker and knocked him down, cutting my knuckles pretty badly against his teeth."[44] But now his mood was tranquil. Never had he spent such a pleasant day; never had Alice looked "sweeter or prettier." He had ushered at Saunders Hall in the morning, lunched at the Porc, ushered again at the Flower Rush, then escorted Alice to two tea-parties in succession. No doubt much of the student body had admired the tall, honey-haired girl strolling around with "that fellow with whiskers and glasses."[45] Now, in the twilight, they sat together watching the sway of tinted lamps in the Yard, and listening to the songs of the Glee Club.

Words, whispered perhaps, passed between Alice and Theodore. At ten o'clock, when the singing ended, they walked over to Memorial Hall and danced till nearly midnight. Then it was time for Alice to go home. Theodore decided, as her carriage-wheels clattered away, that the night was too young for him to go to bed. Accordingly he went to the Porc, and spent a couple of contemplative hours over the billiard-table. He had much to ponder. Alice had rejected him—but in such a way he could not be wholly despondent. She would, he knew, remember him fondly at least through summer, and he had a tacit invitation to resume his suit in the fall.

IF LIGHTFOOT, LIMPING DOWN the gangplank of the Boston–New York freighter, looked forward to a lazy summer on Long Island, he was soon disillusioned. No sooner had Theodore arrived back in Oyster Bay than the horse was put into harness, and trained to trot and go.[46] Mittie Roosevelt, used to her son's sudden enthusiasms, assumed he was merely having fun; it did not occur to her that deadly serious motives lay behind this interest in elegant locomotion. Even his purchase, in August, of a "dog-cart," or tilbury—whose seat was just large enough for two slim people—failed to arouse her suspicions. After all, his twenty-first birthday was approaching, and it was time he learned to drive.

Theodore spent much of the summer trying to imitate his father's prowess with reins and whip—not altogether successfully, for graceful, balanced movements never came easily to him. But he was not discouraged. "I am leading the most delightful life a fellow well could," he wrote, exulting in his "magnificent health and spirits."[47] As usual he passed every spare minute in the open air, rowing, swimming, sailing, shooting (mostly at inanimate targets, out of deference to Alice), and constantly challenging Elliott to physical contests. "As athletes we are about equal; he rows best; I run best; he can beat me sailing or swimming; I can beat him wrestling or boxing; I am best with the rifle, he with the shotgun, &c, &c."[48]

Theodore's diaries do not dwell on the nineteen-year-old Elliott's more obvious superiorities, such as good looks, charm, and sexual attractiveness. That fatally flawed Apollo was still, in the summer of 1879, unaware of the demon that would one day destroy him. An adolescent tendency toward epilepsy had been cured—seemingly—

by the Rooseveltian remedy for all ills, travel. After a trip to Europe and two long stays in Texas he had returned, vigorous and healthy, to take his place as a young banker in New York society.[49] Instantly friends of both sexes flocked to him, as others had done, years before, to Theodore Senior. "Nell" had all of Bamie's poise and none of her severity. He was untouched by Theodore's aggressive egotism. Like Corinne he tended to gush, but his warmth was more genuine. Kindly, open, decent, generous, he indeed was his father's son—were it not for a helpless inability to concentrate on anything but pleasure.

As far as girls were concerned, these faults merely added to his appeal. Even Fanny Smith, a lifelong worshiper of his brother, had to admit that "Elliott as a young man was a much more fascinating person than Theodore Roosevelt."[50]

ON 16 AUGUST THEODORE'S EXCELLENT results arrived from Harvard. He was pleased to note that "in zoology and political economy I lead everybody."[51] This double achievement, in two such diametrically opposed subjects, was enough to reawaken his career dilemma of the previous winter. He had rejected Professor Laughlin's advice to make government, not science, his career. But now, perhaps because Alice had included the effluvia of the laboratory among her reasons for rejecting *him*, he began to wonder if Laughlin had not been right. Actually he had already, as he later confirmed, "abandoned all thought of becoming a scientist."[52] From now on politics, not zoology, would preoccupy those parts of his mind not given over to Alice Lee.

For thirty-six precious hours, in late August, Theodore was able to worship his beloved in body as well as spirit. En route to yet another vacation in Maine, he stopped off in Boston and spent a couple of nights at Chestnut Hill. Alice accompanied him to a beach party, walked with him through the woods, showed off her graceful prowess on the tennis court, and was his partner at a barn dance. She was "so bewitchingly pretty" he could continue north "only by heroic self-denial."[53] Had Island Falls not been beyond the reach of any telegram, Theodore would have undoubtedly canceled his booking with Bill Sewall, and remained at Chestnut Hill to eat lotus fruit with the Lees.[54]

HARSHER PLEASURES AWAITED HIM in Aroostook County, where the first chill of fall was already in the air. Since his first trip to Island Falls in 1878, Theodore had been longing to climb Mount Katahdin, whose silhouette massively dominated the western windows of Sewall's cabin.[55] Forty miles away and 5,268 feet high, Katahdin was the highest mountain in Maine, and was surrounded by some of the most intractable forest in the Northeast. Now the young underclassman felt sufficiently tough and "forest-wise" to answer the challenge on the horizon. Arthur Cutler and his cousin Emlen Roosevelt, who were also vacationing at Island Falls, agreed to join him. After only two days of preparation they helped Sewall and Dow to load up a wagon, and set off southwest into a dank, dripping wilderness.[56]

If nothing else, the events of the next eight days made Cutler withdraw his old doubts about Theodore's stamina. Although conditions were wet and slippery, the young man effortlessly toted a forty-five-pound pack up the ever-steepening mountain. Losing a shoe in a stream, he padded on in moccasins, which protected his feet "about as effectually as kid gloves." Yet despite the pain of tramping over miles of rain-slicked stones, he triumphantly reached the top with Sewall and Dow. Cutler and Emlen remained far below, in a state of collapse.[57] That night, as the rain beat their tents and bedding into a sodden mess, Theodore noted in his diary: "I can endure fatigue and hardship pretty nearly as well as these lumbermen."[58] His fellow New Yorkers could not. As soon as the party got back to Island Falls on 2 September they left exhausted for home.

Having thus, as it were, flexed his muscles, Theodore set off with Bill Sewall on a second expedition, to the Munsungen Lakes, compared to which "our trip to Katahdin was absolute luxury." It included a fifty-mile, six-day voyage up the Aroostook River in a pirogue, or heavy dugout canoe. Fully half the time they had to drag or push the boat through torrential rapids, pausing occasionally to hack their way through beaver dams and log drifts. They spent ten hours a day up to their hips in icy water, stumbling constantly on sharp, slimy stones. "But, oh how we slept at night! And how we enjoyed the salt pork, hardtack and tea which constituted our food!"[59]

By way of relaxing after this bruising expedition, Theodore persuaded Sewall and Dow to take a third jaunt, during which they drove or marched over a hundred miles in three days. Rain fell unceasingly, but Theodore continued to delight in his "superb health" and ability to walk, wrestle, and shoot on near-equal terms with backwoodsmen. When Sewall and Dow finally put him on the Boston train on 24 September, he declared he felt "strong as a bull."[60] The two big men, watching his skinny arm wave them goodbye, may have had their doubts about that—Sewall for years afterward continued to think of him as "frail"—but they could not fail to be awed by his vitality.[61] He had taken them on in their own environment, and proved himself as good as they.

ON THE MORNING AFTER his return to Cambridge, Theodore emerged from breakfast at the Porc and found his new dog-cart outside the door, lamps and lacquerwork gleaming. Lightfoot waited patiently between its curving poles, long since resigned to the indignity of haulage. The staff of Pike's Stable had done a good job: Theodore could see that both horse and cart were in fine condition. His whip stood ready in its sprocket. Neatly folded under the seat lay a rug just large enough to wrap two pairs of touching legs. Climbing up carefully (for the dog-cart had a notoriously erratic center of gravity) he shook the reins and was soon rolling down Mount Auburn Street in the direction of Chestnut Hill.[62]

To his delight, the rig went beautifully, Lightfoot breaking only at the occasional roar of a locomotive. Theodore was conscious of the stares of passersby, and presumed that he was cutting a fine figure: "I really think that I have as swell a turnout as any man."[63] If by *any man* he meant his fellow students, he understated the case; for this was the first dog-cart ever seen at Harvard, and remained the only one throughout his senior year. With such stylish equipage, he could hardly escape the amused notice of his classmates. Hitherto, he had managed to keep his visits to Chestnut Hill fairly secret, but now rumors began to fly.[64] The amorous Don Quixote, spurring Rocinante across the plain of La Mancha, was no more comic a courtier than Theodore, as he wobbled on tall wheels over the Charles River Bridge. In the words of his classmate Richard Welling:

> Some of us were surprised, senior year, when we saw our serious friend Teddy driving a dog-cart, and, between you and me, not a very stylish turnout. Among the fashionables there was in those days an exquisite agony about a dog-cart which stamped it as the summit of elegance. The driver should hold the reins in a rather choice manner as though presenting a bouquet to a prima donna, and the long thornwood whip with its white pipe-clayed lash should be handled in a graceful way, like fly casting, to flick the horse's shoulder. The cart should be delightfully balanced so that, although the horse trotted, the driver's seat would not joggle. The driver was thus serenely perched on his somewhat elevated seat, and holding his whip athwart the lines, acknowledge the salutes of friends by gently raising his whip hand to his hat brim, his poise never for an instant disturbed. In short, in a horse show where the judges were passing upon fine points of equipment and technique, I fear Roosevelt would have been given the gate.[65]

History does not record what Alice Lee thought of this apparition as it creaked to a halt outside the Saltonstalls' house. Presumably she was not as dazzled as Theodore had hoped, for he studiously avoids mentioning her in his diary entry for the day, 26 September 1879: ". . . they were all so heartily glad to see me that I felt as if I had come home." On the next page Theodore writes: "Dr. and Mrs. Saltonstall are just too sweet for anything, and the girls are as lovely as ever."

Something is obviously wrong. For the rest of September, all of October, and most of November, he shows a strange reluctance to refer to Alice, even obliquely. Her name appears but once, in a list of his guests at an opera party on 16 October. Two pages are ripped out just prior to that date. There is also a reduction in the flow of Theodore's perpetual cheerfulness. Yet the evidence is that he continued to drive over to Chestnut Hill, and his relationship with the rest of that sociable community remained as warm as ever. Only Alice, apparently, was cool.

If he was not happy during these first months of his senior year, Theodore was too busy to be depressed. "I have my hands altogether too full of society work," he mildly complained, "being Librarian of the Porcellian, Secretary of the Pudding, Treasurer of the O.K., Vice President of the Natural History Soc., and President of the A.D.Q.; Editor of the *Advocate.*" His diary makes frequent reference to theater parties and suppers—"I find I don't get to bed too early."[66] Although he had purposely arranged a light study schedule (only five courses, as opposed to nine in his junior year), he worked at it six to eight hours a day.[67] He was determined to keep up his three-year average of 82, and in mid-October proudly informed the Roosevelts: "I stand 19th in the class, which began with 230 fellows. Only one gentleman," Theodore added, with a fine regard for social distinction, "stands ahead of me."[68] He was still, for all the influence of Bill Sewall, an unabashed snob. His idea of a good time, during this period of estrangement from Alice, was to pile six fashionable young men into a four-in-hand, "and drive up to Frank Codman's farm where we will spend the day, shooting glass balls &c."[69]

Alice was not at Theodore's side when he turned twenty-one on 27 October 1879. But his adoring family was, and he saw no reason to be despondent. He would get his girl—he knew it. If still not altogether certain about his career, he at least knew roughly what he would like to do, and his achievements to date, whether social, physical, or intellectual, had not dishonored the memory of his father. For once, he could look back at the past without regret, and at the future without bewilderment. Simply and touchingly, he wrote in his diary: "I have had so much happiness in my life so far that I feel, no matter what sorrows come, the joys will have overbalanced them."[70]

SORROWS CAME sooner than he expected. Early in November, Alice's resistance to his advances, hitherto always softened with a hint of future compliance, began to show signs of permanent hardening. Theodore was immediately plunged into a state of sleepless, aching frustration. "Oh the changeableness of the female mind!" he burst out in a letter home, a remark which must have caused the Roosevelts some puzzlement, since he did not go on to explain it.[71] The prospect of failure clearly terrified him. "I did not think I could win her," he afterward confessed, "and I went nearly crazy at the mere thought of losing her."[72]

As usual he kept despair at bay by burying himself in books (for his birthday he had requested "complete editions of the works of Prescott, Motley, and Carlyle") and studying harder than ever.[73] Somehow he managed to conceal his agony from his classmates. Frederick Almy, class secretary, heard Theodore read a paper at the November meeting of the O.K. Society and was impressed by his vigorous, confident manner. "Roosevelt spoke on the machine in politics, illustrating by the recent election in New York. An interesting discussion followed . . . I have a very high opinion of Roosevelt."[74]

As Thanksgiving, the anniversary of his vow, approached, he made a desperate, last-minute effort to press his suit. Alice would "come out" a week after the festival, and become fair game for all the eligible young men in Boston. He reasoned that his best hope lay in bringing their respective families together, enmeshing Alice in such warm webs of mutual affection (for he was sure everybody would get on famously) that she would be powerless to break away. With considerable skill he managed to arrange four such meetings in twenty days. On 2 November Mr. and Mrs. Lee, Alice, and Rose visited New York and were entertained by the Roosevelts; on 17 November Bamie and Corinne visited Chestnut Hill, and the Saltonstalls gave a dinner in their honor. On 18 November the Lees repeated the compliment. Finally, on 22 November, Theodore held an elaborate, thirty-four-plate luncheon in the Porcellian, at which elders of all three families were represented. The rest of the company comprised the most attractive of his Boston girlfriends and the most fashionable of his college chums. Perhaps because of Alice's youth, or because Theodore did not wish to arouse premature suspicions, he relegated her to the secondary position on his left; the place of honor went to a Miss Betty Hooper.[75]

This three-week diplomatic offensive paid off handsomely in terms of family goodwill. The Lees were in reported "raptures" over their New York trip, and his sisters had been effusively welcomed at Chestnut Hill. As for his luncheon, "everything went off to perfection; the dinner was capital, the wine was good, and the fellows all gentlemen."[76] For a few days Theodore basked in the glow of his achievements, then drove out to Chestnut Hill for Thanksgiving hoping that Alice would now look more favorably upon him.

Unfortunately she did not, although she continued, rather heartlessly, to flirt and tease. He returned to Harvard in a melancholy mood. Four days later Alice "came out" in the traditional shower of rosebuds, and Boston's eligible youth began to circle ominously around her. Theodore was a guest at the party, and in the days following could no longer conceal his violent frustration. "See that girl?" he exclaimed at a Hasty Pudding function, pointing across the room at Alice: "I am going to marry her. She won't have me, but I am going to have *her!*"[77]

As winter settled in, and the long evenings dragged out, Theodore felt the loneliness of unrequited love weigh heavily upon him. Unable to find solace in reading books, he began to write one, entitled *The Naval War of 1812*.[78] His insomnia worsened to the point that for night after night he did not even go to bed. He wandered endlessly through the frozen woods around Cambridge, declaiming Swinburne.[79] After one such excursion he refused to return to his rooms. Seriously alarmed, a classmate telegraphed Theodore's family for assistance. Fortunately James West Roosevelt was staying nearby, and rushed to the aid of his stricken cousin. Somehow, the distraught lover was soothed.[80]

He did not see Alice at all during the two weeks prior to his Christmas vacation. Returning to New York on 22 December he threw himself determinedly into the usual family festivities. On Christmas Eve he called on at least ten "very pretty girls," as if to erase from his mind the picture of his beloved. Edith Carow was among them. "She is the most cultivated, best-read girl I know."[81]

All at once, on the day after Christmas, the word "Alice" joyously reappears in his diary. That young coquette had decided to visit New York for a week, accompanied by a retinue of "Chestnut

Hillers." Graciously accepting Theodore's invitation to stay, she permitted him to squire her around town, and his delight knew no bounds. They had "an uproariously jolly time," he told his diary, adding in a more reflective moment that her presence at 6 West Fifty-seventh Street seemed "so natural."[82]

New Year's Day, 1880, dawned calm and sunny, matching Theodore's mood. He drove his guests out to Jerome Park for lunch and an afternoon of dancing.[83] Alice bobbed and swayed enchantingly in his arms, and he sensed that his long agony would soon be over.

> *Sun., Jan. 25* At last everything is settled; but it seems impossible to realize it. I am so happy that I dare not trust in my own happiness. I drove over to the Lees determined to make an end of things at last; it was nearly eight months since I had first proposed to her, and I had been nearly crazy during the past year; and after much pleading my own sweet, pretty darling consented to be my wife. Oh, how bewitchingly pretty she looked! If loving her with my whole heart and soul can make her happy, she shall be happy; a year ago last Thanksgiving I made a vow that win her I would if it were possible; and now that I have done so, the aim of my whole life shall be to make her happy, and to shield her and guard her from every trial; and, oh, how I shall cherish my sweet queen! How she, so pure and sweet and beautiful can think of marrying me I can not understand, but I praise and thank God it is so.[84]

The engagement was kept secret pending family approval. For several days Theodore could not believe his luck. "I still feel as if it would turn out, as it so often has before, and that Alice will repent." But she did not. Now that her defenses were down, he could kiss and cuddle her as often as he wished.[85] In a daze of delight, he rushed to New York to break the news to his family. Mittie Roosevelt was stunned, but, thanks to her prior exposure to Alice, wholly satisfied. The girl had beauty, grace, and humor—qualities for which she herself had been famed in her time. As for Theodore,

Mittie had long since recognized that he, not Elliott, was his father's son: decisive and masterful, a man who knew exactly what he wanted. Right now it was "a diamond ring for my darling."[86] While he shopped for it, Mittie wrote Alice a delicate, violet-scented note, formally welcoming her into the family. The reply came by return of post, and reassured her that Alice, no longer the coquette, was as deeply in love as Theodore.

Chestnut Hill, Feb. 3rd 1880

My Dear Mrs. Roosevelt I feel almost powerless to express my thanks and appreciation of your sweet note received this afternoon, full of such kind assurances of love and welcome, it is more than kind, and feeling so unworthy of such a noble man's love, makes me feel that I do not deserve it all. But I do love Theodore deeply and it will be my aim both to endear myself to those so dear to him and retain his love.

How happy I am I can't begin to tell you, it seems almost like a dream. It is such pleasure to have known all his loved ones, and not to feel that I am going amongst perfect strangers . . . I just long for tomorrow to see Theodore and hear all about his visit home. I was so afraid you might be disappointed when you heard what he went on for, and I assure you my heart is full of gratitude for all your kindness. With a great deal of love, believe me, *Ever yours devotedly,*

ALICE HATHAWAY LEE[87]

There remained the problem of reconciling the Lees to the premature loss of their daughter. Although that amiable couple had no objection to Alice's early engagement, Theodore foresaw "a battle royal" in winning their consent to her early marriage. With his usual regard for the calendar, he hoped to announce the former on Valentine's Day, and celebrate the latter on his birthday, 27 October. Even that eight-month interval would likely be too short for Mrs. Lee.[88] Alice wanted to press for a fall wedding, but he wisely left the date open when negotiating with her father. Pleased at this show of responsibility, George Cabot Lee made the engagement official on 14 February 1880, and Theodore was free to dispatch a series of triumphant announcement notes to his friends. "I have been in love with her for nearly two years now; and have made everything subordinate to winning her. . . ."[89]

Now that Alice was his, Theodore's natural exuberance, so long bottled up, burst out like champagne. His letters and diaries for the months following are awash with adoration. "My sweet, pretty, pure queen, my laughing little love . . . how bewitchingly pretty she is! I can not help petting her and caressing her all the time; and she is such a perfect little sunshine. I do not believe any man ever loved a woman more than I love her."[90] Although the February weather was snowy, he drove constantly to Chestnut Hill, "the horse plunging to his belly in great drifts," impatient to be in the arms of "the purest, truest, and sweetest of all women." When his family arrived in Boston later that month for a round of festive luncheons and dinner parties, Theodore worked himself up to such a pitch of excitement that he went for forty-four hours without sleep.[91]

For all his joy, there came now and again, cold as ice in his stomach, a reminder that he had very nearly failed. "The little witch led me a dance before she surrendered, I can tell you," he confided to his cousin John, "and the last six months have been perfect agony . . . Even now, it makes me shudder to think of some of the nights I have passed."[92] He remained insecure about Alice long after the Lees agreed, in early March, to a fall wedding.[93] "Roosevelt seemed constantly afraid," recalled Alice's cousin, "that someone would run off with her, and threaten duels and everything else. On one occasion he actually sent abroad for a set of French duelling pistols."[94] Planning an Easter visit to New York with Alice, he was naively anxious to impress his local friends at a dinner in her honor: "I want to include everybody, so as to rub up their memories about the existence of a man named Theodore Roosevelt, who is going to bring a pretty Boston wife back to New York next winter."[95]

As the weather softened, and Alice remained faithful, Theodore learned to relax. By 1 April he was able to note smugly that "in spite of being engaged," she was "certainly the belle of the Harvard

Assembly." In order to spend every available minute with her, he resigned many of his official positions, including the vice-presidency of the Natural History Society, neglected his editorship of the *Advocate,* and began to cut recitations freely. His study hours dwindled from thirty-six to fifteen a week. "My marks were so good the first three years that I can afford to be idle now." Already he was bored with scholastic honors. The fact that he had scored 94 and 98 in two semiannuals, written in the same week he successfully proposed to Alice Lee, did not seem remarkable to him.[96]

NOW THAT THEODORE'S romance was common knowledge on the Yard, he not unnaturally became something of a figure of fun. Professor A. S. ("Ass") Hill, his instructor in forensics, was so amused by the "precocious sentimentality" of a Rooseveltian essay that he read it aloud to the class, keeping the name of the author secret. Afterward he waspishly asked Theodore to criticize it, and sat back to enjoy the young man's blushes.[97]

Theodore's dog-cart and dandified appearance (he now sported a silk hat, regarded as the *non plus ultra* of college fashion)[98] did not escape the satire of Owen Wister, who wrote the songs for the D.K.E. theatricals. During one burlesque production of *Der Freischütz,* the chorus launched into a serenade about

The cove who drove
His doggy Tilbury cart . . .
Awful tart,
And awful smart,
With waxed mustache and hair in curls:
Brand-new hat,
Likewise cravat,
To call upon the dear little girls![99]

Wister, gleefully pounding the piano, was unaware that the incensed "cove" himself happened to be in the audience. Next morning, rumors circulated that Teddy Roosevelt was "very angry," and had muttered something about "bad taste." Wister innocently claimed that since Roosevelt's mustache was not waxed, his lyrics were not libelous.[100] He might have added that Theodore had no mustache at all, only whiskers.

But the latter was too much in love to stay angry for long, and looked puzzled when Wister apologized.[101] They soon became fast friends. Theodore was attracted by the sophomore's wit and intelligence, while Wister was one of the first to define the peculiar glow of the mature Rooseveltian personality. During the past few years, this glow had only flickered at sporadic intervals. Now it began to beam forth steadily, throwing Theodore into ever-greater prominence against the muted backdrop of Harvard. "He was his own limelight, and could not help it," Wister wrote many years later. "A creature charged with such a voltage as his, became the central presence at once, whether he stepped on a platform or entered a room."[102]

THE VOLTAGE, OF COURSE, was stimulated by Alice. Its radiance suffuses almost all the diary entries in that spring of 1880.[103] On the fresh April mornings, they played tennis together, she gracefully mobile in her long white dress, he awkward and jerky, clutching his racket halfway up the spine. Later, while Alice sewed, he read to her from Prescott's *Conquest of Peru.* They took endless drives in the dog-cart, with Alice prettily perched beside him in his high seat, as Lightfoot (losing weight rapidly) bowled them along miles of blossom-strewn roads. In the evenings, they sat at whist and listened to the younger Lees practicing the piano. Before bedtime, Theodore generally managed to sneak Alice off for an hour alone in the moonlight. "How I love her! She seems like a star of heaven, she is so far above other girls; my pearl, my pure flower. When I hold her in my arms there is nothing on earth left to wish for; and how infinitely blessed is my lot . . . Oh, my darling, my own bestloved little Queen!"[104]

THEODORE'S ENGAGEMENT seems to have removed the last vestiges of doubt concerning his future. "I shall study law next year, and must there do my best, and work hard for my little wife."[105] He had already made it clear that he considered law a stepping-stone to politics, and confirmed that larger ambition in a conversation with William Roscoe Thayer. The occasion was a meeting of Alpha Delta Phi in Holworthy, shortly before Commencement.

> Roosevelt and I sat in the window-seat overlooking the College Yard, and chatted together in the interval when business was slack. We discussed what we intended to do after graduation. "I am going to try to help the cause of better government in New York City; I don't know exactly how," said Theodore.
>
> I recall, still, looking at him with an eager, inquisitive look and saying to myself, "I wonder whether he is the real thing, or only the bundle of eccentricities he appears."[106]

Theodore was, however, in dead earnest. For his senior thesis he chose the most controversial political subject of the day: it was entitled "Practicability of Giving Men and Women Equal Rights."[107] The very first sentence struck the keynote of his career as a politician. "In advocating any measure we must consider not only its justice but its practicability." Some of his less realistic classmates were shocked by this frank admission that a principle could be both just and impracticable. Yet Theodore made no bones about his real feelings later in the document:

> A cripple or a consumptive in the eye of the law is equal to the strongest athlete or the deepest thinker, and the same justice should be shown to a woman whether she is or is not the equal of man. . . . As regards the laws relating to marriage, there should be the most absolute equality preserved between the two sexes. I do not think the woman should assume the man's name . . . I would have the word 'obey' used not more by the wife than the husband.[108]

By these remarks Theodore laid himself open to charges of effeminacy, and at least one instructor suggested he was too much influenced by "feeling" to be entirely masculine.[109] For the rest of his life he would remain acutely aware of the needs and sensibilities of women. Few things disgusted him more than "male sexual viciousness," or the Victorian conceit that a wife is the servant of her husband's lusts. Although a woman's place was in the home, he believed that the home was superior to the state, and that its mistress was therefore the superior of the public servant. The question of suffrage, as his dissertation made plain, was not so much controversial as unimportant. If women wished to vote, then they should be allowed to do so. Yet he could not resist adding, "Men can fight in defense of their rights, while women cannot. This certainly makes a powerful argument against putting the ballot into hands unable to defend it."[110]

ON 30 JUNE 1880, Theodore Roosevelt graduated from Harvard College as a B.A. *magna cum laude,* twenty-first in a class of 177.[111] His family was present in force, and so was a large contingent from Chestnut Hill. President Eliot placed an embellished diploma in his hand, and murmured the special congratulations due a Phi Beta Kappa. Marching back to his seat in the bright sunlight, with his gown swirling triumphantly and a battery of adoring eyes upon him, Theodore could be excused a moment of self-satisfaction. His academic record was excellent; he was already, at twenty-one, a prominent member of society in Cambridge, Boston, and New York; he had been runner-up in the Harvard lightweight boxing championship; he was rich, pleasant-looking, and, within a limited but growing circle, popular; he was the author of two scholarly pamphlets, a notable thesis, and two chapters of what promised to be a definitive naval history. To crown it all, he was engaged to a beautiful young woman. "Only four months before we get married," he told himself. "My cup of happiness is almost too full."[112]

Yet there was wormwood in his cup, unknown to anybody but the graduate and Dr. Dudley A. Sargeant, college physician. On 26 March, after announcing his engagement, Theodore had undergone a complete physical examination, and had been told to his satisfaction that he had gained twelve pounds since coming to Harvard. But the doctor had other, less satisfactory news. Theodore's heart, strained by years of asthmatic heavings and over-exercise, was in trouble. Far from climbing mountains in Maine, he must in future refrain even from running upstairs. He must live quietly, and choose a sedentary occupation, otherwise, Sargeant warned, he would not live long.[113]

"Doctor," came the reply, "I'm going to do all the things you tell me not to do. If I've got to live the sort of life you have described, I don't care how short it is."

Having spat the wormwood out, Theodore refused to acknowledge that he had ever tasted it. His diary for that night does not even mention the interview, although it is confirmed by Harvard records. Not even Alice Lee, to whom he had promised to tell "everything,"[114] was permitted to know what ailed her future husband. Right through Commencement, Theodore continued to protest his health, happiness, and good fortune. On the following day he could write, with such conviction that every word was heavily underscored, "*My career at college has been happier and more successful than that of any man I have ever known.*"[115]

ALICE JOINED THEODORE at Oyster Bay for the first ten days of July. As he proudly escorted her through the landscapes of his boyhood, he vowed "she shall always be mistress over all that I have."[116] Perhaps this was when the idea of building her a great house overlooking the bay first entered his head. One hill in particular—King Olaf would have called it a *holm,* with its sandy bottom, wooded slopes, and grass-covered crown—he loved above all others. As a teenage ornithologist, he had spent countless hours crouched in its coverts, notating the songs of birds in his own peculiar phonetics—*cheech-ir'r'r', fl'p-fl'p-trkeee, prrrrll-ch'k ch'k* . . . As a Longfellow addict, he had no doubt spent as much time sitting in that hot grass, and seen sails of silk creep over the horizon. Soon he would build a manor on that hill, and live, as Olaf had done, surrounded by his own fields and looking down upon his own ships—well, a rowboat at least. The house would be called Leeholm, after his Queen; and there they would live out their days.[117]

Theodore could indulge such fantasies, in this final summer of boyish irresponsibility, without worrying about such trivia as proprietary rights, mortgages, and deeds of sale. Time enough for them when he took up the duties of a husband and taxpayer. In the meantime, he wished to have fun, and fun meant violent exercise. He would spend three months of such frenetic activity that his heart would simply have to correct itself—or give out in the attempt.

Although Theodore did not state this alarming ambition in so many words, his list of activities for the period makes it quite plain that he intended to keep his promise to Dr. Sargeant. *I'm going to do all the things you tell me not to do.* For the first few weeks at Oyster Bay he swam, rowed, hiked, and played tennis. On 20 July he accompanied Alice, Rose, and Dick Saltonstall to Bar Harbor, Maine, and promptly began to scale mountains, play tennis, bowl, and go for long hikes through the "perfectly magnificent scenery."[118]

Within three days his body began to give off signals of distress, and he fell victim to an attack of *cholera morbus.* "Very embarrassing for a lover, isn't it?" he complained to Corinne. "So unromantic, you know; suggestive of too much unripe fruit."[119] But he was up again next morning, and added dancing to his exercise schedule. Alice's nineteenth birthday, on 29 July, worked him into such a paroxysm of adoration that he collapsed afterward, and the *cholera morbus* struck again. This time Theodore was unable to get up for two days, but Alice nursed him so tenderly he decided he rather liked being sick.[120]

ONE MORE ADVENTURE remained to him as a bachelor: a marathon hunting trip in the West, which he had long been planning with Elliott. "I think it will build me up," he told Mittie, in tacit admission his health was not what it might be.[121] The two young men left New York for Chicago on the night train of 16 August.

Within twenty-four hours, Theodore was gazing through the windows at a horizon wider, and a sky loftier, than any he had ever seen. Lakes as big as seas passed by on his right, farms as big as European countries unrolled to his left. The sheer immensity of

America stirred something in him. For the rest of his life, "big" was to be one of his favorite words. Chicago, which they reached early on the nineteenth, was anticlimactic. "It certainly is a marvellous city," Theodore wrote Bamie, "of enormous size and rich, but I should say not yet crystallized. There are a great many very fine houses; but I should rather doubt the quality of the society."[122]

Anyway it was prairies, not parlors, that he and Elliott had come to see. For the next six weeks they hunted in Illinois, Iowa, and Minnesota with an assortment of guides, not finding very much game, but reveling in the informality of frontier life. "We are dressed about as badly as mortals could be," Theodore boasted, "with our cropped heads, unshaven faces, dirty gray shirts, still dirtier yellow trowsers and cowhide boots."[123] He assured Bamie that his slovenliness was temporary. "We expect to return in three weeks or so. Will you send to 6 W. 57th St. my long travelling bag, with my afternoon suit, 2 changes of underflannels, 6 shirts, 6 pr. silk socks, handkerchiefs, neckties and pin, 2 pairs of low shoes, brushes, razors, and my beaver and my top hat? Also a pair of pajammers . . ." Less than halfway through the trip, the young dandy's thoughts were clearly racing eastward.[124]

Theodore was still too much a New Yorker, and too preoccupied with thoughts of marriage, to enjoy fully this first exposure to the West. His initial excitement dwindled as the weeks dragged by and illness continued to plague him. Although he protested "superb health" in letters home, his diaries record "continual attacks of colic" that made it difficult for him to walk, and asthma so severe he had to sleep sitting up. Other misfortunes combined to aggravate his homesickness and longing for Alice Lee. Both his guns broke, he was bitten by a snake, thrown headfirst out of a wagon, soaked in torrential rainstorms, and half-frozen in a northwesterly gale.[125] Elliott, who had already spent a year in the West, seemed much more at home. Yet beneath the jolly exterior Theodore saw signs of a discontent much deeper than his own. Using as light a touch as possible, he warned the family about it.

> As soon as we got here [Chicago] he took some ale to get the dust out of his throat; then a milkpunch because he was

> thirsty; a mint julep because it was hot; a brandy smash "to keep the cold out of his stomach"; and then sherry and bitters to give him an appetite. He took a very simple dinner—soup, fish, salmi de grouse, sweetbread, mutton, venison, corn, maccaroni, various vegetables and some puddings and pies, together with beer, later claret and in the evening shandigaff. I confined myself to roast beef and potatoes; when I took a second help he marvelled at my appetite—and at bed time wondered why in thunder *he* felt "stuffy" and *I* didn't.[126]

On 24 September the brothers compared their respective game bags. Theodore had shot 203 "items," Elliott, 201.[127] Allowing for seniority, they could call it quits. By now the wind coming off the Great Lakes was bitingly cold, and it was time to go home.

Early on 29 September they arrived in New York. Theodore stopped only long enough to pick up his suitcase of finery before speeding on to Boston. Alice was waiting for him, lovelier than he had ever seen her. She had "a certain added charm that I do not know how to describe; I cannot take my eyes off her; she is so pure and holy that it seems almost a profanation to touch her, no matter how gently and tenderly; and yet when we are alone I cannot bear her to be a minute out of my arms."[128]

THE LAST FEW WEEKS before the wedding were a predictable blur of activity.[129] From Chestnut Hill, Theodore hurried back to New York, and lavished $2,500 on jewelry for his beloved ("I have been spending money like water for these last two years, but shall economize after I am married"). He managed a couple of quick weekends at Oyster Bay, and promised Mittie that he would remain a good son. The enigmatic Edith Carow entertained him at dinner; another old flame, Fanny Smith, was present, and found him "as funny and delicious as ever and wild with happiness and excitement." Then he was again off to Boston, and spent his final weekend as a bachelor on an estate near Salem, "having larks" and chopping down trees in a vain effort to stay calm.

On 26 October, the eve of his wedding, he checked into the Brunswick Hotel, along with a large party of New York friends, and "in wild spirits" tipped Fanny's chair back, until she feared she would do a reverse somersault. Later he went up alone to his room. At midnight he would be twenty-two, and twelve hours later he would be married. Tomorrow there would be another person in his bed. "My happiness is so great it makes me almost afraid."[130]

"I wonder if I won't find everything in life
too big for my abilities."

*Theodore Roosevelt at the time of his assault
on the Matterhorn, 1881.*

CHAPTER 5

The Political Hack

To avenge his father slain
And reconquer realm and reign
Came the youthful Olaf home.

"IT WAS THE DEAREST little wedding," Fanny Smith reported in her diary of 27 October 1880. "Alice looked perfectly lovely and Theodore so happy and responded in the most determined and Theodorelike tones." Bride and groom had emerged from the Unitarian Church, Brookline, into the splendor of a perfect fall afternoon. Indian summer warmed the air and cast a mild glow over the surrounding countryside. Coats and hats were dispensed with on the short drive to Chestnut Hill, and the agreeable holiday mood of a Wednesday wedding spread from carriage to carriage. At the reception in the Lee mansion, sunshine and champagne generated such euphoria that even Edith Carow, who of all the guests had the least reason to celebrate, "danced the soles off her shoes."[1]

The young couple took their departure around four o'clock, and traveled to Springfield, where Theodore had reserved a suite of rooms at the old Massasoit House. Later that evening he noted tersely in his diary: "Our intense happiness is too sacred to be written about."[2]

They journeyed on to New York the next day. There was to be no official honeymoon, only a quiet fortnight together at Oyster Bay. Since Theodore was already registered for the fall and winter terms at Columbia Law School, he could not afford to cut too many classes. Alice was consoled with the promise of a five-month vacation in Europe the following spring.[3]

Mittie Roosevelt had placed Tranquillity at the disposal of the newlyweds. When they arrived, late on Thursday afternoon, they found the house empty save for two maids, an old black groom, and one "melancholy cat." Theodore's rowboat rocked at the jetty. The other houses around the bay were shuttered up, their piazzas strewn with fallen leaves. Wooded hills—flaming red and rusty gold as the setting sun caught them—sealed the little community off from the rest of Long Island. Supper had already been ordered by the thoughtful Bamie. Theodore and Alice had nothing to do but luxuriate in each other's company. For the next two weeks they would spend "hardly an hour of the twenty-four apart."[4]

A SENSE OF DELICIOUS PRIVACY, of port after stormy seas, possessed Theodore as he settled into the domestic routine which he would always consider the height of human bliss. "I am living in dreamland," he told himself.[5] At breakfast Alice prettily presided over the tea-things, "in the daintiest little pink and gray morning dress, while I, in my silk jacket and slippers, sit at the other end of the table." Later she proved herself his equal on the tennis court, and kept pace with him on "long fast walks" through the countryside. There were many excursions, no doubt, up the slopes of Theodore's favorite hill. Alice was persuaded to approve the purchase, for $10,000, of an initial sixty acres overlooking the bay. Together they devoured the newspapers ("Our only intercourse with the outside world") and endlessly discussed "everything . . . from Politics to Poetry." They took afternoon buggy rides over the hills, evening rows across the bay, and feasted on woodcock and partridge. After dinner Alice would curl up in front of a roaring wood fire while Theodore read aloud from the novels of Scott and

Dickens. All through the night her long soft body lay beside his. "How I wish it could last forever!"[6]

MR. AND MRS. THEODORE ROOSEVELT, JR., took up formal residence at 6 West Fifty-seventh Street, New York City, on Saturday, 13 November 1880. They were welcomed back with a "perfect ovation" by the rest of the Roosevelt clan, and Theodore lost no time in assuming the mantle of Elijah. On Sunday, after church, he presided over the traditional family lunch, was "at home" to a variety of relatives and friends in the afternoon, and that evening sat in his father's seat at the Newsboys' Lodging-House Dinner.[7] Before the winter was out, he would inherit two more of Theodore Senior's responsibilities, being elected a trustee of both the Orthopedic Dispensary and the New York Infant Asylum. But the charitable role did not suit him. Many years later he told a friend, "I tried faithfully to do what father had done, but I did it poorly . . . in the end I found out that we each have to work in his own way to do our best; and when I struck mine, though it differed from his, yet I was able to follow the same lines and do what he would have had me do."[8]

Striking that "way" took Theodore a full year, although, as things turned out, it led a mere hundred yards east of his front door. Two other routes temporarily diverted him. The first led three miles south to the Columbia Law School.[9]

EMERGING FROM 6 West Fifty-seventh Street early on the morning of 17 November, Theodore sucked in a lungful of chill, crisp air (marriage had done wonders for his asthma), turned into Fifth Avenue, and marched briskly downtown to 8 Great Jones Street.[10] It was a good forty-five-minute walk, even at the characteristic Rooseveltian gait: arms pumping, toe caps shooting out sideways, every heelfall biting like a pickax.[11] Theodore's first recitation was scheduled for 8:30, and he did not want to miss a word that fell from "the golden lips" of Professor T. W. Dwight, America's most revered legal pedagogue.[12]

The Columbia College Law School, which Dwight had founded in 1858, was little more than a cavernous old house, its floors and walls blotched with tobacco-juice, its windows jammed shut against the traffic-noises of Lafayette Place. Within, an atmosphere of rowdy informality prevailed. Students threw their hats and coats over every available protuberance, argued boisterously in the library, and fought for places in a stuffy little lecture theater. Those who arrived late were obliged to squat around the platform, or wedge themselves onto dusty windowsills, until there was not an inch of standing or sitting space left.[13]

From the moment the white-haired, mildly smiling professor strolled into the room, a cathedral-like hush descended. Dwight was famous for the clarity and persuasiveness of his oratory, the profundity of the questions with which he would every now and again challenge his audience. No conundrum was too knotty for him to untangle, no statute too obscure to exhume and ponder. The thin blood of seven generations of Puritan clergymen, authors, and educators flowed in his veins; his logic was unpolluted by human emotion.[14]

Professor Dwight and his students now discovered that they had in their midst a young man who was impatient with logic, and who, instead of waiting for questions from on high, wished to ask his own. Theodore at Columbia proved to be as harshly persistent an interrupter, as irrepressible a jack-in-the-box, as he had been at Harvard. Time and again he would leap to his feet, glasses flashing, to argue "for justice and against legalism," and express his contempt for the "repellent" doctrine of *caveat emptor.* Why, the young man wanted to know, did this side of the law preclude bargains "which are fair and of benefit to both sides"? He shrilly insisted that the accepted standards of corporation lawyers were incompatible with youthful idealism; they encouraged "sharp practice."[15]

Theodore's pertinacity in raising such subjects vastly irritated a fellow student, Poultney Bigelow. "Roosevelt was then what he was in the White House—an excellent example of the *genus Americanus egotisticus.*" Bigelow may have been a prejudiced witness—those who hated Theodore did so with passion—yet he early detected the future President's lifelong compulsion for center stage. "He was predestined for politics . . . he could not escape the fate of being persistently in the public eye."[16]

Professor Dwight, on the other hand, did not seem to mind Theodore's interruptions. Most of the other students were impressed by the newcomer. He quickly became a favorite, and was accepted as a man with a future, although it was plain to all but himself that he had no future in law. As one classmate dryly put it, "The intricacies of the rule in Shelley's case, the study of feudal tenures as exemplified in the great work of Blackstone, were not the things upon which that avid mind must feed."[17]

All through the winter and spring of 1880–81 Theodore continued to march down Fifth Avenue, Blackstone's *Commentaries* under his arm and a determined expression on his face. "I like the law school work very much," he told himself.[18]

THE SECOND ROUTE that Theodore followed, at the close of his morning classes, led west from the Law School to the Astor Library, on the other side of Lafayette Place. Here he proceeded mysteriously to bury himself in speckled tomes and ancient periodicals. He remained closemouthed about this scholarly activity, not even mentioning it to his diary until March 1881, and then with deliberate vagueness: "Am still working on . . . one or two unsuccessful literary projects."[19]

Just when Theodore became aware of his potential as a writer is unclear. His juvenile letters and diaries had been no more remarkable than those of any intelligent boy; his adolescent notebooks and ornithological pamphlets were strictly scientific; his Harvard themes were laborious, unimaginative, and lacking in "style." Even his eulogies for Theodore Senior and effusions over Alice Lee, while undoubtedly passionate, were expressed in Victorian clichés. Only rarely, as in the stories he used to improvise as a bedridden boy, the humorous letters from Dresden, and the descriptions of birdsong in the Adirondacks, had he shown any flashes of originality. These somehow seem to have convinced him that the name Theodore Roosevelt might one day ornament the spine of this or that leather-bound volume.

From his late teens on he had begun to write, consciously or unconsciously, to an audience. Even the diaries he ostensibly marked "Private" show signs of this urge to communicate. It is impossible to read them at any length without feeling that one is being addressed. Many entries are deliberately prosy and tell Theodore's imagined readers things he does not need to tell himself. Even when he wishes to be genuinely private, he feels the stare of the public, and is obliged to erase paragraphs, tear out whole pages, and curtly announce that some things are "too sacred to be written about."

That other instinct of the born author—the compulsion to write—was also strong in him. Theodore's habit, in moments of joy or sorrow, had always been to reach for a pen, as others might reach for a rosary or a bottle. During the winter of 1879–80, when Alice was driving him to despair, he had begun to write a book, the most technically challenging one he could think of. Now, in the happy winter of 1880–81, he turned again to *The Naval War of 1812*.[20]

Although Theodore protested that the two introductory chapters he had already completed at Harvard "were so dry they would have made a dictionary seem light reading by comparison," he was entitled to be proud of them, for they were a formidable achievement.[21] Before starting the book he had known little about academic research, and less about marine warfare. Merely to master the technicalities of naval strategy and tactics, along with a complex nautical vocabulary, was a task before which any professional historian might quail. To collect and analyze, in terms of comparative firepower, thousands of ballistic and logistic figures (correcting the inaccurate ones *passim*) required the brain of a mathematician—which Theodore did not have. So he had to double-check his calculations until every last discrepancy had worked itself out.

Yet somehow he had managed to do all that—whether successfully or not, the reviewers would have to decide. In the meantime, with his 42 "dry" pages behind him, he could move on to 450 more full of the spray and salt and smoke of real battle.

Despite the enthusiasm with which he took up this work, Theodore was determined not to let his imagination run away with him. He made full use of the research facilities of the Astor Library in an effort to document every sentence of his manuscript. He consulted naval histories published on both sides of the Atlantic, including several French works which he quoted in his own translation. He burrowed through the lives and memoirs of participating admirals. Determined to be scrupulously fair, he consulted such British sources as the *Naval Records, Nile's Register,* and the *London Naval Chronicle.* He sent to Washington for carloads of official captains' letters, logbooks, and shipyard contracts previously untouched by any scholar. He compiled his own construction plans, tactical diagrams, and "tables of comparative force and loss."[22] With these spread out around him, he could ponder such questions as the relationship between a ship armed with long 12s and another presenting 32-pound carronades. Which one would prevail in battle? "At long range the first, and at short range the second," concluded Theodore, who dearly loved a balanced statement. But then the booming of guns in his ears would be interrupted by the library clock chiming three. It was time to march back uptown and take Alice out for her afternoon drive.[23]

Apart from his daily six-mile walk, sleigh-driving was Theodore's only exercise that winter. He went about it with his usual energy, speeding around Manhattan in huge loops, up to thirty miles at a time, while the rest of society sedately circled Central Park. With his "sweet Baby" warmly wrapped in buffalo robes beside him, and Lightfoot's hooves drumming up an exhilarating spray of snow, he would zigzag through the farms and shanties of the Upper West Side until the dark, ice-clogged waters of the Hudson opened out on their left. Spinning north along Riverside Drive, they would admire the snowy Palisades showing in fine relief against the gray winter skies, before curving east across the white fields of Harlem, and south past the great estates of the East River into the pine-forested freshness of Jones' Woods.[24] Emerging at Sixty-eighth Street, they would zigzag toward the mansions of midtown, massed like an interrupted avalanche along the southern fringe of Central Park.

SHOULD THEY PASS Mrs. William Astor's carriage in Grand Army Plaza, Theodore could touch the brim of his beaver with his whip, and know that the gesture would be acknowledged, for the Roosevelt family was eminent enough to be included among the few hundred that majestic lady deigned to recognize. Mrs. Astor's dominance over New York's drawing-rooms was so complete that her word was social law. She was a guest, along with Vanderbilts, Dodges, Harrimans, and Iselins, at Corinne Roosevelt's coming-out party on 8 December.[25] Although the *grande dame* was so stiff with diamonds she could barely turn from one guest to another, she liked what she saw of Theodore and Alice, and invited them to dinner at her austere brownstone on Thirty-fourth Street, whose boards the *nouveaux riches* Vanderbilts were not permitted to tread. As a double seal of her approval, she asked the young couple to her January Ball, the traditional climax of the social season.[26] At this event, and at the scarcely less glittering Patriarch's Ball, and at banquets with Mrs. Stuyvesant Fish, and parties at Delmonico's, and Monday nights at the opera, and at dozens of other receptions, teas, and "jolly little dinners" up and down Fifth Avenue, Theodore and Alice conducted themselves with the grace of natural aristocrats. "Alice is universally and greatly admired," wrote her proud husband, "and she seems to grow more beautiful day by day."[27]

An old friend, separated from the Roosevelts by lesser means, caught sight of them emerging from an opera at the Academy of Music on Fourteenth Street. Theodore had manifestly arrived at the social heights: "I remember thinking what an enormous start he had over youths like myself, whose daily bread depended on their daily effort."[28]

New York at the dawn of the eighties stood poised between the sedate elegance of its past and the fabulous vulgarity of its future. This was at once the age of slippery horsehair furniture and Tiffany glass; of dignified quadrilles and the scandalously sexy waltz; of prephylloxera Burgundies and the harsh, but interesting new Cabernets from California; of copperplate invitations on silver trays and the first crackly telephone messages; of beaux arts filigree decorating old, blocky town houses. Millionaires' Row was not without its vacant lots, and Alva Vanderbilt's vast château at Fifty-second Street—designed to humble Mrs. Astor—was still a skeleton of limestone and marble dust. Not until its last turret was in place, and its doors thrown open to the "splendor seekers," could New York's Golden Age fairly be said to have begun.[29]

Yet already the pace of society was accelerating. For the young

Roosevelts, hardly a night passed without some brilliant affair. Since the opera did not end until 11:30, and balls often continued through dawn, one wonders when Theodore ever found time to sleep. Early in the New Year, after a full day in the law school and the library, a meeting with some old college friends to organize a Free Trade Club, and an evening spent at the Astors', he noted delightedly in his diary, "Every moment of my time occupied."[30] Should a spare moment occasionally present itself, he filled it not with rest but work. Owen Wister has left an anecdote of this period which reads like the opening scene of a Victorian drawing-room comedy. It is the pre-dinner hour; Theodore, standing on one leg at the bookcases in his New York house, is sketching a diagram for *The Naval War of 1812*. In rushes Alice, exclaiming in a plaintive drawl, "We're dining out in twenty minutes, and Teddy's drawing little ships!"[31]

But increasingly, as the season wore on, Theodore used the pre-dinner hour for another, more private activity, of which Mrs. Astor would definitely not have approved. Resplendent in evening dress, he would dash across Fifth Avenue, round the corner of Fifty-ninth Street, and up a shabby flight of stairs.[32]

MORTON HALL, AS THE headquarters of the Twenty-first District Republican Association was grandly called, was a barn-sized chamber over a store.[33] It was furnished with rough benches and spittoons, a raised table and a chair. Two gloomy political portraits completed the decor. Here the cheap lawyers, saloonkeepers, and horsecar conductors who ran Theodore's district—Irishmen, mostly—met together for political meetings once or twice a month. On other nights Morton Hall served as a sort of clubroom where the same clientele could chat informally. During these "bull sessions" Celtic eloquence, punctuated by regular squirts of plug-juice, tended to veer from politics to dirty stories. Theodore, whose distaste for tobacco matched his prudishness, must have winced many times during his first visits in the fall of 1880. He had been by no means welcome, for his side-whiskers and evening clothes made the "heelers" uncomfortable.[34] But he came back again and again, until he was eventually accepted for membership in the association.[35]

When the news of Theodore's unseemly activities leaked out, his family reacted with almost uniform horror. "We thought he was, to put it frankly, pretty fresh," wrote Emlen Roosevelt. "We felt that his own father would not have liked it, and would have been fearful of the outcome. The Roosevelt circle as a whole had a profound distrust of public life."[36] So, too, did his father's friends—bankers, lawyers, businessmen, clubmen. Politics, they assured him from the depths of their leather armchairs, was "low." A gentleman of his upbringing might subscribe to campaign funds—without inquiring too closely as to how the money was spent—might even attend a primary or two, and of course he had a duty to cast his vote on Election Day, providing the weather was fine. But to traffic with men who were "rough and brutal and unpleasant" was decidedly *infra dig*. He should not soil his kid gloves on the levers of political machinery.[37]

Theodore reacted with predictable anger:

> I answered that if this were so it merely meant that the people I knew did not belong to the governing class, and that the other people did—and that I intended to be one of the governing class; and if they proved too hard-bit for me I supposed I would have to quit, but that I certainly would not quit until I had made the effort and found out whether I really was too weak to hold my own in the rough and tumble.[38]

He could, of course, have entered the government the respectable way—by cultivating the society of men in leather armchairs, qualifying as a lawyer himself, and, in ten years or so, running for a seat in the United States Senate. But some instinct told him that if he desired raw political power—and from this winter on, for the rest of his life, he never ceased to desire it—he must start on the shop floor, learn to work those greasy levers one by one.[39] Besides, he had a private score to settle. It had been the New York State Republican machine, still controlled by Boss Roscoe Conkling, that had destroyed Theodore Senior; might not Theodore Junior, by mastering its techniques, use that same machine to avenge him? Among his father's letters, which he kept about him as "talismans against evil,"[40] was one dated 16 December 1877, after Conkling's victory in the Senate. In the tired hand of a dying man, Theodore

Senior had written: "The 'Machine politicians' have shown their colors . . . I feel sorry for the country however as it shows the power of partisan politicians who think of nothing higher than their own interests, and I feel for your future. We cannot stand so corrupt a government for any great length of time."[41]

So the budding socialite turned his back on privilege, and spent more and more time at Morton Hall.[42] Despite the glory he later attained, the clubby set never quite forgave him. He was considered "a traitor to his caste," a man who "should have been on the side of capital."[43] Long after his death, when builders began to convert the Theodore Roosevelt Birthplace into a national shrine, a family elder exclaimed, "I don't know why you are making such a fuss. I used to hate to see him coming down the street."[44]

THE STOUT MAN WHO chaired meetings at Morton Hall, from behind a stout pitcher of iced water, was scarcely more pleased to hear Theodore's feet drumming up the stairs. "Jake" Hess was a self-made, professional politician, and had little use for amateurs in evening clothes.[45] His German-Jewish heritage had not prevented him from elbowing aside many Irish Catholic challengers to win control of the Twenty-first District. A loyal servant of the upstate Republican machine, Hess regularly supplied Albany with loyal, machine-minded Assemblymen. Since the Twenty-first was one of the few "safe" Republican districts in New York City, he was a man of unusual influence, and pompously aware of it.[46]

At first Theodore tried to cultivate Hess, but his efforts were received only with "rather distant affability." The newcomer was forced to mingle instead with the rank and file of the party—and some were rank indeed—acquiring "the political habit" at the very lowest level. For most of the winter of 1880–81 he seemed content with this society.

> I went around there often enough to have the men get accustomed to me and to have me get accustomed to them, so that we began to speak the same language, and so that each could begin to live down what Bret Harte has called "the defective

> moral quality of being a stranger." It is not often that a man can make opportunities for himself. But he can put himself in such shape that when or if the opportunities come he is ready to take advantage of them.[47]

By March he was taking a more active role in party politics, attending a series of primaries in addition to regular meetings, working his way up into the executive committee of the Young Republicans, and presuming to address the association on its new charter.[48]

An opportunity for advancement, he thought, arose early in April. Theodore's only reference to it in his diary was: "Went to Republican Primary; grand row; very hopeless." The story behind this cryptic entry is interesting, since it indicates that his very first political maneuver was in the direction of rebellion and reform. A citizens' movement was under way to introduce a non-partisan Street Cleaning Bill into the State Legislature—then, as always, the cleanliness of New York's streets varied according to who represented which district—and Theodore backed it. He made a speech on behalf of the bill at Morton Hall, and spoke with such force that he won several rounds of applause. By the time he sat down he was the object of at least one man's thoughtful gaze.[49] But the party machine was opposed to the measure; and on 5 May Theodore found himself with only six or seven votes out of three or four hundred.[50]

The young opportunist retired to lick his wounds. He did not go back to Morton Hall that spring. A few days later the law school broke up, Lightfoot was dispatched to the country, and Mittie Roosevelt ordered the blinds drawn at 6 West Fifty-seventh Street. Pausing only to dictate his will, and pack a thousand pounds of luggage, Theodore escorted Alice up the gangplank of the steamship *Celtic* on 12 May 1881. "Hurrah! for a summer abroad with the darling little wife."[51]

HIS EUPHORIA DWINDLED before they were halfway across the Atlantic. "Confound a European trip, say I!" he wrote in his diary. Alice, who had never been overseas before, was so consistently seasick that Theodore exhausted himself taking care of her.[52] But Ireland, which they reached on 21 May, exerted its usual calming influence.[53] They sailed smoothly up the River Lee to Cork, and awoke the following morning, Sunday, to the sound of the Bells of Shandon. Alice recovered immediately, and was able to endure ten days of riding on jaunting cars, ancient trains, and shaggy ponies with sweet equanimity. Meanwhile, Theodore reacted to everything with ears as well as eyes. He praised the birdsong and wildflowers at Castle Blarney, enjoyed the silence and "many-colored mountains" around Killarney, and thrilled to the echoing cliffs of Dunloe's Gap. Unlike most visitors, he investigated some of the uglier aspects of life on the Emerald Isle. A heap of dirty rags on the road to Cork turned out to be a tramp, "insensible from sheer hunger." With the help of some peasants, he revived the man, fed him, and sent him on his way with ten shillings. "A beautiful country," Theodore concluded, "but with a terrible understratum of wretchedness."[54]

By the end of the month, when they embarked on a glassy sea for England, Alice had become the best travelling companion he had ever known. Being athletically inclined, she was game for the most arduous excursions, yet was feminine enough to pretend helplessness while he juggled with suitcases, tickets, and hack-drivers. "Baby enjoys everything immensely," he wrote after a marathon tour of the London galleries, "and has a far keener appreciation of most of the pictures than I have."

Theodore's own taste, on this third exposure to the art of Europe, was cheerfully unsophisticated: "Turner—idiotic." He preferred such sentimental artists as Murillo and Gustave Doré, despite the latter's tendency "to paint by the square mile."[55] A week in Paris, dining deliciously and exploring the caverns of the Louvre; five days in a Venetian palace, with evening rides through the "water-streets," and balcony breakfasts shared with pigeons; an afternoon spent under the "immense, cool, vaulted arches" of Milan Cathedral; four days in the marbled splendor of the Villa d'Este on Lake Como; then north in a rented carriage for a tour of the Alps. Alice, riding on horseback, accompanied Theodore up "a fair-sized mountain" near Samaden, and in consequence spent the next several days nursing various tender areas of her person.[56]

During this lull, early in July, news came that President Garfield had been shot, and was lying in a coma from which he was unlikely to recover. "Frightful calamity for America," wrote Theodore in his diary, adding, ". . . this means work in the future for those who wish their country well."[57]

The assassination of President Garfield was only the latest in a series of political explosions that shook America in the spring and summer of 1881, and whose rumblings followed Theodore across the Atlantic. Fuses had been lit the year before at the Republican National Convention, when the party went into deadlock over the nomination of its presidential candidate. Senator Conkling's machine-minded "Stalwarts," who had grown rich on patronage under Grant, and suffered under the righteous Hayes, wanted the general back in the White House. More independent (but equally corrupt) "Half-Breeds" were united in support of James G. Blaine. It had taken twenty-six ballots before James A. Garfield was nominated as an unpopular compromise. Both factions smoldered in resentment through his election and inauguration in March 1881.[58] Then the first explosion occurred.

IN AN UNCANNY REPETITION of the events of 1877, Garfield named a reform Republican to the Collectorship of Customs for the Port of New York, just as Hayes before him had named Theodore Senior. Boss Conkling was so enraged by this second Presidential slap in the face that on 16 May he resigned his Senate seat, confident that his lieutenants in the New York State Legislature would reelect him and shame Garfield into withdrawing the appointment. No Senator had ever offered so dramatic a challenge to a President, and Theodore, anxiously devouring French and Italian newspapers, kept abreast of developments as best he could.

For a while it seemed that the Boss might win. But then a madman's bullet shattered both Garfield's spine and Conkling's chances.[59] While the President lay dying, Conkling became, by popular consent, the archvillain who had plotted his assassination. This rumor was false. Party leaders in Albany, however, were forced to elect another Senator.

A final stroke of irony, which Theodore had leisure to ponder in his Alpine retreat, was that Garfield's heir apparent was Vice President Chester A. Arthur—the very man whom Theodore Senior had been groomed to replace in 1877. Boss Conkling might be out of power, but as long as his father's old rival sat in the White House, Theodore would be reminded of the uninterrupted power of the machine.

MOVING ON THROUGH Austria and Bavaria, the young man had opportunity to exercise his linguistic abilities, translating German into Italian for the benefit of the carriage driver, and both into English for the benefit of Alice.[60] They found the summer heat of the Bavarian lowlands stifling, and by mid-July Theodore was climbing mountains again. In a period of ten days he "walked up" Pilatus (leaving an exhausted guide halfway down), the Rigi-Grindelwald, and the Jungfrau, confessing only that he felt "rather tired" after the latter. Then, having refreshed himself with a twenty-one-mile hike from Visp to Zermatt, he focused his eager spectacles on the Matterhorn.[61]

The notorious fifteen-thousand-foot peak curved into the sky like a giant scimitar, so steeply pointed that snow either slid off it or blew away in Alpine gales. Unconquered until 1865, the Matterhorn possessed for Theodore "a certain sombre interest from the number of people that have lost their lives on it." This, plus the prestige he would win as one of the few unskilled climbers to ascend it, was enough to tempt him, and the presence of two British mountaineers in his hotel acted as a further goad.[62] Determined to prove that he could climb as well as they could, he set off with two guides on the morning of 5 August.

> At six o'clock in the evening we reached the small hut, half a cavern, where we spent the night; it was on the face of a cliff, up which we climbed by a rope forty feet long, and the floor was covered with ice a foot deep . . . We left the hut at three-forty [A.M.] and, after seeing a most glorious sunrise, which crowned the countless snow peaks and billowy, white clouds with a strange, crimson irradescence, reached the summit at

seven, and were down at the foot of the Matterhorn proper by one. It was like going up and down enormous stairs on your hands and knees for nine hours . . . during the journey I was nearer giving out than on the Jungfrau, but I was not nearly so tired afterwards.[63]

HAVING HAD HIS FILL of exercise for a while, Theodore turned now to mental activity. The manuscript of "that favorite *chateau-en-espagne* of mine," *The Naval War of 1812* formed a bulky part of the Roosevelt luggage, and he worked at it doggedly during his last month in Europe. "You would be amused," he told Bamie from the Hague, "to see me writing it here. I have plenty of information now, but I can't get it into words; I am afraid it is too big a task for me. I wonder if I won't find everything in life too big for my abilities. Well, time will tell."[64]

On 10 September the travelers reached Liverpool,[65] laden with Parisian fashions and presents from the best London shops. Here Theodore's "blessed old sea-captain" uncle, Irvine Bulloch, helped untangle some of the nautical knots in his manuscript.[66] The young author's confidence returned, and he found himself looking forward to the resumption of his legal, literary, and political work in New York.

Summarizing his third trip abroad in twelve years, Theodore wrote Bill Sewall: "I have enjoyed it greatly, yet the more I see the better satisfied I am that I am an American; free born and free bred, where I acknowledge no man as my superior, except for his own worth, or as my inferior, except for his own demerit."[67]

IN THIS HEALTHY FRAME of mind, and feeling superbly healthy in body, the conqueror of the Matterhorn arrived back in New York on 2 October 1881. He lost no time in resuming his tripartite life, although a diary entry for 17 October indicates that his priorities had changed. "Am working fairly hard at my law, hard at politics, and hardest of all at my book." Indeed, Theodore's interest in the first of these activities was steadily waning. He would continue to attend Columbia Law School lectures, on and off, for at least another year, and acquire, almost against his will, a semiprofessional mastery of civil and criminal procedure, corporate and constitutional law, labor contracts, and cross-examination techniques—all highly useful to him in later life. But he found his current ambitions better served (and his soul more soothed) by the contrasted pleasures of politicking and writing.[68]

From 6 October to 8 November it was the former activity that prevailed, since the Twenty-first District was going through its annual throes of returning an Assemblyman to Albany. Theodore did not want to miss a moment of the "rough and tumble." He plunged aggressively into primary work, resolved "to kill our last year's legislator," who was up for renomination.[69] The legislator's name was William Trimble. Like all of Jake Hess's hand-picked Assemblymen, he was a loyal servant of the machine, and a Stalwart through and through. This alone would have been enough to prejudice Theodore against him. The fact that Trimble had voted to oppose his pet cause, the Street Cleaning Bill, added a personal zest to the fight. Accordingly Theodore worked energetically on behalf of independent delegates, and on 24 October, at the preconvention meeting in Morton Hall, he stood up to make a formal protest against Trimble's renomination.[70] Hess listened from behind his pitcher of iced water with the bland patience of a leader who is sure of his delegates. Neither he nor the speaker was aware that the same thoughtful eyes which had rested on Theodore earlier in the year were resting on him again, and that by now their gaze was beady.

The eyes belonged to Joe Murray, one of Hess's Irish lieutenants. Burly, red-faced, taciturn, and shrewd,[71] Murray had his own reasons to stop Trimble, more complex ones than Theodore's. He had been raised in barefoot poverty on First Avenue, and emerged in his teens as the leader of a street gang. In this capacity he had been employed, on a freelance basis, to influence the course of local elections with his fists. Although he worked, in alternate years, for both Republicans and Democrats, his blows on behalf of the former party carried more conviction, so to speak, than those for the latter, and in his early twenties he had been rewarded with the job of ward heeler at Morton Hall. Having thus literally punched his way into politics, Murray revealed unexpected gifts for party organization, and moved up quietly through the ranks until now, in his mid-thirties, he stood at Hess's elbow. Being a philosophical man, he tolerated his leader's arrogance and vanity, content to build up support within the association until the time was ripe to "make a drive" at him.[72]

It had been too early to do that in the spring, when Murray had joined Hess in crushing Theodore's support of the Street Cleaning Bill, but he had not forgotten the young man's courage and outspokenness. During the summer, events had conspired to keep Roosevelt in his mind. The resignation of Boss Conkling, and the assassination of President Garfield, caused a public outcry against machine politicians in general, and Stalwarts in particular. Since Assemblyman Trimble was both, he had been tainted by this unpopularity, and Murray's street instinct warned that if Trimble stood for reelection, the Twenty-first might fall to the Democrats. But when the Irishman expressed his misgivings, Hess had reacted contemptuously. "He'll be nominated anyway. You don't amount to anything."[73]

This was one insult too many for Murray. Unknown to Hess, he had already lined up enough delegates to nominate anybody he chose. All he lacked was a candidate. Two nights later, as he sat listening to Theodore speak at the preconvention meeting, he realized that he had found one. Here was a candidate to beat Trimble, humiliate Hess, and convince the electorate that the bad old days of Republicanism were over. This boy bore the name of one of New York's most revered philanthropists. As an Ivy League man, he could be counted on to bring in "the swells and the Columbia crowd"; as a Knickerbocker, he would generate funds along Fifth Avenue. He was obviously naive and untrained in politics, but that should prove an advantage on the hustings. His manners were pleasing, his face open and ingenuous, and he positively glowed with righteousness. He would be independent of any machine, immune to all bribes; he was honest, elegant, humorous, and a born fighter. What was more, he obviously enjoyed getting up on a chair and shouting at people. Murray decided "it was Theodore Roosevelt or no one."[74]

At the end of the meeting he drew the young man aside and told him that he, too, was opposed to the renomination of Trimble. Casually, the Irishman said that he had been "looking around" for another candidate and thought his search might be over.

"No, I wouldn't dream of such a thing," Theodore said. "It would look as if I had selfish motives in coming around to oppose this man."

Murray could interpret a coy expression as well as anybody. "Well, get me a desirable candidate."

"Oh, you won't have any trouble," replied Theodore, and offered to look for one himself.[75]

The following evening they met again, and Theodore had to admit that he had not found a candidate. But he was still sure he could do so. With only three days to go before the convention, Murray grew impatient.

"Mr. Roosevelt, in case we can't get a suitable candidate, will you take the nomination?"

Theodore hesitated. "Yes, but I don't want it." He was privately suspicious of Murray's motives, and went to seek the reassurance of a mutual friend, Edward Mitchell. "Joe is not in the habit of making statements that he cannot make good," Mitchell told him. "You have fallen in very good hands."[76]

On 28 October 1881, the Assembly Convention met at Morton Hall. Murray sat patiently through a forty-five-minute speech nominating Assemblyman Trimble. Then he rose and simply said, "Mr. Chairman, I nominate Theodore Roosevelt." The convention voted in his favor on the first ballot, with a majority of sixteen to nine.[77] Theodore was just twenty-three years and one day old.

Late that night the nominee wrote in his diary, "My platform is: strong Republican on State matters, but independent on local and municipal affairs." Thus, at the very outset of his political career, he managed to balance party loyalty with personal freedom. The platform he chose was an unstable one, yet he had already found its center of gravity. For the next four decades he would occupy that motionless spot, while the rest of the platform tipped giddily backward and forward, Left and Right.

CONFRONTED WITH Theodore's nomination as a fait accompli, the Roosevelt family rallied to his support with varying degrees of enthusiasm.[78] Wealthy friends of his father offered to help with campaign expenses and published an open letter testifying to his "high character . . . honesty and integrity." The list of signatures on this document, which read like a combination of the *Social Register* and *Banker's Directory*, included that of the eminent lawyer Elihu Root, yet another of Theodore's future Secretaries of State.[79]

Press comment on the nomination was mostly favorable. "Every good citizen has cause for rejoicing," declared *The New York Times*, "that the Republicans of the Twenty-first Assembly District have united upon so admirable a candidate for the Assembly as Mr. THEODORE ROOSEVELT. . . . Mr. Roosevelt needs no introduction to his constituency. His family has been long and honorably known as one of the foremost in this city, and Mr. Roosevelt himself is a public-spirited citizen, not an office-seeker, but one of the men who should be sought for office."

The newspaper went on to note that as Theodore's district was "naturally Republican," he could look forward to "a handsome majority" in the election.[80] This fact may also have been realized by the Democrats. Their candidate was a Dr. W. W. Strew, recently fired from the directorship of Blackwell's Island Lunatic Asylum.[81]

Theodore himself had no doubt that he would be elected. His campaign circular, dated 1 November 1881, was so brief, and bare of promises, as to seem almost arrogant:

> Dear Sir,
>
> Having been nominated as a candidate for member of Assembly for this District, I would esteem it as a compliment if you honor me with your vote and personal influence on Election Day.
>
> Very respectfully,
>
> THEODORE ROOSEVELT[82]

After decades of flowery political appeals, this simple message came as a welcome surprise to the electorate.

For all the favorable trends, Theodore's eight-day campaign was not without its anxious moments. Joe Murray and Jake Hess (who had philosophically agreed to support the Assembly Convention's decision) soon discovered that their candidate had an alarming tendency to speak his mind. It was fortunate that they accompanied him on a personal canvass of the saloons of Sixth Avenue, or, as Theodore recalled in his autobiography, the "liquor vote" might have been lost.

> The canvass . . . did not last beyond the first saloon. I was introduced with proper solemnity to the saloon-keeper—a very important personage, for this was before the days when saloon-keepers became merely the mortgaged chattels of the brewers—and he began to cross-examine me, a little too much in the tone of one who was dealing with a suppliant for his favor. He said that he expected that I would of course treat the liquor business fairly; to which I answered, none too cordially, that I hoped I should treat all interests fairly. He then said that he regarded the licenses as too high; to which I responded that I believed that they were really not high enough, and that I should try to have them made higher. The conversation threatened to become stormy. Messrs. Murray and Hess, on some hastily improvised plea, took me out into the street, and then Joe explained to me that it was not worth my while staying in Sixth Avenue any longer, that I had better go right back to Fifth Avenue and attend to my friends there, and that he would look after my interests on Sixth Avenue.
>
> I was triumphantly elected.[83]

Theodore received the news of his victory—3,490 votes to Strew's 1,989, almost double the usual Republican margin—distractedly. After voting on the morning of 9 November, he had retired to the library at 6 West Fifty-seventh Street and busied himself with his book, which was due at Putnam's by Christmas. Not until an admirer called, "wishing to meet the rising star," did he accept the fact that he was now a professional politician.[84] This sudden change in status seems only to have increased his determination to become, simultaneously, a professional writer. He spent the rest of November working with total absorption on his manuscript, and by 3 December it was in the hands of the publisher.[85]

The Naval War of 1812, which appeared some five months later, was the first and in some ways the most enduring of Theodore Roosevelt's thirty-eight books. Reviewers were almost unanimous in their praise of its scholarship, sweep, and originality. It was recognized on both sides of the Atlantic as "the last word on the subject," and a classic of naval history. Within two years of publication it went through three editions, and became a textbook at several colleges. In 1886, by special regulation, at least one copy was ordered placed on board every U.S. Navy vessel.[86] Eleven years later, when Great Britain was preparing her own official history of the Royal Navy, the editors paid Theodore the unprecedented compliment of asking him to write the section of that work dealing with the War of 1812. For almost a century, *Naval War* would remain the definitive work in its field.[87] Considering the author's youth (he was twenty-one when he began it, and just twenty-three when he finished), his frequent ill health, and many distractions, the book may be considered an extraordinary achievement.

Its merits are as simple as those of any serious piece of academic writing: clarity, accuracy, and completeness, backed by massive documentation. The density of research is such that Theodore often quotes a different authority for every sentence. His impartiality in weighing facts and reaching conclusions is remarkable in view of his burgeoning Americanism. Sentiment is never allowed to interfere with statistics. Admittedly, the first chapters do not make for fascinating reading:

> The 32-gun frigates . . . presented in broadsides 13 long 12's below and seven 24-pound carronades above; the 38-gun frigates, 14 long 18's below and ten 32-pound carronades above; so that a 44-gun frigate would naturally present 15 long 24's below and twelve 42-pound carronades above, as the *United States* did at first. . . .[88]

And so on, for dozens of pages. Clearly he is out to inform, not entertain. And it must be admitted that his own criticism of it as "dry" is justified. The first two chapters, however masterly in their compilation and assortment of figures, are unreadable by all except the most dedicated naval strategists, and the other eight are almost as severe. There is something almost inhuman about the young author's refusal to swashbuckle, taste the triumphs of victory and the pain of defeat, and dramatize character where well he might. Yet there twinkles, every now and again in its gray pages, a flash of sarcastic humor, usually at the expense of historians less scholarly than he:

> James states that she [the *United States*] had but one boy aboard, and that he was seventeen years old—in which case 29 others, some of whom (as we learn from the "Life of Decatur") were only twelve, must have grown with truly startling rapidity during the hour and a half the combat lasted.[89]

Elsewhere he observes that James's remark on the similarity of language spoken by both sides is "an interesting philological discovery that but few will attempt to controvert."[90]

In his search for truth, he does not hesitate to crush such sentimental legends as that of the Battle of Lake Erie. "The 'glory' acquired by it most certainly has been estimated at more than its own worth," he declares, in the course of a long and brilliantly detailed analysis. "The simple truth is . . . the side which possessed the superiority in force, in the proportion of three to two, could not well help winning." Dismissing "stereotyped" arguments that the United States fleet was underarmed and undermanned, he went on to prove, with incontestable figures, that its *weight* of ammunition—i.e., fighting effectiveness—was superior, "as the battle was fought under very short sail, and decided purely by gunnery."[91]

Theodore's very scrupulousness, however, led him to the conclusion that the Naval War of 1812 was a deserved victory for America. Having so decided, he felt no desire to gloat, for a far more important theme preoccupied him: that if the conflict were to be repeated in 1882 the result would undoubtedly be the reverse. The small, efficient, and technically advanced Navy of 1812 was now large, unwieldy, and obsolescent. Writing his preface to the first edition, the young author suddenly cast aside his cloak of academic impartiality and revealed that he was wearing military uniform underneath.

"It is folly," thundered Theodore, "for the great English-speaking Republic to rely for defense upon a navy composed partly of antiquated hulks and partly of new vessels rather more worthless than the old." He urged his compatriots "to study with some care that period of our history during which our navy stood at the highest pitch of its fame . . . to learn anything from the past it is necessary to know, as near as may be, the exact truth—if only from the narrowest motives."[92]

Strategic experts pondered his message at least as far away as Washington, D.C. *The Naval War of 1812* was to have a profound effect upon the attitude of the country to its Navy, not to mention Theodore's future career.[93]

WITHIN THREE DAYS after delivering his manuscript to Putnam's, Theodore was caught up in the whirl and glitter of the new social season. "The going out has fairly begun," he noted on 6 December. "All are at it, from dinners to Balls." He saw that Alice, who had no doubt felt rather neglected in recent months, had her fill of the festivities. She would be seeing even less of him in the New Year, when the legislative session began at Albany. Until his election, they had been thinking of moving into their own house sometime that winter; but now the prospect of leaving her alone for weeks at a time (although he would try to get married digs in Albany, so she could come north occasionally) convinced him they should stay on at 6 West Fifty-seventh Street. The session would be over in the spring, and they could look for a new home then.[94] As to his future beyond that, Theodore professed to be as vague as ever. "Too true, too true; I have become a political 'hack'," he wrote to an ex-classmate. "But don't think I am going into politics after this year, for I am not."[95]

"I intended to be one of the governing class."

Theodore Roosevelt at the time of his election to the New York State Assembly.

CHAPTER 6

The Cyclone Assemblyman

Through the streets of Drontheim
Strode he red and wrathful,
With his stately air.

ASSEMBLYMAN THEODORE ROOSEVELT arrived in Albany in 17-degree weather, late on the afternoon of Monday, 2 January 1882.[1] Alice had gone to Montreal with a party of friends, and would not be joining him for another two weeks. They could look for lodgings then. In the meantime he checked into the Delavan House, a rambling old hotel with whistly radiators, immediately opposite the railroad station. Apart from the fact that it was conveniently located, and boasted one of the few good restaurants in town, the Delavan was honeycombed with seedy private rooms, of the kind that politicians love to fill with smoke; hence it functioned as the unofficial headquarters of both Republicans and Democrats during the legislative season.[2]

The Assembly was not due to open until the following morning, but Roosevelt had been asked to attend a preliminary caucus of Republicans in the Capitol that evening, for the purpose of nominating their candidate for Speaker.[3] He thus had only an hour or two to unpack, change, and prepare to meet his colleagues.

"He was a perfect nuisance in that House, sir!"

The New York State Assembly Chamber in 1882.

Dusk came early, as always in Albany, for the little city straggles up the right bank of the Hudson, and is screened off from the plateau above by a two-hundred-foot escarpment of blue clay. But the western sky was clear, and lit by a rising full moon, when Roosevelt emerged from the Delavan House, and began his walk to the Capitol.[4]

At first he could not see "that building," as it was locally known, for he had to walk south along the river for a block or two before ascending State Street. Yet already he was moving in its monstrous shadow. Roosevelt had probably read, in his *Albany Hand Book,* that the new Capitol was, by common consent, "one of the architectural wonders of the nineteenth century."[5] Whether it was a thing of beauty or not was questionable, but there was no doubt, as the *Hand Book* said, that it was "the grandest legislative building of modern times." Roosevelt's first glimpse of the eleven-million-dollar structure, as he rounded the corner of State and Broadway, and focused his pince-nez uptown, was a thrilling one.

Still not quite finished, the stupendous pile of white granite towered out of mounds of construction rubble at the very top of the hill. The Old Capitol, a Greek Revival hall awaiting demolition, stood a little farther down, obscuring some of Roosevelt's view, yet its dark silhouette merely accentuated the brilliantly lit massiveness looming behind. Jagged against the skyline rose an improbable forest of steeples, turrets, dormers, and gables, all gleaming in the moonlight, for a snowfall the day before had exquisitely etched them out.[6] An architect surveying the Capitol's five stories could successively trace the influence of Romanesque, Italian Renaissance, and French Renaissance styles, with layers of arabesque in between; but to an untutored eye, such as Roosevelt's, the overall effect was of Imperial Indian majesty.[7] Perhaps for the first time the young Assemblyman realized that, as a New York State legislator, he now represented a commonwealth more populous than most of Europe's kingdoms, rich enough and industrious enough to rank alongside any great power.[8]

Inspiring as the sight of his destination was, Roosevelt had to concentrate, for the moment, on the tricky business of getting up there without falling down. The steep sidewalks of State Street, when slicked with frozen snow, were notoriously dangerous, and that night blasts of icy air over the escarpment made them doubly so. All sane Assemblymen, of course, were taking horsecars in this weather, but any such indulgence was abhorrent to Roosevelt. Although the wind-chill factor was well below zero, he wore no overcoat.[9] A man thus unprotected, yet well stoked with Delavan House coffee, might be able to negotiate two or three blocks of State Street without pain; but he will begin to throb before he is halfway to the top, and Roosevelt was undoubtedly hurting in every extremity by the time he crested the hill and ducked into the warmth of the Capitol lobby.[10]

As the pain faded to a glow, and his lenses defrosted, he could make out a labyrinth of stone passages and ground-glass doors through which came the busy clacking of typewriting machines. He was standing on the clerical floor. The halls of power, presumably, were somewhere overhead. To his left the Assembly staircase beckoned. One hundred rapid steps elevated him to the second floor, and the famous Golden Corridor opened out before him. Unquestionably the most sumptuous stretch of interior design in the United States, it formed a dwindling perspective of gilded arches and gorgeously painted pillars. High gas globes picked out the filigree on walls of crimson, umber, yellow, and deep blue, and cast pockets of violet shadow into every alcove. Jardinieres of "exotics," freshly planted to mark the beginning of the legislative season, perfumed the air.[11] Roosevelt might well have imagined himself in Moorish Granada, were it not for a very American hubbub coming from a door at the far end of the corridor. Here fifty-two other Republican Assemblymen awaited him in caucus.[12]

TO SAY THAT Theodore Roosevelt made a vivid first impression upon his colleagues would hardly be an exaggeration. From the moment that he appeared in their midst, there was a chorus of incredulous and delighted comment. Memories of his entrance that night, transcribed many years later, vary as to time and place, but all share the common image of a young man bursting through a door and pausing for an instant while all eyes were upon him—an actor's trick that quickly became habitual.[13] This gave his audience time to absorb the full brilliancy of his Savile Row clothes and furnishings. The recollections of one John Walsh may be taken as typical:

> Suddenly our eyes, and those of everybody on the floor, became glued on a young man who was coming in through the door. His hair was parted in the center, and he had sideburns. He wore a single eye-glass, with a gold chain over his ear. He had on a cutaway coat with one button at the top, and the ends of its tails almost reached the tops of his shoes. He carried a gold-headed cane in one hand, a silk hat in the other, and he walked in the bent-over fashion that was the style with the young men of the day. His trousers were as tight as a tailor could make them, and had a bell-shaped bottom to cover his shoes.
>
> "Who's the dude?" I asked another member, while the same question was being put in a dozen different parts of the hall.
>
> "That's Theodore Roosevelt of New York," he answered.[14]

Notwithstanding this ready identification, the newcomer quickly became known as "Oscar Wilde," after the famous fop who, coincidentally, had arrived in America earlier the same day.[15] At twenty-three, Roosevelt was the youngest man in the Legislature, recognized not only for his boyishness but for his "elastic movements, voluminous laughter, and wealth of mouth."[16] More bitter epithets were to follow in the months ahead, as he proved himself to be something of an angrily buzzing fly in the Republican ointment: "Young Squirt," "Weakling," "Punkin-Lily," and "Jane-Dandy" were some of the milder ones. "He is just a damn fool," growled old Tom Alvord, who had been Speaker of the House the day Roosevelt was born.[17] Nominated again for Speaker that night, Alvord cynically assessed Republican strength in the House as "sixty and one-half members."[18]

Roosevelt had return epithets of his own, and began to record them in a private legislative diary immediately after the 2 January caucus.[19] At first, they were merely superficial, revealing him to be as class conscious as his detractors, but as time went by, and the shabbiness of New York State politics (so at odds with the splendors of the Capitol) became clear to him, his pen jabbed the paper with increasing fury.[20]

"There are some twenty-five Irish Democrats in the House," the young Knickerbocker wrote. "They are a stupid, sodden, vicious lot, most of them being equally deficient in brains and virtue."[21] Eight Tammany Hall Democrats, representing the machine element, drew his especial contempt, being "totally unable to speak with even an approximation to good grammar; not even one of them can string three intelligible sentences together to save his neck." Roosevelt's *bête noire* (and the feeling was reciprocated) was "a gentleman named MacManus, a huge, fleshy, unutterably coarse and low brute, who was formerly a prize fighter, at present keeps a low drinking and dancing saloon, and is more than suspected of having begun his life as a pickpocket."[22]

He was hardly less severe on members of his own party. Ex-Speaker Alvord he instantly dismissed as "a bad old fellow . . . corrupt." Another colleague was "smooth, oily, plausible and tricky"; yet another was "entirely unprincipled, with the same idea of Public Life and Civil Service that a vulture has of a dead sheep." His contempt dwindled reciprocally according to the idealism and independence of the younger members—in other words, those most like himself. Although they could be counted on the fingers of one hand, Roosevelt instinctively sought them out. One in particular caught his eye: "a tall, thin, melancholy country lawyer from Jefferson, thoroughly upright and honest, and a man of some parts."[23]

The melancholy youth was named Isaac Hunt. He, too, was serving his first term in the Assembly. But the two freshmen did not get to meet for several days, owing to a strange state of political paralysis in the House. The situation was succinctly summarized in Roosevelt's diary of 3 January:

> The Legislature has assembled in full force; 128 Assemblymen, containing 61 Republicans in their ranks, and 8 Tammany men among the 67 Democrats. Tammany thus holds the balance of power, and as the split between her and

the regular Democracy is very bitter, a long deadlock is promised us.[24]

His forecast proved correct. The very first piece of business before the House—electing a new Speaker—was stalled by the Tammany members, who refused to give their crucial block of votes to either of the major party nominees. Thus each candidate was kept just short of the sixty-four votes required to win.[25] Clearly the holdouts hoped that one side or the other would eventually make a deal with them, and that the elected Speaker would reward Tammany with some plum committee jobs. Until then, with nobody in the Chair, there could be no parliamentary procedure, and no legislation.

For the first week in Albany, Roosevelt had nothing to do except trudge daily up State Street and answer the roll call in the Assembly Chamber. Then, there being no further business, he would trudge back to the Delavan House and meditate on the "stupid and monotonous" work of politics.[26] Albany was an unattractive place to be bored in: a little old Dutch *burg* separated from New York by 145 miles of chilly river-valley. Back home, in Manhattan, the social season was at its height, and Fifth Avenue was alive with the sounds of witty conversation and ballroom music. Here it was so quiet at night the only sound in the streets was the clicking of telephone wires. There were, of course, several "disorderly houses" for the convenience of legislators, but such places revolted him.

To vent his surplus energy, he went for long walks around town, but the local air was insalubrious, even to a man with healthy lungs. Depending on the vagaries of the breeze, his nostrils were saluted with the sour effluvia of twenty breweries, choking fumes from the Coal Tar and Dye Chemical Works, and brackish smells from the river. Only on rare occasions did chill, pure Canadian air find its way down from the north, bringing with it the piny scent of lumberyards.[27]

ESCAPING TO NEW YORK for his first weekend, Roosevelt put on a cheerful front,[28] but it was plain that his first exposure to government had depressed him. With Alice still away (she had gone to Boston to visit her parents), Elliott abroad, and Mittie sweetly uncomprehending, he unburdened himself to Aunt Annie, mother-confessor to all young Roosevelts. The little lady, now married to a banker, James K. Gracie, held court in her brownstone at 26 West Thirty-sixth Street, surrounded by Bibles and fruitcake. It was on her knee that Teedie had learned his ABCs, and early displayed his contempt for arithmetic; now, twenty years later, Assemblyman Roosevelt returned to complain about Albany. "We talked of his book," she wrote Elliott, "and his political interests. Thee thinks these will only help him in giving him some fame, but neither, he says, will be of *practical* value in his profession . . . he says he must begin again at the beginning in the Spring . . . having gained this *intermediate* experience."[29]

These remarks, and the young man's earlier avowal, "Don't think I am going into politics after this year, for I am not," might be taken with a pinch of salt. Throughout his life, in moments of triumph as well as despair, he would continue to insist he had no future in politics. Relatives and friends soon learned to ignore such protestations, knowing very well that they were insincere, or at best self-delusive. Theodore Roosevelt was addicted to politics from the moment he won his first election until long after he lost his last.

The weekend in New York was sufficiently recuperative for him to bounce back to Albany on Monday, 9 January, with optimistic energy. There was another Republican caucus that night, and although it dealt with the less than fascinating subject of the appointment of Assembly clerks, Roosevelt conscientiously attended. This time he was in even greater sartorial splendor, having dined out somewhere beforehand. Isaac Hunt, the melancholy member from Jefferson County, was standing by the fireplace in the committee room when "in bolted Teddy . . . as if ejected from a catapult."[30]

Deliberately selecting the most prominent position in the room—directly in front of the chairman—Roosevelt sat down and pulled off his ulster. Underneath he was in full evening dress, with gold fob and chain. At the first opportunity he jumped to his feet and addressed the meeting in the affected drawl of Harvard and

Fifth Avenue. "We almost shouted with laughter," Hunt remembered, "to think that the most veritable representative of the New York dude had come to the Chamber." But as Roosevelt continued to speak, "our attention was drawn upon what he had to say because there was a force in his remarks . . . it mollified somewhat his unusual appearance."[31]

Roosevelt was about to sit down again when he caught sight of Hunt by the fireplace. Instantly he made his way over to him. Hunt, too, as it happened, was overdressed; he was sensitive about his rural background and had invested in a custom-made Prince Albert coat by way of disguise. He might as well have saved his money. "You," shrilled Roosevelt triumphantly, "are from the country!"[32] For the rest of that evening he interrogated Hunt on the minutiae of rural politics. His usual practice, after such an interview, was to discard his victim like a well-sucked orange;[33] but something about the young lawyer appealed to him. Hunt, in turn, was charmed. At the end of the caucus the two Assemblymen parted "fast friends."[34] Roosevelt had recruited his first legislative ally.

FOR THE NEXT FIVE WEEKS there was nothing substantial to be allied against. The deadlock over electing a Speaker seemed unresolvable. Roosevelt continued to vent his impatience with vitriolic diary entries and walks that ranged farther and farther out of Albany. He persuaded his new friend to join him on one of these excursions. The long-legged lawyer came back too tired to speak, and went straight to bed. When Roosevelt suggested another tramp, Hunt begged off. "You will have to get somebody else to walk with you. One dose is sufficient for me."[35]

On the second weekend of the session, Roosevelt went to Boston to pick up "the little pink wife," as he was wont to call her.[36] They chose rooms together in a residential hotel on the corner of Eagle and State streets, just across the square from the Capitol. Isaac Hunt had rooms there too, and so saw much of both of them. "She was a very charming woman . . . tall, willowy-looking. I was very much taken with her."[37]

Some older members of the Legislature were less and less taken with Roosevelt. Time, as the deadlock dragged on, hung heavy on their hands, and they began to plot his humiliation. Chief among the bullies was "Big John" MacManus, the ex-prizefighter and Tammany lieutenant whom Roosevelt had so contemptuously characterized in his diary. One day MacManus proposed to toss "that damned dude" in a blanket, for reasons having vaguely to do with the dude's side-whiskers. Fortunately Roosevelt got advance warning. His feelings, with Alice newly installed in Albany, may well be imagined. Marching straight up to MacManus, who towered over him, he hissed, "I hear you are going to toss me in a blanket. By God! if you try anything like that, I'll kick you, I'll bite you, I'll kick you in the balls, I'll do anything to you—you'd better leave me alone." This speech had the desired effect.[38]

There was a second ugly incident, which proved conclusively that Roosevelt was not to be trifled with. Sporting a cane, doeskin gloves, and the style of short pea jacket popularly known in England as a "bum-freezer," he went walking along Washington Avenue with Hunt and William O'Neil, another young Republican Assemblyman. They stopped at a saloon for refreshments, and were confronted by the tall, taunting figure of J. J. Costello, a Tammany member. Some insult to do with the pea jacket (legend quotes it as "Won't Mamma's boy catch cold?") caused Roosevelt to flare up. "Teddy knocked him down," Hunt recalled admiringly, "and he got up and he hit him again, and when he got up he hit him again, and he said, 'Now you go over there and wash yourself. When you are in the presence of gentlemen, conduct yourself like a gentleman.' "

"I'm not going to have an Irishman or anybody else insult me," Roosevelt said later, still bristling.[39]

Now that he and Alice were cozily settled in Albany, his impatience over the deadlock dwindled. It occurred to him that, on the whole, the situation was politically profitable. Since only the infighting of Tammany Hall and regular Democrats prevented the election of a Speaker, nobody could blame the Republicans for holding up legislation. The longer the deadlock persisted, he reasoned, the better his party would look, and the more likely its chances of winning a majority in the next election. On 24 January 1882, he had an opportunity to present this view in the Assembly Chamber. A well-meaning colleague was suggesting that the minority compromise with the majority, and so overwhelm the maverick vote of Tammany Hall. Roosevelt leaped up in silent protest, and the Clerk, acting in lieu of a Speaker, recognized him for the first time.

NO FUTURE PRESIDENT has made his maiden speech in surroundings as inspiring as those framing Theodore Roosevelt that afternoon. Since its completion only three years before, the New York State Assembly Chamber had been acclaimed as the most magnificent legislative hall in the world. Its splendors surpassed even those of the Golden Corridor. "What a great thing to have done in this country!" John Hay had marveled, gazing up at the fabulous vaulted ceiling, a dizzy canopy of vermilion and blue and gold, cleft by ribs of soaring stone. Fifty feet above Roosevelt's head, as he prepared to speak, hung a three-ton ring of granite, keystone of the largest groined arch ever built. Behind him, on the north wall, loomed a vast allegorical mural by William Morris Hunt, *The Flight of Evil Before Good.* With pleasing symbolism it depicted the Queen of Night on a chariot of dark clouds, being driven away by the radiance of Dawn.[40]

Roosevelt's words were, in contrast to this majestic auditorium, deliberately informal, even prosaic. He did not forget that his audience consisted largely of farmers, liquor sellers, bricklayers, butchers, tobacconists, pawnbrokers, compositors, and carpenters.[41] His voice was thin and squeaky as he struggled against the chamber's notorious acoustics, and a general hum of bored conversation.[42]

> It has been said that if the Democrats do not organize the House speedily the Republicans will interfere and perfect the organization. I should very much doubt the expediency of doing this at present. . . .

A newspaperman was struck by Roosevelt's "novel way of inflating his lungs." Between phrases he would open his mouth in a convulsive gasp, dragging the air in by main force.[43] Clearly his asthma was troubling him. At times the slight stammer which friends had noticed at Harvard intruded, and his teeth would knock together as the words fought their way out.[44] "He spoke as if he had an impediment in his speech," said Hunt. "He would open his mouth and run out his tongue . . . but what he said was all right."[45]

> As things are today in New York there are two branches of Jeffersonian Democrats . . . Neither of these alone can carry the State against the Republicans . . . I do not think they can fairly expect us to join with either section. This is purely a struggle between themselves, and it should be allowed to continue as long as they please. We have no interest in helping one section against the other; combined they have the majority and let them make all they can out of it!

There were some scattered bursts of applause, and Roosevelt began to relax.

> While in New York I talked with several gentlemen who have large commercial interests at stake, and they do not seem to care whether the deadlock is broken or not. In fact they seem rather relieved! And if we do no business till February 15th, I think the voters of the State will worry along through without it.

Having said his piece, he abruptly sat down, and was inundated with "many hearty congratulations from the older members."[46] Among these, to his intense amusement, were several representatives of Tammany Hall, who apparently thought he had been speaking on their behalf.[47] That night the *New York Evening Post* reported that he had made "a very favorable impression," an opinion which Roosevelt himself modestly shared.[48] He was less flattered with the *Sun*'s characterization of him next morning as "a blond young man with eyeglasses, English side-whiskers, and a Dundreary drawl." The paper noted sarcastically that Roosevelt's "maiden effort as an orator" had been applauded by his political opponents;

there was a reference to his "quaint" pronunciation of the words "r-a-w-t-h-e-r r-e-l-i-e-v-e-d."[49]

Nevertheless the speech was successful. Roosevelt's advice was accepted by his party, and the deadlock continued.[50]

EARLY IN FEBRUARY the Tammany holdouts finally gave in, and Charles Patterson, Democratic candidate for Speaker, was elected. Announcing his committees on 14 February, Patterson gave Roosevelt a position on Cities. "Just where I wished to be," the young Republican exulted. He was not charmed with his mostly Democratic companions on the committee, one of whom was "Big John" MacManus. "Altogether the Committee is just about as bad as it could possibly be," he decided, with the wisdom of his twenty-three years. "Most of the members are positively corrupt, and the others are really singularly incompetent."[51]

Roosevelt lost no time in making his presence felt on the floor of the House. Within forty-eight hours of his committee appointment he had introduced four bills, one to purify New York's water supply, another to purify its election of aldermen, a third to cancel all stocks and bonds in the city's "sinking fund," and a fourth to lighten the judicial burden on the Court of Appeals.[52] The fact that only one of these—the Aldermanic Bill—ever achieved passage, and in a severely modified form, did not discourage him. He wanted quickly to create the image of a knight in shining armor opposing the "black horse cavalry," his term for machine politicians.[53]

As such, he attracted to his banner a tiny group of independent freshman Republicans, like Isaac Hunt and "Billy" O'Neil, who shared his crusading instincts but lacked his flamboyance. The group's efforts were given wide coverage by George Spinney, legislative correspondent of *The New York Times,* the first of many thousands of journalists to discover that Roosevelt made marvelous copy. The young reformers supplied their leader with research into suspicious legislation, advised him on correct parliamentary procedure, and attempted to suppress his more embarrassing displays of righteousness. Roosevelt's ebullience was amusingly recalled forty years later by Hunt and Spinney, in an interview with the worshipful Hermann Hagedorn:

HAGEDORN	He was cool, was he?
HUNT	No, he was just like a Jack coming out of the box; there wasn't anything cool about him. He yelled and pounded his desk, and when they attacked him, he would fire back with all the venom imaginary. In those days he had no discretion at all. He was the most indiscreet guy I ever met . . . Billy O'Neil and I used to sit on his coat-tails. Billy O'Neil would say to him, "What do you want to do that for, you damn fool, you will ruin yourself and everybody else!"
SPINNEY	You will remember that he was the leader, and he started over the hill and here his army was following him, trying to keep sight of him.
HUNT	Yes, to keep him from rushing into destruction . . .
HAGEDORN	He must have been an entertaining person to have around.
HUNT	He was a perfect nuisance in that House, sir![54]

Roosevelt's behavior on the floor, to say nothing of his high voice and Harvard accent, exasperated the more dignified members of his party. When wishing to obtain the attention of the Chair, he would pipe "Mister Spee-kar! Mister Spee-kar!" and lean so far across his desk as to be in danger of falling over it. Should Patterson affect not to hear, he would march down the aisle and continue yelling "Mister Spee-kar!" for forty minutes, if necessary, until he was recognized.[55]

By the third week of the session proper—his eighth in Albany—Roosevelt had put on a considerable amount of political weight. Actually this weight was an illusion, caused by the delicate balance of power in the House. But he did not hesitate to throw it around. On 21 February he again rose to protest a suggested deal with the opposite side, confident "that enough Independent Republicans would act with me to insure the defeat of the scheme by 'bolting' if necessary." His senior colleagues were aware of this, and the matter was hastily referred to a party caucus that evening. For the next eight hours Roosevelt was besieged by deputations promising him rich rewards if he would withdraw his objections. He declined.[56]

At the caucus a machine Republican spoke eloquently on behalf of the deal. It involved an alliance with the Tammany members (breathing vengeance, now, upon the regular Democrats for denying them committee seats) to take away the Speaker's power of appointment. But this Roosevelt considered to be constitutionally irresponsible and politically demeaning. He wrote afterwards that "as no one seemed disposed to take up the cudgels I responded . . . we had rather a fiery dialogue." His objections were upheld by a narrow vote.

Next morning he woke to find himself, if not famous, at least the hero of some liberal newspapers in New York. "Rarely in the history of legislation here," declared the *Herald*, "has the moral force of individual honor and political honesty been more forcibly displayed." Privately, Roosevelt took pride in the fact that he had managed to impose his will on his party, without embarrassing it on the floor of the House. "I hate to bolt if I can help it," he informed his diary.[57]

As the tempo of legislation picked up, the young reformer became aware of the full extent of corruption in New York State politics. About a third of the entire Legislature was venal, he calculated. He was shocked to see members of the "black horse cavalry" openly trading in the lobbies with corporate backers, and paid particular attention to the bills they were bribed to sponsor—bills worded so ambiguously as to deceive well-meaning legislators. But for every such bill there were at least ten whose corruptive power was all but impossible to monitor in advance.[58] These "strike" bills were introduced to restrict, not favor corporations. They seemed to be in the public interest, and redounded greatly to the credit of their sponsors—who, as Roosevelt succinctly put it, "had not the slightest intention of passing them, but who wished to be paid not to pass them."[59] In other words blackmail, not bribery, was the principal form of corruption in the Assembly.

Roosevelt was confronted with a prime example of such legislation early in March. Representatives of the Manhattan Elevated Railroad asked him to sponsor a bill granting their corporation monopolistic control over the construction of terminal facilities in New York City. Since the sums involved in such construction were huge, the lobbyists said they were "well aware that it was the kind of bill that lent itself to blackmail," and looked to Roosevelt to ensure that it was voted upon honestly. The young Assemblyman scrutinized it carefully. He found that the bill was "an absolute necessity" from the point of view of the city as well as the railroad, and agreed to sponsor it, on condition that "nothing improper" was done on its behalf.[60]

No sooner had the bill come up before the Cities Committee, of which Roosevelt was then acting chairman, than corrupt members, scenting the spoils of blackmail, combined to delay its progress. Exasperated, he decided to force it through. Since the spoilsmen included Big John MacManus and J. J. Costello, he was aware that something more than parliamentary skill might be required:

> There was a broken chair in the room, and I got a leg of it loose and put it down beside me where it was not visible, but where I might get at it in a hurry if necessary. I moved that the bill be reported favorably. This was voted down without debate by the "combine," some of whom kept a wooden stolidity of look, while others leered at me with sneering insolence. I then moved that it be reported unfavorably, and again the motion was voted down by the same majority and in the same fashion. I then put the bill in my pocket and announced that I would report it anyhow. This almost precipitated a riot, especially when I explained . . . that I suspected that the men holding up all report of the bill were holding it up for purposes of blackmail. The riot did not come off; partly, I think, because the opportune production of the chair-leg had a sedative effect, and partly owing to wise counsels from one or two of my opponents.[61]

Chair-legs were of no use in the larger context of the Assembly. Soon, to quote one newspaper, "all the hungry legislators were clamoring for their share of the pie." Roosevelt found himself wholly unable to push the bill any further. He received an embarrassing second visit from the railroad lobbyists, who suggested that some "older and more experienced" Assemblyman might succeed where he had failed. The bill was accordingly taken out of his hands. Within two weeks it received the unanimous approval of the House, and became law.

Roosevelt was aware that its passage had been bought. There was little he could do but fume against "the supine indifference of the community to legislative wrongdoing."[62]

THIS BITTER EXPERIENCE made him act with caution when his services as a crusader were next called upon. Late in March, Isaac Hunt, who had been investigating the dubious insolvency of a number of New York insurance companies, approached him with what seemed like evidence of judicial corruption at the highest level. Receivers, said Hunt, were milking the companies of hundreds of thousands of dollars in unwarranted fees and expenses. In every case, the order allowing such payments had been issued by State Supreme Court Justice T. R. Westbrook. Further investigation revealed that Westbrook's son and cousin were employed by one of the receivers, and that at least $15,000 had already been paid to them.

"We ought to pitch into this judge," said Hunt.[63]

Roosevelt was noncommittal, saying merely that it was "a serious matter" to undertake the impeachment of a Supreme Court Justice. Yet apparently the name Westbrook stirred something in his retentive memory. On 27 December 1881, *The New York Times* had run a story on the acquisition of the giant Manhattan Elevated Railroad by Jay Gould, accusing him of a campaign to depress its stock before purchase.[64] From start to finish, Roosevelt recalled, the transaction had been presided over by this same Judge Westbrook.

A few days later "a thin, anemic-looking, energetic young man" visited the City Desk of *The New York Times* and subjected the editor there to a barrage of questions about the Gould-Westbrook affair. He asked permission to examine documents in *The Times*'s morgue, and pored over them for hours. Still not satisfied, Roosevelt took the editor and the documents home to 6 West Fifty-seventh Street, and continued his questioning there until three in the morning.

The more he probed the sequence of events, the more suspicious he became of the cast of characters. About a year before, State Attorney General Hamilton Ward had sued the Manhattan Elevated as an illegal, fraudulent corporation, and then, reversing himself, merely accused it of insolvency. Judge Westbrook, while publicly agreeing with the former suit, had privately ruled in favor of the latter. Holding court in a variety of eccentric locales, including Attorney General Ward's suite at the Delavan House, he appointed receivers already on Jay Gould's payroll. Finally, when the stock of the railroad had plummeted by 95 percent, Judge Westbrook suddenly declared the company solvent again, and handed it over to Gould. Most damning of all, in Roosevelt's eyes, was an unpublished letter the judge had written the financier, containing the remarkable sentence, "I am willing to go to the very verge of judicial discretion to protect your vast interests."[65]

Returning to Albany on 28 March, Roosevelt told Hunt that he had decided on a resolution demanding the investigation, not only of Judge Westbrook, but of Attorney General Ward as well. "I'll offer it tomorrow."[66]

WHEN THE FAMILIAR, piping call of "Mister Spee-kar!" disturbed the peace of the Assembly Chamber the next day, most of Roosevelt's colleagues assumed that he was rising, as usual, on some exasperating point of order or personal privilege.[67] But the first few words of his resolution quickly shocked them into attention:

> *Whereas,* charges have been made from time to time by the public press against the late Attorney-General, Hamilton Ward, and T. R. Westbrook, a Justice of the Supreme Court of this State, on account of their official conduct in relation to suits brought against the Manhattan Railway, and *Whereas,* these charges have, in the opinion of many persons, never been explained nor fairly refuted . . . therefore *Resolved,* That the Judiciary Committee be . . . empowered and directed to investigate their conduct . . . and report at the earliest day practicable to this Legislature.[68]

His words reverberated "like the bursting of a bombshell," Isaac Hunt remembered forty years later, still awed by Roosevelt's courage. But the echoes had scarcely died before a member of the "black horse cavalry" rose to announce he would debate the resolution. This was a ploy for time, since the resolution was automatically tabled under a mass of other pending legislation, and would remain there until somebody remembered to resurrect it. In the meantime, Roosevelt might be bullied or bribed into forgetfulness.[69]

The young Assemblyman did not lack for "friendly warnings" in the days that followed. His own uncle, James A. Roosevelt, took him to lunch and condescendingly remarked that he had done well at Albany so far. It was a good thing to have dabbled in reform, but "now was the time to leave politics and identify . . . with the right kind of people." Roosevelt asked if that meant he was to yield to corruptionists. His uncle replied irritably that there would always be an "inner circle" of corporate executives, politicians, lawyers, and judges to "control others and obtain the real rewards."

Roosevelt never forgot those words. "It was the first glimpse I had of that combination between business and politics which I was in after years so often to oppose."[70]

On Wednesday, 5 April, he surprised the Assembly by demanding that debate on the Westbrook Resolution begin immediately. He made his motion less than half an hour before adjournment, at a time when most of the "black horse cavalry" had gone forth in search of Albany ale. "No! No!" shouted old Tom Alvord, as the House voted in favor.[71] Having thus won the floor, Roosevelt launched into the first major speech of his career.

"MR. SPEAKER," he began, "I have introduced these resolutions fully aware that it was an exceedingly important and serious task I was undertaking."[72] He was ready, nonetheless, to draw up specific charges against "men whose financial dishonesty is a matter of common notoriety." Just in case anybody wondered whom he meant to accuse of fraud, Roosevelt identified Jay Gould and his associates by name, describing them as "sharks" and "swindlers."

The House, aghast at such blasphemy against the gods of capitalism, fell silent. The only sounds in the chamber were Roosevelt's straining voice, and the rhythmic smack of right fist into left palm.[73]

"A suit was brought in May last, I think, by the Attorney-General against the Manhattan Elevated Railroad . . . declaring the corporation to be illegal . . ." He went on to recount at length the whole shabby story of Ward's and Westbrook's maneuverings in behalf of Jay Gould, and showed how Westbrook, by finally declaring the railroad solvent again, had brought the circle of corruption a full 360 degrees. During his administration of the case, the judge had been so blatant as to hold court in the financier's office—"once even in a private bedroom."

The great clock of the Assembly told Roosevelt that fifteen minutes still remained until adjournment. With luck, those few of his opponents who were present would be unable to fill that time with reasonable debate; if so his resolution might be approved by the stunned and silent majority. Sensing that he had the votes already, he wound up with a rather lame attempt to be humble. He was "greatly astonished" that no investigation had been demanded during the three months since the *Times* exposé, and although "I was aware that it ought to have been done by a man of more experience than myself, but as nobody else chose to demand it I certainly would, in the interest of the Commonwealth of New York . . . I hope my resolution will prevail."[74]

The effect of this speech, according to Isaac Hunt, was "powerful, wonderful."[75] Such direct language, such courageous naming of names, had not been heard in Albany for decades. What was more, Roosevelt's accusations were obviously based on solid research. If a vote had been held then, according to one correspondent, the resolution would have been approved. But Tom Alvord was already on his feet, displaying remarkable agility for a man of seventy years. With gnarled hands knotted on a cane, and his head swaying from side to side, the ex-Speaker suggested that "the young man from New York" needed time to reflect and reconsider. How many bright legislative careers had been ruined, in this very chamber, by just such irresponsible allegations as these! Why, he himself, when young and foolish, had been tempted to do the same. Fortunately, he had refrained. Public reputations were "too precious" to be lightly assailed. . . .[76]

The grandfatherly voice droned on, while the minute hand of the clock crept inexorably toward twelve. At five minutes before the hour Roosevelt asked if the gentleman would "give way for a motion to extend the time."

Alvord's reaction was savage. "No," he shouted, "I will not give way! I want this thing over and to give the members time to consider it!"[77] He continued to maunder on; the clock chimed; the gavel dropped; Roosevelt's resolution returned to the table. Alvord limped out in triumph. "That dude," he snorted. "The damn fool, he would tread on his own balls just as quick as he would on his neighbor's."[78]

THAT EVENING THE CAVERNS of the Delavan House hummed with discussion of Roosevelt's speech, while reporters dashed off the news for front-page headlines in the Thursday papers. "Mr. Roosevelt's charges," wrote the *Sun* correspondent, "were made with a boldness that was almost startling." George Spinney of *The New York Times* complimented him on his "most refreshing habit of calling men and things by their right names," and predicted "a splendid career" for the young reformer. The *World* correspondent, representing the publishing interests of Jay Gould, was dismissive. "The son of Mr. Theodore Roosevelt ought to have learned, even at this early period of his life, the difference between a call for a legislative committee of investigation and a stump speech."[79]

Overnight, both Republican and Democratic machines whirred into silent, efficient action. A secret messenger from Tammany Hall came flying up on the late train, groups of veteran members worked out a strategy to block the "obnoxious resolution," and Gould's representatives in Albany began to lobby behind closed doors.[80]

Next morning, Thursday, Roosevelt called for a vote to lift his resolution from the table. Again, he was outwitted on the floor. The Speaker took advantage of the fact that he had forgotten to say what kind of vote he wanted, and called for members to stand up and be counted. A sea of anonymous heads bobbed quickly up and down. The deputy clerk pretended to count them, recorded a couple of imaginary figures, and the Speaker announced the result: 54 to 50 against.

"By Godfrey!" Roosevelt seethed. "I'll get them on the record yet!"[81]

He waited until much later in the day, when the House was drowsing over unimportant business. This time he demanded a name vote. Forced to identify themselves, the members voted 59 to 45 in favor of considering the resolution.[82] Roosevelt was still short of the two-thirds majority he needed to launch an investigation of Westbrook and Ward, but time, and public opinion, was on his side. Tomorrow, Good Friday, was the beginning of the Easter recess. During the long weekend, newspapers would continue to discuss his "bombshell" resolution, and by the time the Assembly reconvened on Monday evening, members would have heard from their constituents.

THE FORCES OF CORRUPTION, meanwhile, were very anxious that Roosevelt's constituents—the wealthiest and most respectable in the state—should hear something about *him*. Since the young man was maddeningly immune to coercion and bribery,[83] they tried to blackmail him with sex. Walking home to 6 West Fifty-seventh Street one night, he was startled to see a woman slip and fall on the sidewalk in front of him. He summoned a cab, whereupon she tearfully begged him to accompany her home; but he grew suspicious, and refused. As he paid the cabdriver, he took note of the address she gave, and immediately afterward dispatched a police detective to her house. The report came back that there had been "a whole lot of men waiting to spring on him."[84]

THAT EASTER WEEKEND, which saw admiring articles on Roosevelt's Westbrook Resolution appear in newspapers from Montauk to Buffalo, was sufficient to make his name a household word across New York State. At a time of growing disenchantment with the Republican Party (now widely believed to be controlled by men like Jay Gould), he leaped into the headlines, passionate and incorruptible, a defender of the people against the unholy alliance of politics, big business, and the bench. Particularly adoring were wealthy young liberals, such as his former classmates at Harvard and Columbia. "We hailed him as the dawn of a new era," wrote Poultney Bigelow, "the man of good family once more in the political arena; the college-bred tribune superior to the temptations which beset meaner men. 'Teddy,' as we called him, was our ideal."[85]

BY 12 APRIL, when Roosevelt again moved to lift his resolution from the table, public demand for an investigation of Westbrook and Ward was such that the Assembly voted 104 to 6 in its favor. Prominent among the holdouts were J. J. Costello and old Tom Alvord, the latter predicting darkly that certain "gentlemen who had gone after wool would come back shorn."[86] But Roosevelt, whatever the outcome of the investigation, had already scored a major political triumph. As the Judiciary Committee hearings got under way, his personality visibly expanded. The crudely fermenting energy of his early days in Albany sweetened into a bubbling *joie de vivre* that vented itself in exuberant slammings of doors, gallopings up stairs, and shouts of laughter audible, George Spinney guessed, at least four miles away.[87] His hunger for knowledge on all subjects grew to the point that after every Rooseveltian breakfast, hotel waiters had to clear away piles of ravaged newspapers. A reporter who sat nearby recalled that he read these newspapers "at a speed that would have excited the jealousy of the most rapid exchange editor." Roosevelt "saw everything, grasped the sense of everything, and formed an opinion on everything which he was eager to maintain at any risk."[88]

Like a child, said Isaac Hunt, the young Assemblyman took on new strength and new ideas. "He would leave Albany Friday afternoon, and he would come back Monday night, and you could *see* changes that had happened to him. Such a superabundance of animal life was hardly ever condensed in a human [being]."[89]

This new vitality warmed everybody who came in contact with Roosevelt—in particular members of his immediate family. It warmed Alice, lonely in their Albany apartment during the long Assembly sessions; it warmed widowed Mittie and the spinsterish Bamie, coexisting irritably amidst the splendors of 6 West Fifty-seventh Street; it warmed plump, weepy Corinne, as he gave her away in marriage to Douglas Robinson, a man who left her cold;[90] it even warmed Elliott, just returned from India, drinking heavily, and still undecided about his future. All huddled close to the glowing youth in their midst, while Theodore himself reveled in "the excitement and perpetual conflict" of politics, the feeling that he was "really being of some use in the world."[91]

WHAT "USE" HE WAS in Albany became a matter of some debate as the months went by. Not for nothing was he known as "the Cyclone Assemblyman,"[92] being primarily a destructive force in the House. Indeed, Roosevelt seemed better at scattering the legislation of other men than whipping up any of his own. Although he continued to talk loudly of "moral duty," his scruples were usually economic. Halfway through the session the *Tribune* described him as "a watchdog over New York's treasury."[93] Two months later, after the Aldermanic Bill finally achieved passage, the same newspaper remarked: "This is the only bill that Mr. Roosevelt has succeeded in passing through the Legislature; but as he has killed four score [other] . . . bills he is probably satisfied with his record."[94]

Particularly surprising, in view of Roosevelt's later renown as the most labor-minded of Presidents, was his attitude to social legislation. It was so harsh that even the loyal Hunt and O'Neil voted against him on occasion. For instance, he vigorously protested a proposal to fix the minimum wage for municipal laborers at $2.00 a day. "Why, Mr. Speaker, this bill will impose an expenditure of *thousands* of dollars upon the City of New York!"[95] He also fought against raising the inadequate salaries of firemen and policemen. When somebody suggested that such people should at least have parity with civil service workers who got more and lived less dangerously, his response was facetious. "Just because we cannot stop all the large leaks, that is no reason why we should open up all the little ones." Only seven other members agreed with this argument, and the bill was passed overwhelmingly.[96]

He even opposed a bill which sought to abolish the private manufacture of cigars in immigrant tenements—an abuse which turned slummy apartments into even slummier "factories." But in this case Roosevelt proved he was not inflexible: a tour of some of the tenements involved revealed such horrors of dirt and overcrowding that he promptly came out in favor of the measure. "As a matter of practical common sense," he afterward wrote, "I could not conscientiously vote for the continuation of the conditions which I saw."[97]

It should be understood that Roosevelt's attitude toward labor in 1882 was not unusual for a man of his class. Enlightened as he may have been on various outdated aspects of the American dream, he adhered to the classic credo that every citizen is master of his fate.[98] His own fate had been an opulent one, in contrast to that of the average tenement-dweller, but he did not think this unfair. After all, his ancestors had worked their way up from a pig-farm in Old Manhattan.

THE JUDICIARY COMMITTEE did not conclude its investigation of Westbrook and Ward until 30 May, only days before the session of 1882 came to an end. Although the committee's reports were not due to be made public until noon on 31 May, rumors began to circulate in the small hours of the morning that the majority was prepared to recommend impeachment. Roosevelt and Hunt took a straw poll of their colleagues around 3:00 A.M., which indicated that the Assembly would accept this recommendation; yet even at so late an hour, "mysterious influences" were working against them. There was a frantic burst of last-minute bribery, and three pivotal members of the committee agreed to withdraw their signatures from the majority report, to the tune of $2,500 each.[99] Thus in the nine hours preceding the committee's reports to the House, its majority for impeachment was changed to a majority against. The chairman conceded that Judge Westbrook had occasionally been "indiscreet and unwise," but said that he was merely guilty of "excessive zeal" in trying to save the Manhattan Elevated from destruction.[100]

During the reading of this report, Roosevelt was seen writhing with impotent rage.[101] At the first opportunity he jumped to his feet and urged the House to vote nay. He kept his temper well in check, speaking slowly and clearly in a trembling voice, but his choice of words was vituperative. "You cannot by your votes clear the Judge . . . you cannot cleanse the leper. Beware lest you taint yourself with his leprosy!"[102]

He lost control of himself only once in the ensuing debate, when a speaker referred to him as "the reputed father" of the Westbrook Resolution. "Does the gentleman mean to say," Roosevelt yelled, "that the resolution is a bastard?"[103] His anger was to no avail, and the House accepted the committee's findings by a vote of 77 to 35.[104]

Two days later, on 2 June, what *The New York Times* called "the most corrupt Assembly since the days of Boss Tweed"[105] went out of existence. Roosevelt took a rueful farewell of Isaac Hunt, Billy O'Neil, and his other legislative friends, and caught the 7:00 P.M. train to New York, where Alice had already preceded him. Interviewed at Grand Central, he agreed that the session had been a bad one for the Republican party. "There seem to have been no *leaders,*" he said thoughtfully.[106]

Early next morning he and Alice joined the other Roosevelts on the blossoming shores of Oyster Bay.

REVIEWING THE SESSION AT LEISURE that summer (if a schedule including ninety-one games of tennis in a single day can be described as leisurely),[107] Roosevelt had little to regret, and much to look forward to. True, Westbrook and Ward had slipped through his fingers at the last moment, but their venality had been exposed, and his political reputation made. Republican newspapers were loud in his praise, and the one national magazine, *Harper's Weekly,* had congratulated him on "public service worthy of high commendation."[108] Less than two years out of college, still five months shy of his twenty-fourth birthday, he was already a powerful man, knowing more about New York State politics, in expert opinion, than 90 percent of his fellow Assemblymen. A testimonial dinner in his honor was scheduled at Delmonico's; his renomination in the fall was certain, and his reelection probable. Already there were rumors that his name might be put up for party leader.[109] Should the Republicans win a clear majority in the House, that would automatically put him in line for Speaker.

These were pleasant thoughts for a young man to dwell on in hot, lazy weather, as the sun burned his body hickory-brown, and Alice, a vision of white lace and ribbons, snoozed gracefully in the stern of his rowboat, a volume of Swinburne in her lap.

"All huddled close to the glowing youth in their midst."

Alice, Corinne, and Bamie Roosevelt, about 1882.

CHAPTER 7

The Fighting Cock

He was quarrelsome and loud,
And impatient of control.

ON NEW YEAR'S DAY, 1883, Isaac Hunt stood up at the Republican Assembly caucus in Albany and offered the name of Theodore Roosevelt for Speaker.[1] The nomination was approved by acclamation, and Roosevelt could congratulate himself on a political ascent without parallel in American history.[2] To use his own phrase, "I rose like a rocket."[3] A year ago he had been "that damn dude"; now, reelected by a record two-to-one majority, he was his party's choice for the most prestigious office in New York State, other than that of Governor. Yet he was still the youngest man in the Legislature.[4] Already, in scattered corners of the country, his name was being dropped by political prophets. In Brooklyn, the columnist William C. Hudson reportedly wrote that he was destined for "the upper regions of politics." In Iowa, Roosevelt was hailed as "the rising hope and chosen leader of a new generation." At Cornell University, the eminent Dr. Andrew D. White stopped a history lecture to remark, "Young gentlemen, some of you will enter public life. I call your attention to Theodore Roosevelt, now in our Legislature. He is on the right road to success . . . If any man of his age was

"If Teddy says it's all right, it *is* all right."

(Clockwise) Theodore Roosevelt, Walter Howe, George Spinney, Isaac Hunt, and William O'Neil.

ever pointed straight at the Presidency, that man is Theodore Roosevelt."[5]

Such predictions were, of course, as farfetched as they were far-flung. Roosevelt dismissed even his nomination for Speaker as "complimentary."[6] He knew he had no chance of winning. The last state election had been a general disaster for his party. Democrats had captured not only the Assembly, but the Senate and Governorship too. This landslide, in the nation's most powerful legislature, was seen as an omen that the White House, occupied by Republicans since the Civil War, might fall to the opposition in 1884.

The result of the Speakership contest on 2 January emphasized just how much Republican strength in the Assembly had eroded. Voting along party lines, members gave Chapin (D) 84 votes, Roosevelt (R) 41. "I do not see clearly what we can accomplish, even in checking bad legislation," Roosevelt told Billy O'Neil. Still, he had to admit that the title of party leader was preferable to some of the names he had been called in the last session.[7]

There was another future President in Albany that January, and a more likely one, in serious opinion, than the foppish young New Yorker. Two years before, Grover Cleveland had been an obscure upstate lawyer, fortyish, unmarried, Democratic, remarkable only for his ability to work thirty-six hours at a stretch without fatigue. Then, in quick succession, he had served eighteen scandal-free months as Mayor of Buffalo, been nominated for Governor, and been elected to that office with the biggest plurality in the history of New York State. The message of the vote was clear: people wanted clean politicians in Albany, irrespective of party. All this made Roosevelt anxious to see "the Big One," as he was known,[8] in the flesh.

There was plenty of flesh to see. Cleveland, at forty-five, was a man of formidable size, weighing well over three hundred pounds.[9] Although he moved with surprising grace, his bulk, once wheezily settled on a chair, seemed as unlikely to budge as a sack of cement. Interviewers were reassured by the stillness of the massive head, the steady gaze, the spread of immaculate suiting. The Governor was invariably patient and courteous; his first official announcement had been that his door was open to all comers. Yet the slightest appeal to favor, as opposed to justice, would cause the dark eyes to narrow, and evoke a menacing rumble from somewhere behind the walrus mustache: "I don't know that I understand you."[10] Should a foolhardy petitioner blunder on, the sack of cement would suddenly heave and sway, and a ponderous fist crash down on the nearest surface, signifying that the interview was over. Often as not, the nearest surface happened to be Cleveland's arthritic knee. On such occasions everybody in his vicinity scattered.[11]

Few of the Governor's visitors could imagine that Cleveland, behind the closed doors of a tavern, was a jovial beer-drinker, a roarer of songs, a teller of hilarious stories. This "other" Cleveland was known only to his friends in Buffalo, and to a quiet-living widow, whose child he had fathered some six years previously.[12] Roosevelt would find out about the widow one day, and make political hay of her. In the meantime he liked what he saw of Cleveland, and decided to take advantage of that open door as soon as an opportunity presented itself.

HE DID NOT EVEN have to make the first move. Early in the session a summons came for him to visit the Governor and discuss a subject of great mutual interest.[13] Neither man realized, at the time, just how much effect it would have on their future careers.

The matter Cleveland wished to discuss was Civil Service Reform, an explosive political issue. Simply described, it was a nationwide movement aimed at abolishing the traditional system of political appointments, whereby the party in power distributed public offices in exchange for favors—or cash—received. In place of this "spoils system," reformers proposed to institute competitive, written examinations for all civil service posts, making merit, rather than corruption, the basis for selection, and ensuring that a good man, once in office, would remain there, independent of the ins and outs of government.

The movement was fiercely opposed by machine politicians, who maintained that they could not govern without the judicious handing out of political plums. President Garfield's murder by a frustrated office-seeker had caused thousands of idealistic young men, including Theodore Roosevelt, to flock to the reform banner.[14] Reform candidates had been conspicuously successful in the elections of 1882. Congress, paying heed, had passed a bill making 10 percent of all federal jobs subject to written examinations. Governor Cleveland now sought to push similar legislation at Albany.[15]

News that Assemblyman Roosevelt had already introduced a Civil Service Reform Bill in the House caused Cleveland to send for him and his faithful aide Isaac Hunt.[16] The Governor expressed strong support for the Roosevelt bill, and asked how it was doing. Hunt, whose responsibility was to guide the paperwork through the Judiciary Committee, reported that it was hopelessly stalled. Machine politicians in the House had no wish to consider such legislation, and had arranged with their colleagues on the committee to let it die of sheer neglect.

For an hour the three men discussed possibilities of getting the bill reported out, favorably or unfavorably, so that an independent, bipartisan vote could be organized on the floor of the House. Roosevelt left the Executive Office encouraged. It was good to know he had won such powerful support—even if Cleveland did belong to the wrong party.[17]

ALICE DUTIFULLY CAME UPRIVER at the beginning of January to look for another set of rooms with her husband.[18] She seems to have decided—or been persuaded—that she would be better off in New York. With few female friends to visit locally, and, as yet, no child to look after, she indeed had little to detain her. Theodore's duties as Minority Leader, not to mention four very demanding committee jobs,[19] meant that he would be even busier than last year. But every Friday night he would join her in the big city, and stay on through Monday morning. Alice, during her days alone, could enjoy the simple things that gave her pleasure—tennis at Drina Potter's Club, shopping and gossip with Corinne, tea-parties with Mittie and Bamie, concerts and Bible classes with Aunt Annie.[20]

Alice had a house of her own to run now. In October 1882, she and Theodore had moved into a brownstone at 55 West Forty-fifth Street. Fanny Smith, a frequent visitor, found it small but pleasant and full of "fun and talk."[21] The preoccupied Assemblyman, on his weekends in town, admitted there was no place like home. Early in the session he wrote in his diary:

> Back again in my own lovely little home, with the sweetest and prettiest of all little wives—my own sunny darling. I can imagine nothing more happy in life than an evening spent in my cosy little sitting room, before a bright fire of soft coal, my books all around me, and playing backgammon with my own dainty mistress.[22]

For all these blissful interludes, he was never reluctant to return to the more Spartan comforts of a bachelor life in Albany. "He stops at the Kenmore," reported the *New York Herald* solemnly, "and is said to be very fond of fishballs for breakfast."[23]

There is some evidence that Roosevelt, while remaining strictly faithful to his wife, had developed a taste for the "stag" activities enjoyed by Albany legislators, most of whom also left their wives at home in the constituency. "There wasn't anything *vicious* about him," George Spinney hastened to say, ". . . he did not visit any bad houses, but anything and everything else."[24]

Roosevelt's best friends in the capital were still Isaac Hunt and Billy O'Neil, plus a new young Republican from Brooklyn, Walter Howe. Together they formed what their leader called "a pleasant quartette." With George Spinney acting as a non-legislative fifth member, they would occasionally play hookey from the Assembly for a night on the town. By modern standards, these spells of wild abandon were laughably sedate; Roosevelt's disdain for "low drinking and dancing saloons" was marked even in 1883.[25] Since discovering at Harvard that wine made him truculent, he had begun a lifetime policy of near-total abstinence. However an extract from the Hunt/Spinney interviews suggests that a little could go a long way:

SPINNEY They concluded that I was worthy of a dinner, and we had . . . a damned good dinner. Of course we talked and we sang.

HAGEDORN *He* did?
SPINNEY You never heard Theodore sing?
HAGEDORN No, I never did.
HUNT Well, he sang that night.
SPINNEY On top of the table, too.
HUNT With the water bottle, do you remember that?[26]

Here Spinney changes the subject. But he moves on to another anecdote, which indicates that the forces of corruption were still out to besmirch Roosevelt's public image.

SPINNEY What was that story about the cockfight? . . . They put up a job on Roosevelt. Roosevelt liked all sort of athletic sports, and cockfighting was something new to him. . . . Some of them had arranged for a cockfight in Troy, and I think the place was to be pulled by the police. Well . . . the place *was* pulled, but Roosevelt beat it for Albany, and came in puffing and panting into the Delavan House, and telling that he had escaped being pulled in up there . . .
HUNT Next morning some of the fellows had feathers on their coats.[27]

THERE WERE TIMES, during the early months of the session, when Roosevelt seemed not unlike a fighting cock himself. His raucous, repetitive calls of "Mister Spee-kar!," his straining neck, wobbly spectacle ribbons, and rooster-red face were combined with increasing aggressiveness and a fondness for murderous, pecking adjectives. If his opponents were tough, and big enough to fight back, these adjectives could be effective and amusing—as when he denounced Jay Gould's newspaper the *World* as "a local, stock-jobbing sheet of limited circulation and versatile mendacity, owned by the arch thief of Wall Street and edited by a rancorous kleptomaniac with a penchant for trousers."[28] (The paper often lampooned Roosevelt's fashionable attire.) But at other times, and on a more personal level, his words left wounds. As party leader in the Assembly, he admitted to no patience with "that large class of men whose intentions are excellent, but whose intellects are foggy," and attacked them openly on the floor. An Irish Democrat was dismissed as "the highly improbable, perfectly futile, altogether unnecessary, and totally impossible statesman from Ulster."[29] One seventy-year-old Assemblyman, hurt beyond endurance by Roosevelt's incessant vituperation, took the floor, on a point of personal privilege, to defend himself. His refutations were so eloquent that Roosevelt was moved to make a tearful apology. "Mr. Brooks, I surrender. I beg your pardon."[30]

Many of the young man's early gaucheries can be ascribed to that most powerful of political temptations, the desire to see one's name on the front page of tomorrow's newspaper. Ever since the Westbrook affair, reporters had clustered flatteringly around him. They had discovered that the noticeable word ROOSEVELT, besprinkled over a column of otherwise dull copy, was a guarantee of readership. And so, hypnotized by the scratching of shorthand pencils, he talked on. He was unaware that some of his remarks were causing experienced politicians to shake their heads. "There is a great sense in a lot that he says," Grover Cleveland allowed, "but there is such a cocksuredness about him that he stirs up doubt in me all the time."[31]

It was clear that Roosevelt was enjoying himself, and equally clear that he would soon come a cropper. He showed a dangerous tendency to see even the most complicated issues simply in terms of good and evil. As a result, his speeches often sounded insufferably pious. "There is an increasing suspicion," wrote one Albany correspondent, "that Mr. Roosevelt keeps a pulpit concealed on his person."[32] Heretics noted with amusement that, in his theology, God always resided with the Republicans, while the Devil was a Democrat. "The difference between your party and ours," he angrily yelled across the floor one day, "is that your bad men throw out your good ones, while with us the good throw out the bad!" Nor was this enough: "There is good and bad in each party, but while the bad largely predominates in yours, it is the good which predominates in ours!" Such oversimplifications always made him seem rather ridiculous. "When Mr. Roosevelt had finished his affecting oration," the *New York Observer* reported, "the House was in tears—of uncontrollable laughter."[33]

IN FAIRNESS TO ROOSEVELT, it must be admitted that he was under considerable strain when he made the above-quoted remark, on 9 March 1883. A few days before he had reversed his public position on a bill of major importance, and had unleashed an avalanche of bitter personal criticism. For the first time in his career, both friends and enemies seemed genuinely outraged. Even the faithful Billy O'Neil (whose philosophy had always been "If Teddy says it's all right, it *is* all right") split with him on this issue.[34]

The bill was one which proposed to reduce the Manhattan Elevated Railroad fare from ten cents to five. Its grounds were that Jay Gould, owner of the corporation, earned far too much profit—profit which he unscrupulously concealed for the purposes of tax evasion. Any such fare-reducing measure was bound to be enormously popular with the masses, and Roosevelt had given "the Five-Cent Bill" his full support, right from the beginning of the session. If a fellow member had not introduced it, he told the press, he would have done so himself, "for the measure is one deserving of support of every legislator in this city." Both the Assembly and Senate had concurred, and passed the bill by overwhelming majorities. By 1 March it was ready for Grover Cleveland's signature.[35]

But the bill's backers, Roosevelt included, reckoned without the deep and laborious scrutiny that the Governor gave to every measure, no matter how public-spirited it might seem on the surface. Lights in the Executive Office, which rarely went off before midnight, burned into the small hours of 2 March as Cleveland agonized over the Five-Cent Bill. He found it unconstitutional. The state had entered into a contract with Gould allowing the elevated railroad to charge ten cents a ride, and it was honor bound to that contract. If the financier fattened on it, that was the state's fault. Aware that he was risking his political future, the Governor wrote a firm veto. He went to bed muttering, "Grover Cleveland, you've done the business for yourself tonight."[36]

Next day, much to his surprise, he discovered that he was an instant hero. Both press and public praised him for an inspiring act of courage. His veto message declaring that "the State must not only be strictly just, but scrupulously fair" shocked the Assembly into applause.[37] Roosevelt was the first to rise in support of the veto. Full of admiration for Cleveland, he spoke with unusual humility:

> I have to say with shame that when I voted for this bill I did not act as I think I ought to have acted . . . I have to confess that I weakly yielded, partly to a vindictive spirit toward the infernal thieves who have the Elevated Railroad in charge, and partly in answer to the popular voice of New York.
>
> For the managers of the Elevated Railroad I have as little feeling as any man here, and I would willingly pass a bill of attainder on Jay Gould and all of his associates, if it were possible. They have done all possible harm to this community, with their hired newspapers, with their corruption of the judiciary and of this House. Nevertheless . . . I question whether the bill is constitutional . . . it is not a question of doing right to *them*. They are common thieves . . . they belong to that most dangerous of all classes, the wealthy criminal class.[38]

That acid phrase, "the wealthy criminal class," etched itself into the public consciousness.[39] Long after other details of the young Assemblyman's career were forgotten, it survived as an early example of his gift for political invective. For the moment, its sting was such that Roosevelt's audience took little notice of his concluding peroration, in which the future President spoke loud and clear.

> We have heard a great deal about the people demanding the passage of this bill. Now anything the people demand that is *right* it is most clearly and most emphatically the duty of this Legislature to do; but we should never yield to what they demand if it is wrong . . . I would rather go out of politics having the feeling that I had done what was right than stay in with the approval of all men, knowing in my heart that I have acted as I ought not to.

Roosevelt's speech, undoubtedly the best he ever made at Albany, earned him widespread scorn. He was denounced by both hostile and friendly newspapers as a "weakling," "hoodlum," and "bogus reformer."[40] Very few commentators realized that, in openly admitting he was wrong, Roosevelt was in fact a braver man than the Governor. He need not have said anything at all: any fool in the Assembly that morning could see that the majority would accept Cleveland's veto. Roosevelt, as Minority Leader, merely had to record a token vote against it, and his political honor would be intact. Both Hunt and O'Neil urged him to do this, but he was more concerned with personal honor. So it was that on 7 March 1883 he found himself voting, along with Democrats and the hated members of Tammany Hall, to accept the Governor's veto, while members of his "quartette" voted the other way.[41]

On top of this humiliation came the House's decision, on 8 March, to unseat a Roosevelt associate named Sprague, on the suspicion of election irregularities. Roosevelt himself was a member of the Committee of Privileges and Elections, which had recommended that Sprague be allowed to stay. The House rejected its report. At once Roosevelt's self-control cracked, and he furiously announced that he was resigning from the committee. As for the Democratic majority, he waxed Biblical in his wrath. "No good thing will come out of Nazareth . . . Exactly as ten men could have saved the 'cities of the plains,' so these twelve men [who had voted for Sprague] will not save the Sodom and Gomorrah of the Democracy. The small leaven of righteousness that is within it will not be able to leaven the whole sodden lump . . ."[42]

He went on, for almost fifteen minutes. This was the speech which reportedly left his audience "in tears—of uncontrollable laughter." The House refused to accept Roosevelt's resignation, and, ignoring his strident protests, went about its business.[43]

IF ROOSEVELT HAD BEEN a hero to the press before, he now found himself its favorite clown. Democratic newspapers joyfully quoted his "silly and scandalous gabble" and intimated that he, too, was a member of "the wealthy criminal class." He was dubbed "The Chief of the Dudes," and satirized as a tight-trousered snob, given to sucking the knob of an ivory cane. Some of these editorials were undeniably comic.[44] What he read in the *World,* however, was not so funny. Jay Gould's editors cruelly invoked a precious memory: "The friends who have so long deplored the untimely death of Theodore Roosevelt [Senior] cannot but be thankful that he has been spared the pain of a spectacle which would have wounded to the quick his gracious and honorable nature." A short quotation followed:

His sons grow up that bear his name,
Some grow to honor, some to shame—
But he is chill to praise or blame.[45]

Grover Cleveland came to the rescue. Glowing with the praise that had been heaped on him since the veto of the Five-Cent Bill, the Governor could not help being touched by the fate of his innocent Republican ally. Another summons came for Roosevelt to visit the Executive Office and discuss pending Civil Service legislation.[46]

He reported that his Civil Service Bill, long stuck in the Judiciary Committee, was back on the Assembly table at last. (Isaac Hunt had sneaked it out of the committee when the chairman was absent.) Cleveland made him a flattering offer and promise. If the "Roosevelt Republicans" would move the bill off the table, "Cleveland Democrats" would ensure its passage.[47]

Both men were aware that much larger issues were at stake than the mere movement of a bill they happened to care for. Cleveland's victory as Governor had been achieved with the help of Tammany Hall, and for the first few months of his administration he had allowed that corrupt institution to think that he was beholden to it.[48] Yet now he was proposing to force through the Assembly a bill that was anathema to machine politicians, and, what was more, enlisting the aid of Tammany's bitterest enemy in the House. In other words, the Governor was about to destroy the unity he had so recently created in the Democratic party. Roosevelt cannot but have been fascinated by his motives. Did Cleveland, too, feel the groundswell of reform sentiment building up across the land?

ROOSEVELT PROMPTLY MOVED for passage of his Civil Service Reform Bill, and made the principal speech in its behalf on 9 April.

His humilitation of the previous month had reminded him of the value of brevity, but he spoke as forcefully as ever: "My object in pushing this measure is . . . to take out of politics the vast band of hired mercenaries whose very existence depends on their success, and who can almost always in the end overcome the efforts of them whose only care is to secure a pure and honest government."[49]

The immediate reaction to his speech was predictable. A representative of the "black horse cavalry" stood up to say that Roosevelt had "prated a good deal of nonsense." But Governor Cleveland's promise held good: only three Democrats voiced any objection to the bill, to the great mystification of Tammany Hall. However they did so at such length that no action was taken that evening.[50] Tammany mustered its forces somewhat in the days that followed, and was able to delay any progress for several weeks, but the Roosevelt/Cleveland coalition of independents finally triumphed. The Civil Service Reform Bill was sent to the Senate, which passed it on 4 May, the last day of the session.[51]

"And do you know," said Isaac Hunt long afterward, "that bill had much to do with the election of Grover Cleveland. When he came to run for President, the non-partisan liberal-minded citizens, who were not affiliated very strongly with either party, voted for Cleveland." But, Hunt added, "Mr. Roosevelt was as much responsible for that law as any human being."[52]

ROOSEVELT'S OWN RECOLLECTION of his political performance as Minority Leader was that, having risen like a rocket, "I came an awful cropper, and had to pick myself up after learning by bitter experience the lesson that I was not all-important."[53] On another occasion he remarked, "My isolated peak had become a valley; every bit of influence I had was gone. The things I wanted to do I was powerless to accomplish."[54]

The facts do not entirely support this negative view. Although he certainly "came an awful cropper" two-thirds of the way through the session, his legislative record was better than it had been in 1882. His activities on behalf of Civil Service Reform have already been noted. In addition, he helped resurrect the lost Cigar Bill, pushed it through the Assembly, and persuaded a doubtful Governor to sign it into law.[55] During the customary flow of legislation just before adjournment, Roosevelt and his "quartette" were successful in killing many corrupt measures.

He did suffer many defeats during the session, but they were on the whole honorable ones, proving that he was a man who fought for his principles. The fact that the House majority was heavily Irish did not prevent him attacking a bill to appropriate money to a Catholic protectory, on the grounds that church and state must be separate. He fought reform of the New York City Charter, saying that the suggested changes were more corrupt than the status quo; he attempted to raise public-house license fees "to regulate the growing evil in the sale of intoxicating liquors." He objected to bills designed to end the unfair competition of prison and free labor, which he believed preferable to having criminals live in idleness; he even introduced a bill "to provide for the infliction of corporal punishment upon [certain] male persons" at a public whipping-post. (One commentator mischievously predicted that, if this bill became law, Roosevelt would wish to restore "the thumbscrew and rack.")[56]

As for losing "every bit" of his influence, he actually retained all of it, in the opinion of *The New York Times*. "The rugged independence of Assemblyman Theodore Roosevelt and his disposition to deal with all public measures in a liberal spirit have given him a controlling force on the floor superior to that of any member of his party," the paper reported. "Whatever boldness the minority has exhibited in the Assembly is due to his influence, and whatever weakness and cowardice it has displayed is attributable to its unwillingness to follow where he led."[57] Other reform-minded periodicals complimented him, if not quite so fulsomely.[58]

The most interesting appraisal of Roosevelt in the session of 1883 remained unspoken for a quarter of a century. "It was clear to me, even thus early," Grover Cleveland remembered, "that he was looking to a public career, that he was studying political conditions with a care that I have never known any man to show, and that he was firmly convinced that he would some day reach prominence."[59]

ON 28 MAY 1883, three weeks after the Legislature adjourned, the Honorable Theodore Roosevelt was a guest of honor at a bibulous party at Clark's Tavern, New York City. The occasion was a meeting of the Free Trade Club; and although Roosevelt spoke seriously on "The Tariff in Politics," the evening quickly became social. Bumpers of red and white wine and "sparkling amber" flowed freely, as the mostly young and fashionable audience toasted vague chimeras of future reform.[60] Free Trade was in those days a doctrine almost as controversial as Civil Service Reform, and Roosevelt admitted that he was risking "political death" by espousing it.[61] Although he indeed came to regret his speech, he never regretted going to Clark's that hot spring night, for a chance meeting occurred which directly influenced the future course of his life.

There was at the party a certain Commander H. H. Gorringe, who happened to share Roosevelt's dreams of a more powerful American Navy.[62] It was natural that this retired officer should wish to meet the young author of *The Naval War of 1812,* and equally natural that, having discussed nautical matters at length, the two men should turn to another subject of mutual interest—buffalo hunting.

The recent return from India of Elliott Roosevelt, laden down with trophies of Oriental big game, had aroused a great longing in his brother to do something similarly romantic.[63] The papers were full of newspaper articles about hunting ranches in the Far West, where wealthy dudes from New York were invited to come in search of buffalo. By a strange coincidence, Commander Gorringe had just been West, and was in the process of opening a hunting ranch there himself. When Roosevelt wistfully remarked that he would like to shoot a buffalo "while there were still buffalo left to shoot," Gorringe, scenting business, suggested a trip to the Badlands of Dakota Territory.

The Commander said that he had bought an abandoned army cantonment there, at a railroad depot on the banks of the Little Missouri. Although the cantonment was not yet ready to receive paying guests, there was a hotel—of sorts—at the depot, plus a few stores and a saloon where hunting guides might be found and hired, if sufficiently sober. The countryside round about teemed with buffalo, not to mention elk, mountain sheep, deer, antelope, beaver, and even the occasional bear. Gorringe added that he was returning to Little Missouri in the fall. Perhaps Roosevelt would like to come along.[64]

ROOSEVELT WAS QUICK to accept. But he had more pressing matters to consider that spring. Alice had just become pregnant. The news stimulated his old ambition to build Leeholm, the hilltop manor at Oyster Bay. Since his initial purchase of land there, a few weeks after their wedding, he had been too busy with politics to think much about the future; but now the responsibilities of parenthood crowded upon him. He began to plan a house that befitted his stature as a man of wealth, public influence, and proven fertility.[65]

Since he and Alice would live out their days at Leeholm, surrounded of course by numerous children, his first instincts were toward solidity and size. What the manor would *look* like was of less consequence than what it would *feel* like to live in. Apart from Roosevelt's natural penchant for massive walls, heavy oak paneling, and stuffed segments of large animals, he was not, at this stage, interested in decorative details. But he did have "perfectly definite views" as to the general layout of his home.

> I wished a big piazza, very broad at the n.w. corner where we could sit in rocking chairs and look at the sunset; a library with a shallow bay window opening south, the parlor or drawing-room occupying all the western end of the lower floor; as broad a hall as our space would permit; big fire-places for logs; on the top floor the gun room occupying the western end so that north and west it look[ed] over the Sound and Bay.[66]

Questions of health—his own, rather more than Alice's—prevented him from making any more definite architectural plans. The nervous strains of the past winter, aggravated by the excitement of becoming a prospective father, brought about a return of asthma and *cholera morbus.* This time he became so ill that, looking back on the summer of 1883, he described the whole period as "a nightmare."[67] At the beginning of July the family doctor sentenced him to "that quintessence of abomination, a large summer hotel at a watering-place for underbred and overdressed girls"—Richfield Springs, in the Catskill Mountains.[68] Characteristically, Roosevelt chose to drive there with Alice in the family buggy. Settling down amid "a select collection of assorted cripples and consumptives," he submitted patiently to a variety of cures, and relieved his embarrassment in a humorous letter to Corinne.[69]

> The drive up was very pleasant—in spots. In spots it wasn't . . . as we left civilization, Alice mildly but firmly refused to touch the decidedly primitive food of the aborigines, and led a starvling [*sic*] existence on crackers which I toasted for her in the greasy kitchens of the grimy inns. But, on the other hand, the scenery was superb; I have never seen grander views than among the Catskills, or a more lovely country than that we went through afterwards; the horse, in spite of his heaves, throve wonderfully, and nearly ate his head off; and Alice, who reached Cooperstown very limp indeed, displayed her usual powers of forgetting past woe, and in two hours time, after having eaten until she looked like a little pink boa constrictor, was completely herself again. By the way, having listened with round eyed interest to one man advising me to "wet the feed and hay" of Lightfoot, she paralyzed the ostler by a direction "to wet his feet and hair" for the same benevolent object. Personally, I enjoyed the trip immensely, in spite of the mishaps to both spouse and steed, and came into Richfield Springs feeling superbly. But under the direction of the heavy-jowled idiot of a medical man to whose tender mercies Doctor Polk has intrusted me, I am rapidly relapsing. I don't so much mind drinking the stuff—you can get an idea of the taste by steeping a box of sulphur matches in dish water and drinking the delectable compound tepid, from an old kerosene oil can—and at first the boiling baths were rather pleasant; but, for the first time in my life I came within an ace of fainting when I got out of the bath this morning. I have a bad headache, a

general feeling of lassitude, and am bored out of my life by having nothing whatever to do.

By the beginning of August he was, if not fully recovered, at least well enough to retire to Oyster Bay and begin a survey of Leeholm. On the twentieth of that month he bought a further 95 acres of property for $20,000, bringing his total holdings to 155 acres.[70] This, in effect, gave him the whole of the estate he had coveted since boyhood; and even though he afterward resold two large tracts to Bamie, he could still consider himself monarch of all he surveyed.[71] Before the month was out, Roosevelt was seen pacing across the grassy hilltop with his architects, Lamb and Rich, spelling out his "perfectly definite views" for their benefit. Out of this discussion came sketches, crystallizing later into approved blueprints, of an enormous three-story mansion, deep of foundation and sturdy of rafter, with no fewer than twelve bedrooms (poor pregnant Alice must have blanched at that specification) plus plenty of gables, dormers, and stained glass.[72] Although Roosevelt protested he had nothing to do with exterior design, a reader of the blueprints could not help noticing certain resemblances to the Capitol at Albany.

ON 3 SEPTEMBER, Roosevelt kissed his wife good-bye, and loaded a duffel bag and gun case aboard the first of a series of westbound express trains. Alice's emotions, as she watched his beaming, bespectacled face accelerating away from her, may well be guessed. Remembering how ill her "Teddy" had been when he first went West, she was not encouraged by the ravages of his recent illness, still markedly upon him. Last time, at least, he had had Elliott to look after him; now he was alone—for Commander Gorringe had decided, only four days before, not to go. Dakota, to her mind, was a place impossibly remote and inhospitable: "Badlands" indeed, roamed by dangerous animals and even more dangerous men. She could not have contemplated her husband arriving in Little Missouri, where he did not know a single human being, without consternation.[73]

Roosevelt was characteristically optimistic. By the time he reached Chicago he had gotten over his disappointment with Gorringe, and wrote Mittie that he was "feeling like a fighting cock" again.[74] Changing to the St. Paul Express on 6 September, he began the second half of his 2,400-mile journey. When the train crossed the Red River at Fargo, the westernmost limit of his wanderings three years before with Elliott, he knew that he was leaving the United States, and heading west into the empty vastness of Dakota Territory. The landscape was so flat now, as darkness descended, that he was conscious of little but the overwhelming moonlit sky. About eight o'clock the huge spread of the Missouri swam out of the blackness ahead, slid beneath the train's clattering wheels, and disappeared into the blackness behind. For hour after hour, flatness gave way to more flatness, and Roosevelt must surely have tired of pressing his face against the unrewarding glass. Perhaps he slept, lulled by the steady rush of air and wheels. If so, he missed seeing a corrugation on the western horizon, shortly after midnight; then, within minutes, all geological hell broke loose. On both sides the landscape disintegrated into a fantastic maze of buttes, ravines, mudbanks, and cliffs, smoldering here and there with inexplicable fires.[75] Pillars of clay drifted by—more and more slowly now, as the train snaked down into the very bowels of the Badlands. A sluggish swirl of silver water opened out ahead; the train rumbled across on trestles, and stopped near a shadowy cluster of buildings. The time was two in the morning, and the place was Little Missouri.[76]

Roosevelt's heels, as he jumped down from his Pullman car, felt no depot platform, only the soft crackle of sagebrush. The train, having no other passengers to discharge, puffed away toward Montana, and the buttes soon muted its roar into silence. Roosevelt was left with nothing but the trickling sounds of the river, and the hiss of his own asthmatic breathing. Shouldering his guns, he dragged his duffel bag across the sage toward the largest of the darkened buildings.[77]

CHAPTER 8

The Dude from New York

From his window Olaf gazed,
And, amazed,
"Who are these strange people?" said he.

THE BUILDING LOOMED PALE against a black backdrop of buttes as Roosevelt approached. Somebody had given it a coat of white paint, in an ineffective attempt to make it look respectable, and hung out a sign reading PYRAMID PARK HOTEL. Encouraged, Roosevelt hammered on the door until the bolts shot back, to the sound of muttered curses from within.[1] He was confronted by the manager, a whiskery, apoplectic-looking old man. History does not record what the latter said on discovering that his boozy slumbers had been interrupted by an Eastern dude, but it was probably scatological. "The Captain," as he was locally known, had been notorious in steamboat days for having the foulest mouth along the entire Missouri River.[2]

Roosevelt had only to drop the name of Commander Gorringe to reduce his host to respectful silence. He was escorted upstairs to the "bull-pen," a long, unpartitioned, unceilinged room furnished with fourteen canvas cots, thirteen of which already had bodies in them. In exchange for two bits, Roosevelt won title to the remaining

"I shall become the richest financier in the world!"

Antoine-Amédée-Marie-Vincent-Amat Manca de Vallombrosa,
Marquis de Morès.

bed, along with the traditional Western "right of inheritance to such livestock as might have been left by previous occupants."[3] The cot's quilts were rough, and its uncased feather pillow shone unpleasantly in the lamplight;[4] but at two thirty on a cool Dakota morning, to an exhausted youth with five days of train travel vibrating in his bones, it must have seemed a welcome haven.

ROOSEVELT AWOKE EARLY next day. He did not need an alarm clock: breakfast in the Pyramid Park was routinely announced by a yell downstairs, followed by a stampede of hungry guests. There were two tin basins in the lobby, but the seamless sack towel was so filthy as to discourage ablutions. Besides, an aroma of cooking wafting out of the adjoining dining room was too distracting. For all its rough accommodations, the hotel was a famously good place to eat.[5]

Peering out of the dining-room window into the brilliant prairie light, Roosevelt could take stock of Little Missouri, or "Little Misery," as residents pronounced it. Various citizens "of more or less doubtful aspect" were walking about. Next to the hotel was a ramshackle saloon entitled "Big-Mouthed Bob's Bug-Juice Dispensary." It advertised a house specialty, "Forty-Mile Red Eye," guaranteed to scour the alkali dust out of any parched hunter's throat. On the opposite side of the railroad stood a store and three or four shacks, dwarfed by the massive clay outcrop of Graveyard Butte. (A few high crosses, glinting in the sun, explained the butte's name.) Three hundred yards downrail, on the flat bank of the river, were a pair of shabby bungalows, facing each other across the tracks; uprail near the point where Roosevelt's train had disappeared into the bluffs, a section-house sat in the shade of a giant water tank. These few scattered buildings completed what was Little Missouri on 8 September 1883—with the exception of Gorringe's cantonment, a group of gray log huts in a cottonwood grove, about a quarter of a mile downriver.[6] Unimpressive in any context, the tiny settlement was reduced to total insignificance by the buttes hemming it in on both sides of the river, and by Dakota's stupendous arch of sky.

For all its sleepy aspect, Little Missouri was unofficially rated by the Northern Pacific as "the toughest town on the line,"[7] a place where questions of honor—or, more frequently, dishonor—were settled with six-shooters. The nearest sheriff was 150 miles to the east; the nearest U.S. marshal, over 200 miles to the south. The presence of a military detachment, assigned to guard railroad construction gangs from attacks by predatory Sioux, had until recently established some semblance of law and order in the community, but now the soldiers were gone. Only the day before Roosevelt's arrival, a "Golden Spike Special" had passed through town, carrying dignitaries west to Montana for ceremonies marking completion of the Northern Pacific Railroad corridor.[8] Ex-President Grant had been on board, and the glimpse of his profile speeding by was symbolic to Little Missouri's fifty or sixty residents. Uncle Sam had withdrawn his protection from yet another frontier outpost; now the settlement lay open to the conflicting interests of white man and Indian, greed and conservation, law and anarchy, money and guns. A few months would determine whether Little Missouri would survive as a hunting resort, or whether, like so many obsolete railroad towns, it would become a few crumbling sticks in the wilderness.

ROOSEVELT, THAT SUNNY Saturday morning, could not have cared less about Little Missouri's economic future. He had come West to kill buffalo; he was impatient to get out of town and into the Badlands, whose violet ravines beckoned excitingly in all directions. But first a guide must be found. The saloon was not yet open, and the Captain, grouchy from lack of sleep, would not say where else Roosevelt might recruit help. His son, a fat youth with whiskey-red cheeks, apparently inherited, was more helpful. He suggested that Joe Ferris, down at the cantonment, might be willing.[9]

About this time, perhaps, Roosevelt began to realize that hiring a professional guide would not necessarily guarantee him a buffalo. Commander Gorringe, anxious for clients, had doubtless intimated that buffalo were still plentiful in the Badlands, when Roosevelt first met him in May. Actually there *had* been several thousand animals left to shoot then, but the situation soon changed dramatically for the worse. In mid-June a band of excited Sioux, encouraged by the

U.S. Government, had slaughtered five thousand buffalo on the plains just east of the Badlands. Throughout the summer, passengers on the Northern Pacific had blazed away at whatever beasts wandered near the tracks, leaving their carcasses to the successive depredations of skin hunters, coyotes, buzzards, and "bone merchants." Less than a week before Roosevelt's arrival in the Badlands, the Sioux had returned to kill off a herd of ten thousand survivors. Again, the slaughter was carried out with full federal approval; Washington knew that plains bare of buffalo would soon be bare of Indians too.[10]

Joe Ferris's first reaction to Roosevelt's proposal was negative. He was a short, husky young Canadian, built like "the power end of a pile driver." Although his mustache was sad, his eyes were friendly—or was the gloom of the cantonment post store delusive?[11] In his twenty-five-odd years, Ferris had laid railroads, jacked lumber, managed stables, and guided a succession of buffalo hunters through the Badlands, before accepting the job of barn superintendent for Commander Gorringe. For all his out-of-doors background, he was of sedentary disposition; the prospect of another expedition in pursuit of a vanishing species did not appeal to him. Neither, for that matter, did this new dude, with his owlish spectacles and frenzied grin.[12] But the dude proved remarkably persuasive. There was about him the intoxicating smell of money—and Joe Ferris, whose private ambition was to become the first banker in Little Missouri, found himself agreeing to be Roosevelt's guide for the next two weeks.

THE TWO MEN SPENT most of the afternoon loading a buckboard with provisions and hunting equipment. By the time they rolled out of town to the ford just north of the railroad trestle, the sun was already low over Graveyard Butte. Before crossing over to the east bank of the river, they stopped at one of the downrail bungalows to borrow an extra buffalo-gun. Roosevelt had discovered that the hammer of his big Sharps .45-caliber rifle was broken. He had brought a spare Winchester, but Ferris thought the latter was too light to rely on.[13]

The owner of the bungalow stood tall, cold, and quiet as Ferris asked the favor. He was a grizzled, villainous-looking man with pale eyes, a black goatee, and mandarin mustaches dangling below his chin. A pair of revolvers rode easily on his narrow hips.[14] Surprisingly, he agreed to lend the gun without a deposit, and also supplied a new Sharps hammer.

No doubt Roosevelt had plenty of questions to ask about this sinister person as the buckboard splashed across the shallow river. He would have questions, too, about what looked like a rival settlement to Little Missouri, in the process of construction on the sagebrush flats opposite; questions about a giant brick chimney in the midst of the unfinished buildings; questions about a magnificent new ranch house perched on a bluff about half a mile to the southwest, and dominating the entire valley; questions about the crosses on Graveyard Butte (starkly etched now against the setting sun); questions arising out of these questions, and many more besides. It would have taken a harder man than Joe Ferris to withstand the drilling force of Roosevelt's curiosity. The odds are that by the time the buckboard had swung south across the sagebrush flats, Ferris had begun to answer in detail, and that the full story, linking all Roosevelt's objects of inquiry, emerged as they rumbled on upstream in the deepening twilight.

THE MAN IN THE BUNGALOW was Eldridge G. Paddock, *éminence grise* of the Badlands. Long before the Northern Pacific first reached the river in 1880, Paddock had held undisputed sway over the valley's roving population of hunters, trappers, and traders. He had been one of the first to settle near the Little Missouri depot, and quickly became known as "the sneakiest man in town, always figuring on somebody else doing the dirty work for him, and him reap the benefits." Although Paddock was a silent, solitary man, rarely seen to engage in open violence, people who annoyed him had a way of being found with their heads caved in, or with bullets in their backs; he was said to be personally responsible for at least three of the crosses on Graveyard Butte. Yet he was capable of surprising generosity (as Roosevelt had just discovered) and was apparently straight with his friends. All in all, he was an enigmatic character against whom nothing had ever been proven.[15]

Until last winter, Paddock had been content, publicly at least, to flourish as a gambler, guide, and speculator in hunting rights up and down the river. Then, early in the spring, there stepped off the train at Little Missouri a man of unlimited wealth and unlimited gullibility. "I am weary of civilization," declared the stranger.[16] Paddock pounced on him with the sureness of Iago accosting Othello.

The newcomer was a very dark, very handsome young Frenchman, with eagle eyes, waxed mustaches, and military bearing. His name bespoke a lineage both noble and royal, dating back to thirteenth-century Spain: Antoine-Amédée-Marie-Vincent-Amat Manca de Vallombrosa, Marquis de Morès. Local parlance speedily reduced it to "de Moree," and then, as summer wore on, to "that son of a bitch of a Marquis."[17]

De Morès had come to the Badlands to invest in the local beef industry. Although as yet this industry consisted only of six or seven scattered ranches, he seemed sure that he would prosper. "It takes me only a few seconds to understand a situation that other men have to puzzle over for hours," he boasted.[18] Certainly the prospects seemed good, even to the slow-witted. Here, and for thousands of square miles around, were juicy pastures, sheltered bottoms, and open stretches of range whose ability to support countless thousands of bovine animals had been demonstrated over the centuries. Now that the buffalo and red men were on their way out, cattle and white men could move in. The Marquis proceeded to unfold a series of ambitions so grandiose as to stun his buckskinned audience. He would buy up as many steers as the Badlands could produce, plus as many more as the Northern Pacific could bring in from points farther west. He would build a gigantic slaughterhouse in the valley, process his beeves on the spot, and ship the meat East in refrigerated railroad cars. This would save the trouble, expense, and quality loss of transporting cattle on the hoof, resulting in lower prices for the Eastern consumer, higher profits for the Western producer, and untold riches for himself. "I shall become the richest financier in the world!"[19] He was so sure of the scheme's success that he would spend millions—tens of millions, if necessary. With the resultant billions, he would buy control of the French Army, and mount a *coup d'état* for what he believed (apparently with some justification) was his birthright—the crown of France.[20]

The shabby citizens of Little Missouri listened to de Morès with understandable skepticism. All except E. G. Paddock decided they would have nothing to do with the "crazy Frenchman." So, on 1 April 1883, the Marquis crossed over the river, erected a tent on the sagebrush flats, cracked a bottle of champagne over it, and announced that he was founding his own rival town. It would be named Medora, after his wife.[21]

(Roosevelt probably knew, at least indirectly, the lady in question; for that matter, he may even have heard of de Morès before. Medora von Hoffman was, like himself, a wealthy young New York socialite; her father, Louis von Hoffman, was one of the richest bankers on Wall Street. De Morès had wooed the redheaded heiress in Paris, married her in Cannes, and come to live with her in New York in the summer of 1882. For a while, the Marquis had worked at the family bank, but he was of restless disposition, and decided to go West in search of wider horizons. The person who prompted him to visit Little Missouri was none other than that ubiquitous entrepreneur, Commander Gorringe.[22])

Local cynics noted with delight that the date de Morès chose to smash his champagne bottle was April Fools' Day. But the foam had scarcely soaked into the sagebrush before the sounds of construction disturbed the peace of the valley. Gangs of workers began to arrive from St. Paul, and the new town arose with astonishing speed. Higher and faster than anything else soared the Marquis's slaughterhouse chimney, until the citizens of Little Missouri, glancing across the river, could not help but see it. Huge and phallic against the eastern buttes, it stood as a symbol of future glory and the unlimited power of money.[23] When Roosevelt and Ferris rolled past on their buckboard, on 8 September 1883, the slaughterhouse was only two weeks from completion.[24]

Another, more ominous symbol was the Marquis's hilltop ranch house, which he grandiloquently called "Château de Morès." It, too, was nearing completion when Roosevelt drove by. Gray and forbidding, the Château commanded a panorama of both Little Missouri and Medora which could only be described as lordly. This was plainly the home of an aristocrat who regarded himself as far above the vassals in the valley. Roosevelt, if he was not reminded of his own pretensions at Leeholm, may have compared it to the "robber knight" castles he and Alice had seen while cruising down the Rhine, two summers before. "The Age of Chivalry was lovely for the knights," he had mused then, "but it must have at times been inexpressively gloomy for the gentlemen who had to occasionally act in the capacity of daily bread for their betters."[25]

Some inhabitants of the Little Missouri Valley, at any rate, did not intend to become daily bread for the Marquis. Among them were three frontiersmen, Frank O'Donald, Riley Luffsey, and "Dutch" Wannegan. O'Donald had been offered work by de Morès sometime in the spring, but he had refused, saying that he preferred to live on the proceeds of hunting and trapping. Besides, he was an old enemy of E. G. Paddock—and Paddock was already the Marquis's right-hand man. De Morès shrugged and forgot about him. Then one day O'Donald rode home to the hunting-shack he shared with Luffsey and Wannegan, ten miles downriver, and discovered a fence across his path. Inquiries revealed that it had been erected by the Marquis, who was buying up large tracts of public land with Valentine script. O'Donald angrily hacked the fence down. De Morès coolly put it up again. Every time O'Donald and his friends rode up and down the valley, they destroyed the fence, only to find it blocking their path on the way back. Tempers began to rise; threats were shouted across the river. Then, in mid-June, came the final straw. O'Donald heard a rumor—allegedly bruited about by E. G. Paddock—that the Marquis was about to "jump claim" to his hunting-shack. "Whoever jumps us," O'Donald announced publicly, "jumps from there right into his grave."[26]

On Thursday, 21 June, the three frontiersmen arrived in Little Missouri for a long weekend of drinking and shooting. One witness described it as "a perfect reign of terror." The air was thick with promiscuous bullets, and O'Donald, primed with Forty-Mile Red Eye, repeated his threats to shoot de Morès "like a dog on sight." After two days of this, Paddock felt constrained to ride over to Medora and warn the Marquis that his life was in danger. De Morès promptly took the next train east to Mandan, 150 miles away, and reported the situation to a justice of the peace. "What shall I do?" he asked. "Why, shoot," replied the J.P.[27]

The Marquis, who was an expert marksman and no coward (he had already killed two Frenchmen in *affaires d'honneur*),[28] returned nonchalantly to the valley on Monday, 25 June. Waiting for him at the Little Missouri depot were his three rather hung-over enemies. Possibly de Morès stared them down; at all events they allowed him to pass. But later that afternoon, as he stood talking to Paddock outside the latter's bungalow, a bullet cracked past him, missing by less than a yard.[29]

Even then, de Morès somehow retained his European reverence for the law. He telegraphed to Mandan for a sheriff, and retired to Medora to await the next train. It was not due to arrive until Tuesday afternoon. To make sure that his antagonists did not leave town before then, the Marquis posted aides on all the trails leading out of Little Missouri. On Tuesday morning he himself staked out a bluff west of town, overlooking the most likely escape route the frontiersmen would take if they sought to avoid the sheriff. Tension gathered as the hour of the train's arrival approached. Presently the puffing of a locomotive was heard in the east. O'Donald, Luffsey, and Wannegan mounted their horses and rode over to the depot.

As expected, the sheriff was on board the train. Stepping down into the sagebrush, he found himself staring into the barrels of three rifles. When he told the trio he had a warrant for their arrest, O'Donald replied, in classic Western fashion, "I've done nothing to be arrested for, and I won't be taken." With that, they turned and rode out of town. While the sheriff watched indecisively, the frontiersmen headed straight into the ambush de Morès had prepared for them. There were two, apparently simultaneous explosions of gunfire; the three horses collapsed and died; the firing continued; then, with a scream of "Wannegan, oh Wannegan!" Riley Luffsey fell dead, a bullet through his neck. Another bullet smashed into O'Donald's thigh, and Wannegan's clothes were shot to ribbons. They surrendered instantly.

When the dust and smoke cleared, de Morès, Paddock, and two other aides were seen emerging from various hiding-points in the sage. The sheriff arrested all except Paddock, who, having taken care not to be seen participating in the ambush, insisted that the frontiersmen had started the shooting anyway.

At a noticeably sympathetic hearing in Mandan at the end of July, murder charges against the Marquis and his men were dismissed for lack of evidence. There was talk in Little Missouri of lynching de Morès if he ever dared to return to Medora. With characteristic courage he did so immediately; not a hand was laid on him. Construction at Medora went on, and more fences went up in the valley. By the time Roosevelt arrived in the Badlands, a month later, uneasy calm had been restored. But a new cross stood out white and clean on Graveyard Butte, as if in silent protest that Riley Luffsey's death had not been avenged.

This, then, was the story, an authentic tale of the Wild West, that Roosevelt soon came to know by heart, for it was told over and over again in the Badlands, that fall of 1883. Events which the New Yorker could not foresee would one day involve him with all its major characters.

NO SOONER HAD ROOSEVELT and Ferris crested the butte south of Medora and rolled down the far side than a wall of rock screened off the puny outpost of civilization behind them.[30] All memory of the Marquis's grand chimney was obliterated by the craggy immensity opening out ahead. As far as Roosevelt's eye could see, the landscape was a wild montage of cliffs and ravines, tree-filled bottoms and grassy divides. Here and there a particularly lofty butte caught the last rays of the sun, and glowed with phosphorescent brilliance before fading to ashen gray.[31] Nowhere was there any sign of human life, save for an almost invisible wagon trail zigzagging from side to side of the crazily meandering river. Sometimes the trail disappeared completely in meadows of lush, three-foot grass (here, presumably, buffalo once fed); sometimes it ran in straight furrows across beds of dried mud that gave off choking clouds of alkali dust under the horses' hooves.

They had been traveling south steadily for almost an hour before Roosevelt saw the first settler's log house, near the mouth of Davis Creek. Joe Ferris told him it was named Custer Trail Ranch, after the doomed colonel who had camped there in 1876. Another, even earlier expedition had taken this trail in 1864, led by the old Siouxbaiter, General Alfred Sully. It was he who coined the classic description of the Badlands: "hell with the fires out."[32] Seen by Roosevelt in the gloom of early evening, it must indeed have seemed like a landscape of death. There were pillars of corpse-blue clay, carved by wind and water into threatening shapes; spectral groves where mist curled around the roots of naked trees; logs of what looked like red, rotting cedar, but which to the touch felt petrified, cold, and hard as marble; drifts of sterile sand, littered with buffalo skulls; bogs which could swallow up the unwary traveler—and his wagon; caves full of Stygian shadow; and, weirdest of all, exposed veins of lignite glowing with the heat of underground fires, lit thousands of years ago by stray bolts of lightning. The smoke seeping out of these veins hung wraithlike in the air, adding a final touch of ghostliness to the scene. Roosevelt could understand why the superstitious Sioux called such territory *Mako Shika,* "land bad."[33]

Early French trappers had expanded the term to *mauvaises terres à traverser,* "bad lands to travel over." That usage, too, Roosevelt could understand; he and Ferris had to ford the river twice more, and hack through a thicket of cottonwood trees, before arriving at their night stop, a small log hut in a mile-wide valley. This, announced Joe, was the Maltese Cross Ranch, home of his brother Sylvane, and another Canadian, Bill Merrifield.

THE TWO RANCHERS greeted Roosevelt coldly. They did not care for Eastern dudes, particularly the four-eyed variety. (Spectacles, he found out, "were regarded in the Bad Lands as a sign of defective moral character.")[34] Quiet, ill-lettered, humorless, and whipcord-tough, the pair were just beginning to prosper after two years of hunting and ranching on the Dakota frontier. Their herd of 150 head had been supplied by two Minnesota investors on the shares basis customary in those days of "free grass" and absentee owners. In exchange for their management on the range, Sylvane and Merrifield were paid a portion of the profits arising from beef sales. Roosevelt was probably curious about operations at Maltese Cross (the name derived from the shape of the ranch brand), since he himself had some time ago invested five thousand dollars in a

Cheyenne, Wyoming, beef company; but his hosts were not the kind to discuss business with a stranger.[35]

The atmosphere in the one-room cabin continued awkward through supper. Even a game of old sledge, played by lamplight after the table had been wiped over, failed to break the ice. Suddenly some frightful squawks through the log walls distracted them. A bobcat had gotten into the chicken-house, which was jabbed against the side of the cabin. Rushing outside, the four cardplayers joined in a futile chase, and when they returned they were laughing and talking freely at last.[36]

Despite this new friendliness, Sylvane and Merrifield were reluctant to lend Roosevelt a saddle horse for his buffalo hunt. He and Joe had decided to base their operations around Little Cannonball Creek, forty-five miles to the south, in the hope that some stray buffalo might still be found there. Roosevelt did not relish the prospect of having to spend the whole next day jouncing around on the buckboard. He pleaded for a horse, but in vain: the ranchers "didn't know but what he'd ride away with it." Only when he took out his wallet, and offered to buy the horse for cash, did their resistance magically melt.[37]

Noblesse oblige prevented Roosevelt from taking one of the three bunks available in the cabin that night. He simply rolled up in his blankets on the dirt floor, under the dirt roof.[38] Had he known what privations he was to suffer during the next two weeks, even this would have seemed like luxury.

At dawn the next day Roosevelt mounted his new buckskin mare, Nell, and turned south up the valley, with Joe Ferris's wagon rumbling behind. In the clear light of early morning he could see that the Badlands were neither hellish nor threatening, but simply and memorably beautiful. The little ranch house, alone in its bottomland, commanded a magnificent view of westward rolling buttes. Their sandstone caps broke level: flat bits of flotsam on a tossing sea of clay.[39] The nearer buttes, facing the river, were slashed with layers of blue, yellow, and white. In the middle distance these tints blended into lavender, then the hills rippled paler and more transparent until they dissolved along the horizon, like overlapping lines of watercolor. Random splashes of bright red showed where burning coal seams had baked adjoining layers of clay into porcelain-smooth "scoria." Thick black ribs of lignite stuck out of the riverside cliffs, as if awaiting the kiss of more lightning. Their proximity to the Little Missouri told the whole geological story of the Badlands. Here two of the four medieval elements—fire and water—had met in titanic conflict. So chaotic was the disorder, wherever Roosevelt looked, that the earth's crust appeared to have cracked under the pressure of volcanic heat. Millions of years of rain had carved the cracks into creeks, the creeks into streams, the streams into branchlets, the branchlets into veinlets. Each watercourse multiplied by fours and eights and sixteens, until it seemed impossible for the pattern to grow more crazy. Even so, as he rode south, he could see strange dribbles of mud in dry places, and puffs of smoke curling out of split rocks, which signified that water and fire were still dividing the earth between them.

Apart from dense groves of willow and cottonwood by the river, and clumps of dark juniper on the northern-facing slopes, the Badlands were largely bare of trees. A blanket of grass, worn through in places but much of it rich and green, softened the harsh topography. Wild flowers and sagebrush spiced the clean dry breeze—blowing ever hotter as the sun climbed high. Surely Roosevelt's asthmatic lungs rejoiced in this air, as did his soul in the sheer size and emptiness of the landscape. No greater contrast could be imagined to the "cosy little sitting room" on West Forty-fifth Street. Here was masculine country; here the West was truly wild; "here," he confessed many years later, "the romance of my life began."[40]

FOR MILE AFTER MILE, hour after hour, the hunters straggled south over increasingly rugged country. No wagon trail now: six times that morning they had to ford the river as it meandered across their path. About noon they mounted a high plateau, whose views extended west to Montana. Dropping down again into the Little Missouri Valley, they forded the river at least seventeen more times. There were bogs and quicksands to negotiate, and banks so steep the buckboard was in danger of toppling over. The sun was already glowing red in their faces when they sighted their destination, a lonely shack in a meadow at the mouth of Little Cannonball Creek. It was dusk by the time they got there. Lamplight shone invitingly out of the shack's single window.[41]

LINCOLN LANG, a sixteen-year-old Scots lad sporting his first American suntan, was just sitting down to supper with his father, Gregor, when he heard the sound of hooves and wheels outside. Through the window he recognized the burly shape of Joe Ferris, but the skinny figure on horseback was obviously a stranger.[42] Gregor Lang went out to greet his visitors. The boy followed hesitantly, and received one of those photographic impressions which register permanently on the adolescent mind.

> Aided by the beam of light showing through the cabin door, I could make out that he was a young man, who wore large conspicuous-looking glasses, through which I was being regarded with interest by a pair of twinkling eyes. Amply supporting them was the expansive grin overspreading his prominent, forceful lower face, plainly revealing a set of larger white teeth. Smiling teeth, yet withal conveying a strong suggestion of hang-and-rattle. The kind of teeth that are made to hold anything they once close upon . . .
>
> "This is my son, Mr. Roosevelt," [Father] said. Then somehow or other I found both my hands in the solid double grip of our guest. Heard him saying clearly but forcefully, in a manner conveying the instant impression that he meant what he said . . .
>
> "Dee-lighted to meet you, Lincoln!"
>
> . . . Young and all, as I was, the consciousness was instantly borne in upon me of meeting a man different from any I had ever met before. I fell for him strong.[43]

The Langs had been living in the shack for only three weeks. They had spent the summer in Little Missouri, where their presence was somewhat less than welcome, for Gregor Lang had been sent there in an investigative capacity. His employer, a British financier, had been asked to buy shares in Commander Gorringe's Little Missouri Land and Stock Company. Before doing so, the financier felt that some close Scots scrutiny was needed.

Lang had viewed with Presbyterian disapproval the hard drinking and dubious bookkeeping of Gorringe's employees, and his reports back to London were not encouraging. Yet he could see that there was money to be made in the Badlands, and great opportunities to exploit. America had always inspired and challenged this bewhiskered scholarly man. He had named his own son after the Great Emancipator, and here, in "God's own country," freedom beckoned them both. With the blessings—and backing—of the British financier, he had come to Little Cannonball Creek to open a new ranch. As yet it was only a log cabin with sod on the floor and rats in the roof, but a herd was ready to be brought in from Minnesota, Mrs. Lang was on her way across the Atlantic, and his ambitions were large.[44]

Roosevelt, finding Lang to be the first pioneer of intellectual quality that he had met, immediately set about pumping him dry of dreams and practical knowledge. Lang responded readily: his summer among the monosyllabic citizens of Little Missouri had left him starved for good discourse. Long after supper that night, long after Joe Ferris had wearily gone to bed, the two men talked on by the light of the lantern, while wolves howled in the distant buttes, and young Lincoln struggled to keep awake. Never had he heard his father so loquacious, so drawn out by insistent questioning. As for their guest's conversation, it was the most fascinating he had ever heard.[45] Yet the boy, willy-nilly, nodded off at last. So, it is safe to assume, did Gregor Lang, or Roosevelt would have talked all night. Some enormous idea seemed to be taking possession of him, an aspiration so heady it would not let him sleep.

HE SLEPT ENOUGH, at any rate, to be up at dawn. The sound of rain drumming fiercely on the cabin's roof did not deter him from beginning his buffalo hunt immediately. Joe Ferris protested they should wait until the weather cleared, and the Langs warned that he would find the clay slopes round about too greasy to climb. But "he had come after buffalo, and buffalo he was going to get, in spite of hell or high water."[46] At six o'clock Roosevelt and Ferris mounted their horses and rode east into a wilderness of naked, streaming hills.

All day the rain continued. The clay slopes, slimy to begin with, dissolved into sticky gumbo, and finally into quagmires that sucked at the horses' hooves, and squirted jets of black mud over the riders. Tracking was impossible: a buffalo might trot through this landscape and leave deep spoors, but within minutes they would disappear, like holes in dough. Visibility was wretched: no matter how often Roosevelt wiped his swimming spectacles, his vision would blur again, reducing the Badlands to a wash of dark shapes, any one of which might or might not be game. Often as not, a promising silhouette turned out to be a mere mound of clay, topped with a "head" of sandstone.

Eventually they encountered a few deer. Roosevelt fired at a buck from too far away, and missed. Joe Ferris followed up with a shot in a thousand, and brought the bounding animal down. "By Godfrey!" exclaimed his frustrated client. "I'd give anything in the world if I could shoot like that!"[47]

Not until nightfall did they return to the ranch. The Langs, who had been expecting them back for breakfast, looked on in wonder as two clay men dismounted from two clay horses and squelched toward the cabin. Incredibly, Roosevelt was grinning.

HE CONTINUED TO GRIN through four more days of ceaseless rain. Joe Ferris protested every morning, and was on the point of caving in every evening, but Roosevelt seemed incapable of fatigue or despair. "Returning at night, after another day fruitless, all save misery, the grin was still there, being apparently built in and ineradicable. Disfigured with clinging gumbo he might be, and generally was; but always the twinkling eyes and big white teeth shone through."[48]

Not until Lincoln was old and living in another century did he find an adjective that adequately described Roosevelt's energy. The man was "radio-active." Physically he was "none too robust," yet "everything about him was force."[49] When supper was over, and Ferris rolled groaning into bed, the New Yorker would resume his conversation with Gregor Lang, and talk until the small hours of the morning. Lincoln listened for as long as he could, awed by the verbosity of "our forceful guest." Among the subjects covered were aspects of literature; racial injustice; political reform (Lang taking the Democratic, and Roosevelt, the Republican side); the divine right of kings; Abraham Lincoln; the geology of the Badlands; human propagation ("I want to congratulate you, Mr. Lang," Roosevelt said warmly, on learning that the Scotsman was one of fifteen brothers and sisters); hunting; conservation and development of natural resources; social structure and moral order.[50] From the latter discussions young Lincoln deduced the Rooseveltian "view of life" as being

> the upbuilding of a colossal pyramid whose apex was the sky. The eternal stability of this pyramid would be insured only through honest, intelligent, interworking and cooperation, to the common end of all the elements comprised in its structure. Individual elements might strive to build intensively and even high; but never well. Never well, because lacking an adequate base—the united stabilizing support of the other elements—they might never attain to the zenith.[51]

A pyramid built in the air, perhaps, but inspirational to a boy whose first fifteen years had been spent in a society with downward dynamics. "It was listening to these talks after supper, in the old shack on the Cannonball, that I first came to understand that the Lord made the earth for all of us, and not for a chosen few."[52]

AS THE EVENINGS WORE ON, Roosevelt's talk turned more and more to a subject which was clearly preoccupying him—ranching. "Mr. Lang," he said one night, "I am thinking seriously of going into the cattle business. Would you advise me to go into it?"

His host reacted with Caledonian caution. "I don't like to advise you in a matter of that kind. I myself am prepared to follow it out to the end. I have every faith in it . . . As a business proposition, it is the best there is."[53]

Roosevelt had time to ponder this remark during long wet hours on the trail. But on the sixth day of the hunt, the sun finally broke through, and his thoughts returned with fierce concentration to the pursuit of buffalo. If he was passionate before, he became fanatic now.[54] "He nearly killed Joe," Lincoln recalled—with some satisfaction, for the boy did not care for that dour Canadian.[55]

Heading eastward into the rising sun, Roosevelt and his guide soon discovered the fresh spoor of a lone buffalo.[56] For a while it was easy to follow, in earth still soft from rain; but as the day heated up, the ground baked hard, and the tracks dwindled to scratches. The hunters spent half an hour searching the dust of a ravine when suddenly

> as we passed the mouth of a little side coulee, there was a plunge and crackle through the bushes at its head, and a shabby-looking old bull bison galloped out of it and, without an instant's hesitation, plunged over a steep bank into a patch of rotten, broken ground which led around the base of a high butte. So quickly did he disappear that we had not time to dismount and fire. Spurring our horses we . . . ran to the butte and rode round it, only to see the buffalo come out of the broken land and climb up the side of another butte over a quarter of a mile off. In spite of his great weight and cumbersome, heavy-looking gait, he climbed up the steep bluff with ease and even agility, and when he had reached the ridge stood and looked back at us for a moment; while doing so he held his head high up, and at that distance his great shaggy mane and huge forequarter made him look like a lion.

This thrilling vision lasted only for a second; the buffalo was evidently used to the ways of hunters, and galloped off. Roosevelt and Ferris followed his trail for miles but never saw him again.

They found themselves now on the edge of the eastern prairie. "The air was hot and still, and the brown, barren land stretched out on every side for leagues of dreary sameness." At about eleven o'clock they lunched by a miry pool, and then ambled on east, trying to conserve their horses in the midday heat. It was late in the afternoon before they saw three black specks in the distance, which proved to be buffalo bulls. The hunters left their horses half a mile off and began to wriggle like snakes through the sagebrush. Roosevelt blundered into a bed of cactus, and filled his hands with spines. At about 325 yards he drew up and fired at the nearest beast. Confused by its bulk and shaggy hair, he aimed too far back. There was a loud crack, a spurt of dust, "and away went all three, with their tails up, disappearing over a light rise in the ground."

The hunters furiously ran back to their horses and galloped after the buffalo. Not until sunset did they catch up with them. By then their ponies were thoroughly jaded. Flailing with spurs and quirts, Roosevelt closed in on his wounded bull, as the last rays of daylight ebbed away. Fortunately for him, a full moon was rising, and he managed to move within twenty feet of the desperate animal. But the ground underfoot was so broken that his fagged horse could not canter smoothly. His first shot missed. The bull wheeled and charged.

> My pony, frightened into momentary activity, spun round and tossed up his head; I was holding the rifle in both hands, and the pony's head, striking it, knocked it violently against my forehead, cutting quite a gash . . . heated as I was, the blood poured into my eyes.[57] Meanwhile the buffalo, passing me, charged my companion, and followed him as he made off, and, as the ground was very bad, for some little distance his lowered head was unpleasantly near the tired pony's tail. I tried to run in on him again, but my pony stopped short, dead beat; and by no spurring could I force him out of a slow trot. My companion jumped off and took a couple of shots at the buffalo, which missed in the dim moonlight; and to our unutterable chagrin the wounded bull labored off and vanished into the darkness.

The critical thing now was to find water, both for themselves and for their mounts. They had had nothing to drink for at least nine hours. Roosevelt and Ferris led the foaming, trembling animals in search of moisture, and after much wandering found a mud-pool "so slimy that it was almost gelatinous." Parched though they were, "neither man nor horse could swallow more than a mouthful of this water." The night grew chill, and the prairie was too bare to provide even twigs for a fire. Each man ate a horn-hard biscuit (baked, rather too conscientiously, by Lincoln Lang).[58] Then, wrapping themselves in blankets, they lay down to sleep. For pillows they used saddles, lariated—since there was no other tether—to the horses.

It was some time before they could doze off, for the horses kept snorting nervously and peering, ears forward, into the dark. "Wild beasts or some such thing, were about . . . we knew that we were in the domain of both white and red horse-thieves, and that the latter might, in addition to our horses, try to take our scalps."

About midnight the hunters were brutally awoken by having their saddles whipped from beneath their heads. Starting up and grabbing their rifles, they saw the horses galloping frantically off in the bright moonlight. But there were no thieves to be seen. Only a shadowy, four-footed form in the distance suggested that a wolf must have come to inspect the camp, and terrified the horses into flight.

Following the dewy path left by the trailing saddles, they captured both animals, returned to camp, and resumed their interrupted slumbers. But then a cold rain began to fall, and they woke to find themselves lying in four inches of water. Shivering between sodden blankets, Ferris heard Roosevelt muttering something. To Joe's complete disbelief, the dude was saying, "By Godfrey, but this is fun!"[59]

AFTER YET ANOTHER rainy day, so cold it turned Roosevelt's lips blue, and another sunny one, so hot it peeled the skin off his face, even he was willing to return to Lang's ranch and admit failure yet again. He had had an easy shot at a cow buffalo in the rain, but his eyes were so wet he could hardly draw a bead—"one of those misses which a man to his dying day always looks back upon with wonder and regret."[60] Then, in the heat, there had been a somersault that pitched him ten feet beyond his pony into a bed of sharp bushes, and a quicksand that half swallowed his horse. . . . "Bad luck," remarked Joe Ferris afterward, "followed us like a yellow dog follows a drunkard."[61] But Roosevelt still insisted he was having "fun." Indeed, he might well have continued the hunt indefinitely had he not had an important business decision to communicate to his host.

"I have definitely decided to invest, Mr. Lang. Will you take a herd of cattle from me to run on shares or under some other arrangement to be determined between us?"

The rancher was flattered, but regretfully declined. He was already tied to one financial backer, he said, and it would be disloyal to work for another man as well. "I am more than sorry."

Swallowing his disappointment, Roosevelt asked Lang if he could suggest any other possible partners.

"About the best men I can recommend," came the reply, "are Sylvane Ferris and his partner, Merrifield. I know them quite well and believe them to be good, square fellows who will do right by you if you give them a chance."[62]

Roosevelt could not have been enchanted by the prospect of employing two grim Canadians who had looked askance at his spectacles, and had refused to lend him a horse; but he accepted Lang's recommendation. Young "Link" was told to saddle up early next morning and ride to Maltese Cross to fetch them.[63]

MEANWHILE THE HUNT RESUMED. For two more rainy days Roosevelt and Joe combed the Badlands for buffalo, but the elusive animals were nowhere in sight. By now Ferris had come to the grudging conclusion that his client was "a plumb good sort." Garrulous in the cabin, Roosevelt on the trail was quiet, purposeful, and tough. "He could stand an awful lot of hard knocks, and he was always cheerful." The guide was intrigued by his habit of pulling out a book in flyblown campsites and immersing himself in it, as if he were ensconced in the luxury of the Astor Library. Most of all, perhaps, he was impressed by a casual remark Roosevelt made one night while blowing up a rubber pillow. "His doctors back East had told him that he did not have much longer to live, and that violent exercise would be immediately fatal."[64]

Sylvane Ferris and Bill Merrifield were waiting for Roosevelt when he returned to Lang's cabin on the evening of 18 September. After supper they all sat on logs outside and Roosevelt asked how much, in their opinion, it would cost to stock a cattle ranch adequately. The subsequent dialogue (transcribed by Hermann Hagedorn, from the verbal recollections of those present) went like this:

SYLVANE	Depends what you want to do, but my guess is, if you want to do it right, it'll spoil the looks of forty thousand dollars.
ROOSEVELT	How much would you need right off?
SYLVANE	Oh, a third would make a start.
ROOSEVELT	Could you boys handle the cattle for me?
SYLVANE	(*drawling*) Why, yes, I guess we could take care of 'em 'bout as well as the next man.
MERRIFIELD	Why, I guess *so!*
ROOSEVELT	Well, will you do it?
SYLVANE	Now, that's another story. Merrifield here and me is under contract with Wadsworth and Halley. We've got a bunch of cattle with them on shares . . .
ROOSEVELT	I'll buy those cattle.
SYLVANE	All right. Then the best thing for us to do is go to Minnesota an' see those men an' get released from our contract. When that's fixed up, we can make any arrangements you've a mind to.
ROOSEVELT	(*drawing a checkbook from his pocket*) That will suit me. (*Writes check for $14,000, hands it over.*)
MERRIFIELD	(*after a pause*) Don't you want a receipt?
ROOSEVELT	Oh, that's all right.

No photograph survives to record the expressions of the two Scots witnesses to this scene.[65]

Roosevelt was not by nature a businessman. His tendency to spend freely, and invest in dubious schemes on impulse, had long been a source of alarm to the more responsible members of his family, whose shrewd Dutch blood still ran strong.[66] Indeed, as far as financial matters were concerned, Theodore was more of a Bulloch than a Roosevelt. Although he had inherited $125,000 from his father,[67] and was due a further $62,500 when Mittie died, he had since college days lived as if he were twice as wealthy. In 1880, the year of his marriage, his income stood at $8,000, and he had no difficulty in spending every penny—lavishing $3,889 on wedding presents alone. "I'm in frightful disgrace with Uncle Jim," he gaily confessed to Elliott, "on account of my expenditures, which certainly have been very heavy."[68] Yet he made no resolutions to be thrifty. Shortly after the success of *The Naval War of 1812*, he had written a check for $20,000 to buy himself a partnership with its publishers, G. P. Putnam's Sons, but there was only half that amount in his bank at the time, and the check had bounced.[69] He again incurred James Roosevelt's wrath by investing $5,000 in the Cheyenne Beef Company, and had to be dissuaded from sinking a further $5,000 into Commander Gorringe's enterprise. His total income for 1883, swelled by royalties, dividends, and his $1,200 salary as an Assemblyman, would amount to $13,920,[70] yet, with three months of the year remaining, he had just written a check in excess of this amount. He must have had extra funds, for there is no record of the check being returned; still, financial caution was obviously not one of his outstanding characteristics.

Despite Gregor Lang's insistence that the cattle business was "the best there is," Roosevelt must have known he was taking a risk in investing in it. There were huge profits to be made, presumably, but huge expenditures came first, and it would be years before any returns came in. Small wonder that most investors in "the beef bonanza" were Eastern capitalists and European aristocrats, men who could afford to spend—and lose—millions. Roosevelt was a fairly wealthy young man, but his funds were puny in comparison with those of, say, the Marquis de Morès.

What then was the great dream which visibly possessed him during that September of 1883, and committed him to spending one-third of his patrimony in Dakota? It could not have been the mere making of money: as far as he was concerned, he already had enough. The clue may lie in an observation by Lincoln Lang.

> Clearly I recall his wild enthusiasm over the Bad Lands . . . It had taken root in the congenial soil of his consciousness, like an ineradicable, creeping plant, as it were, to thrive and permeate it thereafter, causing him more and more to think in the broad gauge terms of nature—of the real earth.[71]

There was, in this beautiful country, something which thrilled Roosevelt, body and soul. As a child, hardly able to breathe in New York City, he had craved the sweet breezes of Long Island and the Hudson Valley. Here the air had the sting of dry champagne. All his life he had loved to climb mountains and gaze upon as much of the world as his spectacles could take in. Here he had only to saunter up a butte, and the panorama extended for 360 degrees. In recent years, he had spent much of his time in crowded, noisy rooms. Here he could gallop in any direction, for as long as he liked, and not see a single human being. Fourteen thousand dollars was a small price to pay for so much freedom.

IT WAS AGREED that while Sylvane and Merrifield journeyed to Minnesota to break their contract, Roosevelt would remain in the Badlands and await a confirming telegram.[72] On 20 September the ranchers set off downriver, and he and Joe went in search of buffalo yet again. This time they rode west into Montana. About noon, their ponies began to snuff the air. Roosevelt dismounted, and, following the direction of his horse's muzzle, ran cautiously up a valley. He peeped over the rim.

> There below me, not fifty yards off, was a great bison bull. He was walking along, grazing as he walked. His glossy fall coat was in fine trim and shone in the rays of the sun, while his pride of bearing showed him to be in the lusty vigor of his prime. As I rose above the crest of the hill, he held up his

> head and cocked his tail to the air. Before he could go off, I put the bullet in behind his shoulder. The wound was an almost immediately fatal one, yet with surprising agility for so large and cumbersome an animal, he bounded up the opposite side of the ravine . . . and disappeared over the ridge at a lumbering gallop, the blood pouring from his mouth and nostrils. We knew he could not go far, and trotted leisurely along his bloody trail. . . .

And in the next gully they found their prize "stark dead."[73]

Roosevelt now abandoned himself to complete hysteria. He danced around the great carcass like an Indian war-chief, whooping and shrieking, while his guide watched in stolid amazement. "I never saw anyone so enthused in my life," said Ferris afterward, "and by golly, I was enthused myself . . . I was plumb tired out." When Roosevelt finally calmed down, he presented the Canadian with a hundred dollars.[74]

Now they stooped to the "tedious and tiresome" ritual of hacking the bull's huge head off, and slicing fillets of tender, juicy hump meat from either side of the backbone. Then, loading their ponies with the slippery cargo, they rode back home, chanting "paens of victory."[75]

There was feasting that night in the Langs' little cabin. The buffalo steaks "tasted uncommonly good . . . for we had been without fresh meat for a week; and until a healthy, active man has been without it for some time, he does not know how positively and almost painfully hungry for flesh he becomes."[76]

On the morning of 21 September Roosevelt bade farewell to his hosts and began the fifty-mile trek back to Little Missouri, where he would await his telegram from Minnesota. As the buckboard rattled away, and Lincoln Lang caught his last flash of teeth and spectacles, he heard his father saying, "There goes the most remarkable man I ever met. Unless I am badly mistaken, the world is due to hear from him one of these days."[77]

CHAPTER 9

The Honorable Gentleman

Hoist up your sails of silk
And flee away from each other.

"HE'S A BRILLIANT MADMAN born a century too soon," Assemblyman Newton M. Curtis complained, escaping from Theodore Roosevelt's suite in the Delavan House, Albany.[1] Mad or not, Roosevelt had been returned to serve a third term in the New York State Legislature, and was again a candidate for Speaker. With less than twenty-four hours to go before the Republican New Year's Eve caucus, his nomination seemed almost certain.[2] This time the honor would not be complimentary, for his party had recaptured both houses of the legislature with large majorities.[3] To be nominated on 31 December 1883 was to step automatically into the Chair next morning.

Few Assemblymen agreed with Curtis as to Roosevelt's precocity. The novelty of his extreme youth had long since worn off. If he had been a competent party leader at twenty-four, why not Speaker at twenty-five? The candidate himself might be forgiven for thinking that his time for real power had come. All political trends, citywide,

"There is a curse on this house."

Hallway of the Roosevelt mansion at
6 West Fifty-seventh Street, New York City.

statewide, and nationwide, were in his favor. New York State's would-be Republican boss, Senator Warner ("Wood-Pulp") Miller, had cautiously embraced such Rooseveltian principles as municipal reform, purified electoral procedures, and the elimination of unelected political middlemen. At the gubernatorial level, Grover Cleveland had publicly split with Tammany Hall, pledging an independent stance for the rest of his administration. He would obviously like to collaborate with a Speaker as independent as Roosevelt. And in Washington even President Arthur had proved to be surprisingly enlightened. That so notorious a machine politician should now be espousing the cause of Civil Service Reform, and vetoing pork-barrel legislation on moral grounds, must have made Roosevelt think ruefully of the days when "Chet" Arthur, as his father's rival for the Collectorship of New York, had symbolized everything Theodore Senior despised. It was due largely to the President's popularity and undeniable decency that the Republican party had recovered from the humiliations of 1882, and stood a good chance of retaining the White House in 1884.[4]

There is no doubt that Roosevelt passionately wanted to be Speaker. If nominated, he would become the number two elected officer in the nation's number one state—and would play a vital role in what promised to be one of the most exciting election years in American history. As 1883 drew to a close, President Arthur himself was reported to be following events in Albany with anxious interest.[5]

ROOSEVELT HAD BEEN campaigning hard since November. Within days of his reelection, he had dispatched a series of characteristically terse letters to Assemblymen-elect:

> *Dear Sir:* Although not personally acquainted with you, I take the liberty of writing to state that I am a candidate for Speaker. Last year, when we were in the minority, I was the party nominee for that position; and if you can consistently support me I shall be greatly obliged.[6]

To one correspondent, who requested further information, Roosevelt sent a self-description that combined, in one sentence, the words

"Harvard," "Albany," and "Dakota," along with the ringing declaration, "I am a Republican, pure and simple, neither a 'half breed' nor a 'stalwart'; and certainly no man, nor yet any ring or clique, can do my thinking for me."[7]

He followed up many of these letters with personal visits, probing into remote corners of New York State in search of rural supporters. Where he could not go by train, he traveled by buggy; where there were no buggies, he went on foot. Late one evening he arrived at a farm in Monroe County and found his prospect not at home. Undeterred, Roosevelt tramped for miles along the road to Scottsville, hailing every rig that loomed out of the darkness: "Hi, there, is this Mr. Garbutt?" Eventually his persistence was rewarded. He secured not only a vote but a lift back to the station.[8]

IT MAY BE WONDERED why Roosevelt should have to campaign so strenuously for an office to which he was surely entitled, having been Minority Leader in the session of 1883. But at that time the New York Legislature made no such guarantees. There was, besides, serious opposition within his own party. At the state Republican convention in September, Senator Miller had rather rashly promised the job to somebody else—a retired Assemblyman in Herkimer County named Titus Sheard. The constituency had fallen to the Democrats in recent years, and Miller, wishing to do something dramatic to strengthen his leadership, asked Sheard to help him pull Herkimer County "out of the mire." The Senator promised that if Sheard, a respected local citizen, would run for election again—and win—he would be rewarded with the Speakership.[9] Sheard had fulfilled his part of the bargain.

Once again, Roosevelt found himself pitted against the party organization. A *Herald* editorial described the race as a contest between "the young and the good" and "the old and the bad," although most observers agreed that Titus Sheard would make an excellent Speaker, if nominated. Roosevelt, on the other hand, was embarrassed by the endorsement of some anti-Miller Stalwarts in New York—local bosses like John J. O'Brien, Jake Hess, and Barney Biglin. Although he did not like these men, they had considerable political weight, and he could not afford to throw them off. "The frisky Roosevelt colt is showing some mettle," wrote the *Sun* in an article entitled "Candidates' Handicap," ". . . but he is not so well in hand [as Titus Sheard] and is likely to break on the home stretch."[10]

On the contrary, his lead steadily increased right through the last day of the campaign. There was a momentary setback when Isaac Hunt, of all people, treacherously deserted him in favor of the third-running candidate, George Z. Erwin. Another candidate, Billy O'Neil, compensated for this by withdrawing and pledging his own votes to Roosevelt. Then, at 5:00 P.M. on 31 December, Erwin also agreed to withdraw (much to the embarrassment of Hunt, who in later life insisted he had been "for Teddy" all along). With the caucus only three hours away, Roosevelt seemed assured of enough votes to win on the first ballot.[11]

Assemblyman Curtis had already found Roosevelt almost "mad" with the excitement of possible victory. If so, one can only guess at his reaction when the news of Erwin's withdrawal came in from spies down the corridor. But three hours is not too short a time in politics for triumph to collapse into defeat. Roosevelt's Stalwart backers were hastily summoned by Senator Miller, who promised them certain "valuables in the treasury" if they would switch their votes to Sheard.[12] The boss's reputation was at stake, and his bribe was so large as to seduce the entire New York City delegation at once. Roosevelt was still reeling from this blow when the last remaining candidate, DeWitt Littlejohn, also switched to Sheard. By the time Roosevelt trudged up the hill to the caucus room shortly before eight o'clock, it was evident that he was a beaten man. "Mr. Roosevelt had an older and less buoyant look than usual when he dropped wearily into his seat," wrote the *Sun* correspondent. "He has seen a great deal of human nature during the past week, and isn't particularly in love with a public career at present. He made a handsome exit as a candidate in a manly speech, however, and his vote [30 to Sheard's 42] was something to be proud of."[13]

With a graceful final gesture, Roosevelt made the nomination of Titus Sheard unanimous.[14] The caucus broke up, and the tensions of weeks of campaigning dissolved into friendly backslapping and compliments of the season. Some time later the church bells of Albany announced the arrival of 1884. Meanwhile, far away in

New York, the *World*'s presses were drumming out thousands upon thousands of times the ominous sentence, "This will not be a Happy New Year to the exquisite Mr. Roosevelt."[15]

HE WAS PRIVATELY so "chagrined" by his defeat (and by the added annoyance of drawing the second-last seat in the House, on the extreme back row of the northern tier) that his weary, aged look persisted for days. But as the session proceeded, his mood began to improve. He realized that far from being weakened by failure, he was now a more potent political force than ever. "The fact that I had fought hard and efficiently . . . and that I had made the fight single-handed, with no machine back of me, assured my standing as floor leader. My defeat in the end materially strengthened my position, and enabled me to accomplish far more than I could have accomplished as Speaker."[16] Titus Sheard was deferential to his young challenger, and offered him carte blanche in choosing his committee appointments. Roosevelt suggested three: Banks, Militia, and the powerful Cities Committee, of which he was promptly made chairman. Testing his newfound strength, he objected to the clerk Sheard had put under him, and after a short struggle the Speaker capitulated. Roosevelt Republicans were placed in control of all the other important committees. Their exultant leader declared that "titular position was of no consequence . . . achievement was the all-important thing."[17]

He threw himself with zest back into legislative business, working up to fourteen hours a day. Every morning, to speed up his metabolism, he indulged in half an hour's fierce sparring with a young prizefighter in his rooms.[18] "I feel much more at ease in my mind and better able to enjoy things since we have gotten under way," he wrote Alice on 22 January. "I feel now as though I had the reins in my hand." Reading this letter over, he added a discreet postscript: "How I long to get back to my own sweetest little wife!"[19]

THE TRUTH IS that Alice, now in her ninth month of pregnancy, was feeling lonely and somewhat neglected.[20] No sooner had her husband returned from Dakota, and hung up his buffalo-head, than he had plunged into the campaign for reelection; immediately after *that,* he plunged into the Speakership contest. Since 26 December she had seen him only on weekends; even these, now, were being eroded with work and political entertaining.

To avoid having Alice alone at such a time, Roosevelt sublet their brownstone and installed her at 6 West Fifty-seventh Street.[21] Corinne Roosevelt Robinson, who had recently had a baby herself, moved in for a temporary stay at about the same time. The two young women planned to run a nursery for both children on the third floor. With Mittie and Bamie also in residence, Alice was not short of feminine company—nor for affection, since all three women adored her.[22] Yet she obviously longed for the lusty male presence of her spouse. Whenever he arrived from Albany, Alice was waiting at the door. "Corinne, Teddy's here," she would shout happily up the stairs. "Come and share him!"[23]

Alice Lee Roosevelt was now twenty-two and a half years old. Even at this extreme stage of her pregnancy, she was still, by more than one account, "flower-like" in her beauty.[24] Such politicians whom Roosevelt brought home for the weekend were loud in praise of her afterward.[25] Roosevelt himself remained as naively in love with Alice as he had been in Cambridge days. "How I did hate to leave my bright, sunny little love yesterday afternoon!" he wrote on 6 February. "I love you and long for you all the time, and oh *so* tenderly; doubly tenderly now, my sweetest little wife. I just long for Friday evening when I shall be with you again . . ."[26]

However cloying his love-talk, however reminiscent his attitude of David Copperfield's to the "child-wife" Dora, Alice Lee was still, after three years and three months of marriage, his "heart's dearest."[27]

ROOSEVELT HAD PROMISED the electorate that his main concern in the session of 1884 would be to break the power of the machines, both Republican and Democratic, in New York City.[28] As chairman of the Committee on Cities, he was now in a position to push through some really effective legislation. Accordingly he wasted no time getting down to business. "He would go at a thing as if the world was coming to an end," said Isaac Hunt.[29] On 11 January, three days after his appointment, he introduced three antimachine bills in the Assembly. The first proposed a sharp increase in liquor license fees; the second proposed a sharp decrease in the amount of money the city could borrow from unorthodox sources; the third proposed that the Mayor be made simultaneously much more powerful and much more accountable to the people.[30]

It was a foregone conclusion that the liquor license bill would fail, even though Roosevelt had now developed great influence in the Assembly. (The alliance between government and malt, in the late nineteenth century, was as unbreakable as that between government and oil in the late twentieth.) Still, he emerged with his reputation as a crusader enhanced, while in no way sounding like a prohibitionist. Any such image would be fatal to a politician living on so notoriously thirsty an island as Manhattan, with its huge, tankard-swinging German population. "Nine out of ten beer drinkers are decent and reputable citizens," Roosevelt declared. "That large class of Americans who have adopted the German customs in regard to drinking ales and beers . . . are in the main . . . law-abiding."[31]

Roosevelt's second measure achieved passage, and added a needed touch of fiscal discipline to the New York treasury. The third, which he rightly regarded as the most important piece of legislation in the session of 1884, won tremendous popular support—and opposition in the Assembly to match. Grandly entitled "An Act to Center Responsibility in the Municipal Government of the City of New York," it consisted of a mere forty words; but these words, if they became law, were enough to make political eunuchs of the city's twenty-four aldermen. At the moment it was the Mayor who was the eunuch, since the Board of Aldermen enjoyed confirmatory power over all his appointments. Defenders of the status quo invoked the Jeffersonian principle that minimum power should be shared by the maximum number of people.[32] Roosevelt, whose contempt for Thomas Jefferson was matched only by his worship of the autocratic Alexander Hamilton, believed just the opposite. He pointed out that New York's aldermen were, almost to a man, "merely the creatures of the local ward bosses or of the municipal bosses."[33] It was the machine, therefore, which ultimately governed the city; and Roosevelt did not consider that democratic.

His major speech in support of the mayoralty bill, when it came up for a second hearing on 5 February, was so forceful as to create an instant sensation. Roosevelt himself considered it "one of my best speeches,"[34] and the press agreed with him. A sampling of next day's headlines tells the story:

ROOSEVELT ON A RAMPAGE
Whacking the Heads off Republican
Office-Holders in This City

MR. ROOSEVELT'S HARD HITS
Making a Lively Onslaught on New York's Aldermen

TAMMANY DEFEATED
Mr. Roosevelt's Brilliant Assault on Corruption[35]

The speech, as transcribed in black and white by Albany correspondents, loses much of the color which Roosevelt undoubtedly gave it in delivery, for he was by now an accomplished, if awkward, orator. Privately he admitted that "I do not speak enough from the chest, so my voice is not as powerful as it ought to be."[36] Like a violinist without much tone, he had learned to compensate with agogic accents ("Mister Spee-KAR!"), measured phrasing, and percussive noise-effects. Observers noticed his habit of biting words off with audible clicks of the teeth,[37] making his syllables literally more incisive.

One sound in which Roosevelt specialized—and which traveled very well in the cavernous Assembly Chamber—was the plosive initial *p*. He made full use of it in this speech, and since he stood in the back row, one can only feel sorry for the Assemblymen in his immediate vicinity.

"I will ask the particular attention of the House to this bill," said Roosevelt. "It simply proposes that the Mayor of the City of New York shall have absolute power in making appointments . . . At present we have this curious condition of affairs—the Mayor possessing the nominal power and two or three outside men possessing the real power. I propose to put the power in the hands of the men the people elect. At present the power is in the hands of one or two men whom the people did not elect."[38]

Roosevelt's speech, however, was remarkable for more than alliteration—although the *p*s popped energetically to the end. His arguments in favor of an all-powerful Mayor, independent of and unanswerable to the city's two dozen shadowy aldermen, were, to quote *The New York Times*, "conclusive."[39] In reply to criticism that he wished to create "a Czar in New York," Roosevelt said simply, "A czar that will have to be reelected every second year is not much of an autocrat." In any case, he went on, "I would rather have a responsible autocrat than an irresponsible oligarchy." New York's "contemptible" aldermen, whom scarcely any citizen could name, were "protected by their own obscurity." But the Mayor, by virtue of his office, "stands with the full light of the press directed upon him; he stands in the full glare of public opinion; every act he performs is criticized, and every important move that he makes is remembered."[40]

Reporters noted with approval that Roosevelt had lost his youthful tendency to ascribe all evil to the Democratic party. His remarks on municipal corruption were ruthlessly non-partisan. The four aldermen whom he chose to name as vote-sellers to Tammany Hall were all Republicans. "They have made themselves Democrats for hire," said Roosevelt in tones of disgust. "If public opinion does its work effectively . . . no one of them would ever be returned to any office within the gift of the people." He concluded with the extraordinary statement that he did not care if the passage of his bill removed every Republican officeholder from the municipal government—"the party throughout the state and nation would be benefited rather than harmed."[41]

Reading between the lines of this speech, one senses a fierce desire for revenge upon the Republican city bosses who betrayed him when he was about to win the Speakership. Subconsciously, no doubt, Roosevelt was *himself* mounting that autocratic pedestal, to bask "in the full glare of public opinion," while men like O'Brien, Hess, and Biglin skulked in the shadows of "their own obscurity."

Consciously, however, he was sincere in his arguments, and it was generally agreed that what he said made good sense. Rising to reply, the House's ranking Democrat, James Haggerty, admitted that the moral character of New York aldermen was low. His objection to Roosevelt's measure involved "a question of principle."[42] Jeffersonian arguments followed. The debate lasted all day, and, in spite of desperate lobbying by Tammany Hall, ended with a complete rout of the opposition. "The Roosevelt Bill," as it would henceforth be called, was ordered engrossed for a third reading.

NOT CONTENT WITH his three municipal reform bills, Roosevelt simultaneously pushed for an investigation of corruption in the New York City government. This resolution was nothing new. Probes had been launched routinely in the past, and as routinely thrown off by the city's smoothly spinning machine.[43] But Roosevelt felt sure that if he were put in charge of his own investigation, he would be able to jam at least some of the levers. Permission was granted almost immediately by the Assembly. It could not very well have refused, because venality, inefficiency, and waste in New York had again become a national scandal, and an embarrassment to both Democrats and Republicans in this presidential election year. On 15 January Roosevelt found himself chairman of a Special Committee to Investigate the Local Government of the City and County of New York. His colleagues consisted of two Roosevelt Republicans and two sympathetic Democrats, giving him, in effect, a free hand to choose his own witnesses and write his own report.[44]

The committee's hearings began four days later, at the Metropolitan Hotel in New York. Roosevelt symbolically opened the proceedings by calling for a Bible, and in the same breath, for Hubert O. Thompson, Commissioner of Public Works. As a freshman Assemblyman, he had been both repelled and fascinated by Thompson, who seemed to spend most of his time in Albany, and was the successful machine politician par excellence. "He is a gross, enormously fleshy man," Roosevelt wrote then, "with a full face and thick, sensual lips; wears a diamond shirt pin and an enormous seal ring on his little finger. He has several handsome parlors in the

Delavan House, where there is always champagne and free lunch; they are crowded from morning to night with members of assembly, lobbyists, hangers-on, office holders, office seekers, and 'bosses' of greater or less degree."[45] For the last two years Roosevelt had looked on in dismay while Thompson's department more than doubled its expenditures, without any noticeable increase in services.[46] He had no doubt that much of the money was flowing directly into Thompson's pockets.

Now the two men faced each other directly across a rectangular table, and Roosevelt plunged at once into his investigation. But for all the young man's "sharp looks" and energy, it was evident to reporters that he was feeling his way. Thompson, a veteran of many investigations, handled him easily. No sooner had Roosevelt asked his first formal questions than the door opened and a messenger came in with a telegram for the witness. Thompson scanned it, laughed, then read it aloud to the committee. It was a summons to appear at an identical investigation, being conducted simultaneously by the Senate.

"Can I telephone that I am coming down?" he asked.

"Certainly," said Roosevelt, nonplussed. With barely veiled insolence, Thompson turned to the messenger.

"Tell them I will leave here in five minutes," he said, and sat back to enjoy the general laughter at Roosevelt's expense.[47]

ROOSEVELT WAS FORCED to turn his attention to other areas of corruption, but they were so various, and his witnesses so infallible in their pleas of bad memory and reasons for non-appearance, that the investigation languished for several sessions without uncovering any important evidence. He began to fume with frustration, and on 26 January, when the city sheriff suggested a question regarding transportation costs was "going into a gentleman's private affairs,"[48] his anger exploded, and he shot forth a fusillade of angry *p*s.

"You are a public servant," Roosevelt shouted, thumping the table. "You are *not* a private individual; we have a right to know what the expense of your plant is; we don't ask for the expense of your private carriage that you use for your own conveyance; we ask what you, a public servant, pay for a van employed in the service of the public; we have a right to know; it is a perfectly proper question!"[49]

The sheriff meekly supplied the information. But at a subsequent hearing, on 2 February, he was so shocked by the chairman's request to state "how much his office had cost him" that he again pleaded privacy. "This offer threw Mr. Roosevelt into a white heat of passion," reported the *World*, "and he declared that the answer must be given. The Sheriff showed no disposition to reply, and his counsel puffed serenely on his cigar." Roosevelt was forced to accept that the question had indeed been indiscreet, and it took a fifteen-minute recess for him to calm down.[50] Experiences like this disciplined his interrogative technique, and he soon became more effective.

On Monday 11 February the sheriff reluctantly yielded up his books for inspection. Beaming with delight, Roosevelt announced that the committee would stand adjourned for a week, while counsel audited these records.[51]

HE HAD ANOTHER, more private reason for declaring an adjournment. Alice's baby was due at any moment. With luck, the child would be born on Thursday, 14 February—St. Valentine's Day, and the fourth anniversary of the announcement of his engagement. The prospect of such a coincidence was apparently enough to reassure him that there was time for a quick trip to Albany, to see how "the Roosevelt Bill" was doing.

What Alice thought of this desertion on the eve of her first confinement is not recorded, but she could hardly have been pleased—particularly as Corinne was away, and Mittie was in bed with what seemed to be a heavy cold.[52] That left only Bamie in the house to take care of both of them. But with the family doctor in attendance, Mr. and Mrs. Lee installed in the Brunswick, and Elliott only a few blocks away, her husband was not over-concerned. On Tuesday, 12 February, he caught an express train to the capital.

IT WAS A RELIEF for an asthmatic man to get out of New York that morning. For over a week the city had been shrouded in a chill, dense, dripping mist. No wonder Mittie had caught cold. Longshoremen were calling it the worst fog in twenty years.[53] What little light seeped out of streetlamps and shop windows diffused into a universal gray that one reporter compared to the limbo before the Creation. With no sun or stars to pierce the fog (for the skies, too, were veiled) it was difficult to distinguish dawn from dusk, except through the blind comings and goings of half a million workers. Train service was reduced to an absolute minimum, and river traffic canceled but for a few ferries feeling their way past each other. Bridges were jammed with groping multitudes. The all-pervading vapor muffled New York's customary noise to an uneasy murmur, broken only by the hoarse calls of fog-whistles, and the occasional shriek of a woman having her furs torn off by invisible hands. Every brick and metal surface was slimy to the touch; sticky mud covered the streets; the air smelled of dung and sodden ashes. Meteorologists predicted yet more "cloudy, threatening weather,"[54] and a *New York Times* editor wrote despairingly, "It does not seem possible that the sun will ever shine again."[55]

Roosevelt found the weather in Albany clearer, if equally humid, for the entire Eastern seaboard was dominated by a fixed low-pressure system. The Assembly's magnificent fresco *The Flight of Evil Before Good* was beginning to blister, and occasional flakes fell off in the saturated air. Whether from damp rot, or some more fundamental fault, the vaulted ceiling of the chamber was showing ominous cracks, and nervous Assemblymen had taken to walking around, rather than under, its three-ton keystone.[56]

However it would take more than a low-pressure system to affect Roosevelt's natural good humor that Tuesday. With 330 pages of testimony already taken by his Investigative Committee, and the prospect of sensational revelations in the weeks that lay ahead, he was again making front-page headlines. His bill was sure of passage, and (if Alice managed to hold out until Thursday) he would be able personally to guide it through the House on Wednesday afternoon. To speed it on its way through the Senate, a mass meeting of citizens had been called in New York's Cooper Union on Thursday evening.[57] The guest-list was to be a brilliant one: General U. S. Grant himself had agreed to serve as vice-president. All this could only enhance the stature of the Honorable Gentleman from the Twenty-first.

Things were certainly going well for Roosevelt now. He had shed his sophomoric tendencies, along with his side-whiskers, a good while back. The newspapers which had treated him so condescendingly in the past were now uniformly respectful, even admiring, in their tone. Republicans in the House regarded him as their leader *de ipse;* some of the more worshipful members put boutonnieres on his desk every morning. He, for his part, no longer felt snobbish toward his humbler colleagues; on the contrary, he rejoiced in his ability to work "with bankers and bricklayers, with merchants and mechanics, with lawyers, farmers, day-laborers, saloon-keepers, clergymen, and prize-fighters."[58] Except for occasional flare-ups of aggressive temper ("You damned Irishman, what are you telling around here, that I am going to make you an apology? . . . I'll break every bone in your body!"),[59] he was as a rule well-mannered and charming, and, when he chose to be, deliciously comic. Even the melancholy Isaac Hunt took pleasure in his wit. "Through it all and amid it all that humorous vein in him! You would be talking with him and he would strike that falsetto. He did that all the while . . . he was awful funny." Unlike most comedians, Roosevelt also found other people's jokes amusing, and the Assembly Chamber rang often with his honest, high-pitched laughter.[60]

He was never bored, and found entertainment in the dullest moments of parliamentary debate. With a writer's eye and ear, he noted down incidents and scraps of Irish dialogue for future publication. There was Assemblyman Bogan, who "looked like a serious elderly frog," standing up to object to the rules, and, on being informed that there were no rules to object to, moving "that they be amended until there are-r-e!"[61] There was the member who accused Roosevelt, during a legal debate, of occupying "what lawyers would call a *quasi-position* on the bill," only to be crushed by another member rising majestically in his defense: "Mr. Roosevelt knows more law in a wake than you do in a month; and more than that, Michael Cameron, what do you mane by quoting Latin on the floor of the House when you don't know the alpha and omayga of the language?"[62]

He was a connoisseur of mixed metaphors, in which Assembly debate was rich, and took great delight in analyzing them. Of one Democrat's remark that convict labor "was a vital cobra which was swamping the lives of the laboring men," Roosevelt wrote:

> Now, he had evidently carefully put together the sentence beforehand, and the process of mental synthesis by which he built it up must have been curious. "Vital" was, of course, used merely as an adjective of intensity; he was a little uncertain in his ideas as to what a "cobra" was, but took it for granted that it was some terrible manifestation of nature, possibly hostile to man, like a volcano, or a cyclone, or Niagara, for instance; then "swamping" was chosen as an operation very likely to be performed by Niagara, or a cyclone, or a cobra; and behold, the sentence was complete.[63]

Perhaps the best of Roosevelt's Albany stories is his account of the committee meeting whose chairman, having "looked upon the rye that was flavored with lemon peel," fell asleep during a long piece of testimony, and, on waking up, gaveled the witness to order, on the grounds that he had seen him before: "Sit down, sir! The dignity of the Chair must be preserved! No man shall speak to this committee twice. The committee stands adjourned."[64]

AT THE BEGINNING of the morning session of the House on Wednesday, 13 February, Assemblymen were seen flocking around Theodore Roosevelt and shaking his hand.[65] He had just received a telegram from New York, stating that Alice had given birth to a baby girl late the night before. The mother was "only fairly well,"[66] but that was to be expected after the agonies of a first delivery. Roosevelt proudly accepted a father's congratulations and requested leave of absence, to begin after the passage of his other bill that afternoon. "Full of life and happiness," he proceeded to report fourteen other bills out of his Cities Committee.[67] Joy, evidently, must not be allowed to interfere with duty.

Several hours later, a second telegram arrived, and as he read it his face changed. Looking suddenly "worn," he rushed to catch the next train south.[68] No word remains as to the text of the telegram, but it undoubtedly contained a gentler version of the news that Elliott had just given to Corinne at the door of 6 West Fifty-seventh Street: "There is a curse on this house. Mother is dying, and Alice is dying too."[69]

WITH INEXORABLE SLOWNESS, the train crawled down the Hudson Valley into thickening fog. Even in clear weather, the 145-mile journey took five hours; it was anybody's guess how long it would take on this murky evening. There was nothing Roosevelt could do but read and reread his two telegrams, and summon up all his self-discipline against that unmanly emotion, panic. Six years ago last Saturday he had taken another such express to New York, in response to another urgent telegram, and arrived to find his father dead. . . . For hour after hour the locomotive bell tolled mournfully in the distance ahead of him.[70] It was about 10:30 P.M. when the train finally pulled into Grand Central Station. Roosevelt had to search out West Fifty-seventh Street by the light of lamps that "looked as though gray curtains had been drawn around them."[71] When he reached home the house was dark, except for a glare of gas on the third floor.

ALICE, DYING OF Bright's disease, was already semicomatose as Roosevelt took her into his arms. She could scarcely recognize him, and for hours he sat holding her, in a vain effort to impart some of his own superabundant vitality. Meanwhile, on the floor below, Mittie was expiring with acute typhoid fever. The two women had become very close in recent years; now they were engaged in a grotesque race for death.

Bells down Fifth Avenue chimed midnight—St. Valentine's Day at last—then one, then two. A message came from downstairs: if Theodore wished to say good-bye to his mother he must do so now. At three o'clock, Mittie died. She looked as beautiful as ever, with her "moonlight" complexion and ebony-black hair untouched by gray.[72] Gazing down at her, Roosevelt echoed his brother's words: "There *is* a curse on this house."[73] In bewildered agony of soul, he climbed back upstairs and again took Alice Lee into his arms.

Day dawned, but the fog outside grew ever thicker, and gaslight continued to burn in the Roosevelt mansion. About mid-morning, a sudden, violent rainfall miraculously cleared the air, and for five minutes the sun shone on muddy streets and streaming rooftops. The weather seemed about to break, but clouds closed over the city once more. By noon the temperature was 58 degrees, and the humidity grew intolerable. Then, slowly, the fog began to lift, and dry cold air blew in from the northeast. At two o'clock, Alice died.[74]

ROOSEVELT DREW a large cross in his diary for 14 February, 1884, and wrote beneath: "The light has gone out of my life."

THAT EVENING, Cooper Union was packed with thousands of citizens supporting the "Roosevelt Bill," whose passage through the Assembly had been postponed pending his return. Reporters noticed that the "more than usually intelligent audience" included, besides General Grant, ex-Mayor Grace, Professor Dwight, Elihu Root, Chauncey Depew, and two of Roosevelt's uncles, James and Robert. The latter must have known about Theodore's double tragedy, but they kept silent, for the news would not be announced until morning.

Although the real hero of the evening was not there, the hall resounded with cheers at the mention of his name. "Whatever Theodore Roosevelt undertakes," declared Douglass Campbell, the keynote speaker, "he does earnestly, honestly, and fearlessly." The resolution in support of the bill was approved by a tremendous, air-shaking shout of "AYE!"[75]

"SELDOM, IF EVER, has New York society received such a shock as yesterday in [these] sad and sudden deaths," the *World* commented on 15 February. "The loss of his wife and mother in a single day is a terrible affliction," agreed the *Tribune,* "—it is doubtful whether he will be able to return to his labors." The *Herald,* while equally sympathetic to the bereaved Assemblyman, dwelt more on the qualities of the deceased. Mittie was praised for her "brilliant powers as leader of a *salon,*" and for her "high breeding and elegant conversation." Alice, said the paper, "was famed for her beauty, as well as many graces of the heart and head."[76]

In Albany, the House of Assembly paid an unprecedented tribute to its stricken member by declaring unanimously for adjournment in sympathy. Seven speakers, some of them in tears, eulogized the dead women and paid tribute to Roosevelt. "Never in my many years here," declared a senior Democrat, "have I stood in the presence of such a sorrow as this." He said that Alice had been a woman so blessed by nature as to be "irresistible" to any man she chose to love. The House's resolution, adopted by a rising vote, spoke of the "desolating blow" that had struck "our esteemed associate, Hon. Theodore Roosevelt," and expressed the hope that its gesture would "serve to fortify him in this moment of his agony and weakness."[77]

MORE TEARS WERE SHED at the funeral on Saturday, 16 February, in the Fifth Avenue Presbyterian Church. The sight of two hearses outside the door, and two rosewood coffins standing side by side at the altar, was too much for many members of the large and distinguished congregation.[78] Sobs could be heard throughout the simple service. The minister, Dr. Hall, could hardly control his voice as he compared the sad but unsurprising death of a fifty-year-old widow with the "strange and terrible" fate that had snatched away a twenty-two-year-old mother. He cried openly as he prayed for "him of whose life she has been so great a part."[79]

Through all these tears, Roosevelt sat white-faced and expressionless. He had to be handled like a child at the burial ceremony in Greenwood Cemetery.[80] "Theodore is in a dazed, stunned state," wrote Arthur Cutler, his ex-tutor, to Bill Sewall in Maine. "He does not know what he does or says."[81]

THE SHOCK UPON Roosevelt of Alice's wholly unexpected death, coming at a time when he had been "full of life and happiness," was so violent that it threatened to destroy him. Mittie's death served only to increase his bewilderment. He seemed unable to understand the condolences of friends, showed no interest in his baby, and took to pacing endlessly up and down his room. The family were afraid he would lose his reason.[82]

Actually he was in a state of cataleptic concentration on a task which now preoccupied him above all else. Like a lion obsessively trying to drag a spear from its flank, Roosevelt set about dislodging Alice Lee from his soul. Nostalgia, a weakness to which he was abnormally vulnerable, could be indulged if it was pleasant, but if painful it must be suppressed, "until the memory is too dead to throb."[83]

With the exception of two brief, written valedictories to Alice—one private, one for limited circulation among family and friends—there is no record of Roosevelt ever mentioning her name again.[84] The first of these memorials was entered into his diary a day or two after the funeral:

> Alice Hathaway Lee. Born at Chestnut Hill, July 29th 1861. I saw her first on October 18th 1878; I wooed her for over a year before I won her; we were betrothed on January 25th 1880, and it was announced on Feb. 16th;[85] on Oct. 27th of the same year we were married; we spent three years of happiness greater and more unalloyed than I have ever known fall to the lot of others; on Feb 12th 1884 her baby was born, and on Feb. 14th she died in my arms; my mother had died in the same house, on the same day, but a few hours previously. On Feb 16th they were buried together in Greenwood . . . For joy or sorrow, my life has now been lived out.[86]

There were one or two oblique, involuntary references to Alice in conversation during the months immediately following her death, but before the year was out his silence was total. Ironically, the name of another Alice Lee—his daughter—was sometimes forced through his lips, but even this was quickly euphemized to "Baby Lee." Although the girl grew to womanhood, and remained close to him always, he never once spoke to her of her mother.[87] When, as ex-President, he came to write his *Autobiography,* he wrote movingly of the joys of family life, the ardor of youth, and the love of men and women; but he would not acknowledge that the first Alice ever existed.

Others close to Roosevelt naturally took on the same attitude. After his death, their hands went methodically through his correspondence, and all love-letters between himself and Alice—with four trivial exceptions—were destroyed. Whole pages of his Harvard scrapbook, presumably containing souvenirs of their courtship and marriage, were snipped out. Photographs of Alice were torn out of their paper frames. Here and there, handwritten captions that doubtless referred to her are erased so fiercely the page is worn into holes.[88] Only by some miracle did five private diaries, and a handful of letters written to friends, survive to testify to his love for the yellow-haired girl from Chestnut Hill.

IT IS NOW WELL OVER A CENTURY since Alice Hathaway Lee married Theodore Roosevelt, gave birth to his child, and died. Little more than the few facts recorded in this volume will likely ever be known of her. She was, after all, only twenty-two and a half years old at the end. The Roosevelt family, on first meeting her, had found her "attractive but without great depth."[89] She seemed too simple for such a complex person as Theodore. After her death, however, they claimed to have noticed that "abilities lay beneath the surface."[90] Their first, unsentimental impression was surely the more trustworthy.

Only one woman ventured to suggest, many years later, that Alice, had she lived, would have driven Roosevelt to suicide from sheer boredom.[91] The bitterness of this remark is understandable, since it was made by Alice's successor; but one suspects there may be a grain of truth in it. Alice does indeed seem to have been rather too much the classic Victorian "child-wife," a creature so bland and uncomplicated as to be incapable of spiritual growth. Her few surviving letters are sweetly phrased and totally uninteresting. Roosevelt, whose own growth, both physical and mental, was so abnormally paced, could not have been happy married to an aging child.

In his published memorial to Alice, Roosevelt—echoing Dr. Hall—spoke of the "strange and terrible fate" that took her away. Strange, maybe—yet perhaps more kind than terrible. In quitting him so early, she rendered him her ultimate service. In burying her, he symbolically buried his own lingering naïveté. At the time, of course, he felt that he was burying all of himself.

CHAPTER 10

The Delegate-at-Large

Thus came Olaf to his own,
When upon the night-wind blown
Passed that cry along the shore;
And he answered, while the rifted
Streamers o'er him shook and shifted,
"I accept thy challenge, Thor!"

BABY LEE WAS CHRISTENED on Sunday, 17 February 1884, the day after the funeral, and placed in care of Bamie.[1] The latter, now in her thirtieth year, seemed irrevocably headed for spinsterdom, and her sudden acquisition of a golden-haired infant was the only happy event of that bitter weekend. Having thus, within twenty-four hours, interred the past and anointed the future, the Roosevelts addressed themselves to the present.

For all Cutler's statement that Theodore was "in a dazed, stunned state" on Saturday, there is a tough decisiveness about the family's actions during the period immediately following that could only have emanated from him. He set the tone by announcing that he would go back to work at once. "There is nothing left for me except to try to so live as not to dishonor the memory of those I loved who have gone before me."[2]

"Mr. Roosevelt, I'm going to veto those bills!"

Governor Grover Cleveland by Eastman Johnson.

With Alice and Mittie dead, Theodore returning to Albany, and Corinne and Elliott already thinking of moving to the country, it was plain that 6 West Fifty-seventh Street must be sold. The Roosevelt mansion had become increasingly expensive to maintain over the years. Mittie's lavish *soirées,* receptions, banquets, and balls, complete with orchestras and liveried footmen, had considerably eroded the family fortune.[3] Bamie, in her new capacity as surrogate mother, no longer had the time nor the money to keep open house for Astors and Vanderbilts. She agreed to look for a smaller, but equally fashionable home on Madison Avenue, within baby-carriage distance of Central Park. The mansion was put on the market, and in less than a week it was sold. The family was given until the end of April to move out.[4]

Roosevelt simultaneously divested himself of the brownstone on West Forty-fifth Street, the only house he and his wife had ever owned. He could not bear to return there, even to close it up. Bamie was left with the sad task of "dividing everything." Yet on 1 March, just two weeks after Alice's death, Roosevelt signed a contract for the construction of Leeholm, at a total cost, including outbuildings, of $22,135.[5] Construction began immediately, although the weather was so cold Oyster Bay was frozen in ripples. He wanted his manor finished by the summer; why was unclear, since he had no plans to move in. Bamie, ever-resourceful, indefatigable Bamie, would take care of it for him.

"I have never believed it did any good to flinch or yield for any blow," he wrote Bill Sewall. "Nor does it lighten the pain to cease from working."[6] He did not care where he lived, for he intended to spend an absolute minimum of time eating and sleeping. Even in happier days, he had been insomniac and febrile; now his only instinct was to sleep less and labor more. The pain in his heart might be dulled by sheer fatigue, if nothing else. "Indeed I think I should go mad if I were not employed."[7]

And so, on 18 February, the Assemblyman returned to Albany.

HIS ACTIVITIES, through the remainder of the session of 1884, were so prodigious that one gropes, as so often with Theodore

Roosevelt, for an inhuman simile. Like a factory ship in the whaling season, he combined the principles of maximum production and perpetual motion. The naked cliffs of the Hudson Valley must have grown drearily familiar to him, for he commuted constantly in his dual capacity as Assemblyman (on Tuesdays, Wednesdays, and Thursdays) and chairman of the City Investigating Committee (on Fridays, Saturdays, and Mondays). Often as not he got his only sleep on the overnight train. The House was now sitting in the evenings as well as daytime, while the committee's hearings began at ten in the morning and lasted until six.[8]

Thus we find him, on, say, Monday, 25 February, interrogating a New York corrections officer on illegal charges for the transport of prisoners; on Tuesday 26 rising in the Assembly to urge passage of his Municipal Indebtedness Bill; on Wednesday 27 amending a Bill for the Benefit of Colored Orphans, and reporting four bills out of his regular Cities Committee. On Thursday 28 he brings out seven more bills, whose subjects range from security to sewers; on Friday 29 he is back at the New York investigating table, demanding information on clerking procedures in the Surrogate's Court, political patronage in the Bureau of Citations, and research fees in the Bureau of Arrears; next day, Saturday, 1 March, after an exhausting spell of testimony on drunkenness and sex in city jails, he agonizes over, and finally signs, the Leeholm contract. That night he tries to rest, but without much success ("He feels the awful loneliness more and more," Corinne tells Elliott, "and I fear he sleeps little, for he walks a great deal in the night, and his eyes have that strained red look").[9] At 10:00 A.M. on Monday he gavels another investigative session to order; twenty-four hours later, he is in Albany, moving some banking legislation to the third reading, and making a major speech on behalf of his Liquor License Bill; on Wednesday afternoon he reports twelve new bills out of the Cities Committee, and on Thursday night a further seven; in New York next morning, he begins a final long weekend of hearings (his committee's report is due the following Friday). While awaiting counsel's draft of this document, he makes another major speech on municipal government, reports out of various committees a total of thirty-five new bills—the final six on Thursday evening 13 March, as he simultaneously checks every word of the Investigative Report. That night he does not sleep at all, for the text does not satisfy him—it is "a white-washing performance"[10] that ignores his committee's most sensational findings. Roosevelt retires to the Delavan House with 1,054 pages of testimony, summons relays of stenographers, and begins to dictate a new report; when the stenographers wilt in the small hours, he sends them home and takes up the pen himself. He writes on through breakfast; at ten, when the Assembly opens, he transfers his papers there, and continues to write all morning, undisturbed by the roar of debate (although he hears enough to jump to his feet at times and comment on bills before the House). As each sheet of manuscript is finished, it is rushed to the printer. By mid-afternoon the last page is printed and bound, and the 47-page, 15,000-word document is handed in. He delivers a "masterful presentation" on its behalf, introduces nine audacious bills arising from his findings, and concludes with a request for authority to investigate other areas of city government.[11]

NOTWITHSTANDING ROOSEVELT'S other preoccupations, it is probable that he found time to read a front-page article in *The New York Times* on 25 February, for its subject-matter was of intense interest to him. The headlines read DRESSED BEEF IN THE WEST—THE BUSINESS ENTERPRISE OF THE MARQUIS DE MORES, and the copy consisted of an interview with the Frenchman, just arrived at the Hotel Brunswick. Much was made of his elegant city attire, in contrast to the broad sombrero and buckskin suit he wore out West. "The Marquis is a young man of 26, with a clear-cut and refined face and expressive gray eyes. He wears a dark brown mustache and slight sidewhiskers. He went West 18 months ago to organize the dressed beef business on the Northern Pacific Railroad. He put his first slaughterhouse on the Little Missouri. Here it was that the trouble [between himself and the three frontiersmen] occurred. . . ." But de Morès would not discuss "the Buffalo Bill side" of life in Dakota. He was more interested in promoting Medora as a future capital of the beef industry. The little town's population was put at 600, and it already boasted a newspaper, the *Bad Lands Cowboy.* De Morès was prepared to invest a million dollars in his enterprise, and was confident of profitable returns. "In his region, he says, are the most magnificent cattle farms to be found anywhere. Grass-fed cattle keep fat all Winter."[12]

ROOSEVELT'S HYPERACTIVITY did not diminish as the session wore on. If anything it increased, through two more phases of his City Investigation Committee, and two more reports totaling nearly a million words of testimony. The evidence of "blackmail and extortion" in the surrogate's office, "gross abuses" in the sheriff's, "no system whatever" in the Tax and Assessments Department, and "hush money" paid to policemen—interlarded with prison descriptions and brothel anecdotes which make strong reading even today—was so shocking that no fewer than seven of his nine corrective measures were passed by the Legislature.[13]

Since these seven bills called, among other things, for prompt cancellation of the tenure of all New York City department heads, from the bejeweled Commissioner Thompson downward, they aroused frantic opposition in the House, including one free-for-all, on 26 March, which the *Evening Post* called "a scene of uproar and violence to all rules of decency."[14] Hissing, howling Assemblymen ran to and fro, some hiding in the lobby in an effort to break the quorum, others besieging the Clerk's desk with threats and denunciations. "During all this tumult," said Isaac Hunt, "TR was the presiding genius. He was right in his element, rejoicing like an eagle in the midst of a storm."[15]

The uproar was to no avail. All seven bills went on to achieve passage by overwhelming margins, despite parliamentary sabotage by Speaker Sheard.[16] Roosevelt did not, however, pause to enjoy this moment of triumph over his erstwhile rival. A chance for even sweeter revenge—upon Sheard's patron, Senator Warner Miller—lay ahead, at Utica, on 23 April.

UTICA, A SHABBY canal-town in the middle of the Mohawk Valley, was the site of the New York State Republican Convention for 1884. Four delegates-at-large, plus 128 district and alternative delegates, would be chosen for the National Convention at Chicago. When Roosevelt checked into Bagg's Hotel on 22 April, he knew that enormous issues were at stake—issues transcending the convention's provincial locale and rather mundane agenda. Forces had gathered all over the country to nominate James G. Blaine at Chicago, instead of President Arthur, whose political support was eroding.[17] If New York, the President's own state, voted to send a pro-Blaine delegation to Chicago, Arthur might well be deposed after serving less than one full term.

Roosevelt himself supported neither Arthur nor Blaine. The former, if only for his participation in the New York Collectorship struggle of 1877, was *persona non grata* to any son of Theodore Senior. The latter gave off a faint reek of legislative corruption which made the young moralist sniff with disdain. Blaine was a former Speaker of the House and Secretary of State; there was no denying his political stature and magnificent abilities. Yet for fifteen years he had been unable satisfactorily to explain certain improprieties during his Speakership, arising out of a favorable ruling in behalf of a railroad, whose bonds he had subsequently bought. As a result of this apparent self-interest, Blaine had twice been denied the Presidential nomination; but now, in 1884, party regulars seemed disposed to forgive him.[18]

Not so Roosevelt, who early in the New Year had endorsed the third-running candidate, Senator George F. Edmunds of Vermont.[19] Edmunds was honest, industrious, unambitious, and dull, but for these very reasons he appealed to Independent Republicans—the young, idealistic reformers who identified neither with Stalwarts nor Half Breeds. Besides, he happened to suit Roosevelt's present purpose, which was to force the state Convention to elect a pro-Edmunds delegation, and publicly humiliate Boss Miller, who was committed to Blaine.[20] Utica's Grand Opera House promised a suitably theatrical setting for his scenario.

The plot was based on a few simple political facts. There were about five hundred Republicans in town. Roosevelt, as Senator Edmunds's most prominent supporter, would influence the votes of perhaps 70 Independents. The remaining 430-odd votes were evenly divided between Arthur and Blaine.[21] He thus stood in his favorite position—at the balance of power. Could he but persuade the 70 Independents to stand there with him, in a tight group that leaned neither one way nor the other, he would eventually be able to swing the convention in any direction he chose.

No sooner had Roosevelt arrived in the hotel lobby than he was besieged by excited Independents. At least forty of them followed him upstairs, and his suite immediately became known as "Edmunds headquarters." Although the Opera House was not due to open its doors until noon the following day, negotiations began at once, in an atmosphere of whispered secrecy. Messengers sped back and forth between Roosevelt's rooms and those of Boss Miller, representing Blaine, and those of State Chairman James D. Warren, representing President Arthur. Few serious observers believed that the Independent strength would last through the evening. "The Edmunds men . . . are showing their teeth," reported the *New York World*, "and refuse to be coaxed by either side; but they lack organization and may find themselves outwitted."[22]

Actually Roosevelt's organization was very good. He himself was doing the outwitting. By periodically appearing in the corridors to announce, in conversational tones, that he was "no leader" of the Independents and had "no personal ambitions" at Utica, and by giving ambiguous replies to both Blaine and Arthur emissaries, he gave the impression that he was holding on to his seventy votes with difficulty. Miller and Warren thus separately assumed that Roosevelt was bargaining to release them. All the young dude wanted, obviously, was to be made a delegate-at-large. Well, if that was his price . . .

At six o'clock the negotiants emerged for dinner, greeted one another politely, and arranged themselves in enigmatic groups of tables. Newspapermen tried to guess, from the movement of complimentary bottles of champagne, which way the political currents were flowing; but the bottles circulated in all directions. A *Sun* reporter captured something of the tension in the atmosphere.

"Bagg's Hotel is filled to suffocation tonight," he cabled. "There are no Blaine hurrahs, or Arthur enthusiasm, or Edmunds sentiment here. The old party managers are simply . . . groping in the dark for the coming man. There is harmony everywhere; but it is the harmony of men who are afraid of each other."[23]

To Boss Miller's bewilderment, Roosevelt proved no more tractable after dinner than he had been before. He not only rejected an offer to send one Independent delegate-at-large, i.e., himself, to Chicago, along with three Blaine men, but also refused to make the ratio two and two. News of the second rejection, which leaked out about midnight, greatly excited Chairman Warren, who offered the Independents *three* places on the ticket, in exchange for just one Arthur supporter; but Roosevelt also rejected that. At 2:30 A.M., the President's men made their final, humiliating offer, an offer so weak it amounted to capitulation. All four delegates-at-large could be Independents for Edmunds, as long as there was no danger of them ultimately switching to Blaine. Roosevelt graciously accepted, knowing very well who the leader of those delegates would be.[24]

THERE WAS SOMETHING faintly comic, to newspaper reporters, about the sight of machine Republicans filing through the streets next morning in somber black, their tall silk hats shining in the sun. They looked for all the world like mourners at a funeral. Boss Miller walked alone, a large, portly, graying man with troubled eyes.[25] Roosevelt's rejection of his advances last night had stunned and shamed him; his mood today was not improved by an editorial in the *World* calling him "a pigmy" in comparision with his "giant" predecessor, Roscoe Conkling.

Arthur's men were equally sullen and silent as they trooped into the Opera House.[26] There was a round of polite applause for Chairman Warren when he mounted the stage. More applause, rather less polite, greeted Warner Miller. He took an aisle seat next to Titus Sheard on "Wood Pulp Row," the section allotted to Herkimer County. Roosevelt, with his usual unerring sense of timing, waited until all three dignitaries were settled before making his own entrance. Then he stomped briskly down the hall, to the sound of mounting applause "that was taken up by the gallery and prolonged for some moments" after he sat down—a mere yard away from Miller, on the opposite side of the aisle. Casually draping a leg over the chair in front, he allowed his personality to penetrate every corner of the auditorium. From that moment on, there was no doubt as to who was controlling the convention. When Chairman Warren had finished calling the roll, "he simply cast his eye" over toward Roosevelt, who leaped up and proposed that an Edmunds man be nominated temporary chairman of the meeting. The motion was approved.[27]

BY LATE AFTERNOON, when the votes for delegates-at-large were counted, it was plain that Warner Miller had, as the *Sun* correspondent put it, "been pulverized finer than his own pulp." Roosevelt's name led the list with 472 votes. His three colleagues, all Independents, were President Andrew D. White of Cornell University with 407; State Senator John J. Gilbert with 342; and Edwin Packard, a millionaire spice merchant from Brooklyn, with 256. Boss Miller ran fifth with only 243 votes, scarcely half Roosevelt's total, and 6 short of any kind of majority.[28] His humiliation was complete. Word went around that his days as party chief were over.

Flushed with victory, Roosevelt jumped across the aisle and confronted the shaken Senator. According to one reporter, he held out his hand and said, "Time makes all things even. The first of January is avenged."[29] But the reporter was a long distance away, in the press gallery, and got this quote by proxy. Actually Roosevelt's hand was not so much extended as balled in a fist, and his words were rather less printable: "There, damn you, we beat you for last winter!"[30]

"What did you want to say that for?" asked Isaac Hunt afterward. They were walking back to Bagg's Hotel behind Miller, who had somehow torn his trousers coming out of the Opera House, and now looked infinitely pathetic.

"I wanted him to know," Roosevelt replied.

Hunt was not impressed. "Well, I should think he would know without being told."[31]

This exchange in effect ended the three-year friendship of the two young Assemblymen, which had never been the same since Hunt's disloyalty during the Speakership contest. There is no evidence that Roosevelt took any petty offense at his colleague's words. But he knew now that it was time to unrope himself from Hunt, O'Neil, and the other "Roosevelt Republicans," whose horizons extended no further than New York State, and eagerly search out new altitudes, wider vistas. Chicago beckoned, and beyond it the West; could he but rise high enough, he might see his future clear.

"He grew right away from me," Hunt confessed ruefully in old age. "I knew he was born for some great emergency, but what he would do I could not tell . . . I never expected to see him go right up in the heavens."[32]

ROOSEVELT RETURNED TO ALBANY on 24 April to receive the congratulations of his supporters in the Assembly. "For a while," remarked the *Times,* "it was a doubtful question whether the Chamber was being used for legislative purposes or as a Roosevelt reception room."[33] During the next few days he enjoyed such adulation, both public and private, as he had never enjoyed before—and would not experience again for at least a decade. *The New York Times* hailed him as "the victor, the wearer of all the laurels" at Utica, and the *Evening Post,* in the course of a long and flattering editorial, called him "the most successful young politician of our day."[34] Curiosity mounted in Chicago and Washington about the twenty-five-year-old who had almost single-handedly made Senator Edmunds a serious candidate for the Presidency. Arthur Cutler, who kept closely in touch with political trends, and took pedagogic pride in his ex-pupil, assured Bamie, "Theodore's reputation is national and even to us who know him it is phenomenal. Whatever the future may have in store for him, no man in the country has begun his public career more brilliantly."[35]

Two hundred miles away in Boston, Henry Cabot Lodge, another Edmunds supporter and delegate-at-large to Chicago, decided that Roosevelt was a "national figure of real importance,"[36] and made a mental note to cultivate him.

ROOSEVELT'S POST-CONVENTION GLOW was chilled by news that Grover Cleveland was threatening to veto some of his bills for the regulation of New York City. The Assemblyman reacted with understandable shock. He had been so frequent a visitor to the Executive Office recently, and Cleveland had seemed so agreeable to all his legislation, that Roosevelt no doubt expected full cooperation through the concluding weeks of the session. (Only a few days before Utica, *Harper's Weekly* had published a Nast cartoon showing the Governor obediently signing a pile of these same bills in Roosevelt's presence.)[37]

Others, however, had seen signs of a showdown long ago; it was not so much a question of politics as of diametrically opposed personalities. Roosevelt was nervy, inspirational, passionate. He arrived at conclusions so rapidly that he seemed to be acting wholly on impulse, and was impatient when those with more laborious minds did not instantly agree with him.[38] Cleveland, on the other hand, was slow, stolid, objective, almost maddeningly conscientious. No bill was too lengthy, or too complex, for him to scrutinize it down to the last punctuation-mark. His fathomless legal mind absorbed all data indiscriminately, sorted them into logical sequence, then issued an opinion which had about it the finality of a commandment chiseled in marble. One might as well try to sandpaper the marble smooth as to get Cleveland to change his mind.

"I never see those two together," said Daniel S. Lamont, the Governor's secretary, "that I'm not reminded of a great mastiff solemnly regarding a small terrier, snapping and barking at him."[39] William Hudson, of the *Brooklyn Daily Eagle,* used a different metaphor. Cleveland was the Immovable Object, whereas Roosevelt was the Irresistible Force. Any confrontation between them was bound to generate heat—and good copy besides. So when Hudson met Roosevelt in State Street, shortly after his return from Utica, he lost no time in telling him about Cleveland's objections to his city reform bills.[40] The reaction was predictable. "He musn't do that! I can't have that! I won't let him do it! I'll go up and see him at once." With that, Roosevelt turned and began to sprint up the hill. The reporter, scenting a story, hurried after him.

Roosevelt was already pounding on Cleveland's desk when Hudson arrived in the Executive Office. The Governor proceeded to explain that the bills, while admirable in intent, had been too hastily written. They contained several inconsistencies which would render them ineffective as laws. Not the least of these non sequiturs was a clause in the Tenure of Office Bill specifying two different terms, of 4 years and 1 year 11 months respectively, for the same officer. There were sentences in other measures which were incomprehensible even by legal standards; the mere addition of a word or two would repair their logic; he would not sign them as presently drawn. Bristling, Roosevelt declared that "principle" was the main thing, that it was too late to worry about arcane details. "You must not veto those bills. You cannot. You shall not . . . I won't have it!"

At this, Cleveland gathered up all his three hundred pounds and considerable height, visibly mushrooming in his chair. "Mr. Roosevelt, I'm going to veto those bills!" His fist crashed down with such force as to make the Assemblyman seek sanctuary in a chair, muttering something about "an outrage." But Cleveland had already returned to his work. The interview was over.[41]

Thus ended the brief and unlikely political partnership of two future Presidents. They would work together again one day, and for the same cause that preoccupied them in Albany, but their relations would never be as friendly.

ALTHOUGH ROOSEVELT WAS REPORTED to be "beaming with smiles" on his return to the Capitol, he was still privately tortured with sorrow. His colleagues in the House had found him "a changed man" since the double tragedy of 14 February. "You could not mention the fact that his wife and mother had been taken away . . .

you could see at once that it was a grief too deep."[42] There were signs that the pain inside him was increasing, rather than diminishing, due no doubt to its too cruel suppression.

Legislative work was no longer a distraction. He was offered renomination for a fourth term, but refused: he simply could not face the thought of another winter in Albany.[43] With all his soul he longed now to get away from the "dull Dutch town," away from New York with its bitter memories, away to the therapeutic emptiness of the Badlands. Even Chicago, which had so recently seemed such a thrilling prospect, now loomed like a wearisome chore. On 30 April he unburdened himself to the editor of the *Utica Morning Herald,* in an unusually self-revelatory letter.

> I wish to write you a few words just to thank you for your kindness towards me, and to assure you that my head will not be turned by what I well know was a mainly accidental success. Although not a very old man, I have yet lived a great deal in my life, and I have known sorrow too bitter and joy too keen to allow me to become either cast down or elated for more than a very brief period over any success or defeat.
>
> I have very little expectation of being able to keep on in politics; my success so far has only been won by absolute indifference to my future career; for I doubt if any man can realize the bitter and venomous hatred with which I am regarded by the very politicians who at Utica supported me, under dictation from masters who are influenced by political considerations that were national and not local in their scope. I realize very thoroughly the absolutely ephemeral nature of the hold I have upon the people, and a very real and positive hostility I have excited among the politicians. I will not stay in public life unless I can do so on my own terms; and my ideal, whether lived up to or not, is rather a high one.
>
> For very many reasons I will not mind going back into private [life] for a few years. My work this winter has been very harassing, and I feel tired and restless; for the next few months I shall probably be in Dakota, and I think I shall

> spend the next two to three years in making shooting trips, either in the Far West or in the Northern Woods—and there will be plenty of work to do writing.[44]

WHEN HENRY CABOT LODGE and Theodore Roosevelt arrived in Chicago on Saturday, 31 May, they were already close friends. Earlier that month, the thirty-four-year-old Bostonian had written the twenty-five-year-old Knickerbocker, congratulating him on his election as delegate-at-large from New York, and proposing a joint visit to Washington to interview Senator Edmunds before the convention started. On the very day that Roosevelt received this letter, he had been writing a similar one to Lodge, congratulating him, in turn, on *his* election as delegate-at-large from Massachusetts. He accepted Lodge's invitation "with pleasure," and asked him to stay over at 6 West Fifty-seventh Street en route. "We are breaking up house, so you will have to excuse very barren accommodations."[45]

Thus with an exchange of mutual flattery, an evening of echoing conversation in the Roosevelt mansion,[46] and a pilgrimage to the city of their destiny, Lodge and Roosevelt laid the foundation of one of the great friendships in American political history.

At first sight the two men seemed an unlikely pair. Next to the wiry, bouncing, voluble Roosevelt, Lodge was tall, haughty, quiet, and dry. His beard was sharp, his coat tightly buttoned, his handshake quickly withdrawn. His eyes, forever screwed up and blinking, surveyed the world with aristocratic disdain. A heavy mustache clamped his mouth aggressively shut. On the rare occasions when the thin lips parted, they emitted a series of metallic noises which, according to Lodge's whim, might be a quotation from Prosper Mérimée, or a joke comprehensible only to those of the bluest blood and most impeccable tailoring, or a personal insult so stinging as to paralyze all powers of repartee. Only in conditions of extreme privacy would Henry Cabot Lodge unbend an inch or so, and allow the privileged few to call him "Pinky."[47]

Among his own kind, Lodge was said to be a man of considerable wit and charm;[48] but the large mass of humanity, including most of the political establishment, found him repellently cold. By no amount of persuasion could he be made to see any other man's view if it differed from his own. Those who ventured to disagree with him were crushed with sarcasm, or worse still, ignored. Although he had served only two terms in the Massachusetts House of Representatives, as opposed to Roosevelt's three in Albany, "Lah-de-dah Lodge" was already on his way to becoming one of America's most disliked politicians.[49] Yet nobody could deny that he was a man of extraordinary caliber. His promises, once made, were never broken. His treatment of both friends and enemies was unshakably fair. As for his attitude to government, it was as high-minded as a philosopher's.

This latter characteristic, of course, attracted Roosevelt instantly. But the younger man was also drawn to Lodge's mind, which was more erudite than his own. Lodge had not been deprived, by childhood invalidism, of a full classical education. After graduating from Harvard he had become an editor, with Henry Adams, of the *North American Review*, and had collaborated with that august intellectual in a book on the history of Anglo-Saxon law.[50] More recently, he had published biographies of George Cabot (1877), Alexander Hamilton (1882), and Daniel Webster (1883), as well as *A Short History of the American Colonies* (1881). Lodge was now, in 1884, an overseer of Harvard College, chairman of the Massachusetts Republican party, and a candidate for Congress.[51]

No wonder Roosevelt admired this "Scholar in Politics." Lodge, in turn, admired Roosevelt's raw force and superior political instinct. The two had, besides, many things in common: aristocratic manners, wealth, a love of elegant clothes, membership in the Porcellian, early marriages to beautiful women (the Cabot blood shared by both Lodge and Alice Lee was another bond, albeit unspoken), massive egos, and a ruthless ambition.[52] Theirs was a relationship in which occasional clashes of personality merely emphasized identical taste and breeding, as one or two dissonant notes enrich the larger harmonies of a major chord.

NO SOONER HAD ROOSEVELT checked into the Grand Pacific Hotel, New York's headquarters, than newspapermen began to cluster around him. With his "chipper straw hat," "natty cane," and "new, French calf, low-cut shoes" he was "more specifically an object of curiosity than any other stranger in Chicago."[53] Lodge, too, attracted attention with his "crisp, short hair . . . full beard, and an appearance of half-shut eyes."[54]

But it was politics, not appearances, that made reporters cluster around them. Word had spread that they might prove pivotal figures at the convention, beginning Tuesday. Under the patronage of old George William Curtis, the snowy-whiskered Civil Service Reformer and editor of *Harper's Weekly,* Roosevelt and Lodge were leaders of the Independent forces. (They had spent most of the month rounding up Edmunds delegates by mail.)[55] Although their power was too slight to affect the nomination of one clear favorite, they could possibly play two favorites off against each other, and then push the nomination of Senator Edmunds as a compromise. In other words, Roosevelt hoped to repeat his successful Utica performance. The numbers at Chicago were much larger, and the list of candidates longer (at least nine, as of midnight Saturday),[56] but he had at least one trend in his favor: President Arthur and James G. Blaine were running neck and neck, with about three hundred delegates apiece. Edmunds lay third with ninety; all the other dark horses were far behind.

Making the most of their news value, Roosevelt and Lodge announced loudly and repeatedly that they would stay with their candidate until the end. Yet both added *sotto voce,* to at least one reporter, that if either Arthur or Blaine were nominated they, as loyal Republicans, would of course support him.[57] It was a considerable admission, for their ideological rejection of both candidates, especially the "decidedly mottled" Blaine, was total. Editors buried the remarks beneath thousands of words of more frivolous preconvention copy.[58]

IN 1927 NICHOLAS MURRAY BUTLER, president of Columbia University and an old friend of Theodore Roosevelt, remembered the Republican National Convention of 1884 as "the ablest body of men that ever came together in America since the original Constitutional Convention."[59] At the time, it was considered just the opposite—"a disgrace to decency, and a blot upon the reputation of our country," to quote Andrew D. White.[60] Roosevelt himself was unimpressed by most of his fellow conventioneers. Six days of politicking with them were enough to convince him that, often as not, *vox populi* was "the voice of the devil, or what is still worse, the voice of a fool."[61] All the same, he certainly met most of the emerging leaders whose talents Butler so admired, and registered their faces in his photographic memory.[62]

Vastly outnumbering these men of the future were the "Old Guard"—veteran party members who had voted for Frémont and shed their blood for Lincoln and Grant; men who had prospered mightily under the "spoils system" for almost a quarter of a century of Republican power. They held the party and its orthodox ideology so holy that some of them cast their delegate badges in gold.[63] Those from the West, and from Pennsylvania, arrived full of whiskey and love for James G. Blaine; those from the South, and from Wall Street, formed glee clubs to sing the praises of President Arthur. Both groups brought bags of "boodle" to purchase the votes of uncommitted delegates. They looked askance at the Edmunds men, who not only refused to be bought, but sanctimoniously shut up shop on Sunday morning. Independents were promptly accused of having more ice than blood in their blue Northeastern veins, and it became standard procedure, whenever anybody like Henry Cabot Lodge walked by, for members of the Old Guard to turn up their coat collars and shiver ostentatiously.[64]

The "schoolboy" Roosevelt, with his "inexhaustible supply of insufferable dudism and conceit,"[65] aroused their particular scorn, even though they could not help being impressed by his mental powers. One old delegate remarked, after meeting him, that "all the brains intended for others of the Roosevelt family had evidently fallen into the cranium of young Theodore."[66]

To see the Chicago Convention as far as possible through Roosevelt's eyes, it is necessary to remember how desperately he had been driving himself through the last three months, how full of private grief he was, and how he longed during this final crescendo of political bedlam for the silence and solace of the Badlands. The events of the next week may best be visualized through a red blur of fatigue, which thickened as day followed night with barely a pause for sleep.

MIDNIGHT, MONDAY, 2 JUNE. Every room, stairway, and corridor in the Grand Pacific Hotel is crammed with garrulous, perspiring delegates. It takes one reporter a quarter of an hour to fight his way up from the lobby to Arthur headquarters, on the third floor. "All the corrupt element in the Republican party," he notes en route, "seems to be concentrated here working in behalf of Blaine."[67] Brass bands thump in the streets outside, the President's glee clubs roar discordantly, and tabletop orators shout themselves hoarse; but the most omnipresent sound is the soft rustle of "boodle." Thomas Collier Platt of New York, Blaine's unofficial treasurer, is rumored to be paying the highest price for votes. Arthur men are running out of money in the effort to compete with him, and impatiently await the arrival of a $50,000 parcel from New York City.[68] Meanwhile they bolster their bribes with promises of federal jobs. Some wily colored delegates, trading on the white man's traditional inability to distinguish one black face from another, sell themselves over and over to both major candidates, stocking up on free cheese and whiskey, and steadily escalating their prices. The going rate for a black Arkansas vote is already $1,000.

"Niggers," growls one Arthur lieutenant, "come higher at this convention than any since the war."[69]

10:00 A.M., TUESDAY, 3 JUNE. Warm, radiant spring weather.[70] The lake "velvety-violet," the trees along Michigan Avenue dense with new leaves. Atop the arched glass roof of Exposition Hall, a hundred flags flutter and snap. Ten thousand people mill excitedly about: spectator tickets are selling at $40 each.[71]

Inside the hall, an immense, luminous space, so bright with red, white, and blue bunting that at first it sends a tiny stab of pain into the eyes. An acre or more of light cane chairs, banked up row upon row like the seats of a Roman amphitheater. Parterres, galleries, even the high, wide-open windows are already packed with human flesh. Somewhere a band is playing Gilbert and Sullivan. In the distance, at the focal point of the hall, the chairman's podium is a pyramid of flags and flowers. In front of it hangs a portrait of the assassinated Garfield, replacing the traditional martyr's image of Lincoln.[72]

George William Curtis enters on Theodore Roosevelt's arm, at the head of the New York delegation. He is gloomily pleased to note Lincoln's absence. "Those weary eyes . . . are not to see the work that is to be done here," he grunts.[73] After thirty-six hours of intensive lobbying, the Edmunds men know that they have little chance of preventing the nomination of James G. Blaine. For all his shabby past, for all his two previous failures to capture the nomination, and for all his sincere protestations that the Presidency is not for him, the "Plumed Knight" has an inexplicable hold upon both party and public. The mere sight of his boozy, silver-bearded features in a train window is enough to make women weep with adoration, and men vow to God that they will never vote for any other Republican. These same features are now ubiquitous on badges and banners and transparencies all over Chicago—and all over Exposition Hall, as the delegates stream in.

The Independents have one slender hope of averting a Blaine landslide. Late yesterday the news reached them that the Republican National Committee had designated Powell Clayton, a flagrant supporter of Blaine, to be temporary chairman of the convention. Working through the night, Roosevelt and Lodge have built up enough opposition, among Arthur men as well as their own delegates, to defeat Clayton and elect, instead, John R. Lynch, an honorable black Congressman from Mississippi. Should this opposition hold through today's balloting, the convention will at least be assured of neutral guidance from the Chair.[74]

At twenty minutes past noon the enormous building is at last full. The band plays "My Country 'Tis of Thee," and the convention is rapped to order. A chaplain drones the opening prayer. The first item on the agenda is the election of a chairman, and Powell Clayton's name is duly announced. Then, in pin-drop silence, the skinny figure of Henry Cabot Lodge stands up. His grating voice fills the hall. "I move you, Mr. Chairman, to substitute the name of the Hon. John R. Lynch, of Mississippi."[75]

There is a buzz of indignation. Members of the Old Guard protest Lodge's motion. For forty years, roars one delegate, the party has automatically endorsed the National Committee's choice for convention chairman; to suggest somebody else is an act of rank disloyalty. Finally Roosevelt has a chance to rise in support of his friend. Leaping onto a chair and squashing down his wayward spectacles, he begins to speak—with such obvious effort that his body shakes.[76]

> Mr. Chairman, it has been said by the distinguished gentleman from Pennsylvania that it is without precedent to reverse the action of the National Committee . . . there are, as I understand it, but two delegates to this convention who have seats on the National Committee; and I hold it to be derogatory to our honor, to our capacity for self-government, to say that we must accept the nomination of a presiding officer by another body . . .
>
> It is now, Mr. Chairman, less than a quarter of a century since, in this city, the great Republican party organized for victory and nominated Abraham Lincoln, of Illinois, who broke the fetters of the slaves and rent them asunder forever. It is a fitting thing for us to choose to preside over this convention one of that race whose right to sit within these walls is due to the blood and the treasure so lavishly spent by the founders of the Republican party.[77]

This brief speech, interrupted six times by applause, is his only attempt at oratory during the convention. It is praised as "neat and effective," "blunt and manly." But the significance of the fact that Roosevelt, in his maiden speech before a national audience, has sought to elevate a black man will not be fully appreciated for many years.[78]

Lynch is elected by 424 votes to Clayton's 384, a narrow but dramatic victory. Roosevelt, bobbing up and down nervously, accepts congratulations from all over the floor. Judge Joseph Foraker of Ohio is seen engaging him in long and friendly discourse. "I found Mr. Roosevelt to be a young man of rather peculiar qualities," Foraker notes later. "He is a little bit young, and on that account has not quite so much discretion as he will have after a while."[79]

At midnight Roosevelt is still strenuously "booming" for Edmunds. His estimates of the Senator's strength are noticeably larger than anybody else's.[80]

Wednesday, 4 June. A dreary, drizzly day. Routine business in Exposition Hall does not disguise the fact that more and more delegates are pledging themselves to Blaine. The Independents cannot hide their weariness and disillusionment. Only Roosevelt, says the *New York Sun,* is still "bubbling with martial ardor" as he dashes to and fro on behalf of his candidate.[81] All day long, through the evening session, and on into the early hours of Thursday morning, he continues his hopeless battle. He has long since realized that ninety Edmunds men cannot stop the Plumed Knight; their only hope now is to join ranks with those supporting some other reform candidate, such as John Sherman or Robert Lincoln. Meanwhile, both he and Lodge are plotting to delay the final ballot as long as possible, in the hope that Blaine's men will eventually begin to fight each other out of sheer frustration.

Thursday, 5 June. Solid rain and sullen tempers. The delay strategy seems to be working: there are rumors that balloting will not begin until tomorrow, maybe even Saturday. Sporadic fistfights and cane-whackings break out in the Grand Pacific Hotel.[82] By the time Exposition Hall opens its doors, even Roosevelt is too tired to vault to his seat. He plods purposefully down the aisle, surrounded by an anxious crowd of Independents. Later, he is glimpsed "with his arm around some Ohio delegate's neck," tugging restlessly at his mustache and "looking out of the corner of his eyeglasses at the ladies in the east box."[83]

During the long, tension-filled reading of the party platform, and through the hours of irascible debate that follow, Congressman William McKinley of Ohio suddenly emerges as a leading figure in the convention. With unctuous smile and soothing voice, he moves about the floor, quelling arguments before they spread. In the words of Andrew D. White, he is "calm, substantial, quick . . . strong . . . evidently a born leader of men." As McKinley's star brightens, Roosevelt's begins to fade. Exhaustion is setting in. He rises to question a point of procedure, and is crushed by the retort that the point has already been made clear. As he apologizes ("I did not distinctly hear") and sits down, some sparrows fly in from outside and squat mockingly on the gas fixture above his head.[84]

The nominating speeches begin at 7:30 P.M. and continue long past midnight. Twelve thousand pairs of lungs, and forty gas chandeliers, suck more oxygen out of the air than the windows can replenish. Yet Roosevelt remains wide awake throughout the evening's interminable oratory. He writes Bamie afterward:

> Some of the nominating speeches were very fine, notably that of Governor Long of Massachusetts [for Edmunds], which was the most masterly and scholarly effort I have ever listened to. Blaine was nominated by Judge West, the blind orator of Ohio. It was a most impressive scene. The speaker, a feeble old man of shrunk but gigantic frame, stood looking with his sightless eyes toward the vast throng that filled the huge hall. As he became excited his voice rang like a trumpet, and the audience became worked up to a condition of absolutely uncontrollable excitement and enthusiasm. For a quarter of an hour at a time they cheered and shouted so that the brass bands could not be heard at all, and we were nearly deafened by the noise.[85]

If *The New York Times* is to be believed, Roosevelt and Lodge begin another stop-Blaine movement immediately after adjournment, and work right through the night trying to marshal uncommitted delegates "behind some candidate new or old" whom everybody can support.[86]

FRIDAY, 6 JUNE. "Black Friday with the reformers in the Republican party," as one correspondent puts it[87]—begins at 11:30 A.M.

with the slam of Chairman Lynch's gold-ringed gavel. There can be no more delays; the first ballot is called. Amid cheers, hisses, and boos, the secretary announces the tally. With 411 votes required for nomination, James G. Blaine has 334½; Chester A. Arthur, 278; George F. Edmunds, 93.[88]

On the second ballot, Blaine's support increases while that of Edmunds declines. The third ballot brings Blaine within thirty-six votes of the nomination. Even now, Roosevelt will not give up. He starts rushing frantically from delegation to delegation, while Judge Foraker moves to adjourn, so that a final line of defense against Blaine can be organized. The motion is shouted down, but Roosevelt jumps into his chair, yelling for a roll call until he is red in the face. By now the entire hall is reverberating with whistles and catcalls; he continues to shout and gesticulate; when a delegate from New Jersey tells him to "sit down and stop your noise," his temper cracks. "Shut up your own head, you damned scoundrel you!"[89] The Chair rejects his point of order on a technicality. However Roosevelt does succeed, says the *Chicago Tribune,* "in rousing the admiring remarks of the fair sex, who enthused over his 28 [*sic*] years and glasses."[90]

Once again William McKinley pours oil on troubled waters. "Let us have no technical objections. I am as good a friend of James G. Blaine as he has in this convention, and I insist that every man here shall have fair play." The motion to adjourn is voted on, and defeated. Roosevelt sits "pale, jerky, and nervous" as the fourth ballot proceeds. "I was at the birth of the Republican party," murmurs old George William Curtis, "and I fear I am to witness its death."[91]

The sun streams in through high windows, flooding the hall with yellow light. A secretary begins to announce the tally. One Arthur delegate retires to the wings, brushes tears from his eyes, and changes his purple badge for a white one. It is all over.[92] In a hurricane of hats, umbrellas, and handkerchiefs, and what is generally calculated to be the loudest roar in the history of American politics, McKinley pushes smilingly through the crowd. He bends over Roosevelt's chair, asks him to second a motion making the nomination unanimous. Roosevelt shakes his head. McKinley turns to Curtis. The old man shakes his head too.[93]

OUTSIDE, AS THE DELEGATES disperse in the warm afternoon, Roosevelt snaps at a *World* reporter, "I am going cattle-ranching in Dakota for the remainder of the summer and a part of the fall. What I shall do after that I cannot tell you." Asked if he will support the party's choice for President, he replies with angrily flashing spectacles, "That question I decline to answer. It is a subject that I do not care to talk about."[94]

At midnight, he is still too wrought up to sleep. He tells an *Evening Post* editor that, rather than vote for Blaine, he would give "hearty support" to any decent Democrat. More than anything, this rash remark reveals that Roosevelt is politically and physically at the end of his tether.[95] The editor does not print it—yet.

SATURDAY, 7 JUNE. Henry Cabot Lodge heads east to muse on the future; Theodore Roosevelt heads west to forget about the past. He craves nothing so much as the shade of his front porch, the lowing of his own cattle, the soothing scratch of his pen across paper. Yet even at St. Paul, the roar of Chicago pursues him. A reporter from the *Pioneer Press* demands to know if he will accept Blaine's nomination or "bolt." Some sixth sense warns Roosevelt that "bolt" is the most fatal word in American politics. "I shall bolt the Convention by no means," he says at last. "I have no personal objections to Blaine."[96]

With that, Roosevelt changes trains and rumbles off to Little Missouri. A boyhood ambition is rising within him. He will take a rifle, load up a horse, and ride off into the prairie, absolutely alone, for days and days—"far off from all mankind."[97]

"I am going cattle ranching . . . what I shall do after that I cannot tell you."

The first public advertisement of the Maltese Cross brand, 1884.

CHAPTER 11

The Cowboy of the Present

Heart's dearest,
Why dost thou sorrow so?

THE STARS WERE ALREADY PALE in the east as he rode across the river-bottom and struck off up a winding valley.[1] His horse, Manitou, loped effortlessly through a sea of sweet-smelling prairie-rose bushes. Presently the sun's first rays rushed horizontally across the Badlands, kissing the tops of the buttes, and shocking millions of drowsy birds into song.

Among the swelling chorus of hermit thrushes, grosbeaks, robins, bluebirds, thrashers, and sparrows, Roosevelt's acute ear caught one particularly rich and bubbling sound, with "a cadence of wild sadness, inexpressibly touching."[2] He identified it as the meadowlark. Ever afterward, the music of that bird would come "laden with a hundred memories and associations; with the sight of dim hills reddening in the dawn, with the breath of cool morning winds blowing across lowly plains, with the scent of flowers on the sunlit prairie."[3]

Some varieties of birdsong, however much they ravished Roosevelt's ear, aroused in his heart that same sharp, indefinable nostalgia which he had felt as a child, gazing at the portrait of Edith

"New York will certainly lose him for a time at least."

Theodore Roosevelt in his buckskin suit, 1884.

Carow.[4] Ache though he may, he could not escape hearing them in Dakota, in June, a month of prodigious migrations. Nor did he really want to. For four years or more, he had been starved of this, the only kind of music he really understood. In abandoning his natural history studies for Alice Lee, he had stifled the precocious sensitivity to nature that was so characteristic of him as a youth. Now, as a twenty-five-year-old widower, with his second career abandoned—or at least indefinitely postponed—he could reopen his ears to the "sweet, sad songs" of the hermit thrush, the "boding call" of the whippoorwill, and "the soft melancholy cooing of the mourning-dove, whose voice always seems far away and expresses more than any other sound in nature the sadness of gentle, hopeless, never-ending grief."[5]

TWO MAGPIES, perched on a bleached buffalo skull,[6] greeted him as he left the creek and rode through a line of scoria-red buttes. The naked prairie opened out ahead, already hot and shimmering under the climbing sun. Choosing one course at random, he headed south, scanning the horizon for antelope. All he carried, beside his rifle, was a book, a blanket, an oilskin, a metal cup, a little tea and salt, and some dry biscuits. Since arriving in Dakota nine days before, he had eaten nothing but canned pork and starch. Ferris and Merrifield were too busy with the spring roundup to shoot any fresh meat. Roosevelt therefore had good dietetic reasons, as well as his "boyish ambition," for embarking on a trip across the prairie. But his real hunger was for solitude.

> Nowhere, not even at sea, does a man feel more lonely than when riding over the far-reaching, seemingly never-ending plains . . . their vastness and loneliness and their melancholy monotony have a strong fascination for him. The landscape seems always the same, and after the traveller has plodded on for miles and miles he gets to feel as if the distance were really boundless. As far as the eye can see, there is no break; either the prairie stretches out into perfectly level flats, or else there are gentle, rolling slopes . . . when one of these is

> ascended, immediately another precisely like it takes its place in the distance, and so roll succeeds roll in a succession as interminable as that of the waves in the ocean. Nowhere else does one feel so far off from all mankind; the plains stretch out in deathless and measureless expanse, and as he journeys over them they will for many miles be lacking in all signs of life.[7]

Lonely, melancholy, monotony, deathless—these words, especially the first, became obsessive parts of Roosevelt's vocabulary in 1884. There was, however, no shortage of his favorite adjective *manly,* and his favorite pronoun, *I.* While accepting that his first few days on the prairie must have had their moments of anguish (since Alice's death he had not been alone for more than a few hours at a time), one cannot read his descriptions of the trip without sensing his overwhelming delight in being free at last. "Black care," Roosevelt wrote, "rarely sits behind a rider whose pace is fast enough."[8]

He sighted several small bands of antelope that morning. For hours he pursued them, first on foot, then on hands and knees, and finally flat on his face, wriggling through patches of cactus; but the nervous creatures were off before he could draw a bead. After a lunch of biscuits and water, and a snooze in the broiling sun—the only shade available was that of his own hat—he pushed on doggedly. Once horse and rider were very nearly engulfed in a quicksand, "and it was only by frantic strugglings and flounderings that we managed to get over." Roosevelt learned to stay well clear of stands of tall grass in seemingly dry creeks: beneath might lurk a fathomless bed of slime.

He learned, too, that fleeing antelope have a quasi-military tendency to gallop in straight lines, even when intercepted at an angle. Taking advantage of this, he succeeded eventually in rolling over one fine buck "like a rabbit." Cutting off the hams and head, and stringing them to his saddle, he rode on in search of a campsite. Around sunset he found a wooded creek with fresh pools and succulent grass. Turning Manitou loose to browse, Roosevelt lit a fire "for cheerfulness," cut himself an antelope steak, and roasted it on a forked stick. Later he lay on his blanket under a wide-branching cottonwood tree, "looking up at the stars until I fell asleep, in the cool air."[9]

THE SHRILL YIPPING of prairie dogs awoke him shortly before dawn. It was now very chill, and wreaths of light mist hung over the water. Roosevelt reached for his rifle and strolled through the dark trees out onto the prairie.

> Nothing was in sight in the way of game; but overhead a skylark was singing, soaring above me so high that I could not make out his form in the gray morning light. I listened for some time, and the music never ceased for a moment, coming down clear, sweet, and tender from the air above. Soon the strains of another answered from a little distance off, and the two kept soaring and singing as long as I stayed to listen; and when I walked away I could still hear their notes behind me.[10]

On returning to the camp at sunrise, Roosevelt caught sight of a doe going down to the water, "her great, sensitive ears thrown forward as she peered anxiously and timidly around." Gun forgotten, he watched enchanted while she drank her fill. She snatched some hasty mouthfuls of wet grass; presently a spotted fawn joined her. When they left, the pond was taken over by a mallard and her ducklings, "balls of fuzzy yellow down, that bobbed off into the reeds as I walked by."[11]

ROOSEVELT WAS BACK at the Maltese Cross Ranch on 22 June, having spent five days in the wilderness, feeling "as absolutely free as any man could feel."[12] He might have stayed away longer, but he did not wish his venison to spoil in the hot sun. The little log cabin was deserted. Ferris and Merrifield had left for St. Paul, with $26,000 of his money, to purchase a thousand new head of cattle;[13] they would not be back for another month. He felt too restless to settle down and begin the writing he had vaguely planned for summer. Next day he was in the saddle again, riding downriver.[14]

En route he stopped at Medora to pick up some mail, and was able to take his first good look around since returning to the Badlands.[15] The hamlet of last fall, with its giant chimney and scattered, half-finished houses, was now a bustling town of eighty-four buildings, including a hotel which the Marquis de Morès had modestly named after himself. Little Missouri, meanwhile, was already slipping into ghosthood on the other side of the river. Trains no longer stopped there. Medora, clearly, was the future capital of the Badlands.[16]

A spirit of lusty optimism pervaded the place. Roosevelt, tethering Manitou and gazing about him, could not help but respond to it. The beef business was prospering; it had been a mild winter, and plenty of fat steers were ambling to their doom in the slaughterhouse. A record number of calves had been born to replace them—155 at Maltese Cross alone.[17] Daily consignments of dressed meat were being shipped East by the Marquis's Northern Pacific Refrigerator Car Company. Meanwhile, de Morès was spawning new business ideas with codfish-like fertility. He would plant fifty thousand cabbages in the Little Missouri Valley, and force-feed them with his own patented fertilizer, made from offal; he would run a stagecoach line along the eastern rim of the Badlands; he would invest $10,000 in a huge blood-drying machine; he would extend a chain of icehouses as far west as Oregon, so that Columbia River salmon could be whisked, cold and fresh, to New York in seven days; he would open a pottery in Medora to process the fine local clay; he would string a telegraph line all the way south to the Black Hills; he would supply the French Army with a delicious new soup he had invented. . . . As fast as these schemes flourished or failed, the Marquis would think of others.[18]

It is not definitely known whether Roosevelt met the Marquis in Medora that Monday, but they would have had difficulty avoiding each other. De Morès was the most ubiquitous person in town, given to riding up and down the street in a large white sombrero, his blue shirt laced with yellow silk cord, his mustaches prickling haughtily. Tall, wiry, and muscular, he sat his horse more gracefully than any cowboy.[19] Gunmen treated him with scared respect: his reputation as a sharpshooter was exceeded only by the vivacious and redheaded Madame de Morès.[20]

Almost certainly the couple entertained Roosevelt with iced champagne, this being their invariable custom whenever a distinguished stranger came to town. The atmosphere may have been a little stiff at first, for there had been a dispute over grazing rights between the Marquis and Roosevelt's cattlemen during the winter.[21] But it is a matter of record that Roosevelt and de Morès were soon conferring on subjects of mutual interest, and planning a visit to Montana together.[22]

Before continuing his expedition downriver, Roosevelt dropped in at the office of Medora's weekly newspaper, the *Bad Lands Cowboy.* Its editor, a bearded, flap-eared, engaging youth named Arthur Packard, had disquieting news. According to Eastern dispatches, much political vituperation was being lavished on the names Roosevelt and Lodge. The former's railroad interview at St. Paul, stating that he had "no personal objections" to James G. Blaine, and the latter's announcement, on returning to Boston, that he, too, would support the Chicago convention's choice, had enraged the reform press.[23] Clearly they had been expected to follow George William Curtis, and a host of other prominent Independents, out of the Republican party.

Roosevelt showed little interest, merely saying that the St. Paul reporter had misquoted him out of "asininity."[24] Politics must have seemed impossibly remote and irrelevant in Packard's whitewashed, inky-smelling office, with its slugs of type spelling out news of more immediate interest, to do with horse-thievery and the price of fresh manure.[25]

Remounting Manitou, Roosevelt rode out of Medora and headed north into the green bottomlands of the Little Missouri.

THE NEXT ISSUE OF the *Bad Lands Cowboy* briefly reported that a new dude had arrived in town.

> Theodore Roosevelt, the young New York reformer, made us a very pleasant call Monday, in full cowboy regalia. New York will certainly lose him for a time at least, as he is

perfectly charmed with our free Western life and is now figuring on a trip into the Big Horn country . . .[26]

WHEN PACKARD'S NEWS ITEM appeared, Roosevelt was at least thirty miles north, well beyond the farthest reach of ranch settlement. He was looking for "untrodden ground" on which to build a ranch house. The Maltese Cross log cabin, situated only eight miles south of Medora, did not satisfy his present hunger for solitude. A popular pony-trail passed within a few yards of the front door; ten or twelve cowpunchers galloping by every week amounted, as far as he was concerned, to an intolerable amount of traffic noise. Worse still, at least half of them wanted to stop off and pass the time of day.[27] How could a man write with so many interruptions? He wanted to live where the peace of nature was total.

Acting on a tip from a friendly cattleman, Roosevelt kept splashing across the meandering river, heading directly north until he reached a magnificent stretch of bottomland on the left bank. Grass spread smoothly back from the water's edge for a hundred yards, merging into a belt of immense cottonwood trees. This bird-loud grove extended a farther two hundred yards west. Then a range of clay hills, which seemed to have been sculpted by a giant hand as preparatory studies for mountains, loomed steeply into the sky. A distant plume of lignite smoke, glowing pink as evening came on, hinted at the surrounding savagery of the Badlands. No place could be more remote from the world, yet more insulated from the wilderness.[28] Roosevelt knew he had found his "hold" in Dakota.

Here he would build "a long, low ranch house of hewn logs, with a verandah, and with in addition to the other rooms, a bedroom for myself, and a sitting-room with a big fireplace." There would be a rough desk, well stocked with ink and paper, two or three shelves full of books, and a rubber tub to bathe in. Out front, on a piazza overlooking the river, there would be the inevitable Rooseveltian rocking-chair, in which he could sit reading poetry on summer afternoons, or watching his cattle plod across the sandbars. At night, when he came back tired and bloody from hunting, there would be a welcoming flicker of firelight through the cottonwood trees, plenty of fresh meat to eat, and beds spread with buffalo robes. . . .[29]

Of course several practical things had to be done before these dreams were realized. He must first claim the site (the presence of a hunting shack nearby meant he would probably have to buy squatter's rights);[30] he must order many more cattle; he must hire men to build the house and run the ranch for him. As it happened, he already had two recruits for the latter job: his two old friends from the backwoods of Maine, Bill Sewall and Wilmot Dow.

ON 9 MARCH 1884—less than three weeks after burying Alice—Roosevelt had written to Sewall with a rather peremptory invitation to join him in Dakota. "I feel sure you will do well for yourself by coming out with me . . . I shall take you and Will Dow out next August."[31] What persuaded him that a pair of forest-bred Easterners would flourish in the Badlands is unclear, but Sewall and Dow were agreeable. Their motives appear to have been pecuniary. "He said he would guarantee us a share of anything made in the cattle business," Sewall recalled. "And if anything was lost, he would lose it and pay our wages . . . . I told him that I thought it was very one-sided, but if he thought he could stand it, I thought we could."[32] There were minor hindrances, such as mortgages and protesting wives, but Roosevelt settled the former with a check for $3,000, and assured Mrs. Sewall and Mrs. Dow that they could come West in a year, if all went well.[33]

Within a few days of discovering the downriver ranch-site in June, he purchased full rights to both shack and land for $400.[34] Before returning East to pick up Sewall and Dow, he found time to make his scheduled visit to Montana with the Marquis de Morès.[35] The date of this trip was deliberately kept secret, but 26 June seems likely. The Marquis would have found it prudent to be out of town that day, since it was the first anniversary of Riley Luffsey's murder.

The two young men wished to sign on as members of a band of vigilantes, or "stranglers," which had just been organized in Miles City, its purpose being to lynch the horse-thieves currently plaguing the Dakota-Montana border. Fortunately for Roosevelt's subsequent political reputation, their application was refused. Granville Stuart, leader of the vigilantes, told them that they were too "socially prominent" to belong to a secret society.[36]

On 1 July Roosevelt left Medora for New York.[37]

HE FOUND BABY LEE, all blue eyes and blond curls, living with Bamie at 422 Madison Avenue. Henceforth this house would be his pied-à-terre on visits to New York—although Bamie was not keen on the idea of brother and sister sharing the same town address.[38] Much as she loved to look after him, she was afraid they might drift into a cozy, quasi-marital relationship centering around her quasi-daughter. Bamie was a person of fine instinct and disciplined emotions, unlike Corinne, who could never see enough of her "Teddy," and for whom he could never do wrong.[39]

But Bamie need not have worried. Roosevelt showed no desire to remain at No. 422 a moment longer than necessary. Sewall and Dow were ordered to fix up their affairs "at once" and hurry to New York, so that they could leave for Dakota by the end of the month.[40] Then Roosevelt took the ferry to New Jersey for a few days with Corinne. He seemed anxious to stay away from his daughter, who was now almost five months old. (Since going to Dakota he had not asked a single question about the child in his letters home.) No record remains of their reunion. It is known, however, that after leaving New Jersey he took little Alice to Boston to see her grandparents.[41] The visit cannot have been cheerful. At the soonest possible moment he fled Chestnut Hill for Nahant, Henry Cabot Lodge's summer place.[42]

A sentence in one of Aunt Annie Gracie's letters provides a clue, perhaps, to Roosevelt's curious terror of Baby Lee: "She is a very sweet pretty little girl, so much like her beautiful young Mother in appearance."[43]

NOR WAS THIS his only phobia that summer. In New York, Bamie was told to warn him if a certain old family friend came to call, so that he could arrange to be absent.[44] As a married man, he had been able to withstand the cool blue eyes of Edith Carow; but now, widowed and alone, it was as if he feared they might once again find him childishly vulnerable.

ON 11 JULY the Democratic National Convention nominated Grover Cleveland for President of the United States. The Governor was in Albany, working as usual, when at 1:45 P.M. the dull booming of cannons floated through the windows of his office. An aide tried to congratulate him. "They are firing a salute, Governor, for your nomination."

"Do you think so? Well, anyhow, we'll finish up this work."[45]

ROOSEVELT FOUND LODGE depressed during his short stay at Nahant. The extent to which Independent revulsion had gathered against James G. Blaine—and, by extension, against Lodge for supporting him—must have amazed them both. Almost to a man, the intellectual and social aristocracy of Massachusetts had decided to vote for Cleveland. The list of Republican opponents to Blaine contained such names as Adams, Quincy, Lowell, Saltonstall, Everett, and Eliot. These were the same names which had so often been borne on a silver tray into Lodge's parlor. Now, suddenly, the tray was empty, and his friends were snubbing him in the street. Lodge confessed that supporting Blaine was "the bitterest thing I ever had to do in my life." What particularly hurt was the widespread assumption that he had sold his conscience for a Congressional nomination in the fall.[46]

It was time, Roosevelt decided, to come to the aid of his stricken friend. He himself had said nothing publicly since his confession of support for Blaine at St. Paul, except to telegraph an ambiguous denial of the interview from Medora.[47] No sooner had he returned to Chestnut Hill on 19 July than he summoned a reporter from the *Boston Herald* and announced, once and for all, that he, too, would support the Republican presidential ticket.

> While at Chicago I told Mr. Lodge that such was my intention; but before announcing it, I wished to have time to think the whole matter over. A man cannot act both without and within the party; he can do either, but he cannot possibly do both . . .
>
> I am by inheritance and education a Republican; whatever good I have been able to accomplish in public life has been accomplished through the Republican party; I have acted with it in the past, and wish to act with it in the future; I went as a regular delegate to the Chicago convention, and I intend to abide by the outcome of that convention. I am going back in a day or two to my Western ranches, as I do not expect to take any part in the campaign this fall.[48]

He arrived back in New York to find Bamie's doormat piled with abusive letters. "Most of my friends seem surprised to find that I have not developed hoofs and horns," he wryly told Lodge.[49] Harder to take, perhaps, was the criticism of Alice's family, voiced by her uncle, Henry Lee: "As for Cabot Lodge, nobody's surprised at *him;* but you can tell that young whipper-snapper in New York from me that his independence was the only thing in him we cared for, and if he has gone back on that, we don't care to hear any more about him."[50]

Reform newspapers, whose hero Roosevelt had so recently been, were loud in their denunciations of him. The *Evening Post* thundered that "no ranch or other hiding place in the world" could shelter a so-called Independent who voted for the likes of James G. Blaine. Roosevelt sent a mischievous message to the editor, Edwin L. Godkin, accusing him of suffering from "a species of moral myopia, complicated with intellectual strabismus." Godkin, who was a man of little humor, forthwith became his severest public critic.[51]

Roosevelt did not seem to mind his sudden unpopularity. When the rumor that Grover Cleveland was the father of a bastard flashed across the country on 21 July,[52] he could afford to laugh at the Independents who had already bolted to the Governor's side. Although he seemed, in a final interview on 26 July, to be talking only about his life out West, he subtly sounded a favorite theme: that of the masculine hardness of the practical politician, as opposed to the effeminate softness of armchair idealists.

> It would electrify some of my friends who have accused me of representing the kid-glove element in politics if they could see me galloping over the plains day in and day out, clad in a buckskin shirt and leather chaparajos, with a big sombrero on my head. For good healthy exercise I would strongly recommend some of our gilded youth to go West and try a short course of riding bucking ponies, and assist at the branding of a lot of Texas steers.[53]

With that the ex-Assemblyman boarded a train with Sewall and Dow and returned to Dakota.

"WELL, BILL, WHAT do you think of the country?" asked Roosevelt. It was 1 August 1884, and the two backwoodsmen were spending their first night in the Badlands, at the Maltese Cross Ranch.

"I like it well enough," said Sewall, "but I don't believe that it's much of a cattle country."

"You don't know anything about it," Roosevelt protested.

Sewall obstinately went on: "It's the way it looks to me, like not much of a cattle country."[54]

Roosevelt shrugged off this remark. With a thousand new head just arrived from Minnesota ("the best lot of cattle shipped west this year," said the *Bad Lands Cowboy*) and six hundred veterans of last winter browsing contentedly on the river, he could see no reasons for pessimism.[55] The next morning he ordered Sewall and Dow north to the downriver ranch-site, with a hundred head "to practice on." They left under the supervision of a grumpy herder, who was doubtful about Sewall's capacity to stay on his horse. Sewall, jouncing along uncomfortably, allowed that he had more experience "riding logs."[56]

Roosevelt remained behind. There was a certain amount of soothing to be done at Maltese Cross. Merrifield and Ferris had not been pleased to discover, on returning from St. Paul, that a couple of Eastern lumbermen had displaced them in the boss's esteem. Since Roosevelt intended to build his home-ranch downriver, and would spend most of his time there, it was obvious whose company he preferred. Merrifield in particular was a man of easily bruised ego: perhaps to mollify him, Roosevelt asked if he would be his guide in a major hunting expedition later that month.[57]

This was the "trip into the Big Horn country" of Wyoming that he had been excitedly planning since June. "You will probably not hear from me for a couple of months," he warned Bamie, adding with relish, ". . . if our horses give out or run away, or we get caught in the snow, we may be out very much longer—till towards Christmas."[58] He stopped short of telling his nervous sister that he had set his heart on killing the most dangerous animal in North America—the Rocky Mountain grizzly bear.

He wanted to leave within two weeks, but extra ponies had to be found and he was forced to postpone his departure to 18 August. In the interim he roamed restlessly through the Badlands, riding thirty miles south to visit the Langs, and forty miles north to check up on "my two backwoods babies." Exploring his new property with Sewall, he came upon the skulls of two elks with interlocked antlers. "Theirs had been a duel to the death," he decided. It was just the sort of symbol to appeal to him, and he promptly named the ranch-site Elkhorn.[59]

Apart from a touch of diarrhea, brought on by the alkaline water of the Little Missouri, Sewall and Dow seemed to be adjusting well to Dakota, and enjoying their new work. During the day they worked at making Roosevelt's hunting-shack habitable (it would serve as a home until the big ranch house was built), and at night took turns in watching the herd. Sewall still had misgivings about the Badlands as cattle country, while admitting that its "wild, desolate grandeur . . . has a kind of charm."[60]

Roosevelt used almost the same words in his letter to Bamie of 12 August.

> . . . I grow very fond of this place, and it certainly has a desolate, grim beauty of its own, that has a curious fascination

> for me. The grassy, scantily wooded bottoms through which the winding river flows are bounded by bare, jagged buttes; their fantastic shapes and sharp, steep edges throw the most curious shadows, under the cloudless, glaring sky; and at evening I love to sit out in front of the hut and see their hard, gray outlines gradually growing soft and purple as the flaming sunset by degrees softens and dies away; while my days I spend generally alone, riding through the lonely rolling prairie and broken lands.[61]

He spent whole days in the saddle, riding as many as seventy-two miles between dawn and darkness. Sometimes he rode on through the night, rejoicing in the way "moonbeams play over the grassy stretches of the plateaus and glance off the windrippled blades as they would from water."[62] His body hardened, the tan on his face deepened, hints of gold appeared in his hair and reddish mustache. "I now look like a regular cowboy dandy, with all my equipments finished in the most expensive style," he wrote Bamie. His buckskin tunic, custom-tailored by the Widow Maddox, seamstress of the Badlands, gave him particular delight, although its resemblance to a lady's shirtwaist caused some comment in Medora. "You would be amused to see me," he accurately wrote to Cabot Lodge, "in my broad sombrero hat, fringed and beaded buckskin shirt, horse hide chaparajos or riding trousers, and cowhide boots, with braided bridle and silver spurs."[63]

It was probably during these seventeen free-ranging days that Roosevelt had his famous encounter with a bully in Nolan's Hotel, Mingusville, thirty-five miles west of Medora.[64] The incident, which has since become a cliché in a thousand Wild West yarns, is best told in his own words:

> I was out after lost horses . . . It was late in the evening when I reached the place. I heard one or two shots in the bar-room as I came up, and I disliked going in. But there was nowhere else to go, and it was a cold night. Inside the room were several men, who, including the bartender, were wearing the kind of smile worn by men who are making believe to like

> what they don't like. A shabby individual in a broad hat with a cocked gun in each hand was walking up and down the floor talking with strident profanity. He had evidently been shooting at the clock, which had two or three holes in its face.
>
> . . . As soon as he saw me he hailed me as "Four Eyes", in reference to my spectacles, and said, "Four Eyes is going to treat." I joined in the laugh and got behind the stove and sat down, thinking to escape notice. He followed me, however, and though I tried to pass it off as a jest this merely made him more offensive, and he stood leaning over me, a gun in each hand, using very foul language . . . In response to his reiterated command that I should set up the drinks, I said, "Well, if I've got to, I've got to," and rose, looking past him.
>
> As I rose, I struck quick and hard with my right just to one side of the point of his jaw, hitting with my left as I straightened out, and then again with my right. He fired the guns, but I do not know whether this was merely a convulsive action of his hands, or whether he was trying to shoot at me. When he went down he struck the corner of the bar with his head . . . if he had moved I was about to drop on my knees; but he was senseless. I took away his guns, and the other people in the room, who were now loud in their denunciation of him, hustled him out and put him in the shed.

Next morning Roosevelt heard to his satisfaction that the bully had left town on a freight train.[65]

ANOTHER THREAT, from a more powerful adversary, arrived at Elkhorn one day in the form of a letter from the Marquis de Morès. It coolly announced that Roosevelt had no title to the land around his ranch-site. In the summer of 1883 the Marquis had stocked it with twelve thousand sheep; therefore the range belonged to him.[66]

Like most Americans, Roosevelt had a profound contempt for sheep. Not only did the "bleating idiots" nibble the grass so short that they starved out cattle, they were, intellectually speaking, about the lowest level of brute creation. "No man can associate with sheep," he snorted, "and retain his self-respect."[67] In any case, the Marquis's flock had not survived the winter. Roosevelt curtly informed de Morès, by return messenger, that only dead sheep remained on the range, and he "did not think that they would hold it."

There was no reply, but Sewall and Dow were warned to look out for trouble.[68]

ONE MELANCHOLY DUTY awaited Roosevelt before he set off for the Big Horns on 18 August: the collation of some tributes, speeches, and newspaper clippings into a printed memorial for Alice Lee.[69] Having arranged them as best he could, he added his own poignant superscription, under the heading "In Memory of my Darling Wife."

> She was beautiful in face and form, and lovelier still in spirit; as a flower she grew, and as a fair young flower she died. Her life had always been in the sunshine; there had never come to her a single great sorrow; and none ever knew her who did not love and revere her for her bright, sunny temper and her saintly unselfishness. Fair, pure, and joyous as a maiden; loving, tender, and happy as a young wife; when she had just become a mother, when her life seemed to be but just begun, and when the years seemed so bright before her—then, by a strange and terrible fate, death came to her.
>
> And when my heart's dearest died, the light went from my life forever.

The manuscript was sent to New York for private publication and distribution.[70] Roosevelt sank briefly back into total despair. Gazing across the burned-out landscape of the Badlands, he told Bill Sewall that all his hopes lay buried in the East. He had nothing to live for, he said, and his daughter would never know him: "She would be just as well off without me."

Talking as to a child, Sewall assured him that he would recover.

"You won't always feel as you do now and you won't always be willing to stay here and drive cattle."

But Roosevelt was inconsolable.[71]

A MONTH LATER, his mood had improved considerably. "I have had good sport," he wrote Bamie, on descending from the Big Horn Mountains, "and enough excitement and fatigue to prevent over-much thought." He added significantly, "I have at last been able to sleep well at night."[72]

Readers of Roosevelt's diary of the hunt might wonder if by "excitement" he did not mean "carnage." A list culled from the pages of this little book indicates just how much blood was needed to blot out "thought." (Since Alice's death his diaries had become a monotonous record of things slain.)

17 Aug. "My battery consists of a long .45 Colt revolver, 150 cartridges, a no. 10 choke bore, 300-cartridge shotgun; a 45–75 Winchester repeater, with 1,000 cartridges; a 40–90 Sharps, 150 cartridges; a 50–150 double barrelled Webley express, 100 cartridges."

19 Aug. 4 grouse, 5 duck.

20 Aug. 1 whitetail buck, "still in velvet," 2 sage hens.

24 Aug. "Knocked the heads off 2 sage grouse."

25 Aug. 6 sharptail grouse, 2 doves, 2 teal.

26 Aug. 8 prairie chickens.

27 Aug. 12 sage hens and prairie chickens, 1 yearling whitetail "through the heart."

29 Aug. "Broke the backs" of 2 blacktail bucks with a single bullet.

31 Aug. 1 jack rabbit, "cutting him nearly in two."

3 Sept. 2 blue grouse.

4 Sept. 2 elk.

5 Sept. 1 red rabbit, 1 blue grouse.

7 Sept. 2 elk, 1 blacktail doe.

8 Sept. Spares a doe and two fawns, "as we have more than enough meat." Kills 12 grouse instead.

11 Sept. 50 trout.

12 Sept. 1 bull elk, "killing him very neatly . . . knocked the heads off 2 grouse."

13 Sept. 1 blacktail buck "through the shoulder," 1 grizzly bear "through the brain."

14 Sept. 1 blacktail buck, 1 female grizzly, 1 bear cub, "the ball going clean through him from end to end."

15 Sept. 4 blue grouse.

16 Sept. 1 bull elk—"broke his back."

17 Sept. "Broke camp . . . Three pack ponies laden with hides and horns."[73]

Heading back to Dakota with his stinking cargo, Roosevelt killed a further 40 birds and animals on the prairie, making his total bag 170 items in just 47 days.[74]

So much for "excitement." As to "fatigue," he punished himself more severely, during these seven weeks, than ever before in his life. He covered nearly a thousand miles in the saddle and on foot, scorning a "prairie schooner" which accompanied him most of the way. The weather was often brutal, with winds powerful enough to overturn the wagon, and huge hailstones thudding into the earth with the velocity of bullets; but Roosevelt seemed to glory in it, once riding off alone into the rain. He camped in the Big Horns at altitudes of well over eight thousand feet, and at temperatures of well below freezing. Yet for all the thin air in his lungs and the chill in his bones, he pursued elk and bear with the energy of a hardened mountain-man:

> We had been running briskly [after elk] uphill through the soft, heavy loam, in which our feet made no noise but slipped and sank deeply; as a consequence, I was all out of breath and my hand so unsteady that I missed my first shot . . . I doubt if I ever went through more violent exertion than in the next ten minutes. We raced after them at full speed, opening fire; I wounded all three, but none of the wounds were immediately disabling. They trotted on and we panted afterward, slipping on the wet earth, pitching headlong over charred stumps, leaping on dead logs that broke beneath our weight, more than once measuring our full length across the

> ground, halting and firing whenever we got a chance. At last one bull fell; we passed him by after the others, which were still running uphill. The sweat streamed into my eyes and made furrows in the sooty mud that covered my face, from having fallen full length down the burnt earth; I sobbed for breath as I toiled at a shambling trot after them, as nearly done out as could well be.

He kept on going until he had killed the second elk, and pursued the third until "the blood grew less, and ceased, and I lost the track."[75]

Assuredly all this activity left Roosevelt little time to brood. Yet there was at least one final throb of grief. One night in the Big Horns, as bull elks trumpeted their wild, silvery mating-calls,[76] he blurted out to Merrifield the details of his wife's death. He said that his pain was "beyond any healing." When Merrifield, who was also a widower, mumbled the conventional response, Roosevelt interjected, "Now don't talk to me about time will make a difference—time will never change me in that respect."[77]

ON 13 SEPTEMBER, a nine-foot, twelve-hundred-pound grizzly reared up not eight paces in front of him:

> Doubtless my face was pretty white, but the blue barrel was as steady as a rock as I glanced along it until I could see the top of the bead fairly between his two sinister-looking eyes; as I pulled the trigger I jumped aside out of the smoke, to be ready if he charged; but it was needless, for the great brute was struggling in the death agony . . . the bullet hole in his skull was as exactly between his eyes as if I had measured the distance with a carpenter's rule.[78]

Feeling calm and purged, Roosevelt suddenly decided he would, after all, go back East to vote. He might even take part in the last few weeks of the campaign, and make a speech or two for Henry Cabot Lodge. In a letter to Bamie, written at Fort McKinney, Wyoming, on 20 September, he gave his first hint of paternal yearnings for Baby Lee: "I hope Mousiekins will be very cunning: I shall dearly love her."[79]

Impatience began to gather as the expedition creaked slowly homeward over three hundred miles of barren prairie. On 4 October, with seventy-five miles still to go, Roosevelt could stand the pace no longer. Leaving the wagon and extra ponies in care of his driver, he and Merrifield rode the remaining distance non-stop, by night.[80]

He allowed himself just one day to recover (having been in the saddle, almost continuously, for twenty-four hours) before riding another forty miles north to visit Sewall and Dow.[81] They had unpleasant news for him: his forebodings of "trouble," after rejecting the Marquis's claim to the Elkhorn range, had been justified. E. G. Paddock—now more and more the power behind the throne of de Morès—had stopped by the ranch-site in late September, accompanied by several drunken gunmen. Finding Roosevelt away, the gang accepted lunch, sobered up, and rode off well stoked with beans and *bonhomie*. Since then, however, Paddock had begun to declare that the Elkhorn shack was rightfully his. If "Four Eyes" wished to buy it, he must pay for it in dollars—or in blood. Roosevelt, on hearing this, merely said, "Is that so?"[82]

Remounting his horse, he rode back upriver to Paddock's house at the railroad crossing. The gunman answered his knock. "I understand that you have threatened to kill me on sight," rasped Roosevelt. "I have come over to see when you want to begin the killing."

Paddock was so taken aback he could only protest that he had been "misquoted."[83] Next morning Roosevelt left for New York, confident that from now on his ranch-site would be left in peace.

ON 11 OCTOBER, a *Sun* reporter found the former Assemblyman pacing restless and ruddy-faced around the library of 422 Madison Avenue, a glass of sherry in his hand, anxious to discuss campaign politics. "It is altogether contrary to my character," Roosevelt explained, with the frankness that endeared him to all newspapermen, "to occupy a neutral position in so important and so exciting a struggle." He added, rather wistfully, that it was "duty," not ambition, that brought him back East. "I myself am not a candidate for any office whatsoever—for the present at least." The reporter pressed for a comment on Grover Cleveland, and elicited the following exchange, in which Roosevelt's moral disdain for the Governor shone clear:

> Q. What do you think of Mr. Cleveland as a candidate for President of the United States?
>
> A. I think that he is not a man who should be put in that office, and there is no lack of reasons for it. His public career, in the first place, and then private reasons as well. Of these personal questions I will not speak unless forced to, as Mr. Cleveland has always treated me with the utmost courtesy. But if, as I said, it should become necessary for me to discuss personal objections . . .[84]

During his seven subsequent campaign speeches—delivered between 14 October and 3 November, mainly in New York and in Lodge's Massachusetts constituency—Roosevelt avoided the ugly accusations of debauchery which Republicans everywhere were flinging at Cleveland. Respect for that decent gentleman still lurked within him. He managed, however, to make at least one sanctimonious reference to "the immorality of breaking the seventh commandment."[85]

Innuendo of this sort, from a man as genuinely puritanical as Roosevelt, might have been acceptable had it not been flavored with hypocrisy. Cleveland's sexual peccadillo signified little, in national opinion. The Governor had made no attempt to hide the details, and the scandal had begun to die down.[86] On the other hand, Blaine's sins, as a Speaker who had used the powers of office to promote his own portfolio, could not be easily forgotten. There was no question as to which candidate was the morally inferior. Roosevelt's statement that he was a Republican, and therefore bound to support Blaine, was understandable. Yet it could have been made in a letter from Dakota, rather than repeated *ad nauseam* all over the East, on platforms festooned with portraits of a man he despised.[87]

In later years, Roosevelt's support of the Plumed Knight proved to be something of an embarrassment to his admirers, including that most ardent of them, himself. Nobody has ever satisfactorily reconciled Roosevelt's passionate antagonism to Blaine in May and June with his equally passionate partisanship in October and November, although it has been argued that in bowing to the will of the party he was simply acting as a complete political professional.[88] His many statements of support and non-support, his promises of action and threats of inaction, were bewilderingly self-contradictory. No adulterer could more adroitly combine illicit lovemaking with matrimonial obligations than Roosevelt in his relations with both wings of the party in 1884. While seducing the Independents, he promised to remain faithful to the Stalwarts; after abandoning the former, he assured them it was not out of love for the latter.

In his defense it must be said that he never sounded insincere. He genuinely believed that an Edmunds might represent the "good" in politics, but that only a Blaine, as President, could effectively bring that "good" about. Still it is hard to avoid the conclusion of one disgusted classmate: "The great good, of course, was Teddy."[89]

ON 20 OCTOBER Roosevelt was annoyed to read a report, by one Horace White, of his off-the-record, post-convention remarks in a Chicago hotel five months before. White, it turned out, was the journalist to whom he had blustered, late on the night of Blaine's nomination, that "any proper Democratic nomination will have our hearty support." In an obvious attempt to expose Roosevelt as a turncoat, White chose to report the interview now, when the ex-Assemblyman was back in the public eye; to make the blow more personal, he did so in the correspondence columns of *The New York Times.* Roosevelt could do little but protest in a letter of reply that "I was savagely indignant at our defeat . . . and so expressed myself in private conversation." He had "positively refused" to say anything for publication, "nor did I use the words that Mr. White attributes to me."[90] But the damage to his reputation had been done.

He consoled himself, in Boston, with the society of such intellectuals as William Dean Howells, Thomas Bailey Aldrich, and Oliver Wendell Holmes. These men came to a dinner at Lodge's in honor of Roosevelt's twenty-sixth birthday, and he glowed in the radiance of their conversation. "I do not know when I have enjoyed a dinner so much."[91]

As the campaign entered its final week, Blaine seemed poised for inevitable victory. His extraordinary personal magnetism had never been stronger. Audiences everywhere serenaded him with adoring choruses of "We'll Follow Where the White Plume Waves." The stolid Cleveland, meanwhile, droned on about the tariff and Civil Service Reform, trying to ignore catcalls of "Ma! Ma! Where's My Pa? Gone to the White House, Ha Ha Ha!"[92]

Then, in New York on 29 October, a garrulous Presbyterian minister, with Blaine standing at his side, publicly accused the Democratic party of representing "rum, Romanism, and rebellion." The candidate, who was only half-listening, did not react to this *faux pas,* and therefore seemed to condone it. An alert bystander reported the phrase to Cleveland headquarters, just one block away. Within hours it had been telegraphed to every Democratic newspaper in the country. Headlines and handbills amplified the insult a millionfold. Overnight Blaine's support among anti-prohibitionists, Catholics, and Southerners shrank away. In New York alone he lost an estimated fifty thousand votes.[93] On Election Day, 4 November, Grover Cleveland became the nation's first Democratic President in a quarter of a century.

IN A LETTER OF CONDOLENCE to Henry Cabot Lodge, whose bid for Congress had received a humiliating rejection in the polls, Roosevelt raged against "the cursed pharisaical fools and knaves who have betrayed us."[94] Evidently he ascribed the Republican defeat to Independent defectors, although every other political commentator in the country blamed it on the Presbyterian minister. The fact that he and Lodge had helped muster the Independents at Chicago, only to fall in behind the regular Republicans later, did not seem to indicate any betrayal on their part.

But three days after this letter to Lodge, he wrote a *mea culpa* which shows that all his essential decency and common sense had returned, if not yet his optimism.

> Of course it may be true that we have had our day; it is far more likely that this is true in my case than yours . . . Blaine's nomination meant to me pretty sure political death if I supported him; that I realized entirely, and went in with my eyes open. I have won again and again; finally chance placed me where I was sure to lose whatever I did; and I will balance the last against the first . . . I shall certainly not complain. I have not believed and do not believe that I shall ever be likely to come back into political life; we fought a good winning fight when our friends the Independents were backing us; and we have both of us, when circumstances turned them against us, fought the losing fight grimly out to the end. What we have been cannot be taken away from us; what we are is due to the folly of others; and to no fault of ours.[95]

In larger retrospect it may be seen that Roosevelt had done exactly the right thing, obeying the dictates of a political instinct so profound as to be almost infallible. He did not realize his luck, as he miserably returned to Dakota, but a Republican victory might have destroyed his chances of ever becoming President. The grateful Blaine would have offered him a government post, along with all the machine men who supervised the campaign; Roosevelt would thereafter have been associated with the corrupt Old Guard of the nineteenth century, rather than the enlightened Progressives of the twentieth. His decision not to "bolt" after Chicago was equally fortunate. Cleveland would not likely have rewarded him, and later Republican conventions would remember him as a man of doubtful loyalty.

All in all, a Republican defeat was the best thing that could have happened to Roosevelt in 1884. The fact that three alliterative words brought about that defeat only reinforces the conclusion that fate, as usual, was on his side. Not that he could be persuaded to see it that way. "The Statesman (?) of the past," he wrote Lodge from Maltese Cross, "has been merged, alas I fear for good, in the cowboy of the present."[96]

ON 16 NOVEMBER, a spell of "white weather" settled down over the Badlands, as Roosevelt left his southern ranch and headed north to Elkhorn. His progress was slow that morning, for he had a beef herd to deliver to Medora. It was almost two o'clock before he concluded his business in town and rode on alone, with thirty-three miles to go.[97]

The wind in his face was achingly cold, especially on exposed plateaus when it combed grains of snow out of the grass and hurled them at him; the sensation was not unlike being whipped with sandpaper. His lungs (still occasionally troubled by asthma) gasped with every frigid breath, and his eyes throbbed in the glare of the sun. Descent into sheltered bottoms afforded some relief, but he took his life in his hands whenever he rode across the river. The ice was not yet solid. Should Manitou break through and douse him, it would be a serious matter, "for a wetting in such weather, with a long horseback journey to make, is no joke."

Darkness surprised him when he was scarcely halfway to his destination. For a while he cantered along in the starlight, listening to the muffled drumming of his horse's hooves, and "the long-drawn, melancholy howling of a wolf, a quarter of a mile off." Clouds soon reduced visibility to zero, and he was forced to seek shelter in an empty shack by the river. There was enough wood round about to build a roaring fire, but no food to cook; all he had was a paper of tea-leaves and some salt. "I should have liked something to eat, but as I did not have it, the tea did not prove such a bad substitute for a cold and tired man."

At dawn Roosevelt woke to the hoarse clucking of hundreds of prairie-fowl. Sallying forth with his rifle, he shot five sharptails. "It was not long before two of the birds, plucked and cleaned, were split open and roasted before the fire. And to me they seemed most delicious food."[98]

Exactly one month before he had been campaigning on the platform of Chickering Hall in New York, twisting his eyeglasses, catching bouquets, and blushing under the admiring gaze of bejeweled society matrons.[99]

SEWALL AND DOW were felling trees for the ranch house when he galloped down into the Elkhorn bottom a few hours later.[100] He seized an ax to assist them, much to their secret amusement, for Roosevelt was no lumberman. At the end of that day, he was chagrined to overhear Dow report to a cowpuncher: "Well, Bill cut down fifty-three, I cut forty-nine, and the boss, he beavered down seventeen."

"Those who have seen the stump of a tree which has been gnawed down by a beaver," Roosevelt commented wryly, "will understand the exact force of the comparison."[101]

THE COLD WORSENED as they started to erect the walls of the house. For two weeks temperatures hovered around minus 10 degrees Fahrenheit, plummeting at night to 50 degrees below zero.[102] Trees cracked and jarred from the strain of the frost, and the wheels of the ranch wagon sang on the marble-hard ground. Roosevelt's cattle huddled for warmth, with "saddles" of powdered snow lying across their backs and icicles hanging from their lips. He wondered that they did not die. At night the stars seemed to snap and glitter, coyotes howled with weird ventriloquial effects, and white owls hovered in the dark like snow-wreaths.[103]

Tactfully dissuaded from "helping" Sewall and Dow with construction, Roosevelt returned to Maltese Cross and tried to write the book he had been meditating upon all summer. But he was too cold, or too restless, to do more than a few thousand words.[104] He read poetry, roamed the slippery slopes in pursuit of bighorn sheep, broke ponies, lunched at Château de Morès with the Marquis, and—ever the politician—campaigned up and down the valley to organize a Little Missouri Stockmen's Association. On one such trip he managed to freeze his face, one foot, both knees, and one hand.[105]

Despite all this activity, there were periods of depression, stimulated by the bleakness of the weather, which seemed so symbolic of the bleakness in his own life. He sensed a relationship between the iron in his soul and the iron in the landscape. The texture of the frozen soil, its ringing sound-effects, the blue metallic sheen of the Little Missouri, are images which recur obsessively in his writings about Dakota, with constant repetitions of the word *iron, iron, iron.* All these elements synthesized in one magnificent prose-poem, entitled simply "Winter Weather."

> When the days have dwindled to their shortest, and the nights seem never-ending, then all the great northern plains are changed into an abode of iron desolation. Sometimes furious gales blow down from the north, driving before them the clouds of blinding snow-dust, wrapping the mantle of death round every unsheltered being that faces their unshackled anger. They roar in a thunderous bass as they sweep across the prairie or whirl through the naked canyons; they shiver the great brittle cottonwoods, and beneath their rough touch the icy limbs of the pines that cluster in the gorges sing like the chords of an æolian harp. Again, in the coldest midwinter weather, not a breath of wind may stir; and then the still, merciless, terrible cold that broods over the earth like the shadow of silent death seems even more dreadful in its gloomy rigor than is the lawless madness of the storms. All the land is like granite; the great rivers stand still in their beds, as if turned to frosted steel. In the long nights there is no sound to break the lifeless silence. Under the ceaseless, shifting play of the Northern Lights, or lighted only by the wintry brilliance of the stars, the snow-clad plains stretch out into dead and endless wastes of glimmering white.[106]

With the New Year, and spring, and the return of the meadowlark to Dakota, his blood would begin to run warm again.

CHAPTER 12

The Four-Eyed Maverick

Then said Olaf, laughing,
"Not ten yoke of oxen
Have the power to draw us
Like a woman's hair!"

THE *HA-HA-HONK, HA-HONK* of wild geese grew louder in his ears. With unfocused eyes he watched the V-shaped skein flying low and heavily overhead and settling about a mile upriver. Then he hunched again over Bamie's desk and scrawled, in his large, schoolboyish hand, "I took the rifle instead of a shotgun and hurried after them on foot."[1]

Roosevelt had learned, that January of 1885, the old truism that writers write best when removed from the scene they are describing. At Elkhorn and Maltese Cross, he had been too much a part of his environment to re-create it on paper. Fleeing the reality of Dakota just before Christmas, he began to write almost immediately after arriving in New York.[2] During the first nine weeks of the New Year, nearly a hundred thousand words poured from his pen; by 8 March, *Hunting Trips of a Ranchman* was finished. "I have just sent my last roll of manuscript to the printer," he told Cabot Lodge. While modest about the quality of his prose, Roosevelt declared that "the

"Now for the first time he could admire his recently completed house."

Sagamore Hill in 1885.

pictures will be excellent."[3] It is not known whether by this he meant the book's illustrations, or a series of publicity photographs of himself, in the full glory of his buckskin suit.

One of these was chosen as frontispiece, and caused much hilarity when *Hunting Trips* came out.[4]

Bristling with cartridges, a silver dagger in his belt, Roosevelt stands with Winchester at the ready, against a studio backdrop of flowers and ferns. His moccasins are firmly planted on a mat of artificial grass. For some reason his spectacles have been allowed to dangle: although his finger is on the trigger, one doubts if he could so much as hit the photographer, let alone a distant grizzly. His expression combines pugnacity, intelligence, and a certain adolescent vulnerability which touched Lodge, at least, very tenderly.[5]

HUNTING TRIPS WAS PUBLISHED by G. P. Putnam's Sons early in July, and dedicated "to that keenest of Sportsmen and truest of Friends, my Brother Elliott Roosevelt."[6] The first edition, limited to five hundred copies, set new standards of lavishness in Americana. It was printed on quarto-size sheets of thick, creamy, hand-woven paper, with two-and-a-half-inch margins and sumptuous engravings. Bound in gray, gold-lettered canvas, it retailed at the then unheard-of price of $15, and quickly became a collector's item.[7]

The book was well reviewed on both sides of the Atlantic (the British *Spectator* said it "could claim an honorable place on the same shelf as Waterton's *Wanderings* and Walton's *Compleat Angler*"), went through several editions, and was soon accepted as a standard textbook of big-game hunting in the United States.[8] Roosevelt's first published work had also achieved textbook status, yet few critics could have guessed, without comparing title pages, that the same man had written both. Where *The Naval War of 1812* had been scholarly, dry, crammed with sterile statistics, *Hunting Trips* was lyrical, lush, and cheerfully rambling.

It shows signs of being too hastily written. Anecdotes are repeated three times over, purplish tinges mar the otherwise crystal prose, thrilling chapters end in anticlimax. There are examples of

Roosevelt's perennial tendency to praise himself with faint damns. Some zoological details are inaccurate,[9] betraying the fact that the author had, after all, lived only a few parts of one year in Dakota. He is at pains, however, to give the impression that he is a leathery pioneer of many years' standing.[10]

Less than half the text is about hunting as such. Although Roosevelt tells, with tremendous pace and gusto, the story of all his major expeditions, some of the best pages are those in which he muses on the beauty of the Badlands, the simple pleasures of ranch life, the joy of being young and free on the frontier. Except for an occasional outpouring of melancholy adjectives, he gives no indication that he was a brokenhearted man during most of these adventures. On the contrary, there is an abundance of lusty, sensuous images: the carpet-like softness of prairie roses under his horse's hooves, the smell of bear's blood on his hands, the taste of jerked beef after a mouthful of snow, and—most memorably—the warm freshness of a deer's bed, with its "blades of grass still slowly rising, after the hasty departure of the weight that has flattened them down."[11]

Roosevelt's characteristic auditory effects resonate on every page: from the "wild, not unmusical calls" of cowboys on night-herd duty, their voices "half-mellowed by the distance," to the "harsh grating noise" of a dying elk's teeth gnashing in agony. There are, to be sure, some vignettes that make non-hunters gag, such as that of a wounded blacktail buck galloping along "with a portion of his entrails sticking out . . . and frozen solid."[12] But the overwhelming impression left after reading *Hunting Trips of a Ranchman* is that of love for, and identity with, all living things. Roosevelt demonstrates an almost poetic ability to feel a bighorn's delight in its sinewy nimbleness, the sluggish timidity of a rattlesnake, the cool air on an unsaddled horse's back, the numb stiffness of a hail-bruised antelope.

How such a lover of animals could kill so many of them (at the time of writing his lifetime tally was already well into the thousands) is a perhaps unanswerable question.[13] But his bloodthirstiness, if it can be called that, was not unusual among men of his class and generation. Roosevelt hunted according to a strict code of personal morality. He had nothing but contempt for "the swinish game-butchers who hunt for hides and not for sport or actual food, and who murder the gravid doe and the spotted fawn with as little hesitation as they would kill a buck of ten points. No one who is not himself a sportsman and lover of nature can realize the intense indignation with which a true hunter sees these butchers at their brutal work of slaughtering the game, in season and out, for the sake of the few dollars they are too lazy to earn in any other and more honest way."[14]

ROOSEVELT'S ARDUOUS SPELL of writing in the early months of 1885 left him physically and emotionally drained. As usual when he was reduced to this condition, the *cholera morbus* struck, delaying his scheduled departure for Dakota from 22 March to 14 April. Even then he looked so pale and dyspeptic above his high white collar that Douglas Robinson wrote ahead to Bill Sewall, saying that his sisters were worried about him, and asking for reports of his health.[15]

If Sewall was conscientious enough to obey, he would have replied that Roosevelt seemed determined to contract pneumonia after arriving back in Medora. Although the weather was still wintry, the Little Missouri was swollen with dirty thaw-water from upcountry. The only way to cross it was to ride between the tracks of the railroad trestles—unless one chose, like Roosevelt, to negotiate the submerged, slippery top of a dam farther downstream. "If Manitou gets his feet on that dam, he'll keep them there and we can make it finely," he told Joe Ferris.

But halfway across Manitou overbalanced, and to the horror of spectators, horse and rider disappeared into the hurtling river. When they surfaced a few moments later, Roosevelt was seen swimming beside Manitou, pushing ice-blocks out of the horse's way and splashing water in his face to guide him. They made the shore just in time to avoid being swept away completely: the next landing was more than a mile north.[16]

Roosevelt actually enjoyed the experience. A few days later he again swam across the river with Manitou, at a point where there were no spectators to rescue him. "I had to strike my own line for twenty miles over broken country before I reached home and could dry myself," he boasted to Bamie. "However it all makes me feel very healthy and strong."[17]

THE ELKHORN RANCH WAS NOW complete.[18] Roosevelt, exploring its eight spacious rooms, found that they measured up in every way to the descriptions he had already written of them. Bearskins and buffalo robes strewed the beds and couches; a perpetual fire of cottonwood logs reddened the hearthstone; stuffed heads cast monstrous shadows across the rough log walls; there were rifles in every corner, coonskin coats and beaver caps hanging from the rafters. Sturdy shelves groaned with the collected works of Irving, Hawthorne, Cooper, and Lowell, as well as his favorite light reading—"dreamy Ike Marvel, Burroughs's breezy pages, and the quaint, pathetic character-sketches of the Southern writers—Cable, Craddock, Macon, Joel Chandler Harris, and sweet Sherwood Bonner." It was still too cold to sit out in his rocking-chair ("What true American does not enjoy a rocking-chair?"), but he looked forward to many summer afternoons on the piazza, reading or just simply contemplating the view. "When one is in the Bad Lands he feels as if they somehow *look* just exactly as Poe's tales and poems *sound*."[19]

He was pleased to see that his cattle had apparently survived the harsh winter well. "Bill, you were mistaken about those cows. Cows and calves are all looking fine."

Nothing could shake Sewall's habitual pessimism. "You wait until next spring, and see how they look."[20]

Unfazed, Roosevelt sent Sewall and Dow to Minnesota, along with Sylvane Ferris, to help Merrifield bring back an extra fifteen hundred head. This latest purchase, amounting to $39,000, raised his total investment in the Badlands to $85,000, virtually half his patrimony. Coming on top of the $45,000 he had already spent at Leeholm, it made Roosevelt's family as nervous about his finances as about his health. Bamie asked for guarantees that the cattle venture would pay, but got only the unconvincing reply, "I honestly think that it will."[21]

THE NEW HERD ARRIVED in Medora on 5 May, and the bulk of it came north to Elkhorn under Roosevelt's personal supervision. Never before had he attempted to manage so many cattle, and the experience nearly killed him. Since the river was still dangerously high, he was forced to stay clear of the valley, and trek inland. On the third day out the cattle had no water at all. That night they bedded down obediently, but an hour or two later, when Roosevelt and a cowboy were standing guard, a thousand thirst-maddened animals suddenly heaved to their feet and stampeded.

> The only salvation was to keep them close together, as, if they once got scattered, we knew they could never be gathered; so I kept on one side, and the cowboy on the other, and never in my life did I ride so hard. In the darkness I could but dimly see the shadowy outlines of the herd, as with whip and spurs I ran the pony along its edge, turning back the beasts at one point barely in time to wheel and keep them in at another. The ground was cut up by numerous little gullies, and each of us got several falls, horses and riders turning complete somersaults. We were dripping with sweat, and our ponies quivering and trembling like quaking aspens, when, after more than an hour of the most violent exertion, we finally got the herd quieted again.[22]

PALE AND PATHETICALLY THIN, Theodore Roosevelt arrived at Box Elder Creek on 19 May to assist in the Badlands spring roundup. "You could have spanned his waist with your two thumbs and fingers," a colleague remembered. The cowboys looked askance at his toothbrush and razor and scrupulously neat bed-roll.[23] There were the usual jibes about his glasses, which he submitted to with resigned dignity. "When I went among strangers I always had to spend twenty-four hours in living down the fact that I wore spectacles, remaining as long as I could judiciously deaf to any side remarks about 'four eyes,' unless it became evident that my being quiet was misconstrued and that it was better to bring matters to a head at once."[24]

He did not need to knock a man down during the next four weeks to win the respect of the cowboys—although there was one occasion when he told a Texan who addressed him as "Storm Windows" to "Put up or shut up."[25] It soon became apparent that Roosevelt could ride a hundred miles a day, stay up all night on watch, and be back at work after a hastily gulped, 3:00 A.M. breakfast. On one occasion he was in the saddle for nearly forty hours, wearing out five horses, and winding up in another stampede.[26] He roped steers till his hands were flayed, wrestled calves in burning clouds of alkali-dust, and stuck "like a burr" to bucking ponies, while his nose poured blood and hat, guns, and spectacles flew in all directions.[27] One particularly vicious horse fell over backward on him, cracking the point of his left shoulder. There was no doctor within a hundred miles, so he continued to work "as best I could, until the injury healed of itself." It was weeks before he could raise his arm freely.[28]

"That four-eyed maverick," remarked one veteran puncher, "has sand in his craw a-plenty."[29]

THE ROUNDUP RANGED down the Little Missouri Valley for two hundred miles, fanning out east and west at least half as far again. During the five weeks that it lasted, sixty men riding three hundred horses coaxed some four thousand cattle out of the myriad creeks, coulees, basins, ravines and gorges of the Badlands, sorting them into proprietary herds and branding every calf with the mark of its mother. When Roosevelt withdrew from the action on 20 June, he had been with the roundup for thirty-two days, longer than most cowboys, and had ridden nearly a thousand miles.

"It is certainly a most healthy life," he exulted. "How a man does sleep, and how he enjoys the coarse fare!"[30]

Some extraordinary physical and spiritual transformation occurred during this arduous period. It was as if his adolescent battle for health, and his more recent but equally intense battle against despair, were crowned with sudden victory. The anemic, high-pitched youth who had left New York only five weeks before was now able to return to it "rugged, bronzed, and in the prime of health," to quote a newspaperman who met him en route. His manner, too, had changed. "There was very little of the whilom dude in his rough and easy costume, with a large handkerchief tied loosely about his neck . . . The slow, exasperating drawl and the unique accent that the New Yorker feels he must use when visiting a less blessed portion of civilization had disappeared, and in their place is a nervous, energetic manner of talking with the flat accent of the West."[31]

In New York, another reporter was struck by his "sturdy walk and firm bearing."[32] Roosevelt's own habitual assertion that he felt "as brown and tough as a hickory knot" at last carried conviction. All references to asthma and *cholera morbus* disappear from his correspondence. He was now, in the words of Bill Sewall, "as husky as almost any man I have ever seen who wasn't dependent on his arms for his livelihood."[33]

Throughout that summer Roosevelt continued to swell with muscle, health, and vigor. William Roscoe Thayer, who had not seen him for several years, was astonished "to find him with the neck of a Titan and with broad shoulders and stalwart chest." Thayer prophesied that this magnificent specimen of manhood would have to spend the rest of his life struggling to reconcile the conflicting demands of a powerful mind and an equally powerful body.[34]

SUMMER WAS but five days old, and the sea breeze blew cool as Roosevelt's carriage circled Oyster Bay and began to ascend the green slopes of Leeholm. Now, for the first time, he could admire his recently completed house. Huge, angular, and squat, it sat on the grassy hilltop with all the grace of a fort. Bamie's gardeners had planted vines, shrubs, and saplings in an effort to refine its silhouette, but years would pass before leaves mercifully screened most of the house from view.[35]

As Roosevelt drew nearer, its newness and rawness became more apparent. The mustard-colored shingles had not yet mellowed, and the green trim clashed with florid brick and garish displays of stained glass. However, flowers were clustering around the piazza, last year's lawns had come up thick and velvety, and spring rains had washed away the last traces of construction dirt.[36] Roosevelt might be excused a surge of proprietary emotion.

Looking south across the bay toward Tranquillity (rented to others now, but still a symbol, in its antebellum graciousness, of Mittie), he could see the beach where "dem web-footed Roosevelts" used to run down to bathe; the private, reedy channels where he rowed little Edie Carow; the tidal waters where he and Elliott had once joyously battled a snowy northeaster and there, snaking west to the station, was the lane along which Theodore Senior used to speed, his linen duster ballooning out behind him. At nearer points, through the trees, could be seen the summerhouses of cousins and uncles and aunts. If there were some hillside walks, and a tennis court or two, that Roosevelt could not contemplate without being painfully reminded of his honeymoon, he had at last developed the strength to deal with allusive memories.[37]

In token of that strength, he decided that the name Leeholm must be changed. Henceforth his house would commemorate the Indian *sagamore,* or chieftain, who had held councils of war here two and a half centuries before.[38] He would call it Sagamore Hill.

ROOSEVELT ALLOWED HIMSELF eight idyllic weeks in the East during the summer of 1885—his first period of relaxation in two years. Fanny Smith, now married to a Commander Dana and recovering from a miscarriage, was one of the many guests he invited to stay at Sagamore Hill. Although unable to take part in a frenetic schedule of outdoor activities, such as portaging across mosquito-infested mud flats and tumbling down Cooper's Bluff into the sea, she was able to enjoy the stimulating conversation at Bamie's dinner table. "Especially memorable were the battles, ancient and modern, which were waged relentlessly on the white linen tablecloth with the aid of such table-silver as was available." Theodore's penchant for military history made her feel "that Hannibal lived just around the corner."

The entire household went into New York on 8 August to watch

General Grant's funeral parade. Roosevelt himself marched, in his capacity as a captain in the National Guard. "I shall never forget the tense expression on his face as he passed with his regiment," wrote Fanny, "and it seemed to me that the bit of crêpe that floated from his rifle was conspicuous for its size."[39]

Back at Sagamore Hill, Roosevelt indulged in many romps with little Alice, who was now a mass of yellow curls and just learning to walk. Occasionally, perhaps, he strolled through the trees to Gracewood, where Aunt Annie lived, to cuddle little Eleanor Roosevelt, his brother's ten-month-old daughter.[40] On returning home, he could ponder the family motto carved in gold over the wide west door: *Qui plantavit curabit—he who has planted will preserve.*

Roots were forming—fragile ones, exploratory as those of his saplings, yet sure to anchor him permanently someday. Right now his other roots out West seemed lustier and stronger. He was bound to return to his ranch, and would, in time, inhabit many houses, including the grandest in the land; but sooner or later these roots would cause all others to wither, and he would come back more and more to Sagamore Hill. Here hung the hallowed portrait of his father, and various stuffed symbols of his own manhood—the buffalo, the bears, the many antelope heads. The place was loud with the happy squeals of his daughter, the conversation of his friends and relatives. This endearingly ugly house was Home. In it he would live out his sixty years (Roosevelt was already quite sure of that figure)[41] and die.

But for the time being, he was twenty-six, and the Wild West was calling. Urging Bamie to continue her entertainments on his behalf, he caught the Chicago Limited out of New York on 22 August 1885.[42]

NEWSPAPERMEN WERE WAITING to interview Roosevelt at St. Paul and Bismarck as usual, but for some reason they seemed more interested in talking about the Marquis de Morès than about politics. Was it true that he and the Marquis had recently had "a slight tilt," and that their relations were "somewhat strained"?[43]

The only "tilt" Roosevelt could think of—and it was trivial, in his opinion—was a business misunderstanding that had occurred during the spring. He had contracted to sell some cattle to the Northern Pacific Refrigerator Car Company at a price of six cents a pound, but on delivery de Morès had reduced the price to five and a half cents a pound, saying that the market in Chicago was down by that much. Roosevelt, in turn, had insisted that a contract was a contract, irrespective of price fluctuations afterward; but the Marquis remained obdurate. Roosevelt had philosophically taken his cattle back, and let it be known that he would not do business with the Marquis again.[44]

Now, months later, he sought to play down the incident. It was "not true," he said, that the two cattle kings of the Badlands were "looking for each other with clubs." The story of a "tilt" was exaggerated; but why all these questions? He found out soon enough. The Marquis de Morès had just been indicted for murder.[45]

Roosevelt reached Medora on 25 August, and paused only to announce a meeting of his Little Missouri Stockmen's Association on 5 September before hurrying north to discuss the indictment with Sewall and Dow.[46] He already knew the facts. This "murder" was nothing new—merely another skirmish in the legal war that had been waged against de Morès ever since the fatal ambush of 26 June 1883. Charges that the Marquis had killed Riley Luffsey had twice been examined by justices of the peace, and twice dismissed for lack of proof; yet now a grand jury in Mandan had decided there was enough evidence to warrant a trial.[47]

De Morès, who had also been vacationing in the East, arrived in Dakota close on Roosevelt's heels, and gave himself up to the authorities. They told him that "a little matter of fifteen hundred dollars judiciously distributed" would cause the indictment to be withdrawn. "I have plenty of money for defense," he replied haughtily, "but not a dollar for blackmail." He was promptly placed in Bismarck jail.[48]

A SUBTLY TRANSFORMED ranch house greeted the returning proprietor of Elkhorn. There were unmistakable signs of feminine occupation: patches of bright color in the windows, delicate items of laundry hanging up to dry, a new air of neatness and tidiness. Inside,

Roosevelt found Mrs. Sewall and Mrs. Dow, along with Kitty Sewall, "a forlorn little morsel" about the same age as Baby Lee. Dow had brought them all West three weeks before.[49]

Roosevelt was pleased to have more company under his roof. The ranch house was amply big enough for six—so big, indeed, that it needed domestic management. The women, in turn, were anxious to repay him for their free board and lodging. They swept and scrubbed and polished, mended his linen, and at regular intervals sorted out his possessions so he could find what he was looking for.[50] Best of all, they fed him—not as elaborately as Bamie on the polished boards of Sagamore Hill, but from the nutritional point of view probably better. After a dusty morning's work on the range or in the corral he would return ravenous to the Elkhorn table, "on the clean cloth of which are spread platters of smoked elk meat, loaves of good bread, jugs and bowls of milk, saddles of venison or broiled antelope-steaks, perhaps roast and fried prairie chickens with eggs, butter, wild plums, and tea or coffee."[51] Sometimes there were potatoes coaxed from the harsh alkaline soil, jars of buffalo-berry jam, dishes of jelly and cake. Roosevelt's appetite had grown prodigious since his physical transformation in the spring, and he gobbled everything greedily. No doubt he continued to put on weight, but the hard exercise of ranch life kept him, in Bill Sewall's words, "clear bone, muscle, and grit."[52]

GRIT OF ANOTHER SORT was called for on 5 September, when Roosevelt, who had gone to Medora to chair the Stockmen's Association meeting, received the following letter from a jail cell in Bismarck:

> *My dear Roosevelt* My principle is to take the bull by the horns. Joe Ferris is very active against me and has been instrumental in getting me indicted by furnishing money to witnesses and hunting them up. The papers also published very stupid accounts of our quarreling . . . Is this done by your order? I thought you my friend. If you are my enemy I want to know it. I am always on hand as you know, and be-

tween gentlemen it is easy to settle matters of that sort directly.

Yours very truly

Morès

Sept. 3, 1885[53]

Roosevelt's first reaction must have been bewilderment. Despite their little skirmishes over beef prices and grazing rights, he and the Marquis got on fairly well. They had entertained each other at lunch, exchanged books and newspapers, and there had even been an occasion, during a square dance in honor of the spring roundup, when they solemnly took the floor together, and "do-si-do'd" with cowgirls.[54] Yet there was no mistaking the threatening tone of this letter. He could not have read it without a pang of real fear. The Marquis was known to have killed at least two men in duels, and his feats of marksmanship, such as picking off prairie chickens on the wing with a 20–30 Winchester, were legendary.[55] If his letter was, as it seemed, a challenge to arms, Roosevelt would have the choice of weapons; but that was of small comfort to a myopic individual who claimed to be "not more than an ordinary shot."[56] The Marquis's trial was already under way, and if acquitted he might demand satisfaction at once.

Before replying it was necessary to clarify the Frenchman's cloudy umbrage. He obviously believed that Joe Ferris, Roosevelt's old buffalo guide, was bribing witnesses, and with Roosevelt's money. Joe was now a storekeeper in Medora, but he also acted as the unofficial banker of the Badlands. Cowboys would deposit their earnings with him for safekeeping, and withdraw cash from time to time—when they had to go to Bismarck to testify at a murder trial, for instance.[57] The Marquis must be unaware of this. All he *did* know was that Roosevelt had financed Joe's store,[58] and therefore suspected that the same person might well be financing his prosecution.

De Morès also complained about articles publicizing the so-called "tilt." These rumors had been put out by reporters who regularly interviewed Roosevelt at railroad stations farther east: conceivably he could have leaked the stories on his latest trip to New York, knowing that by the time he returned to deny them they would be accepted as fact.

The last and most damaging proof of ill will, as far as de Morès was concerned, was that one of the men to receive money from Joe Ferris before the trial was Dutch Wannegan, a victim of the original ambush, a key prosecution witness, and—for the past year or more—an employee of Theodore Roosevelt.[59]

All these misconceptions might surely be explained away, but how could de Morès ever have imagined that the most decent man in the Badlands was plotting his destruction? Roosevelt, staring dumbfounded at the letter in his hand, knew the notion was preposterous. He discussed his options with Sewall, and said that he was opposed to dueling on principle. But he could not ignore such a challenge; he must answer de Morès in kind. "I won't be bullied by a Frenchman . . . What do you say if I make it rifles?"[60] Sitting down on a log, and flipping the letter over, he scrawled on its back the draft of his reply:

> *MEDORA, DAKOTA,*
>
> *September 6, 1885*
>
> Most emphatically I am not your enemy; if I were you would know it, for I would be an open one, and would not have asked you to my house nor gone to yours. As your final words, however, seem to imply a threat, it is due to myself to say that the statement is not made through any fear of possible consequences to me; I too, as you know, am always on hand, and ever ready to hold myself accountable in any way for anything I have said or done. *Yours very truly*
>
> THEODORE ROOSEVELT[61]

Sewall agreed to act as second, while doubting that the duel would ever take place. "He'll find some way out of it."[62]

A few days later a courier arrived with another message from the

Marquis. Roosevelt showed it to Sewall. "You were right, Bill." De Morès protested that he had implied no threat in his previous letter. He meant, simply, that "there was always a way to settle misunderstandings between gentlemen—*without trouble.*" The tone of this letter was sufficiently conciliatory for Roosevelt to boast later that the Marquis had "apologized."[63]

And so the epic confrontation fizzled out—disappointingly, for those like E. G. Paddock, who had hoped for violence, but decisively in Roosevelt's favor nonetheless. From then on, progress toward organization was rapid in Billings County. Newspapers began to speak of Roosevelt as the likely first Senator from Dakota, when the territory was elevated to statehood.[64]

AUTUMN CAME EARLY to the Badlands, but the cooling air did not prevent the sun from burning every last drop of green juice out of the grass. The prairie became a brittle carpet underfoot, wanting only the spark of a horseshoe on stone—or a tumbling ember of lignite—to erupt into flame.[65] Several times that September, Roosevelt found himself fighting fires on his own range.[66] Similar fires were reported all over Billings County. Stockmen plotted their various locations and grew increasingly suspicious. All the outbreaks were in the "drive" country—a broad strip of grassland lying between the Northern Pacific Railroad and the cattle ranches on either side. This strip, fifty miles wide and hundreds of miles long, had to be crossed by any herd en route to shipping points like Mingusville and Medora. Cattle driven over the blackened wastes shed tons of weight; on delivery they could be sold only as low-grade beef. Clearly it was not nature that so shrewdly sabotaged the profits of stockmen. The fires were being set by Indians, in protest against being deprived of their ancient hunting grounds in the Badlands.[67]

Roosevelt's attitude toward the red man in 1885 was no more tolerant than that of any cowboy. He had publicly explained it in *Hunting Trips of a Ranchman:*

> During the past century a good deal of sentimental nonsense has been talked about our taking the Indians' land. Now, I

> do not mean to say for a moment that gross wrong has not been done the Indians, both by government and individuals, again and again . . . where brutal and reckless frontiersmen are brought into contact with a set of treacherous, vengeful, and fiendishly cruel savages a long series of outrages by both sides is sure to follow. But as regards taking the land, at least from the Western Indians, the simple truth is that the latter never had any real ownership in it at all. Where the game was plenty, there they hunted; they followed it when they moved away to new hunting grounds, unless they were prevented by stronger rivals, and to most of the land on which we found them they had no stronger claim than that of having a few years previously butchered the original occupants. When my cattle came to the Little Missouri, the region was only inhabited by a score or so white hunters; their title to it was quite as good as that of most Indian tribes to the lands they claimed; yet nobody dreamed of saying that these hunters owned the country . . . The Indians should be treated in just such a way that we treat the white settlers. Give each his little claim; if, as would generally happen, he declined this, why, then let him share the fate of the thousands of white hunters and trappers who have lived on the game that the settlement of the country has exterminated, and let him, like these whites, perish from the face of the earth which he cumbers.[68]

One day in early fall Roosevelt set off on another of his solo rides across the prairie.[69] This time he headed northeast. He knew that he was wandering into "debatable territory," where white land bordered on red, and knew of at least one cowboy who had been killed hereabouts by a band of marauding bucks; but this, of course, was more likely to challenge him than deter him. He was crossing a remote plateau when, suddenly, five Indians rode up over the rim.

> The instant they saw me they whipped out their guns and raced full speed at me, yelling and flogging their horses. I was on a favorite horse, Manitou, who was a wise old fellow, with nerves not to be shaken at anything. I at once leaped off him and stood with my rifle ready.

> It was possible that the Indians were merely making a bluff and intended no mischief. But I did not like their actions, and I thought it likely that if I allowed them to get hold of me they would at least take my horse and rifle, and possibly kill me. So I waited until they were a hundred yards off and then drew a bead on the first. Indians—and for the matter of that, white men—do not like to ride in on a man who is cool and means shooting, and in a twinkling every man was lying over the side of his horse, and all five had turned and were galloping backwards, having altered their course as quickly as so many teal ducks.
>
> After this one of them made the peace sign, with his blanket first, and then, as he rode toward me, with his open hand. I halted him at a fair distance and asked him what he wanted. He exclaimed, "How! Me good Injun, me good Injun," and tried to show me the dirty piece of paper on which his agency pass was written. I told him with sincerity that I was glad that he was a good Indian, but that he must not come any closer. He then asked for sugar and tobacco. I told him I had none. Another Indian began slowly drifting toward me in spite of my calling out to keep back, so I once more aimed with my rifle, whereupon both Indians slipped to the side of their horses and galloped off, with oaths that did credit to at least one side of their acquaintance with English.[70]

Although Roosevelt later dimissed this as "a trifling encounter," it is further, perhaps unnecessary proof of his extraordinary courage.[71]

MEANWHILE, THE MURDER TRIAL of the Marquis de Morès was making daily headlines in the Dakota newspapers. Proceedings dragged on for week after week, but little fresh evidence was forthcoming. Neither prosecution nor defense could establish who fired first when the trio of frontiersmen rode into the Marquis's ambush, and whose bullet had killed Riley Luffsey. The Marquis was his own best witness. Tall, calm, and dignified, he spoke in simple sentences that made the testimony of Dutch Wannegan sound maundering and untruthful.[72]

On 16 September Roosevelt passed through Bismarck—en route to the New York State Republican Convention—and briefly visited the Marquis in his jail cell. De Morès sat tranquilly smoking, confident of a favorable verdict. Continuing on to New York, Roosevelt arrived just in time to read the news that the Frenchman had been acquitted.[73]

NOT MUCH NEEDS to be said of Roosevelt's routine activities at the Convention in Saratoga, except that he helped draft the party platform and campaigned unsuccessfully on behalf of a reform candidate for the gubernatorial nomination.[74] Little notice was taken of him during the ensuing county and state campaigns, which ended in general victory for the Democrats. The impression is that he worked with his usual energy and devotion to the reform cause, but without his usual flamboyance.[75] For once he did not need "the full light of the press beating upon him." There was radiance enough in his private life, the radiance of such happiness as he had not known in almost two years. Its secret source lay neither in politics, nor in the adulation of his family and friends, nor in his own superabundant health and vigor. He was in love.

ONE DAY THAT FALL—probably in early October, although the exact date is unknown—Roosevelt returned to his pied-à-terre at 422 Madison Avenue and, opening the front door, met Edith Carow coming down the stairs. For twenty months now, since the death of Alice Lee, he had successfully managed to avoid her. It had been impossible, however, to avoid hearing items of news about his childhood sweetheart, who was still Corinne's closest friend and a regular visitor to Bamie's house on days when he was not in town. He must have known of the rapid decline in the Carow family fortunes, following the death of her improvident father in 1883; of the decision by her mother and younger sister to live in Europe, where their eroded wealth might better support them; of Edith's decision to go with them, having considered, and dismissed, the idea of marrying for money; of her curious aloofness, cloaked behind great sweetness of manner, which frustrated many a would-be beau; of evidence that poor "Edie," at twenty-four, was already an old maid.[76] But that latter item, at least, was mere negative rumor, whereas here, confronting him (had Bamie plotted this deliberately?), was positive reality. Edith was as alarmingly attractive as he had feared—even more so, perhaps, for she had matured into complex and exciting womanhood. He could not resist her.

Nor could Edith resist him. The Theodore she saw was unrecognizably different from the Teedie she knew as a child, or the Teddy of more recent years. He was a mahogany-brown stranger, slim of leg and forearm, inclining to burliness about the head and shoulders. Most changed of all was the bull-like neck, heavy with muscle and bulging out of his city collar as if about to pop its studs. His hair was sun-bleached, and cropped shorter than she had ever seen it, making his massive head look even larger. Only the reddish-brown mustache had been allowed to sprout freely and droop at the corners in approved cowboy fashion. His toothy smile was the same, and the eyes behind the flashing spectacles were still big and childishly blue. But the corrugations of his mobile face had multiplied and were much more deeply etched than she could remember. Edith had to accept the fact that his boyish ingenuousness, which used to be one of his great charms, was gone. In its place were reassuring signs of wisdom and authority.

Theodore, for his part, saw a woman of slender yet appealingly rounded figure, with small hands and feet which assumed semiballetic poses when she hesitated, as then, on a stair, in the knowledge that she was being examined. Whether the scrutiny was friendly or hostile, Edith flinched against it; her privacy was so intense, her sensitiveness so extreme, that she stiffened as if posing for an unwelcome photograph. Her own gaze—when she chose to direct it (for the wide-spaced eyes were usually set at an oblique angle)—was icy blue and uncomfortably penetrating. Its strength belied the general air of softness and shyness, and flashed the unmistakable warning, *hurt me and I will hurt you more.* Her jaw was firm, and her mouth was wide, tightly controlled at the corners. Smiles did not come easily. Yet they did come on occasion, and they transformed her amazingly, for her teeth were pretty, and her cheekbones elegant beneath the peach-like skin. Her most arresting feature, best seen in profile, was a long, sharp, yet classically beautiful nose, of the kind that Renaissance portraitists loved to draw in silverpoint. Here was a person of refinement and steely discipline, yet in the glow of her flesh there was a hint of earthiness, and much sexual potential.[77]

No details are known about the meeting in the hallway, except that it occurred,[78] and that it was, inevitably, followed by others. Whether these encounters were few or many—again the record is blank—they were certainly ardent, for on 17 November Theodore proposed marriage, and Edith accepted him.[79]

THE ENGAGEMENT WAS KEPT a secret, even from their closest relatives. Should the merest whisper of it break out, polite society, just then convening for the season, would be scandalized. Roosevelt, after all, had been only twenty-one months a widower. To post, with such indecent haste, from the arms of Alice Lee to those of Edith Carow—having done the reverse seven years before—was hardly the conduct of a gentleman, let alone a politician famous for public moralizing. At all costs it must seem that Theodore and Edith had merely resumed an old family friendship. Announcement of the engagement must be put off for a year at least.[80] In the meantime they could privately, carefully, adjust to the violent change which had taken place in their lives.

LOVE AND POLITICS were not enough to drain Roosevelt's well of vitality in the fall of 1885. If anything, they intensified its flow. During his free time at Sagamore Hill he threw himself into a new sport, as strenuous and bloodthirsty as any of his Western activities, albeit more elegant: hunting to hounds. He had experimented with it a few times before, but rather disdainfully, for the pursuit of the fox was at that time considered effete and un-American.[81] But now, with the encouragement of Henry Cabot Lodge, an enthusiastic huntsman, he suddenly discovered in it the "stern and manly qualities" that had to justify all his amusements. Long Island's Meadowbrook Hunt was certainly one of the toughest in the world: the Marquis de Morès told Roosevelt that he had never seen such stiff jumping.[82]

Having formally adopted the pink coat, Roosevelt wore it as proudly as his buckskin tunic, and galloped after fox with the same energy he once devoted to buffalo. Often he was "in at the death" ahead of the huntmaster.[83] Although the technique of riding wooded Long Island country was totally different from that he had acquired out West, he showed no fear of coming a serious cropper.

On Saturday morning, 26 October, the hunt met at Sagamore Hill, and after the traditional stirrup cup set off over particularly rough country. High timber obstacles of five feet or more followed one upon another at a frequency of six to the mile. Some of these barriers were post-and-rail fences, as stiff as steel and deadly dangerous: even Filemaker, America's best jumper, began to hang back nervously.[84]

Roosevelt, riding a large, coarse stallion, led from the start. Careless of accidents which dislocated the huntmaster's knee, smashed another rider's ribs, and took half the skin off his brother-in-law's face,[85] he galloped in front for fully three miles. Eventually his exhausted horse began to go lame; at about the five-mile mark it tripped over a wall and pitched over into a pile of stones. Roosevelt's face smashed against something sharp, and his left arm, only recently knit after the roundup fracture, snapped beneath the elbow. Yet he was back in the saddle as soon as the horse was up, and rushed on one-armed, determined not to miss the death. After five or six further jumps the bones of his broken arm slipped past one other, and it dangled beside him like a length of liverwurst; but this, and the blood pouring down his face, did not deter him from pounding across fifteen more fields. He had the satisfaction of finishing the hunt within a hundred yards of the other riders, and returned to Sagamore Hill looking "pretty gay . . . like the walls of a slaughter-house."[86] Baby Lee, who was waiting at the stable for him, ran away screaming from the bloody monster, and he pursued her, chortling.[87]

Washed clean that night, his cut face plastered and his arm in splints, he presided over the Hunt Ball as laird of Sagamore. Edith Carow was his guest,[88] and took her first cool survey of her future home. At midnight, Theodore Roosevelt turned twenty-seven. With his daughter asleep upstairs, his house full of music and laughter, and Edith at his side, he could abandon himself to bliss rendered piquant by pain. Later he wrote to Lodge: "I don't grudge the broken arm a bit . . . I'm always ready to pay the piper when I've had a good dance; and every now and then I like to drink the wine of life with brandy in it."[89]

“Here was a person of refinement . . .
and much sexual potential.”

Edith Kermit Carow at twenty-four.

CHAPTER 13

The Long Arm of the Law

"Death be to the evil-doer!"
With an oath King Olaf spoke;
"But rewards to his pursuer!"
And with wrath his face grew redder
Than his scarlet cloak.

UNABLE TO TEAR HIMSELF away from Edith, Roosevelt remained in the East for a "purely society winter," as he called it, of dinners, balls, and the Opera. At the height of the season, through January and February 1886, he was going out every other night.[1] Fanny Smith Dana saw him often with Edith, yet suspected nothing: to an old family friend they looked as natural together as brother and sister.[2]

What the couple were at pains to conceal in public, they also concealed in private. Page after page of Roosevelt's diary for the period contains nothing but the cryptic initial "E."[3] One can only sigh for the rhapsodies of self-revelation that Alice Lee evoked. But Roosevelt had been a boy then, as much in love with love as with a girl. Now he was a man in love with a woman, and his passion was correspondingly deeper, more dignified. Edith was not the sort of person to encourage rhapsodies, anyway. She disapproved of excess, whether it be in language, behavior, clothes, food, or drink. Too

“We took them absolutely by surprise.”

Deputy Sheriff Roosevelt and his prisoners:
Burnsted, Pfaffenbach, and Finnegan.

much ardor was just as vulgar as too much cream on too many peaches—another Rooseveltian tendency she was determined to restrain. In her opinion, any revelation of the intimacies between lovers, even in a man's diary, was abhorrent. The thought of such details ever becoming public obsessed her, to the point that "burn this letter" became a catch-phrase in her own correspondence. Her influence over Theodore was already sufficient to control his pen in the winter of 1885–86; yet it must be remembered that he, too, had become something of a self-censor. The mature Roosevelt wrote nothing that he could not entrust to posterity. Many of his purportedly "family" letters were quite obviously written for publication. On such occasions he signed himself formally THEODORE ROOSEVELT instead of his usual "Thee."[4] Only in his letters to Edith did he spill out his soul, in the secure knowledge that she would read, understand, and then destroy. By some freak chance one of these love letters has survived. Although written in old age, it is as passionate as anything he ever composed during his courtship of Alice Lee.

They continued to suppress details of their engagement, and in later years Edith even went through family correspondence to weed out every single reference to it.[5] Why she should be quite so secretive is unclear, for it flowered out into a famously successful marriage. Possibly there were quarrels, even estrangements; both she and Theodore were powerful personalities, used to getting their own way. Whatever the case, history must respect their fierce desire for privacy.

As the season proceeded, Roosevelt saw more and more of Edith. He grew bored and restless when forced to socialize without her. "I will be delighted when I get settled down to work of some sort again," he told Henry Cabot Lodge. ". . . To be a man of the world is *not* my strong point."[6] Lodge was now president of the *Boston Advertiser,* had contracted to write a life of George Washington for the prestigious American Statesmen series, and was determined to run again for Congress later in the year. On a trip to New York at the end of January, he projected such an air of purposeful industry that Roosevelt felt ashamed of his own dallying. "I trust that you won't forget your happy-go-lucky friend," he wrote, after Lodge's return to Boston. "Anything connected with your visit makes me rather pensive."[7]

Lodge, meanwhile, had sympathetically pulled a few strings, with the result that Roosevelt also received a commission to write an American Statesmen book.[8] His biography was to be of Senator Thomas Hart Benton, the Western expansionist. It was an ideal subject for a young author of proven historical ability and intimate knowledge of life on the frontier. He accepted with delight, and plunged at once into his preliminary research.

AS FEBRUARY MERGED into March, Roosevelt began to feel neglectful of his "backwoods babies" on the Elkhorn Ranch. They had not seen him for nearly six months, and their morale was surely low: he knew how depressing winter in the Badlands could be. If he did not go West soon, the pessimistic Bill Sewall might work himself into such a state of gloom as to ask for release from his contract. Will Dow would certainly follow suit. With Elkhorn now fully capitalized and turning over satisfactorily, Roosevelt could ill afford to lose either man.

Edith, moreover, would not long detain him in the East. She had confirmed her decision to accompany her mother and sister to Europe in early spring, perhaps because she could not afford to remain behind, or more likely because she knew her absence would remove any lingering doubts Roosevelt might have about marrying her. (He was still racked with guilt about the memory of Alice Lee.) If, by next winter, he was ready to follow her across the Atlantic, a quiet wedding could be arranged in London.[9]

So, on 15 March, after spending ten final days almost entirely with "E," Roosevelt left New York for Medora.[10]

ELKHORN RANCH
March 20th 1886

Darling Bysie [Bamie],

I got out here all right, and was met at the station by my men; I was really heartily glad to see the great, stalwart, bearded fellows again, and they were as honestly pleased to see me. Joe Ferris is married, and his wife made me most comfortable the night I spent in town. Next morning snow covered the ground; but we pushed [on] to this ranch, which we reached long after sunset, the full moon flooding the landscape with light. There has been an ice gorge right in front of the house, the swelling mass of broken fragments having been pushed almost up to our doorstep . . . No horse could by any chance get across; we men have a boat, and even then it is most laborious carrying it out to the water; we work like Arctic explorers.

Things are looking better than I expected; the loss by death has been wholly trifling. Unless we have a big accident I shall get through this all right; if not I can get started square with no debt. . . .

Your loving brother

THEE[11]

THE ABOVE-MENTIONED BOAT was, like Roosevelt's rubber bathtub, an object of some curiosity in the Badlands. There were, to be sure, a few scows tied up at various points along the valley, but often as not their keels rotted away from disuse. For most of the year the Little Missouri was too shallow even for a raft: cowboys galloped across it wherever they chose, barely wetting their horses' bellies. In winter the river froze rapidly, and men and wolves traveled up and down it as if it were a highway.[12]

Only in freak weather, such as that prevailing in March 1886, did the Elkhorn boat really come in useful. Sewall and Dow, who were experienced rivermen, kept it in beautiful trim. Small, light, and sturdy, it was available at a moment's notice whenever they wanted to cross the river for meat, or to check up on their ponies.[13]

Arctic conditions continued for days after Roosevelt's arrival. At night, as he lay in bed, he could hear the ice-gorge growling and grinding outside. Floes were still coming down so thickly that the jam increased rather than diminished. If the ranch house had not been protected by a row of cottonwoods, it would have been overwhelmed by ice.[14] Fortunately a central current of speeding water kept the gorge moving. To prevent the boat from being dragged away, Sewall roped it firmly to a tree.

Early on the morning of 24 March, however, he went out onto the piazza and found the boat gone. It had been cut loose with a knife; nearby, at the edge of the water, somebody had dropped a red woolen mitten.[15]

Roosevelt reacted so angrily on hearing this news that he had to be dissuaded from saddling Manitou and thundering off in instant pursuit of the thieves.[16] A horse, Sewall pointed out, was of little use when the river was walled off on both sides with ice. Roosevelt would never get within a mile of the men in his boat: all they had to do was keep floating downstream (the current was such they could not possibly have gone upstream) until he gave up, or galloped to his death across the gorge. There was only one thing to do: build a makeshift scow and follow them. The thieves probably felt secure in the knowledge that they had stolen the only serviceable boat on the Little Missouri, and would therefore be in no hurry. He had at least an even chance of catching them. Roosevelt agreed, and sent to Medora for a bag of nails.[17]

It was not the value of his loss that annoyed him: the Elkhorn boat was worth a mere thirty dollars. But he was, by virtue of his chairmanship of the Stockmen's Association, a deputy sheriff of Billings County, and bound (at least by his own stern moral code) to pursue any lawbreakers. Besides, he had been intending to use the boat on a cougar hunt that very day, and his soul thirsted for revenge. He knew very well who the thieves were: "three hard characters who lived in a shack, or hut, some twenty miles above us, and whom we had shrewdly suspected for some time of wishing to get out of the country, as certain of the cattlemen had begun openly to threaten to lynch them."[18] Charges of horse-stealing had been leveled against their leader, "Redhead" Finnegan, a long-haired gunman of vicious reputation. (During the previous summer he had blasted half the buildings in Medora with his buffalo-gun, in consequence of a practical joke played on him while drunk.)[19] Finnegan's associates were a half-breed named Burnsted, and a half-wit named Pfaffenbach. All three men must be desperate, or they would never have made a break in such weather; if chased, they would certainly shoot for their lives.

While Sewall and Dow labored with hammers and chisels, Roosevelt, ever the schismatic, began to write *Thomas Hart Benton.* He completed Chapter 1 on 27 March, by which time the boat, a flat-bottomed scow, was ready.[20] But a furious blizzard delayed their departure for three more days. Roosevelt soothed his impatience with a literary letter to Cabot Lodge. "I have got some good ideas in the first chapter, but I am not sure they are worked up rightly; my style is rough, and I do not like a certain lack of *sequitur* that I do not seem able to get rid of." Casually mentioning that he was about to start downriver "after some horse thieves," he added, "I shall take Matthew Arnold along."[21] He also took Tolstoy's *Anna Karenina,* and a camera to record his capture of the thieves. Already he was thinking what a good illustrated article this would make for *Century* magazine.[22]

The story of the ensuing boat-chase was to become, with that of the Mingusville bully, one of Roosevelt's favorite after-dinner yarns.

EARLY ON THE MORNING of 30 March the three pursuers pushed their scow into the icy water.[23] Mrs. Sewall and Mrs. Dow, who were both five months pregnant, worriedly watched them go. The fact that Redhead Finnegan already had six days' start was no reassurance that they would see their menfolk again, for the north country was known to be bleak, and full of hostile Indians.

The boat picked up speed as the river current took it. With Sewall steering, and Dow keeping watch at the bow, there was nothing much for Roosevelt to do. He snuggled down amidships with his books and buffalo robes, determined to have "as good a time as possible."[24] From time to time he would look up from Matthew Arnold and watch the high, barren buttes slide by. They were rimed with snow, yet blotched here and there with rainbow outbursts of yellow, purple, and red. Closer, and on either side, the ice-walls loomed in crazy, glittering stacks. "Every now and then overhanging pieces would break off and slide into the stream with a loud, sullen splash, like the plunge of some great water-beast."

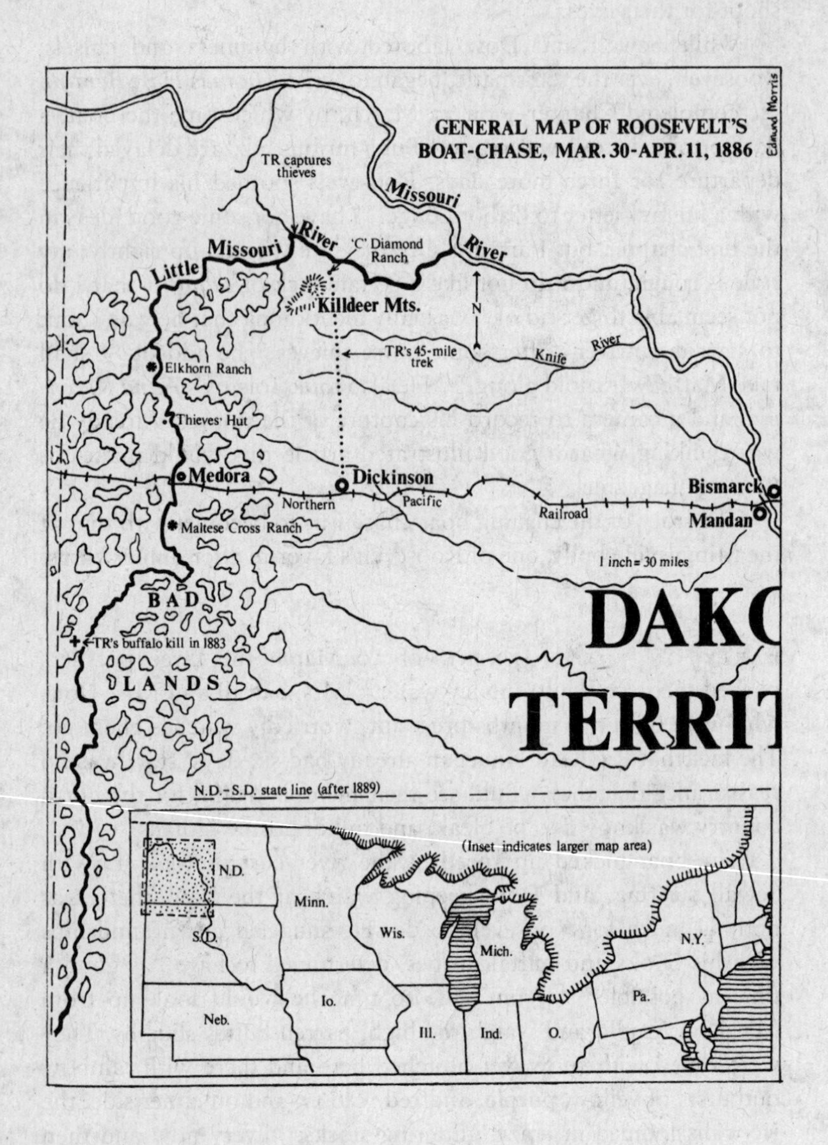
GENERAL MAP OF ROOSEVELT'S BOAT-CHASE, MAR. 30-APR. 11, 1886
Edmund Morris
TR captures thieves
Missouri
River
Little
Missouri
River
'C' Diamond Ranch
Killdeer Mts.
N
TR's 45-mile trek
Knife
River
Elkhorn Ranch
Thieves' Hut
Medora
Dickinson
Bismarck
Mandan
Northern
Pacific
Railroad
Maltese Cross Ranch
1 inch = 30 miles
DAKO
TERRIT
BAD
LANDS
TR's buffalo kill in 1883
N.D.-S.D. state line (after 1889)
(Inset indicates larger map area)
N.D.
S.D.
Minn.
Wis.
Mich.
N.Y.
Pa.
Io.
Neb.
Ill.
Ind.
O.

These sights and sounds were duly memorized for his article.[25] Seeking a simile to describe the shape of the buttes as dusk came on and reduced them to silhouettes, he thought of "the crouching figures of great goblin beasts," then decided that Browning had said it better:

> *The hills, like giants at a hunting, lay*
> *Chin upon hand, to see the game at bay . . .*[26]

Progress was fairly rapid that day and the next, Sewall and Dow poling through stretches of bad water with an expertise no Westerner could match. They would have moved faster had it not been for a freezing wind in their faces, which seemed to bluster ever stronger, no matter which way the river turned. (Sewall was heard grumbling that it was "the crookedest wind in Dakota.")[27] The temperature dropped steadily, and ice began to form on the handles of the poles. The only sign of human life was a deserted group of tepees, sighted on the second day. Of the thieves there was no trace whatsoever. It began to seem as if Finnegan had not headed downriver after all. Then why steal a boat?

They camped, when they were too cold to go on, under whatever shelter they could find ashore, but naked trees afforded little relief from the wind. During the second night, the thermometer reached zero.

Next morning, 1 April, anchor-ice was jostling so thick they could not push on for several hours. They managed to shoot a couple of deer for breakfast, and the hot meat warmed their frozen bodies back to life. Early that afternoon, when they were nearly a hundred miles north of Elkhorn, they rounded a bend, laughing and talking, and almost collided with their stolen boat.[28] It lay moored against the right bank.

> From among the bushes some little way back, the smoke of a campfire curled up through the frosty air . . . Our overcoats were off in a second, and after exchanging a few muttered words, the boat was hastily and silently shoved toward the bank. As soon as it touched the shore ice I leaped and ran up behind a clump of bushes, so as to cover the landing of the

> others, who had to make the boat fast. For a moment we felt a thrill of keen excitement and our veins tingled as we crept cautiously toward the fire . . .
>
> We took them absolutely by surprise. The only one in the camp was the German [Pfaffenbach], whose weapons were on the ground, and who, of course, gave up at once, his companions being off hunting. We made him safe, delegating one of our number to look after him particularly and see that he made no noise, and then sat down and waited for the others. The camp was under the lee of a cut bank, behind which we crouched, and, after waiting an hour or over, the men we were after came in. We heard them a long way off and made ready, watching them for some minutes as they walked towards us, their rifles on their shoulders and the sunlight glittering on their steel barrels. When they were within twenty yards or so we straightened up from behind the bank, covering them with our cocked rifles, while I shouted to them to hold up their hands . . . The half-breed obeyed at once, his knees trembling as if they had been made of whalebone. Finnegan hesitated for a second, his eyes fairly wolfish; then, as I walked up within a few paces, covering the center of his chest so as to avoid overshooting, and repeating the command, he saw that he had no shot, and, with an oath, let his rifle drop and held his hands up beside his head.[29]

Having divested his prisoners of an alarming array of rifles, revolvers, and knives, Roosevelt now found himself in something of a quandary. He could not tie them up, for their hands and feet would freeze off.[30] What was more, Mandan, the first big town downriver, was more than 150 miles away, and the ice-floes ahead were so thick it could be weeks before they got there. With six mouths to feed, and game apparently nonexistent upriver, he was fast running out of provisions.[31] The surrounding countryside, as far as he could see, was uninhabited. There was no question of returning to Elkhorn: the river was nonnavigable in reverse. Any right-minded Westerner, of course, would have executed his prisoners on the spot, then abandoned the boats, and walked back to civilization. But Roosevelt's ethics would not allow that. He was determined to see Finnegan in jail, according to due process of law. His only choice, therefore, was to pole on downriver behind the ice-jam, pray that it would quickly thaw, and maintain a constant guard over the thieves. If this meant losing half a night's sleep every second night, he could stand it.

Now began eight days as monotonous and wearing as any he ever spent. The weather remained so cold that the ice-jam rarely shifted before noon, only to wedge again, like a floating mountain, a few miles farther on. Sometimes they had to fight against being sucked under by the current—all the while keeping an eye on Redhead, who was capable of quick and murderous movement. "There is very little amusement in combining the functions of a sheriff with those of an Arctic explorer," Roosevelt decided.[32]

Game continued scarce. By 6 April the party had nothing to eat but dry flour. They were forced to make soggy, unleavened cakes by dunking fistfuls of it in the dirty water. But Roosevelt's spirits remained high. The strange camaraderie that develops between captors and captives in isolation reached the point where all six men joked and talked freely, "so that an outsider overhearing the conversation would never have guessed what our relations to each other really were." No reference was made to the boat-theft after the first night out.[33]

ROOSEVELT, HAVING FINISHED his volume of Matthew Arnold, proceeded to devour *Anna Karenina,* in between spells of guard duty. He saw nothing incongruous in this. "My surroundings were quite grey enough to harmonize with Tolstoy."[34] The book both attracted and repelled him. His subsequent review of it for Corinne reveals a strange combination of sophistication and naiveté in his critical intellect, plus the insistence that all art should reaffirm certain basic moral values:

> I hardly know whether to call it a very bad book or not. There are two entirely different stories in it; the connection between Levin's story and Anna's is of the slightest, and need not have existed at all. Levin's and Kitty's history is not only very powerfully and naturally told, but is also perfectly

healthy. Anna's most certainly is not, though of great and sad interest; she is portrayed as being prey to the most violent passion, and subject to melancholia, and her reasoning power is so unbalanced that she could not possibly be described otherwise than as in a certain sense insane. Her character is curiously contradictory; bad as she was however she was not to me nearly as repulsive as her brother Stiva; Vronsky had some excellent points. I like poor Dolly—but she should have been less of a patient Griselda with her husband. You know how I abominate the Griselda type. Tolstoy is a great writer. Do you notice how he never comments on the actions of his personages? He relates what they thought or did without any remark whatever as to whether it was good or bad, as Thucydides wrote history—a fact which tends to give his work an unmoral rather than moral tone, together with the sadness so characteristic of Russian writers.[35]

On 7 April Roosevelt struck civilization in the form of a cow camp, and stocked up on bacon, sugar, and coffee. The following day he rode a borrowed bronco fifteen miles to the C Diamond Ranch in the Killdeer Mountains, where he hired a prairie schooner and two horses. The rancher was puzzled as to why he had not strung up his prisoners long since, but agreed to drive them to the sheriff's office in Dickinson, forty-five miles south. Sewall and Dow were to continue downriver to Mandan at their own speed.[36]

Roosevelt elected to walk behind the ranchman's wagon, for he did not trust him. "I had to be doubly at my guard . . . with the inevitable Winchester." They set off on 10 April, the twelfth day of the expedition. By now the long-delayed thaw had begun, and the prairie was a sea of clay:

I trudged steadily the whole time behind the wagon through the ankle-deep mud. It was a gloomy walk. Hour after hour went by always the same, while I plodded along through the dreary landscape—hunger, cold, and fatigue struggling with a sense of dogged, weary resolution. At night, when we put up at the squalid hut of a frontier granger, I did not dare to go to sleep, but . . . sat up with my back against the cabin door and kept watch over them all night long. So, after thirty-six hours' sleeplessness, I was most heartily glad when we at last jolted into the long, straggling main street of Dickinson, and I was able to give my unwilling companions into the hands of the sheriff.

Under the laws of Dakota I received my fees as a deputy sheriff for making the arrests, and also mileage for the three hundred miles gone over—a total of some fifty dollars.[37]

DR. VICTOR H. STICKNEY of Dickinson was just going home to lunch when he met Roosevelt limping out of the sheriff's office.

This stranger struck me as the queerest specimen of strangeness that had descended on Dickinson in the three years I had lived there . . . He was all teeth and eyes. His clothes were in rags from forcing his way through the rosebushes that covered the river bottoms. He was scratched, bruised, and hungry, but gritty and determined as a bulldog . . . I remember he gave me the impression of being heavy and rather large. As I approached him he stopped me with a gesture, asking me whether I could direct him to a doctor's office. I was struck by the way he bit off his words and showed his teeth. I told him I was the only practicing physician, not only in Dickinson, but in the whole surrounding country.

"By George," he said emphatically, "then you're exactly the man I want to see . . . my feet are blistered so badly that I can hardly walk. I want you to fix me up."

I took him to my office and while I was bathing and bandaging his feet, which were in pretty bad shape, he told me the story of his capture of the three thieves . . . We talked of many things that day . . . He impressed me and he puzzled me, and when I went home to lunch, an hour later, I told my wife that I had met the most peculiar and at the same time the most wonderful man I ever came to know.[38]

Relaxing next morning in his Dickinson hotel room, Roosevelt wrote to Corinne: "What day does Edith go abroad, and for how long does she intend staying? Could you not send her, when she goes, some flowers from me? I suppose fruit would be more useful, but I think flowers 'more tenderer' as Mr. Weller would say."[39]

Of course he knew very well when Edith was leaving, and where she was going; but his sisters were not yet in on the secret, and appearances had to be kept up.[40]

HE RETURNED TO MEDORA on 12 April, just in time to witness Billings County's first election as an organized community. Under the supervision of one "Hell-Roaring" Bill Jones, who stood over the ballot-box with a brace of pistols, the votes were cast with a minimum of bloodshed, and a county council duly returned to power. While its first edict, promising "to hang, burn, or drown any man that will ask for public improvements at the expense of the County," could have been worded more diplomatically, it at least voiced sound Republican sentiments, and Roosevelt had every reason to be optimistic about the future of representative government in the Badlands.[41]

THE FOLLOWING DAY, 13 April, he chaired the spring meeting of his Stockmen's Association. The Marquis de Morès was present, yet there was no doubt as to who was the dominant force in the room. Roosevelt conducted the proceedings with iron authority, instantly gaveling to order any speaker who strayed from the subject under discussion. Afterward the stockmen were loud in his praise.[42]

By 18 April, when he arrived in Miles City as a delegate to the much larger Montana Stock Grower's Convention, word of his capture of Redhead Finnegan had spread across the West, and Roosevelt found that he had become a minor folk hero. During his three days there he was "constantly in the limelight," and could report to Bamie, "these Westerners have now pretty well accepted me as one of themselves."[43] No longer was he "Four Eyes," "that dude Rosenfelder," and "Old Hasten Forward Quickly There" (an allusion to the unfortunate order he had yelled at some cowboys shortly after coming to Dakota). Sourdoughs everywhere allowed that he was "one of our own crowd," "not a purty rider, but a hell of a *good* rider," and (highest praise of all) "a fearless bugger."[44]

Roosevelt accepted such compliments graciously, while being careful "to avoid the familiarity which would assuredly breed contempt."[45] Somehow he managed to preserve his gentlemanly status without offending democratic sensibilities—a trick the Marquis de Morès must have envied. Bill Merrifield and Sylvane Ferris thought nothing of moving their mattresses to the loft of the Maltese Cross cabin whenever he came to stay: it was understood that "the boss" liked to sleep alone downstairs.[46] Sewall and Dow were allowed to sit in their shirt-sleeves at the Elkhorn table, but they were expected to address him always as "Mr. Roosevelt." So, for that matter, were his fellow ranchers, some of whom were wealthy enough to consider themselves his social equal. "[Howard] Eaton called him 'Roosevelt' once," Merrifield remembered, "and he turned round and said, 'What did you say.' You bet Eaton never did again."[47] Nobody, of course, dared call him "Teddy," a word which since the death of Alice had become anathema to him. "That was absolutely wrong."[48]

During the spring roundup, which was even more arduous than that of 1885 (five thousand cattle and five hundred horses were involved), Roosevelt put in his fair share of twenty-four-hour days, although he was distracted periodically by *Benton*.[49] The conflict between mind and body which Thayer had forecast had already begun. But Roosevelt insisted that he was having "great fun" and felt "strong as a bear." On 19 June he wrote Bamie: "I should say this free open air life, without any worry, was perfection. I write steadily three or four days, then hunt (I killed two elk and some antelope recently) or ride on the round-up for many more." Although he was wistful for Sagamore Hill, and missed Baby Lee "dreadfully," he decided to remain West all summer.[50]

BENTON, INCREDIBLY, was reported to be complete "all but about thirty pages" by the end of June.[51] It will be remembered that

Roosevelt had only just finished chapter 1 before setting off on his boat-chase on 30 March. A month's hiatus followed: after returning from Dickinson he had been so busy with cattle-politics and hunting that he did not take up his pen again until 30 April. During the next three weeks he must have written the bulk of the 83,000-word volume, for on 21 May he left to join the roundup.[52] From time to time after that, when there was a lull in activity on the range, he would ride into Medora and put in a day or two of literary labor in his room over Joe Ferris's store. Ferris remembered the sound of his footsteps upstairs, as Roosevelt paced up and down, wrestling with obstinate sentences far into the night.[53] "Writing is horribly hard work to me," he complained.[54] On 7 June, when the roundup was at its height, he sent a wry appeal to Henry Cabot Lodge:

> I have pretty nearly finished Benton, mainly evolving him from my inner consciousness; but when he leaves the Senate in 1850 I have nothing whatever to go by; and, being by nature a timid and, on occasions, by choice a truthful man, I would prefer to have some foundation of fact, no matter how slender, on which to build the airy and arabesque superstructure of my fancy, especially as I am writing a history. Now I hesitate to give him a wholly fictitious date of death and to invent all the work of his later years. Would it be too infernal a nuisance for you to hire one of your minions on the *Advertiser* (of course at my expense) to look up his life after he left the Senate in 1850?[55]

Lodge agreed to help, but he begged the fanciful author to check his entire text in a library. As will be seen, Roosevelt did revise the manuscript thoroughly before publication. By then he was sick of it, and doubtful as to its literary value. "I hope it is decent . . . I have been troubled by dreadful misgivings."[56]

HIS MISGIVINGS WERE ONLY partly justified. *Thomas Hart Benton* (Houghton Mifflin, 1887) became Roosevelt's third book in a row to achieve "standard" status, and was considered the definitive biography for nearly two decades.[57] However it did not sell well. Contemporary critics, while generally praising it, had some harsh things to say about the author's "muscular Christianity minus the Christian part."[58] Today the book is dismissed as historical hackwork.

This reputation is not fair. *Benton* may be unread, but it is not unreadable. Certainly there are long stretches of rather dogged narrative, such as the chapters devoted to the politics of nullification and redistribution of federal surplus funds. One can read the volume from cover to cover without finding out what its subject looked like. Secondary characters, such as Andrew Jackson and Daniel Webster, are merely referred to, like names in an encyclopedia. The only personality whose lusty presence stamps every page is that of Theodore Roosevelt. Herein lies the book's main appeal, for its scholarship is so dated as to be spurious now. Roosevelt gleefully discovers many points of common identity with his subject, and in describing them, describes himself. As a testament to his developing political philosophy and theory of statesmanship, *Benton* is sometimes humorous, often entertaining, and, in its great climactic chapter on America's "Manifest Destiny," even inspiring.

The book begins with three brief chapters which explain, in prose hard and clear as glass, the evolution of "a peculiar and characteristically American type" in the West of Benton's boyhood. Since these "tall, gaunt men, with strongly marked faces and saturnine, resolute eyes" were the recent ancestors of his own cowboys, he is able to describe them with unsentimental accuracy.

> They had narrow, bitter prejudices and dislikes; the hard and dangerous lives they had led had run their character into a stern and almost forbidding mould . . . They felt an intense, although perhaps ignorant pride in and love for their country, and looked upon all the lands hemming in the United States as territory which they or their children should one day inherit; for they were a race of masterful spirit, and accustomed to regard with easy tolerance any but the most flagrant violations of law. They prized highly such qualities as courage, loyalty, truth and patriotism, but they were, as a whole, poor, and not

> over-scrupulous of the rights of others. . . . Their passions, once roused, were intense . . . There was little that was soft or outwardly attractive in their character: it was stern, rude, and hard, like the lives they led, but it was the character of those who were every inch men, and were Americans through to the very heart's core.[59]

When young Senator Benton emerges as the spokesman for these people, the parallels between his own and Roosevelt's character grow clear. They are both politicians born to articulate the longings of the inarticulate; scholars able to interpret current events in the light of ancient and modern history; men of "peculiar uprightness," of "abounding vitality and marvelous memory," who stick to their policies with "all the tenacity of a snapping turtle."[60] Yet there are enough psychological dissimilarities between author and subject to keep the tone of the biography healthily critical. Benton is mocked for his humorlessness and pomposity, and sharply reprimanded (along with Thomas Jefferson) for hypocrisy on questions of color. "Like his fellow statesmen he failed to see the curious absurdity of supporting black slavery, and yet claiming universal suffrage for whites as a divine right, not as a mere matter of expediency . . . He had not learned that the majority in a democracy has no more right to tyrannize over a minority than, under a different system, the latter would to oppress the former."[61]

Whenever Roosevelt, in the course of tracing Benton's thirty years in Congress, comes upon one of his own *bêtes noires,* the text fairly crackles with verbal fireworks. Some of these pop-pop harmlessly, as when he castigates President Jefferson as a "scholarly, timid, and shifty doctrinaire," and President Tyler as "a politician of monumental littleness." Others, however, are (or were) genuinely explosive, for example his assertion that "there is no more 'natural right' why a man over twenty-one should vote than there is why a negro woman under eighteen should not."[62]

The most controversial chapter of the book is that devoted to Benton's doctrine of westward expansion, which Roosevelt defines as "our manifest destiny to swallow up the land of all adjoining nations who were too weak to withstand us."[63] The "Oregon" of the 1840s—an enormous wilderness stretching west from the Rockies, and north from California to Alaska—was a prize that both the United States and Britain were entitled to share. But the "arrogant attitude" of Senator Benton, in claiming most of it, "was more than justified by the destiny of the great Republic; and it would have been well for all America if we had insisted even more than we did upon the extension northward of our boundaries." Warming to his theme, Roosevelt declares that "Columbia, Saskatchewan, and Manitoba would, as States of the American Union, hold positions incomparably more important, grander and more dignified than . . . as provincial dependencies of a foreign power . . . No foot of soil to which we had any title in the Northwest should have been given up; we were the people who could use it best, and we ought to have taken it all."[64]

Roosevelt acknowledged, with an almost audible sigh, that the concept of an American Pacifica stretching from Baja California to the Bering Straits was academic in 1886. But this did not detract from Benton's visionary greatness. In attempting to summarize it, the twenty-seven-year-old author became something of a visionary too. He could have been writing about himself, as future President of the United States, rather than the long-dead Senator from Missouri:

> Many of his expressions, when talking of the greatness of our country . . . not only were grandiloquent in manner, but also seemed exaggerated and overwrought even as regards matter. But when we think of the interests for which he contended, as they were to become, and not as they at the moment were, the appearance of exaggeration is lost, and the intense feeling of his speeches no longer seems out of place or disproportionate . . . While sometimes prone to attribute to his country a greatness she was not to possess for two or three generations to come, he, nevertheless, had engrained in his very marrow and fiber the knowledge that inevitably and beyond all doubt, the coming years were to be hers. He knew that, while other nations held the past, and shared with his own the present, yet that to her belonged the

still formless and unshaped future. More clearly than almost any other statesman he beheld the grandeur of the nation loom up, vast and shadowy, through the advancing years.[65]

ROOSEVELT PENNED THE LAST pages of *Benton* at Elkhorn between 29 June and 2 July 1886. He rose every day at dawn, and would stand for a moment or two on the piazza, watching the sun rise through a filter of glossy cottonwood leaves.[66] Then he sat down at his desk, writing as fast as he could while the morning was still cool.[67] By noon the log-cabin was too stuffy to bear, for a crippling heat-wave had struck Dakota. The grass outside, weakened by the late frosts of spring, turned prematurely brown. Mrs. Sewall's vegetable garden began to wilt, despite frantic watering. On 4 July the temperature reached 125 degrees Fahrenheit, and an oven-like wind blew through the Badlands, killing every green thing except for a few riverside trees.[68]

Roosevelt was not on his ranch that morning. Along with half the cowboy population of Billings County, he "jumped" the early freight-train out of Medora, and sped east across the prairie to Dickinson.[69] The little town was celebrating the 110th anniversary of the Declaration of Independence, and he had been chosen as Orator of the Day.

As he neared his destination, he could see people converging upon it from all points of the compass, on foot, on horseback, and in white-topped wagons. The streets of Dickinson itself were filled with "the largest crowd ever assembled in Stark County," most of whom were already very drunk.[70]

At ten o'clock the parade got under way. So many spectators decided to join in that the sidewalks were soon deserted. The Declaration was read aloud in the public square, followed by mass singing of "My Country 'Tis of Thee." The crowd then adjourned to Town Hall for a free lunch. When every cowboy had eaten his considerable fill, the master of ceremonies, Dr. Stickney, introduced the afternoon's speakers. "The Honorable Theodore Roosevelt" stood up last, looking surprisingly awkward and nervous.[71]

With all his boyish soul, he loved and revered the Fourth of July.

The flags, the floats, the brass bands—even Thomas Jefferson's prose somehow thrilled him. This particular Independence Day (the first ever held in Western Dakota) found him feeling especially patriotic. He was filled, not only with the spirit of Manifest Destiny, but with "the real and healthy democracy of the round-up." The completion of another book, the modest success of his two ranches, his fame as the captor of Redhead Finnegan, the joyful thought of his impending remarriage, all conspired further to elevate his mood. These things, plus the sight of hundreds of serious, sunburned faces turned his way, brought out the best and the worst in him—his genuine love for America and Americans, and his vainglorious tendency to preach. To one sophisticated member of the audience, Roosevelt's oration was a cliché-ridden "failure"; yet the majority of those present were profoundly affected by it. Regular roars of applause bolstered the straining, squeaky rhetoric:

> Like all Americans, I like big things; big prairies, big forests and mountains, big wheat-fields, railroads, and herds of cattle too, big factories, steamboats, and everything else. But we must keep steadily in mind that no people were ever yet benefitted by riches if their prosperity corrupted their virtue . . . each one must do his part if we wish to show that the nation is worthy of its good fortune. Here we are not ruled over by others, as is the case in Europe; here we rule ourselves. . . .

Arthur Packard, who was listening intently, noticed that Roosevelt's high voice became almost a shriek as passion took him.[72]

> When we thus rule ourselves, we have the responsibilities of sovereigns, not of subjects. We must never exercise our rights either wickedly or thoughtlessly; we can continue to preserve them in but one possible way, by making the proper use of them. In a new portion of the country, especially here in the Far West, it is peculiarly important to do so . . . I am, myself, at heart as much a Westerner as an Easterner; I am proud, indeed, to be considered one of yourselves, and I address you

> in this rather solemn strain today, only because of my pride in you, and because your welfare, moral as well as material, is so near my heart.[73]

He sat down to a voluntary from the brass band. The audience cheered heartily, but briefly. Everybody was anxious to adjourn to the racecourse and watch the Cowboys take on the Indians.[74]

MUCH LATER THAT DAY Roosevelt and Arthur Packard sat rocking on the westbound freight to Medora, while fireworks popped in the darkening sky behind them. For a while they discussed the speech, which had greatly inspired Packard, and Roosevelt confessed his longings to return to public life. "It was during this talk," Packard said years afterward, "that I first realized the potential bigness of the man. One could not help believing he was in deadly earnest in his consecration to the highest ideals of citizenship."

Roosevelt told Packard that he was thinking of accepting a minor appointment which had been offered him in New York—the presidency of the Board of Health. Henry Cabot Lodge thought the job infra dig, but he was not so sure: he felt he could do his best work "in a public and political way."

The young editor's reaction was immediate. "Then you will become President of the United States."[75]

Roosevelt did not seem in the least surprised by this remark. Indeed, Packard got the impression that he had already thought the matter over and come to the same conclusion. "If your prophecy comes true," he said at last, "I will do my part to make a good one."[76]

THREE DAYS LATER, Roosevelt left unexpectedly for New York. If he hoped to find the Board of Health job open to him, he was disappointed: the incumbent had simply refused to resign, despite an indictment for official corruption.[77] Clearly little had changed for the better in municipal politics.

He spent three weeks checking the manuscript of *Benton* in the

Astor Library, then—yet again—kissed "cunning little yellow headed Baby Lee" good-bye, and headed back to the Badlands in a mood of restless melancholy.[78] It was ironic that at this time of resurgent political ambition he could see "nothing whatever ahead."[79] The city of his birth, his child, his home, his future wife, all lay behind him, pulling his thoughts back East, even as the train hauled him West. Much as he loved Dakota, he knew now that his destiny lay elsewhere: it must have been difficult to escape the feeling that he was traveling in altogether the wrong direction.

Arriving at Medora on 5 August, he found letters from Edith confirming a December wedding in London.[80] From now on he could only count the days that separated him from her.

THE CRIES OF A NEWBORN BABY greeted Roosevelt at Elkhorn next day. Mrs. Sewall had just presented her husband with a son. Mrs. Dow, not to be outdone, produced a son of her own less than a week later.[81] "The population of my ranch," Roosevelt informed Bamie, "is increasing in a rather alarming manner."[82] The squalling of these two new arrivals, not to mention the jam-smeared face of little Kitty Sewall, and Elkhorn's growing air of alien domesticity, seemed to emphasize his bachelor status and growing sense of misplacement. It was as if the house were no longer his own, and he merely the guest of his social inferiors.

Still restless, he hurried off to Mandan, where he witnessed the conviction and sentencing to three years in prison of Redhead Finnegan and the half-breed Burnsted. He withdrew his charge against Pfaffenbach, saying "he did not have enough sense to do anything good or bad." The old man expressed fervent gratitude, and Roosevelt said that was the first time he had ever been thanked for calling somebody a fool.[83]

Notwithstanding his legal triumph, Roosevelt seemed to be under considerable nervous strain during the several days he spent in Mandan. A reporter from the *Bismarck Tribune* remarked on his "facial contortions and rapid succession of squints and gestures."[84] His hosts were surprised to hear him pacing the floor of his room and groaning over and over again, "I have no constancy! I have no constancy!"[85] Evidently Edith's recent letter had evoked once again the guilty memory of Alice Lee.

About this time Roosevelt heard reports of a border clash with Mexico which, in his fertile imagination, seemed likely to lead to major hostilities.[86] Instantly he conceived the idea of raising "an entire regiment of cowboys," and wrote to Secretary of War William C. Endicott notifying him that he was "at the service of the government." From Mandan he beseeched Lodge: "Will you tell me at once if war becomes inevitable? Out here things are so much behind hand that I might not hear the news for a week . . . as my chance of doing anything in the future worth doing seems to grow continually smaller I intend to grasp at every opportunity that turns up." But Secretary Endicott decided to settle the dispute diplomatically, to Roosevelt's obvious disappointment. "If a war had come off," he mused wistfully, "I would surely have had behind me as utterly reckless a set of desperadoes as ever sat in the saddle."[87]

THE HOT AUGUST DAYS dragged on. Plagued by a recurrent "caged wolf feeling," Roosevelt also began to worry about Dakota's continuing drought. It happened to coincide with record new immigrations of cattle, which his Stockmen's Association had tried in vain to prevent. Three years before, when he first came West, the range had been overgrassed and undergrazed; now the situation was reversed.[88] He began to wonder if Sewall's forebodings about the Badlands as "not much of a cattle country" might have been justified.

Between 21 August and 18 September, Roosevelt went with Bill Merrifield on a shooting expedition to the Coeur d'Alene mountains of northern Idaho. His prey this time was "problematic bear and visionary white goat."[89] Although he managed to kill two of the latter—America's rarest and most difficult game—he confessed that he "never felt less enthusiastic over a hunting trip."[90]

On returning to Medora, Roosevelt was "savagely irritated" to read newspaper gossip that he was engaged to Edith Carow. How the secret got out is to this day a mystery. He was forced to write an embarrassed letter of confirmation to Bamie. "I am engaged to

Edith and before Christmas I shall cross the ocean and marry her. You are the first person to whom I have breathed a word on this subject . . . I utterly disbelieve in and disapprove of second marriages; I have always considered that they argued weakness in a man's character. You could not reproach me one half as bitterly for my inconstancy and unfaithfulness as I reproach myself. Were I sure there was a heaven my one prayer would be I might never go there, lest I should meet those I loved on earth who are dead."[91]

HE WAS ANXIOUS NOW to hurry East and console Bamie, who was in agony over the prospect of losing her surrogate daughter. But an urgent matter at Elkhorn detained him. Sewall and Dow had decided, in his absence, that they wanted to terminate their contract and go back to Maine. They had been unable to sell the fall shipment of beeves profitably: the best price Chicago would offer was ten dollars less than the cost of raising and transporting each animal. Both men felt that they were "throwing away his money," and that "the quicker he got out of there the less he would lose."[92]

Roosevelt, as it happened, had reached much the same conclusion. Although he was no businessman, simple figuring told him that his $85,000 investment in the Badlands was eroding away as inexorably as the grass on the range. In any case, he was fast losing his enthusiasm for ranching. Bill Merrifield and Sylvane Ferris could take the Elkhorn herd over; in future he would use the ranch house only as a stopover when checking on his cattle, or as a hunting base. His reaction to Sewall's ultimatum, therefore, was mild. "How soon can you go?"[93]

While the three friends sat squaring their accounts that last week of September, a strange, soft haze settled over the Badlands, reducing trees and cattle to pale blue silhouettes.[94] Weathermen dismissed the haze as an accumulation of fumes from the grass-fires that had smoldered all summer on the tinder-dry plains. Yet its strangeness made cowboys and animals uneasy. Although the heat was still tremendous, old-timers began to lay in six months' supply of winter provisions, muttering that "nature was fixin' up her folks for hard times."[95] Beavers worked double shifts cutting and storing their lengths of willow brush; muskrats grew extra-thick coats and built their reed houses twice the usual height. Roosevelt, casting his ornithologist's eye out of the window, noticed that the wild geese and songsters were hurrying south weeks earlier than usual. He may have heard rumors that the white Arctic owl had been seen in Montana, but only the Indians knew what that sign portended.[96]

SEWALL AND DOW were not ready to move their wives, babies, and baggage out of the ranch before 9 October. By then their impatient boss had already departed for the East. It was left to Sewall to close up the great log cabin and slam the door on what even he, in later life, would recall as "the happiest time that any of us have ever known."[97]

And so silence returned to the Elkhorn bottom, broken only by the worried chomping of beavers down by the river.

CHAPTER 14

The Next Mayor of New York

It is accepted,
The angry defiance,
The challenge of battle!

THE MORNING OF 15 October 1886 was drizzly, and the East River heaved dull and gray as Roosevelt's ferry pushed out from Brooklyn. On Bedloe's Island, far across the Bay, he could mistily make out the silhouette that had been tantalizing New Yorkers for months: an enormous, headless Grecian torso, with half an arm reaching heavenward.[1] But he probably gave it no more than a glance. His mind was on politics, and on this evening's Republican County Convention in the Grand Opera House. He was curious to see who would be nominated for Mayor of New York. The forthcoming campaign promised to be unusually interesting—so much so he had delayed his departure to England until 6 November, four days after the election.

For the first time in the city's history, a Labor party had been organized to fight the two political parties. What was more, it had nominated as its candidate the most powerful radical in America. Roosevelt had met Henry George before—on 28 May 1883, the same night he first met Commander Gorringe[2]—and the little man

"A pale young Englishman . . . with a combination of courtliness and inquisitiveness."

Cecil Arthur Spring Rice at thirty-five.

had hardly seemed formidable. Balding, red-bearded, and runtlike, he was just the sort of "emasculated professional humanitarian" Roosevelt despised.[3] Yet George was famous as the author of *Progress and Poverty* (1879), one of those rare political documents which translate sophisticated social problems into language comprehensible to the ghetto. So simple was the book's language, so inspirational its philosophy to the poor, that millions of copies had been sold all over the world.[4]

Henry George argued that because it takes many poor men to make one rich man, progress in fact creates poverty. The only way to solve this, "the great enigma of our times," was to have a single tax on land, as the most ubiquitous form of wealth. Thus, the more a landlord speculated on Property, the more he would enrich Government, and the more Government would repay Labor, which had produced the wealth in the first place.[5]

Up until 1886, George had been content to propound his single-tax philosophy in print and on lecture platforms (for all his lack of glamour, he was a blunt and effective orator). But the recent rash of angry strikes across the country[6] persuaded him that it was time to submit his principles to the ballot. New York, with its abnormally wide gulf between rich and poor, was the obvious place to start. George let it be known that if thirty thousand workingmen pledged to support him for Mayor, he would run on an independent Labor ticket. Thirty-four thousand pledges flowed in, to the amazement of politicians all over the country. "I see in the gathering enthusiasm [of labor] a power that is stronger than money," George crowed delightedly in his acceptance speech, "something that will smash the political organizations and scatter them like chaff before the wind."[7]

That had been on 5 October, and both Republicans and Democrats had scoffed at the little man's hyperbole. Pledges of support bore, they knew, but fickle relation to actual voting figures: the most George could hope for was fifteen thousand. But now, only ten days later, George's strength was increasing at a truly phenomenal rate. Professional politicians were seriously alarmed. If George, by some political fluke, captured City Hall, he would wield greater power than any former Mayor—thanks to legislation sponsored in 1884 by none other than Assemblyman Theodore Roosevelt.[8]

The latter's first question, when he stepped off the ferry into a group of New York reporters, was about their latest estimate of George's voting strength. The answer, "20,000, and probably much more," surprised and flurried him. After remarking, irrelevantly, that he himself was "not a candidate" for Mayor (not even the most imaginative journalist thought that he might be), Roosevelt hurried uptown to the Union League Club.[9]

DOUBTLESS HE INTENDED to attend the Republican County Convention as an observer. But during the afternoon he was visited by a group of influential Republicans, who, on behalf of party bosses, asked if he would accept the nomination for Mayor. This bombshell took him completely by surprise.[10] As a loyal party man, he could not refuse the honor; as a loyal (and still secret) fiancé, he could not reveal that he had a transatlantic steamship ticket in his pocket. Edith was looking forward to a leisurely, three-month honeymoon in Europe after their wedding, and would surely resent being hurried back to New York so that he could prepare to take office on 1 January. Moreover she was hardly the type to spend the next two years shaking ill-manicured hands at municipal receptions. All this was assuming he won, of course. If he *lost* . . .

But the party bosses were expecting an answer. Roosevelt agreed, "with the most genuine reluctance," to allow his name to be put before the convention.[11] The emissaries departed, leaving him alone. Night came on. He remained ensconced in his club, waiting for the inevitable news from the Opera House.

HE HAD A LOT to think about during those solitary hours. Why had Johnny O'Brien, Jake Hess, Barney Biglin, and all the rest of the machine men offered him this unexpected honor? He was, after all, their ancient enemy. Perhaps they wished to reward him for his support of James G. Blaine in 1884; more likely they hoped he would lure the Independents back into the Republican fold, in order to have a united party behind Blaine—again—in 1888. Or perhaps they imagined (as many did) that he was a millionaire, and might contribute a liberal assessment to the campaign chest.[12] They would soon learn the likelihood of *that:* half his capital was tied up in Dakota, and the interest on the remainder would barely support him and Edith at Sagamore Hill.[13]

A cynical hypothesis which he did not want to consider, but which would come up in the press, was that the party bosses had decided no Republican could win a three-way contest for the mayoralty, and merely wanted a few thousand votes to trade on Election Day.[14] Certainly the campaign odds were against him. The Democrats had just nominated Representative Abram S. Hewitt, a man of mature years, vast wealth, moderate opinions, and impeccable breeding.[15] Hewitt also happened to be an industrialist, famous for his enlightened attitude to labor (during the depression years 1873–78 he ran his steel works at a loss in order to safeguard the jobs of his employees).[16] He would doubtless attract all but the most extreme George followers, along with those Republicans who felt nervous about Roosevelt's youth. Only yesterday, the *Nation* had editorialized: "Mr. Hewitt is just the kind of man New York should always have for Mayor," and Roosevelt's instinct told him the voters would agree on 2 November.[17]

All in all, he concluded, it was "a perfectly hopeless contest, the chance of success being so very small that it may be left out of account . . . I have over forty thousand majority against me." However, there *was* that chance; he had taken on older men before, and beaten them: his pugnacious soul rejoiced at the overwhelming challenge. He would make "a rattling good canvass" for the mayoralty, and would not be disgraced if he ran second. The only disaster would be to run third. But that seemed unlikely: in his opinion Henry George was "mainly wind."[18]

SEVEN BLOCKS AWAY, in the bakingly hot, tobacco-blue auditorium of the Grand Opera House, Chauncey Depew, the Republican party's most unctuous orator, was persuading delegates that the idea of a young mayor for this, "the third city of the world," was a brilliant one. "Every Republican here tonight asks for young blood. I would select a young man whose family has long been identified with good government . . . [cheers and shouts for Roosevelt] . . . He came out of the Legislature with a reputation as wide as the confines of this nation itself." A senior Republican leaped up to protest that the young man was a Free Trader.[19] "If in his experience he has made a mistake," grinned Depew, "he has had the courage to acknowledge it." The protester was booed and hissed out of the hall, and the convention unanimously nominated Theodore Roosevelt for Mayor.[20]

RIGHT FROM THE START the candidate made it clear that he was going to run his own campaign. Establishing himself in luxurious headquarters at the Fifth Avenue Hotel, he informed the party bosses that he would pay "no assessment whatsoever" and would be "an adjunct to nobody."[21] These declarations aroused flattering comments in the press. "Mr. Roosevelt is a wonderful young man," remarked the Democratic *Sun*. Even E. L. Godkin of the *Post* admitted: "If Roosevelt is elected, we have not a word to say against him."[22]

Roosevelt remained sure that he could not win at least through the first four days of the campaign. He explained to Lodge that he was only running "on the score of absolute duty," and hoped to enjoy, if nothing else, "a better party standing" afterward. "The George vote will be very large . . . undoubtedly thousands of my should-be supporters will leave me and vote for Hewitt to beat him."[23] But this did not prevent him from campaigning with all his strength. He worked eighteen-hour days, addressing three to five meetings a night, pumping hands, signing circulars, repudiating bribes, plotting strategy, and on at least one occasion dictating letters and holding a press conference simultaneously.[24]

As usual Roosevelt never minced words. He was determined to meet every issue head-on, even the touchy one of Labor v. Capital. George was so articulate on the left, and Hewitt so persuasive in the center, that Roosevelt might have been well advised to keep his own right-wing views tacit, and concentrate on other subjects; but that was not his style. When a Labor party official accused him of belonging to "the employing and landlord class, whose interests are best served when wages are low and rents are high,"[25] Roosevelt shot back with a contemptuous public letter, dated 22 October 1886.

"The mass of the American people," he wrote, "are most emphatically not in the deplorable condition of which you speak." As for the accusation that he, Roosevelt, belonged to the landlord class, "if you had any conception of the true American spirit you would know that we do not have 'classes' at all on this side of the water." In any case, "I own no land at all except that on which I myself live. Your statement that I wish rents to be high and wages low is a deliberate untruth . . . I have worked with both hands and with head, probably quite as hard as any member of your body. The only place where I employ many wage-workers is on my ranch in the West, and there almost every one of the men has some interest in the profits."

Roosevelt conceded that "some of the evils of which you complain are real and can be to a certain degree remedied, but not by the remedies you propose." But most would disappear if there were more of "that capacity for steady, individual self-help which is the glory of every true American." Legislation could no more do away with them "than you could do away with the bruises which you receive when you tumble down, by passing an act to repeal the laws of gravitation."[26]

To this the Labor man could only reply, "If you were compelled to live on $1 a day, Mr. Roosevelt, would you not also complain of being in a deplorable condition?"[27] But by then Roosevelt's campaign was going so well—to everybody's surprise—that the mournful question was ignored.

ON THE NIGHT of Wednesday, 27 October, Roosevelt's twenty-eighth birthday, bonfires belched in the street outside Cooper Union, reddening the huge building's facade until it glowed like a beacon. For almost an hour, rockets soared into the murky sky, casting showers of light over Lower Manhattan and attracting thousands of curious sightseers. By 7:30 P.M. every seat in the hall was filled, and standing room was at a premium as Republican citizens of New York gathered to ratify the nomination of Theodore Roosevelt for

Mayor. One old politician marveled that he had never seen such a crowd since Lincoln spoke at the Union in 1860.[28]

The guest of honor did not appear until shortly before eight o'clock. He had long ago learned the dramatic effect of delayed entry. In the meantime the audience could feast their eyes on his large crayon portrait, surrounded by American flags and a gilt eagle, and hung around with rich silk banners. It was, as one reporter observed, "a millionaires' meeting." Astors, Choates, Whitneys, Peabodys, and Rockefellers fondled each other's lapels, and discussed "the boy Roosevelt's" remarkable progress in the campaign so far.[29] They had been impressed to read, in various daily papers, such headlines as the following:

(22 Oct.) PIPING HOT—Roosevelt Busy as a Beaver
(23 Oct.) RED HOT POLITICS—The Fight Going on Merrily All Over the City
(24 Oct.) THE ROOSEVELT TIDAL WAVE—Growing Strength of the Candidate
(25 Oct.) ROOSEVELT STILL LEADING
(26 Oct.) CHEERS FOR ROOSEVELT, THE BOY
(27 Oct.) ALL SOLID FOR ROOSEVELT[30]

Not only Republicans were impressed by him. Abram Hewitt himself admitted he would have liked Roosevelt on his team, as president of the Board of Aldermen.[31] The editors of the *Sun*—Democrats to a man—had been moved to print these prophetic words on the eve of the Cooper Union meeting:

> THEODORE ROOSEVELT has gone into the fight for the Mayoralty with his accustomed heartiness. Fighting is fun for him, win or lose, and perhaps this characteristic of his makes him as many friends as anything else. He makes a lot of enemies too, but so does anybody who is fit to live . . . He is getting to be somewhat a shrewder politician . . . and though he is somewhat handicapped by the officious support of the Union League Club, he may do well. It cannot be denied that his candidacy is attractive in many respects, and

he is liable to get votes from many sources. He has a good deal at stake, and it's no wonder that he is working with all the strength of his blizzard-seasoned constitution. It is not merely the chance of being elected Mayor that interests him. There are other offices he might prefer. To be in his youth the candidate for the first office in the first city of the U.S., and to poll a good vote for that office, is something more than empty honor. . . . He cannot be Mayor this year, but who knows what may happen in some other year? Congressman, Governor, Senator, President?[32]

"BLUSHING LIKE a schoolgirl," Roosevelt bounces onstage to brass fanfares and a standing ovation.[33] Somebody shouts, "Three cheers for the next Mayor of New York!" and the auditorium vibrates with noise. It is some minutes before Elihu Root, chairman of the Republican County Committee and the only calm man in the room (with his slit eyes, bangs, and waxlike cheeks, he resembles a Chinese mandarin), introduces Thomas C. Acton as chairman of the meeting. The silver-haired banker steps forward.

"You are called here tonight to ratify the nomination of the youngest man who ever ran as candidate for the Mayor of New York," says Acton. "I knew his father, and wish to tell you that his father did a great deal for the Republican party, and the son will do more . . . [Applause] He is young, he is vigorous, he is a natural reformer. He is full, not of the law, but of the spirit of the law . . ." The chairman begins to flounder, then hits upon a crowd-pleasing phrase. "The Cowboy of Dakota!" he cries. "Make the Cowboy of Dakota the next Mayor!"

This brings about a roar so prolonged that the band has to strike up "Marching Through Georgia" to quell it. Roosevelt, showing all of his teeth, approaches the lectern.

His speech is typically short, blunt, and witty. He begins by noting that Abram Hewitt has predicted "every honest and respectable voter" will support the Democrats. "I think," says Roosevelt, "that on Election Day Mr. Hewitt will find that the criminal classes have polled a very big vote." When the laughter from that dies down, he goes on to counter the outgoing Mayor's charge that he is "too radical" a reformer. "The time for radical reform has arrived," he shouts, "and if I am elected you will have it."

A VOICE You will be elected.
ROOSEVELT I think so, myself! *(Great applause.)*

He castigates his habitual targets, "the dull, the feeble, and the timid good," and proclaims himself a strong man, careless of class, color, or party politics. "If I find a public servant who is dishonest, I will chop his head off if he is the highest Republican in this municipality!"[34]

An effective follow-up speech is made by Richard Watson Gilder, editor of *Century* magazine. He confesses that he has never stood on a political platform before, but is doing so now in order to praise "the best municipal nomination that has been made in my time . . . Mr. Roosevelt is, in my opinion, the pluckiest, the bravest man inside of politics in the whole country."[35] Amid thunderous applause, the nomination is declared ratified.

The candidate shakes hands for twenty minutes until aides drag him from the platform. Outside, in the rain, a large crowd is waiting to serenade him. "I hope to see you all down in the City Hall after January 1, when I am Mayor," says Roosevelt. He bows and he smiles.[36]

AN EXTRAORDINARY HUSH descended on the city's political headquarters next day, 28 October. Everybody except Roosevelt, it seemed, was aboard sight-seeing boats in the Bay, or fighting for a foothold on Bedloe's Island, where, that afternoon, President Cleveland was due to unveil the great Statue of Liberty.[37] Roosevelt, therefore, had a few hours alone at his desk, undisturbed except by a distant thumping of drums, to ponder press reports of his birthday rally, and review his chances for the mayoralty.

While the reports were generally flattering, there was no change in the partisan attitudes of any newspaper. The *Times, Tribune, Commercial Advertiser,* and *Mail & Express* were for him; the

Herald, Sun, World, and *Daily News* were for Hewitt. Only a few smudgy ethnic sheets were for George. The balance, in other words, was fairly even: while Hewitt's newspapers had more readers, Roosevelt's reached more influential people. With his popular momentum increasing, and only five days left to go, it was tempting to believe the *Times*'s headline: "ROOSEVELT SURE TO WIN—THAT'S WHAT LAST NIGHT'S MEETING INDICATES." The *Tribune* carried even more encouraging news, under the headline, "MR. ROOSEVELT'S PROSPECTS—HIS ELECTION NOW DEEMED CERTAIN." It reported that the U.S. Chief Supervisor of Elections, after making an independent survey, projected a total vote of 85,850 for Roosevelt, 75,000 for Hewitt, and 60,000 for George.[38]

Even as he rejoiced in these figures, Roosevelt must have felt a threat in George's amazing total. For a political virgin with no charisma and eccentric, not to say revolutionary views, George had proved to be a redoubtable campaigner. His platform, representing the aspirations of "the disinherited class," was high-toned and reassuringly democratic. Businessmen as well as laborers nodded their heads over such sentences as "The true purpose of government is, among other things, to give everyone security that he shall enjoy the fruits of his labor, to prevent the strong from oppressing the weak, and the unscrupulous from robbing the honest . . . The ballot is the only method by which in our Republic the redress of political and social grievances can be sought."[39] There was no doubt as to George's sincere identity with the working class, nor to his personal honor (he had refused Tammany's offer of a seat in Congress if he would withdraw). One had to admire the dignity with which the little man climbed again and again onto his favorite pedestal, a horse-cart unshackled in the middle of some grimy street. "What we are beginning here," George would yell, at the sea of cloth caps around him, "is the great American struggle for the ending of industrial slavery." Sometimes he would go too far, as when he proclaimed that the French Revolution, "with all its drawbacks and horrors," was "the noblest epoch in modern history," and was "about to repeat itself here."[40] Such inflammatory statements delighted his unlettered listeners, not to mention the nation's anarchists, who looked forward to civil war if George was elected.

Roosevelt had confidence enough in the American democratic system to disbelieve that such a man would ever triumph at the polls. The real danger, as he saw it, was that Henry George's hell-raising image (so like his own, unfortunately) might, come Election Day, turn responsible voters away from *both* of them, in favor of the solid and sober Abram S. Hewitt. Already Democratic papers were chanting the ominous refrain, "A vote for Roosevelt is a vote for George."[41]

However it was not in his nature to think negatively. Hope lay in positive action. From now on he must campaign at an increasing rate, to offset any possible attrition in his lead. By late afternoon, when Republican Committee members began to arrive back from Bedloe's Island, he was already hard at work on his evening's speeches, and autographing colored lithographs of himself.[42]

"IT IS SUCH HAPPINESS to see him at his very best once more," Bamie wrote to Edith in London. "This is the first time since the [1884] Investigation days that he has had enough work to keep him exerting all his powers. Theodore is the only person who has the power (except Father who possessed it in a different way) of making me almost worship him . . . I would never say, or, write this except to you, but it is very restful to feel how you care for him and how happy he is in his devotion to you . . ."[43]

A FAIR IMPRESSION of the pace of Roosevelt's candidacy for Mayor may be gained by following him through one night of his campaign—Friday, 29 October.[44]

At 8:00 P.M., having snatched a hasty dinner near headquarters, he takes a hansom to the Grand Opera House, on Twenty-third Street and Eighth Avenue, for the first of five scheduled addresses in various parts of the city. His audience is worshipful, shabby, and exclusively black. (One of the more interesting features of the campaign has been Roosevelt's evident appeal to, and fondness for, the black voter.) He begins by admitting that his campaign planners had not allowed for "this magnificent meeting" of colored citizens.

"For the first time, therefore, since the opening of the campaign I have begun to take matters a little in my own hands!" Laughter and applause. "I like to speak to an audience of colored people," Roosevelt says simply, "for that is only another way of saying that I am speaking to an audience of Republicans." More applause. He reminds his listeners that he has "always stood up for the colored race," and tells them about the time he put a black man in the chair of the Chicago Convention. Apologizing for his tight schedule, he winds up rapidly, and dashes out of the hall to a standing ovation.[45] A carriage is waiting outside; the driver plies his whip; by 8:30 Roosevelt is at Concordia Hall, on Twenty-eighth Street and Avenue A. Here he shouts at a thousand well-scrubbed immigrants, "Do you want a radical reformer?" "YES WE DO!" comes the reply.[46]

At 9:00 P.M. he is in a ward hall at 438 Third Avenue, where the local boss introduces him as "the Cowboy Candidate." He has had time to get used to this phrase—not that he dislikes it—and jokes that "as the cowboy vote is rather light in this city I will have to appeal to the Republicans." But the audience is more interested in his experiences as deputy sheriff than his views on municipal reform, and Roosevelt makes his escape. He promises to return, as Mayor, with many stories about cowboys, bears, "and other associates in the West."[47]

Now he rattles uptown to Grand Central Station, where a special locomotive (courtesy of New York & Harlem Railroad President Chauncey Depew) is waiting, with steam up, to speed him to Morrisania, in the Bronx. Roosevelt climbs into the observation cab over the boiler; the engine leaps north at sixty miles an hour. For thirteen minutes, red and green lights flash by: all railroad traffic has been halted in his favor. He arrives at Tremont Station only one minute late, and runs into the neighboring hall. Ladies of the 24th Ward present him with an immense floral horseshoe. He says that it is appropriate for a youthful candidate to come to this "young" district of the city. "Three times three cheers for the Boy!" yells someone. Not forgetting his bouquet, Roosevelt jumps back on the train and hurries south across the Harlem River. He reaches the 22nd Assembly District Roosevelt Club in time for his final address of the evening at 10:30 P.M. Then, at last, he can walk home to Bamie's house, where Baby Lee lies sleeping.[48]

Somebody asked him the following morning, Saturday, if he was not exhausted by the pace he was setting himself. "Not in the least!" Roosevelt replied.[49] His wellsprings of energy continued to bubble through the last night of the campaign, but close observers noticed a gradual decline in his confidence of victory. "The 'timid good,' " he exasperatedly wrote Lodge, "are for Hewitt." The word "if" crept frequently into his speeches: "If I am not knifed in the house of my friends I shall win."[50]

KNIVES FLEW thick and fast in those final days, and he could not be sure whether some of the throwers might be his fellow Republicans. A sudden rumor went around that James G. Blaine was coming to lend a hand in the campaign, just when Roosevelt thought he had at last explained away his support of the Plumed Knight in 1884. He was obliged to issue an angry statement that Blaine "had not and would not be invited to speak here."[51] At a large downtown rally for Hewitt, ex–State Senator David L. Foster made a devastating analysis of ex-Assemblyman Roosevelt's democratization of the Board of Aldermen: "The result of this change in the first year of its adoption was that two of them died, five left the country, and about seventeen of them were indicted for crime."[52] Uptown, meanwhile, moonlighting newsboys delivered Democratic newspapers to Republican subscribers, and the slogan "A Vote for Roosevelt is a Vote for George" penetrated into the heart of his traditional constituency.[53]

These same newspapers shrewdly caricatured the "boy" image, knowing that thousands of voters felt nervous about putting a twenty-eight-year-old in charge of America's largest city. "It has been objected that I am a boy," said Roosevelt wearily—he had been hearing the charge for years—"but I can only offer the time-honored reply, that years will cure me of that." He must have been humiliated by a full, front-page cartoon in the *Daily Graphic*, entitled "The Two Candidates," showing Henry George and Abram Hewitt squaring off at each other like giants: only after close inspection did readers perceive the tiny, bespectacled head of Roosevelt peeping out of George's tote-bag.[54]

Most damaging, perhaps, was the *Star*'s publication (on Sunday, 31 October, when the whole city was at home with the papers) of a remark President Cleveland had made as Governor, after vetoing Roosevelt's Tenure of Office Bill: "Of all the defective and shabby legislation which has been presented to me, this is the worst and the most inexcusable."[55] The *World* reprinted this statement on Monday morning, aggravating Roosevelt's embarrassment as his campaign entered its penultimate twenty-four hours.

Evidently sensing defeat now, Roosevelt dropped his hitherto courteous attitude to the opposition. Henry George was "a galled jade," E. L. Godkin was "that peevish fossil," Hewitt's backers were "the same old gang of thieves who have robbed the city for years."[56] Those telltale signs of Rooseveltian frustration, the angry *f*'s and popping *p*'s, reappeared in his oratory: "They [the Democrats] are men who fatten on public plunder—I shall make no promises before election that I will not keep when in office: I propose to turn the plunderers out."[57]

But for the most part he managed to preserve his dignity, as did Hewitt and George in their own contrasting ways. Observers were agreed on Monday night that it had been a splendid contest, fought by men of exceptional quality, inspiring the public to a degree hitherto only seen in presidential years. Substantive issues had been raised and discussed—municipal reform by Roosevelt, social injustice by George, and the dangers of unionized politics by Hewitt. The two latter candidates had, moreover, exchanged a stately series of open letters which expounded the philosophies of Labor v. Capital so brilliantly that Roosevelt himself suggested they should be published in book form. The fact that he could make such a generous proposal, at a time when his own strength was in doubt, is testimony to the elevated mood of all three men. To this day the mayoral campaign of 1886 is regarded as one of the finest in the history of New York.[58]

THE LAST FORECASTS varied widely, with newspapers as usual differing along partisan lines. The *Journal* came nearest to an accurate reflection of the city's enigmatic atmosphere: "Seldom has an election for Mayor of New York presented greater uncertainties on the eve of the voting than the one that will be decided tomorrow. The leaders . . . are at sea."[59]

Through most of the campaign the weather had been cold and drizzly, with curtains of fog drifting around Manhattan, seeming to seal the island off from the outside world. It was still murky when Roosevelt (looking fatigued at last) went to bed on Monday night, but early next morning a meteorological "break" took place. Shortly after dawn, the Statue of Liberty revealed herself above the low fog lying across the Bay. She glowed brilliantly as the sun struck her, and for a while seemed to be standing on a pedestal of cloud.[60] Then a mild breeze whisked the fog away, and New York awoke to Indian summer. The streets, washed clean by weeks of rain, steamed dry in the warmth, and the people turned out en masse to vote.[61]

Peace and good humor prevailed around the ballot boxes. Since the taverns were shut, and the sunshine luxurious, thousands spent the entire day out-of-doors. Rumors as to how the voting was going flashed with near-telegraphic speed from one street corner to another.[62]

As early as 2:00 P.M., secret messages came to Republican headquarters that George's vote was going to be very high and Roosevelt's very low. While the candidate sat innocently by, the party bosses shot back their secret reply: Republicans must vote for Hewitt. At all costs George must be stopped.[63]

The secret, of course, could not long be kept from Roosevelt. His emotions on discovering that he was being "sold out"—even for honorable political reasons—can be imagined. But he maintained a good-humored front, and tried to cheer his drooping staff by telling funny stories. About six o'clock he went out into the bonfire-lit night for dinner with friends. He seemed as buoyant as ever when he returned two hours later. By then it was plain that his defeat had become a rout.[64] The only good news to come his way that evening was a telegram from Boston, announcing that Henry Cabot Lodge had been elected to the Congress of the United States. He shouted with joy, and sent his congratulations by return wire:

AM MORE DELIGHTED THAN I CAN SAY. DO COME ON THURSDAY.

AM BADLY DEFEATED. WORSE EVEN THAN I FEARED.

THEODORE ROOSEVELT.[65]

AFTER A LATE BREAKFAST next morning, Roosevelt went back to his headquarters and found it taken over by "a small army of scrub women." But he seemed reluctant to leave, and sat around until a lone newspaperman poked his head in through the door. "I thought I'd look in to see what they had done with the corpse." Roosevelt responded with a most uncorpselike grin.[66]

By rights the final returns, as headlined that day, should have made him wince. Hewitt had scored 90,552; George, 68,110; Roosevelt, 60,435.[67] These figures were unassailable: the polls had been rigorously supervised. The turnout had been prodigious—20,000 more ballots were cast than during last year's gubernatorial election—yet Roosevelt's votes were 20 percent *fewer* than the Republican total on that occasion. To compound his humiliation, he found that he had run far behind every state and city candidate on the Republican ticket, including those for minor posts on the Judiciary and Board of Aldermen. The *Post* sadistically pointed out that "Mr. Roosevelt's vote is lower than any other Republican vote in the last six years."[68]

The main reason for his poor showing was, of course, the Republican defection to Hewitt, which he estimated at 15,000, and the Democrats at 10,000. What must have rankled was the fact that this defection took place not in the sleazy wards of the East and West Sides (where he proved surprisingly popular) but in the wealthier "brownstone district" he had always regarded as his natural constituency. "I have been fairly defeated," he told a *Tribune* reporter later in the day, as he watched portraits of himself being ripped off the wall and thrown away. "But to tell the truth I am not disappointed at the result."[69]

The evidence is that he was—deeply so.[70] This third political defeat in just over two years became one of those memories which he ever afterward found too painful to dwell on. It rates just one sentence in his *Autobiography.* He talked often in later years of his various campaigns, but that of 1886 was rarely, if ever, mentioned. Once, when he was telling one of his "gory stories," about killing a bear, somebody sympathized out loud for the unfortunate animal: "He must have been as badly used up as if he had just run for Mayor of New York." Roosevelt overreacted. "What do you mean?" he roared, slamming his fists down on the table. It was some time before he could recover himself.[71]

ON THE WHOLE, the press of the day treated him kindly. Republican papers noted that if there had not been a panic swing to Hewitt, Roosevelt would have won. The opposition expressed admiration for his courage against impossible odds. Few editorials displayed any contempt. Even the *Daily Graphic,* which had often poked cruel fun at him, quoted the consolatory lines,

Men may rise on stepping stones
Of their dead selves to higher things . . .

and added: "Reflect on this Tennysonian thought, Mr. Roosevelt, and may your slumbers be disturbed only by dreams of a nomination for the Governorship, or perhaps the Presidency in the impending by and by."[72]

A "Mr. and Miss Merrifield" sneaked up the gangplank of the Cunard liner *Etruria* early on Saturday morning, 6 November. No social reporters were prowling the decks at that hour, or it might have been noticed that the couple bore a marked resemblance to Theodore and Bamie Roosevelt. They had sat up all night writing announcement notes of the engagement and forthcoming wedding; by the time those notes reached their destinations, the *Etruria* would be heading out to sea.[73]

Nobody bothered them that day, and the great ship sailed on schedule at 1:00 P.M.[74] It was not until next morning that a fellow passenger penetrated their disguise. He was a pale young Englishman who approached them with a combination of courtliness and inquisitiveness which they ever afterward associated with the White Rabbit in *Alice*. Might "Miss Merrifield" by any chance be Miss Roosevelt? Bamie, "being well out of sight of land," admitted she was. The young man promptly introduced himself, in the accents of Eton, Oxford, and the Foreign Office, as Cecil Arthur Spring Rice, former assistant private secretary to Lord Rosebery. He said that he was on his way home to England, after spending some "leave" with a brother in Canada.[75]

Spring Rice, generally known as "Springy" or "Sprice," was a born diplomat, and would soon become a professional one. He had a particular way with women. His sharp eye and social instinct had been honed in the best drawing rooms; he invariably picked out and cultivated the most important person in any place, whether it be a Tuscan hill-town or the heaving deck of a transatlantic steamer. Roosevelt, who (despite his ludicrous attempt to look anonymous) emitted an unmistakable glow of power and good breeding, was just such a person. Somehow Spring Rice had found out, through mutual friends in New York, that he would be on board, and had obtained letters of introduction to Bamie.[76]

The Englishman's charm was, in any case, such that he could make friends without any conventional formalities. Roosevelt fell victim to it, while beaming his own charm in return—apparently with even greater effect. Spring Rice was to be, for the rest of his life, one of Roosevelt's most ardent—if amused—admirers. Not only was this American cultured, talkative, and well-connected, he had a certain raw physical force, and a sense of personal direction (for all his recent rejection at the polls) that transcended Spring Rice's own petty ambitions at the Foreign Office. Although Roosevelt was only four months older, he seemed to have lived at least a decade longer. Here was a man worth introducing to his friends at the Savile Club.

By the time the *Etruria* arrived in Liverpool on 13 November, "Springy" had agreed to act as Roosevelt's best man.[77]

LOOKING BACK on the eighteen days he spent in London and the Home Counties before his wedding on 2 December, Roosevelt said he felt "as if I were living in one of Thackeray's novels."[78] Romantically foggy weather added a dreamlike quality to his adventures.[79] Spring Rice's connections afforded him easy entry into British society: he was "treated like a prince . . . put down at the Athenaeum and the other swell clubs . . . had countless invitations to go down in the country and hunt or shoot." For every invitation he accepted there were at least three he turned down—some, such as lunch with the Duke of Westminster or weekends with Lords North and Caernarvon, with real regret. "But I was anxious to meet some of the intellectual men, such as Goschen, John Morley, Bryce, Shaw-Lefèvre . . . I have dined or lunched with them all."[80] So busy was he that he found no time to pay his respects to the American Ambassador, and that gentleman let his displeasure be known.[81]

But Roosevelt had his priorities. No doubt he took frequent strolls through Mayfair to the Bucklands Hotel on Brook Street, where Edith was staying with her mother and sister. No doubt she returned these calls, and sat with him in his rooms in Brown's Hotel on Dover Street; here they discovered "how cosy and comfortable one could be, with a small economical handful of coal in the grate and heavy fog outside."[82]

"You have no idea how sweet Edith is," Roosevelt wrote Corinne in a defensive tone wholly new to him. "I don't think even I had known how wonderfully *good* and unselfish she was; she is naturally reserved and finds it especially hard to express her feelings on paper."[83] He had never had to explain his first wife to anybody, but then Alice Lee had needed no explanation. The complicated, mysterious person who was now preparing to marry him had depths and secrets and silences, like this very fog enshrouding London; it would be years before she disclosed herself fully to him, and even then he might not altogether understand her.

Visibility was so bad on the morning of 2 December that link-bearers had to be hired to guide Roosevelt's carriage to St. George's, Hanover Square. Bamie, arriving separately, found the church itself full of fog. She could not see her brother at the far end of the nave, much less the altar. When she moved into close range she noticed that Spring Rice had, for inscrutable reasons, persuaded him to wear bright orange gloves.[84]

The church was almost empty. Even if hundreds had been in the congregation, the fog would have muffled their whispering. This wedding, unlike Theodore's first, was to be quiet—"as the wedding of a defeated mayoralty candidate should be."[85]

He stood there alone with his orange gloves, waiting for Edith to walk out of the mists behind him.

INTERLUDE

INTERLUDE:

Winter of the Blue Snow, 1886–1887

THE HAZE WHICH HAD HUNG over the Badlands all autumn rose to high altitudes in late October, causing weird "dogs" to glow around the sun and the moon.[1] Then, late on the afternoon of 13 November, it turned white and began to sink again, very slowly, cushioned on the dead still air. Only when it touched the Elkhorn bottom, and sent an icy sting into the nostrils of the cattle, did the whiteness prove to be snow—snow powdered so fine and soft that it hovered for hours before settling.[2]

That night the temperature fell below zero, and a sudden gale came down from Canada, blowing curtains of thicker snow before it. By morning the drifts were piling up six or seven feet deep, and the air was so charged with snow that the cattle coughed to breathe it. Some cows stupidly faced north until the blizzard plugged their noses and throats, asphyxiating them.[3]

The beavers, meanwhile, snuggled down philosophically in their burrows. Thanks to six weeks of overtime chewing, they had cut and stored enough willow-brush to last them several seasons. They could not hear the wind, but as the mud around them froze it

"Their hoofs were locked in ice, and they froze like so many statues."

Dying cow, December 1886. Painted by Charles Russell.

resonated with the growling of ice in the river. When the growling stopped they knew that the Little Missouri had glaciated, and that wolves and lynxes were now patrolling it.[4]

All through November the snow continued to fall—whirling, sifting, billowing across the prairie as rhythmically as waves in the ocean. Lines of violet shadow separated each "roller" from the next. Ever afterward pioneers would call this the Winter of the Blue Snow,[5] the worst in frontier history.

One day in mid-December there was a brief spell of Indian summer. The temperature jumped to 50 degrees Fahrenheit, melting the snow to a depth of six inches. But then subzero weather returned, and the slush became a slabby crust of ice. Cattle hungry for buried grass had to gnaw through it until their muzzles were raw and swollen. Sometimes the crust would split beneath a very heavy steer, and he would drop through it on all fours, lacerating his legs and bleeding to death in the soft snow beneath.[6]

It grew colder and colder. On Christmas Day the mercury stood at minus 35 degrees; on New Year's Day it was minus 41, and still sinking.[7] The first month of the year is traditionally cruel in Dakota—local Indians call it "Moon of Cold-Exploding Trees"—and January 1887 proved to be the coldest in the memory of any man, white or red. Blustery storms alternated with periods of aching calm, but the snowfall rarely ceased. Soon the prairie was covered to a depth of three or four feet. While the lower snow compacted, the powdery flakes on top responded to the slightest breeze. They rolled across the flat country like fog, and on reaching the Badlands tumbled slowly down into cuts and coulees. There they settled in great drifts which piled up, a hundred feet or more, to prairie level, making the broken country seem as smooth as any plain. Ranches—especially the dugout variety—disappeared overnight, with their owners asleep inside them. Thousands of cattle were buried alive.[8]

Beasts nimble enough to escape suffocation emerged wild-eyed on the open range, and began to search for herbage in places where the wind had kept the snow fairly thin. But last summer's drought, aggravated by overstocking, had reduced the grass to stubble. The starving cattle were forced to tear it out and eat the frozen, sandy roots. Then they browsed the bitter sagebrush, gnawing every shred of bark off until the twigs were naked, finally chomping the twigs themselves. When there was nothing left but stumps, the cattle huddled along the railroad, waiting for dropped garbage, and staring at every passing train as if about to stampede aboard.[9]

Then, on 28 January, a blizzard struck which made all previous storms that winter seem trivial. "For seventy-two hours," wrote one survivor, "it seemed as if all the world's ice from Time's beginnings had come on a wind which howled and screamed with the fury of demons."[10] Children wandering out of doors froze to death within minutes, bent by the wind into the fetal position. Women in isolated ranches went mad; men shot themselves and each other. Many cattle exposed on the prairie were too weak to withstand the gale: they simply blew over and died. Others kept their footing, until their hoofs were locked in ice, and they froze like so many statues. Dogies from Texas and yearlings from Iowa, who had not yet experienced the savagery of a northern winter, perished almost without exception, as did bulls and cows heavy with calf. Older range steers, whose coats were shaggier and whose flesh was tougher, survived through February, but they became so mad with cold and hunger that they invaded the streets of Medora, and began to eat tar paper from the sides of the buildings.[11] Townspeople had to nail planks across their windows to prevent desperate steers from thrusting their heads through the glass. Every night the streets echoed with agonized bellowing. There was nothing to do but watch the carcasses pile up in vacant lots, until the snow mercifully shrouded them from view.

At last, on 2 March, when it seemed the Badlands could not possibly hold any more snow, a balmy chinook stole in from the west. Sunshine burned away the haze, and revealed a sky whose bright blue color, coming after a hundred days of monochrome visibility, was a shock to the eyes. Within hours the white landscape began to twinkle with thaw. Rivulets trickled down the slopes, carving cracks in the ice, exposing bits of yellow earth. Gullies and washouts flowed into each other, then sought out the creeks leading down to the river. The air was filled with the sound of running water.[12] About the middle of the month it became a roar. Lincoln Lang hurried to a vantage point near the river, and saw a sight which haunted him through life.

A flood-wave was hurtling down the valley, so full of heavy debris that it battered the cottonwoods like reeds. At first Lincoln could not make out what the debris was: then he understood. "Countless carcasses of cattle [were] going down with the ice, rolling over and over as they went, so that at times all four of the stiffened legs of a carcass would point skyward, as it turned under the impulsion of the swiftly moving current and the grinding ice-cakes. Now and then a carcass would become pinched between two ice-floes, and either go down entirely or else be forced out on top of the ice, to be rafted along . . . carcasses continuously seemed to be going down while others kept bobbing up at one point or another to replace them."[13]

This river of death roared on for days, and still the carcasses jostled and spun. Ranchers estimated their numbers in the thousands, then tens of thousands, then gave up guessing in despair. When the last drifts of snow melted away, and the flood abated, cowboys went out onto the range to look for survivors. Bill Merrifield was among them. "The first day I rode out," he reported, "I never saw a live animal."[14]

In the wake of the cowboys trundled a ghoulish convoy of wagons, not seen in the Badlands since the buffalo massacre of 1883. The wagons were driven by bone pickers in the employ of fertilizer companies. For such men alone the winter had brought wealth. Patiently they began to sort and stack the skeletons of what had been one of the greatest range herds in the world.[15]

Part Two
1887–1901

CHAPTER 15

The Literary Feller

Sing me a song divine
With a sword in every line!

ON 28 MARCH 1887, New York newspapers headlined the return of Theodore Roosevelt and his "charming young wife" to the United States, after a fifteen-week tour of England, France, and Italy.[1] Every reporter commented on how well Roosevelt looked, in contrast to the drained and defeated mayoral candidate of last fall. His face was "bronzed," even "handsome," and he gave off "a rich glow of health" as he strode down the gangplank of the *Etruria*. A certain bearish heaviness was noticeable in his physique (he had put on considerable weight in European restaurants), and several friends were seen to wince as he exuberantly hugged them tight.[2]

Edith's health was rather more delicate than her husband's. In Paris, about halfway through their trip, she had begun to feel "the reverse of brightly," and Theodore had hinted in his next letter home that a honeymoon baby was on its way.[3] This had not stopped them accepting a flood of fashionable invitations during their last weeks in London. There had been Parliamentary visits with members of both Houses (Roosevelt remarking sourly, of some Irish Parnellites, that he had met them before—"in the New York legisla-

"A longing for nobler game soon overwhelmed him."

The Meadowbrook Hunt meeting at Sagamore Hill in the 1880s.

ture"); lunches, dinners, and teas with a variety of British intellectuals; supper with the Prime Minister, Lord Salisbury; and, by way of climax, a sumptuous weekend at Wroxton Abbey in Warwickshire, where the honeymooners slept in the Duke of Clarence's bed and were waited on by powder-wigged servants.[4]

"I have had a roaring good time," Roosevelt told the New York press. Pacing up and down, and tugging excitedly at his pince-nez, he said how glad he was, nevertheless, to be home. Having met "all the great political leaders," and made "as complete a study as I could of English politics," he was convinced that the American governmental system was superior. "Why, Mr. Roosevelt?" asked a *Herald* reporter. "Because a written constitution is better than an unwritten one. Their whole system seemed clumsy. It might do well enough for a social club, but not for a great legislative body."

In answer to the inevitable questions about his political plans, Roosevelt said he had none—at present. "I intend to divide my time between literature and ranching."[5]

HAD HE OPENED HIS MAIL from Medora before talking to the press that afternoon, he might well have dropped the latter option. Vague news of the Dakota blizzards had reached him in Europe, but the true extent of the devastation had become apparent only during his return voyage. Even now, with the spring thaw still going on, Merrifield and Ferris were unable to tell him how many cattle had been lost. They urged him to hurry West and judge the situation for himself.

Roosevelt was plainly anxious to leave right away, but he had to spend at least a week in New York with his wife and sister and "sweet Baby Lee." It was a period of difficult adjustment among them. The decision had been made in Europe that Bamie might not, after all, keep her adored foster daughter.[6] Before remarrying, Theodore had more than once reassured Bamie that the child would stay with her, "I of course paying the expenses."[7] But when Edith heard about the arrangement, she had reacted with surprising vehemence. Little Alice was *her* child now, she insisted, and would live at Sagamore Hill, where she belonged. In a rare display of helplessness,

Roosevelt had thrown up his hands. "We can decide it all when we meet."[8]

What was decided, in those waning days of March, was that to ease the pain of parting, Baby Lee would remain with Bamie for another month. Meanwhile her father would go West, and Edith visit relatives in Philadelphia. Upon their return to New York at the end of April, they would take over Bamie's new house at 689 Madison Avenue, while its mistress went South for a short vacation. By the time she got back in late May the Roosevelts would have opened Sagamore Hill, and they could all move out there for the summer. Together they would spend June and July supervising the delicate task of transferring the child's affections from aunt to stepmother.[9] Not until August, therefore, need Bamie face the prospect of resuming her lonely spinster life.

Bamie accepted that Edith's instinct was the right one—she had never felt entirely secure in her surrogate role—but relations between the two women would never be the same now that they were sisters-in-law. For all their determined sweetness to each other, neither could forget that Bamie had nursed little Alice through her first years of life,[10] and that Bamie had been the first mistress of Sagamore Hill. Corinne, too, was to learn that she now had a formidable rival to her brother's affections and that access to him would henceforth be strictly controlled.[11] It was an ironic reversal for someone who, not so long ago, had served as duenna between Edith and the teenage Theodore.

Two welcome guests at 689 helped smooth things over while negotiations over Baby Lee went on: Congressman Henry Cabot Lodge and "Springy" Spring Rice, now Secretary of the British Legation in Washington. Roosevelt seized on their masculine company with some relief, and lost no time in returning Spring Rice's hospitality of the previous November. The Englishman became an honorary member of the Century Club, which he found as intellectually exclusive as the Savile, and was introduced to an enormous circle of Rooseveltian acquaintances. One morning Whitelaw Reid, the immensely rich and influential owner of the *New York Tribune,* invited the three friends to a political breakfast in his mansion. There, in a magnificent dining hall, paneled with inlaid wood and embossed leather, Roosevelt, Lodge, and Reid gravely discussed whether or not James G. Blaine should again be nominated for the Presidency in 1888. Spring Rice listened in utter fascination. "It was the first real piece of political wire-pulling I had come across," he wrote home afterward. "I am getting quite excited over it."[12]

Not until 4 April was Roosevelt free to go West and find out exactly how poor he was.

HE ALREADY HAD a fairly accurate idea. Or rather, Edith had. That level-headed lady knew that her husband, whatever his other talents, was a financial imbecile.[13] Soon after the wedding she had gone over his affairs with him and discovered that, on the basis of last year's figures alone, they should "think very seriously of closing Sagamore Hill." Then had come the first reports of Dakota blizzards, followed by her attacks of morning sickness. Clearly, if they were to rear their family at Oyster Bay, they would have to "cut down tremendously along the whole line."[14] Roosevelt must learn to live within his income for a change, and begin to pay off his debts. He must sell his enormously expensive hunting-horse, grow his own crops and fodder (for Sagamore Hill was a potentially profitable farm), and stop running the house as a summer resort for friends with large appetites, and thirsts to match.[15]

As to his cattle business, the winter's toll was still a matter of guesswork. Roosevelt could only hope that enough cows would survive to produce at least a token number of healthy calves. In the years ahead he would sell as many beeves as possible for whatever price he could get, and so slowly reduce his losses. Given enough time—and no more freak weather—he might be able to dispose of his entire stock and save most of his $85,000 investment.

But now, as he rode once more out of Medora into the devastated Badlands, all such optimism vanished. "The land was a mere barren waste; not a green thing could be seen; the dead grass eaten off till the country looked as if it had been shaved with a razor." Occasionally, in some sheltered spot, he would come across "a band of gaunt, hollow-flanked cattle feebly cropping the sparse, dry pasturage, too listless to move out of the way." Blackened carcasses lay piled up against the bluffs: he counted twenty-three in a single patch of brushwood. Here and there a dead cow perched grotesquely in the branches of a cottonwood tree, the high snow upon which it once stood having melted away.[16]

Of the once-teeming Elkhorn and Maltese Cross herds, only "a skinny sorry-looking crew" of some few hundred seemed to have survived.[17] He could not find out exactly how many had died until after the spring roundup.

But the roundup was never held. The Little Missouri Stockmen's Association, meeting on 16 April with Roosevelt in the chair, decided that losses were too heavy to merit a general mobilization. There were so few cattle left on the range, ranchers might as well sort them out individually. One search party was dispatched to Standing Rock, in the hope that some thousands of cattle may have migrated south, and returned after three weeks, with exactly two steers.[18]

No official figures, therefore, survive as to the effect of the winter of 1886–87 on the Badlands cattle industry as a whole, nor on Roosevelt in particular. Estimates of the average loss sustained by local ranchers range from 75 percent to 85 percent.[19] Gregor Lang, who began the winter with three thousand head, ended it with less than four hundred. Thanks to the thickly wooded bottoms on both of Roosevelt's properties, his loss was probably about 65 percent. Even so, it was catastrophic.[20] "I am bluer than indigo about the cattle," he wrote Bamie from Medora. "It is even worse than I feared. I wish I was sure I would lose no more than half the money ($80,000) I invested here.[21] I am planning to get out of it." And on 20 April, after attending another gloomy stockmen's meeting in Montana, he wrote Lodge, "The losses are crippling. For the first time I have been utterly unable to enjoy a visit to my ranch. I shall be glad to get home."[22]

THE SPRING AIR WAS WARM, and blades of grass had begun to stipple the bare hills, when Roosevelt left Medora a few days later. But an air of wintry lifelessness still hung over the little cow-town. Already most of its citizens had departed to seek their fortunes elsewhere. Arthur Packard had abandoned the *Bad Lands Cowboy,* and his office was now a fire-blackened ruin. E. G. Paddock had moved to Dickinson, taking the old Pyramid Park Hotel with him on a flatcar. "Blood-Raw John" Warns offered no more "choice Western cuisine" in his Oyster Grotto, and Genial Jim's Billiard Bar had run dry of Conversation Juice. Sad clouds of steam still floated out of Yach Wah's Chinese Laundry, but he, too, would soon pack up his washboards and go.[23]

Most symbolic of all was the shuttered-up bulk of the Marquis de Morès's slaughterhouse. Its doors had closed in November 1886, never to reopen. Even when Medora was booming, the Marquis had been unable to run his giant scheme at a profit. The supply of local steers was simply insufficient, and rangy, refrigerated beef had never appealed to the Eastern consumer.[24] Impatiently shrugging off an estimated loss of $1 million, de Morès had gone off to dig a goldmine in Montana. When last seen—heading East as Roosevelt came West—he had been planning to build a railroad across China.[25]

In less than two years, Medora would become a ghost town, while Dickinson flourished, and a checkerboard of small, fenced-in ranches spread west across the prairie.[26] Roosevelt had foreseen the destruction of Dakota's open-range cattle industry in *Hunting Trips of a Ranchman,*[27] but he had not expected it to come so soon, nor that Nature would conspire to accelerate the process.

Although his Dakota venture had impoverished him, he was nevertheless rich in nonmonetary dividends. He had gone West sickly, foppish, and racked with personal despair; during his time there he had built a massive body, repaired his soul, and learned to live on equal terms with men poorer and rougher than himself. He had broken horses with Hashknife Simpson, joined in discordant choruses to the accompaniment of Fiddlin' Joe's violin, discussed homicidal techniques with Bat Masterson, shared greasy blankets with Modesty Carter, shown Bronco Charlie Miller how to "gentle" a horse, and told Hell-Roaring Bill Jones to shut his foul mouth.[28] These men, in turn, had found him to be the leader they craved in that lawless land, a superior being, who, paradoxically, did not make them feel inferior.[29] They loved him so much they would follow him anywhere, to death if necessary—as some eventually did.[30] They and their kind, multiplied seven millionfold across the country, became his natural constituency.[31] "If it had not been for my years in North Dakota," he said long afterward, "I never would have become President of the United States."[32]

ROOSEVELT'S ASSERTION, on stepping off the S.S. *Etruria,* that he had no political plans "at present" impressed nobody. Yet for once the protestation was true. With a Democratic President in Washington, a Democratic Governor in Albany, and a Democratic Mayor in New York, his prospects for any kind of office were nil, at least through the election of 1888. And there was no guarantee that the Republican party would fare any better then than it had in 1884.

Every day saw a further strengthening of the opposition's grip upon every lever of government.[33] Quietly, ruthlessly, the Civil Service was being purged. Cleveland had promised, upon assuming office, that only those Republicans who were "offensive, indolent, and corrupt" would be dismissed. But the President's aides saw fit to interpret such adjectives loosely: already two-thirds of the entire federal bureaucracy had been replaced.[34]

Although Cleveland was as stiff as ever in public, and openly contemptuous of the press, he had to a certain degree become popular. Labor respected him as the most industrious Chief Executive in living memory. Often as not his was the last light burning on Pennsylvania Avenue, as many a night watchman could testify. Capital admired his conservative attitude to all legislation, from multimillion-dollar appropriations to private pension bills; every Cleveland veto (and there were literally hundreds)[35] meant more wealth in the nation's coffers. Meanwhile that largest and most powerful voting bloc in America, Parlor Sentiment, had canonized the President for his sudden marriage to a pretty debutante half his age—and about one-third of his weight.[36] Mrs. Cleveland was now the country's sweetheart, and would undoubtedly prove a formidable campaign asset in 1888.

Indeed, at this midway point in Cleveland's Administration, the Democratic party seemed assured of another six years in power. For an impatient and idealistic young Republican like Roosevelt, the spring of 1887 was a time of complete frustration.

The message was clear: he must once again forget about politics and seek surcease in literature. For the foreseeable future, he would have to earn a living with his pen.

ONE FINAL POLITICAL HURRAH was permitted him, at Delmonico's Restaurant on 11 May, and he made the most of it. The occasion was the Inaugural Banquet of the New York Federal Club. This organization had been founded in the New Year by some of Roosevelt's mayoral campaign supporters, with the object of keeping Reform Republicanism alive. Its membership consisted largely of young "dudes" from his old brownstone district.[37] They were men he had, on the whole, grown away from, but he could not ignore their support, nor their invitation to be guest of honor.

Originally the dinner was planned as a semiprivate affair of some fifty covers, but when it was announced in the papers an unusual number of ticket applications poured in from Republicans all over the state. The event, remarked *The New York Times,* "bade fair to assume as wide political significance as any this year."[38] A limit was set at 150 admissions, but when Roosevelt arrived at Delmonico's he found over 200 guests sitting at six lavishly appointed tables. The company was, in the words of a *Sun* reporter, "brilliant and distinguished enough to have been a compliment to a veteran statesman."[39]

Roosevelt was introduced after the coffee and cigars as "the man who, had the Republicans stood to their guns last fall, would now be the Mayor of this city." Loud cheers greeted him as he stood up—looking, as he always did when preparing to speak, grim, resolute, tense as a bundle of wire.[40] The knowledge that Edith was watching from the Ladies' Gallery no doubt made him extra conscious of his dignity.

If his fellow diners expected a relaxed and humorous speech—for Charles Delmonico had not stinted on the champagne, and they were in a convivial mood—Roosevelt soon disillusioned them. He began by remarking sardonically that during the mayoralty campaign he had been praised as a party faithful; now, however, he was regarded as a member "of the extreme left." (Here there was some uneasy laughter among senior Republicans.) He proceeded to attack such a wide variety of targets that his listeners must have wondered if there was anything in the State of the Union that he approved of. President Cleveland was castigated for his clumsy English and "sheer hypocrisy" in the cause of Civil Service Reform;[41] the Independent press for its "thoroughly feminine" waywardness and "high-pitched screechings"; the Immigration Department for its unrestricted admission of "moral paupers and lunatics"; the Anti-Poverty Society for being "about as effective as an Anti-Gravitation Society"; anarchists and socialists for inciting labor demonstrators to violence ("there is but one answer to be made to the dynamite bomb, and that can best be made by the Winchester rifle"). For nearly an hour Roosevelt's voice grated through the cigar-smoke. Again and again he hurled insults at the "hysterical and mendacious party of mugwumps," even managing, somewhat anachronistically, to include Presidents Tyler and Johnson in that number "—and they were the most contemptible Presidents we have ever had."

He sat down to considerable applause, although the faces of his listeners registered rather more shock than approval—as if they had been witnessing a bloody prizefight, and were relieved the punishment was over. For all the savagery of Roosevelt's language, his personal force awed the gathering. Chauncey Depew rose to make some flattering follow-up remarks. "Buffalo Bill said to me in the utmost confidence, 'Theodore Roosevelt is the only New York dude that has got the making of a man in him.' " Depew waggishly announced that the evening's other scheduled speakers had all submitted their manuscripts to Roosevelt for checking, "so that when he runs for President no case of Burchard will interfere."[42] This was a reference to the unfortunate preacher whose gaffe had cost James G. Blaine the 1884 election.

Waggish or not, Depew was the first person ever to suggest in public that Roosevelt might be harboring presidential ambitions.[43] The young man's speech made nationwide headlines, and the question of his future was taken up seriously by several Republican newspapers. The *Harrisburg Telegraph* recommended him for Vice-President in 1888, on a ticket headed by Governor Foraker of Ohio;[44] the *Baltimore American* went so far as to nominate him for

President. "Mr. ROOSEVELT," the paper commented, "has a stainless reputation and great personal magnetism. He is a tireless worker, an advocate of real reform in politics, and his speech before the Federal Club fairly reflects his ability to handle the political puzzles with which both parties must deal next year. It may be that the Federal Club have builded wiser than they intended by thus prominently drawing the attention of the country to this vigorous young Republican."[45]

Few out-of-town editors, evidently, realized that Roosevelt was still only twenty-eight, and constitutionally debarred from the greatness they would thrust upon him. The *New York Sun* felt obliged to point out that, "owing to circumstances beyond his control, he will not be able to take the office of President of the United States before 1897."[46]

Major newspapers, of course, paid no attention to such preposterous endorsements. They were (with the single exception of Whitelaw Reid's *Tribune*) harshly disapproving of Roosevelt's "vehement chatter."[47] He was "an immature and poorly posted thinker," wasting "a good deal of breath which he may want someday" on "strained criticism" of the government.[48] Even the *Times,* hitherto his most fervent supporter, admitted the speech had been "most unfortunate and disagreeable."[49] E. L. Godkin of the *Post* wrote that the Republican party no longer had any use for Theodore Roosevelt. "It was a mistake ever to take him seriously as a politician."[50] And on 25 May, *Puck* published a final valedictory:

> Be happy, Mr. Roosevelt, be happy while you may. You are young—yours is the time of roses—the time of illusions . . . You have heard of Pitt, of Alexander Hamilton, of Randolph Churchill, and of other men who were young and yet who, so to speak, got there just the same. Bright visions float before your eyes of what the Party can and may do for you. We wish you a gradual and gentle awakening . . . You are not the timber of which Presidents are made.

THE SPRING OF 1887 settled down on Oyster Bay. Bloodroot and mayflower whitened the slopes around Cove Neck; on

Sagamore Hill, the saplings were feathery green against the sky, noticeably taller than last year. Two woolly horses began to plow the fields behind the house.[51]

Inside, Theodore and Edith unhooked shutters, pulled dust-sheets off beds and sofas, and distributed the latest batch of hunting-trophies from Dakota (already the walls were forested with antlers, and snarling bear-jaws caught the unwary foot). They crammed some very big pieces of oak furniture into the very small dining room, and Edith, insisting that at least one corner of the house should be allowed to look feminine, arranged some rather more delicate furniture in the west parlor.[52]

Theodore's own retreat, which none could visit without his permission,[53] was a pleasantly cluttered room on the top floor, full of guns and sporting books and photographs of his ranches. There was a desk rammed against a blind wall, so that when he sat down to work he would not be distracted by the sight of Long Island Sound brimming blue in the window. Here, sometime early in June, he dipped a steel pen into an inkwell and began to write his fourth book. By the time the nib needed recharging he was already 135 years back in the past, in the New York City of his forebears—

> a thriving little trading town, whose people in summer suffered much from the mosquitoes that came back with the cows when they were driven home at nightfall for milking; while from the locusts and water-beeches that lined the pleasant, quiet streets, the tree-frogs sang so shrilly through the long, hot evenings that a man in speaking could hardly make himself heard.[54]

GOUVERNEUR MORRIS, WHICH Roosevelt worked on steadily throughout the summer of 1887, was a companion biography to his *Thomas Hart Benton* in the American Statesmen series. The critical success of the earlier book had prompted Houghton Mifflin to commission another study of a neglected historical figure. Only one life of Morris had hitherto been published—a ponderous tome now half a century out of date. It was time, the editors felt, for their breezy young author to blow the dust off Morris's letters and diaries, and subject the great New Yorker to a fresh scrutiny.[55]

With his powdered wig and peg-leg, his coruscating wit and picaresque adventures, Morris (1752–1816) was a biographer's dream. There was about him, Roosevelt remarked, "that 'touch of the purple' which is always so strongly attractive."[56] Well-born, well-bred, charming, literate, and widely traveled, he had been a strong believer in centralized government, an aggressive moralist, and a passionate patriot. All these characteristics were shared, to varying degrees, by Roosevelt himself. Yet, as with Benton, there were enough antipathetic elements to keep the portrait objective.

Unfortunately a major obstacle loomed early in Roosevelt's research. "The Morrises won't let me see the old gentleman's papers at any price," he complained to Cabot Lodge. "I am in rather a quandary."[57] Being in no position to pay back his advance, he resolved to make what he could of public documents. Fortunately these were copious,[58] and the complete manuscript was ready for the printer by 4 September.[59]

As HISTORY, the first five chapters of *Gouverneur Morris* are adequate but unrewarding; as biography they are tedious. Roosevelt's lack of family material forces him to weave the thread of Morris's early life (1752–86) into a general tapestry of the Revolutionary period. The resultant cloth is drab, for he seems determined, as in *The Naval War of 1812,* to avoid any hint of romantic color. Only a couple of pages devoted to Morris as the founder of the national coinage are worth reading for their lucid treatment of a complex subject.[60] Matters become more interesting in chapter 6, "The Formation of the National Constitution." Now the author has access to official transcripts, and can ponder the actual speeches of Washington, Franklin, Hamilton, Madison, and the two Morrises (Gouverneur and Robert). "Rarely in the world's history," he concludes, "has there been a deliberative body which contained so many remarkable men."[61]

Morris is presented as the Constitution's most brilliant intellect, as well as its dominant conservative force. Yet the narrative clearly shows why he was doomed never to rise to the first rank of statesmen:

> His keen, masterful mind, his far-sightedness, and the force and subtlety of his reasoning were all marred by his incurable cynicism and deep-rooted distrust of all mankind. He throughout appears as *advocatus diaboli;* he puts the lowest interpretation upon every act, and frankly avows his disbelief in all generous and unselfish motives . . . Morris championed a strong national government, wherein he was right; but he also championed a system of class representation, leaning toward aristocracy, wherein he was wrong.[62]

Nevertheless Morris is commended for his "thoroughgoing nationalism," and for his prophecy of an emergent America whose glories would make the grandest empire of Europe seem "but a bauble" in comparison. Roosevelt also praises his early espousal of the doctrine of emancipation. There are flashes of dry humor, as in the following explanation of Morris's acquisitiveness: "He considered the preservation of property as being the distinguishing object of civilization, as liberty was sufficiently guaranteed even by savagery."[63]

The book comes brilliantly to life in its penultimate section, describing Morris's ten years in London and Paris, 1789–98, and his not-so-neutral participation in the major events of the French Revolution. Roosevelt was doubtless inspired by his own recent stays in those same cities, and his prose sparkles with true Gallic *éclat.* Chapters 7 through 11 are the best stretch of pure biography he ever wrote. Morris's courtly flirtations with Mmes. de Staël, de Flahant, and the Duchesse d'Orléans; his plot to smuggle Louis XVI and Marie Antoinette out of Paris after the fall of the Bastille; the bloody riots of 10 August 1792, when he was the only foreign diplomat left in Paris, and gave sanctuary to veterans of the War of American Independence—all these episodes read like Dumas. Only the occasional jarring reference to municipal corruption in New York City, and sideswipes at the "helpless" Jefferson and that "filthy little atheist" Thomas Paine remind us of the true identity of the writer.[64]

The biography ends with two brief chapters tracing Morris's decline into cantankerous old age. There are hints of certain "treasonous" tendencies during these "discreditable and unworthy" last years (Morris had been part of a Federalist group contemplating secession from the Union in 1812). Yet, in a final-page summary of the whole life, Roosevelt is willing to bestow his highest praise upon Gouverneur Morris. "He was essentially a strong man, and he was American through and through."[65]

REVIEWS WERE NEGATIVE when *Morris* came out the following spring. The *Book Buyer* felt that there had been insufficient character analysis, and complained of some "rather dry" stretches of prose. *The New York Times* commented, "Mr. Roosevelt has no style as style is understood," but allowed that "his meaning is never to be mistaken." The *Dial,* while praising him for "an exceedingly interesting narrative, artistic in its selection, forcible in its pungent expression," called his scholarship "rather more brilliant than sound," and said that his irreverent treatment of the American Revolution, not to mention certain "slurs" upon eminent men of the past, were "beneath the gravity of historical writing."[66] It was generally agreed that *Gouverneur Morris* was clever, patchy, and superficial—a verdict which posterity can only endorse.

ROOSEVELT'S "STRAITENED FINANCES" made the summer of 1887 an uneventful one.[67] He was kept from being too restless by the intensity of his work on *Morris* (the 92,000-word manuscript was researched and written in little over three months). Sometimes he took a day off to row his pregnant wife to a secluded spot in the marshes, where they would picnic and read to each other.[68] For other recreation, he chopped wood, played tennis (winning the local doubles championship and promptly splurging his share of the "cup" on a new Winchester), taught himself the rudiments of polo, and now and then allowed his hunting-horse to "hop sedately over a small fence." There were many wild romps on the piazza with

Baby Lee, who was now an enchantingly pretty little girl of three. His letters are full of fond anecdotes about "the blue-eyed offspring" and "yellow-haired darling."[69]

The only recorded houseguests to Sagamore Hill in 1887 were Bamie, the Douglas Robinsons, and Cecil Spring Rice. Roosevelt's happiness in being remarried and settled at last *en famille* warmed them all, and sent them away glowing. Spring Rice went back to Washington vowing that he liked Theodore "better every day I see him."[70]

By late summer Roosevelt had worked himself into a state of such nervous excitement over *Morris,* and Edith's approaching confinement, that he was felled by a surprise recurrence of asthma. The arrival of an eight-and-a-half-pound baby on 13 September seems to have shocked him back into health. Later that day, in a letter announcing the birth, he proudly added the word "Senior" to his signature.[71]

In October the hunting season got under way. Roosevelt pounded energetically after Long Island fox, but a longing for nobler game soon overwhelmed him. It had been more than a year since he had killed anything substantial. His herds in Dakota offered a convenient pretext for another trip West. Early in November, therefore, he set off with a cousin and a friend for five weeks' ranching and shooting in the Badlands.[72]

Ten days of "rough work" on the range were enough for his two companions, who hurried back to New York on 14 November. He was not sorry to see them go. "As you know," he wrote Bamie, "I really prefer to be alone while on a hunting trip."[73] Little is known about his wanderings during the next three weeks. One can only speculate, but during that solitary period some shock seems to have awakened a long-dormant instinct in Theodore Roosevelt—prompting him to take certain actions immediately after returning East.

The speculation is that as he rode farther and farther afield, he found the Badlands virtually denuded of big game—although he did manage, by an extraordinary fluke, to kill two black-tailed deer with one bullet.[74] Even in 1883 he had been hard put to find any buffalo this side of Montana; a year later the elk and grizzly were gone. In 1885 he had complained that bighorn and pronghorn were becoming scarcer, and in 1886 noticed that some varieties of migratory birds had failed to return to the Little Missouri Valley.[75] All this was due to the white man's guns and bricks and fences. Roosevelt had regretted the loss of local wildlife, but he took the conventional attitude that some dislocation of the environment must occur when civilization enters a wilderness. One day, perhaps, a new balance of nature would be worked out. . . .

Now, in November 1887, it was frighteningly obvious that both the flora and the fauna of the Badlands were facing destruction. There were so few beavers left, after a decade of remorseless trapping, that no new dams had been built, and the old ones were letting go; wherever this happened, ponds full of fish and wildfowl degenerated into dry, crack-bottomed creeks. Last summer's overstocking, together with desperate foraging during the blizzards, had eroded the rich carpet of grass that once held the soil in place. Sour deposits of cow-dung had poisoned the roots of wild-plum bushes, so that they no longer bore fruit; clear springs had been trampled into filthy sloughs; large tracts of land threatened to become desert.[76] What had once been a teeming natural paradise, loud with snorts and splashings and drumming hooves,[77] was now a waste of naked hills and silent ravines.

It would be hard to imagine a sight more melancholy to Roosevelt, who professed to love the animals he killed. For the first time he realized the true plight of the native American quadrupeds, fleeing ever westward, in ever smaller numbers, from men like himself. Ironically, he had always been at heart a conservationist. At nine years old he was "sorry the trees have been cut down,"[78] and his juvenile hobby of taxidermy, though bloody, was in its way a passionate sort of preservation. His teenage slaughter of birds had been scientifically motivated; only as a young adult had he learned to kill for the "strong eager pleasure" of it.[79] Even then he always insisted that a certain amount of hunting by responsible sportsmen was necessary to keep fecund species from multiplying at the expense of others.[80] But by 1887 the ravages of "swinish game-butchers" (and could he, in all conscience, exclude himself from that category?) were plain to see; the only thriving species in Western

Dakota were wolves and coyotes.[81] Roosevelt was now in his twenty-ninth year, and the father of a small son; if only for young Ted's sake, he must do something to preserve the great game animals from extinction.

HE ARRIVED BACK in New York on 8 December, and lost no time in inviting a dozen wealthy and influential animal-lovers to dine with him at 689 Madison Avenue. Chief among these was George Bird Grinnell, editor of *Forest and Stream,* and a crusader against the wanton killing of wildlife on the frontier. He had become Roosevelt's close friend after printing a complimentary review of *Hunting Trips of a Ranchman;* the two men had already spent many evenings together discussing "in a vague way" the threat to various American species. But, as Grinnell afterward explained, "We did not comprehend its imminence and the impending completeness of the extermination . . . those who were concerned to protect native life were still uncertainly trying to find out what they could most effectively do, how they could do it, and what dangers it was necessary to fight first."[82]

Roosevelt now decisively answered these questions. His twelve dinner guests must join him in the establishment of an association of amateur riflemen who, notwithstanding their devotion to "manly sport with the rifle," would "work for the preservation of the large game of this country, further legislation for that purpose, and assist in enforcing existing laws."[83] The club would be named after Daniel Boone and Davy Crockett, two of Roosevelt's personal heroes, and would encourage further explorations of the American wilderness in their honor. Other objectives would be "inquiry into and the recording of observations on the natural history of wild animals," and "the preservation of forest regions . . . as nurseries and reservations for woodland creatures which else would die out before the march of settlement."[84] From time to time the club would publish books and articles to propagate its ideals.

The proposal was approved, and in January 1888 the Boone & Crockett Club was formally organized with Theodore Roosevelt as its president. It was the first such club in the United States, and, according to Grinnell, "perhaps in any country." Membership rapidly grew to a total of ninety, including some of the nation's most eminent scientists, lawyers, and politicians. Through them Roosevelt (who remained club president until 1894) was able to wield considerable influence in Congress.[85]

Among his first acts was to appoint a Committee on Parks, which was instrumental in the creation of the National Zoo in Washington. He ordered another committee to work with the Secretary of the Interior "to promote useful and proper legislation towards the enlargement and better government of the Yellowstone National Park"—then a sick environment swarming with commercial parasites. The resultant Park Protection Act of 1894 saved Yellowstone from ecological destruction. Still other Boone & Crockett committees helped establish zoological gardens in New York, protect sequoia groves in California, and create an Alaskan island reserve "for the propagation of seals, salmon, and sea birds."[86]

When he was not working on these committees himself, Roosevelt joined forces with Grinnell in editing and publishing three fat volumes of wilderness lore, written by club members. *American Big-Game Hunting* (1893), *Hunting in Many Lands* (1895), and *Trail and Camp-Fire* (1897) won acclaim on both sides of the Atlantic, and prompted the establishment of Boone & Crockett–type clubs in England and various parts of the British Empire.[87] A glance at Roosevelt's own contributions as an author shows that he by no means lost his relish for blood sports. It remained strong in him through old age, although an apologist claims "he then no longer spoke of hunting as a pleasure, rather an undertaking in the interest of science."[88] Roosevelt was a complex man, and, as will be seen, his complexity grew apace during the middle years of his life. But as founder and president of the Boone & Crockett Club, he was the prime motivational force behind its conservation efforts.[89]

The most significant, from his own point of view as well as the nation's, was to do not with animals but with forestry. Roosevelt had a profound, almost Indian veneration for trees, particularly the giant conifers he had encountered in the Rockies.[90] Walking on silent, moccasined feet down a luminous nave of pines, listening to invisible choirs of birds, he came close to religious rapture, as many passages in his books and letters attest. Hence, when the American Forestry Association began its struggle to halt the rapid attrition of Western woodlands, Roosevelt threw the full weight of his organization behind it. Thanks to the club's determined lobbying on Capitol Hill, in concert with other environmental groups, the Forest Reserve Act became law in March 1891. It empowered the President to set aside at will any wooded or partly wooded country, "whether of commercial value or not."[91] The time would come when Theodore Roosevelt joyfully inherited this very power as President of the United States. One wonders if he ever paused, while signing millions of green acres into perpetuity, to acknowledge his debt to the youthful president of the Boone & Crockett Club.

ABOUT THE SAME TIME that Roosevelt sat discussing big-game preservation with his dozen dinner guests, President Cleveland dumbfounded Congress with the first Annual Message ever devoted to one subject. The tariff bulked even larger than Civil Service Reform as a political issue in those last days of 1887; as will be seen, the two major parties were diametrically opposed in their attitudes toward it. To provoke a similar division of opinion in the electorate, as Cleveland did by publicly coming out against the tariff, was in effect to decide the result of the next national election, still eleven months off. Republicans reading the text of his message reacted with incredulous joy, while Democrats wondered privately if the Big One had gone mad.[92]

Simply described, the tariff was a system of laws, hallowed for decades by successive Republican administrations, which levied high duties on imported goods in order to protect American industry and provide revenues for the federal government. So vast were these revenues (about two-thirds of the nation's income) that a surplus had been building up in the Treasury every year since 1879. It now waxed enormous,[93] and President Cleveland believed that it posed a malignant threat to the economy. To spend excessive money was wasteful; yet to hoard it, when it could have been in healthy circulation, was even more so. Cleveland, having silently pondered

American tariff schedules for two years, decided that they were "vicious, inequitable and illogical." Congress was instructed to reduce most rates, and abolish others altogether: wool, for example, should be allowed to come in free. The tariff, wrote Cleveland, would be "for revenue only" and not for protection.[94]

By his unfortunate use of the word "free" the President thus laid himself open to charges that he was a Free Trader, while by attacking Protection he identified that comfortable doctrine with the Republican party. "There's one more President for us in Protection," crowed James G. Blaine,[95] leaving few observers in doubt as to which President he had in mind. A wave of optimism spread through the party as bells across the country rang in another election year.[96]

But Roosevelt remained in the pessimistic minority. His political instinct told him the tariff was too complex an issue to divide the electorate neatly.[97] He had to admit that Blaine was a certainty for renomination, and stood at least an even chance of being elected. This made Roosevelt's own hopes for appointive office even more forlorn than they had been the previous spring. President Blaine would be no more likely to favor him than President Cleveland. The Plumed Knight was a man of long memory: he would not forget the rejection of his advances in the mayoral campaign of 1886.

"I shall probably never be in politics again," Roosevelt wrote sadly to an old Assembly friend. "My literary work occupies a good deal of my time; and I have on the whole done fairly well at it; I should like to write some book that would really take rank in the very first class, but I suppose this is a mere dream."

THUS, IN A CRYPTIC CONFESSION dated 15 January 1888,[98] did Roosevelt give his first hint that he was musing the major work of scholarship that would preoccupy him for the next seven years. Four volumes, perhaps eight, would be required to do the subject justice: his theme was enormous but vague. Within its blurry parameters (conforming roughly with the shape of the United States), he began to see heroic figures fighting, moving, pointing in one general direction.

The process of literary inspiration does not admit of much analysis. Writers themselves are often at a loss to say just when or why a given idea takes possession of them. Roosevelt, certainly, never indulged in such speculation.[99] Yet it is possible to mention at least some of the fertilizing influences upon what he proudly called "my *magnum opus.*"[100] In those first weeks of 1888 he happened to be checking through a batch of page proofs from England, comprising several chapters of *The American Commonweath,* by James Bryce, M.P., whom he had met in London the previous winter. Bryce wanted his expert opinion on various passages dealing with municipal corruption. As Roosevelt read the proofs through, he realized that he held a masterpiece in his hands. It was, he decided, the most epochal study of American institutions since that of de Tocqueville; it made his own *Gouverneur Morris* (whose galleys also lay upon his desk) seem pathetically trivial in comparison.[101] Bryce's reference to him, in a footnote, as "one of the ablest and most vivacious of the younger generation of American politicians" was flattering but ironic, given the present stagnation of his political career; it only served to increase his yearning to write a work "in the very first class," which would earn him similar respect as an American historian.[102]

Back of this immediate ambition swirled a mass of past influences, with little in common except their general geographic orientation. Among them were his years in the West, living with the sons and grandsons of pioneers; his belief, inherited from Thomas Hart Benton, that America's Manifest Destiny was to sweep Westward at the expense of weaker nations; his fascination with the racial variety of the West, and its forging of a characteristic frontier "type," never seen in the Old World; his wide readings in Western history; his efforts, through the Boone & Crockett Club, to save Western wildlife and promote Western exploration—all these combined into one mighty concept which (the more he pondered it) he saw he might handle more authoritatively than anyone else. It was nothing less than the history of the spread of the United States across the American continent, from the day Daniel Boone first crossed the Alleghenies in 1774 to the day Davy Crockett died at the Alamo in 1836.[103] He decided to call this grand work *The Winning of the West.*

His first act was to dedicate the book to the ailing Francis Parkman.[104] Like most well-read men of his class, Roosevelt had been brought up on that writer's majestic, seven-volume *History of France and England in North America*. Parkman was a scholar who combined faultless research with the narrative powers of a novelist. With that other sickly, half-blind recluse, William H. Prescott, he wrote sweeping sagas full of color and movement, in which men of overwhelming force bent nations to their will. Roosevelt set out to follow this example. Not for him the maunderings of the "institutional" historians, with their obsessive analyses of treaties and committee reports. He wanted his readers to smell the bitter smoke of campfires, see the sunset reddening the Mississippi, hear the tomahawk thud into bone. While reveling in such detail (which he would meticulously annotate, lest any pedant accuse him of fictionalizing), he would strive for Parkman's epic vision, the ability to show vast international forces at work, whole empires contending for a continent.[105]

BY MID-MARCH he had a contract from Putnam's—committing him rather ambitiously to deliver his first two volumes in the spring of 1889[106]—and he plunged at once into the somewhat rodent-like life of a professional historian. He burrowed through piles of ancient letters, diaries, and newspapers in Tennessee, and unearthed many long-forgotten documents in Kentucky, including six volumes of Spanish government dispatches, and some misspelled but priceless pioneer autobiographies; he inquisitively searched some two or three hundred folios of Revolutionary manuscripts in Washington, and ferreted out thousands of letters by Jefferson, Madison, and Monroe, untouched by previous scholars; he devoured the published papers of the Federal, Virginia, and Georgia governments in New York, and pestered private collectors as far away as Wisconsin and California to send him their papers.[107] By the end of April he had amassed the bulk of his source material, and began the actual writing of *The Winning of the West* on 1 May, at Sagamore Hill.[108]

As always, he found it difficult to marshal his superabundant thoughts on paper. A perusal of the manuscript of Volume One shows what agonies its magnificent opening chapter, "The Spread of the English-Speaking Peoples," cost him. A veritable thicket of verbal debris—interlineations, erasures, blots, and balloons—clogs every page: only the clearest prose is allowed to filter through.[109]

DURING ALL THE SPRING and summer of 1888 Roosevelt complained about the slowness of his progress on *The Winning of the West:* "it seems impossible to write more than a page or two a day."[110] As if from another land, another century, he heard distant shouts that General Benjamin Harrison of Indiana had been nominated by the Republicans for the Presidency—James G. Blaine having withdrawn on the grounds that a once-defeated candidate might, after all, be a burden to the party. Other shouts, even more distant, told him that Grover Cleveland had been renominated by the Democrats. But he paid little attention, and hunched closer over his desk. "After all," he told a friend, "I'm a literary feller, not a politician these days."[111]

To maintain the Sagamore household and bolster Edith's constant sense of financial insecurity, Roosevelt had to earn at least $4,000 in fees and royalties that year.[112] This meant a considerable amount of hackwork over and above his labors on *The Winning of the West.* Scarcely a month, accordingly, passed without at least one book or article from his pen. Although some of these had been written before—or published in a different form—merely to edit and proofread them made heavy inroads upon his time.

A survey of their various titles justifies his growing reputation as a Renaissance man. In February the *North American* printed his "Remarks on Copyright and Balloting," while *Century* put out the first of six splendid essays on ranch life in the West. This series, which included his long-delayed account of the capture of Redhead Finnegan, continued through March, April, May (a month which also saw the publication of his *Gouverneur Morris*), and June. The essays attracted the admiring attention of Walt Whitman, who wrote, "There is something alluring in the subject and the way it is handled: Roosevelt seems to have realized its character—its shape and size—to have honestly imbibed some of the spirit of that wild Western life."[113]

Roosevelt was silent in July and August, but came back resoundingly in September with "A Reply to Some Recent Criticism of America" in *Murray's Magazine*. The piece was a brilliant and erudite attack upon Matthew Arnold and Lord Wolseley ("that flatulent conqueror of half-armed savages") and became the talk of Washington and London. In October, Putnam's put out his *Essays in Practical Politics,* being a reissue, in book form, of two long polemics on legislative and municipal corruption, "Phases of State Legislation" (1884) and "Machine Politics in New York City" (1886). Finally, in December, his six *Century* articles were revised and republished as *Ranch Life and the Hunting Trail,* in a deluxe gift edition, illustrated by Frederic Remington. It was greeted with enthusiastic reviews.[114]

ROOSEVELT'S NONLITERARY ACTIVITIES through 1888 can be briefly summarized. The family man played host to Cecil Spring Rice and "delicious Cabotty," piggybacked little Alice downstairs to breakfast every day, and noted approvingly that young Ted "plays more vigorously than any one I ever saw." He worried sporadically about his brother Elliott, whose health was beginning to deteriorate from too much hard drinking and hard riding with the "fast" Meadowbrook set.[115]

The end of August found Roosevelt the hunter in Idaho's Kootenai country. He spent most of September in the mountains, sleeping above the snow-line without a jacket and feasting lustily on bear-meat. Returning East via Medora, Roosevelt the rancher was able to make some respectable sales of his remaining cattle. But Roosevelt the author was still so hard pressed for money that he rashly accepted an invitation to write a history of New York City for a British publisher. He begged for "a little lee-way . . . to finish up some matters which I *must* get through first."[116]

This referred to *The Winning of the West*. Its text was beginning to drag alarmingly: with six months to go on his contract, he had written only half of Volume One. Vowing to "fall to . . . with redoubled energy," he returned to Sagamore Hill on 5 October[117]—but Roosevelt the politician would not let him sit down at his desk.

The presidential campaign was well under way, and with Cleveland crippled by the tariff controversy, there seemed to be a real chance of a Republican victory. Duty required that he make at least a token appearance for Benjamin Harrison. Actually Roosevelt was more than willing, for he considered the little general an excellent candidate.[118] Despite a total lack of charisma, Harrison was a magnificent orator, capable of enthralling thousands—as long as he did not shake any hands afterward. It was said that every voter who touched his icy flesh walked away a Democrat.[119] Party strategy, therefore, called for maximum public exposure, minimum personal contact, and support appearances by fiery young Republicans like Roosevelt, who could be guaranteed to thaw anybody Harrison had frozen.

On 7 October, after only one day at home, Roosevelt answered the call. Jumping back onto the Chicago Limited, he set off on a speaking tour of Illinois, Michigan, and Minnesota. The sight of crowds and bunting worked its usual magic on him, and he canvassed with great zest. His performance was good enough to establish him, within a week, as one of the campaign's most effective speakers. "I can't help thinking," he wrote Lodge, "that this time we have our foes on the hip."[120]

On 27 October, Theodore Roosevelt turned thirty. Nine days later he heard that his party had won not only the Presidency but the Senate and House of Representatives as well. "I am as happy as a king," he told Cecil Spring Rice, "—to use a Republican simile."[121]

AT LAST, as winter settled down on Sagamore Hill, a measure of tranquillity returned to Roosevelt's life. The sight of snow tumbling past his study window, and the sound of logs crackling in the grate, combined to produce that sense of calm seclusion a writer most prizes—when the pen seems to move across the paper almost of its own accord, and the words flow steadily down the nib, drying into whorls and curlicues that please the eye; when sentences have just the right rhythmic cadence, paragraphs fall naturally into place, and the pages pile up satisfyingly . . . Roosevelt's characteristic interlineations and scratchings-out grew fewer and fewer as the pace of his narrative increased, and inspiration grew.[122]

He worked steadily all though December, finishing Volume One before Christmas.[123] Early in the New Year he moved his family to 689 Madison Avenue. (Bamie, who was traveling in Europe, had placed her house at Edith's disposal.)[124] Seeking refuge from the children, Roosevelt set up a desk at Putnam's, on West Twenty-third Street. For some reason the publishers were in a hurry to get the book out by the middle of June. Chapters of Volume Two were sent upstairs to the composing room as fast as Roosevelt could write them. Meanwhile Volume One was printed and bound on the topmost floors. Later, stacks of both volumes would be cranked downstairs for sale in the retail department at street level—permitting George Haven Putnam to boast that *The Winning of the West* had been in large part written, produced, and marketed under one roof.[125]

Roosevelt scrawled his last line of text on 1 April 1889, and spent the next couple of weeks blearily checking the galleys. With a touch of sadness he wondered "if I have or have not properly expressed all the ideas that seethed vaguely in my soul as I wrote it."[126] But he had little leisure to indulge in self-doubts, for on 27 April Cabot Lodge came up from Washington[127] with a message from the White House.

ONLY A FEW DAYS BEFORE, Roosevelt had written, "I do hope the President will appoint good Civil Service Commissioners."[128] Lodge fully understood the plaintive tone of that remark. Since the beginning of the year he had been trying to get his friend a place in the incoming Administration. Roosevelt had affected nonchalance at first, yet while still engaged on the final chapters of *The Winning of the West,* confessed, "I would like above all things to go into politics."[129] Lodge had tried to persuade Harrison's new Secretary of State—who was none other than James G. Blaine—to appoint Roosevelt as Assistant Secretary, but the Plumed Knight gracefully demurred. In words that proved prophetic, he wrote:

> My real trouble in regard to Mr. Roosevelt is that I fear he lacks the repose and patient endurance required in an Assistant Secretary. Mr. Roosevelt is amazingly quick in appre-

> hension. Is there not danger that he might be too quick in execution? I do somehow fear that my sleep at Augusta or Bar Harbor would not be quite so easy and refreshing if so brilliant and aggressive a man had hold of the helm. Matters are constantly occurring which require the most thoughtful concentration and the most stubborn inaction. Do *you* think that Mr. T.R.'s temperament would give guaranty of that course?[130]

Lodge had reported only the polite parts of this rejection. "I hope you will tell Blaine how much I appreciate his kind expressions," Roosevelt replied.[131]

Lodge had then begun to negotiate directly with the President, urging him to appoint Roosevelt to *some* federal position, no matter how minor, in recognition of his help during the campaign. Several influential Republicans advised the same. Harrison was "by no means eager."[132] Perhaps he remembered the screeching, straw-hatted young delegate at Chicago in 1884, and winced at the idea of having him within earshot of the White House. Eventually he thought of a dusty sinecure that paid little, and promised less in terms of real political power. Ambitious men invariably turned it down; if Roosevelt was crazy enough to want it, he might be crazy enough to make something of it.

Lodge hurried to New York, and, amid the din of the U.S. Government Centennial celebrations,[133] told Roosevelt that Harrison was willing to appoint him Civil Service Commissioner, at a salary of $3,500 per annum. He doubted, however, that his friend would want the post. Such a pittance could only plunge him deeper into financial difficulties; bureaucratic entanglements would interfere with his upcoming book contracts; besides, the work was bound to make him unpopular, for everybody in Washington was heartily sick of the subject of Civil Service Reform.

Roosevelt accepted at once.

A COUPLE OF DAYS LATER the Centennial came to an end with the biggest banquet in American history, held at the Metropolitan

Opera House. About eleven o'clock, after the speeches were over, and $16,000 worth of wine had been drunk, the guests filed out into the crisp spring night. Most were tired and satiated, but one young man seemed anxious to dawdle and talk. His high, eager voice, as he stood on the sidewalk with a group of friends and pointed at the sky, sounded "quite charming" to a passerby, although he occasionally squeaked into falsetto. "It was young Roosevelt," reported the observer. "He was introducing some fellows to the stars."[134]

CHAPTER 16

The Silver-Plated Reform Commissioner

On the deck stands Olaf the King,
Around him whistle and sing
The spears that the foemen fling,
And the stones that they hurl with their hands.

WASHINGTON, D.C., IN THE SPRING of 1889 was, for those who could afford to live there, one of the most delightful places in the world.[1] Seen from various carefully-selected angles, it was a beautiful city, with its broad, black, spotless streets, its marble buildings and sixty-five thousand trees, its vistas of "the silvery Potomac" by day and the illuminated Capitol by night. A visiting Englishman remarked on its air "of comfort, of leisure, of space to spare, of stateliness . . . it looks the sort of place where nobody has to work for his living, or, at any rate, not hard."[2]

This was true above a certain bureaucratic level. Senior clerks and Cabinet officers alike breakfasted at eight or nine, lunched with all deliberate speed, and laid down their pens at four.[3] They then had several hours of daylight left for strolling, shopping, drinking, or philandering (Washington was reputed to be "the wickedest city in the nation")—hours which lengthened steadily as the warm

"Rich and talented people crowded Adams's salon."

Congressman Henry Cabot Lodge, by John Singer Sargent, 1890.

weather approached, and Government prepared to shut down for the summer.

While peaceful, the capital was by no means provincial. Indeed, the decade just ending had seen its transformation from rather shabby respectability to the heights of social splendor. People who spent their summers at Newport and Saratoga were spending their winters in Washington.[4] Some had been drawn by the magnetism of Mrs. Cleveland, now regrettably departed (although imitations of her famous smile lingered on a thousand homelier faces, reminding one correspondent of so many cats chewing wax).[5] Most of Washington's fashionable newcomers, however, were drawn by the desire to be at the power center of an increasingly powerful country. Power, not breeding, was the basis of protocol in this democratic town: there was something wickedly exciting about it. Knickerbockers and Brahmins vied for the company of Western Senators at dinner, laughing at their filthy stories and tolerating their squirts of tobacco-juice; debutantes and newsboys swayed side by side in the horsecars with Supreme Court Justices; the President of the United States could often be seen, a small, bearded, buttoned-up figure, sipping soda in a corner drugstore.[6]

Another significant difference between Washington and most major American cities was the apparent contentment of its working class—particularly now the party of Lincoln was back in control. A thriving *demimonde* offered blacks opportunities for advancement in such government-related industries as prostitution, vote-selling, and land speculation. Here, indeed, were to be found the nation's wealthiest black entrepreneurs, and "colored girls more luscious than any women ever painted by Peter Paul Rubens." They could be seen on a Saturday afternoon strolling in silks and sealskins on the White House lawn, to promenade music by Professor Sousa's Marine Band.[7]

Apart from the several thousands of shanty-dwellers, whose slums could be smelled, if not seen, in the vacant lots behind the great federal buildings, Washington society was prosperous, and graded more by occupation than color. Its unique feature was an ephemeral upper class which turned over every four years, according to the vagaries of politics. Hardly any member of this class, be he diplomat, Congressman, or Civil Service Commissioner, expected to settle permanently in the capital; sooner or later his government would recall him, or his campaign for reelection fail, or a whim of the President leave him jobless overnight.

Servicing the upper class was a middle-to-lower class of realtors, caterers, couturiers, landladies, and servants—all determined to profit by the constant comings and goings of their clients. After every Congressional election, prices rose; after every change of Administration, they soared. But federal pay scales remained fixed at levels set in the 1870s. By 1889 the city had grown so expensive that anybody accepting a fairly senior government job had to have independent means to survive.[8] On the Sunday before Roosevelt's arrival, eight-room houses in the obligatory Northwest sector were being advertised for sale at around $6,500, almost twice a Commissioner's salary. But this was nothing: a thirteen-room house on Pennsylvania Avenue near Nineteenth was $12,500; something more the size of Sagamore Hill, albeit with a much smaller garden, was available on Vermont Avenue for $125,000.[9] Rents were proportionately exorbitant; the pokiest little furnished house would cost him $2,400 a year.[10] Allowing a conservative $1,000 for food, $300 for servants, and $200 for fuel, he could spend every cent of his salary without so much as buying a new suit.[11] On top of that there was Sagamore Hill to maintain, and Edith was pregnant again.

The baby was not due for another five months, but it served as an excuse to keep his family at Oyster Bay at least through November. Meanwhile he could lead a cheap bachelor life in Washington—rent-free, as the vacationing Lodges had placed their house on Connecticut Avenue at his disposal.[12]

So when Roosevelt arrived in town on the morning of Monday, 13 May 1889, he was alone, just like thousands of other hopeful newcomers in the early days of the Harrison Administration. Unlike them, however, he had a desk waiting for him, and a commission, signed by the President of the United States, lying upon it.[13]

IT WAS NOT YET ten o'clock, but the sun was bright and strong. A cool breeze blowing off the Potomac tempered the seventy-degree heat. All Washington sparkled, thanks to torrential rainstorms over the weekend. Fallen locust-blossoms carpeted the sidewalks, rotting sweetly as pedestrians sauntered to and fro. Straw hats and silk bonnets were out in force: summer, evidently, was considered to be a *fait accompli* in the nation's capital, regardless of what the calendar said.[14]

Roosevelt found the Civil Service Commission impressively located in the west wing of City Hall, at the south end of Judiciary Square. Tall Ionic columns rose above a flight of seventeen stone steps, which he could not resist taking at a run.[15] By the time he had crossed the portico and burst into the office beyond, his adrenaline was already flowing.

"I am the new Civil Service Commissioner, Theodore Roosevelt of New York," he announced to the first clerk he saw. "Have you a telephone? Call up the Ebbit House. I have an engagement with Archbishop Ireland. Say that I will be there at ten o'clock."

His clear voice sounded "peculiarly pleasant" as it broke the bureaucratic stillness. Yet it had an incisive edge to it that made the clerk jump to his feet.[16]

Within minutes Roosevelt had taken the oath, and moved into the largest and sunniest of the three Commissioners' offices.[17] Although his gray-haired colleagues, Charles Lyman (Republican) and ex-Governor Hugh S. Thompson of South Carolina (Democrat), were nominally senior to him, he seems to have been accepted, *de ipse,* as leader from the start.[18] Lyman's subsequent election as president of the Commission in no way affected this arrangement. Roosevelt liked both of them, as he did everyone at first, then lost patience with them, as he did with most people sooner or later. Lyman turned out to be "the most intolerably slow of all men who ever adored red tape,"[19] while Thompson was "a nice old boy," but not much else.[20] However Roosevelt managed to keep these opinions private, and the professional harmony among the three was such that some members of Harrison's Cabinet began to worry about it. The last thing they needed, as they began to hand out appointments for services rendered, was an active Civil Service Commission.

IT IS DIFFICULT for Americans living in the first quarter of the twenty-first century to understand the emotions which Civil Service

Reform aroused in the last quarter of the nineteenth. The movement's literature has about it all the faded ludicrousness of Moral Rearmament. How could intellectuals, politicians, socialites, churchmen, and editors campaign so fervently on behalf of customs clerks, Indian school superintendents, and Fourth-Class postmasters? How could they wax so lyrical about quotas, certifications, political assessments, and lists of eligibles? How, indeed, could one reformer entitle his memoirs *The Romance of the Merit System*?[21]

The fact remains that thousands, even millions, lined up behind the banner, and they were as evangelical (and as strenuously resisted) as any crusaders in history. To them Civil Service Reform was "a dream at first, and then a passionate cause which the ethical would not let sleep."[22] Men and women of the highest quality devoted whole careers to it, and died triumphant in the knowledge that, due to their personal efforts, the classified departmental service had been extended by so many dozen places in Buffalo, or that algebraic equations had been deleted from the examination papers of cattle inspectors in Arizona.

For all its dated aspects, Civil Service Reform was an honorable cause, and of real social consequence. It sought to restore to government three fundamental principles of American democracy: first, that opportunity be made equal to all citizens; second, that the meritorious only be appointed; third, that no public servants should suffer for their political beliefs. The movement's power base—admittedly a rickety one—was the Pendleton Act of 1883, which guaranteed that at least a quarter of all federal jobs were available to the best qualified applicant, irrespective of party, and that those jobs would remain secure, irrespective of changes in Administration.[23]

Few converts believed in the above principles more sincerely than Theodore Roosevelt. He had become fascinated with Civil Service Reform shortly after leaving college, and, as an Assemblyman, had helped bring about the first state Civil Service law in the country, closely based on the Pendleton Act. He had joined Civil Service Reform clubs, subscribed to Civil Service Reform journals, and preached the doctrine of Civil Service Reform to numerous audiences. His acceptance of the Commissionership, therefore, seemed natural and inevitable to his colleagues in the movement, although many believed he had sacrificed his political future by doing so.[24] There would be times, during the next six years, when he was tempted to agree with them.

ON THE MORNING after taking his oath of office, Roosevelt went to pay his respects to the President. He was prepared not to like him, for the little general was famously repellent in manner. With his fat cheeks, weak stoop, and small, suspicious eyes, Benjamin Harrison reminded one visitor of "a pig blinking in a cold wind."[25] It was hard to believe that this sour, silent Hoosier possessed the finest legal mind in the history of the White House, or that he was capable of reducing large audiences to tears with the beauty of his oratory.[26] It was even harder to believe the old friend who assured the press, "When he's on a fishing trip, Ben takes his drink of whiskey in the morning, just like anyone else . . . spits on his worm for luck, and cusses when the fish get away."[27]

But during Roosevelt's visit, Harrison made a less dyspeptic impression than usual. He had just returned from a cruise down the Potomac, and looked ruddy and clear-eyed.[28] The President must have given his new Commissioner assurances of support, for Roosevelt was ebullient when he burst out of the Executive Office. He nearly collided with the only other member of the Administration whose personal impetus matched his own: big, bustling, baby-faced John Wanamaker, the Philadelphia retail millionaire and new Postmaster General. Roosevelt recognized him, and the two men exchanged hearty greetings.

Other Cabinet officers were arriving to meet with the President, and Wanamaker introduced Roosevelt all around. There were jokes about the young man's presumed authority over federal jobs. "You haven't any power over my place, anyway," said the Secretary of the Navy, in mock relief. "If I had to pass a civil-service examination for mine," Roosevelt answered, "I would never have been appointed." "I'm glad you realize that," growled the Secretary of Agriculture.[29]

Laughing loudly, the Cabinet filed into Harrison's office, leaving Roosevelt alone with his thoughts. He was aware (as was an unobtrusive reporter) that much cold hostility lurked behind the warm handshakes he had received. John Wanamaker, undoubtedly, would be his major opponent in the fight to enforce Civil Service rules. Wanamaker was a man of charm, pious habits, and magnificent administrative ability; he was also a Republican of the old school, and a staunch defender of the spoils system.[30] The President had rewarded him for his lavish campaign contributions, and Wanamaker believed that all loyal Republicans, great or humble, who had given time and money to the party were entitled to similar recognition. As such he had emerged as the leading "spoilsman" in the Cabinet and a benign foe of all "Snivel Service Reformers."

Roosevelt was already too late to prevent the wholesale looting of Postal Service jobs which had taken place in the first six weeks of the new Republican Administration. (Some said that Harrison had purposely delayed his appointment to allow the Postmaster General a free hand.) The scramble for office was, according to one horrified reformer, "universal and almost unbelievable."[31] Wanamaker's assistant, James S. Clarkson, had been replacing Democratic Fourth-Class postmasters at the rate of one every five minutes. Thousands of newspaper editors who had supported Harrison were put on the government payroll. Even ex-jailbirds whose services had been of the "dirty tricks" variety were rewarded with minor positions. Other Cabinet officers, caught up in the fever, also dispensed largesse. Attorney General William H. Miller was reported to have announced that any aspirant to a federal job must be "first a good man, second a good Republican."[32]

An extension of the Civil Service Law on 1 May—ordered by Cleveland and executed by Harrison—had slowed the pace of looting, but only in the classified quarter of the service. Over the other three-quarters, comprising some 112,000 jobs, Roosevelt had no power whatsoever. His Commission's mandate extended to a mere 28,000 subordinate positions in the departmental, customs, postal, railway mail, and Indian services.[33] Its powers, moreover, were slight. A Commissioner might personally investigate cases of examination fraud in Kansas, or political blackmail in Maine (providing he could find enough money in the budget to get there), but even if the evidence uncovered was flagrant, he could do little more than recommend prosecution to the Cabinet officer responsible. And if that officer were a Wanamaker or a Miller, he might as well save his breath.

Such, at least, had been the attitude of Roosevelt's eight predecessors, who had all been sedentary bureaucrats, content to supervise the marking of countless examination papers. The Civil Service Commission was a pleasant place to drowse, with its large, quiet offices and views of lawns and trees; there was an excellent fried-oyster restaurant across Louisiana Avenue; and if one did not offend any political bigwigs, one was invited to some decent receptions.[34]

Roosevelt would have none of this laissez-faire policy. From the moment he returned from the White House on 14 May, he became a blur of high-speed activity. He mastered the Commission's complex operations within days, throwing off a wealth of new ideas, devouring documents at the rate of a page a glance, dictating hundreds of letters with such hissing emphasis that the stenographer did not need to ask for punctuation marks. Staff and visitors alike were dazed by his energy, exuberance, and ruthless outmaneuvering. "He is a wonderful man," said one caller. "When I went to see him, he got up, shook hands with me, and said, 'So glad to see you. Delighted. Good day, sir, good day.' Then he ushered me to the door. I wonder what I wanted to see him about."[35]

The new Commissioner was not interested in audiences of one. Experience had taught him that he had in abundance the power of mass publicity,[36] that it could be as effective, if not more so, than regular political clout. He intended so to dramatize the good gray cause of Civil Service Reform that the electorate would be forced to take notice of it—and if of himself as well, why, so much the better.

As a preliminary attention-getting exercise, Roosevelt went on 20 May to New York, where the press knew him, to check some recent examinations in the Custom House. He found that various questions had been leaked to favored candidates, at $50 a head, and issued a fiery report accusing the local examinations board of "great laxity and negligence," "positive fraud," and mismanagement for "personal, political, or pecuniary" reasons. The report called for the dismissal of three officials and the criminal prosecution of at least one of them. "This report astonished the spoilsmen," wrote one prominent reformer. "It was the first emphatic notice that the Civil Service Act was a real law and was to be enforced."[37]

Roosevelt returned to the capital and pondered his next move. The Eastern press was watching him now; it was time to get Western newspapers to do the same. On 17 June, therefore, he set off on an investigatory tour of some Great Lakes post offices with Commissioners Lyman and Thompson. Their first scheduled stop, he innocently announced, would be Indianapolis, where there were rumors of incompetence and partisanship involving the local postmaster, William Wallace. It did not take reporters long to realize that Wallace was the close personal friend, and Indianapolis the home city, of the President of the United States.[38]

LUCIUS BURRIE SWIFT, Indianapolis editor of the *Civil Service Chronicle,* was walking downtown on the morning of 18 June when "I saw Theodore Roosevelt coming towards me, his smile of recognition visible half a block away."[39] The two men knew each other well: it had been Swift who originally asked the Civil Service Commission to investigate Postmaster Wallace. While Roosevelt completed his postbreakfast "constitutional," Swift went over the main facts of the case again. Three venal ex-employees of the Post Office, fired some years before by Wallace's Democratic predecessor, had been given their jobs back simply because they were Republicans. One was rumored to be the operator of an illegal gambling den—clearly not the sort of civil servant the Commission should favor.[40]

The investigation, held that afternoon in the Indianapolis Post Office, confirmed the truth of Swift's allegations. "These men must be removed today," Roosevelt exclaimed. Wallace strenuously objected, but Commissioners Lyman and Thompson backed their young colleague up. The postmaster had no choice but to capitulate. He agreed to dismiss the offending employees, and promised that in future he would scrupulously observe the Civil Service law.[41]

Later, when Roosevelt was celebrating at Swift's house, Wallace visited Lyman and Thompson at their hotel. He asked if he might produce "new evidence" exonerating himself before they wrote their final report. The Commissioners agreed, much to Roosevelt's irritation, for he considered Wallace "a well-meaning, weak old fellow," and suspected that he was merely stalling.[42] The evidence, in any case, proved to be worthless. Postmaster Wallace's humiliation was duly headlined in the Indianapolis and Washington newspapers. "We stirred things up well," Roosevelt boasted to Lodge. As for President Harrison, "we have administered a galvanic shock that will reinforce his virtue for the future."[43] Whether Harrison would relish this shock remained to be seen.

TWO DAYS LATER the Commissioners were in Milwaukee, where the evidence of Post Office corruption was so overwhelming as to make Indianapolis seem trivial. Roosevelt got off the train convinced, on the basis of advance information, that Postmaster George H. Paul was "guilty beyond all reasonable doubt,"[44] and as soon as he laid eyes on the man his suspicions were confirmed. "About as thorough-paced a scoundrel as I ever saw," Roosevelt declared. "An oily-Gammon, churchgoing specimen."[45]

The principal testimony against Paul was supplied that afternoon by Hamilton Shidy, a Post Office superintendent and secretary of the Milwaukee Civil Service Board. Before taking the stand, Shidy said he was a poor man, entirely dependent on his job for support. He asked for a promise of protection, which Roosevelt promptly—and rashly—gave.[46] Shidy then went on to describe how Paul had for years "appointed whomsoever he chose" to lucrative Post Office positions. After every such appointment, Shidy was told to "torture" the lists of eligibles so as to make it seem that Paul's men had won their jobs in open examination. On one occasion the postmaster had actually stood looking over his shoulder while Shidy re-marked an examination paper downward. To substantiate his charges, Shidy handed over a sheaf of illegal orders in Paul's own handwriting.[47]

Next morning Roosevelt confronted the fat little postmaster with Shidy's evidence. "Mr. Paul, these are very grave charges, and we should like to hear any explanation you have to make." As he handed them over, item by item, Paul (examining each one disdainfully through his glasses, at arm's length) protested he did not know, or could not remember. "Shidy was the man who was doing all that—you will have to see Shidy." "We are not talking of Shidy," said Roosevelt, "but of what *you* did. Why did you make this appointment? Why did you make that appointment?" "You must ask Shidy," was the nonchalant reply.[48]

The Commissioners did not bother to question Paul at length, for they had more than enough hard evidence to prove his guilt. It would give President Harrison no alternative but to fire him upon their recommendation. A dramatic, high-level dismissal, followed if possible by criminal prosecution, was just the sort of publicity coup Roosevelt wanted in the Midwest. But then Paul blandly announced that his letter of appointment, signed by President Cleveland four years before, had expired. "My term is out. I am simply waiting for my successor to qualify."[49]

At this there was nothing for the Commissioners to do but leave town on the next train. On the way back to Washington they drafted an impotent report. Not until after they had returned, and sent it in, did they discover that Postmaster Paul was a liar. His term of office still had several months to run. A supplemental report was accordingly rushed to the White House—and to the Associated Press.[50] Although the document bore three signatures, its language was unmistakably Rooseveltian.

> For Mr. Paul to plead innocent is equivalent to his pleading imbecility . . . Mr. Paul alone benefitted from the crookedness of the certifications, for he alone had the appointing power . . . He has grossly and habitually violated the law, and has done it in a peculiarly revolting and underhanded manner. His conduct merits the severest punishment . . . and we recommend his immediate removal.[51]

"I HAVE MADE this Commission a living force," Roosevelt rejoiced on 23 June.[52] He was in tremendous spirits, as always after battling the ungodly. There was, as yet, no official reaction to his "slam among the post offices." Some rumblings of displeasure over the Indianapolis affair had been heard down Pennsylvania Avenue, but he doubted the President was really upset. "It is to Harrison's credit, all we are doing in enforcing the law. I am part of the Administration; if I do good work it redounds to the credit of the Administration."[53]

This cheerful optimism was not shared by his Republican friends, nor by Postmaster General Wanamaker, who was reported "enraged" by the press coverage enjoyed by Roosevelt on tour.[54] To investigate discreetly was one thing; to cross-examine senior Post Office executives in public, and express his contempt for them afterward, at dictating speed, was another. Even the loyal Cabot Lodge warned him to keep out of the headlines until he was more settled in his job. "I cry *peccavi,*" Roosevelt replied, "and will assume a statesmanlike reserve of manner whenever reporters come near me."[55]

Reserved or not, he could not quell his bubbling good humor. Things were going particularly well for that other Roosevelt, the man of letters. Volumes One and Two of *The Winning of the West* had been published during his absence, to panegyrical newspaper reviews. "No book published for many years," remarked the *Tribune,* "has shown a closer grasp of its subject, a more thorough fitness in the writer, or more honest and careful methods of treatment. Nor must the literary ability and skill displayed throughout be overlooked. Many episodes . . . are written with remarkable dramatic and narrative power. *The Winning of the West* is, in short, an admirable and deeply interesting book, and will take its place with the most valuable and indispensable works in the library of American history."[56]

He would have to wait for several months for more learned opinions, but in the meantime he could cherish a complimentary letter from the great Parkman himself. "I am much pleased you like the book," Roosevelt wrote in acknowledgment. "I have always intended to devote myself to essentially American work; and literature must be my mistress perforce, for although I enjoy politics I appreciate perfectly the exceedingly short nature of my tenure."[57]

If John Wanamaker had had his way, Roosevelt's tenure would have been the shortest in the history of the Civil Service Commission. The Postmaster General was reluctant—and the President even more so—to fire Postmaster Paul for abuse of the merit system, even though that individual was a Democratic holdover. The precedent thus established would mean that Roosevelt, in future, could demand the dismissal of Republican postmasters for the same reason. In any case, Wanamaker did not like being told what to do in his own department by a junior member of the Administration. His chance for revenge came at the beginning of July, when Roosevelt came to him in great agitation to report that Paul had dismissed Hamilton Shidy for treachery and insubordination. Wanamaker curtly refused to intervene.[58]

This placed Roosevelt in a highly embarrassing position. As Shidy's promised protector, he was in honor bound to find him another federal job. But as Civil Service Commissioner, he was in honor bound to enforce the law. How could he give patronage to a confessed falsifier of government records? How could he, in all conscience, not do so? Wanamaker, of course, understood his dilemma, and knew that the best way out was for him to resign. "That hypocritical haberdasher!" Roosevelt exploded. "He is an ill-constitutioned creature, oily, with bristles sticking up through the oil."[59]

On 10 July a telegram summoned the three Commissioners to the White House. Roosevelt may have wondered if he was about to go the same way as Shidy, but he was pleasantly surprised by Harrison's attitude. "The old boy is with us," he told Lodge. "The Indianapolis business gave him an awful wrench, but he has swallowed the medicine, and in his talk with us today did not express the least dissatisfaction with any of our deeds or utterances."[60]

Fortified by these signs of Presidential approval, Roosevelt was able to persuade the Superintendent of the Census to find a place for Hamilton Shidy in his bureau.[61] Wanamaker philosophically agreed to the transfer, and Roosevelt, feeling that he had settled a gentlemanly debt, doubtless thought no more about it.

DAILY THE SUN GREW hotter, softening the asphalt in the streets and glaring on marble and whitewash. Slum dwellers began to sweep out their shanties, filling the air with acrid dust. Pleasure-boats on the Potomac hoarsely encouraged office-workers to play hooky. Every evening millions of mosquitoes left the marshes south of the White House and fanned out in search of human blood. As August approached, the city's population decreased by almost one-third, and the tempo of government business slowed almost to a standstill.[62]

Roosevelt was unable to prevent the Civil Service Commission from lapsing into what he called "innocuous desuetude." The evidence is he did not try very hard, for his own duties were light. "It is pretty dreary to sizzle here, day after day, doing routine work that the good Lyman is quite competent to attend to himself." He tried to begin his history of New York, but found he could not write. He spent $1.50 on a new volume of Swinburne, read a few voluptuous lines, then threw it away in disgust. "My life," he mourned, "seems to grow more and more sedentary, and I am rapidly sinking into fat and lazy middle age."[63]

Clearly he was in need of his annual vacation in the West. If President Harrison would only hurry up and announce the dismissal of Postmaster Paul, he could take the next train out of town "with a light heart and a clear conscience."[64] But the White House preserved an enigmatic silence. Then, as Roosevelt chafed at his desk, a thunderbolt struck him.

FRANK HATTON, editor of the *Washington Post,* was an ex-Postmaster General and an enemy of Civil Service Reform.[65] He was also a shrewd promoter who knew the value of a running fight in boosting circulation. On 28 July he suddenly decided to launch an attack on Roosevelt. His lead editorial derided the Commissioner as "this young 'banged' (and still to be banged more) disciple of counterfeit reform." He accused Roosevelt of personally condoning many violations of the Civil Service Law, and of misappropriating—or misspending—large sums of federal money. Without being specific as to any recent crimes, Hatton said that "the Fifth Avenue sport" had bribed his way into the New York mayoralty campaign, and made "disreputable" deals with machine politicians.[66]

Nostrils dilated, Roosevelt rushed to the podium to deny these "falsehoods." He was tempted, he said, to use "a still stronger and shorter word."[67] Hatton's reply, published the following day, shrewdly played upon that temptation.

> THE POST regrets that this spangled and glittering reformer, if he is bound to get mad, should not do so in more classic style. You are not a ranchman now, Mr. Theodore Roosevelt . . . Banish your cowboy manners until the end of your trip, which the evening papers announce you are to take in a few days. And, by the way . . . have you made the proper application for a leave of absence, or have you ordered yourself West, that you may have the Government pay your 'legitimate' travelling expenses?
>
> THE POST had an idea that it would bring to the raw the surface of the callow Roosevelt . . . For you to say that the [Civil Service] law has not been violated is to advertise yourself as a classical ignoramus, and the sooner you hie yourself West to your reservation, where you can rest your overworked brain, the more considerate you will be to yourself.
>
> Now, Mr. Commissioner Roosevelt, you can mount your broncho and be off. Personally, THE POST wishes you well. It enjoys you.

On the same day this editorial appeared, Roosevelt bumped into President Harrison, who had doubtless read it with amusement over breakfast. Psychologically the moment was unsuitable for a speech in Western dialect, but Roosevelt, hoping he could persuade Harrison not to take Wanamaker's side in the Paul case, made one anyhow. He quoted the prayer of a backwoodsman battling a grizzly: "Oh Lord, help me kill that b'ar, and if you don't help me, oh Lord, don't help the b'ar."[68] But Harrison reserved the Almighty's right of no reply, and walked on, leaving Roosevelt no wiser than before.

July ended, and August began, with the offending postmaster still in office. Roosevelt vented his frustration in an interview with the *New York Sun,* accusing "a certain Cabinet officer" of working against the cause of Civil Service Reform.[69] Hatton reprinted his words in the *Post,* and commented that if this charge by "the High,

Joint, Silver-Plated Reform Commissioner" was true, it reflected upon the entire Cabinet, and upon President Harrison himself. "It is all very well for this powdered and perfumed dude to be interviewed every day, but what the public would like to know is whom he meant, what Cabinet officer he referred to, when he said that the Civil Service law was being evaded . . . This is a very serious charge for you, Mr. Commissioner Roosevelt, to make against the Administration."[70]

Hatton sent a squad of reporters to ask all the Cabinet members whom they thought Roosevelt was accusing. "I would have to be a mind-reader to guess," said John Wanamaker smoothly.[71]

On 5 August Roosevelt was summoned to the White House and told that God had decided in favor of the grizzly. Rather than dismiss Postmaster Paul outright, Harrison had merely accepted a letter of resignation. "It was a golden chance to take a good stand; and it had been lost," Roosevelt wrote bitterly.[72]

That night he headed West to clear his mind and recondition his body. With unconscious symbolism, he proclaimed himself "especially hot for bear."[73]

JUST AS THE SUN sank behind the Rockies, and dusk crept down into the Montana foothills, he came across a brook in a clearing carpeted with moss and *kinni-kinic* berries.[74] He spread his buffalo-bag across a bed of pine needles, dragged up a few dry logs, and then strolled off, rifle on shoulder, to see if he could pick up a grouse for supper.

Walking quickly and silently through the August twilight, he came to the crest of a ridge and peeped over it. There, in the valley below, was his grizzly. It was ambling along with its huge head down—a perfect shot at sixty yards. Roosevelt fired. His bullet entered the flank, ranging forward into the lungs. There was a moaning roar, and the bear galloped heavily into a thicket of laurel. He raced down the hill in pursuit, but the grizzly disappeared before he could cut it off. A peculiar savage whining told him it had not gone far. Unwilling to risk death by following, he began to tiptoe around the thicket, straining for a glimpse of fur through the glossy leaves. Suddenly they parted, and man and bear encountered each other.

> He turned his head stiffly toward me; scarlet strings of froth hung from his lips; his eyes burned like embers in the gloom. I held true, aiming behind the shoulder, and my bullet shattered the point or lower end of his heart, taking out a big nick. Instantly the great bear turned with a harsh roar of fury and challenge, blowing the bloody foam from his mouth, so that I saw the gleam of his white fangs; and then he charged straight at me, crashing and bounding through the laurel bushes so that it was hard to aim. I waited till he came to a fallen tree, raking him as he topped it with a ball, which entered his chest and went through the cavity of his body, but he neither swerved nor flinched, and at that moment I did not know that I had struck him. He came steadily on, and in another second was almost upon me. I fired for his forehead, but my bullet went low, entering his open mouth, smashing his lower jaw and going into the neck. I leaped to one side almost as I pulled the trigger; and through the hanging smoke the first thing I saw was his paw as he made a vicious side blow at me. The rush of his charge carried him past. As he struck he lurched forward, leaving a pool of bright blood where his muzzle hit the ground; but he recovered himself and made two or three jumps onward . . . his muscles seemed suddenly to give way, his head drooped, and he rolled over and over like a shot rabbit.[75]

Next morning Roosevelt laboriously hacked off the grizzly's head and hide. Somehow, en route back to Oyster Bay, he lost the skull, and had to replace it with a plaster one before proudly laying the pelt at Edith's feet. Of all his encounters with dangerous game, this had been his most nearly fatal; of all his trophies, this—with the possible exception of his Dakota buffalo—was the one he loved best.[76]

ROOSEVELT FOUND HIMSELF something of a literary celebrity in the fall of 1889. His *Winning of the West* was not only a best-seller (the first edition disappeared in little more than a month)[77] but a *succès d'estime* on both sides of the Atlantic. In Britain, where it rated full-page notices in such periodicals as the *Spectator* and *Saturday Review,* Roosevelt was hailed as a historian of model impartiality; the *Athenaeum* went as far as to call him George Bancroft's successor.[78] In America, scholars of the caliber of Fredrick Jackson Turner and William F. Poole praised *The Winning of the West* as a work of originality, scope, and power. Turner called it "a wonderful story, most entertainingly told." He commended the author for his "breadth of view, capacity for studying local history in the light of world history, and in knowledge of the critical use of material."[79] Dr. Poole, representing the older generation of historians, wrote a rather more balanced criticism in *The Atlantic Monthly:*

> *The Winning of the West* will find many appreciative readers. Mr. Roosevelt's style is natural, simple, and picturesque, without any attempt at fine writing, and he does not hesitate to use Western words which have not yet found a place in the dictionary. He has not taken the old story as he finds it printed in Western books, but has sought for new materials in manuscript collections . . . Few writers of American history have covered a wider or better field of research, or are more in sympathy with the best modern method of studying history from original sources; and yet . . . we have a feeling that he might profitably have spent more time in consulting and collating the rich materials to which he had access. . . .
>
> It is evident from these volumes that Mr. Roosevelt is a man of ability and of great industry. He has struck out fresh and original thoughts, has opened new lines of investigation, and has written paragraphs, and some chapters, of singular felicity . . . Mr. Roosevelt, in writing so good a work, has clearly shown that he could make a better one, if he would take more time in doing it.[80]

But the review which, paradoxically, gave Roosevelt the most satisfaction was a vituperative and error-filled notice in the *New York Sun.* Its pseudonymous author accused him of plagiarism and fraud: Theodore Roosevelt could not have written *The Winning of the West* alone. "It would have been simply impossible for him to do what he claims to have done in the time that was at his disposal." Another scholar, at least, must be responsible for the book's voluminous footnotes and appendices.[81]

Roosevelt had no difficulty in guessing the critic behind the pseudonym: James R. Gilmore, a popular historian whose own works had been rendered obsolete by *The Winning of the West*.[82] He sent the *Sun* a long and humiliating rebuttal, identifying Gilmore by name and demolishing his charges, one by one, with ease. In conclusion he offered a thousand dollars to anybody who could prove he had a collaborator. "The original manuscript is still in the hands of the publishers, the Messrs Putnams, 27 West 23rd Street, New York; a glance at it will be sufficient to show that from the first chapter to the last the text and notes are by the same hand and written at the same time."[83]

Gilmore was forced to issue an answer over his own signature.[84] Unable to substantiate any of his charges, or refute any of Roosevelt's answers, he desperately accused the latter of pirating certain "facts" hitherto published only by himself. Roosevelt annihilated him in a letter too long and too scholarly to quote here—unfortunately, for it is a classic example of that perilous literary genre, the Author's Reply. He begged Mr. Gilmore to identify the "facts," if any, that he had unwittingly plagiarized from him, for he did not wish *The Winning of the West* to contain any fiction. In passing he noted that the critic had not taken up his challenge to examine the manuscript. "It makes one almost ashamed to be in a controversy with him. There is a half-pleasurable excitement in facing an equal foe; but there is none whatever in trampling on a weakling."[85]

ROOSEVELT HAD NO SOONER blotted the last line of this letter, in his Washington office on 10 October, than a telegram from Oyster Bay announced the premature birth of his second son, Kermit.[86] He left at once for Sagamore Hill, chartering a special train in order to be at Edith's bedside that night. For the next two weeks he stayed home while she "convalesced," reading to her and trying to conceal his renewed worries about money.[87] The time for their general move to Washington was approaching; how he would finance it he simply did not know.

What was worse, for the first time he felt really insecure in his job. A "scream for his removal"[88] was gathering in the capital. Inevitably, word had gotten out that he had found a favored place for Hamilton Shidy, the Milwaukee informer. Frank Hatton of the *Post* was going to demand a House investigation; the majority of spoilsmen would undoubtedly agree; it was not farfetched to imagine himself being humiliated in a Congressional witness-box just when his wife arrived in town and began to receive Washington society.

Roosevelt put all his faith in the Annual Report of the Civil Service Commission, which would soon become due. It must be so incisive, so powerfully worded, that President Harrison dare not find fault with it; it must serve notice on Congress that Theodore Roosevelt was no mere publicist, but a solid, authoritative Commissioner.

He spent the last days of his thirtieth year working on the report at Sagamore Hill. There was no attempt to consult his colleagues on the Civil Service Commission: he "hardly dare trust" nice, dim Hugh Thompson with such work, and "as for Lyman, he is utterly useless . . . I wish to Heaven he were off."[89] One can almost hear Henry Cabot Lodge sigh as he read those words. After only five months on the Civil Service Commission, Theodore's hunger for absolute power was already asserting itself.

At the end of October, Roosevelt returned to Washington and rented the nearest thing to a decent house he could afford. It was about one-tenth the size of Sagamore Hill, but that could not be helped. At least the location was good—at 1820 Jefferson Place, off Connecticut Avenue. The Lodges, who were at last back in town, lived only a stone's throw away. Until Edith joined him at the end of the year, they would see that he did not starve.

He sent his report to the White House on 14 November,[90] and plunged into the final rounds of a political battle which had involved him, on and off, since early summer. Two formidable rivals—Thomas B. Reed of Maine and William McKinley of Ohio—were fighting for the Speakership of the House. Roosevelt campaigned for the former, having assured the latter he would one day vote for him as President of the United States.[91] McKinley "was as pleasant as possible—probably because he considered my support worthless."[92] When Congress convened on 2 December, Roosevelt had the satisfaction of seeing Reed elected. In the event of a House investigation, he could now count on the support of the most powerful man on Capitol Hill. A few days later, President Harrison added to his sense of security by approving his report and recommending that the Civil Service Commission's budget be increased.[93]

Christmas found Roosevelt at Sagamore Hill with "Edie and the blessed Bunnies," wondering, as he unwrapped his presents, if Bamie was going to give him Motley's *Letters* or Laing's *Heimskringla*.[94] After the holiday he brought his excited family to Washington, installed them at Jefferson Place, and on 30 December read a paper on "Certain Phases of the Westward Movement in the Revolutionary War" to the American Historical Association.

> What funnily varied lives we do lead, Cabot! We touch two or three little worlds, each profoundly ignorant of the others. Our literary friends have but vague knowledge of our actual political work; and a goodly number of our sporting and social acquaintances know us only as men of good family, one of whom rides to hounds, while the other hunts big game in the Rockies. . . .[95]

BENJAMIN HARRISON'S HANDSHAKE was, in the words of one recipient, "so like a wilted petunia"[96] that only a Roosevelt could react warmly to it. The Civil Service Commissioner was noticeably the most ebullient guest at the White House reception on 1 January 1890. He crushed the petunia heartily, and insisted, at some length, that his Chief have a Happy New Year.[97]

Sincere or not, Roosevelt's wishes came true. 1890 was indeed a year of honeyed contentment for the President and his Administration. Republicans were firmly in control of Congress, and thousands of party workers had swarmed, despite frantic net-waving by the Civil Service Commission, back into the federal beehive. The Union was richer by four new states (North Dakota, South Dakota, Montana, and Washington), and two more would soon be admitted (Wyoming and Idaho). All six were firmly committed to the GOP. Political prospects could not be more favorable—at least through the November elections—and as for economic indicators, they were almost too good to be true. "Our country's cornucopious bounty seemed to overflow," sighed one Washington matron forty years later. "Never again shall any of us see such abundance and cheapness, such luxurious well-being, as prosperous Americans then enjoyed."[98]

The new social season, beginning with the President's reception, was correspondingly brilliant and lavish. Roosevelt was already popular enough (even among those Cabinet officers who were his sworn enemies politically) to take his pick of invitations. Delighted to have a young and attractive wife to squire around town, he dined out at least five times a week, going on to all the best suppers and balls. Browsing at random through names dropped in his weekly letters to Bamie, one finds those of the Vice President, the Secretaries of State, War, Navy, and Agriculture, ministers from Great Britain and Germany, a Supreme Court Justice, the Speaker of the House, numerous Senators and Congressmen, the president of the American Historical Association, and two "inoffensive" English peers. While crowding such persons into his own little dining room, Roosevelt was embarrassed at not being able to afford champagne,[99] but nobody, so far as he could see, seemed to mind very much. He and Edith calculated their guest-lists "pretty carefully," trying to maintain the right admixture of power, brains, and breeding.[100]

Gradually, as the season progressed, a group of favored friends began to form. Roosevelt was not so much the leader of this group as its most gregarious member, equally at ease with all.[101] Towering—literally—above the others was Speaker Reed, all six feet two inches and three hundred pounds of him, a vast, blubbery whale of a man, poised on two flipper-like feet. Reed was the cleverest politician in Washington, and the most domineering: his gong-like voice, which filled every corner of the House with ease, could reduce even Roosevelt to silence. Indeed, there was little to be said when the big man had the floor, for he gave off such waves of authority that few men dared contradict him.[102] That February he had already established himself as one of the great Speakers of the House, having just made his historic ruling against members who refused to stand up and be counted. ("The Chair is making a statement of fact that the gentleman is present. Does the gentleman deny it?"[103]) His wit was brilliant and usually cruel. "They never open their mouths," he complained of two House colleagues, "without subtracting from the sum of human knowledge." Asked to attend the funeral of a political enemy, he refused, "but that does not mean to say I do not heartily approve of it."[104] Sooner or later Reed, who kept a diary in French and owned the finest private library in Maine, made his political associates aware of their intellectual ordinariness, but by the same token few questioned his leadership. "He does what he likes," wrote Cecil Spring Rice, "without consulting the Administration, which he detests, or his followers, whom he despises."[105]

Tom Reed came again and again to the tiny house on Jefferson Place, usually with Congressman Henry Cabot Lodge on his arm. Lodge, in turn, escorted Roosevelt as frequently to Lafayette Square, where two small, rich, bearded men lived side by side in a pair of red Richardson mansions. John Hay and Henry Adams were both fifty-two, and both were completing massive works of American history. They were famous for the excellence of their connections, the brilliance of their conversation, and the quality of the guests they invited to dinner. To be entertained by either (or both, for they were virtually inseparable, and liked to call each other "Only Heart") was to count among the intellectual and social elite of Washington.[106] Roosevelt's references gained him instant access to this charmed circle.

Hay, of course, was an old family friend. Two decades had passed since that windy September night when little Teedie Roosevelt first shook his hand; Hay had subsequently distinguished himself as a diplomat, editor, poet, and Assistant Secretary of State under President Hayes. Now he was parlaying his youthful experiences as secretary to Abraham Lincoln into a ten-volume biography clearly destined for classic status.[107] Ill-born but well-married, John Hay was a spectacularly fortunate man.[108] Ruddy with reflected glory, sleek with inherited wealth, he was enough of a personality in his own right to escape censure. No man, with the possible exception of Henry Adams, wrote better letters; not even Chauncey Depew could match his after-dinner wit; no chargé d'affaires bent more gracefully over a lady's hand, or murmured endearments through such immaculate whiskers. If Hay's hidden lips never quite touched flesh, if he winced when slapped on the back, few were offended, for he associated only with those who understood delicacy and nuance. The son of Mittie Roosevelt understood these things very well, and was therefore cordially received.

Henry Adams was rather more formidable. Flap-eared, balding, wizened, secretive, and shy, he looked not unlike one of his own Oriental monkey-carvings. There was also something simian about his behavior, which alternated between bursts of chattering effusiveness and sudden, cataleptic withdrawal. Yet even when sunk nerveless in the depths of a leather armchair, Adams was listening, watching out of the corner of his eye every flicker of activity in his vast drawing room.

It was, perhaps, the most privileged space in the United States, this book-lined chamber with its three huge windows overlooking Lafayette Square. Whichever window one stood at, the White House floated serenely in center frame, as if to remind one that the grandfather and great-grandfather of the little man in the chair had once lived there. Adams himself rarely bothered to glance at the view; he preferred to sit gazing at the marble slabs around his fireplace: "onyx of a sea-green translucency so exquisite as to make my soul yearn . . ."[109] It would be *lèse-majesté* to suggest that he cross the square and pay his respects. Presidents, on the other hand, were welcome to visit him—assuming they could contribute something worthwhile to the conversation. If, like Rutherford B. Hayes, they could not, Adams merely ignored them until they went away.[110]

It was difficult not to be intimidated by Henry Adams. Not only was his blood the bluest in the land, his wisdom was so profound, and his education (a word he loved to use) so universal, that artists, geologists, poets, politicians, historians, and philosophers deferred to him in their respective fields. Roosevelt had only to glance at the proofs of his nine-volume *History of the United States of America, 1801–1817,* which Adams was then checking, to see that here was learning, grace, and fluidity to which he could not hope to aspire. *The Winning of the West* seemed amateurish in comparison. Insofar as a coarse intellect can comprehend a fine one, he had to acknowledge his own inferiority, while preserving a healthy contempt for the older man's vein of "satirical cynicism."[111] His own robust masculinity sensed a certain feminine reticence, a distaste for action and rough involvement, which rescued him from awe. Years after, he would write of Henry Adams and that other "little emasculated mass of inanity,"[112] Henry James, that they were "charming men, but exceedingly undesirable companions for any man not of strong nature."[113]

Adams, for his part, found Roosevelt repulsively fascinating.[114] The young commissioner's vitality was indecent, his finances ridiculous, and he was about as subtle, culturally speaking, as a bull moose; yet there was no denying his originality, and his extraordinary ability to translate thought into deed—with such blinding rapidity, sometimes, that the two seemed to fuse. Roosevelt had "that singular primitive quality that belongs to ultimate matter—the quality that medieval theology assigned to God—he was pure act."[115] He came flying up the steps of 1603 H Street at such a rate that one could sense, as one shrank into one's armchair, the power that drove him. This young man was equally at home on Adams's Oriental hearthrug, the spit-streaked stairway of the Senate, or the sod floor of a cowboy cabin. His self-assurance, as he paced up and down blustering about the "white-livered weaklings" who ran the government, was both amusing and frightening. Adams was to spend the next eleven years waiting for the inevitable moment when Roosevelt moved into the house of his ancestors, marvelling at the momentum, "silent and awful like the Chicago express . . . of Teddy's luck."[116]

The other regular visitors to No. 1603 included Cecil Spring Rice, Clarence King, an eccentric, globe-trotting geologist whose conversation was as coruscating as the specimens clinking in his pockets, and John La Farge—tall, sickly, saturnine, a genius in the difficult art of stained glass, and in the even more difficult art of writing about it. Equally brilliant, though taciturn and absent-minded, was the sculptor Augustus Saint-Gaudens. He was then at work on his masterpiece, the memorial to Mrs. Henry Adams in Rock Creek Cemetery.[117] Senator James Donald Cameron, beetle-browed and gruff, stopped by often, unaware that he was welcome mainly on account of his young wife, Elizabeth, the most beautiful woman in Washington. (Adams was secretly in love with her; so, to a lesser extent, were Hay and Spring Rice; the three men vied with one another in writing sonnets to her charms.) "Nannie" Cabot Lodge was almost as beautiful as Mrs. Cameron, with her sculptured profile and violet eyes. Famous for her tact, she spent much of her time placating those whom her supercilious husband had offended. Many other rich and talented people crowded Adams's salon for good food, good champagne, and good talk—the best, perhaps, that has ever been heard in Washington.[118]

During the season of 1890, Roosevelt's position in this "pleasant gang," as John Hay liked to call it, was distinctly that of junior member. He received more in the way of ideas and entertainment than he could possibly bestow. It may be wondered why he was so immediately popular. Perhaps the clue lies in a remark made by one who did not quite make it into the Adams circle: "There was a vital radiance about the man—a glowing, unfeigned cordiality towards those he liked that was irresistible." Men of essentially cold blood, like Reed and Adams and Lodge, grew dependent upon his warmth, as lizards crave the sun.[119]

Roosevelt's ascent into the stratosphere of Washington society was not accompanied by any easing of his difficulties as Civil Service Commissioner. If anything, they were worse now Congress was in session, for spoilsmen formed a majority in both Houses.[120] President Harrison's request for more money for the Commission met with determined opposition and delay. Meanwhile the agency was so short of clerks it had fallen three months behind in the marking of examination papers. "No department of the Government is run with such absolutely insufficient means as ours," Roosevelt complained to a Congressman, "and I may say also that no officers of corresponding rank to that of the Civil Service Commissioners are so insufficiently paid."[121] But the House was more interested in Frank Hatton's now almost daily editorials charging the Commissioners with inefficiency, corruption, and abuse of the law. While trumpeting the Roosevelt/Shidy affair as evidence of gross favoritism, Hatton also accused Commissioner Lyman of employing a relative who trafficked in stolen examination questions. Clearly something had to be done, and on 27 January Congress ordered a full investigation by the House Committee on Reform in the Civil Service. A prominent spoilsman, Representative Hamilton G. Ewart of South Carolina, was appointed prosecutor, and Frank Hatton chosen to assist him.[122]

As always when confronted with a challenge, Roosevelt instantly took the offensive. He intended so to dominate the hearings that he would be entirely vindicated, and confirmed in the public mind as leader of a just and effective agency. At the preliminary hearing he insisted that any charges against him be separate from those involving Commissioner Lyman. While assuring the committee—repeatedly—that he was "dee-lighted" to be investigated, he "did not want to be tried for other people's faults."[123] This was hardly a compliment to his senior colleagues, but instinct told him that Lyman's case was more embarrassing than his own. Frank Hatton, coming face to face with Roosevelt for the first time, was clearly overawed by his pugnacious gestures and snapping teeth. Afterward the editor announced that he had nothing against Roosevelt personally; he merely wished to expose the weaknesses of the Civil Service Commission as presently constituted. Should the agency be reorganized with only one man at its head, "he would be very glad to see Mr. Roosevelt appointed."[124]

The hearings proper began on 19 February, with a reading of twelve charges indicting the Civil Service Commission of various faults of management and failure to uphold the law. The fourth alleged

> . . . that Theodore Roosevelt, a member of the Commission, secured the appointment of one Hamilton Shidy to a place in

> the Census Bureau, when it was notoriously known to the said Roosevelt that the said Shidy . . . had persistently and repeatedly violated his oath of office in making false certifications and in not reporting violations of the Civil Service law by the postmaster at Milwaukee to the Commission at Washington.[125]

Thanks to a prolonged examination of the charge against Commissioner Lyman, which Roosevelt listened to looking as if he had a bad smell under his nose,[126] his own case did not come up for another week. Finally, on the afternoon of Friday, 28 February, Hamilton Shidy was sworn in.

The hapless clerk confirmed that Roosevelt had promised him protection in exchange for testimony against Postmaster Paul in June 1889. Subsequently "I obtained a position in the Census Office . . . Mr. Roosevelt being particularly friendly and kindly to me in that respect."[127] Sniggers were heard in various parts of the room. Hatton, cross-examining the witness, tricked him into admitting that if he was again asked by a corrupt superior to falsify government records, he would again do so. This was a blow to Roosevelt, who had hoped that Shidy's moral character would stand up to scrutiny. "I do not care to talk to you any more," he told him afterward. "You have cut your own throat."[128]

Hatton made the most of Roosevelt's discomfiture in huge, front-page headlines next morning:

SHIDY PROVES TO BE BOTH A SCOUNDREL
AND A FOOL—
And Roosevelt, knowing his Infamous Character,
Forced him into an Important Position

THE MOST SHAMEFUL TESTIMONY EVER OFFERED
Even Roosevelt Hung his Head in Shame
As the Disgraceful Story was Unfolded.[129]

When the hearings resumed on 1 March, Robert B. Porter, Superintendent of the Census, took the stand. In response to questioning by Prosecutor Ewart, he testified that Roosevelt had once approached him on behalf of a Milwaukee man who had been "unjustly dismissed" for helping the Civil Service Commission with their work, "and he asked if I could find a place in my office for such a man."[130] But Roosevelt had not said a word about Shidy's misdeeds.

EWART If Mr. Roosevelt had told you that this man had persistently violated the law, had stuffed the lists of eligibles, had mutilated the records and made false certifications, would you have appointed him in your bureau?
PORTER I certainly should not.
EWART I know you would not!

Aware that things were not going too well, Roosevelt jumped to his feet.

ROOSEVELT You knew I had made a report on the subject?
PORTER I knew that—
ROOSEVELT And that Shidy and Paul were implicated in that report, and the report was public and that the Postmaster-General had in writing indicated to you his approval of Shidy's transfer, he having known all about my report and having acted upon it?
PORTER That is true, I think.[131]

There was a stir in the room. Roosevelt was clearly willing to drag John Wanamaker into the proceedings. Porter, thoroughly alarmed now, refused to say anything more that might offend the Civil Service Commissioner.

Roosevelt replaced him on the stand and launched into "a brief statement." The next four pages of the printed transcript, hitherto well splotched with white space, are a solid gray mass of impassioned speech. Speaking with such explosive vigor his spectacles seemed in constant danger of falling off, the Commissioner declared that Shidy had been protected only "because he had done right in trying to atone for his wrongdoing." Both Porter and Wanamaker had agreed to the transfer, and both must have been aware of Shidy's record, since the Milwaukee report "had been spread—broadcast—through the press." As for himself, said Roosevelt, his conscience was clear. "The Government *must* protect its witnesses who are being persecuted for telling the truth."[132]

In an openly hostile cross-examination, Ewart harped on the undeniable fact that Roosevelt had glossed over Shidy's background when negotiating his transfer. The witness grew flustered.

EWART When a man commits perjury . . . and when he confesses he has made false certifications and has persistently and repeatedly violated the law, is it your belief as a Civil Service Reformer . . . that he should be reinstated in office?

ROOSEVELT Do you mean in the same position?

EWART The same position, or any position in Government.

ROOSEVELT That would depend on the circumstances of the case.

EWART Take the circumstances of the Shidy case.

ROOSEVELT I mean to say my action was right in the Shidy case . . . (*to the committee, gesticulating*) Mr. Ewart is evidently wishing me to state that if these circumstances arose I would not act as I did then, giving the impression that I was sorry for what I had done. On the contrary, I think I was precisely right, and I am glad I took that stand.[133]

This last declaration, with its rhythmic use of the personal pronoun, has a familiar ring to students of the later Roosevelt. Many times, as he grew older and more set in his ways, he would protest the moral rightness of his decisions; justice was justice "because I did it."[134]

THE CROSS-EXAMINATION continued. How did Roosevelt *know* the Postmaster General had been familiar with his report? "I did not read it aloud to him," Roosevelt replied sarcastically, "but he had acted upon it, and the presumption is fair that he had read it." Commissioner Thompson stood up to make a statement of full support for Roosevelt's actions. But before the old man could say much, the door of the hearing room flew open and in strode John Wanamaker.[135]

The Postmaster General was hurriedly sworn. Although wreathed in smiles as usual, he did not relish being implicated in Roosevelt's testimony, and wished to make it clear that he had been an innocent party to the transfer. Roosevelt had spoken so glowingly of Shidy that he had been happy to agree. "I always express myself as pleased if employment is given to a person that Roosevelt might recommend."[136] If he had only known the *truth* about Shidy, of course . . .

Stung, Roosevelt leaped to the attack.

ROOSEVELT All these facts . . . are in a report that we made to the President of the United States on this matter. You had that report, and had acted upon it, had you not?

WANAMAKER We had the report.

ROOSEVELT And you had acted upon it, had you not?

WANAMAKER How do you mean, "acted upon it"?

ROOSEVELT You referred to it . . . in your letter notifying Mr. Paul that you had accepted his resignation. If there is any doubt in your mind, you can produce the letter, I presume?

WANAMAKER I cannot say how much influence the Civil Service report had upon me . . .

ROOSEVELT Would you send a copy of the letter? . . . My memory is very clear that in that letter you referred to this report.

WANAMAKER I will furnish it with pleasure.[137]

The letter was duly furnished, but with little pleasure, for it proved the accuracy of Roosevelt's memory, as opposed to Wanamaker's convenient amnesia.

Although the hearings dragged on for another week, neither Hatton nor Ewart was able to uncover any evidence of maladministration by the Civil Service Commission. There was a series of interminable examinations by Roosevelt of George H. Paul, who had been brought in from Milwaukee especially for that purpose. The humiliated ex-postmaster sat for three days in his chair, helpless as a trussed turkey, while Roosevelt determinedly pulled out his feathers, one by one. Squawks of protest—that Paul had given all this testimony before and had already suffered amply for it—went unheeded. Roosevelt seemed determined to show the committee what an angry Civil Service Commissioner looked like in action. Not until late in the afternoon of Friday, 7 March, did the chairman tactfully suggest that enough was enough.[138]

EVEN BEFORE the committee filed its formal report, it was plain that Roosevelt had scored a personal triumph. He had dominated the hearings from the first day to the last, and had somehow managed to arouse sympathy for his patronage of "Shady Shidy," as that gentleman was now known. His prestige as Civil Service Commissioner had been greatly enhanced, at the expense of the discredited Lyman and the reticent Thompson. The committee was rumored to be in favor of recommending the creation of a single-headed Commission, with himself the obvious choice as chief, but Roosevelt, surprisingly, opposed this idea, saying that it was attractive but premature. To put a Republican in sole control, he argued, would compromise the Commission's non-partisan image and make it vulnerable to changing majorities in Congress.[139] This was true enough, but sophisticated observers could detect signs of a larger, more long-term ambition in Roosevelt's modesty. He already had all the power the inadequate Civil Service Law allowed him; killing two colleagues off would not increase it. At thirty-one, he could afford to wait a few more years for real power.

Roosevelt himself admitted, later in life, that it was about this time that he began to cast thoughtful eyes upon 1600 Pennsylvania Avenue. "I used to walk by the White House, and my heart would beat a little faster as the thought came to me that possibly—*possibly*—I would some day occupy it as President."[140] Jeremiah Curtin, the translator of Sienkiewicz, happened to catch him in the act one day, during a visit to the White House with Representative Frederick T. Greenhalge of the House Civil Service Committee.

"That man," said Curtin, "looks precisely as if he had examined the building and, finding it to his liking, had made up his mind to inhabit it." "I must make you acquainted with him," replied Greenhalge. "But first listen to a prophecy: when he wants this house he will get it. He will yet live here as President."[141]

MARCH MERGED INTO APRIL, April into May, but the committee, plagued by absenteeism, kept postponing its report. Roosevelt grew impatient and nervous. "It is very important that the present Commission be given an absolutely clean bill of health . . . a verdict against us is a verdict against the reform and against decency."[142] Frank Hatton, too, seemed bothered by the suspense; his editorial attacks on Roosevelt grew hysterical. "This scion of 'better blood,' " he raged, "this pampered pink of inherited wealth . . . this seven months' child of conceited imbecility [is] a sham, a pretender and a fraud as a reformer and a failure as a business man." Eventually the flow of vituperation ceased. "The *Post* . . . having passed the pestiferous Roosevelt between its thumb-nails, drops him and awaits the report of the investigating committee."[143]

As usual in times of stress, Roosevelt distracted himself with literature, and worked doggedly on his long-postponed history of New York City. "How I regret ever having undertaken it!" By way of relaxation he wrote three or four hunting pieces for *Century,* and, by way of duty, some very dull articles on Civil Service Reform. He apologized to George Haven Putnam for having to abandon—temporarily—Volumes Three and Four of his *magnum opus.* "I half wish I was out of this Civil Service Commission work, for I can't do satisfactorily with *The Winning of the West* until I am; but I suppose I ought really to stand by it for at least a couple of years."[144]

HE SPENT ONE of the most important weekends of his life on 10 and 11 May, reading from cover to cover Alfred Thayer Mahan's new book, *The Influence of Sea Power upon History.*[145] Since the publication of his own *Naval War of 1812* he had considered himself an expert on this very subject, and had argued, passionately but vaguely, that modernization of the fleet must keep pace with the industrialization of the economy. But he had never questioned America's traditional naval strategy, based on a combination of coastal defense and commercial raiding. Now Mahan extended and clarified his vision, showing that real national security—and international greatness—could only be attained by building more and bigger ships and deploying them farther abroad. While advocating the constant growth of the American Navy, Mahan paradoxically insisted that its power be concentrated at various "pressure points" which controlled the circulation of global commerce. By striking quickly and sharply at any of these nerve centers, the United States could paralyze whole oceans. Mahan supported his thesis with brilliant analyses of the strategies of Nelson and Napoleon, proving that navies could be more effective than armies in determining the relative strength of nations. He also explained the intricate relationships between political power and sea power, warfare and economics, geography and technology. Roosevelt flipped the book shut a changed man. So, as it happened, did Kaiser Wilhelm II of Germany, when he read it—not to mention various Lords of the British and Japanese Admiralties, and officials throughout the Navy Department of the United States. More than any other strategic philosopher, Alfred Thayer Mahan was responsible for the naval buildup which preoccupied these four nations at the turn of the nineteenth and twentieth centuries; more than any other world leader of the period, Theodore Roosevelt would glory in *The Influence of Sea Power upon History,* both as a title and as a fact.[146]

THE REPORT OF the House committee's investigation, filed 13 June 1890, stated that "the public service has been greatly benefited, and the law, on the whole, well-executed" by all three Commissioners. Charles Lyman was mildly censured for a certain "laxity of discipline" in administrative affairs, while his colleagues received unqualified praise. "We find that Commissioners Roosevelt and Thompson have discharged their duties with entire fidelity and integrity," the document stated.[147] "WHITEWASH!" screamed the *Washington Post,* but most press comment was approving. *The New York Times* and *Evening Post* went so far as to criticize President Harrison and Postmaster General Wanamaker for not supporting the Civil Service Commission. Roosevelt returned with some relief to bureaucratic work.[148] During his first year in office he had attracted a greater glare of publicity than his eight predecessors put together. It was time to retire temporarily to the wings before he was accused of hogging the footlights. Already the *Saturday Globe* was warning: "There is, perhaps, no man in the country more ambitious than this young New York politician."[149]

Once again Washington began to drowse in summer heat. Edith and the children returned to Sagamore Hill; Cecil Spring Rice fled for the cool shores of Massachusetts; Henry Adams prepared to depart for the South Seas. Congress remained in session, with Speaker Reed presiding over the House in flannels and canvas shoes, a yellow scarf around his enormous waist.[150] Roosevelt went to Oyster Bay as often as he could, but pressure of work (for the Commission was still backlogged) continually drew him back. He managed to finish his "*very* commonplace little book" on New York by the beginning of August, and spent the next three weeks feverishly trying to clear his desk. Another Western trip was in the offing, this time to Yellowstone, which he wished to inspect on behalf of the Boone & Crockett Club, but administrative difficulties nearly made him cancel it. "Oh, Heaven, if the President had a little backbone, and if the Senators did not have flannel legs!"[151]

The first of September found Roosevelt in a large family party, including his wife and two sisters, heading West to Medora and the Rockies. Impressed as he was by the splendors of Yellowstone, he reserved his most admiring adjectives for Edith. The sight of that demure, book-loving lady cantering across the prairie on a wiry horse seemed to have shocked him into a renewed awareness of her charms. "She looks just as well and young and pretty as she did four years ago when I married her . . . she is as healthy as possible, and so young-looking and slender to be the mother of those two sturdy little scamps, Ted and Kermit."[152]

WASHINGTON WAS STILL deserted when he got back there in early October. Benjamin Harrison was at home, however, so Roosevelt paid a friendly call. Harrison, who had gotten into the habit of drumming his fingers nervously during their interviews, gave him a frigid reception. Evidently the White House wanted to have nothing further to do with Civil Service Reform. "Damn the President! He is a cold-blooded, narrow-minded, prejudiced, obstinate, timid old psalm-singing Indianapolis politician."[153]

The November Congressional elections were disastrous for the Republican party, due mainly to an unpopular tariff measure which William McKinley had pushed into law at the end of the last session. With prices on manufactured goods rising daily, voters threw the culprit out of office—severely damaging his presidential prospects—and filled the House with the largest Democratic majority in history.[154] Roosevelt, who had never liked the McKinley bill, began to mutter dire predictions about Cleveland recapturing the White House in 1892. But with his family reinstalled in town, and Henry Cabot Lodge by great luck returned to Congress, he found it impossible to be gloomy. Indeed, Roosevelt was conspicuously the most cheerful Republican in Washington that winter. "He continues to wear the nattiest and most stylish grey trousers, and the most boyish hat he can buy," reported a local correspondent, "and he whistles jovially as he legs it down to the rooms of the Civil Service Commission."[155]

Christmas was spent at 1820 Jefferson Place, and Roosevelt rejoiced in the event as much as any of his children:

> Such nice stockings, with such an entrancing way of revealing in their bulging outline the promise of what was inside! They burrowed into them with their eager, chubby little hands, and hailed each new treasure with shouts of delight. Then after breakfast we all walked into the room where the big toys, so many of them! were, on the tables; and I suppose Alice and Ted came as near to realizing the feelings of those who enter Paradise as they ever will on this earth.[156]

That, according to his old friend Mrs. Winthrop Chanler, was the essence of Theodore Roosevelt, at least during his early years in Washington. "Life was the unpacking of an endless Christmas stocking."[157]

"He is evidently a maniac morally no less than mentally."

Elliott Roosevelt about the time of his marriage to Anna Hall.

CHAPTER 17

The Dear Old Beloved Brother

In his house this malcontent
Could the King no longer bear.

IN JANUARY 1891 Roosevelt was forced to turn his attention to "a nightmare of horror"[1] that had been brooding over him for at least three years. His preoccupation with literature, politics, and his own immediate family had caused him to ignore warnings that Elliott Roosevelt was determinedly drinking himself to death. The two brothers, so close in youth, had recently seen very little of each other. Twenty miles of country road, and a yawning social gulf, separated their respective Long Island establishments. At Sagamore Hill the talk was of books and public affairs; at Hempstead, of parties, fashions, and horseflesh. On the rare occasions when the brothers met, friends were struck by the reversal of their teenage roles: where once Theodore had been sickly and solitary, and Elliott an effulgent Apollo, now it was the elder who glowed, and the younger who was wasting away.[2]

It is difficult to say whether Elliott Roosevelt was victim or culprit in his own decline. His misfortunes were physical as well as psychological. Since puberty he had been afflicted with semiepileptic seizures, usually brought on by stress, and when still adolescent discovered that alcohol was an effective depressant.[3] Long before his twenty-first birthday, Elliott was drinking heavily, although his good looks and athletic bearing tended to disguise the fact. After marrying the beautiful but (in Theodore's view) "utterly frivolous" Anna Hall,[4] he had become a confirmed alcoholic. Withdrawal from drink after binges only worsened his tendency to epilepsy. A series of inexplicable sporting accidents, which may have been caused by seizures, progressively wrecked his health. The most serious of these—a fall from a trapeze during amateur theatricals in 1888—temporarily crippled his leg, and he became dependent on laudanum and morphine during the agony of recuperation. There had been a complete physical collapse in 1889, followed by such desperate drinking during the early part of 1890 as to shock even himself into awareness of his impending doom. Swearing never to touch alcohol again, he left the United States for Europe that summer, taking his wife, six-year-old daughter, and baby son with him.[5] From Vienna, in September 1890, came news of the inevitable relapse, followed shortly before Christmas by a *cri de coeur* from Anna.[6] She was pregnant again, and was afraid of spending the winter alone with her unstable husband. If Bamie—ever-willing, ever-capable Bamie—would come over and look after her, Elliott could surely be persuaded to enter a sanitarium for treatment. By the time the baby was born he should be decently dried out, and they could all return happily to New York in time for the next social season.

Although Theodore considered Anna's optimism "thoroughly Chinese," he did see the advisability of Bamie's presence in Vienna.[7] But no sooner had he given his official permission, as head of the family, than a bombshell announcement, on legal stationery, arrived from New York. His brother's seed, apparently, was also sprouting in the body of a servant girl named Katy Mann. She claimed to have been seduced by Elliott shortly before his departure for Europe, and threatened a public scandal if she did not receive financial compensation for her pregnancy.[8]

Roosevelt's reaction to this "hideous revelation" was entirely characteristic. "Of course he was insane when he did it."[9] Alcoholism he believed to be a disease that could be treated and cured. But infidelity was a crime, pure and simple; it could be neither forgiven nor understood, save as an act of madness. It was an offense against order, decency, against civilization; it was a desecration of the holy marriage-bed. By reducing himself to the level of a "flagrant man-swine," Elliott had forfeited all claim to his wife and children. For Anna to continue to live with him now would be "little short of criminal," he told Bamie. "She ought not to have any more children, and those she has should be brought up away from him."[10]

Were it not for Anna's present delicate condition (she was a frail person at the best of times), Theodore would no doubt have ordered Bamie to fetch her home at once. There was nothing to do but let Bamie go over as planned and privately confront Elliott with the news. If nothing else, it might sober him up long enough to commit himself to a sanitarium for treatment. Such an act of voluntary self-incarceration, wrote Theodore, "will serve to explain and atone for what cannot otherwise ever be explained." As souls pass through Purgatory in order to wash away sin, so, presumably, could a repentant Elliott redeem his fit of "insanity."[11] In the meantime Theodore and the lawyers would await the birth of Katy Mann's baby; should any Roosevelt blood be identifiable in it, they would pay her whatever hush-money was necessary.[12]

Bamie sailed for Europe in early February 1891. While she was still on the high seas, Theodore received an affectionate and unsuspecting letter from Elliott. Despite his newfound contempt for "the dear old beloved brother," memories of their happy closeness in the past crowded in on him, and he sank into the deepest gloom. "It is horrible, awful; it is like a brooding nightmare. If it was mere death one could stand it; it is the shame that is so fearful."[13] Much of the "shame," of course, was his own: he felt acute distaste for the role he had inherited as go-between in a shabby paternity suit. If it ever got out that the Civil Service Commissioner was involved in blackmail payments, Frank Hatton would annihilate him. But he saw no other way of protecting his family from a catastrophic scandal.

At the end of February, Bamie wrote to say that Elliott, surprisingly, had already placed himself in the Marien Grund Sanctuary at Graz. He was in a highly excitable state, bursting into tears at the slightest hint of disapproval, so she would wait until he was stronger before telling him about Katy Mann. The incarceration was to last three months. Although Theodore was pessimistic about the effects of so short a stay in so luxurious a retreat, he was relieved for Anna's sake—"Elliott is purely secondary."[14] With neither of his brother's babies due until the spring,[15] he could devote his full attention to Civil Service matters.

IT HAPPENED THAT Roosevelt's family troubles during the early part of 1891 coincided with a period of renewed political difficulties. At times he felt he was "battling with everybody . . . the little gray man in the White House looking on with cold and hesitating disapproval."[16] The struggle was provoked by his efforts to extend the classification of the Civil Service to all offices in the Indian Bureau. Rioting by Sioux in South Dakota reservations, where maladministration and corruption were rife, had forced him to rethink his old paternal attitudes to the red man, and he now tried to persuade Administration officials that Indians should take part wherever possible in agency affairs. "I should take the civilized members of the different tribes and put them to work in instructing their fellows in farming, blacksmithing and the like, and should extend the present system of paid Indian judges and police." But the officials were apathetic, and President Harrison flatly refused to admit that conditions on the reservations were bad.[17]

February saw the usual appropriations crisis in Congress. Republican spoilsmen lobbied to such good effect that for two days the Civil Service Commission was in danger of losing its entire operating budget. Speaker Reed had to use his massive personal influence before the funds were voted on 14 February.[18]

With the departure of Congress in early March, pressure on the Civil Service Commission finally eased, and Roosevelt found himself with little official work to do. His thoughts began to drift toward literature again, for the first reviews of his *History of the City of New York*[19] were flowing in from both sides of the Atlantic.

THE BRITISH CRITICS were complimentary, if not enthusiastic. It was felt that Roosevelt had done as well as could be expected, given the largeness of his subject and the limitations of his space. *New York* was "pleasantly written," remarked the *Spectator,* but as a story it was not inspiring. Roosevelt had been unable to prove that the city's rapid growth had been to any good purpose. "An hour in New York suffices to inform the observing foreigner that it is among the worst-governed, worst-paved, worst-built, and worst-ordered cities in the world." Still, one had to admire Roosevelt's condemnation of municipal corruption and his freedom from "any trace of Chauvinism."[20]

It was left to an American periodical, the *Nation,* to point out that on the contrary Roosevelt was very chauvinistic indeed. The anonymous reviewer sounded a complaint that would be heard with increasing frequency during the next ten years: "Mr. Roosevelt preaches too much. He lays down the singular proposition that a feeling of broad, radical, intense Americanism is necessary if good work is to be done in any direction . . The sooner we get over talking about 'American' systems of philosophy, and ethics, and art, and devote ourselves to what is true, and right, and beautiful, the sooner we shall shake off our provincialism."[21]

The most that can be said of *New York* today is that it is a piece of honorable hackwork, tightly written, unflawed by any trace of originality. One or two passages are of semiautobiographical interest (Roosevelt can never resist injecting himself and his personal opinions into a historical narrative), and his command of urban details is at least as impressive as that of Western material in his earlier histories. The section dealing with the unprecedented tidal wave of immigration that battered New York after the War of 1812 is an early example of Roosevelt's fascination with "ethnic turnover," as he called it. "The public-school system and the all-pervading energy of American life proved too severe solvents to be resisted even by the German tenacity . . . The children of the first generation were half, and the grandchildren in most cases wholly, Americanized—to their own inestimable advantage." There is also a characteristic passage that describes policemen attacking the Draft Rioters "with the most wholesome intent to do them physical harm." Thirty rioters were slain "—an admirable object-lesson to the remainder."[22]

ROOSEVELT WAS WORKING in his office on the afternoon of Tuesday, 24 March—regretting that there was just enough paper on his desk to keep him from *The Winning of the West*[23]—when a Mr. John C. Rose of Baltimore was shown in. Rose was counsel to the Maryland Civil Service Reform League, and as such considered himself a watchdog over the law in his hometown. He had serious irregularities to report.

A Republican primary was scheduled in Baltimore for the following Monday, Rose explained. Its purpose was to elect delegates to the Maryland State Convention, which would in turn establish procedures for the election of delegates to the National Convention in 1892.[24] At the moment things were not going well for the friends of Benjamin Harrison. It looked as if the city might choose an anti-Administration slate; in that case the President could forget about Maryland's votes when he ran for renomination. As a result, the local postmaster and U.S. marshal—both Harrison appointees—were using their offices as emergency campaign chests. Senior federal employees were going around "assessing" subordinates for contributions ranging from $5 to $10 each.[25] This was in open defiance of Section One of the Civil Service Code, prohibiting the solicitation of money for political purposes on government property. The money would certainly be used to bribe election judges on Monday, and there was no saying what other means the pro-Administration forces might use to influence the course of the voting. Rose begged Roosevelt to come down and investigate the situation at once: several witnesses were prepared to testify to the truth of his allegations.[26]

Roosevelt proved oddly coy. Although he did not say as much to Rose, he dreaded another contretemps with the Postmaster General—which would surely occur should he uncover further evidence of politicking in that gentleman's department. Wanamaker had been smarting ever since the Paul/Shidy affair, and if stung once more could be expected to fight tooth and nail for Roosevelt's removal.

Stalling for time, the Commissoner asked Rose to return to Baltimore and put his information in writing. When the letter arrived two days later he sent it on to Wanamaker, suggesting that as most of the allegations therein referred to the Post Office, the Postmaster General should perhaps investigate them himself. Wanamaker declined.[27] Roosevelt felt he had done what he could to protect the Administration, and must now do his duty. With his usual flair for the dramatic, he chose to arrive in Baltimore unannounced, on the morning of Election Day, 30 March.[28]

As he wandered through the noisy wards he saw enough evidence of wanton illegality by federal employees to fill a fleet of police wagons. He tried to maintain an air of official disapproval, but the writer in him could not help rejoicing in scenes and incidents straight out of *Pickwick Papers.* On every sidewalk fists flew and money—taxpayers' money—changed hands, while in house-windows overlooking the street, election judges sat in impassive groups of three, like monkeys who saw, heard, and spoke no evil. Relays of furniture carts rumbled in from all points of the compass, bringing hundreds of rural voters with no apparent connections to the local Republican party. Ward-workers entertained these transients in saloons where the beer flowed freely, compliments of Postmaster Johnson and Marshal Airey. Countless "pudding" tickets (six or seven slips folded together as one) were deposited on behalf of both factions; when a judge objected to this, his two colleagues threw him bodily into the crowd. Elsewhere an anti-Administration worker eliminated three pro-Administration judges by the simple expedient of pulling a blind down over their window. "On account of this excessive zeal," wrote Roosevelt admiringly, "he was taken to the watch-house and fined."[29]

The polls closed at eight o'clock, and although there seemed to be three to four times as many votes as voters, the majority were clearly in favor of the anti-Administration forces. Roosevelt had no comment to make: he was busy interviewing federal employees who had contributed to, or participated in, the day's proceedings.[30] Not one of them saw anything wrong in influencing the course of a political election. "As far as I could find out," Roosevelt recalled, ". . . there seemed to be no question of principle at stake at all, but one of offices merely . . . it was not a primary which particularly affected the interest of private citizens." The civil servants of Baltimore, he added, "were as thorough believers in a system of oligarchical government as if they had lived in Venice or Sparta."[31]

Party reaction to his visit was immediate and violent. On 1 April the Washington correspondent of the *Boston Post* reported: "The removal of Theodore Roosevelt from the Civil Service Commission is among the possibilities of the near future." The President, apparently, was "very mad" with him.[32] Frank Hatton delightedly fanned the flames with a front-page story headlined "TEDDY AT THE POLLS—Helping To Hurt Mr. Harrison—He Is Hand-in-Glove with the Anti-Administration Men." The article alleged that Roosevelt's tour through the wards had caused many government employees to "desert the field," resulting in a humiliating defeat for the Administration. "If the delegation sent to the next nominating convention is anti-Harrison, the President will have nobody to blame more than his Civil Service Commissioner."[33]

On 4 April, an incensed party of Maryland spoilsmen visited the White House to demand Roosevelt's dismissal.[34] Harrison said he would wait for an official report of the investigation before deciding what to do. This was a clear warning to Roosevelt to modify, delay, or even suppress any embarrassing findings.

Aware that he had an ax hanging over him[35]—an ax that threatened to split asunder not only the Civil Service Commission, but the entire Administration—Roosevelt drafted his report with extreme caution. He returned to Baltimore three times, on 6, 13, and 18 April, to gather extra material.[36] Every word of testimony was transcribed by a stenographer, lest the President doubt any of the evidence. Some interviews, despite his efforts to be severe, came out like music-hall dialogue:

Q. How do you do your cheating?
A. Well, we do our cheating honorably.[37]

Although Roosevelt quoted such non sequiturs with relish, the cheerful mendacity of witness after witness gradually sickened him. Out of their own mouths, he wrote, no fewer than twenty-five Harrison appointees stood convicted, and the President should dismiss them at once. His analysis of the evidence contained a typically aggressive plea for the abolition of the spoils system, on the grounds of pure political morality. "Resolved into its ultimate elements, the view of the spoils politician is that politics is a dirty game, which ought to be played solely by those who desire, by hook or crook, to win pecuniary reward [in] the form of money or of office. Politics cannot possibly be put upon a healthy basis until this idea is absolutely eradicated . . . As for the Government office-holder, he must be taught in one way or another that his duty is to do the work of the Government for the whole people, and not to pervert his office for the use of any party or any faction."[38]

In conclusion, Roosevelt noted that Postmaster Johnson had weakly disclaimed responsibility for the politicking of his employees. Such men were loyal, not to him, but to their ward leaders, who had ordered Johnson to hire them in the first place. "This testimony," Roosevelt remarked contemptuously, ". . . shows the utter nonsense of the talk that under the spoils system the appointing officers themselves make the appointments. They do nothing of the kind . . . outside politicians make the appointments for them." There was not enough evidence to warrant indictment of either Johnson or Marshal Airey—although the latter had been seen tearing the coat-buttons off a recalcitrant judge. In an obvious attempt to placate the President, Roosevelt avoided direct censure of either official, but suggested that in future any such politicking by senior civil servants "shall be treated as furnishing cause for dismissal."[39]

THE REPORT OF COMMISSIONER *Roosevelt Concerning Political Assessments and the Use of Official Influence to Control Elections in the Federal Offices at Baltimore, Maryland*[40] was, and remains, a masterpiece in its genre. It was short (146 pages), dense with relevant information, yet so clearly written as to speed both reader and author irresistibly to the same conclusion. Indeed the document was so seductive, not to say seditious, in its indictment of Old Guard Republicanism that Roosevelt himself seems to have had second thoughts about sending it in, or at least to have yielded to the suggestions of Commissioners Lyman and Thompson that he delay its release until the summer vacations, when negative publicity would do the Administration least harm.[41]

As a result, he enjoyed a temporary lull in his "warfare with the ungodly," and drifted into "the pleasant life one can lead in Washington in the spring, if there are several tolerably intimate families."[42] The Roosevelts dined the Reeds; the Reeds responded with lunch; the Hays dined the Roosevelts; and "good, futile, pathetic Springy" entertained everybody at the country club. Theodore and Edith made side trips to Senator Cameron's estate in Pennsylvania, and to William Merritt Chase's art studio in New York, where Carmencita performed the new dance sensation, *flamenco.* April was effulgent, "clear as a bell . . . the flowers in bloom, and the trees a fresh and feathery green." There were moonlight drives along the Potomac, followed by dinner; receptions for "various Dago diplomats," followed by dinner; lazy Saturday lunches and lingering Sunday teas, followed by yet more dinners.[43] Roosevelt, whose body was thickening steadily with age, attempted to lose weight by trotting up Rock Creek in heavy flannels. His Dutch Reformed conscience began to bother him. "I have been going out too much . . . I wish I had more chance to work at my books . . . I don't feel as if I were working to lasting effect."[44]

SOMETIME THAT SPRING he was overjoyed to receive a "temperate, natural, truthful" letter from his brother, whom Bamie had at last told about Katy Mann. It amounted to a total rejection of the girl's story.[45] Naively reassured, Theodore wondered if he should call her bluff. "It is a ticklish business," he told Bamie. "I hate the idea of [a] public scandal; and yet I never believe in yielding a hair's breadth to a case of simple blackmail."[46]

But Katy Mann—who had given birth to a son—was not in the least deterred from pressing her suit. She claimed that Elliott had given her a locket and some compromising letters, which she would be happy to produce in court. Other servants, moreover, were willing to testify that he had been infatuated with her, and that his voice had been heard in her room. "Of course she is lying," Theodore wrote uneasily.[47]

He was still wondering how to proceed when the reports from Europe took on a sudden, alarming turn. Elliott had quit the sanitarium in Graz on some wild impulse, and had dragged Anna, Bamie, and the children to Paris. There he had taken on an American mistress, a Mrs. Evans, begun to drink again, and was occasionally so violent as to frighten Anna into hysterics.[48] Theodore chafed with frustration. Were it not for the fact that his own wife was heavily pregnant, he would have taken the next ship to Paris. He insisted, in a brutally decisive letter dated 7 June, that Elliott must be left to drink himself to death, if necessary, the moment Anna's confinement was over.

> Anna must be made to understand that it is both maudlin and criminal—I am choosing my words with scientific exactness—to continue living with Elliott . . . Do everything to persuade her to come home at once, unless Elliott will put himself in an asylum for a term of years, or unless, better still, he will come too. Once here I'll guarantee to see that he is shut up . . .
>
> Make up your mind to one dreadful scene. Use this letter if you like. Tell him that he is either responsible or irresponsible. If responsible then he must go where he can be cured; if irresponsible he is simply a selfish brutal and vicious criminal, and Anna ought not to stay with him an hour.
>
> Do not care an atom for his threats of going off alone. Let him go . . . What happens to him is of purely minor importance now; and the chance of public scandal must not be weighed for a moment against the welfare, the life, of Anna and the children . . .
>
> If he can't be shut up, and will neither go of his own accord, nor let Anna depart of his free will, then make your plans and go off some day in his absence. If you need me telegraph me, and I (or Douglas [Robinson] if it is impossible for me to go on account of Edith) will come at once. But remember, I come on one condition. I come to settle the thing once and for all . . . You can tell him that Anna has a perfect right to a divorce; she or you or I have but to express belief in the Katy Mann story and no jury in the country would refuse a divorce.

Notwithstanding his threat to uphold Katy Mann in court, Theodore still wanted to believe that the girl was lying.[49] As a gentleman he had to accept his brother's denial until it was proved false. He therefore ordered his representatives "to tell her to go on with her law suit . . . she will get nothing from us." Senior members of the family were alerted to the likelihood of "some pretty ugly matters" surfacing in the press.[50]

At this point another letter arrived from Elliott,[51] reiterating his innocence but authorizing Theodore to pay Katy Mann "a moderate sum" in exchange for a quit claim. The lawyers suggested three thousand dollars, rising to four if necessary.[52] That was much more than Elliott had in mind, but they reminded Theodore that in cases of this kind, involving boozy playboys and humble servant girls, the jury's sympathy was always with the plaintiff. In a letter to "dear old Nell," dated 14 June 1891, Theodore tried desperately to convince his brother—and himself—that the amount was worth paying.

> If you and I were alone in the world I should advise fighting her as a pure blackmailer, yet as things [are] I did not dare . . .
>
> The woman must admit that on her own plea she must have been a willing, probably inviting party. But she has chosen her time with great skill. During that week [of the alleged seduction] you were very sick, and for hours at a time were out of your head, and did not have any clear recollection of what you were doing. You wandered much about the house those nights, alone. She could get testimony that you were often wild and irresponsible, either from being out of your head or from the use of liquor or opiates. At present you are not in any condition to go on the stand and be cross-examined as to your past and your personal habits by a sharp and unscrupulous lawyer. So that however the suit went, it would create a great scandal; and much would be dragged out that we are very desirous of keeping from the public.

This appeal to his brother's sense of reason was rendered academic by a letter from Bamie the next day, saying that Elliott had begun to suffer from *delirium tremens*.[53] Worse news arrived with almost every mail. Elliott no longer denied sleeping with Katy Mann; he merely said "he could not remember" doing so. He refused to be shut up against his will, and threatened to cut Anna off without a penny if she deserted him. Simultaneously he threatened to go off on a long sea voyage as soon as her baby was born.[54] "He is evidently a maniac morally no less than mentally," Theodore wrote in despair.[55]

As the Commissioner pondered each fresh letter and telegram, he could detect a certain animal ruthlessness in Elliott's behavior. What that golden sot really wanted was to have everything—to hold on to his wife and children as symbols of respectability, to drink as much as he liked, sleep with whomever he pleased, and squander his money on himself, rather than alimony and paternity suits.[56] Elliott could not care less about Katy Mann's threats. He knew that the family elders were so afraid of scandal they would silence her at all costs. If he refused to pay her the $4,000, somebody else assuredly would.

Theodore did not doubt this, having already, in an unfortunate gaffe, told Elliott that an uncle was willing to provide the hush-money.[57] He confessed to Bamie on 20 June that he was at his wits' end as to what to advise; he could only insist, ad nauseam, that Anna must come home and not condone Elliott's "hideous depravity" by continuing to live with him "as man and wife."[58] But there seemed little chance of that: Bamie wrote to say that Anna had called longingly for Elliott while giving birth to their son, Hall, on 28 June. "It is dreadful to think of the inheritance the poor little baby may have in him," Theodore wrote somberly—and prophetically.[59]

The thought of Elliott now being free to return to Anna's bed saddened and sickened him. In his opinion, sex between them should cease until Elliott "by two or three years of straight life" had canceled out the sin of adultery.[60] It did not occur to him that Anna, who had no sins to atone for, might be in any way inconvenienced by such an arrangement.

ROOSEVELT'S WORRIES ABOUT Katy Mann, aggravated by nervousness over the political consequences of his Baltimore report (still pigeonholed despite frantic pleas from reformers for its release), plunged him into gloom as June gave way to July. "I am at the end of my career, such as it is," he wrote to Henry Cabot Lodge. ". . . I often have a regret that I am not in with you, Reed, and others in doing the real work." About the only people who seemed to approve of him at the moment were the mugwumps, and he needed none of *their* lisping praises. The "good party men" whose respect he craved seemed to cherish nothing but "bitter animosities" toward him.[61]

His mood was not improved by an awkward business meeting with President Harrison on 1 July. "Throughout the interview he was as disagreeable and suspicious of manner as well might be," Roosevelt wrote Lodge. "He *is* a genial little runt, isn't he?"[62] Actually the meeting had positive results. Harrison approved some new Civil Service rules governing promotions which Roosevelt had been pressing as part of his campaign to root out favoritism in government departments; but the coolness between the two men was such that even their treaties seemed like truces.

ROOSEVELT WAS NOW FREE to leave Washington for the summer, there being little work in his hot, musty office that he could not do at Sagamore Hill. Edith and the children had long since preceded him north, and he missed them so painfully he would look over his shoulder for them on walks through Rock Creek Park. Pausing only to stuff a suitcase with fireworks, he caught the Limited to New York on Friday, 3 July,[63] arriving home in time for the holiday.

It was not a very festive weekend. On Sunday he was obliged to cross the Sound for the funeral of his cousin Alfred—killed horribly under the wheels of a train[64]—and he returned to news that Katy Mann had finally named her price: $10,000. This, Theodore wrote Bamie, was "so huge a sum" that the hoped-for compromise seemed unlikely. The scandal would break any day now, he feared. It was impossible to deny Elliott's culpability: an "expert in likenesses" had seen the baby, and its features were unmistakably Rooseveltian.[65]

Telegrams from Europe crossed his letter to report that Elliott had been inveigled into an inebriate asylum outside Paris. He was now safely under lock and key, and Bamie had persuaded Anna to return to the States without him.[66]

About this time the figure of Katy Mann begins mysteriously to fade from history. The last specific reference to her in Theodore's correspondence is a remark dated 21 July: "Frank Weeks [Elliott's lawyer] advises me that I have no power whatever to compromise in the Katy Mann affair. I suppose it will all be out soon." But the scandal never broke. Evidently the girl got her money, although how much, and when, and who paid it, is unknown.[67]

A SCANDAL OF ANOTHER SORT began to loom on 4 August, when Roosevelt sent advance copies of his Baltimore report to the White House and Post Office Department. Official reaction to the document was best symbolized by Assistant Postmaster General Clarkson, who took one look at it and placed it under lock and key.[68] An abridged form of the report was released for publication on 16 August, and instantly became front-page news.[69] Fortunately both President Harrison and Postmaster General Wanamaker were on vacation, and would not return until early September, by which time Roosevelt planned to be two thousand miles west in the Rockies.[70] The inevitable confrontation between them would thus be delayed until October at least.

Try as he might, Roosevelt could not keep his name out of current headlines. On 17 August, the day after his Baltimore report was broadcast to the nation, the *New York Sun* splashed the following sensational story:

ELLIOTT ROOSEVELT INSANE

His Brother Theodore Applies for a Writ in Lunacy

A Commission [has been] appointed by Justice O'Brien of the Supreme Court to enquire into the mental condition of Elliott Roosevelt, with a view to having a committee

> appointed to care for his person and for his estate. The application was made by his brother, United States Civil Service Commissioner and ex-Assemblyman Theodore Roosevelt, with the approval of Elliott Roosevelt's wife, Anna Hall Roosevelt. . . .
>
> Theodore Roosevelt avers in the papers in the case that the mental faculties of his brother have been failing him for nearly two years. He says he saw him frequently until Elliott went to Europe in July 1890, and he had remarked the gradual impairment of his intellect. His conversation had been rambling and he could not tell a story consecutively . . . During the winter of 1890 he had several bad turns. He became violent and on three occasions threatened to take his own life. He had to be placed in surveillance. Mr. Roosevelt says he is "unable to say how far the result is due to indulgence in drink or other excesses." He alleges that the property of his brother in this State consists of real estate, bonds, stocks, and is worth $170,000.

Substantially the same news item appeared in all the major dailies. Never before had the Roosevelts, that 250-year-old clan of unimpeachable respectability, been tarnished with such shameful revelations.[71] The resentment of family elders against Theodore for having precipitated it may well be imagined, but he was convinced he had done the right thing for Anna and the children. It had been necessary to act hastily before Elliott was released from his French asylum and returned to the United States to claim his property. Even so, the court might not decide in time. "It is all horrible beyond belief," Theodore wrote Bamie. "The only thing to do is go resolutely forward."[72]

All in all, the summer of 1891 must have been a time of anguish for the beleaguered Commissioner. Its only discernible blessing was the birth, on 13 August, of his fourth child and second daughter, "a jolly naughty whacky baby" named Ethel.[73] Even this was saddened by the almost simultaneous death of Wilmot Dow, the younger and more lovable of his Dakota partners. "I think of Wilmot all the time," he wrote. "I can see him riding a bucker, paddling, shooting, hiking. . . ." Solace was to be found out West. At the end of the month he left for Medora and the Rockies.[74]

"As usual, I come back to rumors of my own removal," Roosevelt wrote Lodge on 10 October. But the tone of his letter was spirited. He had killed nine elk in four weeks, and felt "in splendid trim" for a fight.[75] General opinion held that he was too popular to be fired. "Mr. Harrison could be consoled if Mr. Roosevelt would resign," *The New York Times* remarked, "but he will not, and the President will not dare ask him to do so." Amazingly, even Frank Hatton hoped the rumors were not true. "Mr. Roosevelt is a sincere and genuine Civil Service reformer . . . There have been times in the past when [his] ideas of reform did not exactly comingle with those of the *Post,* but . . . it will be a sad day for Civil Service Reform when he steps down and out."[76]

Postmaster Johnson of Baltimore did not share this view. He publicly prayed "that lightning may strike Mr. Theodore Roosevelt."[77] John Wanamaker no doubt added a fervent Amen. It was clearly his responsibility to dismiss the twenty-five Post Office employees who had, by their own testimony, indicted themselves in Roosevelt's report; yet his pride would not let him. Shortly after the pesky Commissioner returned to town, Wanamaker handpicked a team of Postal Department inspectors and ordered them to reinvestigate the Baltimore case "since the evidence gathered so far is inconclusive."[78]

Now it was Roosevelt's turn to be angry. "You may tell the Postmaster-General from me," he roared at a messenger, "that I don't like him for two reasons. In the first place he has a very sloppy mind, and in the next place he does not tell the truth."[79]

Embarrassments crowded in thickly as the year drew to its close—so much so that Roosevelt forgot his own thirty-third birthday. The Maryland Civil Service Reform League complained about his ineffectiveness in securing the twenty-five dismissals, and said a golden opportunity to educate the rest of the country had been lost. Reformers in New York sent word that the law was being abused there just as cynically as it had been in Baltimore. And in Washington, President Harrison brushed aside a plan for new promotion methods in the classified service which Roosevelt had worked on for many months. Instead, Cabinet officers were told they could promote as they pleased, without further reference to the Civil Service Commission—leaving the agency even weaker than before.[80]

Financial worry continued to plague Roosevelt. The expense of maintaining two households, and moving his family back and forth twice a year, had caused an escalation of his debts. Ethel's arrival during the summer had made it impossible to live any longer in the little house on Jefferson Place, so the Commissioner rented a larger establishment at 1215 Nineteenth Street for the new season.

Personal frustration always tended to increase Roosevelt's natural belligerency, and that winter's news of the mob killing of two American sailors in Valparaiso, Chile, made him rampant for war—as he had been in 1886, over the Mexican border incident. To his disgust, the United States merely asked Chile to apologize. An amused John Hay wrote to Henry Adams, "Teddy Roosevelt . . . goes about hissing through his clenched teeth that we are dishonest. For two nickels he would declare war himself, shut up the Civil Service Commission, and wage it sole."[81]

On top of everything, there was the vexatious problem of what to do about Elliott. The insanity suit was getting nowhere, owing to disagreement between the certifying doctors and bickering among various relatives. Elliott had published a denial of his madness in the Paris edition of the *Herald,* and lodged a formal protest with the court in New York.[82] He kept sending "unspeakably terrible" letters to Theodore, some of them penitent, others vituperative. "They are so sane," his brother marveled, "and yet so absolutely lacking in moral sense."[83]

In the last week of November, Roosevelt succumbed to an attack of severe bronchitis, and the doctor warned it might turn to pneumonia. He recovered briefly, only to collapse again in December. Edith ordered him to bed for eight days—his longest recorded confinement since childhood. Although he complained about being treated like "a corpulent valetudinarian," it was plain that he was physically and emotionally spent.[84]

CHRISTMAS WITH "the Bunny chillum" restored him to health, and by New Year's Day his metabolism was running at top speed again. About this time he made a lightning decision to cross the Atlantic and confront his brother with an out-of-court settlement.[85] Instinct told him that Elliott, too, had slipped into despair recently, and that now or never was the time to shock him back to his senses. Elliott had always worshiped him—*Oh, Father will you ever think me a 'noble boy,' you are right about Teedie he is one and no mistake. . . .* [86]—had always craved his authority, even when protesting he could do without it. They must square off again, just as they had in the days when Theodore was "Skinny" and Elliott was "Swelly." *1st Round. Results: Skinny, lip swelled and bleeding. Swelly, sound in every limb if nose and lip can be classed as such . . .* [87] But this time Skinny intended to be the victor.

President Harrison sympathetically granted his request for leave of absence, and he sailed from New York on 9 January 1892. There followed a period of anxious suspense for the family, broken by this triumphant letter from Paris, dated 21 January:

> Won! Thank Heaven I came over . . .
>
> I found Elliott absolutely changed. I was perfectly quiet, but absolutely unwavering and resolute with him: and he surrendered completely, and was utterly broken, submissive, and repentant. He signed the deed, for two-thirds of *all* his property (including the $60,000 trust); and agreed to the probation. I then instantly changed my whole manner, and treated him with the utmost love and tenderness. I told him we would do all we legitimately could to get him through his two years (or thereabouts) of probation; that our one object now would be to see him entirely restored to himself; and so to his wife and children. He today attempted no justification whatever; he acknowledged how grievously he

> had sinned, and failed in his duties; and said he would do all in his power to prove himself really reformed. He was in a mood that was terribly touching. How long it will last of course no one can say. . . .[88]

Part of the agreement was that Elliott, in exchange for the withdrawal of the writ of insanity, would return to the United States and undergo a five-week "cure" for alcoholism at the Keeley Center in Dwight, Illinois. This, coming after his six-month drying-out period at Suresnes, should enable him to start working again and reenter society by degrees. Should he prove himself sober and responsible, he might resume family life sometime in 1894.[89]

Theodore remained in Paris another full week before sailing from Le Havre on 27 January. It seems he wanted to punch every last ounce of immorality out of Elliott. Having done so, he left him to follow one day later, alone on a separate steamer.[90] On 28 January, Elliott's mistress, Mrs. Evans, made the following entry in her diary:

> This morning, with his silk hat, his overcoat, gloves and cigar, E. came to my room to say goodbye. It is all over . . . Now my love was swallowed up in pity—for he looks so bruised, so beaten down by the past week with his brother. How could they treat so generous and noble a man as they have. He is more noble a figure in my eyes, with all his confessed faults, than either his wife or brother. . . .[91]

ROOSEVELT RETURNED HOME on 7 Feburary[92] to find the Civil Service Commission pondering yet another case of political assessments, this time at federal offices in Owensboro, Kentucky.[93] His presence was required in that state as soon as possible, but with the social season at its height he did not feel like immediately embarking on another journey. Elliott had expressed a desire to go south with him at the end of March, after the "Keeley cure" was complete; until then the Owensboro district attorney would simply have to muddle along.

Besides, the Kentucky case served as an exasperating reminder that nothing whatsoever had been done in Baltimore. It was now almost a year since his investigation, and the twenty-five lawbreakers were all still in office, drawing government salaries. John Wanamaker's inspectors had filed their report the previous November, but the Postmaster General would not say whether it confirmed or denied Roosevelt's findings. He also refused to send a copy to the Civil Service Commission, saying that it was an internal document, for his eyes only.[94]

On 8 March, Roosevelt made a special trip to New York in order to shout "Damn John Wanamaker!" at an executive meeting of the City Civil Service Reform Association.[95] Crimson with rage, he launched into an account of the whole case, accusing Wanamaker and Harrison of obstruction of justice. He was sure that the postal inspectors' report would corroborate his own—but how could its findings be made public?

The veteran reformer Carl Schurz made a simple suggestion. Roosevelt must demand a House investigation into the undeniable fact that twenty-five federal employees recommended for dismissal in July 1891 were still on the federal payroll in March 1892. It would be difficult for the House to refuse such a request. Wanamaker would then be obliged to present the inspectors' report as grounds for his inaction; it would become part of the public record, and the Civil Service Reform League would see to it that millions of copies were distributed around the nation. If the document turned out to be a whitewash job, Wanamaker would be humiliated; if it duplicated Roosevelt's original findings, Wanamaker would be destroyed. Either way, the cause of Civil Service Reform would benefit.[96]

ROOSEVELT LOST NO TIME in following Schurz's advice. While awaiting the verdict of the House, he made his planned trip to the South with Elliott, who had agreed to manage Douglas Robinson's estates in Virginia. The two brothers parted affectionately; Elliott declared he was completely cured, and anxious to atone for his misdeeds. Theodore went on to Kentucky, relieved that the long family crisis was over. "It is most inadvisable, on every account, that you and I should have any leading part in Elliott's affairs hereafter," he wrote Bamie, "*especially* as regards his relations with Anna . . . We have done everything possible . . . anything more would simply be interference, would not ultimately help her or him, and would hurt us."[97]

His business in Owensboro did not detain him long; neither did further business in Texas, for in early April he was at the ranch of a friend near the Mexican border. Here he spent two exhilarating days hunting wild hogs on horseback. Running down a band of five on the banks of the River Nueces, he managed to shoot a sow and a boar. "There was a certain excitement in seeing the fierce little creatures come to bay," he mused afterward, "but the true way to kill these peccaries would be with the spear."[98]

THE HOUSE VOTED an investigation of the Baltimore affair by the Civil Service Reform Committee on 19 April 1892. John Wanamaker was asked how soon he could prepare a statement of his official position, and replied that "he would hold himself at the service of the Committee for any date on which Mr. Roosevelt was not to be present."[99]

A special hearing of the Postmaster General was promptly scheduled for Monday, 25 April. Speaking with an air of weary dignity, Wanamaker said that he had not laid eyes on Roosevelt's report until returning from vacation the previous September. Soon afterward Postmaster Johnson had written to him complaining that the document was based on warped evidence. According to Johnson, Commissioner Roosevelt had arrived in Baltimore without warning, and had "frightened" and "bulldozed" Post Office employees into making rash statements that they later begged to withdraw. He had conducted a "star-chamber investigation" in which "men of very ordinary intellect" were denied counsel, and subjected them to a barrage of "leading questions."[100] Wanamaker felt that the men were entitled to be heard on their own behalf, and had ordered his two most senior inspectors to reinvestigate the case. Their report—which he did not happen to have on him at the moment—proved that Roosevelt's victims had not been soliciting election expenses at all; on the contrary, they were merely raising funds for a pool table. It was the official view of his department, therefore, that "the facts do not justify the dismissal of . . . anyone for violation of the Civil Service Law as charged."[101]

Wanamaker, who regularly taught Sunday school in Philadelphia, was at his sanctimonious best in cross-examination. He said that Postmaster Johnson had been "reprimanded" for allowing his men "to give impressions to the Civil Service Commissioner which were not justified by facts." Yet, on the whole, Johnson had done a remarkably good job in enforcing Civil Service rules. "The condition of the Baltimore Post Office is like the millenium in comparison with what it was in the previous Administration." Then Wanamaker launched into a speech which must have made Roosevelt boggle when it appeared in the evening paper:

> I consider myself the highest type of Civil Service man. I have governed the Post Office Department strictly by Civil Service rules . . . It seems to me to be small and trifling business and unworthy of a great Government to discharge a man who declares that he gave five dollars to a pool table . . . And while I have not seen my way clear to order any discharge or indictment . . . I might, if I saw the least thing on the part of these men at the next election to prove that they had not been honest or fair, dismiss them and forty more, if necessary. I am a law-keeper.[102]

Roosevelt's turn came a week later, on 2 May. He made his usual delayed entrance, interrupting testimony by Treasury Secretary Charles Foster, pumping hands right and left, waving aside a proffered chair. While awaiting his turn on the stand he "paced the floor nervously like a caged leopard," and when sworn treated the committee to a series of dazzling grins, some of which clicked audibly. He pulled a typewritten statement from his pocket and read it with gusto.[103]

"In the first place," said Roosevelt, "I stand by my Baltimore report not only in its entirety, but paragraph by paragraph. It is absolutely impossible that my conclusions should be upset, for they are based upon the confessions of the accused persons made at the very time the events took place. It seems to me less a question of judgment in deciding on their guilt than it is a question of interpreting the English language as it is ordinarily used." He offered no apologies for his methods of investigation. "Of course I used leading questions! I have always used them in examinations of this kind and always shall use them . . . to get at the truth."[104]

Having established his own position, Roosevelt turned to an analysis of Wanamaker's. Apparently "the Honorable Postmaster General" (he used this phrase, with heavy sarcasm, no fewer than eighteen times) put more faith in contradictory testimony, prepared after the fact with the help of lawyers, than in verbatim confessions recorded at the scene of the crime. "It is difficult for me to discuss seriously the proposition that a man when questioned as to something which has just happened will lie to his own hurt, and six months afterward tell the truth to his own benefit."

He was glad the Honorable Postmaster General admitted there had been violations of the law in Baltimore during the last Administration, but "if the wrongdoing is not checked it will be found at the end of four years to have been just as great under this Administration." Roosevelt concluded, "I honestly fail to see how there can be a particle of question as to these men's guilt, after reading the evidence that is before you; and if these men are not guilty, then it is absolutely impossible that men ever can be guilty under the Civil Service law."[105]

Before adjournment the committee voted a formal request for the Postmaster General's report. "Ah! I presume I shall be allowed to see that testimony?" said Roosevelt eagerly. When the chairman nodded assent, he was as delighted as a child. "Thanks! Thanks!"[106]

DELIGHT CHANGED TO DISGUST as he read the text of the nine-hundred-page document. Wanamaker's inspectors had not been able to change the basic facts of the case—much of the testimony, indeed, was even more incriminating than before—but they blatantly ignored this evidence in presenting their conclusions. Commissioner

Roosevelt, the report declared, had been "malicious," "unfair," and "partial in the extreme" in his investigation, determined "to deceive or mislead" witnesses for "some political purpose."[107]

Roosevelt reacted to these slurs with a dignity that merely emphasized the depths of his anger. He sent a registered letter to Wanamaker, saying that the Post Office inspectors had cast reflections not only on his actions, but on his motives. "There is no need in commenting on their gross impertinence and impropriety," Roosevelt wrote,

> used as they are by the subordinates of one department in reference to one of the heads of another, who is, like yourself, responsible to the President only. But I have nothing to do with these subordinates. It is with you, the official head, responsible for their action, that I have to deal. By submitting this report without expressly disclaiming any responsibility for it, you seem to assume that responsibility and make it your own. I can hardly suppose this was your intention, but I shall be obliged to treat these statements which in any way reflect on my acts and motives as yours, unless you disavow them with the same publicity with which they were made to the Committee. I therefore respectfully ask you whether you will or will not make such disavowal, so that I may govern myself accordingly, and not be guilty of any injustice.[108]

Roosevelt waited nine days, but Wanamaker made no reply. On 25 May, therefore, he appeared at a final session of the Investigating Committee "with a typewritten statement under his athletic arm and fire in his eye."[109]

HE BEGAN by reading his letter to Wanamaker, to the sound of excited scribbling in the press gallery. Then, in a lucid analysis of the two masses of evidence gathered in Baltimore by himself and Wanamaker's inspectors, he showed that at least two-thirds of the latter was even more damaging than his own. Yet Wanamaker had ignored this evidence in favor of the remaining third, which had obviously been gathered with intent to whitewash. "I have never sheltered myself behind my subordinates," said Roosevelt loftily, "and I decline to let the Postmaster-General shelter himself behind his." He would not accuse Wanamaker of an official cover-up, but "if the investigation in which this testimony was taken had been made with the deliberate intent of shielding the accused, covering up their wrongdoing, and attempting to perjure themselves, so that the [Post] Office could be cleared from the effect of their former truthful confessions, it would have been managed precisely as it actually was managed."

In conclusion Roosevelt noted that the Postmaster General was in the habit of saying he cherished nothing but goodwill toward the Civil Service Commission. "I regret to say that I must emphatically dissent from this statement. Many of his actions . . . during the past two years seem to be explicable only on the ground of dislike of the Commission, and of willingness to hamper its work."[110]

It was a masterly performance. Roosevelt kept tight rein over his temper, let the facts speak for themselves, and stepped from the stand with an air of complete self-assurance. The reaction of the editors of *The New York Times* next morning typified that of honest men across the nation:

> We do not remember an instance in the history of our Government in which an officer of the Government, appointed by the President and charged with independent duties of a most responsible and important character, has felt called upon to go before a Congressional Committee and submit to it statements so damaging to the character of another officer of the Government of still higher rank . . . Nor do we see how Mr. Roosevelt could have refused to do what he has done. He has been forced to it, and by conduct on the part of Mr. Wanamaker that is entirely inexcusable and without any decent motive. It may be said that Mr. Roosevelt has taken upon himself to accuse Mr. Wanamaker of what amounts to untruthfulness . . . That is not a pleasing position to be occupied by a gentleman who is a Cabinet offi-

> cer and a person of conspicuous pretensions to piety. But Mr. Roosevelt showed that Mr. Wanamaker had adopted and acted on statements that he knew were false . . . that he bore himself generally with a curious mingling of smug impertinence and cowardice . . . The exposure he has suffered from Mr. Roosevelt is merciless and humiliating, but it is clearly deserved.

The majority report of the investigating committee, dated 22 June, used even stronger language. It described Wanamaker's testimony as "evasive" and "garbled," and said he was clearly in "desperate straits." The Postmaster General's "extraordinary" failure to act in the Baltimore case indicated "either a determination not to enforce the law or negligence therein to the last degree." As for the testimony taken by his inspectors, it "confirmed and corroborated fully" that taken in the original investigation.[111] The righteousness of the law was upheld, and Theodore Roosevelt could enjoy the sweetest political triumph of his career as Commissioner.

THE STORY OF the rest of the Harrison Administration can be briefly told. At 3:20 A.M. on the morning after the investigating committee filed the above-quoted report, Grover Cleveland was renominated by the Democrats for President of the United States.[112] This news, coinciding as it did with the public disgrace of John Wanamaker, and reports of "scandalous" use of patronage in the renomination of Benjamin Harrison at Minneapolis,[113] came as a signal for all disillusioned reformers to desert the Republican party, as they had in 1884. Although memories of office-looting under the Democrats still lingered, they were neither as recent nor as disturbing as those publicized by the Republican Civil Service Commissioner. "Poor Harrison!" remarked the *New York Sun*. "If he has erred, he has been punished. The irrepressible, belligerent and enthusiastic Roosevelt has made him suffer, and has more suffering in store for him."[114]

Actually Roosevelt ceased to pester the little general through the campaign of 1892, possibly because he knew Mrs. Harrison was dying of tuberculosis. In July he wrote a long, flattering article, "The Foreign Policy of President Harrison," for publication in the 11 August issue of *The Independent*. Although the policy in question was largely that of Secretary of State James G. Blaine, Roosevelt's conclusion, "No other Administration since the Civil War has made so excellent a record in its management of our foreign relations," could not but have gratified his melancholy chief.[115]

Roosevelt enjoyed a renewed burst of literary activity that summer, publishing at least four other major articles on subjects ranging from anglomania to political assessments. He also forced himself to read all of Chaucer, whose lustier lyrics had hitherto made him gag. Even now, he found such tales as the Summoner's "altogether needlessly filthy," but he confessed to enjoying the others.[116] He exercised strenuously to work off the effects of a sedentary winter, galloping through the woods around Washington with Lodge, playing tennis at the British Legation, and whacking polo balls around the green fields of Long Island. "I tell you, a corpulent middle-aged literary man finds a stiff polo match rather good exercise!"[117]

At the beginning of August, Roosevelt left to go West as usual, but official engagements in South Dakota permitted him only a week or two in the Badlands. He was not sorry to leave Elkhorn, for game was scarce and the empty cabin depressed him.[118] Hell-Roaring Bill Jones agreed to drive him south to Deadwood, with Sylvane Ferris as a companion. This trip gave Roosevelt the opportunity to luxuriate in cowboy conversation, of which he had been starved in recent years.[119]

On 25 August, the wagon rolled into Deadwood, and Roosevelt soon discovered that, in spite of his sunburn and rough garb, he was regarded as a visiting celebrity. This was due more, perhaps, to his fame as the captor of Redhead Finnegan than to any relationship with the current Administration. A deputation of citizens waited upon him at his hotel and announced that a mass meeting had been scheduled in his honor that evening. At the appointed hour a band escorted him willy-nilly to the Deadwood Opera House, where he was obliged to open President Harrison's local reelection campaign. There was no point in protesting that as Civil Service Commissioner he was not supposed to take sides in a political contest. Local comprehension of his title was typified by the sheriff of the Black Hills, who remarked genially, "Well, anything civil goes with me."[120]

HE SPENT THE NEXT MONTH on a "tedious but important" tour of the neighboring Indian reservations. The dusty hopelessness of those sprawling communities seems to have wrought a profound change in his attitude to the American Indian. During his years as a rancher, Roosevelt had acquired plenty of anti-Indian prejudice, strangely at odds with his enlightened attitude to blacks. But his research into the great Indian military heroes for *The Winning of the West* had done much to moderate this. Now, touring Pine Ridge and Crow Creek on behalf of the Great White Father, he looked on the red man not as an adversary but as a ward of the state, whom it was his duty to protect. Pity, not unmixed with *honte du vainqueur,* flared into anger when he discovered that even here, in decaying federal agencies and flyblown schools, the spoils system was an accepted part of government. Clerks and teachers testified they were routinely assessed for amounts up to $200 per head by the South Dakota Republican Central Committee, on pain of losing their jobs.[121] Any time now the collectors would be around to seek "contributions" for President Harrison. Roosevelt promptly called a press conference in Sioux City and blasted the "infamy of meanness that would rob women and Indians of their meager wages."[122] He demanded the prosecution of several high Republican officials, and announced that Indians in the classified service "need not contribute a penny" to any future assessments.[123] The wretchedness he saw at Pine Ridge stayed with him long after he returned East. In a speech summing up his career as Civil Service Commissioner under President Harrison, Roosevelt sounded a note of human compassion rare in his early public utterances:

> Here we have a group of beings who are not able to protect themselves; who are groping toward civilization out of the

> darkness of heredity and ingrained barbarism, and to whom, theoretically, we are supposed to be holding out a helping hand. They are utterly unable to protect themselves. They are credulous and easily duped by a bad agent, and they are susceptible of remarkable improvement when the agent is a good man, thoroughly efficient and thoroughly practical. To the Indians the workings of the spoils system at the agencies is a curse and an outrage . . . it must mean that the painful road leading upward from savagery is rendered infinitely more difficult and infinitely more stony for the poor feet trying to tread it.[124]

On 25 October 1892, two days before Roosevelt's thirty-fourth birthday, Mrs. Benjamin Harrison died, adding a final touch of doom to the moribund Republican campaign. The little general had not wanted to be renominated, and now, as grief crippled him, he wanted even less to be reelected. Privately he longed to go back to Indianapolis, but "a Harrison never runs away from a fight."[125] On 8 November, however, his wish for retirement was granted. Grover Cleveland returned to power with a 3 percent majority, thanks to the swing of the reform vote. "Well, as to the general result I am disappointed but not surprised," Roosevelt wrote Lodge. "But how it galls to see the self-complacent triumph of our foes!"[126]

What probably galled him even more (although he did not say it) was the thought that Lodge, who had scored a personal coup in the Massachusetts election, was now in line for a seat in the U.S. Senate, while he would soon have to pack up his bags and return to Sagamore Hill. A few newspapers wanted him to be reappointed,[127] but it was unlikely the Democrats would favor a Civil Service Commissioner who had attacked President Cleveland so sharply in the past. He could scarcely have survived even if Harrison had won; since the Wanamaker affair, Republican spoilsmen had been insisting "in swarms" that Roosevelt must go.[128]

"I . . . have the profound gratification of knowing that there is no man more bitterly disliked by many of the men in my own party," he told a fellow reformer. "When I leave on March 5th, I shall at least have the knowledge that I have certainly not flinched from trying to enforce the law during these four years, even if my progress has been at times a little disheartening."[129]

ANOTHER DEATH SHOOK HIM on 7 December, and plunged the whole family into official mourning. Anna Roosevelt, her frail health broken by two years of humiliation, succumbed to diphtheria at the age of twenty-nine. The last message to Elliott in Virginia was a telegraphed "DO NOT COME."[130] One wonders if this gave any momentary pang to Theodore, who more than anyone else was responsible for their separation.

DURING ITS LAST few months in power, the Harrison Administration was possessed of immortal longings. A robe and a crown, of sorts, became available in the Pacific, and the President hastened to put them on.[131] They belonged to Queen Liliuokalani of Hawaii, who early in the New Year had proclaimed a policy of "Hawaii for the Hawaiians," in an attempt to end half a century of economic domination by the United States. She was immediately deposed in an uprising of native sugar growers, aided by some American marines, and abetted by the American Minister. Within weeks, representatives of the revolutionaries arrived in Washington to negotiate a treaty of annexation. President Harrison complied, although it was unlikely the incoming Democratic Administration would allow the document to get very far in Congress.[132]

Washington society, meanwhile, embraced Hawaii as the theme of the season. Hostesses served lavish *luaus* to their guests, to the whine of native guitars. Fashionable couples, hurrying in furs from one party to another, hummed the latest hit, a serenade to the deposed island Queen:

Come, Liliu-o-kalani,
Give Uncle Sam
Your little yellow hannie . . .[133]

Henry Adams proudly introduced the latest addition to his circle, a four-hundred-pound Polynesian chief named Tati Salmon.

"A polished gentleman," Roosevelt noted approvingly, "of easy manners, with an interesting undertone of queer barbarism."[134]

As the season wore on, a delicious fragrance filled the air, of pineapples and Pacific ozone, of warm dusky flesh and spices. It was the smell of Empire, and none sniffed it more eagerly than Roosevelt. With all his soul, he longed to remain in Washington, where the future of his country was blossoming like some brilliant tropical flower. Amazingly, it seemed that the President-elect bore him no grudge, and might invite him to stay on as Civil Service Commissioner. Benjamin F. Tracy, outgoing Secretary of the Navy, urged him to accept, and in doing so, bestowed a compliment which delighted Roosevelt more than any other he had ever received. "Well, my boy," said Tracy, "you have been a thorn in our side during four years. I earnestly hope that you will remain to be a thorn in the side of the next Administration."[135]

CHAPTER 18

The Universe Spinner

Force rules the world still,
Has ruled it, shall rule it;
Meekness is weakness,
Strength is triumphant!

"WE HAVE BUILT these splendid edifices," roared Grover Cleveland, "but we have also built the magnificent fabric of a popular government, whose grand proportions are seen throughout the world."[1] His eyes flickered back and forth: he was trying to read his notes, seek out an ivory button, and address two hundred thousand people simultaneously. The eyes of the crowd, too, were restless. They shifted from the President's fat forefinger, as it hovered over the button, to the inert fountains, the furled flags, the motionless wheels in the Palace of Mechanic Arts, and the enshrouded statue looming against the fogbanks of Lake Michigan.

"As by a touch the machinery that gives life to this vast Exposition is now set in motion, so at the same instant let our hopes and aspirations awaken forces which in time to come"—Maestro Thomas raised his baton over seven hundred musicians, and for the first moment that morning a hush descended on the Grand Court—"shall influence the welfare, the dignity, and the freedom of mankind,"

"The fair by no means matched the splendor of his own dreams for America."

The Grand Court of the World's Columbian Exposition, Chicago, 1893.

Cleveland intoned, and pressed the button. It was eight minutes past noon, Chicago time, on 1 May 1893.

From the flagstaff crowning the gold-domed Administration Building, three hundred feet above the President's head, Old Glory broke forth, a split second before the lower banners of Christopher Columbus and Spain.[2] Seven hundred other ensigns exploded brilliantly over the White City. The great Allis engine coughed into life, and seven thousand feet of shafting began to move. Fountains gushed so high that umbrellas popped up everywhere; and the folds fell from the Statue of the Republic, revealing a gilt goddess facing west, her arms extended toward the frontier.

The noise accompanying this cataclysmic moment—the first demonstration, on a massive scale, of the generative powers of electricity—was appropriately tremendous. From the lake came the thunder of naval artillery and the shriek of countless steam whistles. Carillons pealed, the orchestra crashed out Handel's *Hallelujah Chorus,* and louder than everything else rose the roaring of the crowd. The war-whooping of seventy-five Sioux added savage overtones. This bedlam continued for ten full minutes; then "America" sounded on massed trombones, and the roaring turned to singing. Even the stolid Cleveland was moved to join in, to the embarrassment of his guest of honor, Cristóbal, duke of Veragua, Columbus's senior living descendant. The little Spaniard stood bowed under the weight of his inherited epaulets, silent in the universal chorus:

Let music swell the breeze,
And ring from all the trees
Sweet freedom's song!

Theodore Roosevelt did not arrive in Chicago for another ten days[3]—his own modest contribution to the World's Fair was a Boone & Crockett Club cabin, dedicated 15 May[4]—but he had little need of music and artillery to swell his love of country. Indeed, this stupendous exposition, whose combination of classical architecture and modern technology so bewildered Henry Adams that he felt the universe was tottering,[5] was to Roosevelt an entirely natural and logical product of American civilization. He was conventionally moved by its grandeur ("the most beautiful architectural exhibit the world has ever seen"),[6] but the Fair by no means matched the splendor of his own dreams for America. These palaces, after all, were carved out of plaster, and would survive, at most, for a couple of seasons; *his* Columbia would burgeon for centuries.

To Adams, sitting with spinning head on the steps of the Administration Building, the World's Fair asked for the first time "whether the American people knew where they were driving." He suspected they did not, "but that they might still be driving or drifting unconsciously to some point in thought, as their solar system was said to be drifting towards some point in space; and that, possibly, if relations enough could be observed, this point might be fixed. Chicago was the first expression of American thought as a unity; one must start there."[7]

Roosevelt felt no need to ask, or answer, such questions. He had long known exactly where the United States was drifting, just as he had throughout life known where he was driving. He came to the White City, gazed cheerfully upon it, then hurried off to Indianapolis on Civil Service Commission business.[8] There was no need to stop and ponder the dynamos, the "new powers" which so mystified Henry Adams, for he felt their energy whirring within himself. Theodore Roosevelt, as the British M.P. John Morley later observed, "was" America[9]—the America that grew to maturity after the Civil War, marshaled its resources at Chicago, and exploded into world power at the turn of the century.

Grover Cleveland's adjectives on Opening Day—*splendid, magnificent, grand, vast*—were no different from those Roosevelt himself had lavished on America in all his books. The symbolism of the flags, and of the little Spanish admiral dwarfed by a three-hundred-pound American President, was pleasing to him, but not revelatory. Nine years before, in his Fourth of July oration to the cowboys of Dickinson, he had hoped "to see the day when not a foot of American soil will be held by any European power," and instinct told him that that day was fast approaching. When it came, it would bring out what some consider the best, what others consider the worst in him. This overriding impulse has been given many names: Jingoism, Nationalism, Imperialism, Chauvinism, even

Fascism and Racism. Roosevelt preferred to use the simple and to him beautiful word *Americanism.*

THE WINNING OF THE WEST, which occupied Roosevelt, on and off, for nearly nine years, was the first comprehensive statement of his Americanism, and, by extension (since he "was" America), of himself. All his previous books had been, in a sense, sketches for this one, just as his subsequent books were postscripts to it, of diminishing historical and psychological interest. One by one, themes he had touched on in the past came up for synthesis and review: the importance of naval preparedness, and effect of ethnic derivations on fighting blood (*The Naval War of 1812*); the identity of native Americans with their own flora and fauna (*Hunting Trips of a Ranchman*); the doctrine of Manifest Destiny (*Thomas Hart Benton*); the need for law and order in a savage environment (*Ranch Life and the Hunting Trail*); the significance of the United States Constitution (*Gouverneur Morris*); the problems of free government (*Essays in Practical Politics*); and the social dynamics of immigration (*New York*).

Nothing written prior to Roosevelt's Presidency shows the breadth of his mind to greater advantage than the introduction to *The Winning of the West,* which makes it clear that his specific subject—white settlement of Indian lands west of the Alleghenies in the late eighteenth century—is but a chapter in the unfolding of an epic racial saga, covering thousands of years and millions of square miles. The erudition with which he traces the "perfectly continuous history" of Anglo-Saxons from the days of King Alfred to those of George Washington is impressive. He draws effortless parallels between the Romanticization of the Celto-Iberians in the second century B.C. and the capture of Mexico and Peru by the conquistadores; between the Punic Wars and the War of the American Revolution; even between the future of whites in South Africa and the fate of Greek colonists in the Tauric Chersonese.

"During the past three centuries," Roosevelt begins, "the spread of the English-speaking peoples over the world's waste spaces has been not only the most striking feature in the world's history, but also the event of all others most far-reaching in its importance."[10] What else but destiny—a destiny yet to be fully realized—can explain the remorseless advance of Anglo-Saxon civilization? The language of what was, in Queen Elizabeth's time, "a relatively unimportant insular kingdom . . . now holds sway over worlds whose endless coasts are washed by the waves of three great oceans." Never in history has a race expanded over so wide an area in so short a time; and the winning of the American West may be counted as "the crowning and greatest achievement" of that mighty movement.[11]

The narrative proper begins in chapter 6 with the first trickle of settlement following Daniel Boone's penetration of the Cumberland Gap in 1765. Roosevelt uses a striking flood metaphor: "The American backswoodsmen had surged up, wave upon wave, till their mass trembled in the troughs of the Alleghenies, ready to flood the continent beyond."[12] As the flood gathers volume, he achieves the effect of ever-widening waves by making his chapters overlap, every one moving farther afield geographically, and further ahead in time. So intoxicated is Roosevelt as he rides these waves that he sweeps uncaring past such solid obstructions as Institutional Analysis and Land Company Proceedings. ("I have always been more interested in the men themselves than the institutions through which they worked," he confessed.)[13] He might have added, "and in action rather than theory." Far and away the best parts of *The Winning of the West* are the fighting chapters. In describing border battles, Roosevelt reveals himself with the utter unself-consciousness which was always part of his charm. He makes no secret of his boyish identification with those gaunt, fierce warriors of the frontier, who were "strong and simple, powerful for good and evil, swayed by gusts of stormy passion, the love of freedom rooted in their very heart's core."[14]

Here is Roosevelt the aggressor, single-handedly killing or crippling seven Indians in the pitch darkness of his pioneer log cabin; wrenching himself from the stake and running naked for five days through mosquito country; trying consecutively to shoot, knife, throttle, and drown a reluctant Chief Bigfoot, while his own brother puts a bullet in his back; advancing upon Vincennes through mile after mile of freezing, waist-deep water; and, in a moment of supreme ecstasy, spurring a white horse over a sheer, three-hundred-foot cliff:

> There was a crash, the shock of a heavy body, half-springing, half-falling, a scramble among loose rocks, and the snapping of saplings and bushes; and in another moment the awe-struck Indians above saw their unarmed foe, galloping his white horse in safety across the plain.[15]

Here, too, is Roosevelt the righteous, assailing the "warped, perverse, and silly morality" that would preserve the American continent "for the use of a few scattered savage tribes, whose life was but a few degrees less meaningless, squalid, and ferocious than that of the wild beasts with whom they held joint ownership."[16] He pours scorn on "selfish and indolent" Easterners who fail to see the "race-importance" of the work done by Western pioneers.[17] Yet Roosevelt is not sentimental about the latter. He shows the tendency of the frontier to barbarize both conqueror and conquered, until such civilized issues as good v. evil, law v. anarchy, are forgotten in the age-old struggle of Man against Man.[18]

> It is a primeval warfare, and it is waged as war was waged in the ages of bronze and iron. All the merciful humanity that even war has gained during the last two thousand years is lost. It is a warfare where no pity is shown to non-combatants, where the weak are harried without ruth, and the vanquished are maltreated with merciless ferocity. A sad and evil feature of such warfare is that the whites, the representatives of civilization, speedily sink almost to the level of their barbarous foes, in point of hideous brutality.[19]

Yet, says Roosevelt, this kind of struggle is "elemental in its consequences to the future of the world." In a paragraph which will return to haunt him, he proclaims:

> The most ultimately righteous of all wars is a war with savages, though it is apt to be also the most terrible and inhuman. The rude, fierce settler who drove the savage from the land lays all civilized mankind under a debt to him. American and Indian, Boer and Zulu, Cossack and Tartar, New Zealander and Maori—in each case the victor, horrible though many of his deeds are, has laid deep the foundations for the future greatness of a mighty people . . . it is of incalculable importance that America, Australia, and Siberia should pass out of the hands of their red, black, and yellow aboriginal owners, and become the heritage of the dominant world races.[20]

Roosevelt the proud saw no reason to retract this passage in later life, for the overall context of *The Winning of the West* makes plain that he regarded any such race-struggle as ephemeral. Once civilization was established, the aborigine must be raised and refined as quickly as possible, so that he may partake of every opportunity available to the master race—in other words, become master of himself, free to challenge and beat the white man in any field of endeavor. Nothing could give Roosevelt more satisfaction than to see such a reversal, for he admired individual achievement above all things. Any black or red man who could win admission to "the fellowship of the doers" was superior to the white man who failed.[21] Roosevelt's long-term dream was nothing more or less than the general, steady, self-betterment of the multicolored American nation.[22]

Of Roosevelt the military man, as revealed in *The Winning of the West,* little need be said. Chapter after chapter, volume after volume, demonstrates his ability to analyze the motives that drive men to battle, to define the mysterious powers of leadership, and weigh the relative strengths of armies. His accounts of the Battle of King's Mountain and the defeat of St. Clair are so full of visual and auditory detail, and exhibit such an uncanny sense of terrain, that it is hard to believe the author himself has never felt the shock of arms. One can only infer from the power and brilliance of the prose that such passages are the sublimation of his most intense desires, and that until he can charge, like Colonel William Campbell, up an enemy-held ridge at the head of a thousand wiry horse-riflemen, he will never be fulfilled.[23]

ROOSEVELT WAS NOT ALONE in his efforts during the early 1890s to define and explore the origins of Americanism. Long before the final volume of *The Winning of the West* was published, other young intellectuals took up and developed his theme that the true American identity was to be found only in the West. The most brilliant of these was Frederick Jackson Turner, who came to the Chicago World's Fair in July 1893 to deliver his seminal address, "The Significance of the Frontier in American History," before an audience of aging, puzzled academics.[24]

Turner had admiringly reviewed Roosevelt's first two volumes in 1889, and had marked in his personal copy a passage describing the "true significance" of "the vast movement by which this continent was conquered and peopled."[25] His thesis—that "the existence of an area of free land, its continuous recession, and the advancement of American settlement westward explain American development"—was identical with that of *The Winning of the West,* albeit expressed more succinctly.[26] But Turner refined away much of the crudity of Roosevelt's ethnic thinking. It was not "blood," but environment that made the American frontiersman unique: he was shaped by the challenge of his situation "at the meeting-point between savagery and civilization." Forced continually to adapt himself to new dangers and new opportunities, as the frontier moved West, he was "Americanized" at a much quicker rate than the sedentary, Europe-influenced Easterner. Consequently, said Turner, it was "to the frontier that the American intellect owes its most striking characteristics."[27] And in listing those characteristics, Turner painted an accurate portrait of somebody not unfamiliar to readers of this biography:

> That coarseness and strength combined with acuteness and inquisitiveness; that practical, inventive turn of mind, quick to find expedients; that masterful grasp of material things,

> lacking in the artistic but powerful to effect great ends; that restless nervous energy; that dominant individualism, working for good and evil, and withal that buoyancy which comes with freedom—these are the traits of the frontier. . . .[28]

Turner closed his great essay on an elegaic note. The Chicago World's Fair marked more than the four hundredth anniversary of the arrival of Columbus in the New World; it coincidentally marked the end of the era of free land. An obscure government pamphlet had recently announced that, since the frontier was now almost completely broken up by settlements, "it cannot . . . any longer have a place in the census reports."[29] This apparently unnoticed sentence, said Turner, made it clear that the United States had reached the limits of its natural expansion. Yet what of "American energy . . . continually demanding a wider field for its exercise"? Turner did not dare answer that question. All he knew was "the frontier has gone, and with its going has closed the first period of American history."[30]

Theodore Roosevelt was not among Turner's drowsy audience that hot summer's day, but he was one of the first historians to sense the revolutionary qualities of the thesis when it was published early in 1894.[31] "I think you have struck some first class ideas," he wrote enthusiastically, "and have put into definite shape a good deal of thought which has been floating around rather loosely."[32] This was hardly the profound scholarly praise which Turner craved; but the older man's warmth, and his promise to quote the thesis in Volume Three of *The Winning of the West,* "of course making full acknowledgement," was flattering.[33] Turner thus became yet another addition to the circle of Roosevelt's academic admirers, and a fascinated observer of his later career.[34] If one could no longer see the frontier retreat, one could have fun watching Theodore advance.

Roosevelt spent much of his time during the years 1893–95 formulating theories of Americanism, partly under the influence of Turner, but mostly under the influence of his own avidly eclectic reading. Gradually the theories coalesced into a philosophy embracing practically every aspect of American life, from warfare to wildflowers.[35] He began to publish patriotic articles with titles like

"What Americanism Means," and continued to write such pieces, with undiminished fervor, for the rest of his life. In addition he preached the gospel of Americanism, ad nauseam, at every public or private opportunity. Ninety-nine percent of the millions of words he thus poured out are sterile, banal, and so droningly repetitive as to defeat the most dedicated researcher. There is no doubt that on this subject Theodore Roosevelt was one of the bores of all ages; the wonder is that during his lifetime so many men, women, and children worshipfully pondered every platitude. Here is an example, taken from the above-named essay:

> We Americans have many grave problems to solve, many threatening evils to fight, and many deeds to do, if, as we hope and believe, we have the wisdom, the strength, and the courage and the virtue to do them. But we must face facts as they are. We must neither surrender ourselves to a foolish optimism, nor succumb to a timid and ignoble pessimism. . . .[36]

And so on and on; once Roosevelt got a good balanced rhythm going, he could continue indefinitely, until his listeners, or his column-inches, were exhausted.

An analysis of "What Americanism Means"[37] discloses that even when dealing with what is presumably a positive subject, Roosevelt's instinct is to express himself negatively, to attack un-Americans rather than praise all-Americans. Imprecations hurled at the former outnumber adjectives of praise for the latter almost ten to one. Selecting at random, we find *base, low, selfish, silly, evil, noxious, despicable, unwholesome, shameful, flaccid, contemptible*—together with a plentiful sprinkling of pejorative nouns: *weaklings, hypocrites, demagogues, fools, renegades, criminals, idiots, anarchists* . . . One marvels at the copious flow of his invective, especially as the victims of it are not identified. It is possible, however, to single out Henry James, that "miserable little snob"[38] whose preference for English society and English literature drove Roosevelt to near frenzy:

> Thus it is for the undersized man of letters, who flees his country because he, with his delicate, effeminate sensitive-

> ness, finds the conditions of life on this side of the water crude and raw; in other words, because he finds that he cannot play a man's part among men, and so goes where he will be sheltered from the winds that harden stouter souls.

In such manner did Roosevelt, with the shrewd instinct of a rampant heterosexual, kick James again and again in his "obscure hurt," until the novelist was moved to weary protest. "The national consciousness for Mr. Theodore Roosevelt is . . . at the best a very fierce affair."[39] James was too courteous to say more in print, but he privately characterized Roosevelt as "a dangerous and ominous jingo," and "the mere monstrous embodiment of unprecedented and resounding Noise."[40]

IT IS A RELIEF to turn from Roosevelt's own spontaneous essays to those prompted by the philosophizing of others, notably the English historian Charles H. Pearson, whose *National Life and Character: A Forecast* appeared in early 1894. Roosevelt wrote a ten-thousand word reply to this work of gentle, scholarly pessimism for publication in the May issue of *Sewanee Review.*[41] It represents altogether the better side of him, both as a man and as a writer, and can be taken as his confident answer to those who, like Pearson and Henry Adams, shuddered at the nearness of the twentieth century.

"At no period of the world's history," says Roosevelt, "has life been so full of interest, and of possibilities of excitement and enjoyment." Science has revolutionized industry; Darwin has revolutionized thought; the globe's waste spaces are being settled and seeded. A man of ambition has unique opportunities to build, explore, conquer, and transform. He can taste "the fearful joy" of grappling with large political and administrative problems. "If he is observant, he notes all around him the play of vaster forces than have ever before been exerted, working, half blindly, half under control, to bring about immeasurable results."[42]

Roosevelt refuses to look at the future through the "dun-colored mists" of pessimism, yet he does not pretend to see it all clearly. "Nevertheless, signs do not fail that we shall see the conditions of our lives, national and individual, modified after a sweeping and radical fashion. Many of the forces that make for national greatness and for individual happiness in the nineteenth century will be absent entirely, or will act with greatly diminished strength, in the twentieth. Many of the forces that now make for evil will by that time have gained greatly in volume and power."

Pearson's theory that "the higher races" cannot long subjugate black and brown majorities finds Roosevelt in complete agreement, for "men of our stock do not prosper in tropical countries." Only in thinly peopled, temperate regions is there any lasting hope for European civilization. A secure future is promised the English-speaking conquerors of North America and Australia, as well as the Russians, who "by a movement which has not yet fired the popular imagination, but which thinking men recognize as of incalculable importance, are building up a vast state in northern Asia."[43] But Europeans hoping "to live and propagate permanently in the hot regions of India and Africa" are doomed. In one of the earliest of his many remarkable flights of historical prophecy (flawed only by an exaggerated time-scale), he writes:

> The Greek rulers of Bactria were ultimately absorbed and vanished, as probably the English rulers of India will some day in the future—for the good of mankind, we sincerely hope and believe in the very remote future—themselves be absorbed and vanish. In Africa south of the Zambesi (and possibly here and there on high plateaus north of it) there may remain white States, although even these States will surely contain a large colored population, always threatening to swamp the whites . . . It is almost impossible that they will not in the end succeed in throwing off the yoke of the European outsiders, though this end may be, and we hope will be, many centuries distant. In America, most of the West Indies are becoming negro islands . . . it is impossible for the dominant races of the temperate zones ever bodily to displace the peoples of the tropics.[44]

Roosevelt is serenely untroubled by Pearson's fear that the black and yellow races of the world will one day attain great economic and military power and threaten their erstwhile masters. "By that time the descendant of the negro may be as intellectual as the Athenian . . . we shall then simply be dealing with another civilized nation of non-Aryan blood, precisely as we now deal with Magyar, Finn, and Basque."[45]

Turning from global to national matters, Roosevelt discusses the phenomenon of the "stationary state," in which a freely developing nation tends to become rigid and authoritarian as its period of upward mobility comes to an end. But again he sees no cause for concern. It is right and proper that the power of government should increase to counteract "the mercilessness of private commercial warfare." As for that other tendency of a maturing civilization, the crowding out of the upper class by the middle and lower, Roosevelt welcomes it as he welcomes all natural processes. Every new generation, he says, will increase the proportion of mechanics, workmen, and farmers to that of scientists, statesmen, and poets, but as long as the aggregate population increases there will be no decline in cultural values. On the contrary, the nation's overall quality will improve, thanks to "the transmission of acquired characters" by an ever-thinning, ever-refining aristocracy.[46] This process "in every civilization operates so strongly as to counterbalance . . . that baleful law of natural selection which tells against the survival of the most desirable classes."[47]

Reducing his focus yet again to the domestic environment, Roosevelt "heartily disagrees" with Pearson's mistrust of Americanized, democratic families. "To all who have known really happy family lives," he writes, "that is, to all who have known or who have witnessed the greatest happiness which there can be on this earth, it is hardly necessary to say that the highest idea of the family is attainable only where the father and mother stand to each other as lovers and friends. In these homes the children are bound to father and mother by ties of love, respect, and obedience, which are simply strengthened by the fact that they are treated as reasonable beings with rights of their own, and that the rule of the household is changed to suit the changing years, as childhood passes into manhood and womanhood."[48]

Roosevelt is making no effort to be metaphorical, but this whole simple and beautiful passage may be taken as symbolic of his attitude to his country and the world. Father is Strength in the home, just as Government is Strength in America, and America is (or ought to be) Strength overseas. Mother represents Upbringing, Education, the Spread of Civilization. Children are the Lower Classes, the Lower Races, to be brought to maturity and then set free.

"We do not agree," Roosevelt concludes, ". . . that there is a day approaching when the lower races will predominate in the world, and the higher races will have lost their noblest elements . . . On the whole, we think that the greatest victories are yet to be won, the greatest deeds yet to be done . . . the one plain duty of every man is to face the future as he faces the present, regardless of what it may have in store for him, turning toward the light as he sees the light, to play his part manfully, as a man among men."[49]

ROOSEVELT WAS CERTAINLY playing his own part manfully when he wrote the above lines in the early spring of 1894. His intellectual activity was as intense as it had ever been. Having published, in late 1893, *The Wilderness Hunter,* the third of his great nature trilogy and arguably his finest book,[50] he was now simultaneously at work on Volumes Three and Four of *The Winning of the West,* planning the never-to-be-written Volumes Five and Six, editing his second Boone & Crockett Club anthology (to which he also contributed scholarly articles), reading Kipling, and addressing a variety of correspondents on subjects ranging from British court procedures to arboreal distinctions between Northern and Southern mammalian species. In addition, he had recently begun a part-time career as a professional lecturer, and took frequent quick trips out of town to speak in New York or Boston on history, hunting, municipal politics, and "the subject on which I feel deepest," U.S. foreign policy.[51]

There was a reason for all this activity, abnormal even by his standards. During the previous summer, Grover Cleveland had presided unhappily over the worst financial panic in American history—a crisis so severe as to make the plaster palaces of Chicago seem but hollow symbols indeed. The nation's steady outflow of gold, caused by a steady rise in imports and monthly purchases of silver by the government (mandatory since the Silver Purchase Act of 1890), could only be stopped by drastic action, and Cleveland had summoned an emergency session of Congress on 7 August 1893. Despite violent opposition from his own party, the President managed to force the repeal of the controversial act on 28 August. He thus saved the nation's credit, but transformed himself overnight into the most unpopular President since James Buchanan.[52] Americans high and low felt the icy threat of bankruptcy that winter, and Roosevelt, still striving vainly to recover from his losses in Dakota, was no exception. His accounts showed a crippling deficit of $2,500 in December 1893; Edith, in her private letters, put the total nearer $3,000.[53] Roosevelt complained that his ill-paid government job was "not the right career for a man without means." The sale of six acres of property on Sagamore Hill, at $400 apiece,[54] brought him temporary security, but Roosevelt knew he would still have to scrabble for freelance pennies during the next few years in order to save his home and educate his children. The birth of a son, Archibald Bulloch, on 10 April 1894, was further cause for concern. "I begin to think that this particular branch of the Roosevelt family is getting to be numerous enough."[55]

Although he professed still to be enjoying his work as Civil Service Commissioner, and to "get on beautifully with the President,"[56] an increasing restlessness through the spring and summer of 1894 is palpable in his correspondence. It would be needlessly repetitive to describe the battles he fought for reform under Cleveland, for they were essentially the same as those he fought under Harrison. "As far as my work is concerned," he grumbled, "the two Administrations are much of a muchness."[57] There were the same "mean, sneaky little acts of petty spoilsmongering" in government; the same looting of federal offices across the nation, which Roosevelt combated with his usual weapons of publicity and aggressive investigation; the same pleas for extra funds and extra staff ("we are now, in all, five thousand papers behind"); the same fiery reports and five-thousand-word letters bombarding members of Congress; the same obstinate lobbying at the White House for extensions of the classified service; the same compulsive attacks upon porcine opponents, such as Assistant Secretary of State Josiah P.

Quincy, hunting for patronage "as a pig hunts truffles," and Secretary of the Interior Hoke Smith, "with his twinkling little green pig's eyes."[58]

All this, of course, meant that Roosevelt was having fun. As Cecil Spring Rice remarked, "Teddy is consumed with energy as long as he is doing something and fighting somebody . . . he always finds something to do and somebody to fight. Poor Cabot *must* be successful; while Teddy is happiest when he conquers but quite happy if he only fights."[59]

He continued utterly to dominate the Civil Service Commission, not without some protest on the part of General George D. Johnston, Hugh Thompson's old and crotchety successor. On several occasions their altercations grew so violent that Roosevelt said only a sense of propriety restrained him from "going down among the spittoons with the general."[60] Things became dangerous when Johnston, who wore a pistol at all times, objected to Roosevelt's office being carpeted before his. Roosevelt had a private talk with President Cleveland, and the general was offered two remote diplomatic posts, in Vancouver and Siam. He refused both, whereupon Cleveland summarily removed him.[61]

This enabled Roosevelt to bring in a new Commissioner, John R. Procter, of Kentucky. Procter was a tall, scholarly geologist and Civil Service Reformer who had caught Roosevelt's eye in the spring of 1893, and whom he had then hoped—in vain—would replace "silly well-meaning Lyman."[62] Now, with Procter in, he at last had "a first-class man" he could groom to take over, and continue his policies as Civil Service Commissioner. Roosevelt was beginning to talk of stepping down after one more winter in Washington, "although I am not at all sure as to what I shall do afterwards."[63]

MANY WRITERS OTHER THAN Henry Adams have compared Theodore Roosevelt's career to that of an express locomotive, speeding toward an inevitable destination. The simile may be extended to describe his two static years under President Cleveland as a mid-journey pause to stoke up with coal and generate a new head of steam. The first signs that he was about to get under way again occurred in the late summer of 1894: there was the lift of a signal, a flickering of needles, the anguish of a personal farewell, a groan of loosening brakes. From now on Roosevelt's acceleration would be continuous—almost frighteningly so to some observers, but very exhilarating to himself.

Sometime during the first week in August, Congressman Lemuel Ely Quigg of New York, an attractive, prematurely grizzled political schemer, dropped a subtle hint regarding Roosevelt's future. What a pity it was, he sighed, that Roosevelt was possessed of "such a variety of indiscretions, fads and animosities" that it would be impossible to nominate him for Mayor of New York in the fall.[64] The odds of a Republican victory in that city were higher than they had been for years; what was more, there seemed to be a good chance of getting a reform ticket elected. Roosevelt rejected Quigg's hint good-humoredly ("I have run once!"), but ambition stirred within him. He had never quite gotten over his failure to capture control of his native city in 1886, and the temptation to try and transcend that failure soon became irresistible. He broached the subject with Edith, but she protested vehemently. To run for Mayor, she said, would require him to spend money they simply did not have, and the prize was by no means assured. Pitiful as his present salary was, it was at least better than the nothing he would earn as a twice-defeated mayoral candidate. Roosevelt miserably told Quigg he would have to think the matter over.[65]

On 7 August, President Cleveland recognized the new Republic of Hawaii,[66] to Roosevelt's grim satisfaction. This meant that the United States at last had a firm ally and naval base in the Pacific, to counter the burgeoning might of Japan. Roosevelt had been fuming for sixteen months over Cleveland's obstinate refusal to sign the annexation treaty prepared for him by President Harrison. "It was a crime against the United States, it was a crime against white civilization."[67] In his opinion the President should now start to build up the Navy, and order the digging of an interoceanic canal in Central America "with the money of Uncle Sam."[68] However Roosevelt knew there was not much chance of that, for the Democrats were "very weak" about foreign policy. "Cleveland does his best, but he is not an able man."[69]

On Monday, 13 August, a telegram arrived to say that Elliott Roosevelt (drinking heavily again and reunited with his mistress in New York) was very ill indeed.[70] Roosevelt, desk-bound in Washington, did not respond: he knew from experience that Elliott would not let any members of the family come near him. There had been many such messages in recent months. "He can't be helped, and he must simply be let go his own gait."[71] The following day Elliott, racked with delirium tremens, tried to jump out of the window of his house, suffered a final epileptic fit, and died. Distraught, Theodore hurried to New York, and saw stretched out on a bed, not the bloated souse of recent years, but the handsome youth of "the old time, fifteen years ago, when he was the most generous, gallant, and unselfish of men."[72] The sight shattered him. "Theodore was more overcome than I have ever seen him," Corinne reported, "and cried like a little child for a long time."[73]

Theodore recovered his equanimity in time to veto "the hideous plan" that Elliott be buried with his wife. Instead, a grave was dug in Greenwood Cemetery, "beside those who are associated only with his sweet innocent youth." At the funeral on Saturday, Roosevelt noted with some surprise that "the woman" and two of her friends "behaved perfectly well, and their grief seemed entirely sincere."[74]

ON 4 SEPTEMBER he started West to shoot a few antelope and ponder the New York mayoralty. He felt depressed and ill, and Dakota's drought-stricken landscape drove him back to Oyster Bay after only two weeks on the range. Edith was still adamantly against his running in October, and Theodore, who was as putty in her hands, decided to turn Quigg down. But this was by no means easy. Quigg was so sure of his acceptance that a special nominating Committee of Seventy had been formed, and was determined to nominate him as a reform candidate; he had to refuse four times before they would accept his decision.[75] He sank into a mood of bitter remorse as his thirty-sixth birthday approached, for he felt himself a political failure. His whole instinct was to run: after well over five years of appointive office he craved the thrill of an election campaign. At all costs he must keep his chagrin private. "No outsider should know that I think my decision was a mistake." Henry Cabot Lodge received the terse explanation, "I simply had not the funds to run."[76] But after a further period of brooding, Roosevelt had to unburden himself to his friend:

> I would literally have given my right arm to have made the race, win or lose. It was the one golden chance, which never returns; and I had no illusions about ever having another opportunity; I knew it meant the definite abandonment of any hope of going on in the work and life for which I care more than any other. You may guess that these weeks have not been particularly pleasant ones . . . At the time, with Edith feeling as intensely as she did, I did not see how I could well go in; though I have grown to feel more and more that in this instance I should have gone counter to her wishes . . . the fault was mine, not Edith's; I should have realized that she *could* not see the matter as it really was, or realize my feelings. But it is one of the matters just as well dropped.[77]

William L. Strong, a middle-aged businessman with little or no political experience, was duly nominated by the Republicans of New York; he ran on a popular reform ticket, and was elected. And so the mayoral campaign of 1894 joined that of 1886 as another of Roosevelt's unspoken, passionate regrets.

RETURNING TO WORK at the Civil Service Commission now was "a little like starting to go through Harvard again after graduating,"[78] and that telltale sign of Rooseveltian frustration, bronchitis, recurred in December. For a week he was confined to his bed. A strange tone of nostalgia for his native city crept into his correspondence, as he obsessively discussed Mayor Strong's appointments and the prospects for real reforms of the municipal government. Shortly before Christmas a message arrived from Strong: would he care to accept the position of Street Cleaning Commissioner in New York?[79]

Roosevelt was "dreadfully harassed" by the offer. Thirteen years before, when he first stood up in his evening clothes to speak at Morton Hall, he had addressed himself to the subject of street cleaning. But something told him that his future lay elsewhere than in garbage collection. He declined with exquisite tact, obviously hoping for a more suitable offer.[80] In the meantime there was more than enough federal business to keep him occupied. President Cleveland had at last begun to extend the classified service; John Procter was responding well to Roosevelt's training; another season of hard work would "put the capstone" on his achievements as Civil Service Commissioner.[81]

THE YEAR 1895 opened snowy and crisp, and Roosevelt plunged into the familiar round of receptions and balls and diplomatic breakfasts, to which he was by now shamelessly addicted. "I always eat and drink too much," he mourned. "Still . . . it is so pleasant to deal with big interests, and big men."[82]

A particularly big interest loomed in February. Revolutionaries in Cuba, Spain's last substantial fragment of empire in the New World, declared war on the power that had oppressed them for centuries. Instantly expansionists in the capital began to discuss the pros and cons of supporting the cause of Cuban independence. Henry Adams's salon at 1603 H Street became a hotbed of international intrigue, with Cabot Lodge and John Hay weighing the strategic and economic advantages of U.S. intervention, and Clarence King rhapsodizing over the charms of Cuban women.[83] Roosevelt, true to form, dashed off a note to Governor Levi P. Morton of New York, begging that "in the very improbable event of a war with Spain" he would be included in any regiment the state sent out. "Remember, I make application now . . . I must have a commission in the force that goes to Cuba!"[84]

As for "big men," he encountered on 7 March a genius greater than any he had yet met, with the possible exception of Henry James.[85] Rudyard Kipling was not quite thirty, but was already the world's most famous living writer,[86] and Roosevelt hastened to invite him to dinner. At first they did not get on too well. Kipling,

Roosevelt wrote, was "bright, nervous, voluble and underbred," and displayed an occasional truculence toward America which required "very rough handling."[87] Kipling's manners improved, and the two men became fond of each other. Roosevelt introduced Kipling to his literary and political acquaintances, escorted him to the zoo to see grizzlies, and to the Smithsonian to see Indian relics. From time to time he thanked God in a loud voice that he had "not one drop of British blood in him." When Kipling amusedly mocked the self-righteousness of a nation that had extirpated its aboriginals "more completely than any modern race has done," Roosevelt "made the glass cases of the museum shake with his rebuttals."[88]

Roosevelt's activity became more and more strenuous as spring approached. He dashed in and out of town on Civil Service Commission business, taught himself to ski, bombarded his friends in the New York City government with advice and suggestions, continued to toil on Volume Four of *The Winning of the West* and collaborated with Cabot Lodge on a book for boys, *Hero Tales from American History.*[89] Friends noticed hints of inner turbulence. He was seen "blinking pitifully" with exhaustion at a dinner for Owen Wister and Kipling,[90] and his tirades on a currently fashionable topic—whether dangerous sports should be banned in the nation's universities—became alarmingly harsh. "What matters a few broken bones to the glories of inter-collegiate sport?" he cried at a Harvard Club dinner. (Meanwhile, not far away in hospital, the latest victim of football savagery lay paralyzed for life.)[91] He declared publicly that he would "disinherit" any son of his who refused to play college games. And in private, through clenched teeth: "I would rather one of them should die than have them grow up as weaklings."[92]

Clearly he was under considerable personal strain. The reason soon became evident. He was torn between his longing to join Mayor Strong's reform administration in New York, and his instinct to stay put until the next presidential election. Toward the end of March he told Lemuel Quigg that he would like to be one of the four New York Police Commissioners, but waxed coy when Quigg said it could be arranged. He dispatched Lodge to New York to discuss the matter further. "The average New Yorker of course wishes me to take it very much," Roosevelt mused on 3 April. "I don't feel much like it myself . . ." On the other hand, it was a glamorous job—"one I could perhaps afford to be identified with."[93] Before the day was out, he had reached his decision:

TO LEMUEL ELY QUIGG WASHINGTON, APRIL 3, 1895

LODGE WILL SEE YOU AND TELL YOU. I WILL ACCEPT SUBJECT TO HONORABLE CONDITIONS. KEEP THIS STRICTLY CONFIDENTIAL.

THEODORE ROOSEVELT[94]

THE APPOINTMENT WAS CONFIRMED on 17 April, by which time Roosevelt was quite reconciled to leaving Washington. "I think it a good thing to be identified with my native city again."[95] Mayor Strong asked him to be ready to take office about the first of May. Roosevelt promptly sent his resignation to President Cleveland.

> I have now been in office almost exactly six years, a little over two years of the time under yourself; and I leave with the greatest reluctance . . . During my term of office I have seen the classified service grow to more than double the size that it was six years ago . . . Year by year the law has been better executed, taking the service as a whole, and in spite of occasional exceptions in certain offices and bureaus. Since you yourself took office this time nearly six thousand positions have been put into the classified service . . . it has been a pleasure to serve on the Commission under you.[96]

"There goes the best politician in Washington," Cleveland said, after bidding him farewell.[97]

All the abrasiveness of recent months melted away as Roosevelt joyfully contemplated his achievements in Washington and the challenge awaiting him in New York. He hated to leave the capital at a time when the trees were dense with blossom, and the slow Southern girls—so different from their quick-stepping Northern sisters!—were strolling through the streets in their light summer dresses, to the sound of banjos down by the river. He was sorry to say good-bye to nice, peevish old Henry Adams, to "Spwing-Wice of the Bwitish Legation,"[98] and Lodge and Reed and Hay and all "the pleasant gang" who breakfasted at 1603 H Street. He would miss the Smithsonian, to which he affectionately donated his pair of Minnesota skis, along with several specimens from the long-defunct Roosevelt Museum of Natural History.[99] Most of all, perhaps, he would miss the Cosmos Club, the little old house on Madison Place where leaders of Washington's scientific community liked to gather for polysyllabic discussions. Ever since Roosevelt's first days as Civil Service Commissioner, when he astonished twenty Cosmos members by effortlessly sorting a pile of fossil-bones into skeletons, with running commentaries on the life habits of each animal, he had been a star attraction at the club.[100] In later life Rudyard Kipling, looking back on these "spacious and friendly days" in Washington, would remember Roosevelt dropping by the Cosmos and pouring out "projects, discussions of men and politics, and criticisms of books" in a torrential stream, punctuated by bursts of humor. "I curled up in the seat opposite, and listened and wondered, until the universe seemed to be going round, and Theodore was the spinner."[101]

CHAPTER 19

The Biggest Man in New York

Bitter as home-brewed ale were his foaming passions.

NEW YORK'S Police Headquarters at 300 Mulberry Street was a squat, square building with a marble facade long since yellowed by the fumes of Little Italy.[1] Many a *stiletto* victim had been carried bleeding up its steep front steps, and countless *padrones* awaiting indictment had glared through its barred basement windows at a little group of reporters lounging on the stoop of No. 303, across the way.

The reporters, in turn, enjoyed one of the more entertaining vistas in Manhattan. Before them stretched a cobbled street, framed on both sides by tenement buildings, and looped around with strings of brilliant laundry. It was an arena always alive with drama, or at least the promise of drama. A sudden singing of the telegraph wires, which untidily connected Police Headquarters with every precinct in the city, might signify riots in Hell's Kitchen, or a brothel-bust in the Tenderloin; sooner or later the latest victims of the law would be delivered in shiny patrol-wagons, and the press would dash across to meet them, pencils and pads at the ready.

Even when Mulberry Street was sunk in Monday-morning calm, as around ten o'clock on 6 May 1895,[2] the stoop-sitters were loath

"Many a *stiletto* victim had been carried bleeding up its steep front steps."

Police Headquarters, Mulberry Street, New York City.

to quit their airy perch for the "newspaper offices" upstairs—actually just stifling cells of the kind that, elsewhere in the neighborhood, sheltered whole families. As long as the breeze did not blow uptown from the reeking slums of Mulberry Bend, a man could enjoy his cigar, play poker, and shout humorous insults at the cop on duty opposite. If the sun grew uncomfortably hot, he could send around the corner for iced oysters at a penny each, or stop a passing *aguajolo* for fresh lemonade.

Lincoln Steffens, the talented young correspondent of the *Evening Post,* was on the stoop that day when Jacob Riis of the *Evening Sun* came out into the street shouting a telephone message. Theodore Roosevelt had just been sworn in as Police Commissioner at City Hall, eighteen blocks south: he and his three colleagues were already on their way to headquarters to relieve the outgoing Commissioners.[3]

The news came as no surprise to Steffens. Riis was an old and worshipful friend of Roosevelt's, and had been gloating over his appointment for weeks. It was the will of God that such a reformer should be chosen to purge the notoriously corrupt New York police. Neither did Riis doubt that his man would become president of the new Police Board. "I don't care who the other Commissioners are. TR is enough."[4]

About half-past ten an interestingly varied quartet walked around the corner. Leading the way was the bull-necked, bull-chested figure of Theodore Roosevelt. Behind him came a dumpy, middle-aged man bearing an uncanny resemblance to Ulysses S. Grant, and a military-looking youth, very tall and very pale, with a nervous vein beating in his temple. The fourth man seemed to walk somehow apart from the other Commissioners, although he was obviously their coequal—a handsome, lounging, bearded dandy of about thirty-five. Steffens identified them in turn as Frederick D. Grant (R), an upstate politician and eldest son of the great general; Avery D. Andrews (D), a graduate of West Point and a rather undistinguished lawyer; and Andrew D. Parker (D), also a lawyer, but one of the cleverest in the city, and a rumored agent of the County Democratic organization.[5]

Roosevelt broke into a run when he caught sight of Riis waiting outside No. 303. As Steffens remembered it,

> He came on ahead down the street; he yelled, "Hello, Jake," to Riis, and running up the stairs to the front door of Police Headquarters, he waved us reporters to follow. We did. With the police officials standing around watching, the new Board went up to the second story . . . TR seized Riis, who introduced me, and still running, he asked questions: "Where are our offices? Where is the Board Room? What do we do first?" Out of the half-heard answers he gathered the way to the Board Room, where the three old Commissioners waited, like three of the new Commissioners, stiff, formal and dignified. Not TR. He introduced himself, his colleagues, with handshakes, and called a meeting of the new Board . . . had himself elected President—this had been prearranged—and then adjourned to pull Riis and me with him into his office.
>
> "Now, then, what'll we do?"[6]

Avery Andrews, writing more than sixty years later, confirmed the accuracy of this account, with the small qualification that Roosevelt's election had *not* been prearranged. "As the senior Commissioner in length of service, I called the meeting to order and nominated Roosevelt as President of the Board; after which I was elected Treasurer."[7] Thus some semblance of bipartisanship was preserved at the outset by distributing control of the Police Department between the two political parties.

"The public," Roosevelt announced in his first presidential statement, "may rest assured that so far as I am concerned, there will be no politics in the department, and I know that I voice the sentiment of my colleagues in that respect. We are all activated by the desire to so regulate this department that it will earn the respect and confidence of the community. . . . All appointments and promotions will be made for merit only, and without regard to political or religious considerations."[8]

ALTHOUGH ROOSEVELT WAS doubtless pleased to have been given pride of place among his colleagues, he found, within two days of taking office, that the honor was merely titular. On 8 May 1895, Mayor Strong approved an Albany bill which substantially altered the power structure of the New York police.[9] Far from elevating the president of the Board above the other Commissioners (as a certain Assemblyman named Roosevelt had suggested in 1884), the Bi-Partisan Police Act depressed him to virtually the same level. Since two Board members were necessarily Republicans, and the other two Democrats, agenda tending to divide the parties would inevitably cause deadlock. Roosevelt knew that these could be resolved only by deal-making or by wrangling. Neither solution appealed to him. The new law, he wrote sarcastically, "modeled the government of the police force somewhat on the lines of the Polish Parliament."[10]

It virtually guaranteed that, contrary to what he had just announced, there was going to be plenty of politics-as-usual in the Police Department, from the Board on down. One of the Act's provisions, frustrating to him as a former campaigner against partisan patronage, was to transfer authority over police examinations from the municipal civil-service commission to a special panel of police officers—each of whom, presumably, would be easily bought. The Act insisted, further, on equal two-party representation while extending the Police Board's control of city elections. This in effect gave the Republican party—a perennial minority in New York municipal affairs—disproportionate clout in "supervising" voter behavior. At the same time, crazily, it seemed designed to thwart any majority decision by the Commissioners. "Lest we should get such a majority, it gave each member power to veto the actions of his colleagues in certain very important matters; and, lest we should do too much when we were unanimous, it provided that the Chief [of Police], our nominal subordinate, should have entirely independent action . . . and should be practically irremovable."[11]

The Chief, moreover, was a formidable figure. Commissioners might come and go, but Thomas F. Byrnes bestrode Mulberry Street with the solidity of a Colossus. At fifty-three, he bade fair to outlast the present Board well into the next century. Byrnes was internationally famous as a detective of almost mystic power, capable of retrieving stolen property at will. "Enough," he would say soothingly to a distraught Fifth Avenue matron, "your diamonds will be delivered at your house within three days." Invariably they were.[12]

Cynical observers, like Lincoln Steffens, noted that such spectacular achievements were the result of a comfortable arrangement with organized crime. The Chief allowed certain lords of the underworld carte blanche, providing their gangs worked regular beats, and cooperated whenever he asked them to return this or that haul for publicity purposes. It was also agreed that the gangs would stay away from the financial district, for Byrnes had another comfortable arrangement with the lords of Wall Street. Capitalists like Jay Gould did not wish to be disturbed by petty bank heists while they went about the larger business of robbing the United States Treasury, and they were prepared to reward Byrnes for his protection with favored stocks and bonds. As a result, the Chief prospered mightily; by 1895 he was worth at least $350,000, according to his own public estimate.[13]

Graft on so majestic a scale could not be expected of other police officers, but Byrnes's example was an inspiration to all, and the corruption elsewhere was proportionate, according to rank. Reporting directly to the Chief were three inspectors, whose corpulent figures and gold-laced uniforms amply symbolized the rewards of office. Then came thirty-five Captains, each of whom controlled a precinct, and the revenues thereof.[14] Officers from high-vice areas like the Tenderloin waxed noticeably richer than their colleagues. However even the poorest precinct was worth several thousand a year if properly organized. A regular system of "taxation" prevailed in most parts of town, whereby the owner of any business, legal or illegal, paid dues based on turnover. Greengrocers would hand over a dollar or two a day for permission to stack fruit on the sidewalk. Owners of gambling houses set aside $15 to $300 a month as insurance against raids. Saloons paid $10,000 for a liquor license; the madam of a brothel might contribute $30,000 over an extended period to her precinct captain, along with more intimate favors upon request.[15]

Another form of corruption—job-peddling—flourished within the Police Department itself. Since there were at least two qualified applicants for every one of the force's thirty-eight thousand positions, certain market values prevailed. In 1894 the going rate for a captaincy was $10,000, although some men had been known to pay

$12,000 to $15,000 in hard currency.[16] At the opposite end of the scale, appointment as a patrolman could be had for $300—even that was much more than most recruits were able to pay. Examining officers explained kindly that the investment would soon be recouped on the beat.[17]

All these sums were a matter of common notoriety when Roosevelt took office. Only four months before, an investigating committee of the New York State Senate, headed by Clarence L. Lexow (R), had published them in a sensational report recommending "an indictment against the Police Department of New York City as a whole." The 10,576-page document, which represented the most searching municipal probe since the days of the Tweed Ring, included a sample police "budget," as follows:

Regular Appropriation	$5,139,147.64
Brothel Contributions	8,120,000.00
Saloon Contributions	1,820,000.00
Gambling-house Contributions	165,000.00
Merchants, peddlers etc.	50,000.00
New Members of Force	60,000.00
Grand Total:	$15,354,147.64

The fact that such figures were now quoted in guidebooks to the city, along with the height of the Statue of Liberty and the length of the Brooklyn Bridge, was indicative of the weary tolerance with which police bribery was regarded.[18]

The memoirs of Commissioners Andrews and Roosevelt differ as to the true extent of corruption in their department in May 1895. Andrews, who had a military fondness for men in uniform, believed that "the great majority of the rank and file were honest and efficient . . . Graft was largely confined to certain senior officers, and their 'wardmen', or graft collectors."[19] Roosevelt expressed himself rather more negatively. "From top to bottom," he wrote, "the New York police force was utterly demoralized by the gangrene . . . venality and blackmail went hand-in-hand with the basest forms of low ward politics . . . the policeman, the ward politician, the liquor seller, and the criminal alternately preyed on one another and helped one another to prey on the general public."[20]

Of course the truth lay somewhere between these two extremes. However both Commissioners, in referring to wardmen and ward politics, emphasized that the Police Department was not in business merely for itself. Its traditional function, indeed, was to finance the city's political machines. Often the person collecting "contributions" around each precinct at the end of the week was not a policeman at all, but an employee of Tammany Hall.[21] The vast sums thus accrued had kept the Democratic organization in power from 1886 (the year Abram Hewitt defeated Theodore Roosevelt for Mayor) until 1894, when mounting disgust over the Lexow hearings swept the reform ticket to victory.

As a result of this near-decade of corrupt domination of New York City politics, Tammany Hall had become so solidly entrenched that Mayor Strong's election seemed but a temporary interruption of the status quo. "Our people could not stand the rotten police corruption," Boss Richard Croker admitted. "They'll be back at the next election; they can't stand reform either."[22]

Croker's confidence was based on the fact that the Police Board also constituted the Board of Elections. This useful quirk in the law gave the four Commissioners power to appoint all election officers, prepare and count all ballots, and preserve order—or willful disorder—at the polls.[23] Croker's last tame Commissioner on Mulberry Street had boasted that "given control of the police, he cared not how the public voted."[24] Croker could have rigged the last election, as he had others in the past; but, being a political realist, he deemed it wiser not to play with the passions aroused by the Lexow investigation. Tammany Hall could afford to put up its shutters for a season or two. Its precinct organization was as perfect as ever, and its financial prospects were excellent. Corruption in the Police Department would continue, Roosevelt or no Roosevelt.[25]

"NOW, THEN, what'll we do?" Roosevelt's impetuous question sounded odd in the ears of the two reporters as they sat in his office on the first day of his Commissionership. "It was just as if we three were the Police Board," marveled Lincoln Steffens, "TR, Riis, and I." Willing as both men were to suggest what and whom Roosevelt might attack—for he was clearly in a fighting mood—they cautioned him to "go a bit slow" at first, and to discuss a program of reform with his colleagues.[26] But Roosevelt knew he could achieve little in this job by proceeding deliberately; it was about as powerful, in constitutional terms, as his last. Once again he must exercise his genius for press relations. Instinct told him that these scribes would be of more use to him than the three Commissioners now waiting in the hallway.[27]

Jacob Riis, at forty-six, was the most influential reporter in the city. A big, rumpled, noisy, sweet-natured Dane, he had been obsessed with social reform ever since his youth as a penniless immigrant on the Lower East Side. (Deep within him he carried the memory of a policeman beating out the brains of his pet dog against the steps of Church Street Station.)[28] In 1890 Riis's documentary book *How the Other Half Lives,* illustrated with his own photographs, had shocked all thinking Americans into awareness of the horrors of the ghetto. Not long after its publication, he had found a card from Theodore Roosevelt on his desk, with the scrawled message, "I have read your book, and I have come to help."[29] A meeting had been arranged, and the Dane, by his own admission, fell in love at first sight.[30] Now, five years later, God had appointed Roosevelt president of the Police Board; the promised help was at hand.

There is no record of Roosevelt's first impression of Lincoln Steffens, but subsequent evidence indicates that he understood the young man shrewdly. Steffens was twenty-nine years old; thin, vain, arrogant, wolfishly ambitious, with the beady eye of a born investigative reporter. He had no false sentiment (unlike Riis, who refused to cover raids on homosexual brothels, on the grounds that "there are no such creatures in this world").[31] Roosevelt knew just how to handle Steffens. A mild scoop every now and again; indulgent nods when he ventured some criticism; a few flattering requests for advice—like "Now, then, what'll we do?"—and the reporter would be his man. In return, Roosevelt could be sure of a constant supply of raw political information, and much useful gossip.[32]

Commissioner Parker was not pleased at having to wait outside Roosevelt's office, and was heard to grumble, "Thinks he's the whole Board." For most of that first day, however, the four new colleagues acted harmoniously. They laughed and chatted together,[33] and each seemed pleased with his agreed-on responsibilities. Parker was given the glamorous and important job of reorganizing the Detective Bureau. Roosevelt showed further confidence in his political integrity by naming him chairman of the Committee of Elections. Grant was made overseer of repairs and supplies, and chairman of the Disciplinary Committee. The military Andrews was asked to draw up a new set of rules designed to tighten efficiency and ensure accountability in the ranks, in addition to his duties as treasurer. Roosevelt, who enjoyed ex officio a seat on all committees, announced that he would concern himself with problems of overall administration, and would act as press spokesman for the entire Board.[34]

JUST HOW SUCCESSFUL he was in the latter capacity may be judged from the following collage of newspaper headlines and cartoon captions, representing his first ten days in office:

ROOSEVELT'S NEW GIRL SECRETARY
The Police Board President Causes Sensation on Mulberry Street

REIGN OF TERROR AT POLICE HEADQUARTERS
Merit Wins Promotion Now—
Political Pulls Frowned Upon

RATTLED—THE DRY OLD POLICE BONES
Kick the Politicians, Lecture the Legislature
Snub the Roundsmen, Warn the Drunken Bluecoats
Abolish the Police Parades, & Stir up
Departmental Surgeons

ROOSEVELT AS JUDGE
The Reform Commissioner Tries Nearly
100 Policemen in One Day
"Pulls" Found Worthless Before the Inquisitor
With Big Teeth and Rasping Voice[35]

A subhead in the *World* summed up the new Commissioner's policy in these words: *Publicity, publicity, publicity.*[36] He seemed determined to expose to general scrutiny every aspect of his department's work, from transcripts of Board meetings to dossiers on the moral fitness of officers for promotion. His habit of inviting reporters to spend the day in his big, bare office made it difficult for the representatives of political organizations to have private speech with him. Whenever the politicians began to whisper, he would deliberately answer "in a voice loud enough to be heard across the room."[37]

The white glare of all this publicity inevitably focused much attention upon Roosevelt the man. A lead article in the *World* of 17 May shows with what clarity he stamped his image on the pages of the press. Although the article purported to describe a routine trial of police officers for infractions of discipline, it dwelt with fascinated relish upon the judge's physical peculiarities, and survives as a documentary portrait of Theodore Roosevelt at thirty-six:

> When he asks a question, Mr. Roosevelt shoots it at the poor trembling policeman as he would shoot a bullet at a coyote. . . . he shows a set of teeth calculated to unnerve the bravest of the Finest. His teeth are very white and almost as big as a colt's teeth. They are broad teeth, they form a perfectly straight line. The lower teeth look like a row of dominoes. They do not lap over or under each other, as most teeth do, but come together evenly . . . They seem to say: "Tell the truth to your Commissioner, or he'll bite your head off."
>
> Generally speaking, this interesting Commissioner's face is red. He has lived a great deal out of doors, and that accounts for it. His hair is thick and short . . . Under his right ear he has a long scar. It is the opinion of all the policemen who have talked with him that he got that scar fighting an Indian out West. It is also their opinion that the Indian is dead.
>
> But Mr. Roosevelt's voice is the policeman's hardest trial. It is an exasperating voice, a sharp voice, a rasping voice. It is a voice that comes from the tips of the teeth and seems to say in its tones, "What do you amount to, anyway?"

> One thing our noble force may make up its mind to at once—it must do as Roosevelt says, for it is not likely that it will succeed in beating him.[38]

Jacob Riis, reporting another trial for the *Evening Sun,* noted how impossible it was for Roosevelt to yield conduct of the court to any of his colleagues. Within a quarter of an hour (although Andrews had the chair) he was putting all the questions and interrupting most of the answers. "Once or twice he turned to Commissioner Andrews and apologized . . . but by the time the third case ended there was no longer any apparent need to do that."[39]

Andrews did not mind being upstaged, and Grant liked nothing so much as to sit and stare into space, but Parker, Roosevelt quickly sensed, needed careful handling. Fortunately the Democrat seemed to prefer working behind the scenes. Immaculate of trouser-leg, dark and glossy of beard, he would loll in his chair with fingers intertwined, smiling easily and often. He projected an air of fashionable languor, coming to work late, leaving early, not bothering to attend many board meetings; yet there was a certain "sinister efficiency"[40] about the way he got things done that Roosevelt greatly admired. "Parker is my mainstay," he wrote Lodge. "He is able and forceful, but a little inclined to be tricky. Andrews is good but timid, and 'sticks in the bark.' Grant is a good fellow, but dull and easily imposed on; he is our element of weakness."[41]

Roosevelt found his new duties "absorbingly interesting,"[42] and threw himself into them with animal vigor. His daily arrival at Mulberry Street became a ritual entertainment for the stoop-sitters of No. 303. About 8:30 he would come around the corner of Bleecker Street, walking with a springy tread, goggling his spectacles enthusiastically at everything around, about, and behind him. There was a rapid increase in pace as he drew near Police Headquarters, followed by a flying ascent of the front steps. Ahead of him in the lobby, a uniformed porter would step into the waiting elevator and reach for its controls; but by that time Roosevelt, feet blurring, was already halfway up the stairs. Arriving on the second floor with no perceptible rise or fall of his chest, he would scurry across the hallway into his office overlooking the street. Here, one morning, a reporter was on hand to note that "He swings the chair, sits down, and takes off his glasses and his hat, all so quickly that he appears to be doing [everything] at once."[43] Replacing the glasses with pince-nez, Roosevelt would "fling his attention" at the first document in front of him. Read, digested, and acted upon, the item would be given to his "girl secretary"[44] for filing, or, often as not, dispensed with in Rooseveltian fashion, i.e., crushed into a ball and hurled to the floor. By the end of the day the area around his desk was ankle-deep in paper jetsam.[45] "I wonder he does not wear himself out," sighed Commissioner Grant.[46]

On 13 May, Roosevelt admitted to Bamie (who was now on an extended stay in London, and had rented him her house at 689 Madison Avenue) that "I have never worked harder than in these last six days." In subsequent letters he altered the clause to read, "the last two weeks," and "the last four weeks."[47] Hard as it was to familiarize himself with every detail of police bureaucracy, there was the intense, additional frustration of finding himself without real administrative authority. "I have to deal with three colleagues, solve terribly difficult problems, and do my work under hampering laws," he wrote, in one of his perennial cries for power. ". . . I have the most important and corrupt department in New York on my hands. I shall speedily assail some of the ablest, shrewdest men in this city, who will be fighting for their lives, and I know how hard the task ahead of me is. Yet, in spite of all the nervous strain and worry, I am glad I undertook it; for it is a man's work."[48] Being congenitally unable to function unless he had some symbols of evil to attack, Roosevelt looked about him for an opponent. As usual he selected the biggest and nearest. "I think I shall move against Byrnes at once," he told Lodge on 18 May. "I thoroughly distrust him, and cannot do any thorough work while he remains.[49]

The Chief of Police was not afraid of righteous persecution. He had survived threats against himself, and against "the business," as policemen were wont to call their profession, many times before. "It will break you," he warned Roosevelt. "You will yield. You are but human."[50]

Yet, for a Colossus, he toppled with surprising ease. Nine days after Roosevelt's declaration, Byrnes was out. The same law which had so recently elevated him to supreme command of the force, also permitted him to retire on full pension, along with any other officer who had served twenty-five years and wished to escape embarrassing questions from the reform Board. Threatened with public investigation, he handed in his resignation on 28 May, and strode heavily out of Police Headquarters. "Men stopped and stood to watch him go, silent, respectful, sad," wrote Lincoln Steffens, "and the next day, the world went on as usual."[51]

A second symbolic departure in the last week of May was that of Inspector "Clubber" Williams. This notoriously brutal officer had earned his nickname cracking skulls on the Lower East Side, while also earning a fortune which he solemnly ascribed to real-estate speculation in Japan. Williams was the pet peeve of Steffens, who told Roosevelt he would love to see him fired. "Well, you will" was the answer.[52]

> A few days later [24 May] TR threw up his second-story window, leaned out, and yelled his famous cowboy call, "Hi yi yi." He often summoned Riis and me thus. When we poked our heads out of my window across the street this time, he called me alone.
>
> "Not you, Jake. Steffens, come up here."
>
> I hurried over to his office, and there in the hall stood Williams, who glared as usual at me with eyes that looked like clubs. I passed on in to TR, who bade me sit down on a certain chair in the back of the room. Then he summoned Williams and fired him; that is to say, he forced him to retire. It was done almost without words. Williams had been warned; the papers were all ready. He "signed there," rose, turned and looked at me, and disappeared.[53]

According to Commissioner Andrews, the resignations of Byrnes and Williams "shook the force from top to bottom." Men in the ranks felt puzzled and insecure in the power vacuum that followed. They hesitated to accept Roosevelt's authority until Acting Chief Peter Conlin, a quiet, colorless ex-inspector, revealed whose side he was on. In the meantime there could be no doubt that the president of the Board had scored a double personal triumph.

Roosevelt boasted publicly that "the work of reforming the force was half done, because it was well begun." The *World* agreed with him. "More than half the difficulty of police reform lay in the principle of corruption inherent in the old machine organization, and firmly established by years of toleration . . . the removal of [Byrnes and Williams] renders the further work of improvement comparatively easy."[54]

Roosevelt now turned his attention to questions of efficiency and discipline in the force. With shrewd flair for melodrama, he chose to begin his investigations at night.[55]

SHORTLY AFTER 2:00 A.M. on 7 June 1895, a stocky, bespectacled figure emerged from the Union League Club and stood on the steps overlooking Fifth Avenue. Although the night was warm, he turned the collar of his evening coat up and pulled a soft hat low over his eyes. Presently a shaggy man in dark green glasses joined him, and the pair began walking eastward along Forty-second Street. Some suspicious club attendants, accompanied by a night watchman, followed them until satisfied that whatever mischief they planned was going to take place somewhere else.

Turning down Third Avenue, Roosevelt and his companion, who was none other than Jacob Riis, walked south as far as Twenty-seventh Street without seeing a single policeman. Second Avenue was better patrolled, in that at least one officer was on the beat. But as the hours wore on, and the searchers continued to prowl around the East Side, it became apparent that New York's Finest were also among its rarest. Roosevelt and Riis were standing outside an all-night restaurant when the owner came out, rapped the sidewalk with a stick, and gazed angrily up and down the deserted street. "Where in thunder does that copper sleep?" he asked, unaware that he was addressing the president of the Police Board.[56]

Later Roosevelt swooped incognito upon a roundsman and two patrolmen conversing outside a corner liquor store. "Why don't you two men patrol your posts?" The loiterers seemed inclined to respond violently until he introduced himself, whereupon they marched off in a hurry.[57] Elsewhere Roosevelt discovered an officer snoring on a butter-tub, and another "partly concealed," as the *Tribune* discreetly put it, "by petticoats."[58]

The result of this expedition was that the Commissioner had six names and numbers entered in his pocketbook by 7:15 A.M., when he returned to Mulberry Street to begin the next day's work. A reporter noted that he looked "tired and worn" as he strode up the steps of Headquarters. Yet he was obviously in a good humor—so much so he could not bring himself to punish the offenders when they were brought before him at 9:30. However he announced afterward that "I certainly shall . . . deal severely with the next roundsman or patrolman I find guilty of any similar shortcomings."[59]

Newspaper coverage that afternoon and the following morning was everything he could have desired. "ROOSEVELT AS ROUNDSMAN" one headline declaimed. "Policemen Didn't Dream the President of the Board Was Catching Them Napping," read another. "He Makes the Night Hideous for Sleepy Patrolmen," reported a third. Even more gratifying were fulsome editorials of praise, in other cities as well as New York. It was generally agreed that "a new epoch" had begun in the Police Department, and that Roosevelt, not Peter Conlin, was its real Chief.[60] The *Brooklyn Times* rejoiced that wanton clubbing of New Yorkers would now decline; no cop would wish his nightstick "to collide with the head of the ubiquitous Theodore." The Washington *Star* suggested that all members of the force should memorize Roosevelt's features, so as to be prepared for trouble whenever teeth and spectacles came out of the darkness.[61]

On his next "night patrol," which took place in the small hours of 14 June, Roosevelt was accompanied by Commissioner Andrews and Richard Harding Davis, the roving correspondent of *Harper's Monthly*.[62] The three young men entered the Thirteenth precinct, on the Lower East Side, soon after midnight, and began a systematic search of its clammy caverns. This was distinctly ghetto territory: ill-lit, badly sanitized, the air around Union Market heavy with the smells of *schmaltz* and blood-soaked kosher salt. Roosevelt, who as president of the Police Board was also a member of the Board of Health, made a note to hasten the closing of the long-condemned slaughterhouse.[63]

What policemen could be seen wandering through pale orbs of

gaslight were all doing their duty conscientiously. "You are to be congratulated, sir," said Roosevelt, materializing in front of a startled sergeant at 1:55 A.M., "this precinct is well patrolled."[64] He visited the station-house men's room and emerged laughing: its graffiti included a sketch of himself prowling the streets.[65]

Clearly the message was getting through to the ranks. The only delinquent discovered on the whole East Side that night was Patrolman William E. Rath, who forsook his beat for an oyster saloon on upper Third Avenue. Here, according to the *Excise Herald,* the following dialogue took place:

ROOSEVELT	(*entering*) Why aren't you on your post, officer?
RATH	(*deliberately swallowing oyster*) What the —— is it to you?
COUNTER MAN	You gotta good nerve, comin' in here and interferin' with an officer.
ROOSEVELT	I'm Commissioner Roosevelt.
RATH	(*reaching for vinegar bottle*) Yes, you are. You're Grover Cleveland and Mayor Strong all in a bunch, you are. Move on now, or—
COUNTER MAN	(*in a horrified whisper*) Shut up, Bill, it's His Nibs, sure, don't you spot his glasses?
ROOSEVELT	(*authoritatively*) Go to your post at once.
	(*EXIT patrolman, running*)[66]

At 3:00 A.M. the night-walkers retired to Mike Lyon's all-night restaurant on the Bowery for steaks, salad, and beer. Little notice was taken of them at first, until an alert reporter identified the two Commissioners, and word spread quickly from table to table. Even the chef came out to stare. Roosevelt was obliged to hold an impromptu press conference before he could proceed with his steak.[67]

Refreshed, he escorted his companions over to the West Side for a tour of the Fifteenth and Nineteenth precincts—the latter being the notorious Tenderloin district. Here things were much less satisfactory. No fewer than seven patrolmen were found to be off their posts, including three who had literally to be awakened to a sense of their duties. Roosevelt jotted down their names and numbers in his pocketbook, and, much later in the day, handed the list to Chief Conlin, saying, "This time there will be no mercy." At the disciplinary hearing he himself appeared as complainant.[68]

These and subsequent nocturnal jaunts delighted the citizens of New York, who for years had been starved of entertaining municipal news. No such eccentric behavior by a public official had ever been recorded. The somnambulant Commissioner was nicknamed Haroun-el-Roosevelt, after the caliph who liked to stalk unrecognized through Baghdad after dark. Cartoons were published of policemen trembling before drugstore displays of false teeth and spectacles.[69] One enterprising peddler showed up on Mulberry Street with a sackload of celluloid dentures, each equipped with a toy whistle and wire tooth-grippers. "This is the way Roosey whistles!" the peddler cried, clipping on a set and hissing convincingly at passersby. The dentures sold as fast as he could fish them out of the bag, and Mulberry Street began to resound with shrilling noises.[70] Whether "Roosey" heard the racket in his second-floor office is unknown, but a Captain Groo quickly emerged from headquarters and arrested the peddler for doing unlicensed business.[71]

Roosevelt inspected the teeth later and allowed that they were "very pretty."[72] With his instinct for public relations, he must have known that the merchandising of one's features, even those most regrettably prominent, is a sure sign of popular acceptance. He had won a wide reputation before, of course, but only in the sense that a few thousand editors, columnists, political observers, and sophisticated newspaper readers across the country knew who he was and what he stood for. But here, in his hand, was the first tactile proof that his "image" was working its way into the folk consciousness of America. These celluloid teeth grinned cheerful news, and he could not but delight in them.

The exact number of midnight patrols Roosevelt took in the summer of 1895 is a mystery. Certainly there were others. But for some reason, after the first two or three, he discouraged the press from publicizing them. Avery Andrews mentions one expedition which Lincoln Steffens was allowed to attend on condition that he did not write about it.[73] Possibly Roosevelt wished to keep the tactical advantage of surprise, knowing that a retinue of reporters would inevitably spread word of his coming and going around the precincts. In any case his daytime activities were by then so controversial as to preclude every inch of available column-space.

Although the nights of vigilance wearied him (each involved going without sleep for about forty hours), he took great pride in them and saw many things that broadened his social understanding.[74] Tramping along what must have been hundreds of miles of silent avenues lit only by corner lamps and the occasional flickering torch of an oyster-cart, he could sense, if not feel, the ache of homelessness and poverty. In alleys and courtyards to left and right, he could gaze through open windows at the hot intimacies of tenement life, and listen to the bedlam of alien conversation. Italian changed to Chinese, German to Yiddish, Russian to Polish as he moved from block to block, until it was a relief to hear even a few words of broken English. Sometimes he cast about for pearls of street wisdom, as when he asked an Italian fruit vendor what possible "monish" could be made selling his wares on a deserted street at dead of night. The vendor cheerfully agreed it was no way to prosper. "W'at I maka on de peanut I losa on de dam' banan'."[75]

"These midnight rambles are great fun," Roosevelt wrote. "My whole work brings me in contact with every class of people in New York . . . I get a glimpse of the real life of the swarming millions."[76]

As always when he was learning something new, he visibly swelled with pleasure and satisfaction. The waiters and patrons at Mike Lyon's Bowery restaurant got used to seeing him drop in at two or three in the morning, tired and hungry yet wreathed in smiles. "It was 'Hello Teddy,' 'How are you Roosevelt?' all over the room," one regular recalled many years later. "Beaming, buoyant, blithe . . . really happy he was in those days."[77]

ROOSEVELT'S HAPPINESS did not remain unalloyed for long. He very soon came up against "an ugly snag" in his efforts on behalf of municipal reform. This was the Sunday Excise Law, a thirty-eight-year-old statute which forbade the sale of intoxicating liquors by saloons on the Sabbath.[78] The law had been reaffirmed in 1892 by a Democratic Legislature, as a gesture to New York State's large but mainly rural temperance vote.[79] In the city it was always honored more in the breach than the observance. Some New York mayors, including William Strong, had threatened total enforcement,[80] but gave up in alarm when they felt the passions any such action aroused. Resistance came from all classes. Slum-dwelling workers were not to be denied their weekend refreshments, after six days and fifty-seven hours of grimy labor. To the large, prosperous German community, a *stein* of lager after *Kirche* was more than a pleasure: it was a folk ritual, hallowed by centuries of tradition in the Old World. As for the "dudes" and "swells," quaffing champagne in the privacy of Fifth Avenue clubs, they could only sympathize with tenement kids scampering through the streets with buckets of ale for the family.

Nevertheless the law existed; it was on the statute books, and Roosevelt, as New York City's chief law enforcement official, sooner or later had to define his attitude toward it. He was not a prohibitionist—although he might well have been, given his own abstemious nature, and the frightful death of Elliott Roosevelt still fresh in his memory. As long ago as 1884, he had warned in the Assembly "that no more terrible curse could be inflicted on this community than the passage of a prohibitory law," and by his deciding vote had killed just such a measure.[81] His objection was practical rather than moral. "It is idle to hope for the enforcement of a law where nineteen-twentieths of the people do not believe in the justice of its provisions." The Sunday Excise Act was only partially prohibitory, but he still considered it "altogether too strict."[82]

Yet suddenly, on 10 June 1895, the President of the Police Board called in his officers and instructed them to "rigidly enforce" the closing of all New York City's saloons between midnight Saturday and midnight Sunday. "No matter if you think the law is a bad one; you must see that your men carry out your orders to the letter."[83]

Announcing his policy to the press, Roosevelt brushed aside suggestions that it was bound to fail and bound to make him personally unpopular:

> I do not deal with public sentiment. I deal with the law. How I might act as a legislator, or what kind of legislation I should advise, has no bearing on my conduct as an executive officer

> charged with administering the law . . . If it proves impossible to enforce it, it will only be after the experiment of breaking many a captain of the police . . .
>
> Moreover, when I get at it, I am going to see if we cannot break the license forthwith of any saloon-keeper who sells on Sunday . . . I shall not let up for one moment in my endeavor to make the police understand that no excuse will be permitted on their part when the law is not observed, and that Sunday by Sunday it is to be enforced more and more rigorously.
>
> This applies just as much to the biggest hotel as to the smallest grog-shop.[84]

It was a declaration of war, harsh and uncompromising, expressed throughout in the first person singular—with the exception of one "we," suggesting that at least a majority of Roosevelt's Board backed him up. As a matter of fact, all four Commissioners believed that the law should be enforced. Roosevelt was particularly gratified by the public support of "my queer, strong able colleague Parker . . . far and away the most positive character with whom I have ever worked on a Commission."[85]

Parker appeared to like him, and Roosevelt was by nature inclined to like everybody at first, so the two men got on excellently. They had many long discussions of the law at Headquarters, often continued over dinner in a nearby restaurant, and Roosevelt never doubted Parker's sincere dedication to municipal reform. Yet something about the affable lawyer made him uneasy. "If he and I get at odds we shall have a battle royal."[86]

ALL HOPES THAT Roosevelt might have been indulging in excise rhetoric evaporated on Sunday, 23 June, when astonished saloonkeepers throughout the city found their premises being invaded and warrants served on them when they refused to close. Even the notorious "King" Callahan, an ex-Assemblyman with powerful political connections, was ordered by a rookie to lock up his establishment on Chatham Square. Callahan liked to boast that he had thrown his front door key into the East River the day he opened for business, and he assumed his visitor was joking. But the rookie, whose name was Bourke, decisively repeated the order; whereupon Callahan knocked him down. Patrons of the saloon joined in stomping the figure on the floor, but Bourke was a wiry youth, and rose to lay out all comers with his nightstick. The King was duly served with a summons to appear in Tombs Police Court.[87]

The seriousness of this gaffe—and Roosevelt's real motive in ordering the saloons closed—became evident when Bourke arrived at the courthouse a couple of days later and found the chamber packed with professional politicians. A Congressman and State Senator stood ready to testify on Callahan's behalf; senior police officials were conspicuously absent. Lincoln Steffens urgently sought out Roosevelt at Headquarters. "Pat Callahan is a sacred person in the underworld, a symbol," he warned. Roosevelt must defend his rookie—even promote him, if the judge found Callahan guilty.[88]

Roosevelt immediately left for the courthouse, but word of his coming preceded him, and Callahan's defense collapsed. Patrolman Bourke was upheld; the witness waived examination and was remanded for trial on two charges of violation and assault. Overjoyed, Roosevelt pumped his rookie by the hand. "Bourke, you have done well. You have shown great gallantry . . . the Board is behind you." He promised to make him a roundsman at the first opportunity.[89] For weeks thereafter Roosevelt boasted about the downfall of King Callahan, with what one reporter described as "a castanet-like ecstasy of snapping teeth."[90]

It soon became clear that Roosevelt's order to close the saloons had very little to do with temperance principles. It was the logical consequence of his mandate—as he saw it—to root out corruption in the police force.[91] Ill-advised as such a crusade against "nineteen-twentieths of the people" might seem in retrospect, his basic reasoning was in the public interest.

Of all the wellsprings of illicit funds in New York City, the corner saloon was the most copious, and the most profitable to all concerned. It profited the liquor sellers with $160,000 worth of "found money" every Sunday. It profited the police, who accepted bribes in order not to enforce the law against them. In particular, it profited Tammany Hall, not only with a percentage of the take, but with a rich harvest of votes upon request—for the saloon was the traditional political center of every neighborhood.[92] A Tammany boss could, with a word to his precinct captain, force the Sunday closing of any establishment which failed to support him; arrests of this kind always increased dramatically in the weeks before Election Day. Sometimes, to make the situation more Byzantine, boss and saloonkeeper were one and the same person. Roosevelt never tired of pointing out that "nearly two-thirds of the political leaders of Tammany Hall have, at one time or another, been in the liquor business."[93]

In 1895 there were between twelve and fifteen thousand saloons in New York City, most of them occupying corner sites with elaborate displays of mahogany and engraved glass. In thirsty neighborhoods, such as Paddy's Market and Germantown, the saloons often occupied all four sides of an intersection. This architectural phenomenon was directly related to the Sunday Excise Law. A corner site meant that even when the front door was locked on Saturday at midnight, there would be at least one open door down the side-street, ostensibly connected with the saloonkeeper's living quarters. The flow of "friends" through this door on Sundays was prodigious. Policemen pretended not to notice the foam on the mustaches of departing guests, although they would conscientiously rattle the front lock and check that all shutters were drawn. Within, under flickering gaslights, business went on as usual.[94]

ROOSEVELT WAS NOT the first authority to invoke the law that year. Ex-Chief Byrnes, for example, had arrested a record 334 saloonkeepers on one Sunday in January. But as Roosevelt pointed out, his victims had been chosen carefully: "The law . . . was enforced with corrupt discrimination." Byrnes would never have permitted the booking of a King Callahan. Now "everybody was arrested alike, and I took especial pains to see . . . that the big men and the men with political influence were treated like every one else."[95]

As a result, 30 June was voted "the Dryest Sunday in Seven Years."[96] Ninety-seven percent of the city's watering-holes were closed, slowing to a trickle the normal Sunday flow of three million glassfuls of beer. Roosevelt bluecoats seemed to be everywhere, waving aside bribes with loathing and writing out summonses at the slightest sign of resistance. Some enterprising saloonkeepers sought to evade the law by serving "meals" with their drinks, in the form of token sandwiches. These were placed on barroom tables, on the tacit understanding they were for display purposes only, and left to curl up at the edges while relays of patrons "washed them down" with liquor.[97]

Roosevelt was sternly disapproving, and ordered his plainclothesmen to monitor all aging sandwiches in future. The legal ratio, he said, was one drink per sandwich, and they were meant to be consumed simultaneously. He congratulated an exhausted Chief Conlin on his success in closing so many saloons, and urged him to even greater efforts. "This must be kept up!"[98]

The following Sunday, 7 July, was not quite so dry, due to a growing awareness of legal constraints placed upon the police. They were forbidden, for example, to search persons or premises without visible evidence of alcohol being drunk and bought. Consequently a strange epidemic of traveling-bags, grip-sacks, and market baskets was observed in the streets of Gotham. Many hundreds of them were carried out of a cigar-store that backed up against Pat Callahan's saloon on Chatham Square. The police knew that a walled, awning-shaded garden connected the two establishments, but they were denied permission to enter. It was announced that the King was entertaining his "friends," and no longer included cops in that category.

In more sophisticated parts of town, coffee-vendors found that a heavy infusion of cognac in every cup greatly increased their sales, while at a German *Biergarten* on Lexington Avenue, requests for "lemon soda," "plain soda," and "cold tea" were met with Rhine wine, gin, and whiskey respectively.[99]

Despite all these ingenious evasions, it soon became apparent that Roosevelt's stranglehold on the saloons was beginning to hurt. The Wine, Beer, and Liquor Sellers' Association, until recently the richest organization in New York, reported that one quarter of its members were facing bankruptcy for lack of Sunday sales; *The New York Times* estimated their average weekend loss as over $20,000 each.[100] Economic shock-waves were felt all over the country. "In his eagerness to close the New York saloons," remarked the *Chicago Tribune*, "Mr. Roosevelt has interfered with the hop-raisers of New York and Washington, with the corned-beef ranchers of the plains, the pigs' feet producers of the West, and the barley-growers of the North. He is in a fair way to cost the American people millions."[101]

Anguished protests came in from Tammany politicians, most notably from ex-Governor David B. Hill, now a United States Senator. In an open letter widely seen as a keynote for the upcoming Democratic state campaign, Hill excoriated New York's "busybody and notoriety-seeking Police Commissioners" for "arbitrary, harsh, and technical" enforcement of the Sunday Excise Law. "A glass of beer with a few crackers in a humble restaurant is just as much a poor man's lunch on Sunday as is Mr. Roosevelt's elaborate champagne dinner at the Union League Club."[102]

On 12 July a Democratic judge handed down the alarming decision that the law, interpreted literally, forbade the sale of *all* drinks on the Sabbath, including milk and lemonade. "ONLY WATER TO DRINK NOW," mourned the *Herald*.[103]

Roosevelt's chance to reply came on 16 July when he faced a large meeting of German-Americans in the Good Government Club at 134 East 115th Street. His audience represented the second-biggest ethnic community in New York City. From Houston Street north to Yorkville, from Third Avenue east to the river, one might walk for miles and not see so much as an English shop-sign. Here lived some 760,000 industrious, beer-drinking burghers, mostly middle-class, sentimentally attached to the Old World, yet fiercely loyal to their adopted country. Economically and politically their votes counted for as much as, if not more than, those of Irish-Americans. Their reaction to Roosevelt's speech—his first major statement as president of the reform Police Board—was therefore eagerly awaited as an indication of how things might go at the next municipal election. Reporters came from as far away as Chicago and Boston to hear it.[104]

The evening began with a complaint, voiced in garbled, guttural English by City Coroner Hoeber, about the Police Board's attitude to the "Continental Sunday." Commissioner Parker (also on the platform) had said immigrants were "welcome" to obey American laws. "He has not got any business to velcome us! Ve are here by right!" Hoeber's language grew so incoherent, as passion took him, that even his fellow Germans laughed; but Roosevelt listened with grave courtesy. Before giving his own prepared speech, he dispelled the specter of ethnic prejudice quickly and bluntly: "I care nothing for the birthplace of those whom I address . . . I speak as an American to fellow-Americans." There was a scattering of shocked applause.[105]

He was always at his best in situations of this kind. Something about united opposition stimulated his adrenaline and accelerated the natural rapidity of his mind. As he launched into the main body of his speech, beginning with a ferocious attack upon Senator Hill, he gave off a clean glow of health and strength. His skin stretched brown and taut around the muscular neck; his eyes shone clear blue through flashing pince-nez; he crouched slightly forward, as if posing for a spring. There was something canine about his eager alertness. A Chicago correspondent, searching for similes, tried "mastiff," but then settled on "greyhound, crossed with a terrier."[106]

> Senator Hill has done me the honor to take me as the antitype of his political methods and political views, and has singled me out for attack in connection with the Excise Law. Senator Hill's complaint is that I honestly enforce the law which he and Tammany put on the statute books . . . [His] assault upon that honest enforcement is the admission, in the first place, that it never has been honestly enforced before, and, in the next place, that he never expected it to be . . . It is but natural that he and Tammany should grow wild with anger at the honest enforcement of the law, for it was a law which was intended to be the most potent weapon in keeping the saloons subservient allies to Tammany Hall.

> With a law such as this, enforced only against the poor or the honest man and violated with impunity by every rich scoundrel and every corrupt politician, the machine did indeed seem to have its yoke on the neck of the people.
>
> But we throw off that yoke, and no special pleading of Senator Hill can avail to make us put it on . . . Where justice is bought, where favor is the price of money or political influence, the rich man held his own and the poor man went to the wall. Now all are treated exactly alike.[107]

With Commissioners Parker and Andrews nodding approval on either side of him, and applause mounting as his sincerity filled the room, Roosevelt argued that honest enforcement of an unpopular law was the most effective way to bring about its repeal. Legislators should think twice in future about passing laws to favor some voters, then neglecting them to please others. Abuse of the statute-book was a mockery of civilization. Inevitably it led to anarchy and violence. Using one of his typically brilliant, if far-fetched analogies, he compared the excise phenomenon with the lynchings phenomenon in the Deep South. In each case the tyranny of a small, powerful mob had brought about a perversion of the law; in each case the authorities accepted the perversion on the grounds that it represented "popular sentiment." To those who advised him to pay heed to the latter, Roosevelt cried: "My answer is that I have to do with popular sentiment only as this sentiment is embodied in legislation." Insisting that he was not against the Germans, nor the Catholics, but acting on behalf of all good Americans, he concluded emphatically: "It is the plain duty of a public officer to stand steadfastly for the honest enforcement of the law."[108]

It was a classic Roosevelt performance: aggression, vehemence, frankness, and authority, expressed in sentences a child could understand. The applause was long and respectful, and he sat down looking "exceedingly pleased" with himself.[109] Commissioner Parker rose to make a few remarks of support, and the evening ended with three hearty Teutonic cheers for the reform Police Board. The Chicago correspondent went home to report that Theodore

Roosevelt was "undeniably the biggest man in New York, if not the most interesting man in public life."[110]

AMONG OTHER SUPERLATIVES lavished on Roosevelt next morning was a telegram from the venerable Senator George F. Hoar, patriarch of the Republican party:

> YOUR SPEECH IS THE BEST SPEECH THAT HAS BEEN MADE ON THIS CONTINENT FOR THIRTY YEARS. I AM GLAD TO KNOW THAT THERE IS A MAN BEHIND IT WORTHY OF THE SPEECH.

"That was pretty good of the old man, was it not?" Roosevelt exulted to Cabot Lodge. "I was really greatly flattered."[111]

In the same letter he acknowledged that his uncompromising attitude had sharply polarized the press. For a couple of months virtually every newspaper in the city had eulogized him—but now, almost overnight, "the *World, Herald, Sun, Journal* and *Advertiser* are shrieking with rage; and the [German-American] *Staats-Zeitung* is fairly epileptic." He could still count on the support of the *Tribune* and *Times,* and also, to his ironic amusement, E. L. Godkin's *Evening Post.* "However I don't care a snap of my finger; my position is impregnable; I am going to fight whatever the opposition is."[112]

If the "yellow," or working-man's press was shrieking then, its clamor rose to levels of real bedlam in the weeks that followed, as the weather grew hotter and the Sunday spigots ran drier. The *World* and *Herald* devoted page after full page to "Teddy's Folly," caricaturing him as a Puritan Dutchman bent on driving innocent citizens out of New Amsterdam. With such active encouragement, about half a million citizens did indeed leave town on Sunday, 21 July, to slake their thirsts in the country pubs of Long Island and New Jersey.[113] They raised their tankards and drank many a bitter toast to Roosevelt's downfall, while Presbyterian ministers and temperance societies sang hymns to his praise.

Controversy builds political stature, and Roosevelt saw no

reason to be alarmed by the extremes of hostility and admiration his name seemed to arouse. Even the *Commercial Advertiser* saw that "the most despised and at the same time the best-loved man in the country" was destined for higher office. "Will he succeed Col. Strong as Mayor; or Levi P. Morton as Governor; or Grover Cleveland as President?"[114]

INSPIRED BY a midnight prowl on 23 July, which found every policeman on the Lower East Side patrolling with clockwork efficiency, Roosevelt announced that the following Sunday, the sixth of his campaign, would be "the dryest New York has ever known."[115] His prophecy proved correct: one newspaper compared the metropolis to the Sahara. A few side-doors were open for privileged customers, but the masses were obliged to go thirsty. Chewing-gum boys reported record sales; bums on the Bowery went into delirium tremens for lack of alcohol; one elderly lady was seen crossing over to Long Island City with an empty beer bucket. Fashionable neighborhoods were deserted as all who could afford to left town for the day. Some well-to-do youths chartered a pleasure-boat, recruited a band and a bevy of girls in white muslin, and cruised off to Idlewild Grove, towing two bargefuls of iced ale.[116]

Roosevelt, relaxing with his family at Oyster Bay, could not be reached for comment, but Commissioner Grant was in the city, and expressed doubt that the poor were really suffering. "Everybody would get on beautifully in hot weather," he suggested, "if they would drink warm weak tea."[117]

At midnight a downtown saloonkeeper named Levy, who had studied the statute-book and found that the hour from 12:00 P.M. Sunday to 1:00 A.M. Monday was not covered by any law, flagrantly opened his doors. Word traveled fast, and for the next hour saloons all over town were brilliant with lights and festivity.[118] "MR. ROOSEVELT IS BEATEN," claimed the *Sun* next morning, but it was plain he was not. The very scrupulousness with which Levy had observed the letter of the law testified to the efficiency of the Police Department in executing it.

As dry Sunday followed dry Sunday through the heat of August, public resentment of Roosevelt smoldered. The English poet John Masefield, then working as a pot-boy in a New York saloon, "often heard men wondering how soon he would be shot."[119] On 5 August a clerk at the post office tore open a suspicious-looking package addressed to Roosevelt, and was startled by "a puff of flame and smoke." Miraculously, all that had exploded was a match-fuse on the wrapper: inside lay a live cartridge embedded in gunpowder.

Roosevelt dismissed the letter-bomb as "a cheap thing," and refused to look at it.[120] The campaign went on.

ROOSEVELT'S ASTONISHING national prestige, so at odds with his unpopularity in New York, continued to grow. "The whole country, it seemed, was talking about Theodore Roosevelt," wrote Avery Andrews. "It liked what he was doing." Word of his exploits spread even to London, where the *Times* described him as a "police Rhadamanthus" ruling Mulberry Street "with undisputed sway." His three colleagues, especially the excellent Parker, were supporting him to a man, and Acting Chief Conlin, although nominally in independent control of the force, was content to obey his orders. Crimes were down, arrests up, corruption clearly on the wane;[121] Roosevelt had every reason to congratulate himself, and did not hesitate to do so.

Familiar signs of self-satisfaction appeared in his behavior. He began to talk in private as if he were on a platform, pausing after every sentence to watch its effect on the listener.[122] His youthful love of flamboyant dress was revived in a summer outfit, the like of which had never been seen at Police Headquarters. It consisted of a straw English boater, a pink shirt, and a black silk cummerbund whose tasseled ends dangled down to his knees.[123] "Bustling, jocose, and rubicund," he would burst into Board meetings and impulsively sweep up piles of documents awaiting action. "These relate to civil service matters. With the Board's permission I will decide them all."[124] The word "I" invaded his speeches to such an extent that the *Herald* took to reproducing it in bold type: the effect on a column of gray newsprint was of buckshot at close range.[125]

The success of Roosevelt's crusade was helped by his early insistence that he was acting out of duty, not bluenosed morality. But the temptation to preach, always strong in him, became irresistible on 7 August, when he appeared at the Catholic Total Abstinence Union's national convention in Carnegie Hall. Sharing the platform with him were Mayor Strong, Commissioner Parker, and a phalanx of clergymen, headed by Archbishop Corrigan of New York. "Big Tim" O'Sullivan, a State Senator from Tammany Hall, represented the forces of iniquity.[126]

After a mass chorus of "While We Are Marching for Temperance," sung to the tune of "Marching Through Georgia," Senator O'Sullivan rose to give the first speech. He had not joined in the singing, and proceeded to make plain his contempt for "the Puritan's gloomy Sabbath." To an uproar of hisses and boos, he declared that the Excise Law discriminated against "the orderly citizen who drinks in moderation," while encouraging the real drunkard to lay in supplies of hard liquor, and souse in front of his family.

Roosevelt's face, during this speech, was a study of majestic disapproval. Throwing aside his prepared text, he followed O'Sullivan to the lectern and soothed the raging audience with a full display of his teeth. "I want to express my gratitude to the Catholic Church," he intoned, "because it stands manfully for temperance, and for a day of rest and innocent enjoyment." The next thirty minutes were devoted to a conversational defense of himself and his policies, remarkable for the roars of applause that greeted every quiet cadence. For the most part it was standard stuff, but Roosevelt inserted paragraphs of temperance rhetoric which worked his seven thousand listeners into a frenzy of righteous fervor. Senator O'Sullivan was mentioned only occasionally, in tones of sympathetic sorrow, as a lost sheep to be mourned by the rest of the flock. "Rub it in to him, Teddy," yelled a voice, and Roosevelt swung into his peroration:

> I hope to see the time when a man will be ashamed to take any enjoyment on Sunday which shall rob those who should be dearest to him, and are dependent on him, of the money he has earned during the week; when a man will be ashamed to take a selfish enjoyment, and not to find some kind of pleasure which he can share with his wife and children.[127]

"Never in my life," he wrote afterward, "did I receive such an ovation." It was fully five minutes before order could be restored. Commissioner Parker ran over to shake his hand, followed by a score of delighted priests. If the *World* is to be believed, Mayor Strong "actually stood up and cheered . . . while State Senator O'Sullivan looked as uncomfortable as any man could possibly look."[128]

Reading the text of Roosevelt's speech eight decades later, one is struck, as so often with his oratory, by the ordinariness of the language which aroused such enthusiasm. Yet the words, banal as they are, are arranged with consummate skill. At no point that evening did he espouse the doctrine of total abstinence; he made no specific condemnation of drink; yet somehow he managed to convince seven thousand diehard prohibitionists that he was wholly on their side. Experts in the study of mass-manipulation techniques could only shake their heads in admiration. "You are rushing so rapidly to the front," wrote Henry Cabot Lodge, "that the day is not far distant when you will come into a large kingdom."[129]

ROOSEVELT WORKED HARDER during the hot months of 1895 than ever before in his life.[130] In addition to a grinding routine of ten- and twelve-hour days, interrupted only by rare weekends at Sagamore Hill, he expounded his board's policy "again and again in packed halls on the East Side . . . with temperatures at boiling point, both as regards the weather and the audiences." Boos greeted his every appearance, but he exuded such charm, vigor, and sincerity (flashing his teeth upon request, and dancing polkas with the girls of the Tee-To-Tum Club) that he usually bowed out to cheers.[131]

Meanwhile the Sunday Closing crusade went on. More and more saloonkeepers decided that their side-door business was not worth the risk of heavy fines and/or loss of license. On 23 August the Liquor Sellers' Association, representing some nine thousand of the city's twelve thousand saloons, came out in favor of total observation of the law, and threatened to expel any members who failed to comply. Its motive, of course, was to make political pressure for repeal overwhelming, but nevertheless the announcement was seen as a psychological victory for Roosevelt. Sunday, 1 September, replaced 28 July as the driest on record.[132]

"There has not been a more complete triumph of law in the municipal history of New York," wrote the London *Times* correspondent. Roosevelt had managed to achieve the impossible by closing the saloons, and getting large crowds of poor people to respect him for it. He himself boasted that he had "never had such a success as in the last four months"—adding the usual disclaimer, "I am not a bit taken in, and . . . shall not be in the least disappointed when it ends."[133]

He scored yet another publicity coup on 25 September, when the United Societies for Liberal Sunday Laws staged a protest parade through Germantown, and sent him a cynical invitation to attend. Few imagined that he would accept. When Roosevelt came drumming up the steps of the reviewing stand on Eighty-sixth Street, Herman Ridder, publisher of the *Staats-Zeitung*, was convinced he was an impostor. "I'll go bail he is the genuine article," laughed the City Comptroller.[134]

The parade, which took two hours to pass by, was a spectacular demonstration of Teutonic irony.[135] Flagstaffs and building facades were draped with purple bunting, symbolizing the death of the "Continental Sunday." The advance guard consisted of a dozen bicyclists with blue noses and bunches of whiskers under their chins, impersonating upstate "hayseed" legislators. Some thirty thousand marchers followed on in leather trousers, Bismarck helmets, and other ethnic paraphernalia. Saloonkeepers rolled by in open carriages, waving bottles of Rhine wine and a poster declaiming, "T'AINT SUNDAY." A gilt wagon carried a pretty *Fräulein* veiled in black, as the mourning Goddess of Liberty. She looked bewildered when Roosevelt loudly applauded her. Another float, labeled "The Millionaire's Club," showed three dress-suited toffs—one with prominent teeth and spectacles—swigging champagne, while behind them two policemen arrested a beer-drinker in working clothes. "As this float passed," reported the *World*, "Mr. Roosevelt looked serious."[136]

For most of the afternoon, however, he beamed with enjoyment. Since he stood on the most prominent part of the platform, it seemed "as if the whole affair were in his honor."[137] Word of his presence spread back down the line, and the paraders twisted their necks to stare at him. One short-sighted veteran peered at the stand

and shouted, "Wo ist der Roosevelt?" The Commissioner leaned forward, thumping his chest, and screamed, "*Hier bin ich!*" At this the marchers, spectators, and everybody on the stand dissolved into helpless laughter. "Teddy, you're a man!" yelled someone in the crowd.[138]

Afterward Roosevelt told his hosts he had never had such fun. "But," he added, "a hundred parades can't swerve us from doing our duty." With that he left, carrying two souvenir banners for the wall of his office: "ROOSEVELT'S RAZZLE-DAZZLE REFORM RACKET" and "SEND THE POLICE CZAR TO RUSSIA."[139]

ROOSEVELT'S PUBLIC TRIUMPHS in the summer and early fall of 1895, coupled with his tireless campaigning on behalf of his board and his party, prompted rumors that he was actively working toward the nation's highest office. The *Commercial Advertiser*'s above-quoted suggestion that he might succeed Grover Cleveland as President was taken up by the *Ithaca Daily News,* which formally endorsed him for the Republican nomination in 1896. In Brooklyn, a certain Reverend A. C. Dixon proclaimed from the pulpit the hope that Theodore Roosevelt might soon enter the White House, "as he incarnates the principles upon which Government is founded."[140] At No. 303 Mulberry Street, Jacob Riis serenely countered all criticism of the Commissioner's high-handed actions with: "Of course! Teddy is bound for the Presidency." What was more, said Riis, Teddy knew it.

"Let's ask him," Lincoln Steffens suggested. The two men dashed across to headquarters and burst into Roosevelt's office. Riis put the question directly. Was he working to be President? The effect, wrote Steffens, "was frightening."

> TR leaped to his feet, ran around his desk, and fists clenched, teeth bared, he seemed about to throttle Riis, who cowered away, amazed.
>
> "Don't you dare ask me that," TR yelled at Riis. "Don't you put such ideas into my head. No friend of mine would ever say a thing like that, you—you—"
>
> Riis's shocked face or TR's recollection that he had few

> friends as devoted as Jake Riis halted him. He backed away, came up again to Riis, and put his arm over his shoulder. Then he beckoned me close and in an awed tone of voice explained.
>
> "Never, never, you must never either of you remind a man at work on a political job that he may be President. It almost always kills him politically. He loses his nerve; he can't do his work; he gives up the very traits that are making him a possibility. I, for instance, I am going to do great things here, hard things that require all the courage, ability, work that I am capable of . . . But if I get to thinking of what it might lead to—"
>
> He stopped, held us off, and looked into our faces with his face screwed up into a knot, as with lowered voice he said slowly: "I must be wanting to be President. Every young man does. But I won't let myself think of it; I must not, because if I do, I will begin to work for it, I'll be careful, calculating, cautious in word and act, and so—I'll beat myself. See?"
>
> Again he looked at us as if we were enemies; then he threw us away from him and went back to his desk.
>
> "Go on away, now," he said, "and don't you ever mention the—don't you ever mention that to me again."[141]

Riis and Steffens were so crestfallen that afterward they did not even mention it to each other. Yet Roosevelt himself could hardly ignore the specter they had raised. He could not stop people addressing him—quite correctly—as "President Roosevelt," and he would have been less than human had his heart not lurched sometimes at the sound of that phrase.

THE NOVEMBER ELECTIONS approached, bringing with them some wintry blasts of political discontent, all seemingly directed at Roosevelt. His anticorruption crusade had been tolerated by the state Republican organization as long as it contributed to the decline of Tammany Hall, but now it began to look as if the reverse effect might be true. There was an ominous contrast between rural and metropolitan voter registrations, the former promising a statewide sweep for the GOP, the latter indicating a Democratic backlash in New York City. Evidently the *World*'s constant presentation of Roosevelt as a reformer gone mad was having its effect. The *Staats-Zeitung*, ignoring his happy appearance at the Liberal Laws parade, accused him of having "a grudge against Irish-Americans and German-Americans." Republican pollsters computed the potential vote loss in each of these communities and blanched. They were not encouraged by Roosevelt's announced intention to police the election fairly. A less virtuous Commissioner might have been persuaded to influence the voting by a combination of intimidation and selective arrests, but that kind of loyal assistance could hardly be expected from "the Patron Saint of Dry Sundays."[142]

Accordingly the Republican Convention at Saratoga endorsed the Excise Law in the vaguest possible terms, hoping to offend neither upstate rural prohibitionists nor thirsty urban workers. Pressure began to build on Roosevelt to moderate his crusade, at least through Election Day. His response was unequivocal and publicly expressed. "The implication is that for the sake of the Republican party, a party of which I am a very earnest member, I should violate my oath of office and connive at lawbreaking . . . Personally, I think I can best serve the Republican party by taking the police force absolutely out of politics. Our duty is to preserve order, to protect life and property, to arrest criminals, and to secure honest elections."[143]

"I shall not alter my course one handsbreadth," he wrote a worried Cabot Lodge, "even though Tammany carries the city by 50,000."[144]

This intransigent attitude had immediate personal consequences. Edward Lauterbach, chairman of the Republican County Committee, issued a statement that the party "was not in any way responsible for Rooseveltism." Lemuel Quigg, who had backed him for Mayor the year before, reproached him for "base ingratitude" and said their friendship was at an end. "He is a goose," Roosevelt commented indifferently. Even Mayor Strong, anxious to placate the German-American lobby, said he should either "let up on the saloon" or quit his post. Roosevelt replied that he would do neither. Strong was enraged but powerless.[145]

Roosevelt put on a cheery front in public, but privately he was depressed by the sudden downturn of his political fortunes. It became increasingly apparent that the city's Republican voters were going to "bolt" in droves, and that he would be held to blame. His support on the Police Board began to erode. "There is considerable irritation," the *World* reported, "because Messrs. Parker, Grant, and Andrews have seemingly lost their identity, and . . . merged into the great and only Theodore Roosevelt." He admitted having some "rough times" with his colleagues. "It has only been by a mixture of tact, good humor, and occasional heavy hitting that I have kept each one in line."[146]

With the abnormal self-control that always restrained his abnormal pugnacity, Roosevelt managed to avoid an open fight with state party leaders. He knew that the organization could not do without his unique talents as a campaigner. Anxious to reaffirm his party loyalty, he stumped for Republican candidates all over the city, speaking two or three times a night, and made side-trips to local hustings in Boston and Baltimore. "I am almost worn out," he wrote on his thirty-seventh birthday. "Thank heaven there is only a week more, and then the exhausting six months will be over, and I can ease up a little, no matter which way the battle goes."[147]

THE BATTLE WENT to the enemy. Although Republicans won overwhelmingly elsewhere in the state, Tammany Hall saw its full slate of municipal candidates elected by landslide margins. Analysis of the polls showed that 80 percent of the German-American vote, hitherto solidly Republican, had gone Democratic.[148] There could hardly have been a more crushing indictment of reform in general, and police reform in particular. The contrast between local and state returns only emphasized Roosevelt's unpopularity in his native city.

He reacted with oblique rage. On 5 November, the same night the returns came in, he wrote to one of his Civil War heroes, General James Harrison Wilson:

> If I were asked what the greatest boon I could confer upon this nation was, I should answer, an immediate war with Great Britain for the conquest of Canada . . . I will do my

> very best to bring about the day . . . I want to drive the Spaniards out of Cuba. I want to stop Great Britain seizing the mouth of the Orinoco. If she does it, then as an offset I want to take the entire valleys of the St. Lawrence, the Saskatchewan, and the Columbia. . . .[149]

Next morning he called in his precinct captains and told them that "The Board will not tolerate the slightest relaxation of the enforcement of the laws, and notably of the Excise Law." But for all this bluster, it was plain his authority had been dealt a mortal blow. Even the loyal *New York Times* doubted that he would ever again mobilize the police as effectively as he had during the long dry summer of 1895.[150]

THE YEAR DREW to a close amid rumors that Mayor Strong had formally asked for Roosevelt's resignation. Both men denied the stories, but Strong was heard to complain at a public banquet, "I thought I would have a pretty easy time until the Police Board came along and tried to make a Puritan out of a Dutchman." The remark was supposed to be jocular—Strong fancied himself as an amateur comedian—but Roosevelt, sitting at the same table, did not find it at all funny.[151]

The pace of his "grinding labor" at Police Headquarters did not slacken. If anything it increased, for he was trying to finish the neglected fourth volume of *The Winning of the West* in between appointments, as well as working full-time on it at weekends. "I should very much like to take a holiday," he confessed, but felt too insecure in his job to leave town for long.

Friends worried about his health, emotional and physical. "He has grown several years older in the last month," William Sturgis Bigelow wrote Henry Cabot Lodge. "At this rate it is only a question of time when he has a breakdown, and when he does it will be a bad one. . . . We shall lose one of the very few really first-class men in the country."[152]

Roosevelt's spirits sank lower as his reserves of physical strength dwindled. "It really seems that there *must* be some fearful shortcoming on my side to account for the fact that I have not one New York City newspaper, nor one New York City politician of note on my side. Don't think," he reassured Lodge, "that I even for a moment dream of abandoning my fight; I shall continue absolutely unmoved from my present course and shall accept philosophically whatever violent end may be put to my political career."[153]

One person who met him during these dark days was Bram Stoker, the author of *Dracula.* After watching Roosevelt in action at a literary dinner table, and afterward dispensing summary justice in the police courts, Stoker wrote in his diary: "Must be President some day. A man you can't cajole, can't frighten, can't buy."[154]

"A man you can't cajole, can't frighten, can't buy."

Theodore Roosevelt as president of the New York City Police Board.

CHAPTER 20

The Snake in the Grass

Eric the son of Hakon Jarl
A death-drink salt as the sea
Pledges to thee,
Olaf the King!

THE ELECTION OF 1895, which cast such sudden shadows over Theodore Roosevelt, threw contrasting beams of light on an old man he had long managed to ignore, but would have to reckon with in future. Thomas Collier Platt was now, after years of powerful obscurity, the undisputed Republican manager of New York State,[1] and a major force in the upcoming Presidential contest.

"The Easy Boss"—as Platt was known for his patient, courteous manner—had entered politics before Roosevelt was born. In 1856 he had been a "campaign troubadour" for John Charles Frémont, the Republican party's first Presidential candidate.[2] He had become a Congressman in 1872, when little Teedie was still stuffing birds on the Nile; he was elected to the U.S. Senate in 1881, about the same time young Theodore first ran up the steps of Morton Hall. Since then the careers of the two men—a quarter of a century apart in age, and diametrically opposed in personality—had intertwined with a closeness remarkable for the fact that they seem never to have actu-

"A decent man *must* oppose him."

Thomas Collier Platt in the 1890s.

ally met.[3] Fortune spotlighted now one, now the other after Roosevelt's election to the New York State Legislature in 1881. Platt was then suffering his darkest hour, having resigned from the Senate in support of Boss Roscoe Conkling's patronage stand against President Garfield. He had failed at reelection, and withdrew into the wings just as Roosevelt took his bow in the Assembly. During the years that followed, Platt worked quietly offstage to assume control of the state Republican organization. In 1884 he had been one of the New York delegates to the Chicago Convention. While Roosevelt campaigned for Edmunds, Platt campaigned for Blaine, seconding his nomination and disbursing large amounts of "boodle" on his behalf. He and Roosevelt had joined forces in making Blaine's nomination unanimous on the final day, but the older man's triumph was the younger man's humiliation. Then it was Roosevelt's turn to retire from public life, while Platt continued his takeover of the organization. Two years later, when Roosevelt ran for Mayor, Platt reluctantly put his machine to work for him. He was disgusted at the "boy" candidate's defeat: like Roosevelt, he preferred not to recall that disaster in later years.[4]

Platt's political luster faded again in 1888, when Benjamin Harrison allegedly promised him a Cabinet post in return for campaign help, only to forget about it after the election. Instead, the Easy Boss had the chagrin of seeing Roosevelt made Civil Service Commissioner, and go on to publicize a cause for which he, Platt, had nothing but contempt.[5] For the next six years he had watched Roosevelt's progress with disapproval, tempered by a certain amount of professional respect.

It had been Platt's organization that swept William Strong into office in 1894, and he was none too pleased when the Mayor appointed Theodore Roosevelt as Police Commissioner. Platt wished to use the Police Board (in its capacity as Board of Elections) to gerrymander the city, as he already had the state; but Roosevelt's gritty idealism began to interfere with the smooth workings of his machine. Roosevelt, in turn, declared that he was "astounded" at Platt's success "in identifying himself with the worst men and worst forces in every struggle, so that a decent man *must* oppose him."[6]

A confrontation between Boss and Commissioner was therefore

inevitable. Both men, in effect, had been preparing for it for eleven years,[7] but they waited until the 1895 election to determine who would have the upper hand. Even then, Platt bided his time. With both houses of the Legislature now firmly under control, he was gearing up his organization for the most massive gerrymander in American history—in which the eradication of a Theodore Roosevelt would be merely incidental. Platt's ambition was to combine old New York (Manhattan and the Bronx) with Brooklyn, Queens, and Staten Island into the metropolis of Greater New York. This would automatically double his powers of patronage. The present Police Department would be abolished, along with those of Fire and Health, and replaced by metropolitan commissions, which he would pack with organization appointees. It went without saying that under such legislation the "side-door saloons" would flourish once more—but on behalf of the Republican party for a change.[8]

Roosevelt had no immediate doom to fear from the Greater New York Bill, for the earliest consolidation date would be 1 January, 1898. But then he began to hear rumors that Platt was drawing up a supplementary bill which would legislate him out of office long before that. Unable to stand the suspense, he asked his old friend and organization contact, Joe Murray, to arrange an interview with the Easy Boss.[9] Early in the New Year word came back that Platt would see him in the Fifth Avenue Hotel on Sunday, 19 January 1896.

LIKE THE LORD, Platt was wont to receive the faithful, and hear their supplications, on the Sabbath. This was not due to any messiah complex on his part: Sunday was simply the most convenient day for out-of-town legislators, big businessmen, and overworked Police Commissioners to visit him. Still, there was something quaintly religious about the little knot of worshipers that gathered every seventh day outside his sanctuary; regular attendants like Quigg, "Smooth Ed" Lauterbach, and Chauncey Depew were nicknamed "Platt's Sunday School Class." After seeing the old man they settled on plush sofas at the end of the corridor to await his decisions. This niche was called the "Amen" corner, on the grounds that no other response was possible once Platt had made up his mind. Presidents Lincoln, Grant, Hayes, Garfield, Arthur, and Harrison had all sat here, as well as James G. Blaine, who, in Platt's opinion, "ought to have been President."[10] Roosevelt might have been excused some feeling of trepidation in following such august predecessors. If not, the sight of the Easy Boss was enough to give any young man pause.

Platt was then in his sixty-third year, and moved (when he moved at all) with the painful majesty of arthritis. Tall, stooped, bearded, and murmuring, he looked like some political Rip van Winkle who had fallen asleep in a more leisurely age, and had woken to find the new one not much to his liking. His handshake was loose, his jaw slack, even his skin seemed tired; it creased down on either side of his nose, and drooped in parchment-like folds over his large sad eyes. Oddly enough, for a man whose desk was always piled with dusty papers and pamphlets, Platt was the perfection of elegance in dress. His suit rippled into place as he rose on his cane, a pearl pin glowed in his silk cravat, and high starched collars scratched against his silvery jowls.[11]

Roosevelt was not deceived by this world-weary image, for Platt was known to be as tough in mind as he was frail in body.[12] After some brief discussion of national affairs—the equivalent, among state politicians, of talk about the weather—the Commissioner asked point-blank if he was to be "kicked out by supplementary legislation after the Greater New York Bill had passed." Platt's reply was equally direct. "Yes." Roosevelt could expect to be unemployed in about sixty days.[13]

Afterward, Roosevelt searched for adjectives to describe the interview. It was, he decided, "entirely pleasant and cold-blooded."[14]

HE ALSO DECIDED that since he was now in "a fair fight" for survival, he would pick up Platt's gauntlet in public.[15] It so happened that the following morning, 20 January, he was due to address the New York Methodist Ministers' Association at 150 Fifth Avenue. Knowing they were sympathetic to his crusade against the saloons, Roosevelt shrewdly presented himself as Christianity's last hope in Gomorrah:

> The other day the most famous gambler in New York, long known as one of the most prominent criminals in this city, was reported as saying that by February everything would again "be running wide open"; in other words, that the gambler, the disorderly-house keeper, and the lawbreaking liquor-seller would be plying their trades once more . . . Undoubtedly there are many politicians who are bent on seeing this . . . they will bend every energy to destroy us, because they recognize in us their deadly foes . . . The politician who wishes to use the Police Department for his own base purposes, and the criminal and the trafficker in vice . . . are quite right in using every effort to drive us out of office. It is for you decent people to say whether or not they shall succeed.[16]

If he had unveiled a giant effigy of Boss Platt with horns and a tail, he could not have more effectively mobilized the ministers. Convinced that Armageddon was at hand, they hurried off to denounce the Easy Boss from pulpits all over the city. The Methodist lobby in Albany warned legislators of "disastrous consequences politically" if they pursued the "foolish and wicked course" of punishing a public servant for doing his duty. Other ecclesiastical, liberal, and independent Republican organizations added their voices, and within forty-eight hours the popular outcry against Platt was deafening. "Roosevelt's a nervy fellow, isn't he?" said Mayor Strong admiringly.[17] Strong was beginning to regret his earlier jibes and threats against Roosevelt, perhaps because he realized that the Commissioner, however controversial, was his only really distinguished appointment. He may also have pondered Richard Croker's widely quoted remark, "Roosevelt is all there is to the Strong Administration, and Roosevelt will make it or break it." At any rate the Mayor was effusive in his approval of Roosevelt's speech, and announced that he would resist any moves against the present Police Board.[18]

On 23 and 24 January *The New York Times* published full details of "the Republican Plot to Oust Roosevelt," identifying Platt and his lieutenants by name, and denouncing them as "contemptible . . . sneaking cowards and hypocrites." The effect of these front-page, double-column articles was to give chapter and verse to Roosevelt's allegations, and draw national attention to the threat of a party split in New York. Platt was severely embarrassed. If he wished to be a force at the upcoming Republican National Convention, he must at all costs preside over a united delegation. His anti-Roosevelt bill was accordingly withdrawn from the Legislature, although it was understood it could be revived at any time.[19]

Roosevelt said he was "delighted" to have been reprieved, but carefully refrained from making any further attacks on Boss Platt. "I shall not break with the party," he confided to Lodge. "The Presidential contest is too important."[20]

Commissioner Andrews also expressed "very great pleasure," and Commissioner Grant rumbled something to the same effect.[21] Only Commissioner Parker was silent.

Coincidentally or not, Roosevelt now discovered that he had an open enemy on the Police Board. A friendly newspaper editor had long ago warned that Andrew D. Parker was "a snake in the grass, and sooner or later he will smite you,"[22] but Roosevelt was so taken in by the man's "sinister efficiency" he had never really believed it. A Republican ward worker had also informed him that "Parker could not be trusted . . . that he was not loyal to him as head of the Commission." Roosevelt laughed. "Not loyal to me? Impossible. Why, only yesterday I boxed with him, and he boxes like a gentleman!"[23] True, there had been an occasion in October 1895 when he heard rumors that Parker was criticizing the dry-Sunday campaign behind his back, while praising it to his face. More recently, Parker had several times lied to him with such "brazen effrontery" as to leave Roosevelt speechless. Yet there had been no direct hostility at Board meetings—not that Parker attended many—and the department continued to operate smoothly well into the New Year.[24] Not until five weeks after Roosevelt's successful appeal to the Methodist ministers did the snake rear up and strike for the first time.

At a routine Board meeting on 28 February 1896, Roosevelt

brought up the routine subject of promotions.[25] Due to mass resignations over the past nine months, by corrupt officers anxious to escape criminal investigation, the force was studded with "acting" inspectors, captains, sergeants, and roundsmen.[26] The Commissioners acted periodically to make at least some of these promotions permanent, and there had been little dissent as to which officers deserved full rank and pay.

Thus, when Roosevelt moved the promotions of Acting Inspectors Nicholas Brooks and John McCullagh, two men known for their decency and efficiency, he doubtless expected the usual unanimous vote. But Commissioner Parker demurred. There were other officers, he said, just as worthy of advancement; for example, an excellent man in the Detective Bureau, which he, Parker, had just finished reorganizing.[27]

Roosevelt protested in dismay. Brooks and McCullagh had been "acting" now for nine months; the force was expecting their immediate promotion; "it was not keeping faith with the men" to delay matters any longer. He insisted that the motion be voted on. Commissioners Andrews and Grant added their ayes to his. Commissioner Parker refused to vote at all.

Had the motion been on some trivial item of agenda, such as the issuance of a mask ball license, or the sale of a police horse, Parker would have been overruled by the majority. But on matters of promotion the Board's "Polish" constitution required a full vote of four—or, three votes plus the written approval of Chief Conlin.[28] Roosevelt was puzzled and frustrated. He did not like to resolve a Board dispute by enlisting the aid of a man in the ranks. However, since Parker was adamant—and remained absent from the next few meetings—the other Commissioners had no choice but to summon Conlin before them on 12 March. They were confident that he would be agreeable. Unlike his formidable predecessor, Chief Byrnes, Conlin was a quiet, unassuming officer who generally did what he was told.[29] Roosevelt asked bluntly if he would recommend the promotion of Brooks and McCullagh. Conlin replied that he would not.[30]

What was more, the Chief went on, he would no longer tolerate promotions or assignments within the force unless they were submitted to him in advance. He had not exercised this, his legal right, in the past, but in future he would insist upon it.

It was evident to the three flabbergasted Commissioners that they were listening to the voice, not of Peter Conlin, but of their absent colleague. For some reason, Parker wished to stop the reorganization of the force, and by some power he had been able to recruit Conlin as his ally. Whatever his motives, the consequences threatened to be serious. Already the failure of Roosevelt's 28 February motion was having its effect on police morale. Some "acting" officers, pessimistic of advancement under a deadlocked Board, refused to act at all until they got job security. Those who did try to give orders found the lack of gold on their sleeves acutely embarrassing. The Commissioners were obliged to pass a resolution on 13 March ordering Conlin to make a formal reply to their request in writing, as required by law.[31]

That very evening Parker was due to dine with Roosevelt at 689 Madison Avenue, in response to a long-standing invitation.[32] Under the circumstances a note expressing polite regrets might have been understandable, but none was forthcoming, and at the appointed hour Parker coolly showed up. It is unlikely either he or his host so much as mentioned the Brooks-McCullagh affair. Their social relations were still cordial,[33] and both men were too well-bred to argue over the dinner table. Besides, there were four other guests, including the Reverend Charles H. Parkhurst, president of the Society for the Prevention of Crime, and Roosevelt's good friend Joseph Bucklin Bishop, an editor of the *Evening Post*. The subjects discussed were mainly political—"Platt, Tammany, reorganization, political treachery, the German vote, etc."[34] Roosevelt must have hogged the conversation as usual, for Parker was in an ill humor by the end of the evening. Walking home with Bishop, he suddenly said, "I wish you would stop him talking so much in the newspapers. He talks, talks, talks all the time. Scarcely a day passes that there is not something from him in the papers . . . and the public is getting tired of it. It injures our work."

Bishop laughed. "Stop Roosevelt talking! Why, you would kill him. He has to talk. The peculiarity about him is that he has what is essentially a boy's mind. What he thinks he says at once, says aloud.

It is his distinguishing characteristic, and I don't know as he will ever outgrow it. But with it he has great qualities which make him an invaluable public servant—inflexible honesty, absolute fearlessness, and devotion to good government which amounts to religion. We must let him work his way, for nobody can induce him to change it."

Parker received this speech in cold silence.[35]

AT NOON THE FOLLOWING DAY Roosevelt telephoned Bishop and invited him to lunch. In the latter's words:

> As soon as we were seated at a narrow table he leaned forward, bringing his face close to mine, and with appalling directness said, "Parker came into my office this morning and said, 'You think Bishop is a friend of yours, don't you?' 'Yes,' I replied. 'Well, you know what he said about you last night? He said you had a boy's mind and it might never be developed.' "
>
> Roosevelt's eye-glasses were within three inches of my face, and his eyes were looking straight into mine. Knowing my man, I did not flinch. "Roosevelt, I did say that. Did he tell you what else I said?" "No, that is what I want to hear." When I told him, he brought his fist down on the table with a bang, exclaiming, "By George, I knew it!" "There, Roosevelt," said I, "is your snake in the grass, of which I warned you—the meanest of mean liars, who tells half the truth."[36]

If nothing else, this incident served to prove Parker's duplicity to Roosevelt. He reacted as he always reacted—aggressively—but, as in a nightmare, found that he had no weapon to wield, no target to hit. Parker continued to stay away from Board meetings, and when Roosevelt rescheduled some to suit his convenience, maddeningly stayed away from those too. Meanwhile Chief Conlin ignored the Board's order to report on Brooks and McCullagh, saying that the Commissioners must resolve their own differences. Roosevelt promptly appealed to the Corporation Counsel for an interpretation of the law, and was told that Parker and Conlin were perfectly within their rights. They could block every major decision of the board for the rest of the century, if they chose. On 24 March, headlines in the yellow press began to mock Roosevelt's impotence: "His the Voice of Authority, But Parker's the Hand that Holds the Rod."[37]

CONSIDERABLE SPACE was devoted to analyses of the deadlock at Mulberry Street that spring, and as reporters did their research some interesting facts came to light. It transpired that Parker had begun to amass power in the department from the day he took office. Quietly establishing control over the Detective Bureau[38]—the most feared in the world, outside of Scotland Yard—he now enjoyed as much potential influence in the underworld as Chief Byrnes had ever done. Just what use, if any, he intended to make of it remained to be seen. His hold over Chief Conlin was traced back to a bargain struck between them the previous year. Apparently Parker had withheld his vote confirming Conlin[39] until that officer was so desperate for permanent rank he had consented to pay the price: a promise of cooperation in any future moves against Roosevelt.

Speculation as to Parker's long-term motives ranged 360 degrees around the political spectrum. The *Herald* noted that Parker and Conlin were both Democrats, and that in the wake of Counsel's ruling they had already begun to change the structure of the precincts, with a fine eye for political detail. "Mr. Parker . . . is calculating the possibilities and probabilities of future elections and future Legislatures . . . Should there ever be a one-headed Commission, and the Democrats in the ascendancy, his friends say, he may be that Commissioner."[40] The *Evening Sun* believed that on the contrary Parker was cooperating with Boss Platt, who, unable to kill Roosevelt with legislation, had crossed party lines in order to cripple him. Parker's reward, presumably, would be some plum job when Greater New York came into being. Other papers speculated that Parker was working for Boss Jimmy O'Brien of the County Democracy, or, alternatively, Boss Richard Croker of Tammany Hall. But Lincoln Steffens, writing in the *Evening Post,* saw the whole thing as a simple clash of personalities. "It is impossible that two men like Mr. Roosevelt and Mr. Parker should long travel the same road. They run on radically divergent tracks. Mr. Parker fights secretively, by choice, while Roosevelt seeks the open . . . Parker rushes swiftly to the punishment of any man. Roosevelt seeks ever a chance to reward and praise. Both are able and obstinate men . . . They were foreordained to disagree, and they did . . . It is idle to say that there is even a semblance of peace in Mulberry Street. There is war and nothing but war in prospect."[41]

ROOSEVELT WOULD HAVE WELCOMED a war of any sort during those early months of 1896. His preference, he confessed to Bamie, ran to the foreign variety.[42] The nation was caught up in great excitement over President Cleveland's Venezuela Message, and pressures were mounting for Congress to recognize the rebellion in Cuba. Roosevelt vigorously championed both causes. He sent a letter of congratulation to the President, and received a long, grateful response. Cleveland, however, seemed unwilling to venture into the Caribbean, much to Roosevelt's disgust. "We ought to drive the Spaniards out of Cuba . . . it would be a good thing, in more ways than one, to do it."[43]

His frustrations over the Police Board deadlock vented themselves in a series of speeches, articles, and open letters aimed at "the peace-at-any-price men," or, more specifically, "beings whose cult is non-virility."[44] The editors of the *Harvard Crimson* were assailed for their "spirit of eager servility toward England," and sternly reminded that John Quincy Adams, the real formulator of the Monroe Doctrine, had been a Harvard man. Students at the University of Chicago were warned that the adult world was "rough and bloody . . . but if you have enough of the lust of battle in you, you will have a pretty good time after all." Elsewhere in the Windy City, in a major address to mark Washington's birthday, he thundered his gospel, "Life is strife," against a backdrop of Stars and Stripes. "There is an unhappy tendency among certain of our cultivated people," Roosevelt went on, "to lose the great manly virtues, the power to strive and fight and conquer." He urged his audience, in the name of Washington, to be ready for the day when America had to uphold its honor "by an appeal to the supreme arbitrament of the sword."[45]

The nonvirile, in reply, made amused reference to his failure to conquer anyone at Police Headquarters. "When a man of marked ability is obviously uncomfortable where he is," wrote a correspondent of the *Evening Post,* "it is a satisfaction to find some place where his energies will have unchecked swing." The writer suggested that Roosevelt should leave immediately for South Africa, where the Boers—"Dutchmen pure and simple"—were fighting a losing battle for control of the Transvaal. "Let him shake from his feet the dust of ungrateful Manhattan . . . let him offer himself as General-in-Chief to President Kruger, and head the staunch conservatives who hold the fort from the Vaal to the Limpopo; perhaps he may succeed in rolling back the British aggressor."[46]

E. L. Godkin, editor of the *Post,* agreed that this was an excellent idea. "Speaking for the American public, we say that, much as we esteem Mr. Roosevelt as a Police Commissioner we think his value to the community would be greatly increased if somehow he could somewhere have his fill of fighting." After two or three campaigns for Kruger, he would be purged, and would be able to resume the life of a dedicated public servant. In barbed sentences that seem to have embedded themselves in Roosevelt's hide, Godkin went on:

> Now, in our opinion, no man—and especially no man of Mr. Roosevelt's bellicose temperament—is qualified to give advice about war who has not seen war . . . The sight of a battlefield is one of the most awful lessons in international ethics which a civilized man can receive . . . Before Mr. Roosevelt sends round the fiery cross among the young men of the country any more, he ought, therefore, to have some personal experience of his own nostrum. Fighting grizzly bears, we can tell him, is child's play compared to facing a battery, or storming a fortification . . . That he would fight like a demon under Kruger, we have no doubt, but he ought

to fight somewhere before he recommends fighting so glibly to our youth.[47]

ROOSEVELT ADMITTED TO hours of deep depression in his job, together with much nervous fatigue as he struggled to break the deadlock at Mulberry Street. "What can I have done? What can I have done? That any man should imagine I could succumb to this hell-born lure?" Commissioners Grant and Andrews were also anxious to promote the two acting inspectors, but Parker continued to object, and Chief Conlin continued to side with him. The deadlock began to look like permanent paralysis. There was no hope of getting remedial legislation through Boss Platt. Grant went to beg his aid, and was politely refused. "I would like to please you, Colonel Grant, but I don't care nearly as much to please you as I do to worry Roosevelt."[48] The old man was obviously looking forward to Roosevelt's early resignation. Grant angrily declared that he would vote for no further promotions until Brooks and McCullagh were confirmed. This only worsened the strain on the president of the Board. "Though I have the constitution of a bull moose," he wrote on 30 March, "it is beginning to wear on me a little."[49]

Later that same day he, Grant, and Andrews made a sudden move to bypass Boss Platt. They jointly petitioned the New York State Legislature to scrap the Bipartisan Act. In its place, the Commissioners proposed a bill that would first, enable a majority of three to override a minority of two, and, second, restore to the Board the independent rights of assignment now enjoyed by Chief Conlin. Roosevelt still had plenty of contacts in Albany, and the new Police Bill came up for consideration within forty-eight hours. Machine Republicans were too slow to organize against it, and a favorable vote was recorded in the Assembly.[50]

Parker moved at once to work up opposition in the Senate. He wrote to warn Boss Platt that Roosevelt was an incorrigible promoter of Democratic policemen. To give the president of the Police Board more power, therefore, would actually reduce Platt's chances of patronage in the upper ranks. Parker went on to say that he himself was just the opposite: a Democratic Commissioner who happened to recommend Republican officers. In proof of this statement he enclosed a list of recent promotions, showing that Roosevelt had favored every Democratic candidate to date.[51]

The list was forwarded to Albany, and Platt's faithful lieutenant, "Smooth Ed" Lauterbach, circulated it among Republican members of the Senate. Roosevelt did not see a copy until 9 April, when he arrived to testify on behalf of his bill before the Senate Committee on Cities. He boggled at the neatly typed document: it was "unqualifiedly false" in almost every particular. Worse still was Parker's insinuation that politics played a part in the advancement process at Mulberry Street. Roosevelt neither knew nor cared which party any policeman he liked belonged to; he conceived of promotion strictly in terms of merit.[52]

Pouncing upon Lauterbach in the Senate corridor, he began to tick off the list's falsehoods, one by one, whereupon Parker (who had also been invited to testify) joined them and insisted they were all true. Both Commissioners were quivering with anger when they adjourned to the nearby hearing room.[53]

In their respective testimonies for and against the Police Bill, they made a study of opposites: Roosevelt barking like a nervous bulldog, Parker feline and purringly sarcastic. The effect of some of his remarks was such that Roosevelt several times leaped up and paced around the room in a vain effort to stay calm. "Of course," Parker drawled after quoting a newspaper attack on himself, given out by some unidentified source at Mulberry Street, "I don't attribute *that* part of the article to Mr. Roosevelt." "Oh, you may, you may," Roosevelt shot back.[54]

His truculence at Albany cost him dear. Although he sent Senate Republicans a convincing rebuttal of Parker's charges, signed by both Andrews and Grant, the Police Bill was reported unfavorably. To add insult to injury, another letter-bomb was waiting for Roosevelt when he got back to headquarters. Had it not been intercepted and defused by detectives, its charge of fine black Chinese gunpowder might have blown his face off.[55]

NOW THAT ROOSEVELT and Parker had made a public spectacle of their hatred for each other, they no longer attempted to conceal it from their colleagues, nor from the force, nor from the reporters who twice weekly attended open sessions of the Police Board. Consequently "the Mulberry Street Affair" became something of a running entertainment for New Yorkers. The popular press treated it as a circulation-boosting suspense serial, and described every new flare-up at headquarters with shrewd attention to dramatic detail. The *Sun* warned its readers to "LOOK OUT FOR EPITHETS—the Row in the Police Board Approaches the Danger Point," while the *Evening News* wondered when "Montague Parker" and "Capulet Teddy" would stop biting their thumbs at each other and engage in armed combat.[56]

The former was too agile an adversary, however, to allow himself to be directly challenged. Whenever Roosevelt seemed to be on the point of exploding, Parker would unfold a deft compliment, or make some unexpected conciliatory gesture, which suddenly relieved the pressure. A case in point occurred on 1 May, when Parker interrupted a regular meeting to announce that it was time for the "annual election" of the president of the Board. There was an amazed silence. Roosevelt said that he "did not understand." Avery Andrews challenged the legality of such a step. Surely a president, once elected, remained so for the duration of the Board? Parker suggested that somebody consult the statute-book. Tension mounted while a clerk flicked the pages over: Parker had never yet been proved wrong on any point of law. Not until the moment of confirmation did Parker propose, with a smile, that Theodore Roosevelt be renominated.[57]

"What are you doing it for?" Lincoln Steffens asked. "Oh, just for ducks," said Parker, "just to see the big bomb splutter, the boss leader of men blow up."[58]

HE CONTINUED TO EVADE Roosevelt so successfully that when the long-threatened explosion came, its victim was not himself but City Comptroller Ashbel P. Fitch. The latter was a waspish, bearded Democrat whose habit of rejecting the Police Department's more questionable bills—such as payment for children reporting Sunday Excise Law violations—was a constant irritation to Roosevelt.

On 5 May the president of the Police Board arrived at City Hall for a meeting of the Board of Estimate, attired in a new tweed suit whose checks, according to the *World,* were "distinctly audible at twenty paces."[59] He was seen to admire himself in a looking-glass before sitting down and facing Fitch across the Mayor's table.

The Comptroller listened impassively while Roosevelt requested that $11,000 of surplus construction funds be transferred to finance his second annual campaign against the saloons, just then beginning. "I doubt that we can do it legally," Fitch replied, and launched into a speech about the "impropriety" of taxpayers' money being used to bribe stool-pigeons on a Sunday.

Roosevelt, his choler visibly rising, explained that policemen could not arrest saloonkeepers for selling liquor illegally without buying it themselves, or paying somebody to buy it for them. The money came out of their own pockets, and they were entitled to be reimbursed. "Yes, yes," Fitch interrupted, "the same old story, we've heard it before."

"If we are brought to a standstill," Roosevelt hissed with clenched fists, "if we have to shut down in our work it is your fault!"

"Oh, stop scolding," said Fitch. He suggested that Roosevelt ask a court for the money. The dialogue, which was transcribed by several eyewitnesses, continued as follows:

ROOSEVELT (*white with rage, jumping to his feet*) You are the one to blame!

FITCH (*lolling back in his chair*) Tush! Tush! I won't discuss the matter with you in this fashion. You're always looking for a fight.

ROOSEVELT I fight when I am attacked!

FITCH (*idly*) Oh, go on, I don't want to fight with you. (*Toys with pencil.*)

ROOSEVELT (*snapping his teeth*) I know you won't fight. You'll run away.

FITCH Well, I wouldn't run away from you, at all events.

ROOSEVELT (*shouting*) You dare not fight!

FITCH Oh, I don't, hey? Just name your weapons. What do you want—pistols?

ROOSEVELT Pistols or anything else! (*Dancing with rage.*)

"At this point," wrote the *World* correspondent, "two reporters who were in the line of fire dropped their notes and dodged under the table." Fitch was no man to challenge lightly, being the unscarred winner of some thirty sword fights at the University of Heidelberg.[60] Fortunately Mayor Strong, who had been listening to the whole exchange with trembling eyelids, made one of the few decisive gestures of his administration. He raised a rheumatic fist and brought it down on the table with a crash.

STRONG (*wincing*) Gentlemen, gentlemen! I warn you right now that if this thing goes on I shall call in the police and have you both arrested.

FITCH Oh, this man Roosevelt is always getting into a row. . . . He had a row with Parker, now he wants a row with me.[61]

The matter was referred to Corporation Counsel, and Roosevelt stalked out in a towering rage. Later he calmed down and told reporters that there would be no duel. But it was too late to avoid headlines, and for days afterward press and public rejoiced in the story. The *Tribune* bet on Roosevelt, who was "always in condition to whip his weight in wildcats," while the yellow press came out strongly for Fitch. The *Evening Post,* anxious as ever to avoid bloodshed, suggested "a meeting in the City Hall plaza with Fire Department hoses at 30 paces," but popular opinion was in favor of a real duel. Offers of seconds—and executors—came in from as far away as Philadelphia, and Fitch was reported to have collected "a small arsenal" of gift weapons.[62] One enormous horse-pistol, adapted to fire peas, putty, and spitballs, was sent to the Mayor by a citizen concerned for his safety. Strong was immensely tickled. "I shall use this at all future Board meetings," he declared.[63]

Actually William Strong had begun to sympathize with his beleaguered Police Commissioner. However much he might regret Roosevelt's hot-headedness, he liked the man, and admired his decency. As for Parker (who had been seen gleefully slapping Fitch on the back after the Board of Estimate meeting),[64] the Mayor regretted ever having appointed him. He had done so in response to intense pressure by the County Democracy, which supported his reform ticket in 1894; and now the taste of that particular compromise was bitter in his mouth. Parker's obstructionism, absenteeism, and indolence had all but halted the work of the Police Department. Morale was sinking steadily, and the crime rate was climbing in proportion. Chief Conlin had become so depressed (while still doggedly supporting Parker) as to request sick leave in Europe. The fifty-five-year-old officer was said to be ready to quit, and wanted only to lead his men in a final parade up Fifth Avenue before handing in his badge.[65]

The worst news, as far as Strong was concerned, was that Parker, casting around for a new ally, had managed to ensnare Commissioner Grant. Both men were now boycotting Police Board meetings,[66] leaving Avery Andrews as Roosevelt's only faithful supporter—and even Andrews was beginning to show signs of polite impatience with the dead-lock.

The final straw came when Roosevelt approached the Mayor with evidence showing that Parker was corrupt. A patrolman named McMorrow had signed an affidavit, dated 20 April 1896, stating that he had bought his appointment for $400, the understanding being that "it was to be done through Commissioner Parker."[67]

Roosevelt was reluctant to publicize this affidavit, since it would seriously damage his Board's reputation for personal honesty, and he could not be entirely sure of the evidence. He asked Strong to intervene. On 20 May, therefore, the Mayor wrote Parker a private letter saying that "the honor of the city" required that he step down, and intimating that certain "sensational" facts would be released to the press if he did not resign within seven days. Parker replied with cold indifference: "I shall serve out my term regardless."[68]

He followed up with an open attack on Roosevelt, for the benefit of a *Recorder* interviewer. "Ever since his appointment as a Police Commissioner . . . he has assumed that he is the Alpha and Omega of the Department . . . For eleven months I have patiently endured this arbitrary assumption of authority . . . Colonel Grant and myself finally decided that, unless Mr. Roosevelt recognized us as possessing equal authority to himself, we would take steps for protecting ourselves."[69]

Mayor Strong allowed the seven-day deadline to pass without releasing the McMorrow statement, but let it be known that Parker had been asked to resign. The news broke on 28 May, just as Chief Conlin returned from Europe to lead the annual parade of New York's Finest.[70]

ROOSEVELT HAD CANCELED last year's event, saying that "we will parade again when we have something to boast about."[71] He was not feeling particularly boastful in the spring of 1896 either, yet there was a lot to be said, psychologically speaking, for a show of unity in the ranks. Despite reports of discontent and renewed corruption from various precincts, he was convinced that "the bulk of the men were heartily desirous of being honest."[72] And if Parker was to be fired (as the Mayor kept promising), the department's moral regeneration would surely continue.

On the first day of June he found himself gripping the rails of a reviewing stand at Fortieth Street and Fifth Avenue. Magnificent sunshine warmed his tails and top hat, and he enjoyed a rare moment of repose as the drumbeats grew louder downtown.[73] His fellow Commissioners were on their best behavior; Mayor Strong beamed kindly upon him; he, in turn, grinned wider and wider at his first sight of the force en masse.

More than two thousand men came up the avenue in wave after wave of blue serge, their white gloves rising and falling like lines of foam, their helmets and brass buttons coruscating. Chief Conlin led the way on an immense bay horse whose coat was rubbed and curried to the sheen of satin. The crowd gave him a thunderous ovation, but saved its biggest roar for the "bicycle squad"—an innovation of Commissioner Andrews—twenty-four burly patrolmen wobbling determinedly along on wheels.[74]

The parade was adjudged a smashing success, and redounded greatly to the credit of "President Roosevelt."[75] At its conclusion he was mobbed by cheering well-wishers, and horses had to be brought in to clear an escape route for him.

BUT THE SOUND OF marching bands had hardly died away before public attention was drawn to renewed hostility between the Commissioners. Amid rumors that Strong had again demanded

Parker's resignation, and again been refused,[76] the Police Board assembled for a regular meeting on Wednesday, 3 June. It proceeded to give the most convincing demonstration yet of its inability to function as an administrative body.

Roosevelt listened stonily while Commissioner Grant offered as a "treaty of peace" a new set of rules governing promotions. He was willing to approve the rules—anything to get the department moving again—but was in no mood to tolerate any more obstructionism from across the table. Only that morning the *Herald* had published a humiliating cartoon of himself being crushed by Parker, in the form of a great, smiling weight, while the caption enquired, "Will the 'Strong' Man Lift It?"[77]

Predictably, Parker waited until both Roosevelt and Andrews had expressed their approval of the rules before subjecting every one to destructive legal analysis. Roosevelt's face darkened to deep red, and beads of sweat stood out on his forehead as the maddening voice droned on, stinging him with insults that passed too quickly for retort. The two men stared steadily into each other's eyes, forgetful of other people in the room, obsessed by their struggle for supremacy.[78]

When Roosevelt spoke in reply, his voice sounded surprisingly deep and guttural, and every word was bitten into precise syllables—a sure sign of danger to those who knew him. One of the items of agenda awaiting discussion was the new police revolver, a .32-caliber, double-action, four-inch Colt. Reporters watched in fascination as the president of the Board absentmindedly fondled it, then, still talking, picked it up and shook it "slowly and impressively" in Parker's face.[79]

On this occasion it was Roosevelt who controlled himself, and Roosevelt who won. After four hours of relentless pressure, Parker, pale with exhaustion, agreed to the adoption of the rules.[80]

BUT HE STILL obstinately refused to confirm the promotions of Brooks and McCullagh, much less resign his commissionership. Mayor Strong, who was prevented by the Power of Removals Act from dismissing him without trial, asked Roosevelt to draw up a list of five formal charges, including "neglected duty, malfeasance, and misfeasance."[81] For some reason the charge of personal corruption was not among them. There was yet another, much more devastating charge, which Roosevelt could have used, had he wanted to. The story, as told by Jacob Riis, sounds apocryphal, but it has been confirmed by two independent sources.[82]

> I was in his office one day [that June] when a police official of superior rank came in and requested private audience with him. They stepped aside and the policeman spoke in an undertone, urging something strongly. Mr. Roosevelt listened. Suddenly I saw him straighten up as a man recoils from something unclean, and dismiss the other with a sharp: "No, sir! I don't fight that way." The policeman went out crestfallen. Roosevelt took two or three turns about the floor, struggling evidently with strong disgust. He told me afterward that the man had come to him with what he said was certain knowledge that his enemy [Parker] could be found that night in a known evil house uptown, which it was his alleged habit to visit. His proposition was to raid it then and so "get square." To the policeman it must have seemed like throwing a good chance away.[83]

If Parker had been caught *in flagrante delicto* he could doubtless have been persuaded to resign: but Roosevelt "struck no blow below the belt."[84]

And so the five formal charges were served, and public hearings set to begin on 11 June in Mayor Strong's office. Elihu Root was appointed prosecutor, and General Benjamin F. Tracy, late of the Harrison Administration and now a Platt intimate, announced he would appear for Parker.[85]

THE "TRIAL," which dragged on sporadically until 8 July, proved to be anticlimactic and dull. The weakness of Roosevelt's charges was apparent from the start,[86] and the evidence, droned out to the whir of electric fans, sounded trivial. It consisted largely of lists of meetings which Parker had missed, and lists of documents he had allowed to pile up on his desk. General Tracy effectively proved that Roosevelt was no slouch at missing meetings himself, when there were lucrative offers to speak out of town.[87] He also suggested that Parker's reluctance to promote Brooks and McCullagh might be justified, and got Roosevelt to admit that as president of the Board he had advanced several ill-qualified men in 1895 simply because they "gave promise of being useful"—in some cases, not even bothering to check their records.[88] One of the few entertaining moments of the proceedings came when Tracy deflated a Rooseveltian tirade thus:

ROOSEVELT	. . . It was a long time before I could make up my mind about Mr. Parker. I struggled against it. I recognized his great ability. But at last I was forced to the conclusion that he was guilty of neglected duty; that he was mendacious, treacherous, capable of double dealing and exercising a bad influence . . .
TRACY	Hasn't the whole trouble come from the fact that you had to yield to Mr. Parker?
ROOSEVELT	No, sir, I would be glad to yield to him if he was right.
TRACY	(*dryly*) You enjoy yielding to a man, don't you?
ROOSEVELT	(*with great energy*) By George, I do, and that's a fact!

"He looked surprised," reported an onlooker, "when the crowd shrieked with laughter." Parker, seated not six feet away, joined in the general mirth.[89]

Mayor Strong made no secret of his dissatisfaction with the evidence presented by the prosecution. In contrast, that of the defense was impressive. Grant and Conlin testified in Parker's praise, and Parker himself made a convincing witness. Relaxed, graceful, and articulate, he cited fact after fact which, in the words of the *Sun*, "made him out as having been exceedingly active in the performance of his duties almost from the hour of his appointment."[90]

Roosevelt's loyal ally, *The New York Times*, was tempted to agree, and forecast that if Strong upheld the prosecution, Parker would be vindicated in court. Most other newspapers expected the Mayor to dismiss the charges once the trial came to an end. As one editor pointed out, the real issue could not be legally considered. It was that "irreconcilable" personality differences made it impossible for Roosevelt and Parker to work democratically together.[91] The only way of resolving it was for one of them to resign; and since both were proud men, that day might be long in coming.

DULL AS THE PARKER trial was, it might have sparked more interest had its first few sessions not coincided with the Republican National Convention in St. Louis. The petty tensions prevailing between prosecution and defense in Mayor Strong's office were as nothing compared with the huge forces then contending on the banks of the Mississippi; yet in a microscopic way they reflected the party struggle. Here was a quiet, kindly man of bland political persuasion (William L. Strong/William McKinley) seeking to transcend the rivalry of an arrogant individualist (Theodore Roosevelt/Thomas B. Reed) and an organization man (Benjamin F. Tracy/Levi P. Morton).

Of the participants in the trial, Roosevelt was by far the most adaptable in his candidate loyalty and the quickest to respond to what was going on in St. Louis. Since at least 1892 he had cherished the idea of electing Reed President of the United States.[92] But his veneration for the Speaker had begun to abate early in the New Year. Reed, he now believed, was not firm enough on financial issues and not aggressive enough in recommending a larger navy. About the same time Roosevelt had found it expedient to campaign in a few delegate primaries for Governor Morton of New York—Boss Platt's personal candidate. While doing so, he kept an uneasy eye on the candidacy of William McKinley. After leaving Congress in 1890 McKinley had twice been elected Governor of Ohio, and the country now seemed ready to forgive him for his harsh policies as Majority Leader. Indeed, the financial panic of 1893 was now widely seen as the result of overreaction to McKinley's wise revisions of the tariff.[93] Although Roosevelt had been favorably disposed toward McKinley in the past at least as a person,[94] he now felt sudden qualms. "It will be a great misfortune to have McKinley nominated," he wrote, in one of the indiscretions Henry Cabot Lodge saw fit to delete from their published correspondence. ". . . If I could tell you all I have learned since his campaign has progressed, you would be as completely alarmed over the prospect of his presidential nomination as I am."[95] That was on 27 February. Less than a month later he had acknowledged "a great wave for McKinley sweeping over the country" and expressed "great disappointment" with Reed. The latter's overbearing personality had alienated a considerable number of professional politicians. Roosevelt might forgive him *that,* but he could hardly approve the tone of a letter his friend sent him in late May, when McKinley emerged as the clear favorite for the nomination. "In a word, dear boy, I am tired of this thing . . . the receding grapes seem to ooze with acid and the whole thing is a farce."[96]

On the eve of the trial, as Lodge prepared to depart for St. Louis, Roosevelt admitted that he was more interested in what happened at the convention than anything else. He told Bamie that he felt "very nervous" about its probable outcome. "McKinley, whose firmness I utterly distrust, will be nominated; and this . . . I much regret."[97] On 18 June 1896, news of the first ballot at St. Louis flashed over the wires to New York: McKinley had scored 661½ votes to Reed's 84½ and Governor Morton's 58.[98]

At once Roosevelt's distrust of the candidate vanished, at least for public purposes. He was due to take the witness box that very day, and used the occasion to make his political sympathies clear:

> Mr. Roosevelt [reported *The New York Times*] attracted the attention of the whole room by appearing with an ivory-colored button, as large as a silver dollar, bearing the portraits of McKinley and [Vice-Presidential nominee] Hobart. The faces could be distinguished across the room. Mr. Roosevelt was very proud of the emblem, which, he said, was the first of its kind to reach New York. All concerned with the case, excepting Mr. Parker, seemed interested in it. Commissioner Roosevelt submitted it to close inspection with infinite good nature and evident gratification.[99]

Only in private did he continue to express reservations. "While I greatly regret the defeat of Reed, who was in every way McKinley's superior, I am pretty well satisfied with the outcome at St. Louis . . . McKinley himself is an upright and honorable man, of very considerable ability and good record as a soldier and in Congress; he is not a strong man however; and unless he is well backed I should feel rather uneasy about him in a serious crisis . . ."[100]

MAYOR STRONG ADDED TO Roosevelt's sense of unease by fleeing New York as soon as the trial was over, saying that he wished to soothe his rheumatism, and consider his verdict, in the mud baths of Richfield Springs. "I will do nothing in the matter for several weeks."[101] Roosevelt was left to ponder the larger implications of McKinley's nomination. He could also look forward to a resumption of hostilities with Commissioner Parker.

A CREEPING DISTASTE for the job of Police Commissioner becomes apparent in Roosevelt's correspondence from the summer of 1896 onward.[102] He had never found the work attractive—"grimy" was his most frequent adjective—yet up until his confrontation with Parker he had exulted in its sheer bruising volume, as a strong man exults in shifting tons of rubble. But the collapse of his legal move against Parker, coinciding as it did with the emergence of William McKinley as the likely next President of the United States, made him realize that he had achieved about as much as he ever would in Mulberry Street. He summed up his feelings in an unusually revealing letter to Bamie, written with an air of finality, as if he had already resigned:

> I have been so absorbed by my own special work and its ramifications that I have time to keep very little in touch with anything outside of my own duties; I see but little of the life of the great world; I am but little in touch even with our national politics. The work of the Police Board has . . .

> nothing of the purple in it; it is as grimy as all work for municipal reform over here must be for some decades to come; and it is inconceivably arduous, disheartening, and irritating . . . I have to contend with the hostility of Tammany, and the almost equal hostility of the Republican machine; I have to contend with the folly of the reformers and the indifference of decent citizens; above all I have to contend with the singularly foolish law under which we administer the Department. If I were . . . a single-headed Commissioner, with absolute power . . . I could in a couple of years accomplish almost all I could desire; but as it is I am one of four Commissioners, each of whom possesses a veto power in promotions . . . Add to this a hostile legislature, a bitterly antagonistic press, an unscrupulous scoundrel as Comptroller . . . However, I have faced it as best I could, and I have accomplished something.[103]

His use of the phrase "a couple of years," while possibly unconscious, is interesting. Projected from his acceptance of the Commissionership in April 1895, it indicates that Roosevelt was looking forward to another offer in April 1897, in other words, about the time the new President would be making appointments.[104]

It was useless to hope for a Cabinet post, such as Thomas B. Reed would have given him; but if he ingratiated himself with McKinley now, and worked hard to ensure his election in November, he might count on some fairly high-level job next spring.

He needed no time to decide which particular appointment to push for. One area of national policy interested him more than any other, in view of what he saw as a gathering threat to American security in the Caribbean and Atlantic.[105] Paging at random through his list of extracurricular activities in the months preceding the convention, one finds him dining with Captain Alfred Thayer Mahan in February; criticizing the weakness of Secretary Herbert's Navy message in March; pumping the German diplomat Speck von Sternburg for "accurate Teutonic information" on world naval affairs in April; and spending "a rather naval week" in May, during which he inspects the *Indiana* from top to bottom, and lunches on the *Montgomery* as she lies in the sun off Staten Island. In between times he reads a life of Admiral James, a two-volume British tome on *Modern Ironclads,* and Lord Brassey's *Naval Annual* for 1896. He maintains a running correspondence with his new brother-in-law, Lieutenant Commander William Sheffield Cowles, USN,[106] writing in June: "Brassey evidently thinks our battleships inferior to the British, because of their 6 inch quick firers . . . I am not at all sure they are right; though I dislike the superimposed turrets."[107]

Finally, in July, he invites an old friend of William McKinley to visit him at Sagamore Hill. She arrives on the first day of August. Although the weather is very hot, he insists on rowing her across the glaring waters of Oyster Bay. As his oars spasmodically rise and fall, he tells her, "I should like to be Assistant Secretary of the Navy."[108]

"The work of the Police Board has . . .
nothing of the purple in it."

New York City Police Commissioners Andrews, Parker, Roosevelt, and Grant.

CHAPTER 21

The Glorious Retreat

Then forth from the chamber in anger he fled
And the wooden stairway shook with his tread.

IN ADDRESSING HIMSELF to Mrs. Bellamy Storer rather than Mr. Bellamy Storer, Roosevelt flatteringly acknowledged that lady's superior political muscle. He had known her since his early Washington days,[1] and had plenty of opportunity to see her in action as a lobbyist for the Roman Catholic Church. Mrs. Storer was a wealthy and formidable matron whose eyes burned with religious fervor, and whose jaw brooked no opposition from anybody—least of all William McKinley, whom she considered to be in her debt. The Presidential candidate had gratefully accepted $10,000 of Storer funds in 1893, when threatened with financial and political ruin. Mrs. Storer was now, three years later, expecting to recoup this investment in the form of various appointments for her near and dear.[2]

Roosevelt knew that she was fond of him, in an amused, motherly sort of way. She tended (like Edith) to treat him as if he were one of her own children. Years later, when events had conspired to embitter her toward him, she wrote that the "peculiar attraction and fascination" of the young Theodore Roosevelt "lay in the fact that he was like a child; with a child's spontaneous outbursts of

"A good-natured, well-meaning, coarse man,
shrewd and hardheaded."

Mark Hanna, sketched the day Theodore Roosevelt went boating with Mrs. Bellamy Storer.

affection, of fun, and of anger; and with the brilliant brain and fancy of a child."[3]

Shrewdly playing upon her maternal sympathies in 1896, he said that his political unpopularity in New York was now so great that the future security of the Roosevelt "bunnies" depended on his getting a high-level post in Washington. Should he fail to negotiate one—or should McKinley (God forbid!) fail to win election, "I shall be the melancholy spectacle . . . of an idle father, writing books that do not sell!"

Mrs. Storer told him that she was "sure" something could be arranged; she and her husband would speak to McKinley in due course.[4] Roosevelt, overjoyed, promised in return to work up support on the Republican National Committee for Bellamy Storer as a Cabinet officer, or Ambassador. The atmosphere in the rowboat grew increasingly cozy, and for the rest of her visit Mrs. Storer basked in Roosevelt's good humor:

> One never knew what he would say next. He was certainly very witty in himself, and he valued wit in others. He used during this period to get on the warpath over Sienkiewicz's novels—*The Deluge* and *Fire and the Sword*—and when he was quite sated with slaughter his face would be radiant and he would shout aloud with delight. He seemed as innocent as Toddy in *Helen's Babies,* who wanted everything to be "bluggy". . . . His vituperation was extremely amusing, and he had a most extraordinary vocabulary . . . Never in our lives have we laughed so often as when Theodore Roosevelt of those days was our host.[5]

FOR ALL THE OPTIMISM flowing out of Sagamore Hill that summer weekend, Roosevelt and the Storers were uncomfortably aware of the proximity, in New York's Waldorf Hotel, of a Cleveland millionaire who could turn their hopes to dust if he felt like it. Marcus Alonzo Hanna was more than McKinley's manager and closest political adviser; he was now the party Chairman as well. In this double role he stood confirmed as the first countrywide political boss in American history.[6] Cynical Democrats were saying that

Hanna, not McKinley, had been nominated at St. Louis; cartoonists depicted the candidate as a limp puppet hanging out of his pocket.

Roosevelt, reacting as usual with electric speed to any new political stimulus, had already been to see Hanna twice. On 28 July, the same day the Chairman arrived in town to set up Republican National Headquarters, he visited him at the Waldorf. In the evening he had returned to dine privately with him and two members of the Executive Committee.[7] A letter to Lodge, dated 30 July, shows how quickly and accurately he summed Hanna up: "He is a good-natured, well-meaning, coarse man, shrewd and hard-headed, but neither very farsighted nor very broad-minded, and as he has a resolute and imperious mind, he will have to be handled with some care."[8]

Roosevelt does not seem to have told the Storers about these two previous meetings with Hanna. Possibly he wished them to follow an independent line with McKinley. At any rate he visited the Chairman again on Monday evening, 3 August, and fulfilled his part of the weekend bargain.[9] Whether he did so quite as forcefully as he afterward implied to Mrs. Storer ("I spoke of Bellamy as *the* man for the Cabinet, either for War or Navy, or else go to France")[10] is doubtful, since Hanna was tired, and in no mood to discuss anything other than ways and means of winning in November. Roosevelt "thought it wise not to pursue the matter further."[11]

Hanna's exhaustion was nervous as well as physical. After nearly two years of working with full-time devotion to secure the nomination of McKinley—at a personal cost of $100,000—he wanted nothing so much as to take a long cruise up the New England coast, and let other Republicans manage the fall campaign. But a certain phenomenon, occurring in Chicago on 10 July, had "changed everything," in his opinion. Alarming predictions of class war, communism, and even anarchy were coming in daily from the West: the political future suddenly seemed fraught with doom.[12] Now was the time for all good men to come to the aid of the party, and Hanna bent his stout body to the task. Word went out from headquarters that he needed all the money and all the stump speakers he could get. Roosevelt, having little of the former, promptly volunteered to be one of the latter.[13]

The phenomenon in Chicago was that of William Jennings Bryan, an obscure thirty-six-year-old ex-Congressman from Nebraska, who by making one speech to the Democratic National Convention had created something akin to an emotional earthquake. Rising to speak on a currency resolution, Bryan had pleaded inspiringly for those rural poor to whom questions of high finance were of less importance than food and shelter. As a result, he was now the Democratic candidate for President, on a ticket so extremely radical as to cause large numbers of his party to bolt. Yet nobody, and certainly not Mark Hanna, discounted the threat he posed to William McKinley. For Bryan had that most potent of all political weapons: a sumptuous, sonorous voice, upon which he played like an open diapason. He also had a natural constituency—the farmers and field-hands of the South, Midwest, and West—not to mention those disadvantaged millions (Riis's "Other Half") who labored in farms and mines, or begged for work at factory doors, and lined up for soup in filthy municipal kitchens. Such people were ravished by his promises of dollars—more dollars for everybody, unlimited silver dollars which could be produced by the simple method of minting them freely and cheaply at a ratio of 16 to 1. The much more expensive gold dollars which McKinley proposed to keep in circulation were just too few to go around—or so Bryan seemed to be saying. His listeners might not quite grasp why one ratio was preferable to another, and phrases like "international agreement for bimetallism" meant little to cornhuskers who had never seen more than a few square miles of Iowa; but they thought they could understand his magnificently vague metaphors, particularly the one with which he had turned Chicago's Coliseum into a howling madhouse:

> You shall not press down upon the brow of labor this crown of thorns, you shall not crucify mankind upon a cross of gold![14]

This was the phenomenon with which Mark Hanna had to deal in August 1896, and it is no wonder that he cut Roosevelt short on the subject of a Bellamy Storer. But he accepted his visitor's offer of campaign help (perhaps the Chairman, in the back of his mind, recalled that other Chicago Convention when he and McKinley had seen this same young man briefly, raspingly capture the attention of seven thousand delegates).[15]

Roosevelt liked Hanna.[16] There was something engagingly piglike about the man, with his snouty nostrils, thick pink skin, and short, trotting steps. His very business was in pig iron, and he had a grunting disdain for fine food and polite conversation. When he laughed (which was often), he snorted, and his language reeked of the farmyard. Yet Hanna's very fleshiness, his love of reaching out and touching, was attractive to someone as physical as Roosevelt. Hanna had none of old Tom Platt's dry secretiveness: he was blunt, honest, friendly, and unassuming, shamelessly addicted to sweets, which he would suck all day in his large loose mouth. But for all his naturalness, the Chairman was obviously a man of calculating intelligence. "X-Rays," wrote one who met him at this time, "are not more penetrating than Hanna's glance."[17]

Surprisingly, for someone with so much power, the Chairman was not corrupt.[18] He had no desire for Cabinet office; his ambition, as he reminded Roosevelt, was to elect McKinley. His love for that placid politician was as frank as it was naive: "He is the best man I ever knew!" Or: "McKinley is a saint."[19] As for the millions he had set out to raise, Hanna was too rich to want anything for himself. He treated campaign contributions much as he did iron ore in his Cleveland foundry—as raw material to be amassed in great quantities for the smelting of something solid. And indeed McKinley had an amusingly metallic quality, with his expressionless, perfectly cast features.[20] Hanna had no doubt that in forging him he had created an ideal President, a man of steel to symbolize the new Industrial Age. The idea of William Jennings Bryan bringing back the Age of Agriculture was more than regressive: it was revolutionary.

Roosevelt could not help but be affected by the Chairman's worried mood. Before their meeting on 3 August he had been confident of a Republican victory in November, but after it he wrote gloomily to Cecil Spring Rice, "If Bryan wins, we have before us some years of social misery, not markedly different from that of any South American republic . . . Bryan closely resembles Thomas Jefferson, whose accession to the Presidency was a terrible blow to this nation."[21]

With that characteristic thrust, he braced himself for the biggest administrative challenge of his career as Commissioner: Bryan's imminent arrival in Manhattan. The Democratic candidate had chosen Madison Square Garden—of all places—to open his campaign on 12 August, and Roosevelt, as president of the Board of Police, would be responsible for protecting his Jeffersonian person.

IT WOULD BE UNFAIR to accuse Roosevelt of deliberately allowing the Bryan meeting to degenerate into a noisy, embarrassing shambles. However, he was conspicuous by his absence from the Garden that night, and supervision of the crowd was left in the hands of a Republican inspector. The police proved remarkably adept at allowing gate-crashers in, and keeping ticket-holders out.[22] Next morning the *Sun* and *News* excoriated "Teddy's Recruits" for gross incompetence and inefficiency, and even *The Times* agreed that the job was "very bunglingly done."[23]

Bryan, however, was the real culprit of the evening. No degree of police efficiency could have altered the fact that he was a stupendous disappointment. For once his oratorical gifts deserted him. Intimidated by the size of his audience, he merely read a prepared text on silver, which dragged on for two hours, to a steady tramp of exiting feet and calls of "Good night, Billy!"[24]

"Bryan fell with a bang," Roosevelt crowed to Bamie. "He was so utter a failure that he dared not continue his eastern trip, and cancelled his Maine and Vermont engagements . . . I believe that the tide has begun to flow against him."[25]

When Bourke Cockran, another celebrated speaker, took over the Garden on 19 August to put the case of gold, Roosevelt was there to prevent any repetition of the previous week's fiasco. He personally supervised all security arrangements, and the evening went off smoothly. It was agreed next morning that the police had "retrieved their reputations."[26]

WITH SEVERAL WEEKS to spare before plunging into his agreed schedule of speaking engagements, Roosevelt decided to go West for his first hunting vacation in two years. But first he was determined to settle once and for all the vexed question of Brooks and McCullagh. Commissioner Parker was still boycotting promotion meetings, and using a variety of other tactics to perpetuate the deadlock. The Mayor's continued reluctance to announce a verdict on the trial charges (Strong hated confrontations, and feebly hoped that Parker had "learned his lesson")[27] made it imperative that something be done.

On the morning after the Cockran meeting Parker happened to be at Police Headquarters, and Roosevelt promptly announced a special session of the Board "for the purpose of acting on the Inspectorship question." Hoping to force Parker into at least a statement of his still-secret objections to the two acting inspectors, Andrews called for a vote on their immediate promotion. He, Roosevelt, and Grant voted aye. Parker, instead of voting, began a monologue of ambiguous dissent, whereupon Roosevelt lost his temper. Andrews quit the meeting in disgust, and even Grant showed signs of vague irritation as the two rivals leaped to their feet and began shaking their fists at each other. Eventually Roosevelt, thinking he had made a point, pounded the table and roared, "Case closed!" Although it manifestly was not, he stormed out of the room. "My, how you frighten me!" Parker called after him, then leaned back in his chair, tilted his head to the ceiling, and laughed for a long time.[28]

The following morning Roosevelt left for North Dakota, clutching in his hand a "new small-bore, smokeless powder Winchester, a 30-166 with a half-jacketed bullet, the front or point of naked lead, the butt plated with hard metal."[29]

DURING THE NEXT THREE WEEKS he grew burly and tanned from sleeping all night in the open and riding all day across the prairie. The Winchester gave him "the greatest satisfaction," he wrote to Bamie. "Certainly it was as wicked-shooting a weapon as I ever handled, and knocked the bucks over with a sledge-hammer."[30]

With his belly full of antelope meat, and the oily perfume of sage in his nostrils, he rejoiced in rediscovering his other self, that almost-forgotten *Doppelgänger* who haunted the plains while Commissioner Roosevelt patrolled the streets of Manhattan. For the thousandth time he pondered the dynamic interdependence of East and West. No force of nature surely, not even the anarchistic Bryan, with his talk of grass growing in the streets of cities,[31] could sunder those two poles, nor for that matter bring them any closer together. American energy lay in their mutual repulsion and mutual attraction. The money men of the East would vote for McKinley, of course. Bryan had already seen he could make no headway there; it was here in the West that the battle between Gold and Silver, Capitalism and Populism, Industry and Agriculture must be fought out.

From talking to his cowboys, and to friends he met in the depot in St. Paul, and to the staff of party headquarters in Chicago, Roosevelt returned to New York on 10 September convinced that "the drift is our way."[32] He serenely articulated his thoughts to an *Evening Post* reporter: "The battle is going to be decided in our favor because the hundreds and thousands of farmers, workingmen, and merchants all through the West have been making up their minds that the battle should be waged on moral issues . . . It is in the West that as a nation we shall ultimately work out our highest destiny."[33]

BUT HIS SURGE OF CONFIDENCE did not last long. By mid-September the "battle" initiative was clearly with the Democrats. A campaign map of the United States showed the frightening smallness of McKinley's constituency (New England, New York, New Jersey, Pennsylvania, and Ohio) as opposed to the vast spread of states loyal to Bryan (the whole South plus Texas, and all of the mountain states). The Democratic candidate seemed to be everywhere, his big body tireless and his melodious voice unfailing. Republican planners, attempting to plot his every whistle-stop, stippled the Midwest with as many as twenty-four new dots a day; in some areas the concentration was so dense as to shade the paper gray.[34] Now the dots were beginning to creep ominously across the Mississippi, into the traditionally Republican plains states, every one of which had been reclassified as doubtful.[35]

Roosevelt, like Hanna, began to feel pangs of real dread. He was "appalled" at Bryan's ability "to inflame with bitter rancor towards the well-off those . . . who, whether through misfortune or through misconduct, have failed in life."[36] Remarks like this suggest that Roosevelt, for all his public attacks upon "the predatory rich," for all his night-walks through the Lower East Side, was congenitally unable to understand the poor. People who lacked wealth, even through "misfortune," had "failed in life."[37]

Their votes, however, mattered, so he threw himself ardently into the campaign. Taking advantage of some space in *Review of Reviews,* which he was supposed to fill with an article on the Vice-Presidency, Roosevelt assailed the Populists (Bryan's third-party backers on the extreme Left) to witty effect:

> Refinement and comfort they are apt to consider quite as objectionable as immorality. That a man should change his clothes in the evening, that he should dine at any other hour than noon, impress these good people as being symptoms of depravity instead of merely trivial. A taste for learning and cultivated friends, and a tendency to bathe frequently, cause them the deepest suspicion . . . Senator Tillman's brother has been frequently elected to Congress upon the issue that he wore neither an overcoat nor an undershirt.[38]

This, and a fiery New York speech criticizing the Democratic platform's bias in favor of unrestricted job action ("It is fitting that with the demand for free silver should go the demand for free riot!")[39] so delighted Republican headquarters that he was sent to barnstorm upstate with Henry Cabot Lodge. In a five-day swing from Utica to Buffalo the two friends spoke to packed, respectful houses, and were encouraged by a general "intent desire to listen to full explanations of the questions at issue."[40]

Before returning to New York and Boston they paid a brief call on William McKinley at his home in Canton, Ohio. Here the Republican candidate was conducting a "front-porch" campaign eminently suited to his sedentary personality. Owing to the convenient ill-health of Mrs. McKinley, he had announced early on that he would eschew the stump. "It was arranged, consequently," writes a contemporary historian, "that inasmuch as McKinley could not go to the people, the people must come to McKinley."[41] The railroads, having much to gain by his election, were glad to cooperate with cheap group excursion rates from all over the country. Every day except Sunday several trainloads of party faithful would arrive in Canton and march up North Market Street to the beat of brass bands. Passing under a giant plaster arch adorned with McKinley's portrait, they would break ranks outside his white frame house and crowd onto the front lawn. The candidate would then appear and listen benignly to a speech of salutation which he had himself edited in advance. In reply, McKinley would read a speech of welcome, then make himself available for handshakes on the porch steps. Occasionally he would invite some favored guests to stay for lunch or dinner.[42]

It is unlikely that Roosevelt and Lodge were granted this privilege. McKinley could hardly forget that they had supported Reed against him for the Speakership in 1890, and for the Presidential nomination earlier that year. "He was entirely pleasant with us," Roosevelt reported to Bamie, "though we are not among his favorites."[43]

ROOSEVELT SPENT the first full week of October on the hustings in New York City, expounding the merits of gold to all and sundry, and trying to persuade a rich uncle to lunch with Mark Hanna. He was amused by the old gentleman's horrified refusal; it was the traditional Knickerbocker disdain for "dirty" politicians.[44] *Nouveau riche* millionaires like James J. Hill and John D. Rockefeller had no such scruples, and the Chairman made the most of their huge contributions. Some 120 million books, pamphlets, posters, and preset newspaper articles poured out of Republican headquarters into all the "doubtful" states, while fourteen hundred speakers, including such luminaries as ex-President Harrison, Speaker Reed, and Carl Schurz, made expense-paid trips into every corner of the country. Masterful, tireless, and increasingly optimistic as this "educational campaign" caught fire, Mark Hanna supervised every itinerary and checked every invoice.[45]

One of the Chairman's tactical decisions was to cancel a plan to send Roosevelt into Maryland and West Virginia. Instead, he was put on Bryan's trail in Illinois, Michigan, and Minnesota during the second and third weeks of the month.[46] Hanna obviously believed him to be an ideal foil to the Democratic candidate: an Easterner whom Westerners revered, an intellectual who could explain the complexities of the Gold Standard in terms a cowboy could understand.

Roosevelt more than justified his faith. Oversimplifying brilliantly, as he sped from whistle-stop to whistle-stop, he spoke in parables and brandished an array of homely visual symbols, including gold and silver coins and odd-sized loaves of bread. ("See this big one. This is an eight-cent loaf when the cents count on a gold basis. Now look at this small one . . . on a silver basis it would sell for over nine cents . . .")[47] En route he discovered that audiences enjoyed his natural gifts of vituperation as much, if not more, than financial argument, so day by day the pejoratives flowed more freely. He scored his biggest success on 15 October in the Chicago Coliseum, where three months before Bryan had made the famous "cross of gold" speech. An audience of thirteen thousand rejoiced as "Teddy"—the name was all but universal now—went about his familiar business of emasculating the opposition.

> It is not merely schoolgirls that have hysterics; very vicious mob-leaders have them at times, and so do well-meaning demagogues when their minds are turned by the applause of men of little intelligence. . . .[48]

Warming to this theme, he compared Bryan and various other prominent free silverites and Populists to "the leaders of the Terror of France in mental and moral attitude." But he added reassuringly that such men lacked the revolutionary power of Marat, Barère, and Robespierre. Bryan, who sought to benefit one class by stealing the wealth of another, wished to negate the Eighth Commandment, while Governor Altgeld of Illinois, having recently pardoned the Haymarket rioters ("those foulest of criminals, the men whose crimes take the form of assassination"), was clearly in violation of the Sixth. Aware that his audience contained a large proportion of college boys, he warned against the seductions of "the visionary social reformer . . . the being who reads Tolstoy, or, if he possesses less intellect, Bellamy and Henry George, who studies Karl Marx and Proudhon, and believes that at this stage of the world's progress it is possible to make everyone happy by an immense social revolution, just as other enthusiasts of a similar mental caliber believe in the possibility of constructing a perpetual-motion machine."[49]

As always, the harshness of Roosevelt's words was softened by his beaming fervor, the sophomoric relish with which he pronounced his insults. For two hours he talked on, juggling his coins and loaves, grinning, grimacing, breathing sincerity from every pore, while the son of Abraham Lincoln sat behind him applauding, and the great hall resounded with cheers.[50] Next morning the *Chicago Tribune* awarded him lead status on its front page, and printed his entire seven-thousand-word speech verbatim, running to almost seven full columns of type. "In many respects," the paper remarked, "it was the most remarkable political gathering of the campaign in this city."[51]

There were one or two column-inches of space left over after Roosevelt's peroration, and into this the editors inserted a filler, reporting an address, elsewhere in the city on the same evening, by an ex-Harvard professor, now head of the Department of Political Economy at the University of Chicago. One wonders with what feelings J. Laurence Laughlin read of the triumph of his former pupil, whom seventeen years before he had advised to go into politics.[52]

ON HIS WAY HOME across Michigan, Roosevelt traveled so closely behind the campaign train of William Jennings Bryan that he was able to gauge local reactions to him at first hand.[53] In one town he actually caught up with Bryan, and stood incognito in the crowd listening to him speak. Although there was no denying the beauty of the voice, nor the power of the eagle eye and big, confident body, he sensed that the average voter was curious rather than impressed. Bryan, he remarked on returning to New York, represented only "that type of farmer whose gate hangs on one hinge, whose old hat supplies the place of a missing window-pane, and who is more likely to be found at the cross-roads grocery store than behind the plough."[54] Yet in spite of encouraging reports of a McKinley swing in the Midwest, "we cannot help feeling uneasy until the victory is actually won."[55]

The last ten days in October saw him hurrying from meeting to meeting in New York, New Jersey, Delaware, and Maryland. In between times he geared the police force to ensure a rigorously honest election. Worn out and apprehensive as 3 November approached, he tried to convince himself that triumph was at hand, that he had done his part to avert "the greatest crisis in our national fate, save only the Civil War."[56]

WILLIAM MCKINLEY was elected President by an overwhelming plurality of 600,000 votes. His electoral college majority was 95; the total amount of votes cast was nearly 14 million. "We have submitted the issue to the American people," telegraphed William Jennings Bryan, "and their will is law."[57] The Democratic candidate could afford to be magnanimous, having racked up some impressive statistics of his own. He had traveled 18,000 miles, addressed an estimated 5 million people, and was rewarded with the biggest Democratic vote in history.[58] When Henry Cabot Lodge wondered if Bryan's party would hesitate before nominating him again, Mark Hanna had a typically vulgar retort. "Does a dog hesitate for a marriage license?"[59]

Hanna was now unquestionably the second most powerful man in America,[60] and Roosevelt, celebrating with him at a "Capuan" victory luncheon on 10 November, felt a sudden twinge of revulsion at the part money and marketing had played in the campaign. "He has advertised McKinley as if he were a patent medicine!"[61] Looking around the room, he realized that at least half the guests were money men. The Chairman might be easy in their company, but he, Roosevelt, was not. "I felt as if I was personally realizing all of Brooks Adams's gloomy anticipations of our gold-ridden, capitalist-bestridden, usurer-mastered future."[62]

But such scruples faded as he basked in the general glow of Republican triumph. McKinley was hailed as "the advance agent of prosperity." Out of a magically cleared sky, the Gold Dollar shone down, promising fair economic weather for the last four years of the nineteenth century.

Roosevelt felt more hopeful than after any election since that of 1888. Then, as now, his party had swept all three Houses of the federal government, and piled up luxurious pluralities in state legislatures. Then, as now, he had campaigned hard for the President-elect, knowing that his efforts would be rewarded. And so he waited with joyful anticipation for news of his appointment as Assistant Secretary of the Navy. It would probably come soon: before November was out, Henry Cabot Lodge and the "dear Storers" traveled separately to Canton to negotiate it.[63]

LODGE GOT THERE FIRST, on 29 November, and lunched with McKinley the next day. He reported the conversation to Roosevelt with some delicacy:

> He spoke of you with great regard for your character and your services and he would like to have you in Washington. The only question he asked me was this, which I give you: "I hope he has no preconceived plans which he would wish to drive through the moment he got in." I replied that he need not give himself the slightest uneasiness on that score. . . .[64]

Only Cabot Lodge, presumably, could make such an assurance with such a straight face. McKinley took it cordially enough, then changed the subject. Lodge felt cautiously optimistic at the end of the interview, "but after all I'm not one of his old supporters and the person to whom I look now, having shot my own bolt, is Storer."[65]

What the latter said to McKinley a day or two later is not of record. It could not have been much, for Storer was understandably more interested in an office for himself. However, his forceful wife, who seems to have already looked beyond the McKinley Administration to some future Roosevelt Administration, was as good as her word. Buttonholing the President-elect after dinner, she pleaded Roosevelt's cause.

McKinley studied her quizzically. "I want peace," he said, "and I am told that your friend Theodore—whom I know only slightly—is always getting into rows with everybody. I am afraid he is too pugnacious."

"Give him a chance," Mrs. Storer replied, "to prove that he can be peaceful."[66]

McKinley received this solicitation as smoothly as he had Lodge's.[67] He had the politician's gift of sending people away imagining that their requests would be granted, and Mrs. Storer, too, sent an optimistic letter to New York.[68] She suggested that Roosevelt now visit McKinley himself, to clinch the appointment. But desperately as he wanted it, pride would not let him:

> I don't wish to go to Canton unless McKinley sends for me. I don't think there is any need of it. He saw me when I went there during the campaign; and if he thinks I am hot-headed and harum-scarum, I don't think he will change his mind now . . . Moreover, I don't wish to appear as a supplicant, for I am not a supplicant. I feel I could do good work as Assistant Secretary, but if we had proper police laws I could do better work here and would not leave; and somewhere or other I'll find work to do.[69]

On 9 December a letter from McKinley arrived on his desk. But it contained nothing more than a polite acknowledgment of the recommendation he had written for Bellamy Storer.[70]

"INDEED, I DO NOT THINK the Assistant Secretaryship in the least below what I ought to have," he wrote fretfully to Lodge.[71] His friend had perceived another obstacle in the way of his appointment, and suspected that it, rather than Roosevelt's belligerency, might be the real reason for McKinley's hesitation. This was the probable reelection, early in the New Year, of Thomas C. Platt to the United States Senate. If Platt won, he would take his old seat in the Capitol on the same day McKinley entered the White House; and since the Republican majority in the Senate hinged on that very seat, McKinley would not dare to offend the Easy Boss by appointing any New Yorker he disapproved of. Lodge had already asked Platt what he thought about Roosevelt as Assistant Secretary, and gotten a negative reaction. "He did not feel ready to say that he would support you, if you intended to go into the Navy Department and make war on him—or, as he put it, on the organization."[72]

It followed, therefore, that if Roosevelt would not ingratiate himself with McKinley, he must ingratiate himself with Platt. One way or another the unhappy Commissioner must eat humble pie. "I shall write Platt at once, to get an appointment to see him," he replied.[73]

The meeting was "exceedingly polite,"[74] but inconclusive. Platt's nomination for the Senate would not come up for another month, so there was no question of a premature deal. The old man was also waiting cruelly to see if Roosevelt would give active support to the nomination. His only rival was Joseph H. Choate,[75] a distinguished liberal Republican who also happened to be Roosevelt's oldest political confidant. At Harvard young Theodore had sought Choate's counsel as a substitute father; Choate had been one of the eminent citizens who backed his first campaign for the Assembly, and had even offered to pay his expenses; after winning, Roosevelt had told Choate, "I feel that I owe both my nomination and my election more to you than to any other one man."[76]

Platt did not have to wait long for enlightenment. A day or two later Choate's aides asked the Police Commissioner to speak for their candidate, and were flatly turned down. On 16 December 1896, when organization men gathered at No. 4 Fifth Avenue to endorse the Easy Boss, Roosevelt was prominently present, and seated at Platt's table.[77]

THE APPROACH OF THE festive season brought deep snow and zero temperatures, cooling the hot flush of politics. Roosevelt retired to Sagamore Hill to chop trees with his children (little Ted, at nine years old, was capable of bringing down a sixty-foot oak, and, though undersized, bore up "wonderfully" during ten-mile tramps). On Christmas Eve the family sleighed down "in patriarchal style" to

Cove School, where Roosevelt played Santa Claus and distributed toys to the village children.[78]

He returned to Mulberry Street on 30 December for the year's final Board meeting, and found Commissioner Parker as tricky and obstructive as ever. After adjournment Roosevelt was moved to an admission of weary respect: "Parker, I feel to you as Tommy Atkins did toward Fuzzy-Wuzzy in Kipling's poem . . . 'To fight 'im 'arf an hour will last me 'arf a year.' I'm going out of town tonight, but I suppose we'll have another row next Wednesday." Parker laughed. "I'll be glad to see you when you get back, Roosevelt."[79]

IN THE NEW YEAR, Roosevelt's longing to be appointed Assistant Secretary was spurred by renewed press criticism of the deadlock at Police Headquarters. Most complaints were directed at Parker, but they also reflected unfavorably on the president of the Board. Editors of all political persuasions agreed that the quarreling between Commissioners was "a discredit" to the department, and "a detriment to public welfare." It was enough, remarked the *Herald,* to make citizens nostalgic for the corrupt but superefficient force of yesteryear. "The simple fact is that this much-heralded 'Reform Board' has proved a public disappointment and a failure."[80] The Society for the Prevention of Crime, which had strongly supported Roosevelt in the past, condemned the Commissioners for "lack of executive vigor" and "indignity of demeanor," while the Rev. Charles H. Parkhurst, in a clear reference to Roosevelt's courtship of Boss Platt, scorned "those who consent, spaniel-like, to lick the hand of their master."[81]

Afraid that some of this publicity would reach the ears of the President-elect, Roosevelt announced on 8 January, "I shall hereafter refuse to take part in any wranglings or bickerings on this Board. They are not only unseemly, but detrimental to the discipline of the force."[82] Commissioner Parker affably agreed to do the same, and a measure of peace returned to Mulberry Street.

Thomas Collier Platt was nominated for the Senate on 14 January 1897, by a Republican caucus vote of 147 to 7. His first reaction, on hearing the news, was to ask for a list of the seven Choate supporters and put it in his pocket. This suggests that Roosevelt had been prudent, if nothing else, in deserting Choate the month before.[83] Platt was duly elected on 20 January, and immediately became a major, if inscrutable factor in Roosevelt's campaign for office.

The Police Commissioner, meanwhile, optimistically prepared himself for his future responsibilities, inviting Alfred Thayer Mahan back to Sagamore Hill, addressing the U.S. Naval Academy on 23 January, and working with concentrated speed on a revised version of his *Naval War of 1812*.[84] The manuscript had been commissioned by Sir William Laird Clowes, naval correspondent of the London *Times* and editor of the official history of the British Navy, then in preparation.[85] Roosevelt inserted "a pretty strong plea for a powerful navy" into his text.[86]

February came and went, with no encouraging news—McKinley was preoccupied with Cabinet appointments and pre-Inaugural arrangements, and Platt remained silent—but Roosevelt continued to hope. "I shall probably take it," he told Bamie, "because I am intensely interested in our navy, and know a good deal about it, and it would mean four years work." He did not see himself surviving a year in his present job, even if obliged to remain.[87]

His truce with "cunning, unscrupulous, shifty"[88] Parker lasted less than five weeks, and by the end of February he was complaining of "almost intolerable difficulty" at Mulberry Street.[89] Commissioner Grant was now firmly allied with Parker, and Roosevelt paused, in a moment of bitter humor, to wonder how so great a general could have produced so lumpish a son. "Grant is one of the most interesting studies that I know of, from the point of view of atavism. I am sure his brain must reproduce that of some long-lost arboreal ancestor."[90]

By 4 March, when William McKinley was inaugurated, the situation at Police Headquarters had become an open scandal. Newspapers that day carried reports of an almost total breakdown of discipline in the force, new outbreaks of corruption, tearful threats of resignation by Chief Conlin, and rabid partisan squabbles between Democratic and Republican officers—echoing those among the four Commissioners, who seemed scarcely able to stand the sight of one another anymore.[91]

"I am very sorry that I ever appointed Andrew D. Parker," Mayor Strong commented sadly. "I am just as sorry that it is beyond my power to remove him from office."[92] A reporter pointed out that he had, nevertheless, the power to find Parker guilty of the charges leveled against him last summer. Strong hesitated for two weeks, then at last, on 17 March, dismissed Parker for proven neglect of duty.[93] But the sentence was subject to gubernatorial approval; so in the meantime Parker smilingly stayed on.

DURING THE REST OF MARCH, and on through the first five days of April, a cast of some twenty-five characters lobbied, fought, bartered, bullied, and pleaded for and against Roosevelt's appointment as Assistant Secretary of the Navy. Lodge acted as coordinator of the pro-Roosevelt group, whose ranks included John Hay, Speaker Reed, Secretary of the Interior Cornelius Bliss, Judge William Howard Taft of Ohio, and even Vice-President Hobart. Mrs. Storer haughtily withdrew when McKinley, who disliked being beholden to anybody, gave her husband the second-rate ambassadorship to Belgium. Mark Hanna was reported favorable to Roosevelt's nomination immediately after the Inauguration, but was so plagued by other rivals for McKinley's favor that Lodge hesitated to approach him.[94] The Chairman had been seen slinging a pebble at a skunk in a Georgetown garden and growling, "By God, he looks like an office-seeker!"[95]

Lodge was at a loss to explain the delay in appointing his deserving young friend. "The only, absolutely the only thing I can hear adverse," he wrote, "is that there is a fear that you will want to fight somebody at once."[96]

This, indeed, was the essence of the problem. In all the welter of contradictory reports, rumors, and ambiguous memoirs surrounding the Navy Department negotiations, one rock constantly breaks the surface: McKinley's belief that once Roosevelt came to Washington he would seek to involve the United States in war. The President wanted nothing so much as four years of peace and stability, so that the corporate interests he represented could continue their growth. He was by nature a small-town son of the Middle West, who shied away from large schemes and foreign entanglements.

(The French Ambassador in Washington found him defensively aware of his own provincialism, "ignorant of the wide world.")[97] But as a Civil War veteran, he had a genuine horror of bloodshed. On the eve of his Inauguration he had told Grover Cleveland that if he could avert the "terrible calamity" of war while in office, he would be "the happiest man in the world." Mark Hanna felt the same. "The United States must not have any damn trouble with anybody."[98]

Roosevelt's response was to send sweet assurances via Lodge to the Secretary of the Navy, that if appointed, he would faithfully execute Administration policies. What was more, "I shall stay in Washington, hot weather or any other weather, whenever he wants me to stay there . . ."[99] No message could have been more shrewdly calculated to appeal to the Secretary, especially the heavy hint about looking after the department in summer. John D. Long, whom Roosevelt knew well from Civil Service Commission days, was a comfortable old Yankee, mildly hypochondriac, who liked nothing so much as to potter around his country home in Hingham Harbor, Massachusetts, and write little books of poetry with titles like *At the Fireside* and *Bites of a Cherry.*[100] Long had been reported nervous about Roosevelt's appointment. "If he becomes Assistant Secretary of the Navy he will dominate the Department within six months!" But now he told Lodge that he would be happy to have the young man aboard, and the pressure on McKinley redoubled.[101]

Senator Platt capitulated in early April, when he was persuaded by his lieutenants that Roosevelt in Washington would be much less of a nuisance to the organization than Roosevelt in New York. The Easy Boss grudgingly told McKinley to go ahead with the appointment, as long as nobody thought that *he* had suggested it. "He hates Roosevelt like poison," remarked a Presidential aide.[102]

And so, on 6 April 1897, Theodore Roosevelt was nominated as Assistant Secretary of the Navy, at a salary of $4,500 a year. Moved almost to tears by the loyalty of his friends, he telegraphed congratulations:

HON. H. C. LODGE, 1765 MASS AVE., WASHINGTON D.C.

SINDBAD HAS EVIDENTLY LANDED THE OLD MAN OF THE SEA

Two days later the Senate confirmed the appointment. Senator Platt was a noticeable absentee from the floor when the vote was called.[103]

ANDREW D. PARKER was greatly amused when news of Roosevelt's imminent departure circulated through Headquarters. "What a glorious retreat!" he exclaimed, and laughed for a long time.[104] Contemptuous to the last, he stayed away from Roosevelt's last Board meeting on Saturday, 17 April. So, too, did Grant, leaving only Avery Andrews to stare across the big table and express polite regrets on behalf of the Police Department. Since there was no quorum, a resolution thanking Roosevelt for his services could not be entered into the minutes. They waited until noon, and then, as Headquarters began to close down for the half-holiday, Roosevelt declared the meeting adjourned. "I am sorry," he said wistfully. "There were matters of importance which I wished to bring up." He shook a few hands, then went into his office to pack up his papers.[105] Chief Conlin did not come in to say good-bye. Later, when Roosevelt walked down the main corridor for the last time, a guard on duty outside Conlin's office threw the door open for him. "No," said Roosevelt, with a gesture of disgust, "I am not going in there." The guard hesitated. "Well, good-bye, Mr. President." "Good-bye," Roosevelt responded, taking his hand. Then, apparently as an afterthought: "I shall be sorry for you when I am gone."[106]

ALTHOUGH THE *WORLD* CLAIMED, with possible truth, that New Yorkers were pleased to see Roosevelt go,[107] few could deny that his record as Commissioner was impressive. "The service he has rendered to the city is second to that of none," commented *The New York Times*, "and considering the conditions surrounding it, it is in our judgment unequaled."[108] He had proved that it was possible to enforce an unpopular law, and, by enforcing it, had taught the doctrine of respect for the law. He had given New York City its first honest election in living memory. In less than two years, Roosevelt had depoliticized and deethnicized the force, making it once more a neutral arm of government. He had broken its connections with the underworld, toughened the police-trial system, and largely eliminated corruption in the ranks. The attrition rate of venal officers had tripled during his presidency of the Board, while the hiring of new recruits had quadrupled—in spite of Roosevelt's decisions to raise physical admission standards above those of the U.S. Army, lower the maximum-age requirement, and apply the rules of Civil Service Reform to written examinations. As a result, the average New York patrolman was now bigger, younger, and smarter.[109] He was also much more honest, since badges were no longer for sale, and more soldierlike (the military ideal having been a particular feature of the departing commissioner's philosophy). Between May 1895 and April 1897, Roosevelt had added sixteen hundred such men to the force.[110]

Those officers he managed to promote before the deadlock began in March 1896 were, with one or two exceptions, men of good quality. They had brought about such an improvement in discipline that even when morale sank to its low ebb a year later, the force was still operating with a fair degree of efficiency. Crime and vice rates were down; order was being kept throughout the city; and police courtesy—a particular obsession of Roosevelt's—had noticeably improved. During the reform Board's administration, he had personally brought about the closure of a hundred of the worst tenement slums seen on his famous night patrols. Patrol-wagon response was quicker; many new station-houses had been built, and other ones modernized; marksmanship scores (thanks to the adoption of the standardized .32 Colt) were climbing; and the "bicycle squad," first of its kind in the world, was being imitated all over the United States and in Europe.[111]

Unfortunately Roosevelt's genius for moral warfare obscured his more practical achievements as Commissioner, both during his tenure and for some time after he left Mulberry Street. An inescapable aura of defeat clouded his resignation.[112] He was the first among his colleagues to quit, having served less than one-third of a six-year term. No matter what he said about "an honorable way out of this beastly job,"[113] the fact remained that he was leaving a position of supreme responsibility for a subservient one. Perhaps that is why Commissioner Parker found his retreat so funny.

Others found it sad—particularly the stoop-sitters of No. 303, who missed him more and more as life on Mulberry Street returned slowly to normal. The next president of the Police Board, Frank Moss, was an ardent reformer who insisted on continuing Roosevelt's policies, but his teeth inspired no metaphors, and his ascent of the front steps of Police Headquarters lacked spectator interest. Board meetings were held twice weekly as usual, but with no "boss leader of men" to blow up at Parker's taunts they were anticlimactic. As the *Harper's Weekly* man remarked, the Roosevelt Commissionership "was never in the least dull." It had been "one long elegant shindy" from the day he took office to the day he resigned.[114]

Ironically, Parker's power began to wane in the months following Roosevelt's departure.[115] His partnership with Frederick D. Grant broke up in June, when the latter resigned in order to rejoin the Army, and was replaced by a Commissioner who naturally sided with Moss and Andrews. On 12 July, Governor Frank S. Black denied Mayor Strong's attempt to oust Parker, saying that the evidence against him was patently "trivial."[116] But this proved a Pyrrhic victory, for the resignation of Chief Conlin on 24 July left Parker without an ally at Headquarters. He was unable to prevent the promotion—at last—of Roosevelt's protégés, Brooks and McCullagh, along with a large number of other worthy officers whose rise had been blocked beneath them. Inspector McCullagh subsequently became Chief, to Roosevelt's great delight.[117] Mayor Strong did not run for reelection in November. As Boss Richard Croker had predicted, the people grew weary of reform, and voted for a return of the old Democracy. By the end of the year it was business as usual at Tammany Hall.[118]

WHAT HAPPENED TO Andrew D. Parker in the years that followed is not known. He vanishes from history as he entered it, a handsome, smiling enigma. The stoop-sitters were never able to agree as to the reason for his poisonous hostility to Theodore

Roosevelt. Riis suggested pure "spite," Steffens the more abstract pleasure of a man who "liked to sit back and pull wires, just to see the puppets jump."[119] Other theories were advanced, of greater and less complexity, but never, it seems, the most fundamental of all: that Parker simply hated Roosevelt and wished to do him ill. Those who loved Roosevelt were so many, and so ardent, that they found it hard to believe that a certain minority always detested him. Parker was of this ilk. He was also, as it happened, the only associate whom Roosevelt never managed to bend to his own will, and, significantly, the only adversary from whom that happy warrior ever ran away.

CHAPTER 22

The Hot Weather Secretary

With his own hand fearless
Steered he the Long Serpent,
Strained the creaking cordage,
Bent each boom and gaff.

THEODORE ROOSEVELT'S WELLSPRINGS of nostalgia for boyhood and youth tended always to surge and spill in moments of self-fulfillment. So, as he prepared to take office as Assistant Secretary of the Navy on 19 April 1897, memories flooded back of his revered uncle James Bulloch, builder of the Confederate warship *Alabama,* and of his mother, who used "to talk to me as a little shaver about ships, ships, ships, and fighting of ships, till they sank into the depths of my soul." Allowing the stream of consciousness to flow unchecked, he recalled how as a Harvard senior he had dreamed of writing *The Naval War of 1812:* "when the professor thought I ought to be on mathematics and the languages, my mind was running to ships that were fighting each other."[1]

The past was still much in his thoughts when he searched for a suitable desk in the Navy Department's storage room. He selected the massive piece of mahogany used by Assistant Secretary Gustavus Fox, another juvenile hero, during the Civil War. Espe-

"No triumph of peace is quite so great as
the supreme triumphs of war."

Assistant Secretary of the Navy Roosevelt at the Naval War College, 2 June 1897.

cially pleasing, to Roosevelt's eye, were two beautifully carved monitors which bulged out of each side-panel, trailing rudders and anchors, and a group of wooden cannons protecting the wooden Stars and Stripes, about where his belly would be when he leaned forward to write.[2] The desk was dusted and polished and carried up to his freshly painted office. When Roosevelt sat down behind it, he could swivel in his chair and gaze through the window at the White House lawns and gardens—a view equally as good as that enjoyed by the Secretary of the Navy himself.[3]

"BEST MAN FOR THE JOB," John D. Long wrote in his diary after his first formal meeting with Roosevelt. Whatever misgivings he may have had about him earlier soon changed to avuncular fondness. The young New Yorker was polite, charming, and seemed to be sincere in promising to be "entirely loyal and subordinate."[4] Long concluded that Roosevelt would be an ideal working partner, amply compensating for his own lack of naval expertise, yet unlikely, on the grounds of immaturity, to usurp full authority.

Certainly the Secretary was everything the Assistant Secretary was not. Small, soft, plump, and white-haired, Long looked and acted like a Dickensian grandfather, although he was in fact only fifty-eight.[5] Nobody would want to hurt, or bewilder, such a "perfect dear"—to use Roosevelt's own affectionate phrase.[6] The mild eyes beamed with kindness rather than intelligence, and they clouded quickly with boredom when naval conversation became too technical. Abstruse ordnance specifications and blueprints for dry-dock construction were best left to specialists, in Long's opinion; he saw no reason to tax his brain unnecessarily.[7] Fortunately Roosevelt had a gargantuan appetite for such data, and could safely be entrusted with them. Long was by nature indolent: his gestures were few and tranquil, and there was a slowness in his gait which regular visits to the corn doctor did little to improve. From time to time he would indulge in bursts of hard, efficient work, but always felt the need to "rest up" afterward. On the whole he was content to watch the Department function according to the principles of laissez-faire.[8]

Roosevelt had no objection to this policy. The less work Long wanted to do, the more power he could arrogate to himself. His own job was so loosely defined by Congress that it could expand to embrace any duties "as may be prescribed by the Secretary of the Navy." All he had to do was win Long's confidence, while unobtrusively relieving him of more and more responsibility. By summer, with luck, he would be so much in control that Long might amble off to Massachusetts for a full two months, leaving him to push through his own private plans as Acting Secretary. But no matter how calculating this strategy, there was nothing insincere about Roosevelt's frequently voiced praises of John D. Long. "My chief . . . is one of the most high-minded, honorable, and upright gentlemen I have ever had the good fortune to serve under."[9]

The American press was largely optimistic about Long and Roosevelt as a team. "Nearly everybody in Washington is glad that Theodore Roosevelt [has come] back to the capital," reported the *Chicago Times-Herald* correspondent. "He is by long odds one of the most interesting of the younger men seen here in recent years." The *Washington Post* looked forward to lots of hot copy, now the famous headliner was back in town. "Of course he will bring with him . . . all that machinery of disturbance and upheaval which is as much a part of his entourage as the very air he breathes, but who knows that the [Navy Department] will not be the better for a little dislocation and readjustment?"[10]

Overseas newspapers, such as the London *Times,* took rather less pleasure in the "menacing" prospect of Roosevelt influencing America's naval policy. With Cuba and Hawaii ripe for conquest and annexation, "what now seems ominous is his extreme jingoism."[11]

Roosevelt knew that President McKinley and Chairman (now Senator) Hanna shared this nervousness, and he was at pains to reassure them, as well as Long, that he intended to be a quiet, obedient servant of the Administration. "I am sedate now," he laughingly told a *Tribune* reporter. All the same he could not resist inserting four separate warnings of possible "trouble with Cuba" into a memorandum on fleet preparedness requested by President McKinley on 26 April. The document, which was written and delivered that same day, could not otherwise be faulted for its effortless sorting out of disparate facts of marine dynamics, repair and maintenance schedules, geography and current affairs. Roosevelt had been at his desk for just one week.[12]

"He is one hell of a Secretary," Congressman W. I. Guffin remarked to Senator Shelby Cullom, unconsciously dropping the qualifier in Roosevelt's title.[13]

SEDATE AS HIS OFFICIAL image may have been in the early spring of 1897, his private activities more than justified foreign dread of his appointment. Quickly, efficiently, and unobtrusively, he established himself as the Administration's most ardent expansionist. A new spirit of intrigue affected his behavior, quite at odds with his usual policy of operating "in the full glare of public opinion." Never more than a casual clubman, he began to lunch and dine almost daily at the Metropolitan Club, assembling within its exclusive confines a coterie much more influential than the old Hay-Adams circle, now broken up.[14] It consisted of Senators and Representatives, Navy and Army officers, writers, socialites, lawyers, and scientists—men linked as much by Roosevelt's motley personality as by their common political belief, namely, that Manifest Destiny called for the United States to free Cuba, annex Hawaii, and raise the American flag supreme over the Western Hemisphere.

This expansionist lobby was not entirely Roosevelt's creation. Its original members had begun to work together in the last months of the Harrison Administration, as America's last frontier fell and Hawaii simultaneously floated into the national consciousness. But their organization had remained loose, and their foreign policy uncoordinated, all through the Cleveland Administration, partly due to the President's own ambivalent attitudes to Hawaii on the one hand and Venezuela on the other. Not until William McKinley took office, amid reports of Japanese ambitions in the Pacific and increased Spanish repression in the Caribbean, did the expansionists begin to close ranks, and cast about for a natural leader.[15]

Whether they chose to follow Roosevelt, or Roosevelt chose to lead them, is a Tolstoyan question of no great consequence given the group's unanimity of purpose. Examples of how he used Captain Alfred Thayer Mahan and Commodore George Dewey to advance his own interest, while also advancing their own, merit separate consideration. Other members of the lobby included Senators Henry Cabot Lodge, William E. Chandler, W. P. Frye, and "Don" Cameron, all powers on the Hill; Commander Charles H. Davis, Chief of Naval Intelligence; the philosopher Brooks Adams, shyer, more intense, and to some minds more brilliant than his older brother, Henry; Clarence King, whose desire to liberate Cuba was not lessened by his lust for mulatto women; and jolly Judge William H. Taft of the Sixth Circuit, the most popular man in town. Charles A. Dana, editor of the *Sun,* and John Hay, now Ambassador to the Court of St. James, represented the Roosevelt point of view in New York and London.[16] Many other men of more or less consequence cooperated with these in the effort to make America a world power before the turn of the century, and they looked increasingly to Theodore Roosevelt for inspiration as 1897 wore on.[17]

THE ASSISTANT SECRETARY of the Navy worked quietly and unobtrusively for over seven weeks before making his first public address, at the Naval War College in Newport, Rhode Island, on 2 June.[18] It turned out to be the first great speech of his career, a fanfare call to arms which echoed all the more resoundingly for the pause that had preceded it. He chose as his theme a maxim by George Washington: "To be prepared for war is the most effectual means to promote peace." This, to Roosevelt's mind, could signify only one thing in 1897: an immediate, rapid buildup of the American Navy.

He dismissed the suggestion that such a program would tempt the United States into unnecessary war. On the contrary, it would promote peace, by keeping foreign navies out of the Western Hemisphere. Should any power be so foolhardy as to attempt invasion, why, that would mean *necessary* war, which was a fine and healthy thing. "All the great masterful races have been fighting races; and the minute that a race loses the hard fighting virtues, then . . . it has lost its proud right to stand as the equal of the best." Roosevelt did not have to remind his listeners that the Japanese, fresh from last year's victory over the Chinese, were in full possession of those virtues, and were even now patrolling Hawaiian waters with an armored cruiser.[19] "Cowardice in a race, as in an individual," he declared, "is the unpardonable sin." During the last two years alone, various "timid" European rulers had ignored the massacre of millions of Armenians by the Turks in order to preserve "peace" in their own lands. Again, Roosevelt did not have to mention Cuba, where Spain's infamous Governor-General Weyler was currently slaughtering the *insurrectos*, to make a point. "Better a thousand times err on the side of over-readiness to fight, than to err on the side of tame submission to injury, or cold-blooded indifference to the misery of the oppressed."

Intoxicated with his theme, Roosevelt continued:

> No triumph of peace is quite so great as the supreme triumphs of war . . . It may be that at some time in the dim future of the race the need for war will vanish; but that time is yet ages distant. As yet no nation can hold its place in the world, or can do any work really worth doing, unless it stands ready to guard its rights with an armed hand.[20]

Aware that his audience consisted largely of naval academics devoted to the theory, rather than the practice, of war, Roosevelt praised teachers, scientists, writers, and artists as vital members of a civilized society, but warned against the dangers of too much "doctrinaire" thinking in formulating national policy. "There are educated men in whom education merely serves to soften the fiber." Only those "who have dared greatly in war, or the work which is akin to war," deserved the best of their country.

By now the Assistant Secretary was using the word "war" approximately once a minute. He was to repeat it sixty-two times before he sat down.

Roosevelt cited fact after historical fact to prove that "it is too late to prepare for war when the time for peace has passed." He poured scorn on Jefferson for seeking to "protect" the American coastline with small defensive gunboats, instead of building a fleet of aggressive battleships which might have prevented the War of 1812. He pointed out that the nation's present vulnerability, with Britain, Germany, Japan, and Spain engaged in a naval arms race, was more alarming than it had been at the beginning of the century. Then, at least, a man-of-war could be built in a matter of weeks; now, naval technology was so complicated that no battleship could be finished inside two years. Cruisers took almost as long; even the light, lethal, torpedo-boat (which he had already made a special priority item in the department)[21] needed ninety days to put into first-class shape. As for munitions, America's current supply was so meager, and so obsolete, that if war broke out tomorrow "we should have to build, not merely the weapons we need, but the plant with which to make them in any large quantity."

Roosevelt chillingly demonstrated that it would be six months before the United States could parry any sudden attack, and a further eighteen months before she could "begin" to return it. "Since the change in military conditions in modern times, there has never been an instance in which a war between two nations has lasted more than about two years. In most recent wars the operations of *the first ninety days* have decided the results of the conflict." It was essential, therefore, that Congress move at once to build more ships and bigger ships, "whose business it is to fight and not to run." Line personnel must be subjected to the highest standards of recruitment and training, while staff officers "must have as perfect weapons ready to their hands as can be found in the civilized world." This new Navy would be more to America's international advantage than the most brilliant corps of ambassadors. "Diplomacy," Roosevelt insisted, "is utterly useless when there is no force behind it; the diplomat is the servant, not the master of the soldier."[22]

Moving into his peroration, he anticipated another great war speech by forty-three years in a eulogy to "the blood and sweat and tears" which heroes must sacrifice for the cause of freedom. He begged his audience to remember that

> there are higher things in this life than the soft and easy enjoyment of material comfort. It is through strife, or the readiness for strife, that a nation must win greatness. We ask for a great navy, partly because we feel that no national life is worth having if the nation is not willing, when the need shall arise, to stake everything on the supreme arbitrament of war, and to pour out its blood, its treasure, and its tears like water, rather than submit to the loss of honor and renown.

ROOSEVELT'S SPEECH WAS PRINTED in full in all major newspapers and caused a nationwide sensation. From Boston to San Francisco, from Chicago to New Orleans, expansionist editors and correspondents praised it, and agreed that a new, defiantly original spirit had entered into the conduct of American affairs.[23] "Well done, nobly spoken!" exclaimed the *Washington Post.* "Theodore Roosevelt, you have found your place at last!" The *Sun* called his words "manly, patriotic, intelligent, and convincing." The *Herald* recommended that readers study this "lofty" speech "from its opening sentence to its close," while the *New Orleans Daily Picayune* said that it "undoubtedly voices the sentiments of the great majority of thinking people." Even such anti-expansionist journals as *Harper's Weekly* found the address "very eloquent and forcible," although the commentator, Carl Schurz, logically demolished Roosevelt's main argument. If too much peace led to softening of the national fiber, Schurz argued, and war led to vigor and love of country, it followed that *prevention* of war would only be debilitating. "*Ergo,* the building up of a great war fleet will effect that which promotes effeminacy and languishing unpatriotism."[24]

Schurz should have left his syllogism there, for it was unanswerable, but he went on to argue dreamily that the United States was so protected by foreign balances of power that no nation dare attack it. This made him sound like one of the naive doctrinaires Roosevelt had criticized in his speech, and served only to justify the Assistant Secretary's warnings. "I suspect that Roosevelt is right," President McKinley sighed to Lemuel Ely Quigg, "and the only difference between him and me is that mine is the greater responsibility."[25]

This startling admission by a Chief Executive personally committed to a policy of non-aggression suggests that Roosevelt had more than mere headlines in mind when he spoke to the Naval War College that June afternoon.[26] His words were obviously intended to create, rather than just influence, national foreign policy. In both timing and targeting, the speech was accurate as a karate chop, for Hawaii and Cuba were the issues of the hour, and the Naval War College was the nerve center of American strategic planning.[27] The isolationists in the Cabinet never quite recovered from Roosevelt's blow, and its shock effects were felt in every extremity of the Administration.

Traditionally, the Naval War College had been founded to give officers advanced instruction in science and history of marine warfare. But during the course of nearly a decade of domination by Alfred Thayer Mahan, it had also become the prime source of war plans for the government.[28] These documents, drawn up by brilliant young Mahanites ambitious to thrust the American Navy into the twentieth century, were submitted for consideration by the Office of Naval Intelligence in Washington, whence they went to the Secretary of the Navy for approval or rejection. Under the conservative Administration of President Cleveland, the Office of Naval Intelligence had acted as a foil to the Naval War College, toning down its more strident proposals, and Secretary Herbert saw to it that such war plans were pigeonholed before they had any effect on national defense policy. Herbert, indeed, was so suspicious of the War College that he had organized a senior board, consisting mainly of Old Guard officers, to keep both it and the Office of Naval Intelligence safely under control.[29]

With the accession of President McKinley, however, the composition of the Board changed radically. A few days after Roosevelt's arrival in the Navy Department, it was ordered to exhume two of the most recent war plans and to produce a new strategy in the light of recent developments in the Pacific and Caribbean. Captain Caspar F. Goodrich, president of the Naval War College, was just beginning to work on this document when Roosevelt chose to deliver his bellicose address to the Staff and Class of '97. There could not possibly have been a stronger hint as to what kind of thinking the new war plan should contain. Roosevelt had, in fact, already sent Captain Goodrich a "Special Confidential Problem" for academic deliberation:

> Japan makes demands on Hawaiian Islands.
>
> This country intervenes.
>
> What force will be necessary to uphold the intervention, and how should it be employed?
>
> Keeping in mind possible complications with another Power on the Atlantic Coast (Cuba).[30]

Such a problem would never exist, he privately informed Captain Mahan, "if I had my way." In an undisguised fantasy of himself as Commander-in-Chief, Roosevelt continued that he "would annex those islands tomorrow. If that was impossible I would establish a protectorate over them. I believe we should build the Nicaraguan Canal at once, and in the meantime that we should build a dozen new battleships, half of them on the Pacific Coast. . . . I would send the *Oregon* and, if necessary, also the *Monterey* . . . to Hawaii, and would hoist our flag over the island, leaving all details for after action." He acknowledged that there were "big problems" in the West Indies, but until Spain was turned out of Cuba ("and if I had my way," he repeated, "that would be done tomorrow"), the United States would always be plagued by trouble there. "We should acquire the Danish Islands. . . . I do not fear England; Canada is hostage for her good behavior . . ."

In the midst of his flow of dictation, recorded at the Navy Department, Roosevelt seems to have noticed that his stenographer's neck was flushing. "I need not say," he hastily went on, "that this letter must be strictly private . . . to no one else excepting Lodge do I speak like this."[31]

It would appear, nevertheless, that he expressed himself almost as strongly to Assistant Secretary of State William R. Day, at least on the subject of Hawaii. So, too, did Lodge and other members of the expansionist lobby. Bypassing Day's senile superior, John Sherman, they persuaded President McKinley to approve a treaty of annexation on 16 June 1897.[32] The treaty was forwarded to the Senate, where Lodge triumphantly undertook to secure its ratification, and Roosevelt rejoiced. It is fair to assume that champagne was drunk in the Metropolitan Club that evening. At last America had joined the other great powers of the world in the race for empire.[33]

THE NEXT MORNING Secretary Long, who was beginning to feel the heat of approaching summer, left town for two weeks' vacation, preparatory to taking his main vacation. Roosevelt was relieved to be alone for a while, since the Secretary had not been at all pleased with his War College speech,[34] and was already resisting pleas for a buildup of the Navy. Beneath the kindly exterior he sensed an old man's obstinacy which gave him "the most profound concern." It would hardly do to have the pace of naval construction slow just as the expansion movement was accelerating. "I feel that you ought to write to him," Roosevelt told Mahan, "—not immediately, but some time not far in the future, explaining to him the vital need for more battleships. . . . Make the plea that this is a measure of peace and not war."[35]

Roosevelt's easy recourse to the world's ranking naval authority, now and on many subsequent occasions in his career as Assistant Secretary, makes it worthwhile to examine their complex relationship or, more accurately, reexamine it, in the light of the enduring belief that the younger man's naval philosophy was inherited from the older. Facts recently uncovered suggest the reverse.[36] In 1881, when the twenty-two-year-old Roosevelt sat writing *The Naval War of 1812* in New York's Astor Library, Mahan had been an obscure, forty-year-old career officer of no particular accomplishment, literary or otherwise. He did not publish his own first book, a workmanlike history of Gulf operations in the Civil War, until two years later, by which time Roosevelt's prodigiously detailed volume was required reading on all U.S. Navy vessels, and had exerted at least a peripheral influence on the decision of Congress to build a fleet of modern warships. Mahan, indeed, was still so unlettered in world naval history that in 1884, when offered an instructorship at the new Naval War College, he asked for a year's leave to study for it. Most of 1885 was spent in the Astor Library, reading the same tomes Roosevelt had already devoured. This research was the basis of Mahan's lecture course at the War College, which in turn became *The Influence of Sea Power upon History* (1890).[37] Long before this masterpiece appeared, however, he had familiarized himself with Roosevelt's theories, to the extent of discussing them with him personally. At least one of the other instructors at the War College, Professor J. Russell Soley, was an enthusiastic Rooseveltian; so, too, was the institution's founder, Admiral Stephen B. Luce. "Your book must be our textbook," Luce told the young author.[38]

Roosevelt's next two histories, *Gouverneur Morris* and *Thomas Hart Benton,* were replete with arguments for a strong Navy and mercantile marine, while *The Winning of the West* propounded visions of Anglo-Saxon world conquest as heady as anything Mahan ever wrote. All of these works predated *The Influence of Sea Power upon History.*

The relative academic prestige of Roosevelt and Mahan altered drastically in the latter's favor after *Sea Power* came out. As has been seen, Roosevelt enthusiastically welcomed the book, reviewing it—and all Mahan's subsequent volumes—with a generosity that could not fail to endear him to the austere, reclusive scholar.[39] During his early years in Washington, he worked to save Mahan from sea duty (which the captain detested) and to increase his backing in government circles.[40]

It is not surprising, therefore, that when the new Assistant Secretary sought to advance his own ambitions in the spring of 1897, he could call upon Mahan in confidence. The fact that their naval philosophies were identical at this point only increased the willingness of one man to help the other.[41]

FINDING HIMSELF IN full, if temporary control of the Navy Department, Roosevelt worked energetically but cautiously, not wanting to jeopardize his chances of being Acting Secretary through most of the summer. He signed with pleasure a letter of permission for general maneuvers by the North Atlantic Squadron in August or September, and told its commanding officer that he would "particularly like to be aboard for a day or two" during gun practice.[42] He continued to dig up Secretary Herbert's suppressed reports, on the grounds that those most deeply buried might yield the most interesting information,[43] ordered an investigation of the management of the Brooklyn Navy Yard,[44] and proposed that some of the great names in American naval history be revived on future warships. He suggested the installation of rapid-fire weaponry throughout the fleet. Horrified when an elderly, bureaucratic admiral boasted about being able to account for every single bottle of red and black ink supplied to ships around the world, Roosevelt initiated a massive campaign to reduce the department's paperwork. Soothingly, he wrote to Long, "There isn't the slightest necessity of your returning."[45]

Undismayed by strong Japanese protest regarding the Hawaii treaty, Roosevelt set his expansionist lobby to work on the subject of Cuba, "this hideous welter of misery on our doorsteps." On 18 June he invited several key Senators to dine at the Metropolitan Club with an envoy recently returned from the island.[46]

Elsewhere on the propaganda front, he played off two publishers—Harpers and G. P. Putnam's Sons—in competition for a volume of "politico-social" essays covering the whole of his career as a speaker and man of letters. Articles on "The Manly Virtues" and "True Americanism" were prominent among them, along with his most ambitious reviews, "National Life and Character," "Social Evolution," and "The Law of Civilization and Decay." For good measure he added his recent address to the Naval War College. "I am rather pleased with them myself," he told Putnam's, the successful bidder.[47] Less robust tastes were repelled by a cumulative impression of jingoism, militarism, and self-righteousness, when the essays came out under the title *American Ideals*.[48] "If there is one thing more than another for which I admire you, Theodore," said Thomas B. Reed, "it is your original discovery of the Ten Commandments."[49]

Henry James, reviewing the volume for a British periodical, expressed mock alarm. "Mr. Theodore Roosevelt appears to propose . . . to tighten the screws of the national consciousness as they have never been tightened before. . . . It is 'purely as an American,' he constantly reminds us, that each of us must live and breathe. Breathing, indeed, is a trifle; it is purely as Americans that we must think, and all that is wanting to the author's demonstration is that he shall give us a receipt for the process." James granted that

Roosevelt had "a happy touch" when he eschewed questions of doctrine for accounts of his own political experiences. "These pages give an impression of high competence. . . . But his value is impaired for intelligible precept by the puerility of his simplifications."[50]

Such criticism, of course, was only to be expected from "white-livered" expatriates, and Roosevelt took no notice of James's remarks, if he even bothered to read them. From now on he would pour out a swelling flood of patriotic speeches and articles, aided by such other expansionists as Mahan, Brooks Adams, and Albert Shaw, until the last remaining dikes of isolationism burst under the pressure.[51]

THE NAVY DEPARTMENT'S new war plan was ready on 30 June, three days before Secretary Long returned from vacation. Roosevelt had no authority to approve it, but it was a document that gladdened his eyes nevertheless. All the more aggressive features of the earlier plans had been restored, and the weaker ones eliminated; in addition there were some new, flagrantly expansionist proposals which proved prophetic to a degree.[52]

In brief, the plan postulated a war with Spain for the liberation of Cuba. Hostilities would take place mainly in the Caribbean, but the U.S. Navy would also attack the Philippines, and even the Mediterranean shores of Europe, if necessary. The Caribbean strategy called for a naval blockade of Cuba, combined with invasion by a small Army force. No permanent occupation of Cuba was suggested, but the plan proceeded to discuss the Philippines, in tones hardly calculated to reassure Republican Conservatives: "we could probably have a controlling voice, as to what should become of the islands when a final settlement [with Filipino rebels] was made."[53]

ROOSEVELT'S METROPOLITAN CLUB CIRCLE widened in the early days of summer to include two new associates—Captain Leonard Wood, the President's Assistant Attending Surgeon, and Commodore George Dewey, president of the Board of Inspection and Survey. He met the former at a dinner party early in June.[54] When he met the latter is not known, but the name "Dewey"

appears in his correspondence for the first time on 28 June.[55] Both men were to play major roles in his life, and he in theirs.

Wood was a doctor by profession and a soldier by choice; he excelled in both capacities. His looks were noble, his physical presence splendid as a Viking's.[56] Tall, fair, lithe, and powerfully muscled, he walked with the slightly pigeon-toed stride of a born athlete, and was forever compulsively kicking a football around an empty lot, the leather thudding nearly flat as he drove it against the wall.

Roosevelt, who as Civil Service Commissioner had won fame as the most strenuous pedestrian in Washington,[57] was impressed to discover that this newcomer could outpace and outclimb him with no signs of fatigue. "He walked me off my legs," the Assistant Secretary told Lodge, with some surprise.[58] Ever the boy, he hero-worshiped Wood (although the doctor was two years his junior) as a fighter of Apaches and a vanquisher of Geronimo. Wood's personality was clear, forceful, honest, and unassuming. Best of all, he was an ardent expansionist, and could not stop talking about Cuba as a wound on the national conscience. Roosevelt decided that this quiet, charming man with excellent military connections (Wood was married to the niece of U.S. Army Commanding General Nelson A. Miles) must needs be cultivated.

Little old Commodore Dewey was a total contrast.[59] Nut-brown, wiry, and vain, he was in his sixtieth year when Roosevelt befriended him, but the size of his personal ambition was in inverse proportion to his age and height. Over three decades of undistinguished peacetime service had not quenched his lust for battle, kindled as a lieutenant under Farragut in the Civil War. Now, with retirement only three years off, Dewey was forced to accept the fact that glory might never be his.[60] Yet the Commodore still bore himself with fierce pride, immaculate in tailored uniform and polished, high-instepped boots. He was without doubt the smartest dresser in the Navy. "It was said of him," wrote one reporter, "that the creases of his trousers were as well-defined as his views on naval warfare."[61] With his beaky nose and restless, caged strut, Dewey looked like a resplendent killer falcon, ready to bite through wire, if necessary, to get at a likely prey.

The Commodore had attracted Roosevelt's admiring attention as long ago as the Chilean crisis of 1891, when he voluntarily bought coal for his ship instead of waiting for official battle orders.[62] Any officer whose instinct was to stoke up *before* a crisis—at his own expense—could be trusted in wartime. Like Wood, Dewey was a dedicated expansionist,[63] lunching and dining daily at the Metropolitan Club; like Wood, he was a man of action rather than thought. Roosevelt began to muse ways of giving him command of the Asiatic Squadron when Rear-Admiral Fred V. McNair retired later in the year.[64]

In the meantime, their friendship ripened. Often, on a sunny afternoon after work, they could be seen riding in Rock Creek Park together.[65]

AT THE BEGINNING OF JULY it was the Assistant Secretary's turn to take a brief vacation. He headed north for a reunion with Edith—pregnant, now, with his sixth child. Distracted as he was with naval affairs and plans for the coming war (whose certainty he never questioned), Roosevelt allowed himself ten days of quiet domesticity at Oyster Bay. The white marble city on the Potomac was all very well, he told Bamie, but "permanently, nothing could be lovelier than Sagamore."[66]

And nothing could be more satisfying than to see his own progeny growing sturdy and sunburned in his own fields. Roosevelt confessed to Cecil Spring Rice that "the diminishing rate of increase" in America's population worried him in contrast to the fecundity of the Slav. Looking around Sagamore Hill, he gave thanks that his own family, at least, had shown valor in "the warfare of the cradle." With various cousins who had come to stay, there were "sixteen small Roosevelts" in his house.[67] Edith, watching him crawling through tunnels in the hay-barn in pursuit of squealing boys and girls, was inclined to put the number one higher.

The eldest cousin was a good-looking lad of fifteen from Groton, named Franklin. He had been invited to Oyster Bay earlier in the year, after a lecture by Roosevelt to his schoolmates on life as a Police Commissioner of New York City. The talk, which kept the boys in stitches of laughter, impressed young Franklin as "splendid." From this summer on he deliberately modeled his career on that of "Cousin Theodore," whom he would always describe as the greatest man he ever knew.[68]

On 11 July, Roosevelt enjoyed one of the privileges of his new job by cruising from Oyster Bay to Newport in a torpedo-boat.[69] The swiftness and responsiveness of the little vessel delighted him. "Like riding a high-mettled horse," he wrote. He did not, like some critics, find its thin-shelled vulnerability a tactical disadvantage: "with these torpedo boats . . . frailty is part of the very essence of their being."[70] Such comments suggest that Roosevelt was not altogether a landlubber, although in general he did prefer the abstract flow of arrows on paper to the heaving, splashing realities of naval movement.

After witnessing some trials at Newport he set off for a tour of the Great Lakes Naval Militia stations in Mackinac, Detroit, Chicago, and Sandusky.[71] His speech to the latter establishment, on 23 July, contained a violent reply to Japan's protest against the annexation of Hawaii. "The United States," Roosevelt thundered, "is not in a position which requires her to ask Japan, or any other foreign Power, what territory it shall or shall not acquire." The *Tribune* called his outburst a "distinct impropriety" and suggested that he "leave to the Department of State the declaration of the foreign policy of this government."[72]

John D. Long, who was a man of delicate nervous constitution,[73] had barely recovered from his subordinate's previous speech to the Naval War College before the news from Sandusky came in. "The headlines . . . nearly threw the Secretary into a fit," Roosevelt told Lodge, "and he gave me as heavy a wigging as his invariable courtesy and kindness would permit."[74]

Abject apologies smoothed the incident over, but Long must have had some scruples about putting Roosevelt in charge of the Department through Labor Day as planned. However the need to resume his vacation was paramount, and on 2 August, Roosevelt found himself installed as "the hot weather Secretary."[75]

HE NOW ENTERED UPON one of those periods of near-incredible industry which always characterized his assumption of new responsibility—whether it be the management of a ranch, the researching of a book, or, as in this case, the administration of the most difficult department in the United States Government.[76] Quite apart from its complex structure, with seven bureaus issuing streams of documents on such subjects as naval law, steam engineering, diplomacy, finance, strategy, education, science, astronomy, and hydrography, there was the huge extra dimension of the Navy itself—a proud, hierarchical institution, traditionally resistant to change and contemptuous of civilian authority.[77] The multiple task of reconciling the various bureaus with one another, and the department with the fleet, while simultaneously dealing with Congress, the White House, the press, and countless industrial contractors was enough to frustrate anybody but a Roosevelt. "I perfectly revel in this work," he exulted to Long. For the first time in his life he had real power in full measure. As Acting Secretary he was answerable only to his chief and President McKinley, both of whom were away from town for at least six weeks. Praying that the latter would come back a few days before the former—since he wished to have a private talk with him—Roosevelt abandoned himself to the drug of hyperactivity. "I am having immense fun running the Navy," he told Bellamy Storer on 19 August.[78]

His industry during that first month confirms Henry Adams's remark, "Theodore Roosevelt . . . was pure act."[79] In just twenty-two days of official duty he managed to write a report of his tour of the Naval Militia; inspect a fleet of first- and second-class battleships off Sandy Hook; expedite a stalled order for diagonal-armor supplies; devise a public-relations plan for press coverage of the forthcoming North Atlantic Squadron exercises; set up a board to investigate ways of relieving the chronic dry-dock shortage; introduce a new post-tradership system; weigh and pronounce verdict upon the Brooklyn Navy Yard probe; surreptitiously backdate a Bureau of Navigation employment form in order to favor a protégé of Senator Cushman Davis; extend his anti-red-tape reforms to cover battleships and cruisers; eliminate the department's backlog of unfilled appointments; draw up an elaborate cruising schedule for the new torpedo-boat flotilla; settle a row between the Bureaus of

Ordnance and Construction; review the relative work programs in various navy yards; draft a naval personnel reform bill, and fire all Navy Department employees who rated a sub-70 mark in the semi-annual fitness reports—all the while making regular reports to the vacationing Secretary, in tones calculated both to soothe and flatter. "I shan't send you anything, unless it is really important," Roosevelt wrote. "You must be tired, and you ought to have an entire rest." He begged Long not to answer his letters, "for I don't want you bothered at all." As for coming back after Labor Day, there was "not the slightest earthly reason" to return before the end of September.[80]

Long, happily pottering about his garden, was more than content to remain away.[81] Ensconced as he was in rural Massachusetts, he probably did not see a lengthy analysis, in the *New York Sun* of 23 August, of European reaction to the expansionist movement in the United States. One paragraph read:

> The liveliest spot in Washington at present is the Navy Department. The decks are cleared for action. Acting Secretary Roosevelt, in the absence of Governor Long, has the whole Navy bordering on a war footing. It remains only to sand down the decks and pipe to quarters for action.

"Yes, indeed," Roosevelt was writing, "I wish I could be with you for just a little while and see the lovely hill farm to which your grandfather came over ninety years ago. . . . Now, stay there just exactly as long as you want to."[82]

IN HIS "SPARE HOURS," as he put it, Roosevelt amused himself by writing and editing another volume of Boone & Crockett Club big-game lore, dictating one of his enormous, prophetic letters to Cecil Spring Rice ("If Russia chooses to develop purely on her own line and resist the growth of liberalism . . . she will sometime experience a red terror that will make the French Revolution pale"),[83] and assembling a series of quotations by various Presidents on the subject of an aggressive Navy. As he read his anthology through, it struck him as a powerful piece of propaganda, and he determined to publish it, after first mailing the text to Long for approval.[84]

The Secretary saw no harm in it, providing that Roosevelt inserted the words "in my opinion" somewhere in the Introduction, to show that it was not an official statement of policy by the Navy Department.[85] An advance copy was sent to President McKinley on 30 August, and in early September the Government Printing Office issued it under the title *The Naval Policy of America as Outlined in Messages of the Presidents of the United States from the Beginning to the Present Day.*[86] It drew admiring comment in most newspapers, "timely" being the adjective most frequently used. Besides being a miniature history of the U.S. Navy, the pamphlet showed a striking similarity of thought between Presidents Washington, Jackson, Lincoln, and Grant on the one hand, and Assistant Secretary of the Navy Roosevelt on the other. No quotations by Thomas Jefferson were deemed worthy of inclusion.[87]

ABOUT THIS TIME Roosevelt added yet another influential voice to his expansionist propaganda machine.[88] William Allen White was not yet thirty, but he was proprietor and editor of a powerful Midwestern newspaper, the *Emporia Gazette,* and had won a national following in 1896 with a diatribe against the Populists, "What's the Matter with Kansas?" Printed first as an editorial in his own paper, then reprinted and distributed in millions of copies by Mark Hanna, the piece had been the single most effective broadsheet of McKinley's campaign.[89] Roosevelt had read the famous editorial with interest. Here was the natural Republican antidote to William Jennings Bryan, and a much better metaphorist to boot. If he could take White in hand and teach him the gospel of expansionism, he would enlarge his own sphere of influence by thousands of readers and thousands of square miles. Roosevelt did not care *who* propounded Rooseveltian views, even if they won glory by doing so: what mattered was that the message got through. When he heard that White was in Washington on a patronage mission, he asked for him to be sent down to the Navy Department.[90]

Blond, red-faced, and pudgy, White looked the typical corn-fed "hick" journalist, yet his intelligence was acute, and his language rich and rolling as the Midwest itself. Their meeting was casual—little more than a handshake and an agreement to have lunch next day—but Roosevelt was so radiant with newfound power that White was unable to sit down for excitement afterward. "I was afire with the splendor of the personality that I had met."[91]

The little Kansan was still "stepping on air" the following afternoon, when Roosevelt escorted him to the Metropolitan Club and signaled for the menu.[92] Both men were compulsive eaters and compulsive talkers, and for the next hour they awarded each other equal time, greed alternating with rhetoric. In old age White fondly recalled "double mutton chops . . . seas of speculation . . . excursions of delight, into books and men and manners, poetry and philosophy."[93]

Roosevelt spoke with shocking frankness about the leaders of the government, expressing "scorn" for McKinley and "disgust" for the "deep and damnable alliance between business and politics" that Mark Hanna was constructing. White, whose worship of the Gold Dollar amounted to religion, flinched at this blasphemy, yet within another hour he was converted:

> I have never known such a man as he, and never shall again. He overcame me . . . he poured into my heart such visions, such ideals, such hopes, such a new attitude toward life and patriotism and the meaning of things, as I never dreamed men had . . . So strong was this young Roosevelt—hard-muscled, hard-voiced even when the voice cracked in *falsetto,* with hard, wriggling jaw muscles, and snapping teeth, even when he cackled in raucous glee, so completely did the personality of this man overcome me that I made no protest and accepted his dictum as my creed.[94]

Later they strolled for a while under the elms of F Street, and when they parted "I was his man." Years later White tried to analyze the elements of Roosevelt's conquering ability. It was not social superiority, he decided, nor political eminence, nor erudition;

it was something vaguer and more spiritual, "the undefinable equation of his identity, body, mind, emotion, the soul of him . . . It was youth and the new order calling youth away from the old order. It was the inexorable coming of change into life, the passing of the old into the new."[95]

WHEN ACTING SECRETARY Roosevelt boarded the battleship *Iowa* on Tuesday, 7 September, the Virginia Capes had long since slipped below the horizon.[96] Apart from a forlorn speck of color floating some twenty-five-hundred yards off—the target for today's gunnery exercises—the world consisted of little but blue sky and glassy water, in which seven white ships of the North Atlantic Squadron sat with the solidity of buildings. Biggest and most sophisticated by far was the eleven-thousand-ton *Iowa*, a masterpiece of naval engineering, and the equal of any German or British battleship. She was so new that she had not yet engaged in target practice, and many of her crew had never even heard her guns fired.

Captain William Sampson welcomed Roosevelt aboard and escorted him to the bridge amid a terrific clamor of gongs. The decks were cleared for action, breakables stowed away, and port-hole-panes left to swing idly as sailors scampered to their stations. Roosevelt, who had just been lunching with the Admiral, looked placid and happy. Word went around that he wanted to see how quickly the "enemy" could be demolished.

The jangling of the gongs gave way to silence, broken only by a general hum of automatic machinery. (It was the constructor's boast that almost nothing on the *Iowa* was done by hand "except the opening and closing of throttles and pressing of electric buttons.")[97] A surgeon distributed ear-plugs to the Acting Secretary and his party.[98] "Open your mouth, stand on your toes, and let your frame hang loosely," he advised.

"Two thousand yards," called a cadet monitoring the ship's course. A few seconds later there was a silent flash of fire and smoke from the 8-inch guns, followed by a thunderous report that shook the *Iowa* from stem to stern. Plumes of spray indicated that the shells were fifty yards short of target. A second salvo landed on range, but slightly to one side. Bugles announced that the *Iowa*'s main battery of 12-inch guns was now being aimed at the floating speck. There was an apprehensive pause, followed by such vast concussions of air, metal, and water that a lifeboat was stove in, and several locked steel doors burst their hinges. Two members of Roosevelt's party, who had forgotten to assume the necessary simian stance, were jerked into the air, and landed clasping each other wordlessly. They were escorted below for ear ointment, while Roosevelt continued to squint at the target through smoke-begrimed spectacles. Had it been a Spanish battleship, and not a shattered frame of wood and canvas, it would now be sinking.

The exercises lasted another two days, and Roosevelt returned to Washington profoundly moved by what he had seen. "Oh, Lord! If only the people who are ignorant about our Navy could see those great warships in all their majesty and beauty, and could realize how well they are handled, and how well fitted to uphold the honor of America."[99]

THE HOT WEATHER CONTINUED until mid-September, and Roosevelt, showing concern for the Secretary's health, suggested that he extend his vacation through the beginning of October. This, however, even John D. Long was unprepared to do, and he sent word that he would be back on 28 September. Roosevelt took the news philosophically, for by then he had realized his ambition to consult with the President as Acting Secretary—not once, but three times.[100]

Hitherto their meetings had been pleasantly impersonal, but now, for some reason, McKinley seemed anxious to flatter him. On 14 September he requested Roosevelt's company for an afternoon drive.[101] He confessed that he had not looked at the *Naval Policy of the Presidents* pamphlet until he saw what press interest it aroused, whereupon he "read every word of it," and was "exceedingly glad" it had been published. McKinley then made the astonishing remark that Roosevelt had been "quite right" to criticize Japan's Hawaiian policy at Sandusky. Finally, he congratulated him on his management of the Navy Department during the past seven weeks. Roosevelt took all this praise with a pinch of salt ("the President," he told Lodge, "is a bit of a jollier"), but he detected nevertheless a "substratum of satisfaction."

Swaying gently against the cushions of the Presidential carriage, relaxed after a day of stiff formalities, William McKinley appeared to best advantage. Locomotion quickened his inert body and statuesque head, and the play of light and shade through the window made his masklike face seem mobile and expressive. Roosevelt could forget about the too-short legs and pulpy handshake, and concentrate on the bronzed, magnificent profile. From the neck up, at least, McKinley was every inch a President—or for that matter, an emperor, with his high brow, finely chiseled mouth, and Roman nose. "He does not like to be told that it looks like the nose of Napoleon," the columnist Frank Carpenter once wrote. "It is a watchful nose, and it watches out for McKinley."[102]

Not until the President turned, and gazed directly at his interlocutor, was the personal force which dominated Mark Hanna fully felt. His stare was intimidating in its blackness and steadiness. The pupils, indeed, were at times so dilated as to fuel suspicions that he was privy to Mrs. McKinley's drug cabinet. Only very perceptive observers were aware that there was no real power behind the gaze: McKinley stared in order to concentrate a sluggish, wandering mind.[103]

Taking advantage of the President's affable mood, Roosevelt touched delicately on the possibility of war with Spain and Japan. McKinley agreed that there might be "trouble" on either front. Roosevelt made it clear that he intended to enlist in the Army the moment hostilities began. The President asked what Mrs. Roosevelt would think of such action, and Roosevelt replied, "this was one case" where he would consult neither her nor Cabot Lodge. Laughing, McKinley promised him the opportunity to serve "if war by any chance arose."[104]

Three days later Roosevelt received an invitation to dine at the White House, and three days after that went for another drive in the Presidential carriage. This time he made so bold as to present McKinley with a Cuban war plan of his own devising. It proposed a two-stage naval offensive, first with a flying squadron of cruisers, then with a fleet of battleships—all dispatched from Key West within forty-eight hours of a formal declaration. If the Army followed up quickly with a small landing force, he doubted that "acute" hostilities would last more than six weeks. "Meanwhile, our Asiatic Squadron should blockade, and if possible take Manila."[105]

BY 17 SEPTEMBER, Roosevelt was beginning to feel guilty about "dear" Secretary Long rusticating in New England, especially when the *Boston Herald* printed a mocking story about his desire to replace the old man altogether. He wrote to Long in quick self-defense, protesting his loyalty and subservience rather too vehemently, and ending with a rueful "There! *Qui s'excuse s'accuse.*"[106] But the Secretary took no offense, and proclaimed his entire satisfaction with Roosevelt at a dinner of the Massachusetts Club in Boston. "His enthusiasm and my conservatism make a good combination," Long said, adding with a twinkle, "It is a liberal education to work with him."[107]

Had Long known what Roosevelt was up to on the eve of his return to Washington, he might have employed stronger terminology. On Monday, 27 September,[108] the Acting Secretary intercepted a letter from Senator William E. Chandler to Long, recommending that Commodore John A. Howell be appointed commander in chief of the Asiatic Station—the very post Roosevelt wanted for Dewey.[109] Howell, though senior, was in his opinion "irresolute" and "extremely afraid of responsibility";[110] the prospect of such an officer leading an attack upon Manila was too depressing to contemplate. With Long due back the following morning, rapid action was necessary.

Roosevelt sent an urgent appeal to Chandler. "Before you commit yourself definitely to Commodore Howell I wish very much you would let me have a chance to talk to you . . . I shall of course give your letter at once to the Secretary upon his return."[111]

Presumably Senator Chandler could not be persuaded, for he withdrew neither his recommendation nor his letter. Throwing all caution to the winds, Roosevelt called in Dewey. "Do you know any Senators?" The Commodore mentioned Redfield Proctor. Roosevelt was delighted, for Proctor had expansionist tendencies and was known to be influential with the President. Dewey must enlist his services at once.[112]

Senator Proctor obligingly went over to the White House and

spoke to McKinley in behalf of the little Commodore. He might have made discreet reference to the fact that Roosevelt also favored Dewey. The President, who took little interest in naval affairs, accepted his advice without question and wrote a memorandum to Secretary Long requesting the appointment.[113]

Long returned to the Navy Department on 28 September and was greatly annoyed to find what political intrigues had been going on in his absence. Tradition required that he appoint the senior officer, and besides he personally favored Howell. But McKinley's memo could not be ignored; and so, to quote the sonorous words of Theodore Roosevelt, "in a fortunate hour for the Nation, Dewey was given command of the Asiatic Squadron."[114]

The Secretary was still in an irritable mood when Dewey called to thank him and apologize for using the influence of Senator Proctor. It had been necessary, Dewey explained, to counteract Senator Chandler's recommendation of Howell. "You are in error, Commodore," snapped Long. "No influence has been brought to bear on behalf of anyone else."

A few hours later Long, in turn, sent apologies to Dewey. It appeared that Senator Chandler had indeed recommended his rival, but the letter "had arrived while he was absent from the office and while Mr. Roosevelt was Acting Secretary and had only just been brought to his attention."

The culprit was serenely unrepentant about his delay in forwarding Senator Chandler's letter, and saw nothing wrong in Dewey's enlistment of senatorial aid. "A large leniency," Roosevelt wrote, "should be observed toward the man who uses influence only to get himself a place . . . near the flashing of the guns."[115]

BY 30 SEPTEMBER, Roosevelt was free to go north for a fortnight's rest at Sagamore Hill. Before leaving he asked the Secretary's permission "to talk to him very seriously about the need for an increase in the Navy." He proceeded to urge the instant construction of six battleships, six large cruisers, seventy-five torpedo-boats, and four dry docks, together with the modernization of ninety-five guns to rapid fire, the laying in of nine thousand armor-piercing projectiles, and the purchase of two million pounds of smokeless powder.

Long could only suggest that Roosevelt list these demands in a memorandum. The Assistant Secretary was eventually persuaded to settle for one battleship.[116]

ROOSEVELT WAS BACK in Washington on 15 October, accompanied by his wife and family. Installing them at 1810 N Street, "a very nice house, just opposite the British Embassy," he set off almost immediately on the campaign trail, stumping in Massachusetts for local candidates, and in Ohio for Senator Hanna.[117] On 27 October he turned thirty-nine.

With November came the familiar, seasonal quickening of his activity, as the days shortened and crisp winds stimulated his blood. The ground of Rock Creek Park grew hard under his hobnailed boots, as he and Leonard Wood strolled their endless visionary miles, talking of Cuba, Cuba, Cuba.[118]

Roosevelt's duties as Assistant Secretary were not numerous enough to divert him, and he began to show signs of intellectual restlessness. He plotted four more volumes of *The Winning of the West,* took Frederic Remington to task for rendering badgers "too long and thin," and yearned for a war with Spain "within the next month."[119] Long sympathetically appointed him president of a board investigating the Navy's most chronic ailment: friction between line and staff personnel.[120] The resultant work load was heavy, yet Roosevelt now toyed with the idea of writing "a historical article on the Mongol Terror, the domination of the Tartar tribes over half of Europe during the Thirteenth and Fourteenth Centuries."[121]

Early in the morning of 19 November he sent joyful news to Bamie: "Very unexpectedly Quentin Roosevelt appeared just two hours ago." Pausing only to enter the boy for Groton, he marched off to work and dictated his most bellicose letter yet, to Lt. Comdr. W. W. Kimball, author of the department's original war plan.[122] "To speak with a frankness which our timid friends would call brutal, I would regard a war with Spain from two standpoints: first, the advisability on the grounds both of humanity and self-interest of interfering on behalf of the Cubans . . . second . . . the benefit done our military forces *by trying both the Navy and Army in actual practice.*"[123]

On 8 December, he heard that Dewey had sailed for the Far East, but by now he was so busy writing the report of his Personnel Board that he paid little attention. The eight-thousand-word document, submitted the following day, proposed a bill for the prompt amalgamation of line and staff, on the grounds that engineers, in an industrial age, could no longer be held separate from or inferior to officers above deck. Roosevelt inserted one of his typical historical parallels, showing how in the mid-seventeenth century sailormen and sea-soldiers had to unite and resolve their differences in much the same way. "We are not making a revolution," he wrote, "we are merely recognizing and giving shape to an evolution."[124]

Secretary Long complimented him highly on the report,[125] as did many naval academics and newspaper editors. The *New York Evening Post* expressed "admiration" for his "grasp and breadth of view" of highly complicated material. "If profound study, evident freedom from bias, and command of the subject could place a report above criticism . . . nothing would be left to do but the enactment by Congress of the proposed bill."[126]

Shortly before Christmas the mammalogist C. Hart Merriam announced that a new species of Olympic Mountain elk had been named *Cervus Roosevelti* in honor of the founder of the Boone & Crockett Club. "It is fitting that the noblest deer of America should perpetuate the name of one who, in the midst of a busy public career, has found time to study our larger mammals in their native haunts and has written the best accounts we have ever had of their habits and chase."[127]

And so the year ended with a crescendo of praise for Assistant Secretary Theodore Roosevelt, who was now recognized to be one of the best-informed and most influential men in Washington.[128] He was also, as the *Boston Sunday Globe* pointed out, by far the most entertaining performer in "the great theater of our national life." But "it would never do . . . to permit such a man to get into the Presidency. He would produce national insomnia."[129]

"From the neck up, at least, McKinley was
every inch a President."

*President William McKinley at the time of
the Spanish-American War.*

CHAPTER 23

The Lieutenant Colonel

"What was that?" said Olaf, standing
On the quarter-deck.
"Something heard I like the stranding
Of a shattered wreck."

THE NEW YEAR was not twelve days old when a riot disturbed the uneasy peace of Havana, Cuba. Spanish officers smashed the presses of four local newspapers critical of the occupying army. The violence lasted about an hour, long enough to convince the nervous U.S. Consul-General, Fitzhugh Lee, that the lives of American residents were in danger. He sent home some urgent dispatches, and the State Department flashed a message to Captain Charles D. Sigsbee of the U.S.S. *Maine,* at Key West, Florida: "TWO DOLLARS."[1]

While Captain Sigsbee pondered that cryptic cable—a prearranged code alerting him to be ready to steam for Cuba at a moment's notice[2]—Assistant Secretary of the Navy Theodore Roosevelt pondered the first press reports of the riot. Next morning, Thursday, 13 January, he went into John D. Long's office and shut the door.[3]

The Secretary was amusedly aware that his subordinate intended

"Now, Senator, may we please have war?"

Wreck of the Maine *in Havana Harbor, February 1898—Old Glory still flying.*

"to abandon everything and go to the front" in the event of war with Spain. Roosevelt had said so at least twice already, but today he was in such fierce earnest that Long wondered if he had not gone "daft in the matter."

Attempting to jolly him back to his senses, the Secretary called him a "crank" and ridiculed his desire to get involved in some "bushwhacking fight" with Cuban mosquitoes. But Roosevelt would not be diverted, as Long noted somewhat pettishly in his diary.

> The funny part of it all is, that he actually takes the thing seriously . . . he bores me with plans of naval and military movement, and the necessity of having some scheme to attack arranged for instant execution in case of an emergency. By tomorrow he will have got half a dozen heads of bureaus together and have spoiled twenty pages of good writing paper, and lain awake half the night. . . . Happily, the latest dispatches of this afternoon are to the effect that everything is quiet again.[4]

Roosevelt soon realized that the "flurry in Havana" was no real threat to American security, but he volunteered his services, just in case, to his friend General C. Whitney Tillinghast II, Adjutant General of New York.

> I believe I can get a commission as a major or lieutenant colonel in one of the National Guard regiments, but I want your help and the Governor's . . . I have served three years in the State Militia (not to speak of having acted as sheriff in the cow country!) and I believe that I would be of some use. . . .[5]

Meanwhile, Edith was lying alarmingly ill at 1810 N Street, having collapsed with suspected typhoid fever nine days before.[6] Roosevelt was "exceedingly put out" by this inconvenience, for it obliged him to cancel a trip to the annual Boone & Crockett dinner in New York. To make matters worse, little Ted was suffering from nervous exhaustion.[7] Roosevelt's own attitude to disease and frailty was the same now, in his fortieth year, as it had been in his fourteenth: if one ignored them long enough, presumably they would go away. No illness, not even the mortal kind, must deter him from leaving for the front at the first hint of war.[8]

But the trumpets did not blow for him that freezing January day. He worked off his frustrations, as the Secretary had predicted, by "spoiling twenty pages of good writing paper," in the form of a memorandum on naval preparedness, and deposited it on Long's desk the following morning.[9] The document was signed *Yours respectfully,* but in its urgency and peremptory statement of facts it read more like a curt set of orders.

Roosevelt warned of "serious consequences" for the Navy Department if it allowed itself to drift unprepared into war. "Some preparation can and should be undertaken, on the mere chance of having to strike . . . the saving in life, money, and reputation by such a course will be very great." He advised—insisted—that vulnerable U.S. cruisers and gunboats currently "scattered about the high seas" be concentrated at strategic points for possible blockade duty in Cuba and the Philippines. This redeployment must begin "at once," since even a fast cruiser like the *Cincinnati* would take thirty days to steam north from South America and would arrive home without any coal. "In other words for the first five or six most important weeks of the war these vessels will be absolutely useless," Roosevelt wrote, temporarily forgetting that war had not yet been declared. Such ships should be recalled "tomorrow," and assembled at Key West, where they could fill up with coal and be ready for instant battle orders.

He was confident that Dewey, his man in Hong Kong, had enough ships to "overmaster" the Spanish Asiatic Squadron, but just to make sure, the vessels now patrolling Hawaii should add their gunpower to the Commodore's. On the Eastern seaboard, "a flying squadron composed of powerful ships of speed and great coal capacity" should be readied for instant dispatch to the Canaries, whence it might attack Cadiz, or slip through Gibraltar by night and destroy Barcelona.

The memorandum ended with rapid-fire demands for more

ammunition, men, and colliers. "When the war comes, *it should come finally on our initiative,* and after we have had time to prepare."

Roosevelt's fine writing-paper was not altogether wasted. Something about his "impetuosity and almost fierceness" persuaded the Secretary to order the *Cincinnati* and several other South Atlantic cruisers into equatorial waters, and station a small force at Lisbon, where it could monitor Spanish naval movements. Meanwhile the formidable North Atlantic Squadron, which Roosevelt had seen in practice the previous fall, joined the *Maine* at Key West (ostensibly to begin "winter exercises") and proceeded to fill up with coal.[10]

Long, surprisingly, went even further than Roosevelt in suggesting to President McKinley that the *Maine* should be detached and sent to visit Havana as "an act of friendly courtesy." McKinley sounded out the Spanish Minister, Enrique Depuy de Lôme, on this subject, and etiquette required His Excellency to express diplomatic delight.[11] The President was, after all, his own accredited host. But de Lôme's private attitude may be judged from a letter he had written to a Spanish friend a few weeks previously. "McKinley is . . . weak and a bidder for the admiration of the crowd, besides being a would-be politician [*politicastro*] who tries to leave a door open behind himself while keeping on good terms with the jingoes of his party."[12]

Unknown to de Lôme, the letter did not reach its destination.[13]

THE *MAINE* DROPPED ANCHOR in Havana Harbor on the morning of 25 January 1898. Spanish officials went aboard in polite but chilly welcome. Captain Sigsbee, not wanting to exacerbate local feelings, announced that there would be no leave for his crew. Contrary to expectations, no demonstrations of welcome or protest broke out in the city, and a relieved Consul-General Lee cabled: "Peace and quiet reign."[14]

ROOSEVELT MIGHT HAVE REACTED more gratefully to the Administration's sudden decision to make a show of naval force had his domestic worries not intensified in the last days of January. Edith was running a constant fever, and could not sleep for the pangs of sciatica; Ted's strange nervous condition was worse, and Kermit, too, was sick.[15] The presence of a squalling two-month-old infant in the house was an added distraction. On top of all this, Roosevelt now discovered that he had personal tax problems in New York. Last summer he had filed an affidavit stating that he was a resident of Manhattan, in order to avoid a heavy assessment in Oyster Bay; in New York, however, his assessment turned out to be even heavier, making him wish he could cancel the original affidavit.[16] Family physicians and accountants were pressed into service, while the Assistant Secretary waited restlessly for further news from Havana. On the last day of the month Henry Cabot Lodge made an eerie prediction: "There may be an explosion any day in Cuba which would settle many things."[17]

For a week nothing happened, then, on 9 February, William Randolph Hearst's sensational *New York Journal* published on its front page the text of Minister de Lôme's undelivered letter, under the banner headline, "WORST INSULT TO THE UNITED STATES IN ITS HISTORY." The paper announced that an agent of the Cuban *insurrectos* had intercepted the letter on the eve of its delivery and sent it to another agent in New York, who in turn gave it to the *Journal* for publication.[18] All possible doubt as to the document's authenticity was avoided by printing it in facsimile.

While ordinary Americans fumed over de Lôme's characterization of their President, students of foreign policy boggled at the implications of his concluding paragraph:

> It would be very advantageous to take up, *if only for effect,* the question of foreign relations, and to have a man of some prominence sent here in order that I may make use of him to carry on a propaganda among the Senators and others in opposition to the [rebel] junta.[19]

In other words, the Spanish Government appeared to be totally cynical in its relations with the United States, and its promises to help secure some sort of autonomous government in Cuba.

To add insult to injury, Minister de Lôme (who at once admitted that he had indeed written the letter) cabled his resignation to Madrid before the State Department had a chance to demand that he be recalled. Thus the United States had to be content with an inadequate Spanish apology, referring, in sarcastic tones, to mail-theft and sensation-mongering newspapers.[20]

That night a highly excited Theodore Roosevelt accosted Mark Hanna and two other Senators at a reception. In his haste to urge war upon them, he did not notice that Hanna was accompanied by Henriette Adler, a young Frenchwoman recently arrived from Paris. Roosevelt launched into a typical fist-smacking harangue, and Mlle. Adler found herself wedged between him and the wall. She tried to follow what he was saying, but was distracted by his flailing right arm, which swept nearer and nearer her bodice. Eventually his elbow ripped off a silken rose and some gauze, whereupon she exclaimed *"Mon Dieu."* Roosevelt, wheeling, made profuse *pardons*. To her alarm, he continued to pour war rhetoric upon her in French, until Nannie Lodge tactfully appeared with a safety pin. The Senators screened Mlle. Adler off, while Roosevelt switched back to English.

It was "a bully idea," he proclaimed, to send the *Maine* to Havana. Senator Hanna said nothing, but stood listening with his jowls sunk on his white tie. Mlle. Adler, decent again, ventured a suggestion that the United States should consider the opinion of other European powers before attempting to crowd Spain out. France and Germany were bound to object to any denial of imperial rights in the New World; she had heard a statement to this effect herself, in Paris only two weeks before.

The Assistant Secretary waved France's scruples aside as unimportant and irrelevant. "I hope to see the Spanish flag and the English flag gone from the map of North America before I'm sixty!" Hanna stared at him. "You're crazy, Roosevelt! What's wrong with Canada?"

Later, in the carriage back home, Mrs. Hanna tried to explain to the dazed Mlle. Adler that Roosevelt, despite his abnormal vehemence, was more "amusing" than violent. But the Senator, chewing on his cigar, thanked God Roosevelt had not been appointed Assistant Secretary of State. "We'd be fighting half the world," he growled.[21]

INCENDIARY TALK WAS COMMON in the days following the *Maine*'s arrival in Havana Harbor, from Henry Cabot Lodge's threatened "explosion" to Mark Hanna's "waving a match in an oil-well for fun,"[22] and the more personal misgivings of Mrs. Richard Wainwright, wife of the cruiser's executive officer: "You might as well send a lighted candle on a visit to an open cask of gunpowder."[23] But as mid-February approached, and life in the Cuban capital drowsed on as normal, even Consul-General Lee began to relax.

On the evening of the fifteenth, tourists aboard the liner *City of Washington,* just arrived in Havana Harbor, leaned on the railings and admired the *Maine*'s sleek white beauty four hundred yards away. The air was hot and motionless, and the harbor scarcely heaved. Its stillness was such that they could hear accordion music coming across the water. Tropic dark came quickly, and the tourists went below to dinner. About two hours later another strand of music sounded from the *Maine:* the sound of a bugler blowing taps. Its melancholy beauty caused Captain Sigsbee, who was writing in his cabin, to lay down his pen and listen until the last echoes died away. He looked at his watch. The time was exactly 9:40 P.M.[24]

ABOUT FOUR HOURS LATER Secretary Long was wakened in his Washington home and handed a telegram. The first sentence alone was enough to banish all further thought of sleep: "MAINE BLOWN UP IN HAVANA HARBOR AT NINE-FORTY TONIGHT AND DESTROYED." Long's eye, running on across the sheet, leaped from phrase to incredible phrase: "MANY WOUNDED . . . DOUBTLESS MORE KILLED OR DROWNED . . . NO ONE HAS CLOTHING OTHER THAN THAT UPON HIM . . . PUBLIC OPINION SHOULD BE SUSPENDED UNTIL FURTHER REPORT." The telegram was signed "SIGSBEE."[25]

Within minutes Long telephoned the White House and ordered a naval attaché to rouse the President. It was not yet two in the morning, and McKinley absorbed the Secretary's news with some difficulty. After hanging up he paced back and forth in front of the bewildered attaché, mumbling slowly to himself, "The *Maine* blown up! The *Maine* blown up!"[26]

Meanwhile, the telegraph wires were still humming, shocking the State Department, Navy Department, and New York newspaper offices into action. In little more than an hour Joseph Pulitzer's *World* had broadcast the first report of the disaster under a four-column headline. Not to be outdone, James Gordon Bennett spread the story across six columns of the *Herald,* and William Randolph Hearst gave it the entire front page of the *Journal.* "This means war," he told his night editors.[27] By dawn the news, complete with a transcript of Captain Sigsbee's report, was thumping onto front porches all over the country, and stimulating newsboys to new heights of shrillness. No doubt some of them repeated McKinley's own phrase, "The *Maine* blown up!" In the face of such a catastrophe, Presidents and paupers spoke with but one voice.

DAWN IN CUBA disclosed that the *Maine* was indeed a total wreck. The explosion, which took place somewhere in the forecastle, had jackknifed the keel up to the level of the bridge, killing 254 men instantly. A further 8 were so badly crushed and burned that they died one by one in hospitals ashore, bringing the death toll to 262. What was left of the ship lay wedged in the mud of Havana Harbor, with only a few blackened parts of the superstructure showing above water.[28]

As to the cause of the explosion, Spanish authorities were apparently no wiser than the Americans. Until the Navy Department's court of inquiry reached Cuba and made its report, there could be no official reaction on either side, beyond expressions of sincere sympathy in Havana. The Governor-General, Ramón Blanco y Erenas, had been seen crying openly in his palace, and the Bishop of Havana spared no expense in giving the dead an elaborate and dignified burial.[29]

Popular opinion in America was surprisingly muted,[30] in contrast to the clamor of the yellow press, thanks to Captain Sigsbee's wise plea for emotional restraint. There was also a widespread suspicion that the explosion had been internal and accidental. Secretary Long shared this view. The *Maine*'s forecastle, after all, had been packed with gunpowder, and its steel-walled magazines, laced around with electric wiring, needed only a short-circuit fire to convert the whole ship into a bomb. Besides, it was hard for thinking people to believe that Spain would deliberately sabotage an American cruiser with a "Secret Infernal Machine," as Hearst's *Journal* alleged.[31] Should the Court of Inquiry prove otherwise, of course, there was no question that the man in the street would expect a declaration of war at once.

This was an alternative President McKinley could hardly bear to contemplate. "I have been through one war," said the ex–Union major. "I have seen the dead piled up, and I do not want to see another."[32]

A RATHER MORE JUNIOR member of the Administration had no such scruples, and no doubts as to who was responsible for the disaster in Havana Harbor. "The *Maine* was sunk by an act of dirty treachery on the part of the Spaniards *I* believe," wrote the Assistant Secretary of the Navy.[33]

ROOSEVELT DOUBTED THAT the Court of Inquiry would be able to prove his theory of Spanish guilt. But he waited "on edge" for its initial findings, in the hope that they would at least absolve the Navy of responsibility for the explosion. Notwithstanding his private judgment, he scrupulously used the word "accident" in departmental correspondence.[34]

Hearst was not so patient. The *Maine*'s burned-out hulk had scarcely cooled before his artists were rendering pictures and diagrams to show exactly where and how the "Infernal Machine" had struck, in response to the push of a plunger on shore. On 18 February, the day before the official inquiry opened, the *Journal* published no fewer than eight pages of "conclusive" data, some of it so detailed that even Captain Sigsbee wondered if the paper did not have secret contacts with the saboteurs.[35] Sales of the paper reached an unprecedented one million that morning. Meanwhile the enterprising Pulitzer bought and dispatched a tugboat to Cuba to learn and report on "the truth." Within a week, his own paper, the *World,* had sold five million copies—"the largest circulation of any newspaper printed in any language in any country."[36]

More responsible newspapers, such as the *Evening Sun,* cautioned readers that the true facts of the disaster were not yet known, and might be slow in coming. The *Maine*'s bow was reported buried so deep in the mud of Havana Harbor that digging would be needed to get at the break. Day after day passed with no announcement by the court, until "Is there anything new about the *Maine*?" became an impatient refrain of everyday conversation. One passenger on a New York electric car was heard to remark that if the Assistant Secretary of the Navy took over the investigation, results would be forthcoming in no time. "Teddy Roosevelt is capable of going down to Havana, and going down in a diving-bell himself to see whether she was stove in or stove out."[37]

A HELPLESS VICTIM of the gathering tension was Edith Roosevelt, whose fever heightened to the point that Roosevelt, for the second time in his life, was confronted with the prospect of death in his bedroom. He confessed that he was so "extremely anxious" about her as to be numb to the full consequences of the *Maine* disaster. As for his son, "Hereafter I shall never press Ted either in body or mind. The fact is that the little fellow, who is peculiarly dear to me, has bidden fair to be all the things I would like to have been and wasn't, and it has been a great temptation to push him."[38]

On the morning of Friday, 25 February, Edith's weakness finally shocked him into seeking the best medical help available.[39] He sent to Johns Hopkins University for Sir William Osler, the great Canadian physician, and left for work as usual, in what torment posterity can only guess.

It so happened that John D. Long was also feeling the strain that morning. Since his violent awakening on the night of the sixteenth, the Secretary had been plagued with insomnia, along with various aches and pains, which he carefully noted in his diary. He had discovered that relief was to be had in "mechanical massage"—a treatment whereby a Washington osteopath strapped him into an electrical contrivance that soothingly jiggled his stomach and legs.[40] Long now felt the need of renewed treatment, so much so that around noon he resolved to take the rest of the day off, leaving Roosevelt in charge of the Department as Acting Secretary.

The "mechanical massage" was most satisfactory, and the Secretary proceeded to visit his corn doctor, after which he "walked about the streets in an aimless way" and finally headed for home,[41] unaware of the cablegram even then winging halfway around the world:

> DEWEY, HONG KONG: ORDER THE SQUADRON, EXCEPT THE MONOCACY, TO HONG KONG. KEEP FULL OF COAL. IN THE EVENT OF DECLARATION WAR SPAIN, YOUR DUTY WILL BE TO SEE THAT THE SPANISH SQUADRON DOES NOT LEAVE THE ASIATIC COAST, AND THEN OFFENSIVE OPERATIONS IN PHILIPPINE ISLANDS. KEEP OLYMPIA UNTIL FURTHER ORDERS.
>
> ROOSEVELT[42]

This momentous message, which Dewey later described as "the first step" toward American conquest of the Philippines,[43] was by no means the only order Roosevelt issued during his three or four hours as Acting Secretary. He sent similar instructions to "Keep full of coal" to squadron commanders all over the world, and to make sure they got it, authorized the Navy's coal-buying agents to purchase maximum stocks. He alerted European and South Atlantic stations to the possibility of war, and designated strategic points where they were to rendezvous in the event of a declaration.[44] He ordered huge supplies of reserve ammunition, requisitioned guns for a project auxiliary fleet, and summoned experts to testify on the firepower of the *Vesuvius*. He even sent demands to both Houses of Congress for legislation authorizing the unlimited recruitment of seamen.[45]

Having thus, in a single afternoon, placed the Navy in a state of such readiness it had not known since the Civil War, Roosevelt wrote a "strictly confidential" letter to warn Adjutant-General Tillinghast of the New York National Guard that the world situation was "sufficiently threatening" to warrant plans for statewide mobilization. "Pray remember that in some shape I want to go."[46]

After work he paid a courtesy call to Secretary Long. If he gave any report on his actions during the last four or five hours, it was of such masterly vagueness that no memorandum of the conversation appears in Long's diary. Yet something about Roosevelt's "enthusiastic and loyal" manner made the Secretary uneasy. "If I have a good night tonight, I shall rather feel that I ought to be back in the Department . . ."[47]

Refreshed by "splendid" slumbers, the Secretary hurried back to work next morning, Saturday, 26 February. He would have gone whether he felt better or not, "because during my short absence I find that Roosevelt, in his precipitate way, has come very near causing more of an explosion than happened to the *Maine* . . . the very devil seemed to possess him yesterday afternoon."[48]

War preparations in the Navy Department were now moving at such a pace that it would take Long days to slow the momentum, let alone stop it. The evidence is that the Secretary did not even try. For all his anger and embarrassment over "action most discourteous to me, because it suggests that there had been lack of attention," Long was forced to defer to the workings of an intellect larger and a political instinct sharper than his own. None of Roosevelt's letters and cables was countermanded. Even the historic order to Dewey was allowed to stand.[49] But Long resolved never to leave Roosevelt in sole charge of the department again. The times were too "trying," and the Assistant Secretary had severe family problems, which could only aggravate "his natural nervousness."[50]

Long did not understand that extreme crisis, whether of an intimate or public nature, had precisely the reverse effect on Theodore Roosevelt. The man's personality was cyclonic, in that he tended to become unstable in times of low pressure. The slightest rise in the barometer outside, and his turbulence smoothed into a whirl of coordinated activity, while a core of stillness developed within. Under maximum pressure Roosevelt was sunny, calm, and unnaturally clear. History was to show that his behavior as Acting Secretary of the Navy on 25 February 1898, was neither nervous nor spontaneous. It was the logical result of ten months of strategic planning, at the Navy Department and at the Metropolitan Club, in his correspondence with Captain Mahan, and on his walks with Captain Wood. "Someday," Roosevelt told the latter confidently, "they will understand."[51]

SIR WILLIAM OSLER examined Edith over the weekend and confirmed that she was "critically ill." There was an abdominal swelling which should be operated on at once.[52] For some unexplained reason Roosevelt ignored this warning and relied instead on more cautious advice. Edith lay wasting with fever for another week, too frail even to stand the sound of his voice reading to her. On 7 March, all opinions concurred that she must undergo surgery or die. He sat holding her hand until ether removed her from him.[53]

The operation revealed an abscess near the hip, and was completely successful.

ROOSEVELT'S CONTEMPT FOR "peace at any price men" rose to new heights as he watched William McKinley trying to avoid war in the weeks following the *Maine* disaster. Certainly the President showed a touching faith in the benign effects of gold currency. His first proposal was that the United States end the Cuban problem once and for all by buying the island outright for $300 million. But Congress showed reluctance to put such funds at his disposal, and the plan was dropped.[54] Then, on 25 February, the same day Roosevelt alerted Dewey to the imminence of war, McKinley reportedly suggested that if the Court of Inquiry found Spain responsible for the loss of the *Maine*, a large cash indemnity would assuage America's grief. Congress did not like this idea either.[55]

"An honest man, but weak," the French Ambassador, Jules

Cambon, remarked of McKinley.[56] By early March, when preliminary divers' reports indicated that a mine might have caused the explosion, the President was desperate enough to use scare tactics. He flabbergasted Joseph Cannon of the House Appropriations Committee with a request for $50 million, saying, "I must have money to get ready for war. I am doing everything possible to prevent war, but it must come, and we are not prepared for war."[57]

McKinley intended this to be his political masterstroke, silencing warmongers in both Washington and Madrid with a sudden display of Presidential decisiveness. At first the move seemed bound to succeed. Congress reacted with such shocked surprise—probably assuming the President was in possession of secret evidence of Spain's hostile intentions—that on 8 March the "Fifty Million Bill" became law without a single dissenting vote.[58] McKinley was authorized to spend the money as he saw fit. Spaniards and Cubans boggled at the wealth of a treasury which could produce such a huge appropriation in extra defense funds with no effect upon its credit. It was announced that the bulk of the appropriation would be given to the Navy Department for a crash program of naval expansion. Construction of three 12,500-ton battleships was to begin immediately, supplemented by sixteen destroyers, fourteen torpedo-boats, and four monitors. In addition, the department could assemble a large auxiliary fleet of ships purchased abroad.[59]

Roosevelt was not as overjoyed as he might have been by the President's apparent conversion to the doctrine of preparedness. Nine months before, at the Naval War College, he had warned against the futility of any such last-minute attempt at naval expansion. The *Maine* Court of Inquiry was due to publish its formal report any day now; if it corroborated his own suspicion of sabotage, "I believe it will be very hard to hold the country."[60] What use would McKinley's construction program be then? His only hope of improving the present strength of the Navy lay in the auxiliary-fleet program.

The ink on the Fifty Million Bill was scarcely dry before Roosevelt and Long began to review all available war vessels on the international market. News that Spain was already bargaining for ships inspired even the Secretary to a sense of urgency, although he continued to hope illogically that the buildup would have some deterrent effect.[61]

Roosevelt was given especial responsibility for purchasing merchant-men suitable for quick conversion into cruisers.[62] Among the many dealers who flocked to his office was one Charles R. Flint, who assessed him as "a young man at the very peak of his truly tremendous physical and mental energy." The Assistant Secretary was obviously in a tearing hurry. Flint started to tell him about the Brazilian ship *Nictheroy*, but Roosevelt knew all about her:

ROOSEVELT What is the price?
FLINT Half a million dollars.
ROOSEVELT (*snapping*) I will take her.
FLINT Good. I shall write you a letter—
ROOSEVELT Don't bother me with a letter. I haven't time to read it.

"We eventually did have a formal contract," Flint noted, ". . . dictated by Mr. Roosevelt. It was one of the most concise and at the same time one of the cleverest contracts I have ever seen. He made it a condition that the vessel should be delivered under her own steam at a specific point and within a specific period. In one sentence he thus covered all that might have been set forth in pages and pages of specifications. For the vessel *had* to be in first-class condition to make the time scheduled in the contract! Mr. Roosevelt always had that faculty of looking through details to the result to be obtained."[63]

EVERY NOW AND AGAIN President McKinley would indulge in a little banter with his Assistant Attending Surgeon, Leonard Wood. "Have you and Theodore declared war yet?"

"No, Mr. President, but we think you should."[64]

McKinley always shook his head when the handsome officer asked to be returned to active duty in the Army. Wood worked off his growing restlessness with more and more violent exercise with Roosevelt. The pair were now inseparable, and Roosevelt began to include Wood in his regular appeals to General Tillinghast. "I have a man here who rendered most gallant service with the regular Army against the Apaches, whom I should very much like to bring in with me if I could raise a regiment."[65]

MID-MARCH CAME and went. Forsythia, magnolia, hyacinths, and tulips sweetened Washington's warming air.[66] Still the Court of Inquiry delayed its *Maine* report. In an atmosphere of mounting political tension, Senator Redfield Proctor of Vermont prepared to deliver a speech on Cuba, which he had just visited.

Proctor, despite his friendly assistance in behalf of Dewey the previous fall, was by no means as "ardent for the war" as Roosevelt supposed. He was a careful, rather colorless politician, respected on all sides as a former Cabinet officer, a friend of big business, and an intimate of President McKinley. When he rose in the Senate on 17 March, the nation listened.[67]

Speaking coldly and dispassionately, Proctor confessed that he had gone to Cuba an isolationist, and returned with views inclining toward armed intervention. For the next several hours he cataloged the horrors he had seen, most notably the barbaric indignities of *reconcentrado* camps, where four hundred thousand peasants were living like pigs and dying like flies. After discussing Spain's promises of "autonomy" with certain eminent Cubans, he was convinced that the authorities would never yield power, and that the *insurrectos* would never cease to fight for it. "To me," he concluded, "the strongest appeal is not the barbarity practiced by Weyler, nor the loss of the *Maine* . . . but the spectacle of a million and a half of people, the entire native population of Cuba, struggling for freedom and deliverance from the worst misgovernment of which I ever had knowledge."[68]

The effect of this toneless speech, after months of fiery oratory for and against war, was so great as to convert large numbers of conservative Senators to the cause of *Cuba Libre*. Even more significantly, Wall Street's hitherto solid resistance to war now began to crumble, while business groups across the country expressed profound concern. Political observers predicted that if McKinley did not intervene upon receipt of the *Maine* report—whatever it said—*Cuba Libre* would become the campaign cry of the Democrats in the fall. "And who can doubt," asked the *Chicago Times-Herald,* "that by that sign . . . they will sweep the country?"[69]

Three days later, on 20 March, the President was confidentially informed that the Court of Inquiry would soon make a "unanimous report that the *Maine* was blown up by a submarine mine."[70] Some inkling of this message must have reached Roosevelt, who vented his wrath in a positively Elizabethan outburst to Brooks Adams. "The blood of the Cubans, the blood of women and children who have perished by the hundred thousand in hideous misery, lies at our door; and the blood of the murdered men of the *Maine* calls not for indemnity but for the full measure of atonement which can only come by driving the Spaniard from the New World."[71]

Events moved rapidly to a climax. On 24 March the Navy ordered squadron commanders to paint their white warships battle-gray.[72] On 25 March the American Minister in Madrid was warned that Spain's presence in Cuba was now considered "unbearable" by the Administration, and that unless an immediate diplomatic settlement was reached "the President . . . will lay the whole question before Congress."[73] And on 26 March, Roosevelt publicly confronted Senator Hanna, one of the last holdouts for peace, at a Gridiron Club after-dinner speech which had the whole capital agog. "We will have this war for the freedom of Cuba," he insisted, and smacked his fist into his palm. Then, wheeling and staring directly at Hanna, he said that "the interests of the business world and of financiers might be paramount in the Senate," but they were not so with the American people. Anyone who wanted to stand in the way of popular opinion "was welcome to try the experiment." Hanna's porcine neck turned purple, and his knuckles tightened on the arms of his chair, as applause filled the room. "Now, Senator," said his neighbor dryly, "may we please have war?"[74]

On 28 March the *Maine* report was finally made public. Although the court made no accusation of Spanish or Cuban guilt (there being absolutely no incriminating evidence), it confirmed that the explosion of the ship's forward magazines had been touched off by an external device, and absolved the U.S. Navy of any "fault or negligence" in the disaster.[75] Within hours a new ominous chant was drowning out calls of *Cuba Libre:*

Remember the MAINE!
To hell with Spain!

ALMOST UNNOTICED, in the general uproar, was a historic memo from Theodore Roosevelt to John D. Long. He wished to draw the Secretary's attention to the "flying machine" of his friend Professor S. P. Langley, having watched it briefly flutter over the Potomac River.[76] "The machine has worked," Roosevelt wrote. "It seems to me worth while for this Government to try whether it will not work on a large enough scale to be of use in the event of war." He recommended that a board of four scientifically trained officers be appointed to examine the strategic and economic aspects of producing flying machines "on a large scale." After some prodding, Secretary Long agreed, and named Charles H. Davis chairman of the board. By the time Davis reported on the "revolutionary" potential of air warfare, the Assistant Secretary had moved on to other things. It would be a long time before Roosevelt was recognized as the earliest official proponent of U.S. Naval Aviation.[77]

HAGGARD, SMUDGE-EYED, drugged, and occasionally tearful as the inevitability of war forced itself upon him, President McKinley managed to maintain statesmanlike decorum at least through the end of March.[78] While Congress debated the *Maine* report, he sent an ultimatum to Madrid courteously demanding a declaration of armistice in Cuba, effective 1 April. His terms stipulated that he be mediator of any subsequent negotiations for peace between the Spanish Government and the *insurrectos*. If no agreement was reached by 1 October (i.e., five weeks before the fall elections), McKinley would assume the role of final arbiter. He also insisted that all *reconcentrado* prisoners be set free, and that Spain cooperate with the United States in relief efforts.[79]

On Thursday, the last day of the month, Queen María Christina's ministers agreed to all points of McKinley's ultimatum except that of armistice. If the *insurrectos* wished to declare a truce themselves, well and good; Spain would not end four centuries of New World dominion with an ignominious acceptance of defeat.[80] McKinley saw no flexibility, only obstructionism, in this reply. After a weekend of sleepless deliberation, he decided, around midnight on 3 April, that he could not afford to gamble with Cuba, or with Congress, or with the Republican party any longer. The will of the American people, reiterated ad nauseam by Assistant Secretary Roosevelt (whom in self-defense, he had finally stopped seeing), must be heeded. McKinley went to bed and next morning began work on a war message to Congress.[81]

THE IMMINENCE OF WAR, like the imminence of death, is enough to give the most ardent soul a momentary pause, to reaffirm basic truths and articulate thoughts long held in suppression. In such frame of mind did Theodore Roosevelt write one of his best letters, to William Sturgis Bigelow, while Madrid pondered McKinley's ultimatum. For once he wrote calmly, reasonably, without any attempt at vulgar bravado:

> I say quite sincerely that I shall not go for my own pleasure. On the contrary if I should consult purely my own feelings I should earnestly hope that we would have peace. I like life very much. I have always led a joyous life. I like thought, and I like action, and it will be very bitter to me to leave my wife and children; and while I think I could face death with dignity, I have no desire before my time has come to go out into the everlasting darkness. . . . So I shall not go into a war with any undue exhilaration of spirits or in a frame in any way approaching recklessness or levity; but my best work here is done.
>
> . . . One of the commonest taunts directed at men like myself is that we are armchair and parlor jingoes who wish to see others do what we only advocate doing. I care very

> little for such a taunt, except as it affects my usefulness, but I cannot afford to disregard the fact that my power for good, whatever it may be, would be gone if I didn't try to live up to the doctrines I have tried to preach.[82]

Bigelow, unimpressed, told Secretary Long that Roosevelt might by the same token "wear no clothes in the street to prove that he is not a negro."[83]

THE PRESIDENT HAD DECIDED to send his war message up to the Hill on Monday, 4 April, but hints from Madrid that further concessions might be made *mañana* caused a postponement until Wednesday the sixth. Belligerents in Congress, who now comprised a majority, did not see why they should have to wait two more days, or for that matter two more hours, before settling with "the butchers of Spain." When the message was postponed a second time, in order to allow for free evacuation of American citizens from Cuba, frustrated legislators crowded the White House so threateningly that McKinley was obliged to lock the precious document in a safe. "By God," one Senator growled to Assistant Secretary of State Rufus Day, "don't your President know where the war-declaring power is lodged?"[84]

As always, Theodore Roosevelt produced the most quotable insult. "McKinley has no more backbone than a chocolate éclair."[85]

7 April was Holy Thursday in Havana. Under lowering skies, bands throughout the city played soothing sacred music. On Good Friday, Roosevelt assured his classmate Bob Bacon that he did not want to annex Cuba, only to free it from "medieval" fiefdom: "Let us fight on the broad grounds of securing the independence of a people who, whether they amount to much or not, have been treated with hideous brutality by their oppressors." On Saturday the American Minister in Madrid was told that at the behest of the Pope, Spain would declare an armistice in Cuba after all. On Easter Sunday, the Minister followed up with a personal appeal to McKinley: "I hope nothing will now be done to humiliate Spain." But on Monday, 11 April, the President finally sent his message to

Congress. Debate still rages as to whether by doing so McKinley confessed his inability to hold the dogs of war any longer, or whether a study of Cuban history persuaded him that Spain's promises were not to be believed. If he wanted peace, why did he not keep the message locked up, and announce that, thanks to the armistice, a diplomatic victory was at hand? If he wanted war, why did he not send in the message sooner? Perhaps the President realized that nothing he thought or said was of much consequence now. America, as Theodore Roosevelt kept saying, "needed" a war. "I have exhausted every effort to relieve the intolerable condition of affairs which is at our doors," McKinley told Congress. "Prepared to execute every obligation imposed upon me by the Constitution and the law, I await your action."[86]

DURING THE WEEK THAT Congress took to debate McKinley's message—pausing, once, to roar out an impromptu chorus of "The Battle Hymn of the Republic"[87]—Roosevelt redoubled his efforts to secure a commission in the Army. There was no question of the Assistant Secretary of the Navy applying for service at sea—"I shall be useless on a ship"—and he was equally determined not to become "part of the garrison in a fort."[88] Preliminary mobilization was ordered on 15 April, well in advance of any declaration of war, and he at once began to pester the Secretary of War, Russell A. Alger, and General-in-Chief Nelson A. Miles. Neither man impressed him. "Alger has no force whatsoever . . . Miles is a brave peacock," he wrote in a new pocket diary. "They both told me they could put 100,000 men in Tampa in 24 hours! The folly, the lack of preparation, are almost inconceivable."[89]

Frustration at the slowness of Congress to act, at his own inability to get a place in any New York regiment, vented itself in further jabs of angry ink. "The President still feebly is trying for peace. His weakness and vacillation are even more ludicrous than painful. . . . Reed . . . is malignantly bent on preventing all preparation for war." Fortunately there was one department in the Administration ready and willing to fight. "Long is at last awake . . . I have the Navy in good shape."[90]

Posterity will not grudge him that boast. The Navy was, indeed, in superb fighting trim as he prepared to resign from office.[91] What it lacked in sheer weight of metal is made up in efficiency and combat toughness. Never before had it been so strategically deployed; never was it so ready for instant action.[92] In comparison, the Spanish Navy, though numerically superior in ships and manpower, was ill-armed, untrained, and grossly mismanaged.[93] Thanks to Roosevelt's ceaseless publicizing of the service, schoolchildren across America could recognize and chant the praises of such romantic vessels as the *Iowa,* the *Oregon,* and the *Vesuvius.* His revolutionary Personnel Report, though not yet enacted into law, had already brought about a new harmony between staff and line officers, easing one of the Navy's most difficult administration problems. His enthusiastic championship of torpedo-boats and submarines, not to mention Professor Langley's "flying machine," had pushed naval technology several years into the future. He had magnified the scope and influence of the Assistant Secretaryship. He had personally set the stage for one of the greatest sea dramas in American history. Most important of all, from the point of view of his later career, he had acquired a fund of naval expertise unmatched by any politician in the country.[94] It would prove a priceless asset when he began to deal with "ships, ships, ships" again, as President of the United States.

At three o'clock in the morning on 19 April 1898, Congress resolved for Cuban independence. Without waiting for the diplomatic niceties of a final ultimatum, rejection, and declaration, the country whooped to war.[95] Roosevelt was surely reminded that he had assumed his duties as Assistant Secretary of the Navy on 19 April 1897. It had taken him exactly one year to bring the war about.

DISCORDANT CRIES OF PROTEST rose above the patriotic din when news leaked out that he had applied for a position on the staff of General Fitzhugh Lee. "What on earth is this report of Roosevelt's resignation?" wrote an agitated Henry Adams. "Is his wife dead? Has he quarreled with everybody? Is he quite mad?" Winthrop

Chanler accepted the last alternative. "I really think he is going mad . . . Roosevelt is wild to fight and hack and hew . . . of course this ends his political career. Even Cabot says this." John D. Long, too, doubted Roosevelt's sanity. "He has lost his head," the Secretary typed sadly in his diary. ". . . He means well, but it is one of those cases of aberration—desertion—vain-glory; of which he is entirely unaware."[96]

Nearly every major newspaper in the country urged Roosevelt to stay on in the Navy Department, where his services were now needed more than ever. Even the *Sun,* while acknowledging "the instinctive glowing chivalry of his nature," lamented the Assistant Secretary's decision. "Is not his work of organizing war infinitely more important to the country than any part, however useful and glorious, which he could play as an officer in the field? . . . We are convinced that it is." One acid opinion, expressed by John Jay Chapman of the reformist periodical *Nursery,* was that "his departure was the cowardly act of a brave man."[97]

But all this clamor only served to convince Roosevelt that he must do what he had to do. Evidently his friends and admirers had never quite believed his vow to fight when the time for battle came. It was therefore vital that he prove himself, once and for all, a man of his word. If he backed down now, what of any future promises he might make to the American people? "I know perfectly well that one is never able to analyze with entire accuracy all of one's motives," he wrote in formal reply to the *Sun.* "But . . . I have always intended to act up to my preachings if occasion arose. Now the occasion has arisen, and I ought to meet it."[98]

ON WEDNESDAY, 20 APRIL, President McKinley signed the Cuba resolution, with its noble disclaimer of any "intention to exercise sovereignty, jurisdiction, or control over said Island," and its promise "to leave the government and control of the Island to its people" once liberation had been achieved.[99] On Thursday the American Minister in Madrid was told that diplomatic relations between the United States and Spain had been severed. On Friday morning before dawn, warships of the North Atlantic Squadron slipped quietly out of Key West Harbor and headed southeast into the Caribbean.[100]

On Saturday the President issued a call for 125,000 volunteers to swell the ranks of the 28,000-man Regular Army. Included in this general summons was an extraordinary provision for three regiments "to be composed exclusively of frontiersmen possessing special qualifications as horsemen and marksmen."[101] Secretary Alger would not have to look far for someone to be colonel of the first regiment, since the nation's most prominent frontiersman, horseman, and marksman was already pounding on his desk at the War Department. That same day, he offered the command to Theodore Roosevelt.[102]

As long ago as 1886 Roosevelt had talked of leading a troop of "harum-scarum roughriders" into battle, without much conviction that such a dream would ever come true. Now, miraculously, it had; fate seemed to be adapting itself to his own peculiar abilities. Here at last was supreme opportunity for personal and military glory. Yet with supreme self-control Roosevelt turned the offer down. He told the Secretary that while he had been a captain in the New York National Guard, he lacked experience in hard military organization. He was sure he could "learn to command the regiment in a month," but that very month might make the difference between fighting at the front or languishing behind and missing the war. He would be happy to serve as lieutenant colonel if the colonelcy went to Leonard Wood.[103]

After some deliberation, Alger accepted this arrangement.[104]

THE FOLLOWING MORNING, Sunday, 24 April, Secretary Long dispatched the order that Dewey had been expecting since Roosevelt's "Keep full of coal" cable of two months before. Within forty-eight hours of receipt the Commodore put out of Hong Kong and vanished into the vastness of the China Sea.[105]

WAR PROPER WAS DECLARED by Spain the same day. Icily formal to the last, the United States replied on 25 April with a declaration backdated to 23 April.[106] But by now Roosevelt was too busy to be bothered with diplomatic trivialities. As chairman of the new Naval War Board, he was responsible for putting into execution the war plan which he had argued before President McKinley the previous September.[107] As second-in-command of the First U.S. Volunteer Cavalry, he had to assist Leonard Wood in recruiting and equipping the new regiment.

Although neither man had yet received his commission, the announcement of their appointments was made on 25 April, and by 27 April sacks of applications were thumping in from all parts of the country.[108] The majority of these applications (which eventually numbered twenty-three thousand, enough for an entire division) were addressed to Roosevelt. He, Secretary Alger, the President, and Congress might imagine Wood to be the true commander of the regiment, but the American public was not fooled. Already Western newspapers were hailing the formation of "Teddy's Terrors," and every day brought a fresh crop of suggested names, all with the same alliterative connotation: "Teddy's Texas Tarantulas," "Teddy's Gilded Gang," "Teddy's Cowboy Contingent," "Teddy's Riotous Rounders" (and then, gradually, as the Lieutenant Colonel let it be known he did not like the nickname), "Roosevelt's Rough 'Uns," and "Roosevelt's Rough Riders." The last name stuck, and was soon common usage. "Colonel Wood," commented the *New York Press,* "is lost sight of entirely in the effulgence of Teethadore."[109]

Wood, fortunately, was an offstage personality who did not mind operating in the shadow that surrounds the spotlight. Roosevelt could grin and posture as much as he liked, as long as he heeded quiet orders coming from the wings. Moving with remarkable speed and efficiency, the colonel completed in two days all the preliminary work of organizing the Rough Riders in Washington. Then, leaving Roosevelt behind to handle Northeastern applications and ensure that his requisitions passed smoothly through the Ordnance and Quartermaster Bureaus, Wood departed for the regimental muster camp in San Antonio, Texas.[110]

LATE ON THE AFTERNOON of 1 May 1898, Americans were stunned to hear of a near-incredible naval victory by an unfamiliar commander in an archipelago on the other side of the world—about ten thousand miles away from what they imagined to be the likely theater of naval operations. In seven hours of stately maneuvers off Manila, George Dewey had destroyed Spain's Asiatic Squadron. Almost every enemy ship was sunk, deserted, or in flames; not one American life had been lost, in contrast to 381 Spanish casualties. The victorious Commodore (who was promptly promoted to Rear-Admiral) modestly ascribed his success to "the ceaseless routine of hard work and preparation" demanded of him by the Navy Department. His government patron lost no time in taking due credit. "You have made a name for the nation, and the Navy, and yourself," wrote Theodore Roosevelt on 2 May. "And I can't say how pleased I am to think that I had any share in getting you the opportunity that you have used so well."[111]

Assured of leaving the Navy Department in triumph, he telegraphed Brooks Brothers for an "ordinary cavalry lieutenant-colonel's uniform in blue Cravenette," and prepared to receive his commission on 6 May. Some instinct to have done with his past, with youth itself now he was nearing forty, caused him to sell off his few remaining cattle and give away his Elkhorn Ranch to Sylvane Ferris. He took out life insurance. He drove his recuperating wife through the blossoming countryside. He wrote a moving farewell to Secretary Long. "I don't suppose I shall ever again have a chief under whom I shall enjoy serving as I have enjoyed serving under you . . . I hate to leave you more than I can say." He acknowledged gifts of maple syrup, poetry, clockwork, and spurs. When he left for San Antonio on 12 May he took the spurs with him.[112] It remained only to win them.

"A man of unbounded energy and force," Secretary Long remarked in his diary. "He thinks he is following his highest ideal, whereas, in fact, as without exception every one of his friends advises him, he is acting like a fool. And, yet, how absurd all this will sound if, by some turn of fortune, he should accomplish some great thing and strike a very high mark."[113]

"Without waiting for diplomatic niceties . . .
the country whooped to war."

A troop of black volunteer soldiers en route to Tampa, 1898.

CHAPTER 24

The Rough Rider

These and many more like these,
With King Olaf sailed the seas.

"THE COMMANDER-IN-CHIEF of the American Army," reported a Madrid newspaper in the early days of the war, "is one Ted Roosevelt, formerly a New York policeman." By way of background information, the paper added that Roosevelt had been "born near Haarlem," but "emigrated to America when young," and was educated at "Harvard Academy, a commercial school." He now went about the country accompanied by a bodyguard of toughs, fittingly known as "rough-rioters."[1]

Commercial or not, Harvard supplied a sizable number of recruits to the First U.S. Volunteer Cavalry, as did the other Ivy League schools and the better clubs of Manhattan and Boston. Roosevelt had enlisted fifty of these "gentleman rankers," as he called them, in order to give the regiment its necessary tone. He made it clear, however, that no man would earn a commission save through bravery and merit, and that once in Texas, "the cowboys and Knickerbockers ride side by side."[2] In choosing them, Roosevelt paid as much attention to physique as ancestry. There was his old classmate Woodbury Kane, a yachty dandy who "fought with the

"This was the rocking-chair period of the war."

Piazza of the Tampa Bay Hotel, early summer 1898.

same natural ease as he dressed."[3] There was Joseph Sampson Stevens, the world's greatest polo player.[4] There were Dudley Dean, the legendary Harvard quarterback; Bob Wrenn, tennis champion of the United States; and Hamilton Fish, ex-captain of the Columbia crew. There were high-jumpers from Yale and football players from Princeton, and huntsmen with names like Wadsworth and Tiffany. For good measure Roosevelt added a Scottish friend of Cecil Spring Rice, and two blue-blooded Englishmen, one of whom insisted on arriving in San Antonio with a delicate walking-stick, in the belief that "cavalrymen carried canes."[5]

The Lieutenant Colonel admitted to some qualms in sending such men to Texas, and their appearance caused much amusement among the more leathery Rough Riders.[6]

ROOSEVELT REACHED San Antonio on the morning of 15 May 1898, wearing a new fawn uniform with canary-yellow trim.[7] The official name of his destination, in the state fair grounds two miles outside of town, was Camp Wood, but a sign at the railroad station already proclaimed, "This Way to Camp of Roosevelt's Rough Riders."[8]

There was a wave of disappointment among the recruits when he arrived at regimental headquarters. "The big objection," recalled one onlooker, "was that he wore glasses."[9] After years in Dakota, Roosevelt was used to this attitude, and if he felt mistrust in their stare, it did not bother him. He gazed back at them through the same offending lenses, with interest but no feelings of novelty. These weather-beaten faces and sinewy, bowlegged bodies were as familiar to him as the aristocratic lineaments of Woodbury Kane (who, he noticed with approval, was cooking and washing dishes for a troop of New Mexicans). He had ridden many a roundup with such men in his youth, and proved himself as tough as they. He had described them intimately in *Thomas Hart Benton* and *The Winning of the West.* As he got to know their thousand names—soon he would memorize every one—time and again it was as if the creatures of his pen were reincarnated before him. Here was young Douglass Campbell, grandson of the man who led the cavalry up King's Mountain in 1780.[10] Here was an Indian named Adair: Roosevelt had spent hours poring over the "ponderous folio" his Cherokee ancestors had written 150 years before.[11] Here was another Indian, named Colbert—perhaps one might trace his origins back to the half-Scottish, half-Chickasaw Colberts who dominated the eastern Mississippi in the eighteenth century. Roosevelt interviewed him and found that he was "as I had supposed, a descendant of the old Chickasaw chiefs."[12] Perusal of the muster-rolls disclosed a Clark and a St. Clair, no Boone but two Crocketts, and several apiece of Adams, Hamilton, and Jackson.[13] Surely, in those early days of dust and mounted drill, the line between past and present (never clearly demarcated in Roosevelt's mind) must have blurred until he found himself galloping, not across the plains of Texas, but over the wooded hills of Revolutionary Kentucky. "More than ever," he confessed to Henry Cabot Lodge, "I fail to get the relations of this regiment and the universe straight."[14]

DAWN AT CAMP WOOD disclosed a flat grassy park, rather the worse for hoofprints, five hundred wedges of dewy canvas, a grove of cottonwood trees, and in the background the sluggish silver of the San Antonio River. A certain surgical precision in the layout of tents, the neatly swept "streets," and gleaming latrines all testified to the medical instincts of the commanding officer.[15] Reveille sounded at 5:30, and within half an hour a thousand bleary men were answering roll call.[16] The range of the accents, from New England drawl to Southwestern twang, from Idaho burr to Pawnee grunt, was matched by an early-morning variety of costume that Wood may have deplored, but Roosevelt cheerfully tolerated. The "Knicks" and Harvard men wore Abercrombie and Fitch shirts and custom leather boots; the polo set wore British breeches, tight at the knee and blossoming around the thighs; the cowboys, who numbered about three-quarters of the total regiment, scorned their Army felt hats for sombreros, and insisted on carrying their own guns.[17]

At 6:10 the ranks broke for stable call—twenty minutes of rubbing down and feeding horses, followed by breakfast. Between

8:30 and 9:30 the animals were watered in the river, then saddled up for mounted drill. This, the main exercise of the day, lasted at least an hour and a half under the climbing sun. Roosevelt was required to supervise it while Colonel Wood occupied himself in the cool of headquarters with problems of requisition and supply. Clouds of dust reduced visibility to nil as the troopers thundered raggedly across the Texas plain. "Our lines were somewhat irregular," Roosevelt admitted when describing the early maneuvers.[18] According to other accounts, there were often no lines at all. It would have taxed the powers of a Genghis Khan to place a thousand individualistic riders, accustomed to the freedom of polo, hunting, and the open range, upon a thousand half-broken horses, and then get them to advance, wheel, fan out, and divide in formation. Roosevelt's high-pitched orders led to endless bucking, biting, striking, and kicking. His first success was rewarded by an anonymous salute of six-shooter fire, causing a stampede into the San Antonio River.[19]

Spare time before "dinner" at 1:30 was usually given over to bronco-busting. Then the horses were put to rest while the men assembled on the parade-ground for skirmish practice, again under Roosevelt's command. High-heeled boots and bandy legs caused further problems of drill: the order to change step often led to a general domino-like collapse of the ranks. When Roosevelt reproved Trooper Billy McGinty for his inability to keep step, the little Oklahoman replied that "he was pretty sure he could keep step on horseback."[20]

By 3:30 a thick coating of dust, mixed with sweat, had rendered the likes of William Tiffany and "Dead Shot" Jim Simpson indistinguishable. Only two spigots of brackish water were available for shower baths, so most men took their soap down to the river.[21]

There followed another stable call at 4:00, and another roll call at 5:00, then the troops reassembled for fifty minutes of dress parade. Scrubbed and spruce in their slouch hats, blue-flannel shirts, brown trousers, leggings, and boots, and sporting loosely knotted neckerchiefs—already the Rough Rider emblem—they looked, in Roosevelt's fond opinion, "exactly as a body of cowboy cavalry should look."[22]

After supper at 7:00, there was night school for both commissioned and non-commissioned officers until final roll call at 8:30. But Roosevelt himself did not allow the "Dismiss" to cut short his military education for the day. With obsessive dedication he carried on by himself. "He was serenely unselfconscious," recalled Quartermaster Coleman. "He would practice giving commands within fifty feet of half the regiment as earnestly as he would have done had he been alone in a desert."[23]

Taps sounded at 9:00. As darkness spread from tent to tent, the Lieutenant Colonel turned up his table lamp and began to write his nightly quota of letters.

> *Dear Mr. President,* This is just a line to tell you that we are in fine shape. Wood is a dandy Colonel, and I really think that the rank and file of this regiment are better than you would find in any other regiment anywhere. In fact, in all the world there is not a regiment I would so soon belong to. The men are picking up the drill wonderfully . . . We are ready now to leave at any moment, and we earnestly hope that we will be put into Cuba with the very first troops; the sooner the better. . . .[24]

Quietness descended over Camp Wood, broken only by the occasional bray of a pack-mule, and the creaking of loose fence-planks, as one by one Roosevelt's Rough Riders squeezed out of bounds and headed for the fleshpots of San Antonio.[25]

IT DID NOT take the men long to size Roosevelt up, to compare him with "Old Poker Face," and find Wood wanting. Although some cowpunchers were put off by the New Yorker's overbearing courtesy ("he was polite almost to the extent of making one uneasy"),[26] they could not help being impressed by his drive. "It was evident to all who met him that he was tremendously ambitious."[27] They noticed that Wood often asked advice, but seldom information; Roosevelt asked information, but never advice.[28] For all the punctilious deference of the older man to the younger, for all Wood's mastery of military bureaucracy (the Rough Riders were easily the best-armed and best-equipped regiment in the Army),[29] there was no doubt, within a week of Roosevelt's arrival, as to whom they considered to be colonel *malgré lui.* Wood knew it, and knew that his superiors in Washington knew it. "I realized that if this campaign lasted for any considerable length of time I would be kicked upstairs to make room for Roosevelt."[30]

Yet the Colonel did not hesitate to exercise authority over his subordinate when he deemed it necessary. Roosevelt was still inexperienced in matters of military discipline, and when Wood heard that he had treated an entire squadron to unlimited beer—apparently as a reward for their improvement in drill—he made a pointed remark over supper "that, of course, an officer who would go out with a large batch of men and drink with them was quite unfit to hold a commission." There was a dead silence. Later Roosevelt visited Wood privately in his tent and confessed to the crime. "I wish to say, sir, that I agree with what you said. I consider myself the damndest ass within ten miles of this camp. Good night."[31]

Toward the end of May it was evident that the Rough Riders had already been forged into a warlike cavalry regiment. In the modest opinion of its Lieutenant Colonel, "it could whip Caesar's Tenth Legion."[32] The speed of this transformation was not altogether surprising, considering the administrative efficiency of the Wood/Roosevelt team, and the fitness and equestrian skills of the troopers (over twenty applicants had been rejected for every one accepted).[33] A local newspaper reported the men "sunburned and . . . impatient to get away." There was not the slightest hint as to where the War Department intended to send them next, or indeed if they would ever get to Cuba. Outbursts of bellicose fervor began to disturb the peace of San Antonio. Two Texan troopers shot a mirrored saloon into smithereens, and the proprietor was too scared to ask for damages. On 26 May, a party of concertgoing Rough Riders were asked to discharge their revolvers discreetly during an outdoor performance of *The Cavalry Charge,* and responded with such gusto that the lights blew out, causing instant pandemonium.[34] "If we don't get them to Cuba quickly to fight Spaniards," Wood remarked, "there is great danger that they'll be fighting one another."[35]

A day or two later the Colonel received a telegram from Washington. He read it expressionlessly, then turned and looked at his second-in-command. Suddenly the two men were hugging each other like schoolboys, while war-whoops resounded through the camp. The Rough Riders had been ordered to proceed to Tampa, Florida, for immediate embarkation on transport ships, "destination unknown."[36]

BEFORE LEAVING SAN ANTONIO the Rough Riders dressed in full uniform and posed in formation for the official regimental photograph. Spread out across the plain, their mounts obedient now and immaculately groomed, they made a majestic military display. But the picture was marred by a slight irregularity of drill: Lieutenant Colonel Roosevelt had absentmindedly allowed his horse to stand a few feet in advance of Colonel Wood's.[37]

THE ROUGH RIDERS STRUCK CAMP at 5:00 A.M. on 29 May 1898. They expected to be off in a matter of hours, but so great was the difficulty of coaxing twelve hundred horses and mules aboard seven different trains that it was after midnight when the last door clanged shut. Somebody then discovered that the passenger cars were missing, and would not be available until dawn; so officers and men lay down in the brush beside the tracks to snatch what sleep they could.[38]

At 6:00 A.M. next morning the Rough Rider convoy finally pulled out of San Antonio. "I doubt," Roosevelt wrote afterward, "if anybody who was on the trip will soon forget it."[39] For four sweltering days the seven trains chugged eastward and southward, strewing a trail of cinders, vomit, and manure across the face of the old Confederacy. Roosevelt, who was in charge of the rear sections, punished all cases of drunkenness severely, "in order to give full liberty to those who would not abuse it."[40] Two or three times a day, as he read his way steadily through Demolins's *Supériorité des Anglo-Saxons,* he sent buckets of hot coffee back to his men to compensate for lack of hot food.[41] But the most eagerly awaited refreshments were free watermelons and jugs of iced beer at stopping-places en route. These were passed through the car windows by "girls in straw hats and freshly starched dresses of many colors," whose beauty some troopers would remember for half a century.[42] No Louisiana village or Mississippi cotton-depot was so remote as to have escaped Rough Rider newspaper publicity: exotic celebrities like Woodbury Kane and Hamilton Fish were requested to appear so often that the cowpunchers took to impersonating them. Everywhere, of course, there were gap-toothed cries for "Teddy."[43]

As he waved at grizzled old Southerners, and they in turn waved the Stars and Stripes back at him, Roosevelt reflected that only thirty-three years before these men had been enemies of the Union.[44] It took war to heal the scars of war; attack upon a foreign power to bring unity at home. But what future war would heal the scars of this one?

ON THE EVENING OF 2 June the seven trains ground to a halt on the pine flats of western Florida, six miles short of Tampa. For some reason railroad employees refused to haul the regiment any farther, so the Rough Riders were forced to complete their journey on horseback, dragging their equipment behind in commandeered wagons. No official welcome awaited them at the sleep-shrouded Fifth Corps campground outside of town; Roosevelt and Wood had to ride through acres of dim tents before stumbling, almost by accident, upon their allotted space.[45]

Next morning they awoke to see the largest gathering of the U.S. Army in four decades. For miles in every direction a pitched city spread out across the savanna. Under the moss-hung pines twenty-five thousand troops, mostly Regulars, were enduring what one of them called "the bane of a soldier's life—waiting for something to happen." Tampa itself lay a mile or so away, shimmering in coastal haze: it looked like some Middle Eastern mirage, with silver domes and minarets.[46]

Half an hour's ride into the freshening sea breeze disclosed that the mirage was real. Here, among mosquito-swamps, derelict shacks, and ankle-deep drifts of sand, stood Henry B. Plant's famous "folly," a five-hundred-room hotel in authentic Moorish style, with its own casino, ballroom, swimming pool, and peacock park. On its street-wide verandah, Army and Navy officers, newspaper correspondents, foreign attachés, and pretty Cuban women rocked in elegant bentwoods, sipping iced tea and champagne.[47]

"This was the rocking-chair period of the war," wrote Richard Harding Davis of the *New York Herald,* himself an indefatigable rocker. "It was an army of occupation, but it occupied the piazza of a big hotel."[48]

Roosevelt dismissed the Tampa Bay Hotel with a single haughty sentence in his own memoir of those days: "We spent very little time there."[49] Actually he spent three nights in its luxurious accommodations, for Edith came down to Tampa, and Colonel Wood discreetly allowed him leave "from before dinner to after breakfast each day."[50] Having attended Edith through much of her recent illness, that gentlemanly officer must have sensed her need to be with Theodore now that she was returned to health and strength.

CONSPICUOUS AMONG THE ELITE who daily crossed the Tampa Bay Hotel lobby was dropsical, gouty old Brigadier General William Rufus Shafter, commander of the Fifth Corps. At three hundred pounds, or one-seventh of a ton, Shafter was barely able to heave himself up the grand stairway;[51] yet President McKinley had chosen him to lead an expeditionary force over the hills of southern Cuba, showing equal faith in the Army's seniority system and its ability to transport ponderous cargo.

"Not since the campaign of Crassus against the Parthians," in Roosevelt's later opinion, "has there been so criminally incompetent a General as Shafter."[52] Yet it was hard in the early days of June 1898 not to sympathize with that harassed officer, for President McKinley was proving an exceedingly erratic Commander-in-Chief. Bent, apparently, on acting as his own Secretary of War, he had been sending Shafter contradictory orders ever since the Battle of Manila. Dewey's overwhelming victory had turned both the President and Secretary Long into war-hawks overnight; their first reaction to the news had been to endorse Roosevelt's naval/military invasion plan, over the objection of Commanding General Miles, on 2 May.[53] General Shafter was ordered to prepare for immediate departure from Tampa (although the Volunteers were still in training), and on 8 May the President had increased the project landing force from ten thousand to seventy thousand. But then McKinley discovered that there was not enough ammunition in the United States to keep such an army firing for one hour in battle, and an urgent cancellation order flew to Tampa.[54] Shafter's force was scaled down to twenty-five thousand by the end of May, and the telegrams from Washington became querulous: "When will you leave? Answer at once." Shafter wired back that he could not sail before 4 June.[55]

Roosevelt happened to ride into town that day, the morning after his midnight arrival in camp. One look at the half-empty transport ships swinging idly at anchor in Tampa Bay—nine miles away at the end of a single railroad track—was enough to convince him, if not General Shafter, that the Fifth Corps would not sail for another few days at least. "No words can paint the confusion," he wrote in his diary on 5 June. "No *head;* a breakdown of both the railroad and military system of the country."[56]

While train after overloaded train jostled for possession of the track, and desperate quartermasters broke open dozens of unmarked cars to see if they contained guns, uniforms, grain, or medicinal brandy, the Rough Riders joined other cavalry regiments at drill on the limitless flats. Richard Harding Davis escorted Edith Roosevelt and a party of foreign attachés to watch some formal exercises on 6 June.[57]

Half-aware that he was witnessing the last great mounted maneuvers in American military history, Davis regretted that more of his countrymen could not be there to enjoy the spectacle. For over an hour two thousand riders galloped back and forth, sweeping through the spindly trees as waves comb through reeds. A cool onshore breeze seemed at times to drive them on, at others to break them up into eddies and ripples of faster and slower motion. The air rang with cheers and the steely percussion of swords (the Rough Riders, flamboyant as ever, brandishing Cuban machetes instead of regulation sabers), and finally, in response to a barked order, the regiments deployed into shoulder-to-shoulder file abreast. "There will be few such chances again," Davis wrote, "to see a brigade of cavalry advancing through a forest of palms in a line two miles long. . . ."[58]

Later that morning Roosevelt received the shocking news that General Shafter had decided to send no horses to Cuba except those belonging to senior officers.[59] What was more, there would be room on the ships for only eight of the twelve Rough Rider troops. If the remaining volunteers wished to charge to glory, they would have to do it on foot.

THE NEXT THIRTY-SIX HOURS were not pleasant for Wood or Roosevelt. They had to decide who would go and who would stay, and had to endure the sight of officers and troopers alike bursting into tears on receiving the bad news. The lucky ones, numbering some 560 men, could hardly bemoan the loss of their horses. "We would rather crawl on all fours than not go."[60]

Coffee was being served at the Tampa Bay Hotel on the evening of Tuesday, 7 June, when General Shafter was summoned to the Western Union office by order of the President of the United States. His instructions, tapped out on a direct line from the White House, were terse: "You will sail immediately as you are needed at destination."[61]

McKinley's urgency was prompted by an agonized cable from Admiral Sampson, who had been blockading the Spanish Cuba Squadron in Santiago Harbor since 1 June: "If 10,000 men were here, city and fleet would be ours within 48 hours." Shafter could only tap back, "I will sail tomorrow morning. Steam cannot be gotten up earlier."[62]

Notwithstanding this guarded reply, the words "sail immediately" ran like an electric shock through the Fifth Corps. By midnight the Rough Riders were packed and waiting with their baggage at the track which had been assigned to them. No train appeared, and after a long period of waiting new orders arrived to proceed to another track. There was no train there, either; but just after dawn some filthy coal-cars hove into sight, and, to quote Roosevelt, "these we seized." The fact that the locomotive was pointing the wrong way did not deter them. "By various arguments" the engineer was persuaded to steam the nine miles to Port Tampa in reverse gear.[63]

Wednesday's sun disclosed what appeared to be a black regiment descending from the coal-cars and jostling for space on the already overcrowded quay. More men kept arriving every few minutes, until the boards groaned with a swarming mass of human freight. Thirty transport ships were taking on the last bales of food and equipment, but it was anybody's guess which regiments were to follow onto what vessel. While the Rough Riders (now mockingly called "Wood's Weary Walkers")[64] stood sweating patiently in the sun, Wood and Roosevelt fanned out in search of Shafter's chief quartermaster, Colonel C. F. Humphrey. "After an hour's rapid and industrious search" they happened upon him almost simultaneously. Humphrey said they were welcome to a transport named *Yucatán,* which had not yet come in to the quay. Wood, sensing a certain lack of interest in the quartermaster's voice, jumped into a passing launch and hijacked the *Yucatán* in midstream. Meanwhile Roosevelt learned that the ship had already been assigned to two other regiments—the 2nd Regular Infantry and the 71st New York Volunteers.

> Accordingly, I ran at full speed to our train; and leaving a strong guard with the baggage, I double-quicked the rest of the regiment up to the boat, just in time to board her as she came into the quay, and then to hold her against the Second Regulars and the Seventy-first, who had arrived a little too late, being a shade less ready than we were in the matter of individual initiative.

Roosevelt listened with polite sympathy to the protests from the quay, but his final argument was conclusive: "Well, we seem to have it."[65] The 71st marched off in a huff, accompanied by a shower of coal from the *Yucatán*'s bunkers.

Presently Roosevelt noticed two photographers standing beside a huge tripod and camera. "What are you young men up to?"

"We are the Vitagraph Company, Colonel Roosevelt, and we are going to Cuba to take moving pictures of the war."

The photographers found themselves being escorted up the gangplank. "I can't take care of a regiment," said nineteenth-century America's greatest master of press relations, "but I might be able to handle two more."[66]

CONSIDERING THE LOGISTICAL problem of moving 16,286 troops along a single stretch of track between 9:00 P.M. Tuesday and 5:00 P.M. Wednesday, the "criminally incompetent" General Shafter did not do too badly. He had no choice but to leave the remainder of his corps behind in Tampa, owing to wild miscalculations of available berth space; as it was the ships were so crammed with men that bodies covered every foot of deck. Convinced that he had done everything that God and gout permitted him, Shafter struggled over the side of his flagship *Segurança* at about 4:30 P.M. and ordered her to lead the way out of the harbor. Then he went below and eased his weary bulk into bed.[67]

The *Segurança* had barely slipped her moorings when a shrilling tug halted her with a telegram:

> WAIT UNTIL YOU GET FURTHER ORDERS BEFORE YOU SAIL. ANSWER QUICK.
> R. A. ALGER, SECRETARY OF WAR.[68]

It transpired that three unidentified warships had been sighted in the Gulf, apparently lying in wait for the invasion fleet.

While the Navy rushed to investigate, Shafter ordered his armada back to quayside. It was out of the question to disembark, since orders to proceed might be received at any minute; so for the next six days sixteen thousand men baked like sardines in their steel ovens.[69]

As if enduring some Ancient Mariner's nightmare, Theodore Roosevelt paced the decks of the *Yucatán,* breathing the stench of dirty men and dying mules. Garbage clogged the quayside canal until it festered in the sun; the drinking-water tanks turned brackish, and Army rations of "fresh beef," when opened, proved to be so disgusting that three out of every four cans were thrown overboard. A move out to midstream on 10 June afforded partial relief, although sharks made swimming hazardous.[70] In any case most of the Rough Riders, having been brought up in the desert, were too transfixed by the sight of seawater to venture into it.[71] Periodically Roosevelt went down to his cabin to vent his wrath in long letters to Henry Cabot Lodge. "I did not feel that I was fit to be Colonel of this regiment . . . but I am more fit to command a Brigade or a Division or attend to this whole matter of embarking and sending the army than many of those whose business it is. . . ."[72]

At last, in the late afternoon of 14 June, the Navy reported that all was safe in the Gulf. Under the bored gaze of three black women, three soldiers, and a gang of stevedores, the largest armed force ever to leave American shores swung out of the bay and steamed southeast into the gathering dusk, until Tampa Light shrank to a pinpoint, wavered, and went out.

CHAPTER 25

The Wolf Rising in the Heart

So into the strait
Where his foes lie in wait,
Gallant King Olaf
Sails to his fate!

NIGHT FELL, and the band of the 2nd Infantry struck up "The Star-Spangled Banner." Almost on cue, General Shafter's invasion fleet lit up like a galaxy, spangling the dark sea from one horizon to the other. Lieutenant Colonel Roosevelt stood with bared head on the bridge of the *Yucatán,* while soldierly emotions surged in his breast. He had no idea where he was being sent—it might not be Cuba at all, merely Puerto Rico—nor what he would be ordered to do when he got there; yet he believed "that the nearing future held . . . many chances of death, of honor and renown." If he failed, he would "share the fate of all who fail." But if he succeeded, he would help "score the first great triumph of a mighty world-movement."[1]

Roosevelt supposed that his fellow Rough Riders could dimly feel what he was feeling, but found that only one of them had enough "soul and imagination" to articulate such thoughts. This was Captain "Bucky" O'Neill, the prematurely grizzled, chain-

"He led these men in one of the noblest fights of the century."

Colonel Roosevelt and his Rough Riders atop San Juan Heights, Cuba.

smoking ex-Mayor of Prescott, Arizona, and a sheriff "whose name was a byword of terror to every wrong-doer, white or red." O'Neill was capable of "discussing Aryan word-roots . . . and then sliding off into a review of the novels of Balzac." He could demonstrate Apache signs which reminded Roosevelt curiously of those used by the Sioux and Mandans in Dakota.[2] He was, in short, a kindred soul, a man to contemplate the night sky with.

"Who would not risk his life for a star?" asked Bucky, as the two officers leaned against the railings and searched for the Southern Cross. The metaphor made up in sincerity what it lacked in originality, and it was duly recorded for quotation in Roosevelt's war memoirs.[3]

For six days the armada steamed southeast across a glassy ocean, under cloudless skies. Its leisurely pace, never more than seven knots, and frequently only four, was caused by the drag of two giant landing-scows and a tank-ship filled with drinking water. Since the thirty-one transport ships varied greatly in power, from big modern liners to iron paddle steamers of Civil War vintage, they straggled farther and farther apart, until the formation was over twenty-five miles long. On one occasion the rear guard lost touch with the vanguard for fourteen hours. Periodically General Shafter would call a halt, while his aides nervously counted ships coming over the horizon astern. Only when the number corresponded with those missing was the expedition allowed to proceed.[4]

The foreign attachés aboard U.S.S. *Segurança* did not know whether to be alarmed or amused at the general's magnificent disdain for enemy torpedo-boats, especially at night. "Had any of these made an attack on the fleet spread over an enormous area, each ship a blaze of lights and with the bands playing at times, a smart Spanish officer could not have failed to inflict a very serious loss," wrote Captain Alfred W. Paget of the British Navy.[5] The American Navy was equally concerned, and the fleet's warship escort made plain its annoyance by megaphone and semaphore; but Shafter spread over an enormous area himself, and was content to let his fleet do the same.

For officers like Roosevelt, who had airy first-class accommodations and wicker easy chairs, "it was very pleasant sailing southward through the tropic seas."[6] But for the men jammed below deck in splintery wooden bunks, breathing the same air as horses and mules—not to mention the effluvia of compacting layers of manure—things were rather less tolerable. There was a chorus of cheers on the morning of 20 June, when the fleet swung suddenly southwest "and we all knew that our destination was Santiago."[7]

A blue line of mountains rose near the *Yucatán*'s starboard bow, looming ever higher as the ship steamed within ten miles of shore. Some peaks rose six thousand feet sheer. Their silent massiveness gave the more thoughtful Rough Riders pause. "Our dreams turned to questions of an immediate concern—what was the enemy like? Would he show much resistance? How good was he in battle?"[8] But the mountains gave off no lethal bursts of smoke, and the fleet continued its coastal cruise across water "smooth as a mill pond." Apprehension changed slowly to bravado: soon the troops were shouting war-cries across the water, and waiting for echoes to roll back.[9]

At noon the fleet came to a halt about twenty miles east of Morro Castle, and a captain from the U.S. Navy blockade squadron (still holding nine Spanish warships in Santiago Harbor) came on board the *Segurança* to escort General Shafter to a rendezvous with Admiral Sampson. It was rumored that the two commanders, after reviewing several possible landing sites nearer the city, would be rowed ashore for a secret council of war with General Calixto García, head of the *insurrectos*.[10]

The *Segurança* steamed off alone, leaving the transport ships to wallow placidly behind at anchor. Hours passed while the invaders gazed their fill upon Cuba, "Pearl of the Antilles," the most beautiful island within reach of the American continent.[11] "Every feature of the landscape," wrote Richard Harding Davis, "was painted in high lights; there was no shading, it was all brilliant, gorgeous, and glaring. The sea was an indigo blue, like the blue in a washtub; the green of the mountains was the green of corroded copper; the scarlet trees were the red of a Tommy's jacket, and the sun was like a lime-light in its fierceness."[12]

Meanwhile, in a palm-thatched hut somewhere along the coast,[13] Shafter, Sampson, and García were perfecting a tripartite plan for the Santiago campaign. It was agreed that the debarkation of troops would be made on the morning of the twenty-second at Daiquirí, eighteen miles east of Santiago. Daiquirí was a mere village, but it had a beach, and a pier of sorts, which should be able to handle Shafter's lifeboats and scows. Starting at dawn, the Navy would bombard the village, as well as several other neighboring seaside settlements, in order to confuse the Spaniards as to which landing point the Army had chosen.[14]

Once the Fifth Corps was safely ashore at Daiquirí, plans called for Shafter to capture the fishing port of Siboney, seven miles farther west, then to march directly up the Camino Real over the hills to Santiago, twelve miles north. This would be the most difficult and dangerous part of the expedition, for enemy defenses were known to be concentrated in those hills. One ridge in particular—known as San Juan Heights—was regarded as almost insuperable,[15] so heavy were its fortifications, and so determined was Spain's General Linares to hold it as the last wall protecting Santiago. If he could keep Shafter's men off at cannon-point for a few weeks, his two most powerful allies—yellow fever and dysentery—would surely lay low all those still standing. But if the *yanquis* by some miracle broke through, Santiago, and Cuba, and the war, and the Western Hemisphere would be theirs.

NOT UNTIL THE EVENING of the following day were battle orders broadcast among the thirty-one transport ships. When the news reached Roosevelt, he entertained the Rough Riders with his patented war-dance, evolved from years of prancing around the carcasses of large game animals. Hand on hip, hat waving in the air, he sang:

> "*Shout hurrah for Erin-go-Bragh,*
> *And all the Yankee nation!*"[16]

Aboard the *Yucatán* a macabre toast was drunk: "To the Officers—may they get killed, wounded or promoted!"[17] Only Roosevelt, presumably, could relish such sentiments to the full. That night, in darkened dormitories that rolled and pitched uneasily in a rising sea, the Rough Riders prepared themselves for invasion. The solemnity of what was about to happen, the likelihood that some soldiers would never sleep again (three hundred Spanish troops were said to be entrenched on the heights above Daiquirí, with heavy guns),[18] made the hours before reveille increasingly suspenseful.

At 3:30 A.M. bugles sounded below decks. In the shadows, men rose whispering, dressed, and donned their bulky equipment: blanket rolls, full canteens, hundred-round ammunition belts, and haversacks stuffed with three days' rations.[19]

Daiquirí was just visible when they emerged on deck in the chill predawn light. It was little more than a notch in the cliffs, with a clutch of corrugated-zinc huts surrounding an old ironworks and a railhead lined with ore-cars. The village appeared to be deserted, but as the Rough Riders looked, a great column of flame leaped up from the ironworks. Evidently the Spaniards intended to destroy Daiquirí's only industrial resource before the *norteamericanos* arrived to exploit it.

Debarkation did not begin for several hours, for the sea was choppy and soldiers had considerable difficulty dropping into boats which rose and sank with the speed of elevators. At about 9:40 A.M. the thunder of naval bombardment was heard from Siboney, seven miles west. One by one the warships along the coast opened fire, until the air was shaking with noise and the zinc roofs were fluttering above Daiquirí like leaves blown in a storm. The flames spread along the ore-cars to the shacks, and bands aboard the truck-cars struck up the expedition's most-requested number: "There'll Be a Hot Time in the Old Town Tonight."[20]

Not until 10:10 A.M. did Shafter silence the guns and order the first landing parties ashore. Some boats headed for the wooden pier, where even greater difficulties arose: now it was like jumping out of an elevator onto a passing floor. The fact that the pier was rotting, and slimy, did not help matters. The soldiers had to wait until high waves lifted them above dock level before leaping, in the knowledge that they would be crushed and ground to pieces if they fell between the boat and the barnacled pilings. Other boats raced for the beach, through tumbling surf, and deposited their passengers on the shingle, some head over heels and cursing.[21]

The problem of getting horses and mules ashore was solved in typical Shafter fashion: they were simply shoved into the sea and left to find the beach for themselves. Some hysterical animals chose to swim instead for Haiti, until a bugler on the beach thoughtfully blew a cavalry call. The horses, according to one witness, "came round to the right and made for the beach like ships answering their helms."[22]

Meanwhile, Roosevelt was supervising the unloading of his two horses, Rain-in-the-Face and Texas. Out of respect to their eminent owner, sailors winched them into the water on booms; but a huge breaker engulfed Rain-in-the-Face, and drowned her before she could be released from harness. Roosevelt, "snorting like a bull, split the air with one blasphemy after another," wrote Albert Smith, the Vitagraph cameraman. The terrified sailors took such care with Texas that she seemed to hang in the air indefinitely, until Roosevelt, losing his temper again, bellowed, "Stop that goddamned animal torture!" This time there was no mishap, and the little horse splashed safely to shore.[23]

According to general orders, the Rough Riders were not due to land until much later in the day, after most of the regulars, but it was soon apparent to Roosevelt that "the go-as-you-please" principle applied to men as well as horses. As luck would have it, his old aide from the Navy Department, Lieutenant Sharp, steamed by in a converted yacht, and offered to pilot the *Yucatán* within a few hundred yards of shore. From this privileged position the Rough Riders landed well in advance of the other cavalry regiments.[24] The *Yucatán* thereupon steamed away, taking large quantities of personal effects with her before any attempt was made to unload them. Roosevelt was left standing on the sand with nothing but a yellow mackintosh and a toothbrush. Fortunately his most essential items of baggage were inside his Rough Rider hat: several extra pairs of spectacles, sewn into the lining.[25] If he was to meet his fate in Cuba, he wished to see it in clear focus.

More than six thousand troops were on Cuban soil by sunset. Not one shot had been fired in Daiquirí's defense; the ruined village was occupied only by a few *insurrectos,* rather the worse for bombardment.

As dusk fell, campfires began to glow along the beach and in the little valley where the Rough Riders were lying on ponchos. At intervals there were shrieks and laughter, as red ants or crabs disturbed their rest;[26] but the tropical air was balmy, the sky filled with comforting stars, and soon everybody except the guards was asleep.

POLITICAL RIVALRY, that most ubiquitous of social weeds, thrives just as fast on tropical islands as in the smoke-filled rooms of northern capitals. By the time the Rough Riders awoke on the morning of 23 June, two generals were already locked in contention for the honor of leading the march upon Santiago.

According to invasion orders, Major General Joseph ("Fighting Joe") Wheeler, commander of the Cavalry Division, was supposed to follow Brigadier General H. W. Lawton of the 2nd Infantry Division to Siboney and remain there to supervise the rest of the landing operation while Lawton established himself farther inland on the Camino Real, or Santiago road. But not for nothing had Fighting Joe earned his nickname, and his reputation of "never staying still in one place long enough for the Almighty to put a finger on him."[27] The fact that Lawton was tall, and had fought for the Union in the Civil War, while Wheeler was five foot two, and had been the leader of the Confederate cavalry, only intensified the latter's ambition to be first to encounter "the Yankees—dammit, I mean the Spaniards."[28] Needless to say, this attitude endeared him to the Rough Riders. "A regular game-cock,"[29] was Roosevelt's opinion of the bristling little general.

Lawton, whose division landed first on the twenty-second, had left for Siboney the same afternoon. Marching at a leisurely pace, he encamped en route and completed his journey next morning. The port (which had been so hastily vacated that tortillas were still steaming over breakfast coals) was reported "captured" at 9:20 A.M., much to Wheeler's chagrin. Only then did he receive the longed-for permission to bring his men on to Siboney.[30]

Doubtless General Shafter expected the cavalry to proceed west at the same comfortable pace as the infantry had the day before. From the moment the bugles sounded "March" in Daiquirí at 3:43 P.M., 23 June,[31] it was plain that Wheeler wanted the Rough Riders in Siboney by nightfall.

Seven miles did not look far on the map, but paper was flat and the Cuban coastline was not. The hard coral road ran up and down precipitous hills, and the heat was blinding enough to incapacitate men in loincloths, let alone military uniform and the heavy accouterments of war. Even when the road leveled off to wind through coconut groves, the entrapped humidity and clouds of insects buzzing over rotten fruit made the exposed slopes seem almost preferable. Soon blanket rolls, cans of food, coats, and even underwear were littering the trail, to be picked up by delighted Cubans.[32]

"I shall never forget that terrible march to Siboney," wrote Edward Marshall of the *New York Journal*. Unlike "Dandy Dick" Davis of the *Herald* (impeccable as usual in a tropical suit and white helmet), Marshall was unable to ride with the officers. He had lost his horse during the debarkation, and had generously offered his saddle to Roosevelt, who had little Texas, but nothing in the way of harness.[33] Roosevelt accepted the gift, but refused to ride "while my men are walking."[34] All the way to Siboney he tramped along in his yellow mackintosh, streaming with perspiration and earning the affectionate respect of his troopers.

"Wood's Weary Walkers"—never had the name seemed more apt—caught up with General Lawton's rear guard, a mile or so above Siboney, just as dusk fell. Without slackening pace, they marched on down the valley. Burr McIntosh of *Leslie's Magazine* asked the commander of the rear guard, Brigadier General J. C. Bates, where they were going. "I don't know," said Bates, peering after them in the dim light. "They have not had any orders to go on beyond us."[35]

If not, they very soon had. Wood encamped his men in a coconut grove well north of Siboney, then rode into the squalid village for a council of war with General Wheeler and his own immediate superior, Brigadier General S.B.M. Young. He learned that Wheeler had made a personal reconnaissance of the Camino Real that afternoon, and had found that the first line of enemy defenses was four miles up-country, at a point where the road crested a spur in the mountains. Fighting Joe's orders were "to hit the Spaniards . . . as soon after daybreak as possible."[36]

While Wood, Wheeler, and Young discussed tactics at headquarters, Roosevelt stayed with the men in camp, eating hardtack and pork and drinking fire-boiled coffee. Rain began to fall. He sat for a couple of hours in his yellow slicker, not bothering to seek shelter. It was at times like this, when lack of seniority excluded him from the decision-making process, that he had leisure to reflect on what he had missed by turning down the offer of the colonelcy. But war had its opportunities. . . .

The sky cleared eventually, and new fires began to blaze as the soldiers stripped off their sweat-drenched, rain-sodden clothes and held them up to dry. Roosevelt strolled over to L Troop, where two of the biggest men in the regiment, Captain Allyn Capron and Sergeant Hamilton Fish, were standing talking. He caught himself admiring their splendid bodies in the flickering glare. "Their frames seemed of steel, to withstand all fatigue; they were flushed with health; in their eyes shone high resolve and fiery desire." Like himself, they were "filled with eager longing to show their mettle."[37]

The pass over the mountains where the Spanish lay in wait was locally known as Las Guásimas, after a clump of *guácima*, or hog-nut trees that grew there. Cuban informants, aware that Americans would have difficulty recognizing these trees in the surrounding jungle, gave General Wheeler a more macabre landmark to search out. There was an approach in the vicinity, scouts said, where the body of a dead guerrilla lay across the trail. Discovery of that body would indicate that the enemy was somewhere in the vicinity[38]—perhaps only a hundred yards ahead.

This was hardly the most sophisticated reconnaissance briefing, but it was good enough for Fighting Joe. Shortly before dawn the next morning, 24 June, his dismounted cavalrymen began a two-

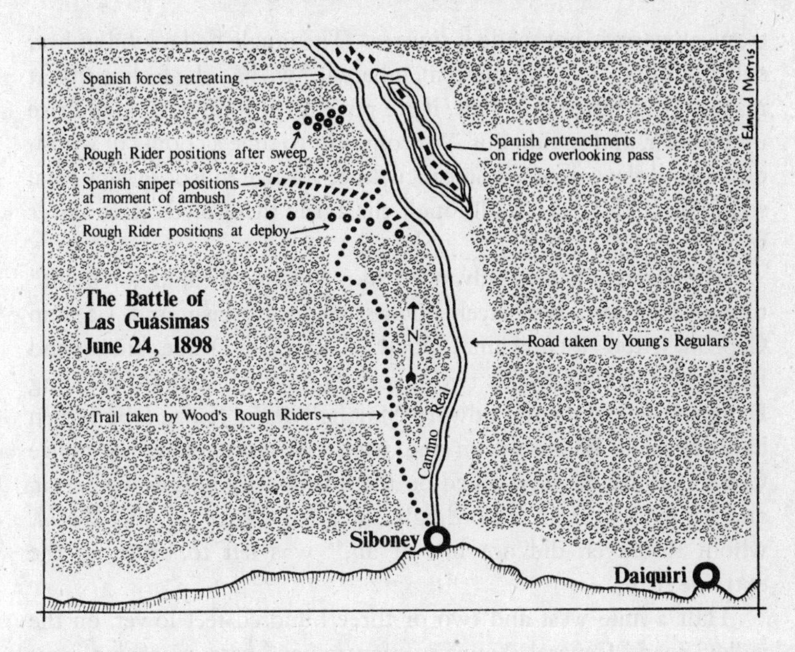

column advance upon Las Guásimas. The right thrust, on the west, was undertaken by General Young and about 470 Regulars, marching directly up the Camino Real. The left thrust, up a high but roughly parallel trail half a mile to the west, was undertaken by Wood and 500 Rough Riders. If Cuban information was correct, trail and road would meet about where the dead guerrilla lay, enabling Young and Wood to deploy, touch flanks, then lead their thousand men against the enemy-held ridge together. Spanish forces were estimated at about 2,000.[39]

Climbing quickly out of the valley at 6:00 A.M., the Rough Riders took their last look at Siboney, seven hundred feet below. Gilded by the sun, half-shrouded in early morning mist, the squalid little port looked almost pretty. It gave off faint sounds, "like blasts from faery trumpets."[40] Evidently Lawton's men were at last waking up.

From this viewpoint the trail led northwest along a forest ridge, the vegetation growing ever taller and thicker until it closed overhead. The Rough Riders found themselves irradiated with chlorophyllic half-light; its effect would have been eerily charming had the tropical warmth not made it sinister. "The jungle had a kind of hot, sullen beauty," one trooper remembered. "We had the feeling that it resented our intrusion—that, if we penetrated too far, it would rise up in anger, and smother us."[41] From time to time a cooing of wood-doves, and the call of a tropical cuckoo, strange to Roosevelt's ears, sounded in the trees,[42] although the birds themselves were never seen.

The Rough Riders advanced like Indians, behind a "point" tipped by those two steely giants, Sergeant Fish and Captain Capron. After them came Wood, flanked by three aides, and Roosevelt, flanked by his two favorite reporters, Richard Harding Davis of the *Herald* and Edward Marshall of the *Journal.* Both men had reported favorably, in the past, on his exploits as Police Commissioner; he now relied on them to glorify him as a warrior, and cultivated them accordingly. Stephen Crane of the *World,* whom Roosevelt did not like at all,[43] was left to bring up the extreme rear.

Half a mile west and two or three hundred feet lower, on the valley road, General Young's infantrymen were marching in a roughly parallel direction. But the intervening vegetation was so dense that they could be neither seen nor heard, save for a bugle-call now and then.[44]

After about an hour's march, Captain Capron came back through the trees to announce that his scout had discovered the body of the dead guerrilla. Wood turned to Roosevelt. "Pass the word back to keep silence in the ranks."[45] Then he disappeared up the trail with Capron, leaving Roosevelt and Marshall to discuss coolly—and disobediently—a lunch they had once had with William Randolph Hearst at the Astor House. Meanwhile the men relaxed on the ground, chewing blades of grass and fanning the stagnant air with their hats.[46]

As Roosevelt talked, his glance fell on some barbed wire curling from a fence to the left of the trail. He reached for a strand, gazed at it with the expert eye of a ranchman, and started. "My God! This wire has been cut today."

"What makes you think so?" asked Marshall.

"The end is bright, and there has been enough dew, even since sunrise, to put a light rust on it . . ."[47]

Just as he spoke, the regimental surgeon came up from behind, riding noisily on a mule. Roosevelt leaped to silence him. Then, as the Rough Riders held their breath, a terrifying sound came winging through the bushes.[48]

MARSHALL, WHO WAS to hear the sound endlessly repeated that day, and would find himself paralyzed from the waist down by it, described it as a *z-z-z-z-z-eu,* rising to a shrill crescendo, then sinking with a moan on the *eu.* It was the trajectory of a high-speed Mauser bullet, standard equipment with Spanish snipers. Bloodcurdling though the sound was, with the concomitant *ping* and *zip* of perforated leaves (enabling a man to judge its approach velocity, and the utter impossibility of getting out of the way in time), the worst moment came when the *z-eu* was followed by a loud *chug,* indicating that the bullet had hit flesh. The force of impact on a man's outstretched arm was enough to spin him around before he thumped in a flaccid heap on the ground. Often as not, a man so struck would rise again after a few minutes, none the worse but for a tiny, cauterized hole; the flaccidity was merely a shock reaction, common to all Mauser victims.[49] But other men lay where they dropped.

The first soldier to be killed by these first rifleshots of the Spanish-American War was Sergeant Hamilton Fish, who fell at the feet of Captain Capron. Then another Mauser took Capron in the heart. So much for their "frames of steel."[50] Six more Rough Riders died in the hail of fire that followed—the most intense, according to one scholarly major, in the history of warfare.[51] Thirty-four men were wounded, many of them repeatedly. Private Isbell of L Troop was hit three times in the neck, twice in the left hand, once in the right hand, and finally in the head.[52] Roosevelt, literally jumping up and down with excitement[53] as he awaited Wood's order to deploy, made no effort to run for cover; somehow the bullets missed him, although one did smack into a tree inches from his cheek, and filled his eyes with splinters of bark.[54]

Wood, whose casual confidence under fire earned him the nickname "Old Icebox," asked Roosevelt to take three troops into the jungle on the right, while three other troops fanned out on the left.

Marshall remained behind, idly curious to see how the Lieutenant Colonel comported himself in battle.

> Perhaps a dozen of Roosevelt's men had passed into the thicket before he did. Then he stepped across the wire himself, and, from that instant, became the most magnificent soldier I have ever seen. It was as if that barbed-wire strand had formed a dividing line in his life, and that when he stepped across it he left behind him in the bridle path all those unadmirable and conspicuous traits which have so often caused him to be justly criticized in civic life, and found on the other side of it, in that Cuban thicket, the coolness, the calm judgment, the towering heroism, which made him, perhaps, the most admired and best beloved of all Americans in Cuba.[55]

Where the shots were coming from even Roosevelt, with his acute hearing, could not tell; he knew only that the snipers were distant and highly placed. Evidently the Spanish, trained in guerrilla tactics by three years of fighting the Cubans, knew exactly where the trail was; but how, since the Rough Riders were camouflaged by trees, did they know *where* to shoot? Much later it transpired that the strange cooing and cuckoo-calls he had heard earlier came from lookouts posted in the jungle, tracking the regiment's progress to the point of ambush.[56]

All at once the trees parted and Roosevelt found himself gazing out over the Santiago road to a razorback ridge on the opposite side of the valley. General Young's men were stationed below, under heavy fire themselves by the sound of it; but thanks to the enemy's smokeless powder he still could not see the entrenchments. It took a newspaperman to point the Spaniards out to him. "There they are, Colonel," cried Richard Harding Davis, "look over there; I can see their hats near that glade." Roosevelt focused his binoculars, estimated the range, and ordered his troops to "rapid fire." Davis joined in with a carbine he had picked up somewhere.[57] The woods, according to Stephen Crane, "became aglow with fighting." In three minutes, nine men were lying on their backs in Roosevelt's immediate vicinity.[58] But the Rough Riders fired back with such blistering accuracy that the Spaniards soon quit their trenches and took refuge in the jungle farther up the ridge.

Unable to pursue them for an impenetrable wall of vines, Roosevelt ordered his men back to the main trail, where the Mausers were whining as viciously as ever. Although he did not fully realize it, he had succeeded brilliantly in his first military skirmish. By engaging and driving back the enemy's foremost flank, he had exposed troops holding the top of the ridge to cross-fire from the entire line of Rough Riders, and frontal attack from General Young's regulars.[59] The way was now open for a final grand charge by all the American forces, with Roosevelt commanding the extreme left, Wood commanding the center, and the regulars on the right advancing under orders from General Wheeler himself. About nine hundred men broke out into the open and ran up the valley (Roosevelt stopping to pick up three Mauser cartridges as souvenirs for his children),[60] their rifle-cracks drowned in the booming of four Hotchkiss mountain-guns. Like ants shaken from a biscuit, some fifteen hundred Spaniards leaped from their rock-forts along the ridge and scattered in the direction of Santiago. "We've got the damn Yankees on the run!" roared Fighting Joe.[61]

By 9:20 A.M. the Battle of Las Guásimas was over. An exhausted major looked at his watch, shook it incredulously, and held it up to his ear. He was sure that the engagement had lasted at least six hours.[62] Actually it had been only two.

A few minutes later the first of General Lawton's infantrymen arrived and found that their services were not needed. Lawton was furious. According to one report he accused Wheeler of deliberately stealing a march on him. "I was given command of the advance, and I want you to know that I propose to keep it, by God, even if I have to put a guard to keep other troops in the rear!"[63] Fighting Joe was philosophical, for he received in due time the congratulations of General Shafter. As long as that leisurely officer remained on board the *Segurança,* Wheeler, not Lawton, was the senior general ashore, and he could issue and interpret orders as he saw fit. For the moment he was satisfied. He had driven back the Spaniards; his bandy-legged cavalry had outmarched the infantry; best of all, he had avenged Appomattox. Such triumph was cheap at a cost of sixteen Americans dead and fifty-two wounded, to Spain's figures of ten and eight.[64] Others, gazing at the sightless eyes of Hamilton Fish, or the shattered spine of Edward Marshall (writhing in agony as he dictated his dispatch to Stephen Crane),[65] might wonder if the Battle of Las Guásimas had been really worth it.

"ONE OBJECT AT LEAST was accomplished," wrote *Leslie's* correspondent Burr McIntosh, whom Roosevelt had also left behind at Siboney. "The names of several men were in the newspapers before the names of several others, and a number of newspaper men, who were sure to write things in the proper spirit, were given the necessary 'tip'."[66] Also the necessary flattery: Roosevelt was quick to cite Richard Harding Davis in his official report, and even tried to get the Associated Press to mention Davis's gallantry while the battle was still going on.[67] Davis, who tended to treat friends as they treated him, responded with laudatory accounts of the battle, earning praise for "Roosevelt's Rough Riders" as its only apparent heroes. In Washington there was talk of promoting Roosevelt to the rank of brigadier general, and in New York a coalition of independent Republicans announced that they intended to nominate him for Governor in September.[68]

Whether the praise was deserved or not, Roosevelt's personal views of his role in the Las Guásimas victory were modest, and remained so always. He liked to joke about his inability to see the enemy, his difficulty running with a sword swinging between his legs, and his policy of firing at any target that was not a tree. However, "as throughout the morning I had preserved a specious aspect of wisdom, and had commanded first one wing and then the other wing, the fight really was a capital thing for me, for practically all the men had served under my actual command, and thenceforth felt enthusiastic belief that I would lead them aright."[69]

IN HIS SPEECH to the Naval War College a year before, Roosevelt had urged America to prepare for "blood, sweat, and tears" when war came. The Battle of Las Guásimas gave the Rough Riders ample opportunity to wallow in all three. Regimental surgeon Bob Church looked, that evening, "like a kid who had gotten his hands and arms into a bucket of thick red paint."[70] Gouts of blood trembled on the leaves along the trail, and plastered whole sheaves of grass together. Fresh blood flowed as Church snipped open Mauser holes in order to dress them. Wherever a casualty lay, the predators of Cuba collected in rings: huge land-crabs shredding corpses with their clattering claws, vultures tearing off lips and eyelids, then the eyeballs, and finally whole faces.[71] But the most despised predators were Cubans themselves, who invariably materialized from the jungle to strip the dead of clothing, equipment, and jewelry, and rummage around for jettisoned food-cans. Was it for these squat, dull-eyed peasants that the flower of America had died?

Compassion, never one of Theodore Roosevelt's outstanding characteristics, was notably absent from his written accounts of Las Guásimas and its aftermath—unless the perfunctory phrase "poor Capron and Ham Fish"[72] can be counted to mean anything. His only recorded emotion as the Rough Riders buried seven of their dead next morning, in a common grave darkened with the shadows of circling buzzards, was pride in its all-American variety: "—Indian and cowboy, miner, packer, and college athlete, the man of unknown ancestry from the lonely Western plains, and the man who carried on his watch the crest of the Stuyvesants and the Fishes." When Bucky O'Neill turned to him and asked, "Colonel, isn't it Whitman who says of the vultures that 'they pluck the eyes of princes, and tear the flesh of kings'?" Roosevelt answered coldly that he could not place the quotation.[73]

His duty, as he saw it, lay with those who were still standing and able to fight. Since landing in Cuba, his men had had nothing to eat or drink but hardtack, bacon, and sugarless coffee. What was left of these heavy comestibles had been dumped during their two forced marches, and due to General Shafter's "maddening" mismanagement of the unloading operation (still in process at Siboney), no fresh supplies were expected for several days. Soon the Rough Riders were forced to scrounge, like Cubans, in the bags of dead Spanish mules.[74]

On the morning of 26 June, Roosevelt got wind of a stockpile of beans on the beach, and marched a squad of men hastily down to investigate. There were, indeed, at least eleven hundred pounds of beans available, so he went into the commissary and demanded the full amount for his regiment. The commissar reached for a book of regulations and showed him that "under sub-section B of section C of article 4, or something like that," beans were available only to officers. Roosevelt had learned enough during his six years as Civil Service Commissioner not to protest this attitude. He merely went outside for a moment, then returned and demanded eleven hundred pounds of beans "for the officer's mess."

COMMISSAR	But your officers cannot eat eleven hundred pounds of beans.
ROOSEVELT	You don't know what appetites my officers have.
COMMISSAR	(*wavering*) I'll have to send the requisition to Washington.
ROOSEVELT	All right, only give me the beans.
COMMISSAR	I'm afraid they'll take it out of your salary.
ROOSEVELT	That will be all right, only give me the beans.[75]

So the Rough Riders got their beans, and the requisition went to Washington. "Oh! what a feast we had, and how we enjoyed it!"[76]

"THE AVERAGE HEIGHT among the Americans," reported a Barcelona newspaper, "is 5 feet 2 inches. This is due to their living almost entirely upon vegetables as they ship all their beef out of the country, so eager are they to make money. There is no doubt that one full-grown Spaniard can defeat any three men in America."[77]

FOR THE LAST SIX DAYS of June the Rough Riders camped in a little Eden on the westward slope of the ridge of Las Guásimas. They washed their bloody uniforms in a stream gushing out of the jungle, learned how to fry mangoes and, when tobacco ran out at a black-market price of $2 a plug, how to smoke dried grass, roots, and manure. The Cubans, if useless for all else, were at least good for rum: a can of Army beef (vintage 1894, according to the label)

was enough to fill one's canteen, and a whole squad could get drunk on the proceeds of one Rough Rider blanket.[78]

Fifth Corps staff, meanwhile, had solved the complicated logistical problem of getting General Shafter finally onshore and bringing him up the Camino Real in a sagging buckboard. Like all obese people, the general felt the heat badly; in addition his gout was worse, and he had contracted a scalp condition which necessitated constant scratching by aides.[79] Not until the morning of 30 June did he venture down from the ridge to explore the terrain still separating his forces from Santiago.[80]

The best vantage point was a hill named El Pozo, to the left of the road where it crossed the river—or, to be more precise, where the river crossed the road. Ascending this hill on the Army's stoutest mule, Shafter gazed across a landscape which the Rough Riders, from their camp in the rear, already knew by heart.

Dense jungle filled the basin in front of him. There were hills to the right and hills to the left—the latter crowned by a fortified village named El Caney. Another ridge of hills rose on the far side of the basin, about a mile and a half away, walling off Santiago in another basin, much wider and lower to the west. The peaks undulated enticingly, exposing whitewashed triangles of the city to view, but their steep facing slopes, and in particular the heavy entrenchments visible all the way along the crest, made it obvious at a glance that they would be, as García had warned, General Linares's last line of defense. These were the San Juan Heights, and that dominant central outcrop, crowned with a blockhouse, was San Juan Hill itself. Since the Camino Real snaked over the range slightly to the right of it, capture of the hill meant possession of the road. Shafter would then be able to mount a land siege of Santiago while Admiral Sampson continued his siege by sea. It would be a matter of time until starvation forced the surrender of the city.

If General Shafter noticed a smaller hill in front of San Juan Heights, cutting off his view of some of the road, he did not consider it worthy of inclusion in his hand-drawn map.[81]

A COUNCIL OF WAR was called in command headquarters early in the afternoon. Shafter looked ill and exhausted by his ascent of El

Pozo—obviously being at the front did not agree with him—but he had a definite plan of campaign worked out, and announced it in peremptory tones. The Fifth Corps would begin the advance upon Santiago immediately, that very evening. (Eight thousand enemy troops were reported to be on their way from another part of the province, to supplement the twelve thousand already in and around Santiago: clearly not a moment must be lost.) The divisions would move along the Camino Real under cover of dusk, and spread out in the vicinity of El Pozo. While Brigadier General J. F. Kent's 1st Infantry and General Wheeler's Cavalry encamped on the flanks of the hill, General Lawton's 2nd Infantry would swing right and march toward El Caney, and bivouac somewhere en route. All forces would then be poised for a big battle which would inevitably begin next morning.[82]

Sitting vast and rumpled in shirt-sleeves and suspenders, his gouty foot wrapped in burlap,[83] Shafter detailed the swift, simple maneuvers he would like to see, or at least hear about, during the day. At dawn General Lawton would assault El Caney and take the fort there, cutting off the northern supply route to Santiago. This should take only about three hours. Meanwhile the other two divisions would launch their own attack upon San Juan Hill, moving through the jungle along Camino Real, and deploying as they approached the foothills. Lawton was to join them on the right as soon as he was free, and the day's action would climax in a massive onslaught on the Heights, plainly inspired by the final charge at Las Guásimas.[84]

The council of war was barely over when a staff officer rode over to Rough Rider headquarters and announced that Generals Wheeler and Young had been felled by fever. Command of the Cavalry Division therefore devolved upon Brigadier General Samuel S. Sumner, and that of Young's 2nd Brigade upon Leonard Wood; "while to my intense delight," wrote Theodore Roosevelt, "I got my regiment."[85] His long-postponed colonelcy had come just in time for the decisive engagement of the Spanish-American War.

ONE SMALL DETAIL which had apparently escaped General Shafter's attention was that mobilization of some sixteen thousand men along a road ten feet wide would cause certain problems, especially as he had ordered the entire Fifth Corps to start marching at 4:00 P.M. A violent rainstorm at 3:30 did not help matters, for it converted the Camino Real into a ditch which squished deeper under every fresh line of boots.[86]

"Darkness came and still we marched," one Rough Rider remembered. "The tropical moon rose. You could almost envy the ease with which this orange ball crossed the sky. It was all we could do to lift our muddy shoes."[87] At last, at about eight o'clock, the dark silhouette of El Pozo loomed up through the trees, and the regiment clambered halfway up its eastern slope. Leaving his men to sleep where they chose, Roosevelt strolled over the brow of the hill and found Wood establishing temporary headquarters in an abandoned sugar factory. Brigadier General and Colonel now, they gazed across at San Juan Heights, and the refracted glow of Santiago's street lights.[88] Then they curled up in their yellow slickers on a bed of saddle blankets and went to sleep.

THE FIRST OF JULY, 1898, which Roosevelt ever afterward called "the great day of my life," dawned to a fugato of bugles, phrase echoing phrase as reveille sounded in the various camps.[89] The morning was Elysian, with a pink sky lightening rapidly to pale, cloudless blue. Mists filled the basin below El Pozo, evaporating quickly as the air warmed, exposing first the crowns of royal palms, then the lower green of deciduous trees and vines. Hills rippled around the horizon to east, west, and north, like a violet backdrop. As the vapor burned away, the effect to Roosevelt was of shimmering curtains rising to disclose "an amphitheatre for the battle."[90]

While his men got up he walked about calmly lathering his face, reassuring the many who had woken afraid.[91] He wore a dark blue shirt with yellow suspenders, fastened with silver leaves, and—in the apparent belief that people might otherwise mistake him for a Regular—a stand-up collar emblazoned with the Volunteer insignia.[92] Breakfast was frugal: a handful of beans, the invariable slabs of fat bacon and hardtack, washed down with bitter coffee. Then the regiment fell in, along with others of Wood's brigade, to await marching orders. Four big guns of the 1st Artillery were hauled up El Pozo and

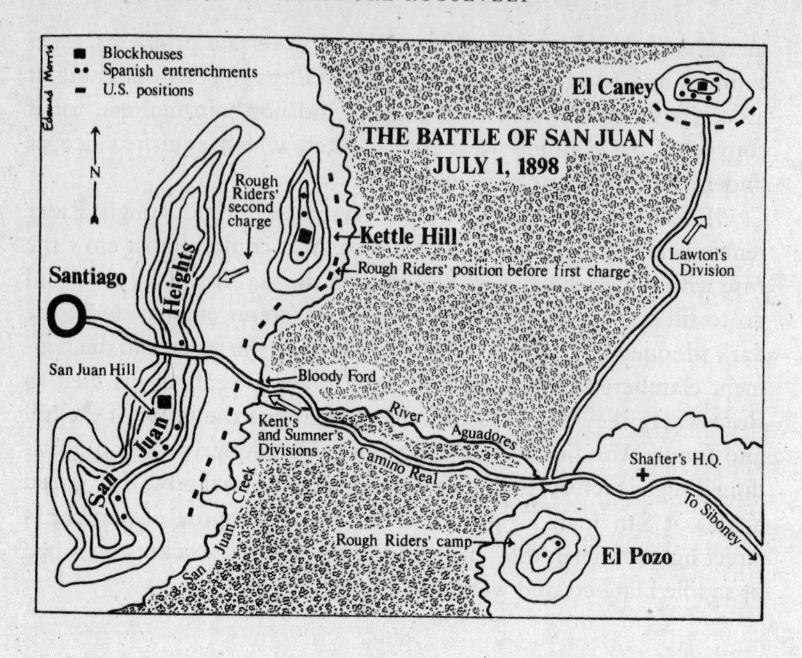

wedged into position. A staff officer came by with the predictable news that General Shafter had been taken ill during the night, and would have to command the battle from his cot.[93] Roosevelt probably paid little attention: he was waiting for the first detonation of Lawton's battery.

It came at 6:30, a sullen roar that rolled over the still-sleeping jungle and sent clouds of birds into the air. Almost immediately the El Pozo battery followed suit, and Roosevelt and Wood became conscious of a white plume of gunsmoke hanging motionless over their heads. Wood barely had time to say "he wished our brigade could be moved somewhere else" when there was a whistling rush from the direction of San Juan Hill, and something exploded in the midst of the white plume. Another shell, another and another: the second explosion raised a shrapnel bump on Roosevelt's wrist, wounded four Rough Riders, and blew the leg off a Regular. The fourth killed and maimed "a good many" Cubans, and perforated the lungs of Wood's horse. Evidently Spanish gunners were as deadly accurate as Spanish riflemen. Roosevelt waited no longer, and hustled his regiment downhill into jungle cover.[94]

About 8:45 the enemy cannonade ceased for no apparent reason—*tortilla* time?—and General Sumner ordered the Cavalry Division to hurry en masse along Camino Real toward San Juan. About where the jungle thinned out, a creek, also called San Juan, crossed the road at right angles; here the Rough Riders were to deploy to the right, and await further orders before moving up the Heights. Shafter's original battle plan had been for them to link up with the 1st Infantry, as soon as General Lawton returned in triumph from El Caney; but the continual booming of guns from that quarter indicated that the fort was holding up much better than anticipated.[95] For strategic purposes, Lawton's aid could now be discounted.

The freshness of the early morning had long since evaporated when Roosevelt, riding on Texas, led his men up the road. But last night's mud was still thick and the jungle gave off insufferable clouds of dank moisture.[96] The heat rose steadily to 100 degrees Fahrenheit, and the sun drilled down with blistering force on sweaty arms and shoulders. Roosevelt's neck, at least, was protected. He had ingeniously attached his blue polka-dot scarf—the unofficial insignia of a Rough Rider—in a semicircular screen dangling from the rim of his sombrero. It fluttered bravely as he trotted along,[97] like the plumes of Alexander the Great; later in the day it would serve him to flamboyant effect.

By now the familiar *z-z-z-z-eu* of Mauser bullets could be heard overhead. They sang louder and louder "in a steady deathly static"[98] as Kent's 1st Regular Brigade, marching just ahead of Roosevelt, approached San Juan Creek. The trees thinned, and suddenly so many thousands of bullets came down, ripping in sheets through grass and reeds and human bodies, that the mud of the crossing turned red, and the water flowing over it ran purple. The Rough Riders wavered, then halted, horrified at the pile-up of bodies in front of them. Ever afterward, this point of deploy was known as Bloody Ford.[99]

As if to improve still further the marksmanship of the Spanish snipers (many of whom were hidden in the high crests of royal palms, completely camouflaged with green uniforms and smokeless powder), an irresistible target was towed down Camino Real: the observation balloon of the Signal Corps. Glistening and wobbling in the sun, it stayed aloft long enough to reconnoiter another crossing five hundred yards to the left, relieving the gruesome bottleneck at Bloody Ford, and gave the cannons on San Juan Heights a precise indication of the position of the advance column.[100]

Plunging frantically across the creek, before the riddled balloon sank and smothered them, the Rough Riders found themselves crouching in a field full of waist-high grass. San Juan Hill rose up directly ahead, its blockhouse and breastworks clearly visible, as were the conical straw hats of entrenched soldiers. Roosevelt's orders were to march to the right, along the bank of the creek, and establish himself at the foot of the little hill that Shafter had overlooked the day before.[101] *He,* however, had not, and saw at once that it represented the nearest and most dangerous holdout of the enemy. Already it was breathing fire at its crest, like a miniature volcano about to erupt, and spitting showers of Mausers. The bullets came whisking through the grass with vicious effectiveness as the Rough Riders crawled nearer. Every now and again a trooper would leap involuntarily into the air, then crumple into a nerveless heap.[102] Roosevelt remained obstinately on horseback, determined to set an example of courage to his men. Now began the worst part of the battle. While the Rough Riders took what cover they could, in bushes and banks below the hill, and in the mosquito-bogs at the edge of the creek, other cavalry regiments fought their way slowly into specified positions to left and right and—humiliatingly—in front of them. The truth was that Roosevelt and his men were being held in reserve by General Sumner,[103] and the new Colonel did not like it one bit. The 1st, 3rd, 6th, and even the black 9th had prior claim to this hill, while General Kent's Infantry Division was awarded the supreme prize of San Juan Hill, now half a mile away on the left front. Orders were orders; Roosevelt could only scrawl an angry note to the (very senior) colonel of his immediate neighbors, the 10th Cavalry. "There is too much firing. Colonel Wood directs that there be no more shooting unless there is an advance. . . ."[104] It is doubtful Wood said any such thing.

Mere spleen could not last through the one and a half hours of military torture that followed. General Sumner was waiting for orders to advance from General Shafter, but General Shafter assumed that any damn fool capable of leading a division would know when to do so without authority. Until this slight misunderstanding was cleared up, the cavalry regiments had to lie in stifling heat and try to stop as few Mausers as possible.[105] Morale sagged as the shrieking projectiles *chugged* into groins, hearts, lungs, limbs, and eyes.[106] Even Roosevelt found it prudent, in this killing hailstorm, to get off his horse and lie low; but Bucky O'Neill insisted on strolling up and down in front of his troop, smoking his perpetual cigarette, as if he were still walking along the sidewalk in Prescott, Arizona. "Sergeant," he said to a protester, "the Spanish bullet isn't made that will kill me." He had hardly exhaled a laughing cloud of smoke before a Mauser shot went *z-z-z-z-eu* into his mouth, and burst out the back of his head. "The biggest, handsomest, laziest officer in the regiment" was dead by the time he hit the ground.[107]

It was now well past noon, and the insect-like figures of General Kent's infantry could be seen beginning a slow, toiling ascent of San Juan Hill. Roosevelt sent messenger after messenger to General Sumner, imploring permission to attack his own hill, and was just about to do so unilaterally when the welcome message arrived: "Move forward and support the regulars in the assault on the hills in front."[108] It was not the total advancement he had been hoping for, but it was enough. "The instant I received the order I sprang on my horse, and then my 'crowded hour' began."[109]

SOLDIERS ARE APT TO recollect their wartime actions, as poets do emotions, in tranquillity, imposing order and reason upon a dreamlike tumult. Roosevelt was honest enough to admit, even when minutely describing his charge up the hill, that at the time he was aware of very little that was going on outside the orbit of his ears and sweat-fogged spectacles.[110] It was as if some primeval force drove him. "All men who feel any power of joy in battle," he wrote, "know what it is like when the wolf rises in the heart."[111]

Yet enough original images, visual and auditory, survive in

Roosevelt's written account of the battle to give a sense of the rush, the roar, the pounce of that vulpine movement.[112] To begin with, there was the sound of his own voice rasping and swearing as he cajoled terrified soldiers to follow him. *"Are you afraid to stand up when I am on horseback?"* Then the sight of a Rough Rider at his feet being drilled lengthwise with a bullet intended for himself. Next, line after line of cavalry parting before his advance, like waves under a Viking's prow. The puzzled face of a captain refusing to go farther without permission from some senior colonel, who could not be found.

Roosevelt: "Then I am the ranking officer here and I give the order to charge." Another refusal. Roosevelt: "Then let my men through, sir." Grinning white faces behind him; black men throwing down a barbed wire fence before him. A wave of his hat and flapping blue neckerchief. The sound of shouting and cheering. The sound of bullets "like the ripping of a silk dress." Little Texas splashing bravely across a stream, galloping on, and on, up, up, up. Another wire fence, forty yards from the top, stopping her in her tracks. A bullet grazing his elbow. Jumping off, wriggling through, and running. Spaniards fleeing from the *hacienda* above. Only one man with him now: his orderly, Bardshar, shooting and killing two of the enemy. And then suddenly a revolver salvaged from the *Maine* leaping into his own hand and firing: a Spaniard not ten yards away doubling over "neatly as a jackrabbit." At last the summit of the hill—his and Bardshar's alone for one breathless moment before the other Rough Riders and cavalrymen swarmed up to join them. One final incongruous image: "a huge iron kettle, or something of the kind, probably used for sugar-refining."[113]

AS HIS HEAD CLEARED and his lungs stopped heaving, Roosevelt found that Kettle Hill commanded an excellent view of Kent's attack on San Juan Hill, still in progress across the valley about seven hundred yards away. The toiling figures seemed pitifully few. "Obviously the proper thing to do was help them."[114] For the next ten minutes he supervised a continuous volley-fire at the heads of Spaniards in the San Juan blockhouse, until powerful Gatlings took over from somewhere down below, and the infantry on the left began their final rush.[115] At this the wolf rose again in Roosevelt's heart. Leaping over rolls of wire, he started down the hill to join them, but forgot to give the order to follow, and found that he had only five companions. Two were shot down while he ran back and roared imprecations at his regiment. "What, are you cowards?" "We're waiting for the command." "Forward MARCH!"[116] The Rough Riders willingly obeyed, as well as members of the 1st and 10th Cavalry. Again Roosevelt pounded over lower ground under heavy fire; again he surged up grassy slopes, and again he saw Spaniards deserting their high fortifications. To left and right, all along the crested line of San Juan Heights, other regiments were doing the same. "When we reached these crests we found ourselves overlooking Santiago."[117]

UNTIL NIGHT FELL, Roosevelt was more interested in looking at the carnage behind him than ahead at the prize city. The trenches were filled with corpses in light blue and white uniforms, most of them with "little holes in their heads from which their brains were oozing"[118]—proof of the killing accuracy of Rough Rider volleys from the top of Kettle Hill. "Look at all these damned Spanish dead!" he exulted to Trooper Bob Ferguson, an old family friend.[119]

Official tallies revealed a fair score of American casualties—656 according to one count, 1,071 according to another. The Rough Riders contributed 89, but this only increased Roosevelt's sense of pride; he noted that it was "the heaviest loss suffered by any regiment in the cavalry division."[120]

"No hunting trip so far has ever equalled it in Theodore's eyes," Bob Ferguson wrote to Edith. "It makes up for the omissions of many past years . . . T. was just revelling in victory and gore."[121]

Roosevelt's exhilaration at finding himself a hero (already there was talk of a Medal of Honor)[122] and, by virtue of his two charges, senior officer in command of the highest crest and the extreme front of the American line, was so great that he could not sit, let alone lie down, even in the midst of a surprise bombardment at 3:00 A.M. A shell landed right next to him, besmirching his skin with powder, and killing several nearby soldiers; but he continued to strut up and down, "snuffing the fragrant air of combat,"[123] silhouetted against the flares like a black lion rampant.

"I really believe firmly now they can't kill him," wrote Ferguson.[124]

SO BEGAN THE SIEGE of Santiago. It was not accomplished without considerable further bloodshed, for the Spanish were found to have retreated only half a mile, albeit downhill, and their retaliatory shells did much damage during the next few days. The city proper was stiffly fortified, with five thousand troops and a seemingly inexhaustible stock of heavy ammunition. Meanwhile the thin blue and khaki line cresting San Juan Heights grew thinner as wounds, malarial fever, and dysentery reduced more and more men to shivering incapacity, and often death. It took less than forty-eight hours for Roosevelt to become desperate should Shafter decide to withdraw for lack of personnel and supplies. Siboney was still clogged with unlisted crates, and each day's rain made it more difficult to haul wagons along the Camino Real. "Tell the President for Heaven's sake to send us every regiment and above all every battery possible," he scribbled to Henry Cabot Lodge. "We are within measurable distance of a terrible military disaster."[125]

On the same day Shafter, blustering out of sheer panic, sent a warning to General José Toral, of the city garrison:

> I shall be obliged, unless you surrender, to shell Santiago de Cuba. Please inform the citizens of foreign countries, and all women and children, that they should leave the city before 10 o'clock tomorrow morning.[126]

Toral's response was to admit a further 3,600 Spanish troops who had somehow managed to elude a watch force of *insurrectos* to the north of the city. That afternoon, while the U.S. Army sweated and sickened in its muddy trenches along the Heights, hostilities suddenly broke out in Santiago Harbor. Admiral Cervera's imprisoned ironclads attempted to rush Admiral Sampson's blockade, with suicidal results. By 10:00 P.M. Shafter was able to inform Washington, "The Spanish fleet . . . is reported practically destroyed." He promptly demanded surrender of the city. Toral replied that a truce might be possible.[127]

There followed a week of uneasy cease-fire as delicate negotiations went on, designed to ensure the capitulation of Santiago at no harm to Spanish honor. On 4 July, bands along the Heights tried to enliven matters with a selection of patriotic tunes (the Rough Riders ensemble contributing "Fair Harvard"), but the music had no charms for men sitting in mud, and it soon died away on the still morning air.[128]

General Toral's dignity was saved by an ingenious compromise worked out on 15 July. The Santiago garrison would surrender in two days if His Excellency, the Commander in Chief of the American forces, would kindly bombard the city (shooting at a safe height above the houses), until all Spanish soldiers had handed in their arms. They might thus be truthfully said to have capitulated under fire.[129] That night the air shook convincingly all over Santiago, and on Sunday, 17 July, the Stars and Stripes was hauled up the palace flagpole, just as church bells rang in the hour of noon.[130] It was time for Spain to begin her withdrawal from Cuba, after four centuries of imperial dominion in the New World. But first, lunch, wine, and *siesta*.

ON MONDAY, 18 JULY, Colonel Theodore Roosevelt—the title was official now[131]—marched with the Cavalry Division over San Juan Hill to a camping ground on the foothills west of El Caney. The move away from the stinking, mosquito-filled trenches was deemed essential because of yellow fever. Already more than half the Rough Riders were, in Roosevelt's words, "dead or disabled by wounds and sickness." But the mosquitoes inland were just as poisonous as those nearer the coast, and his sick list lengthened.[132]

Although mildly diverted by the "curious" fact that "the colored troops seemed to suffer as heavily as the white,"[133] he did not leave the problem to medics or the commissariat. His men must eat and build up their strength for another possible campaign in Puerto

Rico. Accordingly he sent a pack-train into Santiago with instructions to buy, at his expense, whatever "simple delicacies" they could find to supplement the nauseating rations in camp. One Rough Rider claimed that Roosevelt spent $5,000 in personal funds during the next few weeks—an exaggeration no doubt, but it at least indicates the extent of his generosity and concern.[134]

As for himself, he remained healthy and strong as ever—so much so that he proposed to swim in the Caribbean one day with Lieutenant Jack Greenway.[135] The two officers had been invited to Morro Castle by General Fitzhugh Lee, and Roosevelt's attention was drawn to the wreck of the *Merrimac,* some three hundred yards out to sea. It would be fun, he said, pulling off his clothes, to go out and inspect her.

What a colonel suggested, a lieutenant was bound to obey, and Greenway reluctantly agreed to accompany Roosevelt into the water.

> We weren't out more than a dozen strokes before Lee, who had clambered up on the parapet of Fort Morro, began to yell.
>
> "Can you make out what he's trying to say," the old man asked, punctuating his words with long, overhand strokes.
>
> "Sharks," says I, wishing I were back on shore.
>
> "Sharks," says the colonel, blowing out a mouthful of water, "they" stroke "won't" stroke "bite." Stroke. "I've been" stroke "studying them" stroke "all my life" stroke "and I never" stroke "heard of one" stroke "bothering a swimmer." Stroke. "It's all" stroke "poppy cock."
>
> Just then a big fellow, probably not more than ten or twelve feet long, but looking as big as a battleship to me, showed up alongside us. Then came another, till we had quite a group. The colonel didn't pay the least attention. . . .
>
> Meantime the old general was doing a war dance up on the parapet, shouting and standing first on one foot and then on the other, and working his arms like he was doing something on a bet.

Finally we reached the wreck and I felt better. The colonel, of course, got busy looking things over. I had to pretend I was interested, but I was thinking of the sharks and getting back to shore. I didn't hurry the colonel in his inspection either.

After a while he had seen enough, and we went over the side again. Soon the sharks were all about us again, sort of pacing us in, as they had paced us out, while the old general did the second part of his war dance. He felt a whole lot better when we landed, and so did I.[136]

ON 20 JULY, Roosevelt found himself in command of the whole 2nd Brigade. This elevation was due to medical attrition in the higher ranks, rather than his heroism at San Juan, but it was flattering nevertheless. So, too, was the growing flood of letters and telegrams from New York, urging him to consider running for the governorship in the fall. He replied politely that he would not think of quitting his present position—"even for so great an office"—at least "not while the war is on."[137] With preparations for a peace treaty already well under way, the implication of acceptance was obvious, and plots were laid by various Republican groups to entrap him the moment he stepped ashore in the United States.[138]

AT THIS POINT Roosevelt's old genius for political publicity reasserted itself. On or about the last day of July, General Shafter called a conference of all division and brigade commanders to discuss the health situation. All agreed that it was critical, and that the War Department's apparent unwillingness to evacuate the Army was inexcusable. Somebody must write a formal letter stating that in the unanimous opinion of the Fifth Corps staff, a further stay in Cuba would be to the "absolute and objectless ruin" of the fighting forces.[139]

Having reached this agreement, the Regular officers hesitated. None wished to sacrifice his career by offending Secretary Alger or

President McKinley. As the conference's junior officer and a Volunteer, Roosevelt was nudged, or more probably leaped, into the breach. The result was a "round-robin" letter, drafted by himself, and signed by all present, dated 3 August 1898, and handed to the Associated Press.[140]

> We, the undersigned officers . . . are of the unanimous opinion that this Army should be at once taken out of the island of Cuba and sent to some point on the Northern seacoast of the United States . . . that the army is disabled by malarial fever to the extent that its efficiency is destroyed, and that it is in a condition to be practically entirely destroyed by an epidemic of yellow fever, which is sure to come in the near future. . . .
>
> This army must be moved at once, or perish. As the army can be safely moved now, the persons responsible for preventing such a move will be responsible for the unnecessary loss of many thousands of lives.[141]

The document, accompanied by a long and even stronger letter of complaint signed by Roosevelt alone, was published next morning. As predicted, Secretary Alger was enraged. So, too, was the President, whose first inkling of the round-robin came when he opened his morning papers.[142] There were muttered threats in the War Department of court-martialing Roosevelt. Alger vengefully published an earlier letter from Roosevelt to himself, bragging that "the Rough Riders . . . are as good as any regulars, and three times as good as any State troops."[143]

This was a telling blow to any aspiring Governor of New York State. An instant storm of criticism blew up in the press. The *Journal* accused Roosevelt of "irresistible self-assertion and egotism," ill-suited to his "really admirable services in the field." The *Philadelphia Press* remarked that in view of "intense indignation" among the militia, it was unlikely that the New York Republican party could now nominate Theodore Roosevelt for Governor. But many newspapers found equal fault with Secretary Alger, and charged him with treachery in publishing a private letter. The Colonel could surely be excused his overweening pride in his regiment, commented the *Baltimore American;* after all, "he led these men in one of the noblest fights of the century."[144]

Within three days Shafter's army was ordered to Montauk, Long Island.[145]

The Rough Riders sailed out of Santiago Harbor on 8 August, leaving Leonard Wood behind as Military Governor of the city. They were not sorry to see Cuba sink into the sea behind them. In seven weeks of sweaty, sickly acquaintance with it, they had seen it transformed from a tropical Garden of Eden to a hell of denuded trees, cindery fields, and staring shells of houses.[146] The island's bugs were in their veins, the smell of its dead in their nostrils, the taste of its horse meat and fecal water in their mouths. It would be days before the Atlantic breezes, cooling and freshening as they steamed north, swept away this sense of defilement.

Yet the farther Cuba dropped away, the brighter shone the memory of their two great battles—in particular that rush up Kettle Hill behind the man with the flying blue neckerchief. They had done something which orthodox military strategists considered impossible, namely, stormed and captured a high redoubt over open ground, using weapons inferior to, and fewer than, those of a securely entrenched enemy.[147] In doing so they had been the first to break the Spanish defenses; charging on, they had been first to take and hold the final crest overlooking Santiago.

For Roosevelt himself, the "crowded hour" atop San Juan Heights had been one of absolute fulfillment. "I would rather have led that charge . . . than served three terms in the U.S. Senate." And he would rather die from yellow fever as a result than never to have charged at all. "Should the worst come to the worst I am quite content to go now and to leave my children at least an honorable name," he told Henry Cabot Lodge. "And old man, if I do go, I do wish you would get that Medal of Honor for me anyhow, as I should awfully like the children to have it, and I think I earned it."[148]

With fulfillment came purgation. Bellicose poisons had been

breeding in him since infancy. During recent years the strain had grown virulent, clouding his mind and souring the natural sweetness of his temperament. But at last he had had his bloodletting. He had fought a war and killed a man. He had "driven the Spaniard from the New World." Theodore Roosevelt was at last, incongruously but wholeheartedly, a man of peace.

CHAPTER 26

The Most Famous Man in America

From the contending crowd, a shout,
A mingled sound of triumph and of wailing.

IT WAS MONDAY, 15 August 1898. All morning the crowd scattered across the sands of Montauk Point grew larger, as the troopship *Miami* wallowed at anchor three miles out to sea. Soldiers and civilians, women and children, reporters and Red Cross staff squinted over the water, wondering when the Rough Riders would be allowed to disembark. While they waited, a westerly breeze snapped the sails of yachts in the harbor, and swished through the pines of Whithemard Headland.[1] It was this prevailing wind that had determined the selection of Montauk Point as the mustering-out camp for General Shafter's army. Presumably it would blow away whatever yellow-fever bacilli lingered among the troops—wafting them somewhere in the direction of Spain.

Not until nearly noon did the tugs bring *Miami* in, and nudge her sideways against the pier. The crowd peered eagerly at the deep rows of soldiers on board, searching in vain for a hero to recognize. Presently two spectacle-lenses flashed like prisms at the end of the bridge, and "a big bronzed-faced man in a light brown uniform"[2]

"I shall never forget the lustre that shone about him."

Colonel Roosevelt preparing to muster out at Camp Wikoff, Montauk, L.I.

was seen waving his campaign hat. A hundred voices delightedly roared "Roosevelt! Roosevelt! Hurrah for Teddy and the Rough Riders!" Beside him somebody made out a whiskery little general in blue. "Hurrah for Fighting Joe!"[3]

While sailors made the ship fast, an officer on the pier shouted, "How are you, Colonel Roosevelt?" The reply came back in a voice audible half a mile away: "I am feeling disgracefully well!"

There was a pause while Roosevelt allowed the crowd to study the dozens of emaciated faces elsewhere on deck. "I feel positively ashamed of my appearance," he went on, "when I see how badly off some of my brave fellows are." Another pause. Then: "Oh, but we have had a bully fight!"[4]

Laughter and cheers spread from ship to shore and back again.

A QUARTER OF AN HOUR LATER General Wheeler stepped onto the soil of Long Island, toting a Spanish sword so long and heavy its scabbard dragged on the ground. He received a tumultuous welcome, but, to quote Edward Marshall, "when 'Teddy and his teeth' came down the gangplank, the last ultimate climax of the possibility of cheering was reached."[5]

Roosevelt's appearance at close range showed that his claims of rude health were not exaggerated. Three months of hunger, thirst, heat, mud, and execrable food—not to mention that most arduous of human activities, infantry fighting—had not thinned him; if anything, he looked thicker and stronger than when he entrained for San Antonio. He wore a fresh uniform with gaiters and scuffed boots. A cartridge belt encircled his waist, and a heavy revolver thumped against his hip as he "fairly ran" the last few steps onto the dock.[6]

Roosevelt was courteous to the official welcoming party—doffing his hat and bowing to the women on line—but out of the corner of his eye he caught sight of a group of newspapermen, and soon made his way over to them.

"Will you be our next Governor?" a voice cried.

"None of that . . . All I'll talk about is the regiment. It's the finest regiment that ever was, and I'm proud to command it."[7]

While he talked, the Rough Riders were disembarking. To the horror and sympathy of the crowd, they appeared barely able to line up on the dock, let alone march over the hill to Camp Wikoff, a mile or so inland. Their ranks were pitifully decimated. "My God," said one witness, "there are not half of the men there that left."[8]

Roosevelt was enjoying his conversation with the press so much that he paid little attention to the movement of soldiers behind him. His face radiated happiness as he described the feats of the Army's "cracker-jack" regiment, and of himself as its Colonel. "This is a pistol with a history," he said, fondling his revolver affectionately. "It was taken from the wreck of the *Maine*. When I took it to Cuba I made a vow to kill at least one Spaniard with it, and I did. . . ."[9]

WELL MIGHT HE be happy. Theodore Roosevelt had come home to find himself the most famous man in America—more famous even than Dewey, whose victory at Manila had been eclipsed (if temporarily) by the successive glories of Las Guásimas, San Juan, Santiago, and the round-robin which "brought our boys back home."[10] The news that the United States and Spain had just signed a peace initiative came as a crowning satisfaction. Intent as Roosevelt might be to parry questions about his gubernatorial ambitions—thereby strengthening rumors that he had already decided to run—his days as a soldier were numbered.[11] It remained only to spend five days in quarantine, and a few weeks supervising the demobilization of his regiment, before returning to civilian life and claiming the superb inheritance he had earned in Cuba.[12]

Shortly before two o'clock the Colonel strode onto the beach, where the Cavalry Division had formed in double file, and mounted a horse beside General Wheeler. Color Sergeant Wright hoisted the ragged regimental flag, the band crashed out a march, and the Rough Riders trooped off to detention.[13]

MEANWHILE, AT THE OPPOSITE end of Long Island, the man whose power it was to nominate, or not to nominate, Roosevelt for Governor sat pondering the state political situation. Senator Thomas Collier Platt was taking his annual vacation at the Oriental Hotel on Sheepshead Bay.[14] He had been aware since at least 20 July that various groups of Republicans were working up a "Roosevelt boom," but not until yesterday, 14 August, had two trusted lieutenants approached him formally on the subject. These men were Lemuel Ely Quigg, Roosevelt's backer for Mayor in 1894, and Benjamin B. Odell, Jr., chairman of the Republican State Committee. Since Quigg was, in turn, chairman of the New York County Committee, and as forceful as Odell was stubborn, Platt had no choice but to listen while they pleaded the cause of the man he still regarded as "a perfect bull in a china shop."[15]

The Easy Boss knew that something drastic would have to be done to prevent the renomination, at the State Republican Convention in September, of Frank S. Black, New York's present Governor. Black was a faithful protégé whose record victory in 1896 had covered Platt with glory; but he was also anathema to Republican Independents, who accused him, rather unjustly, of gross spoilsmanship in office.[16] This negative reputation might be counterbalanced by positive support for Black in upstate rural areas, were it not for a new scandal which redounded to the Governor's discredit. On 4 August a special investigative committee had reported on "improper expenditures" of at least a million dollars in the state's stalled Erie Canal Improvement project.[17] With the entire multimillion-dollar appropriation already spent, and less than two-thirds of the canal deepened, Platt was severely embarrassed. If he supported Black's bid for reelection he would lay himself and the party open to charges of cynicism and irresponsibility—even though the Governor had not been personally involved in the scandal. If, on the other hand, Platt dropped Black, it would be tantamount to admitting that there had been high-level corruption.[18]

Platt weighed his alternatives, and chose the second, seeing it as the only way he might avoid a Democratic landslide in November. He agreed to let Quigg sound Roosevelt out, but made it clear that the Rough Rider was not his preference for the nomination. "If he becomes Governor of New York, sooner or later, with his personality, he will have to be President of the United States . . . I am afraid to start that thing going."[19]

QUIGG, HOWEVER, was not the first kingmaker to visit Roosevelt at Montauk. On Thursday, 18 August, John Jay Chapman, one of the Independent party's fiercest and brightest idealists, walked up Camp Wikoff's Rough Rider Street in search of the Colonel.[20]

Tall, hook-nosed, flamboyantly scarfed even in the hottest weather, Chapman was a man of near-manic passions, both romantic and intellectual. As testimony to the former, he would brandish the stump of a missing left hand, which he had deliberately burned to a cinder as self-punishment during a stormy love affair.[21] Like Theodore Roosevelt, his friend of many years, he was well-born, Harvard-educated, and drawn equally to politics and literature (his *Emerson and Other Essays* had won the high praises of Henry James).[22] But there the resemblance ended. Chapman could neither compromise, nor join, nor lead; he was a savage loner, fated to work outside the party, a thinker whose pure ideology was unsmirched by practical considerations. Normally Roosevelt despised such people, but Chapman, four years his junior, had such courage and charm as to be permitted the supreme familiarity of "Teddy."[23]

It so happened that in August 1898 Chapman was for the first and only time in his life on the verge of real political power—if he could only persuade Roosevelt to run for Governor on an Independent ticket. The Colonel's popularity, he reasoned, was so great as to seduce large numbers of Republican voters, and would force Boss Platt to nominate him as well, in order to keep those voters within the party. Roosevelt would thus head two tickets, followed on the one by a list of "decent, young Independents" and on the other by machine Republicans. The majority of the electorate, given such a choice, would surely prefer to send Roosevelt to Albany in virtuous company.[24]

It was a beautiful plan, at least in Chapman's enthusiastic opinion. Roosevelt would be almost assured the Governorship, with all voters who were not Democrats united in his favor; the Independents would at one stroke broaden their narrow power base (at present confined largely to the Citizens' Union and Good Government Clubs in New York City) to encompass the whole state; and most important of all, Boss Platt's machine would be destroyed.[25]

Chapman was so sure of himself he allowed Roosevelt "a week to think it over."[26] The Colonel, who had everything to gain as a gubernatorial prospect by remaining silent, accepted this offer with the equanimity of one of his favorite fictional characters, Uncle Remus's Tar Baby.

THE FOLLOWING DAY Lemuel Quigg arrived.[27] Sleek, suave, prematurely gray on either side of his center parting, he made a noticeable contrast to his Independent rival. Yet the language he spoke was equally sweet to Roosevelt's ears.

Quigg "earnestly" hoped to see the Colonel nominated, "and believed that the great body of Republican voters so desired." He and Odell were "pestering" Senator Platt to that effect, but before they pestered further they would have to have "a plain statement" as to whether or not Roosevelt wanted the nomination.[28]

Roosevelt said that he did. But, in view of the fact that Quigg had made no formal offer, this should not be considered a formal reply. He promised, nevertheless, that once in power he would not "make war on Mr. Platt or anybody else if war could be avoided." As a Republican Governor, he would naturally work with the Republican machine, "in the sincere hope that there might always result harmony of opinion and purpose." He reserved the right, however, to consult with whom he pleased, and "act finally as my own judgment and conscience dictated."

Quigg replied that he had expected just such an answer, and would transmit it to Senator Platt.[29]

HAVING THUS AUTHORIZED two secret nomination campaigns (and given tacit approval to the manufacture of ten thousand "Our Teddy for Our Governor" buttons), Roosevelt was free to leave Camp Wikoff on 20 August for a five-day reunion with his family.[30] He smilingly refused to discuss his future with reporters. "Now stop it. I will not say a word about myself, but I will talk about the regiment forever."[31] As a result of this strategy he kept himself in the headlines, while avoiding all political complications. "He is playing the game of a pretty foxy man," said a worried Democratic campaign official.[32]

His trip to Oyster Bay was carefully timed to coincide with the

Republican State Committee meeting in Manhattan. This preconvention assemblage enabled Senator Platt to weigh the relative strengths of Black, Roosevelt, and other potential candidates for the nomination. According to Quigg, the Easy Boss was impressed by reports of Roosevelt enthusiasm in Buffalo and Erie County, which traditionally acted as a pivot between Democratic New York City and the Republican remainder of the state. Informal polls of the thirty-four committeemen showed a large majority in favor of the Colonel.[33] Platt was noncommittal after the meeting, but reporters were quick to infer that Roosevelt would be the party's eventual choice.

At eight o'clock that evening, just as New Yorkers were reading the first reports of Platt's conference, Roosevelt arrived in Oyster Bay amid such bedlam as the little village had never known in its two and a half centuries of existence. Church bells pealed, rockets shot up, cannons and musketry exploded in salute as his train pulled into the station with whistle wide open. The war hero hung out of his window waving his Rough Rider hat, grinning and glowing in the light of a celebratory bonfire. A red, white, and blue banner slung across Audrey Avenue proclaimed the words WELCOME, COLONEL! and fifteen hundred people yelled greetings to "Teddy."[34]

When Roosevelt stepped out onto the platform he was seen to be accompanied by his wife. Edith had gone to Montauk to greet him privately beforehand, and she stood flinching now as the crowd surged forward. This coarse grabbing and grasping, these howls of the detested nickname, presaged ill for whatever hopes she may have had for a quiet return to domestic life at Sagamore Hill. Like it or not, she had to accept that Theodore was now public property. Dreadful as the prospect might have seemed to her, she braced herself for it with all her considerable strength. Smiling and outwardly calm, she followed the Rough Rider as he fought toward their waiting two-seater. Not a few admiring glances followed her. For the rest of his life Roosevelt would have to suffer a ritual greeting whenever he returned to Oyster Bay: "Teddy, how's your 'oman?"[35]

HE SPENT THE NEXT FEW DAYS enjoying the forgotten delights of civilization: cool summer clothes, good food, the conversation of women and children, hot water, clean sheets, green lawns, birdsong. Every night he changed into a tuxedo for dinner and joined his family and guests on the piazza overlooking Long Island Sound. Toying with a glass of Edith's old Madeira, he gazed at the passing lights of pleasure craft and Fall River steamers, and told over and over again to all who would listen the stories of Las Guásimas and San Juan Hill.[36]

A particularly interested auditor was Robert Bridges, editor of *Scribner's*. Four months before, when the Rough Riders were still organizing at San Antonio, Roosevelt had offered Bridges "first chance," ahead of *Century* and *Atlantic*, for the publication of his war memoirs. He suggested that this "permanent historical work" should appear first as a six-part magazine series, beginning in the New Year of 1899.[37] Bridges had accepted with alacrity. Now the editor was pleased to discover that Roosevelt already had the book "blocked out." Not a line had been written, but the Colonel's diary contained scraps of choice dialogue, and the stories he was telling on the piazza were obviously being tested for popular appeal. Bridges expressed concern that politics might delay Roosevelt's reentry into literature, but the author was supremely confident. "Not at all—you shall have the various chapters at the time promised."[38]

On the morning of 24 August, Roosevelt's last before returning to Camp Wikoff, he was waited upon a second time by John Jay Chapman. The Independent leader, who was accompanied by Isaac Klein of the Citizens' Union, requested an answer to his proposal of 18 August. Roosevelt, feeling his power, said he would run as a party regular or not at all. But if the Republicans did honor him with their nomination on 27 September, he would be happy to accept that of the Independents afterward as an "endorsement." He had no objections to the Independents making a preliminary announcement of his acceptance, as long as it was accompanied by a statement of his own making clear the stipulations involved.[39]

This, of course, was all that Chapman and Klein wanted. They happily returned to New York to begin work on a provisional ticket. Chapman had always admired Roosevelt, in the way thinkers follow doers, but now the admiration deepened into reverence. "I shall never forget the lustre that shone about him . . . my companion accused me of being in love with him, and indeed I was. I never before nor since have felt that glorious touch of hero worship. . . . Lo, there, it says, Behold the way! You have only to worship, trust, and support him."[40]

Every day brought new indications that Roosevelt was the coming man of Republican politics, not only in New York State, but across the country as well. National committeemen, Senators, and representatives of far-flung party organizations urged him to run for Governor, and begged his services as a campaign speaker.[41] An envelope adorned with nothing but a crude sketch of him in military uniform was delivered to Oyster Bay, along with sackfuls of other mail.[42] In Chicago several Union Leaguers announced the formation of the "Roosevelt 1904 Club," proclaiming him as the natural successor to President McKinley when that popular executive stepped down after another term. There were some who whispered that he might run, and win, against the President in 1900.[43]

Roosevelt, perhaps remembering his too-rapid boom in the New York mayoralty campaign, announced that he would return to Montauk twelve hours early, on 25 August. He was still an Army officer, not a politician, and "I feel that my place is with the boys."[44]

There followed a week of silence and secrecy while the Colonel nursed his regiment back to health and strength, and Boss Platt's pollsters sounded out opinions on Roosevelt v. Black. One of these pollsters was Isaac Hunt, the gangling reformer of Roosevelt's Assembly days. He reported that only one Republican delegate in three would vote for Black. "Ike," said Platt, "I have sent men all over this state; your report and theirs correspond."[45]

On 1 September, the Easy Boss allowed the first news leaks indicating that he personally favored Roosevelt's nomination. E. L. Godkin of the *Post* chortled over the prospect of two such ill-matched bedfellows coyly climbing into their pajamas. "The humorous possibilities of such a situation are infinite."[46]

Chapman and Klein hurried to Montauk for reassurances that Roosevelt would not "take our nomination and then later throw us down by withdrawing from the ticket." The Colonel's response appears to have been guarded, yet positive enough for Chapman to write on Sunday, 4 September: "We expect to put Roosevelt in the field [soon] at the head of a straight Independent ticket."[47]

ON THE SAME DAY at Camp Wikoff there occurred a symbolic incident highly pleasing, no doubt, to the Roosevelt 1904 Club. President McKinley arrived at Montauk railroad station on a mission of thanks to Shafter's victorious army. As he settled into his carriage with Secretary Alger, he caught sight of a mounted man grinning at him some twenty yards away. "Why, there's Colonel Roosevelt," exclaimed McKinley, and called out, "Colonel! I'm glad to see you!"

Secretary Alger manifestly was not, but this did not prevent the President from making an extraordinary public gesture. He jumped out of the carriage and walked toward Roosevelt, who simultaneously tumbled off his horse with the ease of a cowboy. In the words of one observer:

> The President held out his hand; Col. Roosevelt struggled to pull off his right glove. He yanked at it desperately and finally inserted the ends of his fingers in his teeth and gave a mighty tug. Off came the glove and a beatific smile came over the Colonel's face as he grasped the President's hand. The crowd which had watched the performance tittered audibly. Nothing more cordial than the greeting between the President and Col. Roosevelt could be imagined. The President just grinned all over.
>
> "Col. Roosevelt," he said, "I'm glad indeed to see you looking so well."

Before McKinley reentered the carriage Roosevelt made him promise to visit "my boys."[48]

THE COLONEL CONTINUED to juggle, expertly but dangerously, with the two balls tossed him by Chapman and Quigg. When, on 10 September, the former publicly praised Roosevelt as one "who in his person represents independence and reform," Roosevelt himself announced, by proxy, that he was "a Republican in the broadest sense of the word." He confirmed for the first time that he would accept, but not seek, nomination by his regular party colleagues. Any subsequent nomination by the Independents would of course be "most flattering and gratifying."[49]

To make his position doubly clear, at least to himself, he wrote two letters on 12 September, one to Quigg defining the conditions on which he would accept nomination, the other to the Citizens' Union saying that a new statement that he was still available as an Independent candidate was "all right." The warmth and length of the first letter (thirty-six lines) compared with the curt brevity (two lines) of the second left no doubt as to where his true hopes and sympathies lay.[50] However neither recipient could make this comparison at the time, and both continued to work for Roosevelt's nomination.

THE FOLLOWING DAY, Tuesday, 13 September, was a poignant one for Roosevelt. Demobilization work was complete, and the Rough Riders prepared to muster out, troop by troop. Although the regiment's life had been short—a mere 133 days from formation to dissolution—its rise had been meteoric, leaving an incandescent glow in the hearts of its nine hundred surviving members. Civilian life seemed a dull, even dismal prospect to those who had clerkships and ranch jobs and law school to return to. Yet the glory had to come to an end. At one o'clock bugles rang through the grassy streets of Camp Wikoff, summoning the Rough Riders to their last assembly.[51]

Roosevelt, writing in his tent, was surprised to hear his men lining up outside. He had not expected the mustering out to begin until a little later in the afternoon. But now a group of deferential troopers ducked in out of the sunshine and requested his attendance at a short open-air ceremony.

Emerging, the Colonel found his entire regiment arranged in a square on the plain, around a table shrouded with a lumpy blanket. Nine hundred arms snapped in salute as he stood with brown face flushing. He looked around him and saw tears starting in many eyes; his own dimmed too.[52] Then Private Murphy of M Troop stepped forward and announced in a choking voice that the 1st Volunteer Cavalry wished to present their commanding officer with "a very slight token of admiration, love, and esteem." Murphy struggled to summarize the "glorious deeds accomplished and hardships endured" by the Rough Riders under Roosevelt, while the sound of sobbing grew louder on all sides of the square. "In conclusion allow me to say that one and all, from the highest to the lowest . . . will carry back to their hearths a pleasant remembrance of all your acts, for they have always been of the kindest."[53]

The blanket was whipped away to disclose a bronze bronco-buster, sculpted by Frederic Remington. From thumping hooves to insolently waving sombrero, it was the solid remembrance of a sight seen thousands of times in camp at San Antonio and Tampa, again in Cuba when there were native horses to be rustled, and yet again in Wikoff for the benefit of visitors and envious infantrymen. Roosevelt was so overcome he could only step forward and pat the bronco's coldly gleaming mane.[54] He found his voice with difficulty, forcing the words out:

> Officers and men, I really do not know what to say. Nothing could possibly happen that would touch and please me as this has . . . I would have been most deeply touched if the officers had given me this testimonial, but coming from you, my men, I appreciate it tenfold. It comes to me from you who shared the hardships of the campaign with me, who gave me a piece of your hardtack when I had none, and who gave me your blankets when I had none to lie upon. To have such a gift come from this peculiarly American regiment touches me more than I can say. This is something I shall hand down to my children, and I shall value it more than the weapons I carried through the campaign.[55]

"Three cheers for the next Governor of New York," yelled a voice.

"Wish we could vote for him," came the answering shout.

Roosevelt asked the men to come forward and shake his hand. "I want to say goodbye to each one of you in person."

Company ranks were formed, and the Rough Riders began to pass by their Colonel in single file. Many cried openly as they walked away.[56] "He was the only man I ever came in contact with," confessed one private, "that when bidding farewell, I felt a handshake was but poor expression. I wanted to hug him."[57] Roosevelt had a compliment, joke, recognition, or a ready identification for every man. As he shook the slender fingers of Ivy Leaguers, the rough paws of Idaho lumberjacks, the heavy dark hands of Indian cowpunchers, Roosevelt doubtless reflected, for the umpteenth time, what a microcosm of America this regiment was—or, to use the *World*'s metaphor, what "an elaborate photograph of the character of its founder."[58] Here were game, bristling Micah Jenkins, "on whom danger acted like wine"; Ben Daniels of Dodge City, with half an ear bitten off; languid Woodbury Kane, looking somehow elegant in battle-stained khaki; poker-faced Pollock the Pawnee, smiling for the first and only time in the history of the regiment; and Rockpicker Smith, who had stood up in the trenches outside Santiago and bombarded "them —— Spaniels" with stones. Here, too, were dozens of troopers whom Roosevelt knew only by their contradictory nicknames: "Metropolitan Bill" the frontiersman, "Nigger" the near-albino, "Pork Chop" the Jew, jocular "Weeping Dutchman," foul-mouthed "Prayerful James," and "Rubber Shoe Andy," the noisiest scout in Cuba.[59]

After the last tearful good-bye and promise of everlasting comradeship, Roosevelt's Rough Riders marched off to be paid $77 apiece and discharged. By early evening the first of them were trooping into New York with wild cowboy yells. Within twenty-four hours the 1st U.S. Volunteer Cavalry was dissolved. "So all things pass away," Roosevelt sighed to his old friend Jacob Riis. "But they were beautiful days."[60]

ON SATURDAY, 17 SEPTEMBER, the Colonel (as he would continue to be called throughout his life as a private citizen) braced himself for a prenomination meeting with Senator Platt. Confident as he might be of his new political powers, it was noted that he, not Platt, crossed the gulf between them, namely the East River of Manhattan. He sneaked into the Fifth Avenue Hotel via the ladies' entrance, shortly before three o'clock in the afternoon, looking somber in black and gray, but wearing a defiantly military hat.[61]

Advance word of the meeting had been leaked to the press, along with rumors that Platt was mistrustful of Roosevelt's continued flirtation with the Independents; consequently the hotel's main lobby was thronged with excited politicians and reporters. Anticipation rose as two hours ticked by with no word from the Amen Corner. Some pundits guessed that Platt would insist Roosevelt run as a Republican only, and that Roosevelt would agree, for the very good reason that Platt controlled some 700 of the convention's 971 votes.[62] Others said that the Colonel's boom was already so great that Platt's survival as party boss depended on his favor. Betting on Roosevelt v. Black ran $50 to $20 against the Governor.[63]

A few minutes after five o'clock Roosevelt appeared alone at the top of the grand stairway, hesitating with his habitual sense of drama until the crowd saw him and surged across the intervening space. "I had a very pleasant conversation," he began to say, "with Senator Platt and Mr. Odell—"

An impatient voice interrupted him. "Will you accept the nomination for Governor?"

"Of course I will! What do you think I am here for?"[64]

THUS DID ROOSEVELT proclaim himself both a gubernatorial candidate and an orthodox Republican willing to compromise with, if not actually obey, the Easy Boss. He denied that he had been asked to withdraw from the non-partisan ticket, and the Independents bravely insisted he was still their man, but few doubted that John Jay Chapman would soon receive a "Dear Jack" letter. Sure enough, Roosevelt waited only until the mails reopened on Monday morning.

> I do not see how I can accept the Independent nomination and keep good faith with the other men on my ticket. It has been a thing that has worried me greatly; not because of its

> result on the election; but because it seems so difficult for men whom I very heartily respect as I do you, to see the impossible position in which they are putting me.[65]

Chapman simply refused to believe that the hero of San Juan Hill could write anything so petulant as the last words of this letter. "I know that you are the least astute of men," he shot back. ". . . I am satisfied, however, that you misapprehend the situation and that you never will decline."[66]

On 22 September, Roosevelt sat down to write an icily formal reply. "Dear Mr. Chapman . . . It seems to me that I would not be acting in good faith toward my fellow candidates if I permitted my name to head a ticket designed for their overthrow, a ticket more-over which cannot be put up because of objections to the fitness of character of any candidates, inasmuch as no candidates have yet been nominated."[67]

Was it lingering wistfulness for his own youthful idealism, mingled perhaps with sympathy for the non-partisan workers frantically canvassing upstate in his behalf, that caused him to pigeonhole this letter for three days?[68] Or did he withhold it because he wished to take on as many Independent voters as possible before nudging Chapman overboard? Lack of documentation makes a definite answer impossible. Unpleasant as the latter alternative may be, it is by far the more likely. Wistfulness and sympathy were not characteristics of Roosevelt the politician; a fierce hunger for power was. Clearly, every day he could *seem* to cling to both nominations increased his potential strength at the convention and in the election; the longer he kept Chapman guessing, the less chance the Independents had of finding an adequate replacement.[69]

Whatever his motive, he patiently suffered the abuse of Chapman, Klein, and other desperate Independents. They called him a "broken-backed half-good man," a "dough-face," and—publicly, when he remained obdurate—the puppet of Senator Platt and "standard-bearer of corruption" in New York State. During one meeting, he allegedly "cried like a baby" and "could hardly walk when he left."[70]

Chapman's final argument with Roosevelt, at Sagamore Hill on the afternoon of 24 September, was so violent that the Colonel accused his one-armed aggressor of provoking "an able-bodied man who could not hit back." Chapman stormed out of the house, but returned sheepishly half an hour later to say that the last train for New York had already left Oyster Bay Station. Roosevelt, amused, let him stay for the night and supplied a conciliatory toothbrush. "We shook hands the next morning at parting," wrote Chapman, "and avoided each other for twenty years."[71]

No sooner had Roosevelt decided that he was strong enough to run for Governor on one ticket, than a sensational private revelation threatened to destroy his candidacy overnight. On 24 September headlines in all major newspapers shouted the story:

ROOSEVELT NOT A CITIZEN OF THIS STATE
This Is the Bomb That Gov. Black and His Friends Are Ready to Throw Into the Saratoga Convention[72]

The gunpowder in Black's bomb was an affidavit Assistant Secretary of the Navy Roosevelt had executed just six months before, at the height of his tax problems and worries about his ailing family. It stated that he had been a legal resident of Washington, D.C., since 1 October 1897, when his lease of a Manhattan town house (actually Bamie's place at 689 Madison Avenue) came to an end. This had effectively disqualified him as a New York State taxpayer, saving him from a personalty assessment of $50,000. But it also appeared to disqualify him from the governorship of New York, since the constitution required that all candidates must be "continuous" residents of the state for at least five years prior to nomination.[73]

With only three days to go before the opening of the convention, Boss Platt and Chairman Odell swung into rapid, ruthless action: The party's most eminent lawyers, including Joseph H. Choate and Elihu Root, were called in to analyze the problem. Roosevelt was ordered to stay at home and say nothing to reporters.[74]

The more Choate and Root looked into the case the less they liked it. Not only had Roosevelt declared himself a Washingtonian to escape taxes in New York, he had previously declared himself a New Yorker to escape taxes at Oyster Bay.[75] Cynics might justifiably wonder if the Colonel had since established a residence in Santiago, in order to avoid paying any taxes anywhere.

Choate, perhaps recollecting Roosevelt's disloyalty during his Senatorial bid in 1896, refused to "put himself on record" as to the candidate's fitness for office.[76] Root, too, was "extremely anxious and dubious" about the evidence, until Chairman Odell reminded him that Roosevelt, if elected, would almost certainly bring in a Republican Attorney General on his coattails. There would then be no risk of proceedings *in quo warranto,* and Roosevelt's defense, however flimsy, would stand inviolate.[77]

This was the sort of reasoning that Senator Platt understood. He said that it was the best legal opinion he had heard so far.[78] Roosevelt's nomination would go forward as planned. Root must research, and if necessary invent, enough scholarly argument to reassure the Saratoga Convention that they were in fact voting for a citizen of New York State. Meanwhile he, Platt, would see to it that Root got a delegate's seat, and be recognized as a speaker in advance of the first roll call.[79]

Root philosophically set to work on Roosevelt's affidavits and covering correspondence. Analysis of the latter showed that the candidate was more sinned against than sinning; he had received foolish advice from family lawyers and accountants, despite repeated pleas to them to protect his voting rights. But the cold evidence was embarrassing. Roosevelt had definitely declared himself a resident of another state during the required period of eligibility. Root decided to prepare a brief on varying interpretations of the word *resident,* mixing many "dry details" with sympathetic extracts from Roosevelt's letters, plus a lot of patriotic "ballyhoo" calculated both to obfuscate and inspire.[80]

According to at least two accounts, Roosevelt was nevertheless so depressed about the tax scandal that he went to Platt and suggested that he withdraw his candidacy. "Is the hero of San Juan Hill a coward?" sneered the old man.

"By Gad! I'll run."[81]

ROOSEVELT SPENT SUNDAY, 25 September, relaxing with his family at Oyster Bay, and let it be known that he intended to stay at home through the convention. He was too tired to write more than a few lines to Henry Cabot Lodge: "I have, literally, hardly been able to eat or sleep during the last week, because of the pressure on me."[82]

Conscious of his dignity as a candidate by request, he made no attempt to establish telephone or telegraph connections with the village. He lounged casually in a white flannel suit, napped after lunch, and went for a twilight stroll with Edith. Shortly after sunset the couple changed into evening dress and dined with their children. Then they adjourned to the library, where a fire was crackling, and sat waiting for the first news to come up the hill.[83]

AT 8:30 A MESSENGER BOY arrived on a bicycle and handed Roosevelt a telegram. It was signed by his personal representative at Saratoga.

> READING BY ROOT OF TAX CORRESPONDENCE PRODUCED PROFOUND SENSATION AND WILD ENTHUSIASM. C. H. T. COLLIS

Brave, brilliant Elihu! What *had* the man said? But other telegrams were coming thick and fast now:

> LAUTERBACH FOLLOWS ROOT AND MOST GRATEFULLY TAKES IT BACK. C. H. T. COLLIS

> YOU ARE NOMINATED FOR GOVERNOR. OUR HEARTS ARE WITH YOU. CONGRATULATIONS. ISAAC HUNT—WILLIAM O'NEIL

Ike and Billy! "These two fellows," said Roosevelt, dazedly passing the message to a reporter, "were my right and left bowers when I was in the Legislature." He read the next telegram without comment: it came from his future running mate.

> ACCEPT MY SINCERE CONGRATULATIONS UPON YOUR NOMINATION FOR GOVERNOR. MAY YOUR MARCH TO THE CAPITOL BE AS TRIUMPHANT AS YOUR VICTORIOUS CHARGE UP SAN JUAN HILL. TIMOTHY L. WOODRUFF.[84]

Roosevelt's vote had been an overwhelming 753 to Black's 218. What was more, he had won the approval of all types of constituency, whereas Black attracted mainly urban support. All this bode well for the Colonel as a popular candidate, if not for Republicans in general. He wisely did not exaggerate his chances of election. "There is great enthusiasm for me, but it may prove to be mere froth, and the drift of events is against the party in New York this year. . . ."[85]

ON 4 OCTOBER a committee featuring all the major figures in the state Republican party—with one conspicuous exception—waited upon Roosevelt at Sagamore Hill and formally notified him of his nomination. Senator Thomas C. Platt sent his regrets, saying that he was "indisposed."[86] Arthritic or not, the Easy Boss had no desire to travel as a pilgrim to the Rooseveltian shrine. Candidate and committee were to remember that the party's spiritual center remained the Amen Corner of the Fifth Avenue Hotel.

Roosevelt, for his part, was as determined to assert his own independence. He stood grim and motionless on the piazza as Chauncey M. Depew made the customary flowery address. In reply he read from a typewritten sheet, emphasizing some phrases with particular clarity: "If elected I shall strive so to administer the duties of this high office that the interests of the people as a whole shall be conserved . . . *I shall feel that I owe my position to the people*, and to the people I shall hold myself accountable."[87]

Meanwhile, in Brooklyn, another committee was notifying Judge Augustus van Wyck that he had been selected to run as the Democratic candidate for Governor.[88] Although van Wyck was as obscure as Roosevelt was famous, he boasted an equally clean record, and had the added advantage of belonging to the out-of-power party in a time of corrupt status quo. Boss Richard Croker of Tammany Hall had engineered his nomination, much as Boss Platt had Roosevelt's, yet the Democrat's integrity could not be questioned.[89] By close of business that afternoon, the bookies of Broadway were offering van Wyck at 3 to 5 and finding plenty of takers; one gambler plunked down $18,000 against $30,000 on the judge.[90]

The only even odds, as some wag remarked, were that the next Governor would be a Dutchman.

ONE OF THE FIRST OUTSIDERS to congratulate Roosevelt was William McKinley, who sent a handwritten expression of unqualified good wishes. This letter, said party pundits, "disposed of the rumor that the President regards Colonel Roosevelt as a possible rival two years hence."[91] Yet McKinley could hardly have been reassured by Roosevelt's first campaign speech, in Carnegie Hall on 5 October. It sounded more like the oratory of a Commander-in-Chief than plain gubernatorial rhetoric:

> There comes a time in the life of a nation, as in the life of an individual, when it must face great responsibilities, whether it will or no. We have now reached that time. We cannot avoid facing the fact that we occupy a new place among the people of the world, and have entered upon a new career. . . . The guns of our warships in the tropic seas of the West and the remote East have awakened us to the knowledge of new duties. Our flag is a proud flag, and it stands for liberty and civilization. Where it has once floated, there must be no return to tyranny or savagery . . .[92]

"He really believes he is the American flag," John Jay Chapman remarked in disgust.[93] Senator Platt, who had strongly opposed the Spanish-American War, did not like Roosevelt's imperialistic overtones at all. Neither did any other local party leaders. They noticed an ominous tendency of the candidate to surround himself with khaki-clad veterans, several of whom seemed determined to stump the state with him. Chairman Odell felt that a "Rough Rider campaign" would be undignified and dangerous.[94] Perhaps Roosevelt should go home to Oyster Bay and let Platt's tame newspapers conduct the election.

As a result the Colonel found himself closeted at Sagamore Hill for a period of "absolute sloth" while his managers debated how to proceed through 7 November. The news from upstate was not good.[95] Voters were reported to be apathetic, as well they might be, considering the dullness of the issues. Apart from Democratic accusations of "thievery and jobbery" by Republican canal commissioners, there was little to excite the electorate one way or another. State control of excise rates and licensing fees, state management of the National Guard, state supervision of municipal election bureaus—these were not the sort of subjects to distract a fishmonger's attention from the sporting pages.[96] Indiscreet and irrelevant as Roosevelt's Carnegie Hall address had been, it had at least drummed up a certain amount of enthusiasm. Odell began to regret silencing the candidate so hastily.

On 9 October, Governor Black suggested, in an apparently conciliatory gesture, that Roosevelt be sent to speak in Rensselaer, his own home town. Odell was tempted to agree for the sake of party unity, but hesitated until the evening of the thirteenth, when a second urgent telephone invitation came in from the coordinator of the Rensselaer County Fair. If Roosevelt paid a visit the following morning, said the caller, he would be sure of "a tremendous crowd."[97]

Odell hesitated no longer. He relayed the invitation to Sagamore Hill and received a rather testy message of acceptance. It would be "inconvenient," but Roosevelt would take the early-morning train into town.[98]

So began a day of the drizzly, hopeless kind all political candidates dread.[99] The Colonel arose at dawn and reached New York City at eight. District Attorney William J. Youngs was waiting at Grand Central to escort him north to Albany, where Governor Black expressed the utmost surprise to see them. No advance warning of the visit had been sent, Black insisted. Due to pressure of other engagements, he unfortunately would not be able to accompany them to the fair.

Pausing only to growl that when he next came back to Rensselaer County, it would be as his own campaign manager, Roosevelt returned to the station. As his train rocked and swayed eastward to Troy, he tried to eat a few slippery oysters in the dining car. Six officials in four open carriages were waiting in the rain at Brookside Park Station. The fairground was just far enough away to ensure that Roosevelt was thoroughly soaked en route; when he arrived in front of the main grandstand he found less than three hundred persons idly leaning against the railings.

The candidate did not even deign to step down from his carriage. Five minutes after entering the fairground he left it again, and returned to the station, only to find that his train had disappeared.

NEXT MORNING, SATURDAY, as New Yorkers hooted over Roosevelt's "wild goose chase" (Democratic newspapers saw it as a vengeful prank by Governor Black), the candidate brushed aside Odell's apologies. With little more than three weeks to go before the election, and van Wyck gaining strength daily, it was plain that Republican strategy was not working. The campaign needed drama, and it needed an issue; he, Roosevelt, would supply both.[100]

Sometime during his damp peregrinations the day before, he had read a newspaper interview with Richard Croker in which the Tammany boss had made some amazingly arrogant remarks about the state judiciary. Croker said, for example, that Supreme Court Justice Daly, a respected Democrat with twenty-eight years on the bench, would be opposed by the machine in his bid for reelection. This was because he had recently refused to reappoint a Croker henchman to his staff. Tammany Hall would not endorse any judge who failed to show "proper consideration" for favors received.[101]

Here, in Roosevelt's opinion, was the issue of the campaign. He knew from his youthful experiences with Jay Gould and Judge Westbrook how strongly New Yorkers felt about the corruption of the judiciary. Starting immediately, he intended to stump the state as it had never been stumped before, attacking not van Wyck, but Boss Croker, as a defiler of white ermine.[102]

To make sure he was seen and heard at every whistle-stop, he would take along a party of six Rough Riders in full uniform, including Color Sergeant Albert Wright as flag-waver, Bugler Emil Cassi as herald, and Sergeant "Buck" Taylor, the most garrulous man in the regiment, in case he lost his voice.[103]

Faced with such resolution, Odell could only agree. By the time

Roosevelt's twin-unit Special left Weehawken, New Jersey, at 10:02 on Monday morning, 17 October, his party had been enlarged to include several other aspirants to high state offices, and half a dozen newspaper correspondents.[104]

THE COLONEL MADE seventeen stops that day along 212 miles of the Hudson Valley. Crowds, summoned by blasts from Cassi's bugle, were encouragingly large and enthusiastic, amounting to some twenty thousand in under twelve hours. As he leaned again and again over the rear platform of his private car, he harped on Croker's desire to corrupt the judiciary, mixed in a few stirring calls to Empire, and made some emphatically vague promises to investigate the canal scandal. He soon found that any remark to do with the Rough Riders stimulated applause from old and young, male and female. The citizens of Newburgh were duly reminded of his volunteer status in the war; those of Albany thrilled to the story of San Juan Hill; hecklers at Glens Falls were accused of making more noise than the guerrillas of Las Guásimas.[105] Back in New York, the bookies of Broadway improved their odds in Roosevelt's favor, typically offering $25,000 at 10 to 7, and $5,000 at 5 to 3. Knowledgeable punters said that the market had yet to settle.[106]

During the next two days, 18 and 19 October, the Special steamed around the Adirondacks as far north as Ogdensburg on the St. Lawrence River, then curved south again via Carthage.[107] Roosevelt tailored his speeches (never more than ten minutes long, and seldom repeated) to his audiences with unfailing accuracy. He spoke jerkily and harshly, squinting as though his eyes hurt, yet he radiated a strange, mesmeric power, well described by Billy O'Neil:

> Wednesday it rained all day and in spite of it there were immense gatherings of enthusiastic people at every stopping place. At Carthage, in Jeff. County, there were three thousand people standing in the mud and rain. He spoke about ten minutes—the speech was nothing, but the man's presence was everything. It was electrical, magnetic. I looked in the faces of hundreds and saw only pleasure and satisfaction. When the train moved away, scores of men and women ran

> after [it], waving hats and handkerchiefs and cheering, trying to keep him in sight as long as possible.
>
> . . . Perhaps I measured others by my own feelings, for as the train faded away I saw him smiling, and waving his hat at the people, and they in turn giving abundant evidence of their enthusiastic affection, my eyes filled with tears. I couldn't help it though I am ordinarily a cold-blooded fish not easily stirred like that.[108]

The Colonel returned to New York that evening. During the next thirty-six hours he addressed seven major meetings. His histrionic gifts were everywhere in evidence, particularly when timing his entrances. "Out of the woods came a hero," some warm-up speaker would declaim, and infallibly Roosevelt would sweep onto the platform, waving his military hat to wild cheers.[109] Or he would burst unexpectedly into a German-American *Versammlung* while the chairman barked, "Herr Roosevelt is here!"[110] Wherever he went, Color Sergeant Wright led the way and other Rough Riders brought up the rear, as if Roosevelt were still advancing through the jungles of Cuba.[111] The candidate regaled every audience with a war story or two, discreetly rearranging the facts for rhetorical effect. For example, Bucky O'Neill's celestial musings on the bridge of the *Yucatán* became his "last words" at the foot of Kettle Hill, and acquired expansionist overtones: "Who wouldn't risk his life to add a new star to the flag?"[112]

District leaders meeting with Roosevelt on 21 October discovered that behind the showman lurked a coldly efficient campaign strategist. He was "too strong a man to be susceptible to flattery," asking not for "rosy" forecasts but facts as to where his campaign was weak and what could be done to strengthen it. The district leaders left Republican headquarters "enthusiastic, not so much over the Colonel's personality as his capacity for details. He revealed himself a political fighter very much as he did in the charge of San Juan."[113]

THE ROOSEVELT SPECIAL set off again that Friday afternoon on a quick swing up the Hudson and Mohawk valleys, followed on Monday by a six-day tour of central and western New York State.

It was noticed that the candidate had reduced his Rough Rider escort to two—Sergeant Buck Taylor and Private Sherman Bell of Cripple Creek, Colorado—and had dressed them in mufti, possibly to avoid offending the conservative sensibilities of rural voters.[114] If so, such scruples were groundless. Buck Taylor was listened to with the greatest deference en route, even at Port Jervis, when he pronounced the most resounding *faux pas* of the campaign:

> I want to talk to you about mah Colonel. He kept ev'y promise he made to us and he will to you. . . . He told us we might meet wounds and death and we done it, but he was thar in the midst of us, and when it came to the great day he led us up San Juan Hill like sheep to the slaughter and so will he lead you.

"This hardly seemed a tribute to my military skill," Roosevelt said afterward, "but it delighted the crowd, and as far as I could tell did me nothing but good."[115]

Depot by depot, valley by valley, the little train toiled on through the misty countryside. Roosevelt made sixteen formal speeches that first day, nineteen the second, fourteen the third, fifteen the fourth, eleven the fifth, and fifteen the sixth, plus twelve other impromptu speeches here and there—a total of 102 in all. He hurled them out against the din of brass bands, screaming hecklers, steam whistles, fireworks, and, most deafening of all, hundreds of boot soles clapped together by employees of a shoe factory. Choking cannon fumes greeted him at Lockport and Spencerport, sooty rain sprayed into his face at Tonawanda, and the sulfurous smoke of red flares at Rome made him cough, shout, and cough again until his voice gave out entirely. He pumped the dry hands of tinkers, the greasy hands of cooks, the bandaged hands of stevedores, the sweaty hands of foundry workers. He stood patiently through countless performances of "There'll Be a Hot Time in the Old Town Tonight" (in Middletown, two bands, one black and one white, attempted to play it in counterpoint). He suffered the traditional humiliation of having the train pull out just as he was beginning to speak. He fought off drunks and had war-bereaved mothers cry on his shoulder.[116] In short, he enjoyed himself, as only the true political animal can.

And by all accounts his audiences enjoyed him. During the course of this long tour, Roosevelt so perfected his oratory that he was able at Phoenix to accomplish the most difficult trick in the actor's book, namely, wordless persuasion. Two hundred dour farmers sat on their hands until he stopped in midspeech, leaned over the brake-handle and simply stared at them, wrinkling his face quizzically. "The first man he looked at laughed," reported the *Sun,* "and the next, and the one afterward, and so on, [until] the Colonel and everyone in the crowd was laughing."[117]

At Syracuse, on 27 October, Theodore Roosevelt turned forty.

TWO MORE TRAIN TOURS, of Long Island and southwestern New York, kept him raw-throated through the last hours of election eve, 7 November. Not until midnight could the candidate relax over a copy of *Die Studien des Polybius* as his Pullman rocked homeward.[118] He felt that he had made "a corking campaign," and if the memory of it was tarnished by rumors of $60,000 in last-minute bribes at headquarters, his own image, at least, shone brightly. "There is no denying," the *Troy Times* said, "that Theodore Roosevelt has grown mightily in the public estimation since he appeared in person in the campaign."[119]

The day just beginning would disclose that he had won the governorship of New York State by 17,794 votes—a narrow margin but a decisive one, given the odds of four weeks before.[120] In the opinion of Chauncey Depew, who accompanied him on his six-day sweep, his victory was a triumph of sheer personality over discouraging conditions. Even Boss Platt would admit that Roosevelt was "the only man" who could have saved the party that year. Roosevelt himself was inclined in later life to ascribe his success to the decision to attack not his opponent, but the boss of his opponent.[121] Yet in the first flush of victory he could only invoke fortune. "I have played it with bull luck this summer," he wrote Cecil Spring Rice. "First, to get into the war; then to get out of it; then to get elected. I have worked hard all my life, and have never been particularly lucky, but this summer I *was* lucky, and I am enjoying it to the full. I know perfectly well that the luck will not continue, and it is not necessary that it should. I am more than contented to be Governor of New York, and shall not care if I never hold another office. . . ."[122]

As the last leaves fell around Sagamore Hill he began to dictate his war memoirs, inevitably called *The Rough Riders*. At $1,000 per serial installment (with the prospect of rich book royalties afterward), the work was the most profitable he had ever undertaken. He had also, before Christmas, to deliver eight Lowell lectures at Harvard, for a fee of $1,600; then in the New Year he could start drawing a state salary of $10,000.[123] Affluence stared him in the face. All that was lacking to complete his happiness was "that Medal of Honor," but no doubt it would be forthcoming.

"During the year preceding the outbreak of the Spanish War," Roosevelt intoned, "I was Assistant Secretary of the Navy."[124] Eleven more times before his stenographer reached the end of her first page, he proudly repeated the words *I, my, me.*

CHAPTER 27

The Boy Governor

"Never yet did Olaf
Fear King Svend of Denmark;
This night hand shall hale him
By his forked chin!"

ON THE ICY MIDNIGHT OF Sunday, 1 January 1899, the silence brooding over Eagle Street, Albany, was disturbed by the sound of smashing glass. Theodore Roosevelt, Governor, had stayed out late after dinner (talking too much, as usual), with the result that forgetful servants had locked him out of the Executive Mansion. Unwilling to disturb his sleeping family, he had no choice but to break into his new home.[1]

The noise of tinkling shards on the piazza was full of omens, both for himself and Senator Platt. Their brittle alliance had already undergone a severe strain in the matter of appointments.[2] How long could it last without cracking? Would Roosevelt, indeed, prove to be the "perfect bull in a china shop" that Platt had feared? Few of the professional politicians staying in the capital that night, in preparation for Monday morning's Annual Message,[3] doubted that the first split would come soon.

Roosevelt himself was determined to proceed with the utmost

"It was as if the whole $22-million structure had been built just for him."

The New York State Capitol, Albany, around the turn of the century.

delicacy. He knew that he could achieve next to nothing in Albany without the Senator's help—Platt was, as he phrased it, "to all intents and purposes . . . a majority of the Legislature."[4] Yet if he allowed that majority to control him, as it had Governor Black, he would betray his campaign promises of an independent gubernatorial administration. His duty, as he saw it, "was to combine both idealism and efficiency" by working *with* Platt *for* the people.[5] This was easier said than done, since the interests of the organization and the community were often at variance; but Roosevelt thought he had a solution. "I made up my mind that the only way I could beat the bosses whenever the need to do so arose (and unless there was such a need I did not wish to try) was . . . by making my appeal as directly and emphatically as I knew how to the mass of voters themselves."[6] In other words, he looked as always to publicity as a means to wake up the electorate and ensure governmental responsibility. Men like Platt and Odell did not like to operate "in the full glare of public opinion"; their favorite venues were the closed conference room, the private railroad car, the whispery parlors of the Fifth Avenue Hotel. Roosevelt was willing to meet in all these places with them, but he intended to announce every meeting loudly beforehand, and describe it minutely afterward. He would therefore not be asked to do anything that the organization did not wish the public to know about; but whenever Boss Platt had a reasonable request to make, Roosevelt would gladly comply, and see that the organization got credit for it.[7]

How well this policy would succeed remained to be seen, as the housebreaking Governor climbed into bed, and got what rest he could before beginning his two-year round of official duties.

MONDAY, 2 JANUARY, dawned bright, but so cold that when the band arrived to escort Roosevelt to the Capitol, its brass instruments froze into silence, and the procession advanced only to eerie drumbeats. However, the streets were thronged with the biggest crowd of well-wishers ever seen in Albany, and the bunting on every rooftop was brilliant in the sub-zero air. Roosevelt marched along with many grins and waves of his silk topper, surrounded by a shining phalanx of the National Guard, under the command of Adjutant General Avery D. Andrews.[8]

As he turned the corner of Eagle Street, the white bulk of the Capitol stood out against the sky, as awesomely as it had on that other 2 January when he first walked up the hill as a young Assemblyman, seventeen years before. But then it had been an unfinished pile, with a boarded-up main entrance and mounds of rubble fringing its eastern facade. Now, in place of the rubble, there were lawns and trees, and a new marble stairway, which would have done justice to Cheops, cascading down toward him. Gubernatorial dignity prevented Roosevelt from taking the seventy-seven steps two at a time, as he would invariably do in future. While he mounted with his aides to second-floor level he had leisure to reflect on the improbable series of events that had brought him back to Albany, and the pleasing thought that he would be the first of New York's thirty-six Governors to occupy the completed Capitol.[9] It was as if the whole twenty-two-million-dollar structure had been built just for him.

After briefly seating himself behind a great desk in the Executive Office, where he had once quailed before the wrath of Grover Cleveland, Roosevelt crossed over to the Assembly Chamber. His entrance there aroused none of the old sniggers and inquiries of "Who's the dude?" Instead, both Houses of the Legislature rose to their feet in welcome, and a band crashed out "Hail to the Chief." Even more pleasing, perhaps, was the chorus that greeted him when he took the podium to speak:

> *"What's the matter with Teddy?*
> *HE'S—ALL—RIGHT!"*[10]

Roosevelt's First Annual Message was a short, conventional appeal to practical morality and the manly virtues, worded so as not to antagonize any Republican in the room. Insofar as it said anything specific, it recognized the rights of labor, called for civil service and taxation reform, proposed biennial sessions of the Legislature, and expressed concern over Democratic maladministration in New York City. About the only phrase worth remembering was the Governor's description—or rather self-description—of the ideal public servant: he should be "an independent organization man of the best type."[11] His listeners might have wondered how the two extremes of independence and party loyalty could be combined, but Roosevelt clearly intended to show them. Their applause, therefore, was anticipatory rather than congratulatory, like that of an audience stimulated by the prologue to a suspense drama.

In the corridors afterward the same remark flew back and forth—"What was the boy governor going to do?"[12]

ROOSEVELT'S FIRST MAJOR CHALLENGE was to select a new Superintendent of Public Works. This appointment, the most important in his gift, was a particularly sensitive one in view of last year's "canal steal."[13] Senator Platt had already decided that Francis J. Hendricks of Syracuse was the ideal man, to the extent of actually "naming" him and handing Roosevelt a telegram of acceptance.

Such an arrogant gesture could not go unchallenged. Roosevelt did not hesitate to defend himself.

> The man in question was a man I liked . . . But he came from a city along the line of the Canal, so that I did not think it best that he should be appointed anyhow; and, moreover, what was far more important, it was necessary to have it understood at the outset that the Administration was my Administration and no one else's but mine. So I told the Senator very politely that I was sorry, but that I could not appoint his man. This produced an explosion, but I declined to lose my temper, merely repeating that I must decline to accept any man chosen for me, and that I must choose the man myself. Although I was very polite, I was also very firm, and Mr. Platt and his friends finally abandoned their position.[14]

Actually Platt withdrew only temporarily, and looked on, no doubt with malicious amusement, while the Governor tried to find a substitute for Hendricks. One by one the "really first-class men"

Roosevelt approached expressed regrets.[15] Their reason, unstated but obvious, was that they did not wish to risk the humiliation of nonconfirmation by the Platt-controlled Senate.

The Governor solved the problem by presenting Platt with a list of four suitable candidates and asking his approval of one of them. Colonel John Nelson Partridge was accordingly nominated as Superintendent of Public Works on 13 January 1899. The appointment was widely hailed as "excellent," and indeed turned out to be so.[16] Boss and Governor could congratulate themselves on making a selection that the other approved of. Pride was satisfied, yet there was compromise on both sides.

For the rest of his term Roosevelt would follow this technique of submitting preselected lists to the organization, allowing Senator Platt to make the final choice. With one or two significant exceptions, his appointments were as easy as the Easy Boss could make them.[17] Thus Roosevelt demonstrated what he meant by being "an independent organization man of the best type."

AS FAR AS THE PRESS was concerned, Governor Roosevelt was a window full of sunshine and fresh air. Twice daily without fail, when he was in Albany, he would summon reporters into his office for fifteen minutes of questions and answers[18]—mostly the latter, because his loquacity seemed untrammeled by any political scruples. Relaxed as a child, he would perch on the edge of his huge desk, often with a leg tucked under him, and pour forth confidences, anecdotes, jokes, and legislative gossip. When required to make a formal statement, he spoke with deliberate precision, "punctuating" every phrase with his own dentificial sound effects; the performance was rather like that of an Edison cylinder played at slow speed and maximum volume. Relaxing again, he would confess the truth behind the statement, with such gleeful frankness that the reporters felt flattered to be included in his conspiracy. It was understood that none of these gubernatorial indiscretions were for publication, on pain of instant banishment from the Executive Office.[19]

Unassuming as Roosevelt's press-relations policy may seem in an age of mass communications, it was unprecedented for a Governor of New York State in 1899. "At that time," he wrote in his *Auto-*

biography, "neither the parties nor the public had any realization that publicity was necessary, or any adequate understanding of the dangers of the 'invisible empire' which throve by what was done in secrecy."[20]

His particular concern in these press conferences was to make the electorate aware of what he considered the most ominous of "the great fundamental questions looming before us,"[21] namely, the unnatural alliance of politics and corporations. It was personified by Thomas C. Platt and Mark Hanna—distinguished, generally admirable individuals, yet afflicted with the curious amorality of big businessmen. Both were corporate executives, both were Senators of the United States. To them, capital was king; the corporation was society in microcosm; government was the oil which made industry throb. Just as tycoons were necessary to control the efficiency of labor, so were bosses required to supervise the writing of laws. If tycoon and boss could be combined in one person, so much the better for the gross national product.

The fact that both Hanna and Platt were personally incorrupt did not reassure Roosevelt at all. Their very asceticism, the impartiality with which they distributed corporate contributions for good or ill, disturbed him. Often as not Platt would finance the campaign of some decent young candidate in a doubtful district, and thus prevent the election of an inferior person. But the decent candidate, once in office, would be tempted to show his gratitude by voting along with other beneficiaries of Platt's generosity (or rather, the generosity of the corporations behind Platt); and so, inexorably, the machine grew.[22]

What worried Roosevelt was the inability of ordinary people to see the danger of this proliferation of cogs and cylinders and coins in American life.[23] The corrupt power of corporations was increasing at an alarming rate, directly related to the "rush toward industrial monopoly." In the twenty-five years between the Civil War and 1890, 26 industrial mergers had been announced; in the next seven years there were 156; in the single year 1898 a record $900,000,000 of capital was incorporated; yet in *the first two months of 1899*—Roosevelt's initiation period as Governor—that record was already broken.[24] What chance did women, children, cowboys, and immigrants have in a world governed by machinery? Clearly, if flesh and blood were to survive, all this cold hardness must be grappled and brought under control.

Roosevelt, of course, had been aware since his days as an Assemblyman of the existence of a "wealthy criminal class" both inside and outside politics, but he had never had the legislative clout to do much damage to it. Not until his election as Governor of New York State could he take up really weighty cudgels, and aim his blows shrewdly against "the combination of business with politics and the judiciary which has done so much to enthrone privilege in the economic world."[25] And not until his third month in office would he feel the real power of the organization to resist change.

In the meantime he busied himself with routine gubernatorial matters, making further appointments, discussing labor legislation with union representatives, reviewing the case of a convicted female murderer,[26] approving a minor act or two, and mastering all the administrative details of his job. This was not difficult, thanks to his massive experience of both state and municipal politics. "I am going to make a pretty decent Governor," he assured Winthrop Chanler, adding defensively, "I do not try to tell you about all my political work, for the details would only bother you. It is absorbingly interesting to me, though it is of course more or less parochial."[27] This last adjective was to become obsessive in his correspondence for 1899—almost as if he were ashamed of enjoying legislation to do with the amount of flax threads in folded linen, or the sale of artificially colored oleomargarine.

"Thus far," Henry Adams wrote on 22 January, "Teddy seems to sail with fair wind. What we want to know is whether Platt will cut his throat when the time comes, as he has cut the throat of every man whom he has ever put forward." Roosevelt, meanwhile, protested that Platt was "treating me perfectly squarely . . . I think everyone realizes that the Governorship is not in commission."[28]

He conferred frequently and openly with the old man, traveling down to New York to breakfast with him on Saturday mornings, and lunching or dining as often with organization men like Odell, Quigg, and Root. This, to "silk-stocking" reformers and the *Evening Post,* was the equivalent of "breaking bread with the devil,"[29] but Roosevelt shrugged off their criticism.

> The worthy creatures never took the trouble to follow the sequence of facts and events for themselves. If they had done so they would have seen that any series of breakfasts with Platt always meant that I was going to do something that he did not like, and that I was trying, courteously and frankly, to reconcile him to it. My object was to make it as easy as possible for him to come with me . . . A series of breakfasts was always the prelude to some act of warfare.[30]

The first clash came in March.

On the eighteenth day of that month, Governor Roosevelt told reporters that he would like to see "the adoption of a system whereby corporations in this State shall be taxed on the public franchises which they control."[31] There were, as it happened, four bills in the legislature to do with franchises—three of them awarding rich concessions to gas, tunnel, and rapid-transit companies in Manhattan, and one proposing a general state tax on all such power and traction privileges, in order to replenish the state treasury.[32] It was to the last bill, a measure of Senator John Ford's then languishing in committee, that Roosevelt seemed to be referring. Although his remark was casual, the committee chairman took the hint, and within three days sent the bill to the House with a favorable report.

Roosevelt, delighted, began to push for its passage at once. Here was a measure designed to siphon off some of the money flowing through the politico-corporate machine and return it to the community in the form of increased values for property owners and, possibly, reduced taxes. The organization might be persuaded to agree—Platt himself had suggested that a tax-reform committee be appointed to send some proposals "to the next Legislature." But Roosevelt saw no reason to wait until 1900. Hurrying to New York on 24 March, he invited the Easy Boss to breakfast with him at his pied-à-terre on Madison Avenue next morning.[33]

"I was hardly prepared for the storm of protest and anger which my proposal aroused," Roosevelt wrote afterward.[34] Platt considered the Ford Bill dangerous in the extreme: in its sweeping generalities and "radical" ideas it was "a shot into the heart of the business community" and an "extreme concession to Bryanism."[35] If Roosevelt wished to push such a measure through, the organization would block it. The whole question of tax reform, Platt explained, was too complicated to rush. He repeated his suggestion that a joint legislative committee investigate at leisure, and report in the session of 1900. If Roosevelt agreed to this, Platt promised that some "serious effort would be made to tax franchises."[36]

The Governor capitulated, with real or feigned humility, and on 27 March sent a message to the Legislature recommending that Platt's committee be appointed. He took the opportunity to complain that farmers, market gardeners, tradesmen, and smallholders were bearing a disproportionate burden of taxation in New York State, while franchise-holding syndicates kept every dollar of their profits. "A corporation which derives its power from the State," he declared, "should pay the State a just percentage of its earnings as a return for the privileges it enjoys." Then, in a conclusion which struck many commentators as weakly deferential to Platt, he left it to the proposed committee to decide just how franchises should be taxed, and who should do the taxing.[37]

Since the Ford Bill had specific suggestions on both these points, it was assumed that Roosevelt had given up on the measure. Actually he liked it more and more,[38] although he had one reservation: it empowered local county boards to make assessments, rather than the state. This "obnoxious" clause (which played directly into the hands of Tammany Hall) was sufficient to prevent him speaking out publicly in the bill's favor. But he hinted to various reporters that he would not be sorry to see it pass anyway. On 7 April he risked another Platt "explosion" by telling the editor of the *Sun*, "I shall sign the bill if it comes to me, gladly."[39]

ON 12 APRIL HE WAS surprised to hear that the Senate had mysteriously passed the Ford Bill by a vote of 33 to 11.[40] Whatever Platt's motive in letting Republican members vote for it (perhaps he was making a gesture to placate tax reformers, while still intending to block the measure in the Assembly), Roosevelt now had an excuse to take a public stand. On 14 April he announced that the bill, however imperfect, was beneficial to the community; the Assembly should send it on to him at once for signing.[41] To Platt he guilelessly explained that he had broken silence simply at the request of the Senate Majority Leader, who felt the reputation of the Republican party was at stake. Platt's response was to employ dilatory tactics. The House Taxation Committee promptly pigeonholed the bill and nothing more was heard of it. Meanwhile a rival measure appeared on the floor and was subject to lengthy debate, obviously for purposes of delay.[42]

The end of the session, scheduled for 28 April, was fast approaching, and Roosevelt grew impatient. After four months in office he felt sure enough of his strength to challenge Platt directly. He made up his mind "that if I could get a show in the Legislature the bill would pass, *because the people had become interested* and the representatives would scarcely dare to vote the wrong way."[43] Accordingly he set to work on individual Assemblymen (a task in which he had acquired expertise during his own term as Minority Leader) and used his tame press corps to take daily polls of the increase of likely votes in the House. By noon on 27 April there was a reported majority of twelve in favor of the Ford Bill.[44] All that remained now was to persuade Platt's leaders to bring it out of committee.

As Governor, Roosevelt possessed one formidable weapon which he had hitherto refrained from using: the Special Emergency Message. Under the rules of the Legislature he could use such a ploy to take up any bill out of turn and force it onto the floor.[45] At five o'clock, therefore, when pressure in behalf of the Ford Bill had built up to a maximum in the Assembly, Roosevelt dictated his message demanding its immediate passage.

Speaker S. Fred Nixon, who had received direct orders from Platt "not to pass," simply tore the message up without reading it to the House. He then retired to an anteroom and suffered a nervous collapse.[46]

ROOSEVELT HEARD THE NEWS at seven o'clock next morning, the final day of the session. He reacted much as he had when the Mausers were heard at Las Guásimas. Whether he advanced or retreated now, his political life was in danger. Nixon's rejection of his message, if allowed to go unchallenged, would mean fatal humiliation at the critical moment of his Governorship. What was left of his strength would waste away through the non-legislative months of 1899; when the session of 1900 opened he would be a dead duck, with little hope of renomination by a contemptuous Senator Platt. Meanwhile lobbyists for the big franchise-holders in New York City were warning him that if he sent another message he would "under no circumstances . . . ever again be nominated for any public office," as "no corporation would subscribe" to any future Roosevelt campaign.[47]

Stepping through the barbed wire, the Governor fired off another, more peremptory message:

> I learn that the emergency message which I sent last evening to the Assembly on behalf of the Franchise Tax Bill has not been read. I therefore send hereby another message upon the subject. I need not impress upon the Assembly the need of passing this bill at once. It has been passed by an overwhelming vote through the Senate. . . . It establishes the principle that hereafter corporations holding franchises from the public shall pay their just share of the public burden . . . It is one of the most important measures (I am tempted to say the most important measure) that has been before the Legislature this year. I cannot too strongly urge its immediate passage.[48]

This time he entrusted his personal secretary, William J. Youngs, with delivery, and sent an added threat that if the message were not promptly read he would come over and read it himself. Platt's lieutenants surrendered at once. The Ford Franchise Bill was passed by a landslide vote of 109 to 35, and the Legislature adjourned.[49]

LOOKING BACK OVER the session in the first flush of his victory, Roosevelt felt some relief and no little pride in what he had accomplished as Governor.[50] There had been, beside this recent spectacular achievement, a good deal of progressive legislation,[51] which made up in historical significance what it lacked in contemporary drama. "I got an excellent Civil Service law passed," he boasted, by way of example. This was true enough. The original law which he and Grover Cleveland had engineered in 1883 had been repealed in 1897, for no other reason apparently than to increase Republican spoilsmanship. Cooperating with his old friends at the Civil Service Reform Association, Roosevelt had succeeded in getting a stiff new bill through the Legislature, but only after "herculean labor," and some spontaneous assistance from Senator Platt. The resultant Act was the most advanced for any state in the nation.[52]

Roosevelt also congratulated himself, justifiably, on his labor record.[53] He had supported, fought for, and signed several bills aimed at improving the working conditions in tenement sweatshops; at strengthening state factory-inspection procedures; at limiting the maximum hours to be worked by employed women and children; and at imposing a stricter eight-hour day law upon the state work force, as an example to other large corporations.[54] He consulted widely with union officials—far more than any of his predecessors—and greatly strengthened the state supervisory board to protect industrial workers from exploitation. Fortunately there had been no violent demonstrations to strain his good humor—yet.[55]

There had been one or two blots on Roosevelt's record which time would darken, notably his decision in late February to send a woman to the electric chair for the first time in the history of New York State.[56] This was in spite of the anguished pleas of humanitarians and warnings that the execution would destroy his Presidential chances.[57] The Governor justified his decision by saying that the woman had been fairly convicted of murder, and that in any case sex had nothing to do with the law.[58]

Roosevelt's only major inherited problem, the Erie Canal scandal, was for the time being dormant, thanks to his appointment of Superintendent Partridge and courageous selection of two Democrats to reinvestigate. Critics might complain that the delay was unnecessary, given last year's proof of Republican malfeasance, but few observers doubted that the Governor would prosecute fearlessly if the evidence was upheld.[59]

"All together I am pretty well satisfied with what I have accomplished," wrote Roosevelt. "I do not misunderstand in the least what it means—or rather, how little it may mean. New York politics are kaleidoscopic and 18 months hence I may be so much out of kilter with the machine that there may be no possibility of my renomination. . . ."[60]

Along with *parochial,* the adjective *kaleidoscopic* was increasingly a part of his vocabulary, as he contemplated the rapid shifts of fortune which had marked his recent career. The kaleidoscope continued to shift, ever more rapidly, in the days and months ahead, disclosing sometimes a dazzling perspective to infinity, sometimes dark visions of chaos.

Thus within a month of his boast to Lodge he was confessing to Bamie that he felt "a wee bit depressed"[61]—a Rooseveltian euphemism for submersion in the Slough of Despond. Having had time to reflect, he realized that his early reservations about the Ford Franchise Tax Bill, now lying on his desk for signature, had been well-founded. The local assessment clause was indeed an alarming problem. In New York City, for instance, it meant that Tammany Hall would have the power to tax all the traction companies—or demand vast bribes for leniency. No wonder his oldest corporate friends, including Chauncey Depew, were incensed at his stand.[62] In addition the stock market was down, *The New York Times* accusing him of opportunism, and, worst of all, Senator Platt had hurled the organization's ultimate obscenity at him, albeit in a gentlemanly letter, dated 6 May 1899.

"When the subject of your nomination was under consideration, there was one matter that gave me real anxiety," the Senator wrote. ". . . I had heard from a good many sources that you were a little loose on the relations of capital and labor, on trusts and combinations, and, indeed, on those numerous questions which have recently arisen in politics affecting the security of earnings and the right of a man to run his own business in his own way, with due respect of course to the Ten Commandments and the Penal Code." Now came the imprecation: "I understood from a number of business men, and among them many of your own personal friends, that you entertained various *altruistic* ideas, all very well in their way, but which before they could be put into law needed very profound consideration."[63] Roosevelt knew that in Platt's vocabulary *altruis-*

tic meant *socialistic* or worse.[64] "You have just adjourned a Legislature which created a good opinion throughout the State," the Easy Boss went on loftily. "I congratulate you heartily upon this fact, because I sincerely believe, as everybody else does, that this good impression exists very largely as a result of your personal influence in the legislative chambers. But at the last moment and to my very great surprise, you did a thing which has caused the business community of New York to wonder how far the notions of Populism, as laid down in Kansas and Nebraska, have taken hold upon the Republican party of the State of New York." The letter began to ramble, and concluded with an almost fatherly appeal to the young Governor's discretion. "I sincerely believe you will make the mistake of your life if you allow the bill to become a law," wrote Platt, advising him "with a political experience that runs back nearly half a century"[65] not to sign the bill.

Roosevelt deliberated for twenty-four hours before dictating a reply. He wryly thanked the Senator for the "frankness, courtesy, and delicacy" of his letter, not to mention his cooperation during the legislative season. "I am peculiarly sorry that the most serious cause of disagreement should come in this way right at the end of the session." With tongue firmly in cheek, he assured Platt that he was not "what you term 'altruistic' . . . to any improper degree." As regards the Ford Bill, "pray do not believe that I have gone off half-cocked in this matter." Then he launched into a classic statement of his political philosophy.

> I appreciate all you say about what Bryanism means, and I also . . . [am] as strongly opposed to populism in every stage as the greatest representative of corrupt wealth, but . . . these representatives . . . have themselves been responsible for a portion of the conditions against which Bryanism is in ignorant, and sometimes wicked revolt. I do not believe it is wise or safe for us as a party to take refuge in mere negation and to say that there are no evils to be corrected. It seems to me that our attitude should be one of correcting the evils and thereby showing, that, whereas the populists, socialists and others really do not correct the evils at all . . . the Republi-

> cans hold the just balance and set our faces as resolutely against improper corporate influence on the one hand as against demagogy and mob rule on the other.[66]

In hopes of achieving a "just balance" with Senator Platt, the Governor now made a dramatic offer. He was willing to reconvene the Legislature for a special session, in the hope that the Ford Bill's "obnoxious" assessment clause might be amended. It must be clear to both houses, however, that the essential principle of taxing franchise privileges must stand.[67]

Organization and corporate lawyers welcomed the idea of an amended bill. They obviously intended to shoot it so full of holes that it would hang limp in any breeze of reform. But Roosevelt had a final ultimatum to make to Platt before sending out his summons to the legislators: "Of course it must be understood . . . that I will sign the present bill, if the [amended] bill . . . fails to pass."[68]

The Easy Boss remained silent, and on 22 May the Assemblymen and Senators were back at their desks in the Capitol.

LEAVING NOTHING TO CHANCE, the Governor delivered copies of his ultimatum to the Leader of the Senate and to Chairman Odell, and recruited two of the finest legal consultants in New York State to scrutinize every semicolon that came out of either House. He even arranged for delaying tactics in the event of a recall move, so that he could sign the Ford Bill into law before the pageboys reached his office.[69]

So short, indeed, was the distance between his pen and the document lying open before him that Platt's leaders gave up the attempt to write a new bill more favorable to corporations. All they could do was to insert various strengthening clauses into the original bill, exactly as Roosevelt had intended. No amendment was made without his approval, and the revised measure cleared both Houses in three days. The Governor proudly and accurately described it as "the most important law passed in recent times by any State Legislature." He signed it with a flourish on 27 May, and sat back to enjoy the sweetness of his victory.[70]

Whether he tasted the fruits to the full is doubtful. For all the praise that poured in from the anti-organization press ("Governor Roosevelt," declared the *Herald*, "has given the finest exhibition of civic courage witnessed in this State in many a day"),[71] he only knew that he was tired to his bones. "I have had four years of exceedingly hard work without a break, save by changing from one kind of work to another. This summer I shall hope to lie off as much as possible. . . ."[72]

BUT PRESSURE OF speaking engagements up and down the Hudson Valley kept him away from Oyster Bay until the middle of June. Even then he had only a week at home before setting off West to attend the first Rough Riders reunion in Las Vegas, New Mexico. The two-day celebration, "which I would not miss for anything in the world," was timed to begin on the first anniversary of the Battle of Las Guásimas.[73]

As he journeyed West he pondered again "the relations of capital and labor . . . trusts and combinations."[74] Platt might think him "loose" on these subjects, but they preoccupied him more and more as he contemplated America's entry into the twentieth century. The Ford Bill had been but a step, admittedly a pioneering one, toward resolving the giant inequities of the capitalist system; some future Chief Executive more powerful and visionary than William McKinley must bring about similar legislation on a national scale.

The thought of McKinley made Roosevelt slightly uneasy at present. Ever since taking the oath at Albany he had been receiving demands from the pesky Mrs. Bellamy Storer that he campaign for the promotion to Cardinal of her favorite Archbishop, John Ireland of St. Paul, Minnesota.[75] She imagined that as Governor of New York State he could prevail upon the President to prevail upon the Pope. But Roosevelt was aware of various stately squabbles within the Church, and knew that Ireland was *persona non grata* at the Vatican. He had therefore hedged repeatedly, pleading lack of knowledge, lack of influence, and lack of propriety; but Mrs. Storer would not be put off, and he at last wrote the President a less than enthusiastic plea on her behalf. McKinley's reply, which had arrived a few days before his departure for the West, was a polite refusal to intervene in the affairs of another State.[76]

Behind the politeness lurked a hostility that probably went back to the round-robin incident at the end of the war. (The final installment of *The Rough Riders,* containing Roosevelt's own account of the affair, along with many hints of Administration mismanagement, was currently on the newsstands.) Roosevelt had long since given up hope of being awarded the Medal of Honor: no War Department board was going to recommend his controversial name to the President.[77] But the fact remained that McKinley would probably win a second term in 1900—the election was only eighteen months off—and Roosevelt, if he wished to emerge as a possibility in 1904, must at all costs preserve amiable relations with the White House. On the same day he received McKinley's rejection of his Storer appeal, he had written querulously to Secretary of State John Hay, "I do not suppose the President ever goes to the seaside. It is not necessary to say how I should enjoy having him at Oyster Bay, if possible. . . ."[78]

But as the Governor proceeded west and southwest through Indiana, Illinois, Iowa, Missouri, and Kansas, he realized that he must offer McKinley something more than sea air as an assurance of loyalty. For the embarrassing fact was that huge crowds were waiting to greet him at every station, "exactly as if I had been a presidential candidate."[79]

He found William Allen White was already working for his nomination in Kansas. What the two men said on this subject, during a brief midjourney meeting, is unknown, but White was at least persuaded to avoid setting Roosevelt up as McKinley's rival in 1900.[80] "There is no man in American today whose personality is rooted deeper in the hearts of the people than Theodore Roosevelt," the little editor wrote, as soon as his friend's train was over the horizon. "He is more than a presidential possibility in 1904, he is a presidential probability . . . He is the coming American of the twentieth century."[81]

Eastern newspapers mockingly reprinted this and other Roosevelt-for-President editorials, and suggested that McKinley had better look to his skirts at next year's convention.[82]

AFTER THIRTY-SIX raucous hours at Las Vegas, Roosevelt hurried back to New York on 29 June and announced that he was definitely not a presidential candidate. He urged all Americans to vote for the renomination of William McKinley.[83] With that he adjourned to Oyster Bay, only to be greeted by a garrulous speaker eulogizing him as "the man in whose hands we hope the destinies of our country will be placed." At this his gubernatorial dignity began to collapse. He struggled like a small boy to keep his face straight, but grins broke through, and as the crowd burst into applause, he laughed till he shook.[84]

"NOW AS TO WHAT YOU say about the Vice-Presidency," Roosevelt wrote to Henry Cabot Lodge on 1 July.[85]

Lodge's first words on this interesting subject are unfortunately lost. But it is clear from their surviving correspondence that he considered a vice-presidential nomination in 1900 to be the best assurance of a presidential nomination in 1904.[86] McKinley's last running mate, Garret A. Hobart, was a nice old boy, but in failing health. Rumor had it he would not seek a second term. The President might prefer to select another nice old boy, like John D. Long; on the other hand, the National Convention might prefer Roosevelt, in which case McKinley would undoubtedly bow to its wishes. As Joe Cannon of Illinois once remarked, "McKinley has his ear so close to the ground it's always full of grasshoppers."[87]

"Curiously enough," Roosevelt went on in his letter to Lodge, "Edith is against your view and I am inclined to be for it."[88] There were at least two alternative avenues of approach to the White House. One was to continue his admirable career as Governor of New York, and run for reelection in 1900; unfortunately that would only carry him through the year 1902. By 1904 the people who were shouting for him now might well have forgotten about him: "I have never known a hurrah endure for five years."[89] Another choice would be to succeed Russell A. Alger as Secretary of War; it was an open secret that McKinley wanted to get rid of that embarrassing executive. Roosevelt earnestly wanted the Secretaryship ("How I would like to have a hand in remodeling our army!"),[90] but McKinley had seen enough of his behavior in the Navy Department to look for somebody less forceful.

All in all, therefore, the Vice-Presidency was his best chance of keeping in the national spotlight until 1904. At least it was "an honorable position." But, Roosevelt wrote sadly, "I confess I should like a position with more work in it." There could hardly be an executive position with less.[91]

Tiredness, intensified by his week of railroading, returned as he finished his letter to Lodge. Word went out that the Governor intended a month's rest. Reporters, photographers, and glory-seekers were asked to stay away from Sagamore Hill.

"I don't mean to do one *single* thing during that month," said Roosevelt to his sister Corinne, "except write a life of Oliver Cromwell."[92]

ROOSEVELT'S THIRTEENTH BOOK and third biography, which one friend of the family described as a "fine imaginative study of Cromwell's qualifications for the Governorship of New York," was completed by 2 August.[93] Even allowing for the fact that it was dictated, and that the author spent another month or so revising the manuscript, its speed of composition must be considered something of a record. What was more, Roosevelt did not have the month entirely to himself, as he had planned; McKinley summoned him to the White House for a consultation on the Philippines on 8 July, and he spent three days later in the month at Manhattan Beach trying to restore good relations with Senator Platt.[94] Yet somehow he found time to produce sixty-three thousand words of English history, remarkable for clarity and grasp of detail if not for style.[95] According to his stenographer, William Loeb, the Governor would appear in his study every morning with a pad of notes and a reference book or two, and proceed to talk "with hardly a pause," pouring out dates and place-names as copiously as any college professor. The British military attaché Colonel Arthur Lee, who was Roosevelt's houseguest at this time, remembered him calling in another stenographer and dictating gubernatorial correspondence in between paragraphs of *Cromwell,* while a barber tried simultaneously to shave him. Yet there was no lack of continuity as the author's mind switched to and fro. Robert Bridges came out on 12 August to look at the draft typescript, and remembered one chapter "that could have been printed as it stood, with mere mechanical proof-reading corrections."[96]

Roosevelt, who shared the ability to double-dictate with Napoleon, did not think his intellect was in any way remarkable. "I have only a second-rate brain," he said emphatically to Owen Wister, "but I think I have a capacity for action." When Wister repeated this remark to Lord Bryce many years later, the great scholar was unimpressed. "He didn't do justice to himself there, you know. He had a brain that could always go straight to the pith of any matter. That is a mental power of the first rank."[97]

OLIVER CROMWELL, HOWEVER, has dated even less well than *Thomas Hart Benton* and *Gouverneur Morris*. Unlike those earlier books, it contained no original research. Nor was it short of competitors in the field; even in 1899 it could not compare with the standard lives of the Protector. Reviews were few and apathetic, and the book quickly faded from memory. Yet as a clear, rapid analysis of one leader of men by another, it still has its merits. As with the two previous biographies, *Cromwell* is most interesting when it draws parallels between author and subject. Roosevelt's own analysis of it remains the best and most succinct:

> I have tried to tell the narrative in its bearings upon the later movements for political and religious freedom in England in 1688 and in America in 1776 and 1860. Have endeavoured to show how the movement had two sides; one mediaeval and one modern, and how it failed, just so far as the former was dominant, but yet laid the foundations for all subsequent movements. I have tried to show Cromwell, not only as one of the great generals of all time, but as a great statesman who on the whole did a marvellous work, and who, where he failed, failed because he lacked the power of self-repression possessed by Washington and Lincoln . . . The more I have studied Cromwell, the more I have grown to admire him, and yet the more I have felt that his making himself a dictator was unnecessary and destroyed the possi-

bility of making the effects of that particular revolution permanent.[98]

NOT SURPRISINGLY, Roosevelt's flying visit to the capital prompted instant speculation that McKinley, gratified by his recent announcement of support, intended to name him Secretary of War after all.[99] The secretaryship was indeed discussed at the White House that night—at such length as to lend credence to the rumors—but Roosevelt, showing remarkable self-control, assumed that if the President wanted his advice on War Department management of the Philippine situation, "he should regard me as wholly disinterested." He therefore announced as soon as he stepped into McKinley's office "that I was not a candidate for the position of Secretary of War and could not leave the Governorship of New York now."[100] This protestation seems to have increased McKinley's respect for Roosevelt as a man, if not as an ambitious politician. On 31 July, Secretary Alger stepped down, and the President named Elihu Root to succeed him. Then Vice-President Hobart, though ailing, let it be known that he would like to remain in office indefinitely, so another of Roosevelt's avenues for advancement closed off.[101]

The Governor, setting off for a fall tour of state county fairs, decided to let the kaleidoscope shift for itself for a while.[102] In the New Year, once the legislative season was fairly under way, he would gaze through the prisms again and see if any new perspectives had opened up. For the first time in his adult life he felt no desire to hurry. He was, after all, nearly forty-one, with a growing family (Alice was almost as tall as he was now), a decent income, and a job that he loved. "I do not believe," he told Lodge, "that any other man has ever had as good a time as Governor of New York."[103] Here, within certain geographical and political limits, was the supreme power he had always craved, and the events of last April had shown how well that power became him. Senator Platt, fortunately, had recovered from the Ford Franchise Tax Bill, and was disposed to be "cordial."[104] This augured well for their working partnership through the next session. Roosevelt would live out the nineteenth century in Albany—1900 was not, as so many of his constituents seemed to think, the first year of the twentieth—and try to persuade Platt that he was worth renominating for a second term. "I should be quite willing to barter the certainty of it for all the possibilities of the future."[105]

NIAGARA FALLS. Silver Lake. Chatauqua. Watertown. Riverhead. Otsego City. Mineola. In fair after fair, all through September, Roosevelt waved, spoke, pumped hands, tasted prize-winning pumpkin pies, and basked in the admiration of the public. Whenever he emerged from his train, whenever he walked past an apple tree full of children, he was greeted with shrieks of "Hello, Teddy, you're all right!" or, "Three cheers for the next President!" He had a stock response to the latter: "No, no, none of that, Dewey's not here."[106]

This invariably brought laughter and applause. The hero of Manila Bay, now steaming homeward in glory, had indeed emerged as a dark-horse candidate, despite his own protest, "I would rather be an admiral ten times over." Few professional politicians, Roosevelt included, took the phenomenon seriously.[107]

The *Olympia* was scheduled to enter New York Harbor on 28 September, and cruise up the Hudson next morning, to a welcoming thunder of more ammunition than had been expended to destroy the Spanish fleet. On Saturday, 30 September, Admiral Dewey, President McKinley, Senator Hanna, and thirty-five thousand marchers would proceed down Fifth Avenue to Twenty-third Street, where a seventy-foot triumphal arch, modeled after that of Titus in Rome, gleamed white as a symbol of America's entry into world power. It was to be "the greatest parade since the Civil War," and Roosevelt, as Governor of the Empire State, would ride at its head in top hat and tails.[108]

"I am sorry for I happen to have . . . a particularly nice riding suit, with boots, spurs etc.," he grumbled to Adjutant General Andrews. But when the great day came, he cut an unusually impressive figure in black and gray. Seated on an enormous charger, with his tall hat flashing, he dwarfed the guests of honor rolling behind him in carriages.[109]

A small boy named Thomas Beer happened to be standing in Grand Army Plaza as the parade came round the corner of Fifty-ninth Street and began its descent of the avenue. When Beer wrote the concluding pages of *The Mauve Decade* a quarter of a century later, Roosevelt rode in his impressionistic memory as a figure of strength and promise, great yet uncorrupted by the "disease of greatness," looming head and shoulders above the fin de siècle pageantry all around him:

> A bright dust of confetti, endless snakes of tinted paper began to float from hotels that watched the street . . . Why, you could see everything from here! . . . Brass of parading bandsmen and columns wheeled, turning at the red house to the south. Balconies and windows showered down confetti, and roses were blown. The very generous dropped bottles of champagne . . . The little admiral was a blue and gold blot in a carriage. The President, and the plump senator from Ohio, and all these great were tiny images of black and flesh in the buff shells of carriages in a whirling rain of paper ribbons, flowers, and flakes of the incessant confetti blown everlastingly, twinkling from the high blue of the sky. How they roared! Theodore Roosevelt! The increasing yell came from up the street. A dark horse showed and slowly paced until it turned where now the gilded general stares down the silly city. A blue streamer, infinitely descending from above, curled all around his coat and he shook it from the hat that he kept lifting. Theodore Roosevelt! The figure on its charger passed, and a roar went plunging before him while the bands shocked ears and drunken soldiers struggled out of line, and these dead great, remembered with a grin, went filing by.[110]

And then, on 21 November 1899, Vice-President Hobart died.

CHAPTER 28

The Man of Destiny

Round and round the house they go
Weaving slow
Magic circles to encumber
And imprison in their ring
Olaf the King
As he helpless lies in slumber.

THE PASSING OF Garret Augustus Hobart had several immediate political effects. One was to strengthen Henry Cabot Lodge's strange conviction that Roosevelt should run with McKinley in 1900, in the hope of succeeding him in 1904. He was adamant: "I have thought it over a great deal and I am sure I am right."[1] Most people, including Roosevelt, were puzzled by this attitude. Henry Adams interpreted it cynically. "You may well believe," he wrote Mrs. Cameron, "that Teddy's presidential aspirations are not altogether to Cabot's taste, and that the chapter now opening there, may have its dark adjectives."[2]

Roosevelt's own reaction, now that he was firmly back in office at Albany, was that the Vice-Presidency was "about the last thing for which I would care."[3] When Lodge first mentioned the idea it had admittedly seemed attractive. He loved Washington, loved the

"Don't any of you realize there's only one life between this madman and the Presidency?"

Governor Theodore Roosevelt at the time of his election to the Vice-Presidency.

largeness of its politics in contrast to Albany's "parochial affairs." At that time, too, Platt had been meditating revenge over his sponsorship of the Ford Franchise Tax Bill, and Roosevelt had begun to feel insecure as Governor. But things seemed to be changing for the better. On 11 December 1899, Roosevelt wrote Lodge: "Platt told me definitely that of course he was for me for renomination—that everybody was."[4]

But everybody was not. Even as Platt made his assurances to Roosevelt, representatives of the franchise corporations were urging that the Governor be forced out of Albany and onto the national ticket.[5] They had heard rumors that Roosevelt was plotting further "altruistic" legislation, to do with the limitation of trusts and the preservation of the state's natural resources. Clearly, if the man were permitted to serve another term, he would destroy the economy of New York State.

Senator Platt became sympathetic to these arguments when he saw the proofs of Roosevelt's Annual Message for 1900.[6] Here was provocative language about the need for "increasing a more rigorous control" of public utility companies that had acquired wealth "by means which are utterly inconsistent with the highest laws of morality." The state should be given power to inspect and examine thoroughly "all the workings of great corporations"—where necessary publishing its findings in the newspapers.[7]

Here, too, were suggestions that New York's "defective" lumbering laws should be changed so as to prohibit the dumping of wood-dyes, sawdust, and other industrial products "in any amount whatsoever" into Adirondack streams. There were pleas for the protection of birds, "especially song birds," and eccentric remarks like "a live deer in the woods will attract to the neighborhood ten times the money that could be obtained for the deer's dead carcass." In addition Roosevelt recommended that the liability of management for labor accidents should be increased, and he had harsh things to say about Republican corruption in last year's "canal steal."[8]

The message was, in short, alarmingly radical to a man of Platt's conservative temperament. Even so, he would be inclined to tolerate it (in the knowledge that his lieutenants in the Legislature would not) were Roosevelt not also contemplating the dismissal of Superintendent of Insurance Louis F. Payn. This official, an aging, rat-toothed defender of corrupt businessmen, had once been described by Elihu Root as "a stench in the nostrils of the people of the State of New York."[9]

The Governor was entitled to plenty of animosity toward him, since Payn, a Black supporter, had been responsible for the publication of his embarrassing tax affidavit during the campaign of 1898.[10] There had been little opportunity for revenge during 1899, for Payn's three-year-term appointment was not due to expire until January 1900. But Roosevelt had been marshaling evidence against him for months. He found that the Superintendent had "intimate and secret money-making relations" with New York's biggest insurance companies. Moreover, in the matter of appointments, Payn "represented the straitest sect of the old-time spoils politician." While the evidence was not enough to warrant criminal prosecution, it at least justified the Governor's decision to displace him.[11]

The problem was that the big insurance companies wished Payn reappointed. So, in consequence, did Senator Platt, and so did a majority of the Senate. This practically guaranteed Payn tenure, because until the Senate confirmed Roosevelt's choice of a successor, the superintendent would remain in office under the state constitution.[12]

Roosevelt tried to mollify the Easy Boss by suggesting Francis J. Hendricks as a replacement. Hendricks was the very man Platt had ordered him to appoint as Superintendent of Public Works, back in the fall of 1898. The Senator, as was his wont, listened impassively and said nothing, but when Roosevelt offered the job directly, Hendricks declined "for business reasons."[13] The inference was he had been told not to accept.

Payn, meanwhile, declared his determination to stay, at a press conference on 12 December. "No one has ever charged that I have not performed my duties successfully," he exclaimed in aggrieved tones.[14] During the next couple of weeks the relative positions of Governor and Boss hardened on the issue. "Platt does not want me to fight Payn and feels pretty bitterly about it," Roosevelt told Lodge on 29 December. More ominously, Platt had stopped making promises to protect him from the Vice-Presidency. He now merely quoted other people's opinions that "it would not be a wise move . . . personally." Then, as Albany filled up for the New Year's opening of the Legislature, Roosevelt heard that Platt was telling intimates "that I would undoubtedly have to accept the Vice-Presidency; that events were shaping themselves so that this was inevitable."[15]

ROOSEVELT'S SECOND Annual Message was greeted by most Republican newspapers as "statesmanlike" in its attitude to trusts (thanks to judicious modification of the original text by Elihu Root).[16] Strangely, the conservation section, with revolutionary pleas for a "system of forestry gradually developed and conducted along scientific principles," passed largely unnoticed. Here the Governor was reflecting the views of another expert adviser—Gifford Pinchot, Chief Forester of the United States. Tall, lithe, dreamy-eyed, irresistibly attractive to women, the thirty-four-year-old Pinchot had for years been Roosevelt's main source of ecological information. His theory that "controlled, conservative lumbering" of state and national forests would improve not only the economy, but the forests themselves was enthusiastically pro-pounded in the gubernatorial message.[17] Roosevelt also hinted that a bill to scrap the present five-man Forest, Fish, and Game Board and replace it with a single, progressive commissioner would be forthcoming early in the session.

The Governor disclaimed any personal responsibility for the measure, but its opponents, headed by Senator Platt, were quick to note that it had been prepared by the Boone & Crockett Club, and that both Pinchot and the proposed commissioner, W. Austin Wadsworth, were members of that Rooseveltian organization.[18]

WITHIN A FEW DAYS of his message Roosevelt received word that Judge Charles T. Saxton, another "independent organization man of the best type," was willing to accept the post of Superintendent of Insurance, providing Senator Platt and Charles Odell could be persuaded to forsake Payn. Roosevelt was optimistic. "While I did not intend to make an ugly fight unless they forced me to it, yet if they do force me the fight shall be had."[19]

UNEXPECTED AMMUNITION fell into his hands on 11 January 1900, when a stockholder of the State Trust Company of New York, one of Payn's strongest backers, came to Albany with evidence calculated to embarrass the superintendent and liquidate the company. According to the stockholder's figures, Payn had received $435,000 in loans based on "various unsaleable industrial securities of uncertain and doubtful value, together with what purports to be a certified bank check for $100,000." He petitioned for an immediate investigation of State Trust's books by the Superintendent of Banking, Frederick D. Kilburn.[20]

Roosevelt, showing his usual disregard for niceties of protocol in an emergency, ignored Kilburn and ordered Adjutant General Andrews to conduct the investigation within twenty-four hours. "I had to act at once," he explained to a doubtful Supreme Court Justice.[21] The unspoken implication was that Kilburn, a holdover from the Black Administration, might be rather less willing than Andrews to involve the Superintendent of Insurance in a major scandal.

Andrews had his report ready the next day, 13 January. Although it betrayed signs of hasty and superficial analysis, there was enough evidence of Laocoön-like entanglements between the directors of State Trust and Louis F. Payn for Roosevelt to proceed well-armed to a "bloody breakfast" with Senator Platt. "When I go to war," the Governor confided to a friend, "I try to arrange it so that all the shooting is not on one side."[22]

THE BREAKFAST, which was also attended by Chairman Odell (parchment-pale, glowering and watchful, secretly ambitious to supplant Platt as boss of the party), took place on Saturday, 20 January.[23] It proved to be less of a war than a series of brief preparatory skirmishes. Roosevelt insisted that Payn must be replaced. Platt insisted that Payn would stay. The Governor was sure that Judge Saxton would be an acceptable substitute. The Boss was equally sure he would not. Retreating slightly, Roosevelt produced his usual list of names, "most of whom are straight organization Republicans . . . who would administer the office in a perfectly clean and businesslike manner." Platt waved the list aside with loathing, but allowed Odell to pocket it. Then Roosevelt delivered his ultimatum: the organization had until Tuesday, 23 January, to approve one of the names. If no word was received by then, he would pick his own candidate and send the nomination in as soon as the Legislature opened for business on Wednesday morning.[24] Thanks to the Payn scandal, he felt quite confident there would be enough votes in the Senate to ratify his choice.

Platt's response was to make a public announcement shortly afterward that he believed Roosevelt "ought to take the Vice-Presidency both for National and State reasons."[25]

Judge Saxton gracefully withdrew his conditional acceptance of the nomination, and suggested the Governor again approach Francis J. Hendricks. Roosevelt did so, but had yet to receive a reply when he encountered Platt on the afternoon of the twenty-third. The Senator still refused to consider any other Superintendent of Insurance but Payn, and threatened "war to the knife" if Roosevelt tried to oust him. With only hours to go before his self-imposed deadline expired, the Governor threw caution to the winds. He politely informed Platt that he would send in Hendricks's name in the morning without fail—a massive bluff, considering that Hendricks had not yet given him formal permission to do so.[26]

A little later in the day Odell asked for a final, prewar conference with the Governor. Roosevelt said he could be found at the Union League Club that evening.

If he hoped that Odell would arrive with conciliatory messages, he was soon disillusioned. Platt, he was told, "would under no circumstances yield." If Roosevelt insisted on opposing him, his "reputation would be destroyed," and there would be "a lamentable smash-up" from which he would never recover politically. At this, the Governor got up to go, saying there was nothing to be gained from further talk.

ODELL (*impassive and inscrutable*) You have made up your mind?
ROOSEVELT I have.
ODELL You know it means your ruin?
ROOSEVELT (*walking to the door*) Well, we will see about that.
ODELL You understand, the fight will begin tomorrow and will be carried on to the bitter end.
ROOSEVELT Yes. (*At the door.*) Good night.
ODELL (*as door opens*) Hold on! We accept. Send in Hendricks. The Senator . . . will make no further opposition.

Recollecting this dialogue in his *Autobiography,* Roosevelt commented, "I never saw a bluff carried more resolutely to the final limit."[27] It is not certain whether by this he meant Odell's or his own.

THE FOLLOWING DAY, Wednesday, Hendricks telephoned acceptance, and on Friday afternoon Roosevelt joyfully released news of the nomination to the press. Privately, to his old Assembly colleague Henry L. Sprague, he wrote: "I have always been fond of the West African proverb: 'Speak softly and carry a big stick; you will go far.' "[28]

IN THIS CASE, the Big Stick took him as far as the Republican National Convention in Philadelphia. Although the proceedings there did not open until 19 June 1900, Theodore Roosevelt's trajectory toward the vice-presidential nomination began to accelerate from the moment the New York State Senate confirmed Hendricks as Superintendent of Insurance on 31 January. The very next morning a mysteriously planted article appeared in the *Sun* saying that "representatives of the Republican National Committee" had visited Roosevelt in Albany and urged him to consider acceptance of the nomination. Another mysterious article in the same paper, datelined from Washington, reported that many of the most influential

Republicans in the capital, "including probably a majority of Senators and Representatives," believed him to be "the logical candidate of the party for Vice-President."[29]

It was not difficult for Roosevelt to guess which persons might have provided the *Sun* with this information. "I need not speak of the confidence I have in you and Lodge," the Governor wrote plaintively to Platt that morning, "yet I can't help feeling more and more that the Vice-Presidency is not an office in which I could do anything. . . ."[30] Unfortunately, as he well knew, the newspaper articles were for the most part accurate. He had indeed been visited in Albany by a national committeeman from Wisconsin, who told him that "most of the Western friends of McKinley" thought his name would strengthen the ticket, and that he would be nominated "substantially without opposition" if he agreed to run. The committeeman added that he would be "extremely lucky" to get through 1900 without alienating either the organization men or the Independents forever, and that "it would be tempting Providence to try for two terms."[31]

It was also true that there was a growing vice-presidential boom for the Governor in Washington. Lodge had intensified his efforts to swing the nomination for Roosevelt, to the extent of going to the White House and asking McKinley point-blank for the chairmanship of the convention. The President, taken aback, agreed at once. Lodge also got the impression that McKinley was "perfectly content" to have Roosevelt on the ticket.[32] But then McKinley also seemed to be perfectly content with everything.

Lodge's own correspondence with Roosevelt dangled a tempting bait, conditional on his acceptance of the nomination: the chance to become the first Governor-General of the Philippines. He informed his friend, with what truth one cannot tell, that McKinley would be favorable to the appointment, once the current native insurrection against U.S. rule was crushed.[33] That might take another year or two, during which time Roosevelt, as Vice-President, would remain close to McKinley's elbow, and be available for instant nomination whenever the insurgent general, Emilio Aguinaldo, surrendered.

It so happened that no job, short of the Presidency itself, so appealed to Roosevelt. Convinced as he might be that Cuba deserved its freedom from Spanish rule, he was equally convinced that the Philippines needed the benison of an American colonial administration. "I . . . feel sure that we can ultimately help our brethren so far forward on the path of self-government and orderly liberty that that beautiful archipelago shall become a center of civilization for all eastern Asia and the islands round about. . . ."[34]

However, this bright vision was, he sensed, altogether too remote to pursue by the devious route Lodge recommended. Pressed to give his friend a decision on the Vice-Presidency, he wrote on 2 February: "With the utmost reluctance I have come to a conclusion that is against your judgment." Then, with recourse to his favorite metaphor:

> American politics are kaleidoscopic, and long before the next five years are out, the kaleidoscope is certain to have been many times shaken and some new men to have turned up. . . . Now the thing to decide at the moment is whether I shall try for the Governorship again, or accept the Vice-Presidency, if offered. I have been pretty successful as Governor . . . There is ample work left for me to do in another term—work that will need all of my energy and capacity—in short, work well worth any man's doing . . . But in the Vice-Presidency I could do nothing. I am a comparatively young man yet and I like to work. I do not like to be a figurehead. It would not entertain me to preside in the Senate . . . I could not *do* anything; and yet I would be seeing continually things I would like to do . . . Finally the personal element comes in. Though I am a little better off than the *Sun* correspondent believes, I have not sufficient means to run the social side of the Vice-Presidency as it ought to be run. I should have to live very simply, and would be always in the position of "poor man at a frolic." . . . So, old man, I am going to declare decisively that I want to be Governor and do not want to be Vice President.[35]

Lodge's reaction to this flat refusal was ambiguous, while Senator Platt proved deaf to Roosevelt's heavy hint, "Now, I should like to be Governor for another term. . . ."[36] On 3 February, Roosevelt discovered why. The big insurance companies of New York, furious over his ouster of Payn, had "to a man" joined the franchise corporations already prevailing upon Platt to kick the Governor upstairs. This represented a combined lobbying power of approximately one billion dollars.[37]

After a less-than-reverent meeting in the Amen Corner on 10 February, during which Platt cynically inquired what Roosevelt would do if the convention nominated him by unanimous vote ("I would not accept!" the Governor shot back), Roosevelt made the first public statement of his views two days later. It was both a rejection of the vice-presidential nomination and a plea for renomination as Governor. "And I am happy to say," he concluded, to the puzzlement of many reporters, "that Senator Platt cordially acquiesces in my views in the matter."[38]

If by that he meant the dry statement of support which Platt issued a little later, the Governor showed surprising ignorance of the fine art of political equivocation.

THE STORY OF THE next two months, culminating in the Governor's election as a delegate-at-large to Philadelphia on 17 April, is best expressed in the incomparable image of Thomas Collier Platt: "Roosevelt might as well stand under Niagara Falls and try to spit water back as to stop his nomination by this convention."[39]

President McKinley remained studiously neutral amidst the frantic lobbying for Roosevelt against such minor candidates as Cornelius Bliss, Timothy Woodruff, and John D. Long. Mark Hanna soon emerged as the Governor's principal opponent in Washington, swearing and thumping dramatically on his desk whenever the name Roosevelt was mentioned.[40] Friends were puzzled by the violence of Hanna's antipathy: there was something almost of terror in it. The National Chairman still clung to his massive administrative and patronage powers, augmented by the dignity of his Senate seat, but age and ill health were making him increasingly unstable. Fits of roaring, blind anger alternated with childlike querulousness; the famous warmth seemed to have faded along with the light in his eyes. The truth was that Hanna was no longer sure of his influence on McKinley. His adoration for the podgy little President was such that the slightest hint of coolness depressed him. Recently McKinley had found it necessary to withdraw somewhat from Hanna, who had a habit of trying to run the White House, and he would not even say whether or not he would allow him to remain National Chairman through the convention. Hanna promptly suffered a heart attack.[41]

Roosevelt was neither involved nor particularly interested in the McKinley-Hanna relationship. But Nicholas Murray Butler's news that neither man appeared to favor him for the Vice-Presidency left him oddly "chagrined."[42] He thought the office unsuitable for himself, but did not like to have eminent persons think *him* unsuitable for the office.

Another unsettling influence was the flinty resolution of his best friend to nominate him at Philadelphia, whether he liked it or not. "The qualities that make Cabot invaluable . . . as a public servant also make him quite unchangeable when he has determined that a certain course is right," Roosevelt complained to Bamie. "There is no possible use in trying to make him see the affair as I look at it, because our points of view are different. He regards me as a man with a political career."[43]

During the last week of April the Governor's intransigence toward the nomination began to show subtle signs of change. "By the way," he wrote suddenly to Lodge, "I did *not* say on February 12 that I would not under any circumstances accept the vice-presidency." (Lodge must have been puzzled by this remark, for Roosevelt's exact words to the press had been *It is proper for me to state that under no circumstances could I or would I accept the nomination for the vice-presidency.*) Then, on 26 April, he delivered himself of another public statement, which was markedly looser. "I would rather be in private life than be Vice-President. I believe I can be of more service to my country as Governor of the State of New York."[44]

He explained somewhat shamefacedly to Paul Dana of the *Sun* that he must leave certain avenues open "simply because if it were vital for me to help the ticket by going in, I would feel that the situation was changed."

Dana's own opinion was "If they want you you had better take it."[45]

BY THE END of the legislative session on 8 May, the Governor was having such doubts he decided to visit Washington and check the vice-presidential opinions of various eminent men in the capital. These dignitaries included Senators Foraker and Chandler, Secretaries Root and Long, and President McKinley himself, who gave a dinner in Roosevelt's honor on 11 May.[46]

Accounts vary as to what Roosevelt was told and what he said in reply. Foraker remembered him asking for help in suppressing the nomination at Philadelphia, then returning next day to complain furiously that McKinley and his aides did not want him to run. "There is no reason why they should not want me, and I will not allow them to discredit me. If the Convention wants me, I shall accept."[47]

On the other hand, John D. Long (whom Roosevelt discovered typically taking a postprandial stroll) got the impression that the Governor of New York wished to remain in Albany. This may well have been wishful thinking, because Long badly wanted the nomination himself.[48]

By far the best account of Roosevelt's visit was written by Secretary of State John Hay, to Joseph Bucklin Bishop, after Roosevelt had returned north:

> Teddy has been here: have you heard of it? It was more fun than a goat. He came down with a sombre resolution thrown on his strenuous brow to let McKinley and Hanna know once and for all that he would not be Vice President, and found to his stupefaction that nobody in Washington except Platt had ever dreamed of such a thing. He did not even have a chance to launch his *nolo episcopari* at the Major [McKinley]. That statesman said he did not want him on the ticket—that he would be far more valuable in New York—and Root

said, with his frank and murderous smile, "Of course not—you're not fit for it." And so he went back quite eased in his mind, but considerably bruised in his *amour propre.*[49]

THEODORE ROOSEVELT'S BEHAVIOR at the Republican National Convention in June 1900, while entirely characteristic, was so puzzling as to defy logical analysis. Notwithstanding his genuine repugnance for the Vice-Presidency—it is impossible to read his private letters and not feel it palpably—he seems to have courted the nomination from the moment he stepped off the train in Philadelphia on Saturday the fifteenth. His very presence at the convention was a positive gesture. It would have been easy for him, as Governor, to prevent his nomination as a delegate-at-large, two months before; Lodge had mockingly warned him that to accept delegation was to be nominated; but he had responded that "I would be looked upon as rather a coward if I didn't go."[50]

By this reasoning, mere token attendance would have shown courage enough. Roosevelt could have then sought to deflate his boom by remaining as inconspicuous as possible, in order to avoid attracting the attention of delegates and reporters. But he chose to arrive in town wearing a large, soft, black, wide-rimmed hat, which stood out among Philadelphia's countless straw boaters like a tent in a wheat-field. His fellow delegates-at-large, Senator Platt, Chairman Odell, and Chauncey Depew, noted with amusement how en route to the Hotel Walton he coveted the recognition of the crowd, and kept up a running conversation with the inevitable train of reporters.[51]

Nicholas Murray Butler, who had been sent ahead with express orders to nip any draft-Roosevelt movement in the bud, remembered the galvanic effect of his entrance into the Walton's main lobby. "He walked in . . . with his quick nervous stride and at once the crowd waked up. T.R.'s name was on every lip and the question as to whether or not he should be forced to take the Vice-Presidency pushed every other question into the background . . . All Saturday evening the delegations kept coming and it was perfectly evident to me on Sunday morning that only the most drastic steps would prevent T.R.'s nomination."[52]

The run began with the Kansas delegation, who had been reading William Allen White editorials for a year, and were anxious for the honor of being first to declare in Roosevelt's favor. But the Governor heard they were coming, and ducked out of his suite, leaving word that he would be back "in a few minutes." An hour later the leader of the Kansans, J. R. Burton, traced Roosevelt to Platt's room.

He found the Governor in the act of thumping a table and saying, "I can't do it!" Platt was lying on the sofa, while his son Frank, Benjamin Odell, and "Smooth Ed" Lauterbach sat nearby. Nobody except Roosevelt seemed to mind Burton's intrusion. "Colonel Roosevelt, . . . the delegation from the Imperial State of Kansas is waiting upstairs for you to keep your promise to see them," said the delegate. His colleagues were prepared to forgive his discourtesy, having "the utmost admiration" for him, and were determined to place him before the convention; but if he did not meet with them at once, and choose his own nominator from among them, Burton would take charge of the nomination himself. At this, reported a bystander, Platt looked "friendly." Odell said, "Well, that settles it." And Roosevelt, with a melodramatic sigh, headed upstairs.[53]

Next morning a committee of the still more important Pennsylvania delegation called and also expressed unanimous support for Roosevelt. The California delegation followed on; all day long, as the excitement of conscripting a popular candidate spread through the convention hotels, the flattering flood continued.[54] Roosevelt greeted all comers with expressions of regret that they had ignored his wishes, but he grinned so widely that his complaints lacked somewhat in force. His "resolve" to stand firm began to weaken during the afternoon, and by nightfall it was all but swept away. At 10:30 P.M. a White House observer telephoned McKinley's private secretary, George B. Cortelyou. "The feeling is that the thing is going pell-mell like a tidal wave. I think up to this moment Roosevelt was against it, but they have turned his head." If Senator Mark Hanna had not been spending the weekend out of town, wrote a *Tribune* reporter, the Governor might have withdrawn his statements of non-acceptance there and then.[55]

More calls flashed over the wires—to Haverford, Pennsylvania, where Hanna was dining with a shipping tycoon, and thence to the White House with a plea for McKinley to abandon his neutrality and come out in favor of some other candidate. About midnight a cold reply came back: "The President has no choice for Vice-President. Any of the distinguished names suggested would be satisfactory to him. The choice of the Convention will be his choice; he has no advice to give."[56]

HANNA WAS IN A rage when he returned to the Hotel Walton on Monday, 17 June. McKinley's refusal to advise him on the choice of a running mate was a blow to his prestige, and the first deliberately hostile act of their twenty-four-year-old friendship. All things considered, this was not a good morning for Professor Nicholas Murray Butler to approach the Chairman with what can only be described as an academic piece of advice. The only way to stop the nomination going to Roosevelt, Butler lectured, was to present the convention with another candidate of equally compelling personality. "You cannot beat somebody with nobody." Hanna responded to this epigram with an outburst of profanity, and assured Butler that his precious Governor would not be nominated. He, Hanna, simply would not permit it. When Butler asked whom the Chairman might prefer, Hanna growled something about John D. Long.[57]

The Chairman's mood worsened all morning. "Do whatever you damn please!" he bellowed in response to a routine question. "I'm through! I won't have anything more to do with the Convention! I won't take charge of the campaign!" Somebody tried to soothe him by pointing out that he still controlled the party. "I am not in control! McKinley won't let me use the power of the Administration to defeat Roosevelt. He is blind, or afraid, or something!"[58]

Observers wondered again at the Chairman's strange fear of Roosevelt. Hanna had never liked the man, and his dislike had deepened into something like hatred after the fist-shaking incident at the Gridiron Club in the spring of 1898. But this terror, this premonition of a national disaster should Roosevelt be allowed to stand at McKinley's side, was entirely new. At last Hanna, losing all self-control, blurted it out.

"Don't any of you realize that there's only one life between this madman and the Presidency?"[59]

MAD OR NOT, Roosevelt now posed such a serious threat to all the declared vice-presidential candidates that Hanna was forced to limp into his suite shortly before lunch and ask, once and for all, if he intended to run or not. The Governor would not say. He wondered how he could risk his political future by refusing a popular call. Hanna contemptuously replied that the Roosevelt boom had little to do with popularity. Senator Platt was simply using him as a tool. If Roosevelt really wished to show his so-called independence, he should withdraw promptly, publicly, and finally. That would effectively block any attempt to draft him.

Roosevelt hesitated, then agreed to write a statement of withdrawal at once.[60]

AN HOUR OR SO LATER, while Hanna was alerting the leaders of state delegations to the imminent announcement, Roosevelt sat at lunch with his wife, aides, and a few close friends. Henry Cabot Lodge was there, silent and embarrassed behind an enormous blue silk badge reading "FOR VICE PRESIDENT JOHN D. LONG."[61] It was his duty to wear the emblem, as a member of the Massachusetts delegation, but the irony of the slogan must have grated on the sensibilities of all present.

Butler's account of the luncheon implies that Roosevelt said nothing about his recent decision to issue a final statement of denial. He merely sat and listened while everybody except Lodge pressed him to do just that. Edith Roosevelt was outspoken in her insistence that the Vice-Presidency was wrong for him. Not until after Lodge had left, with a bitter "I must go back and be loyal to Long," did the Governor allow Butler to draft a statement.

The draft was appropriately terse and uncompromising. Edith approved it, and Butler handed it to Roosevelt. "If you will sign that paper and give it out this afternoon, you will not be nominated."

Roosevelt stared at the document, contorting his face, as was his habit in moments of perplexity. He thought he could "improve its phrasing," and crossed over to the desk. Somehow the draft became a new statement entirely in his own handwriting. "Theodore, if that is all you will say, you will certainly be nominated," said Butler, aggrieved. "You have taken out of the statement all the finality and definiteness that was in mine."

At four o'clock Roosevelt's statement obstinately went forth.[62] Thousands of eyes scrutinized it to the last conditional clause, and found nowhere the least hint of a refusal to accept the will of the convention. As far as staving off a draft was concerned, he might as effectively have written the single word "Yes."

> In view of the revival of the talk of myself as a Vice-Presidential candidate, I have this to say. It is impossible too deeply to express how touched I am by the attitude of those delegates, who have wished me to take the nomination. . . . I understand the high honor and dignity of the office, an office so high and so honorable that it is well worthy of the ambition of any man in the United States. But while appreciating all this to the full, I nevertheless feel most deeply that the field of my best usefulness to the public and to the party is in New York State; and that, if the party should see fit to renominate me for Governor, I can in that position help the National ticket as in no other way. I very earnestly hope and ask that every friend of mine in this Convention respect my wish and my judgment in this matter.[63]

"It's a cinch," chuckled one delegate. "All we have to do is go ahead and nominate him."

"And then four years from now—" said another delegate.

"Quite so," said a third.[64]

CHAIRMAN HANNA GAVELED the convention to order in Exposition Hall shortly after noon on Tuesday, 19 June. As the thwacking echoes died away and the band prepared to strike up "The Star-Spangled Banner," Theodore Roosevelt made the most famous of all his delayed entrances. Marching with military purposefulness, but not too quickly, he advanced down the aisle toward the New York delegation, his jaw clenched firm against floating spectacle-ribbons, looking neither to right nor left. Fifteen thousand pairs of eyes admired his broad black hat, so irresistibly reminiscent of Cuba ("that's an Acceptance Hat," somebody quipped),[65] and at least ten thousand pairs of hands applauded him as yells of "We Want Teddy!" swept around the auditorium. Roosevelt took fully two minutes to reach his seat; only then did he stand to attention for the beginning of the anthem. From the podium, Mark Hanna, a temporarily forgotten man, gazed down with disgust. Roosevelt was holding the Acceptance Hat over his heart.[66]

For the rest of the day the convention was anticlimactic and boring. A blight of listlessness, to quote *Harper's Weekly,* hung over the proceedings, intensified by steamy, cabbage-smelling heat wafting from the slums of West Philadelphia. Yet much aggressive activity was going on behind the scenes. Hanna, lobbying like a man possessed, bullied every delegate he could find into promises of support for John D. Long, or Representative Jonathen Dolliver of Iowa—anybody but Theodore Roosevelt. White House observers, fearful that the Chairman would split the party in two, telephoned Washington for advice on Tuesday night. The result was another request for decorum from McKinley: "The President's friends must not undertake to commit the Administration to any candidate. It has no candidate . . . The Administration wants the candidate of the Convention, and the President's friends must not dictate the Convention."[67]

But the true dictators of the convention were not McKinley's friends. Senator Platt, nursing a broken rib, was so confident about the preliminary arrangements he had made in behalf of Roosevelt's nomination that he beat a wheezy retreat on Tuesday night. He left the task of actually creating the nomination in the hands of his old friend, Matthew Quay of Pennsylvania—in Platt's judgment, "the ablest politician this country ever produced."[68]

Quay was happy to undertake the work, not out of any especial love for Roosevelt so much as a deep desire to hurt Mark Hanna. Quay was an ex–United States Senator, and wanted to regain office, but Hanna had blocked his efforts.[69] To strike the Chairman down in front of the National Convention would therefore be sweet revenge; and Platt, by turning Roosevelt over to him, had supplied Quay with an ideal missile.

Few delegates, least of all Roosevelt, took any notice of Quay on Wednesday morning, as he sat short, squat, silent, and Indian-eyed[70] in his light suit at an inconspicuous place in the Pennsylvania delegation. He waited until Roosevelt had escorted Henry Cabot Lodge to the podium as elected chairman of the convention—a moment of great pride to both men—before rising to offer an amendment to the rules. Amid puzzled silence, Quay read a resolution to equalize, and where necessary reduce, the size of delegations at the convention, at a ratio of 1 to every 1,000 votes cast in their home states.[71]

Just what this had to do with nominating Roosevelt for Vice-President none of Platt's aides could tell. But for the first time since the convention opened, there was real noise in the hall.[72] The majority of the delegates from East and West roared approval, while those from the South howled with fear. They realized that Quay's amendment would cut their ranks in half. Republican voting was traditionally light in Dixie. And since most of Chairman Hanna's supporters hailed from the South, "equalization" would in effect neutralize his power over the convention. Quay's true motive dawned on the politically astute: he was not remotely interested in delegate representation; he wanted something from Hanna. Sure enough, the Pennsylvanian suggested that a vote on the amendment be postponed overnight so that "the delegates would have ample time to become familiar with it."[73]

Shortly afterward Hanna was seen crossing over and resignedly asking Quay what his price was. "If you will nominate Roosevelt," said Quay, "I will withdraw the resolution. If you won't, I shall insist upon its coming to a vote, and you know what will happen there."

Hanna did. The resolution would pass on the grounds of simple fairness. He would lose his Southern delegates, and lose control of the convention; there would be no guarantee then even of President McKinley's renomination.

That night Hanna, grimacing at the taste of wormwood, announced that in view of "strong and earnest sentiment . . . from all parts of the country," he would support the nomination of Theodore Roosevelt for Vice-President.

"The best we can do," he told his supporters, "is pray fervently for the continued health of the President."[74]

Roosevelt, meanwhile, sat alone in his hotel room. He had already bowed to the inevitable, and would accept the nomination for what it was worth. Having finished one of the *Histories* of Josephus over the weekend, he was now reading Thucydides.[75]

SHORTLY AFTER TEN O'CLOCK the following morning the icy tones of Cabot Lodge announced that the business before the convention would be the nomination of candidates for President of the United States.

Senator Foraker spoke for an eloquent quarter of an hour on the glories of the McKinley Administration, and was awarded with an ovation that reminded one observer, Murat Halstead, of "the halcyon days of the Plumed Knight." Then eighteen thousand voices joined in the singing of "The Union Forever"—an "incomparably moving" sound even to the dignified correspondent of *Harper's Weekly.* "When one hears that sound one must either sing or cry."[76]

Almost before the delegates resumed their seats, Governor Roosevelt had leaped up beside Lodge to second the nomination. He stared briefly into the eyes of his best friend, while applause rolled around them. Sixteen years before, as young delegates to the convention in Chicago, they had felt the pain of defeat together, and heard predictions of their political ruin; now they were two of the most powerful men in the country, and the party was shouting homage to them. It was a sweet moment—but Lodge's face was distorted with "almost agonized anxiety,"[77] and Roosevelt turned quickly to address the audience.

"Mr. Chairman and my fellow delegates, my beloved Republicans and Americans . . ." An accomplished orator now, he moved confidently through his prepared text, speaking at a torrential speed unusual even for him, his body trembling with the force of his gestures. A man in the audience was reminded of "a graduate in a school of acting";[78] a woman sighed that "he would make a first-class lover . . . from the stage point of view." Here was no soft, hesitant wooer, she felt, "but one who would come at once to the question, and, if the lady repulsed him, bear her away despite herself, as some of his ancestors must have done in the pliocene age. . . ."[79]

While Rose Coghlan dreamed, so did Theodore Roosevelt.

> We stand on the threshold of a new century big with the fate of mighty nations. It rests with us now to decide whether in the opening years of that century we shall march forward to fresh triumphs or whether at the outset we shall cripple ourselves for the contest. Is America a weakling, to shrink from the work of the great world-powers? No. The young giant of the West stands on a continent and clasps the crest of an ocean in either hand. Our nation, glorious in youth and strength, looks into the future with eager eyes and rejoices as a strong man to run a race. . . .[80]

He gazed through his tossing lenses at the thousands of banners, the streamers, the bright balloons, the tricolored bunches of pampas grass, the hanging Stars and Stripes. The whole auditorium looked, said a nearby reporter, like a kaleidoscope.[81]

McKINLEY AND ROOSEVELT were nominated by votes of 926 and 925 respectively—the Governor casting the convention's only vote against himself.[82] After that final gesture to his lost independence, he proclaimed himself a loyal member of the team, and offered his services to Hanna for the duration of the campaign.

The Chairman told him that it would be, as far as McKinley was concerned, a repetition of the campaign of 1896. While the Democratic nominee—William Jennings Bryan, again—stumped the country on behalf of the disadvantaged classes, the President would remain at home in Canton, Ohio, and hold his customary front-porch receptions to visiting deputations. Roosevelt would have to do most of the traveling, and most of the speechmaking; fortunately he was good at both.

The candidate was cheerfully agreeable. "I am as strong as a bull moose," he assured Hanna, "and you can use me to the limit, taking heed of but one thing and that is my throat." He did not wish to seem to be neglecting his duties as Governor of New York, but fortunately "July, August, September, and October are months in which there is next to no work."[83]

All through that quarter of a year, accordingly, Roosevelt crossed and recrossed the country, with such numbing frequency, and such an incessant outpouring of his familiar political philosophy, as to blur the sensibilities of all but a cataloger. Suffice to say that he traveled farther and spoke more than any candidate, presidential or vice-presidential, in nineteenth-century history, with the exception of Bryan himself, four years before. But Bryan in 1900 could not match Roosevelt. By 3 November the Governor had made a total of 673 speeches in 567 towns in 24 states; he had traveled 21,209 miles and spoken an average of 20,000 words a day to 3 million people.[84] The following timetable of one undated campaign day survives from the diary of an aide:

7:00 A.M.	Breakfast
7:30 A.M.	A speech
8:00 A.M.	Reading a historical work
9:00 A.M.	A speech
10:00 A.M.	Dictating letters
11:00 A.M.	Discussing Montana mines
11:30 A.M.	A speech
12:00	Reading an ornithological work
12:30 P.M.	A speech
1:00 P.M.	Lunch
1:30 P.M.	A speech
2:30 P.M.	Reading Sir Walter Scott
3:00 P.M.	Answering telegrams
3:45 P.M.	A speech
4:00 P.M.	Meeting the press
4:30 P.M.	Reading
5:00 P.M.	A speech
6:00 P.M.	Reading
7:00 P.M.	Supper
8–10 P.M.	Speaking
11:00 P.M.	Reading alone in his car
12:00	To bed.[85]

Inevitably, there were moments of ugliness, as when a mob of hired "muckers" assaulted him near Cripple Creek, Colorado, with rocks big enough to crush the iron guards on the caboose. A flying wedge of Rough Riders rescued the candidate from serious harm. William Jennings Bryan haughtily disbelieved reports of the incident, but said it was an outrage "if true."[86]

The Rough Riders, of course, were not above staging a little playful violence themselves, as when a member of the Campaign Special shot a Populist editor for presuming to criticize "mah Colonel." The editor survived,[87] but stories like this revived Roosevelt's forgotten "cowboy" image in the East, much to the delight of cartoonists and humorists. On 13 October, Finley Peter Dunne's barroom philosopher "Mr. Dooley"[88] summarized the campaign thus:

> "Well, sir," said Mr Dooley, "if thayse anny wan r-runnin' in this campaign but me frind Tiddy Rosenfelt, I'd like to know who it is. It isn't Mack, f'r he wint away three weeks ago, lavin' a note sayin' that he'd accipt th' nommynation if twas offered him, an' he ain't been heerd fr'm since. It ain't Bryan . . . 'Tis Tiddy alone that's r-runnin', an' he ain't runnin', he's gallopin'."

Mr. Dooley went on to parody a local account of one of Roosevelt's bipartisan meetings out West.

> At this moment Gov'nor Rosenfelt bit his way through th' throng, an afther bringin' down with a well-aimed shot th' chairman iv th' Dimmycratic commity . . . he spoke as follows: 'Scoundhrels, cowards, hired ruffians, I know ye all well, an' if e'er a wan iv ye comes up to this platform I'll show ye how I feel to'ord ye, an' fellow Raypublicans: This is th' happiest moment iv me life. [A voice: "Kill him."] Nivir bifure have I injiyed so much livin' undher a Constitootion that insures equal r-rights an' no more to wan an' all, an'— excuse me, gents, while I get th' r-red-headed man in th' gal'ry. Got him!

Thanks—an' spreads over the country . . . (Editor's Note: here our rayporther was sthruck on th' back iv th' head with a piece iv castin' . . . But we undherstand that Gov'nor Rosenfelt completed a delightful speech amid gr-reat enthusyasm an' was escorted to th' train be a large crowd. Th' list iv kilt an' wounded will be found in another part iv this paper.)[89]

Comparisons between this piece and, say, the *Chicago Times-Herald* account of Roosevelt's visit to Deadwood, South Dakota, on 3 October prove that Mr. Dooley's imagination was not wholly without basis in fact.[90]

The trip also had its moments of poignancy, as when Roosevelt's train snaked down into the Badlands of North Dakota and stopped at Medora. "The romance of my life began here," said Roosevelt, to nobody in particular. Then, jumping down into the sagebrush, he looked around at the gray buttes, the Little Missouri, and what was left of Medora itself. "It does not seem right," he said sadly, "that I should come here and not stay."[91]

On 6 November 1900, the Republican party won its greatest victory since the triumph of Grant in 1872. McKinley's popular plurality was well over three-quarters of a million, and he swamped Bryan in the Electoral College, 292–155.[92] Much of this favorable vote could be ascribed to the nation's booming economy, and satisfaction with the successful conduct of the war; but the Vice-President-elect was entitled to much of the credit. Party professionals agreed that by his selfless exertions he had earned himself the Presidency in 1904.

If not earlier. "I feel sorry for McKinley," said one Republican campaign worker, as he perused the election results. "He has a man of destiny behind him."[93]

Roosevelt divided the rest of November and December between Albany and Oyster Bay. On the last day of the year his

Governorship came to an end. "I think I have been the best Governor of my time," he claimed, "better either than Cleveland or Tilden."[94] His record had indeed been impressive, seen in the context of history, although the *Evening Post* sneered at his record of "partial and leisurely reform."[95] A wide disparity of other editorial comments indicates that contemporary critics found it difficult, if not impossible, to analyze Governor Roosevelt objectively.

Much of this difficulty arose out of the Roosevelt/Platt relationship, so subtle a combination of enmity and friendliness, clashes and compromise. Conservatives on the one hand, and radicals on the other, simply could not see how two such men could, in effect, be merged into one Governor, and produce legislation so puzzlingly satisfactory to both their traditional constituencies (although of course both regulars and reformers complained that it was neither). The evidence is that Platt himself was confused, and merely trying to make the best of an awkward alliance, whereas Roosevelt, as time would show, knew very well what he was about.

In brief summary, he was responding, along with such other leaders as John P. Altgeld of Chicago, Hazen Pingree of Detroit, and Samuel Jones of Toledo, to the progressive movement then developing in various parts of the country.[96] He had been responding to it, indeed, throughout his career, as a reform Assemblyman in 1882, a reform Civil Service Commissioner in 1889, and a reform Police Commissioner in 1895; but aristocratic paternalism had dominated his thinking until 1898. The war, which brought him confessedly closer to his men than his officers,[97] also awakened his conscience to the needs of those less fortunate, less virile, less intelligent than himself. Having achieved his own military catharsis on San Juan Hill, he was now a politician again, and found himself less interested in battles than in treaties. As such, his two gubernatorial messages could be viewed as social contracts acknowledging the continuing, though waning power of the Old Guard, and promising new powers to the progressives.

If not the first, Theodore Roosevelt was certainly one of the first politicians to act responsibly in view of the changing economics and class structure of late-nineteenth-century America. As such he deserves to be ranked only slightly behind Altgeld and Pingree and

Jones. If his governorship, which lasted only two years (and was subject to enormous distractions in the second), was less spectacular than some, it was spectacular enough in terms of his own membership in the social and intellectual elite. One thinks of his early contempt for unions, for Henry George, for the unwashed Populists, for the rural supporters of William Jennings Bryan. Yet as Governor, Roosevelt had shown himself again and again willing to support labor against capital, and the plebeians in their struggle against his own class.

After 1900, as progressivism rated a capital P and reform governors began to crowd the political landscape, Roosevelt's legislative record would look more and more modest, even cautious. But as a modern historian asks, "who *in office* was more radical in 1899?"[98]

WITH THE TURN of the century came private citizenship again, in preparation for the life of "a dignified nonentity" in his new job.[99] Gratifying though it was to see a collected edition of *The Works of Theodore Roosevelt* put out by G. P. Putnam's Sons, there was also something distressingly final about the fifteen volumes, as if he had already been tombstoned, a strenuous relic of the past.

Apart from boning up in a few issues of the *Congressional Record,* to see how to preside over the Senate, there was really little he could do. The frightening specter of inactivity loomed ahead. To fend it off, he left on 7 January for his first extended hunting trip in years—a chase after cougar in Colorado—and did not get back to Sagamore Hill until 23 February. A week later the Roosevelts headed southward en masse for the Inauguration on 4 March 1901. So did a party of maliciously amused organization men, headed by Senator Platt and the new Governor, Benjamin B. Odell. "We're all off to Washington," said Platt, "to see Teddy take the veil."[100]

Jones. [illegible] only two [illegible] and [illegible] [illegible] [illegible] his own [illegible] [illegible] the social and intellectual [illegible]. One [illegible] of his [illegible] [illegible] Henry George [illegible] [illegible] William Jennings Bryan [illegible] Roosevelt had shown himself again and again willing to support labor against capital, and the peasants in their struggle against their own class.

[illegible]

When [illegible] of the [illegible] private [illegible] appropriation for the [illegible] a dignified [illegible] [illegible] Roosevelt put out [illegible] Putnam's Sons [illegible] something more than about the [illegible] as if he had already [illegible]

[illegible]

[illegible] Senator [illegible] off to Washington [illegible]

EPILOGUE: SEPTEMBER 1901

A strain of music closed the tale,
A low, monotonous, funeral wail,
That with its cadence, wild and sweet,
Made the long Saga more complete.

THEODORE ROOSEVELT'S FORMAL SERVICES to the nation as Vice-President lasted exactly four days, from 4 March to 8 March 1901.[1] The Senate then adjourned until December, and Roosevelt was free to lay down his gavel and return to Oyster Bay. Before doing so he asked Associate Justice Edward D. White for advice on resuming his long-abandoned legal studies in the fall[2]—a sure sign of confusion and pessimism about the future.

It was pleasant, all the same, to relax with his numerous children after so many busy years. Sagamore was at its most beautiful that spring, with spreading dogwood, blooming orchards, and the "golden leisurely chiming of the wood thrushes chanting their vespers" down below.

An old friend, Fanny Smith Dana, visited him that spring. "As always, Theodore was vital and stimulating, but there was a difference. The spur of combat was absent."[3] In May he escorted Edith north to the opening of the Pan-American Exposition in Buffalo, and in July and August made two further restless trips West, to

"He has a man of destiny behind him."

The second Inauguration of William McKinley, 4 March 1901.

Colorado and Minnesota. "I always told you I was more of a Westerner than an Easterner," he explained, rather vaguely, to Lincoln Steffens.[4] In early fall his social schedule began to pick up, and on 4 September 1901, he arrived in Rutland, Vermont, for a short series of speaking engagements.

Sometime that day Roosevelt's eastbound train crossed the tracks of the Presidential Special, bearing William McKinley north to the exposition in Buffalo.[5]

TWO DAYS LATER, on Friday, 6 September, the Vice-President attended an estate luncheon of the Vermont Fish and Game League on Isle La Motte, in Lake Champlain.[6] With a thousand other guests he sat under a great marquee and ate and drank leisurely until about four o'clock. Then, leaving the crowd to follow him, he strolled across the lawns to the home of his host, ex-Governor Nelson W. Fisk. An impromptu reception was planned inside, at which any member of the league might come forward and shake the Vice-President's hand.

Inside the house a telephone shrilled. While Fisk answered it, Roosevelt stood in the sun chatting to one or two companions. Then Fisk appeared at the door and beckoned him in wordlessly. To the puzzlement of other people on the lawn, the door was locked as soon as the Vice-President had stepped through it. Keys were heard turning in all the other doors in the house, and volunteer guards stood at the windows. They would answer no questions as to what was being discussed on the telephone. Yet somehow a realization swept through the crowd that the President had been shot, perhaps killed.

Meanwhile Roosevelt had put down the receiver and was addressing the house company. "Gentlemen, I am afraid that there is little ground for hope that the report is untrue. It comes now from two sources and appears to be authentic." He gave them the facts. A young anarchist had approached the President in Buffalo's Temple of Music with a handkerchief wrapped around his right hand. McKinley, thinking it a bandage, had reached to shake his left hand, whereupon a revolver concealed in the handkerchief blasted two bullets into the President's breast and belly. He was now undergoing exploratory surgery, and the assailant, whose name was Leon Czolgosz, had been apprehended. "Don't let them hurt him," McKinley had murmured before lapsing into deep shock.[7]

While Senator Redfield Proctor apprised the crowd of the details, Roosevelt and his aides left immediately for Buffalo.

McKinley's condition next morning, Saturday, 7 September, gave encouragement to his attending physicians. The breast wound was no more than a gash on the ribs, but the abdominal penetration was deep and serious. Both walls of the stomach had been torn open; the bullet was buried somewhere irretrievable. The most dangerous threat was of gangrene; however there were no visible signs of sepsis.[8]

McKinley was a man of strong constitution, and he rallied amazingly over the weekend. By Tuesday, 10 September, his condition was so improved that Roosevelt (who had comported himself with extraordinary dignity and concern throughout) was told he no longer need remain at the presidential bedside. In fact it would be best, from the point of view of publicity, if he quit Buffalo altogether.[9]

The Vice-President left that afternoon for a short vacation in the Adirondacks, where Edith and the children were waiting for him in a mountain cabin.

HE COULD NOT HAVE CHOSEN a destination more likely to reassure the American people that the national crisis was over, and that his services would not be required in some dread emergency. The cabin stood at Camp Tahawus, "the most remote human habitation in the Empire State," on the slopes of Mount Marcy, highest peak in the Adirondacks. Half a century before, Tahawus had been a little mining community; now, thanks to the enterprise of Roosevelt's wealthy friend and fellow conservationist James McNaughton, it had been transformed into a luxury resort for hunters, fishermen, and climbers.[10]

On arrival at the camp Roosevelt stopped at Tahawus Club, the old village lodging-house, and arranged for two ranger guides to accompany him on an ascent of the mountain, beginning on 12 September.[11] This done, he went on up the slope to his cabin in the trees.

By nightfall on the twelfth, Roosevelt and his climbing party, consisting of Edith, Kermit, ten-year-old Ethel, a governess, James McNaughton, three other friends, and the two rangers, were at Lake Colden, altitude 3,500 feet, where they spent the night in two cabins. The next morning, Friday the thirteenth, was cold and gray: an impenetrable drizzle screened off the mountain above them, and the women and children elected to return to Tahawus. But Roosevelt, who could never resist the highest peak in any neighborhood, in any weather, exhorted his elder male companions to continue climbing with him. Leaving one guide to escort the downward party, he ordered the other to lead his own up into the mists. At about nine o'clock they set off along the cold, slippery trail.[12]

AT 11:52 A.M. ROOSEVELT found himself on a great flat rock, gazing out (could he but see it!) across the whole of New York State. Rolling fog obscured everything but nearer grass and shrubs, yet the sense of being the highest man for hundreds of miles around, cherished by all instinctive climbers, was no doubt pleasing to him. As if in further reward, the clouds unexpectedly parted, sunshine poured down on his head, and for a few minutes a world of trees and mountains and sparkling water lay all around, stretching to infinity.[13]

Roosevelt was not a reflective man, nor was he prone now in his early middle age (he would be forty-three in six weeks' time) to long for the past as much as he used to. But the news of President McKinley's accident, and the unavoidable horrid thrill of being, if only for a few hours, the likely next President of the United States, seems to have temporarily awakened his youthful tendency to nostalgia. Writing to Jacob Riis a few days before, he had said that "a shadow" had fallen across his path, separating him from "those youthful days" which he would never see again.[14]

Here, if ever, was an opportunity to look around him at all these lower hills, and to think of the hills he had himself climbed in life. Pilatus as a boy; Katahdin as an underclassman; Chestnut Hill as a young lover; the Matterhorn in the ecstasy of honeymoon; the Big Horns in Wyoming, with their bugling elks; the Capitol Hill in Albany, that freezing January night when he first entered politics; Sagamore Hill, his own fertile fortress, full of his children and crowned with triumphant antlers; the Hill in Washington where he twice laid out John Wanamaker; that lowest yet loftiest of hills in Cuba, where like King Olaf on Smalsor Horn he planted his shield; now this. Would he ever rise any higher? Or was McKinley's recovery a sign that the final peak he had so long sought would after all be denied him?

Mists rolled in again, and Roosevelt descended five hundred feet to a little lake named Tear-of-the-Clouds, where his party unpacked lunch. It was about 1:25 in the afternoon.[15]

As he ate his sandwiches he saw below him in the trees a ranger approaching, running, clutching the yellow slip of a telegram.[16] Instinctively, he knew what message the man was bringing.

ACKNOWLEDGMENTS

BEFORE LISTING THOSE WHO HAVE CONTRIBUTED in various ways to the writing of this biography, I must single out a few names for special mention. Dr. John Allen Gable, Executive Director of the Theodore Roosevelt Association, minutely scrutinized my manuscript, corrected errors of fact and judgment, and made no attempt to influence my interpretations of TR's character—beyond constructing some logical arguments which I was free to accept or reject. In most cases I accepted them. Those which I rejected are nevertheless so valid that I have incorporated them in my Chapter Notes. My debt to Dr. Gable is large.

So, too, is my debt to Joseph Kanon, who honed the manuscript with the elegant precision of a born editor. To Carleton Putnam, a man I have never met, I express gratitude and admiration for his *Theodore Roosevelt: The Formative Years* (Scribner's, 1958), an essential source for students of TR's youth. It is a tragedy of American biography that this grave, neglected masterpiece was never followed by other volumes. Peggy Brooks and Ann Elmo were the first to suggest, on the basis of a few articles and a screenplay, that I should write a book about TR; if the result bulks somewhat larger than the "short" work they envisioned, my thanks to them have increased proportionately.

I also thank the following, in alphabetical order: John Alsop of Avon, Connecticut, for permission to study his valuable collection of Roosevelt and Robinson papers, now transferred to Harvard;

Georges Borchardt, my agent; John C. Broderick, Chief of Manuscripts at the Library of Congress; the Hon. Alan Clark, M.P., of Saltwood Castle, Kent; Mr. Sheffield Cowles for reminiscences of his uncle TR; Barbara Dailey for hospitality to a starving, snowbound researcher in the Great Blizzard of February 1978; Wallace Dailey for his amazingly efficient work as Curator of the Theodore Roosevelt Collection at Harvard, not to mention his performances of Bach after hours; the late Mrs. Ethel Roosevelt Derby, TR's younger daughter; the European-American Bank, for not blanching at the sight of the word "Writer" on a loan application form; John J. Geoghegan, my publisher, for his patience and generosity; Kathleen Jacklin, Archivist of the Cornell University Libraries; Peter Lacey, *artiorum patronus;* Mrs. Alice Roosevelt Longworth, TR's elder daughter, for contributing many bright fragments of memory to the mosaic of my Prologue; Linda and Noel Rae, for the use of a peaceful house in the country; Larry Remele, Historian/Editor of North Dakota's excellent State Historical Society; Mr. Archibald Roosevelt, son of TR, for uncannily and unconsciously recreating TR's smile for me; Mrs. Philip Roosevelt for showing me letters by and about Alice Lee; Mr. and Mrs. P. James Roosevelt for encouragement, advice, and hospitality; Gary Roth, Curator of Sagamore Hill National Historical Site; Guy St. Clair of the Union League Club; James Terleph, for a psychological critique of my earlier chapters; Angus Wilson for tolerantly answering yet another letter about Rudyard Kipling; and Mitchell York, a highly capable editorial assistant.

Finally I would like to invoke the name of St. Bernard of Clairvaux, who composed the most inspiring of literary aphorisms, "Every word that you write is a blow that smites the Devil."

BIBLIOGRAPHY

THIS BIBLIOGRAPHY LISTS ONLY THE MAJOR SOURCES of information and quotations in *The Rise of Theodore Roosevelt*. The abbreviations preceding each item will be used in the Chapter Notes below. Unpublished sources are coded in capitals, published sources in combined capitals and lower case. Thus ADA. signifies Henry Adams in manuscript, and Ada. Henry Adams in print. All other sources, including dissertations, documents, periodical articles, and minor books, will be cited in full when they first appear in the Chapter Notes. Listings are alphabetical by surname except for Theodore Roosevelt, who appears throughout as TR.

Unpublished material: Papers, Memoirs, and Scrapbooks

ADA. Adams, Henry. Papers in Massachusetts Historical Society, Cambridge.

AND. Andrews, Avery. *Citizen in Action: The Story of TR as Police Commissioner* (typescript) in TRC.

AND.SCR. Andrews, Avery. *Scrapbooks of the New York City Police Department, 1895–97*, 3 vols., in TRC.

BEA. Beale, Howard K. Papers in Mudd Library, Princeton University.

FEN. Fenwick, J. E., compiler. *The White House Record of Social Functions*, 13 vols., in National Archives, Washington, D.C.

FDR. Franklin Delano Roosevelt Library, Hyde Park, New York.

GEO. George, Henry. *Mayoralty Campaign Scrapbooks*, 4 vols., in New York Public Library.

HAG.BLN. Hagedorn, Hermann. "Bad Lands Notes" (research for his *Roosevelt in the Bad Lands* in TRC.

HAY.BR. Hay, John. Papers, Hay Library, Brown University.

LOD. Lodge, Henry Cabot. Papers, including complete TR–Lodge correspondence, in Massachusetts Historical Society. Typed copies of the correspondence, prepared for publication by Lodge and Edith Roosevelt (see Lod. below), reveal occasional blue-penciled bursts of Rooseveltian invective, which I have chosen to restore.

LON. Long, John D. Papers, including diaries, in Massachusetts Historical Society.

PRI.N Pringle, Henry F. Notes for his *TR: A Biography* (see Pri., below).

TRB. Theodore Roosevelt Birthplace, New York City. Unsorted but often valuable collection of Rooseveltiana, including the complete correspondence of TR with his sister Bamie, in photostats and typed copies. This collection was judiciously edited for publication in *Letters from TR to Anna Roosevelt Cowles, 1870–1918* (Scribner's, 1925). Many important letters, such as that of 20 September 1886, describing TR's qualms about remarrying, and a long series to do with the alcoholism and death of Elliott Roosevelt, never saw print. I have preferred to cite the copies, rather than the published versions. TRB also contains many files of interviews, clips, notes, and photographs collected by the indefatigable Hermann Hagedorn. All Roosevelt biographers are indebted to this gentleman, although his hero-worship of TR occasionally got the better of him. To take one small but significant example, the description of TR as an Assemblyman quoted by Isaac Hunt, "He's a brilliant madman born a hundred years too soon" (see Chapter 9), is altered in Hagedorn's stenographic record so that "madman" appears shorn of its offending first syllable.

TRC. Theodore Roosevelt Collection, Harvard College Library, Cambridge, Mass. By far the biggest Roosevelt archive, including most of his 150,000 letters (only 10% of which have been published) either in originals or copies. The voluminous papers of TR's two sisters are also on deposit here, along with stacks of scrapbooks and photographs and an extensive book collection.

TRP. Theodore Roosevelt Papers, Library of Congress, Washington D.C. (L.C.). Mainly incoming and outgoing official correspondence, skimpy for the earlier years covered by this volume, but waxing enormous after 1898.

The above three collections contain the following diaries:

TR.PRI.DI. Theodore Roosevelt: *Private Diaries*, 1878–1885. The most revealing Roosevelt documents to survive. (TRP)

TR.LEG.DI. Theodore Roosevelt: *Diary of Five Months in the New York Legislature*, 1882. (TRB photostat) Reprinted in Mor. (see below).

TR.1886.DI. Theodore Roosevelt: *Diary for 1886*. Enigmatic and fragmentary. (TRC)

TR.WAR.DI. Theodore Roosevelt. *Diary of the Spanish-American War*, 1898. Terse but fascinating. (TRC)

And the following scrapbooks:

TR.HAR.SCR. Theodore Roosevelt. *Harvard Scrapbook*, 1879–80. Stripped of all relics of Alice Lee, but otherwise useful. (TRC)

TR.SCR. Theodore Roosevelt. *Scrapbooks, 1881–1898*. Disorganized and crumbling, but rich in contemporary clips and reviews, which are by no means all flattering. (TRC)

TR.PRES.SCR. Theodore Roosevelt. *Presidential Scrapbooks*, 1901–1909. A prodigious source, used only for the Prologue to this volume. (TRP)

Interviews and Reminiscences

Conversations between the author and Roosevelt's surviving children are cited where relevant in the Chapter Notes, as are interviews conducted by Mary Hagedorn with various members of the Roosevelt family in the 1950s for the Columbia Oral History Project.

COW. Cowles, Anna Roosevelt. Four letter/memoirs to her son Sheffield Cowles, recalling her youth and TR's childhood at 28 East Twentieth Street, plus random recollections of later years. (TRB and TRC)

FRE. French, J. F., interviewer. A collection of verbal reminiscences, mainly political, recorded in the 1920s with TR's old New York Republican Associates. (TRB)

HUN. Hunt, Isaac, and Spinney, George. Verbal reminiscences, mainly of TR's Assembly years, recorded during a dinner with Hermann Hagedorn at the Harvard Club, New York, on 20 Sept. 1923. Typed memorandum, including a supplementary Hunt statement, no date. (TRB)

Published Works

Ada. Adams, Henry. *Letters, 1892–1918,* ed. Worthington Chauncey Ford. Boston, 1938.

Alex. Alexander, DeAlva S. *A Political History of New York State.* Vol. 4: "Four Famous New Yorkers." New York, 1923.

Azo. Azoy, A.C.M. *Charge! The Story of the Battle of San Juan Hill.* New York, 1961.

Bea. Beale, Howard K. *Theodore Roosevelt and the Rise of America to World Power.* Johns Hopkins Press, 1956.

Bee. Beer, Thomas. *Hanna, Crane, and the Mauve Decade.* Knopf, 1941.

Ber. Berman, Jay Stuart. *Police Administration and Progressive Reform: Theodore Roosevelt as Police Commissioner of New York.* Greenwood, 1987.

Bis. Bishop, Joseph Bucklin. *Theodore Roosevelt and His Time.* Scribner's, 1920.

Bur. Burton, David H. *Theodore Roosevelt, Confident Imperialist.* Philadelphia, 1968. Excellent and illuminating.

But. Butt, Archie. *The Letters of Archie Butt, Personal Aide to President Roosevelt,* ed. Lawrence F. Abbot. Doubleday, 1924. A classic.

Cha. Chanler, Mrs. Winthrop. *Roman Spring.* Little, Brown, 1934.

Che. Chessman, G. Wallace. *Governor Theodore Roosevelt.* Harvard U. Press, 1965.

Cly. Clymer, Kenton J. *John Hay: The Gentleman as Diplomat.* U. of Michigan Press, 1975.

Cro. Croly, Herbert. *Marcus Alonzo Hanna: His Life and Works.* Macmillan, 1912.

Cut. Cutright, Paul Russell. *Theodore Roosevelt the Naturalist.* Harpers, 1956. A long overdue addition to the Roosevelt bibliography. Its final pages contain the most moving of all eulogies to TR.

Den. Dennett, Tyler. *John Hay: From Poetry to Politics.* Dodd, Mead, 1933.

Dun. Dunn, Arthur Wallace. *From Harrison to Harding: A Personal Narrative, 1888–1921.* 2 vols. Putnam, 1922.

Gar. Garraty, John A. *Henry Cabot Lodge.* Knopf, 1953.

Gos. Gosnell, Harold F. *Boss Platt and His New York Machine.* U. Chicago Press, 1924.

Gou. Gould, Lewis L. *The Presidency of William McKinley.* Regents Press of Kansas, 1980. A policy-oriented study, importantly supplementing Leech (see below).

Gwy. Gwynn, Stephen, ed. *The Letters and Friendships of Sir Cecil Spring-Rice.* 2 vols. Houghton Mifflin, 1929.

Hag.Boy. Hagedorn, Hermann. *The Boy's Life of Theodore Roosevelt.* Harpers, 1918. Written in cooperation with TR.

Hag.LW. Hagedorn, Hermann. *Leonard Wood: A Biography.* 2 vols. Harpers, 1931.

Hag.RBL. Hagedorn, Hermann. *Roosevelt in the Bad Lands.* Houghton Mifflin, 1921.

Hag.RF. Hagedorn, Hermann. *The Roosevelt Family of Sagamore Hill.* Macmillan, 1954.

Har. Harbaugh, William H. *Power and Responsibility: The Life and Times of Theodore Roosevelt.* Farrar, Straus, and Giroux, 1961.

Hay. Hay, John. *Letters and Extracts* from his diaries, ed. Henry Adams and Mrs. Hay. 3 vols., privately printed, 1908, with initialed names penciled in by Worthington Chauncey Ford, in New York Public Library Rare Book Division.

Her. Herrick, Walter R., Jr. *The American Naval Revolution.* Louisiana State U. Press, 1966.

Igl. Iglehart, Ferdinand Cowle. *Theodore Roosevelt: The Man as I Knew Him.* New York, 1919.

Joh. Johnson, Walter. *William Allen White's America.* New York, 1947.

Jos. Josephson, Matthew. *The President Makers.* New York, 1940. Best account of Henry Cabot Lodge's lifelong career as TR's mentor.

Lan. Lang, Lincoln. *Ranching with Roosevelt.* Lippincott, 1926.

Las. Lash, Joseph P. *Eleanor and Franklin.* Norton, 1971.

Lee. Leech, Margaret. *In the Days of McKinley.* Harpers, 1959. An unsurpassed presidential biography.

Lod. Lodge, Henry Cabot. *Selections from the Correspondence of Theodore Roosevelt and Henry Cabot Lodge, 1884–1918.* Scribner's, 1925.

Loo. Looker, Earle. *The White House Gang.* New York, 1929. A hilarious classic.

Lor. Lorant, Stefan. *The Life and Times of Theodore Roosevelt.* Doubleday, 1959.

Mc.C. McCormick, Richard L. *From Realignment to Reform: Political Change in New York State, 1893–1910.* Cornell U. Press, 1981. Essential background to TR's police commissionership and governorship.

May. May, Ernest. *Imperial Democracy: The Emergence of America as a Great Power.* Harcourt, Brace & World, 1961.

Mil. Millis, Walter. *The Martial Spirit.* New York, 1931.

Morg. Morgan, H. Wayne. *McKinley and His America.* Syracuse U. Press, 1963.

Mor. Morison, Elting E. and Blum, John, eds. *The Letters of Theodore Roosevelt.* 8 vols. Harvard U. Press, 1951–4. A work of formidable scholarship, indispensable to all students of TR.

Morr. Morris, Edmund. *Theodore Rex.* Random House, 2001.

Morr.EKR Morris, Sylvia Jukes. *Edith Kermit Roosevelt: Portrait of a First Lady.* Modern Library edition, 2001.

Nev. Nevins, Allan. *Grover Cleveland.* Dodd, Mead, 1932.

Par. Parsons, Mrs. James Russell (Fanny Smith Dana, *née* Frances Theodora Smith). *Perchance Some Day.* Privately printed memoir, 1951. Copy in TRC.

Pla. Platt, Thomas Collier. *The Autobiography of Thomas Collier Platt.* Edited (and, one suspects, largely written) by Louis J. Lang. New York, 1910. Should be used in conjunction with Gos., above.

Pra. Pratt, Julius W. *The Expansionists of 1898.* Baltimore, 1935.

Pri. Pringle, Henry F. *Theodore Roosevelt: A Biography.* Harcourt, Brace & Co., 1931. Highly prejudiced and selective, but still the best one-volume life of TR.

Put. Putnam, Carleton. *Theodore Roosevelt. Vol. 1: The Formative Years, 1858–1886.* Scribner's, 1958. A neglected masterpiece. See Acknowledgments, above.

Rho. Rhodes, James Ford. *The McKinley and Roosevelt Administrations, 1897–1909.* Macmillan, 1923.

Rii. Riis, Jacob A. *Theodore Roosevelt the Citizen.* Johnson, Wynne Co., 1904.

Rob. Robinson, Corinne Roosevelt. *My Brother Theodore Roosevelt.* Scribner's, 1921. Sentimental and inaccurate, but of prime importance nevertheless.

Sew. Sewall, William Wingate. *Bill Sewall's Story of TR.* New York, 1919.

Ste. Steffens, Lincoln. *Autobiography.* Harcourt Brace, 1936.

Sto. Stoddard, Henry L. *As I Knew Them.* Harpers, 1927.

Sul. Sullivan, Mark. *Our Times: The United States, 1900–1925. Vol. II: America Finding Herself.* New York, 1927.

Tha. Thayer, William Roscoe. *The Life and Letters of John Hay.* Houghton Mifflin, 1915.

TR.Auto Theodore Roosevelt. *An Autobiography.* Macmillan, 1913. I have used the illustrated reprint of March 1914. For all its sins of omission, a fairly complete portrait of TR the man: alternately tender, preachy, humorous, boring, boastful, inspiring, cozy, and sad.

TR.DBY. Theodore Roosevelt. *Diaries of Boyhood and Youth.* New York, 1924. Delightful.

TR.Wks. Theodore Roosevelt. *Works,* ed. Hermann Hagedorn. National Edition, 20 vols. Scribner's, 1926.

Twe.	Tweton, D. Jerome. *The Marquis de Morès, Dakota Capitalist, French Nationalist.* North Dakota Institute for Regional Studies, Fargo, N.D., 1972.
Wag.	Wagenknecht, Edward. *The Seven Worlds of Theodore Roosevelt.* Longmans, Green & Co., 1958. Succeeds more than any other work in capturing the size and complexity of TR. Contains a magnificent bibliography.
Wes.	Westermeir, Clifford P. *Who Rush to Glory: The Cowboy Volunteers of 1898.* Caldwell, Idaho, 1958. Some interesting Western sources.
Whi.	White, William Allen. *Autobiography.* Macmillan, 1946.
Wis.	Wister, Owen. *Roosevelt—The Story of a Friendship, 1880–1919.* Macmillan, 1930.
Woo.	Wood, Fred S., ed. *Roosevelt as We Knew Him: Personal Recollections of 150 Friends.* John C. Winston Co., 1927.

NOTES

References to such general sources as Mor. and TR.Auto are made throughout the Notes. In addition, most chapters refer to sources relevant only to themselves, for example childhood diaries in Ch. 1 and naval studies in Ch. 22. Important sources are cited in full at the beginning of each Note, and are short-listed thereafter. Except where otherwise indicated, all citations of TR's collected letters (Mor.) refer to vols. 1 and 2, which are consecutively page-numbered. Other sources are cited in full *passim;* they, too, are then short-listed. Customary abbreviations like *N.Y.T.* for *The New York Times* are used wherever possible. The following initials identify persons frequently mentioned in the text: TR Sr. and MBR for Theodore's parents; B, E, and C for Bamie, Elliott, and Corinne; EKR for Edith Kermit (Carow) Roosevelt; HCL for Henry Cabot Lodge; CSR for Cecil Spring-Rice; BH, GC, and McK for Presidents Harrison, Cleveland, and McKinley; TCP for Thomas Collier Platt, JDL for John D. Long, and MH for Mark Hanna. The abbreviation "pors." refers to photographs and portraits.

Prologue

Important sources not in Bibliography: Interviews with members of the Roosevelt family. Mrs. Alice Longworth, Nov. 9, 1954, June 2, 1956 (TRB mss.), and in July 1976 with author; Mrs. Ethel Derby, April 1976, with author; Mr. Archibald Roosevelt, Feb. 6, 1976, with author.

Because of the impressionistic nature of this prologue, there are occasional citations from sources dating later than January 1, 1907—but never unless the material quoted is chronologically authentic. For example, William Bayard Hale's *A Week in the White House* was published in 1908, but Hale, as a *New York Times* reporter, had been writing similar descriptions of TR since at least 1903, many of which he transferred verbatim to his book. He may therefore be reliably quoted. On the other hand, all the intimate observations of Archie Butt (see Bibl.) have had to be left out because Butt did not meet TR until after the 1907 Reception.

1. *Washington Herald,* and *Post,* Jan. 2, 1907; *Town & Country,* Jan. 5; clips in Fenwick, 1907. Stoker, Bram, *Reminiscences of Sir Henry Irving* (NY 1906) 237; *N.Y.T.,* Jan. 2, 1907.
2. Fenwick, 1907.
3. Evans, Robert D., *An Admiral's Log* (D. Appleton, 1910) 412.
4. *W. Her.,* Jan. 2, 1907.
5. Ib.; 2 clips. n.d., in Fenwick, 1907.
6. Collage from *W. Her., W. Post,* W. *Evening Star, N.Y. Sun, N.Y.T.,* Jan. 1 and 2, 1907. *Town & Country,* Jan. 5.

7. Ib.
8. Ib.; Fenwick, 1907, qu. W. *Eve Star,* n.d.
9. *Eve Star,* Jan. 2, 1907.
10. Ib., Dec. 31, 1906; *Sun,* same date; *Philadelphia Public Ledger,* Dec. 3, 1906; *Eve. Star,* Jan. 2, 1907.
11. Message to Congress, Dec. 1906, reprinted in TR.Wks.XV. See Dun. II. 3–14 for a list of the legislative achievements in this, "the greatest year in Theodore Roosevelt's life."
12. *Eve. Star,* Dec. 31, 1906; James Thayer Addison to Hermann Hagedorn, Apr. 26, 1921 (TRB).
13. See TR.Auto. 526ff.
14. Speeches at Cuelbra and Colon, Panama, Nov. 16 and 17, 1906.
15. Qu. Har.260.
16. *St. Louis Censor,* Dec. 27, 1906.
17. TRB memo.
18. Mor.6.1605; de Voto, Bernard, ed., *Mark Twain in Eruption,* Harpers, 1940, 8.
19. Qu. Har.303.
20. *Literary Digest,* Dec. 22, 1906; Bea.306–8.
21. Bea, 451; Pri.298. For a full account of the Cuba incident, see Scott, James B., ed., *Robert Bacon: Life and Letters* (NY, 1923) 113 ff.; also Bur.105–8.
22. Bis.I.431.
23. *Eve. Star,* Dec. 31, 1906; Mor.5. 535; *W. Her.,* Jan. 2, 1907; Har.306. See Lane, Ann J., *The Brownsville Affair* (NY, 1971) for an exhaustive and highly critical account of TR's role in this evident miscarriage of justice. The presidential message on the incident, quoted by Joseph Foraker in his *Notes of a Busy Life* (Stewart & Kidd, 1917) is one of TR's most regrettable effusions. He chose not to mention Brownsville in his *Autobiography.*
24. Speech at opening of Pan-American Exhibition, Buffalo, May 20, 1901.
25. Jusserand, Jules, *What Me Befell* (London, 1933) 346; Pri.387.
26. *Harper's Weekly,* July 14, 1906. "Congress has evidenced almost phonographic fidelity to the wishes of the President"—*N.Y. World,* July 2, 1906.
27. Crook, W. H., *Memories of the White House* (Boston, 1911) 298; Scr., TRB; *N.Y. World,* Dec. 30, 1906; Gene Tunney in *Women's Roosevelt Association Bulletin,* 5.6; *Phil. Pub. Ledger,* Dec. 3, 1906.
28. Gwy.1.483.
29. *Rensselaer Independent Republican,* Jan. 1, 1907; London *Times,* Dec. 5, 1906. The message, TR's sixth and longest at 30,000 words, was written throughout in Simplified Spelling. It contained such characteristic Rooseveltisms as "It is out of the question for our people to rise by treading down any of their own number," and the declaration that "wilful sterility," i.e., birth control, "is the one sin for which the penalty is national death. . . . a sin for which there is no atonement." There were at least two discreet suggestions that the Constitution needed amending. "The dominant note," remarked the *Literary Digest* on Dec. 15, 1906, "is a demand for a greater centralization of power."
30. See Schoenberg, Philip E., "The American Reaction to the Kishinev Pogrom of 1903," *American Jewish Historical Quarterly,* Mar. 1974; also Straus, Oscar S., *Under Four Administrations* (Houghton Mifflin, 1922).
31. Unidentified clip, dated June 27, 1907, in TRB.
32. For TR's telegram of acceptance, see Mor.5.524. He separately announced, not without some pangs, that the prize money would be used to establish "a permanent Industrial Peace Committee" in Washington. "Would anybody but Theodore Roosevelt," asked the *Brooklyn Times,* "ever think of dedicating a Christmas windfall of $40,000 for such a purpose?" (*Lit. Dig.,* Dec. 22, 1906).

33. *Eve. Star,* Jan. 1, 1907; *W. Her., W. Post, N.Y. Her.,* Jan. 2; *Florida Times,* Jan. 1, 1907.
34. Hag.RBL.468.
35. *W. Post,* Jan. 2, 1907; Loo.208–13.
36. *W. Her.,* Jan. 2, 1907; Moore, J. Hampton, *Roosevelt and the Old Guard* (Phil., 1925) 176–7.
37. *Eve. Star,* Jan. 1, 1907; Fenwick, *passim; Rand McNally Pictorial Guide to Washington,* 1909.
38. Ib.; Willets, Gilson, *Inside History of the White House* (Christian Herald, 1908) 49, 195–202; *Harper's Weekly,* July 14, 1906.
39. Storer, Maria Longworth, *Theodore Roosevelt the Child* (privately printed, 1921) 27. See Sinclair, David F., "Monarchical Manners in the White House" in *Harper's Weekly,* June 13, 1908.
40. Ib.; Rob.230–3; But.53, 160, 246.
41. Lewis, William D., *The Life of Theodore Roosevelt* (John C. Winston, 1919) 181; Hale, *A Week,* 52; *Harper's Weekly,* Dec. 29, 1906; Edel, Leon, *Henry James: The Master* (London, 1972) 275–6.
42. TR to William Roscoe Thayer (TRB mss.).
43. Bea.7; TRB mss.
44. *Harper's Weekly,* Dec. 29, 1906; "How the President is Protected from Cranks," in *Ladies' Home Journal,* May 1907.
45. *Eve. Star,* Jan. 1, 1907; Willets, *Inside History,* 184; TR to Kermit Roosevelt, Oct. 2, 1903.
46. Pri.475, Wag.61; TRB memo.
47. Mor.3.392; see also "K" in *The American Magazine,* LXV.6. Apr. 1908.
48. Qu. Wag. 224. See also "Cleveland's Opinions of Men" in *McLure's,* XXXII, Apr. 1909: ". . . the most ambitious man and the most consummate politician I have ever seen."
49. Hale, *A Week,* 56; "K" (pseudonym), "The Powers of a Strenuous President," *The American Magazine,* April 1908; James to Edith Wharton, qu. Edel, *James,* 276.
50. *W. Post,* Jan. 2, 1907; un. clip in Fenwick.
51. Hale, *A Week,* 16, 44, 57. For an example of the sort of thing TR found funny, see the account by a White House secretary (*N.Y. Sun,* Jan. 27, 1927) of a letter sent to the President by the former heavyweight champion John L. Sullivan. Requesting leniency for an erring nephew in the U.S. military, Sullivan wrote apologetically, *The boy was always a little wild, he even took to music once.* At this, wrote the secretary, "Roosevelt let out a whoop of laughter and almost had a choking spell. He . . . had to leave his chair and go to the window for air. I never saw a man so convulsed with laughter."
52. Cha.201; Davenport in *Phil. Public Ledger,* n.d., TRB clip.
53. Jusserand, *What Me Befell,* 330.
54. Ib.; also in Memorial Lecture, Oct. 27, 1919, TRB mss. For other anecdotes of TR's Rock Creek Park expeditions, see, e.g., Miles, Nelson M., "Ambassadors at the Court of Theodore Roosevelt," *Mississippi Historical Review,* Sept. 1955; But.119–23; 229.
55. Amos, James, *Theodore Roosevelt: Hero to His Valet* (John Day, 1927) 39–41.
56. Egan, Maurice, *Recollections of a Happy Life* (NY, 1924) 219–220; Loo.152. Others who thought the President insane: Henry Adams (Ada.587) and Marse Henry Watterson (Pri.371).
57. *N.Y. Tribune,* Jan. 2, 1907; Gwy.1.437.
58. Amos, *Valet,* 11; Loo.115; Wag. 173.
59. *Trib.,* Jan. 2, 1907.
60. Bea.5, 13; NYS Legislature, *A Memorial to Theodore Roosevelt* (Feb. 21, 1919) 22; Wag.112. See also TR's Annual Message, Dec. 5, 1906: "Good manners should be an international no

less than an individual attribute . . . we must act uprightly to all men."
61. Mrs. Harper Sibley in TRB mss. (Aug. 10, 1955, interview); Wag.116, 154; But.160.
62. Wag.153, 4; Mor.3.392; Rii.9.
63. Fenwick, 1907; Willets, *Inside History,* 198; *Eve. Star,* Jan. 1, 1907; *N.Y. Her.,* Jan. 2.
64. Bis.1.338.
65. Hale, *A Week,* 116.
66. The only authoritative measurement of TR's height (5'9") is that given in his passport application, 1881 (National Archive). Six years earlier, at age seventeen, he measured himself at 5'8" (see Ch. 2).
67. Physical description from (select list) ib.; Whi.297, also William Allen White, *Masks in a Pageant* (Macmillan, 1928), 284–5; *N.Y. World,* May 17, 1895; But.18 and Amos, *Valet,* 101 (the former estimates TR's shoe size as "4 or 5"); Loo.15; Mike Donovan, Phys. Ed. Director, N.Y. Athletic Club, qu. Colman, *Gossip,* 287–8; pors.
68. Willey, Day Allen, "When You Meet the President," *The Independent,* June 30, 1904; Brooks, Sidney, in *The Reader,* Jan. 12, 1907; Hale, *A Week,* 15–16; *N.Y. World,* May 17, 1895; Wag.8.
69. Hale, *A Week,* 15.
70. Pors; White, *Masks,* 285.
71. Wis.68. The greatest photograph ever taken of TR, by Edward Steichen in 1908, captures all of these subtleties. See *A Life in Photography: Edward Steichen* (Doubleday, 1963) pl.56.
72. White, *Masks,* 284; Julian Street in TRB mss.; Smith, Ira, *Dear Mr. President: The Story of Fifty Years in the White House Mail Room* (NY, 1949) 50.
73. Wag.9–10; Smith, *Dear Mr. President,* 64; Hale, *A Week,* 26–41; see Chs. 4 and 6 for references to this impediment.
74. *N.Y. World,* May 17, 1895; HUN.5.
75. But.7; *Outlook,* Dec. 21, 1895; *Chicago Times-Herald,* July 22, 1895.
76. Loo.17; Street, Julian, *The Most Interesting American,* 10; Ada. 419.
77. John J. Milholland, int. FRE. (TRB).
78. Loo.21.
79. Wells, H.G., *Experiment in Autobiography* (Macmillan, 1934) 648–9.
80. Wells in *Harper's Weekly,* Oct. 6, 1906.
81. Yet see Wag.81 ff. for evidence that TR was on the contrary sensitive to, and not without taste in, the fine arts. Samuel Eliot Morison, in *The Oxford History of the American People* (NY, 1965), praises TR's beautification of Washington during his administrations, his commissioning of Augustus St.-Gaudens to design a new gold coinage, and his sponsorship of the classically elegant postage stamps of 1908 (816). See also the illustrated article "Roosevelt and our Coin Designs," in *Century,* Apr. 1920, for a full account of TR's efforts to give the United States "one coinage at least which shall be as good as that of the Ancient Greeks." The resultant $10 and $20 gold pieces are still regarded as the most beautiful ever produced by the American mint. A $20 coin recently sold for $3,600 at a numismatics auction (*N.Y.T.,* 7.24.77).
82. Wells, *Autobiography,* 649.
83. Howard of Penrith, Lord Esmé, *Theatre of Life* (London, 1936) 2.110.
84. Wag.35; Curtis, Natalie, "Mr. Roosevelt and Indian Music," *Outlook,* CXXI.399–400 and CXX-III.87 ff. (1919); C. Hart Merriam, qu. Sul.3.157; Cut. *passim;* Rob.232.
85. Wag.7. For a modern assessment of TR's mind, see Blum, John M., in *Michigan Quarterly Review,* 1959: "He was, to begin with, perhaps the most learned of all modern residents of the White House . . . He was an intellectual, and he was proud of it."
86. Wag.7.

87. But.87; Wag.8; Amos, *Valet,* 62–3; Booth Tarkington at TR Medal Award ceremony, 1942, TRB mss.
88. HUN.64; Wag.120; Washburn, Charles G., *Theodore Roosevelt: The Logic of his Career* (Houghton Mifflin, 1916) 205; Wag.119; Kipling, Rudyard, *Something of Myself* (London, 1936) 134; TR to Brander Matthews, Dec. 9, 1894.
89. Storer, *Child,* 8; Wis.94; Booth Tarkington (see note 91).
90. Robert E. Livingstone int. FRE. (TRB).
91. Hale, *A Week,* 115–6; see also Wis.47.
92. Straus qu. Wag.107.
93. *N.Y. Trib.,* Jan. 1, 1907; *W. Post,* Jan. 2; Mrs. Longworth, int. Jan. 2, 1956, TRB: "He loved cologne. He'd give us all a sniff of his handkerchief, which was practically saturated with cologne, when he met us in the hall." Apparently TR also liked verbena leaves, "which he would crumple and smell with exquisite pleasure" whenever he found them in fingerbowls. (Ib.)
94. Hale, *A Week,* 16; Donovan, qu. Edna M. Colman, *White House Gossip: From Johnson to Coolidge* (Doubleday, 1927), 287–8: "A plumbline could be dropped from the back of his head to his waist"; *Eve. Star,* Jan. 2, 1906; HUN.70 ("He like to have crushed my hand") and Clark, Chester M., in *St. Nicholas,* Jan. 1908 ("a cordial vise"); un. clip, Nov. 13, 1898, in TRB.
95. Wis.110; Hale, *A Week,* 48, 111; Thwing, Eugene, *The Life and Meaning of Theodore Roosevelt* (NY, 1919) 129, 130.
96. Robert E. Livingstone int. FRE.; Burroughs, John, in *The Life and Letters,* ed. Clara Barrus (Russell & Russell, 1968) 2.146: "He is a sort of electric bombshell, if there can be such a thing." Lewis, E. B., *Edith Wharton* (Harper & Row, 1975) 113, and Mrs. Wharton qu. Wag.109.
97. Amy Belle (Cheney) Clinton to Hermann Hagedorn, Jan. 27, 1949 (TRB).
98. Henry Watterson, un. clip, TRB mss.
99. Spooner qu. Wag. 109; White House appointments diary, TRP; Edel, *James,* 275.
100. Gar.86–7; Muir qu. Wag.109; Rii.131.
101. *Phil. Independent,* June 30, 1904.
102. But.5; Robert E. Livingstone int. FRE.
103. Nicholas Roosevelt, *Theodore Roosevelt: The Man as I Knew Him* (Dodd, Mead, 1967), 56. "It was never safe to contest with him on any question of fact or figures." (HCL in New York State *Memorial,* 1919).
104. Nicholas Roosevelt, *TR,* 56; Wag.74.
105. Ib.; Stanley Isaacs int. May 1, 1956 (TRB). For other examples of TR's memory, see Wis.114; Stoker, *Irving,* 237; Bishop, Joseph B., *Notes and Anecdotes of Many Years* (Scribner's, 1925) 136.
106. *Eve. Star,* Jan. 1, 1907.
107. Moore, *Old Guard,* 178; Fenwick, 1907 has a floor diagram showing crowd movement through the White House.
108. Child qu. Wag.108.
109. *W. Post,* Jan. 2, 1907; *W. Her.,* same date.
110. *W. Post,* Jan. 2, 1907; see Whi.404–5 for TR's post-reception ablutions.
111. Fenwick, 1908; *Guinness Book of World Records* (1978 ed.). Some contemporary sources, e.g. *N.Y. Sun,* Jan. 2, 1907, put the figure as high as 10,000; others, e.g., *Eve. Star,* put it as low as 5,063. Guinness's figure of 8,150 is borne out, in fact slightly exceeded, by *W. Her.,* Jan. 2 (8,513) and the respected *N.Y. Tribune* (8,500) and may be accepted as a fair estimate.
112. The personal details in the follow-

ing section are too numerous, and too ephemeral, for individual citation. Basic sources: Diary (1907) of Kermit Roosevelt in Library of Congress; Longworth, Derby, and Roosevelt interviews listed above. Other sources as cited below.

113. *Naval War* is still considered definitive. See Herr.196; also Gable, John A., *Theodore Roosevelt as Historian and Man of Letters,* intro. to TR's *Gouverneur Morris,* Bicentennial Ed. (Oyster Bay, 1975) *vii.*

114. *Eve. Star,* Jan. 1, 1907; TRP. The subjects covered by these letters range from Choctaw and Chickasaw legislation through *The Song of Roland* to white goats' heads.

115. Mrs. Longworth int. Nov. 1954; Amos, *Valet,* 11; Kermit Roosevelt Diary, Jan. 1, 1907; Day Allen Willey clip, n.d., TRB; Nicholas Roosevelt, *TR,* 55. For TR's half-blindness, which was kept a secret during his term as President, see Morr.355, 653.

116. TR to S. American expedition companion, 1913, memo in TRB mss.

117. Rii.311–2; memo of TR's vice-presidential campaign, TRB mss. (see Ch. 28); Wag.45–6; But.88; Whi.501.

118. Wis.89.

119. W. M. Sims in TR.Wks.VI.xi. In TR Medals file, TRB, Sims recalls TR telling him, after a reprieve from a theatre performance granted by Mrs. Roosevelt, "I have three books, and I am going to read them all tonight."

120. Mor.5, *passim;* TR, *Letters to Kermit* (Scribner's, 1946) *passim;* Rob. 239. Author's guess at 500 other volumes is based on TR's average of one and often two books a day. Those who consider it an inflated estimate should refer to Wag.56, and Mor.3.642–4 for TR's own stupendous reading list for 1902 and 1903, compiled for Nicholas Murray Butler on Nov. 4, 1903. ("Of course I have forgotten a great many, especially ephemeral novels . . . and I have also read much in the magazines.") See also *The Critic,* June 1903: "The President is known as one of the most extensive patrons of the Library of Congress . . . no previous President has ever sent to this institution lists of books so lengthy . . . The President is constantly consulting not only the latest authorities upon subjects which interest him, but also original editions and manuscripts." See also TR to George Haven Putnam, Oct. 6, 1902: "That man Lindsay who wrote about prehistoric Greece has not put out a second volume, has he? Has a second volume of Oman's *Art of War* appeared? If so, send me either or both; if not, then a good modern translation of Niebhur and Momsen or the best modern history of Mesopotamia. Is there a good history of Poland?" (Mor.3.343–5).

121. Mor.5.502; ib.3.557; TR to Mrs. Cadwallader Jones, Oct. 23, 1906 (Derby mss.).

122. Mor.5.549.

123. Ib., 537; *Century,* Jan. 1907. "The Ancient Irish Sagas," which TR wrote to take his mind off Brownsville, is reprinted in TR. Wks.XII.141 ff. See DeeGee Lester, "Theodore Roosevelt, the Ancient Irish Sagas and Celtic Studies in the United States," *Eire-Ireland* 24 (1989) 1.

124. Wag.69.

125. Amos, *Valet,* 151.

1: The Very Small Person

Important sources not in Bibliography: 1. Alsop collection of early Roosevelt family letters (now in TRC). 2. Union League Club of New York, *Theodore Roosevelt Senior: A Tribute* (privately printed, 1878, 1902).

1. The following account of TR's birth is taken from a very detailed letter from Mrs. Martha Bulloch (Mittie Roosevelt's mother) to Mrs. Hillborn West, Oct. 28, 1858 (Alsop).

2. Ib.

3. Ib.; also Morris K. Jesup, qu. Pri.4.
4. Mrs. Bulloch to Mrs. West, July 16, 1859; Put.23.
5. Put.23; TR.Auto.15.
6. Hag.Boy.21.
7. Put.33; Las.4.
8. Rob.4; Put.42–3; TR.Auto.12; News clip, n.d., in TRB, qu. TR "to a friend": see also Rii.445.
9. Louisa Lee Schuyler, qu. Pri.10.
10. Emlen Roosevelt, int. FRE. (TRB mss.); Rob.5; see also Rii.447.
11. *McClure's,* Nov. 1898; Rob.4.
12. TR.Auto.7–8.
13. Ib., 11.
14. Rob.18; Mrs. Joseph Alsop Sr. int., Nov. 22, 1954 (TRB). Lock of MBR's hair in Alsop.
15. Elliott Roosevelt, qu. a Mr. James of North Road, L.I., in Eleanor Roosevelt, ed., *Hunting Big Game in the Eighties* (Scribner's, 1933) 46. See also Par.26.
16. Mrs. Burton Harrison, *Recollections Grave and Gay* (NY, 1911), 278.
17. Mrs. Alsop int.; Rob.18.
18. See, e.g., Rob.18.
19. Roosevelt, Mrs. Theodore, Jr., *Day Before Yesterday* (Doubleday, 1959) 39.
20. The best Roosevelt genealogy in brief is Howard K. Beale, "TR's Ancestry: A Study in Heredity" in *N.Y. Genealogical and Biographical Record,* Oct. 1954. In the fourth generation the family changed the spelling of its name (literally "field of roses") and divided, one line leading down by way of New York City and the Republican Party to President Theodore Roosevelt, the other by way of the Hudson Valley and the Democratic Party to President Franklin D. Roosevelt. Mittie Roosevelt introduced FDR's parents to each other; FDR was TR's fifth cousin. The two branches, usually referred to as the Oyster Bay and Hyde Park Roosevelts, became politically and socially estranged in the early 1920s, despite the marriage of Eleanor of the former and Franklin of the latter. After half a century of family strife, which only Iris Murdoch could do full justice to, the two branches are now, in 1978, attempting reconciliation, and co-sponsoring the publication of a new Roosevelt genealogy.
21. Put.3–6; TR.Auto.1; Rii.435.
22. TR.Auto.1; words and music of *Trippel, trippel toontjes* in TRB.
23. Put.8–9. According to *N.Y. World,* Sep. 22, 1901 (?1907) clip in TRB, Mittie could trace her ancestry back to Edward III of England.
24. Put.8.
25. Emlen Roosevelt, int. FRE.
26. Put.7–9.
27. COW.
28. Bamie (pronounced "Bammie") was also called "Bysie" and "Bye." Corinne was sometimes "Pussie." Elliott later became "Nell." Theodore remained "Teedie" well into his teens, and then became "Thee" (his father's own youthful nickname). For his love-hate relationship with the name "Teddy," see text *passim.*
29. Mrs. Alsop int.; Put.51. Strictly speaking, Mrs. Bulloch and her daughters no longer owned slaves, since they had sold their Roswell, Ga., plantation before moving North in 1856 (Put.21). But, as TR (Auto.5) makes clear, at least two slaves at Roswell remained sentimentally attached to them long after the conclusion of the Civil War. "The only demand they made upon us was enough money annually to get a new 'crittur,' that is, a mule. With a certain lack of ingenuity the mule was reported each Christmas as having passed away, or at least as having become so infirm as to necessitate a successor—a solemn fiction which neither deceived nor was intended to deceive, but which furnished a gauge for the size of the Christmas gift."
30. TR Sr. to MBR, Mar. 1, 1862, qu. Rob.29.
31. William E. Dodge in *A Tribute to TR Sr.,* 17–18. See also TR Sr.'s "Journal" letters to MBR, 1861–2 (microfilm

in TRB). It shows him leaving New York on Nov. 7, 1861, and being introduced to President Lincoln by John Hay the following morning. By November 14 he is working "from six in the morning to one at night."
32. TR Sr. to MBR, Nov. 8, 1861, HAY.BR.
33. Mor.6.966.
34. Annie Bulloch to MBR, Sep. 9, 1861 (Alsop). White House tailors were to have the same problem four decades later. Note: this letter is misquoted in Rob.33.
35. MBR qu. Put.24. "I fancy I can see little Tedie [sic] climbing out of his crib at an incredibly early hour of the morning," TR Sr. replied (Dec. 17, "Journal").
36. Mrs. Bulloch to Mrs. West, July 16, 1859; Put.25–6, 199.
37. On Jan. 8, 1862, qu. Rob.23; ib., 36; Put.26; TR at Bull Run, qu. *N.Y. World,* Nov. 16, 1902: "When the Union and Confederate forces were fighting over these fields I was a little bit of a chap, and nobody seemed to think that I would live."
38. TR Sr.'s "Journal," Dec. 15, 1861, and Jan. 12, 1862. Bamie's spinal ailment was Pott's disease (letter from Anna Roosevelt Cowles to Dr. Russell Hibbs of N.Y. Orthopaedic Hospital, 1928, qu. news clip, no date, in Alsop). She was to remain crippled for life.
39. Put.25.
40. Ste.349–50.
41. TR Sr.'s "Journal," Apr. 1862; Rob.26.
42. Mrs. Longworth Int., Nov. 1954.
43. TR.Auto.12; Mrs. Longworth int.; COW; TR.Auto.8.
44. Ibid.
45. Ib., 7; Put.46.
46. TR.Auto.7.
47. Ib., 11; But.279.
48. Mrs. Alsop int.; COW. TR Sr. left home in early October ("Journal"). Mrs. Bulloch had not sold Roswell willingly; her intention was to buy it back but she could never do so, owing to her dead husband's crippling debts. During the war Roswell was looted, but not destroyed, by Sherman's marchers, and its maintenance during Reconstruction was impeccable. President Theodore Roosevelt made a sentimental pilgrimage there in 1905. Two decades later the young Atlanta journalist Margaret Mitchell visited the plantation on assignment, and is said to have received certain inspirations there. "Bulloch Hall" is now on the register of National Historic Places, and is considered to be one of the most beautiful antebellum houses in the South. In Sep. 1978 it was opened to the public. See Seale, William, "Bulloch Hall in Roswell, Georgia," in *Antiques Magazine at Bulloch Hall.*
49. TR.Auto.11; Rob.17.
50. Ib.; characterization of Aunt Annie based on her diaries and letters in TRC; Rob.17–18; Historic Roswell Inc. release, qu. Bulloch family stories (Dec. 1973); TR.Auto.12.
51. Mor.3.706–8.
52. TR.Auto. 5–6; Lor.37, 48; TR. Auto.6.
53. TR.Auto.5.
54. Bamie in *Women's Roosevelt Association Bulletin,* 1.3 (Apr. 1920); copy of 1858 edition of Livingstone's book in N.Y. Public Library.
55. TR.Auto.18.
56. Ib., 16.
57. Ib., 18, 29.
58. Rob.34; Put.31; TR.Auto.7; Corinne, qu. un. clip, Feb. 16, 1920 (TRB).
59. Rob.36.
60. TR.Auto.14–15.
61. Rob.2.
62. Qu. Hag.Boy.28–29.
63. Qu. Put.30; Par.28; Hag.Boy.45; Gustavus Town Kirby to Corinne, Feb. 26, 1921, Alsop; TR, "My Life as a Naturalist," in TR.Wks.V.385; *WRMA Bulletin* clip, n.d., in TRB.

64. TR.Auto.14–15; memo. n.d., in TRB mss.
65. Mor.1.3.
66. Reprinted in TR.DBY.
67. TR.DBY.4, 3; Hag.Boy.37; Put.57. James and Irvine Bulloch had been refused amnesty because of their personal role in financing, building, and operating the Confederate battleship *Alabama,* which caused an estimated $20 million damage to Union shipping. Although this sanction was later withdrawn, they continued to live in England by choice. Rob.37; Put.57 fn.
68. Put.52–4; Lash, *Eleanor,* 4. In a letter to TR Sr., June 6, 1873, she signs herself "one of your babies."
69. Rob.42; TR.DBY.
70. TR.DBY, 13; Hag.Boy.18; COW; Rob.44; Put.60.
71. Hag.Boy.30.
72. Put.60–1; TR.DBY 15 ff. for the rest of this chapter. Other citations follow.
73. Put.62.
74. Qu. Put.63–4.
75. Ib., 63.
76. One wonders if TR Sr. ever mentioned this incident to Mrs. Sattery at her Night School for Little Italians. Teedie innocently describes at least two other incidents which indicate that his father's charity was not unmixed with contempt. At Pompeii, he tossed pennies at beggars, until one of them "transgressed a rule made by Papa who whiped him till he cried then gave him a sou." And at Sorrento, TR Sr. joined Mr. Stevens in washing the faces of two grimy street urchins with champagne. TR.DBY.156; Rob.49.
77. Contemporary parents might be interested to know what gifts a small boy of good family received a hundred years ago., "I had a beautiful hunt [picture] with all kinds of things in it . . . 2 lamps and an inkstand on the ancient pompeien style and a silver sabre, slippers, a gold helmet and cannon besides the ivory chammois. I have beautiful writing paper, a candle stick on the Antiuke stile. A mosaic 1,500 years old and 3 books, 2 watch cases, 9 big photographs and an ornament and a pair of studs." TR.DBY. 141–2.
78. Rob.47. The Pope was Pius IX.
79. Put.68.
80. COW.

2: The Mind, But Not the Body

1. TR.DBY.235–6.
2. Rob.8–9.
3. TR Sr. to B, Sep. 6, 1870 (TRC).
4. Rockwell, A.D., *Rambling Recollections* (NY, 1920) 261.
5. Rob.50.
6. John Wood in *N.Y. World,* Jan. 24, 1904; COW; Put.72–3.
7. COW; *N.Y. World,* Sep. 4, 1895 (states that Mrs. Gerry, matriarch of the Goelet house, kept cattle there until 1880); also see the Strong, George Templeton, *Diary* (N.Y., 1952) Sep. 26, 1863: "Everybody that passes [Goelet's] courtyard stops to look . . . at his superb peacocks, golden pheasants, silver pheasants, California quail, and so on." Rob.50.
8. Contrast his diary entries of Aug. 1, 1870, with, e.g., Aug. 2, 1871 (TR.DBY.237, 241–2).
9. TR.DBY.247, 254.
10. J. van Vechten Olcott, childhood companion, qu. FRE.
11. Mor.6; Rob.55.
12. TR.Auto.19–20.
13. Ib., 19. See also TR.Wks.5.385.
14. For TR's auditory sensitivity as a teenager, see, e.g., his *Field Notes on Natural History, 1874–75* (TRC). The entire 60-page document is alive with "harsh twitters, wheezy notes, trills and quavers, shrill twitters, chirps, pipings, loud rattling notes, wierd, sad calls, hisses, tap-taps, gushing, ringing songs, rich bubling tones, lisping chirps,

guttural qua, qua's, hissing whistles" etc., etc.
15. TR.Auto.29–30.
16. Hag.Boy.39–40; Put.76; TR.Auto.30. For another boy's recollections of this summer, see Igl.44–8.
17. Put.79–80; Rob.55; TR.Auto.21; TR.DBY. 341, 302.
18. TR.Auto.20; Put.78.
19. TR.DBY.264. From now on, self-evident quotes from this source will not be cited individually.
20. COW; Rob.56.
21. Elliott to TR Sr., Sep. 19, 1873 (FDR).
22. TR.DBY. *passim;* Put.87.
23. Rob.56; COW; Put.88 ff.
24. Put.92.
25. Qu. Rob.56–7.
26. COW; Rob.57.
27. TR.DBY.304.
28. Mor.6.
29. Put.90.
30. Ib., 84, 93.
31. Rob.63; TR.DBY.311–2; Put.93.
32. TR.DBY.313.
33. Ib., 322.
34. Put.102–104; Rob.69.
35. *Encyclopaedia Britannica;* Put.102.
36. Put.103, 108 fn; Rob.70, 80; TR.Auto.22.
37. Mor.10–11.
38. TR.Auto.21; Mor.8.
39. See TR.Auto.23.
40. Rob.72, 84.
41. Mor.9.
42. TR.Auto.22.
43. Put.105.
44. Children of the widow of Mittie's half-brother Stuart Elliott (Put.102 fn.)
45. One anonymous item in this book is worth quoting: *There was an old fellow named Teedie,/Whose clothes at the best looked so seedy/ That his friends in dismay/ Called out "Oh! I say"/ At this dirty old fellow named Teedie.* (Orig. in TRC).
46. Qu. Put.107.
47. Qu. Put.108.
48. Mor.10–11.
49. Put.108.
50. Vierick, Louise, *Success Magazine,* October 1905.
51. Rob.88.
52. TR Sr. to Mittie, July 11, 1873 (TRC). Cutler was a brilliant young Harvard graduate who had left the wool business in order to prepare the children of wealthy families for college. Other Cutler pupils included J. P. Morgan, Harry Payne Whitney, and John D. Rockefeller (Igl.59–60).
53. TR Sr. to Mittie, Oct. 5, 1873. Cornelius van Schaak Roosevelt, who died in 1871, left his four sons, including TR Sr., $10 million in equal shares. (Las. 4.) TR Sr.'s glass business continued to prosper until he sold it in January 1876 (PRI. n.). See Rob.5 for TR Sr.'s founding of the Orthopaedic Hospital.
54. COW; photographs in TRB; fragmentary letter from TR Sr. to Mittie, c. August 1873; another dated Sep. 21.
55. COW; memorandum by Arthur H. Cutler in TRC.
56. TR. Sr. to MBR, Oct. 2, 1874 (TRC).
57. Put.117; Rob.89. *Harper's Weekly,* Sep. 1907, describes Tranquillity as "a fine old house under great trees close to the village." Now demolished.
58. COW; Par. *passim;* Put.119; Rob.95.
59. Qu. Las.3. For TR's bookishness, see Fanny Smith to C, July 1876: "If I were writing to Theodore I would have to say something of this kind, 'I have enjoyed Plutarch's last essay on the philosophy of Diogenes excessively.'" (qu.Rob.96.) Fanny's *Perchance Some Day* (see Par. in Bibl.) is the most charming and the least cloying of Roosevelt family memoirs. Copy in TRC.
60. Par.31 ff.
61. Cutler memorandum. Walt McDougall, in *This Is the Life* (Knopf, 1926,

129–30), remembers TR as the village boys saw him, "undersized, nervous, studious . . . and somewhat supercilious besides." Inevitably known as "Four Eyes," he was game to fight but was forbidden to, on account of his spectacles.

62. Mor.13; Cutler memo.
63. TR to M, Aug. 6, 1896, TRC.
64. TR.DBY.356.
65. Donald Wilhelm, qu. Put.125.
66. Par.28, 140, 29.
67. Ibid.
68. TR to B, Sep. 20, 1886; Cutler memo. TR passed his second round of Harvard entrance exams in the spring of 1876.
69. Rob.90.
70. The phrase is Putnam's, reflecting a conversation he had with Mrs. Joseph Alsop Sr. (Put.170 fn.)

3: The Man with the Morning in His Face

Important sources not in Bibliography:
1. Wilhelm, Donald, *TR as an Undergraduate* (Boston, 1910). Copy in New York Public Library has the added value of irascible marginalia by another classmate, Richard W. Welling.

1. *Boston Daily Advertiser,* Oct. 27, 1876; Pri.31.
2. Wilhelm, *Undergraduate,* 19. Hag. Boy.51–2 confirms this anecdote. See also Woo.1–2.
3. Hag.Boy.15; Prof. Albert Bushnell Hart, TR's classmate, at final Harvard History Lecture (un. clip, 1926, TRB).
4. King, Moses, *Harvard and its Surroundings* (Cambridge, 1880) *passim;* Put.129.
5. Put.131; Grant, Robert, "Harvard College in the Seventies," *Scribner's* May 1897; Thayer, William Roscoe, *TR: An Intimate Biography* (Houghton Mifflin, 1919) 16; Wis.19; Put.130. The majority of the students were Republicans (note in TRB).
6. Qu. Pri.32.
7. Pri.33–4. Put.135–6.
8. Put.136.
9. Mor.42; TR to B, Oct. 15, 1876.
10. Pri.32; qu. Put.131.
11. Wis.12: "he stood out." Montage from Wilhelm, *Undergraduate,* 31, 35, 41, 54, 63; Pri.33; Welling, Richard, "My Classmate TR," *American Legion Monthly,* Jan. 1929; Richard Saltonstall, qu. Put.138; Gilman, Bradley, *Roosevelt the Happy Warrior* (Little, Brown, 1921) 1–2.
12. Welling, "Classmate," 9.
13. Anonymous reminiscence of TR Sr. in Philadelphia *Press,* April 7, 1903. The conversation took place at Moon's Lake, N.Y., in Sept. 1876.
14. Reminiscences of classmates William Hooper and Henry Jackson in HKB.
15. Thomas Perry, qu. Put.140; Hag.Boy.54; Rii.27; Tha.21; PRI.n.
16. Wilhelm, *Undergraduate,* 9.
17. Mor.16; Laughlin, J. Laurence, "Roosevelt at Harvard," *Review of Reviews,* LXX (1924) 393 illus.; diagram by TR in letter to B, Oct. 6, 1876; TR to B, Sep. 30.
18. TR to MBR, Oct. 29, 1876.
19. Mor.23–4.
20. Cut.10; Hag.Boy.54.
21. Mor.26; ib., 23. TR also caused another disturbance this winter, according to Richard Welling: "Part of his initiation into a Harvard secret society was to sit in the gallery of a Boston theatre and applaud loudly during all the quiet moments throughout a performance of *Medea,* a task which he performed with such characteristic zeal that he was speedily invited to decamp." Memo in PRI.n. See also Gilman, *Warrior,* 74.
22. Not to mention a certain Annie Murray. See TR to B, Jan. 22, 1877.
23. Memo by Martha Waldron Cowdin, future wife of Bob Bacon, in TRC. Elsewhere in PRI.n. Mrs. Bacon

remembers TR as "a campus freak, with stuffed snakes and lizards in his room, with a peculiar, violent vehemence of speech and manner, and an overwhelming interest in every thing."

24. TR.Pri.Di. Feb. 8, 1880; ib., Oct. 24, 1878.

25. See Wag.86–88.

26. Put.141; TR.Pri.Di. Apr. 18, 1878.

27. Mor.39; TR to B, Feb. 5, 1877; TR to MBR, Oct. 6, 1876; TR to B, Nov. 12, 1876.

28. Wilhelm, *Undergraduate,* 31; Thayer, *TR,* Mor.25.

29. Gov. Curtis Guild Jr., qu. Wilhelm, *Undergraduate,* 31; John Woodbury, qu. ib., 41.

30. Mor.27.

31. Laughlin, "Harvard," 395–8.

32. Put.139; Thomas Perry, qu. ib.

33. German, 92; Physics, 78; Classical Literature, 77; Chemistry, 75; Advanced Mathematics, 75. His other grades were Latin, 73, and Greek, 58 (Mor.25).

34. Put.169; Mor.28.

35. Ib., 26.

36. Extract from TR's notebook qu. Cut.16–17 (see also Ch. 2, Note 14); TR.Auto.24.

37. "By far the best of the recent lists," wrote the great biologist C. Hart Merriam in *Nuttall Ornithological Society Bulletin.* "It bears prima facie evidence of . . . exact and thoroughly reliable information." See Paul Russell Cutright, "Twin Literary Rarities of TR," *Theodore Roosevelt Association Journal* 12 (1985) 2.

38. Cut.3, 7, 8.

39. TR.Auto.25–6.

40. TR.Pri.Di. May 20, 1878; Mor. 25–6; qu. Put.139.

41. Rob.103.

42. Put.135.

43. Mor.29.

44. Arthur was of course the future President of the United States. This account of the Collectorship crisis is based on Put.146–7 fn., supplemented by Mor.29, and family letters and diaries in TRC.

45. Mor.31.

46. Anna Bulloch Gracie, Diary 1877, TRC.

47. TR.Pri.Di. Jan. 2, Dec. 11, 1878.

48. Ib., Jan. 2, 1878; Put.148.

49. Telegram of TR to A. S. Roosevelt, Feb. 9, 1878 (TRB); *N.Y. World,* Feb. 11, 1878; C to EKR, qu. Put.148; Elliott Roosevelt memorandum in TRC.

50. Igl.39; Anna Bulloch Gracie, Diary Feb. 9, 1878. For tributes to TR Sr., see *N.Y. Telegraph,* Feb. 11; *Nation,* Feb. 14; *Tribune,* Feb. 18; *Harper's Weekly,* Mar. 2, 1878.

51. TR.Pri.Di. Feb. 12, 1878; qu. Put.149; TR.Pri.Di. Mar. 6, Apr. 25, Apr. 30, May 1.

52. Ib., June 9, 1878.

53. Ib., June 19, 1878.

54. Rob.104; TR.Pri.Di. July 11, 14, 1878.

55. Qu. Put.151.

56. Rob.106.

57. TR.Pri.Di. Feb. 23, 1878 (No student, according to Grant, "Seventies," spent more than $2,000 a year in the 70s; most got by on $1,000 or $1,300); TR.Pri.Di. Feb. 28, May 15, 1878; TR to MBR, Mar. 24.

58. TR.Pri.Di. May 23, June 17, 1878.

59. Rob.106.

60. Qu. Put.145; TR.Pri.Di. June 28, 1878.

61. Rob.102; TR.Pri.Di. Aug. 10, 1878.

62. Ib., Aug. 9, 22, 1878.

63. Ib., Aug. 24, 1878. TR justified his cruelty, not very convincingly, by saying that the dog's owner had been warned.

64. Ib., Aug. 26, 1878.

65. Ib., Sep. 1, 1878.

66. Hag.Boy.59; "Bill Sewall Remembers TR" (interview with Alfred Gordon Munro, TRB—un. clip, c.

1901). Sewall told this story rather more confusingly in Sew.2–3 (1919). Putnam accepts the later version, while admitting it to be inconsistent. The earlier tallies with all available supporting evidence, and may be accepted as more reliable.
67. Sew.63.
68. Hag.Boy.60.
69. Qu. Hag.Boy.62.
70. See Morr.140.
71. Put.155; TR.Pri.Di. Sep. 27, June 17, 18, 1878.
72. Mor.25; Put.175–6 fn.
73. Put.175; TR.Pri.Di. Oct. 4, 1878; Mor.25.
74. TR.Pri.Di. Oct. 5, 1878; Mor.35.
75. Put.167.
76. Ib., 166–7.
77. PRI. n.
78. TR.Pri.Di. Oct. 19, 20, 1878.
79. Ib., Nov. 2, 1878; TR.Har.Scr. The menu of ten courses that evening included oysters, turbot, "Mongrel Goose / Young Pig," croustade of venison, canvasback duck / larded quails, Charlotte Russe, Roquefort and olives, sherbet. (Ib.)
80. TR.Pri.Di. Nov. 2, 1878 sic. Some of his classmates corroborate this. "Very little upset him . . . he had the sense to realize his limitations." (James Giddes in PRI. n.) Drinking at Harvard generally was so heavy in the late seventies that two or three students out of every class were expected to die of alcoholism a year or so after graduation. (Ib.)
81. TR.Pri.Di. *passim;* ib. Oct. 2, 1878. A classmate remembered him angrily reprimanding the singer of a risqué song at the Hasty Pudding Club. Edward Wagenknecht remarks: "It is impossible that there can ever have been a more clean-living man than Theodore Roosevelt." (Hagedorn memo, TRB; Wag.87.)
82. Ib., Nov. 28, 1878.
83. Ib., Jan. 25, 1880.

4: The Swell in the Dog-Cart

1. TR to John Roosevelt, Feb. 25, 1880 (privately owned).
2. COW; Par; Mrs. Bacon's statements in TRC; newspaper tributes to Alice, Feb. 1884; letters to B (1884) in TRC.
3. TR.Pri.Di. Nov. 7, 1880.
4. Pri.41–3; Mrs. Bacon's statements; Put.167–8; photographs in TRC; a sample of Alice's hair preserved by TR in Sagamore Hill vaults; TR to John Roosevelt, Feb. 25, 1880.
5. Mor.36.
6. TR to Harry Minot, July 5, 1880, qu. Put.193–4.
7. Rose Lee to Carleton Putnam, qu. Put.166; Pri.42–3; Rob.63.
8. TR to John Roosevelt, Feb. 25, 1880.
9. Mor.36.
10. See Put.178.
11. TR to John Roosevelt, Feb. 25, 1880; Put.173.
12. TR.Pri.Di. Dec. 11, 1879.
13. Ib., Dec. 21, 1878.
14. Mor.34.
15. Wis.12.
16. Cut. 23–25; TR.Pri.Di. Jan. 18, 1879.
17. Laughlin, J. Laurence, "Roosevelt at Harvard," *Review of Reviews,* LXX (1924) 397. Robert Bacon was U.S. Secretary of State, Jan. 27–Mar. 5, 1909.
18. Thayer, William Roscoe, *TR: An Intimate Biography* (Houghton Mifflin, 1919) 20. TR's classmate Frederick Almy recalls TR leading a deputation of students to Harvard President Charles W. Eliot and stammering for some time in the great man's presence. Eventually he forced it out: "Mr. Eliot, I am President Roosevelt." PRI.n. Washburn, Charles G., *TR: The Logic of His Career* (Houghton Mifflin, 1916) says that "at the Pudding we often incited a discussion for the

purpose of rousing 'Teddy.' In his excitement he would sometimes lose altogether the power of articulation, much to our delight. He then had almost a defect in his speech which made his utterance deliberate and even halting." (p.5) References to this impediment are frequent in TR's late teens and early twenties, non-existent thereafter.

19. Put.177.

20. Ib.

21. Put.178. These two remarks, and the fact that TR abandoned his habit of taking field-notes in 1879, suggest that Alice Lee was instrumental in changing TR's vocation to something other than natural history. While admittedly slender, the speculation is borne out by anecdotes indicating that Alice's own interest in the world of animals was minimal. On one occasion she innocently asked Theodore "who had shaved the lions" at a zoo, "being otherwise unable to account for their manes." (Mor.48) John Gable suggests that economic scruples may have caused TR to forego an academic career—but he was after all worth $8,000 p.a. and Alice came of an equally wealthy family.

22. TR.Pri.Di. Jan. 11, 31, 1879; Mor.38.

23. Pors. in TRC; Mor.38. TR's record of expenditures for the years 1877–79 show that dress was always the major item of his budget, exceeding what he spent on board, lodging, education, travel, and sport. Whereas the average Harvard student's total expenditures in the late 1870s was $650 to $850 (even the wealthiest rarely exceeded $1,500) Theodore spent $1,742 in his first year, $2,049 in his second, and $4,113 in his third. See King, Moses, *Harvard and its Surroundings* (Cambridge, 1878); Grant, Robert, "Harvard College in the Seventies," *Scribner's,* May 1897, and TR.Pri.Di. Dec. 31, 1879.

24. The following account of TR's vacation in Maine is drawn from Sew.5–6, Put.159–61.

25. Mor.37.

26. Sew.5.

27. Hag.Boy.59; Mor.37.

28. Sew.6.

29. Sewall to TR, reminding him of their conversation, June 1902, TRP.

30. TR to Mittie, qu. Put.161.

31. TR.Pri.Di. Mar. 15, 1879.

32. TR to B, Mar. 23, 1879; Wis.33.

33. Har.13; Put.144.

34. Wis.4–5.

35. Cut.3, 7, 8.

36. H. E. Armstrong in *The Independent,* Sept. [?], 1902, Presidential Scrapbook, TRP; Richard Welling, "TR at Harvard," *Outlook* clip, n.d., in TRB; Tha.23; Hag.Boy.57–8.

37. TR.Pri.Di. Apr. 2, 1879.

38. Mor.39.

39. TR.Pri.Di. May 8, 1879.

40. Put.174; TR.Pri.Di. May 13, 1879.

41. Put.175.

42. Mor.40.

43. See TR.Pri.Di., Jan. 25, 1880.

44. Ib., June 19, 1879. The following account of Class Day, 1879, owes much to Putnam's treatment in Put.180–2, as well as TR.Pri.Di. June 20.

45. Memo by E in TRC.

46. Put.183.

47. TR.Pri.Di. July 5, 9, 1879.

48. Ib., July 30, 1879.

49. Las. 3–9.

50. Fanny Parsons, note in TRB.

51. TR.Pri.Di. Aug. 16, 1879.

52. Ib., Aug. 18, 1879. TR, dictating his *Autobiography* in 1913, mused for several pages on the reasons behind this decision. See TR. Auto. 25–7.

53. TR to B, Aug. 22, 1879 (TRB); TR.Pri.Di., same date. For an unforgettable photograph of Alice and TR with tennis rackets, evocative of both the bewitcher and the bewitched, see Michael Teague, *Mrs. L: Conversations with Alice Roosevelt Longworth* (New

York, 1981). See also Michael Teague, "Theodore Roosevelt and Alice Lee: A New Perspective," *Harvard Library Bulletin* 33 (1985) 3.

54. Put.183; Mor.40.

55. Put.161.

56. The following account is based on ib., 161–3.

57. TR to B. n.d. (Sep. 4?) TRB.

58. TR.Pri.Di.

59. TR to B, Sep. 14, 1879 (TRB).

60. Put.163.

61. See the impressive analysis of TR's physical feats in Maine in Put.163. The author shows that in a total of 61 days with Sewall, TR marched, paddled, and rode over 1,000 miles through near-virgin wilderness (540 miles on foot), averaging more than 50 miles a day.

62. Mor.41; TR.Pri.Di. May 16, 1879; Put.174, 184 fn.; McCausland, Hugh, *The English Carriage* (London, 1948) *passim;* TR to B (telegram), n.d. but probably early Sep. 1879. (TRB)

63. Mor.41.

64. Pri.43.

65. Welling, Richard, "My Classmate TR," *American Legion Monthly,* Jan. 1929.

66. TR.Pri.Di. Sep. 26, 1879; Put. 184–6; TR.Pri.Di. Oct. 10, 23, 1879.

67. Put.184–5.

68. Mor.41–2.

69. Ib.

70. TR.Pri.Di. Oct. 27, 1879.

71. TR to B, n.d. (Nov. 11, 1879?) TRB.

72. TR to John Roosevelt, Feb. 25, 1880.

73. Mor.41.

74. Qu. Put.178 fn. TR's choice of this subject, at this time of great personal stress, is symbolic. It had been the machine in politics that destroyed his father, whose troubles with it had begun almost exactly two years before; it was the machine in politics that, almost exactly two years later, would launch his own legislative career. (Cf. 238–9).

75. TR.Pri.Di. Nov. 22, 1879.

76. TR to B, n.d. (Nov. 11, 1879?) TRB; TR.Pri.Di. Nov. 22, 1879; Put.187; Thomas Lee, Alice's cousin, to Henry F. Pringle, PRI.n.; TR.Pri.Di. Dec. 2, 1879.

77. Pri.42; see his source, Mrs. Robert Bacon, in PRI.n.

78. Wis.13; Pri.36. The book, which will be discussed later in the text, was prompted by certain inaccuracies in William James's (British) history of the war, which TR found in the Porcellian Library.

79. In 1910, TR recalled reciting "that glorious chorus from *Atalanta in Calydon*" and the despairing lines from *Dolores* beginning "Time turns the old days to derision." "What young man has not, when suffering the pangs of despised love, given vent to his feelings in those words?" George Buchanan, *My Mission to Russia* (Boston, 1923), vol. 1, 88–89.

80. Put.171; Pri.43–4; Corinne Roosevelt Robinson in PRI.n.

81. Put.187; TR.Pri.Di. Dec. 24, 1879; ib., Nov. 16.

82. Put.187.

83. TR.Pri.Di. Jan. 1, 1880.

84. Ib., Jan. 25, 1880. "I have not mentioned a word of it to my diary," TR adds with satisfaction, apropos of his recent torment. "No outsider has suspected it."

85. Ib.; also Feb. 23, 1880.

86. Ib., Jan. 31, 1880; Pri.43; TR.Pri.Di. Feb. 2, 1880.

87. Alice Lee to MBR, Feb. 3, 1880 (typed copy in TRB).

88. TR to B, Mar. 1, 1880 (TRB). The choice of date shows TR's love for parallels and anniversaries in the family. On Oct. 27 he would turn twenty-two, the same age his father had been when *he* was married; Alice would be nineteen, the same as Mittie had been.

89. Mor.43.

90. TR.Pri.Di. Mar. 11, 1880.
91. Qu. Put.189; qu. ib., 190; ib., 189.
92. TR to John Roosevelt, Feb. 25, 1880.
93. Mor.44. They had been reassured by Mittie's offer to accommodate the young couple at 6 West Fifty-seventh Street, at least through the winter of 1880–81.
94. Thomas Lee to Henry F. Pringle, PRI.n. See also Pri.44.
95. Mor.44.
96. TR.Pri.Di. Apr. 1, 1880; Cut.27; Pri.43; TR.Pri.Di. Mar. 25, 1880; Put.185; ib., fn.; Mor.43.
97. Pri.43–4.
98. Mor.42; Grant, "*Seventies.*"
99. Qu. Wis.14–15.
100. Wis.15.
101. Ib.
102. Ib.
103. Mor.45 ff., with TR.Pri.Di. *passim,* form the basis of this paragraph.
104. See also Roosevelt, Nicholas, *TR: The Man as I Knew Him* (Dodd, Mead, 1967) 99 on TR's highly individual tennis style. TR.Pri.Di. July 29, 1880.
105. Ib., Mar. 25, 1880.
106. Thayer, *TR,* 20–1.
107. Welling, "Harvard," offers the most detailed (and negative) analysis of TR's thesis.
108. Qu. ib.
109. Laughlin, "Harvard," 394.
110. See Wag.87–90. TR's thesis qu. Welling, "Harvard."
111. Put.184; *Harvard Register,* July 1880, 143–4; TR.Pri.Di. June 30, 1880. TR's marks in his senior year were lower than those of previous years, but high enough to win him his Phi Beta Kappa key. There had been an attrition of 20 students in his class. In later life TR made light of his academic career, saying only that he was "a reasonably good student"; but as one classmate pointed out, his overall average matched those of Ralph Waldo Emerson and Oliver Wendell Holmes. TR.Auto.25; Wilhelm, Donald, *TR as an Undergraduate* (Luce, 1910) 24. On this Commencement Day, Henry Cabot Lodge marched in the procession as a Marshal, and John D. Long gave the main address.
112. TR.Pri.Di. June 29, 1880.
113. Put.198, Hag.Boy.63; Woo.118. TR kept the secret for thirty-five years. Not until January 1915 did he admit to an old classmate that "when he left college the doctors warned him of weakness of the heart."
114. Hag.Boy.63; TR.Pri.Di. Feb. 10, 1880.
115. Ib., July 1, 1880.
116. Ib., July 4, 1880.
117. Hag.RF.6; TR, *Notes on Some of the Birds of Oyster Bay;* Natural History Notes, *passim;* Mor.73.
118. Qu. Put.200.
119. Mor.45.
120. She managed to take enough time off to win the Mount Desert Ladies' Tennis Tournament.
121. Qu. Put.199.
122. Put.201 ff.; Rob.113; qu. Put.205.
123. TR to MBR, Aug. 25, 1880; Mor.46.
124. TR to B, Sep. 2, 1880 (TRB).
125. TR.Pri.Di. Sep. 1880, *passim;* Put.205–7. E to B, Sep. 12, 1880: "I think he misses Alice poor dear old beloved brother. But I try to keep him at something else all the time."
126. Mor.46.
127. Put.208.
128. Qu. Put.209.
129. TR.Pri.Di. Oct. 6, 1880. This paragraph based on: TR to MBR, Oct. 21, 1880 (TRB); qu. Put.209; ib., 210.
130. TR.Pri.Di. Oct. 13, 1880.

5: The Political Hack

Important sources not in Bibliography:
1. Letters to and from the Roosevelt family and Elliott Roosevelt, traveling

in Europe and the Orient, 1880–1881, in FDR.
1. Par.43; Put.210 and fn.
2. TR.Pri.Di. Oct. 27, 1880. TR's college Bible is marked at the following passage in Prov. V: "Let thy fountain be blessed; and rejoice with the wife of thy youth."
3. Ib.; TR.Pri.Di. Oct. 28, 1880; Put.209.
4. TR to B, Nov. 10, 1880; Mor.47; TR.Pri.Di. Nov. 4, 1880.
5. Ib.
6. Ib., Nov. 1–9, 1880.
7. Ib., Nov. 13–4, 1880. Elliott Roosevelt was not there: he had left on Nov. 7 for an extended tour of Europe and the Orient. See Las. and Roosevelt, Eleanor, ed., *Hunting Big Game in the Eighties* (Scribners, 1933) for accounts of his travels.
8. TR.Pri.Di. Mar. 18, 1881; qu. Rii.36–7.
9. Put.217.
10. TR.Pri.Di. Nov. 17, 1880; MBR to E, Nov. 27, 1880 (FDR).
11. Film footage preserved in the Library of Congress documents TR's rapid walking style.
12. TR.Pri.Di. Nov. 17, 1880; Bigelow, Poultney, *Seventy Summers* (London, 1925) 273; Bar Association of New York, *In Memoriam Theodore William Dwight* (1892).
13. Put.217; Bigelow, *Summers,* 273; Bar Assoc., *Dwight, passim;* "Life in the old Law School," *Columbia Spectator,* Nov. 1, 1878.
14. Bigelow, *Summers,* 273; Put.218; Bar Assoc., *Dwight, passim.*
15. Put.218–9; TR.Auto.55; Bigelow, *Summers,* 273.
16. Bigelow, *Summers,* 273–4.
17. Put.219; Joseph A. Lawson in New York State, *A Memorial to TR* (1919), 53. TR's law notebooks are preserved in the Columbia Law Library (7 vols.).
18. TR.Pri.Di. Nov. 17, 1880 and *passim;* Put.219; TR.Pri.Di. Dec. 4, 1880.
19. Put.221; TR.Pri.Di. Mar. 24, 1881.
20. Ib., May 2, 1881; Put.220. TR's other "literary project" was a beautifully written account of an ornithological sailing expedition during which he and Elliott came near to death in a storm. Entitled *Sou' Sou' Southerly,* it was completed in March 1881 but remained unpublished in TR's lifetime. It finally saw light in *Gray's Sporting Journal* 13 (1988) 3.
21. TR.Auto.24.
22. See TR.Wks.VI for the complete text of *Naval War.* See also "Roosevelt as Historian" in *Evening Post* (N.Y.) Jan. 25, 1919.
23. *Naval War,* ch. 1; MBR to E, Nov. 27, 1880.
24. TR.Pri.Di. *passim* and Jan. 3, 1881; Brown, H. C., ed., *New York in the Elegant Eighties: Valentine's Manual of Old New York* (NY, 1927) *passim;* TR.Pri.Di. Dec. 22, 1880; MBR to E, Dec. 4, 1880 (FDR); Brown, *Valentine's,* 6.
25. Put.228; Churchill, Allen, *The Splendor Seekers* (Grosset & Dunlap, 1974) 63; *New York Times,* Dec. 9, 1880; TR to E, Dec. 6, 1880 (FDR).
26. O'Connor, Richard, *The Golden Summers* (Putnam, 1974) 50–1; MBR to E, Dec. 10, 1880, and Jan. 2, 12, 1881. TR was greatly amused when Mrs. Astor, hearing of the death of the Tsar later in the season, remarked, "Mr. Roosevelt, they are attacking *us* all over the world." (Mor.130) TR.Pri.Di. Jan. 6, 1881; O'Connor, *Summers,* 55–6.
27. TR.Pri.Di. Dec. 1880–Feb. 1881; ib., Dec. 11, 1880.
28. Unidentified contributor to *Harper's Weekly,* Oct. 19, 1901.
29. Brown, *Valentine's, passim.*
30. Churchill, *Seekers,* 68; TR.Pri.Di. Jan. 6, 1881.
31. Wis.24.
32. Leary int., FRE.; TR.Auto.57; Abbot, Lawrence F., *Impressions of TR* (Doubleday, 1919) 36–37.

33. Ib., Pri.59. Morton Hall stood on the south side of 59th St. between Fifth and Madison avenues. The 21st District comprised the area between Seventh and Lexington from 40th to 59th Street south, and between 8th and Lexington from 59th Street north to 86th.
34. TR.Auto.56–7; Pri.46, 59; Leary Int., FRE.; Hag.Boy.66.
35. See TR.Auto.57 for an explanation of the clublike, elective nature of the Republican Association. "As a friend of mine picturesquely phrased it, I 'had to break into the organization with a jimmy.' "
36. Emlen Roosevelt int., FRE. But the Roosevelts, as old Knickerbockers, had been influential in politics until Civil War times. Disdain for grubby politics was a comparatively recent phenomenon, owing much to the Boss Tweed and Grant Administration scandals of the 1870s.
37. Ib.; TR.Auto.57; Thayer, *TR*, 27.
38. TR.Auto.57.
39. Put.248.
40. Rob.106.
41. Cowles Microfilm, TRB.
42. TR.Auto.57.
43. Prof. Albert Bushnell Hart at Farewell History Lecture, Harvard (1926) un. clip, TRB.
44. Savell, Isabelle K., *Daughter of Vermont: A Biography of Emily Eaton Hepburn* (NY, 1952) 106.
45. Put.241; TR.Auto.57; Edward C. Riggs in PRI.n.
46. Put.241; Riggs in PRI. n.
47. TR.Auto.58; TR to Eleanora Kissel Inicutt, June 28, 1901 (TRB); TR.Pri.Di. *passim;* TR.Auto.58.
48. TR.Pri.Di. Mar. 14, 1881.
49. Ib., Apr. 8; Put.241; Hag.Boy.67.
50. TR.Auto.61.
51. Ib.; TR.Pri.Di. May 11, 1881 (baggage list in year-end expenses section); ib., May 12.
52. Ib., May 18, 1881.
53. Mor.47; TR.Pri.Di. May 21, 22, 1881.
54. TR.Pri.Di. *passim;* Put.229; TR to B, May 24, 1881 (TRB).
55. TR.Pri.Di. May 25, 1881; Mor.48–9; TR.Pri.Di. June 1; Mor.48.
56. Ib.; TR.Pri.Di. June 11–27, 1881; Mor.49; TR to B, July 3, 1881 (TRB).
57. TR.Pri.Di. July 5, 6, 1881.
58. Put.244–5; Sto.112 ff.
59. Put.245; Sto.112 ff. The assassin, Charles Guiteau, had shrieked after firing, "I am a Stalwart of the Stalwarts!" For a post-mortem and meticulously detailed day-by-day account of Garfield's last days, see Doyle, Burton T., *Lives of James A. Garfield and Chester A. Arthur* (Washington, 1881).
60. TR.Pri.Di. July 8, 1881.
61. Put.232; TR.Pri.Di. July 15–29, 1881.
62. Mor.49; Put.232. Alice begged one of TR's Harvard classmates, who happened to be staying in Zermatt, to dissuade him from climbing the Matterhorn. But TR was adamant. "I shall climb the mountain." Gilman, Bradley, *Roosevelt the Happy Warrior* (Little, Brown, 1921) 62.
63. Mor.49–50.
64. Mor.50; Put.221.
65. TR's sartorial acquisitions in London included some Savile Row dress suits and (to Mittie's horror) "two or three satin waist coats—purple, pale yellow, and blue and one rich black silk one." She eventually grew to like the last, but "the others *if others wore them* would be very handsome." (MBR to E, Dec. 4, 1881, FDR.)
66. Mor.52; Pri.47; Igl.121–2.
67. Qu. Put.236.
68. For an exhaustive analysis of TR's law studies at Columbia, see Robert B. Charles, "Legal Education in the Late Nineteenth Century, Through the Eyes of Theodore Roosevelt," *The American Journal of Legal History* 37 (July 1993) 3. This article, based on Charles's

discovery of more than 1,100 pages of TR's law notes, is a major corrective to the long-held view of historians that TR lacked legal sophistication.
69. TR.Auto.57; TR.Pri.Di. Oct. 6, 1881.
70. Abbot, *Impressions,* 37–9; Put.241.
71. Hag.Boy.67 ff.
72. Ib.; Put.241; TR.Auto.58–64; Thayer, *TR,* 29.
73. TR.Auto.61; Charles Dumas to Henry F. Pringle, Apr. 2, 1929, PRI.n.; Abbot, *Impressions,* 37–9.
74. Ib., 39; Hag.Boy.70; Abbot, *Impressions,* 40.
75. Abbot's record of this conversation is actually a stenographic transcript of Joe Murray's own account, told in the smoking-car of a train to Saratoga in 1910. It closely tallies with another version by Murray in TRB.
76. Abbot, *Impressions,* 39–41. Mitchell, who later became a U.S. District Attorney, liked to claim in old age that he, not Murray, "was the first person who recognized the practical politician in TR." See *N.Y. Sun,* May 31, 1904. Barney Biglin, another of Hess's lieutenants, also claimed kingmaking honors. TR himself, in his memoirs, settled these and other conflicting claims with a gracious tribute to Joe Murray. "It was not my fight [in 1881], it was Joe's; and it was to him that I owe my entry into politics." As President, TR issued his old patron a card: "Joseph Murray to see me at all times and in all places he may wish to see me." (TR.Auto.61; PRI.n.)
77. TR.Pri.Di. Oct. 28, 1881; Put.244.
78. TR.Pri.Di. Oct. 28, 1881. "We somehow knew the boy was right," a Roosevelt cousin admitted. "We early recognized that Theodore had a great dream in him . . . and that dream was a pure government." Emlen Roosevelt int., FRE.
79. Thayer, *TR,* 30; Sul.385.
80. Facsimile of *N.Y.T.* quote in Lor.190.
81. TR.Pri.Di. Nov. 1, 1881; TR.Har.Scr.
82. Lor.192 (facsimile).
83. Ib.; TR.Auto.61–2.
84. Put.248; un. clip in letter from B to C, 1881 (n.d.) TRC.
85. TR.Pri.Di. Dec. 3, 1881. Around this time TR bought a share of G. P. Putnam's Sons, set up a desk there, and declared himself a "silent partner" in the firm. George Haven Putnam, the president, was doubtful. "Can we think of Roosevelt being silent in any association?" Predictably, TR was soon instructing Putnam in "how to run a publishing business," and producing such a flood of unworkable editorial ideas that his departure for Albany caused sighs of relief. G. H. Putnam in *Century Memorial to Theodore Roosevelt* (New York, 1919), 37. See also Putnam in "Roosevelt, Historian and Statesman," TR.Wks.IX.xvi.
86. Admiral W. M. Sims in TR.Wks.VI. xvii; Bea.4; *N.Y. Tribune,* Oct. 16, 1886. For sample reviews, see *N.Y.T.,* June 5, 1882 ("The volume is an excellent one in every respect"); *Army and Navy Journal,* May 27 ("easy command of material . . . broad reasoning . . . excellent historical perspective . . . masterly manner"); *Philadelphia Bulletin* in TR.Scr. ("a rich contribution to our national history"); N.Y. *Evening Post* in ib. ("remarkable and worthy of high praise"); *Saturday Review* (GB), June 24, 1882 ("very little disposition to national self-laudation . . . none whatever to abuse or depreciate the enemy"). *The Naval War of 1812* is still available (2001) as a Modern Library reprint.
87. Her.196; Gable, John A., *TR as Historian and Man of Letters,* intro. to TR's *Gouverneur Morris,* Bicentennial Ed. (Oyster Bay, 1975), vii.
88. TR.Wks.VI.46–7.
89. Ib., 98.
90. Ib., 32.
91. Ib., 223, 226–8.

92. Ib., 372, 114; Preface.
93. Hag.Boy.61; Sims in TR.Wks. VI.xiv.
94. TR.Pri.Di. Dec. 6, 21, 1881; MBR to E, Dec. 10.
95. Mor.55.

6: The Cyclone Assemblyman

1. TR.Pri.Di. Jan. 2, 1882.
2. Ib.; *Albany Illustrated* (H. R. Page Co., 1892); Phelps, H. P., ed., *The Albany Handbook, 1881 and 1884;* Put.249. The text's assumption that TR stayed at the Delavan House is based on the following facts: it was the depot hotel; it functioned as Albany's political headquarters; lastly, George F. Spinney recalled his presence there later that night. (See HUN. *passim,* and Put.250.)
3. TR.Pri.Di. Jan. 2, 1882.
4. Phelps, *Handbook; Albany Argus,* Jan. 3, 1882. Sunset on Jan. 2 was at 4:40 P.M., the exact time of arrival of the New York express. Other meteorological details from *Albany Argus,* Jan. 1 and 3.
5. Roseberry, Cecil R., *Capitol Story* (ill.), New York State, 1964, 9; Phelps, *Handbook,* 19.
6. *N.Y. Tribune,* Jan. 3.
7. Roseberry, *Capitol,* 31.
8. The last sentence closely follows TR in TR.Wks.XIII. 47.
9. Put.250; *New York Times,* Jan. 3, 1882, states that Jan. 2 was the coldest day of the winter thus far in Albany. "Those who climbed the hill to the Capitol . . . encountered a cold penetrating blast that chilled everything before it."
10. The author, who prides himself on his resistance to cold, followed TR's route in 15-degree weather; although he was well covered, and the day calm, he arrived at the Capitol groaning.
11. Phelps, *Handbook;* Schuyler, Montgomery, "A Dream of the New Albany," *Scribner's,* Dec. 1879; Roseberry, *Capitol,* 45–6. The Golden Corridor is now a row of shabby offices.
12. *Trib.,* Jan. 3, 1882. Some Republicans were missing: the total House strength was 61.
13. See, e.g., But.233.
14. John Walsh in *Kansas City Star,* Feb. 12, 1922.
15. Albany correspondent of the *New York Star,* qu. TRB mss.; Sul.227; *New York Sun,* Jan. 3, 1882.
16. TR.Auto.64; *N.Y. Sun* correspondent (see Note 15).
17. Sul.215; HUN.23; Put.251 n.
18. Isaac Hunt, supplementary statement in HUN.34; Put.251.
19. Citations of this diary refer to the published version in Mor.1469–73.
20. Isaac Hunt has anecdotes concerning the original Ms. of this diary, which startled him considerably when he first read it in TR's Albany room. It struck him as libelous, and indeed TR seems to have been the victim of a libel suit later in the season; whether or not the diary caused it Hunt does not say. See HUN. *passim.*
21. Mor.1470.
22. Ib., 1471.
23. Ib., 1469–73.
24. Ib., 1469.
25. Put.255 gives a typical ballot. (N.B.: his phrase "necessary for choice 61" applies to a day when only 120 members were voting.)
26. Auto.91; Mor.1469.
27. TR.Wks.XIII.57; Phelps, *Handbook,* and *Albany Illustrated, passim.*
28. MBR to E, Jan. 8, 1882 (FDR).
29. Anna Bulloch Gracie diaries in TRC, *passim;* Mrs. Joseph Alsop Sr. in TRB mss.; Anna Bulloch Gracie to E, Jan. 8, 1882 (FDR).
30. HUN.42. Hunt was nearly seventy at the time he recalled this first meeting with TR (see Bibl.). He placed it "in the early part of the first session," saying that the caucus had been called to discuss a proposed Republican-Democratic "deal" regarding appointments. If so, the meeting took place on Feb. 21, 1882. But TR, in his Legislative Diary, Jan. 10, writes enthusiasti-

cally about some fellow-members "from the country," doubtless including Hunt; and since there *was* a caucus on appointments around this time (Put.250) Hunt was probably confusing the one with the other. The author therefore assumes, as Putnam does, that the meeting took place at the earlier caucus. In any case the date matters less than Hunt's vivid memory of TR's appearance and behavior.
31. Hunt, supplementary statement, HUN.32.
32. Ib., 33.
33. Ib. A Harvard classmate recalled to Bradley Gilman how TR had once pounced on him, overwhelmed him with a barrage of questions, then withdrawn as suddenly and picked up something to read. "He was just bored with me. That was all. He had drained me of the information he sought." Gilman, *Roosevelt the Happy Warrior* (Little, Brown, 1921) 49.
34. Hunt, supplementary statement, HUN.33.
35. HUN.75.
36. TR.Pri.Di. Jan. 13, 1882; Mor.56. Elsewhere Alice is, e.g., "Baby," "little darling Alicey," and "poor baby-wife."
37. Pri.48; HUN.22; Hunt, supplementary statement, 23.
38. HUN.50; TR.Auto.65; HUN.84–5. George Spinney told the story of the blanket-tossing incident in ib. The word "balls" was erased from the typed transcript, although five symbolic spaces remain. The story sounds apocryphal, but Spinney reminded TR of it in early January 1907, and the President was highly amused. "That was a mighty good letter of yours and sounded so like the Spinney of twenty-five years ago that it made me laugh as I read it." (Mor.5.559).
39. HUN.85 ff.; supplementary details from James Taylor in TRB mss. Other versions of this incident have TR flattening three toughs at a tavern outside town, and knocking out a Tammany spoiler at the entrance to the Delavan House. All share the Rooseveltian qualities of lightning response to any hostility, and aristocratic contempt for the provoker. See, e.g., Gilman, *Warrior,* 74.
40. Phelps, *Handbook,* 24; Roseberry, *Capitol,* 46 ff. The ceiling is now boarded up.
41. Put.252; Mor.1470.
42. *Albany Press-Knickerbocker,* qu. PRI.n. See TR.Wks.XIV.3 for text of this speech.
43. Ib.
44. *New York Herald,* Feb. 11, 1883.
45. HUN.5.
46. Gilman, *Warrior,* 10.
47. Mor.1470.
48. TR.Pri.Di. Jan. 24, 1882.
49. Facsimile in Lor.193. For another reaction, see *The Criterion,* Jan. 28, 1882: "Mr. Roosevelt made in that brief speech a record for honesty, judgment, and conception of statesmanship that ranks him at once among the leading legislators of his time."
50. Put.257. It may be of interest to note here that six days after TR's maiden speech, his old friend Sara Delano, now married to James Roosevelt of Hyde Park, gave birth to a son, Franklin Delano.
51. TR.Pri.Di. Feb. 14, 1882; Mor. 1471–2.
52. Put.258.
53. TR.Auto.72.
54. HUN.16–26.
55. Put.254–5; Pri.66; John Walsh in PRI.n.
56. Mor.1472.
57. Ib.
58. TR.Auto.72.
59. Ib., 71.
60. Ib., 75.
61. Ib., 75–6.
62. TR.Auto.77.
63. HUN.6–7; Put.261.
64. HUN.8; Put.261.
65. Henry Lowenthal, *N.Y.T.* City Editor, int. FRE; TR.Wks.XIV.7–11; Put.261–70.

66. Hunt, supplementary statement, 1.
67. John Walsh in PRI.n.
68. *New York World,* Mar. 30, 1882.
69. Put.263.
70. TR.Auto.79.
71. Spinney, qu. Put.264.
72. Full text of TR's speech is in TR.Wks.XIV.7 ff.
73. Spinney in Hunt, supplementary statement, 4.
74. Put.265; TR.Wks.XIV.11.
75. HUN.2–4.
76. Spinney, qu. Put.265; *Sun,* Apr. 6, 1882; *Trib, N.Y.T.,* same date.
77. *Sun,* Apr. 6, 1882.
78. Hunt, supplementary statement, 34. (Here, in typed transcript, "balls" is changed to "chickens.")
79. *Sun,* n.d., in TR.Scr.; *N.Y.T.,* n.d., in ib.; *World,* Apr. 7, 1882.
80. *N.Y.T.,* Apr. 6, 7, 1882.
81. Spinney, qu. Put.266.
82. Ib.
83. An associate in the Assembly later estimated that TR "could have made a million dollars if he had wanted to." HUN.75.
84. Pri.73; Put.269.
85. Bigelow, Poultney, *Seventy Summers* (London, 1925) 269.
86. *N.Y.T.,* Apr. 13, 1882.
87. HUN.49. In an interview with Ethel Armes, Sept. 19, 1924, Hunt recalled TR yelling with delight one day, "I have been sued for slander! I am getting on amazingly politically." TRB.
88. Hudson, William C., *Recollections of an Old Political Reporter* (N.Y., 1911) 144–9.
89. Hunt, supplementary statement, 22.
90. Mrs. Joseph Alsop Sr. (Corinne's daughter) int. in TRB mss.
91. Anna Bulloch Gracie's diary, 1882, makes mysterious references to an "illness" of Elliott's (probably a recurrence of his teenage epilepsy attacks), which she first heard about on Mar. 30. "Went to church Holy Communion prayed to God to cure him."
92. Joseph Murray in FRE.; *Morning Journal,* Apr. 29, 1884.
93. *Trib.,* Mar. 22, 1882.
94. Ib., June 3, 1882.
95. Qu. Har.22.
96. *Trib.,* Apr. 28, 1882; Put.300.
97. TR.Auto.69; Put.300.
98. See Hurwitz, Howard L., *TR and Labor in New York State* (NY, 1943) for a negative assessment of TR's labor record in the Assembly, Put.299–305 for a positive. The cigar-bill episode is usually viewed as a turning-point in Roosevelt biographies, largely because TR himself placed so much emphasis on it in his own *Autobiography* (81–3). However the rest of his youthful labor record, not to mention countless contemptuous references to the labor movement in his private letters, indicates that he "matured" in this respect very slowly. It should not be forgotten that TR was an ardent Progressive when he dictated his memoirs in 1913.
99. Clips, TR.Scr.; Hunt, supplementary statement, 2 ff.; HUN.14–20.
100. Clips, TR.Scr.; *Trib.,* June 1, 1882.
101. *World,* June 1.
102. Qu. Put.271.
103. *World,* June 1.
104. Put.272.
105. *N.Y.T.,* June 3, 1882. See comments of individual legislators returning to New York in *Trib.,* June 3.
106. *Trib.,* June 3, 1882; TR.Scr.
107. Mor.56.
108. TR.Scr.
109. Spinney in HUN.41.

7: The Fighting Cock

Important sources not in Bibliography:
1. Hudson, William C., *Random Recollections of an Old Political Reporter* (NY, 1911).

1. *Albany Argus,* Jan. 2, 1883.
2. Pr.74; Put.278–9.
3. TR to TR Jr. in Mor.634–5.

4. See Put.277–9 for an account of TR's re-election campaign. His vote was 4,225 against 2,016, with 67 percent of the ballot—an improvement of 4 percent over his 1882 vote.
5. Shaw, Albert, "TR as Political Leader" in TR.Wks.XIV.xvii; Hudson, *Recollections,* 145; Franklin Matthews in *Harper's Magazine,* Sep. 28, 1901, 984. See also Andrew D. White to Willard Fiske, May 26, 1884: "When you remember that this prodigious series of successes of his have been achieved by a man of . . . college standing . . . you will realize what a striking case it is. In my judgment, nothing has been seen like it in this State since the early days of Seward" (Cornell U. Libraries).
6. TR.Pri.Di. Jan. 1, 1883.
7. *Albany Argus,* Jan. 3, 1883; Put. 278 fn.
8. Hudson, *Recollections,* 251. See Nev. for Cleveland's rise to power.
9. Tugwell, Rexford G., *Grover Cleveland* (NY, 1968) 72. "He is a mass of solid hog," Henry Adams wrote (to C. F. Adams, Jan. 23, 1894). The following physical description of Cleveland is taken from Nev.57–8 and *passim;* Carpenter, Frank G., *Carp's Washington* (McGraw Hill, 1960) 39–41; Wise, John S., *Recollections of Thirteen Presidents* (NY, 1906); pors.
10. Nev.109; Stoddard memo, TRB mss.
11. Hud.143.
12. Nev.57–8; see below, Ch. 11, for details of Cleveland's paternity case.
13. HUN.39.
14. It will be remembered that TR, then touring Europe with Alice, had exclaimed, "This [the assassination] means work in the future for those who wish their country well." Upon returning to New York he began attending meetings of the N.Y. Civil Service Reform Association, and was elected its vice-president just before his departure to Albany. "I am heartily in accord with any movement tending toward the improvement of the 'spoils' system," he wrote in his letter of acceptance, "—or, I should say, its destruction." (TRB mss.)
15. Put.280–1; Nev.123.
16. *New York Times,* Jan. 25, 1883; Ellis, David M. *et al., A History of New York State* (Cornell U. Press, 1967) 369; Nev.123; HUN.40.
17. HUN.40. See also *N.Y. Evening Post,* Jan. 10, 1883: "Mr. Roosevelt . . . has secured to a remarkable degree the confidence of public-spirited citizens of either party."
18. Mor.59. There is some doubt over the date of this letter, which TR marks simply "Albany, Monday evening.": See ib., fn., and Put.274, fn. The latter believes it to be mid-January 1882. But Henry James, whom TR specifically mentions meeting, was not in Boston that January: he had left town on Dec. 26, 1881. James *was* there through New Year's 1883, however; so if TR and Alice had gone to Boston for Christmas, the meeting probably took place sometime during the festive season. Jan. 1, 1883, was a Monday, which would explain TR's advance presence in Albany for the opening of the Legislature. Alice, presumably, joined him on Tuesday or Wednesday, helped him choose rooms, then accompanied him to New York on Thursday, as promised in his letter to Mittie. Note that the letter also mentions his first known reference to meeting with Henry Cabot Lodge.
19. Put.280.
20. Alice's routine reconstructed from the letters of MBR, C, and E, and Anna Bulloch Gracie's diaries in TRC.
21. Anna Bulloch Gracie diary, Oct. 2, 1882; Put.307; Par.44.
22. TR.Pri.Di. Jan. 3, 1883.
23. *New York Herald,* Feb. 11, 1883.
24. HUN.88.

25. Mor.1471.
26. HUN.86 says, "I think the dinner was in 1884." But he adds, "We had our pictures taken before or after." A group portrait of the "quartette" is in TRC, but it manifestly dates from 1883, when TR had lost his side-whiskers, but still retained his center parting. Judging by the solemn expressions of all concerned, the picture was taken "before" the dinner. See p. 171.
27. Ib.
28. Qu. Sul.230.
29. TR.Wks.XIII.48; Ib., XIV.18.
30. Put.305; Hunt, supplementary statement, 33–4.
31. Hudson, *Recollections,* 147. "All the NY dailies gave Roosevelt a good deal of space . . . and he often got on the front page. The *Herald,* especially, sent up an extra man, Thomas J. White, to stand behind him and help develop his career as a reform legislator." (Peter P. McLaughlin, ex-Assemblyman, in FRE.)
32. Put.288.
33. TR.Wks.XIV.21; *Observer,* Mar. 10, 1883 (TR.Scr.).
34. HUN.53; Put.285–6.
35. Put.283–5; Nev.116; *N.Y.T.,* Jan. 8, 1883.
36. Nev.116–7; Put.284; Bis.1.20.
37. *Albany Argus,* Mar. 5, 1883; Put.284; TR.Scr.
38. *Albany Argus* and *N.Y. World,* Mar. 3, 1883.
39. The phrase rated headlines in, e.g., *Chicago Tribune,* May 7, 1883. The paper published a long editorial on "this startling proposition." See also Sul.386.
40. *World,* March 3, 5, 13, 1883; Put.286. But see also *Commercial Advertiser* (Mar. 3) praising TR's "courage and manliness" in this, "the most extraordinary confession that perhaps was ever heard in a deliberative body."
41. *N.Y. Sun,* Mar. 8, 1883; Put.286.
42. TR.Wks.XIV.16–21 for complete text of this speech. Interestingly, TR considered it, not the *mea culpa* of Mar. 2, his "main speech" of the session. (Mor.67.)
43. *Sun,* Mar. 10. TR petulantly declared that even though his resignation had been refused, he would "not do another stroke of work with the Committee." (ib.)
44. See, e.g., *Observer,* Mar. 10, 1883 (TR.Scr.).
45. *World,* Mar. 10, 1883.
46. HUN.38–40.
47. Ib.; Hunt, supplementary statement, 8–9.
48. Nev.112ff.
49. TR.Wks.XIV.23–4; *N.Y.T.,* Apr. 10, 1883.
50. Ib.
51. Nev.123. (But see Put.232. fn.)
52. HUN.39; Nev.123.
53. Mor.3.634.
54. TR to Jacob Riis (Rii.59).
55. TR.Auto.82; Put.302.
56. Put.282; *N.Y.T.,* Mar. 26, 1883; Put.283; TR.Wks.XIV.25; Put.290–1; *Morning Journal,* Feb. 19, 1883.
57. *N.Y.T.,* Mar. 26, 1883.
58. *Harper's Weekly,* Apr. 21, 1883.
59. Parker, George F., *Recollections of Grover Cleveland* (NY, 1911) 250.
60. *N.Y.T.,* May 29, 1883.
61. Ib.
62. Hag.RBL.8–9.
63. See, e.g., MBR to E, Dec. 7, 1880: "Teddie tho' he rejoices with you in your prospects for your Hunt longs to be with you—and walks up and down the room like a Caged Lynx. When Alice appeals to him he smothers her with kisses and tells her he is perfectly happy with her but some time he must go off with his gun instead of pouring [sic] over Brown versus Jenkins etc." (FDR).
64. Hag.RBL.8–9; Put.308–9.
65. See Ch. 5; also Hag.RF.6.
66. TR to Editor, *Country Life in*

America, Oct. 3, 1915 (Sagamore Hill collection).
67. TR to MBR, Sep. 4, 1883 (TRC).
68. Mor.60.
69. The full text of this letter is in Mor.60–1.
70. Anna Bulloch Gracie diary, July 1, 1883; memorandum by Gary Roth, curator, Sagamore Hill National Historic Site; see also Hag.RF.6–7.
71. COW.
72. TR to B, Aug. 25, 1883 (TRB); E to B, Aug. 29 (FDR); MBR to E, Aug. 30 (FDR).
73. TR to MBR, Sep. 4, 1883; Mor.76.
74. Ib.
75. TR's train journey reconstructed from his letters to MBR of Sep. 4 and 8, 1883, and *Official Railways Guide,* July–September 1883. Description of the Badlands on arrival of a stranger from an 1882 travel article in HAG.Bln., and author's own experiences of a midnight visit.
76. TR to MBR, Sep. 8, 1883.
77. TR.Auto.95.

8: The Dude from New York

1. TR.Auto.95.
2. Hag.RBL.10; TR.Auto.95; Lan.52–3.
3. Ib.
4. Ib.
5. Put.320; Lan.53.
6. Hag.RBL.7–8; Lan.48, 56.
7. Brown, Dee, *Trail Driving Days* (Scribner's, 1952) 185.
8. Hag.RBL.48; Put.313.
9. Hag.RBL.10–11.
10. See Put.313–7 for a more detailed account of the destruction of the northern herd, estimated at 1.5 million animals only a decade before. Other details from Lan.23–25. "Bone merchants" were freelance scavengers employed by the big phosphate companies.
11. Hag.RBL.11; Lan. *passim.*
12. Put.321; Hag.RBL.10; 16, 11.
13. Ib., 12; Mor.3.551; see also Put.322–3. Putnam is confused by Hagedorn's mistaken assertion that it was the Winchester that was broken. TR himself confirms, in the letter to John Hay cited above, that the Sharps was faulty.
14. Hag.RBL.12; Put.324; Mor.3.551; HAG.Bln.
15. Lan.70; Put.316; Hag.RBL.49–50; HAG.Bln.; Put.325; Lan.69–70.
16. Hag.RBL.49; Twe.29.
17. Twe. *passim;* Hag.RBL.59; Dr. Stickney in HAG.Bln.; O'Donald, qu. Paddock at trial, Twe.83.
18. Hag.RBL.61.
19. Goplen, Arnold O., "The Career of the Marquis de Mores in the Bad Lands of North Dakota," *North Dakota History,* Jan.–Apr. 1946, 11; Twe. *passim;* Put.351; Howard Eaton in HAG.Bln.; Twe.69, 71.
20. Hag.RBL.336; Twe. *passim.*
21. Qu. Put.351; Goplen, 11; Twe. 111–3.
22. Twe. *passim.*
23. The chimney still stands in Medora, N.D., symbolizing exactly the opposite.
24. Goplen, 17.
25. Mor.50. The text hereafter closely follows Put.353–60. See also Hag.RBL., Twe., and Lan.71–2.
26. Lan.71.
27. *Bismarck Daily Tribune,* qu. Put.355, 356; Hag.RBL.63.
28. Put.538.
29. Ib., 356.
30. This description of the buckboard's trip south to the Maltese Cross ranch is based on Hag.RBL.13; Put.325–6; HAG.Bln.; Lan. *passim;* and personal observations made by the author on a visit to the Badlands in 1974.
31. Lan.46.
32. Ib., 44; Put.325; Schoch, Henry A., *TR National Memorial Park: The Story Behind the Scenery* (National Park Service, 1974) 23.

33. Ib., 4.
34. Hag.RBL.13; TRB memo.
35. Hag.RBL.13–5; HAG.Bln.; Put.321 and *passim;* TR.Auto.95; Put.334.
36. TR.Auto.95–6; Hag.RBL.14.
37. Ib., 16–7. TR, who was no man to hold grudges, forgave their initial distrust of him to the extent of awarding all three men commissions when he became President. Joe Ferris was made Postmaster of Medora; Sylvane Ferris, Land Officer of North Dakota; William Merrifield, Marshal of Montana. (TR.Auto.96).
38. Text follows Putnam's assumption that TR here, as in the nights following, refused to occupy the bunks of his hosts.
39. Hag.RBL.17–8. The following description of the Badlands is based on a personal visit by the author, with touches borrowed from Lan., Hag.RBL., Put., and Schoch *passim.* Note: The Badlands of the Little Missouri (not to be confused with the better-known Badlands of South Dakota) straddle the common border of North Dakota and Montana with an average width of 50 miles. North to south the area measures approximately 225 miles.
40. TR.Pri.Di. Jan. 3, 1883; qu. Put.312.
41. Put.326–8; Hag.RBL.18–9; Lan.83, 101–2.
42. The following section is based on Lan. 100 ff.
43. Ib., 101–2.
44. Put.317–29; Hag.RBL.19; Lan. *passim.* (Gregor Lang bought the cabin, actually an old hunting shack, from Frank O'Donald.)
45. Lan.86, 100 ff.
46. Lan.113. The following account of TR's buffalo hunt is taken primarily from his own narrative in "The Lordly Buffalo" (TR.Wks.I.185–206). Hereafter this source will be abbreviated as "Buffalo." Secondary sources: Hag. RBL.23–46; Put.329–345; HAG.Bln.; Lan.
47. Hag.RBL.24.
48. Lan.113.
49. Ib., 104, 111; Lang, qu. HAG.Bln.
50. Lan.104, 111. Lang states that TR's views on "the race suicide question" were essentially the same in 1883 as those he made famous as President. "I admire the men who are not afraid to propagate their kind as far as they may," he told Gregor Lang—conscious, no doubt, of his own seed swelling in the body of Alice Lee.
51. Lan.109.
52. Lang, qu. Hag.RBL.28.
53. Ib.
54. See Put.339.
55. Lang qu. Hag.RBL.27.
56. From now on text follows TR's own account in "Buffalo."
57. Joe Ferris stated that TR "bled like a stuck pig." (HAG.Bln.) He was, by all accounts, a prodigious bleeder all his life.
58. "Buffalo," 202; Hag.RBL.34 fn.
59. "Buffalo," 202; Hag.RBL.36.
60. "Buffalo," 204–5.
61. Qu. Hag.RBL.37.
62. Lan.116–7.
63. Hag.RBL.41.
64. Ib., 28, 38–9.
65. Qu. Hag.RBL.42–43. (Hagedorn, reconstructing this conversation in 1919, relied on the memories of Sylvane, Merrifield, and Lang.) The deal was later sealed with a contract worked out by Gregor Lang and agreed to by all parties before TR's departure from Dakota. TR signed it on Sep. 27, 1883, in St. Paul, Put.343; see Appendix to Hag.RBL. (original edition) for text.
66. Hag.RBL.39.
67. Following details from Put.337.
68. TR to E, Nov. 28, 1880 (FDR). James A. Roosevelt, elder brother, executor, and trustee of TR Sr., also acted as the family banker.
69. Pri.54.

70. Author's calculation, based on accounts in TR.Pri.Di., 1883.
71. Lan.105.
72. Hag.RBL.44.
73. "Buffalo," 205–6.
74. Hag.RBL.45. Many of TR's guides mention his near-pathological exuberance after killing large game.
75. "Buffalo," 206; Lan.119.
76. "Buffalo," 206. Putnam (p. 338 fn.) points out the problem of reconciling Hagedorn's account with TR's, and both with the few dates that can be confirmed. These are Sep. 8 (TR's letter announcing his arrival to MBR); Sep. 16, confirmed as a Sunday by Joe Ferris in interview; and Sep. 27, confirmed by contract date in St. Paul. Putnam's attempt to straighten out the chronology errs in giving TR five days of rain after arriving at Lang's. It could only have been four. Both he and Hagedorn have TR returning to the kill the day after, i.e., Sep. 21, to behead the carcass; but TR clearly says that the beheading took place on the same day as the kill. All sources agree that the kill took place in the mid-morning, and Lincoln Lang recalls TR and Ferris returning with their "paens of victory" in the *evening;* so they probably did their work on the carcass in between. This would mean that TR left for Little Missouri on Sep. 21, not 22, and allow him at least five nights there, making Hagedorn's "week" seem a little more plausible.
77. Lan.119.

9: The Honorable Gentleman

Important sources not in Bibliography: 1. New York Assembly, *Hearings of the Roosevelt Investigation,* January–April 1884 (Albany, 1884). Copy in Butler Library, Columbia University. 2. Theodore Roosevelt, *In Memory of My Darling Wife* (privately printed, 1884). Only known copy in TRC.

1. HUN.28; Hunt, supplementary statement, 11; *New York Times,* Dec. 27, 1883.
2. Put.368 ff.
3. The figures were 72 to 56 in the Assembly and 19 to 13 in the Senate.
4. This para based largely on Put.365–366. See also Sto.121–2. Senator Miller's nickname referred to his professional involvement in the wood and paper industry of his home county, Herkimer.
5. *New York Sun,* Dec. 28, 1883.
6. Mor.62.
7. Ib. 63.
8. Put.369.
9. Put.370; Hunt, supplementary statement, 11; HUN.27–8.
10. *New York Herald,* Jan. 1, 1884; *N.Y.T.,* same date; *Sun,* Dec. 27, 1883.
11. See Put.371–3, or his source, TR.Scr., for a detailed account of the Speakership contest. *Sun,* Dec. 28, 1883; Put.371; HUN.28; Put.373.
12. HUN.28.
13. Put.373; *Sun,* Jan. 1, 1884.
14. Put.373.
15. *World,* Jan. 1, 1884. (Note: not the *Sun*—Pringle's mistake, which Putnam copied.)
16. TR.Auto.87; *World,* Jan. 2, 1884; MBR to E, Jan. 3, 1884 (FDR); HUN.29.
17. Hunt, supplementary statement, 12; Put.374 and fn.; HUN.29.
18. TR.Wks.XIII.60; TR.Auto.43. These sessions came to an end when TR discovered that Ryan was by profession a burglar, and had been incarcerated in the Albany jail.
19. Mor.64.
20. PRI.n. "Those who knew her then recall that she was somewhat lonely, and that TR's time was too much taken up with politics."
21. Put.377 fn. The house at 55 West Forty-fifth Street was taken over by Elliott Roosevelt and his new bride, Anna Hall.

22. Put.385; Mrs. Longworth int., November 1954. TRB; Mrs. Sheffield Cowles int. Dec. 28, 1954; TRB: Corinne Roosevelt Robinson to Henry F. Pringle, PRI.n.
23. Ib.
24. Ib.; also letters of condolence to Bamie in TRC.
25. Mor.64. One Assemblyman declared he had "never seen anyone look so pretty" as Alice when she begged her husband not to tell the "shaved lion story" (see Mor.48).
26. Ib., 64–5.
27. This phrase, borrowed from Longfellow's *Saga of King Olaf* (IV), was frequently used by TR in connection with Alice Lee.
28. Put.366, 376.
29. HUN.26.
30. See Put.374–6 for an indication of the close relations between the liquor industry and the political machines.
31. HUN.29; Put.374; TR.Wks.XIV. 31.
32. TR.Auto.84; Put.381.
33. Auto.84.
34. Mor.65.
35. *World*, Feb. 6, 1884; *Sun* and *Her.*, same date.
36. Mor.60. Putnam errs in stating (p. 380) that "unhappily, no verbatim record of it exists." The *Herald* (Feb. 6) prints TR's speech in full, and the *World* and *Sun* have detailed paraphrases.
37. E.g., *Sun*, Mar. 9, 1883.
38. *Her.*, Feb. 6, 1884.
39. Qu. Put.380.
40. *Her.*, Feb. 6, 1884.
41. Ib.; see also *World*, same date.
42. Qu. Put.381.
43. See Put.365–8 and 376–7 for municipal background to TR's investigation.
44. Put.376.
45. Mor.1471.
46. Put.376.
47. TR.Scr.; *Her.*, Jan. 20, 1884.
48. *Hearings*, 57–8.
49. Ib.
50. *World*, Feb. 3, 1884.
51. *Evening Post*, Feb. 11; *World*, Feb. 12, 1884.
52. Put.385; Pri.50; PRI.n.
53. *World*, Feb. 14, 1884.
54. *N.Y.T.*, Feb. 13 and 12, 1884.
55. Ib., Feb. 13, 1884. See also *Her.*, Feb. 14, 15; *World*, Feb. 14; *Sun*, Feb. 15; *Trib.*, Feb. 14 *passim.*
56. Put.384; see Roseberry, Cecil R., *Capitol Story* (New York State, 1964) 52 ff., 82 ff.
57. Put.380; *World*, Feb. 15, 1884.
58. Ib.; HUN.52; TR.Wks.XIII.48.
59. HUN.51–2.
60. Hunt, supplementary statement, 33; HUN.50.
61. TR.Auto.91.
62. Ib., 90–1.
63. TR.Wks.XIII.66–7.
64. This story is contained in TR's essay, "Phases of State Legislation," reprinted in TR.Wks.XIII.70–72.
65. See Hunt, supplementary statement, 23.
66. Mor.65.
67. Hunt, supplementary statement, 23; Put.382.
68. HUN.68.
69. PRI.n. Put. (p. 386) has Elliott saying this directly to Theodore; but he contradicts his only source, Pringle, who says the statement was made to Corinne Roosevelt Robinson. Having examined Pringle's own sources—an interview memo and autograph letter in TRC, the author must regretfully conclude that Putnam, usually so meticulous, has here yielded to a romantic temptation.
70. Jacques Offenbach, who traveled this route a few years earlier, had reason to complain of the bell's funereal toll. See Roland van Zandt, *Chronicles of the Hudson*, Rutgers U., 1971.
71. *N.Y.T.*, Feb. 14, 1884.
72. Anna Bulloch Gracie to Archibald Bulloch Sr., May 14, 1884 (TRP).
73. Corinne in PRI.n.

74. *N.Y.T.*, Feb. 15; Put.386.
75. *World, Trib., N.Y.T.*, Feb. 15, 1884.
76. *Her.*, Feb. 15, 1884.
77. TR, *In Memory;* Put.388–9, qu. ib.
78. See *Sun, Her.*, Feb. 17, 1884; HAG.Bln., Put.387–8 for accounts of the funeral. TR Sr.'s funeral service had been held in this same church six years before.
79. Put.387.
80. HAG.Bln.
81. Ib.
82. Cutler to Sewall, HAG.Bln.; C to E, Mar. 4, 1884 (FDR).
83. Mor.6.966; qu. Put.391.
84. Pri.53; Put.390–1.
85. TR's memory is not at fault here. His engagement had been privately announced on Feb. 14, Valentine's Day; but the public announcement was not made until Monday, Feb. 16.
86. TR.Pri.Di. Feb. 16, 1884.
87. Roosevelt, Nicholas, *TR as I Knew Him* (Dodd, Mead, 1967) 24–5. Two recorded mentions of his bereavement to Bill Merrifield and Bill Sewall are noted below (Ch. 11).
88. The scrapbook, with all its mutilations, can be seen in TRC.
89. Corinne to Henry F. Pringle, PRI.n.
90. Ib.
91. Edith Kermit Roosevelt, qu. Mrs. Longworth int., Nov. 9, 1954; TRB memo.

10: The Delegate-at-Large

Important sources not in Bibliography:
1. New York Assembly, *Hearings of the Roosevelt Investigation, January–April 1884* (Albany, 1884). Copy in Butler Library, Columbia University.

1. TR.Pri.Di. Feb. 16, 1884; COW.
2. Mor.66.
3. COW.
4. Ib. It appears that Bamie was given a month's extension of this deadline, since the Roosevelts were still in occupancy at least through the third week in May. See MBR to E, Dec. 10, 1880 (FDR), for a typical account of one of Mittie's parties.
5. COW; Hag.RF.9. This was the actual cost of the house. But TR had also contracted for outbuildings, at an extra cost of $5,160. His land property there represented an investment of $22,500 (after selling of $7,500 worth to Bamie), bringing the total expenditure to $44,635. Memorandum by Gary Roth, curator, Sagamore Hill National Historic Site.
6. TR to Sewall, March 9, 1884 (TRP).
7. COW; Mor.66.
8. Put.393–397 meticulously details all TR's activities from Feb. 25 through Mar. 14.
9. *Hearings,* 416–7, 474, 484, 502, 553, 540–1; C to E, Mar. 4, 1884 (FDR).
10. *Hearings,* 602; HUN.46.
11. HUN.46–7; supplementary statement, 27–28; *Evening Telegram,* Mar. 14; *N.Y. Herald,* Mar. 15; Put.397. TR's report caused an instant furor in the House and in the press. "Sensational Report . . . How the City is Robbed," headlined the *Evening Telegram.* The *World* called it "Roosevelt's Blunderbuss," and the *Commercial Advertiser* warned it was "Dangerous as Dynamite." The *Hour* called it "one of the most excellent pieces of work of its kind that have ever been sent to a legislative body. It is well written, is full of facts, clearly presented, and it fully justifies the investigation." (Mar. 14, 15, 22.) TR.Scr. has the complete text.
12. These facts were repeated, in another interview, by the *Sun* of Feb. 26.
13. Hearings, *passim;* see also Put. 401–11.
14. See Put.396–405 for a more detailed account of TR's efforts on behalf of these bills. Qu. Put.399.
15. Hunt, supplementary statement, 14.
16. Put.397–9.

17. Ib., 415. Arthur, despite his excellent record in the White House, had alienated party conservatives with his support of Civil Service Reform, while failing to convince the reformers that he was sincerely on their side.
18. Put.420–3 minutely analyzes TR's attitude to Blaine at this time.
19. *N.Y.T.*, Jan. 18, 1884.
20. Hunt, supplementary statement, 16; Pri.79. Put.418 fn. agrees that revenge was "unquestionably one object," but suggests that larger political ambitions guided TR.
21. Ib.416.
22. *World*, Apr. 23, 1884. See also *Sun*, *Trib.*, *N.Y.T.*, etc., Apr. 23–5 for general convention coverage. These newspapers, and Put.413–24, provide the basis of the following account.
23. *Sun*, Apr. 23, 1884.
24. Put.417; *Sun*, Apr. 23, 1884.
25. *Sun*, Apr. 24, 1884; *Trib.*, same date.
26. *Sun*, Apr. 24, 1884.
27. *Eve. Post, N.Y.T., Sun*, Apr. 24, 1884. Rochester *Morning Herald*, May 13.
28. *Sun*, Apr. 24, 1884 (See Ch. 9, n. 4). Put.416.
29. *World*, Apr. 25, 1884.
30. HUN.31; Hunt, supplementary statement, 16–17.
31. HUN.31.
32. Ib., 41, 68.
33. *World*, Apr. 25, 1884.
34. *N.Y.T.*, Apr. 25, 1884; *Eve. Post*, Apr. 29.
35. Cutler to B, Apr. 18, 1884 (TRB mss). A more typical press comment: "Theodore Roosevelt has won a brilliant victory by keen intuitions and resolute, swift action, which place him at the front of his party in the state . . . his young head is dizzy tonight with the congratulations being heaped upon him." *Philadelphia Press*, n.d., in TR.Scr. See ib. for the avalanche of praise TR earned at Utica.
36. HCL, Address to Congress, Feb. 9, 1919.
37. See Put.400; Hud.146; HUN. *passim*. *Harper's Weekly*, Apr. 19, 1884.
38. Hud.146.
39. Ib., 147.
40. The following anecdote closely follows ib., 148–9. Hudson, reminiscing many years later, mistakenly writes "Chicago" instead of "Utica," but otherwise his story coincides with legislative and historic facts. See also Put.400–1 and Nev.142.
41. Cleveland proved as good as his word on the Tenure of Office Bill, which he vetoed, to TR's extreme mortification, on May 10, 1884. The other bills were rewritten, repassed, and approved on May 15. For Cleveland's opinion of TR's bill-writing at this time, see below, Ch. 14.
42. *World*, Apr. 25, 1884; Hunt, supplementary statement, 23.
43. Ib., 23 and 6; HUN.73; Lod.21.
44. Mor.66–7.
45. Put.430; Mor.68.
46. "I already had every room empty," B remembered in COW.
47. Description of HCL based on Henry Adams, *The Education of Henry Adams* (Modern Library reprint, 1996), 419–20; Gar.124–8 and *passim;* Wis.153 ff; the unpublished *Autobiography* of Mrs. Joseph Alsop Sr. (Alsop papers, TRC); Howard of Penrith, Lord Esmé, *Theatre of Life* (London, 1936) 2.105; Put.426; Mor.5, 163.
48. Mrs. Joseph Alsop Sr., *Autobiography;* Wis.158.
49. Gar.61.
50. Lodge had lectured at Harvard during the period that TR was there, and met him once or twice at the Porcellian (Lod.25). There was another brief encounter at St. Botolph's Club, Boston, in the winter of 1882/3 (see Ch. 7, n. 18). Apparently they took little notice of each other on these formal occasions.
51. Put.426–7; Pri.88.

52. See Put.426–9 for another, more detailed discussion of their relationship.
53. Put.430; *Sun,* June 2, 1884; *Trib.,* June 4.
54. Un. press clip, qu. Foraker, Joseph, *Notes of a Busy Life* (Stewart & Kidd, 1917) 167.
55. See Mor.69.
56. James G. Blaine, Chester A. Arthur, George F. Edmunds, John A. Logan, John Sherman, Joseph R. Hawley, Robert T. Lincoln (son of the late President), W. T. Sherman (the general, and brother of John), Benjamin Harrison. Harrison withdrew late Saturday night, leaving eight candidates before the Convention.
57. See TR in *Chicago Tribune,* June 1, 1884.
58. Lod.11 implies that he and TR made rather more free with this information than the facts seem to indicate.
59. Qu. Sul.215–6.
60. White, Andrew D., *Autobiography* (Macmillan, 1905) 1.204 ff.
61. See Mor.71. TR's incorrigible optimism made him set the ratio at "fifty-one cases out of a hundred" for *vox deo,* and the remaining forty-nine for *vox diaboli.*
62. The following faces from the album of TR's coming years were visible in the crowd: Benjamin Harrison (50), John D. Long (46), Russell A. Alger (48), Thomas C. Platt (50), Marcus Alonzo Hanna (46), William McKinley (41), Elihu Root (39), Joseph D. Foraker (37), Carl Schurz (55), Chauncey Depew (50). See also Sul.215–6.
63. Sul.215.
64. Put.441; Alex.4.23, TR.Scr.; *Sun,* May 31, June 1–4, 1884; *Chi. Trib.,* June 2.
65. *Sun,* June 2, 1884; un. clips qu. Foraker, *Life,* and in Sul.217.
66. *Sun,* June 2, 1884. See also *Boston Herald* correspondent, qu. *World,* June 9: "He is simply an honest, straightforward young man, with a great big load of brains and a tremendous personal energy, which goes beyond anything I have ever seen . . . all his movements and conversation are of the kind which indicates that he thinks much more rapidly than he can by any human possibility talk."
67. *Sun,* June 2.
68. Ib., and *World,* same date.
69. Ib.
70. *Chi. Trib,* June 4, 1884.
71. Ib.; pictures in New York Public Library Collection. *Sun,* June 4.
72. Collage from various newspapers cited *passim.*
73. *Chi. Trib.,* June 4. According to Andrew D. White, who overheard this remark, it was made on the last day of the Convention, when the portrait of Lincoln dominating the hall was suddenly removed. But contemporary newspapers confirm that Garfield's portrait replaced that of the Emancipator at the beginning of the proceedings.
74. Put.431–2, various newspapers cited *passim.*
75. *Sun,* June 4, 1884; *Chi. Trib., N.Y.T.,* same date; Put.430 fn. and 434.
76. *Sun,* June 4, 1884; Put.434.
77. Mor.72; TR.Wks.XIV.37.
78. *Sun,* June 4, 1884; *World,* same date. (But see *Chi. Trib.,* June 4, ed.) Note that Putnam, whose biography is flawed by occasional racial bias, studiously leaves out the key element in TR's speech (p. 435).
79. Put.435; *Sun,* June 4; Foraker, *Life,* 161. Mrs. Foraker, in her own, excellent autobiography, *I Would Live It Again* (Harpers, 1932), remembers TR at this time as a "scowling and raspily positive" young man whose "fire and point of view" attracted her husband. She notes the irony of the fact that it was a black man that brought them together, and a black regiment (at Brownsville) that caused their spectacular falling-out in 1907.
80. *Sun,* June 4, 1884.
81. Ib., June 5, 1884.

82. Ib., June 6, 1884.
83. *Chi. Trib.*, June 6, 1884.
84. Andrew D. White, *Autobiography*, 1.206–7; *Chi. Trib.*, *Sun*, June 6, 1884.
85. Mor.72. "Governor Long" was John D. Long, TR's future superior at the Navy Department.
86. *N.Y.T.*, June 7, 1884.
87. *Sun*, June 7, 1884.
88. Ib.; see Put.440–1.
89. Ib.; *Sun*, June 7, 1884; HUN.23.
90. *Chi. Trib.*, June 7, 1884. See also Andrew D. White, *Autobiography*, 1.205; other newspapers cited *passim*.
91. Qu. *Sun*, June 7, 1884; qu. Har.40.
92. *Sun*, June 7, 1884; *Chi. Trib.*, same date.
93. *Nation*, June 12, 1884; *N.Y.T.*, June 7.
94. *World*, June 7, 1884. According to the unpublished memoirs of Eugene Hay (LC), TR privately told fellow delegates that he had been sounded out by the Blaine forces as a possible Vice-Presidential candidate.
95. See Put.446.
96. *St. Paul Pioneer Press*, June 9, 1884. See also Put.448. In another careful self-positioning, TR had by now separated himself from the Free Trade Club, which was anathema to protectionist GOP conservatives. "I'm a Republican first; Free Trader afterwards," he wrote a club officer, Poultney Bigelow. Quoted in unpublished biographical sketch of TR by Bigelow in Poultney Bigelow Papers, New York Public Library. (Undated letter, probably Jan. 1884.)
97. TR to B, June 23, 1884 (TRB); TR.Wks.1.152.

11: The Cowboy of the Present

1. TR.Wks.I.150. The following account of TR's solo expedition is taken from his own narrative, "A Trip on the Prairie," first published in *Hunting Trips of a Ranchman* in 1885. Supplementary details from TR. Pri.Di. June 17–22, 1884, and other sources cited *passim*.
2. TR.Wks.I.307–9; 1.2; II.54.
3. Ib.
4. See p. 27.
5. TR.Wks.I.150; 308; 309–10.
6. Apparently TR saw no live buffalo on his peregrinations through the Badlands in 1884. He comments in TR.Pri.Di. only on the countless skulls and skeletons to be seen everywhere. In other words, the future president of the American Bison Society must have killed one of the very last buffalo in Dakota on his hunt the previous fall.
7. TR.Wks.I.149–51; TR to B, June 23, 1884 (TRB); TR.Wks.I.151–2.
8. Ib., 329.
9. Ib., 153–5, 154–7, 158, TR to B, June 23, 1884.
10. TR.Wks.I.161–2.
11. Ib.
12. Put.457; TR to B, June 23, 1884.
13. This commitment raised TR's total investment in Dakota to $40,000, or 20% of his capital. The contract was signed on June 12, 1884.
14. TR.Wks.I.164; Put.457.
15. He had arrived on the night of June 9, and ridden immediately to his ranch.
16. Put. 452; Twe.111. The hotel is still operating under the name "Rough Riders Hotel." Medora, garishly restored and commercialized, is now a major tourist destination in North Dakota. Chateau de Morès survives intact as a state historical site, and the giant chimney of the Marquis's packing plant still looms over town.
17. Mor.73.
18. *Bad Lands Cowboy*, Jan. 5, 1884; Hag.RBL.79, 120; Brown, Dee, *Trail Driving Days* (Scribner's, 1952) 186; Goplen, Arnold O., "The Career of the Marquis de Morès in the Bad Lands of North Dakota," *North Dakota History*, Jan.–Apr. 1946, 40; Twe.69, 71; Brown, *Trail Driving*, 187.

19. Twe. *passim;* Goplen, "de Morès"; *Trail Driving,* 185; Put.362.
20. Goplen, "de Morès," 47.
21. Ferris and Merrifield had refused to allow one of the Marquis's herds to graze on the range opposite Maltese Cross, which according to frontier law "belonged" to their ranch. The Marquis had offered them a $1,500 bribe, which they refused. Hag.RBL. 84–6; Put.451.
22. Hag.RBL.127; Put.460–1.
23. See Gar.79 ff. for Lodge's tribulations and torment after Chicago.
24. *Bad Lands Cowboy,* qu. HAG.Bln.
25. The *Cowboy* office soon became a favorite haunt of TR when he was in town, along with those others who "liked to smell printer's ink and feel civilized." Arthur T. Packard in *Saturday Evening Post,* Mar. 4, 1904.
26. *Bad Lands Cowboy,* qu. HAG.Bln.
27. TR.Wks.271; Hag.RBL.188; HAG. Bn.; Lan.80.
28. Hag.RBL.149; Put.456–7; TR. Auto. 97–8; Sew.18–19. This site, returned to nature, is now the North Unit of the Theodore Roosevelt National Memorial Park. A diorama re-creates it at the Museum of Natural History in New York.
29. TR.Auto.96; photos by TR in TRC; TR.Wks.I.10–11.
30. Put.459; Mor.73.
31. Sew.12.
32. Ib.
33. Ib., 13–4; Sewall in HAG.Bln.
34. Put.459.
35. Hag.RBL.147; Put.461.
36. HAG.Bln. See Hag.RBL.139–147 for an account of Granville Stuart's vigilante movement, also Mattison, Ray H., "Roosevelt and the Stockmen's Association" in *North Dakota History,* XVII.2–3 (Apr.–July 1950). This rough-and-ready form of justice sometimes had unfortunate consequences, as when the vigilantes strung up an innocent man. Their leader did his best to apologize to the widow. "Madam, the joke is on us." Albert T. Vollweiler in *Quarterly Journal of U. North Dakota* 19 (Oct. 1919) 1.
37. *St. Paul Pioneer Press,* July 2, 1884.
38. COW.
39. The family had acquired Alice Lee's habit of calling him by his college nickname. Although the word understandably pained him, it took them some time to relearn the word "Theodore." See Robinson/Cowles/Alsop correspondence, *passim.*
40. Sew.14–15.
41. TR to B, June 23, 1884 (TRB).
42. Put.463–5; COW.
43. Anna Bulloch Gracie to Archibald Bulloch Sr., May 14, 1884 (TRP).
44. Merrifield in HAG.Bln.; Hag. RF.11.
45. Nev.154.
46. Gar.79 ff; Put.464–5.
47. See *N.Y. Evening Post,* June 12, 1884, for text; also Put.448.
48. Elsewhere TR noted that it was "impossible to combine the functions of a guerilla chief with those of a colonel in the regular army; one has the greater independence of action, the other is able to make what action he does take vastly more effective." *Boston Herald,* July 20, 1884; Put.467.
49. Mor.75. The reactions of William Roscoe Thayer may be taken as typical. See his *TR,* 52.
50. Wis.26. TR was blackballed for membership of the Union League Club, which his father had helped found, on June 12, 1884. Not until October 9 did Charles Evarts manage to persuade the club committee to accept him. Irwin, Will et al., *A History of the Union League Club of New York* (Dodd Mead, 1953) 127–8.
51. *Eve. Post* qu. Har.41; Mor.75. John M. Dobson, in "George W. Curtis and the Election of 1884," *New York State Historical Quarterly* 52 (1968) 3, argues

that the GOP's pro-Cleveland mugwumps represented no reformist trend, only anti-Blaine hysteria. Hence TR was justified in declining their embrace.

52. Sample headlines: "A TERRIBLE TALE—DARK CHAPTER IN A PUBLIC MAN'S HISTORY—The Pitiful Story of Maria Halpin and Governor Cleveland's Son." Sample editorial opinion: "We do not believe that the American people will knowingly elect to the Presidency a coarse debauchee who would bring his harlots with him to Washington and hire lodgings for them convenient to the White House." *Buffalo Telegraph* and Charles Dana in the *Sun,* qu. Tugwell, Rexford G., *Grover Cleveland* (NY, 1968) 91–2. For sequel to scandal, see below, n. 86 and text.

53. *Trib.,* July 28, 1884.

54. Hag.RBL.159; Put.471; see also Sew.17.

55. *Bad Lands Cowboy,* July 31, 1884; Mor.73; Hag.159.

56. Sewall qu. Put.471; Hag.RBL.161–2; HAG.Bln.

57. Sewall in ib.; Lincoln Lang on Merrifield in ib.; Lan.67; Put.423.

58. TR to B, Aug. 12 and 17, 1884.

59. Ib.; Put.472–3; TR.Wks.I.420, III.75.

60. Sewall in HAG.Bln.; Sew.19; Put.472–3; Sew.18.

61. TRB.

62. TR to B, Aug. 17, 1884; TR.Wks.I.311.

63. TR burned and bleached quickly and flatteringly. *St. Paul Pioneer Press,* July 2, 1884, described him as already "browned the color of maplewood bark." TR to B, Aug. 12; 1885 newsclip in TRB; Mor.77. According to *N.Y. Her.,* Sep. 22, 1885, TR's equipment included a beautifully embossed, monogrammed, 45-lb. saddle, silver-inlaid bit and spurs, real angora chaps, a braided quirt, and an "exquisite pearl-handled, silver-mounted revolver." Among his many rifles was one inlaid with solid gold plates delicately engraved with hunting scenes.

64. Now Wibaux, Montana. Mingusville was originally so named because its founders were a woman named Minnie and her husband, Gus. TR never specified the exact date of this encounter. Hag.RBL.151–3 places it impossibly in June of 1884; TR's documented movements during that month prove that he would not have had the time to visit Mingusville. Put.251 fn. places the incident in April 1885, while conceding that the evidence is "circumstantial." The author considers August 1884 a far more likely date, for these reasons: TR was at a loose end then; he mentions a shortage of horses in his letter to Bamie, which might explain his search for strays; also both W. Roy Hoffman and Pierre Wibaux, who were living near Mingusville at the time, agree the incident took place "shortly after July 1884." (Hoffman, unpublished autobiography in TRB.) This could only have been between August 1 and 17. TR's assertion that "it was a cold night" causes some problems, but falling temperatures are not unusual in late August, in windswept prairie towns.

65. TR.Auto.124–5. At this point the reader should be reassured that TR, for all his self-esteem, was no braggart. Episodes like the Mingusville story, which seem too "fictional" to be true, occur frequently in his writings. However any scholar who makes any prolonged study of TR discovers that he was almost infallibly truthful. Edward Wagenknecht remarks: "I believe that in general he came as close to telling the truth as any man can come in talking about himself." Elihu Root wrote: "He was incapable of deception, and thoughtless of it." Hostile biographers investigating TR's wilder stories have found them docu-

mented down to the last detail. He was, of course, capable of humorous exaggeration and poetic license, but so is every good story-teller. See Wag.97–103.

66. Hag.RBL.165; Sewall in HAG.Bln.

67. TR.Wks.I.93.

68. Hag.RBL.165–6.

69. Put.391.

70. Only known copy of *In Memory* is in TRC.

71. Sewall in HAG.Bln. (he misdates the year as 1885); see also Sew.47, and Sewall in *Forum,* May 1919. Mrs. Roberts, a Badlands neighbor, remembers TR as "sad and quiet" during these days. (*McCall's,* Oct. 1919.)

72. TR to B, Sep. 20, 1884.

73. TR.Pri.Di. The list is abridged; fragments of text in quotes. (N.B. These dates are adjusted, since TR's diary was an old one, left over from 1883.)

74. His recorded total for 1884 was 227 kills.

75. TR.Wks.I.221. TR's own magnificent account of elk-hunting in the Big Horns is in ib., 212–27. See Put.474–89 for details of the whole expedition. This para. also based on TR.Pri.Di. *passim.*

76. See TR.Wks.I.483 for TR's ecstatic reaction to this elk-music.

77. Merrifield in HAG.Bln.

78. Mor.82.

79. The word "cunning" may best be translated as "cute."

80. For one of TR's finest pieces of atmospheric writing, complete with eerie sound-effects, see his description of this ride in TR.Wks.I.96 or Put.488.

81. TR.Auto.106; Put.490.

82. Ib.; also 460; Hag.RBL.207–8; Sew.21. Text follows Putnam's assumption that confrontation occurred before TR's departure East on Oct. 7, 1884.

83. Hag.RBL.208 (based on Sewall int. in HAG.Bln.).

84. *Sun,* Oct. 12, 1884.

85. See Put.492–3. TR also castigated the Governor for hiring a substitute in the Civil War, conveniently forgetting that Theodore Senior had done the same. (Ib., 498.)

86. "Tell the truth" was Cleveland's message to his friends. The facts of the scandal are these. On Sep. 14, 1874, Maria Halpin, a pretty 36-year-old Buffalo widow, charged Cleveland with the paternity of a son, whom she named Oscar Folsom Cleveland. Although Cleveland could not be sure he was the father (Mrs. Halpin had simultaneous liaisons with several other men), he took full responsibility, noting that he was the only bachelor involved. He refused, however, to marry Mrs. Halpin. The widow promptly took to drink, became unstable, and had to be relieved of Oscar, who was brought up by foster-parents at Cleveland's expense. An enquiry by a respected Buffalo clergyman in 1884 found that "After the primary offense . . . his [Cleveland's] conduct was singularly honorable." See Nev. 162 ff. for full details.

87. Put.493–504 gives a detailed account of TR's campaign for Blaine.

88. Put.500 points out that only three of his seven speeches were for the national ticket as such. John Allen Gable, reviewing this manuscript, writes: "I have no quarrel with what you say about the Blaine campaign. But it is really time to make the point about *professionalism.* As of the Gilded Age, professionals came to dominate politics—pushing aside . . . men who 'stood,' rather than 'ran' for office—the 'Mugwump types' as Richard Hofstadter calls them. TR in 1884 made the choice of being a real professional by being a partisan . . . You will note that in his 1884 speeches he talks mainly about one *party* vs. the other." See also note SI, above.

89. Bigelow, Poultney, *Seventy Summers* (London, 1925) 279.

90. Mor.83; see p. 268, and Put. 446–7.
91. TR to B, c. Oct. 30, 1884 (TRB mss).
92. Sto.129; Put.501–2; Al Smith in PRI.n.
93. Sto.131–4. See also Nev.145.
94. Mor.87.
95. Ib., 88.
96. Lod.I.27.
97. TR.Wks.I.169; Put.508; TR.Wks. I.64. Following account is taken from ib., ff.
98. Ib., 67.
99. See Put.497–8.
100. TR to B, Nov. 23, 1884; TR.Pri.Di. Nov. 18.
101. TR left the Elkhorn site on Nov. 21, and stayed away for the rest of 1884. Anecdote from TR.Auto.98. Notwithstanding the "beavering," he eventually became a skilled woodchopper, and kept the practice up all his life.
102. "I remember the morning we began to put up the walls, the temperature was sixty-five degrees below zero." Sew.25. This sounds like an exaggeration. Still, it is undoubtedly true, as Sewall says, that "No one suffered much from the heat." (ib.)
103. This passage is taken almost verbatim from TR.Wks.I.169.
104. Sewall in HAG.Bln.; Hag.Boy. 109; PRI.n.
105. TR.Wks.I.346. See Put.509–17 for more detail on these winter days. For TR's organization of the LMSA, see ib., and Mattison, "Stockmen's Association." The first meeting was held on Dec. 19, 1884; TR was elected Chairman.
106. TR.Wks.I.341. Note that TR mentions death four times in this passage.

12: The Four-Eyed Maverick

Important sources not in Bibliography:
1. *Bad Lands Cowboy* 1884–1886 (microfilm of all known existing copies in TRB).

1. TR.Wks.I.35.
2. Hag.RBL.233; Put.518. TR also published in the January 1885 issue of *Century* his first article, "Phases of State Legislation" (reprinted in TR.Wks. XIII.47 ff.). It was an admirably detailed and occasionally very funny review of his three years as an Assemblyman, and so impressed James Bryce that he quoted it in his *American Commonwealth* (1888). See below, Ch. 15.
3. Mor.89.
4. See Lor.218–9.
5. Lodge, Journal, Mar. 20, 1885, qu. Put.506.
6. *Hunting Trips of a Ranchman* is reprinted in TR.Wks.I.1–247.
7. Put.519. "Mr. Roosevelt's book is far too sumptuous for the general public," remarked *The Atheneum*, calling it "one of the most beautiful hunting books ever printed." (Sep. 19, 1885.)
8. *New York Mail and Express*, Sep. 14, 1895. There were three American editions and one British, within the first year of publication (*New York Tribune*, Oct. 6, 1886). London reviews were especially complimentary. *The Spectator* (Jan. 16, 1886) noted TR's extraordinary identification with animals outside of the chase, and said that it was "a book to be closed with lingering regret." (Ib.) *Saturday Review* (August 29, 1885) called it "a repertory of thoughtful woodcraft or prairiecraft," whose "cultivated" style and "sumptuous" presentation would make it one of the top ten "sporting classics" of Western literature.
9. Cut.54.
10. It is amusing to note that TR's minute description of the Elkhorn ranch interior, with its flickering firelight, antler-hung walls, and well-stocked shelves, was written at a time when Sewall and Dow had not yet put on the roof.
11. TR.Wks.I.112.

12. Ib., 119. For TR's abnormal sensitivity to sound, see ib., pages 12, 13, 14, 35, 45, 48, 49, 57, 58, 59, 65, 66, 69, 85, 95, 96, 113, 114, 115, 127, 129, 132, 146, 148, 150, 153, 161, 167, 169.
13. The only explanation satisfactory to the author is contained in the last stanza of Oscar Wilde's *Ballad of Reading Gaol.*
14. TR.Wks.I.107.
15. See Hag.RBL.240–1 and the Book of Job, 30.27; also Put.520.
16. Hag.RBL.249–52. The next landing was more than a mile away.
17. TR to B, Apr. 29, 1885 (TRB).
18. Put.520. Sewall (HAG.Bln.) says they all moved in "at the end of April," but since he and Dow were away after Apr. 23 the move must have occurred before that. The ranch house was essentially a huge log cabin, 60′ × 30′ × 7′. It no longer exists, but the site is preserved. See Ch. 11, n. 28.
19. TR.Wks.I.10–11.
20. Qu. Hag.RBL.240.
21. An additional purchase of 52 ponies for $3,275 is included in this total of $85,000. See Put.523 and fn. TR to B, May 17, 1885 (TRB mss.).
22. Put.523; Mor.90; TR.Wks.I.337–8.
23. Put.520; HAG.Bln.
24. TR.Auto.100.
25. Hag.RBL.285; Put.528.
26. TR.Auto.101–6.
27. Put.524–5; Lan.184.
28. TR to B, June 5, 1885; TR.Auto.107; TR.Wks.I.320; Hag. RBL.289–90.
29. Three-Seven Bill Jones (not to be confused with Hell-Roaring Bill Jones), qu. Hag.RBL.279.
30. Lan.185; Put.524; TR to B, June 5, 1885 (TRB mss). TR gives an excellent account of a Badlands round-up in TR.Wks.I.314–340.
31. *St. Paul Pioneer Press,* June 23, 1885.
32. *Trib.,* July 8, 1885.
33. Sew.41. TR was to suffer occasional spells of "wheezing" and "bronchitis" throughout his life, but at such infrequent intervals he can be said to have effectively conquered his asthma.
34. Tha.57. See also below, n. 42.
35. This description of the new house is based on an 1885 photograph in the files of TRB.
36. Other details from Hag.RF.4, Put.532, and TRB picture files.
37. The panorama is now blocked by trees, mostly planted by TR in obedience to the family motto (see p. 299). But in 1885 the hilltop was bare.
38. TR.Auto.328.
39. Par.63.
40. Elliott Roosevelt had married a fragile society beauty, Anna Rebecca Hall, on Dec. 1, 1882. See Las. Ch. 2 for an account of their courtship.
41. HUN.74: "Well, sir, that man planned his life from the start. He told me a good many times that he expected to get his life work done by the time he was sixty." In the last months of his life TR told his sister Corinne that at twenty-one he had decided to live "up to the hilt" until he was sixty, and did not care how soon he died after that. Fate allowed him ten extra weeks.
42. HAG.Bln.; Put.530. "What a change!" commented a reporter who met TR en route. "Last March he was a pale, slim young man, with a thin, piping voice and a general look of dyspepsia . . . He is now brown as a berry and has increased 30 lbs in weight. The voice . . . is now hearty and strong enough to drive oxen." (*Pittsburgh Dispatch,* Aug. 23, 1885, in TR.Scr.)
43. Hag.RBL.340–1; Put.536.
44. Ib.
45. HAG.Bln.; Twe.88.
46. *Bad Lands Cowboy,* May 27, 1885; Put.533.
47. Ib., 536. For more detail, see Twe. *passim.*
48. Hag.RBL.342.
49. *New York Times,* Aug. 22, 1885; Hag.RBL.342–4.

50. Mor.100; Put.533; other details in this and following paras. from HAG.Bln.; also see TR to B, Aug. 30, 1885 (TRB mss.).
51. TR.Wks.I.30.
52. Ib., 295–6; Hag.RBL.310–11; Sewall in *Forum*, May 1919.
53. Photocopy in TRB. See Put.534–5 for details of the LMSA meeting.
54. Twe.106–7; Dakota clip, n.d., in TRB.
55. Put.538.
56. TR.Wks.I.29. Here TR was perhaps being unduly modest. One Badlands veteran told Herman Hagedorn: "Fer a crittur with a squint he were plumb handy with a gun." HAG.Bln.
57. Put.537.
58. Ib.
59. Wannegan had been hired as a "gofer" in the summer of 1884, and was now night-herder at Maltese Cross. "He was a genial soul, and Roosevelt liked him." Hag.RBL.169, 338.
60. Qu. ib., 348. See also Sew.27.
61. Photostat in TRB.
62. The actual letter TR sent de Morès has disappeared, along with almost all of the Marquis's personal papers. It is said to have stipulated "rifles at twelve paces, the adversaries to shoot until one or the other dropped." (Hag.RBL.348.)
63. According to Hagedorn the Marquis also invited TR to dine with him at Chateau de Morès after the trial. (Ib., 349.)
64. See Put.538–542 for a different interpretation.
65. See TR.Wks.I.269–72 on the aridity of the Badlands.
66. See TR.Auto.110–11 for an account of firefighting on the prairie.
67. Put.542; Hag.RBL.350–2.
68. TR.Wks.I.16. In a New York lecture delivered in January 1886, he was openly contemptuous of the red man. "I don't go so far as to think that the only good Indians are the dead Indians, but I believe nine out of every ten are, and I shouldn't like to inquire too closely into the case of the tenth. The most vicious cowboy has more moral principle than the average Indian." (Qu. Hag.RBL.355.) In later years this harsh attitude mellowed considerably. See Wag.229–30 and below, Ch. 17.
69. Text here follows Putnam's assumption "based on circumstantial evidence" that the trip took place during the first two weeks of Sep. 1885. Put.543.
70. TR.Wks.I.371–3.
71. See TR.Auto.54 for TR's own analysis of courage as something that can be acquired "by sheer dint of practicing fearlessness."
72. Qu. Twe.96–7. Also standing trial were the Marquis's aides and ambush partners, Richard Moore, Frank Miller, and E. G. Paddock. All received the same verdict. See Twe.92 ff.
73. Put.542. The exact date of TR's visit to the Marquis (Hag.RBL.344 and Twe.93) is unknown, but Sep. 16 seems almost certain. He was busy with firefighting, hunting, and the LMSA before that. He definitely left Medora on Sep. 16, and would have passed through Bismarck that same evening.
74. See Put.544 ff. for details.
75. Only once, in Brooklyn on Oct. 17, did he allow himself to make a major speech. Text, which contains a slashing indictment of Democratic race discrimination in the South, is in TR.Wks.XIV. 58–67.
76. Hag.RF.11; Put.555.
77. Both descriptions based on contemporary photographs as well as the general portrait of the young Edith in Morr.EKR.
78. Merrifield to Hagedorn, June 1919, TRB memo; Hag.RF.11; Put.557.
79. Hag.RF.426.
80. Sylvia Jukes Morris; see also below, Ch. 13.
81. "A buffalo is nobler game than an anise-seed bag, the Anglomaniacs to

the contrary notwithstanding." TR to Lodge, Mor.77.
82. See TR in *Century,* Jan. 1886, qu. *World,* Oct. 17, 1886; Mor.90.
83. Lod.1.34–5.
84. TR.Wks.II.294–6; *N.Y.T.,* Oct. 27, 1885.
85. TR.Wks.II.296.
86. Ib.; TR.Auto.32; Lod.I.34.
87. Longworth, Alice Roosevelt, *Crowded Hours* (Scribner's, 1933) 4.
88. Edith's presence at the Ball is confirmed by a letter to her from B, Oct. 23, 1886. Derby mss.
89. Lod.I.35.

13: The Long Arm of the Law

1. TR.1886.Di. *passim;* Put.558.
2. Par.65.
3. Put.557–8 discusses the reaction of TR's sisters to his growing intimacy with Edith.
4. See, e.g., his long letter to B summing up the Chicago Convention of 1884 (Mor.70–72). On such occasions he signs himself formally THEODORE ROOSEVELT instead of his more usual "Thee" or "T.R."
5. The period 1884–1886 is a noticeable lacuna in all Roosevelt collections, including those of his two sisters. What letters survive are usually truncated.
6. Mor.94.
7. Put.558; Mor.94.
8. See Gar.56–8 on HCL's relationship with John T. Morse Jr., editor-in-chief of this highly successful publishing venture.
9. See Put.560 for a quote illustrating the bleak mood of Sewall and Dow. Elsewhere he surmises that TR's engagement was open-ended, and that the lovers parted with "considerable uncertainty." There is no evidence of this. Putnam also errs in saying that TR's sisters "knew the situation." As will be seen, they were kept as much in the dark as anybody that spring.
10. Put.559.
11. TRB.
12. TR.Auto.98.
13. Sew.59; TR.Wks.I.381–2.
14. Ib.
15. Ib., 383; Sew.60.
16. Ib., 67.
17. Put.564.
18. Ib., 569 fn.; TR.Wks.I.383.
19. Ib., 384; Hag.RBL.368.
20. Mor.95; TR.Wks.I.385.
21. TR.1886.Di. Mar. 29; Mor.95. The Arnold volume was probably *Discourses in America* (1885).
22. As indeed it did in May 1888. Reprinted in TR.Wks.I.381–98, it forms the basis of the following narrative.
23. TR.1886.Di.; Hag.RBL.373.
24. TR.Wks.I.386–7.
25. Photographs by TR in TRB; TR.Wks.I.387. Unlike most reporters, TR did not need a notebook. Three or four jotted words in his diary, such as "Hung up by ice," were enough for him to write up a whole day with apparently total recall. His account of the boat chase runs to 7,000 words, based on a few dozen words of diary. See extracts from latter in Hag.RBL.371–9.
26. TR.Wks.I.386.
27. TR.1886.Di.; TR.Wks.I.388.
28. Ib., 388–9; Sew.62–3.
29. TR.Wks.I.389–90. Sewall, writing 33 years later (Sew.64–68), is at pains to give the impression that he, not TR, masterminded the capture of the thieves. Put.565–6 contrasts the two accounts.
30. TR.Wks.I.391.
31. There had recently been a big Indian hunt in the lower Little Missouri Valley, and the country was virtually stripped of wildlife. TR.Wks.I.394.
32. TR.1886.Di. Apr. 1–8; TR.Wks.I. 391–3. "If I'd had any show at all, you'd have sure had to fight, Mr. Roosevelt," said Finnegan after his capture, flushing dark with anger. Ib., 395.

33. Ib., 393–5.
34. Ib., 396.
35. Mor.96. TR's opinions of *War and Peace,* which he read (during the round-up!) later that spring, may be quoted here. Predictably he liked the battle scenes, but was irked by Tolstoy's criticisms of the iniquities of war, while failing "to criticize the various other immoralities he portrays . . . he certainly in so far acts as the apologist for the latter, and the general tone of the book does not seem to me to be in the least conducive to morality." (Interestingly, Tolstoy came to feel the same, albeit by more majestic reasoning.) TR fell in love, as all readers do, with Natasha: "her fickleness as portrayed is truly marvellous; how Pierre could ever have ventured to leave her alone for six weeks after he was married I cannot imagine." See Mor.103.
36. TR.1886.Di.; Sew.72–3; TR.Wks.I. 396–7.
37. Ib., 397–8.
38. Dr. Stickney in un. clip, HAG.Bln.
39. Mor.96.
40. Edith was scheduled to leave for Europe on April 24, 1886 (C to B, Mar. 29, 1886).
41. Put.570; Hag.RBL.388–9; TR.Auto. 119. A simple collation of these three sources establishes the election date as Tuesday, Apr. 12, 1886. Edict qu. Hag.RBL.392.
42. See Put.570–1 for LMSA meeting; also Mor.98, *Bad Lands Cowboy,* Apr. 15, 1886.
43. Clay, John, *My Life on the Range* (1924, reprinted NY Antiquarian Press, 1961) 351–2; Put.571–2; TR to B, Apr. 29.
44. HAG.Bln. *passim.* The last compliment was paid TR by Jack Reuter.
45. TR to B, Mar. 28, 1886.
46. HAG.Bln.; Hag.RBL.91.
47. Merrifield int. in HAG. Bln.
48. Ib.
49. Put.579–80; Mor.91 (TR to HCL, June 23, 1886 misdated 1885—see Putnam's fn.).
50. TR to B, June 19, 1886 (TRB); Mor.103.
51. Ib., 105.
52. TR to B, Apr. 29, 1886; Put.578.
53. Hag.RBL.398. According to Sewall in HAG.Bln., TR occasionally suffered from writer's block, and would read pages of manuscript to his men for their opinion.
54. Mor.95.
55. Mor.102 (text slightly amended to conform with original in Mass. Hist. Soc.).
56. Put.579; Mor.108.
57. It was superseded only by W. M. Meig's biography in 1904. *Benton* is reprinted in TR.Wks.VII.1–233.
58. *The Nation,* Mar. 29, 1888. This prestigious journal gave *Benton* a major, 3-column review. Along with the negative comments quoted in text, it praised TR's "lively and energetic development of the Western character" and "many acute and sensible verdicts on the great men of that time." *The New York Times* (May 15) called *Benton* "stirring, argumentative, bold . . . singularly entertaining." Both papers noted TR's tendency to overattack people and policies he disapproved of.
59. TR.Wks.VII.15.
60. Ib., 30; 232; 145.
61. Ib., 79–80.
62. Ib., 156–7. TR nevertheless agreed that "in any purely American community manhood suffrage works infinitely better than would any other system of government . . . in spite of the large number of ignorant foreign-born or colored voters." (Ib.) His views on race and sex discrimination would be labelled "paternalistic" and "chauvinistic" today. Suffice to say they were advanced for his time, and became more so as he grew older.
63. TR.Wks.VII.27.

64. Ib., 172.
65. Ib., 169–70. See Put.574–9 for another review of *Benton.*
66. TR.1886.Di.
67. Hag.RBL.402; HAG.Bln.
68. Sew.16; Hag.RBL.16.
69. Hag.405; Mor.107.
70. *Dickinson Free Press,* July 10, 1886 (TRB); Hag.RBL.406.
71. *Press,* same date; Hag.RBL.407.
72. HAG.Bln.
73. *Press,* same date. The critical listener was Lispenard Stewart (memo in TRB). But see Stickney and Packard in Hag.RBL.409–11, and *Mandan Pioneer,* July 9, 1886: "He made a very favorable impression upon all."
74. *Mandan Pioneer,* same date; Mor.107.
75. Qu. Hag.RBL.583. See also Packard in *Sat. Eve. Post,* May 14, 1905.
76. Hag.RBL.411.
77. As recently as June 28 he had written Bamie: "I cannot tell exactly when I will be home; it will be between the middle of September and the middle of October; make your plans entirely without reference to me." (TRB.) See also Put.581, 583.
78. Hag.RBL.412–3; Mor.107.
79. Ib. 109.
80. TR to B, Sep. 20, 1886.
81. Put.586.
82. TR to B, Aug. 20, 1886.
83. Ib., Sep. 20, 1886; Put.86; Sew.74.
84. *Bismarck Tribune,* Aug. 12, 1886.
85. Qu. Wag.87–8; see also Put.557 and fn.
86. The incident involved the imprisonment, by Mexicans, of an American journalist, and the subsequent killing, by Mexicans, of a U.S. Army officer. Put.586; Mor.158.
87. Put.585–6; Mor.108; TR.Wks.378; Mor.109.
88. Mor.101; Hag.RBL.415–6; TR. Wks.I. 289–90.
89. Mor.109.
90. For an account of this trip, see TR.Wks.I.444–59 and Put.586–8. TR to B, Aug. 20, 1886.
91. See *N.Y.T.,* Aug. 29, for the initial rumor; also a strong denial, evidently inspired by TR, in ib., Sep. 5. TR to B, Sep. 20, 1886. The original of this very important letter appears to have been suppressed. Fortunately the typed transcript survives at TRB. Apparently TR never overcame his dread of the dead Alice Lee's censure. Many years later, "Baby Lee" mused regarding her father's marriages, "He was always so full of guilt." *Washington Post* int., Feb. 12, 1974.
92. TR to B, Sep. 20, 1886; Sew.92; see financial analysis in Put.588–90.
93. Hag.RBL.424–5; Sew.93.
94. Brown, Dee, *Trail Driving Days* (Scribner's, 1952) 224–5.
95. Ib.; Hag.RBL.431.
96. Lan.239–42; Hag.RBL.431; Brown, *Trail Driving,* 225.
97. Put.590; Sew.95.

14: The Next Mayor of New York

Important sources not listed in Bibliography: 1. Nevins, Allan, *Abram S. Hewitt, with Some Account of Peter Cooper* (Harpers, 1935).

1. *New York Times,* Oct. 14, 15, 1886; *Leslie's Illustrated,* Oct. TR had reached Oyster Bay from Dakota on October 8.
2. Alex.144; see Ch. 7. George had been nominated on Sep. 23, 1886.
3. Nevins, *Hewitt,* 467; TR.Wks.VII. 136.
4. Alex.76; Nevins, *Hewitt,* 461–4.
5. Bailey, Thomas A., *The American Pageant* (Boston, 1956) 555; see Barker, C., *Henry George* (1955).
6. Nevins, *Hewitt,* 461; Condon, Thomas J., "Politics, Reform, and the Election of 1886," *New-York Historical Society Quarterly,* Vol. 44.4 (Oct. 1960) 367. 1886 was a year of great unrest in the labor movement. In all,

about 1,500 strikes occurred across the country, crippling at least 10,000 establishments. Chicago was chosen by the half-million strong Knights of Labor as a focal point of a number of May Day strikes. That city was also, unfortunately, home to several hundred anarchists, who used the strikes to further their own violent aims. The Knights therefore became associated, in the public mind, with communist subversives. Tensions built up rapidly in Chicago, and on May 4, at a labor meeting in Haymarket Square, somebody threw a dynamite bomb which killed seven policemen and wounded seventy bystanders. TR's reaction to this incident was typical. "My men here in Dakota are hardworking, laboring men, who work longer hours for no greater wages than the strikers; but they are Americans through and through; I believe nothing would give them greater pleasure than a chance with their rifles at one of the mobs . . . In relation to the dynamite business they become more furiously angry and excited than I do. I wish I had them with me, and a fair show at ten times our number of rioters; my men shoot well and fear very little." Nevins, *Hewitt,* 463–1; Alex.74 ff.; Bailey, *Pageant,* 537–9; Put.603; Mor.100.

7. GEO., un. clip, Oct. 6, 1886.

8. *World,* Sep. 26, 1886; Alex.112; see Ch. 9.

9. *New York Journal,* Oct. 16, 1886.

10. Mor.111; *New York Tribune,* Oct. 16, 1886.

11. Mor.111.

12. *World,* Oct. 17, 1886; Mor.111. The local Republican party was somewhat embarrassed for funds in 1886. Before turning to TR, the bosses had considered nominating such millionaires as William H. Astor and Cornelius Vanderbilt. (GEO., un. clip.)

13. See below, Ch. 15.

14. See, e.g., *New York Star,* Oct. 17, 1886; Alex.79; *Sun,* Oct. 21.

15. Nevins, *Hewitt,* is the standard biography.

16. Nevins, *Hewitt,* 465; *Encyclopaedia Britannica,* 1970 ed., 11.467.

17. E. L. Godkin in *The Nation,* Oct. 14, 1886. "Der's no use tryin'," TR's old backer Joe Murray said of a youthful Roosevelt supporter. "Yer can nominate him, but yer can't elect him." Asked why not, Murray explained, "Why, if he were elected mayor, der boys [Hess, Biglin, *et al.*] wouldn't have peace day or night—and dey knows it." A. W. Callisen to TR, May 14, 1916 (TRP).

18. Mor.111–2, 115.

19. *Star,* Oct. 16, 1886; *Trib.,* same date; *N.Y.T.,* Oct. 17.

20. Ib.; *Trib.,* Oct. 16. See Mor.110–11 for TR's acceptance letter.

21. *Sun,* Oct. 21, 1886; *Eve. Post,* same date.

22. Ib., Oct. 27, 1886.

23. Mor.112–3.

24. See TR.Wks.XIV.70–1.

25. Mor.114.

26. *Star,* Oct. 28, 1886.

27. *N.Y.T.,* Oct. 28, 1886; *Journal, Mail and Express,* same date.

28. *N.Y.T.,* Oct. 28, 1886; *Star,* same date.

29. *Telegram, Mail and Express, Trib., N.Y.T., Journal.*

30. GEO. *passim.* TR's double-dictation technique was as follows. While reporters scribbled down his answer to a question, he would dictate some rapid sentences to his stenographer; while she scribbled those, he turned his attention to the next press question, apparently with no loss of continuity on either side. (*Mail and Express,* Oct. 18, 1886.)

31. Ib.

32. *Sun,* Oct. 26, 1886.

33. The following account of the Cooper Hall meeting is based on *N.Y.T.,* Oct. 28, 1886; supplementary

details from *Trib., Star, World,* same date.
34. *N.Y.T.,* Oct. 28, 1886.
35. *Commercial Advertiser,* Oct. 27, 1886.
36. *World,* Oct. 28.
37. *Daily News, Trib.,* Oct. 29, 1886.
38. See TR's own Oct. 28 analysis in Mor.8.1426. See also *Trib.,* Nov. 4, 1886, for his confession that there was a mid-campaign moment when victory seemed possible.
39. Alex.71.
40. Ib., 71; Nev.460–2; GEO. clip., un., Oct. 5, 1886; Nev.464.
41. *Daily Graphic,* Oct. 22, 1886. This slogan was repeatedly bandied by Democratic newspapers as the campaign progressed.
42. *Trib.,* Oct. 29.
43. B to Edith in Europe, Oct. 23, 1886. (Derby mss.)
44. The following narrative based on *N.Y.T.,* Oct. 29, 1886; *Trib.,* same date.
45. See ib.: "Mr. Roosevelt has given much attention to the colored men, among whom he is a favorite."
46. Ib.
47. Ib.; *N.Y.T.,* Oct. 29, 1886.
48. Bamie had relocated earlier in the year to 689 Madison Avenue.
49. *Mail and Express,* Oct, 30, 1886.
50. *World,* Oct. 31, 1886. Hewitt, in appealing for Republican votes, suavely played on TR's fears. "I trust that at some future time he will receive the reward due to his energy, his ability, and his character, but he has made a mistake. He has allowed himself to be the tool of designing men." Qu. Nevins, *Hewitt,* 468.
51. *Sun,* Oct. 31, 1886.
52. *Her.,* Oct. 31, 1886.
53. GEO. *passim.*
54. *Journal,* Oct. 26, 1886; *Daily Graphic,* Nov. 1.
55. Lincoln, Charles T., ed., *Messages from the Governors,* VII, 1072, qu. Nevins, *Hewitt,* 142.
56. *Her.,* Oct. 31, 1886; *Trib.,* Oct. 29.
57. *Her.,* Oct. 31, 1886.
58. *Mail and Express,* Oct. 30, 1896; Nevins, *Hewitt,* 463; Condon, "Election of 1886," 363.
59. For a more optimistic election-eve forecast, see *Trib.,* Nov. 1, 1886.
60. *Telegram,* Nov. 3, 1886.
61. GEO. clip, un., Nov. 3, 1886.
62. *Her.,* 3.
63. Nevins, *Hewitt,* 468.
64. This was TR's first defeat at the polls. He would not suffer another such until 1912.
65. *Sun,* Nov. 3, 1886; Lod.150.
66. *Sun,* Nov. 4, 1886; *World,* same date.
67. Alex.82. Nevins's figures differ slightly at 90,466, 67,930, and 60,477. Historically, the average Republican Mayoral vote was 98,715 (*Eve. Post,* Nov. 3, 1886).
68. Alex.82–3; *Eve. Post,* Nov. 3, 1886.
69. *Trib.,* Nov. 4, 1886.
70. "I do not disguise from myself that this is the end of my political career," TR told Robert Underwood Johnson. The poet wrote many years later: "I cannot remember to have seen a man so cast down by political defeat." Johnson in TR.Wks.X.342.
71. Luther B. Little int. FRE. See also Alex.83, and Abbot, Lawrence F., *Impressions of TR,* 6: "I never heard him talk about it—as he was glad to do about his other political experiences."
72. *Daily Graphic,* Nov. 3, 1886. For sample range of other comments, see *Comm. Adv.,* Nov. 3; letter to *Eve. Post,* Nov. 5; F. B. House int. FRE. Other recommended reading: Hurwitz, Howard L., *TR and Labor in New York State,* 1880–1900, and Condon, "Election of 1886."
73. *N.Y.T.,* Nov. 7, 1886; COW; see also Mor.115. The *Times* erroneously reported next day that Corinne and her husband, Douglas Robinson, sailed

with them too. Why TR was at such pains to conceal his departure, now that the campaign was over, is a mystery. Perhaps he merely felt weary of crowds and fuss. The formal news of his engagement certainly caused a sensation. Elliott, who saw TR off, went on to a society wedding afterward and found the congregation buzzing with conversation, not about the bride and groom, but about Edith and Theodore. (E to B, Nov. 10, 1886, FDR.)

74. *N.Y.T.*, Nov. 7 and 8, 1886.

75. All from COW.

76. Portrait of CSR from Gwy. *passim;* Roosevelt family letters; COW.; Cha.

77. *N.Y.T.*, Nov. 14, 1886; TR.Auto. 33; COW.

78. TR.Auto.33.

79. COW.

80. Gwy.48. "Roosevelt was surprised to find that Henry George's campaign for the Mayoralty had been widely publicized in Britain, and that he in consequence was something of a celebrity." *Her.*, Mar. 28, 1887. Mor.116–7. George Joachim Goschen, Liberal Cabinet minister, just about to become Lord Randolph Churchill's successor as Chancellor of the Exchequer. John Morley, Liberal statesman and distinguished literary biographer (for his later opinion of TR, see Prologue). James Bryce, statesman, scholar, and one of the most brilliant conversationalists in England. He was then engaged on his classic *The American Commonwealth*. (See Ch. 15.) Morley and Bryce were to become TR's lifelong friends.

81. COW.

82. Ib. TR's and Edith's addresses are on their marriage certificate, reproduced in Lor.240. Under "Rank or Profession" TR wrote: "Ranchman."

83. Mor.117.

84. COW; Gwy.48. Both men were nearly late for the ceremony, having been "intensely occupied in a discussion of the population of an island in the Southern Pacific." (Bamie, qu. Gwy.48).

85. TR to William Sewall, TRB memo. Apparently, TR's quietude did not last. For an amusing anecdote about his too-exuberant Americanism in London, see Harris, Frank, *Contemporary Portraits* (New York, 1915), 266–68.

Interlude

Important sources not listed in Bibliography: 1. Mattison, Ray H., "The Hard Winter and the Range Cattle Business," *Montana Magazine of History,* Vol. 1.4 (Winter, 1950). This is authority for all the chronological details in the following account, supplemented by *Dickinson Press* and *Mandan Pioneer* coverage, October 1886–March 1887. Files in North Dakota State Historical Society.

1. Brown, Dee, *Trail Driving Days* (Scribner's, 1952) 224–5; Lan.245–6.

2. Mattison, "Winter," 10 ff.; Lan.24 ff.

3. Put.592; Lan.242 ff.; HAG.Bln.

4. TR.Auto.98.

5. Earl Henderson, pioneer, in Fifty Years in the Saddle Club, *Looking Back Down the Trail,* Vol. 1 (Watford City, N.D., 1963) 230.

6. Mattison, "Winter," 11.

7. Ib.

8. Brown, *Trail Driving,* 225; Lan. 242–3; Mattison, "Winter," 12; "A Dakota Blizzard," anonymous article in *Atlantic,* Dec. 1888.

9. TR.Wks.I.346–7; Mattison, "Winter," 12.

10. Brown, *Trail Driving,* 225.

11. "A Dakota Blizzard"; Hag. RBL.435–6; TR.Wks.I.346; Brown, *Trail Driving,* 225.

12. *Bismarck Tribune,* Nov. 1886, qu. Hag.RBL.430; TR.Wks.I.347; *Mandan Pioneer,* Jan. 28, 1887; Hag.RBL.435; Mattison, "Winter," 12; Lan.259.

13. Ib.; Hag.RBL.436–8; Mattison, "Winter," 14; HAG.Bln; Lan.594.
14. Qu. HAG.438.
15. Hag.RBL.439; Clay, John, *My Life on the Range* (NY Antiquarian Press, 1961) 179. See Robinson, Elwyn B., *History of North Dakota* (U. of Nebraska Press, 1966) 190–6 for the effect of the winter on the economy of the Dakotas. For details of its particular effect on TR's business, see below.

15: The Literary Feller

1. This, the fourth of TR's pre-presidential trips to Europe, was, with a fifth quick visit to Paris in 1892, to make TR the most widely traveled Chief Executive since John Quincy Adams. The Roosevelts' honeymoon itinerary was as follows. After the wedding they crossed the Channel to begin "an idyllic three weeks trip" south to Provence via Paris and Lyons. They made their "leisurely way" from Hyères along the French and Italian Rivieras by carriage to Pisa, then visited Florence and Rome before moving south to Naples, which they reached on Jan. 16, 1887. After exploring Sorrento and Capri they began to move north again, revisiting Rome early in February before going on to Venice, where they took moonlit gondola rides and witnessed that rarest and most beautiful of phenomena, a Venetian snowstorm. They crossed over to Milan, whose pillared Cathedral reminded TR of Rocky Mountain forests. In Paris he decided he was too poor to order a cellarful of claret for Sagamore Hill, yet splurged on three days of classical riding lessons at an *école d'équitation*. The Roosevelts returned to London about Feb. 23, 1887, and after three weeks in that city sailed from Liverpool on March 19. TR to B, Dec. 3, 1886–Mar. 12, 1887; also Lod.52–3.
2. *New York Times, Herald, Sun, Tribune,* all Mar. 28, 1887. See also TR to C re his "daily overeating," Mor.118–9.
3. Ib., 123.
4. Ib., 123–6; TR to B, Mar. 12, 1887.
5. *Trib.*, Mar. 28, 1887; *Her., N.Y.T., Sun,* same date.
6. See TR to B, Jan. 10, 1887.
7. TR to B, Sep. 20, 1886. In fact he insisted. "Theodore has against my will insisted on my keeping Baby," Bamie wrote Nannie Lodge on Nov. 2, 1886.
8. TR to B, Jan. 10, 1887.
9. TR to B, Apr. 16 and May 16, 1887.
10. Nor, apparently, could Alice. She loved Bamie extravagantly always, while preserving at best an ambiguous relationship with Edith. In old age Alice remarked sadly that "Auntie Bye did talk about my mother to me . . . none of the others ever mentioned her." (Int. Nov. 9, 1954, TRB.)
11. Ib.
12. Rixey, Lilian, *Bamie: TR's Remarkable Sister* (David McKay, 1963) 68; Gwy.60–1.
13. See Wag.210–16.
14. TR to B, Jan. 3, 1887. The words are Theodore's, but the thoughts are manifestly Edith's.
15. Ib. The hunting horse, at least, won a reprieve, for TR became quite maudlin about it. See Mor.119. EKR, meanwhile, had to operate Sagamore Hill on a budget of something like half of what B had spent there. (Hag.RF.15.)
16. TR.Wks.I.347; TR to W. Sewall, qu. Hag.RBL.441; Lan.246; Hag.RBL. 438.
17. Ib., 441; TR.Wks.I.347. Over the years he had bought a total of 3,000 head (Put.523 fn.), which reproduction probably raised to around 4,000 in 1886. One authority, Elwyn B. Robinson in *History of North Dakota*, puts the total as high as 5,000.
18. Lan.259; Mattison, Ray H., "The Hard Winter and the Range Cattle Business," *Montana Magazine of History,* Vol. 1.4 (Winter, 1950) 18.

19. Put.594; Lan.246–59; *North Dakota History,* Vol. 17.3; Mattison, "Winter," *passim.*
20. TR.Wks.I.347; author's estimate; Put.594. TR told a fellow-rancher he was "utterly crushed by the fearful tragedy." Hoffman, W. Roy, *TR: His Adventuring Spirit* (unpublished ms. in TRB) qu. Pierre Wibaux, 311.
21. Mor.126. Actually the figure was in excess of $85,000. See Put.523 fn. and 588 fn. TR had himself predicted during the fall of 1886 that an overall loss of 50% would affect the range cattle industry should a harsh winter strike the overgrazed Badlands. See TR.Wks.I.290. Not for twelve years did he finally manage to extricate himself. During that period Merrifield and Ferris succeeded, by judicious management, in reducing his loss to $20,292. Put.595. But in 1887 any such relief seemed inconceivable.
22. Mor.127.
23. Lan.259; *Dickinson Press,* Jan.–April 1887, *passim;* Hag.RBL.451–2; Put.595–6; Lan.263; Twe.111–5; HAG. Bln.
24. *Dickinson Press,* May 7, 1887; Clay, John, *My Life on the Range* (NY Antiquarian Press, 1961) and Twe. *passim.*
25. Twe.70; Hag.RBL.450; John Goodall, pioneer, qu. Fifty Years in the Saddle Club, *Looking Back Down the Trail,* 288. Soon after TR arrived home, he must have read that the Marquis had been arrested in New York for nonpayment of business debts. See, e.g., *Sun,* May 20, 1887. De Morès bought his way out of this and other American entanglements, escaping to Europe later that summer. He returned to the Badlands only once, but like TR came only to hunt. After visits to India and China he settled in his native country and became an arch-reactionary, fighting on behalf of French royalists to overthrow the Republican government. He was for a while an ardent disciple of Boulanger. Later the Marquis decided that Jews were responsible for France's economic and social ills. In May 1892 he was seen, immaculate in tails and top hat, throwing spitballs at Juliette de Rothschild's wedding. Tiring once more of "civilization," he went in 1896 to Morocco, hoping to promote a Franco-Islamic alliance against the British Empire. While crossing the Sahara en route to Sudan he was ambushed and killed by a band of Tuaregs. Brave to the end, de Morès left a circle of dead tribesmen around him before collapsing into the sand. His funeral in Paris was a public event. In its front-page obituary, *Le Figaro* commented: "Morès was always marvellously optimistic . . . everywhere that he went was like a novel of chivalry . . . he was the classic man of action, officer, agitator, or colonial of old France." *Le Siècle* viewed him somewhat differently. "Morès was a dangerous madman." For a full account of the Marquis's later years, see Twe.
26. Robinson, *History of N.D.,* 190–6.
27. TR.Wks.I.17.
28. TR.Auto.111–2; Dantz, qu. HAG. Bln.; Merrifield, qu. ib. ("Roosevelt had a great weakness for bad men."); Erskine, Gladys S., *Bronco Charlie: A Saga of the Saddle* (NY, 1934) 231–2; Hag.RBL.116. "I can't tell why in the world I like you," TR told Hell-Roaring Bill Jones, "for you're the nastiest-talking man I ever heard."
29. On Apr. 15, 1897, TR was re-elected as chairman of the Little Missouri Stockmen's Association. *Dickinson Press,* Apr. 16. See also Put.528.
30. As early as August 1886, at the time of the Mexican war scare, the cowboys were anxious to follow TR into battle. See TR.Wks.I.378.
31. See, e.g., TR's famous letter of Aug. 9, 1903, to John Hay, in Mor.3.547 ff.

32. Vollweiler, Albert T., "Roosevelt's Ranch Life in North Dakota," *U. North Dakota Quarterly Journal* 9.1 (Oct. 1918).
33. See Alex.102–4.
34. Fourth-Class Postmasters were fired by the thousands, effecting a complete purge in two years; all 85 IRS inspectors were replaced, as were 100 of the nation's 111 Customs Collectors. (Alex.102.)
35. GC vetoed 413 bills in his first Administration. (Ib. 114.)
36. The wedding took place on June 2, 1886. See Nev.
37. *N.Y.T.*, May 11, 1887.
38. Ib.; *World*, May 12, 1887.
39. *N.Y.T.*, May 12, 1887; *Sun*, May 15. For a list of notables attending, see *Trib.*, May 12.
40. The following account of TR's speech is collated from *N.Y.T.*, *Trib.*, *World*, *Sun*, *Her.*, *Eve. Post*, and *Daily Graphic*, May 12–16, 1887.
41. TR grudgingly allowed that GC had made some good appointments to the U.S. Treasury, and was taken aback by an unexpected burst of applause. Nev.367.
42. *Trib.*, May 12, 1887.
43. Interestingly, Depew himself was a Presidential candidate at that time, and his remarks were interpreted by some as a put-down of the youthful TR.
44. Qu. *Sun*, May 16, 1887.
45. Ib.
46. Ib.
47. *N.Y.T.*, May 13, 1887.
48. Un. clip, TRB; *N.Y.T.*, May 13, 1887.
49. Ib.
50. *Eve. Post*, May 13, 1887.
51. *N.Y.T.*, May 15, 1887; TR.Auto. 329–30; TR to B, May 21, 1887.
52. Lod.55; Hag.RF.15.
53. TR to B, Feb. 12, 1887.
54. TR.Wks.VII.241; Mor.131.
55. *N.Y.T.*, May 6, 1888. See Gar.56 for an alternate explanation of editor-in-chief Morse's decision to commission the book. *Morris* is reprinted in TR.Wks.VII.235–470, and in a recent special edition by the Theodore Roosevelt Association of Oyster Bay, N.Y. (1975). This edition carries an introduction by John A. Gable, "Theodore Roosevelt as Historian and Man of Letters," vii–xxiv.
56. Lod.57. See also Mor.7.175.
57. Lod.55. See also Gable, "Historian," x.
58. Ib.
59. Mor.131.
60. TR.Wks.VII.306.
61. Ib., 324.
62. Ib., 328.
63. Ib., 329, 456, 336.
64. Ib., 459, 421.
65. Ib., 464, 459, 469.
66. *The Book Buyer*, May 1888; *N.Y.T.*, May 6; *Dial*, May 1888. For a more positive review, see *The Critic*, July 21: "We are struck with the author's wide, if not profound reading of purely European political and general literature . . . crisp and even classic English . . . freely strung pearls of thought . . . sparkling on every page." The *Boston Advertiser* came up with a telling line in its review of Apr. 4: "He [TR] seems to have been born with his mind made up." The line may have been contributed, tongue-in-cheek, by the paper's owner, Henry Cabot Lodge.
67. Mor.119.
68. TR to C, June 8, 1887 (TRB photostat).
69. Rob.130; TR to B, Sep. 9, 1887; TR to C, June 8, Lod.57; TR to B, Aug. 20; Rob.130.
70. Gwy.67. This remark echoes one made privately by HCL, two years before in his diary: "The more I see him, as the fellow says in the play, the more and more I love him." Qu. Put.506.
71. TR to B, Sep. 11, 1887; ib., Sep. 13, 1888.

72. As *persona non grata* in political circles, TR had taken no part in the New York State fall campaign, and his departure West was obviously timed to spare him the agony of witnessing another Democratic landslide in the election on Nov. 8. "The Republican party seems moribund," he despairingly wrote afterward. (To B, Nov. 20, 1887.)
73. TR to B, Nov. 13, 1888. The cousin was West Roosevelt, and the friend Frank Underhill.
74. TR.Wks.I.409.
75. Ib., 79; Lan.223–4.
76. Ib., 222–4. Lincoln Lang was an early and passionate conservationist, far ahead of his time. It was his considered opinion that TR was so sickened by the environmental damage suffered by the Badlands in 1886 (*before* the Great Blizzard) that he had decided to give up the cattle business "several months before he actually did." (Ib., 225.)
77. See Clay, *Life on the Range*, 43.
78. TR to MBR, Apr. 28, 1868 (see Ch. 1).
79. TR.Wks.II.160.
80. See Cut. *passim* for TR's early conservationist instincts.
81. Lan.223–4.
82. TR to B, Nov. 20, 1887; Grinnell in TR.Wks.I.xiv–xvii.
83. Rules qu. in TR's own description of the Club, *Harper's Weekly*, Mar. 1893.
84. Ib.; Grinnell in TR.Wks.I.xvii; TR in *Harper's Weekly*, Mar. 1893.
85. Cut.70; TR.Wks.I.xvii–i.
86. Cut.70–3; TR in *Harper's Weekly*, Mar. 1893.
87. Cut.78; TR.Wks.I.xviii.
88. Eugene Swope, curator Roosevelt Bird Sanctuary at Oyster Bay, to Helen Elizabeth Reed (TRC).
89. Cut.79.
90. See TR to B, Feb. 12, 1887.
91. The eminent historian David Seville Muzzey, writing in 1927, called the act "one of the most noteworthy measures ever passed in the history of this nation." Qu. Cut.72.
92. See Nev.383 ff.
93. $55 million on Dec. 1, 1887. By the end of the fiscal year 1888 it was expected to grow to $140 million. Nev.375.
94. See Sto.152.
95. Ib., 153.
96. Nev.395.
97. Mor.136; Lod.62; Har.73.
98. Mor.136. TR had made a similar confession to HCL about a year earlier (Lod.51), but had failed to act upon it. Mor.705.
99. Although once, when writing the first chapter of *Benton*, he described it as "an outline I intend to fill up." Mor.94.
100. E.g., Mor.141.
101. Ib., 134–5; also 133. *Commonwealth* was duly proclaimed a masterpiece when it appeared in December 1888, and is regarded as such to this day.
102. Bryce, James, *The American Commonwealth* (N.Y., 1888) I.540–2, II.103, 119, 173, has extensive quotes from TR's essays on legislative and municipal corruption.
103. Later the theme was extended still further, to include the more recent settlements of New Mexico and Arizona, covering two full centuries of American history.
104. Mor.140.
105. See Gable, "TR as Historian," xi–xxiv for a modern historiographical assessment of TR. *The Winning of the West* is extensively discussed below, in Ch. 18.
106. Mor.140; also see below.
107. TR's trip to the South lasted from Mar. 21 to about Apr. 3, 1888; he visited Washington at least twice, in late January and early March.

108. Mor.197.
109. The manuscript of *The Winning of the West* is now in the New York Public Library.
110. TR to B, July 1, 1888.
111. TR to Brander Matthews, Oct. 5, 1888.
112. See TR to B, Oct. 13, 1889, when he complains that his new income of $3,500 will be "700/800 dollars" less than his income as a writer in 1888.
113. Norton, Charles Eliot, *Walt Whitman as Man, Poet, and Friend* (Boston, 1919), 216.
114. Lod.56; See *N.Y.T.*, Nov. 30, 1888: "Cleverly told, very handsome and interesting." Also *The Book Buyer*, Dec. 1888: "To a most readable style of writing Mr. Roosevelt adds a thorough familiarity with his subject, happily combining accuracy with entertainment."
115. TR to B, July 13, 1888.
116. Mor.145–9; TR to B, Sep. 18, 1888.
117. Ib.; Mor.147.
118. Mor.142.
119. Pla.252: ". . . he was as glacial as a Siberian stripped of his furs."
120. Mor.148; Tha.84.
121. Mor.149.
122. Manuscript in New York Public Library.
123. TR to B, n.d., 1888.
124. COW.
125. George Haven Putnam in TR.Wks.IX.xv; see also Mor.197.
126. Mor.163.
127. Ib., 156.
128. Ib.
129. Lod.74.
130. Gar.104; Har.74.
131. Mor.154.
132. Lod.76; HCL to W. R. Thayer, Oct. 7, 1919.
133. There is a good account of these celebrations in the *Sun*, May 1, 1889.
134. Ib.; Foraker, Mrs. Julia, *I Would Live It Again* (Harpers, 1932) 167–8.

16: The Silver-Plated Reform Commissioner

Important sources not listed in Bibliography: 1. 51st Congress, 1st session, *Report of the House Committee on Civil Service Reform,* Serial #2823, Document #2445 (1890). Hereafter cited as *House Report* 1. 2. Foulke, William D., *Fighting the Spoilsmen: Reminiscences of the Civil Service Reform Movement* (Putnam, 1919).
1. The following description is based on the unexcelled reporting of "Carp" (Frank G. Carpenter, Washington correspondent of the *Cleveland Daily Leader*) excerpted in *Carp's Washington* (McGraw-Hill, 1960). Other details from Green, Constance McLaughlin, *Washington—Capital City, 1879–1950* (Princeton U. Press, 1962) Vol. 2 *passim;* contemporary guidebooks.
2. G. W. Steevens, qu. Green, *Washington,* 77.
3. Ib., 77–8.
4. Green, *Washington,* 12.
5. Carpenter, 102.
6. Ib., 8, 296–7.
7. Ib., 110, 306, 329, 80 ff.
8. See, e.g., Gar.104.
9. *Washington Post,* May 12, 19, 1889.
10. Green, *Washington,* 13.
11. Figures projected from those qu. ib., 80.
12. See Lod.77.
13. Washington *Star,* May 13, 1889; ib., May 19. The appointment was made official on May 7, 1889.
14. W. *Star,* May 13, 1889.
15. The author may be forgiven this surmise. If anything was at all times predictable about TR, it was his habit of taking stairs two—or even three—at a time. William Loeb, Jr., his godson, remembers him in gouty old age, thun-

dering upstairs with boyish energy. "I didn't know any other adults that *ran* upstairs. The ones I knew generally walked." (To author, Feb. 28, 1975.) The location of the Civil Service Commission (henceforth CSC) is given in Halloran, Matthew F., *The Romance of the Merit System* (Washington, 1929) 51–2 and 166–7. Note that Pringle's location (Pri.121) is incorrect. The CSC did not move to Eighth and E until later.

16. Halloran, *Romance,* 56.

17. *W. Star,* May 13, 1891.

18. Bis.I.46. Within ten months of becoming Commissioner, TR's effective power in the agency was estimated as "two-thirds" by the *Chicago Morning News* (Mar. 28, 1890) and "seven-eighths" by another paper (TR.Scr.).

19. Mor.192. At various points in the TR/Lodge correspondence Lyman is "dreary," "mushy," and "a chump." (Oct. 27, 1889; Aug. 23, Sep. 23, 1890.)

20. TR to B, n.d., 1889 (TRB).

21. See Halloran, n. 15 above.

22. Thayer, William Roscoe, *TR: An Intimate Biography* (Houghton Mifflin, 1919) 88.

23. For the early history of Civil Service Reform up to and including TR's Commissionership, see Sageser, A. Bower, "The First Two Decades of the Pendleton Act," *Nebraska University Studies,* Vols. 34–35 (1934–35); White, D., *The Republican Era, 1869–1901* (Macmillans, 1958); van Riper, Paul, *History of the USCSC* (Evanston, Ill., 1958); Hoogenboom, Ari, "The Pendleton Act and the Civil Service," *American Historical Review,* 64.2 (Jan. 1959).

24. Mor.57, 154, 153. Foulke, *Spoilsmen,* 12.

25. W. *Star,* May 14, 1889; Wise, John S., *Recollections of Thirteen Presidents* (NY, 1906) 200.

26. See Sto.164; also 181–4; Depew, Chauncey, *My Memories of Eighty Years* (Scribner's, 1922) 133–4.

27. Qu. Carpenter, 305.

28. *W. Post,* May 15, 1889.

29. W. *Star,* May 14; *W. Post,* May 15, 1889.

30. Ib.; Har.78; Pri.123. Carl Schurz wrote that Wanamaker's appointment "was the first instance in the history of the Republic that a place in the Cabinet had been given for a pecuniary consideration." Sageser, "Two Decades," 135.

31. Foulke, William D., *Lucius Burrie Swift* (Bobbs-Merrill, 1930) 39.

32. Ib., 41; Pri.123.

33. Foulke, *Spoilsmen,* 11–12; USCSC, *Sixth Report* (1889).

34. Bis.I.45; Halloran, *Romance,* 52–5.

35. Ib., 76.

36. It is amusing for those familiar with TR's love of making delayed entrances to follow the shrewd build-up of suspense that preceded his arrival in Washington. Although he had long since accepted the Commissionership, he deliberately avoided telling his colleagues when he would report for duty. The press daily enquired as to TR's whereabouts, and the Commissioners daily replied that they did not know. Lyman even exclaimed, rather irritably, that he still had "no intimation" whether TR would indeed take the job. Consequently, when the laggard arrived at last, on May 13, his oath-taking rated front-page headlines in that evening's paper, along with the information that he had established himself in the CSC's largest office. See *W. Star,* May 8, 9, 10, and 13, 1889.

37. Mor.8.1429; *N.Y. Tribune,* May 22, 1889; Foulke, *Spoilsmen,* 13.

38. Mor.165; *W. Star,* June 18, 1889; Foulke, *Swift,* 37; Foulke, *Spoilsmen,* 13. According to the *N.Y. Evening Post,* June 19, Wallace was BH's old law partner.

39. W. *Star,* June 19, 1889; Foulke, *Swift,* 37.

40. Foulke, *Spoilsmen,* 13–14; *Swift,* 37.
41. Foulke, *Spoilsmen,* 14; see also W. *Star,* June 19, 1889.
42. Mor.165, 166.
43. Ib.
44. *Milwaukee Daily Journal,* June 20, 1889; *House Report 1,* 307.
45. Lod.79.
46. *House Report 1,* 150, 161.
47. Ib., 324, 326, and *passim.*
48. Ib., 220, 263, 303.
49. Ib., 303.
50. W. *Post,* June 25, 1889, has text of the first report; *House Report 1,* 324 ff. has text of the second. See also ib., 175.
51. Ib., 327.
52. Mor.167.
53. Ib., 168.
54. Sample editorial opinion, in *Chicago Morning News,* June 26, 1889: "One of the conspicuous successes of President Harrison's administration is the Hon. Teddy Roosevelt . . . More power to him! He has made various spoilsmen of his party as mad as hornets, and he seems to be glad of it." TR.Scr. give a good idea of the publicity surrounding his Midwestern "slam": it made headlines as far away as San Francisco.
55. Mor.168–9.
56. N.Y. *Trib.,* June 30, 1889.
57. Mor.173.
58. *House Report 1,* 177–80. See also testimony below.
59. TR to HCL, July 11, 1889. A fair example of the invective which Lodge deleted when preparing his correspondence with TR for publication. See Bibl., LOD.
60. Mor.171–2.
61. *House Report 1,* 150.
62. Details from Carpenter, 237–8; W. *Post* and *Star,* July–Aug. 1889, *passim.*
63. Mor.169, 172, 177, 174.
64. Ib., 172.
65. Ib., fn.
66. *N.Y. Herald,* July 28, 1889; W. *Post,* July 29, 1889.
67. Reprinted in W. *Post,* July 31, 1889.
68. W. *Post,* Aug. 1, 1889; Mor.182; Sievers, Harry J., *Benjamin Harrison* (New York, 1960), III, 86.
69. *Sun,* Aug. 1, 1889.
70. W. *Post,* Aug. 2 and 3, 1889.
71. Ib., Aug. 5, 1889.
72. W. *Star,* Aug. 5, 1889; Mor.1. 185–6. An intimate of the Harrison Administration remarked at this time that TR was altogether too fond of talking to the press. L. T. Michener to E. W. Halford, Aug. 9, 1889.
73. Mor.182.
74. The following two paras. are taken almost verbatim from TR.Wks.II. 240–1.
75. Ib.
76. Ib., 242; TR, qu. Cut.51.
77. Mor.175.
78. See Utley, George B., "TR's *The Winning of the West:* Some Unpublished Letters," *Mississippi Valley Historical Review,* XXX (1944) 469.
79. *Dial,* Vol. X.112 (Aug. 1889).
80. *Atlantic Monthly,* Nov. 1889. See Utley, "TR's WW," 499 ff. for TR's rueful but appreciative response, and for his subsequent relations with Poole. See, for other assessments of TR the historian, Har.53–61 and 526; Lasch, Christopher, ed., *WW by TR* (NY 1963) intro.; Wish, Harvey, *American Historians: A Selection* (NY, 1962); Gable, John A., "TR as Historian and Man of Letters," cited Ch. 15, n. 55. For other contemporary reviews of *WW,* see *N.Y.T.,* July 7, 1889; *New Englander and Yale Review,* 52 (1890); and *The Critic,* Aug. 3, 1889, which predicted that *WW,* with all its faults, "will rank among American historical writings of the first order."
81. *Sun,* Sep. 22, 1889; Mor.188–90.
82. Mor.188 fn.
83. Ib., 192.
84. *Sun,* Oct. 6, 1889.
85. The complete texts of both TR's letters are in Mor.194–7.

86. TR to B, Oct. 15, 1889.
87. Hag.RF.18; EKR to TR re finances, *passim* (Derby mss.); TR to B, Oct. 13, 1889.
88. Cecil Spring-Rice, qu. Gwy.101.
89. Lod.196; Mor.199.
90. USCSC, *Sixth Report* (1889).
91. Dun.I.20. Early in the year, Congressman Reed had obligingly helped Lodge in his attempts to get TR a place in the government. For the relationship of the two most charismatic figures in late-nineteenth-century American politics, see R. Hal Williams, "'Dear Tom,' 'Dear Theodore': The Letters of Theodore Roosevelt and Thomas B. Reed," *Theodore Roosevelt Journal* 20 (1995) 3–4.
92. Lod.88.
93. St.177; Mor.210.
94. TR to B, Oct. 13, 1889.
95. Ib., Dec. 31; Utley, "TR's *WW*," 505; Mor.200.
96. Foraker, Julia, *I Would Live It Again* (Harpers, 1932) 133.
97. See *W. Post,* Jan. 2, 1890.
98. Sto.235; Foraker, *Again,* 7.
99. Mor.3.486.
100. TR to B, Feb. 13, 1890.
101. Adams, Henry, *The Education of Henry Adams,* ed. Ernest Samuels (Houghton Mifflin, 1974) 332; Den.339.
102. See, e.g., Pla.214–5; Foraker, *Again,* 170; Gar.109; Butler, Nicholas Murray, *Across the Busy Years* (Scribner's, 1940) 297–8; Sto.189.
103. Qu. Sto.190.
104. McCall, Samuel W., *Thomas B. Reed* (Houghton Mifflin, 1914) 248; character sketch, anon., TRB mss.
105. McCall, *Reed,* 147–8; Gar.109; Butler, *Years,* 297–8; Gwy.105.
106. Tha.55; Den.119. See J. B. Moore to Tyler Dennett, Nov. 18, 1929, Tyler Dennett Papers, LC, on the "distinctly effeminate" interdependence of Hay and Adams.
107. Hay, John, with John G. Nicolay, *Abraham Lincoln: A History,* 10 vols., 1890; Adams, Henry, *History of the United States from 1801 to 1817,* 9 vols., 1889–91.
108. "Good luck," he wrote toward the end of his life, "has pursued me like my own shadow."—to Henry Adams, July 14, 1901.
109. Qu. Samuels, Ernest, *Henry Adams* (Harvard, 1958–64) II.262.
110. Ib., 3.32.
111. Mor.6.1490.
112. TR to HCL, Feb. 15, 1887 (LOD.).
113. Mor.6.1490.
114. This portrait, and that of Hay above, is the author's own, based on his reading of the private and published words of Adams, Hay, and TR, as well as their respective biographies.
115. Adams, *Education,* 417.
116. Ada.350.
117. Adams's wife, a precociously intelligent woman with manic-depressive tendencies, had committed suicide in December 1885. See Samuels, *Adams,* II.270–276.
118. Samuels, *Adams,* III *passim;* Cater, Harold, ed., *Henry Adams and His Friends* (Houghton Mifflin, 1947) intro., *passim;* Gwy. *passim.* See also Lacey, Michael J., "The Mysteries of Earth-Making Dissolve: A Study of Washington's Intellectual Community and the Origins of American Environmentalism in the Late Nineteenth Century," Ph.D. diss., George Washington University, 1979.
119. Adams actually asked TR to live rent-free in his house with him in 1889, and was rather put out when the Commissioner declined to do so. See also Samuels, Adams, II.414; Cha.195.
120. At the White House, E. W. Halford, the President's secretary, thoughtlessly introduced TR to one of the leading Republican spoilsmen. A violent quarrel ensued, and would have led to fisticuffs had Halford not intervened. Halford in "R's Introduction to

Washington," *Leslie's Magazine,* Mar. 1, 1919.
121. Mor.210.
122. Williams, Cleveland, "TR, Civil Service Commissioner," U. Chicago dissertation, June 1955, 86.
123. *W. Post,* Jan. 21, 1890.
124. Ib.
125. *House Report 1,* 2. Other details covering the hearing are taken from Washington papers covering the proceedings, mainly *Post* and *Star.*
126. *W. Post,* Feb. 27, 1890.
127. *House Report 1,* 150.
128. *W. Post,* Mar. 1, 1890; *House Report 1,* 153, 191. Dr. Shidy was hurriedly fired by the Census Bureau.
129. *W. Post,* Mar. 1, 1890.
130. *House Report 1,* 163.
131. Ib., 164–5.
132. Ib., 165–6; 168–71.
133. Ib., 174–5.
134. See Wag.148–9, 203–7.
135. *House Report 1,* 177.
136. Ib., 178.
137. Ib., 179–80.
138. Ib., 313.
139. Williams, "TR, CSC," 87. The Committee, nevertheless, went ahead with its recommendation; but the House did not agree. White, *Republican Era,* 326.
140. TR (1912) qu. Sto.7.
141. Statement by J. J. Leary in TRB mss. There is another version of this anecdote (which Greenhalge confirmed) in Halloran, *Romance,* 85. The latter, however, appears to misdate it as 1891. Greenhalge must surely have made the remark in 1890, around the time he was personally encountering TR at the hearings. TR's political stock was high then; as will be seen, it fell precipitately in 1891.
142. Mor.220.
143. *W. Post,* May 6, 1890. It may have been the morning after this editorial that TR was seen pacing up and down outside the Post Office building, waiting for Hatton to show up. "I want to punch his head." Dun.I.19.
144. Mor.215; 211. TR's "The Merit System versus the Patronage System" (*Century,* Feb. 1890) may be taken as his definitive statement on Civil Service Reform. It is reprinted in TR.Wks.XIV. 99 ff.
145. Mor.221. TR knew Mahan slightly, having met him in 1887. Their relationship, which was to develop apace during the 1890s, will be analyzed in Ch. 22.
146. See Chs. 22 and 23; also O'Gara, Gordon Carpenter, *TR and the Rise of the Modern Navy* (Princeton U. Press, 1969) for TR's Presidential naval policies.
147. *House Report 1,* v. Sageser, "Two Decades," 146, says that Lyman was censured unjustly. The facts of the case indicate otherwise.
148. See ib., 146 for an analysis of the media blitz following the committee's report.
149. Ib.; *N.Y. Saturday Globe,* Mar. 8, 1890.
150. Gwy.106.
151. Mor.229, 230; Cut.72.
152. COW; Mor.233. Edith Roosevelt had just turned 29.
153. Mor.234; Sullivan, Mark, *The Education of an American* (Doubleday, 1938), 272–74; TR to HCL, Oct. 4, 1890 (LOD.).
154. Sto.215. The majority was 255 to 88.
155. Mor.236; *Boston Evening Transcript,* Oct. 30, 1890.
156. TR to B, Dec. 26, 1890.
157. Cha.195.

17: The Dear Old Beloved Brother

Important sources not listed in Bibliography: 1. *Report of Commissioner Roosevelt concerning Political Assessments and the use of Official Influence to Control Elections in the Federal Offices at Baltimore, Md.* (USCS, Government Printing Office, May 1891). Hereafter cited as *Baltimore Report.* 2. 52nd Congress, 2nd session, *Report of the House Committee on Reform in the Civil Service, June 21, 1892,* Misc. Doc. #289, Report #1669. Hereafter cited as *House Report* 2.

1. TR to B, May 23, 1891.

2. See Las.30 ff. for an account of E's life as a Hempstead "swell." Wise, John S., *Recollections of Thirteen Presidents* (NY, 1906) 244.

3. Las.8. "He became a drunkard because he was an epileptic . . . in the family we understood that." Mrs. Longworth int., Nov. 1954, TRB.

4. See p. 132; also TR to B, May 10, 1890, when he says that E has been drinking for "a dozen years." TR to B, Apr. 30, 1890.

5. *Sun, World,* Aug. 18, 1891, also Las.30–4.

6. COW; Las.36; TR to B, *passim,* 1891.

7. TR to B, Jan. 25, 1891.

8. TR to B, *passim,* 1891, and below.

9. TR to B, Jan. 25, 1891; ib., Mar. 1.

10. See Wag.87–8; TR to B, Mar. 1, 1891.

11. Ib., Jan. 25, 1891. For other examples of TR's curious, neo-Christian morality, see Wag.85–92.

12. Ib., and below.

13. TR to B, Feb. 22, 1891; ib., Feb. 15.

14. Ib., Mar. 1, 1891; COW; also Las.34 ff.

15. The legitimate baby was due in late June 1891. For lack of evidence we can only assume that the illegitimate baby was due in March or April 1891, E having departed for Europe the previous July (*Sun,* Aug. 17, 1891). It may have been due earlier, but as Katy Mann began her legal action only in January 1891, her pregnancy was surely not far advanced.

16. Mor.237.

17. Mor.238. BH eventually yielded to TR's entreaties, and extended the rules to cover a token 626 places in the Bureau. See below for TR's further efforts on behalf of reservation Indians.

18. Reed was an advocate of the spoils system, and his campaign for favorable votes during the appropriations crisis surprised many colleagues. "Well, I didn't know *you* were in love with Civil Service Reform," said a Tennessee member. "I don't like it straight," Reed admitted, "but mixed with a little Theodore Roosevelt, I like it well." *Columbus* (*O.*) *Press,* May 8, 1892.

19. New York ("Historic Towns" Series, Longmans, Green & Co., 1891—issued simultaneously in New York and London). Reprinted in TR.Wks.X.339–547.

20. *Spectator,* Sep. 5, 1891. Other reviews in TR.Scr.

21. *The Nation,* May 14, 1891.

22. TR.Wks.X.512ff., 514, 529.

23. TR to B, Mar. 22, 1891.

24. Mor.284, 283.

25. *W. Post,* Mar. 30, 31, and Apr. 3, 1891. These amounts were by no means trivial in the 1890s, when clerks like Hamilton Shidy earned $720 per annum, or $14 a week.

26. Mor.284.

27. Ib.; Williams, Cleveland, "TR, Civil Service Commissioner," U. Chicago dissertation, June 1955, 43.

28. *House Report* 2, 1. TR went down for a preliminary investigation on Mar. 28, but seems to have kept his plans to return a secret. The press was taken completely by surprise—see *W. Post,* Mar. 31 and Apr. 3, 1891.

29. *Baltimore Report,* 7 and *passim.* TR was still rejoicing in the primary's Dickensian aspects a year later—see *W. Post,* May 26, 1892.

30. Charles Joseph Bonaparte, president of the Maryland Civil Service Reform League, assisted TR in these interviews, and also took a part in the

drafting of the final report. See Eric F. Goldman's unfinished "Charles J. Bonaparte, Patrician Reformer: His Earlier Career," *Johns Hopkins U. Studies in Historical and Political Science,* Series LXI, No. 2 (1943).

31. *Baltimore Report,* 2, 4.

32. *Boston Post,* Apr. 1, 1891; *W. Post,* qu. *Sun,* Apr. 14; *Civil Service Chronicle,* May 1891.

33. Goldman, *Bonaparte,* 25. See TR. Scr. for nationwide reaction.

34. *W. Post,* Apr. 3, 1891.

35. Metaphor taken from *C. S. Chronicle,* May 1891.

36. During the session of Apr. 6, TR sent out for some sandwiches, and was puzzled when the office boy delivered them without a bill. "But I want to pay for them," said the Commissioner, holding out a dollar. "You can keep the change." The boy backed off in terror. "No, sir, I am not receiving any money on Government property." *W. Post,* Apr. 7, 1891.

37. *Baltimore Report,* 3.

38. Ib., 4–5.

39. Ib., 126, 3, 139; *C. S. Chronicle,* Apr. 1891; *Baltimore Report,* 16.

40. Not to be confused with TR's earlier report on the Baltimore Post Office (Aug. 1, 1889) reprinted in Mor.177 ff.

41. See n. 69 below for sample reactions when it did appear. Har.78 implies, incorrectly, that it was President Harrison who pigeon-holed the report—no doubt because TR himself (Mor.242) was at pains to give that impression. Actually the document, dated May 1, was not even sent to Harrison until early in August (*C. S. Chronicle,* May 1892). BH approved its release in mid-August. *N.Y. Tribune,* Aug. 17, 1891.

42. TR to B, May 5, 1891.

43. Ib., *passim,* and Apr. 26, 1891.

44. Mor.243.

45. TR to B, n.d., 1891.

46. Ib., May 10.

47. Undated, mutilated letter from TR to B, probably early May 1891; another, probably late June.

48. TR to B, June 7, 1891; Las.36–7.

49. TR to B, June 14, 1891.

50. TR to E, June 24, 1891.

51. The letter has not survived, but its contents can be inferred from references in subsequent letters from TR to B and E.

52. TR to B, n.d., probably late June 1891.

53. See TR to B, June 17, 1891; also July 12.

54. Ib., June 20, 1891; June 17; later letters, *passim.*

55. Ib., June 17, 1891.

56. He was currently spending at the rate of $1,500 a month, or $18,000 a year, against an estimated $15,000 in income. Las.34 and 21.

57. TR to E, June 14, 1891. The uncle was James K. Gracie, husband of Aunt Annie.

58. TR to B, June 20 and July 2, 1891.

59. Ib., July 12 and 2, 1891. Hall Roosevelt drank himself to death in 1941 at the age of fifty.

60. Ib., July 2, 1891.

61. Goldman, *Bonaparte,* 25; Mor.255. HCL was now in his third term at Congress, and was one of the most influential members of the House. Sto.183 and Gar. *passim.*

62. TR to HCL, July 1, 1891 (edited version in Mor.256).

63. TR to B, July 8, 1891.

64. Ib.

65. TR to B, July 8, 21, 12, 1891. Apparently TR also went to look at the baby, with Douglas Robinson, on July 13.

66. Ib., July 12, 1891. How B managed to get E shut up is unclear. He seems to have consented at first (ib.), but afterwards claimed he had been "kidnapped." (Las.37.)

67. TRB mss.

Postscript: In a letter prompted by the first edition of this biography, Katy Mann's granddaughter reported that Katy never married. She took no pains to conceal the parentage of her son, who was named Elliott Roosevelt Mann. Money left in trust for the child by Elliott Senior apparently never reached the family, which has remained bitter for generations. Eleanor Mann Biles to author, July 6, 1981.

68. *C.S. Chronicle,* May 1892; *W. Post,* Sep. 2, 1891 (Wanamaker was on vacation).

69. See, e.g., *N.Y. Tribune* and *Times,* Aug. 17, 1891. Sample editorial quote, from *N.Y. Evening Post,* same date: "All that he says is true, and furnishes the most startling picture yet presented to the President of the fruits of his policy in violating his Civil Service Reform pledges."

70. *W. Post,* Sep. 1, 1891; Mor.259.

71. *Sun,* Aug. 17, 1891; see also *N.Y.T., World, Trib.,* same date.

72. TR to Douglas Robinson, Aug. 6, 1891; TR to B, Aug. 22.

73. At the time of writing, December 1977, Ethel Roosevelt Derby has just died at Oyster Bay.

74. TR to B, Sep. 1, 1891.

75. Mor.261. Cut.58 says that the excessive butchery of this trip was to prove an embarrassment to TR in later years. It was, nevertheless, the only recorded instance of the mature TR breaking his own controlled-hunting rules. "The horror about poor Elliott" may have had something to do with it. As can be seen in a passage deleted from his letter to HCL of Oct. 10, 1891 (LOD.), the worry was still very much with him when he returned to Washington.

76. *N.Y.T.,* Nov. 29, 1891; *W. Post,* Sep. 2, 1891.

77. *N.Y.T.,* Nov. 29, 1891.

78. *W. Post,* Sep. 2, 1891.

79. Foulke, William D., *Fighting the Spoilsmen* (Putnam, 1919) 25–6.

80. TR to B, Oct. 28, 1891; Goldman, *Bonaparte,* 26; Mor.265–6 (the reports turned out to be false); ib., 258; Williams, "TR, CSC," 85.

81. EKR to TR, *passim* (Derby mss.); Hay to Adams, Jan. 6, 1892, ADA.

82. Las.38; TR to B, *passim; N.Y. Herald,* Aug. 22, 1891.

83. TR to B, Sep. 1, 1891.

84. TR to B, Nov. 27 and Dec. 13, 1891.

85. Ib., Dec. 22, Jan. 3, 1892.

86. E (age 15) to TR Sr., Mar. 6, 1875, qu. Las.7.

87. E's sporting notes (1873), TRC.

88. TR to B, Jan. 21, 1892.

89. Las.38–39; TR to B, Feb. 13, 1892.

90. Author's surmise, based on TR's letter announcing departure plans, Jan. 21, 1892.

91. Fragment in Anna Hall Roosevelt papers, FDR.

92. The exact dates of TR's trip to Paris have long been uncertain, due to an extraordinary combination of misdatings in the surviving correspondence. For example, his letter to B announcing the trip is dated "January 3, 1891" in the TRB typed transcripts, and his next letter to her from Paris, quoted above, is dated "June 21st 1891." To make matters more complicated, his letter to Spring-Rice, beginning "When I was in Paris," is dated in Mor.270 as "Jan. 25, 1892." The correct dates should be, consecutively, Jan. 3, Jan. 21, and Feb. 25, 1892. Recently discovered letters of EKR to her mother, Gertrude Tyler Carow, confirm that TR left New York on Jan. 9, and arrived back home on Feb. 7, 1892. TRC.

93. See Mor.270.

94. *House Report* 2, 1–3. See also TR to Bonaparte, Jan. 4, 1892: "My devoted friend, Mr. Wanamaker, has not dared to have published the report of his inspectors."

95. Before giving vent to this imprecation, he checked to see there were no reporters in the room.

96. George Haven Putnam in Century Association, *TR Memorial Addresses,* (NY, 1919) 40–3; also in Putnam, *Memories of a Publisher* (NY, 1915) 141–2. Putnam does not give the date, but since the incident obviously occurred in the period preceding the House Investigation, March 8 seems most likely. TR paid a visit to NY on that date, arriving in the evening, as Putnam remembers. He remained in NY on Mar. 9 and 10, but was otherwise engaged on those nights. (TR to B, *passim.*)
97. Las.39; TR to B, Feb. 13, 1892.
98. See "A Peccary-Hunt on the Nueces," TR.Wks.275–84. One of TR's best pieces, full of visual and auditory details. Note how few lines are devoted to the actual chase, the rest being taken up with zoological observations and some beautiful nature-writing.
99. *House Report* 2, 1; Putnam in *Memorial Addresses,* 43.
100. *House Report* 2, 12.
101. Ib., 2.
102. Ib., 5, 7, 9.
103. Ib., 25; *W. Post,* May 3, 1892.
104. *House Report* 2, 25–6.
105. See ib., 25–36, 27, 36.
106. *W. Post,* May 3, 1892.
107. *House Report* 2, 60; *N.Y.T.,* May 26, 1892; Mor.281–2; *Sun,* May 13.
108. See Mor.281–2 for complete text. TR sent a copy of this letter to BH, "with the utmost confidence that you will recognize the propriety of my action."
109. *House Report* 2, 59; *W. Post,* May 26, 1892.
110. *House Report* 2, 60, 63.
111. *N.Y.T.,* May 26, 1892. See TR.Scr. for more reactions, and Bis.II.48–9; *House Report* 2, iii–v.
112. *W. Post* Extra Edition, June 23, 1892.
113. BH won on the first ballot, due largely to the support of thousands of his own appointees. Foulke, *Spoilsmen,* 31–2.
114. Sageser, "Two Decades" (cited in Ch. 16, n. 2) 150 and *passim* confirms that publicity was the CSC's main weapon during the Harrison Administration. *Sun,* qu. Foulke, *Spoilsmen,* 32. As Har.78 points out, in matters other than Civil Service Reform, Wanamaker's was the most distinguished Postmaster Generalship since the Civil War. The man was an imaginative innovator, and "a near administration genius." (Ib.) He has suffered much from TR's shrewd attacks upon him, even allowing for the fact that right was on the younger man's side. Today Wanamaker's handling of the Baltimore affair would be construed as obstruction of justice. It is interesting to note that he, at least in later life, bore TR no ill-will. He tried once to analyze the latter's "masterful greatness," and wrote that its secret lay "in the fact that no insincerity lurked behind his ever-welcoming smile." Qu. Appel, J. H., *A Business Biography of John Wanamaker* (NY, 1930) 255.
115. See Mor.293; TR.Wks.XIV.141.
116. Mor.275–7.
117. Ib., 277, 290; Lod.122. For a description of TR the polo player, see *Harper's Weekly,* July 20, 1892.
118. Mor.289; TR to B, Aug. 11, 1892.
119. See Mor.3.547–63 for an account of the exquisite dialogue between Jones and Ferris. Their "lunatic story" became one of TR's favorite after-dinner recitations. John Hay was so charmed by this and other Rooseveltian stories of the Old West that he begged him to commit it to paper. The result was a 9,000-word letter which, along with two other classic examples of TR the raconteur, have been separately published under the title *Cowboys and Kings* (Harvard U. Press, 1954).
120. Mor.290; ib., 3.553. The sheriff's name was Seth Bullock. He later

became one of the more exotic members of TR's "Tennis Cabinet."
121. Williams, "TR, CSC," 51.
122. Un. clip, Sep. 15, 1892, TR.Scr. See also Herbert Welsh, *Civilization Among the Sioux Indians* (Philadelphia Office of the Indian Rights Association, 1893) 4–7.
123. USCSC, *11th Report,* 164–5.
124. The text of this magnificent speech is in TR.Wks.XIV.156–68. See also Hagan, William T., "Civil Service Commissioner Theodore Roosevelt and the Indian Rights Association," *Pacific Historical Review,* 44.2 (May 1975) 187 ff. Hagan protests that TR's contribution to the improvement of the Indian Service as CSC "has been ignored too long." He shows how TR acted in concert with Herbert Welsh, of the I.R. Association, to root out injustice and corruption on the reservations, and offer more government employment to Indians. Later Welsh recommended TR to President McKinley as Commissioner of Indian Affairs. "His hold upon the public, his knowledge of the subject, would make him, perhaps, the most valuable man in the country." As a result of his CSC work, TR was "the best-informed man on Indian affairs to occupy the White House since the Civil War." Ib., 199–200.
125. Sto.179.
126. Mor.295.
127. Gar.129ff.; see, e.g., the *Charleston News & Courier,* qu. *N.Y.T.,* Nov. 27, 1892.
128. Foulke, *Spoilsmen,* 24.
129. Ib., 33.
130. Las.44.
131. See Foraker, Julia, *I Would Live It Again* (Harpers, 1932) 188.
132. See Gar.150.
133. Foraker, *Again,* 188.
134. Mor.304.
135. See Carl Schurz to TR, Jan. 4, 1893, qu. Bis.I.52; Pri.131; Har.79; Mrs. Bellamy Storer in *Harper's Weekly,* June 1, 1912.

18: The Universe Spinner

1. *Chicago Tribune,* May 2, 1893. The following description of the opening of the World's Fair is taken largely from this newspaper, supplemented by the *World* and *Sun* of the same date; Northrup, H. D., *The World's Fair as Seen in a Hundred Days* (Philadelphia, 1893) and Rand McNally's *The World's Columbian Exposition Reproduced* (Chicago, 1894).
2. Nineteenth-century Americans unhesitatingly accepted the Discoverer as Spanish, just as today he is generally believed to have been an Italian. For what appears to be the last word on the subject, see Morison, Samuel Eliot, *The European Discovery of America: The Southern Voyages* (NY, 1974) 6–8.
3. TR to B, Apr. 26, 1893.
4. Wis.36.
5. Adams, Henry, *The Education of Henry Adams* (Houghton Mifflin, 1974) 340.
6. Mor.320.
7. Adams, *Education,* 343.
8. Mor.317. TR had recently been retained by Cleveland as Civil Service Commissioner, after handing in his formal resignation at the beginning of the new Administration. Although he explained the act was prompted by his desire "to relieve the President any embarrassment and . . . to get back to his books," he did not need much persuading to stay. See *New York Times,* May 4, 1893, and Mor.314.
9. Morley in 1903, qu. TRB mss.
10. TR.Wks.VII.3.
11. Ib., 3, 7.
12. Ib., 111.
13. Mor.440.
14. TR.Wks.VII.108.
15. Ib., 380, 403–4, 377–9, 331, 279.

16. Ib., 57.
17. Ib.
18. See Cut.36–7 and Bur.14 on TR's observations of the rule of tooth and claw in nature.
19. Ib., 58.
20. Ib., 57–8.
21. See Bea.31.
22. For examples of Commissioner Roosevelt's abhorrence of racial discrimination in hiring practices, see Mor.373, 381, 402; also TR.Wks.XIV. 165. In 1954, Edmund Wilson, reviewing Vols I and II of Mor., remarked: "It is impossible to go through the correspondence of Roosevelt's early official life without being convinced that he pretty consistently lived up to this principle." Wilson, "The Pre-presidential TR" in *Eight Essays* (NY, 1954) 211.
23. TR.Wks.X.479–509.
24. See Billington, Ray Allen, *Frederick Jackson Turner* (Oxford U. Press, 1973) *passim* for the genesis and presentation of Turner's great thesis.
25. *The Dial*, August 1889 (see p. 462). See also Jacobs, Wilbur R., *The Historical World of Frederick Jackson Turner* (Yale, 1968) 4. Jacobs says that Turner wrote an unpublished essay, "The Hunter Type," in 1890, "based almost entirely upon the early volumes of *The Winning of the West.*" The essay depicted a Rooseveltian warrior-hero of the border, represented as an evolutionary American type. Massive, scholarly reading went into the subsequent preparation of "Significance," but it may well be, as Jacobs suggests, that *WW* "provided the inspiration for his frontier thesis." For a full account, see Billington, *Turner*, 83–4, 108–25.
26. Qu. ib., 127. See also Knee, Stuart E., "Roosevelt and Turner: Awakening in the West," *Journal of the West* 17 (1978) 2.
27. Lasch, Christopher, ed., *WW by TR* (NY, 1963) xii; qu. Billington, *Turner*, 128.
28. Turner, Frederick Jackson, *Frontier and Section: Selected Essays*, ed. Ray Allen Billington (Prentice-Hall, 1961) 61.
29. Ib., 37.
30. Ib., 62.
31. See Billington, *Turner*, 129–30.
32. Mor.363.
33. Ib.
34. See Billington, Turner, *passim* for further details of the TR/Turner relationship.
35. See Wag.44.
36. *Forum*, Apr. 1894; TR.Wks.XIII. 13–26, 151.
37. Ib., 13–26.
38. Qu. Wag.63.
39. TR.Wks.XIII.20; James, Henry, *The American Essays*, ed. Leon Edel (Vintage Books, 1956).
40. Edel, Leon, *Henry James: The Master* (London, 1972) 275–76. Overhearing TR characterize an unidentified contemporary novelist, possibly James, as "a malignant pustule," George Kennan reflected, "If this young Civil Service Commissioner fully develops his capacity for hatred and his natural gift for denunciation, he will be, in the maturity of his powers, an unpleasant man to encounter." Kennan, *Misrepresentation in Railroad Affairs* (Garden City, NY, 1916), 49.
41. Reprinted in TR.Wks.XIII.200–222.
42. Ib., 203.
43. Ib., 206.
44. Ib., 208–9.
45. Ib., 214.
46. Ib., 216.
47. Ib. For TR's enlightened interpretation of Social Darwinism, see his review of Benjamin Kidd's *Social Evolution* (NY, 1894), published in *North American Review*, 161.94–109 (July 1895) and reprinted in TR.Wks.XIII. John M. Blum exhaustively and brilliantly dis-

cusses this and other aspects of TR's intellectual development in an essay, "TR: The Years of Decision," printed as Appendix IV to Mor.2.1484–94.

48. TR.Wks.XII.219.

49. Ib., 222.

50. Space does not permit an extended description of this richly detailed, sweet-natured book. Suffice to say it has all the freshness of observation of *Hunting Trips of a Ranchman*, even less slaughter than *Ranch Life and the Hunting Trail*, and an abundance of original zoological information. The chapter on the life habits of the grizzly bear marked a definite contribution to science: TR was by now recognized as the world authority on this and other large Western species. There are several delicious comic episodes, notably the story of Fowler and the Turk, and the dialogue overheard by TR on the Brophy ranch in 1884, as well as one of his finest lyrical pieces, inspired by the all-night song of a Tennessee mockingbird. See TR.Wks.II.330–4, 327–30, and 52–5. For sample reviews in 1893, see *Nation*, Aug. 14; *St. Paul Press*, Aug. 22; *Edinburgh National Observer*, Dec. 30.

51. Mor.367; Wag.304; TR to B, Nov. 6, 1893; Mor.391, 409. TR accepted no fees for lectures on Civil Service Reform. These he considered part of his job.

52. Pri.157.

53. Mor.342–3; see also n. 56, below.

54. Mor.343. The land was sold to his uncle James A. Roosevelt. It reduced to 30 acres the original estate he bought during his first marriage. TR to B, Jan. 28, 1893; EKR to Emily Carow, May 19, 1894; Mor.306.

55. Ib., 343, 376; see also TR to B, Apr. 15, 1894, and EKR to B, Jan. 10 and June 6, 1894 (TRC). The extent of TR's embarrassments may be gathered from his suggestion to Bamie, who had a habit of understamping her letters, that she buy "a pair of scales and a copy of the postal regulations," so as to save him the 20-cent collect charge. TR to B, April 1, 1894.

56. Mor.345.

57. Ib., 340; TR to HCL, July 4, 1893 (LOD.).

58. Mor.389, 323, 335; TR to B, June 20, 1893. A memo sent to Secretary Smith suggests that the hostility may have been mutual. See Mor.328.

59. Cecil Spring Rice to Elizabeth Cameron, July 2, 1891 (ADA.).

60. Foulke, William D., *Fighting the Spoilsmen* (Putnam, 1919) 40.

61. On Nov. 28, 1893. Foulke, *Spoilsmen*, 38–40; Mor.317. See also ib., 341; Foulke, William D., *Lucius Burrie Swift* (Bobbs-Merrill, 1930) 69.

62. Halloran, Matthew F., *The Romance of the Merit System* (Washington, D.C., 1929) 77; TR to HCL, June 8, 1893 (LOD.).

63. Mor.343; see also ib., 396.

64. Mor.393. See Woo.19 for an earlier example of TR's reaction to suggestions that he again run for Mayor.

65. TR to HCL, Oct. 11, 1894 (LOD.); EKR to Emily Carow, 1894 *passim* (Derby mss.).

66. Sto.223.

67. TR to B, qu. Bea.47.

68. Mor.379, 409. See also Bea.46–7. This is not the first mention of the Canal by TR. He had been interested in France's attempt to build a waterway at Panama since his Dakota days. Among his papers in TRP there is a copy of a U.S. Government *Special Intelligence Report on the Progress of the Work on the Panama Canal During the Year 1885*. The document contains much technical prose, thoughtfully penciled by TR.

69. Mor.384; TR to B, Feb. 25, 1894.

70. Ib., Aug. 18, 1894.

71. Ib.; also July 29, 1894. Elliott had, for example, severely burned himself that February by accidentally tipping

an oil lamp over his naked body. In May he had spent the night in a police cell, being too incoherent to say where he lived. In July he had driven into a lamppost while blind drunk and been catapulted onto his head, incapacitating himself.

72. C to B, Aug. 15, 1895 (TRC); TR to HCL, Aug. 18, 1894 (LOD.).

73. TR wrote to HCL afterward: "I confess I felt more broken than I had thought possible." Aug. 18, 1894, LOD. To B in England he wrote that Elliott "would have been in a straight jacket had he lived forty-eight hours longer. . . . he had been drinking whole bottles of anisette and green mint, besides whole bottles of raw brandy and champagne, sometimes half a dozen a morning . . . He was like some stricken, hunted creature; and indeed he was hunted by the most terrible demons that ever entered a man's body and soul." Aug. 18, 1894, TRB.

74. Ib. Elliott's companions at Greenwood were Alice Lee and Mittie Roosevelt. See also Las.56–7. Elliott had been living with Mrs. Evans at 313 West 102 Street under the names of "Mr. and Mrs. Eliot." TR to B, n.d., 1894; *World,* Aug. 16, 1894. According to Lash (who does not identify the woman), she had a house in New England, and was not with him when he died. This is puzzling, in view of TR's remark to B (Aug. 18) that E "would not part with the woman" in his last days. Either Lash is mistaken, or E had *two* mistresses, which seems unlikely. At any rate the winding up of his affairs produced circumstances of some absurdity. Katy Mann made an appearance, bastard in arm, to claim further damages; then Mr. Evans arrived, while the lawyer was negotiating with his wife, and threatened both parties with a loaded revolver. Mrs. Evans eventually received a settlement of $1,250. TR to B, Aug. 18 and 25.

75. Ib., Aug. 24, 1894; Lod.134; Mor.399. For a further description of this hunting trip, see Mor.410–11. TR to HCL, Oct. 11, 1894 (LOD.).

76. TR to B, Oct. 22, 1894; Mor.400.

77. Mor.8.1433.

78. Ib.

79. Ib., 410; HCL to his mother, Dec. 9, 1894 (LOD.); see Mor.418–9 and ff.; ib., 417.

80. Ib.; see p. Ch. 5; also Put.241. TR's letter of reply has not survived, but its contents can be inferred from his supplementary letters to Carl Shurz and Jacob Riis (Mor.418–20).

81. Ib., 417–20.

82. Ib., 428.

83. Gar.180; see Samuels, Ernest, *Henry Adams: The Major Phase* (Harvard, 1964) 164 ff.

84. Mor.426.

85. Ib., 433. The date of this first meeting with Kipling has been the subject of some confusion, since Mor.370 puts TR's letter describing the occasion (a dinner at the Bellamy Storers') in 1894, and Kipling, in *Something of Myself* (London, 1936) 131, vaguely remembers it as 1896. The correct date—March 7, 1895—is made obvious by other references in TR's letters. See, e.g., Mor.433, 436, 439.

86. *Encyclopaedia Britannica* (1970) 13.382.

87. Mor.370.

88. Ib., 448, 439; Kipling, *Something,* 131–3.

89. Mor.247; TR.Wks.IX contains the text of *Hero Tales.*

90. Wis.40.

91. *Manchester* (NH) *Telegram,* Feb. 11, 1895 (TR.Scr.).

92. Ib.; Storer, Mrs. Bellamy, *In Memoriam Bellamy Storer* (privately printed, 1923) 22. This was, of course, the era of "red-meat" football—infinitely more bloody than anything seen today. Eye-gouging and multiple fractures, sustained in real on-field fights, were

routine. Football grew redder and meatier until TR himself, as President, was revulsed and called for reforms. See "Walter Camp," *American Heritage,* XI.6, Oct. 1961.
93. See Mor.437, 9.
94. Ib.
95. Ib., 442.
96. Ib., 444. Sageser, A. Bower, "The First Two Decades of the Pendleton Act," Nebraska U. Studies, Vols. 34–35 (1934–35) prints a table showing the growth of the classified system under Commissioner TR. Opinions of the latter's effectiveness in office vary widely. Leonard D. White in *The Republican Era, 1869–1901* (Macmillan, 1958) points out that for all TR's boasts about doubling the classified service, the service as a whole was growing so fast that the number of patronage positions *increased* steadily through the rest of the century. He allows, however, that the Roosevelt team was "one of the strongest commissions in the whole history" of the CSC. TR's genius for publicity was, in the opinion of this author, his greatest contribution to the good gray cause. See the *Civil Service Chronicle* of May 1895, which praises his ability to throw dazzling light on the hitherto shady patronage practices of professional politicians. Through his courage and his flamboyance, he had spread "an educational process . . . across the country," resulting in a general desire for reforms in all areas of public business. "He is the only man in the Harrison Administration who has won permanent national fame." The view of the CSC itself expressed in *Letters of TR, Civil Service Commissioner* (Washington, 1958) 125, is unequivocal: "Theodore Roosevelt probably contributed more to the development and extension of the civil service than any other person in the history of the United States."
97. Gardiner, A. G., *Pillars of Society* (London, 1913), 238.
98. TR to B, June 17, 1895; Cha.204.
99. Theodore Roosevelt Association, *Journal,* Winter/Spring 1976; Cut.34.
100. *Sun,* June ?, 1889 (TR.Scr.). TR used to joke that the real reason he came to Washington was his "desire to mingle with members of the Cosmos Club and discuss with them congenial topics." (Ib.)
101. Kipling, *Something,* 132; Kipling qu. Tha.II.333.

19: The Biggest Man in New York

1. The following description of Mulberry Street is based on pictures and text in *Shepp's New York City Illustrated* (Globe, Philadelphia, 1894); *King's Handbook of New York,* 1893; Scrapbooks, "Mulberry Street," in the New York Public Library; Riis, Jacob, *The Making of an American* (NY, 1902) *passim;* Ste.197–265.
2. *New York Evening Post,* May 6, 1895.
3. Ste.257; see also *Eve. Post,* May 6, 1895; AND.30–3.
4. Ib.
5. *Eve. Post,* May 6, 1895. Physical descriptions taken from sketches in *World,* May 7; group portrait in *Review of Reviews,* May 20; various other pors. in TRB. Personal details from AND.16, 30–1; AND.Scr. For more on Grant, see Perling, I. J., *Presidents' Sons* (New York, 1947), 178–79.
6. Ste.257–8; Brant, Donald Birtley, Jr., "TR as New York City Police Commissioner," unpublished dissertation (Princeton, 1964) in TRB, 10; AND.32.
7. Andrews quoted Steffens's story verbatim in his memoirs. One of the Republican members was by courtesy entitled to the presidency, since the appointing Mayor was of that party. According to Steffens in the *Post* that evening, Grant announced that he

wanted the honor to go to TR; this was obviously at Strong's request.
8. TR qu. Ber.47. Berman observes that such a statement at such a time, coming from so prominent a public figure, "clearly marked a radical departure" from old-style Police Headquarters policies. The hopes that it raised among reformers, however, were dashed by passage of the Bi-Partisan Police Act. (See below.)
9. Richardson, James F., *The New York Police: Colonial Times to 1901* (Oxford U. Press, 1970) 244. See ib. 214 ff., and the more recent scholarship of Ber. 35–41, for background to this bill.
10. TR was, by virtue of his sweeping investigation of the city government in 1884, intimately familiar with all phases of police operation. See, e.g., his "Machine Politics in New York City," (1886) in TR.Wks.XII.30. "Polish" quote from ib., 123.
11. Ber.35–36; TR.wks.XII.123. TR and his three colleagues and the Chief all earned the same salary: $5,000 (*New York Times,* May 7, 1895). Richardson, *Police,* 212; AND.35; *New York Herald* and *World,* May 28.
12. Ber.51; Ste.221.
13. Richardson, *Police,* 210; Ber.51.
14. AND.7.
15. Ib., 19; 8; Ste.254; *King's Handbook; Shepp's NYC,* 410 ff; New York State, *Report and Proceedings of the Senate Committee Appointed to Investigate the Police Department of the City of New York* (Albany, 1895, reprinted Arno/*N.Y.T.,* 1971) 28 ff.
16. *Sun,* May 12, 1895; *Shepp's NYC,* 413; *Report,* 49; AND.7; TR.Wks.XIII. 119; TR.Auto.178.
17. *Report,* 29; AND.7.
18. *Report,* 1–76; Ber.23–29; Brant, "TR, PC," 5; *Shepp's NYC,* 410–3.
19. AND.11.
20. TR.Wks.XIII.119.
21. *Report,* 16; *Shepp's NYC,* 413; AND.11.
22. Ste.256.
23. AND.18–9, 141 ff; see also *Trib.,* May 23, 1895, on former election corruption.
24. Richardson, *Police,* 231; AND.13; *Report,* 16–19.
25. The Lexow Committee asserted that "honest elections had no existence, in fact, in the city of New York." Qu. Richardson, *Police,* 233. Myers, Gustavus, *The History of Tammany Hall* (NY, 1901) 333; Connable, Alfred, and Silverfarb, Edward, *Tigers of Tammany* (NY, 1967) 197–214; *Report,* 15–61; AND.10.
26. Steffens, *Autobiography,* 258.
27. Ib.
28. Riis, *Making,* 70–3.
29. Rii.131; Riis, *Making,* 328; TR.Auto.174. "*How the Other Half Lives* had been to me both an enlightenment and an inspiration," TR wrote in ib. ". . . I wished to help him in any practical way to try to make things a little better. I have always had a horror of words that are not translated into deeds, of speech that does not result in action."
30. Riis, *Making,* 328.
31. See Kaplan, Justin, *Lincoln Steffens* (Simon & Schuster, 1974) 57; Steffens, *Autobiography,* 223.
32. See Stein, Harry H., "Theodore Roosevelt and the Press: Lincoln Steffens," *Mid-America,* 54.2 (Apr. 1972). This essay convincingly demonstrates TR's mastery of the media by providing a documented case history of his dealings with one reporter over a long period. After TR became President, he ignored Steffens for two years, until the journalist became nationally famous; he then took him up again, manipulating him with consummate skill and no little hypocrisy. Stein's essay should be read as an antidote to the Steffens *Autobiography,* which suggests that the author had a powerful influence on TR.
33. Ste.258; *Eve. Post,* May 6, 1895.

34. Ib.; Richardson, *Police,* 249; New York City Police Department, *Minutes of the Board,* 1895–7 (TRB) 1–2.
35. *World,* May 10, 1895; *Evening World,* same date; *World,* May 11; *Journal,* May 17; *World,* May 17.
36. *World,* May 22, 1895. The *Journal,* May 21, noted "the constant splurge made over what Mr. Roosevelt does or says." Also AND.67–9.
37. See, e.g., Ste.261–2. *N.Y.T.,* July 21, 1895.
38. *World,* May 17, 1895. No other explanation of TR's scar has ever been offered. It shows up clearly in numerous photographs.
39. *Eve. Sun,* May 8, 1895.
40. Ib.; *Sun,* June 27, 1896, quoting TR.
41. TR to HCL, May 18, 1895 (LOD.).
42. Mor.457.
43. *N.Y.T.,* July 23, 1895.
44. Miss Minnie Gertrude Kelly is insinuatingly described in the *World,* May 10, 1895, as "young, small, and comely, with raven-black hair and . . . a close-fitting gown." TR's motives in hiring her were of the highest, however. She was to "take the place of two men employed by the previous President, at a saving of $1,200 a year." Apparently the arrival of Miss Kelly, a family friend of the Roosevelts and a protégée of Joe Murray, "quite took the breath out of the old stagers in the Mulberry Street barracks." Hitherto headquarters staff had been exclusively male. (Ib.)
45. Photographs of TR working survive as evidence of this curious habit. See, e.g., Bis.I.60.
46. Wise, John S., *Recollections of Thirteen Presidents,* 246.
47. TR to B, May 19, 1895; ib., June 2.
48. Mor.456, 458.
49. Ib.; *World,* May 17, 1895.
50. Rii.130; AND.36.
51. AND.78–9; Ber.51–53; Ste.261. See also *N.Y.T.,* May 29, 1895.
52. Ste.206–14, 263; AND.79–80.
53. Ib.; *N.Y.T.,* May 25, 1895.
54. *World,* June 3, 1895.
55. Jacob Riis, in *Outlook,* June 22, 1895, confirms that what follows was TR's own idea.
56. Account of the night walk based on Riis, *Making,* 330–2; *Trib.,* June 8, 1895; *World,* same date; AND.Scr.; TR.Scr.
57. *World, Trib.,* June 8, 1895; AND.57.
58. *Trib.,* June 8, 1895.
59. *World, Trib.,* June 8, 1895.
60. *Eve. Sun,* June 8; *Philadelphia Times,* n.d., AND.Scr.
61. *Brooklyn Times,* Washington *Star,* June 8, 1895.
62. Davis (31) and TR had met in Washington on Dec. 6, 1892. They did not get on too well at first. TR's insistence that Americans should approve of all things American prompted Davis to ask if that included "chewing tobacco and spitting all over the floor." TR replied sarcastically that it did, and what was more, he always made a point of sitting with his feet on the table when dining at the British Legation. (Mor.299.) After that their relationship improved. Davis later contributed much to the Roosevelt legend.
63. *Trib.,* June 15, 1895; *Recorder, Commercial Advertiser,* same date; AND.54.
64. *Press,* June 15, 1895.
65. Ib.
66. *Excise Herald,* June 29, 1895; AND. confirms the report by quoting it.
67. *Sun, World, N.Y.T.,* June 15, 1895.
68. *Press, N.Y.T., Commercial Advertiser,* June 15, 1895.
69. AND.Scr.; TRB clips, 1895; *Sun,* Mar. 24, 1896.
70. Ib. For another, very funny anecdote about "Teddy's Teeth," see Edward Marshall, "The Truth about Roosevelt," *The Columbian Magazine,* June 1910.
71. Ib.
72. Pri.138.

73. AND.62. See *World,* Aug. 22, for an account of a daytime prowl.
74. EKR to Emily Carow, n.d., TRB mss.; Mor.462; TR.Auto.205.
75. Rii.145.
76. Mor.463.
77. Bernard McCann int. FRE.; James Burke, ex–Lyon's waiter, ib.
78. Mor.464; Brant, "TR, PC," 33.
79. Ib., 34.
80. *N.Y.T.,* Jan. 16, 1895.
81. TR.Wks.XIV.27; Mor.466.
82. Ib.; also 464.
83. *Evening Telegraph,* June 11, 1895.
84. TR.Wks.XIV.181.
85. Mor.463.
86. Ib.
87. TR.Auto.197–9; *Advertiser,* June 25, 1895; Ste.264; AND.113–8; *N.Y.T.,* June 24, 1895.
88. *N.Y.T.,* June 25, 1895; TR.Auto. 199; *P.D. Minutes,* 3; Ste.264.
89. AND.115.
90. *Journal,* July 12, 1895.
91. TR.Auto.197.
92. TR.Auto.196; Richardson, *Police,* 251; John R. Voorhis, former Police Commissioner, int. FRE.
93. Brant, "TR, PC," 35; New York Police Department, *Annual Report,* Dec. 31, 1897, 38; TR.Wks.XII.129.
94. TR.Auto.194; AND.105–7.
95. *N.Y.T.,* Jan. 15, 1895; TR.Auto. 194–6; see also AND.137.
96. *World,* July 1, 1895.
97. *N.Y.T.,* July 1, 1895; *Journal,* July 26. AND.137 says that "fully half the force" was employed to administer the Sunday law. *Her.,* July 2.
98. Ib.
99. *Comm. Adv.,* July 8, 1895.
100. *N.Y.T.,* July 18, 1895.
101. Qu. *Journal* (ed.), July 26, 1895.
102. *N.Y.T.,* July 12, 1895; *Her.,* July 13; see also Mor.466.
103. *Her.,* July 13, 1895.
104. AND.123.
105. Un. clip, TRB; *Her.,* July 17, 1895.
106. *Chicago Times-Herald,* July 22, 1895.
107. *Her.,* July 17. Author's italics.
108. Ib.; un. clip, TRB.
109. *Her.,* July 17, 1895.
110. *Chicago Times-Herald,* July 22, 1895.
111. Mor.469.
112. Ib.
113. *Her.,* July 24, 1895.
114. *Comm. Adv.,* July 25, 1895.
115. *Sun,* July 25, 1895; *N.Y.T.,* July 27.
116. *World,* July 29, 1895.
117. Ib.
118. Ib.
119. Spark, Muriel, *John Masefield* (London, 1953) 38; John Masefield to Hermann Hagedorn, Mar. 25, 1952 (TRB mss.); Igl.111–2. The man who attempted to kill TR in 1912 was a saloonkeeper from New York City. He testified that he first became aware of his future victim during this season of dry Sundays in 1895. *N.Y.T.,* Oct. 15, 1912.
120. *Journal,* Aug. 6, 1895.
121. AND.137–8; *Boston Herald,* July 21, 1895 ("They do not seem to understand Theodore Roosevelt very well in his native city"); see also *Review of Reviews* clip, n.d., in TR.Scr.: ". . . From San Francisco to New Orleans to Bangor and Minneapolis the daily newspapers are giving him the space that is allotted to the most important subject before the people." London *Times,* Aug. 10, 1895; Mor.472–3.
122. *Trib.,* Aug. 22, 1895.
123. Pri.136, qu. *World,* July 23, 1895; Rii.29.
124. *N.Y.T.,* Aug. 6, 1895; AND.73.
125. *Her.,* Aug. 14, 1895. "It was a blemish due less to egotism," Andrews comments mildly (p. 69), "than to the recognition that, in effect, he was actually the Board." See also *Journal,* July 12.
126. "Big Tim represented the morals

of another era," TR wrote in his *Autobiography.* "That is, his principles and actions were very much those of a Norman noble in the years immediately succeeding the Battle of Hastings." (192.)

127. All from *World,* Aug. 8, 1895.

128. Mor.475; *World,* Aug. 8, 1895.

129. HCL to TR, Aug. 31, 1895.

130. TR to B, *passim;* see also AND.34, Mor.486.

131. Ib., 475; *Her.,* Sep. 6, 1895.

132. *N.Y.T.,* Aug. 24, 1895.

133. TR to B, Sep. 8, 1895. Statistical and other documentary assessments of TR's crusade in behalf of the Excise Law are given in Ber.105–16.

134. *Trib.,* Sep. 26, 1895. This was, of course, before the age of the press photograph.

135. The following description based on *World,* Sep. 26, 1895, also *Trib., Her.,* same date.

136. *World,* Sep. 26, 1895.

137. Ib.

138. *Her.,* Sep. 26, 1895. The warmly admiring tone of this article shows that the yellow press was not blind to TR's merits.

139. Ib., *Trib.,* same date.

140. *N.Y.T.,* July 22, 1895.

141. Ste.258–60.

142. See, e.g., AND.172. Mor.484; AND.141 ff.; also *Trib.,* May 23, 1895; Har.85.

143. See Mor.477; TR.Wks.XIV.184; TRB clips.

144. Mor.490.

145. Ib., 485–89. See also ib., 488, TR.Wks.XIV.212, and *Journal,* Jan. 31, 1896, for details of this quarrel, which was later patched up. (Mor.496).

146. Ib., 483, 485; *Outlook,* Oct. 10, 1895; Mor.480, 490; see *Trib.,* Sep. 12, *World,* Oct. 29, and *Journal,* Jan. 31, 1896, for sample articles on TR's election policies. *World,* Aug. 19, 1895; Mor.493.

147. Ib., 481, 487, 489, 493; TR to B, Oct. 27, 1895.

148. AND.176 puts the German vote-loss alone at 30,000. Har.85.

149. Unpublished letter, Nov. 5, 1895, in TRB mss. Specifically, it deals with the Venezuela border dispute between the U.S. and Great Britain, which was then approaching its crisis point.

150. *N.Y.T.,* Nov. 7, 1895; AND.176–7.

151. *Journal,* Nov. 22, 1895; *Sun,* Dec. 14. Mor.500.

152. TR to B, Dec. 1, 1895; Bigelow to HCL, Nov. 23, 1895, qu. in Murakata, Akiko, "Selected Letters of Dr. William Sturgis Bigelow," Ph.D. diss., George Washington University, 1971, 84. Notwithstanding Bigelow's fears, TR avoided collapse, and Volume IV of *WW* was finished by Dec. 23. See Mor.499–504.

153. Ib., 503.

154. Stoker, Bram, *Reminiscences of Sir Henry Irving* (NY, 1906) II, 236. Charles Eliot Norton used similar words, about this time, to the English journalist David Alec Wilson. "I'll tell you what, if Roosevelt lives, he'll be President of the United States . . . He is a strong and able man, who is not to be bought." Wilson, *East and West* (Methuen, 1911) 262.

20: The Snake in the Grass

1. Pla.295; Gos.48–59.

2. Pla.8.

3. Gos.1 says Platt and TR had political relations with each other since the mid-80s, but does not specify any actual meetings. Pla.178, 193 says essentially the same, again without mentioning any personal contact. The unreliable Louis J. Lang in his appendix to ib. (522) says without documentation that TR, George F. Edmunds, and George W. Curtis met with Platt in New York "a few days before the Republican National Convention" in 1884. This is possible, but improbable, since TR and HCL made a special journey to Washington at that time to meet Edmunds *there;* no contemporary letters or news-

papers mention the New York meeting. TR's letters to HCL in 1895 give the strong impression that Platt was a personal stranger to him. The best account of their early relationship remains Gos.29–72.

4. Ib., 29–30, 32–3; see Chs. 10, 14.

5. Gos.34.

6. Ib. 230; Ber. 36; Lod.I.144.

7. See Pla.178, 183; Gos.229–31; AND.18–19; Pla.527.

8. See Mor.482, 476; Pla.300 ff.; *New York Times*, Jan. 24, 1896; AND.78.

9. Mor.499; *N.Y.T.*, July 8, 1896. Murray was now Excise Commissioner of New York.

10. Gos.57; TR.Auto.294; Pla.488.

11. Description of Platt based on pors. in Pla., *passim*, and Library of Congress; Sto.168; un. clip by EGR, Sep. 7, 1919, in TRB; White, William Allen, "Platt," in *McLure's* 18.146 (Dec. 1901); Thompson, Charles Willis, *Party Leaders of the Time* (NY, 1906) 105; Chessman, G. Wallace, *Governor TR* (Harvard, 1965) 7 ff.

12. See, e.g., his open letter to Governor Levi P. Morton, dated Jan. 3, 1896, in which he dresses the Governor down with the assurance of a headmaster punishing a schoolboy. (Pla.307–10.)

13. *N.Y.T.*, July 8, 1896; Mor.509. This legislation proposed to transfer from Mayor Strong to Governor Morton the power to hire and fire Police Commissioners. Morton was then in Platt's debt, as the latter had undertaken to secure him the Presidential nomination in July. He could thus be relied on to dismiss TR promptly—and with a certain amount of satisfaction, for Morton was irked by the Commissioner's support of Thomas B. Reed for the Presidency. See *N.Y.T.*, Jan. 23, 1896; Mor.499.

14. Mor.509.

15. *N.Y.T.*, July 8, 1896.

16. Ib., Jan. 23, 1895; text in TR.Wks.XIV.215–6.

17. Igl.115–6; *Journal*, Jan. 21, 1896. See *Sun*, Jan. 23, 1896. Connable, Alfred, and Silverfarb, Edward, *Tigers of Tammany Hall* (NY, 1967) 215; *N.Y.T.*, Jan. 24, 1896.

18. *Herald*, Jan. 22, 1896. A letter from TR to Strong dated Jan. 21, 1896, confirms that their relations were "cordial" again. (Municipal Archives, Strong Mss.)

19. AND.186. Brant, Donald Birtley, "TR as New York City Police Commissioner" (unpublished dissertation, Princeton, 1964), reports it surfacing again in March.

20. *N.Y.T.*, Jan. 24, 1896; Mor.509.

21. *N.Y.T.*, Jan. 23, 1896.

22. Bis.I.62.

23. *Sun*, June 27, 1896, quoting TR. John J. Milholland, a Republican yard worker, also warned TR that "Parker could not be trusted . . . that he was not loyal to him as head of the Commission." "Not loyal to me?" TR exclaimed. "Impossible!" (Int. FRE.)

24. *N.Y.T.*, July 8, 1896; Mor.504–5; see *World*, Feb. 18, 1896.

25. *Sun*, Mar. 29, 1896. The account of the police promotions crisis of 1896, which begins here and occupies much of the chapter, is distilled from so many sources, and is itself so simplified (for the record was complicated by myriad questions of procedure and board-room politics) that documentation of every sentence will be fatal to the clarity of the whole. Major sources, however, are cited throughout. In general the story is based on New York City Police Department, *Minutes of the Board*, 1896 (TRB); the comprehensive reporting of *N.Y.T.*; AND.Scr; AND.92 ff; TR to B and HCL, *passim*; supplementary details from *Sun*, *World*, *Eve. Post*, and *Journal*.

26. *World*, Mar. 13, 1896.

27. *Herald*, Mar. 15, 1896.

28. Ib.; *N.Y.T.*, Mar. 18, 1896.

29. AND.66; on p. 93 he remarks that Conlin "was never a strong character."

30. *World*, Mar. 13, 1896; *Journal*,

Mar. 28. For Conlin's personal view of the matter, see Ste.280.
31. See AND.202; *World,* Mar. 13, 1896; P.D. *Minutes,* 604.
32. TR to B, Mar. 15, 1896. The following anecdote is undated in its source, Bis.I.62–3. However TR and Parker both confirm that the dinner took place in their testimony of July 8 and 9, 1896 (*N.Y.T.,* July 9 and 10) and mention Bishop's presence. Furthermore TR specifically states that Parker was invited on March 13 "to meet" Bishop. It follows that Parker and Bishop could not have met at any previous dinner in TR's house; since TR was in no mood to invite Parker ever again after March 13, the anecdote may be conclusively inserted here.
33. Parker, testimony July 8, 1896 (*N.Y.T.,* July 9).
34. TR to B, Mar. 15, 1896.
35. Bis.I.63.
36. Ib., 63–4.
37. P.D. *Minutes,* 614; *N.Y.T.,* Mar. 19, 1896; *Journal,* Mar. 24.
38. *Her.,* Mar. 15, 1895.
39. *Journal,* Mar. 24, 1896.
40. *Her.,* Mar. 15, 1895.
41. *Evening Post,* Mar. 24, 1896.
42. TR to B, Jan. 19, 1896.
43. See Ch. 19, n. 149, and Mor.504 n. The Venezuela affair was not settled until November 1896. For Cleveland's reply to TR's letter ("It seems to me that you and I have both been a little misunderstood recently") see Bis.I.69. Mor.522.
44. Lod.204; TR qu. by Talcott Williams in *Century Memorial to TR,* 74; Mor.509.
45. Ib., 505–6; *Chicago Tribune,* Feb. 23, 1895.
46. *Eve. Post,* Jan. 14, 1896.
47. Ib.
48. TR to B, Feb. 2, 1896; Lod.213.
49. *N.Y.T.,* June 6, 1896; Mor.503.
50. *Eve. Post,* Apr. 1, 1896; see *Commercial Advertiser,* Apr. 4.
51. Mor.525.
52. *Journal,* Apr. 11, 1896; AND.193; Mor.525–6; *N.Y.T.,* Apr. 17. AND.194 confirms.
53. Mor.525; *Journal,* Apr. 10, 1896.
54. Ib. TR's childhood friend, Fanny Smith Parsons, was watching from the gallery, and regretted that he did not behave to better effect. (Par.112.)
55. See Mor.524–32. *Her.,* Apr. 15, 1896.
56. *Sun,* Apr. 16, 1896; *Evening News,* Apr. 19.
57. *Eve. Post,* May 1, 1896.
58. Ste.276.
59. *World,* May 6, 1896. The following account is taken from two articles in this newspaper, plus others in the *Her., Comm. Adv., Eve. Post, Journal, Trib.,* and *N.Y.T.,* same date.
60. *Journal,* May 6, 1896.
61. *World,* May 6, 1896.
62. *Trib.,* May 6, 1896; *Eve. Post,* May 6; *Sun,* n.d. (TR.Scr.); *Her.,* May 7.
63. Ib.; *N.Y.T.,* May 7, 1896.
64. TR to B: "I am on pretty good terms with the old boy now, and he is trying to turn Parker out." June 1, 1896. *Press,* May 7.
65. AND.30–1; *Comm. Adv.,* June 2, 1896; *N.Y.T.,* Apr. 22; *Recorder,* Apr. 28.
66. *Recorder,* May 20, 1896. See also Ste.276.
67. A copy of this statement, with TR's covering letter, is in the New York Municipal Archives, Strong Mss.
68. Ber. 117–18; TR to B, June 1, 1896, also Apr. 26: "Unfortunately I cannot be sure of Parker's financial honesty . . . I feel very uneasy lest he compromises." Andrews memo, TRB.
69. *Recorder,* May 21?, 1896 (TR.Scr.).
70. *Sun,* May 28, 1896.
71. P.D. *Minutes,* 17; AND.148.
72. TR.Wks.XIII.126.
73. The following account is taken from *Sun* and *Her.,* June 2, 1896, plus various artists' sketches in TRB.

74. The mid-nineties marked the peak of the "bicycle boom" in the United States, and the proliferation of two-wheelers in New York City streets, combined with wagons and carriages, caused serious traffic jams long before the advent of the automobile. See AND.146–52; also TR.Auto. 187–8.
75. See, e.g., *Her.*, June 2, 1896.
76. *Eve. World*, June 3, 1896.
77. Ib.; *Her.*, same date.
78. *Eve. World*, June 3, 1896; *World*, June 4.
79. Ib.
80. Ib.
81. *Trib.*, June 9. The day before, this paper had become the first to call for Parker's resignation. According to Jessup, Philip C., *Elihu Root* (Dodd, Mead, 1938) I.190–191, TR and Andrews drew up the charges together, although they publicly denied this.
82. Max Fishel, *Eve. World* reporter, int. FRE. Jan. 1922, TRB; see also TR.Scr.
83. Riis, Jacob, *Making of an American* (NY, 1902) 334–5.
84. Ib.
85. AND.199; Gos.68.
86. See *Trib.*, June 9, 1896; *World*, June 10.
87. *N.Y.T.*, June 22, 1896. This newspaper contains the fullest session-by-session account of the Parker trial, and its issues of June 12, 13, 19, 22, July 3, 8, and 9 form the basis of the following summary. Other sources: AND.198–9; TR.Scr.
88. *World*, July 8, 1896; AND.158 agrees TR was too hasty in promotion procedures.
89. *World*, July 8, 1896; Mor.546.
90. *Her.*, June 26, 1896; *Sun*, July 3.
91. *N.Y.T.*, July 10, 13, 1896.
92. See, e.g., Lod.212; Pri.158. It will be remembered that TR had helped make Reed Speaker in 1889 (Ch. 16), and doubtless expected to be rewarded with a Cabinet post if he helped make him President.
93. Rho.12.
94. TR, qu. Dun.20.
95. TR to HCL, Feb. 27, 1896 (LOD.).
96. TR to B, Mar. 21, 1896 (TRB); Pla.212–4; qu. Pri.159.
97. Lod.222; Mor.543.
98. *N.Y.T.*, June 19, 1896; Rho.16–17.
99. *N.Y.T.*, July 19, 1896.
100. Mor.543.
101. *N.Y.T.*, Aug. 11, 1896; *World*, Aug. 3.
102. *Her.*, July 22, 1896: "Henceforth it will be war to the knife in the councils of the heads of the Police Department."
103. Mor.545.
104. This is confirmed in Mor.556 and Lod.229.
105. See Lod.214.
106. Mor.512, 519; TR to B, Apr. 26; Mor.542, 544. Bamie Roosevelt had amazed her family by marrying Commander Cowles in November 1895. She was then in her forty-first year. See Rixey, Lillian, *Bamie: TR's Remarkable Sister* (David McKay, 1963) 86–7.
107. Mor.544.
108. Storer, Maria Longworth (Mrs. Bellamy), "How Theodore Roosevelt Was Appointed Assistant Secretary of the Navy," *Harper's Weekly*, 56 (June 1, 1912). See also ib., *Theodore Roosevelt the Child* (privately printed, 1921) 15. Mrs. Storer dated this visit "in July 1896" and said that it lasted "several days." Her memory was slightly in error, since TR in a letter to B, Aug. 2, 1896, writes: "The dear Storers are spending Sunday with us." They probably arrived Saturday evening, Aug. 1, and left Monday morning, Aug. 3.

21: The Glorious Retreat

1. TR to CSR, Jan. 16, 1893. See also Storer, "How Theodore Roosevelt,"

Harper's Weekly, 56 (June 1, 1912), *Theodore Roosevelt the Child,* 15.
2. See Lee.58–60 and Mott, T. Bentley, *Myron T. Herrick, Friend of France* (NY, 1924) 72–74 for details of McKinley's "debt" to the Storers. His financial situation was entirely honorable in that he had endorsed the notes of a friend, totalling $130,000, believing that they would be paid off. The financial panic of 1893 caused the notes to fail, and McK took it upon himself to redeem them.
3. Storer, *Child,* 1.
4. Ib., 15.
5. Storer, "How TR Was Appointed," also see subsequent text. Ib.
6. Mark Hanna's arrival had been widely reported in the local papers, e.g., *New York Times,* July 29. See Rho.2 for his "comet-like" entry into the political scene. For the early relationship of MH and McK, see Lee.66–9; Rho.9–11; Morg.52 ff.
7. *N.Y.T.* and *Tribune,* July 29, 1896.
8. Mor.552. The adjective "coarse" was changed to "rough" by HCL when editing this letter for publication.
9. Ib., 556; *Trib.,* Aug. 4, 1896. Aug. 3 was formal opening day at HQ. The suggestion that TR was being evasive about the two July 28 visits to MH is prompted by the tone of his letter describing the Aug. 3 visit to the Storers: "The day after you left I saw Mark Hanna, and *after I thought we had grown intimate enough, the chance arriving,* I spoke of Bellamy . . ." (author's italics). It seems odd he should write of Hanna thus as a stranger, having dined with him *à quatre* only six days before.
10. Mor.556.
11. *Trib.,* Aug. 4, 1896; Mor.556.
12. Rho.10, 17–8; Whi.157; TR to B, Aug. 2, 1896. John Hay, visiting HQ at this time, remarked on the nervousness of the general atmosphere. Tha.150.
13. *World,* July 31, 1896; *Trib.,* Aug. 4; Mor.226–7, 230; Pri.160.
14. Boorstin, Daniel J., ed., *An American Primer* (U. Chicago Press, 1966) II.573 ff. gives the complete text of Bryan's speech.
15. *Trib.,* Aug. 5 and 6, 1896, reports that MH was having difficulty attracting "name" speakers who would be effective over a wide area of the country. TR was emphatically in this category.
16. Whi.329. TR told Hanna's biographer that the Chairman had "not a single small trait in his nature." Cro.361. In TR.Auto.157 TR wrote with a trace of wistfulness, "I do not think he ever grew to like me."
17. Description of MH based on sketch reproduced at beginning of this chapter; other sketches and pors. in *Review of Reviews,* XIV.4. (Oct., 1896). Prose sources: White, William Allen, *Masks in a Pageant* (Macmillan, 1928) 155 ff.; Whi.292; *N.Y.T.,* July 29, 1896; *World,* ib., and July 30; Murat Halstead in *R. of Rs.,* cited above; Rho., Sul., Sto., and Bee., *passim.*
18. Rho.12; Whi.292; Morg.230,253.
19. Ib., 219; Rho.10.
20. See McK to MH, Nov. 12, 1896, qu. Cro.229; also ib., 221. Although the National Committee ended the campaign with a considerable surplus, MH refused to accept reimbursement of the $100,000 he had spent before the Convention. For McK's metallic quality, see Tha.III.78; White, *Masks,* 175.
21. MH's despondency lasted at least through mid-August. Cro.219. TR to B, Aug. 2, 1896; Mor.554.
22. *Sun,* Aug. 13, 1896.
23. TR was very defensive about this bad publicity. See Lod.230. Certainly the huge size of the crowd and high temperatures (New York was in the middle of a heat wave) must be counted as extenuating circumstances. Other newspapers guardedly praised the security arrangements, and the Democratic National Committee sent a formal note of thanks to Chief Conlin. Even so, there were some peculiar goings-on

which the Police Department never satisfactorily explained. George Spinney, TR's old reporter friend from Albany days, was told that "the doors is locked" when he presented his press pass. Spinney protested, and was instantly arrested on a charge of disorderly conduct. *World,* Aug. 13, 1896. Several other eminent citizens and newsmen suffered the same treatment, as did many members of the general public. These were all "mysteries of reform," the *Sun* editors remarked, "to which Mr. Theodore Roosevelt had better apply his intellect without delay." Ib., Aug. 14.

24. Ib., Aug. 13, 1896.

25. TR to B, Aug. 15, 1896.

26. Mor.558; *Herald,* Aug. 20, 1896.

27. *N.Y.T.,* July 13, 1896.

28. *Sun,* Aug. 21, 1896; *N.Y.T., World,* same date. The *Times* editorially accused Parker of "intolerable impudence and bravado," and said he had "wrought inestimable harm on the Police Department and to the whole cause of municipal reform in this city." Aug. 21, 1896.

29. TR to B, Sept. 13, 1896.

30. Ib.

31. See Boorstin, *Primer,* II.581.

32. TR to B, Sep. 13, 1896; to HCL, Mor.559; *N.Y.T.,* Sep. 11. There were two GOP headquarters, one in Chicago and one in New York.

33. TR to *Evening Post* reporter, c. Sep. 11, 12, 1896. (TR.Scr., n.d.)

34. *R. of Rs.,* XIV.4 (Oct. 1896). This periodical gives good monthly summaries of the campaign. See also ib., 5 (Nov. 1896).

35. Ib., see also Cro.; Rho.20 ff.

36. Cro.209; TR to B, Sep. 13.

37. See also TR to B, Aug. 2, 1896; Pri.162–3.

38. TR.Wks.XIII.153.

39. To the Sound Money League, Sep. 11, 1896. Text in TR.Wks.XIV.25–7. The Chicago platform contained a plank "which condemned the use of the injunction in labor disputes and deplored the judicial invalidation of the income tax." Pri.163.

40. Lod.236–7; TR to B, Oct. 4, 1896.

41. Ib. The visit probably occurred on Oct. 2 (Lod.237). Cro.215.

42. Lee.88; Cro.215–6; Rho.25.

43. See Ch. 16. TR to B, Oct. 4, 1896.

44. Ib., Oct. 11, 1896.

45. *R. of Rs.,* XIV.4 (Oct. 1896); Cro.217–8.

46. For a good recent account of the campaign, see Morg.209–248. Lod.237.

47. Pri.163–4; TR.Wks.XIV.258–79.

48. *Chicago Tribune,* Oct. 16, 1896; TR.Wks.XIV.258.

49. Ib.; also 265, 264–5.

50. *Chicago Tribune,* Oct. 16, 1896.

51. Ib.

52. Ib.; see also Ch. 4.

53. TR to *Sun* reporter, Oct. 28, 1896. On Oct. 17, TR and Bryan addressed simultaneous meetings in Detroit.

54. *Sun,* ib.

55. *N.Y.T.,* Oct. 18, 1896. *Sun,* Oct. 28.

56. TR to B, Oct. 22 and 26, 1896; ib., Nov. 1; Mor.566.

57. Rho.29; Stoddard, Henry L., *Presidential Sweepstakes* (Putnam, 1948) 110.

58. Rho.28.

59. Bee.552.

60. Whi.292.

61. Mor.566; Bee.523. Hanna had, for better or worse, laid the foundations of modern campaign spending by systematically assessing banks and large corporations at ½ of 1% of their capital. Cro.220. His largest benefactor—John D. Rockefeller—gave $250,000. The total GOP campaign cost $3,350,000, a staggering sum in those days. Pri.163.

62. Mor.566. TR, in this letter, uses the adjective "Jew" when describing the bankers. It is the only hint, if hint it be, of anti-Semitism in his vast correspondence, and it pales into insignificance beside the remarks typical of his class and kind, for instance those constantly exchanged by John Hay and Henry Adams. See Wag.230. TR later appointed at least one of his "Jew" fellow-guests at the Victory luncheon, Isaac Seligman, to high state office (Mor.566), and as President he relied much on the counsel of another, Jacob Schiff.

63. TR to B, Aug. 2, 1896.

64. Lod.240; ib., 241.

65. Ib., 242.

66. Storer, "How TR Was Appointed."

67. Ib. For an insight into McK's true feelings about the Storers, see Mott, *Herrick*, 72–4.

68. As late as 1921, Mrs. Storer was convinced McK had said, "I will do this to please you," but, as will be seen, he could not have said anything of the kind.

69. Mor.569.

70. Storer, *Child*, 25.

71. Mor.570.

72. TR's negotiations with and around TCP during the next three months are fully described in Lod.244–66. Gos.172; Morg.267; Lod.244. When HCL asked what "war" TCP had in mind, the Easy Boss replied that TR would interfere with his patronage in the Brooklyn Navy Yard. Ib., 245.

73. Ib., 247; see also Mor.569.

74. Ib., 572.

75. Gos.171–2.

76. See Mor.34; 55–58; Choate to TR, Oct. 31, 1881 (facsimile in Lor.192). Mor.59.

77. Lod.249; Pri.169; *Her.*, Dec. 17; Mor.572. In fairness to TR it must be said that he would have come out for Choate if forced to a decision—see ib. Nevertheless, his refusal to speak for his old patron, and his tacit endorsement of TCP, must be regarded as proof of his ruthless ambition and invariable policy of working with the organization whenever possible and expedient.

78. TR to B, Dec. 20, 1896; ib., Nov. 29; ib., Dec. 26.

79. *Morning Advertiser*, Dec. 31, 1896.

80. *Eve. Post*, Jan. 1, 1897; *Her.*, Dec. 31, 1896.

81. Qu. *Her.*, Jan. 9, 1897; qu. Pri.169.

82. *Eve. Post*, Jan. 8, 1897.

83. Ib.; Gos.171. Fourteen years later, when TCP came to write his *Autobiography*, the memory of those seven dissenters still rankled. Pla.348.

84. TR to B, Jan. 24, 1897; ib., Feb. 28.

85. *The Royal Navy*, 7 vols. (London, 1897–1903). TR's volume, which he finished writing during the first week of March (TR to B, Mar. 7, 1897), was published under the title *The War with the United States, 1812–1815*. For a complimentary British review, see *The Atheneum*, Dec. 28, 1901.

86. Lod.255.

87. Mor.582.

88. TR to B, Feb. 28, 1897.

89. Ib.

90. TR to T. R. Lounsbury, Mar. 9, 1897, qu. Brant, Donald Birtley, Jr., "TR as New York City Police Commissioner," unpublished dissertation (Princeton, 1964) 66.

91. See, e.g., *Eve. Post*, Mar. 1, 1897; *World, Commercial Advertiser*, Mar. 4; *Her.*, Mar. 6; see also TR in Mor.662.

92. *Sun*, Mar. 2, 1897.

93. Ib.; *Her.*, Mar. 18, 1897.

94. TR/HCL correspondence in Lod. *passim:* Lod.253.

95. Bee.525 (wrongly dated after Ambassador Cassini's arrival in Washington, June 1898).

96. Lod.253. There were, of course, other objections to TR's appointment. Senator Chandler of New Hampshire, for example, considered him overqualified. Secretary Long concurred with this view. Morg.262.

97. Tabouis, Geneviève, *Jules Cambon: Par l'un des Siens* (Paris, 1938), 84 (author's translation).

98. Rho.41; Bee.529.

99. Lod.I.262.

100. Long had been a Congressman

during TR's CSC days, and was a regular guest with TR at Thomas B. Reed's dinner table. McCall, Samuel W., *Thomas B. Reed* (Houghton Mifflin, 1914) 143. For TR's first respectful impression of him as an orator at the 1884 Chicago Convention, see Ch. 10.

101. HCL in Woo.43; E.G.R. in un. clip, Aug. 31, 1919, TRB; Lee.137.

102. Mott, *Herrick,* 74. Pri.169 says that TCP was "singularly dull" not to have seen this before. The Easy Boss may have been many things, but he was not dull. His reasons for objecting to TR's appointment were perfectly logical, and he made no secret of them. In the first place he felt that TR, as Assistant Secretary, would interfere with his powers of patronage at the Brooklyn Navy Yard. In the second, he was annoyed that McK's previous New York appointments—Secretary of the Interior Cornelius Bliss and Ambassador to France Horace Porter—were both of them anti-organization men. TR would make a third; and since McK was unlikely to give any more appointments to the Empire State, TCP felt that his organization, which had worked so hard on behalf of the President, had been slighted. Hence he refused to approve of TR. Of course TCP had other, less public reasons. He hoped (vainly) that TR would buy his approval by persuading Mayor Strong to replace him with a Commissioner friendly to the organization. Finally, this writer would suggest that TCP was simply exercising his political muscle. Not many Senators get a chance to say "no" to a President in the early days of their relationship, and the Roosevelt affair gave TCP an ideal opportunity to bully McK a little. "Anybody but that fellow!" he exploded when the President mentioned TR to him. Myron Herrick's account (Mott, 72–74) shows how deferentially McK was forced to treat the old man. TCP was further soothed with a series of prize plums, including the Collectorship of New York. His own account of the affair, in Pla.540 ff., is patently untruthful. See Lod.244–5, 261, 263–4, and Lee.137.

103. Paullin, Charles O., *Paullin's History of Naval Administration, 1775–1911* (U.S. Naval Institute, 1968) 369; Lod.266.

104. N.Y. *World,* Apr. 9, 1897.

105. *N.Y.T.,* Apr. 18, 1897.

106. Ib. See also *Eve. Sun,* Apr. 17, 1897, and Rii.29.

107. *World,* Apr. 8, 1897. Mayor Strong, for one, did not publicly regret TR's departure. But see *N.Y.T.,* Apr. 16 for the eulogies of those who did.

108. *N.Y.T.,* Apr. 8, 1897.

109. AND.144; Brant, "TR, PC," 31; TR in his resignation letter to Strong, Mor.595; AND.40–1; *Mail & Express,* May 1, 1897; AND.86–8; *World,* May 22, 1895. See also TR's very funny compilation of specimen entrance examination answers in Mor.578–81, and Wis.51–2 for a good Civil Service List anecdote.

110. New York Police Department, *Annual Reports,* 1895 and 1897; Richardson, James F., *The New York Police: Colonial Times to 1901* (Oxford U. Press, 1970) 91; AND.86–89; Mor.600. See also "Who'll be a Bluecoat?" in *World,* August 1, 1895, for TR's recruitment policies, and Ber. 60–62 on "the military analogy."

111. Mor.596; TR to Strong, ib., 594; Richardson, *Police,* 260 ff.; AND.44, 65–6, 144–56; Brant, "TR, PC," 31, 76; *Trib.,* Sep. 12, 1895. See also Hurwitz, Howard L., *TR and Labor in New York State* (Columbia U. Press, 1943) 116 and *passim.* Not all of these achievements can be ascribed directly to TR, but as president of the Board, and member ex officio of all its committees, he undoubtedly deserves principal credit. In moral achievement, certainly, he stood alone. See E. L. Godkin to TR,

modestly quoted in TR.Auto.408, Ber. 120–21, and Avery Andrews's last word: "It may truthfully be said that Theodore Roosevelt at no time in his career fought more effectively for the basic principles of free government than he fought for them as New York Police Commissioner." AND.9.

112. See, e.g., *N.Y.T.* ed., Apr. 8, 1897: "We cannot consider it [the Assistant Secretaryship] in any sense a promotion."

113. The actual date of TR's resignation was Apr. 19, 1897. Mor.594. Igl.121., quoting TR.

114. *Harper's Weekly,* May 2, 1897.

115. AND. *passim.*

116. Municipal Archives, Strong mss. Most newspapers, and many eminent lawyers, concurred with this verdict, while still urging Parker to resign. See, e.g., *N.Y.T.,* July 13, 1897.

117. AND.207; Mor.660–1.

118. Che.14–15; Pri.150–1; see Mor. 711 for TR's disgusted reaction.

119. Ste.275.

22: The Hot Weather Secretary

Important sources not in Bibliography: 1. Grenville, John A. S., "American Preparations for War with Spain," in *Journal of American Studies* (GB) 1968.2(1). 2. Karsten, Peter, "The Nature of 'Influence': Roosevelt, Mahan, and the Concept of Sea Power," in *American Quarterly,* 1971.23(4). A convincing reassessment of the early TR/Mahan relationship; required reading for all students of TR's political methods. (See also Turk, Richard W., *The Ambiguous Relationship: Theodore Roosevelt and Alfred Thayer Mahan* (Greenwood Press, 1987). 3. Nicholson, Philip Y., "George Dewey and the Expansionists of 1898," in *Vermont History,* 1974.42(3). 4. Paullin, Charles Oscar, *Paullin's History of Naval Administration 1775–1911* (U.S. Naval Institute, Annapolis, 1968). 5. Spector, Ronald, *Admiral of the New Empire* [Dewey] (Louisiana State U., 1974). 6. Sprout, Harold and Margaret, *The Rise of American Naval Power, 1776–1918* (Princeton, 1966). In this revised version of their classic history, the authors anticipate Karsten *op. cit.* by lowering their assessment of Mahan's influence vis à vis TR's.

1. Mor.599; TR.Auto.12; But.291; Igl.121–2.

2. *New York Times,* May 2, 1897. (This desk is now preserved at TRB.)

3. *Harper's Weekly,* May 7, 1897.

4. LON. Apr. 9, 1897; Mor.588; But. 40.

5. "Rightly or wrongly Uncle John [Sherman, Secretary of State] and Long are considered and treated as senile."—Elizabeth Cameron to Henry Adams, Mar. 4, 1898 (ADA).

6. Mor.604.

7. "I make it a point not to trouble myself overmuch to acquire a thorough knowledge of the details pertaining to any branch of the service . . . the range is so enormous I could make little progress, and that is a great expense of health and time, in mastering it." Long, Journal, Feb. 2, 1897.

8. Pau.428; Intro to Lon; LON. *passim;* pors.

9. Pau.369, 429; Mor.608.

10. Chicago *Times-Herald,* Apr. 7, 1897; *Washington Post,* Apr. 8.

11. London *Times,* Apr. 8.

12. Clip dated "May 1897" in TR.Scr.; Mor.602–3.

13. Cullom int. *N.Y. World* news clip, n.d. [1897], in Pratt Scrapbook (TRB).

14. Mor.626; Nicholson 217.

15. See Pra. for a negative but invaluable account of the movement.

16. Bea.22–3; Gar.182; Mor.608, 621; Sam.3.161–3; Millis, Walter, *Arms and Men* (N.Y., 1956), 169; Jos., Chapter 2; Nicholson, 217; Mor.621; Her.197.

17. Spr.225; Nicholson, *passim.*

18. TR.Works.XIII.182–99.
19. Mor.601.n. Japan had despatched the cruiser *Naniwa Kan* to Hawaii in mid-April, fearful that an annexation move by the U.S. would threaten the rights of some 25,000 Japanese citizens in the islands. See also Pra.217–220, May.127.
20. TR.Wks.XIII.185–6.
21. Pittsburgh *Dispatch*, Sep. 12, 1897; *Sun*, May 22.
22. TR.Wks.XIII.199.
23. Bis.1.77; TR.Scr. *passim.*
24. *W. Post,* n.d., TRB; *Sun,* June 3, 1897; *Herald,* ib.; *Daily Picayune,* June 7; *Harper's W.*, June 19.
25. L.E.Q. to H. L. Stoddard, Feb. 15, 1919, TRB.
26. Millis, *Arms*, 169–70; Spr.226; Lee. 149.
27. Spr.202 ff.; Bur.44. See also Millis, *Arms,* 166–7; Pra.212 ff.
28. This para. based largely on Grenville.
29. Pau.416; Grenville. (Herbert was not against naval expansion per se; his scruples were in the area of foreign policy. See Spr.218–20.)
30. Mor.617–8.
31. Mor.607. (Mahan had recently retired from NWC, but continued to influence it.)
32. Bea.57, Mor.622; Pra.217–9; Morg.295; Mor.627–8.
33. For details of this international race, see Bur.28 ff., Bea.14 ff.
34. Mor.623.
35. Mor.622–3.
36. The following account of the early relationship between TR and Mahan is based largely on Karsten, *passim.*
37. Millis, *Arms,* 155–6 (the adjective "workmanlike" is his).
38. Luce to TR, Feb. 13, 1888, qu. Karsten, 588; see also ib., 225–6.
39. See, e.g., TR.Wks.XII.264–72; ib., 372–79; XIV.309.
40. Karsten, 591.
41. Bur. points out that despite their earlier similarity of views, Mahan was always the nautical professional, arguing that the Navy was the engine of national greatness, whereas TR was the political professional, arguing that national greatness necessitated a strong Navy. See also Turk, Richard L., *The Ambiguous Relationship: Theodore Roosevelt and Alfred Thayer Mahan* (Greenwood, 1987).
42. Mor.627–8.
43. Ib., 628–9. (But TR was not above "confiscating and filing" documents himself—for example a list of official complaints that threatened to slow his pet torpedo-boat construction program. See Mor.630.)
44. Mor.628. It will be remembered that this was just where Boss Platt had worried that TR might interfere with organization patronage.
45. Mor.629–631; see also TR to B, Apr. 30, 1897.
46. Bea.57–60.
47. Mor.624, 635.
48. Reprinted in TR.Wks.XIII.
49. Qu. Sul.389.
50. *Literature,* Apr. 23, 1898, qu. Edel, Leon, *Henry James: The American Essays* (N.Y., 1956). (For a favorable review of *Ideals,* see *Harvard Grad. Mag.*, March 1898.)
51. See Bea.474 for a sample list of TR's contributions; also Pra.222; also, e.g., Mor.622.
52. Grenville 36–7; Mor.627. The entire next para. based on Grenville. He prints the war plan as an appendix, 41–47.
53. Grenville, 43. (He notes that this plan also contained the first known war plan against Japan, anticipating War Plan Orange by some sixteen years.)
54. TR to EKR, June 18, 1897, qu. Hag. LW. 1.138; see also TR.Wks.XI. xiii.
55. Mor.652.
56. Descr. taken from Hag.LW. *passim;* Holme, John G., *Life of Leonard Wood* (N.Y., 1920), 6; pics. and pors. in TRB.

57. See N.Y. *Tribune,* May 10, 1894.
58. Lod.285. Wood had come to Washington in Sep. 1895 as Assistant Attending Surgeon to President Cleveland. Hag.LW.1.133.
59. Descr. taken from Spector, *passim;* Nicholson, *passim;* pics. and pors.
60. Nicholson, 214; Spector 30–39 for background.
61. Qu. Clemens, Will M., *The Life of Admiral GD* (N.Y., 1899), 73.
62. TR.Auto.216.
63. Nicholson, 221 (but Spector disagrees).
64. Spector, 32.
65. Ib., 36.
66. TR to B, Aug. 17, 1897.
67. Mor.620, 649. (See Roosevelt, Nicholas, *TR: The Man as I Knew Him* (Dodd, Mead, 1967) for one child's memory of these summers at Sagamore Hill.)
68. Mor.625; Las.118–9, 167; Asbell, B., *The FDR Memoirs* (NY, 1973). Like TR, FDR went to Harvard, edited a college newspaper, studied at Columbia Law School, entered the State Legislature in his twenties, and then became successively Assistant Secretary of the Navy, Governor of New York, and President of the United States. He also married TR's niece.
69. TR to B, July 10, 1897.
70. These Rooseveltian comments actually date from a similar torpedo-boat ride in the second week of May (*Sun,* May 22), but seem quite relevant here. For admiring press comments on his report on the torpedo-boats, see ib., and *W. Post,* May 23.
71. Mor.635; see *Sun,* Aug. 10, for TR's report of this tour.
72. *Herald,* July 24; *Tribune,* July 27. (Ib., July 31, prints a letter saying TR was misquoted, but TR himself admitted to Lodge that the speech was reported "with substantial accuracy." Mor.637.)
73. Lee.106. Long had suffered a nervous breakdown in 1896.
74. Mor.637.
75. TR's own phrase. See TR to Bellamy Storer, Sep. 2, 1897; also Mor.691.
76. Pau.365.
77. Ib.; see also chart 4, "The Navy Department," in Mor.627; see Karsten, Peter, *The Naval Aristocracy* (N.Y., 1972), on the Navy as a social phenomenon in 19th-century America.
78. Mor.655, 673.
79. Adams, Henry, *The Education of HA* (Houghton Mifflin, 1974), 417.
80. Mor.637–65 *passim.*
81. LON. diaries *passim.*
82. Mor.662. Reading through TR's correspondence with Long during the summer of 1897, one cannot help noticing how scrupulous he was in upholding the Secretary's dignity. The letters, for all their amusing insistence that Long extend his vacation, are models of frankness and courtesy. See Mor.639–64.
83. Ib., 647.
84. Ib., 652, 4, 61.
85. Ib., 664.
86. *Sun,* Sep. 5, 1897; *Proceedings of the U.S. Naval Institute* (23) 509 ff. (1897).
87. TR.Scr. For sample comment, see *Sun* and *Boston Journal,* Sep. 5, 1897.
88. Whi.299 speaks of "that summer day" in describing his first meeting with TR, but elsewhere refers to it as "autumn." Late August or early September seem most likely.
89. Reprinted in Boorstin, Daniel, ed., *An American Primer,* U. Chicago Press (1966), Vol. 2, 584 ff.
90. These paras. based on Whi.296–9; also Joh. *passim.*
91. Whi.297.
92. White (ib.), writing in the late 1930s, says the lunch took place at the Army and Navy Club. This is probably a slip of memory, given TR's fondness for the Metropolitan Club, not to mention its double lamb chops, which White nostalgically describes. TR's

papers for the period are full of Metropolitan chits for double lamb chops: he seems to have had an insatiable passion for the dish.
93. Whi.298.
94. Ib., 297–8.
95. Ib.
96. The following account is taken from the *Herald,* Sep. 9, and *Sun,* Sep. 9 and 24, 1897.
97. Charles H. Cramp. qu. Pau.397.
98. The party included Frederic Remington, the artist, as well as two reporters carefully selected by TR as part of his naval public-relations effort.
99. Mor.680.
100. Mor.675, 90; see TR to HCL, Sep. 24, Mor.689.
101. Ib., 676. The account of the following conversation comes entirely from this letter.
102. Carpenter, Frank, *Carp's Washington* (McGraw-Hill, 1960), 179.
103. Descr. of McKinley based on Whi.292, 333–5; Carpenter, 27; John Hay to HA, Oct. 20, 1896 (Hay.3.78); Bee.480; pics. and pors. For the President's extraordinary gaze, see, e.g., Lor.360 and the last por. in Morg; also LaFollette qu. Lee.38–9: "The pupils of his eyes would dilate until they became almost black, and his face, naturally without much color, would become almost like marble."
104. Mor.677.
105. TR to B, Sep. 17; Mor.685, 717; Karsten, 592. (Ib. notes how closely TR's plan matched the actual course of the war.)
106. Mor.682–9.
107. Un. clip, TR.Scr.
108. Senator Chandler's letter was dated Sep. 25 (TRP), but since that was a Saturday, it follows that it would have been neither delivered nor read until Monday Sep. 27, the date of TR's reply.
109. The following account is based on Nicholson, 223–6, plus other sources as cited below.
110. Mor.691.
111. Ib., 691–2.
112. TR.Auto.216.
113. Sprout, 224; Nicholson, 226.
114. Mor.692, 915; TR.Auto.217.
115. Dewey, George, *Autobiography,* 169–70; TR.Auto.216. Although the main facts of Dewey's appointment, as detailed above, are borne out by many sources, there is some ambiguity about the time-sequence of events postdating Long's return on Sep. 28. According to Spector, 38, it was not until Oct. 16 that Senator Proctor reported McK's favorable response to his appeal. But Dewey (*Autobiography*) and Nicholson, 224–26, both imply that things were settled on the day that Long returned. If so, TR would only have delayed Sen. Chandler's letter by a few hours, until the Secretary recognized Dewey's appointment as a fait accompli. It is hardly possible that he could have held on to the letter until Oct. 16. Whatever the case, there can be no doubt that TR was in large part responsible for making Dewey C-in-C of the Asiatic Squadron, and for the infinitely larger consequences of that appointment. (Spector, 32–9; Bea.63; Mor.822–3, 915; Nicholson, 227.)
116. Mor.694–7, 710.
117. Lod.286; TR to B, Oct. 17 and 28; Mor.702–9.
118. TR.Wks.XI.xi.
119. Mor.750, 66, 713, 707.
120. Pau.459.
121. Mor.713; TR to B, Nov. 30, 1897.
122. Grenville, 35.
123. Mor.1.717 (italics mine).
124. Qu. Pau.460.
125. Mor.790.
126. *Eve. Post,* Jan. 4, 1898. See Bur.49 and TR.Wks.XIV.427–37 for more on the Personnel Bill.
127. *Proceedings of the Biological Society of Washington,* XI.271–5 (Dec. 17, 1897).
128. See Woo.45 ff.
129. Sep. 19, 1897.

23: The Lieutenant Colonel

Important sources not listed in Bibliography: 1. Paullin, Charles Oscar, *Paullin's History of Naval Administration 1775–1911* (U.S. Naval Institute, 1968).
1. Mil.93.
2. The *Maine* had been in Key West since December 15 of the previous year, "under confidential instructions to proceed at once to Havana in the event of local disturbances which might threaten American safety." (Ib.) The Consul-General, Fitzhugh Lee, was given responsibility for determining when that moment might be. "Two dollars" was to be followed by a second code message, upon receipt of which Captain Sigsbee would leave for Havana instantly. (Ib.) See also May.135.
3. The following account of TR's interview with JDL is taken from the latter's Journal, Jan. 13, 1898, in LON. Extracts from the Journal are published in Mayo, Lawrence S., ed., *America of Yesterday* (Atlantic Monthly Press, 1923) and Long, Margaret, ed., *The Journal of John D. Long* (Rindge, N.H., 1956).
4. Long, Journal, Jan. 13, 1898, LON.
5. Mor.758. TR also wrote on the same day to Col. Francis Vinton Greene in a similar vein.
6. Mor.755; TR to B, Jan. 9, 1898.
7. TR to B, Jan. 17, 1898; Mor.767. For a chilling anecdote about TR's determination to make a "fighter" out of Ted, see Bradley, John, ed., *Lady Curzon's India: Letters of a Vicereine* (N.Y., 1985), 133.
8. This attitude has become a characteristic of the Roosevelt family as a whole. But.146.
9. Mor.759–63 has the text of this memo.
10. Ib., 760.
11. Ib., Mor.763; Her.209, 206–7; Mil.93; May.137.
12. De Lôme qu. May.137. See also Mil.58; Morg.356.
13. Mil.97–8.
14. Ib., 95–6; Her.210.
15. TR to B, Jan. 20, 25, 27, 1898; Mor.767.
16. Mor.765, 766, 767.
17. See Pri.203 ff. Pra.226, quoting HCL.
18. Morg.356; *N.Y. Journal,* Feb. 9, 1898.
19. De Lôme qu. Mil.98.
20. See ib., 98–9; Gov. 73–74; Morg. 356–9.
21. This anecdote is based on Bee.546 ff. Beer's own source was Mlle. Adler's precisely-dated account of the meeting with TR, which he found in her brother's papers.
22. MH qu. Bee.548.
23. Mrs. Wainwright qu. Her.210.
24. Mil.96, 100–1; Her.212; Azo.12–14.
25. Long, Journal, Feb. 16, 1898, LON.; Mil.102.
26. Ib., 102; Lee.166.
27. Brown, Charles H., *The Correspondents' War* (NY, 1967), 120–1. Ib., ff., gives the fullest account of press coverage of the *Maine* tragedy.
28. Mil.105; Her.214; ib., 212 (author's copy has "88" survivors, an obvious typographical mistake for "8"). Because the explosion was forward, only two of the dead were officers.
29. Mil.104, 106.
30. See May.139–41.
31. Long, Journal, Feb. 17, 1898, LON.; see Lee.166; Mil.108, *N.Y. Journal,* Feb. 17.
32. Hag.LW.I.141.
33. Mor.775. This was a private letter, written to Benjamin J. Diblee on Feb. 16, as "a Jingo" and "one Porc man to another." TR was of course scrupulous about expressing such opinions in public.
34. Mor.775, 783. See, e.g., ib., 773–4.
35. *N.Y. Journal,* Feb. 17, 1898; Brown, *Correspondents,* 123; Her.217; Mil.108.

36. Ib.; also 110.
37. *Sun*, Feb. 22, 1898; un. clip in TRB.
38. TR to B, Feb. 19, 1898; Mor.783; ib., 785, 804.
39. Mor.785.
40. Long, Journal, *passim*, LON. See, e.g., ib., Feb. 25, 1898.
41. Ib.
42. Mor.784–5.
43. Dewey qu. TR.Auto.218. Mil.87 and Her.12 concur.
44. It will be remembered that the Atlantic Squadron was already menacingly moored off Key West. Her.209.
45. Long, Journal, Feb. 26, 1898, LON.; Dewey, qu. TR.Auto.218; Bea.61–2; Her.219–20; Mil.112; see also Gar.186.
46. Mor.784.
47. Long, Journal, Feb. 25, 1898, LON.
48. Ib., Feb. 26, 1898.
49. Not only that, but JDL confirmed it the following day with a redundant order echoing TR's own words: "Keep full of coal, the very best that can be had." Perhaps the Secretary wished to give the impression that TR had been anticipating his own policy. In any case, TR was entirely within his rights to act the way he did on Feb. 25. A written memorandum of JDL, dated Apr. 21, 1897, states specifically: ". . . You will, at all times when the Secretary of the Navy shall be absent from the Department, whether such absence shall continue during the whole or any part of an official day, perform the duties of the Secretary of the Navy and sign all orders and other papers appertaining to such duties." (TRP.)
50. Long, Journal, Feb. 26, 1898, LON.
51. See, e.g., Bea.61–3; Her.220; Mor.784 fn. For a critical view, see Lee.169. The fallacy that HCL helped TR draft his Dewey telegram has been laid to rest by Gar.186. TR.Wks.XII. xviii. Modern historians tend to agree with Dewey as to TR's seminal role in bringing about the Battle of Manila. "The Assistant Secretary," writes Howard K. Beale, "had seized the opportunity given by Long's absence to insure our grabbing the Philippines without a decision to do so by either Congress or the President, or at least of all the people. Thus was important history made not by economic forces or democratic decisions but through the grasping of chance authority by a man with daring and a program." (Bea.63.)
52. Mor.786, 787.
53. Ib., 790.
54. May.149–150.
55. Ib., 148–9.
56. Tabouis, *Jules Cambon*, author's translation.
57. Mil.115, Morg.363–4.
58. May.149; Morg.364; Mil.117. Of course this is not to say there were not many absentees. The actual vote was 311–0 in the House, 76–0 in the Senate.
59. Morg.364; Her.223.
60. Mor.789.
61. Long, Journal, Mar. 8, 1898, LON.; see Her.223–4 for details of the naval expansion program. Morg.364; May.149.
62. The following anecdote is taken from Flint, Charles R., "I Take a Hand in Combining Railroads and Industries," *System*, Jan. 22, 1922.
63. The *Nictheroy* arrived ahead of schedule, was rechristened *Buffalo*, and did good service in the Philippines. Flint, "I Take a Hand," 31.
64. Wood in TR.Wks.XI.xvi.
65. Hag.LW.I.141. Dun.266 describes Wood as McK's "favorite." Mor.792.
66. Elizabeth Cameron to Henry Adams, March 21, 1898, ADA.
67. TR.Auto.216; Mil.123; Her.225; Pra.246; Rho.51; Mil.123.
68. Proctor qu. Rho.51–2.
69. Rho.52; May.144–5; Morg.365; Pra.246 ff; Mil.124.
70. Rho.53.
71. Mor.798.
72. Herrick, *Naval Revolution*, 230.
73. Rho.53.
74. Bee.551; *Evening Telegraph*, Mar.

27, 1898; *Chicago Chronicle,* Mar. 29. Hanna's personal opinion, which he never altered, was "War is just a damn nuisance." Bee.554.

75. Mil.127; Her.214–216. For text of the report, see Senate Exec. Docs., 55th Cong., 2nd Session, No. 207. Herrick has a good analysis of the evidence, and reveals that there was considerable dissent among members of the court before the unanimous verdict was reached. In 1911 another U.S. Court of Inquiry, which obtained funds to raise the *Maine,* upheld the findings of the first. There remained, however, a considerable amount of doubt in the minds of many impartial analysts, due to the inconclusive nature of the evidence. As the Spanish-American War faded from memory into history, the U.S. grew increasingly embarrassed about its assumption of Spanish guilt in 1898. According to Weems, J. E., *The Fate of the Maine* (NY, 1941), TR's fifth cousin Franklin D. Roosevelt made a lame attempt to atone for it in 1935 by sending Madrid a Navy Department statement absolving Spain of all suspicion. The *Maine* disaster remains an unexplained mystery to this day, although contemporary opinion is that the explosion was accidental. See Rickover, Adm. Hyman, *How the Battleship Maine Was Destroyed* (Washington, 1976).

76. Kipling, Rudyard, *Something of Myself* (London, 1936); EKR to TR Jr., July 13, 1927, Library of Congress.

77. Mor.799; ib., 806; Levine, Isaac Don, *Mitchell: Pioneer of Air Power* (NY, 1943) 20. Samuel Pierrepont Langley was the head of the Smithsonian Institution, and had become friendly with TR during his Cosmos Club days. The Langley flying machine, or "aerodrome," was demonstrably capable of powered, unmanned flight over distances of up to one mile. Kipling, in *Something of Myself,* recalls accompanying TR to one of Langley's experimental launchings, which unfortunately ended with a nosedive into the Potomac. Gen. Greely, Chief of the U.S. Signal Corps, was another enthusiastic Langley backer, and worked with Assistant Secretary Roosevelt to set up the Davis Board. $50,000 was eventually appropriated by Congress for further Langley experiments, none of which were successful. TR and Greely were assisted in the Senate by John Mitchell of Wisconsin, father of Gen. Billy Mitchell, the air power visionary of the 1920s.

78. The best and most sympathetic account of McKinley's pre-war agony is in Gov. 76–90. See also Lee.181; Kohlsaat, H. H., *From McKinley to Harding* (Scribner's, 1923) 66; Rho.31.

79. See May.153.

80. Rho.63; Mil.131.

81. JDL found the President bleary and befuddled from lack of sleep on Apr. 14. Long, Journal, same date, LON. Mil.133; Mor.812, and, e.g., 812: "I have preached the doctrine to him [McK] in such plain language that he will no longer see me!" (TR to W. Tudor, Apr. 5, 1898.) Also *Sun,* Mar. 29 d.l., TR.Scr.: "Of all the executive officers with whom Mr. McKinley has held consultations . . . there has been only one who has not ceased to use every endeavor to influence the President . . . to end the Cuban trouble without further delay." The same article praises TR's loyalty, but says that McK found him embarrassingly outspoken: "He has been set down as too radical for further advice." For more on McK's war message, see Mil.133–4; Morg. 368–72; also Rho.63–4; May.153–4.

82. Mor.802–3. For a more labored, public explanation of his views, see ib., 816–8.

83. Bigelow in Long, John D., *Papers* (Mass. Hist. Soc., 1939) Vol. 78, 103.

84. Rho.61; Morg.372; Mil.135.

85. Rho.57.
86. Un. clip, TR.Scr.; Mor.814; Mil.137–8; Morg.373–4; Rho.63–4.
87. Ib., 143.
88. Mor.812; TR.Wks.XI.6. (This volume of ib. contains the complete text of *The Rough Riders,* and will be cited henceforth as *RR.*)
89. Azo.23; TR.War.Di. Apr. 17, 1898.
90. *RR*.6; TR.War.Di. Apr. 16, 17, 19, 1898.
91. See TR.Auto.226.
92. Her.12; Sprout, Harold and Margaret, *The Rise of American Naval Power* (Princeton, 1966) 231; Bea.63; Bur.47–8.
93. Her.234–5 balances out the two fleets, showing how Spanish naval strength existed largely on paper.
94. Morison, Samuel Eliot, *The Oxford History of the American People* (Oxford, 1965) 802; Her.204 (TR drafted the Congressional bill arising out of his Personnel Bill himself; it was finally passed in 1899); Paullin, *History,* 429; Bea.63; Woo.43ff.
95. Mil.143–4; Hag.LW.I.143.
96. *Sun,* Apr. 17 and 18, 1898; Ada.172; Winthrop Chanler to Margaret Chanler, Apr. 29, 1898, qu. Cha.285; Long, Journal, Apr. 25, LON.
97. *McClure's,* Nov. 1898. *Sun,* Apr. 18; Chapman qu. Howe, M. A. de Wolfe, *John J. Chapman and His Letters* (Houghton Mifflin, 1937) 134.
98. Mor.817. John Hay, at least, understood TR's need to fight. "You obeyed your own daemon," he wrote sympathetically. Tha.2.337.
99. Rho.66.
100. Mil.144, 145; Her.231.
101. Mil.148; Hag.LW.I.145. The idea of a southwestern volunteer cavalry regiment had been formally suggested to the Secretary of War in early April by Governor Miguel Otero of New Mexico. See Wes. Ch.1 for background.
102. *Sun,* Apr. 25 d.l., TR.Scr.; Hag. LW.I.145.
103. *RR*.6.
104. Hag.LW.I.145 says that it was Wood's understanding that Alger was going to offer him a command anyway, the idea being that he and TR should each have a regiment. See also TR.Auto.222–3.
105. JDL's message: "War has commenced between the United States and Spain. Proceed at once to Philippine Islands. Commence operations at once, particularly against the Spanish fleet. You must capture vessels or destroy. Use utmost endeavors." Qu. Mil.149. There is some question as to the exact authorship of this cable. See Lee.192. Rho.71.
106. Azo.23.
107. See Paullin, *History,* 432–3 for details of Naval War Board; also Her.227–8. The war plan was not, as is commonly supposed, one TR submitted to Mahan on Mar. 16, 1898. That document was drafted by President Goodrich of the Naval War College, whom TR considered an inferior strategic thinker. While flatteringly allowing Mahan to work on Goodrich's plan, TR continued to refine his own, "a plan which pretty fairly matched that of the actual war." Karsten, Peter, "The Nature of 'Influence': Roosevelt, Mahan, and the Concept of Sea Power," *American Quarterly,* 1971.23(4). See also Grenville, John A. S., "American Preparations for War with Spain," *Journal of American Studies* (GB) 1968.2(1), *passim;* TR to Mahan, Mor.796, 797, 798 (note the chilly politeness of the last letter, where Mahan has overstepped himself).
108. Hag.LW.I.145–6; *RR*.7.
109. Wes.34; see also Mil.218.
110. Hag.LW.I.151; ib., 146–7.
111. Mil.171; Her.236–7; Rho.71–3; ib., 74; Mor.822–3. See also May.220: "Only a few prescient Europeans had even guessed that the war might extend to Spain's Philippine possessions. The best informed writers had not credited

the American navy with such enterprise and efficiency." In 1902 JDL tried, not very convincingly, to discount TR's large responsibility for the success of the Battle of Manila. He claimed, in the privacy of his Journal (Jan. 3), that ". . . of my own notion I took [Dewey's] name to the President and recommended the assignment." Long had no choice but to recommend it, in that the President had already asked for it. He also denied as "a lie" the story that TR armed Dewey at the last minute with a special despatch of ammunition, but TR never made any such claim. Her.206 shows that JDL was actually obstructive of TR's support plans for Dewey in early 1898. See Mil.150 fn.; Bea.63; Alfonso, Oscar S., *TR and the Philippines* (NY, 1974).

112. Mor.822; TR.War.Di. May 6, 1898; Mor.823, 824, 831, 825 (for JDL's equally fulsome letter to TR, see Bis.I.104), 823; TR.War.Di. May 12.

113. Long, Journal, Apr. 25, 1898, LON.

24: The Rough Rider

Important sources not in Bibliography: 1. Davis, Richard Harding, *The Cuban and Porto Rican Campaigns* (Scribner's, 1898). 2. Cosmas, Graham A., *An Army for an Empire: The U.S. Army in the Spanish-American War* (U. Missouri Press, 1971).

1. *Sun* clip. n.d., TR.Scr.

2. TR.Wks.XI.8. (This vol. of ib. contains complete text of *The Rough Riders.* Henceforth cited as *RR.*) TR was able to accept only one application in ten from his alma mater. Leonard Wood, too, was a Harvard man. Other sources: TR to B, May 5, 1898; *RR.*10–11; Wes.56–7, qu. *Denver Evening Post,* May 4.

3. *RR.*10; Wis.7–8.

4. Jones, Virgil Carrington, *Roosevelt's Rough Riders* (Doubleday, 1971) 35; *RR.*9; Stallman, R. W., *Stephen Crane: A Biography* (NY, 1968) 385.

5. TR to B, May 5, 1898; *RR.*8–10, 27–30; Wes.56–7; Cosby, Arthur S., "A Roosevelt Rough Rider Looks Back," unpublished ms., 1957, TRC, 27.

6. *RR.*10.

7. TR.War.Di. May 15, 1898; Jones, *Rough Riders,* 35; Hag.LW.I.151–2.

8. Wes.79; Hag.LW.I.151.

9. Ib., 152; Jones, *Rough Riders,* 36.

10. *RR.*10. "Why, he knows every man in the regiment by name"—a Rough Rider qu. in *McLure's Magazine,* Nov. 1898; *Sun,* May 8.

11. *RR.*16.

12. Ib.

13. Jones, *Rough Riders,* 282–340 has a complete alphabetical roster of the regiment.

14. Mor.832.

15. Hag.LW.I.147; Cosby, "A RRR Looks Back," 25; *RR.*22; pics in TRC.

16. The following timetable of a typical day at Camp Wood is based on a letter of George Hamner (d. Feb. 6, 1973) to his sweetheart, qu. in Walker, Dale, "The Last of the Rough Riders," *Montana,* XII.3 (July 1973) 43–4.

17. Cosby, "A RRR Looks Back," 36.

18. *RR.*23–4; Cosby, "A RRR Looks Back," 39; see also Wes.80. Mounted drill usually took place at the nearby Mission of San Jose, where there was more space available. Ib., 80.

19. Prentice, Lt. Royal A., "The Rough Riders," *New Mexico Historical Review,* 26.4 (Oct. 1951) and 27.1 (Jan. 1952) 269.

20. Ib., 264; *RR.*18–19.

21. Cosby, "A RRR Looks Back," 39; Jones, *Rough Riders,* 39.

22. *RR.*25.

23. Ib., 22; Hall, Thomas W., *The Fun and Fighting of the Rough Riders* (NY, 1899) 42.

24. Mor.832.

25. Prentice, "The RRs," 267: "After the day's work was done there would be

hardly a man left in camp, as each troop had its own gateway."
26. Hall, *Fun and Fighting,* 42.
27. Ib.
28. This sentence is taken nearly verbatim from ib., 43.
29. See Wes.77; Hag.LW.I.145–6.
30. "Theodore has already a great hold on them—before long he will be able to do anything he likes with them." Robert Ferguson to Douglas Robinson, c. May 15, 1898 (Alsop Papers, TRC). Wood qu. Hag.LW.I.157.
31. Jones, *Rough Riders,* 37; TR qu. Hag.LW.I.154. This incident seems mild enough now, but in those pre-prohibition days it was a serious breach of military discipline. The modern equivalent would be for an officer to join his men after drill for a friendly joint of marijuana. "Nectar," sighed one trooper, "never tasted as good as that beer." Prentice, "The RRs," 267.
32. *RR*.25; Mor.832. Arthur S. Cosby, a late recruit who arrived in camp on May 26, was impressed by the regiment's flawless performance during mounted drill. "It was a fine sight to see these men marching their mounts in formation or launching on thunderous gallops—all at quick response to the nasal, high-pitched commands of Col. Roosevelt." Cosby, "A RRR Looks Back," 29. TR qu. *Sun* clip, n.d., TR.Scr.
33. Har.103.
34. Wes.83; *Chicago Tribune,* May 27, 1898 ("Teddy's Terrors Cut Up High Jinks at San Antonio"), qu. Wes.82. Jones, *Rough Riders,* 43, says that two thousand shots were fired.
35. Wood qu. Hag.LW.I.149.
36. Jones, *Rough Riders,* 43; Hag. LW.I. 155; Azo.54–5.
37. See Lor.304–5.
38. TR.War.Di. May 29, 1898; Cosby, "A RRR Looks Back," 39 ff; *RR*.34; see also Jones, *Rough Riders,* 44.
39. *RR*.32. The Rough Rider Special consisted of 25 day coaches, 2 Pullmans, 5 baggage cars, 8 box cars, and 60 livestock cars. Sections traveled about a mile apart. Jones, *Rough Riders,* 43.
40. *RR*.35.
41. See *RR*.32 for TR's amused rejection of Demolins's military thesis.
42. Cosby, "A RRR Looks Back," 45.
43. See Wes. *passim* for an indication of the depth and extent of this coverage through the West and South. Cosby, "A RRR Looks Back," 43–6; *RR*.34–5; Hall, *Fun and Fighting,* 68–74; *Sun,* d.l. Waldo, Fla., June 2, 1898.
44. *RR*.35.
45. Cosby, "A RRR Looks Back," 49. The exact point was Ybor City. *RR*.36.
46. Prentice, "The RRs," 272; Mor.834; Davis, *Campaigns,* 46.
47. Cosby, "A RRR Looks Back," 50, mentions a pleasant breeze on June 2, tempering the 90-degree heat. Davis, *Campaigns,* 46 and *passim; RR*.37; Mil.241; Azo.38; Brown, Charles H., *The Correspondents' War* (NY, 1967) 206 ff; pics in TRB and TRC.
48. Davis, *Campaigns,* 50.
49. *RR*.37.
50. Mor.835.
51. Cosmas, *An Army,* 193. According to Shafter's chief commissary, the General "couldn't walk two miles in an hour, just beastly obese." Qu. ib.
52. Mor.849. Cosmas, *An Army,* 193–4, in the most balanced opinion of Shafter, points out that the General was a distinguished career soldier, a recipient of the Medal of Honor, and a man whose mental quickness belied his bulk. However "his worst failing as a commander . . . was a lack of experience in organizing and maneuvering large formations. Never, before taking command at Tampa, had he directed so many men—25,000 infantry, cavalry and artillery—in an independent campaign."
53. Ib., 103–9, 124.

54. Azo.35; Brown, *Correspondents' War,* 202; full details in Cosmas, *An Army,* 123–5.
55. Ib., 129; Azo.54–5.
56. Mil.245; TR.War.Di., June 5, 1898.
57. See Gen. Miles, qu. Mil.245; also Cosmas, *An Army,* 195–6. Mor.834; Davis, *Campaigns,* 83.
58. Ib., 82–3 is the basis of this description, supplemented by details from Cosby, "A RRR Looks Back," *passim.* According to TR in Mor.834, the foreign attachés expressed "great wonder" at the performance and training of the Rough Riders. Generals Miles and Wheeler also reviewed the regiment at this time "and unhesitatingly said it is the finest volunteer regiment they ever saw . . . never had they known a regiment, either regular or volunteer, to have learned so much in one month's service. . . ." Santa Fe (N.M.) correspondent, qu. Jones, *Rough Riders,* 53–4.
59. Mor.835; *RR.*37; Cosmas, *An Army,* 196. At first TR was under the impression that the horses would be sent on afterward, but this soon proved to be a hollow expectation.
60. *RR.*37; Mor.836. C, H, I, and M Troops stayed behind.
61. Azo.57.
62. Her.239; Azo.58, 57; see also Mil.246.
63. *RR.*38–9; Cosby, "A RRR Looks Back," 59–60.
64. Ib., 60; Frank Brito, qu. Walker, Dale, "The Last of the Rough Riders," *Montana,* XII.3 (July 1973) 44; *Baltimore Sun,* June 11, 1898.
65. *RR.*39–40. See also Mor.841; Azo. 60; Cosmas, *An Army,* 195–6 for details of the administrative foul-up.
66. Smith, Albert E., *Two Reels and a Crank* (NY, 1952) 57. Elsewhere Smith speaks of "the camera's hypnotic effect on Mr. Roosevelt." If Smith is to be believed, TR even halted on the advance to San Juan to pose for a final, heroic newsreel sequence. "It was not until then that we began to appreciate the full scope of his perception in the field of public relations." Ib., 148.
67. See Azo.63 for breakdown of total force. Brown, *Correspondents' War,* 274. See also Mil.246: "It is a testimonial to General Shafter's understanding of his men that orders which in almost any other army in the world would have spelled a disaster ended up with a brilliant success." Brown, *Correspondents' War,* 276; Mil.248.
68. Azo.61.
69. Ib., 62–3; TR.War.Di. June 8–14, 1898; Mor.836–43, *passim; RR.*40–2.
70. Walker, "Rough Riders," 44; Azo.62–3.
71. *RR.*14.
72. Azo.63; Davis, *Campaigns,* 86; *RR.*42; McIntosh, Burr, *The Little I Saw of Cuba* (NY, 1898), 44–5. The *Yucatán* approached Egmont Keys about sunset on May 13, narrowly avoiding a collision with the *Matteawan* on the way. McIntosh, a *Leslie's* photographer, captured the incident on film, and left an interesting footnote to history: "Had the vessel not been brought to a halt the instant she was, it is highly probable that there would have been no Rough Rider deeds to record in Cuba . . . Thirty-five hundred pounds of dynamite, which was later to be associated with the dynamite gun, rested in her bow." The final distance separating the two ships was a mere three feet. Ib., 38–44.

25: The Wolf Rising in the Heart

Important sources not in Bibliography: 1. Davis, Richard Harding, *The Cuban and Porto Rican Campaigns* (Scribner's, 1898). 2. McIntosh, Burr, *The Little I Saw of Cuba* (NY, 1898). 3. Marshall, Edward, *The Story of the Rough Riders* (NY, 1899).

1. Mor.843; TR.Wks.I.43. Ib. contains the text of *The Rough Riders,* and is

henceforth cited as *RR*. The former source, written on the morning of June 15, 1898, makes it plain that the thoughts expressed in the latter are those of the night of June 14. Morison, incidentally, errs in identifying TR's addressee as Corinne Roosevelt Robinson. Actually he was writing to his wife. EKR later copied out the letters, minus personal paragraphs, for circulation among members of the family. Original copies in TRB.
2. Mor.843; also *RR*.12, 27, 44–5.
3. Ib., 45.
4. Descriptions of the voyage to Cuba are given in Mor.843–4; *RR*.42–6; Hag.LW.I.160; Davis, *Campaigns*, 89–98; Mil.255–8; Azo.64–8; Ranson, E., "British Military and Naval Observers in the Spanish-American War," *Journal of American Studies* (GB) 3.1 (July 1969). Following three paragraphs based on these sources.
5. Ranson, "British Observers," 40. "At night the fleet was as conspicuous as Brooklyn or New York, with the lights of the bridge included." Davis, *Campaigns*, 90–1.
6. Ib., 90–1; *RR*.43.
7. Cosby, Arthur S., "A Roosevelt Rough Rider Looks Back," unpublished ms., 1957, TRC, 64; Ranson, "British Observers," 38; *RR*.46; Azo.60.
8. The mountains were the Sierra Maestra range. Hag.LW.I.160; Cosby, "A RRR Looks Back," 74.
9. Same two sources.
10. Azo.69; Davis, *Campaigns*, 102; ib., 102–112.
11. Jones, Virgil Carrington, *Roosevelt's Rough Riders* (Doubleday, 1971) 86; war picture-books in TRC. The superlative in praise of Cuba's beauty of course no longer applies.
12. Davis, *Campaigns*, 108.
13. The hut was at Asserraderos, twenty miles east of Santiago.
14. Battle orders, qu. Davis, *Campaigns*, 113. Azo.68; Mil.260–2.
15. Azo.68.
16. Jones, *Rough Riders*, 92.
17. Azo.72.
18. Mil.262.
19. Jones, *Rough Riders*, 92–100; McIntosh, *Cuba*, 56; Azo.73.
20. McIntosh, *Cuba*, 57; Davis, *Campaigns*, 115–7; Azo.73; Mil.265; Jones, *Rough Riders*, 100.
21. Davis, *Campaigns*, 117–9; Azo.73; Jones, *Rough Riders*, 65–6.
22. Stephen Bonsal, *N.Y. Herald* correspondent, qu. Brown, Charles H., *The Correspondents' War* (NY, 1967) 307.
23. Smith, Albert, *Two Reels and a Crank* (NY, 1952) 57.
24. Mil.267; *RR*.46.
25. Pri.184–5. Just to make sure, TR took twelve extra pairs of spectacles to Cuba.
26. Ranson, *British Observers*, 42; Cosby, "A RRR Looks Back," 77; McIntosh, *Cuba*, 64; Prentice, Lt. Royal A., "The Rough Riders," *New Mexico Historical Review*, 26–4 (Oct. 1951) and 27.1 (Jan. 1952) 30.
27. Azo.82, 31.
28. Ib.; Pri.189.
29. *RR*.50.
30. Azo.78–9; Mil.270. The details of Wheeler's advance to the front are rather confused. Mil.270 has him riding to Siboney at the head of the entire Cavalry Division on the afternoon of June 2. Azo.79 accepts this account. But Davis, *Campaigns*, 136 specifically states that the General reconnoitred the country beyond Siboney that afternoon, and had a plan for the next day's maneuvers worked out by the time Wood and TR arrived. Marshall, who took part in the march from Siboney, confirms (*Story*, 83). TR, in *RR*.50, says that the 1st and 10th Cavalry left Daiquiri before the Rough Riders; it therefore seems that Wheeler must have left with those regiments, much earlier in the day.
31. McIntosh, *Cuba*, 82.

32. Mar.78–83; Jones, *Rough Riders,* 112.
33. Marshall, *Story,* 78. Marshall had been amazed by the violence of TR's reaction when the *Yucatán* steamed off without unloading a saddle for Texas. "His wrath was boiling, his grief was heartbreaking." (Ib.)
34. Jones, *Rough Riders,* 111.
35. McIntosh, *Cuba,* 69.
36. Mil.270–1; *RR.*51; Davis, *Campaigns,* 136; Freidel, Frank, *The Splendid Little War* (Little, Brown, 1958) 100; *RR.*52, 57.
37. Marshall, *Story,* 88–9; *RR.*51–2.
38. Brown, *Correspondents' War,* 313; Hag.LW.162.
39. The following account of the Battle of Las Guásimas is based on these primary sources: Cosby, "A RRR Looks Back"; Marshall, *Cuba,* 90; Davis, *Campaigns,* 138–72; *RR.*53–72; TR.Auto.245 ff; Mor.844–6; and Hag.LW.I.163–170, which is itself based on Wood's written account of the fight. Secondary sources: Azo.; Freidel, *Splendid Little War;* Mil.; Brown, *Correspondents' War;* Crane, Stephen, *War Dispatches,* ed. R. W. Stallman and E. R. Hageman (N.Y.U. Press, 1964). Crane saw nothing of the fighting.
40. Marshall, *Story,* 91.
41. Stephen Crane, writing from the opposite point of view, said that the Rough Riders looked like "brown flies" as they swarmed up the bluff. Cosby, "A RRR Looks Back," 82.
42. *RR.*56.
43. See Stallman, R. W., *Stephen Crane: A Biography* (NY, 1968) for a full analysis of the relationship of TR and Crane.
44. Davis, *Campaigns,* 139.
45. *RR.*104 (TR says the body was "Cuban"); Azo.86; Davis, *Campaigns,* 141.
46. Ib., 142; Marshall, *Story,* 99–100; Davis, *Campaigns,* 141.
47. Marshall, *Story,* 99–100.
48. Ib. Most other sources, including several defensively cited by TR in Ch. IV of *RR.*, say that the first shots did not come until *after* Wood had deployed the Rough Riders against the enemy. However all these sources represent a revisionist view of events, since the Rough Riders were much embarrassed by reports that they had been ambushed (as indeed they were). The author chooses to follow Marshall, who was with TR when the first shot came, and who had especial reasons for remembering the Battle of Las Guásimas with clarity.
49. Marshall, *Story,* 119–21, 124.
50. Azo.90. The statistic of course refers to military, rather than naval, operations.
51. Hagedorn memo, "Wood under Fire," TRB mss.
52. *RR.*68–9.
53. Marshall, *Story,* 104.
54. Mor.844.
55. Azo.91; see also Hag.LW.I.164–7 (Wood afterward confessed that he had been thinking much of the time about life insurance); Marshall, *Story,* 104.
56. *RR.*57–8; Marshall, *Story,* 110. TR insisted afterward that the sounds *were* bird calls at least "until we came right up to the Spanish lines." *RR.*56. But Edward Marshall (93) and Stephen Crane, who had been in Cuba much longer than he, recognized the calls. "Ah, the wood-dove!" wrote Crane, "the Spanish guerrilla wood-dove which had presaged the death of gallant marines at Guantanamo!" Crane, *Dispatches,* 156. One senses a certain ornithological embarrassment in TR's disclaimer, not to mention unwillingness to admit that he had been victim of an ambush.
57. Davis, *Campaigns,* 149 points out that Wood had to plot all his tactical movements by ear, being unable to see more than two or three of his own troops at a time, let alone the enemy. *RR.*59; Mil.116.

58. Crane, *Dispatches,* 157; Davis, *Campaigns,* 146.
59. Ib.
60. Hag.LW.I.165. The best overall accounts of the battle are Freidel, *Splendid Little War,* 102–9, and Azo.83–85.
61. Davis, *Campaigns,* 148–9; Azo.95.
62. Azo.95.
63. Lawton, qu. Azo.96.
64. *RR.*50; Azo.83, 95.
65. See Stallman, *Crane,* 383; Crane, *Dispatches,* 158.
66. McIntosh, *Cuba,* 89–90.
67. Brown, *Correspondents' War,* 321–2.
68. McIntosh, *Cuba,* 117; see *New York Times,* June 27, 1898, "Rough Riders Prove Heroes" for sample press treatment. Not one of the article's six headlines made reference to any other regiment. For gubernatorial announcement, see ib., June 28.
69. See, e.g., TR.Auto.245 ff.; Foulke, William D., *A Hoosier Autobiography* (NY, 1922), 119. TR.Auto.245.
70. Cosby, "A RRR Looks Back," 87.
71. Davis, *Campaigns,* 167; *RR.*68; un. clip, TR.Scr.
72. Mor.844.
73. *RR.*70. Capt. Capron's body was buried separately. See *N.Y.T.,* June 27, 1898, for another account of the hilltop funeral.
74. Mor.845, 846; *RR.*67. See Ranson, "British Observers," for details of the landing operation.
75. Copy entitled "Progressive Principles" in TRB. See also slightly different version in TR.Auto.257–8.
76. Mor.845. TR carried one sack of the beans back to camp himself, over eight miles of jungle road. EKR to Emily Carow, Aug. 8, 1896 (Derby mss.).
77. Qu. Wes.79.
78. Mor.845; Cosby, "A RRR Looks Back," 93; Davis, *Campaigns,* 176; Azo.99–101.
79. Ranson, *British Observers.*
80. Davis, *Campaigns,* 183; Freidel, *Splendid Little War,* 122; Azo.102. The following descriptions of the battlefield of San Juan are based on prose sources as quoted, plus sketches, maps, and photographs, in, e.g., Lor.312–15; Freidel, *Splendid Little War, passim,* and Spanish-American war picture book collection in TRC.
81. See Davis, *Campaigns,* 174 for copy of Shafter's map. It was, in the opinion of one foreign attaché, so "laughably inadequate" that the Battle of San Juan was fought almost blind. Ranson, "British Observers," qu. Arthur Lee.
82. Azo.104; Davis, *Campaigns,* 183; Freidel, *Splendid Little War,* 120; Hag.LW.I.173.
83. Pri.193.
84. Azo.104–5; Freidel, *Splendid Little War,* 122 ff; Hag.LW.I.173–4.
85. Davis, *Campaigns,* 188; Hag.LW.I. 172–3; TR.Auto.245.
86. Davis, *Campaigns,* 190; Azo.107.
87. Cosby, "A RRR Looks Back," 96–7.
88. *RR.*74. The promotions were of course unofficial, and the titles "Acting" until the confirmation and notification from Washington; but wartime conditions made such formalities irrelevant.
89. TR to Hermann Hagedorn, Harvard Club, Aug. 14, 1917: "San Juan was the great day of my life. I rose over those regular army officers like a balloon."
90. *RR.*72; Cosby, "A RRR Looks Back," 98; McIntosh, *Cuba,* 120; Davis, *Campaigns,* 193; Azo.107; Freidel, *War,* 144 ill.; *RR.*75.
91. Cosby, "A RRR Looks Back," 98.
92. Description by Howard Chandler Christy, war artist, qu. Brown, *Correspondents' War,* 338. (TR on June 30, 1898: author assumes he was wearing the same clothes, having slept in them overnight.)
93. *RR.*74; Azo.110–11, 147.
94. Ib., 110; *RR.*75. The commander of Lawton's battery was Captain Allyn

Capron, father and namesake of the victim of Las Guásimas. *RR*.76.

95. Azo.115; Davis, *Campaigns*, 200 ff.; Hag.LW.I.174.

96. Azo.116. TR to EKR, July 30, 1898.

97. Davis, *Campaigns*, 217. The reporter describes TR and Gen. Hawkins, leader of Kent's division, as the most conspicuous figures on the battlefield. But whereas the white-haired general "was so noble a sight that you felt inclined to pray for his safety," the blue-scarfed colonel, "mounted high on horseback, and charging the rifle-pits at a gallop and quite alone, made you feel that you would like to cheer." (Ib.) See also Marshall, *Story*, 187.

98. Azo.117–8; Cosby, "A RRR Looks Back," 103.

99. *RR*.77; Azo.118.

100. Davis, *Campaigns*, 189, 208; *RR*.81; Azo.120–1; *RR*.77; Cosby, "A RRR Looks Back," 103–4.

101. *RR*.77; Cosby, "A RRR Looks Back," 33; Freidel, *War*, 157 ill.

102. Cosby, "A RRR Looks Back," 104, 78; Davis, *Campaigns*, 204–12.

103. *RR*.79.

104. *RR*.78 TR qu. Azo.126.

105. *RR*.79–80; Davis, *Campaigns*, 207; Azo.127; Freidel, *War*, 157.

106. Davis, *Campaigns*, 204; Mor.853. Lt. Royal Prentice, "Rough Riders," 34, remembers the fusillade as "a solid sheet of bullets and shells . . . it appeared that nothing could live to get over the top."

107. *RR*.80; Marshall, *Story*, 203.

108. Azo.135; *RR*.81.

109. *RR*.81.

110. See, e.g., RR.84, and TR.Auto. 245: "Memory plays funny tricks in such a fight [as San Juan], where things happen quickly, and all kinds of mental images succeed one another in a detached kind of way, while the work goes on. . . ."

111. TR.Wks.XII.306.

112. The following collage is based on *RR*.82 ff.; TR.Auto.247 ff.; Mor.847, 856–7. See also the eyewitness accounts reprinted by TR in TR.Auto., Appendix B to Ch. VII. There is some confusion as to whether TR killed his man on the first hill (Kettle), or the second (San Juan). The overwhelming weight of evidence is that he did so on Kettle. See Mor.853, TR to HCL: "Did I tell you that I killed a Spaniard with my own hand when I led the storm of the first redoubt?" TR to EKR, July 3, 1898 (TRB transcript) confirms. But TR prints a letter by Maj. M. J. Jenkins in TR.Auto.274, saying that the kill was on San Juan, and TR himself in *RR*.89 includes it in his account of the second charge. Close analysis of his language, however, indicates that he was indulging in a sort of flashback to the first. Maj. Jenkins must simply have been mistaken, and TR careless in printing his testimony.

113. "Jack-rabbit" quote: R. H. Ferguson to EKR (using TR's own words), July 5, 1898. See also n. 119 below. *RR*.86.

114. Ib.; Davis, *Campaigns*, 218; *RR*.86.

115. *RR*.87. The Rough Riders' cross-fire was extremely deadly: see below.

116. *RR*.88; Hall, *The Fun and Fighting of the Rough Riders* (NY, 1899) 34.

117. *RR*.90; TR.Auto.248; ib., Appendix B to Ch. VII. Memo of John H. Parker to Stanley Allen, *The Register*, Feb. 14, 1938 (TRB); See also Mor.856–7, and Davis, *Campaigns*, 220 ff.

118. *RR*.89.

119. R. H. Ferguson to EKR, July 5, 1898. TR's exultation, however excessive, must be considered in the light of undeniable atrocities by the other side during the Battle of San Juan. See Davis, *Campaigns*, 208, on the sharpshooters who methodically pumped bullets into

the surgeons, Red Cross personnel, litter-bearers, and even the wounded themselves at Bloody Ford Hospital; also Mor.858. As for the sheer hatred of the enemy which battle instinctively inspires, see Cosby, "A RRR Looks Back," 101, on his reaction to the fusillade at Kettle Hill: "Now we were hating mad—anger began to wriggle through our minds—and on down through our arms and hands." But TR's killing triumph lasted well beyond the date of final victory. Isaac Hunt, his old Assembly colleague, heard him talk about "doubling up" the Spanish soldier in later years, and "it made cold chills run down my back. He told it about like . . . I would talk about shooting a squirrel." HUN.90. See also Wag.250.

120. Azo.144; *RR*.101, 100. During four and a half months of official existence, the Rough Riders attained a 37% casualty rate, highest of any regiment in the war (1 out of every 3 dead, wounded, or diseased).

Note: TR's heroism on San Juan Heights has been called into question by some historians, but an eloquent contemporary tribute to it, written by Admiral French E. Chadwick, on the eve of the tenth anniversary of the battle, is available in Maguire, Doris D., *French Ensor Chadwick: Selected Letters and Papers* (Washington, D.C., 1981), 462–63.

121. R. H. Ferguson to EKR, July 5, 1898.

122. Within a week, Gen. Wheeler had agreed to send a formal Medal of Honor recommendation to Washington. Mor.850.

123. Mor.853; TR.Auto.250; Prentice, "Rough Riders," 46; R. H. Ferguson to EKR, July 5, 1898; Hall, *Fun and Fighting*, 218.

124. R. H. Ferguson to EKR, July 5, 1898.

125. *RR*.110 ff.; Freidel, *War*, 120 ff. and 185; Azo.140; Mor.846. Azo.151–2 quotes Shafter's letter to Secretary Alger, threatening withdrawal.

126. Freidel, *War*, 191.

127. Ib., 179; Shafter qu. Azo.155.

128. Ib., 156; Hall, *Fun and Fighting*, 218.

129. Azo.157–8.

130. Ib., 160.

131. Although TR did not formally accept his full colonelcy until July 31 (*Herald*, Sep. 25, 1898), his commission had already been issued on July 11 and sent to him in Cuba. (Ib.)

132. Mor.853; TR.War.Di. July 3; Mor.851. TR's only known ailment in Cuba was a bout of dysentery. EKR to Emily Carow, Aug. 14, 1898 (Derby mss.).

133. *RR*.135.

134. See Mor.858–9; ib., 855; *RR*.133, 136. *McClure's*, Nov. 1898, qu. an anonymous Rough Rider.

135. Mor.851. The lieutenant appears in the photograph at the beginning of this chapter, standing immediately behind TR's right shoulder.

136. Greenaway qu. J. J. Leary in TRB mss.

137. Mor.861; ib., 860.

138. See Che.18–19.

139. *RR*.138, 142.

140. The authors of the document, TR included, were carefully vague about how it came into the hands of the Associated Press correspondent. Leonard Wood claimed that he handed the round-robin to Gen. Shafter, who affected a lack of interest in it. The document was ostentatiously left lying on the table between them, whereupon the A.P. man seized it and transmitted it to the U.S. by cable. TR wrote that he also handed his supplementary letter to Shafter, who waved it away in the same fashion. "I, however, insisted on handing it to him, whereupon he shoved it toward the correspondent . . . who took hold of it, and I released my hold."

TR.Auto.252; ib., fn.; Hag.LW.I.201; Wes.240; Mil.352.

141. Full text of both documents: Mor.864–66. See also TR's letter to HCL on the subject, which is full of genuine passion. Mor.862–3.

142. Mil.352; Morg.394. Cosmas, *An Army,* 294, 305 blames McK for the delay.

143. Mor.859. Secretary Alger also made public his sarcastic reply to TR's letter: "I suggest that, unless you want to spoil the effects and glory of your victory, you make no invidious comparisons. The Rough Riders are no better than the other volunteers. They had an advantage in their arms, for which they ought to be grateful." Mor.860 fn. Alger later apologized to TR. See TR.Auto. Ch. VII, Appendix A, "A Manly Letter."

144. Clips, n.d., in TRB clips file. For sample sympathetic comment on TR, see *Chicago Tribune,* August 5, 1898.

145. *RR*.145. It of course seemed, to the general public, that TR's round-robin was responsible for the pull-out order. Actually Alger had issued the order on Aug. 3, the day *before* all the newspaper publicity. TR was not averse to the accidental glory thus gained. See Freidel, *War,* 296; Cosmas, *An Army,* 258.

146. Freidel, *War,* 298; Hag.LW.I.183; war picture book collection, TRC.

147. Mor.852.

148. Mor.861, 862. John D. Long, who had deplored TR's decision to resign as Assistant Secretary of the Navy in his Journal, Apr. 25, 1898 (Ch. 23), turned back to that entry many years later and wrote a superscription; "P.S. Roosevelt was right and we his friends were all wrong. His going into the army led through to the Presidency."

Historical Note: In 2000, President Clinton, responding to heavy pressure from the Roosevelt family and the Theodore Roosevelt Association, posthumously granted TR his Medal of Honor. TR's own mature feeling about the medal was expressed in 1907, when he declined honorary membership in the United States Medal of Honor Club: "I was recommended for it by my superior officers in the Santiago campaign, but I was not awarded it; and frankly, looking back at it now, I feel that the board which declined to award it took exactly the right position." Mor.5.865.

26: The Most Famous Man in America

1. *New York Times* and *Evening Post,* Aug. 16, 1898.

2. *New York Herald,* Aug. 16, 1898.

3. Ib.

4. Ib.; also above-quoted sources.

5. Marshall, Edward, *The Story of the Rough Riders* (NY, 1899) 240.

6. *Her.,* Aug. 16, 1898; *N.Y.T., Eve. Post,* same date.

7. *Her.,* Aug. 16, 1898. According to Lovell H. Jerome, one of TR's gubernatorial backers, he was cautioned not to say anything about politics even before he disembarked. Int. FRE.

8. *N.Y.T.,* Aug. 16, 1898.

9. *Eve. Post,* Aug. 16, 1898; Marshall, *Story,* 240; *Commercial Advertiser,* Aug. 16; *Her.,* same date.

10. *World,* Aug. 28: "Travelling men of all shades and classes declare him more talked about than any man in the country."

11. The peace protocol was signed on Aug. 12, 1898. For gubernatorial rumors, see, e.g., *Her.,* Aug. 17.

12. The last phrase is taken almost verbatim from Marshall, *Story,* 240.

13. *N.Y.T.,* and *Eve. Post,* Aug. 16, 1898.

14. Che.7. With this first citation the author wishes to express his debt to the definitive—and only—study of Governor Theodore Roosevelt. Without Chessman's indispensable work (itself a

condensation of a lengthy dissertation, preserved in TRC) the following three chapters of the present biography could not have been written in their present form. For some afterthoughts by Chessman on the structure and conclusions of his book, see the *Theodore Roosevelt Association Journal,* Vol. I.1, Winter-Spring 1975.
15. Che.18–19; ib., 20; HUN.55.
16. Che.18.
17. Ib., 11–12, 16.
18. Ib., 16–17.
19. See TR.Auto.279; also Che.7–24 for an extended treatment of Platt's meeting with Quigg. *Her.,* Aug. 17, 1898; Quigg to TR, Mar. 19, 1913, qu. Mor.1475.
20. Che.26.
21. Howe, M. A. de Wolfe, *John Jay Chapman and His Letters* (Houghton Mifflin, 1937) 1–8; Cha.248–9; Che.26.
22. See Edel, Leon, ed., *American Essays of Henry James* (NY, 1956) 240–1.
23. Howe, *Chapman,* 469.
24. Cha.248; Chapman to Mrs. Chapman, Sep. 14, 1898, qu. Mor.1475.
25. Che.32; Howe, *Chapman,* 142–3; Che.27; Mor.1474–5.
26. Chapman qu. Che.29.
27. Quigg came either in response to TR's telegram of Aug. 17, 1898, or as a result of his own previous suggestion, which the telegram confirmed. Whatever the case, TR "particularly wanted" to talk over matters with Platt's lieutenant.
28. TR.Auto.280–1.
29. Ib.; Che.29–30.
30. *Her.,* Aug. 17, 1898; Hag.RF.58; Che.26. TR had received an advance discharge from quarantine on Aug. 17.
31. *Her.,* Aug. 17, 18.
32. *N.Y.T.,* Aug. 20, 1898.
33. See juxtaposition of Rooseveltian and Republican news in, e.g., *N.Y.T.,* Aug. 21, 1898. Che.34; *Her.,* Aug. 21.
34. Ib.; Hag.RF.58–9.
35. EKR's emotions are inferred from a letter to Emily Carow, c. Aug. 25, 1898, excerpted in TRB mss. *Her.,* Aug. 21; Hagedorn memo, TRB.
36. See *Her.,* Aug. 22, 1898; *World,* Aug. 24.
37. See Mor.852.
38. Robert Bridges in *Eve. Post,* Jan. 1919 (n.d.), TRB.
39. Mor.1475. Che.27 fn. points out that both Mor. and Howe, *Chapman,* are wrong in describing this as the first TR/Chapman meeting. See *New York Tribune,* Aug. 19, 1898, for confirmation. How.465; Che.33.
40. Howe, *Chapman,* 142.
41. See, e.g., *World,* Aug. 28, 1898; *Her.,* Aug. 22, 23, 24; *World,* Aug. 24.
42. There is a photostat of this envelope in TRB.
43. *World, Sun,* Aug. 27, 1898; *Her.,* Oct. 6.
44. Ib., Aug. 25, 1898.
45. HUN.55.
46. Che.35; *Eve. Post,* Sep. 1, 1898.
47. Howe, *Chapman,* 143; Mor.1476; Chapman qu. ib.
48. Un. clip (*Her.?*), Sep. 5, 1898, TRB.
49. *Her.,* Sep. 10, 1898; *Eve. Post,* same date; Che.38.
50. See Mor.874 fn; *N.Y.T.,* Sep. 26, 1898; Mor.875.
51. Jones, Virgil Carrington, *Roosevelt's Rough Riders* (Doubleday, 1971) 276. The following account is based on *Her.,* Sep. 14, Marshall, *Story,* 247–51, and random clip files in TRB.
52. Marshall, *Story,* 247–251.
53. Ib., *Her.,* Sep. 14, 1898.
54. Ib.
55. TR's entire speech is reprinted in *RR.*157–8 fn.
56. *Her.,* Sep. 14, 1898; TRB clips.
57. Private Bill Bell, un. clip, c. Nov. 1, 1898, TRB.
58. *World,* June 26, 1898.
59. Characterizations from *RR. passim.*
60. *Her.,* Sep. 14, 1898; Rii.200.
61. *N.Y.T.,* Sep. 18, 1898; Che.42.

62. See, e.g., *Her.*, *N.Y.T.*, Sep. 16, 1898. *Eve. Post*, Sep. 17.
63. See, e.g., *Her.*, Sep. 14, 1898. *N.Y.T.*, Sep. 16.
64. *Eve. Post*, Sep. 18, 1898; *Her.*, same date. Quigg was also present. During this conversation with the press, TR evoked for the first time an image he would one day make famous: "I feel like a bull moose." Williams, Talcott, in *Century Memorial to TR*, 73.
65. *N.Y.T.*, Sep. 20, 1898; Mor.876.
66. Howe, *Chapman*, 469.
67. Mor.877.
68. Che.45.
69. For a different interpretation, see Mor.1476–1478.
70. Howe, *Chapman*, 143; Chapman, qu. ib., 139–141.
71. Cha.248, Chapman qu. Howe, *Chapman*, 143. Further sidelights into the early relationship of TR and Chapman are available in the Chapman Papers, Houghton Library, Harvard (letters to Mrs. Chapman, Aug. 1898 ff.). TR, significantly, did not mention his negotiations with the Independents in his *Autobiography*, except to say there was "a lunatic fringe" in the party that attempted to "force" him upon Platt, and campaigned against him afterwards. (TR.Auto.282.)
72. *Her.*, Sep. 24, 1898; see *Sun*, same date, for full statement of facts. Chessman, G. Wallace, "Theodore Roosevelt's Personal Tax Difficulty," *New York History*, 34.54–63 explores this complicated matter in great detail. See also Pri.203–4, and n. 75 below.
73. The date of TR's Washington affidavit was Mar. 21, 1898. *Sun*, Sep. 26.
74. Che.46.
75. On Aug. 24, 1897. Mor.878. The facts of TR's tax embarrassment are briefly these: From 1880 to 1894 inclusive he voted and paid taxes on personal and real property in Oyster Bay, except during his three terms as a New York City Assemblyman, 1882–84. After being made Police Commissioner in 1895 he rented Bamie Roosevelt's house at 689 Madison Avenue, and declared it his legal residence. While thenceforth voting and paying taxes in New York City, he maintained Sagamore Hill as a country home, and for two years paid extra taxes in Oyster Bay, although there was no need for him to do so. In 1897, however, his personalty assessment in Oyster Bay was increased from $2,000 to $12,000, causing the first of his two affidavits in order to avoid that "perfectly absurd" liability. He was then, of course, already living in bachelor digs in Washington as Assistant Secretary. Not until October 1, 1897, did his lease on Bamie's Manhattan house expire; and the following month, when his family at last joined him in Washington, he moved into the house opposite the German Embassy. It then became a question of deciding whether to declare yet another legal residence, or revert to his old status in Oyster Bay. There was not time between Oct. 1 and the November elections for him to qualify as a voter in Oyster Bay, and TR was so preoccupied with Navy matters during the next critical months that he seems to have forgotten about the whole residence question. Only in January 1898, when he was notified that he had been assessed a hefty $50,000 as an absentee resident of New York City, did he hastily issue his second affidavit, declaring himself a resident of Washington. All this was done on the advice of family advisers, notably Douglas Robinson, John E., and James Roosevelt. However the understanding was, when he left for Cuba, that steps would be taken to restore him permanently to the rolls of Oyster Bay—even if that meant paying taxes in two places at once. But the person responsible for this step, his uncle James, died before undertaking it, and TR again forgot about his resi-

dence problems in the excitement of the war. Here matters rested until Tammany Hall delivered the "bomb" affidavit of March 21 to Governor Black's supporters. *Sun,* Sep. 26, 1898; TR to Root, Platt, and Nicholas M. Butler, Mor.878–9; Che.46–7.
76. Che.48.
77. Ib.; Gos.192.
78. Ib.
79. Ib.; Pla.370–3; *Sun,* Sep. 29, 1898; *Trib.*, Sep. 28.
80. See Mor.878–9; *Trib.*, Sep. 28, 1898. Che.46–8.
81. Pla.367; HUN.59. TR paid his taxes—$995.28—on Oct. 3, 1898. *Trib.*, Oct. 4.
82. *Sun,* Sep. 26, 1898; Mor.880.
83. *Trib.*, Sep. 28, 1898; *Her.*, same date.
84. *Sun,* Sep. 28, 1898. See *Trib.*, Sep. 28 for verbatim report of what Root did say. *Her.*, Sep. 28. The nominating speech was made by Chauncey Depew. "I have done that a great many times in conventions," he wrote in his *Memories of Eighty Years,* "but have never had such a response." (162).
85. *Trib.*, Sep. 28, 1898; Mor.881.
86. *Her.*, Oct. 5, 1898.
87. Ib.; *N.Y.T.*, same date. Author's italics.
88. *Her.*, Sep. 5, 1898. Van Wyck was the brother of Robert W. van Wyck, Mayor of New York.
89. Che.50–1.
90. *Her.*, Sep. 6, 1898.
91. See Mor.882 for TR's reply to McK. *Her.*, Sep. 6, 1898.
92. TR.Wks.XIV.290–1. See *Her.*, Sep. 6, 1898, for audience reaction.
93. Howe, *Chapman,* 470.
94. TR.Auto.280; Mor.883; Che.54; ib., 59–60; Odell int. FRE. See Gos.131–8 for an account of TCP's manipulation of various periodicals.
95. TR on Oct. 7, 1898, qu. Hagedorn in TRB memo; *Her.*, Oct. 15.
96. See Che. *passim.*
97. *Trib.*, Oct. 10, 1898; two *Herald* clips, both dated Oct. 15, in TRB.
98. Ib.
99. The following account of TR's campaign day is based on "Roosevelt On A Wild Goose Chase," article in *Her.*, Sep. 15, 1898.
100. Ib., and Sep. 16, 1898; Gos.142.
101. *Her.*, Oct. 15, 16, 1898; *Trib.*, Oct. 23; Che.57–8. TR had been aware for some time that Judge Daly would not receive the Democratic nomination, and had seen to it that he appeared on the Republican ticket. He considered this nomination "a great card for us." Che.57.
102. *Her.*, Oct. 16, 1898; Che.59.
103. *Her.*, Oct. 18, 1898; Che.60.
104. Ib.; Gos.141–2.
105. *Her.*, Oct. 18, 1898; *World,* same date.
106. *Her.*, Oct. 18, 1898.
107. Che.61.
108. *Her.*, Oct. 18, 1898; O'Neil qu. Mor.896.
109. Che.63; *Sun,* Oct. 21, 1898.
110. Ib.
111. TRB clips, *passim.*
112. *Sun,* Oct. 21, 1898; cf. p. 634.
113. *Press* clip, n.d., in TRB; see, e.g., TR's chivvying of Quigg in Mor.887.
114. *Sun,* Oct. 25, 1898.
115. Ib.; Clarke, John Proctor, "Random Recollections of Campaigning with Roosevelt," TRC; TR.Auto.127.
116. *Sun,* Oct. 25, 26, 27, 29, 30, 1898.
117. Ib., Oct. 29, 1898.
118. Che.66; Rii.203–7.
119. Mor.918; Pla.537–8; *Troy Times,* Nov. 5, 1898, qu. Gos.143.
120. Ib., 149. TR scored 661,715 to van Wyck's 643,921. The narrowness of TR's margin (17,794) can be gauged by contrasting it with Gov. Black's in 1896—787,516 votes to a Democratic total of 574,524. Ib.
121. Che.68, qu. Depew and Platt; TR.Auto.282.
122. Mor.888.

123. EKR to Emily Carow, June 22, 1900, TRC. TR's Lowell Lectures are described by Rev. William E. Barton in "Theodore Roosevelt: An Address," pamphlet, 1919, in the Walter Merriam Pratt collection (TRB). "They were the most popular Lowell Lectures I have heard."
124. Original manuscript of *The Rough Riders* in New York State Library, Albany.

27: The Boy Governor

1. Par.123.
2. See TR.Auto.293–4, and below.
3. Because January 1, 1899, fell on a Sunday, TR and other elective officials had taken their oaths in the Secretary of State's office shortly after noon on Sat., Dec. 31, 1898. *Sun,* Jan. 1.
4. TR.Auto.286.
5. Ib.
6. Ib., 290.
7. Obvious as such a publicity policy may seem in this media-conscious age, it was near-revolutionary in the shadowy world of New York State politics at the end of the nineteenth century. A comprehensive study of TR's whole career as a publicist has yet to be written: should any skilled historian undertake the project, it would be of revelatory significance and interest.
8. *Sun,* Jan. 3, 1899.
9. See Roseberry, Cecil R., *Capitol Story* (New York State, 1964) 9, and *passim.*
10. *Sun,* Jan. 3, 1899.
11. See *Public Papers of Theodore Roosevelt, Governor* (Albany, 1899–1900) 248–9; Gos.196; Pri.209; and Che. *passim* for discussion of various aspects of this Annual Message.
12. New York State Legislature, *A Memorial to Theodore Roosevelt,* Feb. 21, 1919, 37.
13. TR.Auto.295. Superintendent G. W. Aldridge had asked to be suspended while certain charges purporting to involve him in the "canal steal" were being investigated. Gos.208.
14. TR.Auto.294–5.
15. Che.72; Mor.891–902.
16. Gos.209; Che.72–3, 178–9. TR had private doubts about Partridge at first ("I do not think he is a very strong man"), but they turned out to be unfounded. The superintendent effected a 25% saving in public works expenses by Oct. 1, 1899, and was singled out by the *Eve. Post* to be a model state official. Che.178–9.
17. Youngs, William J., "A Short Résumé of the Administration of Theodore Roosevelt [Governor]," TRP., 4; Gos.209–14; Har.114; Che.73. See ib., *passim,* for analyses of other gubernatorial appointments. TR's only personal indulgences were the selection of his old mentor, Joe Murray, as First Deputy in the Public Works Dept., Avery D. Andrews as Adjutant-General, and some impoverished Rough Riders to unimportant sinecures.
18. Che.75; Har.122.
19. Secretary William J. Youngs declared that "the happiest moments of the Governor's administration were the 15-minute talks with reporters, morning and afternoon." Un. clip, c. June, 1900, entitled "Studies in American Character, No. 5," TRB. See also Che.75, quoting *Brooklyn Eagle,* Jan. 4, 1899, and *Albany Argus,* June 6, 1899. This description of TR in press conference is also based on the reminiscences of reporters who knew him well, notably Joseph B. Bishop and J. J. Leary.
20. TR.Auto.285.
21. Ib., 289. The following three paragraphs are based on ib., 283–93.
22. Ib., 285.
23. Ib., 289.
24. The preceding four sentences closely follow Che.158–9.
25. TR.Auto.292.
26. For TR's handling of the Martha

Place case, see Mor.938 ff., and n. 56, below.

27. See calendar in Mor.1498 ff. for a list of TR's day-to-day business as Governor. Mor.918.

28. Ada.208; Mor.902.

29. TR.Auto.297; Mor.1498 ff.; Wis.70.

30. TR.Auto.297–8. See also Che.76.

31. TR qu. Che.133.

32. Gos.196; Che.133–7. Ib., 132, says TR was not necessarily referring to the Ford Bill, but at any rate "favored some positive step toward franchise tax that year." Since there was no other franchise-tax legislation on the books, and in view of TR's own hurry to get such a law passed in 1899, it is difficult to see what other measures he could have had in mind. TR did, nevertheless, express grave doubts about at least one of the Ford Bill's clauses. (See text below.) For the full story of TR's works on the franchise bills, see Che. Ch. 6, "The Honest Broker."

33. Gos.197; Che.135, 137, 133. TR's pied-à-terre was 689 Madison Ave., where Bamie (now Mrs. Sheffield Cowles, and a mother) delighted to play hostess for him. COW. Occasionally TR took TCP to breakfast at Corinne's house, 422 Madison Ave. Rob.185.

34. TR.Auto.308.

35. Gos.198; TCP qu. Che.138; for complete text of TCP's views on the Ford Bill, see *William Barnes v. Theodore Roosevelt: Case on Appeal* (Walton, N.Y., 1917) 2368 ff.

36. TCP qu. Che.138.

37. Che.138; Gos.196; *Public Papers,* 54–7; Gos.197; Che.139.

38. *New York Herald,* qu. Che.139; Mor.982, 1006.

39. TR.Auto.312; Che.140; Mor.982. Three days after this, TR was in Chicago as guest of honor at the Appomattox Day meeting of the Hamilton Club. Mor.1499. Here he delivered his famous "Strenuous Life" speech, the definitive statement of his pre-presidential philosophy. It is reprinted in TR.Wks.XIII.

40. Che.140.

41. Ib.; *New York Tribune,* Apr. 15, 1899.

42. Che.141.

43. TR.Auto.311. Gos.197: "He kept talking to the newspaper men about its desirability." See, e.g., *Trib.,* Apr. 15, 1899.

44. See Che.75 on TR's use of reporters as legislative contacts. Ib., 143.

45. TR.Auto.308.

46. Ib., 311–2; Che.143–4; Mor.1007; TR.Auto.312.

47. Ib; Mor.1008.

48. *Public Papers,* 1899, 89.

49. TR.Auto.312.

50. See his letter to HCL, Apr. 17, 1899, Mor.997–8.

51. For an excellent brief summary, see Har.114–121.

52. Mor.997; *New York Times,* Apr. 29, 1899; Che.79.

53. See Che.200–25 for a largely favorable review of TR's labor policies as Governor; Hurwitz, Howard L., *TR and Labor in New York State, 1880–1900* (Columbia U. Press, 1943) *passim* for a more negative assessment.

54. Mor.998; Har.120–121.

55. Ib. But see Che.215 ff. for TR's subsequent difficulties with labor groups, and ib., 221 for his overreaction to the Croton Dam riots in April 1900.

56. Martha Place, a resident of Brooklyn, was found guilty of killing her stepdaughter and attacking her husband with an axe. Although she claimed not to remember the murder, state medical examiners informed Roosevelt that she was sane. She was executed on March 20, 1899.

57. Mor.950: "As for Mrs. Place, you can rest assured that the last thing that will influence me will be any statement that no man can become President if he

allows a woman to be executed. In the first place, being myself sane, I have no thought of becoming President. In the next place, I should heartily despise the public servant who failed to do his duty because it might jeopardize his own future." (TR to Francis W. Jones, Feb. 21, 1899.)

58. Mor.938.

59. See Che.177 ff. for an extended discussion of this subject.

60. Mor.998. For a compact modern assessment of the governorship of Theodore Roosevelt, within the larger context of New York politics, see McC. 157–63. According to McCormick, TR took "moderate but creative" steps toward addressing the burgeoning phenomenon of interstate corporate combinations. His policy innovations were few, but his rhetoric galvanizing, and "his management of economic issues notably anticipated—though it did not inaugurate—twentieth-century methods of governance." (158) TR's instincts remained conservative (and actually friendly toward entrenched corporate interests), even as his antitrust rhetoric heated up. He was notable for his "fear of class politics," and determinedly democratic in weighing the conflicting claims of special-interest groups—as shown in his open-minded, moderately reformist attitude to labor. (160) Although his main legislative achievement was indeed the Ford Franchise Act, he really only "vitalized" the issue it entailed. The best that can be said overall of TR's gubernatorial administration, in McCormick's view, is that he pointed New York State "toward a political accommodation with the powerful, clashing interests of an industrial society." (163)

61. Ib., 999. See also TR to C. Grant LaFarge, May 1, 1899, TRP.

62. See Che.147; *N.Y.T.*, May 5, 1899.

63. TR.Auto.309. Author's italics.

64. Ib.

65. Ib., 309–10; Gos.148; see *Barnes v. Roosevelt*, 2368–2375 for complete text.

66. Mor.1004–1009. "These two letters," TR wrote in his *Autobiography*, "express clearly the views of the two elements of the Republican party, whose hostility gradually grew until it culminated, thirteen years later." (311) For a more extended version of TR's views at the time, see his address on "The Uses and Abuses of Property" (Buffalo, May 15, 1899), in TR.Wks.XIV.321–9.

67. Mor.1004–1009. Che.150 says that the idea of recalling the Legislature was first suggested to TR by corporation counsel on May 11, 1899. But TR's letter to TCP clearly shows that he had been thinking along the same lines as early as May 8.

68. Mor.1011.

69. TR's legal experts were Judge William N. Cohen and Prof. E.R.A. Seligman of Columbia University. Che.151–2.

70. See Mor.1017 for TR's account of the frantic activities of TCP's representatives. Che.152, 153; Mor.1017.

71. *Her.*, May 26, 1899.

72. Mor.1017.

73. Ib., 1501, 1018.

74. See Che.160. TR discussed the subject with at least two editors en route.

75. See Mor.954 ff. The first few requests came through Mr. Bellamy Storer, but he was at no time anything more than a mouthpiece for his formidable wife. Mrs. Bellamy Storer soon lost patience with his lack of success, and began to negotiate with TR herself.

76. Mor.954, 968, 971–2, 1001, 1015, 1019.

77. See Mor.893, 894, 901, 902, 919 esp., 935, 1395 for TR's desperate attempts to secure the Medal of Honor; also Appendix B to Ch. VII of TR.Auto., which shows how his failure still rankled in 1913.

78. See Lod.I.399; also Mor.1021.

79. Ib., 1022.
80. White wrote many years later that he began this work—with TR's full approval—in 1898, even before the gubernatorial election. "He did not want to be Governor of New York. He wanted to be President of the United States." Whi.327.
81. *Emporia Gazette,* June 26, 1899. See also Kohlsaat, H. H., *From McKinley to Harding* (Scribner's, 1923) 76 ff. for anecdotes of this trip. He says that at several stops along the way crowds brandished "Roosevelt in 1904" cards.
82. See, e.g., *N.Y.T.,* June 29, 1899.
83. In July 1969 Jesse Langdon attended the seventieth and last Rough Rider Reunion at Las Vegas. His two surviving comrades, Frank Brito and George Hamner, were too ill to join him. Walker, Dale, "The Last of the Rough Riders," *Montana,* XII.3 (July 1973). TR on McK's renomination: see *N.Y.T.,* June 30, 1899; *Trib.,* same date.
84. *World,* July 5, 1899; *N.Y.T.,* same date.
85. Mor.1023.
86. See Chessman, G. Wallace, "Theodore Roosevelt's Campaign Against the Vice-Presidency," *The Historian,* XIV.2 (Spring 1952).
87. Trad.; see, e.g., Morg.225.
88. Mor.1023.
89. Ib.
90. Ib., 918.
91. Ib., 1023. See Young, K. H., and Lamar Middleton, *Heirs Apparent* (NY, 1948), and Williams, Irving G., *The Rise of the Vice-Presidency* (NY, 1956) for indications of how insignificant the office really was at the end of the nineteenth century.
92. Mor.1024; un. clip, TRB, c. July 1, 1899; Rob.195. Note: Corinne wrongly places the date of *Cromwell*'s composition in 1900.
93. Probably Elihu Root, qu. Arthur Lee in TR.Wks.X.169–70.
94. Mor.1043; ib., 1046; *World,* July 9, 1899; Mor.1038–9, 1502.
95. Ib., 1043, 1046. TR exceeded his word quota from Scribner's by some twenty thousand words. The serial purchase price was $5,000, plus 15% in book royalties. Ib., 1049.
96. *Eve. Post* article, "Roosevelt the Ideal Contributor," n.d., but c. Feb. 1919, TRB; Mor.1053; Lee in TR.Wks.X.170.
97. Wis.65–6.
98. Mor.1047.
99. See *Trib.,* July 9, 1899; *N.Y.T.,* July 16. See also TR to HCL, July 21, Mor.1036–9, for a complete account of the meeting with McK.
100. Mor.1037. TR was particularly scrupulous as the meeting had in fact been suggested by himself, in a letter to Secretary of State Hay on July 1, 1899. See Mor.1024–5. His intention was to advise that Maj.-Gen. Francis V. Greene be put in command of the entire U.S. force in the Philippines, and that Maj.-Gen. Leonard Wood be given similar powers in Cuba. Mor.1025.
101. Secretary Long, who attended the meeting, was at any rate impressed. "I believe Roosevelt to be thoroughly honest, and his ambition is one for the good of the service. Sometimes, I distrust his judgment, but he is so above all purely selfish and dishonorable intentions that I esteem him very highly." Journal, July 8, 1899, LON. As for TR's reaction to the accession of Elihu Root to the Secretaryship of War, see Mor.1041. His letter of congratulation is a startlingly cold document, avoiding direct compliments. It betrays more than a hint of anger that circumstances prevented TR himself being offered the position. Mor.1036.
102. Ib., 1062. Ib., 1052–3 gives TR's upstate itinerary.
103. Ib., 1062.
104. Ib.
105. Ib.
106. See, e.g., *World,* July 5, 1899; *N.Y.T.,* Oct. 2.
107. See Spector, Ronald, *Admiral of*

the New Empire (Louisiana State U., 1974) 111. Dewey was said by his family and friends to be a Republican (he remained mum on the subject himself) so TR naturally assumed that, as a loyal officer, he would support the renomination of his Commander-in-Chief. When Dewey subsequently announced he would, indeed, run for President, and under the Democratic banner, TR's fury knew no bounds. Spector, *Admiral,* 106 ff., tells the full story of Dewey's act of hubris.

108. Ib., 104–5; Bee.261.

109. TR had been hoping to ride in boots and breeches, as befitted a Colonel of Cavalry, but his brother-in-law Douglas Robinson protested that it would be "unwise, and . . . undignified." Mor.1072.

110. Bee.261–2.

28: The Man of Destiny

1. See HCL to TR, Dec. 7, 1899, Lod.I.424. EKR to B, n.d., from Albany: "I think exactly as you do about the v.p. for Theodore—Cabot has a strange bias about it." HCL to TR, July 12, 1899, LOD.

2. Ada.275. See Jos. *passim* on HCL's kingmaking role in TR's life: "Much might be said of his strange behavior in this [vice-presidential] affair." Ib. 108.

3. Mor.1112.

4. Ib., 1104.

5. Ib., 1166; TR.Auto.318.

6. A copy of the Message was sent to TCP by TR on Dec. 19, 1899.

7. Che.167–9. Even Elihu Root jibbed at the line about morality, and pointed out that most of the grand fortunes in America belonged to people whose industry and imagination had conferred "great benefits" on the community. "There is altogether too general an impression," he chided TR, "that it is immoral to acquire wealth." Dec. 13, 1899, qu. Che.170.

8. Extracts from the Message are quoted in TR.Auto.324–5. Che.206; Pri.211.

9. Che.94–5; Gos.207. See ib., 59–61 for Payn's background.

10. Pri.212.

11. Che.92; TR.Auto.300. Significantly, TR chose to launch his investigation of Payn on May 27, 1899, the day of his big triumph on the Ford Bill. "If there has been any iniquity," he wrote Secretary Youngs, "I wish we could discover it." Che.93–4.

12. TR.Auto.300.

13. Che.95–6.

14. *Evening Post,* Dec. 13, 1899.

15. Mor.1122–3.

16. Che.172, 166–70.

17. Ib., 172; TR.Auto.325; Che.251; Mor.1320; Par.127; Pinkett, Harold T., *Gifford Pinchot, Private and Public Forester* (U. Illinois Press, 1970) 34, 53; Che.250. See Appendix A, "Conservation," to Ch. 8 of TR.Auto., 323–325.

18. *Public Papers of Theodore Roosevelt, Governor* (Albany, 1900) 35–7; *N.Y.T.* clip, n.d., TRB; Che.251–3; Cut.86–8. For Pinchot's early and later relations with TR, see Pinchot, Gif-ford, *Breaking New Ground* (Harcourt Brace, 1947); Pinkett, *Pinchot;* Hays, Samuel P., *Conservation and the Gospel of Efficiency: The Progressive Conservation Movement, 1890–1920* (NY, 1959). See Che.242–53 for a fuller discussion of TR's environmental reforms at Albany. "All that I later strove for in the Nation in connection with conservation," wrote TR in his *Autobiography,* "was foreshadowed by what I strove to obtain for New York State when I was Governor." (299).

19. Che.98; Mor.1131, 1130.

20. Che.99–100.

21. Mor.1131.

22. Che.74, 101–3; *Eve. Post,* Jan. 19, 1900; TR. qu. Che.106.

23. Pors.; FRE. int; Mor.1504. TR's complex relations with Odell (which

lasted well into his presidency) are tracked by McC., *passim.*

24. Mor.1135–6; TR.Auto.302–3; Che. 107–108.

25. Mor.1136.

26. Che.108; TR.Auto.303.

27. Ib. See also Che. 109. Ib. doubts that this meeting took place on the evening specified by TR, without offering any convincing proof that it did not.

28. Ib.; Mor.1141.

29. *Sun,* Feb. 1, 1900; see also Mor.1157 fn.

30. Ib., 1157.

31. Ib., 1139–40.

32. Gar.213; Lee.530.

33. HCL was Chairman of the Senate Committee on the Philippines. LOD.I. 404; Lee.338. For a clear-eyed analysis of the vexed subject of U.S. response to the Philippines insurrection, see Gov. 187–89.

34. Mor.1343. See Bur.63 ff. for a short but excellent discussion of TR's relations with the Philippines. Alfonso, Oscar S., *Theodore Roosevelt and the Philippines* (NY, 1974) is the only book-length treatment of the subject.

35. Mor.1160–1. TR sent a similarly strong but courteous refusal to the Republican National Committeeman Henry Clay Payne. Ib., 1162.

36. Mor.1157.

37. Ib., 1161; *New York Tribune,* June 21, 1900.

38. *World,* Feb. 11, 1900; see *Trib.*, Feb. 13, 1900.

39. Platt qu. Quigg, cit. Mor.1337. TR's "rivals" included such minor figures as Cornelius Bliss, Timothy Woodruff, and John D. Long.

40. Mor.489–50; Butler, Nicholas M., *Across the Busy Years* (Scribner's, 1940) 226.

41. Lee.531–5.

42. Butler, *Years,* 226.

43. Mor.1276.

44. *Trib.*, Feb. 13, 1900; *New York Herald,* Apr. 27.

45. Mor.1278; Dana to TR, Apr. 17, 1900, TRP.

46. Mor.1291; *Trib.*, May 12, 1900.

47. Foraker, Joseph, *Notes of a Busy Life* (Stewart & Kidd, 1917) 91–2. Foraker also claimed that McK said to him: "I hope you will not allow the convention to be stampeded for Roosevelt for Vice-President." Qu. Lee.532. In view of the fact that TR and Foraker were bitter enemies later in life, this and the anecdote quoted in the text should be taken with caution.

48. Long, Journal, May 10, 1900: "Personally, if I could be made Vice-President tomorrow, I should like it because of the honor." LON. There are many other such wistful references in Long's Journal and letters.

49. Tha.II.342.

50. Mor.1264. TR had received similar warnings from Benjamin Odell and others. Ib.; Odell int. FRE.

51. Butler, *Years,* 227; sketch, un. newspaper, in TRB; Pla.384 ff.

52. Butler, *Years,* 227.

53. Burton later attained the twin distinction of serving in the U.S. Senate and in a Federal prison. Ib., 228. Anecdote from Lafayette B. Gleason int. FRE. See also Butler, *Years,* 228. Robert B. Armstrong of the *Chicago Record,* who was eavesdropping outside on a fire escape, remembered the scene somewhat differently. TR, he wrote, was sitting on a wooden chair. Rising in a rage, as the others in the room sought to persuade him, he allegedly lifted the chair high and smashed it to the floor. Then he sighed, and capitulated. Memo in TRB.

54. Butler, *Years,* 228; Lee.536.

55. *Trib.*, June 21, 1900. Olcott, Charles S., *The Life of William McKinley* (Houghton Mifflin, 1916) II.271 ff.; see also Lee.536; Morg.494.

56. Lee.536; Olcott, *McKinley,* II.274.

57. Sto.248; Butler, *Years,* 229.

58. Lee.537.

59. See Pri.220; *Trib.*, June 21, 1900. Lee.537.
60. Olcott, *McK*, II.274–6; Morg.494–5; *Trib.*, June 21, 1900; Lee.537.
61. Butler, *Years*, 229.
62. Ib., 230–1; Lee.537.
63. Reprinted in Mor.1337.
64. Pri.221; *Her.*, June 20, 1900.
65. *N.Y.T.*, June 20, 1900; Olcott, *McKinley*, II.275–6.
66. *N.Y.T.*, June 20, 1900.
67. *Harper's Weekly*, June 30, 1900; Morg.495; Lee.538; McK qu. Morg. 496.
68. Marshall, Dexter, "The Real Story of How Roosevelt was Named for the Vice-Presidency," *New York Press*, Dec. 8, 1907, is the source of much of the ensuing account. See also Mor.1338 fn; Pla.241 on Quay. Others echoed TCP's opinion. See Abbot, Lawrence F., *Impressions of TR* (Doubleday, 1919) 46; Sto.168.
69. Pri.222.
70. Quay had some Indian blood. See the moving account of his death in TR.Auto.158–161. Other descriptive material from Marshall, "The Real Story."
71. Ib.
72. Ib.
73. Ib. See ib. for Quay's further motives in using this victory to get himself back into the Senate.
74. *Her.*, June 21, 1900; Watson, James E., *As I Knew Them: Memoirs* (Indianapolis, 1936), 58.
75. Albert Shaw, qu. Rii., memo in TRB; Rob.196.
76. *World*, June 21, 1900; *Her.*, June 22; *Harper's Weekly*, June 30.
77. *World*, June 22, 1900; Mor.1340.
78. *World*, June 22, 1900.
79. "Rose Coghlan's Vivid Pen-Picture," in ib. Miss Coghlan was herself an accomplished actress.
80. Entire speech reprinted in TR.Wks. XIV.342–5.
81. *World*, June 22, 1900.
82. *Her.*, June 22, 1900.
83. Mor.1342; ib., 1343.
84. TR's entire campaign itinerary is given in Mor.1508–10. *Philadelphia Record*, Nov. 4, 1900; *Her.*, Oct. 21. Bryan's comparative figures were: 546 speeches, 493 towns, 18 states, 2,500,000 people addressed. For an extended discussion of the political issues raised by TR in the campaign, see Har.136–43.
85. Thwing, Eugene, *The Life and Meaning of TR* (Current Literature, 1916) 257.
86. *Sun*, Sep. 27, 1900; *Trib.*, same date.
87. TR.Auto.127.
88. See Scharf, Barbara C., *Mr. Dooley's Chicago* (Doubleday, 1977) for early relationship of TR and Finley Peter Dunne.
89. *Harper's Weekly*, Oct. 13, 1900.
90. See *Chicago Times-Herald*, Oct. 21, 1900. Less factual, and considerably more annoying to TR, were persistent press rumors that he was often drunk on tour. Similar rumors, stimulated by his high color and constant air of excitement, were to dog him for the next decade. *Harper's Weekly*, Dec. 7, 1901; Ickes, Harold L., *Autobiography of a Curmudgeon* (New York, 1943), 55. See also Morr.82.
91. Hag.RBL.466.
92. Lee.559; Pri.226; Mor.507.
93. Milholland int., FRE; Thayer, William R., *Theodore Roosevelt: An Intimate Biography* (Houghton Mifflin, 1919), 157. See also Dun.I.355. For an almost identical expression of foreboding, in the words of one of Roosevelt's oldest friends, see Par.136.
94. Qu. Pri.214.
95. See Har.129–30 for a modern confirmation of TR's boast. *Eve. Post* qu. Che.300.
96. In preparing this summary the author acknowledges the scholarly assistance of John Allen Gable, histo-

rian of the progressive movement and author of *The Bull Moose Years: Theodore Roosevelt and the Progressive Party* (National University Publications, 1978).

97. "While I know I need not say to my officers in what a deep regard I hold them, they will not mind my saying that just a little bit closer come the men." TR's farewell address to the Rough Riders, Sep. 13, 1898, TR.Wks.XI.157 fn.

98. John Allen Gable in letter to the author.

99. TR qu. Morg.508.

100. Mor.3.6–7. Milholland int. FRE.

Epilogue: September, 1901

1. See Mor.4.1343 ff. for a calendar of TR's Vice-Presidency.

2. Washburn, Charles G., *TR: The Logic of His Career* (Houghton Mifflin, 1916) 39.

3. Par.137. (See Hag.RF.108 ff. for TR's domestic activities through the fall of 1901.)

4. Par.137; TR.Auto.338. TR to Steffens, Aug. 8, 1901 (Columbia U., Steffens Papers).

5. Mor.3.1345; Morg.518.

6. The following account is taken from the reminiscence of Frank Lester Greene, one of TR's friends in the Fish and Game League, as recorded in Woo.81 ff.

7. Olcott, *McK*, II.316.

8. Ib.

9. Pri.231; Hagedorn memo, TRB mss. Secretary of State John Hay received similar assurances that McK was recovering, and proceeded to write a circular letter communicating the good news to all U.S. Embassies. "I thought it might stop the rain of enquiries from all over the world. After I had written it the black cloud of foreboding, which is always over my head, settled down and enveloped me and I dared not send it." Hay to Henry Adams, Sep. 19, 1901, ADA.

10. The following description of TR's expedition up Mount Marcy is based on these sources: Tahawus Club Guest Book, memoranda by George G. Wheelock, club president, and Beverly R. Robinson, member, Sep. 12, 1901; *World*, Sep. 15, 1901; Noah La Casse, int. Harry V. Radford, *Forest Leaves*, Winter 1904; TR.Auto.364; TR to J. J. Leary, Leary Notes, TRB; Hagedorn Notes, TRB; letter from Julia Hill, local resident, in ib.; reminiscences of EKR in *Women's Roosevelt Memorial Association Bulletin* (Fall 1933); Harmes, Edward A., "2.15 A.M.," article in *The Adirondac*, Nov.–Dec. 1963; Taylor, Dorothy, "Noah La Casse, Presidential Hiking Mate," *Adirondack Life*, 1972.3(2) 9–11. Scenic material from ib., 1972.3(1) 37, and 1973.4(3) 40.

11. Taylor, "La Casse."

12. EKR in *WRMA Bulletin;* Radford, La Casse int.

13. Ib.; Hagedorn Notes; Taylor, "La Casse."

14. Rii.76.

15. Radford, La Casse int.

16. Ib.; TR.Auto.364. La Casse testified that TR "became very calm" as he watched the ranger approach. TR to Leary: "I instinctively knew he had bad news . . . I wanted to become President, but I did not want to become President that way."

ILLUSTRATIONS

Theodore Roosevelt at the time of his Harvard entrance examinations, 1876. Frontispiece
Theodore Roosevelt Collection, Harvard College Library.

Theodore Roosevelt receives the American people on New Year's Day. xii
Brown Brothers.

Martha Bulloch Roosevelt at twenty-two. 2
Brown Brothers.

Theodore Roosevelt Senior, aged about forty-five. 31
Author's Collection.

Theodore Roosevelt the Harvard freshman, 1877. 55
Theodore Roosevelt Birthplace National Historic Site, New York.

Alice Hathaway Lee when Theodore Roosevelt first met her. 81
Theodore Roosevelt Association.

Alice Lee, Theodore Roosevelt, and Rose Saltonstall on their "tintype spree." 84
Alice Sturm Collection, privately held.

Theodore Roosevelt at the time of his assault on the Matterhorn, 1881. 114
Theodore Roosevelt Association.

Theodore Roosevelt at the time of his election to the New York State Assembly. 139
Theodore Roosevelt Association.

The New York State Assembly Chamber in 1882. 141
New York Public Library.

Alice, Corinne, and Bamie Roosevelt, about 1882. 167
Theodore Roosevelt Association.

Assemblymen Roosevelt, Howe, Spinney, Hunt, and O'Neil. 169
Theodore Roosevelt Association.

Antoine-Amédée-Marie-Vincent-Amat Manca de Vallombrosa, Marquis de Morès. 188
North Dakota State Historical Society.

Hallway of the Roosevelt mansion at 6 West Fifty-seventh Street, New York, 1880s. 214
Sagamore Hill National Historic Site.

Governor Grover Cleveland. Painting by Eastman Johnson. 236
New York State Library.

The first public advertisement of the Maltese Cross brand, 1884. 260
Theodore Roosevelt Association.

Theodore Roosevelt in his buckskin suit, 1884. 262
Theodore Roosevelt Collection, Harvard College Library.

Sagamore Hill in 1885. 290
Theodore Roosevelt Association.

Edith Kermit Carow at twenty-four. 312
Sagamore Hill National Historic Site.

Deputy Sheriff Roosevelt and his prisoners. 314
Theodore Roosevelt Association.

Cecil Arthur Spring Rice at thirty-five. 340
Theodore Roosevelt Birthplace.

Dying cow, December 1886. Painting by Charles Russell. 364
Montana Stockgrowers Association.

The Meadowbrook Hunt meeting at Sagamore Hill in the 1880s. 372
Theodore Roosevelt Association.

Congressman Henry Cabot Lodge, by John Singer Sargent, 1890. 401
National Portrait Gallery.

Elliott Roosevelt about the time of his marriage to Anna Hall. 437
Franklin Delano Roosevelt Library.

The Grand Court of the World's Columbian Exposition, Chicago, 1893. 471
Avery Architectural Library, Columbia University.

Police Headquarters, New York City, 1890s. 495
New York Public Library.

Theodore Roosevelt as president of the New York City Police Board. 533
Theodore Roosevelt Association.

Thomas Collier Platt in the 1890s. 535
Theodore Roosevelt Birthplace.

New York City Police Commissioners Andrews, Parker, Roosevelt, and Grant. 562
Theodore Roosevelt Association.

Mark Hanna on 2 August 1896. 564
New York Public Library.

Assistant Secretary Roosevelt at the Naval War College, 2 June 1897. 589
Theodore Roosevelt Association.

President William McKinley at the time of the Spanish-American War. 617
Sagamore Hill National Historic Site.

Wreck of the *Maine,* Havana Harbor, February 1898. 619
Sagamore Hill National Historic Site.

A troop of black volunteers en route to Tampa, 1898. 645
Theodore Roosevelt Association.

Piazza of the Tampa Bay Hotel, early summer 1898. 647
Theodore Roosevelt Collection.

Colonel Roosevelt and his Rough Riders atop San Juan Heights, Cuba. 662
Theodore Roosevelt Association.

Colonel Roosevelt preparing to muster out at Camp Wikoff, Long Island. 696
Theodore Roosevelt Collection.

The New York State Capitol, Albany, late nineteenth century. 724
New York Public Library.

Theodore Roosevelt at the time of his election to the Vice-Presidency. 748
Theodore Roosevelt Association.

The second Inauguration of William McKinley, 4 March 1901. 776
Theodore Roosevelt Collection.

INDEX

Page numbers in *italics* refer to illustrations.

Acton, Thomas C., 347
Act to Center Responsibility in the Municipal Government of the City of New York (1884), 220–24
Adair, John M., 649
Adams, Brooks, 576, 593, 601, 635
Adams, Henry, xvii, xxvi, xxvii, 250, 423, 435, 455, 486, 493, 593, 606, 640, 730, 747
  at Chicago World's Fair, 472–73
  described, 424
  salon of, 425–26, 468–69, 490
  TR as seen by, 425
Adams, John Quincy, 545
Adams, Mrs. Henry, 426
Adler, Henriette, 624–25
African Americans, *see* blacks
Aguinaldo, Emilio, 755
Airey (U.S. Marshal), 444, 446
Alabama, CSS, 588
Albany Hand Book, 142
Aldermanic Bill (1882), 152, 163
Aldrich, Thomas Bailey, 284
Alfred, King, 474
Alger, Russell A., 639, 642, 643, 659, 691–92, 705, 741, 744
Allotment Commissioners, 9
Almy, Frederick, 100
Alpha Delta Phi, 107
Altgeld, John P., 574, 772–73
Alvord, Tom, 144, 145, 158, 159–60, 162
American Big-Game Hunting (Boone & Crockett Club), 389
American Commonwealth, The (Bryce), 392
American Forestry Association, 390
American Historical Association, 421, 422
American Ideals (T. Roosevelt), 601–2
Americanism, 29, 136, 442, 473–75, 478–81
  frontier and, 478–79
  other terms for, 473–74
  as TR's personal philosophy, 479–81
  in TR's writings, 474–75, 479–80
  Turner's influence on, 478–79
  in *Winning of the West,* 474–75
American Statesmen series, 315–16
"Ancient Irish Sagas, The" (T. Roosevelt), xxxiv
Andrews, Avery D., 496–97, 500, 503, 505, 507, 509, 511, 520, 523, 530, 540, 541, 547, 548, 552, 553, 562, 562, 570, 584, 586, 726, 745, 752
Anna Karenina (Tolstoy), 319
  TR's review of, 323–24
Anti-Poverty Society, 380
Apache Indians, 603, 634, 663
Apponyi, Albert, xxx
Armenians, Turkish massacre of, 594
Arnold, Matthew, 319, 323, 395
Arthur, Chester A., 69, 129, 215, 241–43, 251, 252, 253, 254, 258, 538
Asiatic Squadron, Spanish, 621, 644
Asiatic Squadron, U.S., 604, 612–13
  Dewey assigned command of, 613–14
Assembly, New York State, *see* New York State Assembly
Associated Press, 411, 676, 692
Astor, Mrs. William, 121–22, 123
Astor Library, 119, 120–21, 599
Athenaeum, 418

Atlantic Monthly, 418, 703
At the Fireside (Long), 583
Australia, in colonialist racial theories, 477, 482
Autobiography (T. Roosevelt), 4, 233, 356, 728–29, 754

Bacon, Bob, 61, 64, 68, 86, 638
Badlands, Dakota Territory, 316, 454, 465
 boat chase in, 317–24
 as campaign stop in election of 1900, 771
 end of TR's cattle business in, 644
 in *Hunting Trips of a Ranchman,* 292
 ice incident and, 293–94
 ruin of cattle industry in, 375–78
 spring roundups in, 295–96, 327, 376
 TR's capital investment in, 294–95, 337, 375–76, 485
 TR's 1883 trip to, *see* Badlands trip of 1883
 TR's 1884 trip to, *see* Badlands trip of 1884
 TR's 1887 trip to, 386–88
 TR's 1896 trip to, 570–71
 TR's physical and spiritual transformation in, 296–97
 TR's popularity in, 377–78
 Winter of the Blue Snow in, 363–67
 see also Elkhorn Ranch
Bad Lands Cowboy, 239, 267–68, 273, 377
Badlands trip of 1883, 187–212
 buffalo killed in, 211–12
 failed hunts in, 202–3, 205–9
 Ferris hired for, 190–91
 inspiration for, 182–83
 Little Missouri in, 189–90, 194, 195
 terrain encountered in, 199–201
 TR's cattle-ranching investment in, 204–5, 208–11
 TR's journey to, 185–86
Badlands trip of 1884, 261–69, 273–74, 286
 antelope killed in, 264
 down-river ranch site claimed in, 268–69, 274, 276
 Elkhorn site in, 274, 276
 encounter with bully in, 275–76
 Medora visit in, 266–67
 TR's need for solitude in, 263–64
Balfour, Arthur James, xviii
Ballantyne, R. M., 16
Baltimore American, 380–81, 693
Balzac, Honoré de, 663
Bancroft, George, 418
Bardshar, Henry, 686
Barère de Vieuzac, Bertrand, 574
Bates, J. C., 669
Beer, Thomas, 746
Belgium, Storer's ambassadorship to, 582
Bell, Sherman, 720
Bellamy, Edward, 575
Benefit of Colored Orphans Bill (1884), 238
Bennett, James Gordon, 626
Benton, Thomas Hart, 316, 383, 392
 TR contrasted with, 330–32
Bigelow, Poultney, 118, 162
Bigelow, William Sturgis, xxi, 531, 637–38
Big Horn country hunting trip, 274–75, 277–80
 animals killed in, 278–79, 280
Biglin, Barney, 216, 222, 342
Billings County, Dakota Territory, 1886 city council election in, 326
Bi-Partisan Police Act (1895), 498, 547–48
Bishop, Joseph Bucklin, 542–43, 759
Bismarck Tribune, 335
Bites of a Cherry (Long), 583
Black, Frank S., 586, 699, 702, 704, 709, 714, 716–17, 725, 750, 752
blacks, xv, xvii, 466
 at 1884 Republican National Convention, 253, 255
 1886 New York City mayoral election and, 350–51
 see also race relations
Blaine, James G., 128, 241–43, 251, 252, 254, 256, 258–59, 267, 282–85, 342, 352, 375, 380, 391, 394, 465, 536, 538
 on TR, 397–98
Blanco y Erenas, Ramón, 626
Bliss, Cornelius, 582, 757
Board of Health, New York City, 334, 509
Bogan (New York assemblyman), 227
Bonner, Sherwood, 294
Book Buyer, 385
Boone, Daniel, 388, 392, 475

Boone & Crockett Club, 388–89, 392, 435, 472, 484, 607, 616, 620, 751
Boston Advertiser, 315, 328
Boston Herald, 271, 613
Boston Post, 444–45
Boston Sunday Globe, 616
Bourke (policeman), 515
Brassey, Lord, 561
Bridges, Robert, 703, 742–43
Brooklyn Daily Eagle, 246
Brooklyn Navy Yard, 601, 606
Brooklyn Times, 509
Brooks (New York assemblyman), 175
Brooks, Nicholas, 541, 542–43, 547, 554, 556, 570, 586
Browning, Robert, 321
Bryan, William Jennings, 568–69, 571–75, 576, 608, 768–71, 773
"cross of gold" speech of, 567, 574
Bryce, James, 358, 392, 743
Buchanan, James, 485
Bulloch, Annie, *see* Gracie, Annie Bulloch
Bulloch, Archibald, 8
Bulloch, Irvine, 130
Bulloch, James, 7–8, 588
Bulloch, Mrs. (TR's grandmother), 9
Burchard (preacher), 380
Bureau of Arrears, New York State, 238
Bureau of Citations, New York State, 238
Bureau of Construction, U.S., 606–7
Bureau of Navigation, U.S., 606
Bureau of Ordnance, U.S., 606–7
Burnsted (Badlands criminal), *314,* 318–19, 335
Burroughs, John, 294
Burton, J. R., 761
Butler, Nicholas Murray, 251–52, 758, 760, 762, 763–64
Byrnes, Thomas F., 498–99, 506, 516, 541, 544

Cable, George Washington, 294
Cabot, George, 250
Caernarvon, Lord, 358
California, conservation of sequoia groves in, 389
Callahan, Pat "King," 514–15, 516, 517
Cambon, Jules, 631–32
Cameron, Elizabeth, 426, 747
Cameron, James Donald, 426, 447, 593
Cameron, Michael, 227
Campbell, Douglass (grandfather), 230, 648–49
Campbell, Douglass (grandson), 648
Campbell, William, 478
Camp Wood, 648–51
Canada, 598, 624
"Candidates Handicap" (*New York Sun*), 217
Cannon, Joseph G., xiv, 632, 741
Capron, Allyn, 670, 672–73, 677
Carmencita (dancer), 447
Carow, Edith (TR's second wife), *see* Roosevelt, Edith Kermit
Carpenter, Frank, 612
Carroll, Lewis, 45
Carter, Modesty, 377
Cassi, Emil, 717
Castro, Cipriano, xxviii
Catholic Total Abstinence Union, 524
Cavalry Charge, The (play), 652
C Diamond Ranch, 324
Celtic (steamship), 126
Century, xxxiv, 319, 348, 394, 395, 433, 703
Century Club, 374
"Certain Phases of the Westward Movement in the Revolutionary War" (T. Roosevelt), 421
Cervera, Pascual, 688–89
Chandler, William E., 593, 613, 614, 759
Chanler, Mrs. Winthrop, 436
Chanler, Winthrop, 640–41, 730
Chapin, Alfred Clark, 170
Chapman, John Jay, 641, 699–701, 703, 704–6, 709–11, 715
Charles Dickens, A Critical Study (Gissing), xxxiii
Chase, William Merritt, 447
Chaucer, Geoffrey, 465
Cheyenne Beef Company, 210
Chicago, University of, 545
Chicago Times-Herald, 591, 635, 771
Chicago Tribune, 258, 518, 575
Chicago World's Fair (1893), 470–73, *471,* 478–79
Child, Richard Washburn, xxxi
Children's Aid Society, 4
Chilean crisis of 1891, 455, 603–4
Choate, Joseph H., 579, 580–81, 711–12
Church, Bob, 677
Churchill, Lord Randolph, 381
Cigar Bill (1883), 180–81

Cincinnati, USS, 621, 622
Citizens' Union, 700, 703, 706
City Civil Service Reform Association, 458
City of Washington (tour ship), 625
Civil Service Act (Pendleton Act) (1883), 405, 407, 409, 414, 416, 432
Civil Service Chronicle, 409
Civil Service Commission, 400–436, 485, 489, 491
 annual report of, 420–21
 Baltimore investigation and, 443–46, 450–51, 452, 454–55, 457–64
 in Cleveland Administration, 485–86
 Indianapolis Post Office corruption and, 409–10, 412
 mandate of, 407–8
 neglected budget of, 426–27, 441
 New York Customs House examinations and, 408–9
 Paul/Shidy affair and, 410–13, 415, 420, 427–33, 434, 443
 threatened budget cuts to, 441, 466
 TR's appointment as head of, 397–98
 TR's first day at, 404
 TR's reappointment to, 469
 TR's resignation from, 492
 Washington Post editorials on, 414–16, 433
Civil Service reform, 54, 69, 171, 180, 182, 215, 284, 390, 398, 404–5, 414, 433, 436, 454, 585
 Cleveland's commitment to, 378
 in Harrison Administration, 407
Civil Service Reform Association, 735
Civil Service Reform Bill (1883), 172, 179–80
Civil Service Reform League, 458
Civil War, U.S., 8–10, 13, 588, 599, 603, 668
Clarence, Duke of, 373
Clarkson, James S., 407, 452
Clark's Tavern, Free Trade Club meeting at, 181–82
Clayton, Powell, 254, 255
Cleveland, Frances Folsom, 378, 402
Cleveland, Grover, xxi, 180, 236, 285, 348, 353, 411, 436, 469, 487, 489, 492, 522, 527, 583, 592, 597, 726, 735, 772
 described, 170–71
 at Chicago World's Fair, 470–72
 Civil Service Reform as commitment of, 378, 380
 elected President, 284
 Five-Cent Bill and, 176–77, 178
 as Governor of New York, 171–72
 illegitimate child of, 272, 282
 Nast cartoon of, 246
 nominated for President, 271
 in panic of 1893, 484–85
 reelected President, 467
 renominated for President, 394, 464
 in split with Tammany Hall, 215
 in tariff controversy, 390–91, 396
 on TR, 175, 181
 TR's confrontation with, 246–47
 Venezuela Message of, 545
Clowes, William Laird, 581
Cockran, Bourke, 569–70
Codman, Frank, 99
Cody, Buffalo Bill, 380
Coghlan, Rose, 768
Colbert, Benjamin H., 649
Coleman, Quartermaster, 651
Collis, C.H.T., 713
Columbia Law School, 116, 117–19, 130–31
Columbus, Christopher, 472, 479
Committee of Seventy, 488
Congress, U.S., xvii, xix, 172, 389, 391, 421, 441, 591, 629
 Fifty Million Bill passed by, 632
 McKinley's war message to, 637–38
 in onset of Spanish-American War, 631–32, 634–35, 639–40
 see also House of Representatives, U.S.; Senate, U.S.
Congressional Record, 773
Conkling, Roscoe, 69, 124, 128–29, 132, 243, 536
Conlin, Peter, 509, 511, 517, 523, 553, 581, 584
 Byrnes replaced as police chief by, 507–8
 in controversy over police promotions, 541–44, 547, 552, 556
 resignation of, 586
conservation:
 in creation of Boone & Crockett Clubs, 388–90
 1887 Badlands trip and, 386–88
 national legislation for, 389–90

in TR's Annual Message of 1900, 749, 751
Constitution, U.S., 7, 474
Coolidge, W. W., 90
Cooper, James Fenimore, 16, 294
Cooper Union, 345–46
Corrigan, Michael Archbishop, 524
Cortelyou, George B., 761
Cosmos Club, 493
Costello, J. J., 149, 155, 162
County Democracy, 544, 551–52
Cowles, William Sheffield, 561
Craddock, Charles Egbert, 294
Crane, Stephen, 672, 674, 676
Crockett, Davy, 388, 392
Croker, Richard, 501, 539, 544, 586, 714, 717, 718
Cromwell, Oliver, 742–43
Cuba, xvi, 531, 591, 592, 593, 597, 598, 601, 602, 621, 636–37, 755–56
rebellion against Spain in, 490, 545, 594, 634
in TR's war plan, 612–13
see also Spanish-American War, prelude to
Cuba Squadron, Spanish, 657
Cullom, Shelby, 592
Curtin, Jeremiah, 432–33
Curtis, George William, 251, 254, 258–59, 267
Curtis, Newton M., 213, 217
Custer Trail Ranch, 197
Cutler, Arthur Hamilton, 48–49, 75, 96, 231, 235, 245
Czolgosz, Leon, 778

Daly, Justice, 717
Dana, Charles A., 593
Dana, Commander, 298
Dana, Fanny Smith, 50, 51–52, 95, 112–13, 115, 172–73, 298–99, 313, 775
Dana, Paul, 758–59
Daniels, Ben, 708
Darwin, Charles, 481
Davenport, Homer, xxii
Davis, Charles H., 593, 636
Davis, Cushman, 606
Davis, Richard Harding, 509, 655, 656–57, 664, 669, 672, 674, 676
Day, Rufus, 638
Day, William R., 598
Declaration of Independence, 332
Delaware, 1896 presidential campaign in, 576
Delmonico, Charles, 379
Deluge, The (Sienkiewicz), 565
Democratic National Conventions:
of 1884, 271
of 1896, 567
Democratic party, New York, 178, 179, 180, 219–20, 222, 307, 341, 343, 501
and election of 1883, 170
Westbrook Resolution and, 160–61
see also New York City mayoral elections; New York State gubernatorial elections; Tammany Hall
Democratic party, U.S., 378, 487
and election of 1890, 436
tariff controversy and, 390
see also elections, U.S.
Demolins, Edmond, 653
Depew, Chauncey, 230, 343–44, 351, 380, 424, 537, 714, 736, 760
De Quincey, Thomas, xxxiii
Dewey, George, 593, 602–4, 616, 621, 642, 745
appointed commander of Asiatic Squadron, 613–14
background of, 603
at Manila Bay, 643–44, 655, 698
TR's friendship with, 604
TR's historic orders to, 629–30
Dial, 385
Dickens, Charles, 45, 116–17
Dickinson, Lowes, xxxiii
Dill, Samuel, xxxiii
Dixon, A. C., 527
Dolliver, Jonathan, 765
Dow, Mrs. Wilmot, 269, 301, 319, 335
Dow, Wilmot, 88–89, 96–97, 269, 270, 273–74, 277, 281, 287, 294, 300, 301, 316, 317, 319–21, 324, 327, 337–38, 453–54
Dracula (Stoker), 531
Dunne, Finley Peter, 770
Dwight, T. W., 117–19, 230

Eaton, Howard, 327
Edmunds, George F., 241, 243, 245–46, 249, 251, 252, 254, 256, 257, 258, 283, 536

Edward VII, King of England, xviii
election of 1896, U.S., 534, 560, 608, 712, 768
  Republican National Convention in, 540, 557–59
  results of, 576–77
  TR as possible presidential candidate in, 527–28
  TR's campaign in, 565–66, 569, 571–75
election of 1900, U.S., 704
  results of, 771
  TR as possible presidential candidate in, 740–42
  TR's campaign in, 769–71
  TR's vice-presidential candidacy supported in, 754–58, 760–64
  see also Republican National Convention of 1900
elections, U.S.:
  of 1856, 534
  of 1860, 346
  of 1872, 534, 771
  of 1876, 54–56
  of 1880, 128
  of 1881, 534
  of 1882, 172, 215
  of 1884, 170, 215, 240–41, 267, 271–72, 280, 281–84, 342, 352, 378, 380, 398, 464, 536
  of 1886, 315, 326, 354–55
  of 1888, 342, 378, 390–91, 394, 396, 536, 577
  of 1890, 422, 436, 557, 573
  of 1892, 436, 464–67, 557
  of 1895, 528–30, 534, 537
  of 1896, *see* election of 1896, U.S.
  of 1897, 578–79, 615
  of 1900, *see* election of 1900, U.S.
  of 1904, 740, 771
  see also New York City mayoral elections; New York State gubernatorial elections
Eliot, Charles William, 57, 108
Elizabeth I, Queen of England, 475
Elkhorn Ranch, 281, 286–87, 294, 316, 337
  boat stolen from, 317–18
  given to Sylvane Ferris, 644
  living arrangements at, 300–301, 335
  ruin of, 363–67, 373, 375–76
  see also Badlands, Dakota Territory
Elliott, John, 45
Elliott, Maud, 45
Ellis, Ralph, 68
Emerson and Other Essays (Chapman), 700
Emporia (Kans.) *Gazette,* 608
Endicott, William C., 336
Erie Canal Improvement project, 699, 735
Erwin, George Z., 217
Essays in Practical Politics (T. Roosevelt), 395, 474
Etruria (ocean liner), 356, 357, 371, 378
Evans, E., 447, 457
Ewart, Hamilton G., 427, 429–30, 431
Excise Herald, 510

Farragut, David, 603
Ferguson, Bob, 687–88
Ferris, Joe, 192, 194, 197, 199, 201, 202–5, 207–8, 211–12, 293, 317, 328
  TR's hiring of, 190–91
  in TR's misunderstanding with de Morès, 301, 302–3
Ferris, Sylvane, 198–99, 208–9, 211, 263, 265, 273–74, 294, 327, 337, 373, 465, 644
Fiddlin' Joe, 377
Fifth Corps, U.S., 654, 656, 657, 665, 679–81, 691
Fifty Million Bill (1898), 632
Filemaker (horse), 310
Finnegan, Redhead, *314,* 318–23, 326, 333, 335, 394, 465
Fire and the Sword (Sienkiewicz), 565
First U.S. Volunteer Cavalry, *see* Rough Riders
Fish, Hamilton, 648, 654, 670, 672–73, 676, 677
Fish, Mrs. Hamilton, 19
Fish, Mrs. Stuyvesant, 122
Fisk, Nelson W., 777
Fitch, Ashbel P., 549–51
Five-Cent Bill (1883), 176–78, 179
Flahant, Madame de, 384
Flight of Evil Before Good, The (Hunt), 150, 226
Flint, Charles R., 633
Foraker, Joseph, 255–56, 258, 380, 759, 767
Ford, John, 731

Ford Franchise Tax Bill (1899), 731–34, 736–38, 744, 749
assessment clause of, 736
revised, 738
TR's correspondence with Platt on, 736–38
"Foregoing Ant, The" (T. Roosevelt), 18
Foreign Office, British, 357
"Foreign Policy of President Harrison, The" (T. Roosevelt), 465
Forest and Stream, 388
Forest, Fish, and Game Board, 751
Forest Reserve Act (1891), 390
Foster, Charles, 460
Foster, David L., 352
Foulke, William Dudley, xxxiii
Fox, Gustavus, 588
France, Spanish-American War and, 624
Franklin, Benjamin, 383
Free Trade Club, 123, 182
Frémont, John Charles, 252, 534
French Revolution, 349, 384, 607
frontier, 592
Americanism and, 478–79
closing of, 478–79
race struggle in, 476–77
Frye, W. P., 593

García, Calixto, 664–65, 679
Garfield, James A., 127–28, 132, 171–72, 254, 536, 538
George, Henry, 575, 773
in 1886 New York City mayoral election, 339–42, 343, 344, 349–50, 352–55
Germany, Imperial, 595, 624
Geronimo, Chief, 603
Gilbert, John J., 244
Gilder, Richard Watson, 348
Gilmore, James R., 419
Gissing, George, xxxiii
Godkin, Edwin L., 272, 344, 353, 381, 521, 546–47, 704
Good Government Club, 518–19, 700
Goodrich, Caspar F., 597–98
Gorringe, H. H., 182–83, 185, 186, 187, 189, 190, 191, 194, 202, 210, 339
Goschen, George, 358
Gould, Jay, 156, 158–59, 160, 162, 174, 176–77, 179, 499, 717
Gouverneur Morris (T. Roosevelt), 382–85, 392, 394, 474, 600, 743
assessment of, 383–85
reviews of, 385
Government Printing Office, 608
G. P. Putnam's Sons, 135, 138, 210, 393, 395, 397, 419, 601, 773
Grace, William Russell, 230
Gracie, Annie Bulloch, 9, 10, 11, 22, 40, 172, 270, 299
marriage of, 147
as TR's tutor, 14–15
Gracie, James K., 147
Grant, Frederick D., 496, 503, 505, 506, 522, 530, 540, 541, 547, 548, 552, 554, 562, 570, 581, 584, 586
Grant, Ulysses S., 54, 128, 190, 226, 230, 252, 298–99, 496, 538, 608, 771
Great Britain, 136, 331, 389, 417–18, 434, 531, 595, 598
Greater New York Bill (1896), 537, 538
Great Lakes Naval Militia, 605–6
Greek View of Life, The (Dickinson), xxxiii–xxxiv
Greenhalge, Frederick T., 432–33
Greenway, Jack, 689–90
Gridiron Club, 635, 762
Grinnell, George Bird, 388–89
Groo, Captain, 511
Guffin, W. I., 592

Hagedorn, Hermann, 152–53, 174, 209
Haggerty, James, 223
Hale, Edward Everett, xviii
Hale, William Bayard, xxviii
Hall, Dr., 231, 234
Halstead, Murat, 767
Hamilton, Alexander, 7, 220, 250, 381, 383
Hanks, C. S., 90–91
Hanna, Mark, 564, 567, 571, 573–74, 576, 582, 583, 591, 608, 609, 615, 624, 635, 729, 745, 768
described, 568
as nationwide political boss, 565–66
Quay's deal with, 765–66
TR on, 566
TR's vice-presidential candidacy opposed by, 757–58, 761–63, 765–66
Hanna, Mrs. Mark, 624
Harper's (publisher), 601

Harper's Monthly, 509
Harper's Weekly, xxvi, 165, 246, 251, 586, 596, 765, 767
Harris, Joel Chandler, 294
Harrisburg Telegraph, 380
Harrison, Benjamin, 394, 397–98, 410–14, 415, 416, 420, 421, 426, 434–36, 441, 443, 445, 451, 452, 454, 455, 456, 458, 464, 465, 466, 468, 486, 536, 538, 573
  described, 396, 406–7
Harrison, Caroline Lavinia Scott, 464–65, 467
Harrison, Mrs. Burton, 5
Harrison Administration, 403, 421–22, 445, 464, 468, 592
Hart, Albert Bushnell, 56
Harte, Bret, 125–26
Harvard Advocate, 90, 99, 105
Harvard Athletic Association, 90
Harvard Club, 491
Harvard Crimson, 87, 545
Harvard Natural History Society, 86, 105
Harvard University, 54–56, 57, 63
  Porcellian Club of, 77, 79, 100, 250
  Rough Rider recruits from, 646, 649
  TR's academic career at, 64–65, 68, 73, 77, 86, 90, 92, 95, 99, 105, 107–8
  TR's championship boxing bout at, 90–91
  TR's description of life at, 61–62
  TR's fellow students at, 57–60, 77–78
  TR's preparation for, 47, 49, 50
Hasty Pudding Club, 57, 86, 101
Hatton, Frank, 414–16, 420, 427–28, 431, 433, 440, 445, 454
Hawaii, 468, 591, 592, 597, 601, 611, 621
  annexation of, 598–99, 605
  U.S. recognition of, 487
Hawthorne, Nathaniel, 294
Hay, John, xxviii, 10, 150, 426, 455, 490, 493, 582, 593, 740, 759–60
  background of, 423–24
  described, 424
  TR's first meeting with, 30–32
Hayes, Rutherford B., 54, 56, 68–69, 128, 423, 424, 538
Haymarket riot, 574
Hearst, William Randolph, 623, 626, 627, 672
Hendricks, Francis J., 727, 750, 753, 754
Herbert, Hilary, 560, 597, 600
Hero Tales from American History (Lodge and T. Roosevelt), 491
Hess, Jake, 125, 131–32, 134–35, 216, 222, 342
Hewitt, Abram S., 343, 344, 346, 347, 349–50, 352–55, 501
Hill, A. S. "Ass," 105
Hill, David B., 518, 519–20
Hill, James J., 573
History of France and England in North America (Parkman), 393
History of the City of New York (T. Roosevelt), 382, 433, 435, 441–42, 474
History of the United States of America, 1801–1817 (H. Adams), 425
Hoar, George F., 521
Hobart, Garret A., 558, 582, 741, 745, 746, 747
Hoeber (New York City coroner), 519
Hoffman, Louis von, 194
Hoffman, Medora von, 194
Holmes, Oliver Wendell, 284
Hooper, Arthur, 61, 68
Hooper, Betty, 100
Houghton Mifflin, 382–83
House of Representatives, U.S., xvii
  Appropriations Committee of, 632
  Baltimore affair investigated by, 459–63
  Civil Service Reform Committee of, 427, 459
  and election of 1888, 396
  Reed as Speaker of, 421, 422–23, 435
  Shidy affair hearings of, 427–33, 434
  see also Congress, U.S.
Howard, Esmé, xxvii
Howe, Walter, 169, 173
Howell, John A., 613–14
Howells, William Dean, 284
How the Other Half Lives (Riis), 502
Hudson, William C., 168, 246–47
Humphrey, C. F., 658
Hunt, Isaac, 145, 147–48, 149, 151, 152, 153, 156–59, 162–65, 168, 169, 172, 173–74, 178, 179, 180, 217, 220, 240, 704, 713
  end of TR's friendship with, 244–45
Hunt, William Morris, 150

Hunting in Many Lands (Boone & Crockett Club), 389
Hunting Trips of a Ranchman (T. Roosevelt), 289–92, 377, 388, 474
 assessment of, 291–92
 Indians episode in, 304–6

Idaho, 395
 statehood of, 422
immigration, 380, 442
Immigration Department, U.S., 380
Independent, 465
Independent party, 699–701, 703–5, 706, 709–11
India, in Pearson's racial theory, 482
Indiana, USS, 560
Indian Bureau, U.S., 441
Indians:
 Civil Service Commission and, 441, 466
 TR's attitude toward, 304–6, 441, 466
 in TR's writings, 474–77
Influence of Sea Power upon History, The (Mahan), 433–34
 TR's influence on, 600
In Memoriam (Tennyson), 68
"In Memory of My Darling Wife" (T. Roosevelt), 277
Institute of 1770, 86
Interior Department, U.S, 389
interoceanic canal, 487, 598
Iowa, USS, 610–11, 640
Ireland, John, 404, 739
Irving, Washington, 294
Isbell, Thomas J., 673
Ithaca (N.Y.) *Daily News,* 527

Jackson, Andrew, 329, 608
Jackson, Harry, 61
Jacobs, William Wymark, xxxiii
James, Admiral, 561
James, Henry, xx, xxi, xxx, 425, 490, 700
 American Ideals reviewed by, 601–2
 TR on, 480–81
James, William (naval historian), 137
James, William (philosopher), 68
Japan, 434, 487, 592, 594, 595, 612
 discrimination against immigrants from, xvi–xvii
 U.S. Hawaiian policy protested by, 601, 605, 611
Jay, August, 40–41
Jefferson, Thomas, 220, 330, 333, 384, 393, 568, 595, 608
Jenkins, Micah, 708
Jews, persecution of, xviii
jingoism, 473, 591
Johnson, Andrew, 380
Johnson (Baltimore Postmaster), 444, 446, 454, 459–60
Johnston, George D., 486
Jones, Bill "Hell-Roaring," 326, 377, 465
Jones, Samuel, 772–73
Jörn Uhl (Frenssen), xxxiii
Josephus, 767
Jusserand, Jean Jules, xviii

Kane, Woodbury, 646–48, 654, 708
Kent, J. F., 680, 684–86
Kilburn, Frederick D., 752
Kimball, W. W., 615
King, Clarence, 425, 490, 593
King's Mountain, Battle of, 477, 648–49
Kipling, Rudyard, 484, 490–91, 580
 on TR, 493
Klein, Isaac, 703, 710
Kruger, Paul, 546

Labor party, U.S., 339, 341, 344–45
labor relations, 378, 735, 739, 749, 773
 in 1886 New York City mayoral campaign, 341, 344–45, 353
La Farge, John, 425–26
Lafayette, Marquis de, 7
Lake Erie, Battle of, 137
Lamb and Rich, 185
Lamont, Daniel S., 246
Lang, Gregor, 201–5, 274, 376
Lang, Lincoln, 201–5, 207, 211, 274, 366–67
 on TR's view of life, 203–4
Lang, Mrs. Gregor, 202
Langley, S. P., 636, 640
Las Guásimas, Battle of, 670–77, *671,* 698, 739
Laughlin, J. Laurence, 86, 89, 95, 575
Lauterbach, Edward, 529, 537, 548, 713, 761
"Law of Civilization and Decay, The" (T. Roosevelt), 601
Lawton, H. W., 668, 669, 671, 680, 682, 683
Lee, Alice Hathaway, *see* Roosevelt, Alice Hathaway Lee

Lee, Arthur, 742
Lee, Fitzhugh, 618, 622, 625, 640, 690
Lee, George Cabot, 78, 100, 101, 104, 225
Lee, Henry, 272
Lee, Mrs. George Cabot, 100, 101, 225
Leeholm estate, 237, 238, 294
  becomes Sagamore Hill, 297–98
Leslie's Magazine, 669, 676
Levy (saloonkeeper), 522
Lexow, Clarence L., 500, 501
Liberal Laws parade, 526–27, 529
Life of Oliver P. Morton (Foulke), xxxiii
Life of St. Patrick, xxxiii
Lightfoot (TR's horse), 74, 92, 94, 97, 106, 121, 126, 184
Liliuokalani, Queen of Hawaii, 468
Linares, Arsenio, 665, 679
Lincoln, Abraham, xviii, 9, 10, 12, 60, 204, 252, 254, 255, 346, 423, 538, 608, 743
Lincoln, Mary Todd, 12
Lincoln, Robert, 256
Liquor License Bill (1884), 238
Littlejohn, Dewitt, 217
Little Missouri, Dakota territory, 189–90, 194, 195, 266
Little Missouri Stockmen's Association, 287, 300, 318, 326, 336, 376
Livingstone, David, 15
Lodge, Henry Cabot, xxii, xxx, 246, 259, 267, 270, 271, 272, 280, 282, 309, 374, 375, *401,* 412, 420, 423, 426, 465, 490, 493, 531, 540, 579, 612, 736, 760, 766
  described, 249–50
  elected to Congress, 354–55, 436
  elected to Senate, 467
  in expansionist lobby, 593, 598
  explosion in Cuba predicted by, 623, 625
  Hawaii annexation and, 598–99
  at Republican National Convention of 1884, 251, 254–55, 256, 257
  TR's *Benton* commission and, 315–16
  TR's Civil Service Commission appointment and, 397–98
  TR's correspondence with, 275, 284–86, 289–91, 311, 315–16, 319, 328, 334, 336, 344, 352, 376, 383, 396, 410, 413, 451, 454, 467, 489, 505, 506, 521, 525, 529, 532, 558, 566, 578, 583, 603, 611, 649, 660, 688, 693, 713, 741–42, 749–50, 758
  in TR's 1896 campaign, 572–73
  TR's friendship with, 249–50, 767
  TR's Navy Department appointment and, 577–78, 582–83
  TR's Police Board appointment and, 491–92
  TR's vice-presidential nomination and, 741–42, 747–79, 755–57, 758, 763
Lodge, Nannie, xxvii, xxxiii–xxxiv, 426, 624
Loeb, William, 742
Lôme, Enrique Depuy de, 622, 623–24
London Naval Chronicle, 121
Long, John D., 257, 583, 590–91, 599, 601, 602, 605–7, 611, 615, 616, 618–20, 621, 622, 625, 626, 627, 629, 630, 632, 638, 639, 641, 644, 655, 759, 762, 763
  described, 590
  Dewey's appointment and, 613–14
  as possible vice-presidential candidate, 741, 757, 765
  TR's "flying machine" memorandum to, 636
Longfellow, Henry Wadsworth, xxxiii, 16, 109
Longworth, Alice Lee Roosevelt (Baby Lee) (TR's daughter), xiii, 299, 310, 335, 352, 358, 395, 436, 744
  Anna Roosevelt as surrogate mother to, 235, 237, 270, 373–74
  birth of, 228–29
  christening of, 235
  TR and, 231–32, 280–81, 327, 385–86
Louis XVI, King of France, 384
Lowell, James Russell, 294
Luce, Stephen B., 600
Luffsey, Riley, 195, 196, 197, 269, 300, 306
Lyman, Charles, 404, 409–10, 414, 420, 427, 428, 432, 434, 446, 486
Lynch, John R., 254–55
Lyon, Mike, 510, 512

Macaulay, Thomas Babington, xxx
McCullagh, John, 541, 542–43, 554, 556, 570, 586
McGinty, Billy, 650

"Machine Politics in New York City" (T. Roosevelt), 395
McIntosh, Burr, 669, 676
McKinley, Ida Saxton, 572, 612
McKinley, William, xvi, 258–59, 421, 436, 560, 563, 567, 571, 591–92, 596, 597, 606, 608, 609, 617, 656, 704, 705, 715, 739, 741, 742, 755, 758, 762
  and annexation of Hawaii, 598–99
  assassination of, 777–80
  Cuba resolution signed by, 641
  described, 612
  Dewey's appointment and, 614
  1896 "Front-Porch" campaign of, 572–73
  elected President, 576
  emergence of, 256–57
  as erratic Commander-in-Chief, 655–56
  Hanna as political manager of, 565–66
  inauguration of, 581, 776
  nominated for presidency, 558–59
  and onset of Spanish-American War, 622, 626, 627, 631–39
  political career of, 557
  renomination of, 768
  Root named War Secretary by, 744
  TR's Navy Department appointment and, 577–78, 582–83
  TR's Navy Department meetings with, 611–13
  TR's opposition to candidacy of, 557–58
  TR's round-robin letter and, 691–92
  ultimatum to Spain issued by, 636–37
  war message to Congress of, 637–39
MacManus, "Big John," 145, 149, 152, 155
McMorrow (policeman), 552
McNair, Fred V., 604
McNaughton, James, 778–79
Maddox, Widow, 275
Madison, Dolley, xxxi
Madison, James, 383, 393
Mahan, Alfred Thayer, 433–34, 560, 581, 593, 597, 598, 601, 631
  career of, 599–600
  TR's influence on, 600
Maine, USS, 618, 622, 624
  sinking of, 625–26
Maltese Cross Ranch, 198, 265, 266, 268, 273, 287, 376
Mandan Indians, 663
Manhattan Elevated Railroad, 154–57, 159, 165, 176
Manifest Destiny, 329, 330–31, 333, 392, 474, 592
Manila, Battle of, 643–44, 655, 698
Manitou (TR's horse), 261, 264, 266, 267, 286, 293–94, 305, 318
"Manly Virtues, The" (T. Roosevelt), 601
Mann, Katy, 439, 440, 447–49, 450, 451–52
Marat, Jean Paul, 574
María Christina, Queen of Spain, 636
Marie Antoinette, Queen of France, 384
Marroquín, José Manuel, xxviii
Marryat, Frederick, 16
Marshall, Edward, 669, 697
Marvel, Ike, 294
Marx, Karl, 575
Maryland, 1896 presidential campaign in, 576
Maryland Civil Service Reform League, 443, 454–55
Masefield, John, 523
Massachusetts:
  election of 1884 in, 271, 282
  election of 1892 in, 467
  election of 1897 in, 615
Massachusetts Club, 613
Massachusetts House of Representatives, 250
Masterson, Bat, 377
Mauve Decade, The (Beer), 746
Mayoralty Bill (Roosevelt Bill) (1884), 220–24
Meadowbrook Hunt, 310, 372
Mérimée, Prosper, 249
Merriam, C. Hart, 616
Merrifield, Bill, 198–99, 208–9, 211, 263, 265, 273–74, 280, 281, 294, 327, 336, 367, 373
Merrimac, CSS, 690
Metropolitan Club, 592, 599, 601, 602, 604, 609, 631
Mexico, 336, 455, 474
Miami (troopship), 695
Miles, Nelson A., 603, 639, 656
Miller, Bronco Charlie, 377

Miller, Warner "Wood-Pulp," 215, 216, 217, 240, 241, 243–44
Miller, William H., 407
Milton, John, xxxiii
Milwaukee Civil Service Board, 410
Minkwitz, Anna, 44, 46–47, 52
Minkwitz family, 44–47
Minot, Harry, 65, 68, 77, 88
Missionary Travels and Research in Southern Africa (Livingstone), 15
Mitchell, Edward, 133
Modern Ironclads, 561
Monocacy, USS, 629
Monroe, James, 393
Monroe Doctrine, 545
Montana, 416
  statehood of, 422
Montana Stock Grower's Convention, 326
Monterey, USS, 598
Montgomery, USS, 560–61
Morès, Antoine-Amédée-Marie-Vincent-Amat Manca de Vallombrosa, Marquis de, *188,* 193–97, 210, 239–40, 269, 287, 310, 326, 327
  failed cattle business of, 377
  murder charge against, 300, 306–7
  TR's land-rights disputes with, 266–67, 276–77, 281
  TR's misunderstanding with, 299–304
Morès, Madame de, 267
Morgan, Mrs., 61
Morley, John, xxiv, 358, 473
Morris, Gouverneur, 382–84, 385
Morris, Robert, 383
Morton, Levi P., 490, 522, 557, 558
Morton Hall, 123–26, 131, 133, 490
Moss, Frank, 586
Muir, John, xxx
Muller-Ury, Adolfo, xxv
Municipal Indebtedness Bill (1884), 238
Murphy, William S., 707
Murray, Joe, 131–35, 537
Murray's Magazine, 395

Napoleon I, Emperor of France, 434
Nation, 343, 442
National Guard, New York, 299, 620, 630, 642, 716, 726
"National Life and Character" (T. Roosevelt), 601
National Life and Character: A Forecast (Pearson), 481
National Zoo, 389
Natural History (Wood), 18
"Natural History on Insects" (T. Roosevelt), 18, 20
Naval Policy of America as Outlined in Messages of the Presidents of the United States from the Beginning to the Present Day (T. Roosevelt), 607–8, 611
Naval Records, 121
Naval War Board, 643
Naval War College, *589*
  Mahan at, 598–99
  TR's speech at, 593–96, 597, 601, 605, 632, 676
Naval War of 1812, The (T. Roosevelt), xxxii, 182, 210, 383, 433, 474, 588, 599
  assessment of, 137–38
  publishing of, 135–36
  revised version of, 581
  textbook status of, 291
  in Wister satire, 123
  writing of, 101, 120–21, 130
Navy, British, 136
Navy, Spanish, 640
Navy, U.S., 182, 487, 593, 595, 606, 621, 629–30, 640, 660, 664
  Mahan's influence on, 434
  Naval War of 1812 as influence on, 137–38
Navy Department, U.S., 434, 565, 588–616, 621, 630, 741
  and annexation of Hawaii, 598–99
  Brooklyn Navy Yard investigation and, 601, 606
  bureaucratic structure of, 606
  conflict between line and staff officers of, 616, 640
  Court of Inquiry of, 626–27, 631–32, 634–36
  expansionist lobby and, 592–93, 598, 601, 602–4
  foreign reaction to TR's appointment to, 592
  Great Lakes Naval Militia tour and, 605–6

Iowa gunnery inspection tour and, 610–11
Naval Policies of the Presidents issued by, 607–8
press coverage of TR's appointment to, 591
as source of war plans, 597–98, 602
TR appointed assistant secretary of, 583–84
TR's achievements in, 640
TR's ambition to be secretary of, 561
TR's desk at, 588–90
TR's initiatives in, 600–601, 605–7
TR's lobbying for appointment to, 577–78, 579, 582–83
TR's Naval War College address and, 593–96, 597, 599, 601, 605
TR's resignation from, 640
Nelson, Horatio, 434
New Jersey, 1896 presidential campaign in, 571, 576
New Orleans Daily Picayune, 596
Newsboys' Lodging-House Dinner, 117
newspapers, *see* press; *specific newspapers*
New York City, 491, 726
charter of, 181
corruption probe in, 223–25
Customs House exams corruption in, 408–9
elections of, *see* New York City mayoral elections
Platt's gerrymandering attempt in, 536–37
TR as Police Commissioner of, *see* Police Board, New York City
TR's history of, 382, 433, 435, 441–42, 474
New York City Board of Health, 334, 599
New York City mayoral election of 1886, 339–56, 379–80, 391, 487, 489, 501, 536, 551–52, 699, 704
black voters in, 350–51
George's candidacy in, 339–42, 343, 344, 349–50, 352–55
labor relations in, 341, 344–45, 353
press coverage of, 344, 346–49, 352–53, 356
projected vote totals in, 349
Republican County Convention in, 339, 342
results of, 354–55
TR nominated in, 342, 343–48
TR's disappointment in, 355–56
TR's platform and campaign in, 349, 350–52
New York City mayoral elections:
of 1886, *see* New York City mayoral election of 1886
of 1894, 536
of 1897, 586
New York Commercial Advertiser, 348, 521, 522, 527
New York Daily Graphic, 352–53, 356
New York Daily News, 349, 569
New York Evening News, 549
New York Evening Post, 151, 240, 245, 259, 272, 344, 355, 381, 434–35, 496, 521, 544–45, 546, 551, 571, 616, 704, 730
New York Evening Sun, 496, 505, 628
New York Federal Club, 379–81
New York Herald, 154, 173, 216, 230–31, 349, 373, 455, 518, 521, 523, 544, 554, 580, 596, 626, 655, 669, 672, 739
New York Infant Asylum, 117
New York Journal, 353–54, 521, 623, 626, 627–28, 669, 672, 692
New York Mail & Express, 348
New York Methodist Ministers' Association, 538
New York National Guard, 299, 620, 630, 642, 716, 726
New York Observer, 175–76
New York Press, 643
New York Recorder, 552
New York Saturday Globe, 435
New York Star, 353
New York State, 571
Capitol building of, 724, 726
Cleveland as Governor of, 171–72
elections of, *see* New York State gubernatorial elections
Republican machine of, 124, 125, 126
Sunday Excise Law enacted by, 512–13
TR as legal resident of, 711–12
TR's growing fame in, 161–62

New York State Assembly, 140–81, 213–23, 237–40, 245, 547
Aldermanic Bill in, 152, 163
Banks Committee of, 218
Chamber of, *141*, 150, 226
Cigar Bill in, 180–81
Cities Committee of, 152, 155, 218, 219–20, 228, 238
Civil Service Reform Bill in, 172, 179–80
cockfight incident and, 174
corruption and, 154–55, 165
and election of 1881, 131, 134–35
and election of 1883, 170
Five-Cent Bill in, 176–78, 179
Ford Franchise Bill passed by, 732–34
Judicial Committee of, 172, 179
Manhattan Elevated Railroad bill in, 154–56
Militia Committee of, 218
municipal bills in, 220–24, 238
Privileges and Elections Committee of, 178
speakership contests in, 168–70, 213–17, 218
Sprague's ouster from, 178
Taxation Committee of, 733
TR as minority leader in, 180–81, 216
TR nominated for, 133–34
TR's Albany stories and, 227–28
TR's behavior on floor of, 153
TR's first appearance in, 140–44
TR's first speech in, 150–52
TR's legislative diary of, 144–45, 149, 173
TR's vituperative style in, 174–75
Westbrook Resolution in, 156–64
New York State gubernatorial election of 1898, 691, 711–22, 759
Independents in, 699–701, 703–6, 709–11
judiciary corruption as issue in, 717–18
Platt and, 698–99, 701–2, 708–9
Rensselaer fiasco in, 716–17
Republican Convention in, 699, 712–14
residency controversy in, 711–12
results of, 721–22
Tammany Hall and, 714, 717
TR's speeches in, 715, 718–21
TR's train-tour campaign in, 718–21
New York State gubernatorial elections:
of 1883, 170
of 1885, 355
of 1896, 699
of 1898, *see* New York State gubernatorial election of 1898
of 1900, 741, 749
New York State Legislature, 128, 216, 240, 547
corruption in, 154–57
Street Cleaning Bill in, 126
New York State Senate, 7, 170, 176, 180, 226, 500, 536, 547, 548, 728, 732, 750, 754
New York Sun, 160, 217, 242–43, 244, 256, 281, 344, 346, 349, 379, 381, 415, 418–19, 452–53, 464, 521, 522, 544, 549, 556, 569, 593, 596, 607, 641, 754, 755, 758
New York Supreme Court, 156
New York Times, 134, 152, 156, 159, 160, 165, 181, 222, 226, 245, 257, 283, 348, 349, 379, 381, 385, 434, 454, 463–64, 518, 521, 523, 531, 539, 556–57, 558, 569, 584, 736
New York Tribune, xvii, 163, 230, 348, 349, 355, 374, 381, 412, 509, 521, 551, 591, 605, 761
New York World, 160, 174, 178–79, 217–18, 225, 231, 242, 243, 259, 349, 353, 504–5, 508, 521, 525, 526, 529, 530, 550, 551, 626, 628, 672, 708
Nicaragua, TR's plans for interoceanic canal in, 598
Nictheroy (ship), 633
Nile's Register, 121
Nixon, S. Fred, 733–34
Nobel Prize, xviii
North, Lord, 358
North American Review, 250, 394
North Atlantic Squadron, U.S., 600, 606, 622, 641–42
North Dakota, statehood of, 422
Northern Pacific Railroad, 190, 191, 239, 304
Northern Pacific Refrigerator Car Company, 266, 300
Notes on Some of the Birds of Oyster Bay (T. Roosevelt), 66
Nursery, 641
Nuttall Ornithological Society, 86

O'Brien, John J., 216, 222, 342, 544
O'Brien, Justice, 452–53
Odell, Benjamin B., Jr., 699, 701, 709, 712, 715–17, 725, 730, 738, 751–54, 760, 761, 773
"Ode to Indifference" (Pellew), 57
O'Donald, Frank, 195–96
Office of Naval Intelligence, 597
Oglethorpe, James Edward, 8
Ohio:
  election of 1896 in, 571
  election of 1897 in, 615
O.K. Society, 100
Oliver Cromwell (T. Roosevelt), 742–44
Olympia (ship), 629, 745
O'Neil, William, 149, 152, 163, 165, *169*, 170, 173, 176, 178, 217, 245, 713, 718–19
O'Neill, Bucky, 661–63, 677, 685
Oregon, USS, 598, 640
Orléans, Duchess d', 384
Orthopedic Dispensary, 117
Osler, William, 628, 631
O'Sullivan, Tim, 524, 525
Ouida, 16
Outlook, xxiv
Oyster Bay, N.Y., 49–50
  see also Sagamore Hill

Packard, Arthur, 267–68, 333–34, 377
Packard, Edwin, 244
Paddock, Eldridge G., 191–93, 194, 195–96, 281, 304, 377
Paget, Alfred W., 663
Paine, Thomas, 384
Panama Canal, xv
Panamanian Revolution, xiv–xv
Pan-American Exposition (1901), 775
Panic of 1893, 484–85, 557
Parker, Andrew D., 496, 502, 505, 514, 519, 520, 523, 524, 525, 530, 558, 562, 586–87
  Bishop and, 542–43
  corruptness of, 552–54
  Detective Bureau and, 503, 551, 554
  formal charges against, 555–57
  Police Bill and, 547–48
  Strong's attempted dismissal of, 581–82
  TR's conflict with, 540–49, 551–57, 559, 570, 580, 581–82, 584
Parkhurst, Charles H., 542, 580
Parkman, Francis, 393, 412
Park Protection Act (1894), 389
Partridge, John Nelson, 728, 735
Patterson, Charles, 152, 153
Paul, George H., 410–11, 413, 414, 415, 416, 428, 431–32
Payn, Louis F., 750–54, 757
Pearson, Charles H., 481–83
Peffer, William Alfred, xxviii
Pellew, George, 57
Pendleton Act (1883), *see* Civil Service Act
Pennsylvania, election of 1896 in, 571
Perry, Thomas, 68
Peru, conquistadores in, 474
Pfaffenbach (Badlands criminal), *314*, 318–19, 322, 335
"Phases of State Legislation" (T. Roosevelt), 395
Philadelphia Independent, xxx
Philadelphia Press, 692
Philippines, 602, 613, 621, 629, 742, 744
  insurrection against United States in, xvi, 755–56
Pinchot, Gifford, 751
Pingree, Hazen, 772–73
Pitt, William, 381
Plant, Henry B., 654–55
Platt, Frank, 761
Platt, Thomas Collier, 253, *535*, 544, 547, 548, 568, 704, 729, 730, 735, 742, 760, 773
  attempted ouster of TR by, 536–40
  described, 538
  elected to Senate, 580–81
  Ford Franchise Tax Bill and, 731–34, 736–38, 749
  Hendricks appointment issue and, 727–28
  Payn appointment and, 749–53
  political career of, 534–36
  TR's 1898 gubernatorial campaign and, 698–99, 701–2, 708–9, 712, 714–15, 721
  TR's Navy Department appointment and, 578–79, 583, 584
  TR's vice-presidential nomination and, 755, 757, 761, 763, 765
  TR's working relationship with, 723–25, 728, 731, 744–45, 772
Poe, Edgar Allan, xxxiii, 294

Police Bill (1896), *see* Bi-Partisan Police Act
Police Board, New York City, 470–587
annual police parade and, 553
assessment of TR's tenure on, 584–85
Byrnes's ouster and, 506–7, 508
city elections and, 498, 501, 503, 528–30, 569, 576
corruption problems in, 499–501
letter-bomb incidents and, 523, 548
Liberal Laws parade and, 526–27, 529
Platt's attempted ouster of TR from, 536–40
powers of, 497–98, 506
press and, 502, 503–4, 519, 521–22, 544, 551, 556–57, 580
Sunday Excise Law enforced by, 512–29, 538–39
TR elected president of, 497
TR renominated as president of, 549
TR's appointment to, 491–92
in TR's conflict with Parker, 540–49, 551–57, 559, 570, 580, 581–82, 584
in TR's confrontation with Fitch, 549–51
TR's disillusionment with, 559–60
TR's night patrols and, 508–12
TR's presidential ambition and, 527–28
TR's resignation from, 585–86
Police Department, New York City:
corruption in, 496, 499–501
Mulberry Street headquarters of, 494–96, 495
power structure of, 497–98
Polk, Doctor, 184
Pollock, William J., 708
Poole, William F., 418
Populists, 572, 574, 608, 737, 773
Porcellian Club, 77, 79, 100, 250
Porter, Robert B., 428–30
Portsmouth Peace Conference (1905), xxiii
Post Office, U.S., 409
Power of Removals Act, 554–55
"Practicability of Giving Men and Women Equal Rights" (T. Roosevelt), 107
Prescott, William H., 393
press:
Alice Roosevelt's death reported in, 230–31
1884 Republican National Convention covered in, 250–51, 258–59
1884 Republican New York Convention covered in, 242–43
1886 New York City mayoral election covered in, 334, 346–49, 352–53, 356
Federal Club speech in, 380–81
Naval War College speech in, 596
Police Board and, 502, 503–4, 519, 521–22, 544, 551, 556–57, 580
in prelude to Spanish-American War, 623, 626, 627–28, 635
TR satirized in, 178–79
TR's governorship covered in, 728–29, 733, 739
on TR's Navy Department appointment, 591
on TR's nomination for New York State Assembly, 134
TR's relations with, 154, 174–76, 178–79, 502, 503–4, 728–29, 733, 739
Procter, John R., 486, 489
Proctor, Redfield, 613–14, 634, 778
Progress and Poverty (George), 341
progressive movement, 772–73
Proudhon, Pierre, 575
Puck, 381
Puerto Rico, possible Rough Rider campaign in, 689–90
Pulitzer, Joseph, 626, 628
Punic Wars, 474
Pure Food Act (1906), xv
Putnam, George Haven, 397, 433

Quay, Matthew, 765–66
Quigg, Lemuel Ely, 487–88, 491–92, 529, 537, 596, 699, 701–2, 705–6, 730
Quincy, Josiah P., 485–86

race relations:
frontier and, 476–77
Pearson's theory of, 481–83
in TR's writings, 482–84
see also blacks
Rain-in-the-Face (TR's horse), 667
Ranch Life and the Hunting Trail (T. Roosevelt), 395, 474

Rath, William E., 510
Reed, Thomas B., 421, 422–23, 426, 435, 441, 451, 493, 557, 573, 582, 601, 639
Reid, Mayne, 16
Reid, Whitelaw, 374–75, 381
"Remarks on Copyright and Balloting" (T. Roosevelt), 394
Remington, Frederic, 395, 615, 707
Rensselaer County Fair, 716
"Reply to Some Recent Criticism of America, A" (T. Roosevelt), 395
Report of Commissioner Roosevelt Concerning Political Assessments and the Use of Official Influence to Control Elections in the Federal Offices at Baltimore, Maryland, The (T. Roosevelt), 446, 450–51, 452
Republican County Committee, 347, 529, 699
Republican County Convention (1886), 339, 342
Republican Maryland State Convention (1891), 443
Republican National Committee, 254, 565, 754
Republican National Convention of 1884, 241, 249–59, 536
  balloting at, 256, 258
  blacks in, 253
  Independent campaign against Blaine in, 252, 254, 256–57
  McKinley's emergence in, 256–57
  nominating speech in, 257
  Republican Old Guard in, 252, 255
  TR's speech in, 255
  vote buying in, 253
Republican National Convention of 1900, 741, 754, 757, 760–68
  Hanna-Quay deal in, 765–66
  TR nominated in, 768
  TR's address to, 767–68
  TR's entrance into, 764–65
  TR's vice-presidential candidacy supported in, 760–64
  TR's withdrawal statement in, 763–64
Republican National Conventions:
  of 1880, 128
  of 1884, *see* Republican National Convention of 1884
  of 1892, 443
  of 1896, 540, 557–59
  of 1900, *see* Republican National Convention of 1900
Republican New York State Conventions:
  of 1884, 240–44
  of 1885, 307
  of 1895, 529
  of 1898, 699, 712–14
Republican party, Massachusetts, 250
Republican party, New York, 227, 341, 343, 498, 528
  Federal Club and, 379–80
  New York State machine of, 69, 124, 125, 126, 129, 160–62, 165, 166, 219–20, 222–23
  Speaker deadlock and, 149–50
  see also New York State gubernatorial elections
Republican party, U.S., 215, 267, 378
  and election of 1884, 284–86
  and election of 1888, 396
  and election of 1890, 436
  and election of 1896, 576–77
  tariff controversy and, 390–91
  see also elections, U.S.
Republican State Committee, 699, 701–2
Review of Reviews, 572
Richardson, Mrs., 60, 62
Richfield Springs, N.Y., 184–85
Ridder, Herman, 526
Riis, Jacob, xxx, 496–97, 501–2, 505, 507, 555, 587, 708, 779
  TR's confrontation with, 527–28
  in TR's night patrols, 508–9
Robespierre, Maximilien, 574
Robinson, Corinne Roosevelt (TR's sister), 8, 18, 19, 22, 23, 33, 72, 74, 95, 100, *167*, 172, 219, 225, 229, 237, 238, 270, 307, 374, 386, 487
  childhood of, 17
  coming-out party of, 122
  in foreign tour of 1872, 38, 40, 43
  illness of, 11, 21
  marriage of, 163
  personality of, 50
  TR's correspondence with, 58, 65, 68, 184–85, 323–24, 326, 358, 742
Robinson, David, xvii
Robinson, Douglas, 163, 293, 386, 448, 458
Rockefeller, John D., 573

Rockwell, A. D., 32
Romance of the Merit System, The (Halloran), 405
Roman Society from Nero to Marcus Aurelius (Dill), xxxiii
Roosevelt, Alfred (TR's cousin), 451
Roosevelt, Alice Hathaway Lee (TR's first wife), 79, *81*, 87–88, 91, 119, 120, 140, 147, 166, *167*, 184, 185, 226, 237, 250, 263, 264, 309, 313, 316, 336
- in Albany, 148, 149, 163, 172, 173
- coming-out of, 101
- death of, 229–32
- described, 80–82
- in European tour of 1881, 126–27
- in group photograph, 83–85, *84*
- honeymoon of, 116–17
- in New York society, 122–23
- pregnancy and childbirth of, 183, 218–19, 225, 228–29
- TR's courtship of, 83–86, 88, 90, 92–94, 97–102, 315
- TR's engagement to, 101–5, 106, 109
- TR's first meeting with, 78, 80
- TR's lifelong silence on, 232–33
- TR's marriage proposal to, 93–94
- TR's reaction to death of, 231–32
- TR's relationship with, 91–92, 98–99, 219
- TR's written memorials to, 232, 234, 277
- wedding of, 115

Roosevelt, Alice Lee (TR's daughter), *see* Longworth, Alice Lee Roosevelt
Roosevelt, Anna (Bamie) (TR's sister), xxxii, 8, 10, 13, 60, 95, 100, 116, 163, *167*, 172, 185, 219, 225, 245, 272, 295, 297, 299, 301, 307, 308, 350, 352, 397, 452, 711
- Alice Lee Roosevelt in care of, 235, 237, 270, 373–74
- childhood of, 17
- Edith Roosevelt's relationship with, 374
- in European tour of 1869, 25, 29
- in foreign tour of 1872, 36, 39, 43
- illness of, 11, 21
- personality of, 50
- Spring Rice met by, 356–57
- at TR and Edith Roosevelt's wedding, 358
- TR's correspondence with, 77, 88, 111, 130, 257, 274–75, 278, 280–81, 294, 316–17, 326–27, 335, 336–37, 376, 386, 422, 440, 449–50, 453, 459, 506, 545, 558, 559–60, 569, 570, 573, 604, 615, 736, 758

Roosevelt, Anna Hall (TR's sister-in-law), 439, 440–41, 447–48, 450, 452–53, 459, 468
Roosevelt, Archibald Bulloch (TR's son), 485
Roosevelt, Corinne (TR's sister), *see* Robinson, Corinne Roosevelt
Roosevelt, Cornelius van Schaak (TR's grandfather), 7
Roosevelt, Edith Kermit (TR's second wife), xix, xxii–xxiii, 27, 50, 51, 65, 101, 112, 115, 261–63, 271, 298, 311, 342, 343, 350, 379, 382, 397, 417, 421, 422, 448, 451, 455, 563, 612, 656, 687, 775, 778–79
- Alice Lee Roosevelt and, 373–74
- Anna Roosevelt's relationship with, 374
- childhood of, 22
- as First Lady, xxxi
- honeymoon of, 371–73
- illness of, 620, 623, 628, 631, 655
- personality of, 308–9, 313–15
- pregnancies and childbirths of, 371, 375, 385, 386, 403, 419–20, 453, 485, 604, 615
- TR's bid for mayor opposed by, 487–89
- TR's correspondence with, 315, 335, 336
- TR's fame and, 702
- TR's first meeting with, 307–8
- TR's relationship with, 22, 52–53, 62–63, 74, 82–83, 315, 435, 604
- TR's secret engagement to, 309, 312, 313, 315, 326, 336–37
- TR's vice-presidential candidacy opposed by, 741, 763
- wedding of, 357, 358–59

Roosevelt, Eleanor (TR's niece), 299
Roosevelt, Elliott (TR's brother), 8, 22, 23, 44, 52, 74, 103, 147, 182, 185, 210, 225, 229, 237, 238, 298, 437, 447–48, 468
- alcoholism of, 111–12, 163, 395, 438–40, 447–50, 457

athleticism of, 94
childhood of, 17, 46, 48, 49
death of, 488, 513
epilepsy of, 438–39
in foreign tour of 1872, 38, 43
Hunting Trips dedicated to, 291
illnesses of, 11, 21, 94–95, 438–39, 449–50
insanity suit and, 452, 453, 455–57
paternity suit and, 439–40, 447, 451–52
personality of, 50, 95
TR compared with, 94
in Western hunting trip, 110–12, 186
Roosevelt, W. Emlen (TR's cousin), 5, 75, 96, 124
Roosevelt, Ethel (TR's daughter), 453, 455
Roosevelt, Franklin D. (TR's cousin), 604–5
Roosevelt, Hall (TR's nephew), 450
Roosevelt, James A. (TR's uncle), 158, 210
Roosevelt, James West (TR's cousin), 101
Roosevelt, Kermit (TR's son), 435, 779
birth of, 419–20
illness of, 623
Roosevelt, Martha Bulloch (Mittie) (TR's mother), 2, 30, 32, 36, 43, 44, 46, 47, 49, 94, 102–3, 110, 112, 116, 126, 147, 163, 172, 210, 219, 226, 237, 298
ancestry of, 7–8
Confederate sympathies of, 9, 13–14
death of, 229, 230–32
described, 5–6
in European tour of 1869, 23–25
as invalid, 21
TR's birth and, 3–4
TR's correspondence with, 19–20, 61, 186
Roosevelt, Quentin (TR's son), xix, xxii, xxiii, 615
Roosevelt, Theodore:
abstemiousness of, 79, 123, 173, 513, 525
adolescence of, 36–37, 45–46
Albany stories of, 227–28
Americanism of, *see* Americanism
ancestry of, 6–8
art enjoyed by, 29, 127
as assemblyman, *see* New York State Assembly
as Assistant Navy Secretary, *see* Navy Department, U.S.
attempted blackmailing of, 161
birth of, 3–4
in boat chase, 317–24, *320*
as born leader, 46
boyhood diary of, 20, 22–23, 25–28
in cartoons, xxv–xxvi, 174, 352–53, 503, 511, 554, 704, 770–71
as Civil Service Commissioner, *see* Civil Service Commission
class consciousness of, 144–45, 292–93
college writing of, 64, 107
combat account of, 685–87
conservationist ethos awakened in, 386–88
courage of, 158, 306
dee-lighted as speech mannerism of, xxi, xxvi, xxix, xxx, 201
delayed entrances of, 143–44, 243–44, 346, 460, 719, 764–65
depression of, 288, 547
as deputy sheriff, 317–24, *320*
double-dictating ability of, 743
early education of, 14–15, 34, 39, 44, 147
early natural-history writings of, 18–19
elected Vice-President, 771
in European tour of 1869, 21–27
in European tour of 1881, 126–27, 129–30
exercise as passion of, xxii, xxiv, 32–34, 38, 73–74, 110, 121, 465
fame of, 161–62, 523, 698, 702
familiarity discouraged by, xxiii, 327
family motto of, 299
as father, xxii–xxiii, 12, 299, 579–80, 604–5
father's chastising of, 12–13
father's philanthropy unsuited for, 117
finances and income of, 210–11, 294–95, 337, 375–76, 385–86, 394, 398, 455, 485, 487, 489, 721, 744
first gun of, 34
first military skirmish of, 673–75
first political campaign of, 133, 134–35

Roosevelt, Theodore (*cont'd*):
first printed work of, 65–66
as folk hero, 326–27
as genius, xxvi–xxvii
as Governor of New York, *see* Roosevelt, Theodore, as Governor of New York
at Grant's funeral, 298–99
in grief for father, 70–72, 73, 75, 78–79
in grief for first wife, 247–49, 277–78
hack writing by, 394–95
at Harvard, *see* Harvard University
Henry James's characterization of, 481
humor and wit of, xxii, xxiii, xxviii, 40, 45–46, 51, 137, 227, 384, 565, 572
on Indians, 304–6, 441, 466
interrogation technique of, 224–25
language studies of, 34, 44–45, 47, 129
as law student, 116, 117–18, 130–31
letter-bombs sent to, 523, 548
life view of, 204–5
liveliness and *joie de vivre* of, 10–11, 104, 152, 162–63
memory of, xxx, 17, 22, 80, 156, 252
Mrs. Bellamy Storer's maternal relationship with, 563, 565
nature and natural history as interests of, 17–19, 33, 263, 292–93, 386, 389–90
Navy Department position as ambition of, 561
new species of elk named for, 616
New York World's documentary portrait of, 504–5
nicknames of, xxvi, 4, 163, 511
onset of political career of, 123–26
as orator, 150–51, 175–76, 221, 333–34, 353, 525, 575, 719, 767
orinthology as passion of, xxvii, 17, 36, 38, 41–42, 65–67, 109, 261
party loyalty vs. personal freedom balanced by, 133
personal magnetism and charm of, xxiv, xxviii–xxx, 51, 227, 475, 609–10
physical and spiritual transformation of, 296–97
physical appearance of, *see* Roosevelt, Theodore, physical characteristics and activities of
as Police Commissioner, *see* Police Board, New York City
political philosophy of, 737–38
poor misunderstood by, 571–72
Pope met by, 28
possible scientific career as dilemma for, 67, 87–89, 95, 106–7
as possible senator from Dakotas, 304
power loved by, xvii, 124, 420, 710, 744
predictions of presidential career for, 47, 51–52, 168–70, 334, 433
presidential ambition of, 380–81, 432–33, 521–22, 527–28, 704
press relations of, 154, 174–76, 178–79, 502, 503–4, 728–29, 733, 739
as professional historian, 393
as professional lecturer, 484, 722
as proponent of naval aviation, 636
prudishness of, xxix, 63, 123, 465
purported "family" letters of, 315
race relations in writings of, 482–84
reading habits of, xxvi–xxvii, xxxii–xxxiii, xxxiv, 15–16, 32, 34, 38, 64, 294, 479
as reform minded, 126, 158
senior thesis of, 107
simplified spelling advocated by, xxxiii
social legislation opposed by, 163–64
in Spanish-American War, *see* Rough Riders
in speakership contest, 215–17, 218
speaking style of, xxiv–xxv, xxvii–xxviii, 728
"speak softly" adage of, xvi, 754
"stag" activities of, 173–74
Stickney's description of, 325
storytelling ability of, xxii, 17, 83
taxidermy as interest of, 34, 67
temper of, 56, 59, 165, 227
Thayer's description of, 297
in torpedo-boat cruise, 605
as "traitor to his caste," 125
twenty-sixth birthday of, 284
twenty-seventh birthday of, 311
vows to marry Alice Hathaway Lee, 83–85, 100

women's rights advocated by, 107–8
worldview of, 483–84
as writer, 18–19, 66–67, 119–20, 135–36, 289–93, 315, 389, 391–92, 394–97, 465, 482–84, 742
Roosevelt, Theodore, as Governor of New York:
assessment of, 772–73
county-fair tour and, 744–45
First Annual Message of, 723, 726–72
Ford Franchise Tax Bill and, 731–34, 736–38
Hendricks's appointment and, 727–28
Payn appointment debate and, 749–54
political support for, 676, 691, 698
press coverage of, 728–29, 733, 739
progressive legislation and, 734–36
Second Annual Message of, 749, 751
vice-presidential nomination and, 740–42, 747–49, 751, 753; *see also* election of 1900, U.S.
Roosevelt, Theodore, physical characteristics and activities of:
asthma of, 4, 8, 11–12, 17, 20, 23, 24–26, 29, 32, 35, 42, 46, 51, 72, 75, 83, 89, 111, 151, 183–85, 286, 297, 386
body-building, xxiv, 32–34, 35, 47, 62
boxing, 35, 49–50, 61, 62, 83, 90–91, 218
bull neck of, xxv, 174, 297, 308, 496, 519
dress of, 63–64, 88, 105, 111, 116, 123, 147–48, 149, 251, 262, 275, 291, 310, 325, 358–59, 436, 523, 549–50, 644, 648, 681, 695–97, 703, 709, 745–46, 760, 765
energy of, xxi, xxiv, 17, 59, 83, 121, 203–4, 297, 352, 505–6
facial features of, xxv, 36, 51, 174, 275, 297, 308, 496, 504, 519
first hunting attempts, 39–40, 42
first spectacles of, 34–35
first Western hunting trip, 110–12
fist-pounding habit of, xxv, 159, 635
fox hunting, 309–11, 386
hearing ability of, 35, 65–66, 109, 261
heart problem of, 108–9, 110
horseback riding, 41, 385
ill health of, 4, 11, 16, 20–21, 23, 46, 51, 64, 74, 108–9, 110, 183–85, 287, 293, 297, 386, 455–56, 488, 489
injuries of, 296, 310–11
laugh of, xxii, 227
Maine hunting trips, 75–77, 88–89, 95–96
mountain climbing, 129–30, 778–80
myopia of, 34–35
near-fatal grizzly encounter, 416–17
physical and spiritual transformation of, 296–97
physical development and form of, xxiv, 32, 36–37, 51, 297, 371, 447, 496, 697
pince-nez of, 373, 506, 519
prodigious eating of, 301, 490
singing ability of, 62
spectacles of, 295–96
teeth of, xxv–xxvi, 36, 51, 63, 201, 202, 325, 504, 511, 524, 609
voice of, xxi–xxii, xxvi, 36, 83, 150, 153, 165, 333, 380, 399, 404, 504, 554, 609, 686, 697
weight gained by, 301, 371, 447
whiskers of, 71, 88, 106, 123, 227
Roosevelt, Theodore, speeches of:
on Civil Service reform, 179–80
at Dickinson 4 July celebration, 332–34, 473
in election of 1884 campaign, 282
in election of 1886 campaign, 347–51, 353
in election of 1888 campaign, 396
in election of 1896 campaign, 572, 574–75
in election of 1898 campaign, 715, 718–21
in election of 1900 campaign, 769–70
on Excise Law, 518–21, 524–25, 538–39
at Federal Club, 379–81
First Annual gubernatorial Message, 723, 726–27
first as assemblyman, 150–52
first before national audience, 255
first public, 87
at Good Government Club, 518–21
to Great Lakes Naval Militia, 605–6
at Gridiron Club, 635
on Harrison Administration, 466–68
on Liquor License Bill, 238

Roosevelt, Theodore, speeches of (*cont'd*):
on Mayoralty Bill, 221–22
at Naval War College, 593–96, 597, 599, 601, 605, 632, 676
oversimplification in, 175–76
in parting from Rough Riders, 707–8
as professional lecturer, 484
at Republican National Convention of 1884, 282
at Republican National Convention of 1900, 767–68
Second Annual gubernatorial Message, 749, 751
in speakership campaign, 217
on Sprague's ouster, 178
on Street Cleaning Bill, 126
on "Tariff in Politics," 182
on veto of Five-Cents Bill, 177–78
on war with Spain, 635
Washington's Birthday, 545–46
wealthy criminal class phrase in, 177–78
on Westbrook Resolution, 158–59
Roosevelt, Theodore, Sr. (TR's father), 4, 19, 21, *31*, 47–48, 59, 67, 119, 179, 241, 298
in Civil War, 8–10, 16
Customs Collectorship nomination and, 68–69, 124–25, 128, 215
death of, 69–70
estate of, 210
in European tour of 1869, 23, 25, 27, 29
in foreign tour of 1872, 36, 38, 41, 43, 44, 46
Hay introduced to TR by, 30–32
personality and background of, 4–5
philanthropy of, 4–5, 117
TR chastised by, 12–13
TR's grief for, 70–73, 75, 78–79
Roosevelt, Theodore, III (Ted) (TR's son), 388, 395, 435, 436, 579, 628
birth of, 386
illness of, 620–21, 623
Roosevelt, West (TR's cousin), 48, 75
Roosevelt Bill (Mayoralty Bill) (1884), 220–24
Roosevelt family foreign tours:
of 1869, 21–29
of 1872, 35–45
of 1881, 126–27, 129–30
Roosevelt Museum of Natural History, 18, 19, 33, 493
Roosevelt 1904 Club, 704, 705
Root, Elihu, 134, 230, 347, 555, 711–12, 713, 730, 751, 759–60
named War Secretary, 744
Payn described by, 750
Rose, John C., 443
Rosebery, Lord, 357
Rosenvelt, Klaes Martenszen van, 6–9
Rough Riders (First U.S. Volunteer Cavalry), xix, 646–94, *662*
in Battle of Las Guásimas, 670–77, *671*, 698, 739
in Battle of San Juan Heights, *see* San Juan Heights, Battle of
at Camp Wood, 648–52
casualties of, 673–74, 687
command structure of, 642
in convoy to Tampa, 653–54
creation and naming of, 642, 643
in debarkation at Daiquiri, 665–68
in debarkation at Montauk Point, 695–98
in departure from Cuba, 693
and election of 1900, 770
en route to Cuba, 661–64
first reunion of, 739
McKinley's visit to, 705
in march to Siboney, 668–69
mustering out of, 706–8
neckerchief emblem of, 650, 683
official regimental photograph of, 653
recruits to, 646–49
in siege of Santiago, 688–89
in Tampa, 654–60
TR's *Merrimac* swim and, 690–91
TR's parting gift from, 707
TR's parting speech to, 707–8
TR's procurement of eleven hundred pounds of beans for, 677–78
TR's promotion to colonel, 680
TR's round-robin letter on, 692–93, 698, 740
Wheeler-Lawton rivalry and, 668
Rough Riders, The (T. Roosevelt), 722, 740
Rubens, Peter Paul, 402
Rumania, Jews persecuted in, xviii
Russia, Imperial, 607
Jews persecuted in, xviii

Sagamore Hill, *290*, 311, 374, 375, 403, 775
Meadowbrook Hunt at, 311, *372*
naming of, 297–98
sale of property from, 485
summer of 1887 at, 385–86
as TR's permanent home, 299
TR's retreat in, 382
Saga of King Olaf (Longfellow), 16, 75
Saint-Gaudens, Augustus, 426
St. Louis Censor, xv
St. Paul Pioneer Press, 259
Salisbury, Lord, 373
Salmon, Tati, 468–69
Saltonstall, Leverett, 78, 98
Saltonstall, Mrs. Leverett, 91, 98
Saltonstall, Richard, 68, 77–78, 110
Saltonstall, Rose, 78, 85, 100, 110
Sampson, William T., 610, 657, 664–65, 679, 688–89
San Juan Heights, Cuba, 665, 679, 681, 684
San Juan Heights, Battle of, 678–87, *682*, 698
artillery bombardment in, 681–82
Bloody Ford in, 683–84
casualties in, 687
onset of, 682–83
TR's charge up Kettle Hill in, 685–86
TR's courageous example in, 684, 687–88
U.S. council of war in, 679–80
Santiago, siege of, 688–89
Sargeant, Dudley A., 108–9, 110
Sargent, John Singer, *401*
Saturday Review, 418
Savile Club, 357, 374
Saxton, Charles T., 751, 753
Schurz, Carl, 458, 573, 596
Scotia (steamer), 21, 22
Scott, Sir Walter, xxxiii, 23, 116–17
Scribner's, 703
Secret Service, xx
Segurança (ship), 659, 663, 664, 675
Senate, U.S., xvii, 68, 69, 315, 328, 578–79, 635, 773, 775
and annexation of Hawaii, 598–99
and election of 1888, 396
Lodge elected to, 467
Platt elected to, 580–81
Proctor's speech on Cuba in, 634
see also Congress, U.S.
71st New York Volunteer Regiment, U.S., 658
Sewall, Kitty, 301, 335
Sewall, Mrs. William, 269, 301, 319, 332, 335
Sewall, William, 99, 231, 278, 293, 297, 300, 301, 303, 304, 327
in capture of Badlands gunmen, 319–21, *320*, 324
in Maine, 75–76, 78, 88–89, 95–97
TR's cattle business with, 269, 270, 273–74, 277, 281, 287, 294, 316, 317–18, 336, 337–38
TR's correspondence with, 130, 237
Sewanee Review, 481
Shafter, William Rufus, 655–59, 661, 663–67, 669, 675, 679–83, 685, 688, 689, 705
Sharp, Lieutenant, 667
Shaw, Albert, 602
Shaw-Lefèvre, Charles, 358
Sheard, Titus, 216–17, 218, 240, 243
Sherman, John, 256, 598
Shidy, Hamilton, 410–11, 413, 420, 427–32
Short History of the American Colonies, A (Lodge), 250
Sienkiewicz, Henryk, 565
Signal Corps, U.S., 684
"Significance of the Frontier in American History, The" (Turner), 478
Sigsbee, Charles D., 618, 622, 625, 626, 627–28
Silver Purchase Act (1890), 485
Simpson, Hashknife, 377
Simpson, Jim "Dead Shot," 650
Sioux Indians, 190–91, 198, 441, 472, 663
Smith, Albert, 667
Smith, Fanny, *see* Dana, Fanny Smith
Smith, Hoke, 486
Smith, Rockpicker, 708
Smithsonian Institution, 491, 493
"Social Evolution" (T. Roosevelt), 601
Society for the Prevention of Crime, 542, 580
Soley, J. Russell, 600
Sousa, John Philip, 402
South Africa, 474, 546
South Dakota, statehood of, 422
South Dakota Republican Central Committee, 466

Spain, 472, 592, 595, 598, 602, 612, 615, 620, 627, 635, 698
Cuban rebellion against, 490, 545, 591, 634
Navy of, 640
in onset of Spanish-American War, 623–24, 641; *see also* Spanish-American War, prelude to
U.S. ultimatum to, 636–37
war declared on United States by, 642
Spanish-American War, xviii–xix, 639–41, 740
Battle of Las Guásimas in, 670–77, *671*, 698, 739
Battle of Manila Bay in, 643–44
Battle of San Juan Heights in, *see* San Juan Heights, Battle of
peace initiative signed in, 698
rocking-chair period of, 655
siege of Santiago in, 688–89
Spain's declaration of war in, 642
TR's war plans adapted for, 655–56
Spanish-American War, prelude to, 618–41
Court of Inquiry on *Maine* sinking in, 626–27, 631–32, 634–35
"*Cuba Libre*" cry in, 634–35
Cuban independence supported by Congress in, 639–40
Cuban officers' riot in, 618–20
Fifty Million Bill in, 632
McKinley's war message to Congress in, 637–39
Maine disaster in, 625–28, 631–33, 635
press coverage in, 623, 626, 627–28, 635
Proctor's Senate speech in, 634
TR's agitation for war in, 624–25
TR's orders to Dewey in, 629–30
TR's preparedness memorandum in, 621–22
TR's readiness order in, 629–30
U.S. Naval redeployment in, 621–22, 632–33
U.S. ultimatum to Spain in, 636–37
"speak softly and carry a big stick," xvi, 754
Special Committee to Investigate the Local Government of the City and County of New York, 223–25, 226, 238–39, 240
Spectator, 291, 418, 441–42
Spinney, George, 152, 160, 162, *169*, 173–74
spoils system, 171, 252, 407, 445–46, 466
see also Civil Service reform
Spooner, John, xxx
Sprague, Henry L., 178, 754
Spring Rice, Cecil, xxii, *340*, 358, 374, 386, 395, 396, 423, 425, 426, 435, 447, 486, 493, 568, 604, 607, 648
described, 356–57
Staats-Zeitung, 521, 526, 529
Staël, Madame de, 384
State Department, U.S., 605, 618, 624, 626
State Trust Company of New York, 752
Statue of Liberty, 348, 354
Steffens, Lincoln, 11, 496–97, 499, 501–2, 507, 511, 515, 527–28, 544–45, 549, 587, 777
Sternburg, Speck von, 560
Stevens, Joseph Sampson, 648
Stickney, Victor H., 332
TR described by, 325
Stoker, Bram, 531
Storer, Bellamy, 563, 565–567, 577–78, 582, 606
Storer, Mrs. Bellamy, 561, 563, 564, 565–66, 577–78, 582, 739
Straus, Oscar Solomon, xviii, xxviii–xxix
Street Cleaning Bill (1891), 126, 131–32
Strew, W. W., 134, 135
Strong, William L., 489, 491, 497–98, 501, 513, 522, 524, 525, 529, 531, 536, 539, 551–57, 559, 570, 582, 586
Stuart, Granville, 270
Studien des Polybius, Die, 721
Sturgis, Russell, 48
Stuyvesant, Pieter, 8
Sully, Alfred, 197–98
Summer Birds of the Adirondacks, The (T. Roosevelt), 65–66, 67
Sumner, Samuel S., 680, 683–85
Sunday Excise Law, 512–14, 516, 518, 519–20, 524, 529, 531, 549
Supériorité des Anglo-Saxons (Demolins), 653
Swift, Lucius Burrie, 409
Swinburne, August, 414

Tacitus, xxxiii
Taft, William Howard, xvi, xxii, 582, 593
Tammany Hall, 145–46, 149–50, 151, 154, 178, 179, 180, 222–23, 349, 518, 519, 528, 544, 586
Cleveland's split with, 215
and election of 1895, 530
and election of 1898, 714, 717
police corruption and, 501, 516
Westbrook Resolution and, 160–61
Tampa Bay Hotel, *647*, 654–55
"Tariff in Politics, The" (T. Roosevelt), 182
tariffs, 182, 436, 557
Cleveland and, 390–91, 396
Tarkington, Booth, xxviii
Taylor, Buck, 717, 720
Teddy bears, xvii
Tee-To-Tum Club, 525
Tennyson, Alfred, Lord, 68
Tenure of Office Bill (1884), 247, 353
Texas (TR's horse), 667, 683, 686
Thayer, Nathaniel, 40–41
Thayer, William Roscoe, 87, 90, 107, 327
TR described by, 297
Theodore Roosevelt Birthplace, 125
Thomas Hart Benton (T. Roosevelt), 327–32, 382, 600, 648, 743
assessment of, 328–32
Manifest Destiny as theme of, 329, 330–31, 474
writing of, 319, 327–28, 332, 334–35
Thompson, Hubert O., 223–24, 240
Thompson, Hugh S., 404, 409–10, 420, 430–31, 432, 434, 446, 486
Thompson, W., 75
Thucydides, xxxiii, 324, 767
Tiffany, William, 650
Tilden, Samuel J., 772
Tillinghast, C. Whitney, II, 620, 630, 633–34
Tillman, Benjamin R., 572
Times (London), xviii, 526, 581, 591
Tocqueville, Alexis de, 392
Tolstoy, Leo, 319, 323–24, 574
Toral, José, 688, 689
Tracy, Benjamin F., 469, 555–56, 557
Trail and Camp-Fire (Boone & Crockett Club), 389
Trevelyan, George Otto, xxx, xxxiii
Trimble, William, 131, 132, 133
Trollope, Anthony, xxxiii
Troy (N.Y.) *Times*, 721
"True Americanism" (T. Roosevelt), 601
Tudor, Mr. and Mrs., 62
Tunney, Gene, xvii
Turks, Armenians massacred by, 594
Turner, Frederick Jackson, 418, 478–79
Twain, Mark, xv, xxii
Tweed, William Marcy "Boss," 165
Twenty-first District Republican Association, 123
22nd Assembly District Roosevelt Club, 351–52
"Two Candidates, The" (newspaper cartoon), 352–53
Tyler, John, 330, 380

Under Two Flags (Ouida), 16
Union League Club, 342, 346, 508, 518, 704, 753
United Societies for Liberal Sunday Laws, 526–27, 529
United States Naval Academy, 581
Utica (N.Y.) *Morning Herald*, 248

Vanderbilt, Alva, 122
van Wyck, Augustus, 714, 717
Vatican, 739
Venezuela, Cleveland's ambivalent attitude toward, 592
Venezuela Message, 545
Veragua, Cristóbal, Duke of, 472
Vermont Fish and Game League, 777
Vesuvius, USS, 629, 640
Vienna Exposition (1872), 36
Vitagraph Company, 658

Wadsworth, James, xv
Wadsworth, W. Austin, 751
Wainwright, Mrs. Richard, 625
Wallace, William, 409–10
Walsh, John, 144
Wanamaker, John, 406–7, 412–13, 416, 429–31, 435, 443, 467, 780
Baltimore investigation and, 452, 454, 458, 459–64
Wannegan, Dutch, 195–96, 303, 307
Ward, Hamilton, 157, 159, 161–62, 164, 165
War Department, U.S., 642, 652, 691, 692, 740, 744

Warns, "Blood-Raw" John, 377
War of American Independence, 384, 385, 474
War of 1812, 136, 137–38, 595
Warren, James D., 242
Washington, D.C., 400–403
Washington, George, xviii, xx, 315, 383, 474, 546, 593, 608, 743
Washington *Evening Star,* xiv
Washington Post, 414–16, 420, 433, 434, 454, 591, 596
Washington *Star,* xvi–xvii, 509
Washington State, statehood of, 422
Webster, Daniel, 250, 329
Weeks, Frank, 452
Welling, Richard, 58–59, 98
Wells, H. G., xxvi, xxvii
West, Judge, 257
Westbrook, T. R., 156, 157, 159, 161–62, 164–65, 717
Westbrook Resolution, 156–64
Westminster, Duke of, 358
Weyler, Valeriano, 594, 634
Wharton, Edith, xxix
"What Americanism Means" (T. Roosevelt), 479–80
"What's the Matter with Kansas?" (White), 608
Wheeler, Joseph "Fighting Joe," 668, 669–70, 675–76, 680, 697
White, Andrew D., 168–70, 244, 252, 257
White, Edward D., 775
White, Horace, 283
White, William Allen, xxv, 740, 761
  on TR's charisma, 609–10
  TR's first meeting with, 608–9
"White House Gang," xxiii, xxiv
Whitman, Walt, 493, 677
Wilde, Oscar, 144
Wilderness Hunter, The (T. Roosevelt), 484
Wilhelm II, Kaiser of Germany, xvii, 434
Williams, "Clubber," 507, 508
Wilson, James, xxxi
Wilson, James Harrison, 530–31
Wilson, Woodrow, xv
Wine, Beer, and Liquor Sellers' Association, 518, 525
Winning of the West (T. Roosevelt), xxxii, 391–97, 412, 425, 443, 466, 600, 648
  Americanism as theme in, 474, 479
  as bestseller, 417–18
  chapters on combat in, 475–76
  dedication and opening chapter of, 393–94
  influences on, 392
  inspiration for, 391–92
  introduction of, 474–75
  military analysis in, 477–78
  race struggle in, 476–77
  reviews of, 412, 417–19
  source material for, 393
  writing of, 395–97, 484, 491, 531, 615
Winter of the Blue Snow (1886–1887), 363–67
"Winter Weather" (T. Roosevelt), 288
Wister, Owen, xxv, xxxiii, 123, 491, 743
  TR satirized by, 105–6
  TR's boxing bout described by, 90–91
  TR's friendship with, 106
Wolseley, Lord, 395
women's rights, 107–8
Wood, J. G., 16, 18
Wood, Leonard, 602–3, 604, 615, 669, 670, 671–75, 680–82, 684, 693
  described, 603
  personality of, 643
  as Rough Riders commander, 642, 650–55, 657, 658
  TR's relationship with, 633–34
Woodruff, Timothy L., 713, 757
Works of Theodore Roosevelt, The (T. Roosevelt), xxxii, 773
Wrenn, Bob, 648
Wright, Albert, 698, 717, 719
Wyoming, statehood of, 422

Yellowstone National Park, 389, 435
Young, S.B.M., 669–70, 671, 672, 674, 675, 680
Young Republicans, 126
Youngs, William J., 716, 734
Yucatán (transport ship), 658, 659, 661, 664, 665, 667, 719

ABOUT THE AUTHOR

EDMUND MORRIS was born in Nairobi, Kenya, in 1940. He was schooled there, and studied music, history, and literature at Rhodes University, Grahamstown, South Africa. After leaving Africa at the age of twenty-four, he worked for six years as an advertising copywriter in London and New York. He became a full-time writer in 1972. His first book, *The Rise of Theodore Roosevelt,* began life as a screenplay. It was published in 1979 and won the Pulitzer Prize and National Book Award. In 1985, Morris was appointed the official biographer of President Ronald Reagan. The resultant work, *Dutch: A Memoir of Ronald Reagan* (1999), was and remains controversial because of its revolutionary narrative technique. *Theodore Rex* (2001), the second volume of Morris's Roosevelt trilogy, won the Los Angeles Times Book Award for biography. Before completing his trilogy with *Colonel Roosevelt,* Morris published a short life of Beethoven.

He lives in New York and Kent, Connecticut, with his wife and fellow biographer, Sylvia Jukes Morris.

ABOUT THE TYPE

This book was set in Sabon, a typeface designed by the well-known German typographer Jan Tschichold (1902–74). Sabon's design is based upon the original letter forms of Claude Garamond and was created specifically to be used for three sources: foundry type for hand composition, Linotype, and Monotype. Tschichold named his typeface for the famous Frankfurt typefounder Jacques Sabon, who died in 1580.